Adolescence

2

Ninth Edition

Adolescence

Laurence Steinberg
Temple University

McGraw Hill

Connect
Learn
Succeed™

The McGraw·Hill Companies

Connect
Learn
Succeed™

ADOLESCENCE, NINTH EDTION
International Edition 2011

Published by McGraw-Hill, an imprint of The McGraw-Hill Companies, Inc., 1221 Avenue of the Americas, New York, NY 10020. Copyright © 2011, 2008, 2005, 2002, 1999 by The McGraw-Hill Companies, Inc. All rights reserved. No part of this publication may be reproduced or distributed in any form or by any means, or stored in a database or retrieval system, without the prior written consent of The McGraw-Hill Companies, Inc., including, but not limited to, in any network or other electronic storage or transmission, or broadcast for distance learning.

Some ancillaries, including electronic and print components, may not be available to customers outside the United States.

10 09 08 07 06 05 04 03 02 01
20 15 14 13 12 11
CTP   COS

When ordering this title, use ISBN: 978-125-900742-2 or MHID: 125-900742-1

Printed in Singapore

www.mhhe.com

For Wendy and Ben

About the Author

LAURENCE STEINBERG, Ph.D., is the Distinguished University Professor and Laura H. Carnell Professor of Psychology at Temple University. He graduated from Vassar College in 1974 and from Cornell University in 1977, where he received his Ph.D. in human development and family studies. He is a Fellow of the American Psychological Association and former President of the Society for Research on Adolescence and the Division of Developmental Psychology of the American Psychological Association. Dr. Steinberg has been on the editorial boards of many major journals, including *Developmental Psychology* and *Child Development,* where he served as Associate Editor. He chairs the National Academies' Committee on the Science of Adolescent Health and Behavior, and has been a frequent consultant to state and federal agencies and lawmakers on child labor, secondary education, and juvenile justice policy. His work was cited numerous times by the U.S. Supreme Court in its 2005 landmark decision that abolished the juvenile death penalty.

Dr. Steinberg is one of the most highly cited scholars in the field of developmental psychology. His own research has focused on a range of topics in the study of contemporary adolescence, including parent–adolescent relationships, adolescent employment, high school reform, juvenile crime and justice, and adolescent brain development. He has been the recipient of numerous honors, including the John P. Hill Award for Outstanding Contributions to the Study of Adolescence, given by the Society for Research on Adolescence; the Society for Adolescent Medicine's Gallagher Lectureship; and, from the American Psychological Association, the Urie Bronfenbrenner Award for Lifetime Contribution to Developmental Psychology in the Service of Science and Society, the Award for Distinguished Contributions to Research in Public Policy, and the APA Presidential Citation. In 2009, he was named as the first recipient of the Klaus J. Jacobs Research Prize for Productive Youth Development, one of the largest prizes ever awarded to a social scientist.

Dr. Steinberg also has been recognized for excellence in research and teaching by the University of California, the University of Wisconsin, and Temple University, where he was honored in 1994 as one of that university's Great Teachers. He has taught undergraduate and graduate courses in adolescence for more than 35 years and has served as the doctoral advisor to more than 35 students, many of whom have gone on to become influential scholars in their own right in the field of adolescence.

In addition to *Adolescence*, Dr. Steinberg is the author or co-author of more than 300 scholarly articles on growth and development during the teenage years, as well as the books *You and Your Adolescent; When Teenagers Work: The Psychological and Social Costs of Adolescent Employment* (with Ellen Greenberger); *Crossing Paths: How Your Child's Adolescence Triggers Your Own Crisis* (with Wendy Steinberg); *Beyond the Classroom: Why School Reform Has Failed and What Parents Need to Do* (with B. Bradford Brown and Sanford Dornbusch); *The 10 Basic Principles of Good Parenting* (which has been published in 10 languages); *Rethinking Juvenile Justice* (with Elizabeth Scott); and the textbooks *Development* (with Deborah Lowe Vandell and Marc Bornstein) and *Lifespan Development* (with Marc Bornstein, Deborah Lowe Vandell, and Karen Rook). He is co-editor of *Studying Minority Adolescents: Conceptual, Methodological, and Theoretical Issues* (co-edited with Vonnie McLoyd) and the *Handbook of Adolescent Psychology* (co-edited with Richard Lerner).

Brief Contents

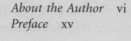

Contents

Preface

I BEGAN MY GRADUATE WORK at Cornell University in 1974, just as the field of adolescence was beginning to emerge as a distinct area of study within the discipline of human development. My mentors were two scholars who have probably influenced the contemporary study of adolescence more than anyone else: John Hill, who modernized the scientific study of adolescence and was the founding president of the Society for Research on Adolescence, and Urie Bronfenbrenner, who was the father of the ecological perspective on human development. There is a lot of each of these great thinkers in this book. Its organization comes directly from Hill's framework for the study of adolescence, and the perspective is indisputably ecological.

I've taught adolescent development at both the undergraduate and graduate levels for more than 35 years, and I know firsthand how exhilarating and exasperating teaching adolescence can be. Every student comes into class an expert; for many of them, adolescence wasn't very long ago. No good instructor wants to squelch the interest and curiosity most students bring with them when they first come into a class. But no conscientious teacher wants to see students leave with little more than the preconceptions they came in with and an even firmer conviction that social scientists who study human development are out of touch with the "real" world.

Urie Bronfenbrenner once wrote that the science of child development had found itself caught between "a rock and a soft place"—between rigor and relevance. Teachers of adolescent development find

themselves in the same boat. How do you present scientific research on adolescent development in ways students find interesting, believable, relevant, and worth remembering when the term is over? I hope this book will help.

My goals for this book are fourfold: to provide students with the most current, most thorough coverage of the scientific literature on adolescent development; to help students understand how the context in which adolescents come of age shapes the way in which they develop; to help students see how what they are learning about adolescence can be applied to improve the lives of young people and their families; and, most importantly, to get students to really think about what adolescence is and why it is a unique period in the human life span. For some, this understanding will make them better teachers, health care providers, or counselors, because they will really grasp how adolescents are different from children and from adults and how they should take these differences into account when they interact with youth. For some, this will mean being smarter researchers, because they will know the research literature and the importance of separating science from stereotype. For some, this will mean designing better programs or policies that affect young people, because they will understand what adolescents need to grow up healthy. And for most, this understanding will mean being better mothers and fathers, because they will know what to expect and how to respond as their sons and daughters mature from childhood into adulthood.

Adolescent Development in Context

If there is a guiding theme to *Adolescence*, it is this: Adolescent development cannot be understood apart from the context in which young people grow up. Identity crises, generation gaps, and peer pressure may be features of adolescent life in contemporary society,

but their prevalence has more to do with the nature of our society than with the nature of adolescence as a stage in the life cycle. In order to understand how adolescents develop in contemporary society, students need first to understand the world in which adolescents live and how that world affects their behavior and social relationships. I have therefore devoted a good deal of attention in this book to the contexts in which adolescents live—families, peer groups, schools, neighborhoods, and work and leisure settings—to how these contexts have changed and are changing, and to how these changes are transforming the nature of adolescence.

A Few Words About Diversity

Perhaps the greatest expansion of knowledge during the past decade has been about adolescents from ethnic minority groups, from disadvantaged communities, and from parts of the world other than North America. This has permitted increased coverage in this edition of the ways in which development during adolescence is affected by culture, class, and region.

Authors take different approaches to handling issues of diversity. Whereas some choose to present this material in a separate chapter on ethnicity or culture, I am not convinced that this is the best way to help students understand when, how, and why patterns of adolescent development vary across ethnicity and region of the world. Moreover, the literature on psychological development of ethnic minority and non-American adolescents has expanded so rapidly during the past 15 years that it would be impossible to provide adequate coverage of this material in just one chapter.

Others take what I think of as the "travelogue" approach, sprinkling boxes on the nature of adolescence in various ethnic groups or different parts of the world (the more remote and exotic, the better) throughout the text, in which they discuss adolescence as if everyone from that culture or country were the same. I think it is both patronizing and misleading to take this approach. (As a character in the Woody Allen movie *Annie Hall* said sarcastically, "I just love being reduced to a cultural stereotype.") There isn't any such thing as "the" Mexican adolescent or "the" Indian adolescent, any more than there is such a thing as "the" American adolescent.

My approach is to integrate discussions of ethnicity and culture throughout *every single chapter,* focusing not only on ethnic differences in development but also on similarities that cut across adolescents from different social, economic, and cultural backgrounds. There are important differences in the experiences of adolescents from different backgrounds, to be sure, but, as I point out often in the book, many studies indicate that influences on adolescent development are far more similar than different across ethnic and cultural groups. Factors that influence school achievement, risky sexual behavior, and drug use, for instance, are virtually identical across ethnic groups. In other words, "diversity" doesn't necessarily equal "difference." In fact, one of the consequences of the globalization of adolescence that

has taken place in the last decade is that technological innovation has made adolescence more similar around the world, not more different.

My emphasis is on getting students to think critically about whether and why ethnicity matters, rather than simply assuming that it does. So, while you will not find a separate chapter labeled "culture" or "ethnicity" in this book, you will find extensive and thoughtful discussions of such issues as ethnic identity, ethnicity and family relationships, cross-ethnic peer relations, ethnic differences in achievement, ethnic differences in sexuality, and ethnic differences in problem behaviors, as well as comprehensive coverage of research on adolescent development in the context of economic disadvantage. I treat gender in a similar fashion. Gender influences virtually *every* aspect of adolescent development. That's why I discuss it in *every* chapter.

About the Ninth Edition

The material in each chapter has been thoroughly updated. Nearly 800 new studies have been cited since the eighth edition alone—studies that my research assistant and I culled from the several thousand we reviewed to prepare for this edition. We work from a list of about 50 scientific journals from the fields of psychology, education, sociology, psychiatry, economics, law, neuroscience, medicine, history, and anthropology, and we review the abstract of every single article involving adolescents published since the last edition of the textbook. If the abstract looks interesting, I read the entire article and decide whether it contains information that students need to know. I focus on incorporating studies that break new ground (like studies of brain development), change the way the field thinks (like studies of why aggressive adolescents are often popular), or update existing findings with more recent samples or newer methods (like studies of media use). The current edition also reflects a lot of new research I came across while co-editing the latest edition of the *Handbook of Adolescent Psychology,* which was published just a year before I began revising this edition.

Like the field of adolescence itself, some things about this book have changed very little over the years, and others have been completely transformed. In addition to the increase in our knowledge about adolescents from different cultural groups and different parts of the world, which, as noted earlier, is included in every chapter, our understanding of adolescent brain development, risk taking, popularity, ethnic identity, extracurricular participation, romance, spirituality, and media use (including use of the Internet) has expanded substantially since the last edition. All of these topics have received new or expanded coverage.

As I worked on the previous edition, I came to the conclusion that it was unwise to include any important material in a boxed insert, because instructors told me that students often skipped over these. I haven't seen any evidence since then that has persuaded me to return to using boxes, and in fact I've heard that today's instructors are even more negative about them than they had been in the past. Based on positive feedback I've received from users, I've retained the use of interim summaries—called "Recaps"—and thought-provoking questions—called "Food for Thought." Many instructors use the "Food for Thought" questions as a launching pad for class discussions or as essay questions on examinations.

I also worked especially hard to shorten this edition a bit. With the addition of more and more research with each edition—a development that has been necessary because of the explosion of scientific knowledge about adolescence—the text had simply become too long. I've tried my best to cut the book's length without dropping essential coverage and while still making room for new material.

Organization and Learning Aids

The overall organization of this book has not changed since the previous edition. Specifically, the chapters about psychosocial development during adolescence are separate from those about the contexts of adolescence. In this way, the psychosocial concerns of adolescence—identity, autonomy, intimacy, sexuality, and achievement—are presented as central developmental concerns that surface across, and are affected by, different settings.

This book contains an Introduction and 13 chapters, which are grouped into three parts: the fundamental biological, cognitive, and social changes of the period (Part 1); the contexts of adolescence (Part 2); and psychosocial development during the adolescent years (Part 3). The Introduction presents a model for studying adolescence that serves as both the organizational framework for the text and an overview of some of the basic disciplinary perspectives on the period. I have found the framework to be extremely helpful in teaching adolescent development, and I highly recommend using it. However, if the model does not fit with your course outline or your own perspective on adolescence, it is possible to use the text without using the framework. Each chapter is self-contained, and so it is not necessary to assign chapters in the sequence in which they are ordered in the text. Most users of this book assign the chapters in the order in which they appear, but some assign the chapters in a sequence that pairs an aspect of psychosocial development with the context that most influences it (for example, "Schools" with "Achievement," or "Peer Groups" with "Intimacy"), and that has worked well for them.

Theory and Methods

Although the Introduction reviews how different disciplines (such as psychology, sociology, anthropology, and history) approach the study of adolescence, it does not provide detailed examinations of particular theories or research methods. My preference is to integrate material on theory and methods when it is most relevant, in a way that shows students how research and theory are related. At the beginning of the chapter on intimacy, for instance, several perspectives on close relationships (for example, attachment theory and Sullivan's perspective on psychosocial development) are presented, and then the relevant research is examined. Similarly, the research methods and tools employed in the study of adolescence are discussed in the context of specific studies that illustrate the powers—or pitfalls—of certain strategies.

Supplements

FOR THE INSTRUCTOR

The supplements for the ninth edition have been carefully revised and updated by Elizabeth Cauffman and Jordan Bechtold, both of the University of California, Irvine. The instructor resources for the new edition include an Instructor's Manual, Test Bank, and Power-Point presentations for each chapter. All of these supplements can be found on the text's password-protected Online Learning Center at www.mhhe.com/steinberg9e. Ask your McGraw-Hill representative for access information.

FOR THE STUDENT

The student Online Learning Center features chapter-by-chapter multiple choice, true/false, and essay questions that allow students to test their understanding of the text. For access go to www.mhhe.com/steinberg9e.

 **CourseSmart eBook** This book is available as a Course-Smart eBook. CourseSmart is a new way to find and buy eTextbooks. At CourseSmart you can save up to 50% off the cost of a print textbook, reduce your impact on the environment, and gain access to powerful web tools for learning. CourseSmart has the largest selection of eTextbooks available anywhere, offering thousands of the most commonly adopted textbooks from a wide variety of higher education publishers. CourseSmart eTextbooks are available in one standard online reader with full text search, notes and highlighting, and email tools for sharing notes between classmates. For further details contact your sales representative or go to www.coursesmart.com.

Acknowledgments

Revising a textbook at a time when so much new information is available is a challenge that requires much assistance. Over the years, my students (as well as many who have written to me from other institutions) have suggested numerous ways in which the text might be improved, and I have learned a great deal from listening to them. I am especially grateful to Hilary Hodgdon, who ably tracked down and organized much of the new research published in the three years between editions. I also acknowledge with appreciation the following colleagues, whose feedback on the eighth edition helped make this one better:

Maria R. Chavira, *Maricopa Community College*

Kendall Cotton Bronk, *Ball State University*

A. K. Ganzel, *Cornell College*

Janet Gebelt, *Westfield State College*

Julia A. Graber, *University of Florida*

Jana Hunzicker, *Bradley University*

Julie M. Hupp, *The Ohio State University–Newark*

Shelley Dean Kilpatrick, *Southwest Baptist University*

William Kimberlin, *Lorain County Community College*

Frances Haemmerlie Montgomery, *Missouri University of Science and Technology*

Narina Nuñez, *University of Wyoming*

Julie A. Osland, *Wheeling Jesuit University*

Barry M. Wagner, *The Catholic University of America*

Nanci Stewart Woods, *Austin Peay State University*

I also wish to thank my colleagues at McGraw-Hill, including Mike Sugarman, publisher; Krista Bettino, sponsoring editor; Meghan Campbell, managing editor; Stephanie Kelly, development editor; Pam Cooper, marketing manager; Anne Fuzellier, production editor; and Ashley Bedell, designer.

In addition, I am grateful to the many colleagues and students across the country who took the time during the past 25 years to send me comments and suggestions based on their firsthand experiences using *Adolescence* in the classroom. They have improved the text with each edition.

I wrote the first edition of this book when I was teaching at the University of California, Irvine, sitting at a desk in a small alcove of a tiny 1930s beach cottage a few blocks from the ocean, with our Springer Spaniel, Oscar, at my feet each day. This revision was written under similar circumstances, although in the guest bedroom of a different Southern California house and with a different Springer, named Smuckers, after the dog in a favorite Seinfeld episode, close at hand (and a slightly loopy Cocker Spaniel named Lucy burrowed under the guest bed). Like his predecessor, Smuckers showed little interest in the book, but his presence was always reassuring.

Laurence Steinberg

Adolescence

The Study of Adolescent Development

The oddest question I have ever been asked during the 35 years that I have been studying adolescent development is this: "Do you believe that someone would need to be capable of formal operational thinking in order to build an IED?" As you will learn in Chapter 2 of this book, formal operational thinking is, according to one theory of adolescence, the highest level of cognitive development, which is not attained until early adolescence (Kuhn, 2009). And, as you probably know from the news, an IED is an improvised explosive device, a homemade bomb often planted along the roadside in an effort to attack the enemy.

This unusual question was posed to me during a pretrial investigation held at Guantánamo Bay, where I was serving as an expert witness in a case involving a detainee who had been accused of building and setting IEDs in eastern Afghanistan, as an assistant to Al Qaeda and Taliban operatives, and throwing a hand grenade that killed an American soldier. Omar Khadr, the detainee, was 15 when he was captured by American soldiers (Glaberson, 2007). Omar had been interrogated for many months, first in Afghanistan and later at Guantánamo Bay, where he was still being held, nearly seven years after his capture.

Omar's defense team, which had retained me, was planning to argue in court that a 15-year-old should not have been interrogated using the same methods used for adults and should not have been held to the same level of criminal responsibility that applied to someone who was older. The prosecutor questioning me was looking for evidence that Omar, by virtue of his bomb-building ability, demonstrated adultlike cognitive maturity, which argued in favor of treating him as an adult and viewing his responses during the interrogation as no different from those an adult would have provided.

The Omar Khadr case is certainly the most unusual one in which I have been involved, but the central issue for discussion is one that my collaborators and I have grappled with for the past 15 years: Where, on the basis of scientific study, should we draw the line between adolescence and adulthood? This is not just an abstract, academic exercise. How we answer this question has far-reaching ramifications for society and, of course, for teenagers. How old does someone have to be in order to be tried and sentenced as an adult for a crime he has committed? At what age should a pregnant adolescent be able to obtain an abortion without parental permission? How old should individuals have to be to obtain contraception, see a psychologist, or have cosmetic surgery without their parents knowing? Have we picked the right ages in deciding where to draw the line as to who can drive, see R-rated movies, or buy cigarettes? Is there an age by which you think individuals are mature enough to make these sorts of decisions on their own? Or should we have different ages for different decisions? And how should we respond to young offenders—even those like Omar Khadr? "Do the adult crime, do the adult time" may sound fair from the perspective of crime victims, but does it make sense in light of what we know about adolescent development?

FOOD FOR THOUGHT

In 2005, the U.S. Supreme Court ruled that imposing capital punishment for crimes committed before the age of 18 was unconstitutional, thereby abolishing the so-called juvenile death penalty. What do you think about this decision? Should 16- and 17-year-olds who commit serious crimes be punished the same way as adults who commit comparable offenses?

A Multidisciplinary Approach to Adolescence

What is the nature of adolescents' identity development in a changing world? How should society deal with problems of youth unemployment, underage drinking, teenage pregnancy, and juvenile crime? What is the best way to prepare young people for the work, family, and citizenship roles of adulthood?

Answering these questions requires a thorough understanding of adolescents' psychological development; and in this book, we will examine how—and why—people's hopes and plans, their fears and anxieties, and their questions and concerns change as they grow into adulthood. Answering these difficult questions requires more than an understanding of the ways in which individuals change psychologically as they move through adolescence, though. It also requires knowledge of how they develop physically, how their brain matures, how their relationships with others change, how as a group they are viewed and treated by society, how adolescence in our society differs from adolescence in other cultures, and how the nature of adolescence itself has changed over the years. In other words, a complete understanding of adolescence in contemporary society

One significant aspect of transition from childhood into adolescence is the young person's entry into the labor force.

depends on being familiar with biological, social, sociological, cultural, and historical perspectives on adolescence (Dahl & Hariri, 2005).

In this book, we will look at adolescence from a *multidisciplinary* perspective—a perspective that draws on a variety of disciplines. Each provides a view of adolescence that, in its own way, helps further our understanding of this period of the life cycle. We will look at contributions to the study of adolescence made by biologists, psychologists, educators, sociologists, historians, and anthropologists. The challenge here is not to determine which perspective on adolescence is best, but to integrate contributions from different disciplines into a coherent and comprehensive viewpoint on the nature of adolescent development in contemporary society.

The Boundaries of Adolescence

Let's begin with a fairly basic question: When does adolescence begin and end? Perhaps we can gain some insight into this question by examining the word itself.

The word *adolescence* is derived from the Latin *adolescere,* which means "to grow into adulthood" (R. Lerner & Steinberg, 2009). In all societies, adolescence is a time of growing up, of moving from the immaturity of childhood into the maturity of adulthood, of preparation for the future (Larson, Wilson, & Rickman, 2009; Schlegel, 2009). **Adolescence** is a period of transitions: biological, psychological, social, economic. During adolescence, individuals become interested in

sex and become biologically capable of having children. They become wiser, more sophisticated, and better able to make their own decisions. They become more self-aware, more independent, and more concerned about what the future holds. They are permitted to work, to get married, to drive, and to vote. Think for a moment about how much you changed between elementary school and college. I'm sure you'll agree that the changes you went through were remarkable.

For the purposes of this book, adolescence is defined, roughly speaking, as the second decade of the life span. Although at one time "adolescence" may have been synonymous with the teenage years (from 13 to 19), the adolescent period lengthened considerably in the 20th century, both because physical maturation occurs earlier (you'll read about this in the next chapter) and because so many individuals delay entering into work and marriage until their mid-20s (Settersten, Furstenberg, & Rumbaut, 2005). It therefore makes more sense to think of adolescence as beginning around age 10 and ending in the early 20s.

As you can see in Table I.1, there are a variety of boundaries we might draw between childhood and adolescence, and between adolescence and adulthood. Whereas a biologist would place a great deal of emphasis on the attainment and completion of puberty, an attorney would look instead at important age breaks designated by law, and an educator might draw attention to differences between students enrolled in different grades in school. Is a biologically mature fifth-grader

adolescence   The second decade of life.

TABLE I.1 The boundaries of adolescence. One problem that students of adolescence encounter early is a fundamental one: deciding when adolescence begins and ends, or what the boundaries of the period are. Different theorists have proposed various markers, but there is little agreement on the issue. Here are some examples of the ways in which adolescence has been distinguished from childhood and adulthood that we shall examine in this book. Which boundaries make the most sense to you?

Perspective	When Adolescence Begins	When Adolescence Ends
Biological	Onset of puberty	Becoming capable of sexual reproduction
Emotional	Beginning of detachment from parents	Attainment of separate sense of identity
Cognitive	Emergence of more advanced reasoning abilities	Consolidation of advanced reasoning abilities
Interpersonal	Beginning of shift in interest from parental to peer relations	Development of capacity for intimacy with peers
Social	Beginning of training for adult work, family, and citizen roles	Full attainment of adult status and privileges
Educational	Entrance into junior high school	Completion of formal schooling
Legal	Attainment of juvenile status	Attainment of majority status
Chronological	Attainment of designated age of adolescence (e.g., 10 years)	Attainment of designated age of adulthood (e.g., 21 years)
Cultural	Entrance into period of training for ceremonial rite of passage	Completion of ceremonial rite of passage

an adolescent or a child? Is a 20-year-old college student who lives at home an adolescent or an adult? There are no right or wrong answers to these questions. It all depends on the boundaries we use to define the period. Determining the beginning and ending of adolescence is a matter more of opinion than of absolute fact.

Rather than argue about which boundaries are the correct ones, it makes more sense to think of development during adolescence as involving a *series* of transitions from immaturity into maturity (Settersten et al., 2005). Some of these passages are long and some are short; some are smooth and others are rough. And not all of them occur at the same time. Consequently, it is quite possible—and perhaps even likely—that an individual will mature in some respects before he or she matures in others. The various aspects of adolescence have different beginnings and different endings for every individual. An individual can be a child in some ways, an adolescent in other ways, and an adult in still others.

early adolescence   The period spanning roughly ages 10–13, corresponding roughly to the junior high or middle school years.

middle adolescence   The period spanning roughly ages 14–17, corresponding to the high school years.

late adolescence   The period spanning roughly ages 18–21, corresponding approximately to the college years.

emerging adulthood   The period spanning roughly ages 18–25, during which individuals make the transition from adolescence to adulthood.

EARLY, MIDDLE, AND LATE ADOLESCENCE

Although adolescence may span a 10-year period, because so much psychological and social growth takes place during this decade, most social scientists and practitioners argue that it makes more sense to view the adolescent years as composed of a series of stages than as one single stage. The 11-year-old whose time and energy is wrapped up in hip-hop, Facebook, and basketball, for example, has little in common with the 21-year-old who is involved in a serious romance, worried about pressures at work, and looking for an affordable apartment.

Social scientists who study adolescence usually differentiate among **early adolescence** (about ages 10–13), **middle adolescence** (about ages 14–17), and **late adolescence** (about ages 18–21). These divisions, as you may have guessed, correspond to the way our society groups young people in educational institutions; they are the approximate ages that customarily mark attendance at middle or junior high school, high school, and college. In discussing development during adolescence, we will need to be sensitive not only to differences between adolescence and childhood, or between adolescence and adulthood, but also to differences among the various phases of adolescence itself. Some writers also have suggested that a new phase of life, called **emerging adulthood** (Arnett, 2004) or "youthhood" (Côté, 2000), now characterizes the early and mid-20s. However, despite the popularity of this idea in the mass media, there is little evidence that this is a universal stage of life or that the majority of young people in their mid-20s are in some sort of psychological or social limbo (Côté & Bynner, 2008; M. J. Shanahan, Porfeli, Mortimer, & Erikson, 2005). Indeed, what is most striking about the transition from adolescence to adulthood today is just how many different pathways there are. Some individuals—those we might label "emerging adults"—spend their 20s single, dependent on their parents, and bouncing from job to job, while others leave adolescence and go straight into marriage, full-time employment, and economic independence (Osgood, Ruth, Eccles, Jacobs, & Barber, 2005). As you'll see in Chapter 3, the pathways through adolescence and into adulthood are equally varied.

FOOD FOR THOUGHT

What boundaries make the most sense to you? How would you draw the line between childhood and adolescence? Between adolescence and adulthood?

RECAP

- The study of adolescence draws on different disciplines, including psychology, biology, sociology, anthropology, and education.
- *Adolescence* comes from the Greek word meaning "to grow into adulthood."
- There is no single accepted way to define the beginning or end of adolescence—it has different boundaries depending on how one chooses to define the period.
- Most social scientists distinguish among three stages of adolescence: early (10–13), middle (14–17), and late (18–21).
- Some writers have suggested that a new phase of life, called "emerging adulthood," now characterizes the early and mid-20s.

A Framework for Studying Adolescent Development

In order to organize information from a variety of different perspectives, this book uses a framework that is based largely on a model suggested by the late psychologist John Hill (1983). The framework is organized around three basic components: (1) the fundamental changes of adolescence, (2) the contexts of adolescence, and (3) the psychosocial developments of adolescence.

THE FUNDAMENTAL CHANGES OF ADOLESCENCE

What, if anything, is distinctive about adolescence as a period in the life cycle? According to Hill, three features of adolescent development give the period its special flavor and significance: (1) the onset of puberty, (2) the emergence of more advanced thinking abilities, and (3) the transition into new roles in society. We refer to these three sets of changes—biological, cognitive, and social—as the *fundamental changes* of adolescence. And they are changes that occur universally; virtually without exception, all adolescents in every society go through them.

▌ **Biological Transitions**   The chief elements of the biological changes of adolescence—which collectively are referred to as **puberty**—involve changes in the young person's physical appearance (including breast development in girls, the growth of facial hair in boys, and a dramatic increase in height for both sexes) and the development of the ability to conceive children (Susman & Dorn, 2009).

Chapter 1 not only describes the biological changes that occur in early adolescence but also examines how puberty affects the adolescent's psychological development and social relationships. The adolescent's self-image, for example, may be temporarily threatened by marked changes in physical appearance. When your body and face are changing, not surprisingly, the way you look at yourself changes as well. In addition, relationships inside the family are transformed by adolescents' greater need for privacy and their interest in forming intimate relationships with peers. Girls may suddenly feel uncomfortable about being physically affectionate with their father, and boys with their mother. And, of course, adolescents' friendships are altered by newly emerging sexual impulses and concerns. In short, puberty is not just a biological event.

▌ **Cognitive Transitions**   The word *cognitive* is used to refer to the processes that underlie how people think about things. Memory and problem solving are both examples of cognitive processes. Changes in thinking abilities, which are dealt with in Chapter 2, make up the second of the three fundamental changes of the adolescent period. The emergence of more sophisticated thinking abilities is one of the most striking changes to take place during adolescence. Compared with children, for example, adolescents are much better able to think about hypothetical situations (that is, things that have not yet happened but might, or things that may not happen but could) and about abstract concepts, such as friendship, democracy, or morality (Kuhn, 2009). As you'll read, groundbreaking research

puberty   The biological changes of adolescence.

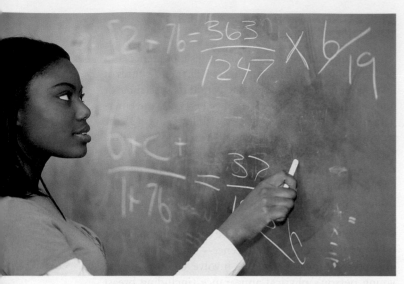

The implications of the cognitive changes of adolescence are far-reaching.

on brain development is beginning to shed light on the ways in which these and other changes in thinking during adolescence result from the maturation of particular brain regions and systems.

The implications of these cognitive changes are also far-reaching. The ability to think more capably in hypothetical and abstract terms affects the way adolescents think about themselves, their relationships, and the world around them. We will see, for example, that teenagers' abilities to plan ahead, argue with their parents, solve algebraic equations, and resolve moral dilemmas are all linked to changes in the way they think. Even the way day-to-day decisions are made is affected. For the first time, individuals become able to think in logical ways about what their life will be like in the future, about their relationships with friends and family, and about politics, religion, and philosophy.

▌ **Social Transitions**   All societies distinguish between individuals who are thought of as children and those who are seen as ready to become adults. Our society, for example, distinguishes between people who are "underage," or minors, and people who have reached the age of majority. Not until adolescence are individuals permitted to drive, marry, and vote. Such changes in rights, privileges, and responsibilities—which we'll examine in Chapter 3—constitute the third set of fundamental changes that occur at adolescence: social changes. In some cultures, the social changes of adolescence are marked by a formal ceremony—a **rite of passage.** In most contemporary industrialized societies, though, the

rite of passage   A ceremony or ritual marking an individual's transition from one social status to another, especially marking the young person's transition to adulthood.

transition is less clearly marked. But, everywhere, a change in social status is a universal feature of adolescence (Schlegel, 2009).

FOOD FOR THOUGHT

In contemporary industrialized society, we do not have formal ceremonies that designate when a person has become an "adult." Do we have more informal ways to let individuals know when they have made the transition?

As the young person's treatment by society changes, so do relationships around the home, at school, and in the peer group. Changes in social status also permit young people to enter new roles and engage in new activities, such as marriage and work, that dramatically alter their self-image and relationships with others. The adolescent, on the verge of becoming an adult, has important decisions to make and new options to choose among. Even something as simple as being able to drive has implications for the adolescent's relationships with parents and friends.

RECAP

- The three features of adolescence that make the period unique are called the "fundamental changes of adolescence."
- One fundamental change is biological and involves the physical changes of puberty.
- A second fundamental change is cognitive and involves changes in thinking abilities.
- The third fundamental change is social and involves changes in the way that society defines the individual.

THE CONTEXTS OF ADOLESCENCE

Although all adolescents experience the biological, cognitive, and social transitions of the period, the *effects* of these changes are not uniform for all young people. Puberty makes some adolescents feel attractive and self-assured, but it makes others feel ugly and self-conscious. Being able to think in hypothetical terms makes some teenagers thankful that they grew up with the parents they have, but it prompts others to run away in search of a better life. Reaching 18 prompts some teenagers to enlist in the military or apply for a marriage license, but for others, becoming an adult is frightening and unsettling.

If the fundamental changes of adolescence are universal, why are their effects so varied? Why aren't all individuals affected in the same ways by puberty, by cognitive development, and by changes in social and legal status? The answer lies in the fact that the psychological impact of the biological, cognitive, and social changes of adolescence is shaped by the environment in which the changes take place. In other words, psychological development during adolescence is a product of the interplay between a set of three very basic, universal changes and the context in which these changes are experienced. According to the **ecological perspective on human development,** whose main proponent was Urie Bronfenbrenner (1979), we cannot understand development without examining the settings, or context, in which it occurs. I always laugh to myself when parents ask me how their children are going to be affected by puberty, because the only honest answer I can give them is "It depends."

Consider, for example, two 14-year-old girls growing up in neighboring communities. When Diane went through puberty, around age 13, her parents responded by restricting her social life because they were afraid she would become too involved with boys and neglect her schoolwork. Diane felt her parents were being unfair and foolish. She rarely had a chance to meet any boys she wanted to date, because all the older boys went to the high school across town. Even though she was in the eighth grade, she was still going to school with fifth-graders. And she couldn't meet anyone through work, either, because her school would not issue work permits to any student under the age of 16.

Maria's adolescence was very different. For one thing, when she had her first period, her parents took her aside and discussed sex and pregnancy with her. They explained how different contraceptives worked and made an appointment for Maria to see a gynecologist in case she ever needed to discuss something with a doctor. Although she was still only 14 years old, Maria knew that she would begin dating soon, because in her community, the junior and senior high schools had been combined into one large school, and the older boys frequently asked the younger girls out. In addition, since there was no prohibition at her school against young teenagers working, Maria decided to get a job; she knew she would need money to buy clothes if she were going to start dating.

Two teenage girls. Each goes through puberty, each grows intellectually, and each moves closer in age to adulthood. Yet each grows up under very different circumstances: in different families, in different schools,

One of the most important contexts for adolescent development is the peer group.

with different groups of peers, and in different communities. Both are adolescents, but their adolescent experiences are markedly different. And, as a result, each girl's psychological development will follow a different course.

Diane's and Maria's worlds may seem quite different from each other. Yet the two girls share many things in common, at least in comparison to two girls growing up in different parts of the world or in different historical eras. Imagine how different your adolescence would have been if you had grown up a century ago and, instead of going to high school, had been expected to work full-time from the age of 12. Imagine how different it might be to grow up 100 years from today. And imagine how different adolescence is for the teenager whose family is very poor than for one whose family is wealthy. It is impossible to generalize about the nature of adolescence without taking into account the surroundings and circumstances in which young people grow up.

For this reason, the second component of our framework is the *context* of adolescence. In modern societies, there are four main contexts in which young people spend time: families, peer groups, schools, and work and leisure settings. But it is not enough to consider these settings in isolation, because they themselves are located within a neighborhood or community, which influences how they are structured and what takes place

ecological perspective on human development   A perspective on development that emphasizes the broad context in which development occurs.

in them. It would be naïve, for example, to discuss the impact that "school" has on adolescent development without recognizing that a school in an affluent suburb is likely very different from one in the inner city or in a remote rural area. Moreover, the community in which these settings are located is itself embedded in a broader context that is shaped by culture, geography, and historical forces (Bronfenbrenner, 1979). The nature and structure of these contexts—both proximal and distant—dramatically affect the ways in which the fundamental changes of adolescence are experienced. To the extent that one adolescent's world differs from another's, the two young people will have very different experiences during the adolescent years.

Most social scientists interested in adolescent development study young people in one setting at a time. Researchers traditionally have looked at family relations or at peer relations, at school or at work, at home or in the community. Increasingly, however, researchers have begun to acknowledge the linkages among the different contexts of adolescence, and they are beginning to ask questions about the nature of these connections. Instead of asking how adolescents are affected in the home environment, for example, studies might ask how events in the home environment affect events in the peer group.

This change in orientation reflects, in part, the increased importance of the ecological perspective on development (Bronfenbrenner, 1979). From this perspective, we focus not only on the developing individual but also on the interrelations between the individual and his or her contexts, and on the interconnections among the contexts themselves. According to Bronfenbrenner, the ecology of adolescent development can be thought of as having four distinct levels: (1) each of the immediate settings in which adolescents live (such as the family and the school), which he calls **micro-systems;** (2) the system of relations between these immediate settings (such as the family–peer group link and the home–school link), which he calls the **meso-system;** (3) the settings that do not contain the adolescent but that affect him or her indirectly (such as

the parent's workplace), which he calls the **exo-system;** and (4) the broader context of culture and historical time (such as the country and era in which an adolescent lives), which he calls the **macro-system.**

FOOD FOR THOUGHT

Think about the context in which you went through adolescence, and compare it to that in which your parents went through the same period of development. How do these contexts differ from each other? What difference might it have made for psychological development?

Although young people growing up in modern America share some experiences with young people all over the world, their development is distinctly different from that of young people in other societies, especially those in less affluent and less industrialized nations, because their families, peer groups, schools, work settings, and social institutions are different (Larson et al., 2009). In other words, the contexts of adolescence are themselves shaped and defined by the larger society in which young people live. In this book, we'll be especially interested in how the contexts of adolescence have changed in contemporary industrialized society and what the implications of these changes are for adolescent development. Key contexts include the following:

▌ **Families**   Adolescence is a time of dramatic change in family relationships (Laursen & Collins, 2009). In addition, frequent moves, high rates of divorce, and increasing numbers of single-parent households have altered aspects of family life in contemporary America. In Chapter 4, we examine how changes in the family system, and in the context of family life, affect young people's psychological development.

▌ **Peer Groups**   Over the past 100 years, the peer group has come to play an increasingly important role in the socialization and development of teenagers (B. Brown & Larson, 2009). But has the rise of peer groups in contemporary society been a positive or negative influence on young people's development? In Chapter 5, we discuss how peer groups have changed adolescence, for better and for worse.

▌ **Schools**   Chapter 6 examines schools as a context for adolescent development. Contemporary society depends on schools to occupy, socialize, and educate adolescents. But how good a job are schools doing?

---

micro-systems   In the ecological perspective on human development, the immediate settings in which adolescents develop, such as the family or the peer group.

meso-system   In the ecological perspective on human development, the layer of the environment formed by two or more immediate settings, as in the home–school linkage.

exo-system   In the ecological perspective on human development, the layer of the environment that does not directly contain the developing person but that affects the setting in which the person lives.

macro-system   In the ecological perspective on human development, the outermost layer of the environment, containing forces such as history and culture.

What should schools do to help prepare adolescents for adulthood? And how should schools for adolescents be structured (Elmore, 2009)? These are three of the many difficult questions we will be examining.

▌ **Work, Leisure, and the Mass Media**   In Chapter 7, we look at the most important after-school influences on adolescent development: part-time jobs (Staff, Messersmith, & Schulenberg, 2009), extracurricular activities (Mahoney, Vandell, Simpkins, & Zarrett, 2009), the mass media (Roberts, Henriksen, & Foehr, 2009), and, of course, the Internet (Valkenburg & Peter, 2009).

RECAP

- According to Urie Bronfenbrenner's ecological perspective on human development, we cannot understand development without examining the settings, or context, in which it occurs.
- Although the fundamental biological, cognitive, and social changes of adolescence are universal, their effects depend on the context in which they take place.
- The immediate, or proximal, contexts of adolescent development are the family, the peer group, school, and work and leisure settings, including mass media and the Internet.
- What takes place in these immediate settings is influenced by the broader context in which they are contained, including the community, the culture, and the historical era in which people grow up.

PSYCHOSOCIAL DEVELOPMENT OF ADOLESCENCE

The third, and final, component of our framework concerns the major *psychosocial developments* of adolescence—identity, autonomy, intimacy, sexuality, and achievement—as well as certain psychosocial problems that may arise in adolescence. Social scientists use the word **psychosocial** to describe aspects of development that are both psychological and social in nature. Sexuality, for instance, is a psychosocial issue because it involves both psychological change (that is, changes in the individual's emotions, motivations, and behavior) and changes in the individual's social relations with others.

Of course, it is not only during the adolescent years that concerns about identity, autonomy, intimacy, sexuality, and achievement arise, and psychological or social problems can and do occur during all periods of the life cycle. These five sets of issues are present throughout the life span, from infancy through late adulthood. They represent basic developmental challenges that all people face as they grow and change: (1) discovering and understanding who they are as individuals—**identity,** (2) establishing a healthy sense of independence—**autonomy;** (3) forming close and caring relationships with other people—**intimacy;** (4) expressing sexual feelings and enjoying physical contact with others—**sexuality;** and (5) being successful and competent members of society—**achievement.**

Although these issues are not unique to adolescence, development in each of these areas takes a special turn during this stage. Understanding how and why such psychosocial developments take place during adolescence is a special concern of social scientists interested in this age period. We know that individuals form close relationships before adolescence, for example, but why is it that intimate male-female relationships first develop during adolescence? We know that infants struggle with learning how to be independent, but why during adolescence do individuals need to be more on their own and make some decisions apart from their parents? We know that children fantasize about what they will be when they grow up, but why is it that these fantasies are not transformed into serious concerns until adolescence?

Part Three of this book discusses changes in each of the five psychosocial areas and examines several common psychosocial problems.

▌ **Identity**   Chapter 8 deals with changes in identity, self-esteem, and self-conceptions. In adolescence, a variety of important changes in the realm of identity occur (Côté, 2009). The adolescent may wonder who he or she really is and where he or she is headed. Coming to terms with these questions may involve a period of experimentation—a time of trying on different personalities in an attempt to discover one's true self. As you will read, the adolescent's quest for identity is a quest

psychosocial   Referring to aspects of development that are both psychological and social in nature, such as developing a sense of identity or sexuality.

identity   The domain of psychosocial development involving self-conceptions, self-esteem, and the sense of who one is.

autonomy   The psychosocial domain concerning the development and expression of identity.

intimacy   The psychosocial domain concerning the formation, maintenance, and termination of close relationships.

sexuality   The psychosocial domain concerning the development and expression of sexual feelings.

achievement   The psychosocial domain concerning behaviors and feelings in evaluative situations.

Sexuality is a central psychosocial issue of adolescence.

not only for a personal sense of self but also for recognition from others and from society that he or she is a special, unique individual.

Autonomy Adolescents' struggle to establish themselves as independent, self-governing individuals—in their own eyes and in the eyes of others—is a long and occasionally difficult process, not only for young people but also for those around them, especially their parents. Chapter 9 focuses on three sorts of concerns about autonomy that are of special importance during adolescence: becoming less emotionally dependent on parents (McElhaney, Allen, Stephenson, & Hare, 2009), learning to make independent decisions (W. A. Collins & Steinberg, 2006), and establishing a personal code of values and morals (Eisenberg, Morris, McDaniel, & Spinrad, 2009).

Intimacy During adolescence, important changes take place in the individual's capacity to be intimate with others, especially with peers. As we'll see in Chapter 10, during adolescence, for the first time, friendships emerge that involve openness, honesty, loyalty, and exchange of confidences, rather than simply a sharing of activities and interests (B. Brown & Larson, 2009; W. Collins & Steinberg, 2006). Dating takes on increased importance, and as a consequence, so does the capacity to form romantic relationships that are trusting and loving (Connolly & McIssac, 2009).

Sexuality Sexual activity generally begins during the adolescent years (Diamond & Savin-Williams, 2009). Becoming sexual is an important aspect of development during adolescence—not only because it transforms the nature of relationships between adoles-

cents and their peers but also because it raises a range of difficult questions for the young person. Chapter 11 discusses these concerns, including efforts to incorporate sexuality into a still-developing sense of self, the need to resolve questions about sexual values and morals, and the need to come to terms with the sorts of relationships into which the adolescent is prepared—or not prepared—to enter. We also look at sex education, contraceptive use, sexually transmitted diseases, and adolescent childbearing.

Achievement Chapter 12 examines changes in individuals' educational and vocational behavior and plans. Important decisions—many with long-term consequences—about schooling and careers are made during adolescence. Many of these decisions depend on adolescents' achievement in school, on their evaluations of their own competencies and capabilities, on their aspirations and expectations for the future, and on the direction and advice they receive from parents, teachers, and friends (Eccles & Roeser, 2009).

Psychosocial Problems Historically, the scientific study of adolescence has focused much attention on the problems that some young people have during this time, despite the fact that most adolescents move through the period without getting into serious trouble (Steinberg & Morris, 2001). In Chapter 13, we'll look at three sets of problems typically associated with adolescence: drug and alcohol use and abuse (Chassin, Hussong, & Beltran, 2009), delinquency and other "externalizing problems" (Farrington, 2009), and depression and other "internalizing problems" (Graber & Sontag, 2009). In each case, we examine the prevalence of the problem, the factors believed to contribute to its development, and approaches to prevention and intervention.

FOOD FOR THOUGHT

Of the five psychosocial issues just described, which posed the most challenges for you as a teenager?

RECAP

- Five main psychosocial issues are especially important in adolescence.
- Identity involves changes in the ways individuals see, evaluate, and think about themselves.
- Autonomy involves the development of emotional, behavioral, and moral independence.
- Intimacy involves the development of the ability to form close and satisfying relationships with others.

- Sexuality involves the development of the ability to express sexual feelings and enjoy physical contact with others.
- Achievement involves the development of beliefs and abilities that permit one to be a competent and successful member of society.
- Some individuals experience psychological problems during adolescence—most commonly depression, delinquency, and substance abuse—although the majority of individuals move through the period without serious difficulties.

Theoretical Perspectives on Adolescence

The study of adolescence is based not just on empirical research but also on theories of development. You will read more about different theories of adolescence throughout this book, but an overview of the major ones may be helpful.

I find it useful to organize theoretical perspectives on adolescence around a question that has long dominated discussions of human development: How much is due to "nature," or biology, and how much is due to "nurture," or the environment? Some theories of adolescence emphasize biology, others emphasize the environment, and still others fall somewhere between the two extremes (see Figure I.1). The purpose of this brief overview is not to argue for one approach over another, but rather to demonstrate how each of these views has helped us gain a better understanding of the nature of adolescence. We'll begin with a look at the most extreme biological perspectives and work our way across a continuum toward the other extreme—perspectives that give primacy to the role of the environment.

BIOSOCIAL THEORIES

The fact that biological change during adolescence is noteworthy is not a matter of dispute—how could it

be, when puberty is such an obvious part of adolescence? But how important this biological change is in defining the psychosocial issues of the period is something that students of adolescence disagree about. Theorists who have taken a biological or, more accurately, "biosocial" view of adolescence stress the hormonal and physical changes of puberty as driving forces. The most important biosocial theorist was G. Stanley Hall (1904), considered the "father" of the scientific study of adolescence.

■ **Hall's Theory of Recapitulation** G. Stanley Hall, who was very much influenced by the work of Charles Darwin, the author of the theory of evolution, believed that the development of the individual paralleled the development of the human species, a notion referred to as his theory of recapitulation. Infancy, in his view, was equivalent to the time during our evolution when we were primitive, like animals. Adolescence, in contrast, was seen as a time that paralleled the evolution of our species into civilization. For Hall, the development of the individual through these stages was determined primarily by instinct—by biological and genetic forces within the person—and hardly influenced by the environment.

The most important legacy of Hall's view of adolescence is the notion that it is inevitably a period of "storm and stress." He believed that the hormonal changes of puberty cause upheaval, both for the individual and for those around him or her. Because this turbulence was biologically determined, it was unavoidable. The best that society could do was to find ways of managing the young person whose "raging hormones" would invariably lead to difficulties.

Although scientists no longer believe that adolescence is an inherently stressful period or that the hormonal changes of puberty cause emotional problems, much contemporary work continues to emphasize the role that biological factors play in shaping the adolescent experience. More than 100 years ago, in fact, Hall speculated about brain maturation, hormonal influences on behavior, and changes in patterns of sleep during adolescence—all very hot topics in the study of adolescence today (Dahl & Hariri, 2005). Current work in the biosocial tradition, also influenced by Hall and

Theoretical Perspectives on Adolescence

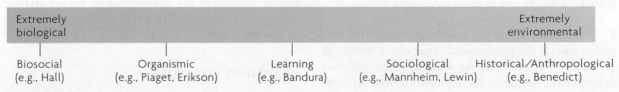

Extremely biological				Extremely environmental
Biosocial (e.g., Hall)	Organismic (e.g., Piaget, Erikson)	Learning (e.g., Bandura)	Sociological (e.g., Mannheim, Lewin)	Historical/Anthropological (e.g., Benedict)

FIGURE I.1 Theories of adolescence range from the extremely biological, like that of G. Stanley Hall, to the extremely environmental, like that of Ruth Benedict.

his followers, explores the genetic bases of individual differences in adolescence and the evolutionary bases of adolescent behavior.

ORGANISMIC THEORIES

Our next stop on the continuum is in the domain of what are called "organismic" theorists. Like biosocial theorists, organismic theorists stress the importance of the biological changes of adolescence. But unlike their biosocial counterparts, organismic theories also take into account the ways in which contextual forces interact with and modify these biological forces.

If you have had previous course work in developmental psychology, you have undoubtedly encountered the major organismic theorists, for they have long dominated the study of human development more generally. Three of these theorists, in particular, have had a great influence over the study of adolescence: Sigmund Freud (1938), Erik Erikson (1968), and Jean Piaget (Inhelder & Piaget, 1958). Although these theorists share in common an organismic orientation, the theories they developed emphasized different aspects of individual growth and development.

■ **Freudian Theory** For Freud, development was best understood in terms of the psychosexual conflicts that arise at different points in development. Like Hall, Freud saw adolescence as a time of upheaval. According to Freud, the hormonal changes of puberty upset the psychic balance that had been achieved during the prior psychosexual stage, called "latency." Because the hormonal changes of puberty were responsible for marked increases in sex drive, the adolescent was temporarily thrown into a period of intrapsychic crisis; and old psychosexual conflicts, long buried in the unconscious, were revived. Freud and his followers believed that the main challenge of adolescence was to resolve these conflicts and restore a psychic balance. Although the process was driven by the hormonal changes of puberty, the specific conflicts faced by the young person were seen as dependent on his or her early experiences in the family.

Sigmund Freud himself actually had very little to say specifically about adolescence. But his daughter, Anna Freud (1958), extended much of her father's thinking to the study of development during the second decade of life. This work has been carried on by neo-Freudians such as Peter Blos (1979), whose theories of adolescent autonomy we explore in detail in Chapter 9.

■ **Eriksonian Theory** In Erikson's theory, the emphasis was on the psychosocial crises characteristic of each period of growth. Like Freud, Erikson believed that internal, biological developments moved the individual from one developmental stage to the next. But unlike Freud, Erikson stressed the psychosocial, rather

than the psychosexual, conflicts faced by the individual at each point in time. Whereas Freud emphasized the development of the id—that part of the psyche believed to be dominated by instinctual urges—Erikson emphasized the development of the ego—that part of the psyche believed to regulate thought, emotion, and behavior.

Erikson proposed eight stages in psychosocial development, each characterized by a specific "crisis" that arises at that point in development because of the interplay between the internal forces of biology and the unique demands of society. In Erikson's theory, which we look at in detail in Chapter 8, adolescence is seen as a period that revolves around the identity crisis, a crisis that is shaped both by the changes of puberty and by the specific demands that society places on young people to make decisions about the future. According to Erikson, the challenge of adolescence is to resolve the identity crisis and to emerge with a coherent sense of who one is and where one is headed.

■ **Piagetian Theory** Freud and Erikson both emphasized emotional and social development. For Jean Piaget, in contrast, development could best be understood by examining changes in the nature of thinking, or cognition. Piaget believed that, as children mature, they pass through stages of cognitive development, and in each stage, from birth to adolescence, their ways of thinking are qualitatively distinct. In his view, understanding the distinctive features of thought and reasoning at each stage can give us insight into the overall development of the individual at that point in time.

In Piaget's theory, which is discussed in detail in Chapter 2, adolescence marks the transition from concrete to abstract thought. According to this model, adolescence is the period in which individuals become capable of thinking in hypothetical terms, a development that permits a broad expansion of logical capabilities. As you will see, many of the familiar changes in behavior that we associate with adolescence have been attributed to these changes in cognitive abilities. Piaget's views have been applied to the study of moral development, social development, and education.

As is the case with the other organismic theories, Piaget's theory of cognitive development emphasizes the interplay between biological and contextual forces. The development of abstract thinking in adolescence, for example, is influenced both by the internal biological changes of the developmental period and by changes in the intellectual environment encountered by the individual.

LEARNING THEORIES

As we move across the theoretical continuum from extreme biological views to extreme environmental ones, we encounter a group of theories that shift the emphasis from biological forces to environmental ones. Whereas organismic theorists tend to emphasize the interaction between biological change and environmental demands, learning theorists stress the context in which behavior takes place. The capacity of the individual to learn from experience is assumed to be a biological given that is in place long before adolescence. What is of interest to learning theorists is the content of what is learned.

Learning theorists are not especially developmental in their approach and, as a consequence, have little to say specifically about adolescence as a developmental period. Indeed, for learning theorists, the basic processes of human behavior are the same during adolescence as during other periods of the life span. But learning theorists have been extremely influential in the study of adolescent development because they have helped us understand how the specific environment in which an adolescent lives can shape his or her behavior.

▌ **Behaviorism** There are two general categories of learning theorists. One group, known as behaviorists, emphasizes the processes of reinforcement and punishment as the main influences on adolescent behavior. The main proponent of this view was B. F. Skinner (1953), whose theory of operant conditioning has had a tremendous impact on the entire field of psychology. Within an operant conditioning framework, reinforcement is defined as the process through which a behavior is made more likely to occur again, whereas punishment is defined as the process through which a behavior is made less likely to occur again. From this vantage point, adolescent behavior is nothing more or less than the product of the various reinforcements and punishments to which the individual has been exposed. An adolescent who strives to do well in school, for example, does so because in the past she or he has been reinforced for this behavior or has been punished for not behaving this way. Similarly, a teenager who continues to experiment with risky behavior is being reinforced for this sort of activity or punished for being especially cautious.

▌ **Social Learning Theory** A related approach is taken by social learning theorists such as Albert Bandura (Bandura & Walters, 1959). Social learning theorists also emphasize the ways in which adolescents learn how to behave, but in contrast to behaviorists, they place more weight on the processes of modeling and observational learning. According to these theorists, adolescents learn how to behave not simply by being reinforced and punished by forces in the environment but also by watching and imitating those around them. As is clear throughout the text, social learning approaches to adolescence have been very influential in explaining how adolescents are affected by the child-rearing methods employed by their parents and by the influence, or pressure, of their peers. From this vantage point, an adolescent who strives to do well in school or who takes a lot of risks is probably imitating peers, family members, or actors portrayed in the mass media.

SOCIOLOGICAL THEORIES

The emphasis of the biosocial, organismic, and learning theories is mainly on forces within the individual, or within the individual's specific environment, that shape development and behavior. In contrast, sociological theories of adolescence attempt to understand how adolescents, *as a group,* come of age in society. Instead of emphasizing differences among individuals in their biological makeups or their experiences in the world, sociological theorists focus on the factors that all adolescents or groups of adolescents have in common by virtue of their age, gender, ethnicity, social class, or some other demographic factor.

▌ **Adolescent Marginality** Sociological theories of adolescence often have focused on relations between the generations and have tended to emphasize the difficulties young people have in making the transition from adolescence to adulthood, especially in industrialized society. Two themes have dominated these discussions. One theme, concerning the marginality of young people, emphasizes the difference in power that exists between the adult and the adolescent generations. Two important thinkers in this vein are Kurt Lewin (1951) and Edgar Friedenberg (1959). Although the view that adolescents are "second-class citizens" was more influential 50 years ago than today, contemporary applications of this viewpoint stress the fact that many adolescents are prohibited from occupying meaningful roles in society and therefore experience frustration and restlessness. Some writers have noted that many of the problems we associate with adolescence have been created, in part, by the way in which we have structured the adolescent experience and isolated young people from adults (R. Epstein, 2007).

A modification of this view focuses on differences within the adolescent population. According to this viewpoint, the adolescent's social class, or socioeconomic status, as it is formally known, structures his or her experience of growing up. Theorists such as August Hollingshead (1949/1975) and Robert Havighurst (1952) have emphasized the fact that the experience of adolescence differs markedly as a function of the young person's family background. They argue that it is impossible to generalize about the "nature" of adolescence because it varies so much depending on the resources of the adolescent's family.

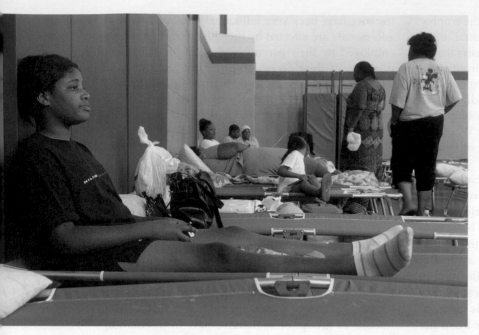

Dramatic historical events, such as a major hurricane, can transform the nature of adolescence.

▌ Intergenerational Conflict The other theme in sociological theories of adolescence concerns intergenerational conflict, or as it is more commonly known, the generation gap. Theorists such as Karl Mannheim (1952) and James Coleman (1961) stressed the fact that adolescents and adults grow up under different social circumstances and therefore develop different sets of attitudes, values, and beliefs. As a consequence, there is inevitable tension between the adolescent and the adult generations. Some writers, like Coleman, have gone so far as to argue that adolescents develop a different cultural viewpoint—a counterculture—that may be hostile to the values or beliefs of adult society. We'll look more closely at this idea in Chapter 5.

Although sociological theories of adolescence clearly place the emphasis on the broader context in which adolescents come of age, a theme of inevitability still runs through their approach. Mannheim, for example, believed that because modern society changes so rapidly, there will always be problems between generations, because each generation grows up with different experiences and beliefs. American adults who were teenagers in the late 1960s, for instance, when "sex, drugs, and rock 'n' roll" was the mantra, may find themselves arguing with their children, who may have come of age during a time of extreme political conservatism, such as the 1980s. Similarly, Lewin believed that marginality is an inherent feature of adolescence because adults always control more resources and have more power than young people.

HISTORICAL AND ANTHROPOLOGICAL THEORIES

Our final stop on the continuum takes us to the extreme environmental position. Historians and anthropologists who study adolescence share with sociologists an interest in the broader context in which young people come of age, but they take a much more relativistic stance. Historical perspectives, such as those offered by Glen Elder (1980), Joseph Kett (1977), and Thomas Hine (1999), stress the fact that adolescence as a developmental period has varied considerably from one historical era to another. As a consequence, it is impossible to generalize about such issues as the degree to which adolescence is stressful, the developmental tasks of the period, or the nature of intergenerational relations. Historians would say that these issues all depend on the social, political, and economic forces present at a given time. Even something as basic to our view of adolescence as the "identity crisis," they say, is a social invention that arose because of industrialization and the prolongation of schooling. Prior to the Industrial Revolution, when most adolescents followed in their parents' occupation, people didn't have "crises" over who they were or what they were going to do in life.

▌ Adolescence as an Invention One group of theorists has taken this viewpoint to its logical extreme, arguing that adolescence is *entirely* a social invention (Bakan, 1972). They believe that the way in which we divide the life cycle into stages—drawing a boundary between childhood and adolescence, for example—is nothing more than a reflection of the political, economic, and social circumstances in which we live. They point out that, although puberty has always been a feature of human development, it was not until the rise of compulsory education that we began treating adolescents as a special and distinct group. This suggests that social conditions, not biological givens, define the nature of adolescent development. We noted earlier that contemporary writers debate whether a new phase of life, "emerging adulthood," actually exists. Writers who believe that different stages of life are social inventions would say that if emerging adulthood does exist, it does so because society has made it so, not because people have really changed in any fundamental way.

▌ Anthropological Perspectives A similar theme is echoed by anthropologists who study adolescence, the most important of whom were Ruth Benedict (1934) and Margaret Mead (1928/1978). Benedict and Mead, whose work is examined in Chapter 3, pointed out that societies vary considerably in the ways in which they view and structure adolescence. As a consequence, these thinkers viewed adolescence as a culturally defined experience—stressful and difficult in societies that saw it this way, but calm and peaceful in societies that had an alternative vision. Benedict, in particular, drew a distinction between continuous and discontinuous societies. In continuous societies (typically, nonindustrialized societies with little social change), the transition from adolescence to adulthood is gradual and peaceful. In discontinuous societies (typically, industrialized societies characterized by rapid social change), the transition to adulthood is abrupt and difficult. In Chapter 3, we'll look at whether the nature of development differs for individuals in continuous versus discontinuous societies.

FOOD FOR THOUGHT

Some writers have argued that the stage of life we call adolescence is a social invention. What do they mean by this? Could you say this about other periods of development? Is infancy a social invention? Is middle age?

RECAP

- Theoretical perspectives on adolescence range from those that emphasize the role of biology to those that emphasize the role of the environment.
- Biosocial theorists view development in adolescence as the inevitable outcome of the physical changes of puberty. Hall believed that adolescence was necessarily a period of storm and stress.
- Organismic theorists like Freud, Erikson, and Piaget view development as the product of an interaction between biology and the environment. Freud and his followers emphasized the internal psychological conflicts brought on by puberty. Erikson viewed adolescence as a time of "identity crisis." Piaget emphasized the development of abstract thinking.
- Learning theorists like Skinner and Bandura view development in adolescence as the result of exposure to forces that reinforce, punish, or model particular behaviors.
- Sociological theorists focus more on the ways in which adolescents as a group, rather than as individuals, are treated by society. They emphasize differences between the adolescent and adult generations in power, attitudes, and values.

- Historical theorists focus on the ways in which adolescence differs during different periods. They emphasize the fact that adolescence is at least in part a social "invention," whose characteristics depend on the way in which young people are viewed at that point in time.
- Anthropological theorists emphasize the diversity of adolescent experiences across different cultures. Like historical theorists, they believe that the nature of adolescence is determined by the conditions under which people grow up.

Stereotypes Versus Scientific Study

One of the oldest debates in the study of adolescence is whether adolescence is an inherently stressful time for individuals. As we noted earlier, G. Stanley Hall, who is generally acknowledged as the father of the modern study of adolescence, likened adolescence to the turbulent, transitional period in the evolution of the human species from savagery into civilization. Long before Hall, in the 18th century, the French philosopher Jean-Jacques Rousseau had described adolescence by drawing an analogy to a violent storm. "As the roaring of the waves precedes the tempest, so the murmur of rising passions announces the tumultuous change. . . . Keep your hand upon the helm," he warned parents, "or all is lost" (Rousseau, 1762/1911, pp. 172–173).

Although neither Hall nor Rousseau had any scientific evidence that adolescence was any more stormy than childhood or adulthood, their portrayal of teenagers as passionate, troubled, and unpredictable persists today. One 12-year-old girl I was counseling told me that her mother had been telling her that she would go through a difficult time when she turned 14—as if some magical, internal alarm clock was set to trigger storm and stress on schedule.

The girl's mother wasn't alone in her view of adolescence, of course. Sometime this week, turn on the television or go to a movie and note how teenagers are depicted. If they are not portrayed as troublemakers—the usual role in which they are cast—adolescents are depicted as sex-crazed idiots (if they are male), giggling fools (if they are female), or tormented lost souls, searching for their place in a strange, cruel world (if they aren't delinquent, sex-crazed, or giggling). It's not only fictionalized portrayals of teenagers that are stereotyped—studies of local newscasts find that the majority of stories on youth are about violence (Dorfman, Woodruff, Chavez, & Wallack, 1997; Gilliam & Bales, 2001). Scholars, too, have been influenced by this viewpoint—a disproportionate number of scientific studies of adolescents have focused on young people's problems rather than their normative development (Steinberg & Morris, 2001).

Adolescents are one of the most stereotyped groups in contemporary society and, as a consequence, are one of the most misunderstood (Males, 1998). These stereotypes have important implications for how teenagers are treated—by teachers, by shopkeepers, and by parents. One study, for example, measured mothers' general beliefs about adolescence to see how well these preconceptions predicted how they raised their own teenager (C. Buchanan, 2003). The more likely a mother was to believe that teenagers are conforming, risk taking, and rebellious, the more likely she was to expect adolescence to be difficult for her own child—regardless of her own child's actual behavior. In contrast, the more likely a mother was to believe that adolescents as a group are kind and moral, the more likely she was to expect that she would have a positive relationship with her own child. This finding is important because, as you'll read in Chapter 4, parent–teenager relations are influenced by the expectations they have about each other. For example, one recent study found that mothers' beliefs about their teenagers' likely alcohol use may actually lead to increases in their child's drinking (Madon, Willard, Guyll, Trudeau, & Spoth, 2006).

The tremendous growth of the scientific literature on adolescence over the past two decades has, fortunately, led to more accurate views of normal adolescence among practitioners who work with young people (Stoller, Offer, Howard, & Koenig, 1996), although a trip to the "Parenting" section of your local bookstore will quickly reveal that the storm-and-stress stereotype is still alive and well (Steinberg, 2001). (I once saw a book titled *Surviving Your Dog's Adolescence*!) Today, most experts do not dismiss the storm-and-stress viewpoint as entirely incorrect but do see the difficulties that some adolescents have as due largely to the cultural context within which they grow up. Studies show that adolescents are more stressed in contemporary industrialized societies, for example, than they are in nonindustrialized, traditional ones, although this may change as globalization brings some of the more stressful aspects of adolescence to less industrialized parts of the world (Larson et al., 2009). Indeed, one of the most striking trends of the past several decades is that globalization has made adolescence in different parts of the world increasingly similar (National Research Council, 2005).

You have no doubt come into this course with many convictions of your own about adolescence. These beliefs are based in part on your own experiences as a teenager (C. Buchanan & Holmbeck, 1998) and in part on the images of adolescents to which you have been exposed over the years—on books, in film, and in television. As several writers have pointed out, even social scientists' portrayal of teenagers is influenced by the broader social and historical context in which they work. To the extent that we *want* to see adolescents as different from adults, we exaggerate the differences between teenagers and their elders and portray young people as "out of control due to hormonal storms" (Lesko, 1996, p. 157). During periods of economic downturn, for instance, when jobs are scarce, scholars depict adolescents as immature, unstable, and undereducated, whereas during periods of war, the same age group is portrayed as mature, responsible, and competent (Enright, Levy, Harris, & Lapsley, 1987). Presumably, these characterizations serve a broader, if hidden, agenda—during depressions, there are fewer jobs to go around, and adults may "need" to see adolescents as incapable of working, whereas the reverse is true during wartime, when adolescents are needed to take on jobs and serve in the military.

The truth of the matter is that most characteristics of adolescence as a developmental stage have both positive and negative elements (A. Siegel & Scovill, 2000). Young people's willingness to challenge authority, for instance, is both refreshing (when we agree with them) and bothersome (when we do not). Their propensity to take risks is both admirable and frightening. Their energy and exuberance is both exciting and dangerous.

In many respects, then, whatever "story" adult society tells about adolescence at any given moment is one that portrays young people in a way that best serves the needs of adults. Adolescent "irresponsibility" is cast in a favorable light by advertisers trying to sell soft drinks (e.g., our product will make you as carefree and fun loving as a teenager), but in a negative light in order to justify policies like mandating community service for high school students or spending money to build more juvenile detention facilities. Today's calls for treating youthful offenders as adults—"adult time for adult crime"—have more to do with politicians' desires to take advantage of public concerns about crime than with any real changes that have taken place in young people themselves (E. Scott & Steinberg, 2008).

Sadly, recent public opinion polls indicate that American adults today view adolescents very negatively, describing them as rude, irresponsible, wild, and disrespectful (Public Agenda, 1999). Part of this is due, no doubt, to the overly negative picture of adolescents presented in the contemporary mass media, which exaggerates the prevalence of adolescents' involvement in crime, drug use, promiscuous sex, and various forms of risk taking (Males, 1998). Unfortunately, there are signs that as globalization has spread these images beyond America, stereotypes of adolescents have become more negative around the world (Larson et al., 2009). There is even an obscure word for the irrational fear of adolescents: **ephebephobia!**

One of the goals of this book is to provide you with a more realistic understanding of adolescent development in contemporary society—an understanding that reflects the best and most up-to-date scientific knowledge. As you read the material, you should think about your personal experiences as an adolescent, but you should also try to look beyond them and be willing to question the "truths" about teenagers that you have grown accustomed to over the years. This does not mean that your experiences were not valid, or your recollections inaccurate. Rather, your experiences as a teenager were the product of a unique set of forces that have made you the individual you are today. The person who sits next to you in class—or the person who right now, in some distant region of the world, is thinking back to his or her adolescence—was probably exposed to different forces than you were and probably had a different set of adolescent experiences as a consequence.

FOOD FOR THOUGHT

If adolescence is not inevitably a period of storm and stress, why is it so often portrayed this way?

RECAP

- Adolescents are one of the most stereotyped groups in society.
- Many stereotypes about adolescence are excessively negative, portraying teenagers as sex-crazed, foolish, irresponsible, difficult, or troubled.
- The scientific study of adolescence has not provided evidence in support of these stereotypes.
- One goal of this book is to foster an objective understanding of adolescence that is grounded in solid research and theory.

ephebephobia   The irrational fear of adolescents.

The Fundamental Changes of Adolescence

Biological Transitions

According to an old joke, there are only two things in life that one can be sure of—death and taxes. To this brief list, we might add puberty—the physical changes of adolescence—for, of all the developments that take place during the second decade of life, the only truly inevitable one is physical maturation. Not all adolescents experience identity crises, rebel against their parents, or fall madly in love, but virtually all undergo the biological transitions associated with maturation into adult reproductive capability.

Puberty, however, is considerably affected by the context in which it occurs. Physical development is influenced by a host of environmental factors, and the timing and rate of pubertal growth vary across regions of the world, socioeconomic classes, ethnic groups, and historical eras. Today, in contemporary America, the average girl reaches **menarche**—the time of first menstruation—at about age 12½. But among the Lumi people of New Guinea, the typical girl does not reach menarche until after 18 years of age (Eveleth & Tanner, 1990). Imagine how that five-year difference transforms the nature of adolescence. Picture how different high school would be if sexual maturation did not occur until after graduation!

Physical and sexual maturation profoundly affects the ways in which adolescents view themselves and are viewed and treated by others. Yet the social environment exerts a tremendous impact on puberty and its psychological and social consequences; indeed, as you will read in this chapter, the social environment even affects the timing of puberty (that is, whether a person matures early or late). In some societies, pubertal maturation brings with it a series of complex and public initiation rites that mark the passage of the young person into adulthood, socially as well as physically. In other societies, recognition of the physical transformation from child into adult takes more subtle forms. Parents may merely remark, "Our little boy has become a man," when they discover that he needs to shave, or "Our little girl has grown up," when they learn that she has gotten her first period. Early or late maturation may be cause for celebration or cause for concern, depending on what is admired or derogated in a given peer group at a given point in time. The fifth-grader who is developing breasts might be embarrassed, but the ninth-grader who has not developed breasts might be equally self-conscious.

In sum, even the most universal aspect of adolescence—puberty—is hardly universal in its impact on the young person. In this chapter, we examine just how and why the environment in which adolescents develop exerts its influence even on something as fundamental as puberty.

Puberty: An Overview

Puberty derives from the Latin word *pubertas,* which means "adult." Technically, the term refers to the period during which an individual becomes capable of sexual reproduction. More broadly, however, puberty encompasses all the physical changes that occur in the growing girl or boy as the individual passes from childhood into adulthood.

Puberty has three chief physical manifestations:

1. a rapid acceleration in growth, resulting in dramatic increases in both height and weight;
2. the development of primary sex characteristics, including the further development of the gonads (sex glands), which results in hormonal changes that ultimately enable reproduction; and
3. the development of secondary sex characteristics, including changes in the genitals and breasts, and the growth of pubic, facial, and body hair.

Each of these sets of changes is the result of developments in the endocrine and central nervous systems, many of which begin years before the external signs of puberty are evident—some occur even before birth. Puberty may appear to come on suddenly, judging from its external signs, but in fact it is part of a gradual process that begins at conception (Susman & Dorn, 2009). You may be surprised to learn that no new hormones are produced and no new bodily systems develop at puberty. Rather, some hormones that have been present since before birth increase, and others decrease.

THE ENDOCRINE SYSTEM

The **endocrine system** produces, circulates, and regulates levels of hormones in the body. **Hormones** are

---

menarche   The time of first menstruation, one of the most important changes to occur among females during puberty.

endocrine system   The system of the body that produces, circulates, and regulates hormones.

hormones   Highly specialized substances secreted by one or more endocrine glands.

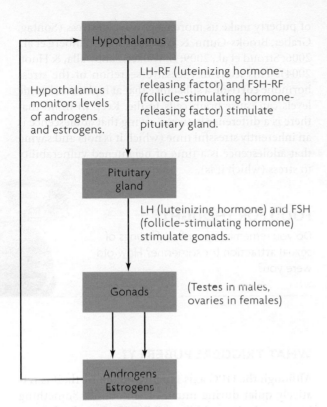

FIGURE 1.1 Levels of sex hormones are regulated by a feedback system (the HPG axis) composed of the hypothalamus, pituitary gland, and gonads. (Grumbach et al., 1974)

highly specialized substances that are secreted by one or more endocrine glands and then enter the bloodstream and travel throughout the body. **Glands** are organs that stimulate particular parts of the body to respond in specific ways. Just as specialized hormones carry "messages" to particular cells in the body, so are the body's cells designed to receive hormonal messages selectively. Many of the hormones that play important roles at puberty carry their instructions by activating very specific types of neurons in the brain, called **gonadotropin-releasing hormone (GnRH) neurons** (Sisk & Foster, 2004).

■ **The Hormonal Feedback Loop** The endocrine system receives its instructions to increase or decrease circulating levels of particular hormones from the central nervous system, mainly through the firing of GnRH neurons in the brain. The system works like a thermostat. Hormonal levels are "set" at a certain point, which may differ depending on the stage of development, just as you might set a thermostat at a certain temperature (and use different settings during different seasons or different times of the day). By setting your room's thermostat at 60°F, you are instructing your heating system to go into action when the

temperature falls below this level. Similarly, when a particular hormonal level in your body dips below the endocrine system's **set point** for that hormone, secretion of the hormone increases; when the level reaches the set point, secretion temporarily stops. And, as is the case with a thermostat, the setting level, or set point, for a particular hormone can be adjusted up or down, depending on environmental or internal bodily conditions.

Such a **feedback loop** becomes increasingly important at the onset of puberty. Long before early adolescence—in fact, before birth—a feedback loop develops involving the **pituitary gland** (which controls hormone levels in general), the **hypothalamus** (the part of the brain that controls the pituitary gland, and where there is a concentration of GnRH neurons), and the **gonads** (in males, the **testes**; in females, the **ovaries**), which release the "sex" hormones—**androgens** and **estrogens**. This feedback loop is known as the **HPG axis** (for Hypothalamus, Pituitary, Gonads) (see Figure 1.1). Although you may think of androgens as "male" hormones and estrogens as "female" hormones, both

glands Organs that stimulate particular parts of the body to respond in specific ways to particular hormones.

gonadotropin-releasing hormone (GnRH) neurons Specialized neurons that are activated by certain pubertal hormones.

set point A physiological level or setting (e.g., of a specific hormone) that the body attempts to maintain through a self-regulating system.

feedback loop A cycle through which two or more bodily functions respond to and regulate each other, such as that formed by the hypothalamus, the pituitary gland, and the gonads.

pituitary gland One of the chief glands responsible for regulating levels of hormones in the body.

hypothalamus A part of the brain that controls the functioning of the pituitary gland.

gonads The glands that secrete sex hormones: in males, the testes; in females, the ovaries.

testes The male gonads.

ovaries The female gonads.

androgens A class of sex hormones secreted by the gonads, found in both sexes, but in higher levels among males than females following puberty.

estrogens A class of sex hormones secreted by the gonads, found in both sexes, but in higher levels among females than males following puberty.

HPG (hypothalamic-pituitary-gonadal) axis The neurophysiological pathway that involves the hypothalamus, the pituitary gland, and the gonads.

types of hormones are produced by each sex, and both are present in males and females at birth. During adolescence, however, the average male produces more androgens than estrogens, and the average female produces more estrogens than androgens (Susman & Dorn, 2009).

The hypothalamus responds to the levels of sex hormones circulating in the body. Your HPG axis is set to maintain certain levels of androgens and estrogens. When these levels fall below the set points, the hypothalamus no longer inhibits the pituitary, thus permitting it to stimulate the release of sex hormones by the gonads, and other puberty-related hormones by the adrenal gland. When sex hormone levels reach the set point, the hypothalamus responds by inhibiting its stimulation of the pituitary gland. As you will see, puberty occurs when it does because several different signals—genetic as well as environmental—instruct the brain to change the set point (Sisk & Foster, 2004). Just as you might change the setting on your heating thermostat automatically every November 1, or when your utility bill has become too expensive, your brain is constantly monitoring a variety of signals and adjusting your hormonal set points in response.

■ **Adrenarche**   During and just before puberty, the pituitary also secretes hormones that act on the thyroid and on the adrenal cortex as well as hormones that stimulate overall bodily growth. The release of these substances is also under the control of the hypothalamus. The thyroid and adrenal cortex, in turn, secrete hormones that cause various bodily changes to take place at puberty. Research also indicates that early feelings of sexual attraction to others—most individuals, in America and around the world, report that their first sexual attraction took place at the "magical age of 10," before they went through puberty—may be stimulated by maturation of the adrenal glands, called **adrenarche** (Herdt & McClintock, 2000). Changes at puberty in the brain system that regulates the adrenal gland are also important because this is the brain system that controls how we respond to stress (Del Giudice, Angeleri, & Manera, 2009). One reason adolescence is a period of great vulnerability for the onset of many serious mental disorders is that the hormonal changes

of puberty make us more responsive to stress (Sontag, Graber, Brooks-Gunn, & Warren, 2008; Steinberg et al., 2006; Stroud et al., 2009; E. Walker, Sabuwalla, & Huot, 2004). This leads to excessive secretion of the stress hormone **cortisol,** a substance that at high and chronic levels can cause brain cells to die. Keep in mind that there is a difference between saying that adolescence is an inherently stressful time (which it is not) and saying that adolescence is a time of heightened vulnerability to stress (which it is).

FOOD FOR THOUGHT

Do you remember your first feelings of sexual attraction for someone? How old were you?

WHAT TRIGGERS PUBERTY?

Although the HPG axis is active before birth, it is relatively quiet during much of childhood. Something happens during middle childhood, though, that reawakens the HPG axis and signals it that the body is ready for puberty. Some of this is due to a clock whose "puberty alarm" is set very early in life by information coded in the genes (as you will read, the age at which someone goes through puberty is largely inherited). But some of the reawakening of the HPG axis at puberty is due to multiple signals that tell the brain it is time to "get the childbearing show on the road." These signals indicate whether there are sexually mature mating partners in the environment, whether there are sufficient nutritional resources to support a pregnancy, and whether the individual is physically mature and healthy enough to begin reproducing.

For example, some evidence suggests that rising levels of a protein produced by fat cells, **leptin,** may be the most important signal, at least in females (Susman & Dorn, 2009). This idea is consistent with observations that individuals may not go through puberty until they have accumulated a certain amount of body fat. Research also shows that stress, illness, nutritional deficiencies, excessive exercise, and excessive thinness can all delay the onset of puberty (Susman & Dorn, 2009). The signal carried by rising levels of leptin instructs the hypothalamus to stop doing things that have been inhibiting puberty (Sisk & Foster, 2004). As a result of these genetic and signaling processes, the GnRH neurons are excited, and the hypothalamus initiates a cascade of hormonal events that ultimately results in sexual maturation.

adrenarche   The maturation of the adrenal glands that takes place during adolescence.

cortisol   A hormone produced when a person is exposed to stress.

leptin   A protein produced by the fat cells that may play a role in the onset of puberty.

Excessive exercise can delay the onset of puberty among girls.

HOW HORMONES INFLUENCE ADOLESCENT DEVELOPMENT

Hormones play two very different roles in adolescent development: an **organizational role** and an **activational role** (Coe, Hayashi, & Levine, 1988). Most people understandably think that changes in behavior at puberty result from changes in hormones that occur at that time. But this is only partially correct. Long before adolescence—in fact, before birth—hormones shape, or *organize*, the brain in ways that may not be manifested in behavior until childhood or even adolescence. Generally, until about eight weeks after conception, the human brain is "feminine" unless and until it is exposed to certain "masculinizing" hormones, like testosterone. Because levels of testosterone are higher among males than females while the brain is developing, males usually end up with a more "masculinized" brain than females. This sex difference in brain organization predetermines certain patterns of behavior, many of which may not actually appear until much later (Collaer & Hines, 1995). Studies of sex differences in aggression, for example, show that even though some of these differences may not appear until

adolescence, they likely result from the impact of prenatal hormones, rather than from hormonal changes at puberty.

In other words, the presence or absence of certain hormones early in life may "program" the brain and the central nervous system to develop in certain ways and according to a certain timetable later on (Sisk & Foster, 2004). Because we may not see the resulting changes in behavior until adolescence, it is easy to conclude, mistakenly, that the behaviors result from hormonal changes that take place at the time of puberty. In reality, however, exposure to certain hormones before birth may set a sort of alarm clock that does not go off until adolescence. Just because the alarm clock rings at the same time that puberty begins does not mean that puberty *caused* the alarm to go off.

Many changes in behavior at adolescence occur, however, because of changes in hormone levels at puberty; these hormonal changes are said to *activate* the changes in behavior. For instance, the increase in certain hormones at puberty is thought to stimulate the development of secondary sex characteristics, such as the growth of pubic hair. Other hormonal changes at adolescence, controlled by the adrenal gland, may stimulate an increase in individuals' sex drive (McClintock & Herdt, 1996).

Still other changes during puberty are likely to be results of an *interaction* between organizational and activational effects of hormones (Collaer & Hines, 1995). Hormones that are present during the development of the fetus may organize a certain set of behaviors (for example, our brains may be set up to have us later engage in sexual behavior), but certain changes in those hormones at puberty may be needed to activate the pattern; that is, individuals may not become motivated to engage in sex until puberty.

RECAP

- Puberty has three main physical manifestations: a rapid acceleration in growth, the development of primary sex characteristics, and the development of secondary sex characteristics.
- Puberty is regulated by a hormonal feedback loop that includes the hypothalamus, the pituitary gland, and the gonads.

organizational role (of hormones)   The process through which early exposure to hormones, especially prenatally, organizes the brain or other organs in anticipation of later changes in behavior or patterns of growth.

activational role (of hormones)   The process through which changes in hormone levels, especially at puberty, stimulate changes in the adolescent's behavior, appearance, or growth.

- Many important changes at puberty involve a process called adrenarche, which involves the regulation of the adrenal gland rather than the gonads.
- The onset of puberty is triggered by several factors, including a biological "alarm" that is coded in the individual's genes and various environmental signals, which let the body know that it is ready to begin reproduction.
- Physical and behavioral changes at puberty result from two different hormonal processes: organizational, which take place long before adolescence, and activational, which result from changes in hormones when puberty takes place.

Somatic Development

The effects of the hormonal changes of puberty on the adolescent's body are remarkable. Consider the dramatic changes in physical appearance that occur during early adolescence. The individual enters puberty looking like a child but within four years or so has the physical appearance of a young adult. During this relatively brief period, the average individual grows about 10 inches taller, matures sexually, and develops an adult-proportioned body. Along with many other organs, the brain changes in size, structure, and function at puberty, a series of developments we'll discuss in Chapter 2.

CHANGES IN STATURE AND THE DIMENSIONS OF THE BODY

▌ **The Adolescent Growth Spurt** The simultaneous release of growth hormones, thyroid hormones, and androgens stimulates rapid acceleration in height and weight. This dramatic increase in stature is referred to as the **adolescent growth spurt.** What is most incredible about the adolescent growth spurt is not so much the absolute gain of height and weight that typically occurs but the speed with which the increases take place.

adolescent growth spurt   The dramatic increase in height and weight that occurs during puberty.

peak height velocity   The point at which the adolescent is growing most rapidly.

epiphysis   The closing of the ends of the bones, which terminates growth after the adolescent growth spurt has been completed.

Think for a moment of how quickly very young children grow. At the time of **peak height velocity**—the time at which the adolescent is growing most rapidly—he or she is growing at the same rate as a toddler. For boys, peak height velocity averages about 4 inches (10.3 centimeters) per year; for girls, it's about 3.5 inches (9.0 centimeters). One marker of the conclusion of puberty is the closing of the ends of the long bones in the body, a process called **epiphysis,** which terminates growth in height. Puberty is also a time of significant increase in weight—nearly half of one's adult body weight is gained during adolescence (Susman & Dorn, 2009).

Figure 1.2 shows just how remarkable the growth spurt is in terms of height. The graph on the left shows changes in absolute height and indicates, as you would expect, that the average individual grows throughout infancy, childhood, and adolescence. As you can see, there is little gain in height after age 18. But look now at the right-hand graph, which shows the average increase in height per year (i.e., the *rate* of change) over the same age span. Here you can see the acceleration in height at the time of peak height velocity.

Figure 1.2 also indicates that the growth spurt occurs, on average, about two years earlier among girls than boys. In general, as you can see by comparing the two graphs, boys tend to be somewhat taller than girls before age 11; then girls tend to be taller than boys between ages 11 and 13; and finally, boys tend to be taller than girls from about age 14 on. You may remember what this was like during the fifth and sixth grades. Sex differences in height can be a concern for many young adolescents when they begin socializing with members of the opposite sex, especially if they are tall, early-maturing girls or short, late-maturing boys.

FOOD FOR THOUGHT

Think back to a time when the girls in your elementary school class tended to be taller than the boys. What impact, if any, did this have on social relationships?

Much of the height gain during puberty results from an increase in torso length rather than in leg length. The sequence in which various parts of the body grow is fairly regular. Extremities—the head, hands, and feet—are the first to accelerate in growth. Then accelerated growth occurs in the arms and legs, followed by torso and shoulder growth. As one classic article put it, "A boy stops growing out of his trousers (at least in length) a year before he stops growing out of his jackets" (J. Tanner, 1972, p. 5).

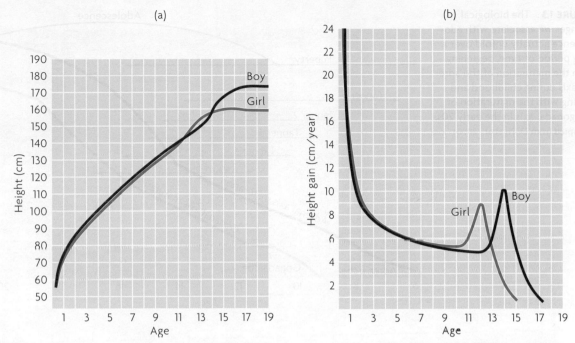

FIGURE 1.2 (a) Height (in centimeters) at different ages for the average male and female youngster. (b) Gain in height per year (in centimeters) for the average male and female youngster. Note the adolescent growth spurt. (Adapted from Marshall, 1978)

Young adolescents often appear to be out of proportion physically—as though their nose or legs were growing faster than the rest of them. This is because different parts of the body do not all grow at the same rate or at the same time during puberty. This can lead to an appearance of awkwardness or gawkiness in the young adolescent, who may be embarrassed by the disproportionate growth of different body parts. It is probably little consolation for the young adolescent going through the awkward phase to be told that an attractive balance probably will be restored within a few years, but fortunately, this is what usually happens.

■ **Sex Differences in Muscle and Fat** The spurt in height during adolescence is accompanied by an increase in weight that results from an increase in both muscle and fat, but there are important sex differences in body composition. Before puberty, there are relatively few sex differences in muscle development and only slight sex differences in body fat. In both sexes, muscular development is rapid during puberty, but muscle tissue grows faster in boys than girls. In contrast, body fat increases for both sexes during puberty, but more so for females than for males, especially during the years just before puberty. For boys, there is actually a slight decline in body fat just before puberty. The end result of these sex differences is that boys finish adolescence with a muscle-to-fat ratio of about 3 to 1, but the comparable ratio for girls is approximately 5 to

4. This has important implications for understanding why sex differences in strength and athletic ability often appear for the first time during adolescence. According to one estimate, about half of the sex difference in athletic performance during early adolescence results simply from the difference in body fat (Smoll & Schutz, 1990).

It is tempting to attribute sex differences in athletic performance purely to changes in body fat and to hormonal factors, because androgens, which increase during puberty in males at a much faster rate than in females, are closely linked to growth in aspects of the body that influence athletic ability. But with age, environmental factors like diet and exercise become increasingly important influences on sex differences in physical performance (Smoll & Schutz, 1990). There are strong social pressures on girls to curtail "masculine" activities—including some forms of exercise—at adolescence, and studies show that girls are more likely than boys to markedly reduce their physical activity in preadolescence, with a very large proportion of adolescent girls failing to meet national guidelines for exercise (Goran et al., 1998; Savage & Scott, 1998). Moreover, adolescent girls' diets, especially those of Black girls, are generally less adequate nutritionally than the diets of boys, particularly in important minerals like iron (R. Johnson, Johnson, Wang, Smiciklas-Wright, & Guthrie, 1994). Both factors could result in sex differences in exercise tolerance. In other words, sex differences in physical

FIGURE 1.3 The biological changes we associate with adolescence actually unfold over a long period of time, beginning with the maturation of the adrenal axis during childhood and ending with the maturation of the gonadal axis in the early 20s. (Adapted from Dorn et al., 2006)

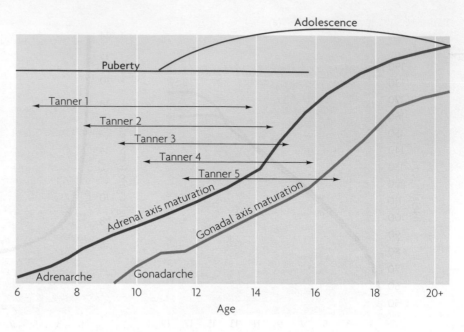

ability are influenced by a variety of factors, of which hormonal differences are but one part of a complex picture.

Body Dissatisfaction Among Adolescent Girls

The rapid increase in body fat that occurs among females in early adolescence frequently prompts young girls to become overly concerned about their weight—even when their weight is within the normal range for their height and age (Smolak, Levine, & Gralen, 1993). Although the majority of girls diet unnecessarily during this time in response to the increase in body fat, the girls who are most susceptible to feelings of dissatisfaction with their bodies during this phase of development are those who mature early, begin dating early, and come from relatively more affluent families (Smolak et al., 1993). Girls who spend a lot of time talking about their looks with their friends are especially vulnerable to feelings of body dissatisfaction. In fact, for girls, it is comparing themselves with their friends, and not just being exposed to media portrayals of thinness, that leads to dissatisfaction (Carlson Jones, 2004). In contrast, boys' feelings about how they look revolve around how muscular they are and do not seem to be affected by comparisons with peers.

There are also important ethnic differences in the ways in which adolescent girls feel about their changing bodies (Yates, Edman, & Aruguete, 2004). Black adoles-

cents seem less vulnerable to these feelings of body dissatisfaction than other girls (Nishina, Ammon, Bellmore, & Graham, 2006), and consequently they are less likely to diet, presumably because of ethnic differences in conceptions of the ideal body type. Even among Black girls, however, dieting is common in early adolescence (Halpern & Udry, 1994). As you will read later in this chapter, many studies point to adolescence as the period of greatest risk for the development of eating disorders such as anorexia and bulimia.

FOOD FOR THOUGHT

Given the nature of sex differences in the physical changes of puberty, is body dissatisfaction inevitable among adolescent girls? Can anything be done to make young women feel better about their appearance?

SEXUAL MATURATION

Puberty brings with it a series of developments associated with sexual maturation. In both boys and girls, the development of the **secondary sex characteristics** is typically divided into five stages, often called **Tanner stages,** after the British pediatrician who devised the categorization system. Figure 1.3 shows the relative timing of the somatic and hormonal changes of puberty.

Sexual Maturation in Boys

The sequence of developments in secondary sex characteristics among

secondary sex characteristics The manifestations of sexual maturity at puberty, including the development of breasts, the growth of facial and body hair, and changes in the voice.

Tanner stages A widely used system that describes the five stages of pubertal development.

TABLE 1.1   The sequence of physical changes at puberty

Boys		Girls	
Characteristic	Age of First Appearance (Years)	Characteristic	Age of First Appearance (Years)
1. Growth of testes, scrotal sac	10–13½	1. Growth of breasts	7–13
2. Growth of pubic hair	10–15	2. Growth of pubic hair	7–14
3. Body growth	10½–16	3. Body growth	9½–14½
4. Growth of penis	11–14½	4. Menarche	10–16½
5. Change in voice (growth of larynx)	About same time as penis growth	5. Underarm hair	About two years after pubic hair
6. Facial and underarm hair	About two years after pubic hair appears	6. Oil- and sweat-producing glands	About same time as underarm hair
7. Oil- and sweat-producing glands, acne	About same time as underarm hair		

Source: B. Goldstein, 1976.

boys is fairly orderly (see Table 1.1). Generally, the first stages of puberty involve growth of the testes and scrotum, accompanied by the first appearance of pubic hair. Approximately one year later, the growth spurt in height begins, accompanied by growth of the penis and further development of pubic hair—now of a coarser texture and darker color. The five Tanner stages of penis and pubic hair growth in boys are shown in Figure 1.4.

The emergence of facial and body hair are relatively late developments. The same is true for the deepening of the voice, which is gradual and generally does not occur until very late adolescence. During puberty, there are changes in the skin as well. The skin becomes rougher, especially around the upper arms and thighs, and there is increased development of the sweat glands, which often gives rise to acne, pimples, and increased oiliness of the skin.

During puberty, there are slight changes in the male breast—to the embarrassment of many boys. Breast development is largely influenced by the estrogen hormones. As noted earlier, both estrogens and androgens are present in both sexes and increase in both sexes at puberty, although in differing amounts. In the male adolescent, the areola (the area around the nipple) increases in size, and the nipple becomes more prominent. Some boys show a slight enlargement of the breast, although in the majority of cases this is temporary.

Other, internal changes occur that are important elements of sexual maturation. At the time that the penis develops, the seminal vesicles, the prostate, and the bulbourethral glands also enlarge and develop. The first ejaculation of seminal fluid generally occurs

about one year after the beginning of accelerated penis growth, although this is often determined culturally rather than biologically, since for many boys first ejaculation occurs as a result of masturbation (J. Tanner, 1972). One interesting observation about the timing and sequence of pubertal changes in boys is that boys are generally fertile (i.e., capable of fathering a child) before they have developed an adultlike appearance. As you will read in the next section, the opposite is true for girls.

Sexual Maturation in Girls   The sequence of development of secondary sex characteristics among girls (shown in Table 1.1) is less regular than it is among boys. Generally, the first sign of sexual maturation in girls is the elevation of the breast—the emergence of the so-called breast bud. In about one-third of all adolescent girls, however, the appearance of pubic hair precedes breast development. The development of pubic hair in females follows a sequence similar to that in males—generally, from sparse, downy, light-colored hair to denser, curlier, coarser, darker hair. Breast development often occurs concurrently and generally proceeds through several stages. In the bud stage, the areola widens, and the breast and nipple are elevated as a small mound. In the middle stages, the areola and nipple become distinct from the breast and project beyond the breast contour. In the final stages, the areola is recessed to the contour of the breast, and only the nipple is elevated. The female breast undergoes these changes at puberty regardless of changes in breast size. For this reason, changes in the shape and definition of the areola and nipple are far better indicators of sexual

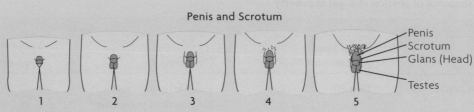

Penis and Scrotum

—Penis
—Scrotum
—Glans (Head)
—Testes

1   2   3   4   5

Stage 1:   The infantile state that persists from birth until puberty begins. During this time the genitalia increase slightly in overall size but there is little change in general appearance.

Stage 2:   The scrotum has begun to enlarge, and there is some reddening and change in texture of the scrotal skin.

Stage 3:   The penis has increased in length and there is a smaller increase in breadth. There has been further growth of the scrotum.

Stage 4:   The length and breadth of the penis have increased further and the glans has developed. The scrotum is further enlarged and the scrotal skin has become darker.

Stage 5:   The genitalia are adult in size and shape. The appearance of the genitalia may satisfy the criteria for one of these stages for a considerable time before the penis and scrotum are sufficiently developed to be classified as belonging to the next stage.

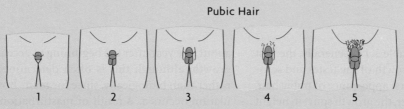

Pubic Hair

1   2   3   4   5

Stage 1:   There is no true pubic hair, although there may be a fine velus over the pubes similar to that over other parts of the abdomen.

Stage 2:   Sparse growth of lightly pigmented hair, which is usually straight or only slightly curled. This usually begins at either side of the base of the penis.

Stage 3:   The hair spreads over the pubic symphysis and is considerably darker and coarser and usually more curled.

Stage 4:   The hair is now adult in character but covers an area considerably smaller than in most adults. There is no spread to the medial surface of the thighs.

Stage 5:   The hair is distributed in an inverse triangle as in the female. It has spread to the medial surface of the thighs but not elsewhere above the base of the triangle.

FIGURE 1.4   **The five pubertal stages for penile and pubic hair growth.** (From Morris & Udry, 1980)

maturation among adolescent girls than is breast growth alone. The five Tanner stages of breast and pubic hair growth in girls are shown in Figure 1.5.

As is the case for boys, puberty brings important internal changes for adolescent girls that are associated with the development of reproductive capacity. In girls, these changes involve development and growth of the uterus, vagina, and other aspects of the reproductive system. In addition, there is enlargement of the labia and clitoris.

As is apparent in Table 1.1, the growth spurt is likely to occur during the early and middle stages of breast and pubic hair development. Menarche, the beginning of menstruation, is a relatively late development that reflects the culmination of a long series of hormonal changes

(Dorn et al., 1999). Generally, full reproductive function does not occur until several years after menarche, and regular ovulation follows menarche by about two years (Hafetz, 1976). Unlike boys, therefore, girls generally appear physically mature before they are fertile.

FOOD FOR THOUGHT

Think about the changes in secondary sex characteristics that take place at puberty in humans. Why might we have evolved so that puberty occurs outside as well as inside the body?

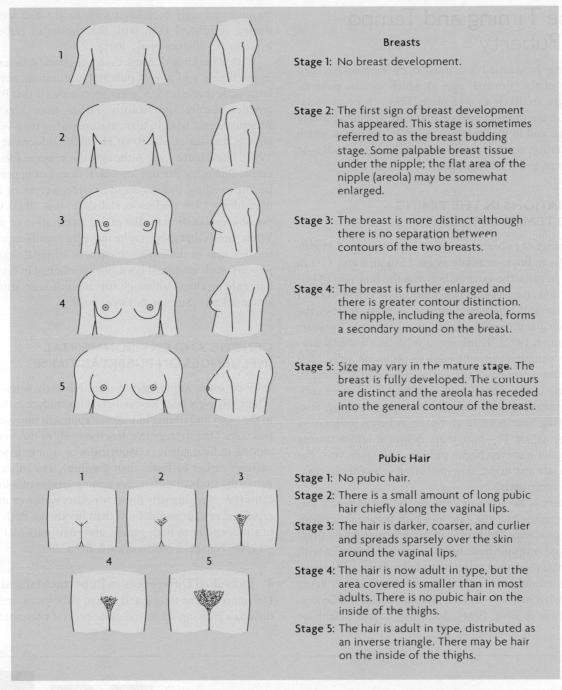

Breasts

Stage 1: No breast development.

Stage 2: The first sign of breast development has appeared. This stage is sometimes referred to as the breast budding stage. Some palpable breast tissue under the nipple; the flat area of the nipple (areola) may be somewhat enlarged.

Stage 3: The breast is more distinct although there is no separation between contours of the two breasts.

Stage 4: The breast is further enlarged and there is greater contour distinction. The nipple, including the areola, forms a secondary mound on the breast.

Stage 5: Size may vary in the mature stage. The breast is fully developed. The contours are distinct and the areola has receded into the general contour of the breast.

Pubic Hair

Stage 1: No pubic hair.

Stage 2: There is a small amount of long pubic hair chiefly along the vaginal lips.

Stage 3: The hair is darker, coarser, and curlier and spreads sparsely over the skin around the vaginal lips.

Stage 4: The hair is now adult in type, but the area covered is smaller than in most adults. There is no pubic hair on the inside of the thighs.

Stage 5: The hair is adult in type, distributed as an inverse triangle. There may be hair on the inside of the thighs.

FIGURE 1.5   The five pubertal stages for breast and pubic hair growth. (From Marshall & Tanner, 1969)

RECAP

- The adolescent growth spurt, which takes place about two years earlier among girls than boys, involves a rapid increase in height and weight.
- Puberty brings with it changes in ratio of muscle to fat, with marked gender differences in the way in which body composition changes. The increase in fat, which is greater among females than males, is a source of concern to many girls.
- Sexual maturation in both sexes is measured according to Tanner stages, which are used to chart the development of secondary sex characteristics.

The Timing and Tempo of Puberty

You may have noted that, thus far, no mention has been made of the "normal" ages at which various pubertal changes are likely to take place. This is because variations in the timing of puberty (the age at which puberty begins) and in the tempo of puberty (the rate at which maturation occurs) are so great that it is misleading to talk even about average ages.

VARIATIONS IN THE TIMING AND TEMPO OF PUBERTY

The onset of puberty can occur as early as age 7 in girls and 9½ in boys, or as late as age 13 in girls and 13½ in boys. In girls, the interval between the first sign of puberty and complete physical maturation can be as short as a year and a half or as long as six years. In boys, the comparable interval ranges from about two to five years (J. Tanner, 1972). Think about it: Within a totally normal population of young adolescents, some individuals will have completed the entire sequence of pubertal changes before others have even begun. In more concrete terms, it is possible for an early-maturing, fast-maturing youngster to complete pubertal maturation by age 10 or 11—two years before a late-maturing youngster has even begun puberty, and seven years before a late-maturing, slow-maturing youngster has matured completely!

There is no relation between the age at which puberty begins and the rate at which pubertal development proceeds. The timing of puberty may have a small effect on one's ultimate height or weight, however, with late maturers, on average, being taller than early maturers as adults, and early maturers, on average, being somewhat heavier—at least among females (St. George, Williams, & Silva, 1994). Adult height and weight are far more strongly correlated with height and weight during childhood than with the timing of puberty, however (Pietiläinen et al., 2001).

Within the United States, there are ethnic differences in the timing and rate of pubertal maturation. Several large-scale studies of U.S. youngsters indicate that Black females mature significantly earlier than Mexican American girls, who, in turn, mature earlier than White girls (Chumlea et al., 2003; Herman-Giddens et al., 1997) (see Figure 1.6). Although the reasons for this ethnic difference are not known, it does not appear to be due to ethnic differences in income, weight, or area of residence (S. E. Anderson, Dallal, & Must, 2003). One possible explanation for the earlier maturation of non-White girls is that they may be more frequently exposed to chemicals in the environment that stimulate earlier puberty, such as animal hormones contained in certain hair care products, although this has not been studied systematically (Susman & Dorn, 2009).

GENETIC AND ENVIRONMENTAL INFLUENCES ON PUBERTAL TIMING

Why do some individuals mature relatively early and others relatively late? Researchers who study variability in the onset and timing of puberty approach the issue in two ways. One strategy involves the study of differences among individuals (i.e., studying why one individual matures earlier or faster than another). The other involves the study of differences among groups of adolescents (i.e., studying why puberty occurs earlier or more rapidly in certain populations than in others). Both sets of studies point to both genetic and environmental factors (Ge, Natsuaki, Neiderhiser, & Reiss, 2007).

■ **Individual Differences in Pubertal Maturation** Differences in the timing and rate of puberty among individuals growing up in the same general environment

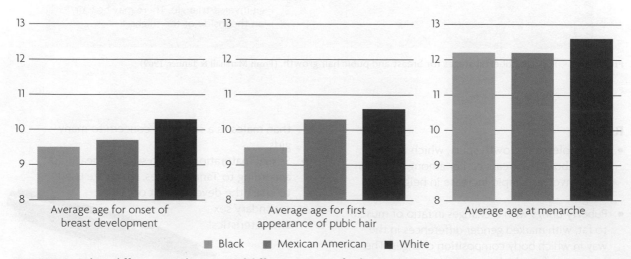

FIGURE 1.6   Ethnic differences in the timing of different aspects of puberty. (From Wu, Mendola, & Buck, 2002)

result chiefly, but not exclusively, from genetic factors. Comparisons between individuals who are genetically identical (identical twins) and individuals who are not indicate that the timing and tempo of an individual's pubertal maturation are largely inherited (Dick, Rose, Pulkkinen, & Kaprio, 2001; Mustanski, Viken, Kaprio, Pulkkinen, & Rose, 2004).

Despite this powerful influence of genetic factors, the environment plays an important role. In all likelihood, every individual inherits a predisposition to develop at a certain rate and to begin pubertal maturation at a certain time. But this predisposition is best thought of as an upper and lower age limit, not a fixed absolute. Whether the genetic predisposition that each person has to mature around a given age is actually realized, and when within the predisposed age boundaries she or he actually goes through puberty, is subject to the influence of many external factors. In this respect, the timing and rate of pubertal maturation are the product of an interaction between nature and nurture, between one's genetic makeup and the environmental conditions under which one has developed.

By far the two most important environmental influences on pubertal maturation are nutrition and health. Puberty occurs earlier among individuals who are better nourished throughout their prenatal, infant, and childhood years. Not surprisingly, then, whereas girls who are taller or heavier than their peers mature earlier (St. George et al., 1994), delayed puberty is more likely to occur among individuals with a history of protein and/or caloric deficiency. Chronic illness during childhood and adolescence is also associated with delayed puberty, as is excessive exercise. For example, girls in ballet companies or in other rigorous training programs often mature later than their peers (Frisch, 1983). Generally, then, after genetic factors, the most important determinant of the timing of puberty is the overall physical well-being of the individual from conception through preadolescence (Susman & Dorn, 2009).

■　**Familial Influences on Pubertal Timing**　Interestingly, a number of studies suggest that social factors in the home environment may influence the onset of maturation, especially in girls; in contrast, boys' pubertal maturation has not been consistently linked to family functioning. Puberty occurs somewhat earlier among girls who grew up in father-absent families, in less cohesive or more conflict-ridden households, or with a stepfather (Ellis, 2004). One explanation for the finding that distant family relations may accelerate pubertal maturation is that distance in the family may induce a very small amount of stress, which, in turn, may affect hormonal secretions in the adolescent (Belsky, Steinberg, Houts, Friedman, DeHart, et al., 2007). Puberty may be sped up by *small* amounts of stress; a great deal of stress, however, is likely to slow maturation. In addition, the presence of a stepfather may expose the adolescent girl to **pheromones** (a class of chemicals secreted by animals that stimulate certain behaviors in other members of the species) that stimulate pubertal maturation. In general, among humans and other mammals, living in proximity to one's close biological relatives appears to slow the process of pubertal maturation, whereas exposure to unrelated members of the other sex may accelerate it.

Although it may seem surprising that something as biological as puberty can be influenced by factors in the social environment, scientists have long known that our social relationships can indeed affect our biological functioning. One of the best-known examples of this is that women who live together—such as dormitory roommates—find that their menstrual periods begin to synchronize over time (C. Graham, 1991; McClintock, 1980).

FOOD FOR THOUGHT

Why might the timing of puberty in girls be more influenced by social factors than is the case among boys?

■　**Group Differences in Pubertal Maturation**　Researchers typically study group differences in puberty by comparing average ages of menarche in different regions. Most of these studies have indicated that genetic factors play an extremely small role in determining group differences in pubertal maturation (Eveleth & Tanner, 1990). Differences among countries in the average rate and timing of puberty are more likely to reflect differences in their environments than differences in their populations' gene pools (Morabia, Costanza, & World Health Organization, 1998).

The influence of the broader environment on the timing and tempo of puberty can be seen in more concrete terms by looking at two sets of findings: (1) comparisons of the average age of menarche across countries and (2) changes in the average age of menarche over time. (Although menarche does not signal the onset of puberty, researchers often use the average age of menarche when comparing the timing of puberty across different groups or regions, because it can be measured more reliably than other indicators.)

First, consider variations in the age of menarche across different regions of the world. Menarche generally is earlier in countries where individuals are less likely to be malnourished or to suffer from chronic disease. For example, in western Europe and in the United

pheromones　A class of chemicals secreted by animals that stimulate certain behaviors in other members of the species.

FIGURE 1.7   The age at menarche has declined considerably over the past 150 years. This decline is known as the **secular trend**. (Adapted from Eveleth & Tanner, 1990)

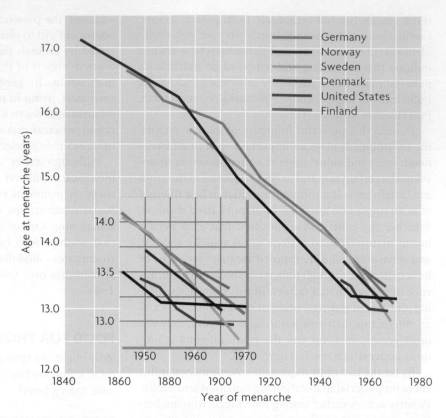

States, the median age of menarche ranges from about 12½ to 13½ years. In Africa, however, the median age ranges from about 14 to 17 years. The range is much wider across Africa because of the greater variation in environmental conditions there.

▌ **The Secular Trend**   We can also examine environmental influences on the timing of puberty by looking at changes in the average age of menarche over the past two centuries. Because nutritional conditions have improved during the past 150 years, we would expect to find a decline in the average age at menarche over time. This is indeed the case, as can be seen in Figure 1.7. This pattern, known as the **secular trend,** is attributable not only to improved nutrition but also to better sanitation and better control of infectious diseases. In most European countries, maturation has become earlier by about three to four months per decade. For example, in Norway 150 years ago, the average age of menarche may have been about 17 years. Today, it is between 12 and 13 years. Similar declines have been observed over the same period in other industrialized nations and, more recently, in developing countries as well. The secular trend is less well documented

among boys, in part because there is no easily measured marker of puberty, like menarche. But there is some evidence that the age of onset of puberty among American boys may have dropped very slightly during the second half of the 20th century (Karpati, Rubin, Kieszak, Marcus, & Troiano, 2002; Slyper, 2006).

Scientists disagree about whether the secular trend has continued in the United States in recent years and, if so, whether the trend toward earlier puberty is greater in some ethnic groups than in others (Susman & Dorn, 2009). According to the recent report of an expert panel of scientists (Eulinget al., 2008), there is evidence, among girls, of a continued decline in the age of puberty as indexed by breast development and menarche, but not as indexed by genital maturation or the appearance of pubic hair. In general, the average age of menarche among American girls dropped by about two and a half months between the 1960s and 1990s (see Figure 1.8), most probably because of increased rates of obesity (S. E. Anderson, Dallal, & Must, 2003) or changes in diet (Slyper, 2006), a decline that has been especially marked among Black girls (Chumlea et al., 2003). The panel concluded that there was no evidence for a comparable decline among boys. One reason for these discrepancies is that puberty can be measured in many ways (Dorn, Dahl, Woodward, & Biro, 2006), and what we conclude about the average age of puberty depends on what indicator is used. Because the development of pubic hair (which is influenced by androgens)

secular trend   The tendency, over the past two centuries, for individuals to be larger in stature and to reach puberty earlier, primarily because of improvements in health and nutrition.

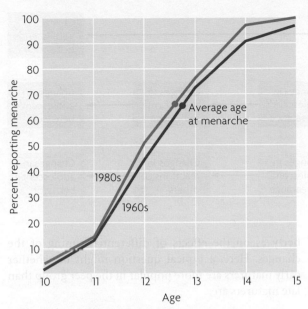

FIGURE 1.8 The age at which American girls have their first period (menarche) continued to drop in the late 20th century. (From Anderson, Dallal, & Must, 2003)

is affected by different factors than is menarche (which is influenced by estrogen and progesterone), patterns of change over time in each would not necessarily be identical (Biro, Huang, et al., 2006). In general, though, most scientists agree that any changes in the average age of puberty have been much less dramatic in recent decades than they were in the early 20th century, when the average age of menarche dropped by about four months every decade.

FOOD FOR THOUGHT

Some studies indicate that the secular trend has been more dramatic among females than males. Why might this be the case?

RECAP

- The timing of puberty, as well as the rate at which it occurs, is highly variable.
- The timing of puberty is influenced by both genetic and environmental factors. Among the most important environmental influences are health and nutrition. Generally, individuals who are healthier and better nourished begin puberty at a relatively younger age than their less healthy or more poorly nourished peers.
- Some evidence suggests that girls growing up in single-parent families, stepfamilies, or families in

which there is a high level of conflict go through puberty somewhat earlier than their peers.
- The age at which puberty occurs has declined over time, a phenomenon known as the "secular trend." In the United States, it appears that this trend has continued among girls, but not among boys.

The Psychological and Social Impact of Puberty

Puberty can affect the adolescent's behavior and psychological functioning in a number of ways (Brooks-Gunn, Graber, & Paikoff, 1994) (see Figure 1.9). First, the biological changes of puberty can have a direct effect on behavior. Increases in testosterone at puberty are directly linked, for example, to an increase in sex drive and sexual activity among adolescent boys (Halpern, Udry, & Suchindran, 1996). (The impact of hormonal change on girls' sex drive and sexual activity is more complicated, as you'll see in Chapter 11.)

Second, the biological changes of puberty cause changes in the adolescent's self-image, which, in turn, may affect how he or she behaves. For example, a boy who has recently gone through puberty may feel more grown up as a result of his more adultlike appearance. This, in turn, may make him seek more independence from his parents. He may ask for a later curfew, a larger allowance, or the right to make decisions about things that previously were decided by his parents. As we will see later in this chapter, the physical changes of puberty often spark conflict between teenagers and their parents, in part because of the ways in which puberty affects the adolescent's desire for autonomy.

Finally, biological change at puberty transforms the adolescent's appearance, which, in turn, may elicit changes in how *others* react to the teenager. These changes in reactions may provoke changes in the adolescent's behavior. An adolescent girl who has recently matured physically may find herself suddenly receiving the attention of older boys who had not previously paid her much heed. She may feel nervous about all the extra attention and confused about how she should respond to it. Moreover, she must now make decisions about how much time she wishes to devote to dating and how she should behave when out on a date.

Young people's reactions to the changes brought on by puberty, and others' reactions to them, are influenced by the broader social environment, in which messages about physical attractiveness, sexuality, and sexual maturation change, often markedly, from era to era. Although it is difficult to imagine an era in which

FIGURE 1.9 The biological changes of puberty can affect the adolescent's behavior in at least three ways.

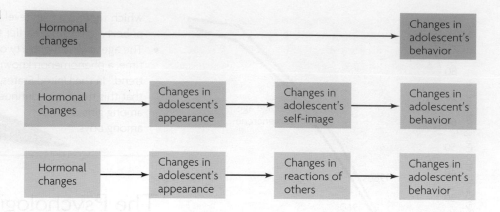

adolescents, especially girls, did not obsess about their shape, size, and sexual allure, adolescent females' preoccupation with their body is a relatively recent phenomenon, created largely by marketers of clothing, undergarments, cosmetics, weight loss programs, and "feminine" products (Brumberg, 1997). Contemporary society's views of puberty and physical maturation are expressed through television commercials, newspaper and magazine advertisements, and depictions of young adolescents in films and other media. People cannot help but be influenced by these images, and the expectations they associate with puberty, as well as the meaning they give it, determine the reactions puberty brings out in them.

Researchers have generally taken two approaches to studying the psychological and social consequences of puberty. One approach is to look at individuals who are at various stages of puberty, either in a **cross-sectional study** (in which groups of individuals are compared at different stages of puberty) or in a **longitudinal study** (in which the same individuals are tracked over time as they move through the different stages of puberty). Studies of this sort examine the impact of puberty on young people's psychological development and social relations. Researchers might ask, for example, whether youngsters' self-esteem is higher or lower during puberty than before or after.

A second approach compares the psychological development of early and late maturers. As noted previously, there is large variation in pubertal timing, and individuals of the same chronological age, who are in the same grade in school, may be at very different stages of puberty. Researchers have been tremendously interested in whether the timing of puberty affects the adolescent's psychological development. The focus of these studies is not so much on the absolute impact of puberty as on the effects of differential timing of the changes. Here, a typical question might be whether early maturers are more popular in the peer group than late maturers are.

THE IMMEDIATE IMPACT OF PUBERTY

Studies of the psychological and social impacts of puberty indicate that physical maturation, regardless of whether it occurs early or late, affects the adolescent's self-image, mood, and relationships with parents. As you will see, however, the short-term consequences of puberty may be more taxing on the adolescent's family than on the adolescent.

Puberty and Self-Esteem Although research suggests that puberty can be a potential stressor with temporary adverse psychological consequences, this is true only when it is coupled with other changes that necessitate adjustment (Simmons & Blyth, 1987). In this respect, the impact of puberty on adolescents' psychological functioning is to a great extent shaped by the social context in which puberty takes place (Susman & Dorn, 2009). The impact of puberty on mental health varies by gender and across ethnic groups, with girls more adversely affected than boys, and with White girls, in particular, at greatest risk for developing a poor body image (J. Siegel, Yancey, Aneshensel, & Schuler, 1999). Given the premium in contemporary society placed on thinness, the increase in body dissatisfaction among White girls that takes place at puberty is, not surprisingly, linked to specific concerns that girls have about their hips, thighs, waist, and weight (Rosenblum & Lewis, 1999). Interestingly, the way adolescents feel about their physical appearance when they begin adolescence remains remarkably stable over time, regardless of whether their actual attractiveness changes (Rosenblum & Lewis, 1999).

Puberty and Adolescent Moodiness Although an adolescent's self-image can be expected to change during a time of dramatic physical development,

cross-sectional study   A study that compares two or more groups of individuals at one point in time.

longitudinal study   A study that follows the same group of individuals over time.

self-esteem or self-image can also be reasonably stable, with long and sturdy roots reaching back to childhood. For this reason, some researchers have turned their attention to the impact of puberty on more transient states, such as mood. One reason for this focus is that adolescents are thought to be moodier, on average, than either children or adults. One study, in which adolescents' moods were monitored repeatedly by electronic pagers, for example, showed that their moods fluctuate during the course of the day more than the moods of adults do (Csikszentmihalyi & Larson, 1984). Many adults assume that adolescent moodiness is directly related to the hormonal changes of puberty (C. Buchanan, Eccles, & Becker, 1992). Is there any scientific evidence that the hormonal changes of puberty cause adolescents to be moody or, for that matter, that these hormonal changes affect the adolescent's psychological functioning or behavior at all?

According to several comprehensive reviews of research on hormones and adolescent mood and behavior, the direct connection between hormones and mood is not very strong (C. Buchanan et al., 1992; Flannery, Torquati, & Lindemeier, 1994). When studies do find a connection between hormonal changes at puberty and adolescent mood or behavior, the effects are strongest early in puberty, when the process is being "turned on" and when hormonal levels are highly variable. For example, studies indicate that *rapid increases* in many of the hormones associated with puberty—such as testosterone, estrogen, and various adrenal androgens—may be associated with increased irritability, impulsivity, aggression (in boys) and depression (in girls), especially when the increases take place very early in adolescence. One interpretation of these findings is that it is not so much the absolute increases in these hormones during puberty but their rapid fluctuation early in puberty that may affect adolescents' moods. Once the hormone levels stabilize at higher levels, later in puberty, their negative effects appear to wane (C. Buchanan et al., 1992). There is also evidence, discussed in Chapter 2, that important changes take place around the time of puberty in regions of the brain that play major roles in the processing of emotion, although the specific ways in which hormones contribute to this are not yet fully understood (E. Nelson, Leibenluft, McClure, & Pine, 2005).

Even so, most researchers agree that the impact of hormonal change on mood and behavior in adolescence is greatly influenced by environmental factors (A. Booth, Johnson, Granger, Crouter, & McHale, 2003; Susman, 1997). For example, although rapid increases in hormones early in puberty are associated with depressed mood in girls, it turns out that stressful life events, such as problems in the family, in school, or with friends, play a far greater role in the development of depression than do hormonal changes (Brooks-Gunn, Graber, & Paikoff,

Contrary to widespread belief, there is little evidence that the hormonal changes of puberty contribute in a dramatic way to adolescent moodiness.

1994). Similarly, while high levels of testosterone have been associated with impulsivity and aggression and low levels with depression, these associations are weaker among adolescents who have positive family relationships (A. Booth et al., 2003).

Interestingly, not only is there little evidence that adolescents' moodiness results from the "storm and stress" of raging hormones, but there is also research that questions the very idea that adolescents are inherently moodier than children. Psychologists Mihaly Csikszentmihalyi and Reed Larson (1984; Larson & Lampman-Petraitis, 1989) had teenagers carry electronic pagers, and the researchers paged them periodically throughout the day. When the adolescents were paged, they filled out forms noting how they were feeling, what they were doing, where they were, and whom they were with. By looking at changes in mood across activities and settings, the researchers were able to determine the correlates of adolescent moodiness.

Their findings suggest that adolescent mood swings parallel their changes in activities. Over the course of a day, a teenager may shift from elation to boredom, back to happiness, and then to anger. But these shifts in mood

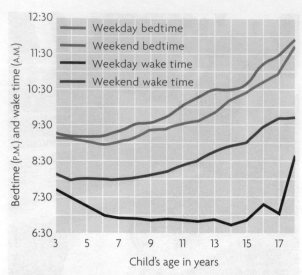

FIGURE 1.10   Children's weekday and weekend bedtimes and wake times, by age. (Adapted from Snell et al., 2007)

appear to have more to do with shifts in activities—elated when seeing a girlfriend, bored in social studies class, happy when having lunch with friends, and angry when assigned extra work at the fast-food restaurant—than with internal, biological changes (Schneiders et al., 2006). More important, comparisons of youngsters ages 9–15 did not show increases in moodiness during the transition into adolescence.

Puberty and Changes in Patterns of Sleep

One fascinating finding on hormones and behavior in adolescence concerns adolescents' sleep preferences (Fredriksen, Rhodes, Reddy, & Way, 2004). Many parents complain that their teenage children go to bed too late in the evening and sleep in too late in the morning, a pattern that begins to emerge in early adolescence (see Figure 1.10). It now appears that the emergence of this pattern—called a **delayed phase preference**—is driven by the biological changes of puberty (Carskadon, Acebo, Richardson, Tate, & Seifer, 1997).

Falling asleep is caused by a combination of biological and environmental factors. One of the most important is the secretion of a hormone in the brain called **melatonin.** Melatonin levels change naturally over the course of the 24-hour day, mainly in response to the amount of light in the environment. Feelings of sleepiness increase and decrease with melatonin levels—as melatonin rises, we feel sleepier, and as it falls, we feel more awake. Over the course of the day, we follow a sleep–wake cycle that is calibrated to changes in light and regulated by melatonin secretion.

delayed phase preference   A pattern of sleep characterized by later sleep and wake times, which usually emerges during puberty.

melatonin   A hormone secreted by the brain that contributes to sleepiness.

During puberty, the time of night at which melatonin levels begin to rise changes, becoming later and later as individuals mature physically. In fact, the nighttime increase in melatonin starts about two hours later among adolescents who have completed puberty than among those who have not yet entered puberty (Carskadon & Acebo, 2002). As a result of this shift, individuals become able to stay up later before feeling sleepy. In fact, when allowed to regulate their own sleep schedules (as on weekends), most teenagers will stay up until around 1:00 A.M. and sleep until about 10:00 A.M. Because the whole cycle of melatonin secretion is shifted later at puberty, this also means that adolescents who have gone through puberty are more sleepy early in the morning than those who are still prepubertal.

Falling asleep is affected by the environment as well—as you know, it is much easier to fall asleep when a room is dark than when it is bright. But when pre-adolescents get into bed at night, they tend to fall asleep very quickly—even if there is something that they want to stay up for—because their melatonin levels are already high. After going through puberty, though, because of the delayed timing of the increase in melatonin, it is easier for individuals to stay up later, so that if there is something more exciting to do—surf the Internet, watch a DVD, talk on the phone—it is not difficult to remain awake (Taylor, Jenni, Acebo, & Carskadon, 2005), and some scientists believe that many adolescents' sleep deprivation stems directly from overuse of computers and cell phones (Punamäki, Wallenius, Nygård, Saarni, & Rimpelä, 2007). Thus, the tendency for adolescents to stay up late is due to the interaction of biology (which delays the onset of sleepiness) and the environment (which provides an impetus to stay up). This shift in sleep preferences, to a later bedtime and a later wake time, begins to reverse around age 20, but at a slightly earlier age among females than males (Roenneberg et al., 2004).

If getting up early the next day were not an issue, staying up late would not be a problem. Unfortunately, most teenagers need to get up early on school days, and the combination of staying up late and getting up early leads to sleep deprivation and daytime sleepiness. The shift in the timing of the melatonin cycle contributes to this, because the decrease in melatonin that takes place in the middle of the night happens later after puberty than before. This means that when teenagers get out of bed early in the morning, their melatonin levels are relatively higher than they are at the same time of day for preadolescents. Indeed, one study found that adolescents were least alert between the hours of 8:00 and 9:00 A.M. (when most schools start) and were most alert after 3.00 P.M., when the school day is over (R. Allen & Mirabell, 1990). Sleep researchers estimate that, because of early school start times, adolescents get two fewer hours of sleep per night when the school year begins than they did during the preceding summer months (Hansen, Janssen, Schiff, Zee, & Dubocovich, 2005). This has prompted some communities to delay their school starting time for teenagers (Mitru, Millrood, & Mateika, 2002).

Interestingly, the tendency for individuals to go to bed later as they become teenagers has become stronger over the past 30 years (Iglowstein, Jenni, Molinari, & Largo, 2003), perhaps because the availability of television, the Internet, and other mass media during late-night and early-morning hours has increased (Van den Bulck, 2004). This suggests that the late-night hours kept by many adolescents are at least somewhat voluntary, made easier by the changes in the sleep centers of the brain. (There is also evidence that exposure to light depresses melatonin secretion, so that staying up late with the lights on will delay the rise in melatonin even more.) Whatever the explanation, because teenagers' wake time has not changed, but their bedtime has gotten later, today's teenagers get significantly less sleep than their counterparts did several decades ago. Excessive daytime sleepiness is rampant among American teenagers, a finding that has been replicated in several countries, including Japan and Taiwan (Gau, Soong, & Merikangas, 2004; Ohida et al., 2004).

Although individuals' preferred bedtime gets later as they move from childhood into adolescence, the amount of sleep they need each night remains constant, at around nine hours. Yet, one study of more than 3,000 Rhode Island high school students found that only one fifth of the students got at least eight hours of sleep on an average school night and that nearly half got seven hours or less (Wolfson & Carskadon, 1998). A more recent study of Chicago middle school students found, similarly, that the average eighth-grader got about seven hours of sleep on school nights (Fredriksen et al., 2004). There is now a clear consensus among scientists that most teenagers are not getting enough sleep and that inadequate sleep is associated in adolescence with poorer mental health (Fuligni & Hardway, 2006), more frequent injuries (Lam & Yang, 2007), being overweight (Snell, Adam, & Duncan, 2007), and poorer school performance (Fredriksen et al., 2004). In the Rhode Island study, for example, students who were earning grades of C or lower were going to bed 40 minutes later and sleeping about 25 minutes less each night than their classmates whose grade point averages were B or better. The students with poorer grades also reported staying up con-

Important changes in the sleep cycle take place after puberty. This "delayed phase preference" causes adolescents to want to stay up later at night and makes them feel more tired in the early morning hours.

siderably later on weekends than they did on school nights; other studies find higher rates of problem behavior among adolescents who prefer to stay up later (Susman et al., 2007). Despite many adolescents' belief that catching up on their sleep on weekends will make up for sleep deprivation during the week, research indicates that having markedly different bedtimes on weekends versus weekdays contributes to further sleep-related problems (Wolfson & Carskadon, 1998). (Actually, the best thing teenagers can do to avoid problems waking up on school days is to force themselves to get up at the same time on the weekend as on school days, regardless of how late they have stayed up.) Not surprisingly, sleep-related difficulties among teenagers are also linked to the consumption of caffeine (Pollack & Bright, 2003) and tobacco (Patten, Choi, Gillin, & Pierce, 2002), both of which are stimulants. About 10% of teenagers report chronic insomnia (E. Johnson, Roth, Schultz, & Breslau, 2006), which increases the risk of other psychological problems (R. Roberts, Roberts, & Duong, 2008).

FOOD FOR THOUGHT

Some policymakers have called for delaying the time at which the high school day begins, in view of new studies on changing patterns of sleep during adolescence. Do you think this is a good idea?

▌ Puberty and Family Relationships   Research into the impact of puberty on family relationships has pointed to a fairly consistent pattern, namely, that puberty appears to increase conflict and distance between parents and children. You should be aware, however, that the "distancing" effect of puberty on adolescent–parent relationships is not as strong in single-parent homes (E. Anderson, Hetherington, & Clingempeel, 1989) and not as consistently observed in ethnic minority families (Molina & Chassin, 1996; Sagrestano, McCormick, Paikoff, & Holmbeck, 1999). Among White families, however, several studies show that as youngsters mature from childhood toward the middle of puberty, emotional distance between them and their parents increases, and conflict intensifies, especially between the adolescent and his or her mother (Laursen, Coy, & Collins, 1998; Ogletree, Jones, & Coyl, 2002). The change that takes place is reflected in an increase in "negatives" (e.g., conflict, complaining, anger) and, to a lesser extent, a decrease in "positives" (e.g., support, smiling, laughter) (e.g., Flannery et al., 1994; Holmbeck & Hill, 1991). Although negative interchanges may diminish after the adolescent growth spurt, adolescents and their parents do not immediately become as close as they were before the adolescents entered puberty. Interestingly, puberty increases distance between children and their parents in most species of monkeys and apes, and some writers have suggested that the pattern seen in human adolescents may have some evolutionary basis (Steinberg & Belsky, 1996).

Because this connection between pubertal maturation and parent–child distance is not affected by the age at which the adolescent goes through puberty—in other words, the pattern is seen among early as well as late maturers—it suggests that something about puberty in particular may transform the parent–child bond. To date, we do not know whether this effect results from the hormonal changes of puberty, from changes in the adolescent's physical appearance, or from changes in adolescent psychological functioning that, in turn, affect family relationships. Moreover, because few studies of family relationships at puberty have examined multiple aspects of adolescent development simultaneously, it is difficult to say whether the patterns of change in family relationships that many studies have found do, in fact, result from puberty and not from some other change taking place at the same time in the adolescent or in the parent (Paikoff & Brooks-Gunn, 1991).

Whatever underlying mechanism is involved, one interpretation of these studies is that developments occurring around the time of puberty can upset interpersonal balances that are established during childhood, causing temporary periods of disruption in the family system. During a son's or daughter's childhood, families develop patterns of relationships that are comfortable and workable, but they may find that puberty disrupts the patterns to which they have grown accustomed. They have developed a certain way of discussing things and a certain way of including the children in discussions. But as the children go through puberty, they may want to be treated more like adults and have a greater say in family decisions. Consequently, families may experience a temporary period of conflict or tension when sons and daughters enter early adolescence. It may take some time for the individual and the family to achieve a new equilibrium that takes into account the changes brought on by puberty.

▌ Pubertal Maturation and Peer Relationships
Puberty may have an effect on relationships in the peer group, too. One study of adolescents' social networks—the people they are most likely to see and spend time with—found that adolescents who were physically mature were less likely than their less developed peers to name adults as people who were important to them, and they were more likely to name other adolescents (Garbarino, Burston, Raber, Russell, & Crouter, 1978). This finding suggests that pubertal maturation may play an important role in shifting adolescents' interests and energies toward the peer group. Boys and girls who are physically mature are more likely than less mature age-mates to be involved in cross-sex romantic activities such as having a boyfriend or girlfriend or going out on dates (Compian, Gowen, & Hayward, 2004), although this depends on the social norms of the adolescent's peer group and the prevailing expectations about the age at which teenagers should begin dating (Dornbusch et al., 1981; Gargiulo, Attie, Brooks-Gunn, & Warren, 1987). Interestingly, pubertal maturation is *not* associated with having platonic relationships with other-sex peers (Compian et al., 2004).

THE IMPACT OF SPECIFIC PUBERTAL EVENTS

Several studies have focused specifically on adolescents' attitudes toward and reactions to particular events at puberty, such as girls' reactions to menarche or breast development and boys' reactions to their first ejaculation.

In general, most adolescents react positively to the biological changes associated with puberty, especially those associated with the development of secondary sex characteristics. One study of adolescent girls' attitudes toward breast development, for example, found that the majority of girls greeted this change positively (Brooks-Gunn, Newman, Holderness, & Warren, 1994).

Adolescent girls' attitudes toward menarche are less negative today than they appear to have been in the past (J. Lee, 2008), a change that may be attributable to the increase in information about menstruation in schools and in the media in recent years (Merskin, 1999). In general, among today's adolescent girls, menarche is typically accompanied by gains in social maturity, peer prestige, and self-esteem—as well as by heightened self-consciousness (Brooks-Gunn & Reiter, 1990). Nevertheless, many young women have developed a negative image of menstruation before reaching adolescence, and they enter puberty with ambivalent attitudes about menarche—a mixture of excitement and fear (S. Moore, 1995). Generally speaking, girls whose mothers are helpful and matter-of-fact in their response to menarche report the most positive memories of the experience (J. Lee, 2008).

Interestingly, one set of studies indicates that a strong negative bias toward menstruation before menarche may actually be associated with greater menstrual discomfort. Menstrual symptoms are reported to be more severe among women who expect menstruation to be uncomfortable, among girls whose mothers lead them to believe that menstruation will be an unpleasant or uncomfortable experience, and in cultures that label menstruation as an important event. In Mexico and in China, for example, where attitudes toward menarche may be especially ambivalent, menarche may have an adverse effect on girls' mental health, an effect not generally observed in the United States (Benjet & Hernandez-Guzman, 2002; Tang, Yeung, & Lee, 2003). In addition, girls who experience menarche early, relative to their peers, or who are otherwise unprepared for puberty report more negative reactions to the event (Koff & Rierdan, 1996; Tang, Yeung, & Lee, 2004).

Far less is known about boys' reactions to their first ejaculation, an experience that we might consider analogous to menarche in girls. Although most boys are not very well prepared for this event by their parents or other adults, first ejaculation does not appear to cause undue anxiety, embarrassment, or fear. Interestingly, however, in contrast to girls, who generally tell their mothers shortly after they have begun menstruating and tell their girlfriends soon thereafter, boys, at least in the United States, do not discuss their first ejaculation with either parents or friends (Gaddis & Brooks-Gunn, 1985; J. Stein & Reiser, 1994). In other cultures, the event may be experienced somewhat differently. For example, one study of first ejaculation among adolescent boys in Nigeria found not only that boys were not upset by the event but also that they told their friends about the experience very soon after it occurred (Adegoke, 1993). Cultural differences in boys' responses to their first ejaculation are likely related to differences in how cultures view masturbation. As is the case with girls and menarche, boys' reactions to their first ejaculation are more positive when they have been prepared for the event (J. Stein & Reiser, 1994).

Because of wide variability in the timing and tempo of puberty, individuals of the same chronological age can have very different physical appearances.

THE IMPACT OF EARLY OR LATE MATURATION

Adolescents who mature relatively early or relatively late stand apart from their peers physically and may, as a consequence, elicit different sorts of reactions and expectations from those around them. Moreover, individual adolescents may be all too aware of whether they are early or late relative to their age-mates, and their feelings about themselves are likely to be influenced by their comparisons. One recent study found that early-maturing adolescents were more likely to be "pseudomature"—wishing they were older, hanging around with older peers, less involved in school, and more oriented toward their peers (Galambos, Barker, & Tilton-Weaver, 2003). Indeed, adolescents' *perceptions* of whether they are an early or a late maturer are more strongly related to their feelings about their physical maturation than whether they actually are early or late (Dubas, Graber, & Petersen, 1991). Further, adolescents' behavior is related to how old they feel, not simply to how physically mature they are (Galambos, Kolaric, Sears, & Maggs, 1999). Nevertheless, early and late maturers are often treated differently by others and view themselves differently, and they may, as a result, behave differently. As we shall see, however, early and late maturation have different consequences in the immediate present and in the long run, different consequences in different contexts, and, most important, different consequences for boys and girls.

▌ Early Versus Late Maturation Among Boys
Over the past 50 years, research on boys' pubertal timing has consistently shown that early-maturing boys

feel better about themselves and are more popular than their late-maturing peers (Graber, Lewinsohn, Seeley, & Brooks-Gunn, 1997; M. C. Jones & Bayley, 1950). Consistent with this, boys who are more physically mature than their peers report more frequent feelings of positive affect, attention, strength, and being in love (Richards & Larson, 1993). Interestingly, studies of boys with delayed puberty indicate that their feelings of competence, especially in the realms of work and sports, increased following the administration of hormone treatments (Schwab et al., 2001).

At the same time, however, early-maturing boys are more likely than their peers to get involved in antisocial or deviant activities, including truancy, minor delinquency, and problems at school (W. A. Collins & Steinberg, 2006). They are also more likely to use drugs and alcohol and engage in other risky activities (Dick, Rose, Pulkkinen, & Kaprio, 2001; Drapela, Gebelt, & McRee, 2006; Wichstrom, 2001), even as young adults (Biehl, Natsuaki, & Ge, 2007). Interestingly, although all adolescents are adversely affected by being bullied by their peers, the impact of victimization is greater for early maturers, perhaps because being picked on when one is larger than average is all the more embarrassing (Nadeem & Graham, 2005). The impact of early maturation on adolescents' antisocial behavior is comparable among Black, Mexican American, and White boys (Cota-Robles, Neiss, & Rowe, 2002). One reasonable explanation is that boys who are more physically mature develop friendships with older peers and that these friendships lead them into activities that are problematic for the younger boys (Andersson & Magnusson, 1990). Once involved with these older peer groups, the early maturers' higher rate of delinquency and substance use increases over time through their social contacts (Silbereisen et al., 1989). Thus, early puberty seems to play a role in the initiation, but not intensification, of substance use.

Clearly, early-maturing boys enjoy some psychological advantages over late maturers during early adolescence, when some boys have matured physically but others have not. But what about later during adolescence, when the late maturers have caught up? At least one study points to some interesting advantages for late-maturing boys, despite their initially lower popularity. Although early and late maturers exhibit similar psychological profiles before they enter adolescence, during the time of pubertal onset, and one year later as well, late maturers show significantly higher ratings on measures of intellectual curiosity, exploratory behavior, and social initiative. While they are in the midst of puberty, early maturers experience more frequent and more intense temper tantrums and depression (Ge, Brody, Conger, Simons, & Murry, 2002; Ge et al., 2003).

Why might this be? One explanation is that late maturers have the advantage of a longer preadolescent period, giving them more time to "prepare" psychologi-

cally for the onset of puberty (Peskin, 1967). This preparation may be important if, as noted earlier, rapid increases in hormones at puberty provoke changes in mood. Many theorists believe that the middle-childhood and preadolescent years are extremely important periods for the development of coping skills—skills that prove valuable during adolescence and adulthood. Although puberty by no means marks the end of the growth of coping abilities, it does come as an abrupt interruption to the more relaxed preadolescent era. Later puberty, and hence a longer preadolescence, might allow for coping skills to develop more fully before adolescence. This may account in part for the apparently better coping skills demonstrated by late maturers—not only during puberty but, as you will read, during adulthood as well.

Do the psychological and interpersonal differences that are observed between early and late maturers during adolescence persist into adulthood? In order to answer such questions, a series of follow-up studies some 25 years later looked at the adult personalities of males who had been studied during adolescence (Livson & Peskin, 1980). At age 38, the early maturers were more responsible, cooperative, self-controlled, and sociable. At the same time, though, they had grown up to be more conforming, conventional, and humorless. The late maturers, in contrast, remained somewhat more impulsive and more assertive but turned out to be more insightful, inventive, and creatively playful. What had happened?

One interpretation is that, because of their more adultlike appearance, the early-maturing boys were pushed into adult roles earlier than their peers. They were more likely to be asked to assume responsibility, to take on leadership positions, and to behave in a more grown-up manner; consistent with this, other studies have found that early maturing boys are, as men, more successful in work and marriage (Taga, Markey, & Friedman, 2006). But this early press toward adulthood may have come too soon and may have stifled a certain amount of creativity and risk taking.

Have you gone to any gatherings of former high school classmates? Did you discover that some of the people whom you remembered as being extremely mature and socially successful during high school had turned out to be not all that interesting? Perhaps too much leadership, responsibility, social success, and maturity during the high school years interferes with the sort of psychological development that makes for interesting and creative adults. As we shall see in a later chapter, many psychologists believe that adolescents may benefit in the long run from having an extended period of time during which they are *not* being pushed into adulthood.

▌ Early Versus Late Maturation in Girls   In contrast to the generally positive impact that early maturation has on the psychological well-being of boys, early-maturing girls have more emotional difficulties than their peers, including lowered self-image and higher rates of depression, anxiety, eating disorders, and panic attacks (W. A. Collins & Steinberg, 2006; Mendle, Turkheimer, & Emery, 2007; Natsuaki, Biehl, & Ge, 2009; Stice, Presnell, & Bearman, 2001). These difficulties seem to have less to do with the direct effects of hormones and more to do with the ways in which standing apart from their peers physically affects girls' feelings about their appearance and social relationships with other adolescents (Mendle et al., 2007). There is also evidence that early maturation in girls is associated with higher emotional arousal (Graber, Brooks-Gunn, & Warren, 2006).

Given the role of social factors in linking early maturation and girls' psychological distress, it is no surprise that the ultimate impact of early maturation on the young girl's feelings about herself appears to depend on the broader context in which maturation takes place. For example, studies of American girls generally find that early-maturing girls have lower self-esteem and a poorer self-image, because of our cultural preference for thinness and our ambivalence about adolescent sexuality (Brooks-Gunn & Reiter, 1990). In Germany, however, where sex education is more open and attitudes toward adolescent sexuality are less conflicted, early-maturing girls are found to have *higher* self-esteem (Silbereisen, Petersen, Albrecht, & Kracke, 1989).

Interestingly, even *within* the United States, the impact of physical maturation appears to depend on the social context in which teenagers live (Dyer & Tiggemann, 1996). One study of suburban Chicago youngsters, for example, found that girls' body image was significantly higher in one community than in another—despite comparable levels of physical maturation between the two groups. One factor that differentiated the two communities was "cliquishness": In the more cliquish high school, girls were less satisfied with the way they looked, perhaps because cliquish girls place more emphasis on physical appearance in determining popularity (Richards, Boxer, Petersen, & Albrecht, 1990).

Although some early-maturing girls may have self-image difficulties, their popularity with peers is not jeopardized. Indeed, some studies indicate that early maturers are more popular than other girls, especially, as you would expect, when the index of popularity includes popularity with boys (Simmons, Blyth, & McKinney, 1983). Interestingly, one study of girls with delayed puberty found that hormone treatments improved girls' perceptions of their romantic appeal (Schwab et al., 2001). Ironically, it may be in part because the early maturer is more popular with boys that she reports more emotional upset: Early pressure to date and, perhaps, to be involved in a sexual relationship may take its toll on the adolescent girl's mental health. Consistent with this, research indicates that early-maturing girls are more vulnerable to emotional distress when they have relatively more other-sex friendships (Ge, Best, Conger, & Simons, 1996) and when they are in schools with older peers (for example, sixth-graders who are in a school that has seventh- and eighth-graders, too) (Blyth, Simmons, & Zakin, 1985). Again, we see the importance of context.

Psychologists have offered several explanations for the fact that early maturation appears to be harder on girls than boys. One explanation might be termed the "maturational deviance" hypothesis (Simmons & Blyth, 1987). Simply put, youngsters who stand far apart from their peers—in physical appearance, for instance—may experience more psychological distress than adolescents who blend in more easily. Because girls mature earlier than boys, on average, early-maturing girls mature earlier than both their male and female peers. This makes them stand out at a time when they would rather fit in and, as a result, may make them more vulnerable to emotional distress. This explanation would also account for the lower self-esteem of late-maturing boys, who deviate toward the other extreme.

A second explanation for the sex difference in the impact of early maturation focuses on "developmental readiness." If puberty is a challenge that requires psychological adaptation by the adolescent, perhaps younger adolescents are less ready to cope with the challenge than older ones. Because puberty occurs quite early among early-maturing girls, it may tax their psychological resources. Early maturation among boys, because it occurs at a later age, would pose less of a problem. This also helps to explain why late-maturing boys seem better able than early maturers to control their temper and their impulses when they are going through puberty: They are relatively older and psychologically more mature (Peskin, 1967). If the developmental readiness hypothesis is true, both girls and boys should experience more difficulty if they are early maturers than if they are on time or late, but the difficulty should be temporary. This appears to be the case among boys (for whom the negative effects of early puberty occur during puberty itself, but then fade), but not for girls (for whom the negative effects of early puberty persist) (Ge et al., 2003).

A final explanation for the relatively greater disadvantage of early maturation for girls concerns the cultural desirability of different body types (Petersen, 1988). Early maturation for girls means leaving behind the culturally admired state of thinness. As noted previously, among girls, the ratio of fat to muscle increases dramatically at puberty, and many girls are distressed when they mature because they gain weight. Early maturers experience this weight gain at a time when most of their peers are still girlishly thin. One interesting study showed that in ballet companies—where thinness

FIGURE 1.11 Early-maturing girls are more likely to use tobacco, alcohol, and other drugs than girls who mature on time or late. (From Dick et al., 2000)

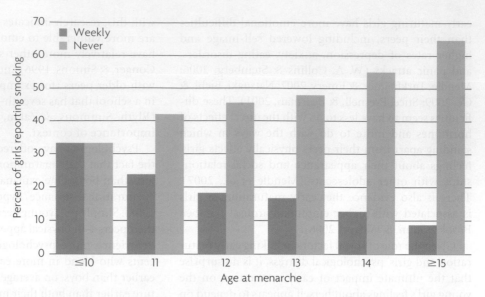

is even more important than in the culture at large—late maturers, who can retain the "ideal" shape much longer than earlier maturers, have fewer psychological problems than even on-time girls (Brooks-Gunn & Warren, 1985). In contrast, at puberty, boys move from a culturally undesirable state for males (short and scrawny) to a culturally admired one (tall and muscular). Early maturers enjoy the special advantage of being tall and muscular before their peers—a special benefit in a society that values males' athletic prowess—and therefore are more likely to react well to puberty. The fact that the effects of early maturation on girls' self-esteem vary across cultures suggests that contextual factors need to be taken into account in explaining this pattern of sex differences.

Whatever the explanation, it's important for parents and school counselors to bear in mind that early-maturing girls are at heightened risk for psychological problems, at least in the United States. Unfortunately, as long as our culture overvalues thinness and encourages the view that females should be judged on the basis of their physical appearance rather than their abilities, values, or personality, the risks of early puberty will probably endure. Adults can help by being supportive, by helping the early-maturing girl recognize her strengths and positive features—physical and nonphysical alike—and by preparing her for puberty before it takes place.

Like their male counterparts, early-maturing girls are also more likely to become involved in problem behavior, including delinquency and drugs and alcohol use; are more likely to have school problems; and are more likely to experience early sexual intercourse (Dick, Rose, Viken, & Kapris, 2000; Stice, Presnell, & Bearman, 2001; Wichstrøm, 2001) (see Figure 1.11). This is true in Europe and the United States (Silbereisen et al., 1989) and across ethnic groups within the United

States (Deardorff, Gonzales, Christopher, Roosa, & Millsap, 2005). These problems appear to arise because early-maturing girls are more likely to spend time with older adolescents, especially older adolescent boys, who initiate them into activities that might otherwise be delayed (Haynie, 2003; Magnusson, Statin, & Allen, 1986). Girls with a history of problem behavior prior to puberty appear most susceptible to the adverse effects of early maturation (Caspi & Moffitt, 1991).

Again, however, it is important to consider the role of context in interaction with pubertal change. Although early-maturing girls generally are more likely to engage in delinquent behavior than their late-maturing peers, a study of New Zealand youngsters indicates that this may hold true only for girls who attend coeducational high schools (Caspi, Lynam, Moffitt, & Silva, 1993). Early-maturing girls in all-female schools are no more likely than late maturers to be involved in delinquent activities, presumably because there are far fewer opportunities for delinquency in same-sex schools. Thus, while early puberty may predispose girls toward more frequent and earlier deviance, this predisposition may be realized only in an environment that permits the behavior—such as a school that places early-maturing girls in close contact with older boys. Similarly, among both boys and girls, the impact of early maturation on problem behavior or depression is accentuated when adolescents have many stressful life events, live in disadvantaged urban neighborhoods, or have harsh and inconsistent parents (Ge, Brody, Conger, Simons, & Murry, 2002; Ge, Conger, & Elder, 2001; Obeidallah, Brennan, Brooks-Gunn, & Earls, 2004).

One study of the adult personalities of women who were either early or late maturers suggests some interesting parallels between the personality development of early-maturing girls and late-maturing boys (Peskin, 1973). Both sets of youngsters may have self-esteem problems during adolescence, but both appear to be somewhat more psychologically advanced than their peers during adulthood. Like the late-maturing boys, the early-maturing girls may be forced to develop coping skills during adolescence that have some long-term positive effects.

At the same time, however, more recent research indicates that the earlier involvement of early-maturing girls in problem behavior may adversely affect their long-term educational achievement and mental health. In one study of Swedish girls, for example, the researchers found that the school problems of early-maturing girls persisted over time, leading to the development of negative attitudes toward school and lower educational aspirations. In young adulthood, there were marked differences between the early- and late-maturing girls' levels of education; for example, the late-maturing girls were twice as likely as early-maturing girls to continue beyond the compulsory minimum number of years of high school (Magnusson et al., 1986). In a different study of American girls, researchers found that women who had been early maturers reported higher levels of psychological distress and were more likely than others to have experienced a serious mental disorder at some point in adolescence or young adulthood (Graber, Seeley, Brooks-Gunn, & Lewinsohn, 2004).

FOOD FOR THOUGHT

Consider the research on the psychological consequences of early versus late maturation in males and females. Most of this research has been done in the United States. Are the effects of being early, on time, or late likely to be similar in different parts of the world?

RECAP

- Although going through puberty in and of itself is not ordinarily stressful, some evidence suggests that adolescents may be moodier during periods of rapid changes in pubertal hormones. In general, though, stress in the environment is a much stronger influence on adolescent mental health than is puberty.

- Important changes in patterns of sleep take place at puberty. As the result of the emergence of a "delayed phase preference," after puberty, adolescents tend to stay up later at night and sleep later in the morning.

- Family relationships frequently become temporarily more strained and distant during the early stages of puberty.

- Among boys, early maturation is associated with popularity, higher self-esteem, and more self-

confidence, but also with higher rates of problem behavior.

- Among girls, early maturation is associated with higher rates of problem behavior, with psychological distress, and with emotional difficulties.

- In both sexes, the impact of early or late maturation depends on the social context in which it takes place.

Eating Disorders

Although a variety of nutritional and behavioral factors can lead to weight gain during adolescence, weight gain sometimes results directly from the physical changes of puberty. Not only does the ratio of body fat to muscle increase markedly during puberty, but the body's **basal metabolism rate**—the minimal amount of energy one uses when resting—also drops about 15%. A person's weight is partly dependent on this rate.

Because adolescence is a time of dramatic change in physical appearance, teenagers' overall self-image is very much tied to their body image. In light of the tremendous emphasis that contemporary society places on being thin, particularly for females, the normal weight gain and change in body composition that accompany puberty leads many adolescents, especially girls, to become extremely concerned about their weight.

OBESITY

Many adolescents, of course, have legitimate concerns about being overweight. The easiest way to determine whether someone is overweight is to calculate his or her **body mass index (BMI),** which is done by dividing the person's weight, measured in kilograms, by the square of the person's height, measured in meters. Individuals are considered obese if their BMI is at or above the 95th percentile for people of the same age and gender, at great risk for obesity if their BMI is at or above the 90th percentile, and overweight if their BMI is at or above the 85th percentile (Zametkin, Zoon, Klein, & Munson, 2004). (Charts showing the BMI cutoffs for males and females of different ages can be found at www.cdc.gov/growthcharts.) Using this definition, more than one sixth of adolescents in the United States are obese (Ogden, Carroll, & Flegal, 2008), and another 15% are

basal metabolism rate   The minimal amount of energy used by the body during a resting state.

body mass index (BMI)   A measure of an individual's body fat, the ratio of weight to height; used to gauge overweight and obesity.

FIGURE 1.12   The rate of obesity among American adolescents has more than tripled since 1970. (From Institute of Medicine, 2006)

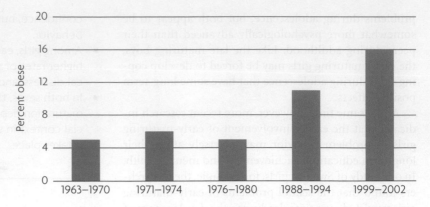

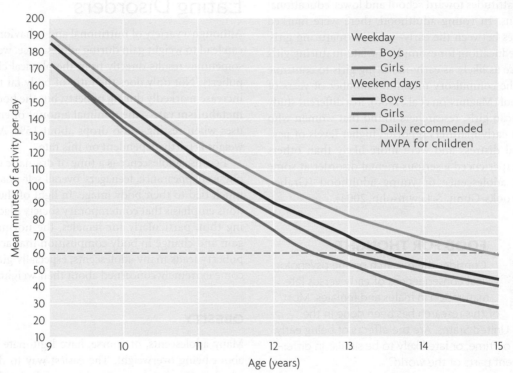

FIGURE 1.13   Between ages 9 and 15, there is a dramatic decline in the amount of time individuals spend in moderate-to-vigorous physical activity (MVPA). (Nader et al., 2008)

at great risk for obesity, a rate that has *tripled* since 1980 (Institute of Medicine, 2006) (see Figure 1.12). Compared to their peers in the mid-1960s, the average 15-year-old boy today is 15 pounds heavier, and the average 15-year-old girl is 10 pounds heavier—increases that are far greater than could possibly be due to changes in height. Obesity is now considered the single most serious public health problem afflicting American teenagers, and, unfortunately, there is no evidence that the situation is getting any better (Ogden, Carroll, & Flegal, 2008).

▌ **Influences on Obesity**   Current research indicates that obesity is a result of the interplay of genetic and environmental factors (Zametkin et al., 2004). Obesity is especially prevalent among poor youth and

among Black, Latino, and Native American adolescents (Miech et al., 2006; K. A. T. Wickrama, Wickrama, & Bryant, 2006). There is also worrisome evidence that, with each successive generation born in the United States, Latino youth show increasingly poorer nutrition (M. L. Allen et al., 2007).

Research on the psychological consequences of obesity has not led to consistent conclusions, in part because the psychological correlates of being overweight vary across ethnic groups, with more adverse correlates seen among White and Hispanic than among Black adolescents (BeLue, Francis, & Colaco, 2009). And while some studies show higher levels of psychological distress (such as depression and low self-esteem) among obese individuals, many studies show no such effect, and some research indicates that depression leads to obesity, rather than vice versa (Zametkin et al., 2004). In addition, the long-term psychological consequences of obesity in adolescence appear to be greater for females than males (M. Merten, Wickrama, & Williams, 2008); one study found, for example, that obese girls were less likely to enter college than other girls, but that no such pattern existed among boys (Crosnoe, 2007). Nevertheless, because nearly 80% of obese adolescents will be obese adults, obesity during adolescence places the individual at much higher risk for other health problems, including hypertension (high blood pressure), high cholesterol levels, and diabetes (Institute of Medicine, 2006).

Although genetic factors are important contributors, the dramatically increased prevalence of adolescent obesity over such a short time period indicates that the problem has strong environmental causes. Indeed, it is not at all difficult to understand why so many American adolescents today are overweight. Studies show that too many adolescents eat far too much high-calorie, high-fat food (drinking far too many sugary soft drinks and consuming far too much junk food), and too few are physically active (spending far too much time with television, video games, or the computer). One recent study of American youth (Nader, Bradley, Houts, McRitchie, & O'Brien, 2008) found that the amount of time individuals spend in moderate-to-vigorous physical activity falls from 3 hours per day at age 9 to only 49 minutes on weekdays and only 35 minutes on weekend days at age 15 (see Figure 1.13). The combination of inadequate exercise and poor nutrition is a recipe for obesity (Institute of Medicine, 2006).

▌ **Preventing and Treating Obesity** Much recent attention has focused on the availability of unhealthy foods and beverages in and near American schools. One study of 500,000 California adolescents found that students attending schools that were in close proximity to fast-food restaurants were significantly more likely to be overweight (B. Davis & Carpenter, 2009). Manufacturers of high-calorie and high-fat foods also have been criticized for marketing these products to younger children, because food preferences are known to develop largely during early childhood (Institute of Medicine, 2006). Of course, although schools and advertisers undoubtedly influence what children and adolescents eat and drink, the bulk of what children and adolescents put into their mouths comes from their own homes. Taken together, these studies indicate that preventing obesity will require multifaceted efforts involving parents, the mass media, food and beverage manufacturers, restaurants, and schools.

Research has also evaluated a variety of approaches to individual weight loss, including behavioral therapy designed to gradually alter patterns of diet and exercise and medications designed to promote weight loss. Sev-

Obesity is by far the most common eating disorder among adolescents.

eral evaluations indicate that the combination of behavior modification and weight loss medication is more effective than either component by itself (Berkowitz, Wadden, Tershakovec, & Cronquist, 2003; Chanoine, Hampl, Jensen, Boldrin, & Hauptman, 2005). Although there is evidence suggesting that some weight loss programs work, there is wide variability in success rates depending on the nature of the program (Stice, Shaw, & Marti, 2006). Radical approaches to weight control—fad diets and the like—actually increase, rather than decrease, obesity (Stice, Presnell, Shaw, & Rohde, 2005).

ANOREXIA NERVOSA AND BULIMIA

Health care professionals are concerned not only about adolescents who are obese but also about adolescents who have unhealthy attitudes toward eating and toward their body image (S. French, Story, Downes, Resnick, & Blum, 1995). Only about one-fourth of American adolescents are highly satisfied with their body (A. Kelly, Wall, Eisenberg, Story, & Neumark-Sztainer, 2005). Egged on by advertisers, who promote the idea that "thin is beautiful"—middle-class White girls define bodily perfection as being 5 feet 7 inches tall and weighing 110 pounds—many adolescents respond to normal bodily changes at puberty by dieting, often unnecessarily (Brumberg, 1997). More than half of all adolescent girls consider themselves overweight and have attempted to diet (M. Fisher et al., 1995). One recent study found that 14% of female college undergraduates were so concerned about eating that they were embarrassed at buying a chocolate bar in a store (Rozin, Bauer, & Catanese, 2003). Gender differences in concerns about weight emerge long before adolescence (Phares, Steinberg, & Thompson, 2004).

█ **Disordered Eating**   Psychologists use the term **disordered eating** to refer to unhealthy eating attitudes and behaviors. Disordered eating can range from unnecessary preoccupation with weight and body image to full-blown clinical eating disorders, such as anorexia and bulimia. Research shows that disordered eating is associated with a range of stress-related psychological problems, including poor body image, depression, alcohol and tobacco use, and poor interpersonal relationships (S. French et al., 1995; Graber, Brooks-Gunn, Paikoff, & Warren, 1994; Neumark-Sztainer, Story, Dixon, & Murray, 1998). It is not clear, however, whether these problems precede or follow from disordered eating (Leon, Fulkerson, Perry, Keel, & Klump, 1999).

In contemporary America, as the expression goes, one can never be too rich or too thin. Studies of magazines aimed at women and adolescent girls reveal clear and consistent messages implying that women cannot be beautiful without being slim and promoting a range of weight loss products. Between 1970 and 1990, moreover, images presented in these magazines' advertisements changed, with the "ideal" body shape becoming slimmer and less curvaceous (Guillen & Barr, 1994). Exposure to commercials containing images of females with idealized thin bodies increases girls' dissatisfaction with their own bodies (Hargreaves & Tiggemann, 2003). Interestingly, among Hispanic girls, those who are more acculturated ("Americanized") are significantly more likely to develop disordered eating than those who are less acculturated (Gowen, Hayward, Killen, Robinson, & Taylor, 1999). Girls whose mothers have body image problems are especially likely to engage in extreme weight loss behaviors (Ogle & Damhorst, 2003), as are those who report more negative relationships with their parents (Archibald, Graber, & Brooks-Gunn, 1999). Ironically, research indicates that adolescents' attempts to control their weight through intensive dieting, the use of laxatives and appetite suppressants, and deliberate vomiting lead to weight *gain,* not loss (Stice, Cameron, Killen, Hayward, & Taylor, 1999).

Not everyone is genetically or metabolically meant to be as thin as fashion magazines tell people they should be, however. Some young women become so concerned about gaining weight that they take drastic—and dangerous—measures to remain thin. Some go on eating binges and then force themselves to vomit to

avoid gaining weight, a pattern associated with an eating disorder called **bulimia.** In the more severe cases, young women who suffer from an eating disorder called **anorexia nervosa** actually starve themselves in an effort to keep their weight down. Adolescents with these sorts of eating disorders have an extremely disturbed body image: They see themselves as overweight when they are actually underweight. Some anorexic youngsters may lose between 25% and 50% of their body weight. As you might expect, bulimia and anorexia, if untreated, lead to a variety of serious physical problems; in fact, nearly 20% of anorexic teenagers inadvertently starve themselves to death.

Anorexia and bulimia each began to receive a great deal of popular attention during the 1980s, because of their dramatic nature and their frequent association in the mass media with celebrities. Perhaps because of this attention, initial reports characterized these eating disorders as being of epidemic proportion. Although unhealthy eating and unnecessary dieting are prevalent among teenagers, careful studies indicate that the incidence of genuine anorexia and genuine bulimia is rather small (M. Fisher et al., 1995). Fewer than 0.5% of adolescents are anorexic, and only about 3% are bulimic (American Psychiatric Association, 1994). Rates among females are substantially higher than among males—clinically defined anorexia and bulimia are 10 times more prevalent among adolescent girls than boys (Jacobi, Hayward, de Zwaan, Kraemer, & Agras, 2004), although the female-to-male ratio is substantially smaller when less severe forms of these disorders are considered (Muise, Stein, & Arbess, 2003; Ricciardelli & McCabe, 2004).

█ **Body Dissatisfaction**   Although the incidence of anorexia and bulimia is small, the proportion of adolescents who are unhappy with their body shape or weight is not. In one study, for example, more than one third of girls whose weight was considered normal by medical and health standards believed that they were overweight—including 5% who actually were *underweight* by medical criteria. (In contrast, fewer than 7% of normal-weight boys and no underweight boys described themselves as being overweight.) In this study, more than 70% of the girls reported that they would like to be thinner than they are (as opposed to one third of the boys), and more than 80% said that being thinner would make them happier, more successful, and more popular (Paxton et al., 1991). Dissatisfaction with body shape and weight is likely to lead to the development of eating problems (Attie & Brooks-Gunn, 1989), depression (Stice & Bearman, 2001; Stice, Hayward, Cameron, Killen, & Taylor, 2000), and the initiation of smoking (Austin & Gortmaker, 2001; Fulkerson & French, 2003; Stice & Shaw, 2003). According to a recent

disordered eating   Mild, moderate, or severe disturbance in eating habits and attitudes.

bulimia   An eating disorder found primarily among young women, characterized by a pattern of binge eating and self-induced vomiting.

anorexia nervosa   An eating disorder found chiefly among young women, characterized by dramatic and severe self-induced weight loss.

study, more than half of high school girls engaged in some form of unhealthy behavior (e.g., fasting, smoking, vomiting after eating, using diet pills) in order to lose weight (Croll, Neumark-Sztainer, Story, & Ireland, 2002). Taken together, these findings have led some writers to suggest that we think about disordered eating on a continuum, ranging from dieting that may be perfectly sensible and healthy, to disordered eating that is unhealthy but not psychopathological (i.e., at a level requiring treatment) to full-blown anorexia or bulimia (Tyrka, Graber, & Brooks-Gunn, 2000).

Unfortunately, many girls gain weight during puberty, and for early adolescent girls, being overweight is highly correlated with being seen as unattractive by others (Rosenblum & Lewis, 1999). Despite adults' wishes that girls not place so much emphasis on being thin, research indicates that the widespread belief among adolescent girls that being slim will increase their popularity, especially with boys, is in fact based in reality (Halpern, Udry, Campbell, & Suchindran, 1999). That is, the pressure girls feel to be thin in order to attract boys does not just come from television, movies, and magazines—it comes from their actual experience. Indeed, one recent analysis found that, regardless of a girl's ethnicity, each 1-point increase in a young woman's BMI (an index of the degree to which she is overweight) was associated with a 6% decrease in the probability of her being in a romantic relationship (Halpern, King, Oslak, & Udry, 2005). In that study, a 5-foot 3-inch girl who weighed 110 pounds was twice as likely to date as a girl of the same height and level of pubertal maturity who weighed 126 pounds.

▌ Prevalence and Causes of Anorexia and Bulimia　Initial reports on the prevalence of disordered eating among adolescent girls led to the conclusion that eating disorders were especially common among affluent, suburban, White, and Asian American girls (e.g., Condit, 1990). More recent studies do not support this contention, however. Contemporary research indicates that disordered eating and body dissatisfaction have been reported among poor as well as affluent teenagers and among Black and Hispanic as well as Asian and White youngsters (Jacobi et al., 2004). Although less is known about the causes and consequences of body dissatisfaction among adolescent males, evidence suggests that many contemporary adolescent boys feel pressure to be especially muscular and engage in unhealthy behaviors, such as anabolic steroid use, in order to develop an appearance that is more similar to the idealized male body type (Ricciardelli & McCabe, 2004). Moreover, body dissatisfaction is predictive of dieting, unhealthy weight control behaviors, and binge eating among males as well as females, re-

gardless of whether they are actually overweight (Crow, Eisenberg, Story, & Neumark-Sztainer, 2006; Neumark-Sztainer, Paxton, Hannan, Haines, & Story, 2006).

A recent analysis of historical and cross-cultural trends in the prevalence of anorexia and bulimia points to important differences between the two disorders (Keel & Klump, 2003). Whereas anorexia has been observed all over the world, bulimia has been reported almost exclusively in Western cultures or in cultures exposed to strong Western influences. And whereas anorexia has increased in prevalence steadily over time, the prevalence of bulimia increased significantly between 1970 and 1990 but has declined somewhat since then—interestingly, paralleling trends in females' reported body dissatisfaction, which also peaked in the early 1990s, despite the fact that individuals' BMI continued to increase (Cash, Morrow, Hrabosky, & Perry, 2004). This suggests that bulimia is a much more culturally determined disorder than is anorexia. Consistent with this, the degree to which anorexia is an inherited disorder is far more comparable from one culture to another than is the case for bulimia.

Several theories have been proposed to account for the onset of anorexia and bulimia during adolescence (see Jacobi et al., 2004, for a review). Traditional views emphasized psychological factors and, in particular, aspects of the parent–child relationship. Early writers who observed patterns of dysfunctional relationships in families with anorexic girls proposed that anorexia is related to the adolescent's attempts to assert her autonomy within an overly controlling family system in which parents are overprotective and highly critical (e.g., Minuchin, Rosman, & Baker, 1978). According to a recent comprehensive review of studies of risk factors for eating disorders, however, evidence in support of these theories is sparse, and the same familial factors that have been proposed to cause eating disorders have been shown to influence a wide variety of psychological disorders (Jacobi et al., 2004). In addition, longitudinal studies have shown that negative family relationships often follow from, rather than precede, the onset of disordered eating, raising questions about which causes which (Archibald, Linver, Graber, & Brooks-Gunn, 2002).

A second school of thought views eating disorders as part of a more general syndrome of psychological distress. Many studies have pointed to links between eating disorders and other serious mental health problems, such as depression, obsessive-compulsive disorders, or substance abuse; many anorexic and bulimic women display such psychological problems along with their eating disorder (D. French et al., 2001; Jacobi et al., 2004; Stice, Burton, & Shaw, 2004). These studies suggest that anorexia and bulimia may be best understood not as independent or unique disorders, but as particular manifestations of a more general underlying psychological problem—called "internalized distress"—that can be displayed in a variety of ways. (As you'll see in Chapter 13, many different psychological disorders in adolescence occur together, or "covary.") In support of this view, some evidence suggests that the same medications that are successful in treating depression and obsessive-compulsive disorder are useful in treating bulimia (but, interestingly, not anorexia) (Walsh et al., 2006).

Finally, because anorexia and bulimia are 10 times more common in females than males, broader social forces are probably a main factor in the development of these eating disorders (Keel & Klump, 2003). Research indicates, for example, that girls who are early maturers and early daters are likely to report greater dissatisfaction with their body and to be at greater risk for disordered eating (Cauffman & Steinberg, 1996; Smolak, Levine, & Gralen, 1993; Swarr & Richards, 1996); that girls who perceive that they are under pressure to be thin or who have accepted thinness as an ideal toward which to strive are more susceptible to eating disorders (Stice & Whitenton, 2002); and that girls who turn to popular magazines, such as *Seventeen, Sassy,* and *Glamour,* for information about dieting and appearance are more likely to have a high drive for thinness, low body satisfaction, and disturbed patterns of eating (D. C. Jones, Vigfusdottir, & Lee, 2004; M. Levine, Smolack, & Hayden, 1994). As noted earlier, cultural influences on the development of bulimia are especially strong.

Adolescents' beliefs about ideal body types are also shaped by the people they spend time with. One interesting study showed, for example, how bulimia became socially "contagious" in a college sorority (Crandall, 1988). This researcher found that over the course of the academic year, women's eating behavior became more and more like that of their sorority friends—even in a sorority in which binge eating was the norm. Other research indicates that girls' attitudes toward eating and dieting are influenced by the attitudes of their parents (especially their mothers) and friends (E. R. Mackey & La Greca, 2008; Mukai, 1996; Ogle & Damhorst, 2003; Paxton, Eisenberg, & Neumark-Sztainer, 2006). Being teased about one's weight is especially likely to lead to disordered eating, as well as symptoms of depression (M. E. Eisenberg, Neumark-Sztainer, Haines, & Wall, 2006; Haines, Neumark-Sztainer, Eisenberg, & Hannan, 2006).

Just because cultural conditions contribute to the development of disordered eating doesn't mean that individual characteristics do not play a role as well. Cultural conditions may predispose females more than males toward anorexia and bulimia, and girls and young women who have certain genetic vulnerabilities, psychological traits (such as proneness to depression or low self-esteem), physical characteristics (such as early pubertal maturation), familial characteristics (such as strained relations with parents), or social concerns (such as a strong interest in dating) may be more likely to develop problems (e.g., Cauffman & Steinberg, 1996; S. Frank & Jackson, 1996; Ricciardelli & McCabe, 2001). The onset of eating disorders, like so many aspects of adolescent development, is likely the product of a complex interaction between individual and contextual factors.

A variety of therapeutic approaches have been employed successfully in the treatment of anorexia and bulimia, including individual psychotherapy and cognitive-behavioral modification, group therapy, family therapy, and, more recently, antidepressant medications (Agras, Schneider, Arnow, Raeburn, & Telch, 1989; Condit, 1990; Killian, 1994). The treatment of anorexia often requires hospitalization initially in order to ensure that starvation does not progress to fatal or near-fatal levels (E. Mitchell, 1985).

FOOD FOR THOUGHT

Although obesity is a far more prevalent disorder than either anorexia or bulimia, until fairly recently, obesity attracted far less media attention. Now, however, childhood obesity is constantly in the news. Why do you think this change in media coverage has taken place?

RECAP

- The most common eating disorder in adolescence is obesity. About one in six American adolescents are obese, and another one in six are at great risk for obesity. Obesity is associated with a wide array of serious health problems.
- Anorexia and bulimia are eating disorders that do not appear until adolescence and that are far more prevalent among females than males.
- Many girls with anorexia or bulimia develop the disorder as a result of dissatisfaction with the way in which their body has changed following puberty, especially within a culture that idealizes thinness among women.
- Anorexia and bulimia are often accompanied by other emotional problems, such as depression, anxiety, or obsessive-compulsive disorder.

Physical Health and Health Care in Adolescence

Although puberty is undoubtedly the most important biological development of adolescence, concerns about the physical health and well-being of young people are far broader than those involving reproductive maturation. In the past two decades, the field of **adolescent health care** has grown rapidly, as health educators and health care practitioners have come to better understand that the health care needs of adolescents differ from those of children and adults in important respects (P. Williams, Holmbeck, & Greenley, 2002).

THE PARADOX OF ADOLESCENT HEALTH

Adolescence is a paradox as far as physical health is concerned. On the one hand, adolescence is one of the healthiest periods in the life span, characterized by a relatively low incidence of disabling or chronic illnesses (such as asthma or cancer), fewer short-term hospital stays, and fewer days in which individuals stay home sick. Nonetheless, in the United States, nearly 1 in 15 adolescents has at least one disabling chronic illness, with the main causes of disability being mental disorders such as depression, respiratory illnesses such as asthma, and muscular and skeletal disorders such as arthritis (Özer & Irwin, 2009). Fortunately, in the past 50 years, rates of death and disability resulting from illness and disease during adolescence have decreased substantially, and new medical technologies and better health care delivery have improved the physical well-being of children, especially those with chronic illnesses and disabling medical conditions (P. Williams et al., 2002). Adolescents are far less likely than individuals of any other age to seek and receive medical care through traditional office visits to practitioners, however; and there are large socioeconomic and ethnic disparities in adolescents' access to health care, with poor and ethnic minority youths far less likely to have adequate health insurance and health care access than affluent or White youths (Ozer & Irwin, 2009).

The most virulent threat to adolescent health comes from unhealthy behaviors (such as drug use), violence (both self-inflicted and inflicted by others), and risky activity (such as unprotected sexual intercourse or reckless driving) (P. Williams et al., 2002). In some senses, then, many of the improvements in preventing and treating the traditional medical problems of the period—those having to do with chronic illnesses—have been offset by what some scientists call the "new morbidity and mortality" of adolescence (Hein, 1988). Contributors to this new morbidity and mortality include accidents (especially automobile accidents), suicide, homicide, substance abuse (including tobacco and alcohol use), and sexually transmitted diseases (including AIDS).

CAUSES OF MORTALITY IN ADOLESCENCE

The contrast between the old and new mortalities of adolescence is readily apparent. Fifty years ago, illness and disease accounted for more than twice as many deaths among teenagers as violence or injury, but the reverse is true today. A recent analysis of the causes of mortality among adolescents and young adults indicates that unintentional injuries are the leading cause of death worldwide, followed by AIDS, infectious disease, homicide, and suicide, in that order (Blum & Nelson-Mmari, 2004). According to recent estimates, approximately 45% of all teenage deaths in the United States result from car accidents and other unintentional injuries, and another 27% are a result of homicide or suicide (Ozer & Irwin, 2009). Adolescents are involved in more driving accidents than adults, primarily because they are less experienced behind the wheel (at any age, new drivers are more likely to have accidents than seasoned drivers), but also because they are more likely to take chances while driving (Cvijanovich, Cook, Mann, & Dean, 2001; Dee & Evans, 2001; Harré, 2000). Two of the most important contributors to serious car accidents involving teenage drivers are driving at night and driving with other teenagers in the car (Simons-Morton, Hartos, Leaf, & Preusser, 2005). This finding has led many states to implement graduated driver-licensing programs, which place restrictions on when and with whom teenagers can drive until they have gained sufficient experience; these programs have reduced automobile fatalities (Foss, Feaganes, & Rodgman, 2001; Shope, Molnar, Elliott, & Waller, 2001). One piece of good news: Although alcohol contributes greatly to automobile accidents among young drivers, the rate of alcohol-related traffic fatalities among young people has dropped dramatically in recent years (Dee & Evans, 2001).

The consensus among health care experts, then, is that the most significant threats to the health of today's youths arise from psychosocial rather than from natural causes (Ozer & Irwin, 2009). Unlike some other periods of the life span (such as infancy or old age), when we are more vulnerable to disease and illness, in adolescence most health problems are preventable. Moreover, patterns of diet, drug use, and exercise established during adolescence persist into adulthood (P. Williams et al., 2002). As a result of this recognition, the focus in the field of adolescent health has shifted away from traditional medical models (in which the emphasis is on the assessment, diagnosis, and treatment of disease) and

adolescent health care   A field of study and health care devoted to understanding the health care needs of individuals during the second decade of life.

toward more community-oriented, educational approaches (in which the emphasis is on the prevention of illness and injury and the promotion of good health) (National Research Council and Institute of Medicine, 2009).

FOOD FOR THOUGHT

Although most adolescent health problems are caused by teenagers' own behavior, getting adolescents to change how they live has proven remarkably difficult. Why do you think this is the case?

In other words, instead of asking how we can best treat sick adolescents, experts in adolescent health care are now asking how we can encourage adolescents to take the steps necessary to prevent illness and disability. Current efforts include providing teenagers with education about alcohol and drug use, accident prevention, safe sex, and proper nutrition, as well as encouraging health care professionals to do more direct screening for risky health practices among their adolescent patients. As one group of experts put it, "Don't ask, they won't tell" (Blum, Beuhring, Wunderlich, & Resnick, 1996, p. 1767).

PROMOTING ADOLESCENT HEALTH

As many experts point out, health behavior is influenced by a number of factors, of which knowledge is only one component (e.g., H. Leventhal & Keeshan, 1993). Changes in the context in which adolescents live (such as the accessibility of handguns or the availability of tobacco, alcohol, and illicit drugs) must accompany changes in adolescents' knowledge and understanding if lasting health promotion is to be accomplished (Nation et al., 2003). For example, recent investigations of the impact of changing one element of the broader context of adolescent health—the legal drinking age—have found that raising the age leads to a significant decline in accidental death rates among young automobile drivers and pedestrians, as well as in the rates of unintentional injuries not involving cars and homicides (N. Jones, Pieper, & Robertson, 1992; Kypri et al., 2006). Similarly, the single most effective policy for reducing teen smoking has been raising the price of cigarettes (Gruber & Zinman, 2001), and the prevalence of adolescent smoking is a direct function of the number of retail outlets selling tobacco in their immediate neighborhood (Novak, Reardon, Raudenbush, & Buka, 2006).

Improving the health of young people is an especially important concern among those working with adolescents who are poor or from ethnic minority groups, because these youngsters are at greater risk for many of the old and new morbidities and mortalities of adolescence (Ozer & Irwin, 2009). Non-White youngsters, for example, are relatively more likely than White youngsters to suffer from a chronic illness (Ozer & Irwin, 2009), to be obese or to have high blood pressure or high cholesterol levels (National Heart, Lung, and Blood Institute Growth and Health Study Research Group, 1992), to be physically inactive (Wolf et al., 1993), to be victims of violent crimes (Earls, Cairns, & Mercy, 1993), to contract AIDS (Sells & Blum, 1996), to die from drowning (Warneke & Cooper, 1994), and to be murdered (Sorenson, Richardson, & Peterson, 1993). Homicide is the leading cause of death for Black adolescents, accounting for almost half of all deaths among Black youth. American Indian/Alaska Native males have a suicide rate higher than that of any other racial/ethnic group. Yet, despite their generally poorer health, minority youngsters are less likely to have access to sources of medical care, less likely to visit the doctor when ill, and less likely to have health insurance (Ozer & Irwin, 2009).

The combination of poor health and limited access to health care is even more concentrated among the sizable proportion of adolescents who live in poverty, a disproportionate number of whom are from ethnic minority backgrounds (Klerman, 1993). There is now convincing evidence that the links between health and socioeconomic status are strong and pervasive across different sorts of health problems, with physical and mental health problems increasing linearly as one moves down the socioeconomic ladder (Adler et al., 1994; Keating & Hertzman, 2000). Because increases in the size of the adolescent population over the next several decades worldwide will be concentrated among poor and minority youth (Fussell & Greene, 2002), the most daunting challenge facing health care providers and policymakers will be finding ways of minimizing or even eliminating the socioeconomic and ethnic disparities in health and health care that currently exist around the world (Call et al., 2002; Ozer & Irwin, 2009).

RECAP

- The most important physical health problems afflicting adolescents have behavioral rather than natural causes.
- The leading cause of mortality among adolescents around the world is unintentional accidents.
- Experts in adolescent health care argue that it is important to focus on changing adolescents' behavior in order to prevent health-compromising activities and encourage health-promoting ones.

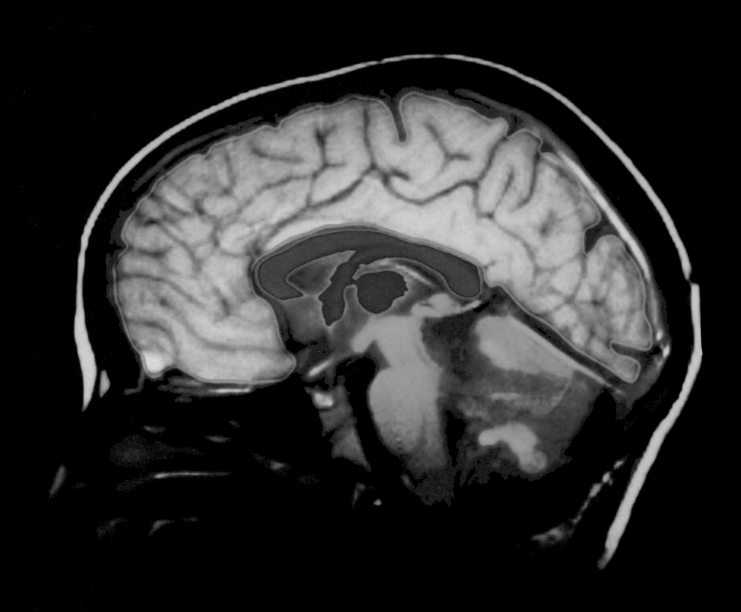

Cognitive Transitions

CHANGES IN COGNITION, or thinking, represent the second of three fundamental changes that occur during adolescence—the others being the biological changes of puberty and the transition into new social roles. Like developments in the other two domains, the cognitive transitions of adolescence have far-reaching implications for the young person's psychological development and social relations. Indeed, the expansion of thought during adolescence represents as significant an event and as important an influence on the adolescent's development and behavior as puberty. In the view of some writers, adolescence is a critical period for the development of more complex and sophisticated ways of reasoning about the world (Kuhn, 2009).

In recent years, scientists have made tremendous gains in understanding brain maturation during adolescence through the use of imaging techniques that permit us to look inside the adolescent brain, just as an X-ray permits physicians to look directly at bones. We now have a good idea of how the brain changes during the adolescent years and the implications of these changes for behavioral, emotional, and, of course, cognitive development. Later in this chapter, we'll look at brain maturation in adolescence in detail. But let's begin by simply describing how adolescents think and, more importantly, how their thinking differs from that of children.

Changes in Cognition

Most people would agree that adolescents are "smarter" than children. Not only do teenagers know more than children—after all, the longer we live, the more opportunities we have to acquire new information—but they actually think in ways that are more advanced, more efficient, and generally more effective. This can be seen in five chief ways:

1. Adolescents are better able than children to think about what is possible, instead of limiting their thought to what is real.
2. Adolescents are better able than children to think about abstract things.
3. Adolescents think more often than children about the process of thinking itself.
4. Adolescents' thinking, compared to children's, is more often multidimensional, rather than limited to a single issue.
5. Adolescents are more likely than children to see things as relative, rather than as absolute.

Let's look at each of these advantages—and some of their implications for adolescents' behavior—in greater detail.

THINKING ABOUT POSSIBILITIES

Adolescents' thinking is less bound to concrete events than is that of children. Children's thinking is oriented to the here and now—that is, to things and events that they can observe directly. But adolescents are able to consider what they observe against a backdrop of what is possible. Put another way, for the child, what is possible is what is real; for the adolescent, what is real is just a subset of what is possible. Consider how individuals think about themselves. Children generally do not wonder, the way adolescents often do, about how their personalities might change in the future, or how their lives might be affected by different career choices, or how they might have been different had they grown up under different circumstances. As a young child, you simply are who you are. But as an adolescent, who you are is just one possibility of who you could be.

This does not mean that children are incapable of imagination or fantasy. Nor does it mean that children are unable to conceive of things being different from the way they observe them to be. Rather, the advantage that adolescents enjoy over children when it comes to thinking about possibilities is that adolescents are able to move easily between the specific and the abstract, to generate alternative possibilities and explanations systematically, and to compare what they actually observe with what they believe is possible.

The adolescent's ability to reason systematically in terms of what is possible comes in handy in a variety of mathematical, scientific, and other problem-solving contexts. For instance, the study of mathematics in junior and senior high school (algebra, geometry, and trigonometry) often requires that you begin with an abstract or theoretical formulation—for example, "the square of a right triangle's hypotenuse is equal to the sum of the squares of the other two sides" (the Pythagorean theorem). This theorem, after all, is a proposition about the possible rather than the real. It is a statement about all *possible* right triangles, not just triangles that you might actually observe. In mathematics, you learn how to apply these theorems to concrete examples (that is, real triangles). Scientific experimentation—in biology, chemistry, and physics—also involves the ability to generate possibilities systematically. In a chemistry experiment in which you are trying to identify an unknown substance by performing various tests, you must first be able to imagine alternative possibilities for the substance's identity in order to know what tests to conduct.

The adolescent's use of this sort of thinking is not limited to scientific problem solving. We see it in the types of arguments adolescents employ, in which they are better able than younger children to envision and therefore anticipate the possible responses of an opponent and to have handy a counterargument or series of counterarguments (R. Clark & Delia, 1976). Many parents believe that their children become more argumentative during adolescence. What probably happens, though, is that their children become *better arguers*. An adolescent does not accept other people's points of view unquestioningly—including his or her parents' viewpoints—but instead evaluates them against other theoretically possible beliefs. As you'll see in Chapter 4, this improvement in the adolescent's intellectual ability likely contributes to the bickering and squabbling that often occur between teenagers and their parents (Smetana, 1989).

FOOD FOR THOUGHT

In what ways did your high school classes take advantage of the advanced thinking abilities that develop in adolescence? In what ways were opportunities to do this missed?

■ **Deductive and Inductive Reasoning** One manifestation of the adolescent's increased facility with thinking about possibilities is the development of **deductive reasoning.** Deductive reasoning is a type of logical reasoning in which you draw logically necessary conclusions from a general set of premises, or givens. Consider the following problem:

All hockey players wear mouth guards.
Kim is a hockey player.
Does Kim wear a mouth guard?

Individuals who reason deductively understand that the correct conclusion (that Kim wears a mouth guard) necessarily follows from the first two statements. No additional knowledge about hockey or about Kim is necessary to reach the correct answer. Adolescents are also better able than children to recognize when a logical problem does not provide sufficient information and to respond by saying that the question can't be answered with any certainty. Suppose we were to change the problem to read like this:

All hockey players wear mouth guards.
Kim is wearing a mouth guard.
Is Kim a hockey player?

If you answer this type of question quickly, without thinking it through, you might say that Kim is indeed a hockey player. But, in fact, this is not necessarily the case. Whereas children are easily fooled by such problems, adolescents are more likely to say that there is no way of knowing whether Kim plays hockey, because we are not told that the *only* people who wear mouth guards are hockey players. One reason for their superior performance on these sorts of problems is that adolescents are better able to catch themselves before they incorrectly answer the question and pause a moment before responding (Daniel & Klaczynski, 2006). Interestingly, the ability to stop yourself before acting automatically (and perhaps incorrectly) is controlled by a region of the brain that has been shown to mature during adolescence (Luna, Garver, Urban, Lazar, & Sweeney, 2004).

Often in life, we make educated guesses even though our hunches cannot be supported by deductive reasoning. Consider the following problem:

Kim, John, Julie, Tom, Liz, and Kendra are hockey players.
Kim, John, Julie, Tom, Liz, and Kendra all wear mouth guards.
Do all hockey players wear mouth guards?

This problem cannot be solved using deductive reasoning because no certain answer to the question necessarily follows from the first two statements. Instead, this problem is likely to be solved using **inductive reasoning,** in which an inference is made based on the accumulated evidence. For this problem, your answer to the question would likely vary depending on how many people were listed in the first two statements, your knowledge of hockey, your own experience playing contact sports, and so on. And rather than being certain of your answer, you would have different degrees of confidence in your conclusion depending on the amount of information you had. In other words, whereas the conclusions derived from deductive inferences are guaranteed to be true by virtue of their inherent logic, conclusions derived from inductive inferences vary in their likelihood of being true (Galotti, Komatsu, & Voelz, 1997). Inductive reasoning is used by people of all ages, even very young children (Jacobs & Portenza, 1991). Indeed, we all use inductive reasoning in everyday situations (for example, you find out that many of your classmates have gotten poor grades on a test, so you start to worry that you will, too). Deductive reasoning is seldom used before adolescence, however. Indeed, the development of deductive

deductive reasoning A type of logical reasoning in which one draws logically necessary conclusions from a general set of premises, or givens.

inductive reasoning Reasoning that involves drawing an inference from the evidence that one has.

reasoning is seen by many researchers as the major intellectual accomplishment of adolescence (Klaczynski & Narasimham, 1998; Morris & Sloutsky, 2001).

▌ Hypothetical Thinking Related to the development of deductive reasoning is the emergence of hypothetical, or "if-then," thinking. In order to think hypothetically, you need to see beyond what is directly observable and apply logical reasoning to anticipate what might be possible. The ability to think through hypotheses is an enormously powerful tool. Being able to plan ahead, to see the future consequences of an action, and to provide alternative explanations of events are all dependent on being able to hypothesize effectively.

Thinking in hypothetical terms also permits us to suspend our beliefs about something in order to argue in the abstract. Being capable of assuming a hypothetical stance is important when it comes to debating an issue, since doing so permits us to understand the logic behind the other person's argument without necessarily agreeing with its conclusion. Playing devil's advocate, for example—as when you formulate a position contrary to what you really believe in order to challenge someone else's reasoning—requires the ability to think in hypothetical terms. Studies show that prior to adolescence, individuals have difficulty in dealing with propositions that are contrary to fact, unless they are part of a larger fiction (Markovits & Valchon, 1989). For example, a 7-year-old would have trouble answering the question "Where would flying cows build nests?" He might say, "Cows don't fly," unless he had heard about flying cows in a story that was clearly fantasy-based.

Of course, hypothetical thinking also has implications for the adolescent's social behavior. It helps the young person to take the perspective of others by enabling him or her to think through what someone else might be thinking or feeling, given that person's point of view ("If I were in that person's situation, I would feel pretty angry"). Hypothetical thinking helps in formulating and arguing a viewpoint, because it allows adolescents to think a step ahead of the opposition—a cognitive tool that comes in quite handy when dealing with parents ("If they come back with 'You have to stay home and clean up the garage,' then I'll remind them about the time they let my sister go out when *she* had chores to do"). And hypothetical thinking plays an important role in decision making, because it permits the young person to plan ahead and to foresee the consequences of choosing one alternative over another ("If I go out for the soccer team, then I am going to have to give up my part-time job"). As we will see, scientists now believe that the development of the ability to think ahead is closely tied to the maturation of a region of the brain that changes dramatically during adolescence (Steinberg, 2005a).

THINKING ABOUT ABSTRACT CONCEPTS

The appearance of more systematic, abstract thinking is the second notable aspect of cognitive development during adolescence. We noted earlier that children's thinking is more concrete and more bound to observable events and objects than is that of adolescents. This difference is clearly evident when we consider the ability to deal with abstract concepts—things that cannot be experienced directly through the senses.

For example, adolescents find it easier than children to comprehend the sorts of higher-order abstract logic inherent in puns, proverbs, metaphors, and analogies. When presented with verbal analogies, children are more likely than adolescents to focus on concrete and familiar associations among the words than on the abstract, or conceptual, relations among them.

Consider the following analogy:

Sun : Moon : : Asleep : ?

a. Star

b. Bed

c. Awake

d. Night

Instead of answering "awake"—which is the best answer of the four—children would be more likely to respond with "bed" or "night," since both of these words have stronger associations with the word "asleep." It is generally not until early adolescence that individuals are able to discern the abstract principles underlying analogies—in the one above, the principle involves opposites—and therefore solve them correctly (Sternberg & Nigro, 1980).

The adolescent's greater facility with abstract thinking also permits the application of advanced reasoning and logical processes to social and ideological matters. This is clearly seen in the adolescent's increased facility and interest in thinking about interpersonal relationships, politics, philosophy, religion, and morality—topics that involve such abstract concepts as friendship, faith, democracy, fairness, and honesty. As some writers have pointed out, the ability to think abstractly may prompt many adolescents to spend time thinking about the meaning of life itself (Hacker, 1994). The growth of social thinking—generally referred to as "social cognition"—during adolescence is directly related to the young person's improving ability to think abstractly. Later in this chapter, we will examine the ways in which social thinking improves in adolescence.

THINKING ABOUT THINKING

A third noteworthy gain in cognitive ability during adolescence involves thinking about thinking itself, a process sometimes referred to as **metacognition.** Metacognition often involves monitoring your own cognitive activity during the thinking process—for example,

metacognition The process of thinking about thinking itself.

when you consciously use a strategy for remembering something (such as *Every Good Boy Deserves Fun,* for the notes of the treble clef in music notation) or when you appraise your own comprehension of something you are reading before going on to the next paragraph. Studies show that using such strategies significantly aids adolescents in problem-solving situations (Chalmers & Lawrence, 1993). In addition, interventions designed to improve adolescents' metacognitive skills have been shown to enhance reading, writing, test taking, and performance on homework (W. Williams et al., 2002). Not only do adolescents "manage" their thinking more than children do, but they are also better able to explain to others the processes they are using. Adolescence is an important time for changes in our understanding of what knowledge is and how it is acquired (Schommer, Calvert, Gariglietti, & Bajaj, 1997). When asked, adolescents can explain not only *what* they know but *why* knowing what they know enables them to think differently and solve problems more effectively (Reich, Oser, & Valentin, 1994). In addition, adolescents are much better able than children to understand that people do not have complete control over their mental activity. One study found, for example, that adolescents and adults were much more likely than children to understand that it is impossible to go for a long period of time without thinking about anything, that we often have thoughts that we do not want to have, and that unwanted thoughts we try to get rid of often return (Flavell, Green, & Flavell, 1998).

Another interesting way in which thinking about thinking becomes more apparent during adolescence is in increased introspection, self-consciousness, and intellectualization. When we are introspective, we are thinking about our own emotions. When we are self-conscious, we are thinking about how others think about us. And when we intellectualize, we are thinking about our own thoughts. All three processes play an important role in the adolescent's psychological growth. As we'll see in Chapter 8, for example, these processes permit the sorts of self-examination and exploration that are important components of the young person's attempt to establish a coherent sense of identity.

FOOD FOR THOUGHT

What metacognitive tools do you use to aid in your own studying?

❚ Adolescent Egocentrism   These intellectual advances may occasionally result in problems for the young adolescent, particularly before she or he adjusts

Adolescent egocentrism brought on by the cognitive changes of the period can contribute to a heightened sense of self-consciousness.

to having such powerful cognitive tools. Being able to introspect, for instance, may lead to periods of extreme self-absorption—a form of "adolescent egocentrism" (Elkind, 1967). Adolescent egocentrism results in two distinct problems in thinking that help to explain some of the seemingly odd beliefs and behaviors of teenagers (Goossens, Seiffge-Krenke, & Marcoen, 1992).

The first, the **imaginary audience,** involves having such a heightened sense of self-consciousness that the teenager imagines that his or her behavior is the focus of everyone else's attention. For example, a teenager who is going to a concert with 4,000 other people may worry about dressing the right way because "everybody will notice." Given the cognitive limitations of adolescent egocentrism, it is difficult indeed to persuade the young person that the "audience" is not all that concerned with his or her behavior or appearance. According to a recent study (Rankin, Lane, Gibbons, & Gerrard, 2004), feelings of self-consciousness, which on average are more intense among girls than boys, increase during early adolescence, peak around age 15, and then decline, presumably as the adolescent gains more social confidence. And evidence from recent studies of brain maturation suggests that the parts of the brain that process social information—such as perceptions of what others are thinking—undergo significant change during early adolescence, just when self-consciousness is increasing (E. Nelson, Leibenluft, McClure, & Pine, 2005; Sebastian, Burnett, & Blakemore, 2008).

imaginary audience   The belief, often brought on by the heightened self-consciousness of early adolescence, that everyone is watching and evaluating one's behavior.

A second problem resulting from adolescent egocentrism is called the **personal fable.** The personal fable revolves around the adolescent's egocentric (and erroneous) belief that her or his experiences are unique. For instance, an adolescent whose relationship with a girlfriend has just ended might tell his sympathetic mother that she could not possibly understand what it feels like to break up with someone—even though breaking up is something that most people have experienced plenty of times during their adolescent and young adult years. In some respects, adherence to a personal fable of uniqueness provides some protective benefits, in that it enhances adolescents' self-esteem and feelings of self-importance. Sometimes, however, holding on to a personal fable can be dangerous, as in the case of a sexually active adolescent who believes that pregnancy simply won't happen to her or a reckless driver who believes that he will defy the laws of nature by taking hairpin turns at breakneck speed.

Although it had once been thought that much of the risk-taking behavior engaged in by adolescents was due in part to teenagers' heightened susceptibility to the personal fable, researchers have found it difficult to confirm that egocentrism actually peaks in early adolescence. In fact, certain aspects of adolescent egocentrism, such as the personal fable, may persist through the adult years (Frankenberger, 2000; Goossens et al., 1992; Quadrel, Fischhoff, & Davis, 1993). Ask any *adult* cigarette smoker if she or he is aware of the scientific evidence linking cigarette smoking with heart and lung disease, and you'll see that the personal fable is quite common among many individuals who have long since left adolescence.

Why have studies failed to find that egocentrism is greater in adolescence than at other ages? One problem with many studies of adolescent egocentrism is that they rely on fairly simple questionnaires to assess rather complicated belief systems invoked in real-life situations (Alberts, Elkind, & Ginsberg, 2007). For example, it is easy to imagine that the same adolescent who is worried about being seen by "everyone" at a rock concert might not endorse a questionnaire item that reads "When I am at a concert, I think everyone in the audience is looking at me." One explanation for this discrepancy is that adolescent egocentrism is an emotional and social phenomenon, not a cognitive one. Another is that adolescents are overly concerned about what others think of them not because they are intellectually compromised, but because, in the highly social world in which they live, other peoples' opinions actually have genuine and important consequences (J. Bell & Bromnick, 2000). It's like the old joke: "Just because you're paranoid doesn't mean that people aren't following you."

FOOD FOR THOUGHT

Think back to your own adolescence. Can you recall times when you experienced an imaginary audience? Do you think this happened more when you were younger than it does now?

THINKING IN MULTIPLE DIMENSIONS

A fourth way in which thinking changes during adolescence involves the ability to think about things in a multidimensional fashion (Huizenga, Crone, & Jansen, 2007; Kuhn, 2009). Whereas children tend to think about things one aspect at a time, adolescents can see things through more complicated lenses. For instance, when a certain hitter comes up to the plate in a baseball game, a preadolescent who knows that the hitter has a good home-run record might exclaim that the batter will hit the ball out of the park. An adolescent, however, would consider the hitter's record in relation to the specific pitcher on the mound and would weigh both factors, or dimensions, before making a prediction (perhaps this player often hits homers against left-handed pitchers but strikes out against righties).

The ability to think in multidimensional terms is evident in a variety of situations. Obviously, adolescents can give much more complicated answers than children to questions such as "Why did the Civil War begin?" or "How did Jane Austen's novels reflect the changing position of women in European society?" Thorough answers to these sorts of questions require thinking about several dimensions simultaneously.

The development of a more sophisticated understanding of probability is also made possible by an improved ability to think in multidimensional terms. Suppose I give you a set of blue and yellow beads. Now I ask you to divide them into two containers so that the containers have different numbers of beads overall but the probability of reaching into a container and picking a blue bead is the same for each. In order to do so, you would have to vary the number of blue beads *and* the number of yellow beads between the two containers, because the probability of drawing a blue bead is a function of both the number of blue beads and the number of yellow beads. It is not until early adolescence that individuals can solve this sort of problem successfully (Falk & Wilkening, 1998).

As is the case with other gains in cognitive ability, the increasing capability of individuals to think in multiple dimensions also has consequences for their

---

personal fable   An adolescent's belief that he or she is unique and therefore not subject to the rules that govern other people's behavior.

behavior and thinking outside of academic settings. Adolescents describe themselves and others in more differentiated and complicated terms ("I'm both shy and extroverted") and find it easier to look at problems from multiple perspectives ("I know that's the way you see it, but try to look at it from her point of view"). Understanding that people's personalities are not one-sided or that social situations can have different interpretations, depending on one's point of view, permits the adolescent to have far more sophisticated—and far more complicated—self-conceptions as well as relationships with other people.

■ **Sarcasm and *South Park***   One interesting manifestation of adolescents' ability to look at things in multiple dimensions concerns the development of children's understanding of sarcasm. As an adult, you understand that the meaning of a speaker's statement is communicated by a combination of what is said, how it is said, and the context in which it is said. If I turned to you during a boring lecture, rolled my eyes, and said, in an exaggeratedly earnest tone, "This is the most interesting lecture I've ever heard," you would know that I actually meant just the opposite. But you would know this only if you paid attention to my inflection and to the context, as well as the content, of my statement. Only by attending simultaneously to multiple dimensions of speech can we distinguish between the sincere and the sarcastic. Because our ability to think in multidimensional terms improves during adolescence, we would predict improvements as well in the ability to understand when someone is being sarcastic.

In one study designed to look at this question, children, adolescents, and adults were presented with different stories, in which an interaction between two people was followed by a remark that was sincere, deliberately deceptive, or sarcastic (Demorest, Meyer, Phelps, Gardner, & Winner, 1984). The participants in the study were then asked what the true meaning and intent of the remark were. Before the age of 9, children had difficulty picking out sarcastic remarks. Individuals' understanding of sarcasm increased somewhat between ages 9 and 13 and continued to increase during the adolescent years.

Why do young adolescents laugh hysterically when characters in movies aimed at their age group say things like "He said 'erector set'"? Adolescents' increased facility in thinking along multiple dimensions permits them to appreciate satire, metaphor, and the ways in which language can be used to convey multiple messages, as in double entendres—expressions that have two meanings, one of them typically rude or crude. Teenagers' newfound ability to use and appreciate sarcasm and satire helps to explain why shows like *The Simpsons, South Park,* and *The Family Guy* have always had such strong appeal in this age group. (Not to mention that they are often pretty funny to adults, too. Our son's

school once summoned his class's parents to watch an "offensive" episode of *South Park,* to show us how our children were being harmed by television; the demonstration ended prematurely, though, because we parents were laughing too hard.)

ADOLESCENT RELATIVISM

A final aspect of cognition that changes during adolescence concerns a shift from seeing things in absolute terms—in black and white—to seeing things as relative. Compared to children, adolescents are more likely to question others' assertions and less likely to accept "facts" as absolute truths.

This increase in relativism can be particularly exasperating to parents, who may feel as though their adolescent children question everything just for the sake of argument. Difficulties often arise, for example, when adolescents begin seeing parents' values that they had previously considered absolutely correct ("Moral people do not have sex before they are married") as completely relative ("Welcome to the twenty-first century, Dad").

Adolescents' belief that everything is relative can become so overwhelming that they may become extremely skeptical about many things (Chandler, 1987). In fact, once adolescents begin to doubt the certainty of things that they had previously believed, they may come to believe that everything is uncertain, that no knowledge is completely reliable. Some theorists have suggested that adolescents pass through such a period of extreme skepticism on the way toward reaching a more sophisticated understanding of the complexity of knowledge.

RECAP

- One of the most important changes in thinking during adolescence is the increased ease with which individuals think about what is possible or hypothetical.
- Being able to think about what is possible, and not just what is real, is reflected in improvements in deductive reasoning—reasoning that is based on principles of logic.
- Adolescence is a time of improvements in thinking about abstract concepts.
- During adolescence, individuals become better able to engage in "thinking about thinking," or metacognition.
- Compared with children, adolescents are better able to think in multiple dimensions.
- Adolescents often go through a stage of relativistic thinking, during which they question the validity of absolutes.

Theoretical Perspectives on Adolescent Thinking

Although there is general agreement that adolescents' thinking is different and more advanced than children's in the ways we have just described, there is far less consensus about the processes underlying the cognitive differences between children and adolescents. Part of the lack of agreement stems from the fact that no one single factor distinguishes thinking during adolescence from thinking during childhood (Keating, 2004). And part of the lack of agreement stems from the different points of view that theorists have taken toward the issue of cognitive development in general. Because researchers working from different theoretical perspectives have posed different research questions, used different tasks to measure cognitive growth, and emphasized different aspects of cognitive activity, their studies provide different, but still theoretically compatible, pictures of mental development during adolescence.

The two theoretical viewpoints that have been especially important are the Piagetian perspective and the information-processing perspective. Although these two views of adolescent thinking begin from different assumptions about the nature of cognitive development in general, they each provide valuable insight into why thinking changes during adolescence (Kuhn, 2009).

THE PIAGETIAN VIEW OF ADOLESCENT THINKING

▌ **Piaget's Theory of Cognitive Development**
Generally, theorists who adopt a Piagetian perspective and take a **cognitive-developmental view** of intellectual development argue that cognitive development proceeds through a fixed sequence of qualitatively distinct stages, that adolescent thinking is fundamentally different from the type of thinking employed by

children, and that during adolescence, individuals develop a special type of thinking that they use in a variety of situations.

According to Piaget, cognitive development proceeds through four stages: (1) the **sensorimotor period** (from birth until about age 2), (2) the **preoperational period** (from about age 2 until about age 5), (3) the period of **concrete operations** (from about age 6 until early adolescence), and (4) the period of **formal operations** (from adolescence through adulthood). Each stage is characterized by a particular type of thinking, with earlier stages of thinking being incorporated into new, more advanced, and more adaptive forms of reasoning. According to Piaget, transitions into higher stages of reasoning are most likely to occur when the child's biological readiness and the increasing complexity of environmental demands interact to stimulate more advanced thinking.

Piagetian theorists believe that the use of abstract logical reasoning—the foundation of formal-operational thinking—is the chief feature of adolescent thinking that differentiates it from the type of thinking employed by children. This is not unlike the claim, discussed earlier, that the ability to use deductive reasoning is the defining feature of adolescent cognition. We noted that adolescents' thinking can be distinguished from the thinking of children in several respects—among them, in thinking about possibilities, in thinking multidimensionally, and in thinking about abstract concepts. The connection between these types of thinking and the development of formal operations is clear: In order to think about alternatives to what really exists, in order to think in multidimensional terms, and in order to systematically think about concepts that are not directly observable, you must have a system of reasoning that works just as well in abstract, imagined, and complicated situations as it does in concrete ones.

▌ **The Growth of Formal-Operational Thinking**
The development of formal thinking appears to take place in two steps. During the first step, characteristic of early adolescence, formal thinking is apparent, but it has a sort of "Now you see it, now you don't" quality to it. Young adolescents may demonstrate formal thinking at some times but at others may think only in concrete terms; they may use formal operations on some tasks but not on others; they may reason formally under some but not all testing situations (Markovits et al., 1996). It is not until middle or even late adolescence that formal-operational thinking becomes consolidated and integrated into the individual's general approach to reasoning (Markovits & Valchon, 1990).

While virtually all adolescents have the potential to develop formal-operational thinking, and most can and do demonstrate it from time to time, not all adolescents (or, for that matter, all adults) develop

---

cognitive-developmental view   A perspective on development, based on the work of Piaget, that takes a qualitative, stage-theory approach.

sensorimotor period   The first stage of cognitive development, according to Piaget, spanning the period roughly between birth and age 2.

preoperational period   The second stage of cognitive development, according to Piaget, spanning roughly ages 2–5.

concrete operations   The third stage of cognitive development, according to Piaget, spanning the period roughly between age 6 and early adolescence.

formal operations   The fourth stage of cognitive development, according to Piaget, spanning the period from early adolescence through adulthood.

Improvements in selective attention and divided attention enable adolescents to tune out interference and focus on the task at hand.

formal-operational thinking or employ it regularly and in a variety of situations. At least some research suggests that adolescents who as children had more secure relationships with their parents are more likely to display formal thinking than their insecure peers (Jacobsen, Edelstein, & Hofmann, 1994), as are young people who have received explicit instruction in deductive reasoning (Morris & Sloutsky, 1998). Consistent with the notion that certain types of instruction may facilitate the development of formal reasoning, one analysis of French students' reasoning abilities found that adolescents in the 1990s performed significantly better than their counterparts who were tested 20 or 30 years earlier, a change that must be related to changes in schooling (Flieller, 1999).

More important, the extent to which formal-operational thinking is displayed consistently by an individual depends a great deal on the conditions under which his or her reasoning is assessed (Overton, 1990). It is important, therefore, to differentiate between *competence* (that is, what the adolescent is capable of doing) and *performance* (that is, what the adolescent actually does in the assessment situation). Much research, on adults as well as adolescents, indicates that gaps between individuals' logical reasoning abilities and their actual use of logical reasoning in everyday situations are very large, with everyday decision making fraught with logical errors that cannot be explained by cognitive incompetence (Klaczynski, 2000, 2001). For example, if asked whether they would rather try to pull a lucky lottery ticket from an envelope of 10 tickets, of which only 1 is lucky, versus an envelope of 100 tickets, of which 10 are lucky, most people select the second option—even though, if quizzed, they know that the

mathematical odds of pulling a lucky ticket are identical in the two scenarios.

Although its influence has waned considerably over the past three decades (see Bjorklund, 1997; Keating, 2004), the Piagetian perspective on cognitive development during adolescence has stimulated a great deal of research on how young people think (Lourenço & Machado, 1996). Where the perspective falls short is in its claim that cognitive development proceeds in a stagelike fashion and that the stage of formal operations is the stage of cognitive development characteristic of adolescence (Kuhn, 2009). In fact, very little research supports this view. Rather, research suggests that advanced reasoning capabilities develop gradually and continuously from childhood through adolescence and beyond, in more of a gradual fashion than was proposed by Piaget (that is, more like a ramp than like a staircase). Rather than talking about a stage of cognitive activity characteristic of adolescence, then, it is more accurate to depict these advanced reasoning capabilities as skills that are employed by older children more often than by younger ones, by some adolescents more often than by others, and by individuals when they are in certain situations (especially familiar ones) more often than when they are in other situations (Kuhn, Garcia-Mila, Zohar, & Andersen, 1995).

THE INFORMATION-PROCESSING VIEW OF ADOLESCENT THINKING

Whereas Piaget attempted to describe adolescent thinking as a whole, and to use one overarching concept—formal operations—to characterize the period, others have tried to identify the specific abilities that improve as individuals move from childhood into adolescence and beyond. Just what is it about the ways adolescents think about things that makes them better problem solvers than children? This question has been the focus of researchers working from a second theoretical vantage point: the **information-processing perspective.**

Studies of changes in specific components of information processing have focused on five areas in which improvement occurs during adolescence: attention, working memory, processing speed, organization, and metacognition. Studies show that improvements in all of these areas take place as individuals move from childhood through adolescence, mainly during the first half of the adolescent decade (Demetriou, Christou, Spanoudis, & Platsidou, 2002; Keating, 2004). Taken together, these gains help to explain why adolescents are better than children at abstract, multidimensional, and hypothetical thinking.

■ **Attention**   First, there are advances in the individuals' ability to pay attention. Improvements are seen both in **selective attention,** in which adolescents must focus on one stimulus (such as a reading assignment) and tune out another (such as the electronic beeping of a younger brother's video game), and in **divided attention,** in which adolescents must pay attention to two sets of stimuli at the same time (such as studying while listening to music) (Higgins & Turnure, 1984; Schiff & Knopf, 1985). Improvements in attention mean that adolescents are better able than children to concentrate and stay focused on complicated tasks, such as reading and comprehending difficult material (Casteel, 1993). There also is considerable evidence that the ability to inhibit an unwanted response (for instance, stopping yourself from looking up at a commercial that suddenly appears on the television in the corner of the room while you are reading) improves during early and middle adolescence (Kuhn, 2009). This improvement is likely linked to maturation of brain systems that govern impulse control (Luna et al., 2001, 2004).

■ **Memory**   Second, during adolescence, memory abilities improve. This is reflected both in **working memory,** which involves the ability to remember something for a brief period of time, such as 30 seconds, and in **long-term memory,** which involves being able to recall something from a long time ago (Keating, 2004). When we think of the importance of memory in problem solving, we typically think of having to retrieve facts that we deliberately have memorized—one aspect of long-term memory. For example, can you recall the name of the stage of thinking that precedes the stage of formal operations in Piaget's theory? (If not, refer to page 64.)

But working memory is extremely important in problem solving as well. For example, in order to answer multiple-choice questions, you need to be able to remember each option long enough to compare it with the other choices as you read them. Think for a moment of how frustrating it would be to try to solve a multiple-choice problem if, by the time you had read the final potential answer, you had forgotten the first one! Studies show that working memory skills for both verbal and visual information increase between childhood and adolescence and over the course of adolescence (Hale, Bronik, & Fry, 1997). Improvements in working memory coincide with the continued maturation of brain regions during adolescence that are responsible for this aspect of cognition (Conklin, Luciana, Hooper, & Yarger, 2007; Klingberg, 2006; O'Hare, Lu, Houston, Bookheimer, & Sowell, 2008).

FOOD FOR THOUGHT

Suppose you were designing a curriculum for early adolescents. Would you emphasize different things if you were more Piagetian in your orientation than if you leaned more toward information-processing perspectives?

information-processing perspective   A perspective on cognition that derives from the study of artificial intelligence and attempts to explain cognitive development in terms of the growth of specific components of the thinking process (such as memory).

selective attention   The process by which we focus on one stimulus while tuning out another.

divided attention   The process of paying attention to two or more stimuli at the same time.

working memory   That aspect of memory in which information is held for a short time while a problem is being solved.

long-term memory   The ability to recall something from a long time ago.

■ **Speed**   A third component of information processing that may be closely related to the observed improvements in thinking is an increase in the sheer speed of information processing (Kail & Ferrer, 2007). Regardless of the type of cognitive task employed, researchers find that older adolescents process the information necessary to solve the problem faster than early adolescents, who, in turn, process information faster than preadolescents. This fact would certainly help explain age differences in performance on timed tests, such as standardized achievement tests. Generally, the increase in the speed of information processing that occurs with age becomes smaller over the course of adolescence. Therefore, the difference in speed between a 9-year-old and a 12-year-old is greater than that between a 12-year-old and a 15-year-old, which, in turn, is greater than that between a 15-year-old and an 18-year-old (see Figure 2.1) (Kail & Ferrer, 2007). In fact, speed of processing does not appear to change very much between middle adolescence and young adulthood (Brahmbhatt, McAuley, & Barch, 2008; Hale, 1990).

■ **Organization** A fourth type of information-processing gain seen in adolescence involves improvements in individuals' organizational strategies (Siegler, 1988). Adolescents are more "planful" than children— they are more likely to approach a problem with an appropriate information-processing strategy in mind and are more flexible in their ability to use different strategies in different situations (Plumert, 1994). The use of mnemonic devices (such as using HOMES to remember the names of the Great Lakes—Huron, Ontario, Michigan, Erie, and Superior) and other organizational strategies helps to account for differences in the performance of older and younger children on tasks requiring memory (A. Brown, 1975). For instance, think for a moment about how you approach learning the information in a new textbook chapter. After years of studying, you are probably well aware of particular strategies that work well for you (underlining, highlighting, taking notes, writing in the margins), and you begin a reading assignment with these strategies in mind. Because children are not as "planful" as adolescents, their learning is not as efficient. Developmental differences in levels of planning during childhood and adolescence can be seen quite readily by comparing individuals' approaches to the guessing game 20 Questions. With age, individuals' strategies become increasingly more efficient—when guessing the name of a person, an adolescent might begin by asking whether the person is dead or alive, whereas a young child might just start throwing out the names of specific people (Drumm & Jackson, 1996).

■ **Metacognition** Finally, individuals' knowledge about their own thinking processes improves during adolescence. We noted earlier that one of the most important gains in adolescence is in the realm of metacognition— thinking about thinking. Adolescents are more likely than children to think about their own thoughts—a tendency, as we saw, that helps to explain their greater self-consciousness. One explanation for this emphasizes adolescents' greater sensitivity to social information. But from an information-processing perspective, adolescents' heightened self-consciousness results from advances in basic metacognitive abilities. For the first time, the adolescent is capable of "thinking about thinking about thinking." Once you begin thinking

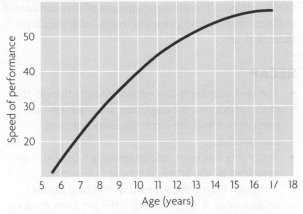

FIGURE 2.1 Speed of information processing increases markedly between ages 5 and 15 and then begins to level off. (Adapted from Kail & Ferrer, 2007)

about what other people might think you are thinking, it is hard to avoid becoming self-conscious.

Of course, advances in metacognition are more a blessing than a curse. Because adolescents are better able to think about their own thoughts, they are much better at monitoring their own learning processes (Crone, Somsen, Zanolie, & Van der Molen, 2006; Kuhn, 2009). For example, during the course of studying, adolescents are more able than children to step back and assess how well they are learning the material. Doing this enables them to pace their studying accordingly—to speed up and skim the material if they feel that they are learning it easily or to slow down and repeat a section if they feel that they are having a hard time. Recent studies of brain maturation indicate that brain systems that are active when individuals are monitoring their own performance continue to mature throughout adolescence and early adulthood, which may play a role in the development of metacognition (Ladouceur, Dahl, & Carter, 2007).

Most basic information-processing skills, like working memory or attention, as well as logical reasoning abilities, increase throughout childhood and early adolescence and then level off around age 15 (Gathercole, Pickering, Ambridge, & Wearing, 2004; Keating, 2004; Luciana, Conklin, Hooper, & Yarger, 2005). In other words, by the time they have turned 15, adolescents are just as proficient as adults in these basic skills. Where adolescents of this age are lacking, relative to adults, and where cognitive development continues beyond age 15 and into young adulthood, is in more sophisticated cognitive skills, such as planning ahead or judging the relative costs and benefits of a risky decision, and in the coordination of cognition and emotion, when feelings might interfere with logical reasoning (for example, when you have to make a decision when you are angry or when faced with peer pressure). In fact, much of what we have learned about brain maturation in adolescence—the subject of the next section—leads to the conclusion that the development of these advanced abilities may not be complete until individuals reach their mid-20s.

RECAP

- The two dominant theoretical perspectives in the study of adolescent cognition are the Piagetian perspective and the information-processing perspective.
- According to Piaget, adolescence is a period characterized by the stage of formal operations.
- Although Piaget theorized that thinking during adolescence is qualitatively different from thinking during childhood, research shows that changes in cognition during this time are more gradual.
- The information-processing perspective focuses on the specific components of thinking, such as memory and attention, and asks whether and to what extent these improve in adolescence.
- In general, there are major improvements in basic cognitive processes in early adolescence, but by the time individuals have reached age 15 or so, their basic thinking and reasoning abilities are comparable to those of adults.

The Adolescent Brain

Until fairly recently, attempts to link the changes in adolescent thinking described in the previous section with changes in the brain were not very fruitful. Although it had been believed that improved intellectual functioning in adolescence would be reflected in larger brain size, the brain reaches its adult size by age 10, making it impossible that changes in thinking during adolescence are due to sheer increases in the size or volume of the brain (Paus, 2009). For many years, scientists could not find links between physical changes in the brain and improvements in cognitive functioning during adolescence.

functional magnetic resonance imaging (fMRI)   A technique used to produce images of the brain, often while the subject is performing some sort of mental task.

diffusion tensor imaging (DTI)   A technique used to produce images of the brain that shows connections among different regions.

brain structure   The physical form or shape of the brain.

brain function   Patterns of brain activity.

electroencephalography (EEG)   A technique for measuring electrical activity at different locations on the scalp.

All this changed about ten years ago. Since 2000, there has been an explosion in research on adolescent brain development, and the speed with which our understanding of adolescent brain development has grown has been breathtaking (Spear, 2009).

Improvements in the methods used to study brain maturation—including studies of brain growth and development in other animals (because all mammals go through puberty, it is possible to study "adolescent" brain development in other species), studies of changes in brain chemistry in humans and other species, and postmortem studies of brain anatomy—have advanced the field in important ways (Giedd, 2008; Paus, 2009). But the major contribution to our understanding of what takes place in the brain during adolescence has come from studies using various imaging techniques, especially **functional magnetic resonance imaging (fMRI)** and **diffusion tensor imaging (DTI)**. These techniques allow researchers to take pictures of individuals' brains and compare their anatomy and activity. Some aspects of brain development in adolescence are reflected in changes in **brain structure** (for instance, certain parts of the brain are relatively smaller in childhood than adolescence, while others are relatively larger), whereas others are reflected not so much in the brain's structure but in changes in **brain function** (for instance, adolescents may use different parts of the brain than children when performing the same task) (e.g., Wang, Huettel, & De Bellis, 2008; O'Hare, Lu, Houston, Bookheimer, & Sowell, 2008).

Using DTI, scientists are able to see the ways in which various regions of the brain are connected and compare patterns of interconnections among people at different ages (e.g., Klingberg, 2006). This allows us to better understand how "communication" patterns linking different regions of the brain change with development. By using fMRI, researchers can examine patterns of activity in various regions of the brain while individuals are performing a variety of tasks (for example, recalling a list of words, viewing photos of friends, or listening to music). Participants in an fMRI study are asked to perform tasks on a computer while they are lying inside a brain scanner. With this setup, it is possible to study both how patterns of brain activity differ during different tasks (for example, when we are actively reading versus being read to) and whether people of different ages show different patterns of brain activity while performing the very same task. In our lab, for instance, my collaborators and I are studying how patterns of brain activity vary when individuals perform tasks either alone or with their friends watching them, and whether the ways in which the presence of friends changes brain activity differs between teenagers and adults.

Scientists have also studied age differences in patterns of brain activity using **electroencephalography (EEG)**, which measures electrical activity at different locations on the scalp. EEG can be used to examine changes in electrical activity—called **event-related potentials (ERP)**—in response to different stimuli or events (Segalowitz & Davies, 2004). Scientists often compare ERPs between people of different ages to determine when, if at all, patterns of brain activity undergo developmental change (e.g., Bishop, Hardiman, Uwer, & von Suchodoletz, 2007).

▌ **Are Male and Female Brains Different?**   Many popular books claim that there are important differences between the brains of adolescent boys and girls (and, for that matter, adult men and women). Research indicates, however, that differences between the genders in brain structure and function are very small and unlikely to explain differences between males and females in the way they behave or think (Paus, 2009; Spear, 2010). In general, male brains are about 10% larger than female brains (even accounting for the fact that male bodies, on average, are bigger than females'), but as noted above, there is no relation between sheer brain size and intellectual functioning, so it is unlikely that this small difference in size has any practical significance. In addition, there are few sex differences in the size of specific brain regions or structures—some parts of the brain are slightly larger among females, and some are slightly larger among males. By and large, the similarities between males and females in brain structure and function—before, during, and after adolescence—are far more impressive than the differences.

WHAT CHANGES IN ADOLESCENCE?

In order to understand how the brain changes in adolescence, it is necessary to have a little background on how the brain works more generally.

▌ **How Your Brain Works**   Your brain contains approximately 100 billion **neurons,** which are cells that carry information by transmitting electrical charges across the body and brain as well as back and forth within the brain by means of chemicals called **neurotransmitters.** The two neurons do not actually touch; there is a minuscule gap between them, called a **synapse.** When the electrical charge travels through a neuron, it stimulates the release of neurotransmitters, chemicals that carry the signal across the synapse from one neuron to the next. Any time we perceive something (e.g., feel an itch), move something (e.g., scratch the itch), or process information (e.g., wonder where the itch came from), this process of electrical transmission is involved.

A key process in early brain development is the development of connections—synapses—between neurons. By age 2, a single neuron may have 10,000 con-

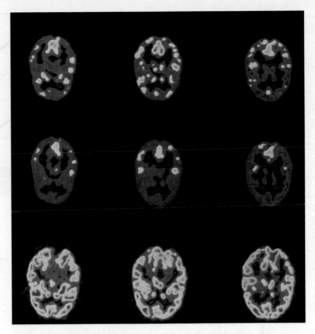

Advances in brain-imaging technology have contributed to our understanding of of how the brain changes at adolescence. These images are created through a process known as functional magnetic resonance imaging, or fMRI.

nections to other neurons. The formation of some synapses is genetically programmed, but others are formed through experience. The rate of synapse formation peaks at about age 1 and slows down in early childhood, but the development of new synapses continues throughout life as we learn new skills, build memories, acquire knowledge, and adapt to changing circumstances. The more a synapse is used, the stronger its electrical pathway becomes.

Initially the brain produces many more connections among cells than it will use. At 1 year of age, the number of synapses in the infant brain is about *twice* the number in the adult brain (Couperus & Nelson, 2006). However, soon after birth unused and unnecessary synapses start to be eliminated, a process called **synaptic pruning.** As a general rule, we tend to assume that "more is better," but that's not the case here. Imagine a meadow between two patches of forest. Hundreds of

event-related potentials (ERP)   Changes in electrical activity in areas of the brain in response to specific stimuli or events.

neurons   Nerve cells.

neurotransmitters   Specialized chemicals that carry electrical impulses between neurons.

synapse   The gap in space cbetween neurons, across which neurotransmitters carry electrical impulses.

synaptic pruning   The process through which unnecessary connections between neurons are eliminated, improving the efficiency of information processing.

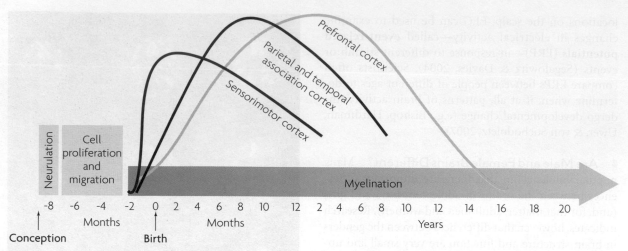

FIGURE 2.2   Gray matter density in different brain regions. Synaptic pruning takes place in different brain regions at different ages. (From Casey et al., 2005)

lightly trodden paths connect one side to the other (the unpruned brain). Over time people discover that one path is more direct than others. More people begin using this path more often, so it becomes wider and deeper. Because the other paths are not used any more, the grass grows back and those paths disappear. That's what synaptic pruning is like.

The elimination of synapses continues through adolescence and is normal and necessary to development and functioning. Just as pruning a rose bush—cutting off weak and misshapen branches—produces a healthier plant with larger flowers, so synaptic pruning enhances the brain's functioning. Synaptic pruning makes the brain more efficient by transforming an unwieldy network of small pathways into a better organized system of "superhighways."

Generally, the development of synapses is characterized by a period of growth (when more and more synapses are created) followed by a period of decline (when more and more synapses are eliminated). When we plot the density of synapses over time, we see a ∩-shaped curve—or, more accurately, a series of ∩-shaped curves that peak at different ages, depending on the specific region of the brain. That is, although synaptic pruning takes place throughout infancy, childhood, and adolescence, different regions of the brain are pruned at different points in development. As a rule, the brain regions in which pruning is taking place at a particular point in development are the regions associated with the greatest changes in cognitive functioning during that stage.

myelination   The process through which brain circuits are insulated with myelin, which improves the efficiency of information processing.

prefrontal cortex   The region of the brain most important for sophisticated thinking abilities, such as planning, thinking ahead, weighing risks and rewards, and controlling impulses.

Myelination is another key process in brain development. Initially, neurons are "nude," but over development, white fatty tissue, called myelin (and often referred to as white matter), encases the projections of neurons (often referred to as gray matter) that interconnect them. Myelin, which acts a little like plastic insulation around an electrical wire, increases the speed of neural impulses and so improves information transmission. Myelination occurs in waves, beginning in the prenatal period and continuing into young adulthood (Paus, 2009). Unlike synapses, with their ∩-shaped pattern of growth, white matter increases throughout childhood and adolescence, well into adulthood, although at different rates in different regions of the brain at different points in development. As with synaptic pruning, examining *where* myelination is occurring most dramatically at a particular point in development provides clues about the aspects of cognitive functioning that are changing most at that stage.

Changes in Brain Structure During Adolescence
During adolescence, the brain is "remodeled" through synaptic pruning and myelination in particular brain regions (Spear, 2009). As Figure 2.2 illustrates, the part of the brain that is pruned in adolescence is the **prefrontal cortex,** the region of the brain most important for sophisticated thinking abilities, such as planning, thinking ahead, weighing risks and rewards, and controlling impulses (Casey, Tottenham, Liston, & Durston, 2005). One recent study found a relation between intelligence and patterns of synaptic growth and pruning in the cortex, with relatively more intelligent adolescents showing a more dramatic and longer period of production of synapses before adolescence and a more dramatic pruning of them after (P. Shaw et al., 2006).

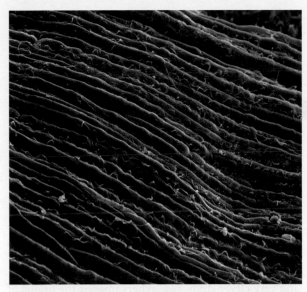

Myelination increases the speed of neural impulses and so improves information transmission. The amount of myelin in the brain increases throughout childhood and adolescence, well into adulthood.

Structural brain change in adolescence is not just about gray matter, however. There is also continued myelination of the prefrontal cortex throughout adolescence, which also leads to many cognitive advances (Paus, 2009; Spear, 2009). Although scientists initially focused on the decrease in gray matter as the main feature of structural change in the brain at adolescence, there has been increasing interest in the importance of the increase in white matter, which reflects improved connectivity within and across brain regions (Paus, 2009; Spear, 2009). Connectivity between the prefrontal cortex and the **limbic system,** an area of the brain involved in the processing of emotions, social information, and reward and punishment, lead to improvements in our ability to regulate our emotions and coordinate our thoughts and feelings (Steinberg, 2008).

▌ **Changes in Brain Function During Adolescence**
Accompanying these changes in the structure of the brain during adolescence are changes in how the brain functions.

We now know that full structural maturation of the prefrontal cortex is not complete until the mid-20s (Casey et al., 2005; Hooper, Luciana, Conklin, & Yarger, 2004; Paus, 2009; Santesso & Segalowitz, 2008). Of special importance are developments in the **dorsolateral prefrontal cortex,** the outer and upper areas of the front of the brain, which is important for skills such as planning ahead and controlling impulses (Casey et al., 2005); the **ventromedial prefrontal cortex,** the lower and central area of the front of the brain, which is important for more gut-level, intuitive decision making, and which has strong connections with the limbic system, where emotions and social information are pro

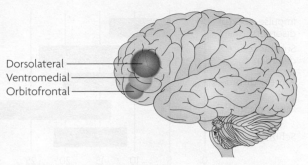

FIGURE 2.3 Three regions of the frontal cortex that undergo major change in adolescence are the dorsolateral prefrontal cortex, the ventromedial prefrontal cortex, and the orbitofrontal cortex.

cessed (Bechara, 2005); and the **orbitofrontal cortex,** the area of the brain directly behind the eyes, which is important for evaluating risks and rewards (Galvan et al., 2006) (see Figure 2.3).

The two most important changes in brain function involving the prefrontal cortex in adolescence both lead to greater efficiency in information processing (Spear, 2010). First, patterns of activation *within* the prefrontal cortex generally become more focused. For instance, in experiments in which participants are presented with a rapid succession of images and asked to push a button when a certain image appears, but refrain from pushing it when a different image appears, adolescents are less likely than children to activate prefrontal regions that are not relevant to performing the task well. Second, over the course of adolescence, individuals become more likely to use multiple parts of the brain simultaneously and coordinate activity *between* prefrontal regions and other areas, including the limbic system. This is especially important on difficult tasks, where the task demands may overtax the prefrontal cortex working alone, and especially on tasks that require self-control, where it is necessary to coordinate thinking and feeling. This simultaneous recruitment of multiple brain regions working as a "team" is made possible by the increased connectivity between brain regions, which we discussed earlier.

A different type of functional change involves patterns of change, especially in the limbic system, in levels

limbic system　An area of the brain that plays an important role in the processing of emotional experience, social information, and reward and punishment.

dorsolateral prefrontal cortex　The outer and upper areas of the front of the brain, important for skills such as planning ahead and controlling impulses.

ventromedial prefrontal cortex　The lower and central area at the front of the brain, important for gut-level decision making.

orbitofrontal cortex　The region of the brain located directly behind the eyes, important for the evaluation of risk and reward.

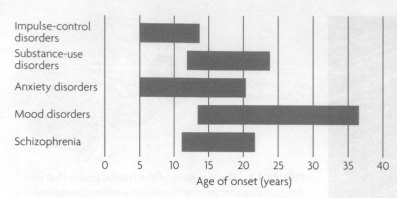

FIGURE 2.4 The age of onset of most common psychiatric disorders is somewhere between the ages of 10 and 20. New research on adolescent brain development helps explain why this is the case. (Paus et al., 2008)

of several neurotransmitters, including **dopamine** (which plays an important role in our experience of reward) and **serotonin** (which plays an important role in the experience of different moods), in many areas of the brain. These changes, which occur around puberty, make individuals more emotional, more responsive to stress, and more likely to engage in reward seeking and sensation seeking (Ernst et al., 2005; Galvan, Hare, Voss, Glover, & Casey, 2007; Silk et al., 2009; Spear, 2009). They are also thought to increase individuals' vulnerability to substance abuse, because they seek higher levels of reward; depression, because of their increased vulnerability to stress; and other mental health problems, because of their easily aroused emotions, including anger and sadness (see Figure 2.4) (Gunnar, Wewerka, Frenna, Long, & Griggs, 2009; Paus, Keshavan, & Giedd, 2008; Steinberg et al., 2006; Stroud et al., 2009).

Importantly, these changes in the functioning of the limbic system occur relatively early in adolescence, in contrast to developments in the prefrontal cortex, which, as you now know, are still ongoing in early adulthood. This relatively late maturation of the prefrontal cortex, particularly compared to the changes that take place in the limbic system at puberty, has been the subject of much discussion among those interested in risk taking and behavioral problems in adolescence, because this gap in timing may help explain the dramatic increase in risky behavior that takes place between childhood and adolescence (Spear, 2009; Steinberg, 2008). In essence, the brain changes in ways that may provoke individuals to seek novelty, reward, and stimulation several years before the complete maturation of the brain systems that regulate judgment, decision making, and impulse control. In the words of one team of writers, it's like "starting the engines with an unskilled driver" (C. Nelson et al., 2002, p. 515).

Changes in the limbic system in early adolescence may also help explain why adolescents' concerns about what their peers think increase during this time, because the limbic system is important for the processing of social information (E. Nelson et al., 2005). Conceivably, this could make adolescents more susceptible to peer pressure, a topic we'll look at in Chapter 9. In one recent and very clever study, researchers imaged the brains of adolescents who thought they were participating in a Facebook-style task, networking with other teenagers who were being imaged at the same time in different locations (Guyer, McClure-Tone, Shiffrin, Pine, & Nelson, 2009). (Inside the fMRI equipment was a computer screen, on which the researchers could show any images of their choosing.) While being imaged, the adolescents were shown pictures of the other teenagers and asked to rate how interested they were in chatting with them online. The adolescents, who were told that their own photograph was "posted" online, received what they thought was feedback from the other teenagers. In reality, though, no other teenagers were connected to the network, and the feedback the adolescents received was rigged to be positive (interested in chatting) half the time and negative (not interested in chatting) half the time. When the adolescents were told that other teenagers were interested in them, areas of their brain known to be sensitive to rewards like food and money were activated, suggesting that social rewards may be processed during adolescence in ways similar to the ways in which we process other types of rewards.

Other research indicates that sensitivity to others' emotions increases during adolescence. For instance, individuals' ability to recognize subtle changes in others' facial expressions improves during adolescence (L. A. Thomas, De Bellis, Graham, & LaBar, 2007). Although this increased attentiveness to other people's emotions likely has a number of benefits (it may make teenagers more socially skilled, for example), it also appears that adolescents are more easily distracted than adults by others' emotional expressions. In one experiment, researchers presented adolescents whose brains were being scanned with a mixed sequence of one of four types of images (red circles, scrambled images, neutral faces, and sad faces); the adolescents were asked to indicate when pictures of the red circle appeared (L. Wang, Huettel, & De Bellis, 2008). Unlike adults, who had been

dopamine   A neurotransmitter especially important in the brain circuits that regulate the experience of reward.

serotonin   A neurotransmitter that is especially important for the experience of different moods.

studied using the same paradigm (L. Wang, McCarthy, Song, & LaBar, 2005), adolescents showed heightened activation when viewing the sad faces, which interfered with their ability to pay attention to the appearance of the red circles. An important implication of this research for parents is that yelling at a teenager in an angry voice may not be an especially effective means of getting the adolescent to listen, because the teenager may end up paying more attention to the angry emotion than to the content of what the parent is saying.

FOOD FOR THOUGHT

New research shows that brain systems governing things like impulse control, planning ahead, and balancing risk and reward are still maturing during late adolescence. Should we, as a result, rethink laws that regulate the age at which individuals are allowed to do certain things? Some have argued, for instance, that the new research raises questions about whether we should let individuals drive when they are 16 or serve in the military when they are 18. What's your opinion?

IMPLICATIONS FOR ADOLESCENT BEHAVIOR

▌ **Correlation Is Not Causation** It is important to keep in mind that evidence of a correlation between changes in brain structure or function and changes in adolescent behavior does not necessarily mean that the first is necessarily causing the second (Kuhn, 2009; Paus, 2009). One important hallmark of brain development in adolescence is that the brain is very malleable, or "plastic," and its development is affected by experience as well as biology and, most probably, by the interaction between the two (M. Thomas & Johnson, 2008). For instance, individuals may inherit genes that direct the brain to develop in certain ways during adolescence, but whether these genes are actually expressed (that is, whether they actually result in observable behavior) may depend on the environment. Studies have found, for example, that individuals who have a genetic predisposition to develop depression become depressed only if they are exposed to a certain degree of life stress. People with the same genetic profile, but without the stress exposure, have no higher rates of depression than those without the genetic vulnerability (Caspi et al., 2003).

It is also the case that adolescents' behavior affects their brain development. An obvious illustration of this relationship, which we will look at in Chapter 13, involves the impact of alcohol and other drugs on the brain, but there are other, more subtle examples as well. As mentioned earlier, the process of synaptic pruning, for example, is influenced by experience: Repeated activation of a specific collection of neurons as a result of engaging in a particular behavior will actually result in structural changes that strengthen the connections among those neurons, which in turn will make them function more efficiently. For example, practicing the same task over and over again makes it easier and easier to perform the task each time.

Although scientists agree about the ways in which the structure and function of the brain change during adolescence, the implications of these changes for adolescent development are still the subject of a great deal of ongoing research and considerable speculation, because few studies have directly linked changes in brain images with changes in thought, emotion, or behavior. One question that is often asked is when adolescents begin to think like adults. As you now know, brain science alone cannot answer this question, because it depends on which aspects of thinking one is concerned about. When it comes to relatively more sophisticated cognitive abilities, such as thinking ahead, envisioning the future consequences of a decision, balancing risks and rewards, or controlling impulses—all of which are governed mainly by the prefrontal cortex—research on brain maturation certainly suggests that these capabilities are still developing well after individuals enter their 20s. But when it comes to more basic abilities, such as those involving memory, attention, and logical reasoning, especially under optimal conditions, brain and behavioral studies indicate that the average 15-year-old performs no worse than the average adult. Where we draw the boundary between adolescence and adulthood—at least as far as cognitive development is concerned—should probably depend on why the boundary is being drawn and on what specific abilities are relevant to the behavior in question (Steinberg, Cauffman, Woolard, Graham, & Banich, 2009).

RECAP

- New imaging techniques, especially functional magnetic resonance imaging (fMRI), have enabled scientists to chart changes in the structure and function of the brain in adolescence.
- Among the most important structural changes to take place in adolescence is the elimination of unnecessary synapses, a process called synaptic pruning, particularly in the prefrontal cortex.
- A second important structural change involves increased myelination of the brain, which permits more efficient connections within and between brain regions. Along with synaptic pruning, myelination is thought to lead to improvements in many advanced thinking abilities.

- Adolescence is also a time of changes in brain function. Two specific changes involving the prefrontal cortex are noteworthy: First, activation within the prefrontal cortex becomes more focused during adolescence, and the activation of irrelevant brain areas declines. Second, activity in the prefrontal cortex becomes increasingly coordinated with activity in other parts of the brain.
- Another important functional change in the brain at adolescence involves changes in levels of several neurotransmitters in the limbic system. This is thought to increase sensation seeking and emotional arousal and to make adolescents more sensitive to emotional stimuli and social information.
- The combination of heightened sensation seeking and a still-maturing prefrontal cortex may make adolescence a period of experimentation with risky activity.
- It is important to remember that the relation between brain development and psychological development is a two-way street. The adolescent brain is very malleable, and experiences shape its structure and function.

Individual Differences in Intelligence in Adolescence

For the most part, theorists who have studied adolescent cognitive development from either a Piagetian or an information-processing framework, or through brain research, have focused on the universals in adolescent intellectual growth. These theorists ask, How does thinking change as individuals move into adolescence? What processes drive cognitive development as children become teenagers? What cognitive competencies do all adolescents share?

In contrast, other theorists have been more interested in studying individual differences in intellectual abilities. They ask, How can we account for different patterns of intellectual growth within the adolescent population? How large are individual differences in intelligence in adolescence? Are some adolescents brighter than others? If so, why, and in what ways?

THE MEASUREMENT OF IQ

To answer questions about the relative intelligence of individuals, psychologists have had to devise ways of assessing intelligence—no easy feat given the considerable disagreement over what "intelligence" really is. Today, the most widely used measures are intelligence tests, or IQ (for "intelligence quotient") tests. Among these tests are the Stanford-Binet, the Wechsler Intelligence Scale for Children (WISC-IV), and the Wechsler Adult Intelligence Scale (WAIS-III). An individual's IQ is computed by dividing his or her mental age by his or her chronological age and then multiplying the result by 100.

The IQ test is one of the most widely used—and most widely misused—psychological instruments. Initially developed in France in 1905, the first intelligence test was devised in response to the French government's interest in better predicting which children would and would not profit from formal schooling. Although the test—and the many others that would be developed over the years—was designed to yield a measure of "intelligence," it was devised with a very specific type of intelligence in mind: the type it takes to succeed in formal education. Even the best IQ tests used today measure only a very specific type of intelligence.

An individual's performance on an IQ test is usually presented not as a raw score but as a relative score in comparison to the scores of other individuals of the same age and generation. Comparison scores are collected every so often, so that the comparison group for individuals taking the test at any given time is valid, representative, and up-to-date. The score of 100 is used to designate the midway point. An IQ score below 100 indicates a poorer test performance than half of the comparison group; a score above 100 indicates a better performance than half the comparison group. In other words, the higher an individual's IQ, the smaller the number of age-mates who perform equally or better on the same test.

Although an individual's score on an intelligence test is often reported in terms of her or his overall IQ, intelligence tests actually comprise a series of tests, and it is usually possible to look at performance in different areas independently. The WISC-IV and the WAIS-III, for example, each contain two groups of tests: verbal tests, which include measures of vocabulary, general information, comprehension, and arithmetic abilities, and performance tests, which include measures of memory, perceptual reasoning, and picture completion.

The IQ test represents only one of many ways of assessing intelligence in adolescence. Indeed, many theorists have argued that its exclusive focus on "school smarts"—the sorts of abilities that are related to scholastic success—yields a one-sided picture of what it means to be an intelligent person. Two of the better-known attempts to expand on this narrow definition come from the work of Robert Sternberg (1988) and Howard Gardner (1983). Many of Sternberg and Gardner's ideas formed the basis for the best-selling book *Emotional Intelligence,* by journalist Daniel Goleman (1995).

Critics of standardized testing argue that these tests measure just one type of intelligence — "school smarts"—and neglect other, equally important skills, such as emotional intelligence, creativity, and "street smarts."

TYPES OF INTELLIGENCE

▌ **Sternberg's "Triarchic" Theory** Sternberg proposed a triarchic, or three-part, theory of intelligence. He argued that a thorough assessment of an individual's intellectual capabilities requires that we look at three distinct but interrelated types of intelligence: (1) componential intelligence, which involves our abilities to acquire, store, and process information (as described in the previous section about information processing); (2) experiential intelligence, which involves our abilities to use insight and creativity; and (3) contextual intelligence, which involves our ability to think practically. Componential intelligence is closest to the type of intelligence measured on traditional intelligence tests. Experiential intelligence is closest to what we call "creativity." And contextual intelligence is closest to what we might call "street smarts." All individuals have all three types of intelligence, but some individuals are stronger in one respect than in others. You probably can think of individuals who are good test takers but who are not particularly creative or sensible. According to Sternberg's model, these individuals would be high in componential intelligence but low in experiential and contextual intelligence.

More importantly, Sternberg's view forces us to look at individuals who are not good test takers but who are creative or street smart as being just as intelligent as individuals who score high on IQ tests—but intelligent in a different way. Sternberg argued that society needs individuals with all types of intelligence and that it is time we started assessing—and encouraging— experiential and contextual intelligence as much as we do componential intelligence (D. Matthews & Keating, 1995).

▌ **Gardner's Theory of Multiple Intelligences** Howard Gardner's theory of multiple intelligences also stresses that there is more to being smart than being "book smart." Gardner proposed that there are seven types of intelligence: verbal, mathematical, spatial, kinesthetic (having to do with movement), self-reflective, interpersonal, and musical. According to his view, for example, outstanding athletes such as basketball great LeBron James or soccer legend Mia Hamm have a well-developed kinesthetic intelligence, which allows them to control their bodies and process the movements of others in extraordinary ways. Although conventional tests of intelligence emphasize verbal and mathematical abilities, these are not the only types of intelligence that we possess—nor are they the only types that we should value.

FOOD FOR THOUGHT

What particular intellectual strengths do you have that might not be picked up by conventional measures of intelligence?

INTELLIGENCE TEST PERFORMANCE IN ADOLESCENCE

Although the existence of different forms of intelligence is a popular idea, most research in the psychometric tradition has employed traditional IQ tests to investigate the nature of intelligence during adolescence. Assessments based on IQ tests have been used to examine two seemingly similar but actually very different questions: (1) How *stable* are IQ scores during adolescence? and (2) Do the sorts of mental abilities that are assessed via intelligence tests *improve* during adolescence?

It is easy to confuse these questions, because at first glance, they seem to be asking the same thing. But consider this: Individuals' IQ scores remain remarkably stable during the adolescent years; yet, during the same period, their mental abilities improve dramatically. Although this might seem contradictory, it is not. Studies of stability examine changes in individuals' *relative* standing over time, whereas studies of change examine changes in individuals' *absolute* scores.

Take height, for example. Children who are taller than their peers during middle childhood are likely to be taller than their peers during adulthood as well; children who are average in height remain so throughout childhood and adulthood; and children shorter than their peers at one time are likely to be shorter than their peers later on. Height, therefore, is a very stable trait. But this does not mean that individuals don't grow between childhood and adolescence.

Like height, scores on intelligence tests are characterized by high stability and a good deal of change during childhood and adolescence. To the first question posed above—about how stable IQ scores are during adolescence—the answer, then, is very stable. Youngsters who score higher than their peers on intelligence tests during early adolescence are likely to score higher throughout the adolescent years. In fact, recent research indicates that certain measures of intellectual performance taken during the first year of life—not IQ tests, but measures of speed of information processing—are significantly predictive of IQ test performance in early adolescence (S. Rose & Feldman, 1995). This does not mean, however, that individuals' intellectual performance remains fixed or is not susceptible to change—as you will see in a moment.

A 10-year-old boy whose score is average for his age would have an IQ of about 100. If his score were stable—that is, if he remained average in comparison with his peers—his IQ would remain at about 100. Even if he became more intelligent over time, as any normal child would, his IQ score probably would not change very much, because the score would always reflect his performance relative to his peers. If his abilities increased at the same rate as his age-mates', his relative standing would not change. In other words, when an individual's IQ scores are fairly stable, a graph of those scores over time produces a relatively straight horizontal line. For most individuals, this is indeed what happens. Although some individuals show fluctuation in IQ scores between childhood and adolescence, ultimately, most adolescents end up with IQ scores that are not very different from their scores as children. In one study, for example, the average amount of change over a 7-year period (from age 7 to age 13) was only 5 IQ points among *all* of the individuals whose scores fluctuated to *any* degree, which is not a change of much practical significance (Moffitt, Caspi, Harkness, & Silva, 1993).

In absolute terms, however, do mental abilities increase during adolescence? Figure 2.5 shows the growth of mental abilities as assessed by standardized tests. As you can see, abilities assessed by conventional IQ tests increase dramatically through childhood and adolescence, reaching a plateau sometime in mid-to-late adolescence. (It is no coincidence that this plateau occurs at around the same age as that for information processing, because IQ test performance depends a lot on information-processing abilities.) Thus, despite the fact that IQ scores remain stable over time, individuals do become smarter as they get older—a fact that argues strongly in favor of educational interventions, especially in early childhood, because they have been shown to improve intellectual performance during adolescence (B. C. Campbell, Pungello, Miller-Johnson, Burchinal, & Ramey, 2001). In addition, research shows that extended schooling during adolescence itself enhances individuals' performance on standardized tests of intelligence (Ceci & Williams, 1999). Whereas individuals who had dropped out of school early showed unchanging—and relatively lower—scores on intelligence tests during adolescence, students who remained in school, especially those in the more advanced tracks, showed impressive gains in verbal ability over time. As you read in the previous section, on brain maturation in adolescence, scientists believe that much of the synaptic pruning that takes place in the frontal lobe during the mid-adolescent years is affected by experience (Casey, Tottenham, Liston, & Durston, 2005).

■ Disappearing Sex Differences Studies that compare the performance of males and females on

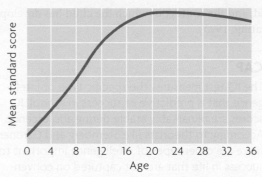

FIGURE 2.5   The growth of mental abilities from birth to age 36, as measured by standardized IQ tests. (Adapted from Bayley, 1949)

various tests of intelligence have found few reliable sex differences. Although it was once the case that males performed better on tests of mathematical ability, and females on tests of verbal ability, these sex differences disappeared about 20 years ago (Jacklin, 1989). The only reliable sex difference in mental abilities during adolescence is in the area of spatial ability, where males outperform females by a slight margin. You may recall taking standardized tests in which you were asked to imagine how an irregular three-dimensional object would appear if it were rotated in certain ways; this is a test of spatial ability. The male advantage on many tests of spatial performance emerges before age 10 and is more or less constant during the adolescent years (Voyer, Voyer, & Bryden, 1995).

CULTURE AND INTELLIGENCE

▌ **Vygotsky's Perspective**   Much of our current thinking about the nature of intelligence has been influenced by the work of the late Russian psychologist Lev Vygotsky (1930/1978), who emphasized the broader context in which intellectual development occurs. According to this view, it is essential that we understand the nature of the environment in which an adolescent develops in terms of its demands for intelligent behavior and its opportunities for learning. Individuals develop and use intellectual skills not simply as a function of their cognitive maturation but also in response to the everyday problems they are expected to solve. Young street merchants in Brazil, for example, who might not perform well on standardized tests of math knowledge, nevertheless use sophisticated mathematical skills during transactions with customers (Guberman, 1996). The very same children who perform poorly on school-based tests of knowledge may excel when faced with an equally challenging test of competence in the real world—such as figuring out the most efficient

route between school and home through a dangerous neighborhood.

Vygotsky argued that children and adolescents learn best in everyday situations when they encounter tasks that are neither too simple nor too advanced, but just slightly more challenging than their abilities permit them to solve on their own. Within this so-called **zone of proximal development,** young people, through close collaboration with a more experienced instructor (whether an adult or another child), are stimulated to "reach" for the more advanced level of performance. The role of the instructor is to help structure the learning situation so that it is within the reach of the student—a structuring process called **scaffolding.** If you watch good parents, teachers, or coaches at work, you will probably observe a great deal of scaffolding.

▌ **Culture-Fair Testing**   Studying cognitive development in context clearly points out the problems in measuring intelligence through standardized testing. Indeed, the problem of defining intelligence adequately is perhaps no more readily apparent than when issues of ethnic or racial differences in intelligence are raised. In general, studies find that Black and Hispanic youngsters typically score lower on standardized IQ tests than do their White peers (Anastasi, 1988). But how are we to interpret this finding? Does this mean that minority youngsters are less "intelligent" than White youths? Or does it mean that the tests used to assess intelligence are unfairly biased against minority children?

In general, experts have leaned toward the latter explanation. They point out that IQ tests, which were initially developed and standardized for populations of individuals of European descent, are loaded with questions that reflect the experiences and values of middle-class Whites. These critics suggest that White individuals would do similarly poorly on intelligence tests designed by and for ethnic minority individuals (Miller-Jones, 1989). In addition, language differences between minority and nonminority youths (especially if English is not the minority youngster's first language) may lead to apparent differences in intelligence when the testing is performed in English. These criticisms have lead to calls for **culture-fair tests**—intelligence tests that attempt to reduce sources of

zone of proximal development   In Vygotsky's theory, the level of challenge that is still within the individual's reach but that forces an individual to develop more advanced skills.

scaffolding   Structuring a learning situation so that it is just within the reach of the student.

culture-fair tests   Standardized tests that do not, by virtue of their construction, favor one cultural or ethnic group over another.

ethnic or cultural bias. Such tests tend to be based less on verbal skills (thus avoiding the language problems of many tests) and more oriented toward the sorts of items included on the performance scales of traditional IQ tests.

One fascinating study of the SAT demonstrates how a relatively simple change in the way the test is scored can significantly reduce the gap between White and ethnic minority test takers (Freedle, 2003). The researcher hypothesized that the items with the greatest cultural bias would be the easier items on the test, because these items refer to concepts that are likely learned outside school, where culture plays a strong role in influencing what children learn. In contrast, more difficult items are more likely to refer to concepts that are learned in school, where cultural differences between students with respect to what they learn are much smaller, because students in the same class use the same textbooks and are exposed to the same curriculum (although tracking can certainly introduce ethnic differences into what students are exposed to in school). For example, an item using the word "golf" would be considered an easy item, because it is a common word, yet adolescents from different cultural groups likely have different degrees of familiarity with the sport. Although an item with the infrequently used word "anathema" (which means someone or something that is detested) would be considered hard, it is not one that most people are exposed to in everyday life, and most adolescents familiar with the word would have learned it in a more culture-neutral context. Sure enough, when the researcher compared SAT scores of ethnic minority and White students using two different scoring procedures—one that used the whole test, and one that used only the difficult items—ethnic differences in performance changed.

Even with the advent of culture-fair testing, the notion that there is such a "thing" as intelligence and that it is the same in all cultural and ethnic groups is a difficult one to swallow. The skills that contribute to intelligent behavior in a nonindustrialized farming and hunting community, or on the streets of an inner-city community, are likely very different from those that contribute to intelligence in a high school science class. Yet the standardized tests used in assessing intelligence place nearly exclusive emphasis on the intellectual skills that are chiefly helpful in educational settings. It is essential for practitioners to keep in mind that any assessment of a youngster's intelligence must take into account the nature and purpose of the test used, the circumstances of the assessment, the background of the child, and the context in which the child has developed (Keating, 1995).

RECAP

- The IQ test measures the specific type of intelligence that is predictive of success in school. IQ scores are remarkably stable during adolescence.
- According to theorists like Sternberg and Gardner, there are other types of intelligence important to success in life that are not captured on conventional IQ tests.
- Sex differences in intellectual abilities have largely disappeared and are limited to differences in spatial ability.
- Experts agree that it is essential to view and assess intelligence in a way that takes into account the cultural context in which the adolescent has grown up. An important influence on this perspective has been Vygotsky.

Adolescent Thinking in Context

Just as it is important to ask how the broader context influences adolescents' cognitive development, it is also important to ask how their cognitive development influences their interactions with their environment. After all, most of the thinking adolescents do occurs in everyday situations, not just when they are taking tests designed to see how able they are.

As our understanding of adolescent thinking has expanded, researchers have begun to look beyond laboratory experiments and standardized tests to examine how the cognitive changes of adolescence actually affect teenagers' day-to-day thoughts and actions. Do advances in deductive reasoning or information-processing abilities make a difference in the real world? To answer this question, psychologists and educators have studied the practical side of adolescent thinking in three domains: in social situations, in risk taking, and in the classroom.

SOCIAL COGNITION IN ADOLESCENCE

Many of the examples of adolescent thinking that we have looked at in this chapter have involved reasoning about scientific problems or physical objects. But the same sorts of gains in intellectual abilities that are observed in young people's thinking in these realms are apparent in their reasoning about social phenomena. **Social cognition** involves such cognitive activities as

---

social cognition The aspect of cognition that concerns thinking about other people, about interpersonal relations, and about social institutions.

thinking about people, social relationships, and social institutions (Smetana & Villalobos, 2009).

It is not difficult to imagine that adolescents' advanced abilities in thinking about possibilities, thinking in multiple dimensions, and thinking about abstract concepts make them more sophisticated when it comes to reasoning about social matters. Compared with those of children, adolescents' conceptions of interpersonal relationships are more mature, their understanding of human behavior is more advanced, their ideas about social institutions and organizations are more complex, and their ability to figure out what other people are thinking is far more developed. As we shall see in subsequent chapters, gains in the area of social cognition help account for many of the psychosocial advances typically associated with adolescence—advances in the realms of identity, autonomy, intimacy, sexuality, and achievement. Individual differences in social cognitive abilities also help explain why some adolescents have more social problems than others (Dodge, Coie, & Lynam, 2006; Fontaine, Yang, Dodge, Pettit, & Bates, 2009).

Research on social cognition during adolescence includes many topics, but four of the most often studied concern (1) social perspective taking; (2) individuals' thinking about social relationships; (3) individuals' conceptions of laws, civil liberties, and rights; and (4) individuals' understanding of social conventions (Smetana & Villalobos, 2009).

▌ **Social Perspective Taking**   During preadolescence and adolescence, individuals develop a more nuanced understanding of other people's personalities and psychological states. Whereas children tend to use fairly global and concrete descriptors, like gender and age, when asked to describe others, adolescents are more likely to describe people in terms of such things as interests, personality characteristics, and attitudes. As they develop a more sophisticated **theory of mind,** the ability to understand that others have beliefs, intentions, and knowledge that may be different from one's own, they are better able to interpret the feelings of others and to infer their motives and feelings, even when specific information of this sort is not directly observable (Choudhury, Blakemore, & Charman, 2006).

Related to these gains in understanding other people are considerable improvements in adolescents' **social perspective taking**—the ability to view events from the perspective of others. According to Robert Selman (1980), who has studied this aspect of development extensively, children become better able as they grow older to recognize that others may view an event from a different, but equally valid, perspective. Not only are adolescents more capable of discerning another person's perspective on some issue or event, but they are also better able to understand that person's perspec-

Improvements in social cognition during adolescence lead adolescents to think in more sophisticated ways about themselves and their relationships.

tive on their own point of view. Interestingly, the fact that individuals' ability to look at things from another person's perspective increases in adolescence does not mean that individuals become more tolerant of the beliefs of those with whom they disagree. People's tolerance for diversity in viewpoint depends more on the particular issue involved than on age (Wainryb, Shaw, Laupa, & Smith, 2001).

According to Selman, the development of social perspective taking progresses through a series of stages. In the preadolescent stage, youngsters can put themselves in others' shoes but do not yet see how the thoughts and feelings of one person may be related to the thoughts and feelings of another. During early adolescence, with the progression into what Selman calls **mutual role taking,** the young adolescent can be an objective third party and can see how the thoughts or actions of one person might influence those of another. In thinking about two friends, for instance, an adolescent at this level would be able to look at the friends' relationship and see how each person's behavior affects the other's.

Later in adolescence, perspective taking achieves an in-depth, societal orientation. The adolescent at this

theory of mind   The ability to understand that others have beliefs, intentions, and knowledge that may be different from one's own.

social perspective taking   The ability to view events from the perspective of others.

mutual role taking   In Selman's theory, the stage of social perspective taking during which the young adolescent can be an objective third party and can see how the thoughts or actions of one person can affect those of another.

level understands that the perspectives which people have on each other are complicated, are often unconscious, and are influenced by larger forces than individuals can control—including each person's position in society or within a social institution. For example, you are able to understand that your perspective on the instructor teaching your class is influenced not only by your own personality and by the instructor's but also by forces inherent in the professor–student relationship. Ultimately, adolescents' gains in social-perspective-taking abilities lead to improvements in communication, as they become more capable of formulating arguments in terms that are more likely to be understood by someone whose opinion is different. As you will read in Chapter 4, this gain in perspective taking may change the dynamics of adolescents' relationships with their parents—for better (because adolescents are able to see more things from their parents' point of view) and for worse (because adolescents may use these advanced social cognitive abilities to challenge their parents' authority) (Smetana & Villalobos, 2009).

▌ **Thinking About Relationships**   These improvements in social perspective taking, in turn, lead to changes in the way that adolescents think about relationships with peers and parents. One topic that researchers have been especially interested in concerns adolescents' beliefs about peer exclusion (Leets & Sunwolf, 2005). All other things equal, children believe that it is wrong to exclude peers from social activities (i.e., whether to invite the whole class or just one's close friends to a birthday party). With age, however, as adolescents' understanding of group dynamics becomes more sophisticated, they begin to take into account other considerations, like loyalty, social status, the activity context, and the reason for excluding some individuals but not others. For example, one study found that adolescents who were members of high-status peer crowds (e.g., jocks) judged excluding other teenagers from peer groups as less wrong than did individuals who were members of low-status peer groups (e.g., druggies) (Horn, 2003). On the other hand, adolescents become more likely, with age, to believe that social exclusion on the basis of gender orientation or ethnicity is wrong (Killen, Henning, Kelly, Crystal, & Ruck, 2007).

Changes in adolescents' understanding of social relationships also transform their beliefs about authority, which has important implications for their relationships with parents and other adults (Smetana & Villalobos, 2009). With age, adolescents increasingly distinguish between moral issues (such as whether it is acceptable to steal from someone else) and conventional ones (such as

whether one eats dessert before or after the main course). Although the stereotype of adolescents is that they increasingly reject the authority of adults, research shows that what happens instead is that adolescents increasingly distinguish between issues that authority figures have the right to regulate and issues that are their own personal choices. As adolescents begin to make these distinctions, they may come to question their parents' authority in various contexts. Issues that had been viewed as matters of right and wrong start to seem like matters of personal choice and, as such, beyond the bounds of parental authority (Cumsille, Darling, Flaherty, & Martínez, 2009). For example, parents' rules about things like the cleanliness of the adolescent's bedroom or how late she or he can stay up on school nights, which had been accepted as matters of right and wrong, start to seem like arbitrary conventions that are open to debate. As we'll see in Chapter 4, one main source of conflict between adolescents and their parents involves which issues parents have legitimate authority over and which they do not. Similar changes occur in adolescents' beliefs about their teachers' authority (Smetana & Bitz, 1996). For instance, adolescents understand that teachers have the right to demand that students show up for class on time and sit quietly if asked, but believe that students should be able to decide where they sit in class or during lunch.

▌ **Social Conventions**   The realization that individuals' perspectives vary, and that their opinions may differ as a result, leads to changes in the ways that adolescents approach issues regarding social conventions (Smetana & Villalobos, 2009). During middle childhood, **social conventions**—the social norms that guide day-to-day behavior, such as waiting in line to buy movie tickets—are seen as arbitrary and changeable, but adherence to them is not; compliance with such conventions is based on rules and on the dictates of authority. When you were 7 years old, you might not have understood why people had to wait in line to buy movie tickets, but when your parents told you to wait in line, you waited. By early adolescence, however, conventions are seen as arbitrary and changeable in terms of both origins and enforcement; conventions are merely social expectations. As an adolescent, you begin to realize that people wait in line because they are expected to, not because they are forced to. Indeed, young adolescents often see social conventions as *nothing but* social expectations and, consequently, as insufficient reasons for compliance. You can probably imagine youngsters in their midteens saying something like this: "Why wait in a ticket line simply because other people are lined up? There isn't a *law* that forces you to wait in line, is there?"

Gradually, however, adolescents begin to see social conventions as the means by which society regulates people's behavior. Conventions may be arbitrary, but we follow them because we share an understanding of

social conventions   The norms that govern everyday behavior in social situations.

how people are expected to behave in various situations. In fact, high schoolers see conventions as so ingrained in the social system that individuals follow them partly out of habit. We wait in line for theater tickets not because we want to comply with any rule, but because it is something we are accustomed to doing.

Ultimately, individuals come to see that social conventions serve a function in coordinating interactions among people. Social norms and expectations are derived from and maintained by individuals' having a common perspective and agreeing that, in given situations, certain behaviors are more desirable than others, because such behaviors help society and its institutions function more smoothly. Without the convention of waiting in line to buy movie tickets, the pushiest people would always get tickets first. Older adolescents can see that waiting in line not only benefits the theater by keeping order but also preserves everyone's right to a fair chance to buy tickets. In other words, we wait in line patiently because we all agree that it is better if tickets are distributed fairly.

▍ **Laws, Civil Liberties, and Rights** As is the case with individuals' developing understanding of relationships between people, over the course of adolescence individuals also become more nuanced in the way they think about the relationship between the individual and society. Most research on adolescents' beliefs about rights and civil liberties comes from studies of Western, middle-class youth, and it is important to be cautious about generalizing the findings of these studies to young people from other cultures. Nevertheless, even in collectivist cultures that place less emphasis on the rights of the individual than is the case in America, adolescents become increasingly likely to believe that there are some freedoms—like freedom of speech and freedom of religion—that should not be restricted (Smetana & Villalobos, 2009). That said, research also finds that, with age, teenagers come to believe that there are situations in which it may be legitimate to restrict individual rights to serve the benefit of the community. For instance, one recent study of Muslim and non-Muslim Dutch youth found that, although both groups favored freedom of speech in general, Muslim youth were relatively more likely to reject freedom of speech that might be offensive to God or their religion, whereas non-Muslim youth were more likely to reject the rights of minority groups to burn the Dutch flag during political demonstrations (Verkuyten & Slooter, 2008).

Researchers have also looked at changes in adolescents' beliefs about their rights to be taken care of (called "nurturance rights") and their rights to make their own decisions (called "self-determination rights") (Ruck et al., 1998). In general, there are few changes in individuals' endorsement of nurturance rights as they get older— that is, adolescents are just as likely as children to believe that parents have an obligation to provide food,

clothing, and other types of support—but that support for self-determination rights (e.g., the right to keep a private diary) increases markedly over the course of adolescence. As is the case with support for basic individual rights, like the right to free speech or religion, the growth in support for self-determination rights is seen among adolescents from a diverse array of Western and non-Western cultures (Cherney & Shing, 2008).

Several themes cut across the research findings from studies of different aspects of social cognition—the way we think about people, relationships, conventions, and rights. First, as individuals move into and through adolescence they become better able to step outside themselves and see things from other vantage points. Second, adolescents are better able to see that the social "rules" we follow (in the family, at school, and in broader society) are not absolute and are therefore subject to debate and questioning. Third, with age, adolescents develop a more differentiated, more nuanced understanding of social norms; yes, individuals are entitled to certain rights, but there are some situations under which it might be appropriate to curtail them. Yes, it is generally wrong to exclude others, but sometimes social exclusion is justifiable.

These gains in social cognition help to account for gains in social competence during adolescence. As you will see in Chapter 10, adolescents who have more sophisticated social cognitive abilities (for example, more advanced perspective-taking abilities) actually behave in more socially competent ways (N. Eisenberg, Morris, McDaniel, & Spinrad, 2009; L. Lenhart & Rabiner, 1995). Although there is more to social competence than social cognition, being able to understand social relationships is an important component of social maturity.

▍ **Adolescent Wisdom** One of the most important ways in which improvements in social cognition are manifested during adolescence is in the development of wisdom. *Wisdom* has been defined as rich knowledge about life that permits "exceptional insight, judgment, and advice about complex and uncertain matters" (Pasupathi, Staudinger, & Baltes, 2001, p. 351). Wisdom requires social-perspective-taking skills that do not develop until mid-adolescence. In a recent study of the development of wisdom, individuals between the ages of 14 and 37 were interviewed about a series of dilemmas, concerning complex interpersonal problems or the meaning of life, that required sophisticated insight, reasoning, and judgment but that did not have clear-cut solutions. One such dilemma was this: "A teenager learns that his or her parents want to divorce. What could one or the teenager do and think in such a situation?" The interviews were transcribed and coded for the presence of various aspects of wisdom. Although we tend to associate the development of wisdom with adulthood rather than adolescence, the researchers found that wisdom increased steadily between the ages of 14 and 25, and then leveled off. In other words, it is during the transition between adolescence and adulthood that individuals acquire the sort of wisdom we associate with age (Pasupathi et al., 2001).

ADOLESCENT RISK TAKING

A second practical application of research into adolescent thinking involves the study of adolescent risk taking. In Chapter 1, you read that many of the health problems of adolescence are the result of behaviors that can be prevented—behaviors such as substance abuse, reckless driving, and unprotected sex. The Centers for Disease Control and Prevention, a federal agency that monitors the health of Americans, now surveys American teenagers annually and asks whether they had engaged in various behaviors during the previous 30 days (Centers for Disease Control and Prevention, 2008). Risk taking is common among adolescents. Recent surveys have revealed, for example, that although most high school students regularly use a seat belt, of those teenagers who ride motorcycles, 33 percent report rarely or never wearing a helmet, and of those who ride bicycles, 85 percent report rarely or never wearing a helmet. Close to one third of both sexes have been passengers in cars driven by intoxicated drivers, and one tenth have driven while drinking (Centers for Disease Control and Prevention, 2006; Ozer & lrwin, 2009). In general, risk taking is much more common among males than females, although some evidence suggests that this gender gap has been narrowing over time (Abbott-Chapman, Denholm, & Wyld, 2008; Byrnes, Miller, & Schafer, 1999).

Some writers have suggested that we look at these behaviors as resulting from decisions that adolescents make—for instance, decisions to drink alcohol, to drive fast, or to have intercourse without using contraception—and that we need to better understand the cognitive processes behind such decision making. One line of research has attempted to examine whether adolescents make risky decisions because of deficiencies in their developing cognitive abilities (Furbey & Beyth-Marom, 1992).

▌ Behavioral Decision Theory   A number of writers have looked at adolescent risk taking from a perspective called **behavioral decision theory** (Fischhoff & Quadrel, 1995; Kahneman, Slovic, & Tversky, 1982; Reyna & Farley, 2006). In this perspective, which draws heavily on economics, decision making is a rational process in which individuals calculate the costs and benefits of alternative courses of action and behave in ways that maximize the benefits and minimize the costs (Gruber,

2001). According to this theory, all behaviors, including risky ones, can be analyzed as the outcome of a process involving five steps: (1) identifying alternative choices, (2) identifying the consequences that might follow from each choice, (3) evaluating the costs and benefits of each possible consequence, (4) assessing the likelihood of each possible consequence, and (5) combining all this information according to some decision rule (Beyth-Marom, Austin, Fischhoff, Palmgren, & Jacobs-Quadrel, 1993).

So, for example, an adolescent girl who is trying to decide whether to accept a ride home from a party with friends who have been drinking will (1) identify the choices (to accept the ride or not), (2) identify the consequences ("If I accept the ride, and we get into an accident, I could be seriously hurt, but if I don't accept the ride, my friends will make fun of me for being a 'loser'"), (3) evaluate the desirability of each consequence ("Appearing like a 'loser' to my friends is bad, but being in an accident would be terrible"), (4) assess the likelihood of each consequence ("My friends probably won't really change their opinion of me just because I turn down the ride, and my friend who is driving is so drunk that he really might get into an accident"), and (5) combine all the information according to some decision rule ("All things considered, I think I won't take the ride").

From the perspective of behavioral decision theory, then, it is important to ask whether adolescents use different processes than adults in identifying, estimating, and evaluating behavioral options and consequences. If risky decisions are the result of faulty information processing—in attention, memory, metacognition, or organization, for example—perhaps it would make sense to train adolescents in these basic cognitive abilities as a means of lessening their risk taking.

As we have seen, however, adolescents, at least by the time they are 15 or so, make decisions using the same basic cognitive processes that adults use (Beyth-Marom et al., 1993; Furbey & Beyth-Marom, 1992). This is true even for issues as complicated as deciding whether to abort a pregnancy (C. Lewis, 1987). The major gains in the cognitive skills that affect decision making appear to occur between childhood and adolescence, rather than between adolescence and adulthood (Steinberg & Cauffman, 1996). Thus, educating adolescents in how to make "better" decisions is not likely to reduce risk taking (Steinberg, 2007).

FOOD FOR THOUGHT

What risky behavior did you engage in during adolescence that you would be reluctant to engage in today? If you did, why do you think you took those risks? What has changed that has made you more risk averse?

---

behavioral decision theory   An approach to understanding adolescent risk taking, in which behaviors are seen as the outcome of systematic decision-making processes.

▌ Do Adolescents Really Feel Invulnerable? A second possibility that is often suggested is that adolescents are more likely to feel invulnerable—more likely, that is, to subscribe to the personal fable that they will not be harmed by potentially harmful activities. However, as you read earlier, there is no evidence for the widely held belief that adolescents are more likely to subscribe to personal fables than are adults (Quadrel, Fischhoff, & Davis, 1993). More importantly, studies indicate that young adolescents are *less* likely than young adults to see themselves as invulnerable—if anything, young adolescents *overestimate* the risks involved in potentially harmful behavior (Millstein & Halpern-Felsher, 2002). By middle adolescence, individuals have begun to underestimate their likelihood of being hurt by potentially harmful activities, but they are no more likely to do this than adults (Quadrel et al., 1993). There is no evidence, for example, that adolescents are worse at perceiving risks than adults are (Van Leijenhorst, Westenberg, & Crone, 2008). Interestingly, however, research indicates that adolescents vary far more than adults in how they interpret words and phrases used to describe risk—words like "probably," "likely," or "a very low chance"—suggesting that health educators and practitioners should not take for granted that an adolescent's understanding of a message about risk is what they think it is (Biehl & Halpern-Felsher, 2001; Mills, Reyna, & Estrada, 2008). Similarly, just because an adolescent says that she knows that having "safe sex" can protect her against sexually transmitted diseases doesn't necessarily mean that she knows the specific behaviors that constitute safe sex (Reyna & Farley, 2006).

▌ Age Differences in Values and Priorities If adolescents use the same decision-making processes as adults, and if adolescents are no more likely than adults to think of themselves as invulnerable, why, then, do they behave in excessively risky ways? One answer may involve the different ways in which adolescents and adults evaluate the desirability of different consequences (S. Moore & Gullone, 1996). For example, an individual's decision to try cocaine at a party may involve evaluating a number of different consequences, including the legal and health risks, the pleasure the drug may induce, and the way in which he or she will be judged (both positively and negatively) by the other people present. An adult and an adolescent may both consider all these consequences, but the adult may place relatively more weight on the health risks of trying the drug, while the adolescent may place relatively more weight on the social consequences of not trying it. Although an adult may see an adolescent's decision to value peer acceptance more than health as irrational, an adolescent may see the adult's decision as equally incomprehensible. Behavioral decision theory reminds us that all decisions—even risky ones—can be seen as rational

Recent research on cognitive development in adolescence has been aimed at understanding the thinking behind risk-taking behavior.

once we understand how an individual estimates and evaluates the consequences of various courses of action.

One very important difference between adolescents and adults, for instance, is that, when weighing the costs and benefits of engaging in a risky behavior, adolescents are more attuned to the potential rewards than adults are (Ben-Zur & Reshef-Kfir, 2003; Cauffman et al., 2010; Millstein & Halpern-Felsher, 2002). This difference is consistent with what we now know is taking place in the limbic system around the time of puberty. One recent study of delinquents found, for instance, that adolescents' criminal activity was more strongly related to their beliefs about the potential rewards of the activity (for example, being seen as "cool") than to their perceptions of the activity's riskiness (for example, the chances of being arrested) (Matsueda, Kreager, & Huizinga, 2006). As several writers have pointed out, this has important implications for the prevention of risky behavior among adolescents. It may be more important to convince adolescents that the rewards of a risky activity are small (for example, that few people will actually look up to someone for being violent) than to persuade them that the costs are large (for example, that being incarcerated will be terrible).

In all likelihood, of course, neither adolescents' nor adults' decisions are always made in as straightforward or rational a way as suggested by behavioral decision theory. Nevertheless, this approach has opened up a new way of thinking about adolescent risk taking. Instead of viewing risky activities as the result of irrational or faulty judgment, experts are now trying to understand where and how adolescents obtain the information they use in reaching their conclusions, and how accurate the information is. If, for example, adolescents underestimate the likelihood of getting pregnant

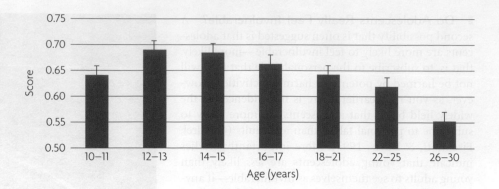

FIGURE 2.6 Self-reported sensation seeking increases between childhood and adolescence and declines between adolescence and adulthood. (Steinberg et al., 2008)

following unprotected sex, sex education efforts might focus on teaching teenagers the actual probability. (Of course, this presumes that adolescents' decisions about whether to have sex are made rationally, which may not be the case [P. Levine, 2001].)

Emotional and Contextual Influences on Risk Taking

We should also keep in mind that emotional and contextual factors, as well as cognitive ones, contribute to adolescent risk taking (Dahl, 2008; Rivers, Reyna, & Mills, 2008; Seguin, Arseneault, & Tremblay, 2007). Several researchers have noted that adolescents may differ from adults in important ways that are not captured by measures of logical reasoning, such as susceptibility to peer pressure, impulsivity, orientation to the present rather than the future, or reward seeking (Cauffman et al., 2010; Steinberg et al., 2008; Steinberg et al., 2009). With respect to emotional factors, for example, studies show that individuals who are high in reward seeking and **sensation seeking**—that is, who seek out novel and intense experiences—are more likely to engage in various types of risky behaviors than their peers (C. A. Johnson et al., 2008; D. Miller & Byrnes, 1997), and that both reward seeking and sensation seeking are higher during adolescence than childhood or adulthood (Cauffman et al., 2010; Steinberg et al., 2008) (see Figure 2.6).

The context in which individuals spend time matters, too (Boyer, 2006). Keep in mind that a good deal of adolescents' risk taking takes place in contexts in which they are unsupervised by adults and exposed to tremendous peer pressure to engage in risky behavior (Byrnes, 1997; Crockett, Raffaelli, & Shen, 2006). As noted earlier, individuals' susceptibility to peer pressure is higher during early and middle adolescence than later, suggesting that one reason for teenagers' greater risk taking is the fact that they spend so much time in the peer group (Steinberg & Monahan, 2007). Most adolescent risk taking, including delinquency, drinking, and reckless behavior, occurs when other teenagers are present (Steinberg, 2008).

The effect of peers on adolescent risk taking is clearly evident in studies of driving accidents. As Figure 2.7 shows, having multiple passengers in the car increases the risk of crashes dramatically among 16- and 17-year-old drivers, significantly among 18- and 19-year-old drivers, and not at all among adults. Consistent with this, in one recent experiment, in which adolescents, college undergraduates, and adults who were either alone or in a room with their friends played a video driving game that permitted risky driving—for instance, driving through an intersection after a traffic light had turned yellow—found that the mere fact of having friends watching their performance increased risk taking among adolescents and undergraduates, but not adults (M. Gardner & Steinberg, 2005). In that study, the presence of peers also increased adolescents' stated willingness to take all sorts of risks, including shoplifting, stealing, and allowing friends to bring drugs into their house. Contrary to popular belief, alcohol is not the main contributor to the increased rate of automobile accidents among teenagers—in fact, adolescents are *less* likely to drink and drive than adults. Driving with other teenagers in the car and speeding are far more important factors (A. Williams, 2003).

Reducing Adolescent Risk Taking

Generally speaking, the most common approach to reducing adolescent risk taking is through classroom-based education programs designed to teach adolescents about the dangers of various activities (e.g., smoking, unprotected sex, drinking and driving), about making better decisions, and about resisting peer pressure to engage in risky activity. As you will read in later chapters, however, the evidence that these programs work is very shaky. If, as we have seen, adolescents do not seem to be ignorant about the risks of these activities or deficient in the ways in which they make decisions, it does not seem likely that efforts to change their knowledge or decision making will result in very much risk reduction. And if recent research on brain maturation is pointing to reasons for the inherent vulnerability of adolescence—the combination of heightened sensation seeking and immature impulse control—perhaps it

sensation seeking The enjoyment of novel and intense experiences.

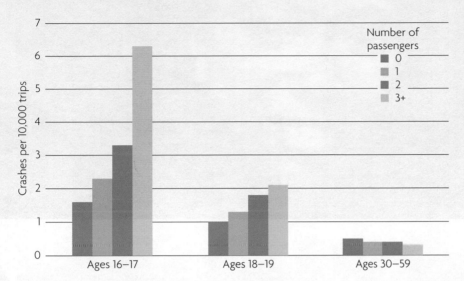

FIGURE 2.7 Crash rates are significantly higher when teenage drivers have passengers in the car. This is less true for college-age drivers and not at all true for middle-aged adults, however. (Williams, 2003)

makes sense to rethink our approach to the problem (Steinberg, 2007).

One alternative approach might focus on limiting adolescents' opportunities to put themselves in risky situations. For example, because we know that adolescents are more likely to have automobile accidents when they have teenage passengers in the car or drive at night, limiting the situations under which teenagers are permitted to drive, especially after they are newly licensed, would give adolescents that coveted driver's license but limit risky driving. It is also possible to reduce adolescent risk taking through economic policies. For example, although anti-tobacco education has met with only limited success, increases in the cost of cigarettes have dramatically reduced the rate of teen smoking. Thus, raising the price of tobacco or alcohol would likely diminish adolescents' use of these products, because adolescents generally do not have a great deal of money and would therefore be sensitive to increases in the cost of smoking or drinking (Gruber, 2001). Another possibility would be to make risky substances harder for adolescents to obtain, by more strictly enforcing policies that prohibit stores from selling tobacco and alcohol to minors, limiting the supply of illegal drugs, or enforcing laws that limit adolescents' access to firearms. Yet a third possibility would be to make the penalties for engaging in certain risky behaviors, like reckless or drunk driving, more severe, and in so doing increase the salience of the potential costs of engaging in the risky behavior. Finally, to the extent that sensation seeking may be a normal part of adolescence, perhaps we can figure out how to provide safe outlets for this motivation. Not all risk taking is bad, after all. The challenge for parents, educators, and policymakers is to find ways to permit adolescents to take risks without putting themselves in situations in which they can hurt themselves.

RECAP

- Contemporary researchers have been interested in the ways in which the cognitive changes of adolescence play out in everyday activities.
- One domain in which improvements in thinking are evident is the realm of social cognition. Adolescence is a time of increased understanding of other people, social relationships, social conventions, and personal rights.
- Scientists who have examined the underlying reasons for the higher rate of risk taking among adolescents have noted that this is not due to deficiencies in basic cognitive abilities. More likely causes are age differences in priorities, in psychosocial factors, and in the contexts in which adolescents and adults spend time.

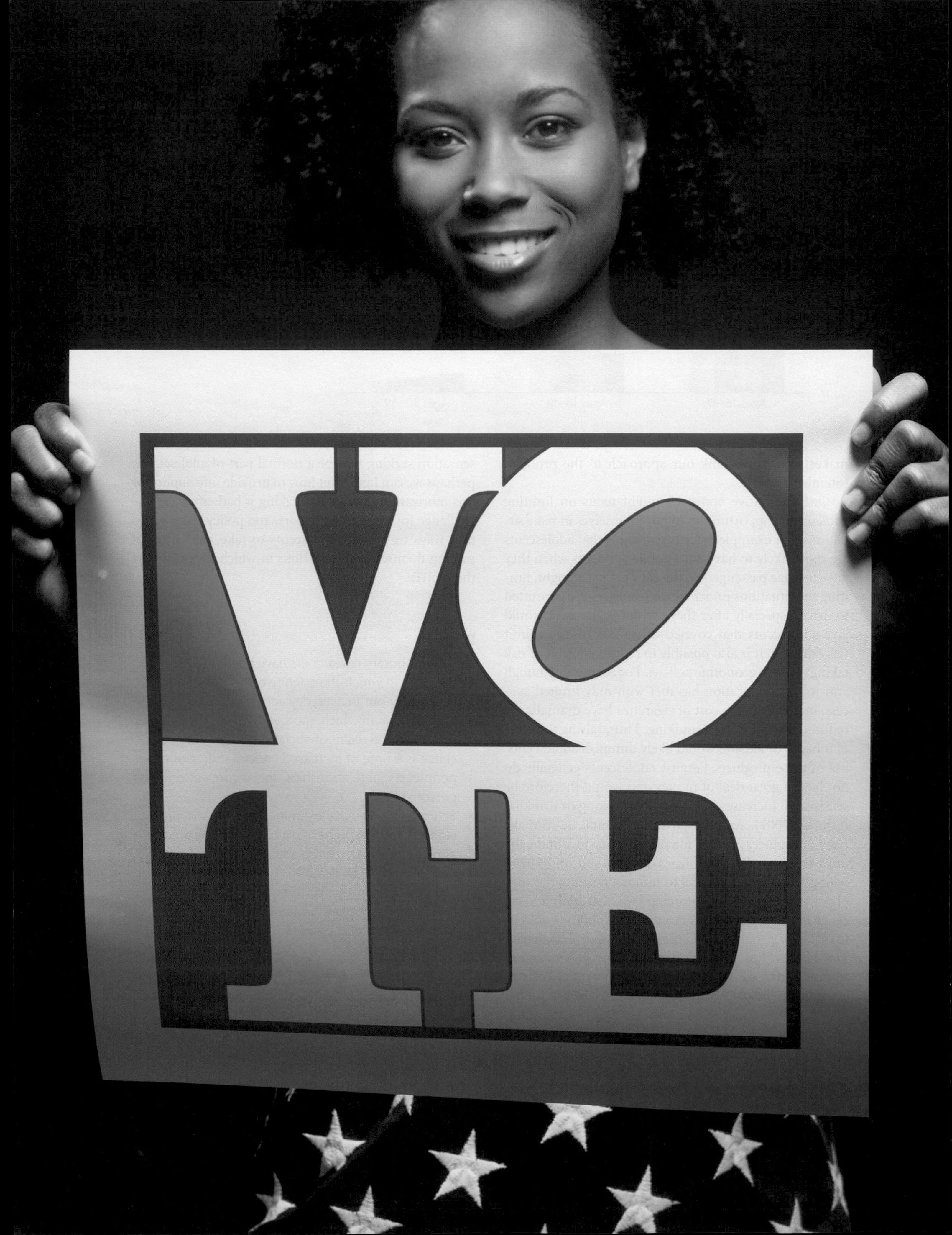
VOTE

Social Transitions

WHAT EVENTS IN YOUR LIFE told you—and others around you—that you were no longer a child and had finally become an adolescent? Was it when you turned 13? Finished elementary school? Went to your first boy–girl party? Were allowed to be out at the mall without an adult?

And what signaled, or will signal, that you are an adult? Turning 18? Turning 21? Getting your first full-time job? Getting your driver's license? Graduating from college? Getting your first apartment? Getting married?

Each of these social transitions is not just an event. Each is also a source of information—to the individual and those in his or her life—about the individual's stage of development. Parents may treat their children differently once they start high school, even if their appearance and behavior haven't changed. Neighbors might look at a child who has grown up next door differently once they see him or her driving. Adolescents may feel differently about themselves once they have started working at a "real" job.

In all societies, adolescence is a period of social transition for the individual. Over the course of the adolescent years, the individual ceases to be viewed by society as a child and comes to be recognized as an adult. This chapter is about the ways in which individuals are redefined during adolescence and the implications of this process for psychological development. Although the specific elements of this social passage from childhood into adulthood vary across time and space, the recognition that the individual's status has changed—a **social redefinition** of the individual—is universal.

In this chapter, we will look at a third fundamental feature of adolescence—changes in the way in which society defines who that person is and determines what rights and responsibilities she or he has as a result. Along with the biological changes of puberty and changes in thinking abilities, changes in social roles and social status constitute yet another universal feature of development during adolescence. As you will read, some theorists have argued that the nature of adolescent development is far more influenced by the way in which society defines the economic and social roles of young people than by the biological or cognitive changes of the period.

The study of social transitions in adolescence provides an interesting vehicle through which to compare adolescence across different cultures and historical epochs. Puberty, after all, is pretty much the same everywhere (although its timing and meaning may vary across contexts). Abstract thinking and logical reasoning don't differ from one society to the next (although *what* people think and reason about certainly does). The social transitions of adolescence are not the same, however. Although the existence of a social passage from childhood into adulthood is universal, considerable differences exist between the processes of social redefinition in industrialized society and those in more traditional cultures. In examining some of these differences, you will come to understand better how the way in which society structures the transition of adolescents into adult roles influences the nature of psychosocial development during the period.

Social Redefinition and Psychosocial Development

Like the biological and cognitive transitions of adolescence, the social transitions have important consequences for the young person's psychosocial development. In the realm of identity, for example, attainment of adult status may transform a young woman's self-concept, causing her to feel more mature and to think more seriously about future work and family roles. Similarly, an individual may feel older and more mature the first time he or she reports to work, goes into a bar, drives without an adult in the car, or votes. In turn, these new activities and opportunities may prompt self-evaluation and introspection.

Becoming an adult member of society, accompanied as it is by increases in responsibilities and freedom, also has an impact on the development of autonomy, or independence. In contrast to the child, the adolescent-turned-adult faces a wider range of decisions that may have serious long-term consequences (Woolard & Scott, 2009). An individual who has reached the drinking age, for example, must decide how to handle this new privilege. Should he go along with the crowd and drink every weekend night, follow his parents' example and abstain from drinking, or chart a middle ground? And in return for the privileges that come with adult status, the adolescent-turned-adult is expected to behave in

social redefinition   The process through which an individual's position or status is redefined by society.

a more responsible fashion. For example, receiving a driver's license carries with it the obligation of driving safely. Thus, the attainment of adult status provides chances for the young person to exercise autonomy and to develop a greater sense of independence.

Changes in social definition often bring with them changes in relationships with others. Social redefinition at adolescence is therefore likely to raise new questions and concerns for the young person about intimacy—including such matters as dating and marriage. Many parents prohibit their children from dating until they have reached an "appropriate" age, and not until the **age of majority** (the legal age for adult status) are individuals allowed to marry without first gaining their parents' permission. In certain societies, young people may even be *required* to marry when they reach adulthood, entering into a marriage that may have been arranged while they were children (Schlegel, 2009).

Changes in status at adolescence also may affect development in the domain of sexuality. In contemporary society, for example, laws governing sexual behavior (such as the definition of statutory rape) typically differentiate between individuals who have and have not attained adult status. By becoming an adult in a legal sense, the young person may be confronted with the need for new decisions about sexual activity. One problem continuing to face contemporary society is whether sexually active individuals who have not yet attained adult legal status should be able to make independent decisions about such adult matters as abortion and contraception (Woolard & Scott, 2009).

Finally, reaching adulthood often has important implications in the realm of achievement. For instance, in contemporary society, individuals can hold informal jobs, like babysitting, when they are still young, but it is not until adult work status is attained (typically at age 16 in the United States) that young people can enter the labor force as full-time employees. And not until young people have reached a designated age are they permitted to leave school of their own volition. In less industrialized societies, becoming an adult typically entails entrance into the productive activities of the community. Together, these shifts are likely to prompt changes in the young person's skills, aspirations, and expectations.

FOOD FOR THOUGHT

Which fundamental change of adolescence—biological, cognitive, or social—do you think has the most powerful effect on psychological development? Why?

RECAP

- Changes in social definition—in how society views the individual—constitute a third set of fundamental changes that define adolescence.
- Although societies vary in how the transition from childhood to adulthood is signified, all cultures have some way of recognizing that the individual's rights and responsibilities have changed once he or she becomes an adult.
- Changes in social definition may have profound effects on development in the realms of identity, autonomy, intimacy, sexuality, and achievement.

The Elongation of Adolescence

One of the most striking aspects of the social transition experienced by adolescents today is the sheer length of the time it takes to travel from childhood to adulthood. By virtually any indicator, adolescence lasts longer today than ever before, because young people go through puberty (one marker of the beginning of adolescence) earlier and enter into adult roles of work and family (one way to define the end of adolescence) later. Although this is more true in industrialized societies than in developing ones, there is evidence that adolescence lasts longer in developing countries as well (Larson, Wilson, & Rickman, 2009).

In previous eras, when puberty occurred around age 15 and individuals left school and went to work just a few years later, adolescence, at least by these markers, lasted only a few years. Today, in contrast, young people are caught between the world of childhood and the world of adulthood for an extremely long time, often longer than a decade, and frequently with only a vague sense of when—and how—they become adults. Indeed, in the minds of many social scientists who study adolescence in modern society, the social passage of young people into adult roles is too long, too vague, and too rocky (Chisholm & Hurrelmann, 1995; S. Hamilton & Hamilton, 2009; Nightingale & Wolverton, 1993). And, as we shall see, the passage from adolescence into adulthood is especially difficult for young people growing up in poverty, in part because social institutions that once enabled poor youth to make a successful transition into adulthood no longer provide sufficient support (S. Hamilton & Hamilton, 2009). In today's economy, making a smooth and successful transition into adult

age of majority The designated age at which an individual is recognized as an adult.

work and family roles is challenging enough for individuals who graduate from college, but it has become incredibly difficult for those who only complete high school and almost impossible for those without a high school diploma.

The lengthening of adolescence as a developmental period has had important implications for how young people see themselves, relate to others, and develop psychologically. Consider just a few examples:

- Parents used to "launch" their children from home very close to the age of puberty. As a consequence, individuals spent very little time living under the same roof with their parents once they had become sexual beings. In contemporary society, however, individuals live with their parents long after they have become sexually mature. What impact might this have on parent–child relationships?

- Adolescents today probably aren't any less emotionally mature than they were 100 years ago—if anything, growing up under many of the pressures to which individuals are exposed in today's world has made them more mature at a younger age. But because the cost of living independently has increased so rapidly, adolescents' economic "maturity" (that is, their ability to support themselves without help from their parents) lags far behind their psychological maturity (that is, their ability to behave responsibly). What implications does this have? How does it feel to be an adult psychologically but a child financially?

- One of the main reasons that adolescence has been lengthened is that much more formal education is now necessary in order to make a successful transition into adult work roles. School, however, is not something that all individuals enjoy equally. How might forcing all adolescents to follow the same pathway into adulthood benefit some but not others?

FOOD FOR THOUGHT

The time between the age when individuals become sexually mature and when they marry was much shorter in previous generations than it is today—because sexual maturity takes place so much earlier now and marriage takes place so much later. As a result the admonition to "wait until you're married" to have sex was probably a lot easier to do 150 years ago than it is today. Do you agree?

inventionists   Theorists who argue that the period of adolescence is mainly a social invention.

RECAP

- The length of adolescence as a developmental period has increased dramatically due to the earlier onset of puberty and the prolongation of formal education, which delays many of the role transitions that mark the beginning of adulthood.

- Many observers of adolescence in contemporary society believe that the transition into adulthood is too long, too vague, and too disorderly and that this has had harmful effects on adolescents' development and well-being, especially those for whom formal schooling is not a fulfilling experience.

Adolescence as a Social Invention

Many writers have argued that adolescence, as a period in the life cycle, is mainly a social invention (e.g., Fasick, 1994; Lapsley, Enright, & Serlin, 1985). These writers, often referred to as **inventionists,** point out that, although the biological and cognitive changes characteristic of the period are important in their own right, adolescence is defined primarily by the ways in which society recognizes (or does not recognize) the period as distinct from childhood or adulthood.

Many of our images of adolescence are influenced by the fact that society draws lines between adolescence and childhood (for instance, the boundary between elementary and secondary school) and between adolescence and adulthood (for instance, the age at which one can hold a job). Inventionists stress that it is because we see adolescence as distinct that it exists as such. They point to other cultures and other historical periods in which adolescence has been viewed very differently. Many of these theorists view the behaviors and problems characteristic of adolescence in contemporary society, such as delinquency, as a consequence of the particular way that adolescence is defined and young people are treated, rather than the result of the biological or cognitive givens of the period. As you know, this is an entirely different view from that espoused by writers such as G. Stanley Hall, who saw the psychological changes of adolescence as driven by puberty and, as a result, by biological destiny.

THE "INVENTION" OF ADOLESCENCE

Have there always been adolescents? Although this may seem like a simple question with an obvious answer, it is actually a very complicated issue. Naturally, there have always been individuals between the ages of 10 and 20, or who just passed through puberty, or whose frontal lobes were still maturing. But according to the inventionist view, adolescence as we know it in contemporary society did not really exist until the Industrial Revolution of the mid–19th century (Fasick, 1994). Prior to that time, in the agricultural world of the 16th or 17th century, children were treated primarily as miniature adults, and people did not make precise distinctions among children of different ages ("child" referred to anyone under the age of 18 or even 21). Children provided important labor to their families, and they learned early in their development the roles they were expected to fill later in life. The main distinction between children and adults was based not on their age or their abilities but on whether they owned property (Modell & Goodman, 1990). As a consequence, there was little reason to label some youngsters as "children" and others as "adolescents"—in fact, the term *adolescent* was not widely used prior to the 19th century.

▌ The Impact of Industrialization   With industrialization came new patterns of work, education, and family life. Adolescents were among those most dramatically affected by these changes. First, because the economy was changing so rapidly, away from the simple and predictable life known in agrarian society, the connection between what individuals learned in childhood and what they would need to know in adulthood became increasingly uncertain. Although a man may have been a farmer, his son would not necessarily follow in his footsteps. One response to this uncertainty was that parents, especially in middle-class families, encouraged adolescents to spend time within societal institutions, such as schools, preparing for adulthood. Instead of working side by side with their parents and other adults at home, as was the case before industrialization, late-19th-century adolescents became increasingly more likely to spend their days with their peers, preparing for the future. As you will read in later chapters, this change was one factor that led to the increased importance of peer groups and youth culture.

Inventionists are quick to point out that the redefinition of adolescence as a time of preparation rather than participation suited society's changing economic needs as well (Fasick, 1994). One initial outcome of industrialization was a shortage of job opportunities, because machines were replacing workers. Although adolescents provided inexpensive labor, they were competing with adults for a limited number of jobs. One way of protecting adults' jobs was to remove adolescents from the labor force, by turning them into full-time students. To accomplish this, society needed to begin discriminating between individuals who were "ready" for work and those who were not. And although there was little factual basis for the distinction, society began to view adolescents as less capable and more in need of guidance and training—as a way of legitimizing what was little more than age discrimination. Individuals who earlier in the century would have been working next to adults

were now seen as too immature or too unskilled to carry out similar tasks—even though the individuals themselves hadn't changed in any meaningful way.

A less cynical view of the events of the late 19th century emphasizes the genuine desire of some adults to protect adolescents from the dangers of the new workplace, rather than the selfish desire to protect adults' jobs from teenagers. Industrialization brought with it worrisome changes in community life, especially in the cities. Many factories were dangerous working environments, filled with new and unfamiliar machinery. The disruption of small farming communities and the growth of large urban areas was accompanied by increases in crime and in "moral degeneracy." **Child protectionists** argued that young people needed to be kept away from the labor force for their own good. In addition to the rise of schools during this time, the early 20th century saw the growth of many organizations aimed at protecting young people, such as the Boy Scouts and other adult-supervised youth clubs (Modell & Goodman, 1990).

▌ The Origins of Adolescence as We Know It Today   For whatever the reason, it was not until the late 19th century—little more than 100 years ago—that adolescence came to be viewed as it is today: a lengthy period of preparation for adulthood, in which young people, in need of guidance and supervision, remain economically dependent on their elders. This view started within the middle class—where parents had more to gain by keeping their children out of the labor force and educating them for a better adulthood—but it spread quickly throughout society. Because the workplace has continued to change in ways that make the future uncertain, the idea of adolescence as a distinctive period of preparation for adulthood has remained intact. Adolescence, as a transitional stage between childhood and adulthood, now exists in virtually all societies (Larson et al., 2009).

FOOD FOR THOUGHT

In your view, is adolescence mainly a social invention?

Two other modifications of the definition of adolescence also gave rise to new terminology and ideas. The first of these concerns the use of the term **teenager,** which was not employed until about 50 years ago. In

child protectionists   Individuals who argued, early in the 20th century, that adolescents needed to be kept out of the labor force in order to protect them from the hazards of the workplace.

teenager   A term popularized about 50 years ago to refer to young people; it connoted a more frivolous and lighthearted image than did "adolescent."

Although adolescence was invented during the late 19th century, it was not until the middle of the 20th century that our present-day image of the teenager was created. Making an important contribution to this image were the mass media—magazines such as Seventeen *cultivated the picture of the happy-go-lucky teenager as a way of targeting advertisements toward an increasingly lucrative adolescent market.*

contrast to "adolescent," "teenager" suggests a more frivolous and lighthearted age, during which individuals concern themselves with such things as cars and cosmetics. An important social change that led to the development of the concept of teenager was the increased affluence and economic freedom enjoyed by American adolescents during the late 1940s and early 1950s (Fasick, 1994; Hine, 1999). Advertisers recognized that these young people represented an important consumer group and, with the help of new publications such as *Seventeen* magazine, began cultivating the image of the happy-go-lucky teenager as a means of targeting ad campaigns toward the lucrative adolescent market (Osgerby, 2008; Palladino, 1996). Interestingly, although the image of the American teenager—fun-loving, irresponsible, and independent—now appears all over the world, in some societies it is viewed favorably, while in others it is held up as an example of what adults do *not* want their children to become (Larson et al., 2009).

A second term whose acceptance grew as a result of social change is **youth,** which was used long before "adolescent." But, prior to industrialization, youth had a vague, imprecise meaning and could refer to someone

youth   Today, a term used to refer to individuals ages 18–22; it once referred to individuals ages 12–24.

as young as 12 or as old as 24 (Modell & Goodman, 1990). Gradually, and during the 1960s in particular, the growth of the college population and the rise in student activism focused attention on individuals who were somewhere between adolescence and young adulthood—those from 18 to 22. Many adults referred to the changes they saw in attitudes and values among college students as the "youth movement." One theorist went so far as to argue that youth is a separate stage in the life cycle, psychologically as well as chronologically distinct from adolescence and adulthood (Keniston, 1970). Indeed, many college students are unsure about whether they are adolescents or adults, since they may feel mature in some respects (for example, keeping up an apartment or being involved in a serious relationship) but immature in others (for example, having to depend on parents for economic support or having to have an advisor approve class schedules). Although it may strike you as odd to think of 22-year-olds as adolescents, the lengthening of formal schooling in contemporary society has altered the way we define adolescence, because the majority of young people continue their education past high school and are forced to delay their transition into many adult work and family roles (Furstenberg, 2000). By this definition, many 22-year-olds (and many individuals who are even older) are still not yet adults.

FOOD FOR THOUGHT

Historians agree that social conditions during the second half of the 19th century led to the creation of adolescence as we know it today. What changes in the nature of adolescence have taken place since that time? How might adolescence change in the 21st century?

EMERGING ADULTHOOD: A NEW STAGE OF LIFE OR A LUXURY OF THE MIDDLE CLASS?

The transition to adulthood has become so delayed in many industrialized societies that some have suggested that there is a new stage in life—emerging adulthood—that may last for some individuals until their mid-20s (Arnett, 2004). The main proponent of this idea has been psychologist Jeffrey Arnett, who contends that the period from ages 18 to 25 is neither adolescence nor adulthood, but a unique developmental period in its own right, characterized by five main features:

1. the exploration of possible identities before making enduring choices;

2. instability in work, romantic relationships, and living arrangements;

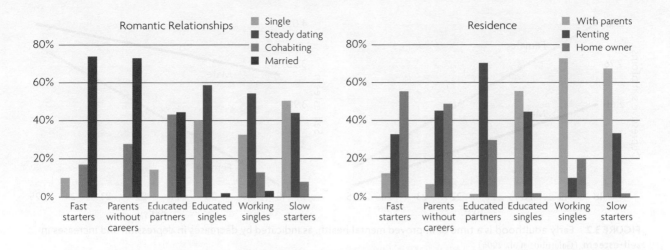

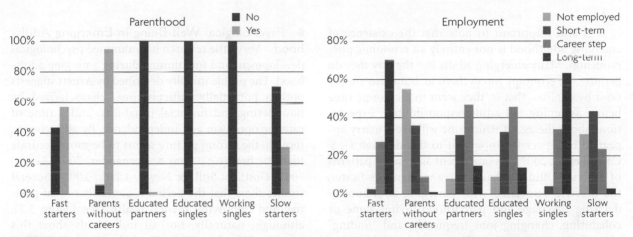

FIGURE 3.1   It is difficult to generalize about lifestyle patterns followed in early adulthood. One study found six distinct clusters that varied in their relationships, living arrangements, employment, and transition to parenthood. (Osgood et al., 2005)

3. a focus on oneself and, in particular, on functioning as an independent person;

4. the subjective feeling of being between adolescence and adulthood; and

5. the subjective sense that life holds many possibilities.

■ **Is Emerging Adulthood Universal?**   This profile certainly describes many young people in contemporary society, particularly those whose parents can foot the bill while their "emerging adults" are figuring out what they want to do with their lives. As Arnett himself points out (2000), however, emerging adulthood does not exist in all cultures—in fact, it exists in very few (the United States, Canada, Australia, New Zealand, Japan, and the more affluent nations of Western Europe). A recent study of Chinese college students, for instance, found that the majority feel they have reached adult status in their early 20s (L. J. Nelson, Badger, & Bo, 2004). And even within countries in which there are significant numbers of emerging

adults, the majority of individuals cannot afford to delay the transition from adolescence into full-fledged adulthood for a half decade. Several recent analyses indicate that there is a great deal of variability among people in their mid-20s with respect to the dimensions of emerging adulthood. As one team of researchers put it, "It is a mistake to think that a sample of youth in their midtwenties are all emerging adults" (e.g., M. J. Shanahan, Porfeli, Mortimer, & Erickson, 2005, p. 251). According to one study of Michigan working- and middle-class youths in their mid-20s (Osgood, Ruth, Eccles, Jacobs, & Butler, 2005), for example, six distinct lifestyle patterns, each characterized by different degrees of commitment to adultlike work, romantic, and residential arrangements, were evident: fast starters (12%), parents without careers (10%), educated partners (19%), educated singles (37%), working singles (7%), and slow starters (14%) (see Figure 3.1). The group that most resembled emerging adults, the "educated singles," made up about 40% of the sample.

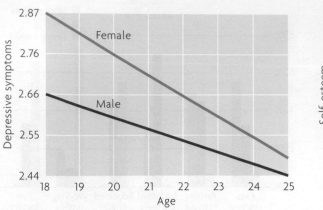
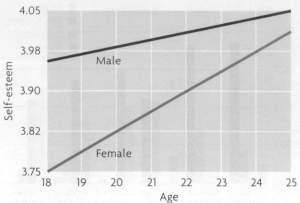

FIGURE 3.2 Early adulthood is a time of improved mental health, as indicated by decreases in depression and increases in self-esteem. (Galambos et al., 2006)

It is also important to note that the existence of emerging adulthood is not entirely an economic phenomenon. Many emerging adults live the way they do because the economy forces them to, but many simply do it by choice—that is, they want to take some time before assuming full adult responsibilities. Expectations about the age at which one will likely marry appear to be especially important to this decision (J. S. Carroll et al., 2007). As one recent analysis of patterns of marriage and residential arrangements indicates, the lifestyle associated with emerging adulthood—delaying marriage and parenthood, living alone or cohabiting, changing jobs frequently, and "finding" oneself—is more prevalent in some communities than in others. The researchers, using U.S. census data, looked at differences between states in patterns of marriage, household formation, and so forth (Lesthaeghe & Neidert, 2006). They found that in some states a substantial number of individuals appeared to be living the life of the quintessential emerging adult, but in other states this was not very common. In particular, young adults in states that are generally more politically and socially conservative were far less likely to follow the emerging-adulthood pattern than those who lived in more liberal states. This suggests that the existence of emerging adulthood may have a lot to do with values and priorities.

FOOD FOR THOUGHT

What do you think of the concept of "emerging adulthood"? If it is a choice, rather than an inevitable consequence of economic change, why do you think some, but not all, people choose it?

Psychological Well-Being in Emerging Adulthood Very little research has examined psychological development and functioning during emerging adulthood. The profile initially described by Arnett suggests both a potentially difficult time, characterized by floundering and financial instability, and a time of carefree optimism and independence. By all accounts, though, the second picture seems to be more accurate than the first (e.g., Arias & Hernández, 2007; Arnett, 2007; Gottlieb, Still, & Newby-Clark, 2007). Several studies show that the period is generally one of positive and improving mental health (see Figure 3.2), although, naturally, not all individuals show this pattern (Galambos, Barker, & Krahn, 2006; H. K. Kim, Capaldi, & Stoolmiller, 2003).

One recent study followed a national sample of American youths from age 18 to their mid-20s. The researchers compared four groups of individuals: (1) those who reported positive well-being across the entire interval, (2) those who reported negative well-being across the entire interval, (3) those whose well-being started low but increased, and (4) those whose well-being started high but decreased (Schulenberg, Bryant, & O'Malley, 2004). (There also was a large group whose well-being was average to begin with and stayed that way.) They then looked to see whether these patterns of well-being over time were related to indicators of individual functioning, by rating whether individuals had been succeeding, maintaining, or stalling as they moved into adulthood (see Table 3.1). Three main findings emerged. First, over 80% of the sample showed great stability in their well-being over the period. This is consistent with findings from many other studies indicating that psychological functioning in childhood and adolescence is highly predictive of success later in life (e.g., M. J. Shanahan & Bauer, 2004). That is, success in one stage (doing well in high school) usually leads to success in the next stage (getting into a good college), and some

TABLE 3.1 Descriptions of developmental task domains

Domain	Succeeding	Maintaining	Stalling
Education	• Graduated from 4-year college by age 26, or • Expected to graduate from 2-year college and received 2-year degree	• Expected to graduate from 4-year college and received 2-year degree, or • Did not expect 2- or 4-year degree and did not receive either degree, or • Expected 2-year degree and did not receive 2-year degree by age 26	• Expected 4-year college degree and did not receive either 2- or 4-year degree by age 26
Work	• No unemployment at age 22 or 26, and • Working 10+ months/year at full-time job by age 26, and • High job confidence at age 26	• Neither succeeding nor stalling (e.g., homemaker or otherwise not working and not looking for work outside home)	• Some unemployment at age 22 and/or 26, and • Low job confidence at age 26
Financial autonomy	• Self and/or spouse providing all resources at age 26	• Some resources come from other than self or spouse (and not stalling)	• At age 26, less than half of support is from self and/or spouse, and/or • Live with parents and receive some financial help (>20%) from them
Romantic involvement	• At age 26, married or engaged (with or without cohabitation), and • No divorce history	• At age 26, cohabiting, or • Dating more than once a month, and/or • Divorced, but remarried	• At age 26, not married, not engaged not cohabiting, and • Dating once a month or less
Peer involvement	• Goes out two or more times a week for fun and recreation at age 22 and age 26	• Neither succeeding nor stalling	• Goes out one or fewer times a week for fun and recreation at age 22 and age 26
Substance abuse avoidance (healthy coping/lifestyle)	Four indicators of substance use: cigarettes (current use), binge drinking (past 2 weeks), marijuana (current use) and other illicit drugs (12-month use): • No substance use at any age (18, 22, 26)	• Some substance use, but less than stalling	• Use of two or more substances at all three ages (18, 22, 26), and/or • Use of three or more substances at age 26
Citizenship	• Three indicators reported at age 22 and age 26: social conscience, charity, and awareness of social/political events • Measures indicate at least one strong connection at age 22 and at least two strong connections at age 26	• Measures indicate some strong connections but not as frequent as at succeeding level	• Measures indicate no strong connections at age 26

Source: Schulenberg et al., 2004.

95

basic "resources" predict success throughout the life span—if you want to succeed in life, make sure you have a high IQ, money, and good parents (e.g., K. Burt, Obradović, Long, & Masten, 2008; Masten, Burt, & Roisman, 2004). Second, for more than a sixth of the sample, this period was one of substantial change in mental health—about 7% of the sample were well-functioning adolescents whose mental health declined, and another 10% were troubled adolescents who became "exemplary" young adults. Finally, experiences in the domains of work, romance, and citizenship—but not in the domains of school or finances—were especially linked to changes in well-being. Other studies have also found that success in the worlds of work and romance are related to well-being during this time (Galambos et al., 2006).

Has a new stage of life actually arisen? How widespread does a pattern of behavior have to be for us to conclude that a new stage of development has emerged? Does emerging adulthood exist if it is common in Boston or Berkeley, but not in Biloxi, Baghdad, or Beijing? It is hard to say. "Midlife" is a stage that we take for granted in contemporary America but that doesn't exist everywhere, or at least, not as we think of it (Schweder, 1998). Nevertheless, the notion that individuals go through a distinct and unique set of psychological transitions during middle age has become widely accepted (if perhaps less supported by hard evidence than journalists and other writers in the popular media suggest).

Clearly, on average, in some parts of the world, and in some segments of society, the transition between adolescence and adulthood has been lengthened—that much is indisputable. More individuals attend college than in previous eras, which delays their entrance into the world of work, and more postpone getting married, which delays their settling into a more stable lifestyle. But whether this means that the psychological functioning of 23-year-olds who follow this pattern of a delayed and prolonged transition is significantly different from that of 23-year-olds who transition from college directly into full-time employment and marriage is anyone's guess, because it hasn't been studied. Whether a *psychological* stage of emerging adulthood really exists has yet to be established (Côté, & Bynner, 2008). For example, even though the transition into adult work and family roles has been delayed in many segments of society, there is no evidence that this has been accompanied by a comparable prolongation into adulthood of problem behaviors typically associated with late adolescence, such as crime or substance abuse (Hayford & Furstenberg, 2008). In other words, it is entirely possible that economic forces have delayed the transition into *social* adulthood (i.e., the roles that people occupy) but have not affected the transition into *psychological* adulthood.

Note that when we say that adolescence (or the teenager, or youth, or emerging adulthood) is in part a social invention, we do not mean that its significance is in any way diminished or that it is somehow less real than if it were an entirely biological phenomenon. Democracy, after all, is a social invention, too, but its creation and development have had profound effects on the way that we live. As with other social inventions, the notion that there should be a distinct period of adolescence has endured over time and has had important and concrete repercussions. But as with other social constructs, the nature of adolescence changes over time, and it will continue to change as we revise our notions of what it means to grow from childhood into adulthood.

RECAP

- Inventionists argue that adolescence is more a social invention than a biological or cognitive phenomenon.
- Our conception of adolescence—whether it exists as a separate period and what its nature is—is determined largely by forces in the broader social environment. Changes in the broader environment, therefore, can change the very nature of adolescence.
- Adolescence as we know it today is largely a product of the Industrial Revolution of the late 19th century.
- Some writers have suggested that a new stage of life, called emerging adulthood, has arisen in recent years. Evidence for the existence of emerging adulthood as a widespread phenomenon is mixed.
- Although there is not a great deal of research on psychological development during the years immediately following adolescence, several studies indicate that for most people, especially those who successfully move into adult work and romantic roles, this is a time of increasing well-being and positive mental health.

Changes in Status During Adolescence

Changes in social definition at adolescence typically involve a two-sided modification in the individual's status. On the one hand, the adolescent is given certain privileges and rights that are typically reserved for the society's adult members. On the other hand, this increased power and freedom generally are accompanied by increased expectations for self-management, personal responsibility, and social participation.

DRAWING A LEGAL BOUNDARY

With the attainment of adult status, the young person is often permitted more extensive participation in the community's decision making. Among the Navajo, for example, it is only after a formal **initiation ceremony** that adolescents are considered members of the Navajo people and are permitted full participation in ceremonial life (Y. Cohen, 1964). In contemporary America, attaining the age of majority brings the right to vote. But along with this increased power usually come new obligations. In most societies, young adults are expected to serve their communities in cases of emergency or need, and in many cultures, training for warfare is often demanded of young people once they attain adult status (Benedict, 1934).

In most societies, not until adult status is attained is the young person permitted to participate in a variety of activities that are typically reserved for adults. Gambling, purchasing alcoholic beverages, and seeing X-rated films are but three of the many privileges we reserve in America for individuals who have reached the legal age of adulthood.

Once an adolescent is designated as an adult, she or he is also subject to a new set of laws and will be treated differently by the society's legal institutions than would be a child. In some instances, attaining adult status brings with it more lenient treatment under the law, whereas in others, it may be associated with harsher treatment. In the United States, for example, certain activities that are permissible among adults, such as not showing up for school (truancy) or leaving one's home without informing others (running away), are considered offenses when they are committed by young people. (Indeed, we use the term **status offense** to refer to a behavior that is problematic because of the young person's *status* as a juvenile.) As a college student, you cannot be legally punished for not showing up for class, as would have been the case when you were in high school; and if you decide you don't want to return home when you are on a break, you don't have to, at least not as far as the law is concerned. Certain crimes, when committed by a minor, are adjudicated in a separate **juvenile justice system,** which operates under different rules and principles than the **criminal justice system** that applies to adults. Although being tried in the juvenile justice system usually results in a less severe sanction than being found guilty of the same crime in adult court, this,

During the mid-1990s, many states changed their laws to permit adolescents accused of violent crimes to be tried as adults.

interestingly, is not always the case (Kurlychek & Johnson, 2004).

The legal regulation of adolescent behavior in the United States has been quite controversial in recent years. Part of the problem is that development during adolescence is so rapid and so variable between individuals that it is difficult to know at what chronological age a line should be drawn between legally viewing someone as an adult and viewing him or her as a child (Woolard & Scott, 2009; E. Scott & Steinberg, 2008). This problem is compounded by the fact that we draw the boundary at different places for different purposes (for example, driving at 16, voting at 18, buying alcohol at 21, and so on). This inconsistency makes it hard to point to any specific age and say with certainty that there is consensus about where the legal boundary should be drawn.

initiation ceremony   The formal induction of a young person into adulthood.

status offense   A violation of the law that pertains to minors but not adults.

juvenile justice system   A separate system of courts and related institutions developed to handle juvenile crime and delinquency.

criminal justice system   The system of courts and related institutions developed to handle adult crime.

FOOD FOR THOUGHT

At what age do you think we should draw the line between legal adolescence and legal adulthood? Should this age be the same for all activities, or should different activities have different age boundaries?

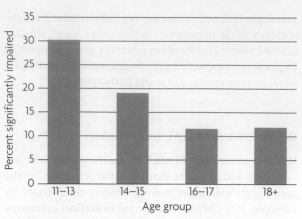

FIGURE 3.3   Significant numbers of juveniles under the age of 16 may not be competent to stand trial as adults. Shown are the proportions of individuals at different ages whose trial competence is as impaired as mentally ill adults who have been found incompetent. (Grisso et al., 2003)

■   **Adolescents as Criminal Defendants**   There is especially great disagreement about how we should view and treat young people who commit serious violent offenses (E. Scott & Steinberg, 2008). Should juveniles who commit crimes be viewed as less blameworthy than adults because they are less able to foresee the consequences of their actions or resist the pressure of others to engage in antisocial activity? Or should we hold adolescents and adults to the same standards of criminal responsibility? If a youngster has committed a violent crime, should he or she be treated as a child (and processed as a delinquent) or tried as an adult (and processed as a criminal)? Should young teenagers and adults who are convicted of the same crime receive the same penalties? As noted in the Introduction to this book, in 2005, the U.S. Supreme Court raised the age at which individuals can be exposed to the death penalty from 16 to 18 (*Roper v. Simmons,* 2005).

One issue that arises in cases in which a juvenile might be tried as an adult is whether the adolescent is competent to stand trial. In the United States, it is not permissible to try someone in a criminal proceeding if the individual does not understand the charges against him or her, does not understand the nature of the trial, or is unable to make reasoned decisions about the case (for example, whether to take the stand in his or her own defense). Historically, questions about a defendant's competence to stand trial have been raised only in cases in which the individual is mentally ill or mentally retarded. Now that more and more juveniles are being tried as adults at younger and younger ages, however, experts have asked whether some young defendants may be incompetent to stand trial simply because of cognitive or emotional immaturity. One recent study of this issue examined the competence to stand trial of a large sample of individuals between the ages of 11 and 24 (Grisso et al., 2003). The researchers found that about one third of those ages 13 and younger, and one fifth of 14- and 15-year-olds, were as impaired in their abilities to serve as a competent defendant as were mentally ill adults who had been found not competent to stand trial (see Figure 3.3). This study suggests that courts should not assume that younger adolescents, even those who are not mentally ill or retarded, are necessarily competent to be tried as adults and that juveniles' competence

to stand trial should be evaluated before their cases can be heard in adult court. Research also indicates that juveniles are less likely than adults to understand their rights when being questioned by the police, more likely to confess to a crime than remain silent, and less likely to discuss disagreements with their attorneys (Redlich, Silverman, & Steiner, 2003; Viljoen, Klaver, & Roesch, 2005).

INCONSISTENCIES IN ADOLESCENTS' LEGAL STATUS

Many other issues surrounding the legal status of adolescents in the United States remain vague and confusing. Two U.S. Supreme Court cases indicate just how inconsistent our views of adolescents' status are (Moshman, 1993). In one case, *Hazelwood v. Kuhlmeier,* the Court ruled that a public high school can censor articles written by students for their school newspaper, on the grounds that adolescents are so "immature" that they need the protection of "wiser" adults. Yet the same Court also ruled, in *Board of Education v. Mergens,* that students who wanted to form a Bible study group had the right to meet on campus because high school students are "mature" enough to understand that a school can permit the expression of ideas that it does not necessarily endorse. Similarly, in *Hodgson v. Minnesota,* the Court ruled that, because of their maturity, adolescents do not need to obtain parental consent to get an abortion. Yet the Court also ruled, in *Roper v. Simmons,* that adolescents should not be subject to the death penalty, because their immaturity makes them less responsible for their criminal behavior (and therefore less "punishable") (Steinberg, Cauffman, et al., 2009).

There are many other examples of this sort of inconsistency. For example, courts have ruled that teenagers have the right to obtain contraceptives without their parents' approval. But they also have upheld laws forbidding adolescents access to cigarettes or to magazines that, although vulgar, are not considered so obscene that they are outlawed among adults (Zimring, 1982). As you know, the age at which adolescents are permitted to engage in various adult behaviors—driving, voting, drinking, viewing R-rated movies, smoking—varies considerably from one domain to the next. Is there a pattern to this inconsistency? In general, legal decisions tend to set the age boundary high, in order to restrict the behavior of adolescents when the behavior in question is viewed as potentially damaging to the young person (for example, buying cigarettes), but have supported the concept of adolescent autonomy and set the age boundary low when the behavior is viewed as having potential benefit (for example, having access to contraceptives) (E. Scott & Steinberg, 2008).

RECAP

- Changes in the individual's social definition at adolescence typically involve changes in status. When they become adults, individuals are given greater privileges but are expected to take increased responsibility for self-management and participation in adult society.
- An especially controversial issue concerns whether juveniles who commit serious crimes should be treated as children or tried as adults.
- In contemporary America, there is great inconsistency in where we draw age boundaries between childhood and adulthood. Different ages are used for different purposes.

The Process of Social Redefinition

Social redefinition during adolescence is not a single event but, like puberty or cognitive maturation, a series of events that often occur over a relatively long time. In contemporary America, the process of redefinition typically begins at age 15 or 16, when the young person is first permitted to drive, to work, and to leave school. But in most states, the social redefinition of the adolescent continues well into young adulthood. Some privileges of adulthood, such as voting, are not conferred until the age of 18, and others, such as purchasing alcoholic beverages, are not conferred until the age of 21,

five or six years after the redefinition process begins. Even in societies that mark the social redefinition of the young person with a dramatic and elaborate initiation ceremony, or rite of passage, the social transformation of the individual from child into adult may span many years, and the initiation ceremony may represent just one element of the transition (Markstrom & Iborra, 2003). In fact, the initiation ceremony usually marks the beginning of a long period of training and preparation for adulthood and not the adolescent's final passage into adult status (Y. Cohen, 1964).

In many cultures, the social redefinition of young people occurs in groups. That is, the young people of a community are grouped with peers of approximately the same age—a cohort—and move through the series of status transitions together. One of the results of such age-grouped social transitions is that very strong bonds are formed among youngsters who have shared certain rituals. In many American high schools, for example, attempts are made to create class spirit or class unity by fostering bonds among students who will be graduated together. In many Latino communities, adolescent girls participate together in an elaborate sort of "coming-out" celebration, called the **quinceañera.** On college campuses, fraternities and sororities may conduct group initiations that involve difficult or unpleasant tasks, and special ties may be forged between "brothers" or "sisters" who have pledged together.

COMMON PRACTICES IN THE PROCESS OF SOCIAL REDEFINITION

Although the specific ceremonies, signs, and timetables of social redefinition during adolescence vary from one culture to another, several general themes characterize the process in all societies.

▮ **Real or Symbolic Separation From Parents** First, social redefinition usually entails the real or symbolic separation of young persons from their parents. In traditional societies, this may take the form of a practice known as **extrusion:** During late childhood, children are expected to begin sleeping in households other than their own. Youngsters may spend the day with their parents but spend the night with friends of the family, with relatives,

cohort A group of individuals born during the same general historical era.

quinceañera An elaborate sort of "coming-out" celebration for adolescent girls that is practiced in many Latino communities.

extrusion The practice of separating children from their parents and requiring them to sleep in other households, part of the process of social redefinition at adolescence in many societies.

In many nonindustrial societies, a formal initiation ceremony is used to mark the beginning and end of adolescence.

or in a separate residence reserved for preadolescents (Y. Cohen, 1964). In America, during earlier times, it was customary for adolescents to leave home temporarily and live with other families in the community, either to learn specific occupational skills (as apprentices) or to work as domestic servants (Kett, 1977). Interestingly, the "placing out" of adolescents from their parents' home often coincided with puberty (which, as you now know, occurred at a much later age at this time in history) (M. Katz, 1975). In contemporary societies, the separation of adolescents from their parents takes somewhat different forms. They are sent to summer camps, to boarding schools, or, as is more common, to college.

▎ **An Emphasis on Differences Between the Sexes**   A second aspect of social redefinition during adolescence entails the accentuation of physical and social differences between males and females (C. Ford & Beach, 1951; Schlegel & Barry, 1991). This accentuation of differences occurs partly because of the physical changes of puberty and partly because adult work and family roles are generally highly sex-differentiated. Many societies separate males and females during religious ceremonies, have individuals begin wearing sex-specific articles of clothing (rather than clothing permissible for either gender), and keep males and females apart during initiation ceremonies.

Still, in many non-Western societies today, the privileges extended to males and females once they have reached puberty are so different that adolescence often is an entirely different phenomenon for boys and girls

(Larson et al., 2009). Examples of the differential treatment of adolescent boys and girls in non-Western cultures abound, but in general, girls' behavior is more subject to the control of adults, whereas boys are given more freedom and autonomy. Girls are expected to remain virgins until marriage, for example, whereas boys' premarital sexual activity is tolerated. Girls are expected to spend time preparing for domestic roles, whereas boys are expected to acquire vocational skills for employment outside the home. And formal schooling is far less available to girls than to boys, especially in rural societies.

The separation of males and females in adolescence is not limited to non-Western societies. In earlier times in America (and to a certain extent in many other industrialized societies today), during adolescence, males and females were separated in educational institutions, either by excluding adolescent girls from secondary and higher education, grouping males and females in different schools or different classrooms, or having males and females follow different curricula. In present-day America, many of these practices have been discontinued because of legal rulings prohibiting sex discrimination, but some elements of accentuated sex differentiation and sex segregation during adolescence still exist—for example, in residential arrangements, styles of dress, athletic activities, and household chores. And many contemporary ceremonies designed to recognize the young person's passage into adulthood are either limited to one sex or the other (for example, debutante balls or the quinceañera, each of which is for young women) or somehow differentiate between males and females (for example, the **Bar Mitzvah** and the **Bas Mitzvah** ceremonies for Jewish males and females, respectively).

▎ **The Passing on of Information From the Older Generation**   A third aspect of social redefinition during adolescence typically entails the passing on of cultural, historical, and practical information from the adult generation to the newly inducted cohort of young people. This information may concern (1) matters thought to be important to adults but of limited utility to children (for example, information about the performance of certain adult work tasks), (2) matters thought to be necessary for adults but unfit for children (for example, information regarding sex), or (3) matters concerning the history or rituals of the family or community (for example, how to perform certain ceremonies). In traditional societies, initiates are often sent to some sort of "school" in which they are instructed in the productive activities of the community (hunting, fishing, or farming). Following puberty, boys and girls receive instruction about sexual relations, moral behavior, and societal lore (M. Fried & Fried, 1980; N. Miller, 1928).

In contemporary society, too, adolescence is a time of instruction in preparation for adulthood. Elementary

Bar (Bas) Mitzvah   In Judaism, the religious ceremony marking the young person's transition to adulthood.

school students, for example, are generally not taught a great deal about sexuality, work, or financial matters; such course work is typically reserved for high school students. We also restrict entrance into certain "adult" activities (such as sexually explicit movies) until adolescents are believed old enough to be exposed to them.

Because formal initiation ceremonies are neither very common nor very meaningful in modern society, students sometimes overlook important similarities between the processes of social redefinition in traditional and contemporary societies. Practices like extrusion or **scarification**—the intentional creation of scars on some part or parts of the body, often done as part of an initiation ceremony—may seem alien to us. But if we look beneath the surface, at the meaning and significance of each culture's practices, we find many common threads. In contemporary society, for example, although we do not practice anything as "alien" as scarification, we do have our share of body rituals, which often are not seen until adolescence and which might seem equally alien to someone unfamiliar with our society: the punching of holes in earlobes or other parts of the body (ear or body piercing), the scraping of hair from faces or legs (shaving), the permanent decoration of skin (tattoos), and the application of brightly colored paints to lips, eyes, and cheeks (putting on makeup).

FOOD FOR THOUGHT

Social redefinition in contemporary society is often so familiar that we overlook it. Can you think of examples of social definition practices within your personal experience that parallel practices in more traditional cultures?

RECAP

- Certain themes are common to the process of social redefinition across many societies. These include the real or symbolic separation of young people from their parents, the accentuation of differences between males and females, and the passing on of cultural, historical, or practical information deemed important for adulthood.
- Although these themes are more explicit in the formal initiation ceremonies practiced in traditional societies, they are evident in the process through which individuals are redefined in contemporary industrialized society as well.

Variations in Social Transitions

Different societies recognize and orchestrate the passage into adult status at different times and in different ways. In this respect, although the presence of social redefinition in a general sense is a universal feature of adolescent development, there is considerable diversity in the nature of the transition. Examining social redefinition from cross-cultural and historical perspectives provides a valuable means of contrasting the nature of adolescence in different social contexts. Two very important dimensions along which societies differ in the process of social redefinition are in the explicitness, or clarity, of the transition and in the smoothness, or continuity, of the passage.

VARIATIONS IN CLARITY

Initiation ceremonies are in many ways religious ceremonies. As such, they are most often employed in societies in which a shared religious belief unites the community and structures individuals' daily experiences. Universal, formal initiation ceremonies therefore have never been prevalent in U.S. society, largely because of the cultural diversity of the population and the general separation of religious experience from everyday affairs.

There are, however, factors other than the presence of formal rites of passage that determine how clear the transition into adult status is to young persons and to society. One such factor concerns the extent to which various aspects of the status change occur at about the same time for individuals and during the same general period for adolescents growing up together (Elder, 1980). When transitions into adult work, family, and citizenship roles occur close in time, and when most members of a cohort experience these transitions at about the same age, the passage into adulthood takes on greater clarity. If all young people were to graduate from high school, enter the labor force, and marry at the age of 18, this age would be an implicit boundary between adolescence and adulthood, even without a formal ceremony. But when different aspects of the passage occur at different times, and when adolescents growing up in a similar environment experience these transitions in different order and along different schedules, the boundary between adolescence and adulthood becomes cloudier.

■ **The Clarity of Social Redefinition in Contemporary Society** When did you become an adolescent? When did you (or when will you) become

---

scarification   The intentional creation of scars on some part or parts of the body, often done as part of an initiation ceremony.

Formal rites of passage from adolescence to adulthood are rare in contemporary society. Certain cultural ceremonies—like the quinceañera, a coming-of-age celebration for young women in some Latino communities—are about as close as we come in today's society.

an adult? If you are like most individuals in contemporary society, your answers to these questions will not be clear-cut. One study, for example, found that, when asked, "Do you feel that you have reached adulthood?" nearly half of all 12- to 17-year-olds and nearly three-fifths of 18- to 25-year-olds answered, "Yes and no" (Arnett, 2000). We have no formal ceremonies marking the transition from childhood into adolescence, nor do we have any way to mark the passage from adolescence into adulthood. Although in many religious, cultural, and social groups, the young American adolescent may undergo an initiation ceremony of sorts—the confirmation, the Bar or Bas Mitzvah, the quinceañera, and the coming-out parties of debutantes are some examples—rarely does such a rite have much significance outside the youngster's family, circle of friends, or religious community. School graduation ceremonies perhaps come the closest to universal rites of passage in contemporary society, but school graduation does not bring with it many meaningful or universal changes in social status, responsibilities, or privileges. As a result, social redefinition in contemporary society does not give adolescents any clear indication of when their responsibilities and privileges as an adult begin. As we noted earlier, laws governing the age at which individuals can and cannot do "adult" activities are inconsistent. In many states, for example, the age for starting employment is 15; for driving, 16; for attending restricted (R-rated) movies without parents, 17; for voting, 18; and for drinking, 21. In some states, the age at which someone can be tried as an adult for a serious violent crime is as low as 10 (Hartney, 2006).

In short, we have few universal markers of adulthood—adolescents are treated as adults at different times by different people in different contexts. A young person may be legally old enough to drive, but his parents may feel that 16 is too early and may refuse to let him use the family car. Another may be treated like an adult at work, where she works side by side with people 3 times her age, but be treated like a child at home. A third may be viewed as an adult by her mother but as a child by her father. It is little wonder, in light of the mixed and sometimes contradictory expectations facing young people, that for many adolescents the transition into adult roles is sometimes a difficult passage to navigate.

▌ **Adolescents' Views of Themselves**   Because contemporary society does not send clear or consistent messages to young people about when adolescence ends and adulthood begins, young people living within the same society can have widely varying views of their own social status and beliefs about age-appropriate behavior (Arnett, 1994; Nurmi, 1993). For this reason, it is instructive to ask people what they think defines the transition to adulthood, as a way of gauging the way in which adult status is conceptualized by the broader society. Psychologist Jeffrey Arnett has examined conceptions of adulthood in contemporary North America and has contrasted them with the ways in which adult status has been viewed in other cultures and at other points in time (Arnett, 1998). His analysis points to three interesting trends.

First, in modern industrialized society, adolescents place relatively less of an emphasis than is the case in traditional societies on the attainment of specific roles (for example, worker, spouse, parent) as defining characteristics of adulthood and relatively more emphasis on the development of various character traits indicative of self-reliance (for example, responsible, independent, self-controlled) (Kenyon, Rankin, Koerner, & Dennison, 2007). Parents of young people similarly emphasize psychosocial maturity as the defining feature of reaching adulthood (E. Nelson et al., 2007).

Consistent with this, in one recent study of individuals ages 17–29, the best predictor of subjective age—that is, what age they *felt* they were, regardless of how old they actually were—was their level of psychosocial maturity (Galambos, Turner, & Tilton-Weaver, 2005). Among contemporary American youths, for instance, "accepting responsibility for one's self" is the most frequently mentioned criterion for being an adult; among Inuit adolescents in the Canadian Arctic, the most important is the establishment of a marriage-like relationship by moving into a separate household with a prospective mate. Of the role-related transitions viewed as important among contemporary youth, being able to support oneself financially was the most important defining criterion of adulthood (Arnett, 1998). Perhaps for this reason, less than one-third of college undergraduates see themselves unambiguously as adults. Interestingly, indicators of entering into adultlike roles of romantic partner and worker at age 20—basically, successfully holding down a job and being involved in an emotionally close romantic relationship—are not especially good predictors of later adult competence, according to a longitudinal study that tracked individuals from age 20 to age 30 (Roisman, Masten, Coatsworth, & Tellegen, 2004). Far better predictors of later adult success were more "adolescent" indicators of competence—doing well in school, having an active social life, and staying out of trouble.

Second, over time, there has been a striking decline in the importance of family roles—marriage and parenthood—as defining features of the transition from adolescence to adulthood. In early American society, for example, the role of head of household was an especially important indicator of adult status for males, and taking on the roles of wife and mother defined adulthood for females. In contrast, in Arnett's surveys of contemporary youth, in which he asked whether certain accomplishments were necessary for an individual to be considered an adult, only 17% of the respondents indicated that being married was necessary, and only 14% indicated that it was necessary to become a parent (Arnett, 1998).

Finally, the defining criteria of adulthood have become more or less the same for males and females in contemporary industrialized society, unlike the case in traditional societies or during previous eras. In nonindustrialized cultures, the requirements for male adulthood were to be able to "provide, protect, and procreate," whereas for females, the requirements for adulthood were to care for children and run a household. Contemporary youth, in contrast, view the various indicators of adult status as equally important (or equally unimportant) for males and females (Arnett, 1998).

Given the absence of clear criteria that define adult status in contemporary North America, it is not surprising that, among people of the same age, some may feel older than their chronological age-mates, while others may feel younger. How old an adolescent feels affects his or her behavior, with adolescents who feel older spending more time with other-sex peers, feeling more autonomous, spending more time with antisocial peers, and engaging in more problem behavior (Galambos, Kolaric, Sears, & Maggs, 1999). Psychologist Nancy Galambos has been interested in changes in individuals' subjective age and, more specifically, in when individuals make the transition from feeling older than they really are (as most teenagers do), to feeling younger than they really are (as most adults do) (Galambos et al., 2005). In her research on Canadian youth, Galambos found that this shift takes place around age 25, for both males and females.

The Clarity of Social Redefinition in Traditional Cultures

Unlike the case in contemporary society, social redefinition during adolescence is clearly recognized in most traditional cultures. Typically, the passage from childhood into adolescence is marked by a formal initiation ceremony, which publicly proclaims the young person's assumption of a new position in the community (C. Ford & Beach, 1951). For boys, such ceremonies may take place at puberty, at a designated chronological age, or at a time when the community decides that the individual is ready for the status change. For girls, initiation is more often linked to puberty and, in particular, to the onset of menstruation. In both cases, the initiation ceremony serves to ritualize the passing of the young person out of childhood and, if not directly into adulthood, into a period of training for it.

In many initiation ceremonies, the adolescent's physical appearance is changed, so that other members of the community can distinguish between initiated and uninitiated young people. For example, new types of clothing may be worn following initiation, or some sort of surgical operation or scarification may be performed to create a permanent means of marking the individual's adult status. Unlike the case in contemporary society, where we often can't tell who is a juvenile and who is an adult by physical appearance alone, in most traditional societies, there is no mistaking which individuals are adults and which are still children. We have grown accustomed to seeing teenagers who try to dress like adults, and adults who try to dress like teenagers, but such a state of affairs would be highly uncommon in traditional cultures.

The Circumcision Controversy

One practice involving the physical transformation of the adolescent that has generated a great deal of controversy is circumcision. **Circumcision** is a procedure in which some part of the genitals is cut and permanently altered. There are important differences between male and female circumcision. In the United States, male circumcision, in which the foreskin around the penis is removed during infancy, is very common and is performed both for religious reasons (mainly among Jews) and for health reasons, because male circumcision is associated with decreased risk of urinary tract infections and sexually transmitted diseases, including HIV infection. There is no evidence that men are harmed emotionally by being circumcised, and complications from the procedure are minimal and far fewer than the health risks associated with not being circumcised (Tobian et al., 2009).

Female circumcision, which involves the cutting or removal of the clitoris and, often, the labia, is rarely

circumcision　A procedure in which some part of the genitals is cut and permanently altered.

practiced outside of North Africa (where, in some countries, such as Mali, Somalia, and Egypt, virtually all women have been circumcised, usually during childhood or preadolescence). Unlike male circumcision, female circumcision—some have called it "genital mutilation"—has no associated health benefits and carries many risks, including infection and chronic pain during urination, menstruation, and sexual intercourse. After circumcision, it is virtually impossible for a woman to achieve an orgasm during sex (Althaus, 1997). Many international groups, citing female circumcision as a human rights violation, have called for a worldwide prohibition against the practice.

▌ The Clarity of Social Redefinition in Previous Eras   Two old friends meet on the street. The first one asks, "How's your wife?" The second one replies, "Compared to what?"

What is the transition to adulthood like today? Well, compared to what? We often use the **baby boom** generation—individuals who were adolescents in the late 1950s and 1960s—as an implicit point of comparison when characterizing today's young people, perhaps because the baby boom generation has provided the basis for so many of the images of modern family life that are deeply embedded in our cultural psyche. (How often have you heard someone use the television show *Leave It to Beaver,* which ran from 1957 to 1963, as a comparison point in discussions of family life?) But the baby boomers' transition to adulthood was highly unusual in many respects. Let's look at life in 1960, during the middle of *Leave It to Beaver*'s run on television, as an example:

- In 1960, the average age of marriage was 20 for women and 22 for men; today, it is 26 and 28, respectively (U.S. Census Bureau, 2009).

- In 1960, about 20% of 22-year-old women and about 30% of 22-year-old men lived with their parents; in 2005, the figures were 35% and 45% (U.S. Census Bureau, 2005).

- In 1960, a very high proportion of adolescents went directly from high school into the military or full-time employment, and only one-third of American high school graduates went directly to college; today, nearly 70% do (Bureau of Labor Statistics, 2009).

In other words, in 1960, three key elements of the transition to adulthood—finishing school, moving out of the parents' home, and getting married—all occurred

relatively early, and all took place within a fairly constricted time frame. By that standard, today's transition to adulthood looks excessively long and vaguely defined. Indeed, one recent study of patterns of schooling, work, romance, and residence during emerging adulthood found that individuals frequently move back and forth between periods of independence and dependence. This suggests that the progression from adolescence to adulthood today not only is long but also occurs in fits and starts (P. K. Cohen, Chen, Hartmark, & Gordon, 2003). It's little wonder that 60% of people in their mid-20s today don't know whether they are adolescents or adults.

Compared to the situation 50 years ago, then, today's transition to adulthood is long and rocky. But the transition into adulthood was just as disorderly and prolonged during the 19th century. According to historian Joseph Kett (1977), many young people at that time moved back and forth between school, where they were viewed as children, and work, where they were viewed as adults. Moreover, timetables for the assumption of adult roles varied considerably from one individual to the next, because they were highly dependent on family and household needs rather than on generally accepted age patterns of school, family, and work transitions. An adolescent might have been working and living away from home, but if his family needed him—because, let's say, someone became ill—he would leave his job and move back in with his parents. During the middle of the 19th century, in fact, many young people were neither enrolled in school nor working, occupying a halfway stage that was not quite childhood but not quite adulthood (M. Katz, 1975). And age at first marriage was just about the same among males at the turn of the 20th century (26) as it is today (28); age at first marriage among females actually is much older today (26) than it was a century ago (22) (U.S. Census Bureau, 2009b). Although the notion of "emerging adulthood" may ring true today, it is by no means a new phenomenon. At least in industrialized societies, the brief and clear transition into adulthood experienced by many baby boomers in the mid–20th century was the exception, not the rule. It's important not to lose sight of that.

VARIATIONS IN CONTINUITY

The well-known anthropologist Ruth Benedict (1934), after surveying many different societies, pointed out that a second way in which the process of social redefinition varies across cultural and historical contexts is along the dimension of *continuity*—the extent to which the adolescent's transition into adulthood is gradual or abrupt. Gradual transitions, in which the adolescent assumes the roles and status of adulthood bit by bit, are referred to as **continuous transitions.** Transitions that are not so smooth, in which the young person's

---

baby boom   The period following World War II, during which the number of infants born was extremely large.

continuous transitions   Passages into adulthood in which adult roles and statuses are entered into gradually.

entrance into adulthood is more sudden, are referred to as **discontinuous transitions.** For example, children who grow up working on the family farm and continue this work as adults have a continuous transition into adult work roles. In contrast, children who do not have any work experience while they are growing up and who enter the labor force for the first time when they graduate from college have a discontinuous transition into adult work roles.

▌ The Continuity of the Adolescent Passage in Contemporary Society

In contemporary society, we tend to exclude young people from the world of adults; we give them little direct training for adult life and then thrust them rather abruptly into total adult independence. Transitions into adulthood in contemporary society are therefore more discontinuous than in other cultural or historical contexts. Consider, for example, three of the most important roles of adulthood that individuals are expected to carry out successfully— the roles of worker, parent, and citizen. In all three cases, we find that adolescents in contemporary society receive little preparation for these positions.

For instance, young people are segregated from the workplace throughout most of their childhood and early adolescent years, and they receive little direct training in school relevant to the work roles they will likely find themselves in as adults. As you will read in Chapter 7, the sorts of jobs available to teenagers today, such as working the counter of a fast-food restaurant, bear little resemblance to the jobs they will hold as adults. The transition into adult work roles, therefore, is fairly discontinuous for most young people in industrialized society, and, according to many employers, a high proportion of young people leave school without adequate preparation for the workplace.

All modern societies face the challenge of helping young people move from the world of school into the world of work, but societies vary in how they approach this issue (Shanahan, Mortimer, & Krueger, 2002). Numerous writers (e.g., Kazis, 1993; Rosenbaum et al., 1992; Stern, Finkelstein, Stone, Latting, & Dornsife, 1994) have argued that many individuals have difficulty making this transition successfully because only one acceptable way of making this passage actually exists— through higher education—and not all individuals can, or want to, make the transition via this route. Studies have found, for example, that most high school counselors steer all students toward college, regardless of their interests or plans (Krei & Rosenbaum, 2001). As you will read in Chapter 6, this is one reason that many American students enroll in college but drop out before obtaining their degree.

Is it possible to create a route from high school to adult work that doesn't involve college? Many critics of the American educational system say that there is. They point out that in other industrialized countries high school students have many options other than going to college, including, most importantly, entering into a formal **youth apprenticeship;** this provides structured, work-based learning that will likely lead to a high-quality job. Typically, a high school student combines time in an apprenticeship with time in school as he or she gradually makes the transition from school to work. Among the most successful models of youth apprenticeships are those developed in Germany, in which young people during their last few years of high school can spend one or two days per week in school and the remainder of the week at a job supervised by master workers (S. Hamilton & Hamilton, 2009). Unlike American high school students, who have difficulty finding good jobs after graduation, German graduates who complete a youth apprenticeship program usually enter a high-quality job within a few days of finishing school (Rosenbaum et al., 1992). Although some writers have questioned whether the German model can be directly copied in the United States, there is hope that some version of an apprenticeship system can be developed. At the very least, some critics have argued that, for many young people in the United States, high school as it now exists lasts far too long (Botstein, 1997).

The transition of young people into adult family roles is even more abrupt than is their transition into work roles. Before actually becoming parents, most young people have little training in child rearing or other related matters. Families are relatively small today, and youngsters are likely to be close in age to their siblings; as a result, few opportunities exist for participating in child care activities at home. Schools generally offer little, if any, instruction in family relationships and domestic activities. And with childbirth generally taking place in hospitals rather than at home, few young people today have the opportunity of observing a younger sibling's birth.

Passage into adult citizenship and decision-making roles is also highly discontinuous in contemporary Western society. Adolescents are permitted few opportunities for independence and autonomy in school and are segregated from most of society's political institutions until they complete their formal education. Young people are permitted to vote once they turn 18, but they receive little preparation for participation in government and community roles prior to this time.

It is little surprise, then, that some young people today have difficulty in assuming adult roles and

discontinuous transitions   Passages into adulthood in which adult roles and statuses are entered into abruptly.

youth apprenticeship   A structured, work-based learning experience that places an adolescent under the supervision of a skilled adult.

responsibilities. Instead of being gradually socialized into work, family, and citizenship positions, adolescents in modern society typically are segregated from activities in these arenas during most of their childhood and youth. Yet young people are expected to perform these roles capably on reaching the age of majority. With little experience in meaningful work, adolescents are expected to find, get, and keep a job immediately after completing their schooling. With essentially no training for marriage or parenting, they are expected to form their own families, manage their own households, and raise their own children soon after they reach adulthood. And without any previous involvement in community activities, they are expected on reaching the age of majority to vote, pay taxes, and behave as responsible citizens.

▌ The Continuity of the Adolescent Passage in Traditional Cultures

The high level of discontinuity found in contemporary America is not characteristic of adolescence in traditional societies. Consider the socialization of young people in Samoa, described in detail by the late anthropologist Margaret Mead in her classic book *Coming of Age in Samoa* (1928/1978). From early childhood on, Samoan youngsters are involved in work tasks that have a meaningful connection to the work they will perform as adults. They participate in the care of younger children, in the planting and harvesting of crops, and in the gathering and preparation of food. Their entrance into adult work roles is gradual and continuous, with work tasks being graded to their skills and intelligence. They are charged with the socialization of their infant brothers and sisters, particularly during middle childhood, when they are not yet strong enough to make a substantial contribution to the community's fishing and farming activities. Gradually, they are taught the fundamentals of weaving, boating, fishing, building, and farming. By the time they reach late adolescence, Samoan youngsters are well trained in the tasks they will need to perform as adults.

Such continuity is generally the case in societies in which hunting, fishing, and farming are the chief work activities. As Mead observed, the emphasis in these societies is on informal education in context rather than on formal education in schools. Children are typically not isolated in separate educational institutions, and they accompany the adult members of their community in daily activities. Adolescents' preparation for adulthood, therefore, comes largely from observation and hands-on experience in the same tasks that they will carry out as adults. Typically, boys learn the tasks performed by adult men, and girls learn those performed by adult women. When work activities take adults out of the community, it is not uncommon for children to accompany their parents on these expeditions (N. Miller, 1928).

As Reed Larson and his colleagues (Larson et al., 2009) have pointed out, however, modernization and globalization have made the transition from adolescence to adulthood longer and increasingly more discontinuous all over the world. As successful participation in the workforce increasingly has come to require formal education, parents have become less able to provide their children with advice on how best to prepare for adulthood. Increasingly, school, rather than hands-on experience in the workplace, is how individuals all over the world are expected to prepare for adult work (National Research Council, 2005). How these changes are affecting the psychological development of young people in developing countries is a question that researchers are only now beginning to examine. It is very likely, however, that many of the familiar psychological struggles that have up until now been characteristic of adolescence in modern, industrialized societies—developing a sense of identity, choosing among occupational alternatives, and renegotiating relationships with one's parents, to name just three—are becoming more common among young people all over the world.

FOOD FOR THOUGHT

Many commentators have remarked on the tremendous discontinuity characteristic of the adolescent transition in modern society. But in light of the nature of adult roles in contemporary society, is it really possible to make the transition more continuous than it currently is? If so, what changes would you recommend?

▌ The Continuity of the Adolescent Passage in Previous Eras

During earlier periods in American history, the transition into adult roles and responsibilities began at a younger age and proceeded along a more continuous path than generally is the case today. This is especially true with regard to work. During the 18th century and the early 19th century, when many families were engaged in farming, a good number of adolescents were expected to work on the family farm and to learn the skills necessary to carry on the enterprise. Boys often accompanied their fathers on business trips, learning the nuances of salesmanship and commerce (Kett, 1977)—a pattern reminiscent of that found in many traditional societies.

Many other young people left home relatively early—some as early as age 12—to work for nonfamilial adults in the community or in nearby villages (M. Katz, 1975; Kett, 1977). Even as recently as the mid–19th century, young adolescents commonly worked as apprentices, learning skills and trades in preparation for the work roles of adulthood; others left home temporarily to work as servants or to learn domestic skills. The average 19th-century youngster in Europe or America left school well before the age of 15 (Chisholm & Hurrelmann, 1995; Modell, Furstenberg, & Hershberg, 1976).

However, census data and historical documents—such as letters, diaries, and community histories—indicate that although adolescents of 100 years ago took on full-time employment earlier in life than they typically do today, they were likely to live under adult supervision for a longer period than is usual in contemporary society. That is, although the transition into work roles may have occurred at a younger age in the 19th century than in the 20th, this transition was made in the context of semi-independence rather than complete emancipation (M. Katz, 1975; Kett, 1977; Modell & Goodman, 1990). This semi-independent period—which for many young people spanned the decade from about ages 12 to 22, and often beyond—may have increased the degree of continuity of the passage into adulthood by providing a time during which young people could assume certain adult responsibilities gradually (M. Katz, 1975). The semi-independence characteristic of adolescence in the 19th century had largely disappeared by 1900, however (Modell & Goodman, 1990). It is worth noting, though, that although many contemporary commentators (and many college graduates) complain about the increasing prevalence of unpaid internships as a bridge between college and full-time paid employment (e.g., Kamenetz, 2006), this transitional pathway into the world of adult work is not unlike what existed in the 19th century.

Socialization for family and citizenship roles may also have been more continuous in previous eras. Living at home during the late-adolescent and early-adult years, particularly in the larger families characteristic of households 100 years ago, contributed to the preparation of young people for future family life. It was common for the children in a family to span a wide age range, and remaining at home undoubtedly placed the older adolescent from time to time in child-rearing roles (President's Science Advisory Committee, 1974). As opposed to today's adolescents, who typically have little experience with infants, adolescents 100 years ago were more likely to have fed, dressed, and cared for their younger siblings. They were also expected to assist their parents in maintaining the household (Modell et al., 1976), which no doubt benefited young people when they eventually established a home separate from their parents. This pattern also likely strengthened sex-role stereotypes, because leaving their parents' home earlier and living independently before marriage encourages young women to develop less traditional attitudes, values, and plans than those of their counterparts who live with their parents as young adults (Waite, Goldscheider, & Witsberger, 1986). Interestingly, individuals from single-parent homes, stepfamilies, adoptive families, and

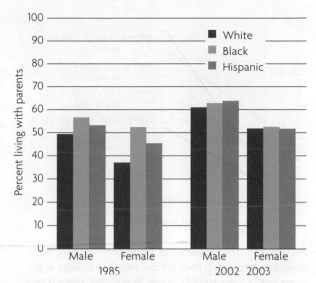

FIGURE 3.4 In general, a higher proportion of young adults (ages 20–22) live with their parents today than was the case two decades ago. (Hill & Holzer, 2007)

foster homes tend to leave home at an earlier age than do their peers whose biological parents remain married (Aquilino, 1991; B. Mitchell, Wister, & Burch, 1989).

■ **Current Trends in Home Leaving** Recent reports of changes in home leaving are noteworthy, however, and suggest that this aspect of the transition into adulthood may be changing in many industrialized countries. On average, individuals are living with their parents longer today than in recent years (see Figure 3.4). More than 55% of all Americans ages 20 to 22 (more than 60% of males, and about 50% of females) either live with or are supported by their parents (C. Hill & Holzer, 2007). Most experts attribute this trend to the increased costs of housing and transportation, which make it difficult for individuals to move out of their parents' home (or give up their parents' financial support) and establish a separate residence. A similar trend is evident in western Europe, where there was a substantial increase during the 1980s in the proportion of youth who were living with their parents well into their mid-20s (Chisholm & Hurrelmann, 1995). One potentially positive consequence of the increase in young adults living at home is that the usual rise in alcohol and drug use seen when adolescents go off to college (Fromme, Corbin, & Kruse, 2008) is not nearly as great when individuals continue to live with their parents (White, Fleming, Kim, Catalano, & McMorris, 2008) (see Figure 3.5). Not surprisingly, the presence of parents tends to put a damper on partying.

How living with their parents in late adolescence affects psychological development and mental health likely depends on the extent to which this experience is seen as normative within the cultural group. In the United States, where a premium is placed on becoming

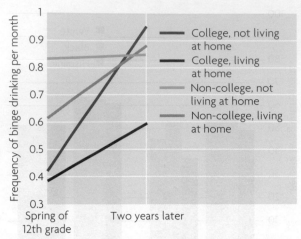

FIGURE 3.5 The frequency of binge drinking more than doubles when high school seniors go off to college and move out of their parents' home. In contrast, there is very little change in binge drinking after high school graduation among non-college youth or among college students who continue to live with their parents. (White et al., 2008)

independent from one's parents, living at home may have a negative impact on a young adult's well-being and contribute to conflict in the parent–adolescent relationship. One study of middle-class Black young women found that those who had left home had relatively better relationships with their parents (Smetana, Metzger, & Campione-Barr, 2004). Among Asian and Hispanic young adults, who are more likely to have been raised in a culture that places special importance on family obligations, however, living with one's parents in late adolescence and early adulthood may be characterized by positive feelings and close family relationships (Fuligni & Pedersen, 2002). In one recent study of adolescents in the People's Republic of China, a sense of family obligation was associated with more positive family relationships and better school performance (Fuligni & Zhang, 2004), although other studies, of American adolescents, have found that family obligations can detract from school performance (Tseng, 2004).

The current impact of the economy on adolescents' home leaving reaffirms the importance of looking at the broader context in defining what normal adolescence is. In 1960, because it was the exception for adolescents to live at home past high school, we tended to view individuals who did so as being less independent or less mature than their peers. But now that living at home has become the norm, we no longer view it as an index of maturity. Above all, we need to keep in mind that, because adolescence is in part defined by society, its nature changes along with society.

Recent economic changes in many postindustrial societies have had a particularly strong effect on the expectations and plans of working-class adolescents

(Bettis, 1996) and those living in rural areas (Crockett & Bingham, 2000). Many such teenagers are anxious and uncertain about their future, given the shrinking number of well-paying, blue-collar jobs and the limited economic opportunities for individuals without a college degree. Rural adolescents, especially those with high aspirations, often face a difficult choice between leaving their community in search of better opportunities and staying near home, where social supports are stronger (M. Johnson, Elder, & Stern, 2005).

Historic events, such as the economic recession of the early 1980s, the 2003 war in Iraq, and Hurricane Katrina, may temporarily alter the nature of the adolescent passage and may produce exceptions to general historical trends. One such event was the Great Depression of the early 1930s. Sociologist Glen Elder, Jr., has examined the impact of growing up during this era on adolescents' behavior and development (Elder, 1974), and many of his findings are relevant to the issue of continuity in the adolescent passage. Elder looked at the data collected during the Depression as part of a longitudinal study of individuals living in Oakland, California. Members of the group Elder focused on were born between 1920 and 1921 and thus were preadolescents during the worst years of the Depression.

Elder found that youngsters whose families experienced economic hardship during these years were more likely to be involved in adultlike tasks at an earlier age than were their more privileged peers. Boys, for example, were more likely to work and to help support their families; girls were more likely to play a major role with household chores; and both boys and girls were more likely to marry and enter into full-time employment relatively early. Thus, some aspects of the semi-independent stage of adolescence that had become uncommon by 1930 may have reappeared during the Depression. For many youngsters growing up during this period, the adolescent passage may have resembled that of an earlier era.

Research on contemporary German and Polish youngsters by Rainer Silbereisen and colleagues (Silbereisen, Schwarz, Nowak, Kracke, & von Eye, 1993) indicates that, even today, growing up under adversity is associated with an earlier transition into adult roles and behaviors. Whether "earlier" means "better" is a matter of some debate, however. As you'll read in Chapter 8, some writers believe that adolescents profit psychologically from having a relatively long period of time to develop without being burdened by adult responsibilities.

It will be interesting to see how the dramatic economic downturn that took place in 2009 altered the nature of the transition into adulthood and, if so, whether this affected adolescents' psychological development. It is not clear whether this crisis, like the Great Depression, forced young people to grow up faster (because their families needed their help) or, alternatively, actually slowed their development (because economic conditions limited opportunities to enter the labor force and establish independent residences).

RECAP

- The process of social definition varies from society to society in terms of its clarity.
- In most traditional societies, adolescence is marked by a formal initiation ceremony and specific rites of passage. In contemporary industrialized society, however, the transition from childhood into adulthood is vague and poorly defined.
- Contemporary adolescents are more likely to define adulthood with respect to psychological achievements than to role transitions.
- Societies vary in the extent to which the passage into adulthood is continuous or discontinuous. In a continuous passage, the adolescent assumes the roles and status of adulthood bit by bit, with a good deal of preparation and training along the way. In a discontinuous passage, the adolescent is thrust into adulthood abruptly, with little prior preparation.

The Transition into Adulthood in Contemporary Society

We do not know for certain whether today's prolonged and discontinuous passage into adulthood impedes or enhances adolescents' psychosocial development. Much probably depends on whether the adolescent has access to the resources necessary for such a protracted transition. Indeed, many commentators have noted that there is not one transition into adulthood in contemporary America, but three very different transitions: one for the "haves," one for the "have-nots," and one for those who are somewhere in between (Furstenberg, 2006). As one writer recently put it:

> The lack of societal support for [the] most vulnerable youth stands in stark contrast to the extensive support provided to the best situated, most-likely-to-succeed young adults—the 25 to 30 percent of all youth who attend four-year colleges and obtain bachelor's degrees.
>
> The great majority of these youth are embedded in networks—families, friends, and communities—that provide guidance, support, and help, both financial and otherwise, when they face the crises that are an inevitable part of the transition. The majority live in households with higher incomes. Beyond what their parents provide, society invests billions of dollars in these youth and provides them with an extensive support system. . . . While students attending two-year colleges have fewer

support services, they too benefit from a system designed to aid their development and transition. Colleges also convey to their students a sense of being special, a message that is rarely, if ever, conveyed to vulnerable youth, who are ignored at best and demonized at worst. (Wald, 2005, pp. ix–x)

Observers of adolescence in America have suggested that the discontinuity in the passage into adulthood has become so great that many youngsters, especially those not bound for college, are having tremendous problems negotiating the passage into adult roles (National Research Council, 1993; Osgood, Anderson, & Shafer, 2005). One national commission found that society had so neglected the needs of non-college-bound adolescents that its report called them "The Forgotten Half" (William T. Grant Foundation, 1988). Another prestigious panel, in a disheartening report, estimated that about one-quarter of American 10- to 17-year-olds are at risk of failing to lead productive adult lives (National Research Council, 1993).

These observers point to problems that the most vulnerable young people in society face in developing a coherent sense of identity, establishing a healthy sense of autonomy, and making informed decisions about commitments to family and work. They note that the lack of clarity and continuity in the transition into adulthood may contribute to some of the problems faced by adolescents in contemporary society and may also contribute to some of the problems faced by contemporary society in dealing with young people. Many social scientists believe that our relatively high rates of divorce, family violence, youth unemployment, juvenile delinquency, and teenage alcoholism stem in part from the confusing and contradictory nature of the passage into adulthood in modern society (National Research Council, 1993).

As we look to the future, we can point to two specific societal trends that are reshaping the nature of the transition from adolescence to adulthood (Mortimer & Larson, 2002). First, as I have noted throughout this chapter, the length of the transitional period is increasing. As the labor force continues to shift toward jobs that demand more and more formal education, the amount of time individuals need to spend as economically dependent students will increase, which will delay their assumption of all sorts of adult roles, including family roles. (One of the reasons that individuals are marrying at a later age today than in the past is that it takes longer to accumulate enough wealth to establish a separate residence or start a family.) Today, the transition between childhood and adulthood takes longer than it did in the past century. Tomorrow, however, it will take even longer.

Second, as success in the labor force comes to be more and more dependent on formal education, the division between the haves—those who have access to money, schools, and information technology—and

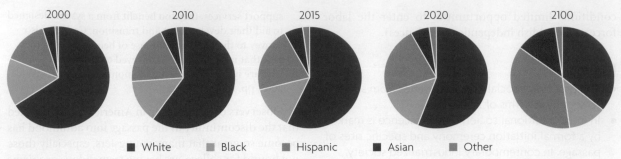

FIGURE 3.6   The ethnic composition of the United States will continue to change dramatically over the 21st century. (Federal Interagency Forum on Child and Family Statistics, 2005)

have-nots—those who are poor, less well educated, and cut off from important resources, will grow. This division will be seen both between countries (that is, the nature of adolescence will differ markedly in wealthy and poor nations) and within countries (that is, within any given country, adolescence will differ markedly between the affluent and the poor). Already in the United States, for example, we can see dramatic differences in what it means to be an adolescent when we compare young people growing up in suburban affluence with those growing up in urban or rural poverty, or when we compare relatively more privileged adolescents with those whose transition to adulthood is impeded by mental illness, disability, severe learning problems, or involvement with the foster care or justice systems (Osgood et al., 2005). One extremely important international trend concerns different birthrates in different parts of the world: Because the birthrate in poor and developing countries is so much higher than it is in wealthy nations, the distribution of the world's adolescents is changing dramatically. As we move further into the 21st century, relatively fewer and fewer of the world's teenagers will come from affluent parts of the world, and relatively more and more will live in impoverished countries (Larson et al., 2009).

SPECIAL TRANSITIONAL PROBLEMS OF POOR AND MINORITY YOUTH

No discussion of the transitional problems of young people in America today would be complete without noting that youngsters from some minority groups—Black, Hispanic, and American Indian youth, in particular—have more trouble negotiating the transition into adulthood than do their White and Asian counterparts. This is due to many factors, including poverty, discrimination, segregation, and disproportionate involvement with the justice system (Garcia Coll et al., 1996; McLoyd et al., 2009; Osgood et al., 2005).

Youngsters from minority backgrounds make up a substantial and growing portion of the adolescent population in America. At the beginning of this century, about two-thirds of American adolescents were White. Today, about 21% of American adolescents are Hispanic, 14% Black, 5% Asian or Pacific Islanders, 3% biethnic youth, and 1% American Indian and Native Alaskan youth. In other words, close to 45% of American adolescents are from ethnic minority groups. By the end of this century, the U.S. Census Bureau estimates that nearly two-thirds of American adolescents will be non-White and that Hispanic adolescents will be the largest ethnic group in the country (see Figure 3.6).

Many American adolescents were not born in the United States, of course. One curiosity within studies of ethnic minority youth and the transition to adulthood concerns the better-than-expected mental health and school performance of immigrant adolescents in the United States. For reasons not entirely understood, foreign-born adolescent immigrants generally have better mental health, exhibit less problem behavior, and perform better in school than do adolescents from the same ethnic group who are native-born Americans (Fuligni, Hughes, & Way, 2009). Indeed, one of the most interesting findings to emerge from research on immigrant adolescents is that their "Americanization" appears to be associated with worse, not better, outcomes. For example, the longer a foreign-born adolescent has lived in the United States, the more likely he or she is to smoke cigarettes or binge drink (Gfroerer & Tan, 2003). Similarly, a study of Latino adolescents in Los Angeles found that those who spoke English exclusively (an index of Americanization) were more likely to drink alcohol, smoke cigarettes, and engage in sexual intercourse than were those who spoke a mixture of English and Spanish, who, in turn, were more likely to engage in these behaviors than those who spoke Spanish exclusively (Ebin et al., 2001) (see Figure 3.7).

One possible reason for this is that when adolescents from immigrant families become more Americanized, family conflict and increased distance between adolescent and parents may result, leading, in turn, to problem behavior (McQueen, Getz, & Bray, 2003). For example, highly Americanized Asian adolescents

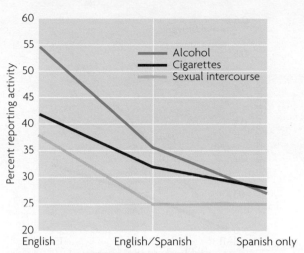

FIGURE 3.7 Latino adolescents who are relatively more acculturated, as indexed by their primary language, are more likely to engage in problem behavior than those who are less acculturated. (Ebin et al., 2001)

who have strong attachments to their parents are not at heightened risk for problems (Hahm, Lahiff, & Guterman, 2003).

THE EFFECTS OF POVERTY ON THE TRANSITION INTO ADULTHOOD

Of all the factors that may impair youngsters' ability to move easily between adolescence and adulthood, poverty is at the top of the list. Poverty is associated with failure in school, unemployment, and out-of-wedlock pregnancy, all of which contribute to transitional difficulties (Guldi, Page, & Stevens, 2007; McLoyd et al., 2009; Schoon et al., 2002). Because minority youngsters are more likely than other teenagers to grow up in poverty, they are also more likely to encounter transitional problems during middle and late adolescence.

Experiencing poverty during adolescence has an especially negative effect on adolescents' school achievement (McLoyd et al., 2009). As you will see in later chapters, school dropout rates are much higher among Hispanic and American Indian teenagers than among other groups, and college enrollment is lower among Black, Hispanic, and American Indian youth. In addition, unemployment is much higher among Black, Hispanic, and American Indian teenagers; Black and Hispanic youth are more likely to be victimized by crime and exposed to violence; and rates of out-of-wedlock births are higher among Black and Hispanic teenagers than among White teenagers. All these factors disrupt the transition into adulthood by limiting individuals' economic and occupational success. Poverty impedes the transition to adulthood among all teenagers, regardless of race, of course; but because minority youth are more likely to grow up poor, they are also more likely to have transition problems.

WHAT CAN BE DONE TO EASE THE TRANSITION?

A variety of suggestions have been offered for making the transition into adulthood smoother for all young people, especially those who are not college-bound, including restructuring secondary education, expanding work and volunteer opportunities, and improving the quality of community life for adolescents and their parents. Some groups have called for expanded opportunities in the workplace as a way of making the high school years more of a "bridge" between adolescence and adulthood (Kazis, 1993). Others have suggested that adolescents be encouraged to spend time in voluntary, nonmilitary service activities—such as staffing day care centers, working with the elderly, or cleaning up the environment—for a few years after high school graduation so that they can learn responsibility and adult roles (Children's Defense Fund, 1989; McLellan & Youniss, 2003). Still others have pointed out that adolescents cannot come of age successfully without the help of adults and that programs are needed to strengthen families and communities and to bring adolescents into contact with adult mentors (Sánchez, Esparza, & Colón, 2008). Overall, most experts agree that a comprehensive approach to the problem is needed and that such an approach must simultaneously address the educational, employment, interpersonal, and health needs of adolescents from all walks of life (Dryfoos, 1990).

▌ Mentoring In recent years, there has been growing interest in mentoring programs for at-risk adolescents, many of whom have few relationships with positive adult role models (DuBois, Holloway, Valentine, & Cooper, 2002; Rhodes, 2004). Adolescents who lack positive adult role models are more likely to have psychological and behavioral problems (Bryant & Zimmerman, 2003; K. F. Parker & Reckdenwald, 2008; M. Zimmerman, Bingenheimer, & Notaro, 2002).

Mentoring programs seek to pair adults with young people through community- or school-based efforts designed to facilitate positive youth development, improve academic achievement, and deter antisocial behavior. Evaluations of mentoring programs indicate that they have a small, but significant positive effect on youth development. On average, adolescents who have been mentored are less likely to have problems in school and at home, less likely to use drugs and alcohol, and less likely to get into trouble with the law (Rhodes & Lowe, 2009). Not surprisingly, the impact of mentoring varies as a function of characteristics of the mentor, the young person, and their relationship (DuBois, Holloway, et al., 2002; Rhodes & Lowe, 2009). In general, mentoring tends to be more successful when the mentor maintains a steady presence in the youth's life over an extended period (at least two years), has frequent contact with the youngster, and involves the adolescent in a wide range of recreational, social, and practical activities (Langhout, Rhodes, & Osborne, 2004; Roth, Brooks-Gunn, Murray, & Foster, 1998). It is important to note, however, that although mentoring may benefit adolescents, other influences in their lives are also important, and mentoring alone is not sufficient to meet the needs of at-risk youth (DuBois & Silverthorn, 2005). One potentially important influence, to which we now turn, is the neighborhood in which the adolescent lives.

RECAP

- There are three very different "transitions" to adulthood in contemporary America, one for the haves, one for the have-nots, and one for those who are somewhere in between the extremes.
- The discontinuous and prolonged nature of the adolescent passage in contemporary society has caused difficulties for many of today's youth, especially poor minority youth living in pockets of concentrated poverty.
- Mentoring programs have a small, but significant positive effect on the development of at-risk adolescents, but mentoring alone is not sufficient to help poor adolescents make a successful transition to adulthood.
- Most experts agree that a comprehensive approach to the problem is needed and that such an approach must simultaneously address adolescents' educational, employment, interpersonal, and health needs.

The Influence of Neighborhood Conditions on Adolescent Development

One factor contributing to the especially worrisome situation of poor and minority youth in the United States is that poverty has become much more concentrated over the past 40 years, with greater and greater clustering of poor families into economically and racially segregated communities. In response to this, a number of researchers have turned their attention to the study of the ways in which neighborhoods influence adolescent development (T. Leventhal, Dupéré, & Brooks-Gunn, 2009). Although other characteristics of neighborhoods in addition to poverty certainly could potentially affect adolescents' development (for example, the ethnic composition, crime rate, or availability of social service programs), far more is known about the effects of neighborhood poverty than about any other neighborhood factor. Exposure to neigh-

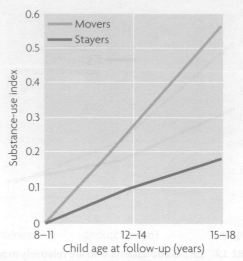

FIGURE 3.8   Contrary to expectation, in an experiment designed to study neighborhood effects, poor adolescents whose families were moved to more affluent neighborhoods increased their use of alcohol and illicit drugs. (Fauth et al., 2007)

borhood poverty is an especially prevalent problem among non-White adolescents. Close to 90% of all residents of the poorest neighborhoods in the United States are from ethnic minority groups (National Research Council, 1993).

Studying neighborhood influences on adolescent development is tricky business. Because poor families tend to live in poor neighborhoods, it is not always easy to separate the effects of neighborhood disadvantage from the effects of family disadvantage. To do this, researchers have had to compare adolescents whose family situations are similar, but who live in very different types of neighborhoods. This is not always easy to do—as you can imagine, few affluent families live in poor neighborhoods, and few poor families live in affluent ones.

There is also the problem of cause and effect. If families in a good neighborhood seem to be functioning better than families in a poor one, it might simply reflect the fact that better-functioning families choose to live in better neighborhoods (rather than indicate that the neighborhood actually influenced family functioning) (Boyle, Georgiades, Racine, & Mustard, 2007). There have been a few experiments in which the researchers took this into account, by randomly assigning families from poor neighborhoods to either remain where they were living or be relocated into more advantaged neighborhoods, and then tracking the psychological development and behavior of adolescents in the two groups. These studies have found mixed effects of relocation, with some studies showing positive effects, others showing no effect, and some actually showing negative effects (J. R. Kling, Ludwig, & Katz, 2005; T. Leventhal, Fauth, & Brooks-Gunn, 2005; Ludwig, Duncan, & Hirschfield, 2001) (see Figure 3.8).

FIGURE 3.9 Neighborhood conditions influence adolescents' development by shaping the norms to which adolescents are exposed; by influencing the quality of the relationships they have with others, including their parents; and by facilitating or limiting adolescents' and families' access to economic and institutional resources.

How can we account for the finding that relocating poor families to more affluent neighborhoods actually may have negative effects on adolescents' behavior? According to one team of researchers, there are several possible explanations (Fauth, Leventhal, & Brooks-Gunn, 2007). First, adolescents from poor families that moved may have encountered more discrimination in the new neighborhoods than in their old ones. Second, although it is generally true that advantaged communities have more resources than disadvantaged ones, it is possible that poor families who moved to more affluent neighborhoods actually may have had less access to community resources than they did in their old neighborhoods. Third, adolescents who moved to more advantaged neighborhoods may have ended up feeling more disadvantaged than their peers who remained in poor communities because the adolescents who moved compared their life circumstances to those of their more affluent peers. Finally, there is some evidence that parents in poor neighborhoods may monitor their children relatively more vigilantly because they worry about crime and other dangers; as you'll read in Chapter 4, adolescents who are more closely monitored tend to have fewer problems.

Despite these cautions, evidence suggests that growing up in a poor neighborhood has negative effects on adolescent behavior, achievement, and mental health and that these effects are above and beyond those attributable to growing up in a poor family or attending a poor school (Harding, 2003; T. Leventhal et al., 2009). Adolescents growing up in impoverished urban communities are more likely than their peers from equally poor households but better neighborhoods to be sexually active at an earlier age, to bear children as teenagers, to become involved in criminal activity, and to achieve less in, or even drop out of, high school—factors that, as you will read in later chapters, seriously interfere with the successful transition into adulthood (Dupéré, Lacourse, Willms, Leventhal, & Tremblay, 2008; T. Leventhal & Brooks-Gunn, 2004; K. A. S. Wickrama, Merten, & Elder, 2005). Interestingly, the absence of affluent neighbors, rather than the presence of poor neighbors, seems to place

adolescents in impoverished communities at greatest risk (Duncan, 1994; Ensminger, Lamkin, & Jacobson, 1996; T. Leventhal & Brooks-Gunn, 2004). Although virtually all neighborhood research has focused on urban adolescents, studies find that growing up in poor rural communities also places adolescents at risk (Farmer et al., 2003).

PROCESSES OF NEIGHBORHOOD INFLUENCES

How might neighborhood conditions affect the behavior and development of adolescents? Three different mechanisms have been suggested (T. Leventhal et al., 2009) (see Figure 3.9).

Collective Efficacy First, neighborhood conditions shape the norms that guide individuals' values and behaviors. Poverty in neighborhoods breeds social isolation and social disorganization, undermining a neighborhood's sense of **collective efficacy**—the extent to which neighbors trust each other, share common values, and count on each other to monitor the activities of youth in the community (Sampson, Raudenbusch, & Earls, 1997). As a consequence, it is easier for deviant peer groups to form and to influence the behavior of adolescents in these communities. Rates of teen pregnancy, school failure, and antisocial behavior are all higher in neighborhoods that have low levels of collective efficacy (Ainsworth, 2002; Bowen & Bowen, 2002; Herrenkohl et al., 2000; Karriker-Jaffe, Foshee, Ennett, & Suchindran, 2008; Sampson, 1997; Sampson & Laub, 1994; Tolan, Gorman-Smith, & Henry, 2003). Living in a neighborhood high in collective efficacy— where adults monitor the behavior of all adolescents, not just their own—is especially important for adolescents whose parents are themselves not very vigilant (Browning, Leventhal, & Brooks-Gunn, 2005).

collective efficacy A community's social capital, derived from its members' common values and goals.

A variety of psychological and social problems are more common among adolescents who grow up amidst poverty.

Some writers (e.g., J. Crane, 1991; R. Simons, Johnson, Beaman, Conger, & Whitbeck, 1996) suggest that, under conditions of low collective efficacy, social problems are contagious—they spread from one adolescent to another in a pattern not unlike a disease epidemic. To the extent that poverty increases behavior problems, for example, adolescents living in poor neighborhoods will come into contact with deviant peers more often. Adolescents who associate with delinquent peers are more likely to be drawn into criminal and delinquent activity (R. Simons et al., 1996). Similarly, adolescents who live in neighborhoods characterized by high rates of teenage childbearing grow up exposed to large numbers of peers who are relatively more tolerant of this behavior, which affects their own attitudes toward premarital childbearing (Baumer & South, 2001; South & Baumer, 2000). Adolescents who see nothing but poverty and unemployment in their communities have little reason to be hopeful about their own future, and they may feel that they have little to lose by having a baby, dropping out of school, or becoming involved in criminal activity (D. Kirby, Coyle, & Gould, 2001; LeBlanc, 2003). Interestingly, neighborhood poverty has an impact on adolescents' sexual behavior and decisions about whether to abort a pregnancy—with those living in poor neighborhoods more likely to be sexually active at an early age and to have the baby—but not on their likelihood of getting pregnant or using contraception (Cubbin, Santelli, Brindis, & Braveman, 2005; South & Baumer, 2001). The impact of living amidst low collective efficacy is especially bad among individuals who are impulsive or insensitive to the feelings of others (Dupéré, Lacourse, Willms, Vitaro, & Tremblay, 2007; M. Meier, Slutske, Arndt, & Cadoret, 2008).

The Impact of Stress Second, the stresses associated with poverty undermine the quality of people's relationships with each other. Poverty, we know, interferes with parents' ability to be effective parents (Goosby, 2007). Psychologist Vonnie McLoyd, who has done extensive research on the impact of poverty on Black youth, has shown in numerous studies that both the financial strain and the neighborhood stress associated with poverty undermines the quality of parenting in a family, which, in turn, leads to adolescent maladjustment (McLoyd et al., 2009). Indeed, across all ethnic groups, poverty is associated with harsh, inconsistent, and punitive parenting, and these factors, in turn, are linked to adolescent misbehavior (Bradley, Corwyn, Pipes McAdoo, & Garcia-Coll, 2001; Gutman, McLoyd, & Tokoyawa, 2005; Ramirez-Valles, Zimmerman, & Juarez, 2002). When parents are not effective in supervising and monitoring their teenagers, for example, and when teenagers have little social support from parents or other adults, the teenagers are more likely to associate with antisocial peers and get into trouble (see Figure 3.10) (Chung & Steinberg, 2006; J. P. Hoffman, 2003; Lynam et al., 2000; Tolan, Gorman-Smith, & Henry, 2003). As a consequence, the link between family poverty and delinquency is even stronger among poor families living in poor neighborhoods (Hay, Fortson, Hollist, Altheimer, & Schaible, 2007).

Consistent with this, the harmful effects of exposure to negligent or harsh parenting are even more pronounced in disadvantaged neighborhoods (J. M. Beyers, Bates, Pettit, & Dodge, 2003; Brody et al., 2003; Browning, Leventhal, & Brooks-Gunn, 2005; H. Cleveland, 2003; Knoester & Haynie, 2005; Roche, Ensminger, & Cherlin, 2007). Studies of whether the impact of good parenting is affected by neighborhood conditions have not yielded consistent results. Some studies show that good parenting is more effective in good neighborhoods (e.g., R. Simons, Simons, Burt, Brody, & Cutrona, 2005), while others show the reverse (M. J. Cleveland, Gibbons, Gerrard, Pomery, & Brody, 2005).

The impact of poverty on levels of neighborhood violence is especially devastating. Adolescents who grow up in poor neighborhoods are far more likely than other youth to be exposed to chronic community violence, and repeated exposure to violence and other types of stress increases the risk of behavioral, emotional, and even physical health problems (Farrell & Sullivan, 2004; D. O'Donnell, Schwab-Stone, & Ruchkin, 2006; Shahinfar, Kupersmidt, & Matza, 2001; H. Stevenson, 1998). Perhaps not surprisingly, adolescents who grow up in poor neighborhoods are more likely to interpret ambiguous situations as threatening and to show increases in blood pressure and heart rate as a consequence, placing them at risk for heart disease (E. Chen, Langer, Raphaelson, & Matthews, 2004).

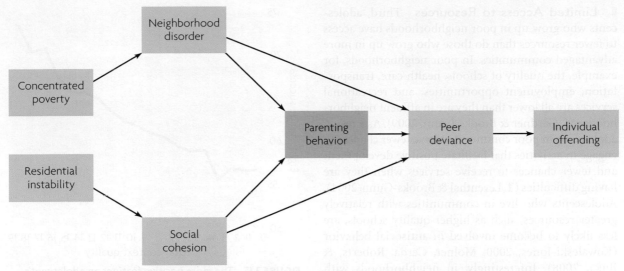

FIGURE 3.10 Neighborhood disadvantage diminishes parental effectiveness, which leads adolescents to affiliate with deviant peers and get involved in crime and delinquency. (Chung & Steinberg, 2006)

Exposure to violence is pervasive in poor neighborhoods. In one recent study of a high-risk sample of New York City adolescents, the researchers found that 93% had seen someone get beaten badly, 75% had seen someone get knifed, 92% had seen someone get shot, and 77% had seen someone get killed. In addition, 78% reported that they had lost a close friend due to violence, and 85% reported losing someone they knew from the neighborhood to violence (D. Wilkinson & Carr, 2008). Here is one 16-year-old's account of an experience that has become all too common in many inner-city neighborhoods:

Rashard: We was in the projects. He had beef with some kids around the corner, another rival, over a drug spot and as we sat on the gates . . . them kids from around the corner came from both ways. . . . you see, it's hard for me to talk about it [respondent is crying]. And . . . they came from both ways and they pulled out guns from every angle and they just let off and my friend got shot in the head with a .44, magnum.

Interviewer: And what happened, how did you escape that situation?

Rashard: I was on my side [and I] jumped off the gate . . . as they were shooting, I ducked, I ran for dear life, that's the only thing I could tell you. It happened so fast, it ain't like I could tell you no whole war story. (D. Wilkinson & Carr, 2008, p. 1035)

Adolescents who themselves have been exposed to violence are more likely to engage in violent behavior, to think about killing themselves, and to report symptoms of depression, posttraumatic stress disorder, hopelessness, and substance abuse (Allwood & Bell, 2008; Bolland, Lian, & Formichella, 2005; Gorman-Smith & Tolan, 1998; Ruchkin, Henrich, Jones, Vermeiren, & Schwab-Stone, 2007; Youngstrom, Weist, & Albus, 2003). One recent study found that witnessing gun violence *doubles* an adolescent's risk for committing violence in the future (Bingenheimer, 2005).

Not all adolescents who are exposed to violence are equally affected, of course; among the factors that help protect against the harmful effects of exposure to violence are having parental support and, especially among Black youth, strong religious beliefs (Aceves & Cookston, 2007; Benhorin & McMahon, 2008; Brookmeyer, Henrich, & Schwab-Stone, 2005; Fowler, Ahmed, Tompsett, Jozefowicz-Simbeni, & Toro, 2008; Kliewer et al., 2006; S. T. Li, Nussbaum, & Richards, 2007; Pearce, Jones, Schwab-Stone, & Ruchkin, 2003; Rosario, Salzinger, Feldman, & Ng-Mak, 2008).

FOOD FOR THOUGHT

Inner-city neighborhoods typically come to mind when we think of adolescents growing up in poverty, but many poor adolescents live in rural, not urban, areas. In what ways is poverty different for urban versus rural youth? How might this affect the nature of adolescence in each type of community?

■ **Limited Access to Resources**   Third, adolescents who grow up in poor neighborhoods have access to fewer resources than do those who grow up in more advantaged communities. In poor neighborhoods, for example, the quality of schools, health care, transportation, employment opportunities, and recreational services are all lower than they are in affluent neighborhoods (M. Gardner & Brooks-Gunn, 2009). As a result, adolescents in poor communities have fewer chances to engage in activities that facilitate positive development and fewer chances to receive services when they are having difficulties (T. Leventhal & Brooks-Gunn, 2004). Adolescents who live in communities with relatively greater resources, such as higher-quality schools, are less likely to become involved in antisocial behavior (Kowaleski-Jones, 2000; Molner, Cerda, Roberts, & Buka, 2008). Interestingly, in neighborhoods with higher levels of resources and greater feelings of cohesion, adults' beliefs about teenagers tend to be more favorable, probably because the casual interactions that take place between adults and adolescents in these settings are more positive (Zeldin & Topitzes, 2002). The presence of institutional resources, then, often goes hand in hand with the presence of positive social relationships.

Most of the effects of neighborhoods on adolescent development are indirect, transmitted through the impact of the neighborhood on the more immediate settings in which adolescents spend time (Cantillon, 2006; Chung & Steinberg, 2006; D. J. Jones, Forehand, Brody, & Armistead, 2002; Teitler & Weiss, 2000). For example, neighborhood disorder affects the way that parents behave, and this, in turn, affects adolescents' development and mental health. Consistent with the ecological perspective on human development discussed in the Introduction, then, neighborhoods influence individuals by transforming what takes place within the more immediate contexts that are embedded in them.

Is one setting—the family, the peer group, the school—a more influential transmitter of neighborhood effects than others? A study by Thomas Cook and his colleagues shows that no single context alone provides a complete explanation of why some adolescents have an easier time making a successful transition into adulthood than do others (Cook, Herman, Phillips, & Settersten, 2002). Each setting contributes modestly and independently to the course of adolescent development, and it is the cumulative impact of multiple contexts that matters most. As Figure 3.11 illustrates, the greater the number of positive features an adolescent's environment contains, the better off he or she will be. By the same token, the more sources of contextual risk an adolescent is exposed to, the greater his or her chances are of developing problems (Morrison, Gutman, Sameroff, & Eccles, 2002; D. J. Jones et al.,

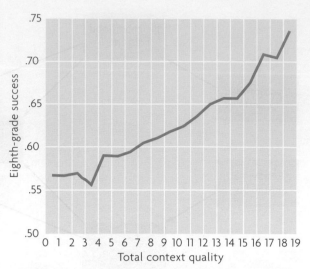

FIGURE 3.11   The more positive features an adolescent's context contains, the more likely he or she is to succeed. (Cook et al., 2002)

2002; Prelow, Danoff-Burg, Swenson, & Pulgiano, 2004; Prelow & Loukas, 2003).

In the next set of chapters, we'll look in detail at the immediate contexts in which adolescents spend time—the family, the peer group, the school, and work and leisure settings—and at the features of each that help or hinder healthy adolescent development.

RECAP

- Neighborhoods affect adolescents through three interrelated processes: by influencing the sorts of norms to which adolescents are exposed, by altering the nature of interpersonal relationships inside and outside the family, and by facilitating or limiting adolescents' access to economic and institutional resources.

- To date, most research on neighborhood influences has focused on the impact of growing up in a poor neighborhood, which has been shown to have adverse effects on adolescents' development, above and beyond the adverse effects of growing up in a poor family.

- Exposure to violence is an especially severe problem for adolescents in poor neighborhoods.

- The impact of the neighborhood on adolescent development occurs through the neighborhood's influence on the more immediate settings in which adolescents spend time.

- The more positive features an adolescent's context contains, the more likely he or she is to succeed.

The Contexts of Adolescence

Families

THE NEXT TIME you are in a bookstore, take a look at the books in the section on parent–adolescent relationships. Judging from the titles—ones like *Why Do They Act That Way?*; *Get Out of My Life, But First, Could You Drive Me and Cheryl to the Mall*; *I'm Not Mad, I Just Hate You*; and *Yes, Your Teen Is Crazy*—you would think that stress and strain between teenagers and their parents is commonplace, even normal. In contrast to advice books on infancy, which emphasize normative development, books for parents of teenagers tend to focus on problems (Steinberg, 2001). This is unfortunate, for two reasons. First, as you'll read, the stereotype presented in these writings isn't true. And second, the more parents believe in the stereotype of adolescents as difficult, the more they expect their own child to conform to it, and the worse their relationship with their teenager becomes (Jacobs, Chin, & Shaver, 2005). In other words, parents' beliefs that they are going to have a difficult time with their child once he or she enters adolescence can become what psychologists call a **self-fulfilling prophecy**—an expectation that is realized because parents act in ways that make it happen.

In truth, scientific studies indicate that, on average, there is very little emotional distance between young people and their parents (Laursen & Collins, 2009). Although some adolescents and their parents have serious interpersonal problems, the overwhelming majority of adolescents feel close to their parents, respect their parents' judgment, feel that their parents love and care about them, and have a lot of respect for their parents as individuals (Steinberg, 2001). In fact, one fifth of American teenagers say that their top concern is that they don't spend *enough* time with their parents; ironically, less than one tenth of parents say that *their* top concern is that they don't spend enough time with their kids (YMCA, 2000).

To be sure, there are times when adolescents and parents have their problems. But there are times when younger children and their parents have problems, and when adults and their parents do, too. No systematic studies demonstrate that family problems are any more likely to occur during adolescence than at other times in the life span. Most research indicates that among the 25% of teenagers and parents who report having problems, about 80% had problematic relations during childhood (Rutter, Graham, Chadwick, & Yule, 1976). Only about 5% of families who enjoy positive relations during childhood can expect to develop serious problems during adolescence.

In this chapter, we'll look at the family as a context for adolescent development, with three broad questions in mind. First, how do relationships in the family change during adolescence—that is, what is the effect of adolescence on the family? Second, how are adolescents affected by their experiences in the family—in other words, what is the effect of the family on adolescents? And third, how have changes in family life during the past half century affected the adolescent experience?

FOOD FOR THOUGHT

Portrayals of adolescent–parent relationships in the popular press suggest that the period is much more difficult and unpleasant than research indicates. Why might there be a "disconnect" between what research finds and what the public is led to believe?

Is Conflict Between Teenagers and Parents Inevitable?

It is impossible to discuss adolescents' relationships with their parents without talking about parent–adolescent conflict, a topic that not only dominates popular writings on this stage of life but also has been the focus of decades of research by scholars of adolescence (Laursen & Collins, 2009).

THE GENERATION GAP: FACT AND FICTION

Most people believe that adolescents and adults hold different values and attitudes, a phenomenon known

self-fulfilling prophecy   The idea that individuals' behavior is influenced by others' expectations for them.

as the **generation gap,** and that this is a constant source of difficulty for young people and their parents. However, this is not the case. Systematic studies of teenagers and their parents find that they usually have surprisingly similar beliefs about such things as the importance of hard work, educational and occupational ambitions, and the personal characteristics and attributes that they feel are important and desirable (Knafo & Schwartz, 2003). Indeed, when it comes to basic, core values—concerning religion, work, education, and so on—diversity *within* the adolescent population is much more striking than are differences between the generations. Why is this so? Because adolescents and their parents share a common social, regional, and cultural background, and these are the factors that shape our central beliefs.

Although there is not much of a generation gap when it comes to core values, there is often a gap between the generations in matters of personal taste, most clearly evident in styles of dress, preferences in music, and patterns of leisure activity (Laursen & Collins, 2009). The explanation for a gap of this sort is not surprising: Unlike basic values, which develop gradually over time and are shaped from an early age, preferences and tastes for things like clothing, music, and hairstyles are far more transitory and subject to current fads and fashions. Adolescents are more likely to be influenced by their friends than by their parents in these matters, and as a consequence, disagreements and differences in opinion between old and young often result. Because adolescents spend a great deal of time with their friends (and because a good deal of that time is spent in social activities in which taste in clothes, music, and so on is especially important), teenagers' preferences are likely to be shaped to a large measure by forces outside the family.

WHAT DO ADOLESCENTS AND PARENTS USUALLY FIGHT ABOUT?

If parents and teenagers typically don't argue over "big" issues, what do they fight about? Studies find that they squabble about things like teenagers' curfews, leisure time activities, clothing, and the cleanliness of their rooms. These have been the major sources of disagreement in families with teenagers for at least as long as scientists have been studying the issue (Steinberg, 2001). And, although conflict between adolescents and parents over these mundane matters is generally less frequent in ethnic minority than in White families, the topics of disagreement are similar across ethnic groups and cultures (Barber, 1994; Smetana, Daddis, & Chuang, 2003). A recent study of adolescents in the People's Republic of China and Hong Kong, for example, found that the most common sources of conflict between adolescents and parents were everyday issues, such as time spent on

schoolwork, household chores, and choice of friends (Yau & Smetana, 2003).

Why do parents and teenagers argue over such mundane matters? According to research by psychologist Judith Smetana (1995, 2000; Smetana & Asquith, 1994), a major contributor to adolescent–parent bickering is the fact that teenagers and their parents define the issues of contention very differently—a finding that has been replicated across many cultural and ethnic groups (Smetana & Villalobos, 2009). Parents view many issues as matters of right and wrong—not necessarily in a moral sense, but as matters of custom or convention. Adolescents, in contrast, are likely to define these same issues as matters of personal choice. A mother who disapproves of her daughter's outfit says, "People just don't dress that way to go to school." The daughter responds, "*You* wouldn't dress this way for school, but *I* do."

■ **Rebels With a Cause** Contrary to stereotype, though, adolescents rarely rebel against their parents just for the sake of rebelling (Darling, Cumsille, & Martínez, 2007). In fact, they are willing to accept their parents' rules as legitimate when they agree that the issue is a moral one (whether it is permissible to cheat on a school test) or one involving safety (whether it is permissible to drink and drive), but they are less inclined to accept their parents' authority when they view the issue as personal (what clothes to wear to a party) (Jackson, 2002; Smetana & Daddis, 2002). In other words, rather than resisting all of their parents' attempts to make and enforce rules (the stereotype that many people have of teenagers), adolescents draw distinctions between parental rules that they think their parents have a right to make (for instance, having to let their parents know what time they'll be home after going out) and rules that they think are out of bounds (for example, having to keep their bedroom orderly), a distinction that in many ways is quite understandable (Smetana & Villalobos, 2009). Of course, there are differences among adolescents in the extent to which they believe their parents have the authority to regulate various sorts of decisions; adolescents who see parents as having more legitimate authority have fewer behavior problems (Cumsille, Darling, Flaherty, & Martínez, 2009; Darling, Cumsille, & Martínez, 2008).

As you'll read, conflict between parents and children increases during early adolescence. One reason for this is that, with time, adolescents see more and more issues that they previously saw as legitimate for their parents to regulate (for example, how late they can stay up on school nights) as matters of personal choice—a finding that has been replicated in numerous parts of the world,

---

generation gap The popular phrase for the alleged conflict between young people and adults over values and attitudes.

One source of conflict between parents and teenagers involves differences in the way they define issues. Making sure that the adolescent's bedroom is tidy is seen by parents as an area over which parents should have jurisdiction. Teenagers, however, tend to see their bedroom as their own private space and decisions about neatness as matters of personal choice.

including North America, South America, and Asia, and among both White and Black adolescents in the United States (e.g., Hasebe, Nucci, & Nucci, 2004; Milnitsky-Sapiro, Turiel, & Nucci, 2006; Smetana, 2005). Adolescents whose parents attempt to regulate what they believe are personal issues are more likely to describe their parents as being overly controlling. Perhaps because of this, the effects of feeling psychologically controlled by their parents, which has a negative impact on adolescents' mental health, are very different from the effects of feeling that their parents want to know where they go and what they do, which has a positive impact (Hasebe, Nucci, & Nucci, 2004; Padilla-Walker, 2008; Silk, Morris, Kanaya, & Steinberg, 2003; Smetana, Campione-Barr, & Daddis, 2004; Smetana & Daddis, 2002).

In other words, teenagers and their parents often clash more over the definition of the issue (e.g., whether something is a safety issue versus a matter of personal choice) than over the specific details. The struggle, then, is over who has the authority—and whose jurisdiction the issue falls into. Because early adolescence is a time when adolescents' reasoning abilities are changing, the ways that individuals understand family rules and regulations change as well. As a consequence of normal cognitive development, a 9-year-old child who is willing to accept his parents' views—who doesn't

question his mother when she says, "We do not leave clothes on the floor"—grows into an adolescent who understands that some issues are matters of personal choice, rather than social convention ("It's my room, so why should it bother you?"). One manifestation of this change in perspective is an increase, with age, in adolescents' willingness to lie to their parents. In one study, in which adolescents were presented with hypothetical situations and asked whether it was acceptable to lie to one's parents about a personal matter (e.g., dating someone one's parents didn't like), about half of the younger adolescents (12- to 14-year-olds) said it was acceptable to lie, whereas more than 80% of the older adolescents (15- to 17-year-olds) did (S. A. Perkins & Turiel, 2007).

RECAP

- Although popular books for parents of teenagers present adolescence as a problematic time for the family, the notion that a wide gap exists between the generations in fundamental values is largely a myth.
- When parents and adolescents disagree, it tends to be over mundane, day-to-day issues, not over major values or priorities.
- Many disagreements between parents and teenagers stem from the different perspectives that they bring to the discussion: The same issues that parents see as matters of right or wrong may be seen by adolescents as matters of personal choice.
- Conflict between parents and children may increase in early adolescence because adolescents change their perspective on many issues that they had previously viewed as ones their parents had legitimate authority to regulate.

Family Relationships at Adolescence

Although it is incorrect to characterize adolescence as a time of high conflict in most families, it is important to keep in mind that adolescence is nevertheless a period of change and reorganization in family relationships and daily interactions (Laursen & Collins, 2009). As they develop, adolescents spend increasingly less time in family activities, especially in activities with the family as a group (see Figure 4.1) (Larson, Richards, Moneta, Holmbeck, & Duckett, 1996).

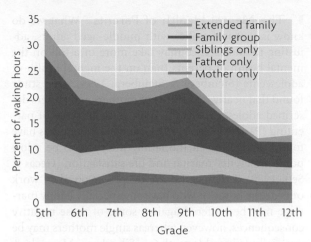

FIGURE 4.1 Age differences in the amount of time adolescents spend with family members. (Larson et al., 1996)

A TIME OF REORGANIZATION AND CHANGE

According to **family systems theory,** relationships in families change most dramatically during those times when individual family members or the family's circumstances are changing, since it is during these times that the family's previously established equilibrium, or balance, will be upset. Not surprisingly, one period in which family relationships usually change a great deal is adolescence. One study of interactions between adolescent boys and their parents found that the peak time for this equilibrium to be upset was around age 13 or 14; the researchers speculate that, because some of this transformation may be driven by puberty, in families with girls, this "disequilibrium" is more likely to occur earlier, around age 11 or 12 (Granic, Hollenstein, Dishion, & Patterson, 2003).

The specific concerns and issues characteristic of families at adolescence arise not just because of the changing needs and concerns of the young person but also because of changes in the adolescent's parents and in the needs and functions of the family. You already have some understanding of the biological, cognitive, and social changes adolescents go through and how these may affect the family system. But to fully understand family relationships during the adolescent years, we must also take into account characteristics of the adolescent's parents and of families at this stage as well.

THE ADOLESCENT'S PARENTS AT MIDLIFE

Because people typically have their first child around age 30, most parents are in their early 40s when the first child enters early adolescence. Some research suggests that this time of life can be a potentially difficult time for many adults, whether they have children or not. In-

deed, some theorists have gone so far as to describe it as a time of **midlife crisis** (D. Levinson, 1978).

Midlife Meets Adolescence If we look at the nature of the midlife crises in some detail, we find that the developmental concerns of parents and adolescents are complementary (Steinberg & Steinberg, 1994). First, consider the issue of biological change. At the same time that adolescents are entering into a period of rapid physical growth, sexual maturation, and, ultimately, the period of the life span that society has labeled one of the most physically attractive, their parents are beginning to feel increased concern about their own bodies, about their physical attractiveness, and about their sexual appeal (R. Gould, 1972). One mother of an early-adolescent girl once remarked, in an interview with my research staff, that it was jarring to realize that when she and her daughter walked down the street, men now looked at her daughter, and not at her.

A second overlap of crises concerns perceptions of time and the future. At the same time that adolescents are beginning to develop the capability to think systematically about the future and do, in fact, begin to look ahead, their parents are beginning to feel that the possibilities for changes in their own lives are limited. Before midlife, individuals tend to measure time in terms of how long they have been alive; after midlife, they are more likely to see things in terms of how much longer they have to live (Neugarten & Datan, 1974). One reason for this shift may be that at midlife adults are reminded of their mortality because they see their own parents aging. Whatever the reason, it is not hard to imagine that the naïve optimism of adolescence may clash with the hardened pragmatism of middle age.

Finally, consider the issue of power, status, and entrance into the roles of adulthood. Adolescence is the time when individuals are on the threshold of gaining a great deal of status. Their careers and marriages lie ahead of them, and choices may seem limitless. For their parents, in contrast, many choices have already been made—some successfully, others perhaps less so. Most adults reach their "occupational plateau"—the point at which they can tell how successful they are likely to be—during midlife, and many must deal with whatever gap exists between their early aspirations and their actual achievements (R. Gould, 1972). In sum, for adolescents, this phase in the family life cycle is a time of boundless horizons; for their parents, it is a time of

family systems theory A perspective on family functioning that emphasizes interconnections among different family relationships (such as marital, parent–child, sibling).

midlife crisis A psychological crisis over identity believed to occur between the ages of 35 and 45, the age range of most adolescents' parents.

For many adults, their child's adolescence coincides with their own passage through midlife. Not all adults experience a "midlife crisis," but for many, this is a time of heightened introspection and self-doubt. The collision of adolescence and midlife may make the period an especially challenging one in some families.

coming to terms with choices made when they were younger.

This overlap of crises is likely to have an impact on family relationships (Hamill, 1994; Steinberg & Steinberg, 1994). A father who is worried about his own physical health may suddenly feel uncomfortable about playing tennis each weekend with his growing son, as they did for years when the boy was younger. An adolescent girl with big plans for the future may find it difficult to understand why her father seems so cautious and narrow-minded when she asks him for advice. An adolescent boy may find his mother's constant attention annoying; he doesn't see that, to her, his interest in independence signifies the end of an important stage in her career as a parent. The adolescent's desire for independence appears to be especially stressful for parents (Steinberg & Steinberg, 1994).

This generalization about the collision of adolescence and midlife must be tempered by the fact that recent decades have seen important changes in both the age at which individuals marry and the age at which they have their first child. The average age at marriage has increased, and proportionately more couples today are delaying childbearing until they have become established in their careers. As a consequence, adults tend to be older today when their children reach adolescence than was the case two decades ago. Although psychologists have studied the impact of this change on parents' relationships with their infants (e.g., Parke, 1988), we do not know how being an older parent affects relationships during adolescence.

The Mental Health of Parents   What we do know is that in families with middle-aged adults, adjusting to adolescence may take more of a toll on the mental health of parents than on the mental health of adolescents (Steinberg & Steinberg, 1994). One study found that nearly two-thirds of mothers and fathers described adolescence as the most difficult stage of parenting (Pasley & Gecas, 1984), and several studies have found this period in the family life cycle to be a low point in parents' marital and life satisfaction (Gecas & Seff, 1990). Parents who are deeply involved in work outside the home or who have an especially happy marriage may be buffered against some of these negative consequences, however, whereas single mothers may be especially vulnerable to them (Silverberg, Marczak, & Gondoli, 1996; Silverberg & Steinberg, 1990; Steinberg & Steinberg, 1994). In fact, a strained relationship between a midlife parent and his or her adolescent child may drive the parent to devote relatively more time to work (Fortner, Crouter, & McHale, 2004).

By the way, the notion that mothers' mental health declines when they enter the "empty nest" stage is a myth, especially among mothers. Parents' mental health is worse when their teenage children are living at home than it is once they have moved out, and when children leave home, it is fathers, not mothers, who typically feel the greatest sense of loss (Steinberg & Steinberg, 1994).

FOOD FOR THOUGHT

Many studies have found that marital satisfaction is lower when parents' first-born child is a teenager than at any other point in the marriage. Why do you think this might be?

CHANGES IN FAMILY NEEDS AND FUNCTIONS

It is not only individual family members who undergo change during the family's adolescent years. The family as a unit changes as well in its economic circumstances, its relationship to other social institutions, and its functions.

One of the most important changes is financial, with family finances likely to be strained during adolescence. Children grow rapidly during puberty, and clothing for adolescents is expensive. Keeping up with the accoutrements of the peer culture—the DVDs, cosmetics, clothes, cell phones, computers, and electronics—may push a family budget to the limit. Many families also begin saving money for large anticipated expenditures, such as the adolescent's college education. And in some families, parents may find themselves having to help support their own parents at a time when their children are still economically dependent. The financial demands placed on parents in the "sandwich generation" (that is, sandwiched between their adolescent children and their aging parents) require considerable adjustment.

In addition to these financial pressures, the adolescent's family must cope with the increasing importance of the peer group (Larson & Richards, 1994). During the early stages of the life cycle, the child's social world is fairly narrow, and the family is the central setting. During late childhood and early adolescence, however, the peer group becomes a setting in which extremely close ties are forged, and parents and adolescents may argue about the teenager's reluctance to give up time with her or his friends for family activities. How adolescents and parents adjust to this shift in orientation is likely to vary across ethnic groups, since certain cultures are more likely to stress family obligations—like helping with household chores—than others (Fuligni, Yip, & Tseng, 2002; Hardway & Fuligni, 2006; S. Lee, 2001). Different expectations between immigrant parents and teenagers are a significant source of stress for adolescents and parents alike, especially when the adolescent is more Americanized and the parents are less so, a phenomenon known as **generational dissonance** (Choi, He, & Harachi, 2008; D. R. Crane, So, Larson, & Hafen, 2005; Phinney & Ong, 2002; Weaver & Kim, 2008). Recent studies of Mexican American families, for example, have found that stress and family conflict are higher in Latino families with relatively more acculturated adolescents (Gonzales, Deardoff, Formoso, Barr, & Barrera, Jr., 2006; C. R. J. Martinez, Jr., 2006). Different expectations about the adolescent's social life can cause problems between newly arrived immigrants and their teenagers, as this Chinese mother of a 15-year-old girl explains:

> Sometimes some of her male friends called. After she hung up the phone I often asked her, 'Who is he?' She then answered, 'My male classmates.' I asked her, 'Why is he calling you every night?' then she said I was overpowering her and even intruding into her privacy. I said 'I'm just asking. Is there any problem?' I asked her, 'Are you dating? He does not have to call and ask you about homework every night, does he?' She then said, 'We are just chatting.' I said, 'If you guys are having casual conversations, does he have to call her every night?' Since then, her male friends dared not call her. (Qin, 2008, p. 27)

Finally, important changes in family functions also take place during adolescence. During infancy and childhood, the functions and responsibilities of the family are fairly clear: nurturance, protection, and socialization. While all these roles are still important during adolescence, adolescents are in need of support more than nurturance, of guidance more than

protection, and of direction more than socialization. Making the transition from the family functions of childhood to the family functions of adolescence is not necessarily easy, especially in contemporary society, where preparation for adulthood—one of the chief tasks of adolescence that was once carried out primarily by the family—is increasingly performed by other institutions, such as the school. Many families may feel at a loss to figure out just what their role during adolescence is.

TRANSFORMATIONS IN FAMILY RELATIONS

Together, the biological, cognitive, and social transitions of adolescence; the changes experienced by adults at midlife; and the changes undergone by the family during this stage in the family life cycle set in motion a series of transformations in family relationships. In most families, there is a movement away from patterns of influence and interaction that are asymmetrical and imbalanced toward ones in which parents and adolescents are on a more equal footing. And some evidence suggests that early adolescence—when this shift toward more egalitarian relationships first begins—may be a time of temporary disruption in the family system.

■ **Changes in the Balance of Power** Studies of family interaction suggest that during early adolescence young people begin to try to play a more forceful role in the family, but parents may not yet acknowledge adolescents' input. As a result, young adolescents may interrupt their parents more often but have little impact. By middle adolescence, however, teenagers act and are treated much more like adults. They have more influence over family decisions, but they do not need to assert their opinions through interruptions and similarly immature behavior (Grotevant, 1997).

Increases in the assertiveness and influence of adolescents as they get older are consistent with their changing needs and capabilities. To adapt to the changes triggered by the child's entrance into adolescence, family members must have some shared sense of what they are experiencing and how they are changing. Yet studies show that in many families parents and children live in "separate realities," perceiving their day-to-day experiences in very different ways (Larson & Richards, 1994). A mother and son, for example, may have a conversation about schoolwork, and while she may experience the conversation as a serious discussion, he may perceive it as an argument. One recent study of Black

generational dissonance Divergence of views between adolescents and parents that is common in families of immigrant parents and American-born adolescents.

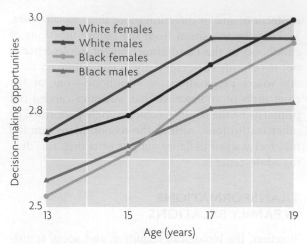

FIGURE 4.2   Parents generally give adolescents greater opportunity to make decisions as they get older, although the pattern of change varies by race and gender. (Gutman & Eccles, 2007)

families, in which mothers, teenagers, and researchers all rated a videotape of the mother and teenager having a discussion, found that the teenagers rated their mother's behavior far more negatively than did either the mother or the researcher (Campione-Barr & Smetana, 2004). One interesting finding to emerge from recent research on brain maturation in adolescence is that young adolescents may be especially sensitive—perhaps even overreactive—to the emotional signals given off by others. A parent may speak to an adolescent in a serious voice, but the adolescent may experience it as anger (E. Nelson, Leibenluft, McClure, & Pine, 2005).

■ **The Role of Puberty**   The adolescent's biological and cognitive maturation likely plays a role in unbalancing the family system during early adolescence. Several researchers have demonstrated that family relationships change during puberty, with bickering between adolescents and their parents increasing, and closeness between adolescents and their parents diminishing (Baer, 2002; Goede, Branje, & Meeus, 2009; Larson, Richards, Moneta, Holmbeck, & Duckett, 1996; McGue, Elkins, Walden, & Iacono, 2005).

Although puberty seems to distance adolescents from their parents, it is not associated with familial "storm and stress," and rates of outright conflict between parents and children are not dramatically higher during adolescence than before or after (Laursen, Coy, & Collins, 1998). Rather, disputes between parents and teenagers are typical of the sorts of arguments people have when a more powerful person (in this case, the parent) is trying to get a less powerful one (in this case, the adolescent) to do something (Adams & Laursen, 2001). Similarly, the diminished closeness is more likely to be manifested in increased privacy on the part of the adolescent and diminished

physical affection between teenagers and parents, rather than any serious loss of love or respect between parents and children (Laursen & Collins, 2009). Research suggests that the distancing that takes place between parents and teenagers in early and middle adolescence is temporary, however, and that parent–child relationships may become less conflicted and more intimate during late adolescence (Thornton, Orbuch, & Axinn, 1995). Nevertheless, studies indicate that the more frequent bickering characteristic of early adolescence may take a modest toll on parents' mental health (Steinberg, 2001), and at least one study found that individuals who reported more conflict with their parents during adolescence had more mental health problems in late adolescence and young adulthood (Herrenkohl, Kosterman, Hawkins, & Mason, 2009).

Patterns of conflict and closeness in the family at adolescence may vary across ethnic groups. One study found that in Asian households, there is an increase in conflict, as in non-Asian families, but not until later in adolescence (Greenberger & Chen, 1996). Another study, comparing Black families with White families, found that White parents tended to give adolescents relatively more autonomy over decisions, although opportunities for adolescent decision making increased in both ethnic groups over time (see Figure 4.2) (Gutman & Eccles, 2007).

Because the disagreements parents and adolescents have typically revolve around issues of parental control, patterns of squabbling and bickering will likely vary across cultural groups whose timetables for adolescent independence differ. Patterns of conflict and closeness in immigrant families may therefore differ as a function of the family's degree of acculturation. One recent study of Mexican American families found higher rates of parent–adolescent cohesion during mid-adolescence among more highly acculturated families (Baer & Schmitz, 2007). Conversely, conflict is less frequent, and cohesion higher, in households where teenagers and their parents communicate in their native language (Tseng & Fuligni, 2000).

In any event, it is probably fair to say that the first half of adolescence may be a somewhat more strained and distant time for the family than earlier or later, although this may be more true in the case of firstborns than in the case of later-borns, perhaps because parents may learn from experience (L. Shanahan, McHale, Osgood, & Crouter, 2007). Part of the problem may be that conflicts between teenagers and parents tend to be resolved not through compromise but through one party giving in or walking away, neither of which enhances the quality of the relationship or contributes to the adolescent's or the parent's well-being (Laursen & Collins, 1994; C. Tucker, McHale, & Crouter, 2003b).

▌ **Violations of Expectations** Several researchers have studied changes in adolescents' cognitive abilities and how these changes may reverberate throughout the family. We noted earlier in this chapter that changes in the ways adolescents view family rules and regulations may contribute to increased conflict between them and their parents (Smetana, 1989). Research also indicates that early adolescence is a time of changes in youngsters' views of family relationships and in family members' expectations of each other (Lanz, Scabini, Vermulst, & Gerris, 2001). For example, one study asked adolescents of different ages to characterize their actual and ideal families in terms of how close and dominant different family members were (S. Feldman & Gehring, 1988). With age, the gap between adolescents' actual and ideal portraits widened, indicating that as they became older, adolescents became more aware of their families' short-comings—at least in comparison to what they believed a perfect family was like.

Psychologist W. Andrew Collins (1990) has examined changes in children's and parents' expectations for each other during adolescence and how "violations" of these expectations can cause family conflict. A child may enter adolescence expecting that it will be a time of great freedom, for example, whereas the parents may view the same period as one in which tighter reins are necessary. Alternatively, another child, perhaps influenced by television sitcoms portraying happy families, may imagine that adolescence will be a time of increased closeness and shared activities in the family, only to find that his or her parents have been looking forward to having time to themselves. It is easy to see how differences in expectations about what adolescence is going to be like can escalate into arguments and misunderstandings. When questioned about whether adolescents were expected to disclose secrets to their parents, for example, adolescents' expectations for secrecy were much greater than parents' (Smetana, Metzger, Gettman, & Campione-Barr, 2006). For this reason, psychologists have been studying what sorts of beliefs children and parents have about adolescence, what influences these beliefs, and where they turn for sources of information (Steinberg, 2001; Whiteman & Buchanan, 2002).

SEX DIFFERENCES IN FAMILY RELATIONSHIPS

In general, differences between the family relations of sons and daughters are minimal. Although there are occasional exceptions to the rule, sons and daughters report similar degrees of closeness to their parents, similar amounts of conflict, similar types of rules (and disagreements about those rules), and similar patterns of activity. And observational studies of interactions between par-

Adolescents fare better when their parents are warm and firm, a style known as authoritative parenting.

ents and adolescents indicate that sons and daughters interact with their parents in remarkably similar ways (Steinberg & Silk, 2002).

On the other hand, teenagers relate very differently to mothers and to fathers. Across many ethnic groups and cultures, adolescents tend to be closer to their mother, to spend more time alone with their mother, and to feel more comfortable talking to their mother about problems and other emotional matters; as a consequence, mothers tend to be more involved than fathers in their adolescents' lives (Updegraff, McHale, Crouter, & Kupanoff, 2001; S. K. Williams & Kelly, 2005). Fathers often rely on mothers for information about their adolescent's activities, but the reverse is uncommon (Crouter, Bumpus, Davis, & McHale, 2005; Waizenhofer, Buchanan, & Jackson-Newsom, 2004). Fathers are more likely to be perceived as relatively distant authority figures who may be consulted for objective information (such as help with homework) but who are rarely sought for support or guidance (such as help with problems with a boyfriend or girlfriend) (Crockett, Brown, Russell, & Shen, 2007). Interestingly, adolescents also fight more often with their mothers than with their fathers and perceive mothers as more controlling, but this does not appear to jeopardize the closeness of the mother–adolescent relationship (Shek, 2007). Relationships between adolescents and their mothers are more emotionally intense in general, and this intensity has both positive and negative manifestations (Apter, 1990; Larson & Richards, 1994).

RECAP

- Transformations in family relations are sparked by the biological, cognitive, and social maturation of the adolescent; by the changes parents face at midlife; and by changes in the needs and functions of the family.
- Adolescence is a time of reorganization in family relationships, with adolescents gaining increasingly more power and becoming increasingly more assertive.
- Many of the changes in family relations that occur at adolescence affect the psychological well-being of the adolescent's middle-aged parents as well as the teenager; indeed, in some regards, adolescence may be a more difficult time for the parents than the teenager.
- Although the family relations of adolescent males and females are very similar, studies show that mothers and fathers have very different relationships with their teenagers.

Family Relationships and Adolescent Development

Thus far, we have looked at the sorts of issues and concerns faced by most families during the adolescent years. In our focus on those experiences that all families share, however, we have not addressed the very important questions of how relationships differ from family to family and whether these differences have important consequences for the developing adolescent. Some parents are stricter than others. Some adolescents are given a great deal of affection, while others are treated more distantly. In some households, decisions are made through open discussion and verbal give-and-take; in others, parents lay down the rules, and children are expected to follow them. To what extent are different patterns of family relationships associated with different patterns of adolescent development? Are some styles of parenting more likely to be associated with healthy development than others?

parental responsiveness One of the two important dimensions of parenting; responsiveness refers to the degree to which the parent responds to the child's needs in an accepting, supportive manner.

parental demandingness One of two important dimensions of parenting; demandingness refers to the degree to which the parent expects and insists on mature, responsible behavior from the child.

Before we try to answer these questions, several cautions are in order. Although our tendency is to see children's behavior as the result of their parents' behavior, socialization is actually a two-way, not a one-way, street (W. A. Collins, Maccoby, Steinberg, Hetherington, & Bornstein, 2000). Just as parents affect their adolescents' behavior, adolescents affect their parents' behavior (Ge, Conger, Lorenz, Shanahan, & Elder, 1995; J. Lerner, Castellino, & Perkins, 1994). One nine-year longitudinal study found, for example, that adolescents' and parents' negative feelings toward each other had a reciprocal relationship over time—the more negative adolescents felt, the more this led to negative feelings on the part of their parents, and vice versa (K. Kim, Conger, Lorenz, & Elder, 2001).

In addition, various types of parenting affect different adolescents differently. For example, although it is well established that adolescents whose parents are hostile or aloof are more likely to exhibit antisocial behavior (e.g., Dobkin, Tremblay, & Sacchitelle, 1997), the link between negative parenting and adolescent problem behavior is stronger among teenagers who are temperamentally more impulsive; in contrast, among adolescents who are temperamentally more introverted, the same sort of parenting leads to anxiety and depression (Stice & Gonzales, 1998; Van Leeuwen, Mervielde, Braet, & Bosmans, 2004). Furthermore, adolescents who have a greater genetic risk for developing problems (by virtue of their family history) are more likely to evoke from their parents the sort of behavior that has been shown to lead to the development of behavior problems (O'Connor, Deater-Deckard, Fulker, Rutter, & Plomin, 1998).

PARENTING STYLES AND THEIR EFFECTS

There are a variety of ways to characterize parents' behavior toward their children. One of the most useful approaches derives from the work of psychologist Diana Baumrind (1978). According to her work and that of others in this vein, two aspects of the parent's behavior toward the adolescent are critical: parental responsiveness and parental "demandingness" (Maccoby & Martin, 1983). **Parental responsiveness** refers to the degree to which the parent responds to the child's needs in an accepting, supportive manner. **Parental demandingness** refers to the extent to which the parent expects and demands mature, responsible behavior from the child. Parents vary on each of these dimensions. Some are warm and accepting, while others are unresponsive and rejecting; some are demanding and expect a great deal of their child, while others are permissive and demand very little.

▌ **Four Styles of Parenting** Because parental responsiveness and demandingness are more or less independent of each other—that is, it is possible for a parent to be demanding without being responsive, and vice versa—it is possible to look at various combinations of these two dimensions (see Figure 4.3). Many studies of parents and children indicate that the four-fold classification scheme presented in Figure 4.3 is very important in understanding the impact of parents' behavior on the child, and psychologists have given labels to the four different prototypes presented in the figure.

Parents who are both responsive and demanding are authoritative. **Authoritative parents** are warm but firm. They set standards for the child's conduct but form expectations that are consistent with the child's developing needs and capabilities. They place a high value on the development of autonomy and self-direction but assume the ultimate responsibility for their child's behavior. Authoritative parents deal with their child in a rational, issue-oriented manner, frequently engaging in discussion and explanation over matters of discipline. Authoritative parents strive to raise a child who is self-reliant and who has a strong sense of initiative.

Parents who are very demanding but not responsive are authoritarian. **Authoritarian parents** place a high value on obedience and conformity. They tend to favor more punitive, absolute, and forceful disciplinary measures. Verbal give-and-take is not common in authoritarian households, because the underlying belief of authoritarian parents is that the child should accept without question the rules and standards established by the parents. They tend not to encourage independent behavior and, instead, place a good deal of importance on restricting the child's autonomy. Authoritarian parents place a premium on obedience.

A parent who is very responsive but not at all demanding is indulgent. **Indulgent parents** behave in an accepting, benign, and somewhat more passive way in matters of discipline. They place relatively few demands on the child's behavior, giving the child a high degree of freedom to act as he or she wishes. Indulgent parents are more likely to believe that control is an infringement on the child's freedom that may interfere with healthy development. Instead of actively shaping their child's behavior, indulgent parents are more likely to view themselves as resources for the child. Indulgent parents tend to be especially concerned with raising a happy child.

Parents who are neither demanding nor responsive are indifferent. **Indifferent parents** try to do whatever is necessary to minimize the time and energy they must devote to interacting with their child. In extreme cases, indifferent parents may be neglectful. They know little about their child's activities and whereabouts, show little interest in their child's experiences at school or with friends, rarely converse with their child, and rarely consider their child's opinion when making decisions. Rather than raising their child according to a set of

FIGURE 4.3 A scheme for classifying parenting types. (From Maccoby and Martin, 1983)

beliefs about what is good for the child's development (as do the other three parent types), indifferent parents structure their home life primarily around their own needs and interests.

▍ The Power of Authoritative Parenting Few areas of research in the field of adolescent development have received as much attention as the link between what parents do and how adolescents turn out, and the findings of this body of work are amazingly consistent (Steinberg, 2001). Generally, young people who have been raised in authoritative households are more psychosocially mature than peers who have been raised in authoritarian, indulgent, or indifferent homes. Adolescents raised in authoritative homes are more responsible, self-assured, creative, intellectually curious, socially skilled, and academically successful. Adolescents raised in authoritarian homes, in contrast, are more dependent, more passive, less socially adept, less self-assured, and less intellectually curious. Adolescents raised in indulgent households are less mature, less responsible, and more conforming to their peers. Adolescents raised in indifferent homes are often impulsive and more likely to be involved in delinquent behavior and in precocious experiments with sex, drugs, and alcohol (W. A. Collins & Steinberg, 2006). Although it generally is not a good thing for parents to disagree about how they raise their teenager, studies show that it is better to have at least one authoritative parent than two nonauthoritative ones who happen to be consistent (Fletcher, Steinberg, & Sellers, 1999; McKinney & Renk, 2008; L. Simons & Conger, 2007).

authoritative parents Parents who use warmth, firm control, and rational, issue-oriented discipline, in which emphasis is placed on the development of self-direction.

authoritarian parents Parents who use punitive, absolute, and forceful discipline, and who place a premium on obedience and conformity.

indulgent parents Parents who are characterized by responsiveness but low demandingness, and who are mainly concerned with the child's happiness.

indifferent parents Parents who are characterized by low levels of both responsiveness and demandingness.

TABLE 4.1   The 10 basic principles of good parenting

Several years ago, after reviewing decades of research on parenting and child development, I came to the conclusion that we really did know what sort of parenting is most likely to help children and adolescents grow up in healthy ways. I summarized this evidence in a book called *The 10 Basic Principles of Good Parenting* (Steinberg, 2005b). Here's what all parents, regardless of their child's age, should keep in mind:

1. What You Do Matters
2. You Can Not Be Too Loving
3. Be Involved in Your Child's Life
4. Adapt Your Parenting to Fit Your Child
5. Establish Rules and Set Limits
6. Help Foster Your Child's Independence
7. Be Consistent
8. Avoid Harsh Discipline
9. Explain Your Rules and Decisions
10. Treat Your Child With Respect

Source: Steinberg, 2005b.

The evidence linking authoritative parenting and healthy adolescent development is remarkably strong, and it has been found in studies of a wide range of ethnicities, social classes, and family structures, not only within the United States (e.g., Bean, Barber, & Crane, 2006; R. Clark, Novak, & Dupree, 2002; Cleveland, Gibbons, Gerrard, Pomery, & Brody, 2005; S. Kim & Ge, 2000; Luthar & Latendresse, 2005; Matza, Kupersmidt, & Glenn, 2001) but also in parts of the world as diverse as Iceland (Adalbjarnardottir & Hafsteinsson, 2001), the Czech Republic (Dmitrieva, Chen, Greenberger, & Gil-Rivas, 2004), India (Carson, Chowdhury, Perry, & Pati, 1999), China (Pilgrim, Luo, Urberg, & Fang, 1999), Israel (Mayseless, Scharf, & Sholt, 2003), Switzerland (Vazsonyi, Hibbert, & Snider, 2003), and Palestine (Punamäki, Qouta, & Sarraj, 1997). Indeed, the evidence favoring authoritative parenting is so strong that some experts have suggested that the question of which type of parenting benefits teenagers the most need not be studied anymore (see Table 4.1) (Steinberg, 2001). Furthermore, research shows that educational programs designed to teach parents how to be more responsive and more demanding are effective in fostering healthy adolescent development and behavior (e.g., Brody, Murry, et al., 2006; Connell & Dishion, 2008; Herrenkohl, Hill, Hawkins, Chung, & Nagin, 2006).

At the other extreme, parenting that is indifferent, neglectful, hostile, or abusive has been shown consistently to have harmful effects on adolescents' mental health and development, leading to depression and a variety of behavior problems (Buehler, 2006; Coley, Medeiros, & Schindler, 2008; Hoeve et al., 2008; Pittman & Chase-Lansdale, 2001). Severe psycholog-

ical abuse (excessive criticism, rejection, or emotional harshness) appears to have the most deleterious effects (Dube et al., 2003; Haj-Yahia, Musleh, & Haj-Yahia, 2002; Rohner, Bourque, & Elordi, 1996).

How Authoritative Parenting Works   Why is authoritative parenting associated with healthy adolescent development? First, authoritative parents provide an appropriate balance between restrictiveness and autonomy, giving the adolescent opportunities to develop self-reliance while providing the sorts of standards, limits, and guidelines that developing individuals need (Rueter & Conger, 1995a, 1995b). Authoritative parents, for instance, are more likely to give children more independence gradually as they get older, which helps children develop self-reliance and self-assurance. Because of this, authoritative parenting promotes the development of adolescents' competence (Glasgow, Dornbusch, Troyer, Steinberg, & Ritter, 1997; Steinberg, Elmen, & Mounts, 1989) and enhances their ability to withstand a variety of potentially negative influences, including life stress (Barrera, Li, & Chassin, 1995; McCabe, 1997; Pearce, Jones, Schwab-Stone, & Ruchkin, 2003; Wagner, Cohen, & Brook, 1996) and exposure to antisocial peers (Galambos, Barker, & Almeida, 2003; C. Mason, Cauce, Gonzales, & Hiraga, 1994; Mounts & Steinberg, 1995; Walker-Barnes & Mason, 2004).

Second, because authoritative parents are more likely to engage their children in verbal give-and-take, they are likely to promote the sort of intellectual development that provides an important foundation for the development of psychosocial maturity (Rueter & Conger, 1998; Smetana, Crean, & Daddis, 2002). Authoritative parents, for example, are less likely than other parents to assert their authority by turning adolescents' personal decisions (such as over what type of music they listen to) into "moral" issues (Smetana, 1995b; Smetana & Asquith, 1994). Family discussions in which decisions, rules, and expectations are explained help the child understand social systems and social relationships. This understanding plays an important role in the development of reasoning abilities, role taking, moral judgment, and empathy (N. Eisenberg, Morris, McDaniel, & Spinrad, 2009; Krevans & Gibbs, 1996).

Third, because authoritative parenting is based on a warm parent–child relationship, adolescents are more likely to identify with, admire, and form strong attachments to their parents, which leaves them more open to their parents' influence (Bogenschneider, Small, & Tsay, 1997; Darling & Steinberg, 1993; K. Mackey, Arnold, & Pratt, 2001; Mounts, 2002; T. Sim, 2000). Adolescents who have had warm and close relationships with their parents are more likely, for example, to have similar attitudes and values (Brody, Moore, & Glei, 1994). Adolescents who are raised by nonauthoritative parents, in contrast, often end up having friends their parents disapprove of, including those involved in problem behavior (Adamczyk-Robinette, Fletcher, & Wright, 2002; J. Kim, Hetherington, & Reiss, 1999; Knoester, Haynie, & Stephens, 2006).

FOOD FOR THOUGHT

Our discussion has focused mainly on the consequences of growing up with parents who use different styles of parenting. But what makes parents choose the sort of parenting they use? Why are some parents authoritative but others not?

Finally, the child's own behavior and temperament may play a role in shaping parenting practices (Albrecht, Galambos, & Jansson, 2007; Beaver & Wright, 2007; W. L. Cook, 2001; Stice & Barrera, 1995). Children who are responsible, self-directed, curious, and self-assured elicit from their parents warmth, flexible guidance, and verbal give-and-take. In contrast, children who are irritable, aggressive, dependent, or less psychosocially mature may provoke parents' behavior that is excessively harsh, passive, or distant (Huh, Tristan, Wade, & Stice, 2006; Lengua, 2006; Rueter & Conger, 1998). Parents may enjoy being around children who are responsible, independent, and willing to tell them about their activities and whereabouts, and they may treat them more warmly as a result. Thus, although evidence suggests that active parental monitoring does deter adolescent problem behavior (Coley, Votruba-Drzal, & Schindler, 2008; Fletcher, Steinberg, & Williams-Wheeler, 2004; Hair, Moore, Garrett, Ling, & Cleveland, 2008; Lahey, Van Hull, D'Onofrio, Rodgers, & Waldman, 2008; Waizenhofer et al., 2004), some of what often appears to be "effective parental monitoring" may actually be the end result of a parent–adolescent relationship in which the adolescent willingly discloses information to the parent (Kerr & Stattin, 2000; Soenens, Vansteenkiste, Luyckx, & Goossens, 2006; Stattin & Kerr, 2000; Warr, 2007). In contrast, children who are continually acting up make their parents short-tempered, impatient, or distant. In one recent study, for instance, the researchers found that when parents had little knowledge of their adolescent's behavior, this led to an increase in delinquency, but that increases in delinquency, in turn, led to decreases in parental knowledge (Laird, Pettit, Bates, & Dodge, 2003) (see Figure 4.4). In other words, the relationship between adolescent competence and authoritative parenting may be the result of a reciprocal cycle in which the child's psychosocial maturity leads to authoritative parenting, which, in

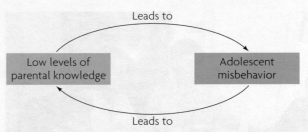

FIGURE 4.4 The relation between parenting and adolescent behavior is often reciprocal. (Adapted from Laird et al., 2003)

turn, leads to the further development of maturity (J. Lerner, Castellino, & Perkins, 1994; Repetti, 1996). In contrast, nonauthoritative parenting may lead to the development of emotional and behavioral problems, which may lead parents to disengage even more (Burke, Pardini, & Loeber, 2008; Dishion, Nelson, & Bullock, 2004).

ETHNIC DIFFERENCES IN PARENTING PRACTICES

A number of researchers have asked whether parents from different ethnic groups vary in their child rearing and whether the relation between parenting styles and adolescent outcomes is the same across different ethnic groups. These, of course, are two different questions: The first concerns average differences between groups in their approaches to parenting (for example, whether ethnic minority parents are stricter than White parents), whereas the second concerns the correlation between parenting practices and adolescent adjustment in different groups (for example, whether the effect of strictness is the same in ethnic minority families as it is in White families).

In general, researchers find that authoritative parenting, as defined earlier in this chapter, is less prevalent among Black, Asian, or Hispanic families than among White families, no doubt reflecting the fact that parenting practices are often linked to cultural values and beliefs (Dornbusch, Ritter, Liederman, Roberts, & Fraleigh, 1987; Smetana & Chuang, 2001; Yau & Smetana, 1996). Nevertheless, even though authoritative parenting is less common in ethnic minority families, its effects on adolescent adjustment are beneficial in all ethnic groups (Amato & Fowler, 2002; Knight, Virdin, & Roosa, 1994; C. Mason, Cauce, Gonzales, & Hiraga, 1996; Vazsonyi & Belliston, 2006; Vazsonyi, Trejos-Castillo, & Huang, 2006; Walker-Barnes & Mason, 2001). In other words, ethnic minority youngsters benefit from parenting that is responsive and demanding, just as their nonminority peers do.

Research also indicates that authoritarian parenting (high in demandingness but low in responsiveness) is more prevalent among ethnic minority than among White families, even after taking ethnic differences in

Family relationships often differ across ethnic groups.

socioeconomic status into account (Chao, 1994; Dornbusch et al., 1987; Steinberg, Lamborn, Dornbusch, & Darling, 1992). As opposed to research on authoritative parenting, however, which suggests similar effects across ethnic groups, research on authoritarian parenting indicates that the adverse effects of this style of parenting may be greater among White youngsters than among their ethnic minority counterparts (Chao, 1994; Morrison Gutman et al., 2002; Lamborn, Dornbusch, & Steinberg, 1996; Ruiz, Roosa, & Gonzales, 2002; Schweingruber & Kalil, 2000; Steinberg, Lamborn, Darling, Mounts, & Dornbusch, 1994). Several explanations have been offered for this finding.

First, because ethnic minority families are more likely to live in dangerous communities, authoritarian parenting, with its emphasis on control, may not be as harmful and may even offer some benefits (Steinberg, Blatt-Eisengart, & Cauffman, 2006). Second, as several researchers (Chao, 2001; Gonzales, Cauce, & Mason, 1996) have pointed out, the distinction between authoritative versus authoritarian parenting may not always make sense when applied to parents from other cultures. For example, non-White parents frequently combine a very high degree of strictness (like White authoritarian parents) with warmth (like White authoritative parents) (Formoso, Ruiz, & Gonzales, 1997; Jackson-Newsom, Buchanan, & McDonald, 2008; Smetana & Gaines, 2000; Supple, Peterson, & Bush, 2004). Because most of the research on parenting and adolescent development has been conducted by White researchers, other ethnic groups' approaches to child rearing (which appear very controlling, but which are neither aloof nor hostile) may be mislabeled as authoritarian (Gonzales, Cauce, & Mason, 1996). Similar arguments have been made about the misinterpretation

of strictness among American parents who are conservative Protestants (Gunnoe, Hetherington, & Reiss, 1999, 2006; Wilcox, 1998). Nevertheless, it is important to keep in mind that the conclusion to be drawn from these studies is not that authoritarian parenting is better than authoritative parenting for ethnic minority adolescents, but rather that it is not as harmful in these groups as it has been shown to be among White adolescents (W. A. Collins & Steinberg, 2006).

AUTONOMY AND ATTACHMENT IN THE ADOLESCENT'S FAMILY

Several studies of conversations between adolescents and their parents have examined factors in the nature of parent–adolescent communication that contribute to healthy adolescent development. In these studies, families were asked to discuss a problem together, and their interaction was videotaped and later analyzed. Generally, families with psychologically competent teenagers interact in ways that permit family members to express their autonomy and individuality while remaining attached, or connected, to other family members (McElhaney, Allen, Stephenson, & Hare, 2009; Rathunde, 1996; Silverberg, Tennenbaum, & Jacob, 1992). In these families, verbal give-and-take is the norm, and adolescents (as well as parents) are encouraged to express their own opinions, even if this sometimes leads to disagreements. At the same time, however, the importance of maintaining close relationships in the family is emphasized, and individuals are encouraged to consider how their actions may affect other family members (Rueter & Conger, 1995a, 1995b). Indeed, adolescents who are permitted to assert their own opinions within a family context that is secure and loving develop higher self-esteem and more mature coping abilities. Adolescents whose autonomy is squelched are at risk for developing feelings of depression and low self-esteem, whereas those who do not feel connected are more likely than their peers to develop behavior problems (Aquilino & Supple, 2001; Barber, 1996; Bender et al. 2007; McElhaney, Allen, Stephenson, & Hare, 2009).

In other words, adolescents appear to do best when they grow up in a family atmosphere that permits the development of individuality against a backdrop of close family ties (Grolnick, Kurowski, Dunlap, & Hevey, 2000; Walsh, Shulman, Bar-On, & Tsur, 2006). In these families, conflict between parents and adolescents can play a very important and positive role in the adolescent's social and cognitive development, because individuals are encouraged to express their opinions in an atmosphere that does not risk severing the emotional attachment (McElhaney, Allen, Stephenson, & Hare, 2009). Perhaps for this reason, adolescents whose perceptions of their family differ from those of their parents a little bit are better adjusted than those whose views are either identical to their parents' or extremely divergent (Feinberg, Howe, Reiss, & Hetherington, 2000).

ADOLESCENTS' RELATIONSHIPS WITH SIBLINGS

▌ **The Nature of Sibling Relationships in Adolescence**   Sibling relationships during adolescence have characteristics that set them apart both from relationships with parents and relationships with friends (East, 2009). In one study, young adolescents were asked to rate several types of relationships along similar dimensions. Adolescents rated their sibling relationships similarly to those with their parents with regard to measures of companionship and importance, but sibling relationships were rated more like friendships with respect to power, assistance, and their satisfaction with the relationship (Furman & Buhrmester, 1985).

FOOD FOR THOUGHT

Did you grow up with siblings? How did your relationship with them change as you moved through adolescence?

Young adolescents often have emotionally charged relationships with siblings that are marked by conflict and rivalry, but also by nurturance and support (Lempers & Clark-Lempers, 1992). As children mature from childhood to early adolescence, sibling conflict increases (Brody, Stoneman, & McCoy, 1994), with adolescents reporting more negativity in their sibling relationships than in their relationships with peers (Buhrmester & Furman 1990) and less effective conflict resolution than with their parents (C. Tucker, McHale, & Crouter, 2003a). Over the course of adolescence, adolescents' relationships with siblings, and especially with younger siblings, become more egalitarian but also more distant and less emotionally intense (Buhrmester & Furman, 1990; A. Cole & Kerns, 2001), although patterns of change in sibling relationships differ between same-sex and mixed-sex dyads (see Figure 4.5). As Figure 4.5 indicates, in same-sex dyads, intimacy increases between preadolescence and middle adolescence, and then declines somewhat. In mixed-sex dyads, the pattern is the opposite: intimacy drops between preadolescence and mid-adolescence, and then increases. In fact, by late adolescence, mixed-sex siblings are closer than are same-sex siblings, although both types of relationships become closer as individuals move into

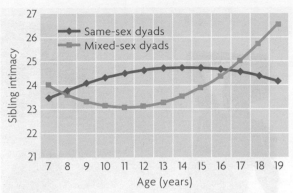

FIGURE 4.5   Patterns of change in intimacy between siblings differ between same-sex and mixed-sex dyads. (Kim et al., 2006)

young adulthood (Scharf, Shulman, & Avigad-Spitz, 2005). Despite these changes over time, there is considerable stability in the quality of sibling relationships between childhood and adolescence, and siblings who are relatively closer during middle childhood are relatively closer as adolescents (J. Dunn, Slomkowski, & Beardsall, 1994)

▌ **A Network of Relationships**   Several researchers have uncovered important links among parent–child, sibling, and peer relations in adolescence, and these findings indicate that it is helpful to think of the adolescent's interpersonal world as consisting of a web of interconnected relationships. The quality of the parent–adolescent relationship influences the quality of relations among brothers and sisters (e.g., East & Khoo, 2005; K. L. Hoffman, Kiecolt, & Edwards, 2005; L. S. Matthews & Conger, 2004; Paley, Conger, & Harold, 2000; Reese-Weber, 2000). Harmony and cohesiveness in the parent–adolescent relationship are associated with less sibling conflict and a more positive sibling relationship (East, 2009). In contrast, adolescents who experience maternal rejection and negativity are more likely to display aggression with siblings.

By the same token, children and adolescents learn much about social relationships from sibling interactions, and they bring this knowledge and experience to friendships outside the family (East, 2009; McCoy, Brody, & Stoneman, 1994; Updegraff, McHale, & Crouter, 2000). In poorly functioning families, aggressive interchanges between unsupervised siblings may provide a training ground within which adolescents learn, practice, and perfect antisocial and aggressive behavior (Bank, Reid, & Greenley, 1994; Criss & Shaw, 2005; Snyder, Bank, & Burraston, 2005). The reverse is true as well—the quality of adolescents' relationships with their friends influences how they interact with their siblings (Kramer & Kowal, 2005).

The quality of the sibling relationship affects not only adolescents' peer relations but also their

Because siblings live in close proximity to each other, they have added opportunities for both positive and negative interactions.

adjustment in general (Seginer, 1998; Stocker, Burwell, & Briggs, 2002). Positive sibling relationships contribute to adolescents' academic competence, sociability, autonomy, and self-worth (e.g., Hetherington et al., 1999; Kim, McHale, Crouter, & Osgood, 2007; Yeh & Lempers, 2004). Having a close sibling relationship can partially ameliorate the negative effects of not having friends in school (East, 2009), and siblings can serve as sources of advice and guidance (Kolburn Kowal & Blinn-Pike, 2004; C. Tucker, Barber, & Eccles, 1997; C. Tucker, McHale, & Crouter, 2001). Of course, siblings can influence the development of problems as well (Bank, Burraston, & Snyder, 2004; K. Conger, Conger, & Scaramella, 1997). For example, younger sisters of childbearing adolescents are relatively more likely to engage in early sexual activity and to become pregnant during adolescence (East, Reyes, & Horn, 2007). Siblings also influence each other's drug use and antisocial behavior (e.g., Ardelt & Day, 2002; Bullock & Dishion, 2002; Haynie & McHugh, 2003).

Behavioral Genetics and Adolescent Development

One topic of interest to researchers who study adolescents and their siblings concerns how closely siblings resemble each other in various characteristics, such as intelligence, personality, and interests. Recent advances in the study of **behavioral genetics** have provided new insights into this issue, as well as a host of others concerning the joint impact of genes and environment on development.

Researchers examine this issue by studying adolescents who are twins, to see whether identical twins are more similar than fraternal twins (e.g., McGue, Elkins, Walden, & Iacono, 2005); by studying adolescents who have been adopted, to see whether adopted adolescents are more like their biological parents than like their adoptive parents (e.g., Abrahamson, Baker, & Caspi, 2002; Deater-Deckard & Plomin, 1999); and by studying adolescents and their siblings in stepfamilies, to see whether similarity between siblings varies with their biological relatedness (e.g., Hetherington, Reiss, & Plomin, 1994; Neiderhiser et al., 2004). In addition to examining whether and how much given traits are genetically versus environmentally determined, researchers also ask how these two sets of factors interact (for example, whether the same environment affects people with different

behavioral genetics   The scientific study of genetic influences on behavior.

genetic makeups in different ways, or whether people with different genetic makeups evoke different reactions from their environment) (W. A. Collins, Maccoby, Steinberg, Hetherington, & Bornstein, 2000).

GENETIC AND ENVIRONMENTAL INFLUENCES ON ADOLESCENT DEVELOPMENT

In studies of genetic and environmental influences on adolescent development, researchers distinguish between two types of environmental influences. **Shared environmental influences** are factors in the environment that individuals, such as siblings, have in common and that make the individuals similar in personality and behavior. **Nonshared environmental influences** are factors in the environments of individuals that are not similar and that, as a consequence, make the individuals different from one another (Plomin & Daniels, 1987). In studies of siblings, nonshared environmental influences can include factors within the family as well as outside of it. For example, if two siblings are treated very differently by their parents, this would be considered a nonshared environmental influence. Indeed, some evidence suggests that this sort of nonshared environment—that is, the nonshared environment that results from people having different experiences within what would appear to be the same context—may be the most important (Turkheimer & Waldron, 2000). Studies indicate that both genetic and nonshared environmental influences, such as differential parental treatment, peer relations, and school experiences, are particularly strong in adolescence. In contrast, shared environmental factors, such as family socioeconomic status or the neighborhood in which two siblings live, are less influential (McGue, Sharma, & Benson, 1996; Pike et al., 1996).

Studies have revealed that genetic factors strongly influence many qualities that previously had been assumed to be shaped mainly by the environment. Aggressive behavior is especially driven by genetic influences, although shared and nonshared environmental influences on adolescents' antisocial behavior, including aggression, also have been found (S. A. Burt, McGue, Kreuger, & Iacono, 2007; Deater-Deckard & Plomin 1999; Eley, Lichenstein, & Stevenson, 1999; Spotts, Neiderhiser, Hetherington, & Reiss, 2001). Genetic factors also have been linked to emotional distress in adolescence, such as risk for suicide and depression (Jacobson & Rowe, 1999). Research also has found strong genetic influences on adolescent competence, self-image, and intelligence. Adolescents' self-conceptions also are moderately heritable, with little evidence for shared environmental influences (S. McGuire, Neiderhiser, Reiss, Hetherington, & Plomin, 1994; S. McGuire et al., 1999).

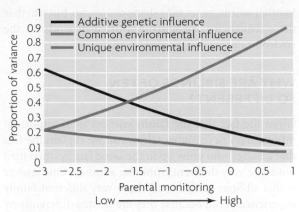

FIGURE 4.6 Genetic influences on smoking are much stronger among adolescents whose parents do not monitor their behavior closely. (Dick et al., 2007)

Intelligence in adolescence (as indexed by IQ) is also under strong genetic control, with genetic influences compounding over time and ultimately becoming more influential than the family environment. Interestingly, the maturation of brain regions associated with complex reasoning becomes increasingly under genetic control over time (Lenroot & Giedd, 2008). However, genetic influences on intelligence are stronger in families with highly educated parents, consistent with the general notion that the influence of genes is typically higher in more favorable environments (Rowe, Jacobson, & Van den Oord, 1999). Genetic influences on school performance, in contrast to intelligence, are more modest (Loehlin, Neiderhiser, & Reiss, 2005; Teachman, 1997).

It is important to emphasize that the same genes may have different effects on adolescent development in different contexts (W. A. Collins et al., 2000). Consider the following findings from recent studies:

- Genetic influences on sexual activity are stronger when adolescents attend schools in which a higher proportion of students are having sex at an early age (Guo, Tong, & Cai, 2008).
- Genetic influences on antisocial behavior are stronger among adolescents who have delinquent peers (Beaver, DeLisi, Wright, & Vaughn, 2009).
- Genetic influences on depression are stronger among adolescents exposed to family conflict (F. Rice, Harold, Shelton, & Thapar, 2006).
- Genetic influences on smoking are stronger among adolescents whose parents do not monitor them closely (Dick et al., 2007) (see Figure 4.6)

shared environmental influences Nongenetic influences that make individuals living in the same family similar to each other.

nonshared environmental influences The nongenetic influences in individuals' lives that make them different from people they live with.

In other words, genes may shape *tendencies*, but whether these tendencies are actualized often depends on the environment.

WHY ARE SIBLINGS OFTEN SO DIFFERENT?

Given the fact that the family context is an important influence on development, how can we explain the fact that siblings who grow up in the same family often turn out to be very different from one another? One answer is that siblings actually may have very different family experiences, both because they are treated differently by their parents and because they often perceive similar experiences in different ways (Feinberg & Hetherington, 2000; O'Connor, Hetherington, Reiss, & Plomin, 1995; C. Tucker, McHale, & Crouter, 2003b). For example, one brother may describe his family as very close-knit, while another may have experienced it as very distant. One girl may describe her family life as plagued with argument and conflict, while her sister describes it as peaceful and agreeable. In other words, even though we may assume that children growing up in the same family have shared the same environment, this is not necessarily the case.

As you might expect, unequal treatment from mothers or fathers often creates conflict among siblings (Brody, Stoneman, & Burke, 1987) and is linked to a variety of problems, such as depression, antisocial behavior, and early pregnancy (East & Jacobson, 2003; Reiss et al., 1995). Studies also show that differences in siblings' real and perceived family experiences are related to different patterns of development (E. Anderson, Hetherington, Reiss, & Howe, 1994; Barrett-Singer & Weinstein, 2000; K. Conger & Conger, 1994; Mekos, Hetherington, & Reiss, 1996). In general, better-adjusted adolescents are more likely than their siblings to report that they had close relationships with their parents, that their relations with brothers or sisters were friendly, that they were involved in family decision making, and that they were given a high level of responsibility around the house (Daniels, Dunn, Furstenberg, & Plomin, 1985; L. Shanahan, McHale, Crouter, & Osgood, 2008).

Despite this evidence for differential treatment and its potentially adverse influence on adolescent development, adolescents report that 75% of parental treatment is not differential. Interestingly, studies show that adolescents, especially as they get older, generally appreciate the reasons for parents treating siblings differently and that sibling relationships are strained only when this differential treatment is per-

ceived as unfair (Feinberg, Neiderhiser, Simmens, Reiss, & Hetherington, 2000; Kowal & Kramer, 1997).

Oddly, treating siblings differently may actually be a good thing for parents to do, so long as each sibling is treated well. There is some evidence that when siblings are treated differently by their parents, they get along better—presumably because this differential treatment makes them feel unique and lessens **sibling rivalry** (Feinberg, McHale, Crouter, & Cumsille, 2003). Perhaps you have a brother or sister whom you resemble more than you'd like—so much, in fact, that you've had a hard time establishing your own personality. When siblings feel this way, they often deliberately try to be different from each other—a phenomenon known as **sibling deidentification.** An adolescent whose brother or sister is a star athlete, for instance, may shun sports and focus on cultivating other types of talents, perhaps in academics or in the arts, a strategy that will diminish feelings of competition. Differential treatment by parents may have similar consequences.

In addition to having different experiences inside the family, siblings also may have very different experiences outside the family—at school, with friends, in the neighborhood. These contexts provide yet another source of nonshared environmental influence. Because factors other than the family environment shape adolescent development and behavior, siblings may turn out very different if they have divergent experiences outside the home.

▌ **Adolescents and Adoption** Studies of the psychological development of adolescents who have been adopted have yielded mixed and often contradictory results. On average, adopted individuals show relatively higher rates of delinquency, substance use, psychological difficulties, and poorer school performance, but the magnitude of the difference between adopted and nonadopted adolescents is small, especially when other factors, like family resources, are taken into account (B. Miller, Fan, Christensen, Grotevant, & van Dulmen, 2000; Slap, Goodman, & Huang, 2001; Sun, 2003). One reason for the mixed results and relatively modest effects is that there is a good deal of variability among adopted adolescents in their adjustment and in their feelings about being adopted. For instance, adopted adolescents who are preoccupied with having been adopted are relatively more alienated from and mistrustful of their adoptive parents (J. K. Kohler, Grotevant, & McRoy, 2002).

FOOD FOR THOUGHT

The proportion of adolescents growing up as only children has increased substantially in recent decades. How might growing up without siblings influence development in adolescence?

---

sibling rivalry   Competition between siblings, often for parental attention.

sibling deidentification   The process through which siblings deliberately try to be different from each other.

RECAP

- Researchers have examined genetic and environmental influences by studying identical and fraternal twins, adolescents who have been adopted, and adolescents and their siblings in stepfamilies.

- Researchers distinguish between two types of environmental influences: shared environmental influences, which make individuals in the same environment similar, and nonshared environmental influences, which make them different.

- Although genetic influences on a wide range of characteristics have been documented, adolescent development is the product of the interaction between genetics and environment.

- Siblings often differ from each other because they have different experiences both inside and outside the family and because they sometimes deliberately strive to be different.

The Adolescent's Family in a Changing Society

THE CHANGED AND CHANGING NATURE OF FAMILY LIFE

In America and in many other industrialized countries, the family has undergone a series of profound changes during the past half century that have diversified its form and, as a result, adolescents' daily experiences. Increased rates of divorce and childbearing outside of marriage, as well as a changing international economy and accelerating geographic mobility, have dramatically altered the world in which children and adolescents grow up. Although some of the most striking trends in family life slowed during the early 1990s, they

did not reverse by any means. The divorce rate and proportion of single-parent families, which skyrocketed during the 1970s and 1980s, stabilized at their historically high levels at the beginning of the 1990s and have changed relatively little since then (Hernandez, 1997; Kilborn, 1996).

Questions about whether these changes have weakened the family's influence over young people or, in one way or another, have harmed young people, continue to generate heated debate. According to some observers, the all-too-familiar problems of young people—low achievement test scores, high rates of alcohol and drug use, sexual precocity, violence in schools—have been due to changes in the family (e.g., Cornwell, Eggebeen, & Meschke, 1996). Others, less pessimistic, note that today's families are strong in their own ways and that it is the quality of relationships in the adolescent's life, not the number of adults in his or her household, that matters most (Parke & Buriel, 1998; Weisner & Garnier, 1995). According to many, supporting and strengthening today's families—in all their diversity—is more important than wringing our hands over the passing of the family forms of the 1950s.

Just how dramatic have the changes in American family life been over the past half century? Consider four of the most important indicators of family circumstances: divorce, single parenthood, remarriage, and poverty.

▌ **Divorce**   As Figure 4.7 shows, the divorce rate increased markedly beginning in the 1960s, rising steadily, and at times rapidly, until 1980. Although this rate declined during the 1990s, it is estimated that about a third of all first marriages that occurred between 1990 and 2000 will likely end in divorce or separation within the first 20 years (B. Stevenson & Wolfers, 2007). As a consequence, about 30% of all American children born during the late 1990s—today's teenagers—will experience their parents' divorce and will spend approximately five years in a single-parent household before turning 18

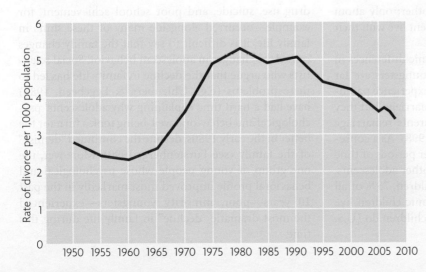

FIGURE 4.7   The divorce rate in America increased steadily during the 1970s, remained stable for several years, and began declining in the mid-1980s. (Tejada-Vera & Sutton, 2009)

Poverty often diminishes the quality of parenting in a household, which adversely affects adolescent development.

(Hetherington, Henderson, & Reiss, 1999). It is important to keep in mind, however, that the divorce rate varies considerably among people with different levels of education—divorce is much more common among college graduates than nongraduates (Hurley, 2005).

Single Parenthood In addition to adolescents who live in a single-parent household as a consequence of their parents' divorce, a sizable percentage of youngsters will spend time in a single-parent household from birth; indeed, today, the number of American children in single-parent households who live with a parent who has never married is about the same as the number who live with a parent who has been married and divorced (Fields, 2003). Keep in mind, though, that a substantial number of adolescents who are classified as living in single-parent households actually live with more than one adult, often with the unmarried partner of the child's parent (Fields, 2003). When youngsters live with only one of their biological parents, either in single-parent or in two-parent households, it is usually with the mother; only about 15% of children who live with one parent live with their father (U.S. Census Bureau, 2006).

There are important racial and ethnic differences in these patterns of family life. Black youngsters are far more likely than other youngsters to experience parental divorce and to be born outside of marriage, but they are far less likely to experience their parents' remarriage (Hetherington, Bridges, & Insabella, 1998). As a consequence, Black adolescents spend longer periods of time in single-parent households than do other adolescents. Whereas close to 80% of all Asian children, 75% of all White children, and 67% of all Hispanic children live with two parents, only 35% of Black children do (U.S. Census Bureau, 2006).

Remarriage Because more than three fourths of divorced men and two thirds of divorced women remarry, the majority of youngsters whose parents separate also experience living in a stepfamily at some time. Of the young people living in two-parent families, a substantial number—close to 15%—live with only one of their biological parents (Hernandez, 1997). And, because the divorce rate is higher for second marriages than first marriages, the majority of youth whose parents remarry will experience a *second* divorce. Moreover, because divorces generally occur faster in remarriages—one fourth happen within five years—many children confront a second divorce before they have finished adapting to having a stepparent (Hetherington et al., 1999).

Poverty Finally, approximately 16% of all children in the United States grow up in abject poverty, and an additional 22% grow up in low-income families (National Center for Children in Poverty, 2002). Although the proportion of children living in poverty declined during the 1990s, it began to rise again in 2000. Perhaps more importantly, the gap between the very poor and the very wealthy has widened substantially in the past 30 years (Hernandez, 1997). Poverty, as we noted in Chapter 3, is much more likely to touch the lives of non-White children; approximately 30% of Black and Hispanic children grow up in poverty. One reason for the large disparity in poverty rates between White and non-White children, in fact, is the racial disparity in rates of single parenthood: Because non-White children are more likely to be raised in single-parent homes, they are more likely to be poor (Hernandez, 1997).

To what extent has the changed nature of the American family changed the nature of adolescent development? How do divorce, single parenthood, remarriage, and poverty affect adolescents' development?

Many individuals are certain that the answer to these questions is, "For the worse." But before we jump to this conclusion, it is important to raise two considerations. First, although increases in adolescents' problems between 1950 and 1980—as indexed by such indicators as drug use, suicide, and poor school achievement, for example—occurred alongside many of these shifts in family life, it is difficult to say that the family changes *caused* the changes in adolescent behavior. Social scientists who argue that the decline in family life has led to these problems (e.g., Uhlenberg & Eggebeen, 1986) have had a hard time explaining why adolescents' psychological and behavioral well-being took a turn for the better in the early 1980s, despite the continued "demise" of the family (see Furstenberg, 1990). Moreover, the one group of young people whose psychological and behavioral profile improved most markedly in the past 10 years—poor, minority youngsters—experienced the most dramatic "decline" in family life during this time.

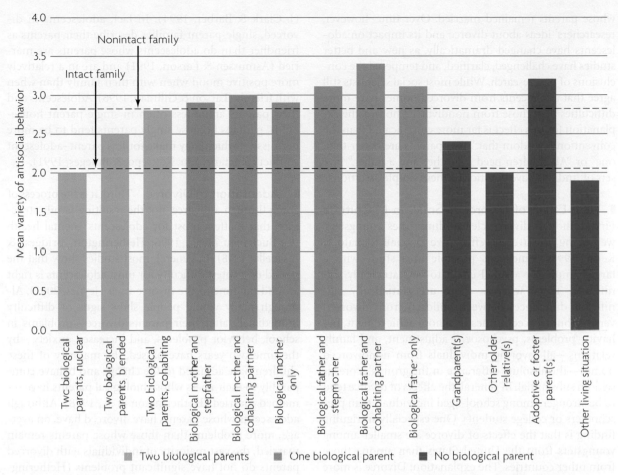

Notes: N = 8,330. Estimates are weighted. The dashed lines represent the means for a traditional binary measure of family structure, in which an "intact" family is headed by two biological parents, irrespective of whether it is a nuclear, blended, or cohabiting family. A "nonintact" family includes all other family living situations.

FIGURE 4.8   Adolescents' antisocial behavior varies as a function of their family structure. (Apel & Kaukinen, 2008)

Second, because the conditions under which divorce, single parenthood, and remarriage take place vary tremendously from family to family, it is hard to generalize about their effects on adolescents. (In contrast, it is relatively easy to generalize about the effects of poverty on adolescents, which are almost always negative.) For some young people, divorce may bring a welcome end to family conflict and tension; for others, it may be extremely disruptive psychologically. Some young people living with only their mother actually see their father more often than do their peers who live in homes where the father ostensibly is present (D. N. Hawkins, Amato, & King, 2006).

It is also the case that broad categories of family structures (e.g., "intact," "single-parent," etc.) often combine types of households that are very different in other respects. Take a look at Figure 4.8, which shows rates of antisocial and delinquent behavior across different types of households (Apel & Kaukinen, 2008). The first three columns all show "intact" families, where adolescents live with both biological parents. But as you can see, adolescents whose biological parents are cohabiting have a rate of antisocial behavior that is

40% higher than those whose biological parents are married and a rate of antisocial behavior that is about the same as adolescents who live in households with a biological mother and no other adult. Similarly, adolescents from "intact" families who live with both biological parents in so-called families where one or both of the parents has a child from a prior marriage generally have a fairly high rate of problems, despite their living with both biological parents (Halpern-Meekin & Tach, 2008). In other words, variations *within* different family structures are likely to be more important than the differences among them. This is readily apparent when we look at how adolescents are affected by parental divorce.

ADOLESCENTS AND DIVORCE

At one time, any discussion of adolescents and divorce would likely have started with the assumption that living with one parent was not as good as living with two and, consequently, that children whose parents divorced would be at a distinct disadvantage relative to those whose parents remained married. Over time, however, researchers' ideas about divorce and its impact on adolescents have changed dramatically, as new and better studies have challenged, clarified, and tempered the conclusions of past research. While most social scientists still agree that adolescents from divorced homes have more difficulties than those from nondivorced homes, the explanation for this effect is far more complicated than the conventional wisdom that "Two parents are better than one" or "All children need a mother and a father." Five sets of findings have questioned these simple assertions.

▌ The Effect of Divorce Is Small in Magnitude

First, although divorce clearly diminishes youngsters' well-being, the average effect size is small (Amato & Keith, 1991a), and it is possible in a study with a large sample for a small effect to be statistically significant. Thus, whereas there are statistically significant differences between children from divorced versus nondivorced homes in school achievement, behavior problems, psychosocial adjustment, and family relations—all favoring individuals from nondivorced homes—the absolute difference in the groups' scores is seldom substantial. In general, the effects of divorce tend to be stronger among school-aged individuals than preschoolers or college students. One especially intriguing finding is that the effects of divorce are smaller among youngsters from the United States than among those from other countries. The explanation: Divorce is more common in the United States than abroad; and as a consequence, American children from divorced homes are less likely to be stigmatized and more likely to have access to psychological services, such as counseling, that may attenuate the negative impact of family disruption.

▌ Quality Matters

Second, the quality of the relationships the young person has with the important adults in her or his life matters more than the number of parents present in the home (C. Buchanan, Maccoby, & Dornbusch, 1996; Hines, 1997; Mandara & Murray, 2000; McKeown et al., 1997). Adolescents from stepfamilies, for example, have as many, if not more, problems than those from single-parent homes, even though adolescents in stepfamilies have two parents in the home (P. Allison & Furstenberg, 1989; Hetherington et al., 1999; J. P. Hoffman, 2002; Jeynes, 1999). In addition, youngsters from single-parent families that have not experienced divorce (for example, youngsters who have lost a parent through death, or youngsters with a single mother who never married) have fewer difficulties than their counterparts from divorced or remarried homes (Demo & Acock, 1996). Finally, adolescents in two-parent homes do not always have warm and close relationships with their parents. Indeed, adolescents living in father-absent homes have higher self-esteem than adolescents who live in two-parent homes but who feel that their father has little interest in them (J. Clark & Barber, 1994). In fact, adolescents in divorced, single-parent families describe their parents as friendlier than do adolescents whose parents are married (Asmussen & Larson, 1991) and are in a relatively more positive mood when with their family than when with friends (Larson & Gillman, 1996). Adolescents and their parents argue less often in single-parent households, perhaps because single parents tend to be more permissive, which may make for less parent–adolescent conflict (Smetana, Yau, Restrepo, & Braeges, 1991).

▌ Adaptation to Divorce

Third, it is the process of going through a divorce, not the resulting family structure, that matters most for adolescents' mental health (C. Buchanan et al., 1996; Hetherington, Bridges, & Insabella, 1998). In general, most studies show that the period of greatest difficulty for most adolescents is right around the time of the divorce itself (Jeynes, 2001). Although many young people show signs of difficulty immediately after their parents divorce—problems in school, behavior problems, and increased anxiety—by the time two years have passed, the majority of these children have adjusted to the change and behave comparably to their peers whose biological parents have remained married (Hetherington et al., 1998). Although adolescents whose parents have divorced have, on average, more problems than those whose parents remain married, the vast majority of individuals with divorced parents do not have significant problems (Hetherington et al., 1998).

▌ Conflict and Stress

Fourth, research has linked the adverse consequences of divorce to a number of factors not specifically due to having a single parent (Hetherington et al., 1998). These include the exposure of the children to marital conflict (Amato & Keith, 1991a; Forehand et al., 1991; Vandewater & Lansford, 1998), disorganized or disrupted parenting (Forehand, Thomas, Wierson, Brody, & Fauber, 1990; Hetherington et al., 1992; Shucksmith, Glendinning, & Hendry, 1997), and increased stress in the household, often due to loss of income (Hetherington et al., 1998; Pong & Ju, 2000; Sun & Li, 2002; Thomson, Hanson, & McLanahan, 1994). As you will read, adolescents living in two-parent families in which no divorce has occurred are also harmed by marital conflict, disrupted parenting (especially parenting that is too lenient, too harsh, or inconsistent), and loss of income. In other words, the adverse temporary effects of divorce or remarriage on youngsters' well-being appear to reflect the heightened conflict, disorganization, and stress surrounding the event, not the divorce or remarriage per se. The most important pathway through which divorce may adversely affect adolescent adjustment is via its direct and indirect impact on the quality of parenting to which the child is exposed (Amato & Sobolewski, 2001; Hetherington et al., 1998).

Genetic Influences Finally, although some of the apparent effects of parental divorce are the result of exposure to such stressors as marital conflict or disorganized parenting (S. A. Burt, Barnes, McGue, & Iacono, 2008; Frisco, Muller, & Frank, 2007), some of the differences between adolescents whose parents have divorced and those whose parents have not are due to genetic differences between the teenagers. At least part of the reason that adolescents from divorced homes have more problems than their peers is that they have inherited from their divorced parents some of the same traits that influenced their parents' divorce (O'Connor, Caspi, DeFries, & Plomin, 2000). Adults who divorce are different from those who do not with respect to many traits that have strong genetic origins—such as aggression, antisociality, and predispositions to different sorts of emotional and behavioral problems, like depression—and these traits are passed on from parents to children (D'Onofrio et al., 2006).

Individual Differences in the Effects of Divorce There also are differences among children in how vulnerable they are to the short-term effects of divorce. In general, immediate problems are relatively more common among boys, younger children, children with a difficult temperament, children who do not have supportive relationships with adults outside the immediate family, and youngsters whose parents divorce during childhood or preadolescence as opposed to before or after (Davies & Windle, 2001; K. Rodgers & Rose, 2002).

Studies of Black youth indicate that social support from friends and relatives outside the family may be an especially important resource for inner-city children growing up in single-parent homes (Lamborn & Nguyen, 2004; C. Mason, Cauce, Gonzales, Hiraga, & Grove, 1994; Pallock & Lamborn, 2006; Salem, Zimmerman, & Notaro, 1998; R. Taylor, 1996; R. Taylor & Roberts, 1995). Support from kin, in particular, appears to increase single parents' effectiveness in child rearing, and this, in turn, tends to limit adolescents' misbehavior. This support can come from relatives living apart from, or within, the adolescent's household. For example, several studies of Black youngsters have found that children growing up in home environments that include a grandparent as well as a parent fare significantly better than those growing up in single-parent homes or in stepfamilies. These studies, as well as others, remind us that relatives other than parents may play an extremely important role in adolescents' lives, especially within ethnic groups that historically have placed a great deal of importance on maintaining close ties to extended family members. Single parenthood and extensive contact with the extended family have been salient features of Black family life for more than 100 years (Ruggles, 1994), which may explain why, generally speaking, the relations between adjustment and divorce are generally weaker among Black adolescents

FIGURE 4.9 The effects of exposure to marital conflict are both direct and indirect through its negative impact on parenting.

than among adolescents from other backgrounds (Heard, 2007; Kowaleski-Jones & Dunifon, 2006).

THE SPECIFIC IMPACT OF MARITAL CONFLICT

Although divorce is generally associated with short-term difficulties for the adolescent, several studies show that at least some of the differences between adolescents from divorced versus nondivorced homes were present before the parents divorced (Sun, 2001). In one sample of British youngsters who were followed from birth into adulthood, 7-year-olds whose parents eventually divorced had more educational and behavioral problems than did 7-year-olds whose parents did not divorce (Cherlin, Chase-Lansdale, & McRae, 1998; B. Elliott & Richards, 1991). One explanation for this is that children in the households that later divorced were exposed to higher levels of marital unhappiness and conflict and strained parent–child relationships, both of which are known to increase children's difficulties (Amato & Booth, 1996; Forehand, Neighbors, Devine, & Armistead, 1994) (see Figure 4.9). Children's maladjustment, in turn, adversely affects the quality of their parents' marriage, creating a vicious cycle (Cui, Donnellan, & Conger, 2007).

The recognition that exposure to marital conflict, apart from and in addition to divorce itself, has harmful effects on children's development has prompted many researchers to study why and how the quality of the adolescent's parents' marriage affects teenagers' mental health and behavior (Cui, Conger, & Lorenz, 2005; Erel & Burman, 1995; S. Feldman & Fisher, 1997; Fincham, 1994; Harold & Conger, 1997; M. Rogers & Holmbeck, 1997). Several conclusions have emerged from this research. First, children are more adversely affected by marital conflict when they are aware of it than when it is more covert (S. Feldman & Wentzel, 1995; Harold & Conger, 1997). For this reason, marital conflict is particularly harmful when it is especially hostile, physically violent, or frightening (Buehler et al., 1998; Gordis, Margolin, & St. John, 1997; Harold & Conger, 1997; Osofsky, 1995). Exposure to overt marital conflict and domestic violence has been linked to a wide range of adolescent problems, including depression (especially in girls) and aggression and delinquency (especially in boys) (Davies & Lindsay, 2004; Harold & Conger, 1997; Krishnakumar & Buehler, 1996; H. Sim & Vuchinich, 1996).

Second, children are more negatively affected when the marital conflict leads to feelings of insecurity or self-blame. Adolescents who blame themselves for their parents' conflict, whose feelings of security are challenged, or who are drawn into their parents' arguments are more likely to feel anxious, depressed, and distressed (Buehler, Lange, & Franck, 2007; Buehler & Welsh, 2009; Davies & Cummings, 1994; Grych, Raynor, & Fosco, 2004; Tschann et al., 2002).

Finally, marital conflict more adversely affects the adolescent when the conflict disrupts the quality of the parent–child relationship (Amato & Sobolewski, 2001). Adolescents are directly affected by exposure to their parents' conflict, to be sure, but several studies have found as well that tension between spouses spills over into the parent–child relationship, making mothers and fathers more hostile, more irritable, and less effective as parents (Bradford, Vaughn, & Barber, 2008; Buehler, Benson, & Gerard, 2006; Cui & Conger, 2008; Doyle & Markiewicz, 2005; A. Mahoney, Donelly, Boxer, & Lewis, 2003). As you will read later in this chapter, adolescents who perceive their parents as hostile or uncaring are more likely to report a wide range of emotional and behavioral problems than are their peers.

FOOD FOR THOUGHT

Based on the available research, what advice would you give to parents of teenagers who are considering divorce?

THE LONGER-TERM EFFECTS OF DIVORCE

Social scientists have also looked at the longer-term (more than two or three years) consequences of divorce. These studies, for example, might look at elementary school children whose parents divorced when their child was in preschool, or at adolescents whose parents split up during the youngster's elementary school years. Presumably, if the adverse effects of divorce are solely attributable to the immediate problems of adjusting to a new household structure, or due to exposure to intense marital conflict before and during the divorce, these effects will dissipate within a few years.

Research on the longer-term consequences of parental divorce has yielded very interesting findings. Some studies show that individuals whose parents divorce during preadolescence and adolescence often demonstrate adjustment difficulties later, even after two or three years (e.g., Hetherington, 1993). The problems typically seen in greater frequency among individuals from divorced homes include higher rates of drug and alcohol use, more behavior problems, precocious sexual activity, and poorer school performance (P. Allison & Furstenberg,

1989; Hetherington & Stanley-Hagan, 1995; Sandefur, McLanahan, & Wojtkiewicz, 1992), poorer interpersonal relationships with members of the other sex in late adolescence and young adulthood, including more negative attitudes toward marriage and higher rates of divorce (Summers, Forehand, Armistead, & Tannenbaum, 1998; Tasker & Richards, 1994; Wallerstein & Blakeslee, 1989) and, with the exception of Black and Hispanic males, lower levels of occupational attainment as adults (Amato & Keith, 1991b). Some research indicates that individuals whose parents divorced during childhood or adolescence continue to have adjustment problems well into their 30s (Cherlin et al., 1998). These effects do not appear to be ameliorated by parental remarriage; adolescents from stepfamilies score similarly, or worse, on measures of longer-term adjustment, as do adolescents from single-parent, divorced homes (P. Allison & Furstenberg, 1989; Hetherington et al., 1998).

Sleeper Effects   To what can we attribute these "sleeper" effects—effects of divorce that may not be apparent until much later in the child's development? Two possible explanations come to mind. The first is that the ways in which adjustment difficulties might be expressed may not surface until adolescence. For example, social scientists believe that increased drug use and higher rates of early pregnancy are consequences of the lower level of parental monitoring in divorced homes (e.g., Dornbusch et al., 1985; McLanahan & Bumpass, 1988; M. R. Moore & Chase-Lansdale, 2001). But because younger children—even poorly monitored ones— are unlikely to use drugs or be sexually active, no matter what their family background, the effect of the poor monitoring is not seen until adolescence, when individuals might begin using drugs and having sex.

A second explanation concerns the particular developmental challenges of adolescence (S. J. Steinberg, Davila, & Fincham, 2006). Adolescence is a time when individuals first begin experimenting with intimate sexual relationships. If having one's parents divorce or being exposed to marital conflict affects one's conceptions of relationships or views of romantic commitment (Tasker & Richards, 1994; Woodward, Fergusson, & Belsky, 2000), it makes sense that some of the effects of early parental divorce will not be manifested until the adolescent begins dating and gets seriously involved in romantic relationships. These initial forays into intimate relationships may recall old and difficult psychological conflicts that had remained latent for some time (Wallerstein & Blakeslee, 1989).

CUSTODY, CONTACT, AND CONFLICT FOLLOWING DIVORCE

After a divorce, do adolescents fare better or worse in different kinds of living arrangements? Does contact with the nonresidential parent contribute to the adolescent's well-being?

Studies indicate that it is the nature of the relationship between the adolescent's divorced parents, and not which one he or she lives with, that makes a difference (C. Buchanan et al., 1996; D. Downey, Ainsworth-Darnell, & Dufur, 1998; Hetherington et al., 1998). In the years immediately following a divorce, children may fare a bit better in the custody of the parent of the same sex, but these effects are not long-lasting; over time, both male and female adolescents fare equally well either in dual custody or in the sole custody of their mother (C. Buchanan et al., 1996; Donnelly & Finkelhor, 1992; D. Downey, 1995). More important, especially for adolescents who have dual residences, are two factors: whether the ex-spouses continue to fight and place the child between them, and whether the adolescent's discipline is consistent across the two households. Adolescents whose parents have a congenial, cooperative relationship and who receive consistent and appropriate discipline from both homes report less emotional difficulty and fewer behavioral problems than those whose parents fight or are inconsistent with each other (C. Buchanan et al., 1996; Coiro & Emery, 1996; Donnelly & Finkelhor, 1992; R. Simons, Whitbeck, Beaman, & Conger, 1994).

Adolescents whose parents have divorced also vary in the extent to which they have contact with the parent they no longer live with, typically their father. Generally, contact between adolescents and their father following a divorce diminishes very quickly after the father moves out and continues to decline over time, especially among men who remarry or enter into a new romantic relationship (Stephens, 1996). Generally speaking, adolescents who have regular postdivorce contact with their father have fewer problems (e.g., Coley & Medeiros, 2007; V. King & Sobolewski, 2006), but not all studies have reached this conclusion, and some have concluded that it is healthy adolescent functioning that is influencing fathers' involvement, rather than the reverse (D. N. Hawkins, Amato, & King, 2007). More important than the father's involvement in and of itself may be the level of conflict between the divorced parents and the nature of the adolescent's relationship with the father before the divorce (Amato & Rezac, 1994; Hetherington & Stanley-Hagan, 1995; S. D. Stewart, 2003; Videon, 2002). Adolescents benefit from contact with their nonresidential parent when conflict between their parents is minimal, but suffer from such contact when parental conflict is intense. Similarly, adolescents benefit when they have frequent contact with a nonresidential parent with whom they had a close relationship when their parents were married, but suffer from contact with one with whom they didn't get along prior to the divorce. One consistent finding, though, is that financial support from fathers is associated with less problem behav-

ior and higher academic achievement (Furstenberg, Morgan, & Allison, 1987; Menning, 2002).

▌ What Divorced Parents Tell Their Teenagers

Psychologist Susan Koerner and colleagues have examined the sorts of disclosure that takes place between recently divorced mothers and their children (Koerner, Jacobs, & Raymond, 2000; Koerner, Wallace, Lehman, Lee, & Escalante, 2004). To the researchers' surprise, mothers were equally likely to talk to sons and daughters, and their conversations were similar, consistent with a point made earlier—namely, that for the most part adolescent males and females are treated similarly. Koerner has been especially interested in two topics of conversation: the mother's complaints about and anger toward her ex-husband and the mother's concerns about finances (both common concerns among recently divorced women).

Among mothers who disclosed these sorts of feelings, an important motive for doing so turned out not to be the mother's need for a confidante, but rather her desire to shape her daughter's impression of her and the circumstances surrounding the divorce. Here's one example:

> I talk to her about anything. Complaints I have about her father. [Alison] thinks the divorce is all my fault. Her Dad has been absent for two years. He called on occasion and sent presents on Christmas and B-Days. While he was gone Alison turned him into some sort of God in her mind. Now that he has returned to the area he wants little or nothing to do with his kids. When Alison complains, I make statements like, "Alison, you're starting to see the side of your Dad that I was married to" or "He never gave me any time either." (Koerner et al., 2000, p. 305)

Not all mothers shared their feelings about these topics with their child. As one put it:

> I try really hard not to say anything negative about my ex-husband to my children. We agreed when we got divorced to always do what was best for our children. So far, so good. (Koerner et al., 2000, p. 305)

Consistent with other research indicating that adolescents fare worse when they are drawn into their divorced parents' conflict, adolescents whose mothers complain to them about their ex-husbands or discuss their financial concerns report more psychological distress, in the form of anxiety, depression, tension, and psychosomatic complaints. It's not hard to see why. As several adolescents explained:

> I was thinking, my gosh, my dad doesn't care about me—he's not paying it [child support]! I felt like going and calling my dad and yelling at him because I think he doesn't care about it. (11-year-old daughter, quoted in Koerner et al., 2004, p. 52)

> My mom constantly rags on and on about how my dad is such a jerk and won't pay her as much as she thinks he should. It disturbs me incredibly because my dad is very

Studies show that each time a family goes through a marital transition, such as divorce or remarriage, the adolescent is placed at some risk for minor adjustment difficulties.

kind when I visit him and I don't think my mom is fair. (15-year-old son, quoted in Koerner et al., 2004, p. 52)

My mom talks to me about how we don't have extra money. I don't really like to hear how little money we have.... I feel sad and kinda angry when we talk about money cause before the divorce this topic never, really came up to talk about.... (13-year-old daughter, quoted in Koerner et al., 2004, p. 52)

REMARRIAGE

Adolescents growing up in stepfamilies—especially if the remarriage occurred during early adolescence rather than childhood—often have more problems than their peers, a finding that holds regardless of whether the stepparents are legally married or cohabiting (Hetherington et al., 1999; Manning & Lamb, 2003). For example, youngsters growing up in single-parent homes are more likely than those in intact homes to be involved in delinquent activity, but adolescents in stepfamilies are even more at risk for this sort of problem behavior than are adolescents in single-parent families (Dornbusch et al., 1985; Steinberg, 1987). This results, in part but not entirely, because they are exposed to a "double dose" of marital conflict—normal, everyday conflict between the parent and stepparent and additional conflict between ex-spouses (T. Hanson, McLanahan, & Thomson, 1996; MacDonald & DeMaris, 1995)—and because they are exposed to a new set of potentially difficult issues that arise in the blending of children from two different marriages (Hetherington et al., 1999).

Like the short-term effects of divorce, the short-term effects of remarriage vary among children, although not necessarily in the same ways. In general, girls have more difficulty in adjusting to remarriage than do boys, and older children have more difficulty than younger ones (Hetherington, 1993; V. Lee, Burkham, Zimiles, &

Ladewski, 1994; Needle, Su, & Doherty, 1990; Vuchinich, Hetherington, Vuchinich, & Clingempeel, 1991; Zimiles & Lee, 1991). One explanation for this is that both boys and younger children have more to gain from their mother's remarriage than do girls or older children, who may have become accustomed to having a single mother (Hetherington, 1991). Over time, however, gender differences in adjustment to remarriage disappear, and in remarriages that last more than five years, the adjustment of male and female children is similar (Hetherington et al., 1999). One interesting finding, especially in light of the growing number of young adults who depend on their parents' financial support, is that remarried parents and stepparents are less inclined than other parents to provide money to their children over the transition to adulthood (Aquilino, 2005).

Difficulties Adjusting to Parental Remarriage
Remarriage during the adolescent years may be extremely stressful when families are unable to accommodate the new stepparent relationship. Given what we know about family reorganization and change during adolescence, having to integrate a new type of relationship into a family system that is already undergoing a great deal of change may be more than some families can cope with (Kurdek & Fine, 1993). Many adolescents find it difficult to adjust to a new authority figure moving into the household, especially if that person has different ideas about rules and discipline, and particularly if the new authority figure is not legally married to the child's biological parent (C. Buchanan et al., 1996; Hetherington et al., 1999). This appears to be especially true when the adolescent in question is already somewhat vulnerable, either because of previous psychological problems or because of a recent divorce or other stressful event.

By the same token, many stepparents find it difficult to join a family and not be accepted immediately by the children as the new parent. Stepparents may wonder why love is not forthcoming from their stepchildren, who often act critical, resistant, and sulky (Vuchinich et al., 1991). Although many stepfathers and their adolescent stepchildren establish positive relationships, the lack of a biological connection between stepparent and stepchild—coupled with the stresses associated with divorce and remarriage—may make this relationship especially vulnerable to problems (Hetherington et al., 1999). Adolescents in remarried households fare better when their stepparent can establish a consistent, supportive, authoritative style of discipline (Crosbie-Burnett & Giles-Sims, 1994; C. Henry & Lovelace, 1995; Hetherington et al., 1999).

This research underscores the need—particularly as remarriage becomes a more common part of American family life—to understand the special problems that may arise in the course of family reorganization. Several studies indicate that children's adjustment declines somewhat each time they must cope with a change in their family's household composition (e.g., Adam & Chase-Lansdale, 2002; Albrecht & Teachman, 2003; K. Kim, Conger, et al., 2003; J. B. Kirby, 2006), in part because parenting may become less effective during each family transition (Forgatch, DeGarmo, & Knutson, 1994; Kurdek & Fine, 1993). Given the fact that the benefits of authoritative parenting are just as strong in divorced and remarried families as they are in other homes, experts believe that clinicians who work with families that have undergone marital transitions should help parents learn and adopt this parenting style (Hetherington et al., 1999).

One factor that seems to make a very big difference in the adjustment of children in stepfamilies is the nature of the relationship they have with their noncustodial parent—that is, the biological parent with whom they do not live. Children in stepfamilies fare better when there is consistency in discipline between their custodial and noncustodial parents and when they have a good relationship with the noncustodial parent, especially in the years immediately following the remarriage (E. Anderson, 1992; Bray, Berger, Tiuch, & Boethel, 1993; C. Buchanan & Maccoby, 1993; Gunnoe, 1994). Having a close relationship with the noncustodial parent does not appear to undermine the relationship with the custodial parent (C. Buchanan & Maccoby, 1993), nor does it undermine the relationship between the adolescent and the stepparent (Yuan & Hamilton, 2006). Indeed, studies find that adolescents who feel close to *both* their father and stepfather have better outcomes than those who feel close to one but not the other (V. King, 2006; Risch, Jodl, & Eccles, 2004).

ECONOMIC STRESS AND POVERTY

In recent years, and in light of the recent economic downturn, there has been an upsurge in interest in the relationship between parents' unemployment and adolescents' well-being—in particular, in the ways in which adolescents' mental health is affected by changes in their family's financial situation. To date, the studies of family income loss and adolescent adjustment suggest a number of parallels with the research on divorce and remarriage.

▌ **The Effects of Financial Strain** Like divorce, income loss tends to be associated with disruptions in parenting, which, in turn, lead to increases in adolescent difficulties, including a diminished sense of mastery, increased emotional distress, academic and interpersonal problems, and delinquency (Barrera et al., 2002; R. Conger, Conger, Matthews, & Elder, 1999; Cui, Conger, Bryant, & Elder, 2002; Kloep, 1995). Although males and females alike are adversely affected by their family's economic problems, the pathways through which this occurs may differ between the sexes. For girls, financial difficulty is likely to lead to more demands for maturity and increased responsibility around the house (perhaps to assume some of mother's duties while she works or looks for employment) (Elder, 1974; Flanagan, 1990). This may contribute to their developing more pessimistic expectations about their own occupational futures, since they may find it difficult to envision a satisfying career outside the home (Galambos & Silbereisen, 1987). For boys, in contrast, disruptions in family finances seem to lead to more frequent conflict, especially with fathers (Elder, van Nguyen, & Caspi, 1985; Flanagan, 1990). Boys whose fathers have been laid off may lose respect for them and challenge their authority. The resulting disruption in family functioning may lead to more involvement in problem behavior and heightened irresponsibility.

A series of studies of rural families during the American farm crisis of the 1980s by sociologists Rand Conger and Glen Elder sheds light on some of the processes through which economic strain on the family can adversely affect adolescents' psychological development (R. Conger et al., 1999; R. Conger, Ge, Elder, Lorenz, & Simons, 1994; Elder, Conger, Foster, & Ardelt, 1992; Ge & Conger, 1995) (see Figure 4.10). Financial strain increases mothers' and fathers' feelings of depression, worsens parents' marriages, and causes conflicts between parents and adolescents over money. These consequences, in turn, make parents more irritable, which adversely affects the quality of their parenting. Studies show that parents under economic strain are less involved, less nurturing, harsher, and less consistent in their discipline (McLoyd, 1990).

The family climate created by economic strain puts adolescents at risk for a variety of problems. As you now know, adolescents who are exposed to harsh, uninvolved, and inconsistent parenting are at greater risk for a wide range of psychological and behavioral problems. When adolescents are repeatedly exposed to marital conflict—especially when it is not resolved—they are more likely to become aggressive and depressed (Cummings, Ballard, El-Sheikh, & Lake, 1991). And when adolescents themselves are the recipients of aggressive parenting, they are likely to imitate this behavior in their relationships with siblings (K. Conger, Conger, & Elder, 1994) and peers (S. T. Williams, Conger, & Blozis, 2007), and, later, in their own marriage (Straus & Yodanis, 1996) and with their children (R. Simons, Whitbeck, Conger, & Chyi-In, 1991).

▌ **The Impact of Chronic Poverty** Researchers have also studied the impact on adolescents of growing up amidst chronic economic disadvantage (McLoyd et al., 2009). In general, persistent poverty, like temporary economic strain, undermines parental effectiveness, making mothers and fathers harsher, more depressed, less vigilant, less consistent, and more embroiled in conflict. These consequences all have negative effects on adolescent adjustment, which are manifested in increases in anxiety and depression, more frequent conduct problems, and diminished school performance

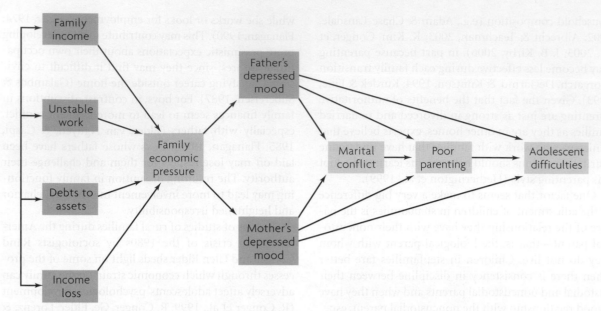

FIGURE 4.10 Economic strain affects adolescent adjustment via several pathways. (Conger et al., 1993)

(R. Conger, Patterson, & Ge, 1995; S. Kim & Brody, 2005; R. Taylor, Rodriguez, Seaton, & Dominguez, 2004; Wadsworth & Compas, 2002).

Interestingly, there appear to be few differences in the behavior, values, or family relationships between adolescents in families that are on welfare and those that are not, calling into question the notion that welfare undermines parental effectiveness, contributes to adolescents' development of undesirable beliefs and values about work, or encourages problem behavior among teenagers (Kalil & Eccles, 1998). At the same time, studies of the impact of requiring women who have been on welfare to enter the labor force find very few effects—positive or negative—on adolescent development or behavior (Chase-Lansdale et al., 2003). Some evidence suggests that adolescents whose mothers have been required to go off public assistance and go to work show somewhat worse school performance as a result, but this effect is most pronounced when the adolescent has a younger sibling, presumably because of the added household responsibilities the mother's employment created for the teenager (Gennetian et al., 2004).

Growing up poor affects adolescents' mental health in a variety of ways. As we discussed in Chapter 3, poor adolescents are more likely to be exposed to violence (Sheidow, Gorman-Smith, Tolan, & Henry, 2001), to feel more alienated from school (Felner et al., 1995), and to be exposed to high levels of stress (Felner et al., 1995; Masten, Miliotis, Graham-Bermann, Ramirez, & Neeman, 1993). Although few scientific studies have been conducted on homeless adolescents, research suggests that these youngsters share many of the same problems with other youth who experience chronic poverty, including higher rates of depression and suicidal thoughts, academic difficulties, and behavior problems (Masten et al., 1993; Unger, Kipke, Simon,

Montgomery, & Johnson, 1997; Whitbeck, Hoyt, & Bao, 2000; Zima, Wells, & Freeman, 1994). An estimated 5% of American adolescents experience at least one night of homelessness each year (Ringwalt, Greene, Robertson, & McPheeters, 1998).

FOOD FOR THOUGHT

Most research on economic conditions, family functioning, and adolescent development has focused on poverty. Do you think there are negative effects of growing up under extreme *affluence*?

Studies of families living in poverty also tell us what parents living in poor neighborhoods can do to help protect their children from the adverse consequences of growing up in poor inner-city or rural neighborhoods (Brody, Stoneman, & Flor, 1996; Early & Eccles, 1994; Elder & Ardelt, 1992; Furstenberg, 1996; Jarrett, 1995). In general, families fare better when they have adequate sources of social support (Mason, Cauce, Gonzales, Hiraga, & Grove, 1994; R. Taylor, 1996; R. Taylor & Roberts, 1995) and when they have strong ties to religious institutions (Brody, Stoneman, Flor, & McCrary, 1994; Brody et al., 1996). In addition, two specific sets of family management strategies employed by parents in poor neighborhoods seem to work: promotive strategies, which attempt to strengthen the adolescent's competence through effective child rearing within the home environment or through involving the child in positive activities outside the home, and restrictive strategies, which attempt to minimize the child's exposure to dangers in the neighborhood (Crosnoe, Mistry, & Elder,

2002; Furstenberg, Cook, Eccles, Elder, & Sameroff, 1999; Jarrett, 1995). Studies indicate that a combination of promotive strategies and moderately (but not overly) restrictive strategies may be especially beneficial to adolescents living in impoverished communities. Although adolescents in poor neighborhoods benefit from consistent parental monitoring—perhaps even from monitoring that is more vigilant than that used by families in more advantaged communities—they do not thrive when their parents exercise excessive control (McCarthy, Lord, Eccles, Kalil, & Furstenberg, 1992).

RECAP

- Four demographic trends that have changed the nature of family life in adolescence have been increases in rates of divorce, single parenthood, remarriage, and poverty.
- Research on divorce indicates that the period of greatest difficulty for adolescents whose parents divorce is the time immediately after the event and that this is largely attributable to the exposure of the child to marital conflict, disrupted parenting, and family stress.
- It is the nature of the relationship between the adolescent's divorced parents, and not which one he or she lives with, that makes a difference.
- Because adolescents' mental health suffers somewhat each time their family situation changes, young people growing up in stepfamilies are at even greater risk for problems than their peers in single-parent, divorced homes.
- Research on economic strain and its impact on adolescents indicates that the main effects of financial stress are transmitted to the adolescent through the negative impact they have on parents' mental health and marital relations.

The Importance of the Family in Adolescent Development

As you have seen, there is considerable diversity among families with adolescents—diversity in background, in income, in parenting style, and in household composition. Yet no factor seems to influence adolescent adjustment more than the quality of relationships at home (Garnefski, 2000). As one team of experts concluded on the basis of a comprehensive study of the lives, behavior, and health of 90,000 American teenagers:

Across all of the health outcomes examined, the results point to the importance of family and the home environment for protecting adolescents from harm. What emerges most consistently as protective is the teenager's feeling of connectedness with parents and family. Feeling loved and cared for by parents matters in a big way. (Blum & Rinehart, 2000, p. 31)

Study after study finds that adolescents who believe their parents or guardians are there for them—caring, involved, and accepting—are healthier, happier, and more competent than their peers, however health, happiness, or competence is assessed. This conclusion holds true regardless of the adolescent's sex, ethnicity, social class, or age, and across all types of families, whether married or divorced, single-parent or two-parent, rich or poor (Dornbusch, Erickson, Laird, & Wong, 2001). This has led many psychologists, including myself, to call for widespread efforts to increase the quality of parenting that children and adolescents receive as a way of preventing emotional and behavioral problems and promoting healthy development (Kumpfer & Alvarado, 2003). As I have written elsewhere, we know what the basic principles of good parenting are (Steinberg, 2005b). The challenge facing us is to figure out how best to disseminate this information to the people who need it most—parents.

Despite the tremendous growth and psychological development that take place as individuals leave childhood on the road toward adulthood, despite society's pressures on young people to grow up fast, despite all the technological and social innovations that have transformed family life, and contrary to claims that parents don't really make a difference—that by adolescence, parents' influence is overshadowed by the peer group or the mass media (e.g., J. R. Harris, 1998)—adolescents continue to need the love, support, and guidance of adults who genuinely care about their development and well-being. Being raised in the presence of caring and committed adults is one of the most important advantages a young person can have in life.

RECAP

- No factor seems to influence adolescent adjustment more than the quality of his or her relationships at home.
- Even after reaching adolescence, young people continue to need the love, support, and guidance of adults who genuinely care about their development and well-being.
- We know what the basic principles of good parenting are. The challenge facing us is to figure out how best to disseminate this information to parents.

Peer Groups

IT IS ABOUT 8:00 A.M. A group of teenagers congregates in the hallway in front of their first-period classroom, discussing their plans for the weekend. As the first-period bell sounds, they enter the classroom and take their seats. For the next 4 hours (until there is a break in their schedule for lunch), they will attend class in groups of about 25 adolescents to 1 adult.

At lunch, the clique meets again to talk about the weekend. They have about 45 minutes until the first afternoon period begins. After lunch, they spend another 2 hours in class—again, in groups of about 25 adolescents and 1 adult. The school day ends, the clique convenes yet again, and they go to someone's house to hang out for the rest of the day. Everyone's parents are working; they are on their own. At about 6:00 P.M., they disperse and head home for dinner. A few will talk on the phone that night. Some will get together to study. And they will see one another first thing the next morning.

Adolescents in modern society spend a remarkable amount of time with their peers. High school students in the United States and Europe spend twice as much of their time each week with peers as with parents or other adults—even discounting time in class (B. Brown & Larson, 2009; Larson & Verma, 1999). Virtually all adolescents spend most of each weekday with their peers while at school, and the vast majority also see or talk to their friends in the late afternoon, in the evening, and over the weekend (Larson & Verma, 1999). And studies show that adolescents' moods are most positive when they are with their friends, that time spent with friends becomes more rewarding over the course of adolescence, and, as Figure 5.1 illustrates, that teenagers' moods become more positive over the course of the week, as the weekend approaches (Larson & Richards, 1991, 1998).

American society is highly age segregated. From the time youngsters stop spending their full day at home—certainly by age 5, but for many, as early as the first year of life if they go to a day care center—until they graduate from high school at age 18 or so, they are grouped with children their own age. Other than relatives, they have little extended contact with people who are older or younger. Because schools play such an important role in determining children's friendships, age grouping carries over into after-school, weekend, and vacation activities. In contemporary society, **peer groups**—groups of people who are roughly the same age—have become an increasingly important context in which adolescents spend time (J. Harris, 1995). Indeed, the rise of peer groups in modern society gives adolescence in contemporary society some of its most distinctive features.

For these reasons, understanding how adolescent peer groups form and what takes place within their boundaries is critical to understanding adolescent development in contemporary society. No discussion of adolescent identity development is complete without an examination of how and why teenagers derive part of their identity from the group they spend time with. No discussion of the development of autonomy is complete without consideration of how adolescents learn to be independent decision makers when they are with their friends. No discussion of intimacy is complete without an understanding of teenagers' cliques and how they are formed. No discussion of adolescent sexuality is complete without an examination of how, and when, peer groups change from same-sex groups to mixed-sex groups. And no discussion of the development of achievement in adolescence can ignore the role that friends play in influencing each other's attitudes toward school.

FIGURE 5.1 As the weekend approaches and adolescents anticipate spending more time with their friends, their mood takes a marked turn for the better. (Larson & Richards, 1998)

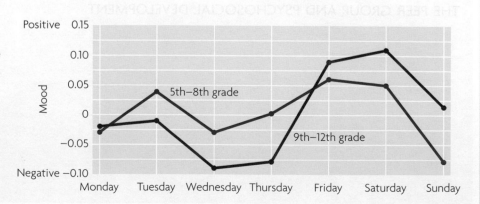

peer groups   Groups of individuals of approximately the same age.

The Origins of Adolescent Peer Groups in Contemporary Society

Contact between adolescents and their peers is found in all cultures, of course. But not all societies have peer groups that are as narrowly defined and age segregated as those in contemporary industrialized societies (B. Brown, 2004; Larson & Verma, 1999).

AGE GRADING AND COMPULSORY EDUCATION

Educators first developed the idea of free public education, with students grouped by age—a practice known as **age grading**—in the middle of the 19th century. Thus, they established an arrangement that would encourage the development and maintenance of age-segregated peer groups. It was not until the second quarter of the 20th century, however, that most adolescents were directly affected by educational age grouping. Attending elementary school may have been common before 1900, but until 1930 or so, high school was a luxury available only to the affluent. In other words, adolescent peer groups based on friendships formed in school were not prevalent until well into the 20th century.

▶ FOOD FOR THOUGHT

Has the increase in the number of adolescents in single-parent households had any impact on the rise of peer groups in modern society?

CHANGES IN THE SIZE OF THE YOUTH POPULATION

Perhaps the most important factor influencing the rise of adolescent peer groups in contemporary society was the rapid growth of the teenage population between 1955 and 1975. Following the end of World War II, many parents wanted to have children as soon as possible, creating what has been called the postwar **baby boom.** The products of this baby boom became adolescents during the 1960s and early 1970s, creating an "adolescent boom" for about 15 years. The size of the population ages 15–19 nearly doubled between 1955 and 1975 and, more importantly, rose from less than 7% of the total population to well over 10%. During the mid-1970s, in fact, more than 1 out of every 6 Americans was a teenager!

This trend turned downward in 1975, and the relative size of the adolescent population decreased until 1995. But during the last decade of the 20th century—when the products of the baby boom began raising adolescents of their own—the size of the teenage population began

Contemporary society is very age-graded. Even when they are in activities outside school, adolescents tend to be with same-aged peers.

increasing once again. In the year 2000, the population of 15- to 19-year-olds in the United States numbered about 20 million. An additional 20 million individuals were between ages 10 and 14 at that time, meaning that as we entered the 21st century, approximately 1 in 7 individuals in the United States were adolescents. The proportion of the U.S. population that is adolescent is estimated to remain at about this level through the next half century (U.S. Census Bureau, 2000). Keep in mind, though, that patterns of change in the size of the adolescent population vary considerably around the world, mainly because of different birthrates.

Social scientists track the size of the adolescent population for several reasons. First, changes in the number of adolescents may warrant changes in the allocation of funds for social services, educational programs, and health care, since adolescents' needs are not the same as those of children or adults. Second, changes in the size of the adolescent population have implications for understanding the behavior of cohorts. A cohort is a group of individuals born during a particular period, such as the baby boomers (born in the late 1940s and early to mid-1950s), "Gen X" (born in the early 1970s), the "Millennial generation" (the adolescent children of the baby boomers, born in the 1980s and early 1990s, also known as "Generation Y"), or "Generation Z" (born during the 1990s, and sometimes referred to as iGeneration, because of the growth of the Internet during their time) (see Table 5.1). Baby boomers, for example,

age grading   The process of grouping individuals within social institutions on the basis of age.

baby boom   The period following World War II, during which the number of infants born was extremely large.

TABLE 5.1 Cohorts, periods, and ages

Cohort Name	Became Young Adults (16–30)	Key Events at That Time	in Census Year											
			1900	1910	1920	1930	1940	1950	1960	1970	1980	1990	2000	2010
Generation Z	2002–2025	Internet explosion												16–24
Millennial generation	1992–2015	Information era: economic growth and global politics											16–24	25–30
Gen X	1982–2005	Reagan era: economic polarization, political conservatism										16–24	25–30	
Late baby boomers	1972–95	Watergate era: economic recession, employment restructuring									16–24	25–30		
Early baby boomers	1962–85	Hippies: social movements, campus revolts								16–24	25–30			
Happy days generation	1952–75	Family and conformity: baby boom and Cold War/McCarthy era							16–24	25–30				
Happy days/greatest generation	1942–65	Family and conformity: baby boom and Cold War/McCarthy era						16–24	25–30					
Greatest generation/children of Great Depression	1932–55	Hard times: economic depression and World War II					16–24	25–30						
Children of Great Depression	1922–45	Hard times: economic depression and World War I				16–24	25–30							
Lost generation	1912–35	World War I and Roaring Twenties, Prohibition			16–24	25–30								
. . .	1902–25	Age of invention and World War I		16–24	25–30									
. . .	1892–1915	Age of invention, urbanization	16–24	25–30										

were members of a very crowded cohort, which meant that during their adolescence, in the late 1960s and early 1970s, they encountered a relatively high degree of competition for places in college, jobs, and so on. The size of this cohort also meant that it could attract a great deal of public attention, from politicians to advertisers. In contrast, members of Gen X, who were adolescents in the late 1980s and early 1990s, were members of a much smaller cohort, with less competition among individuals but also with far less clout. Because Gen Z, today's teenagers, is considerably larger than Gen X, it will likely be much more influential.

RECAP

- In contemporary society, adolescents spend a great deal of time with age-mates, or peers.
- Peer groups are a far more important influence on adolescent development today than in previous eras, when age segregation was not as pervasive.
- Many factors contributed to the rise of peer groups during the 20th century, including the spread of compulsory secondary education and changes in the relative size of various cohorts of adolescents.

Many adults have worried whether there is a distinct youth culture that is counter to mainstream values.

The Adolescent Peer Group: A Problem or a Necessity?

Is the rise of peer groups in modern society a problem that needs to be remedied, or is it an inevitable—perhaps even necessary—part of life in contemporary America? This question has sparked some of the hottest debates in the study of adolescence over the past 25 years (B. Brown & Larson, 2009). On one side are those who claim that age segregation has led to the development of a separate youth culture, in which young people maintain attitudes and values that are different from—even contrary to—those of adults. On the other side are those who argue that industrialization and modernization have made peer groups more important, that adults alone can no longer prepare young people for the future, and that peer groups play a vital role in the socialization of adolescents for adulthood (J. Harris, 1995). Let's look at both sides of the debate.

IS THERE A SEPARATE YOUTH CULTURE?

The belief that age segregation has fueled the development of a separate—and troublesome—youth culture

was first expressed about 50 years ago, by sociologist James Coleman, whose book *The Adolescent Society* (1961) presented the findings of an extensive study of the social worlds of 10 American high schools. Many of Coleman's concerns have echoed repeatedly over the past 5 decades. When adults today complain about the questionable morals and poor character of today's young people, they are saying nothing different from what Coleman and other commentators were asserting in the middle of the 20th century (and what adults said about them, when *they* were teenagers). Indeed, there probably hasn't been a generation of adults that didn't complain about young people.

Coleman worried specifically about the relatively low value adolescents placed on academic success. Although the parents he surveyed felt that academic achievement should be a priority, the adolescents lived in a social world where academic success was frowned on, where doing well in school did not earn the admiration of peers, and where wealth, athletic ability (for boys), and good looks (for girls) mattered most.

One recent team of researchers used a combination of questionnaires, observation, and interviews to see just how much had changed since Coleman's original study, especially in light of the changing ethnic composition of American society (Garner, Bootcheck, Lorr, & Rauch, 2006). They assessed the social climate of seven schools that varied with respect to their size; the ethnic and socioeconomic composition of the student body; and whether they were inner-city, suburban, or semirural. The researchers concluded that there were both similarities and differences between what they found and what Coleman described. The combination of physical attractiveness, athletic ability, and money was still associated with popularity, and middle-class values, supported by parents and teachers alike, were still dominant. Academic success was valued, but an atmosphere of anti-intellectualism prevailed, and doing well in school clearly was not a pathway to popularity, as Coleman and more recent researchers have found (Bishop, 1999; Steinberg, 1996).

Other things were different, though, especially in communities that were not composed mainly of White, middle-class families. In these schools, the student body was fragmented into crowds defined largely by ethnicity and social class; there was often tension among crowds as well as strong opposition to middle-class culture among some crowds. In some senses, the diversification of American society changed the adolescent "society" in similar ways. An important lesson here is that the world of adolescents usually reflects the broader context at that time.

▌ Do Adolescents Inhabit a Separate World?

According to some observers, age segregation has so strengthened the power of the peer group that American adolescents have become alienated from and unfamiliar with the values of adults. In this view, problems such as youth unemployment, teenage suicide, juvenile delinquency, drug and alcohol use, and premarital pregnancy can be attributed to the rise of peer groups and the isolation of adolescents from adults. Many observers of the adolescent scene note that all these problems have increased dramatically since the 1940s, as peer groups have become more prominent and age segregation has become more prevalent (e.g., Bronfenbrenner, 1974). Their argument is that the increase in adolescents' problems can be directly linked to the rise in the power of adolescent peer groups.

As B. Bradford Brown (Brown & Larson, 2009), an expert on adolescent peer groups, has noted, however, the nature and strength of adolescent peer influence varies a great deal from one historical period to the next and from one context to another. One study of Canadian adolescents, for example, found that the majority of students preferred to be remembered as outstanding students (rather than as great athletes or popular adolescents), and other studies have found that students' preferences for how they will be remembered vary a great deal by sex, age, and their place in the social structure of the school (B. Brown, 1990).

▌ Has the Youth Culture Harmed Adolescents?

These cautions notwithstanding, it is obvious that peers play a more important role in the lives of adolescents in modern society than they did in previous eras. But has the rise of adolescent peer groups really caused so many problems?

This question is very difficult to answer. While age segregation certainly has increased over the past 60 years,

society has changed in other ways during this same time—ways that may also have contributed to increases in such problems as crime and drug use. In many regards, the world is a far more stressful place to grow up in now than it was in the past. Families move every few years. Divorce is commonplace. Adolescents experience enormous pressures from parents, peers, and the mass media (Meyer, 1994). More importantly, as you will read in later chapters, rates of many adolescent problem behaviors—crime and drug use are good examples—have fluctuated considerably over the past three decades, but there has not been a reversal of the trend toward age segregation. If age segregation were the "true" cause of adolescents' problems, this would not be the case.

To be sure, contemporary adolescents spend more time in peer groups than adolescents did in past eras. But we do not know if today's young people are any more susceptible to the influence of their friends than their counterparts were previously, nor do we know if teenagers are any worse off because peer groups have come to play a more prominent role. Moreover, adolescents exert both positive and negative influences on each other, and it is simply incorrect to describe the peer group as a monolithic, negative influence (B. Brown, 2004). Peer pressure is a mixed blessing: On the one hand, most teenagers feel that their friends are likely to pressure them *not* to use drugs or to engage in sexual activity, but adolescents report a good deal of pressure to drink, and very few adolescents report that their friends pressure them to do well in school (B. Brown, Clasen, & Eicher, 1986; Steinberg, 1996).

But this debate about whether peer groups are a good or bad thing may be moot. Peer groups are inevitable by-products of modernization. Some theorists even have suggested that peers have become essential to the transmission of cultural information (J. Harris, 1995).

THE NEED FOR PEER GROUPS IN MODERN SOCIETY

The family is a less influential institution today than it was in the past. In less industrialized societies, political, economic, and social institutions revolve around the family. Occupation, choice of spouse, place of residence, treatment under the law, and participation in community governance are all tied to who one's relatives are. Individuals' family ties determine with whom they can trade and how much they pay for various commodities. In short, how adults are expected to behave depends on which family they come from.

▌ Particularistic Versus Universalistic Norms

Because not all adults are expected to behave in the same manner in these kinship-based societies and therefore have to learn somewhat different sets of norms, it is not possible to educate or socialize all young people in one large group. Norms for behavior that vary from person to person are called **particularistic norms.** In societies in which norms are particularistic, grouping adolescents by age and sending them off to school is not an effective strategy for socializing them for adulthood, since their family background, not their age, determines what their rights and responsibilities are. The socialization of adolescents in kinship-based societies is best accomplished in family groups, where elders can pass on the family's particular values and norms to their younger relatives.

In contemporary societies, things are different. Generally, all individuals are expected to learn the same set of norms, because the rules governing behavior apply equally to all members of the community. These norms are called **universalistic norms.** Whom you may marry, what kind of work you do, where you live, and how you are treated under the law are not based on family lineage. The norms that apply to you apply to everyone.

Under these circumstances, it is not wise to limit the socialization of adolescents to the family, because doing so does not ensure that all youngsters will learn the same set of norms (J. Harris, 1995). In societies that require individuals to learn universalistic norms, it is more efficient to group by age all the individuals who are to be socialized (Eisenstadt, 1956). Teaching is better done in schools than left up to individual families. One of the reasons we have driver education classes, for example, is that our rules for driving are universalistic—the same for everyone—and we need to make sure that individuals learn a common set of regulations, not simply the ones their parents teach them.

As the family has become a less important political and economic institution, universalistic norms have come to replace particularistic ones. And this has required a change in the way in which adolescents are prepared for adulthood. Not only has modernization created age groups, but it has also made them absolutely necessary. Without some kind of age grouping in schools, it would be impossible to prepare young people for adulthood.

FOOD FOR THOUGHT

Can you think of examples from your own experience that support the argument that age-graded peer groups are a necessary, even beneficial, influence on adolescent development? Has this had any effect on relationships between adolescents and adults?

RECAP

- Social scientists have long debated whether the prominent role played by peer groups in the socialization of young people is a cause for concern or celebration.
- Some commentators have suggested that the rise of peer groups has contributed to the development of a separate youth culture that is hostile toward adult values. Others point to the necessary and valuable educational role played by peer groups in rapidly changing societies like ours.
- Peer groups are especially important in societies that are governed by universalistic norms, where individuals are educated mainly outside the family.

The Nature of Adolescent Peer Groups

CHANGES IN PEER GROUPS DURING ADOLESCENCE

Visit any elementary school playground, and you will see that peer groups are an important feature of the social world of childhood. But even though peer groups exist well before adolescence, during the teenage years they change in significance and structure. Four specific developments stand out (B. Brown, 1990; B. Brown & Larson, 2009).

▌ **In What Ways Do Peer Groups Change?** First, as noted earlier, there is a sharp increase during adolescence in the sheer amount of time individuals spend with their peers and in the relative time they spend in the company of peers versus adults. If we count school as a setting in which adolescents are mainly with agemates, well over half of the typical American adolescent's waking hours are spent with peers, as opposed to only 15% with adults—including their parents (a good deal of the remaining time is spent alone or with a combination of adults and age-mates). Indeed, during the transition into adolescence, there is a dramatic drop in the amount of time adolescents spend with parents; for boys, this is mainly replaced by time spent alone, whereas for girls, it is replaced by time alone and time with friends (see Figure 5.2) (Larson & Richards, 1991). There

particularistic norms Guidelines for behavior that vary from one individual to another; more commonly found in less industrialized societies.

universalistic norms Guidelines for behavior that apply to all members of a community; more common in industrialized societies.

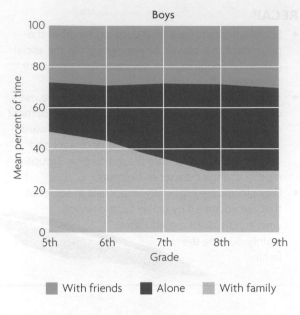

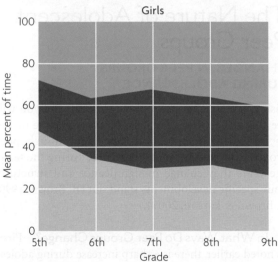

FIGURE 5.2   There are significant changes in how individuals spend leisure time during early adolescence. (Larson & Richards, 1991)

are important ethnic and gender differences in patterns of time use, however. For example, the decline in time spent with family members and the dramatic increase in time spent with peers in early adolescence are more striking among White girls than among boys or Black youth (Larson, Richards, Sims, & Dworkin, 2001).

Second, during adolescence, peer groups function much more often without adult supervision than they do during childhood, partly because adolescents are more mobile and partly because they seek, and are granted, more independence (B. Brown, 1990). Groups of younger children typically play in the presence of adults or in activities organized or supervised by adults (for example,

sex cleavage   The separation of boys and girls into different cliques, common during late childhood and early adolescence.

Little League or Brownies), whereas adolescents are granted far more independence. A group of teenagers may go off to the mall or the movies on their own or congregate at the home of someone whose parents are absent.

Third, during adolescence, increasingly more contact with peers is with other-sex friends. During childhood, peer groups are highly sex segregated, a phenomenon known as **sex cleavage.** This is especially true of peer activities of children in school and other settings organized by adults, although somewhat less so of their more informal activities, such as neighborhood play (Maccoby, 1990). During adolescence, however, an increasingly larger proportion of an individual's significant others are other-sex peers, even in public settings (B. Brown, 2004).

Finally, whereas children's peer relationships are limited mainly to relatively small groups—at most, three or four children at a time, for example—adolescence marks the emergence of larger collectives of peers, or crowds. In junior high school cafeterias, for example, the "popular" crowd sits in one section of the room, the "brains" in another, and the "druggies" in a third (see Eder, 1985). These crowds typically develop their own minicultures, characterized by particular styles of dressing, talking, and behaving. Studies show that it is not until early adolescence that individuals can confidently list the various crowds in their schools and reliably describe the stereotypes that distinguish the different crowds from one another (B. Brown, Mory, & Kinney, 1994).

■ **What Causes Peer Groups to Change?**   These changes in peer relations have their origins in the biological, cognitive, and social transitions of adolescence. Puberty, as we have seen, stimulates adolescents' interest in other-sex relationships and serves to distance them from their parents, which helps to explain why adolescents' social networks increasingly include more other-sex peers and fewer adults. The cognitive changes of adolescence permit a more sophisticated understanding of social relationships, an understanding that may allow the sort of abstract categorization that leads to grouping individuals into crowds. And changes in social definition may stimulate changes in peer relations as a sort of adaptive response: The larger, more anonymous social setting of the secondary school, for instance, may force adolescents to seek out individuals whom they perceive as having common interests and values, perhaps as a way of re-creating the smaller, more intimate groups of childhood (B. Brown, 2004). Instead of floundering in a large, impersonal high school cafeteria, the adolescent who belongs to the "cheerleader" crowd, or even the "nerds," may head directly for her or his place at a familiar table.

CLIQUES AND CROWDS

To better understand the significance of peer relations during adolescence, it is helpful to think of adolescents'

Adolescents usually belong to at least one clique, a close group of about a half dozen friends, usually of the same age and sex.

peer groups as organized around two related, but different, structures (B. Brown & Larson, 2009). **Cliques** are small groups of between 2 and 12 individuals—the average is about 5 or 6—generally of the same sex and, of course, the same age. Cliques can be defined by common activities (for example, the "drama" group or a group of students who study together regularly) or simply by friendship (e.g., a group of girls who have lunch together every day or a group of boys who have grown up together). The importance of the clique, whatever its basis, is that it provides the main social context in which adolescents interact with one another. The clique is the social setting in which adolescents hang out, talk to each other, and form close friendships. Some cliques are more open to outsiders than others (that is, the members are less "cliquish"), but virtually all cliques are small enough that the members feel they know each other well and appreciate each other more than people outside the clique do (B. Brown & Larson, 2009).

■ **How Cliques Structure Social Networks** One study of the structure, prevalence, and stability of cliques among 9th-graders in five different high schools within a large American school district illustrated the ways in which cliques structure adolescents' friendship networks (Ennett & Bauman, 1996). Based on interviews with students over a 1-year period, the researchers categorized adolescents as *clique members* (individuals

who have most of their interactions with the same small group of people), *liaisons* (individuals who interact with two or more adolescents who are members of cliques, but who themselves are not part of a clique), and *isolates* (individuals who have few or no links to others in the network). Three interesting patterns emerged. First, despite the popular image of adolescents as "cliquish," fewer than half the adolescents in any school were members of cliques. Second, girls were more likely than boys to be members of cliques, whereas boys were more likely than girls to be isolates (see also Urberg, Değirmencioğlu, Tolson, & Halliday-Scher, 1995). Finally, adolescents' positions in their school's social network was relatively stable over time: Adolescents who were members of cliques in the 9th grade were clique members in 10th grade; 9th-grade isolates remained, for the most part, isolates one year later. This does not mean that the composition of specific cliques is stable—typically, it is not—only that individuals who were members of some clique at one point of time were members of some clique 1 year later. In other words, there is stability in adolescents' tendency to join cliques, but not in the makeup of particular groups (B. Brown, 2004). In one study, about 75% of seventh-graders were members of cliques and about 15% were isolates; very

cliques Small, tightly knit groups of between 2 and 12 friends, generally of the same sex and age.

few were liaisons or connected to just one other adolescent in a dyad (A. M. Ryan, 2001). Not surprisingly, the more recently a student has arrived at a school, the less "well connected" he or she is likely to be; developing a social network is especially hard on students whose families move frequently (South & Haynie, 2004).

▎**How Adolescents Sort Into Crowds** Cliques are quite different in structure and purpose from crowds. **Crowds** are based on "the identification of adolescents who share a similar image or reputation among peers, or who have a common feature such as ethnicity or neighborhood, even if they do not consider each other friends or spend much time interacting with each other" (B. Brown, 2004). In contemporary American high schools, typical crowds include "jocks," "brains," "nerds," "populars," and "druggies." The labels for these crowds may vary from school to school ("nerds" versus "geeks," "populars" versus "preps"), but their generic presence is commonplace, at least in the United States, Canada, Australia, and, with the exception of the "jock" crowd, most western European countries (Arnett, 2002; Delsing, ter Bogt, Engels, & Meeus, 2007). (The jock crowd is seldom found in European schools because athletic events are typically organized around clubs located in the community rather than school teams.) If you grew up in one of these countries, you can probably recognize these different types of crowds from your own school experience. In contrast to cliques, crowds are not settings for adolescents' intimate interactions or friendships but instead serve three broad purposes: to locate adolescents (to themselves and to others) within the social structure of the school, to channel adolescents into associations with some peers and away from others, and to provide contexts that reward certain lifestyles and disparage others (B. Brown, Dolcini, & Leventhal, 1995; B. Brown & Larson, 2009; B. Brown, Mory, & Kinney, 1994).

Membership in a crowd is based mainly on reputation and stereotype, rather than on actual friendship or social interaction. This is very different from membership in a clique, which, by definition, hinges on shared activity and friendship. In concrete terms, and perhaps ironically, an adolescent does not have to actually have "brains" as friends, or hang around with "brainy" students, to be one of the "brains." If he dresses like a "brain," acts like a "brain," and takes honors courses, then he is a "brain" as far as his crowd membership

goes. The images adolescents have of various crowds in their schools are often highly stereotyped and caricatured, and adolescents tend to inflate the positive qualities of their own crowd while exaggerating the negative qualities of others (Mory, 1992).

The fact that crowd membership is based on reputation and stereotype can be very difficult for individual adolescents, who—if they do not change their reputation early on in high school—may find themselves stuck, at least in the eyes of their peers, in a crowd that they do not wish to belong to (or that they do not see themselves as a part of) (B. Brown, Freeman, Huang, & Mounts, 1992). This also means that some individuals can be members of more than one crowd simultaneously, if their reputation is such that they fit into them (B. Brown, 2004; Mory, 1994). According to recent estimates, close to half of high school students are associated with one crowd, about one third are associated with two or more crowds, and about one sixth do not clearly fit into any crowd (B. Brown, 2004). Although an adolescent's closest friends are almost always members of the same clique, some of them may belong to a different crowd, especially when one crowd is close in lifestyle to the other (Urberg et al., 1995). Thus, for example, a "brain" will have some friends who are also "brains" and some who are "nerds" but few, if any, who are "druggies" (B. Brown et al., 1994).

More importantly, crowds are not simply clusters of cliques; the two different structures serve entirely different purposes. Because the clique is based on activity and friendship, it is the important setting in which the adolescent learns social skills—how to be a good friend, how to communicate effectively, how to be a leader, how to enjoy someone else's company, or even how to break off a friendship that is no longer satisfying. In contrast, because crowds are based more on reputation and stereotype than on interaction, they probably contribute more to the adolescent's sense of identity and self-conception—for better and for worse—than to his or her actual social development.

CHANGES IN CLIQUE AND CROWD STRUCTURE OVER TIME

Studies of the structure of adolescents' peer groups often make use of a research technique called **participant observation.** In this approach, the researcher establishes rapport with a group of individuals in order to infiltrate and eventually join the group. In *Inside High School* (Cusick, 1973), which, incidentally, provided much of the material for the movie *Fast Times at Ridgemont High,* the author pretended to be a newcomer to the community and attended high school for a year to learn more about the adolescents' social world. As an observer who is also a participant, the researcher can observe the group's behavior under conditions that are

---

crowds Large, loosely organized groups of young people, composed of several cliques and typically organized around a common shared activity.

participant observation A research technique in which the researcher "infiltrates" a group of individuals in order to study their behavior and relationships.

more natural and more private than would otherwise be the case. Overhearing a 10-minute conversation in a high school locker room often can be more informative than interviewing a student for 3 hours.

How Romance Changes the Peer Group

Observational studies of young people indicate that there are important changes in the structure of cliques and crowds during the adolescent years, driven in large measure by the increased importance of romantic relationships (e.g., Connolly, Furman, & Konarski, 2000; Kuttler & La Greca, 2004). During early adolescence, adolescents' activities revolve around same-sex cliques. Adolescents at this stage are not yet involved in "partying" and typically spend their leisure time with a small group of friends, playing sports, talking, or simply hanging out.

Somewhat later, as boys and girls become more interested in one another romantically—but before romantic relationships actually begin—boys' and girls' cliques come together. This is clearly a transitional stage. Boys and girls may go to parties or hang out together, but the time they spend there actually involves interaction with peers of the same sex. When young teenagers are still uncomfortable about dealing with members of the other sex, this setting provides an opportunity in which they can learn more about other-sex peers without having to be intimate and without having to risk losing face. It is not unusual, for example, at young adolescents' first mixed-sex parties, for groups of boys and girls to position themselves at other sides of a room, watching each other but seldom interacting.

The peer group then enters a stage of structural transformation. As adolescents become interested in romance, part of the group begins to split off into mixed-sex cliques, while other individuals remain in the group but in same-sex cliques. This shift is usually led by the clique leaders, with other clique members following along. For instance, a clique of boys whose main activity is playing basketball may discover that one of the guys they look up to has become more interested in going to mixed-sex parties Saturday nights than in hanging out with the guys and playing video games. Over time, they will begin to follow his lead, and their all-male activities will become more infrequent. A recent observational study of middle-school dances over the course of the academic year found that the integration of boys' and girls' peer groups increased over time, but that this occurred mainly among physically attractive adolescents (no surprise, because being good-looking contributes to status in the peer group) (see Figure 5.3) (Pellegrini & Long, 2007).

During middle adolescence, mixed-sex and mixed-age cliques become more prevalent, and in time, the peer group becomes composed entirely of mixed-sex cliques (Cooksey, Mott, & Neubauer, 2002). One

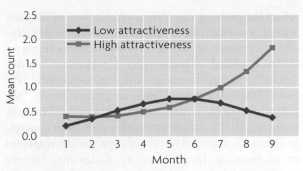

FIGURE 5.3 Intermingling of boys' and girls' peer groups increases during early adolescence, but it starts first among physically attractive adolescents, who often are clique leaders. Mean count = mean number of interactions with other-sex peer groups. (Pellegrini & Long, 2007)

clique might consist of the drama students—male and female students who know each other from acting together in school plays. Another might be composed of four girls and four boys who like to drink on weekends. The preppies—male and female—might make up a third.

Finally, during late adolescence, peer crowds begin to disintegrate. Pairs of adolescents who see themselves as couples begin to split off from the activities of the larger group. The larger peer group is replaced by loosely associated sets of couples. Adolescents begin to shift some of their attention away from friends and toward romantic partners (Kuttler & La Greca, 2004). Groups of couples may go out together from time to time, but the feeling of being in a crowd has disappeared. This pattern—in which the couple becomes the focus of social activity—persists into adulthood.

When viewed from a structural point of view, the peer group's role in the development of intimacy is clear. Over time, the structure of the peer group changes, in keeping with adolescents' changing needs and interests. As we'll see in Chapter 10, the adolescent's capacity for close relationships develops first through friendships with peers of the same sex. Only later does intimacy enter into other-sex relationships. Thus, the structure of the peer group changes during adolescence in a way that parallels the adolescent's development of intimacy: As the adolescent develops increasing facility in intimate relationships, the peer group moves from the familiarity of same-sex activities to contact with other-sex peers, but mainly in the safety of the larger group. It is only after adolescent males and females have been slowly socialized into dating roles—primarily by modeling their higher-status peers—that the safety of numbers is no longer needed and adolescents begin pairing off.

Changes in Crowds

There also are changes in peer crowds during this time. Many of these changes reflect the growing cognitive sophistication of the adolescent. For example, as adolescents mature intellectually, they come to define crowds more in terms of abstract, global characteristics ("preppies," "nerds," "jocks") than in terms of concrete, behavioral features ("the ballet crowd," "the Play Station crowd," "the kids who play basketball on 114th Street") (O'Brien & Bierman, 1988). As you know, this shift from concrete to abstract is a general feature of cognitive development in adolescence. In addition, as adolescents become more cognitively capable, they become more consciously aware of the crowd structure of their school and their place in it (B. Brown, 2004).

Over the course of adolescence, the crowd structure also becomes more differentiated, more permeable, and less hierarchical, which allows adolescents more freedom to change crowds and enhance their status (B. Brown, 2004; Horn, 2003). For example, in a study of peer crowds in one small Midwestern city, the researcher found that over the course of adolescence, the crowd structure shifted between middle school, early high school, and late high school (Kinney, 1993). During middle school, there was a small in-group ("trendies") and a larger out-group ("dweebs"). During early high school, there was one high-status crowd ("trendies"), two other socially acceptable crowds ("headbangers" and "normals"), and two less desirable groups ("grits" and "punkers"). And during late high school, the status differences among "trendies," "normals," and "headbangers" were negligible, and "hybrid" crowds (for example, "grit-headbangers") were common. This change over time permitted some individuals who were low in status during middle school to "recover" during high school.

▌ The Transformation of the Nerds

In one fascinating study of the day-to-day experiences of "nerds" and their interactions with other students, sociologist David Kinney conducted an **ethnography** of the social interaction and peer culture in a high school in a small Midwestern city. In contrast to survey or experimental research, which is typically quantitative in nature (that is, the data collected can be quantified), ethnographic research is qualitative. The researcher spends a considerable amount of time observing interactions within the setting, interviewing many adolescents, and writing up field notes, much as an anthropologist would do in studying a foreign culture. Ethnographic approaches can be extremely useful in studying social relationships, because they provide rich, descriptive data.

Here, for example, is an excerpt of an interview Kinney conducted with two students who had been "nerds" in middle school:

Ross: And middle school—

Ted: We were just nerds. I mean—

Ross: Yeah—

Ted: People hated us.

Ross: Well, they didn't hate us, but we weren't—

Ted: Popular. Which was either you were popular or you weren't.

Ross: In middle school it's very defined. There's popular people and unpopular people. It's just very—rigid. You were popular or unpopular. That's it.

Ted: And there wasn't people that were in between.

Ross: Oh no!

Ted: You just had one route [to becoming popular], and then there was the other. And we were the other, and—basically you were afraid of getting laughed at about anything you did because if you did one thing that was out of the ordinary, and you weren't expected to do anything out of the ordinary, then you were laughed at and made fun of, and you wouldn't fit the group at all, and then, of course, you were excluded and then you didn't even exist.

Ross: You got "nuked," so to speak. (Kinney, 1993, p. 27)

Kinney discovered, however, that many individuals who had been "nuked" in middle school had managed to transform themselves from "nerds" into "normals" sometime during high school. For some, this transition was accomplished because the high school peer structure was more differentiated and more permeable. As opposed to middle school, where there were only two groups—the popular and the unpopular—in high school, there were more socially acceptable groups with which to affiliate. For others, the transition to "normal" came about through gains in self-assurance that came with physical and social development. And for still others, the transformation was facilitated by the development of a more cognitively sophisticated, confident view of the social hierarchy—one that permitted them to reject the premise that whatever the "trendies" valued was necessarily desirable.

In essence, the transformation of "nerds" to "normals" was enabled by a combination of factors both within the context (for example, the increasing differentiation and permeability of the peer crowd system) and within the adolescent (for example, the physical, cognitive, and social maturation of the individual)

---

ethnography A type of research in which individuals are observed in their natural settings.

(B. Brown, 1996). Kinney's study, as well as other ethnographies of peer groups, reminds us of the potential for growth and change during the adolescent years, even for individuals who begin the period at a social disadvantage.

■ **The Waxing and Waning of Crowds**   As crowds become more salient influences on adolescents' view of their social world, they come to play an increasingly important role in structuring adolescent social behavior (B. Brown & Larson, 2009). By 9th grade, there is nearly universal agreement among students in a school about their school's crowd structure, and students' assessment of the strength of peer group influence is very high. Between 9th and 12th grades, however, the significance of the crowd structure begins to decline, and the salience of peer pressure wanes.

In one study, students were presented with several scenarios asking if it was all right to exclude someone from a school activity (cheerleading, basketball, student council) because the person was a member of a certain crowd ("jock," "gothic," "preppie") (Horn, 2003). They were also asked whether it was acceptable to deny individuals resources (for example, a scholarship) on the basis of their crowd membership. Consistent with the decline in the salience of peer crowds between mid- and late adolescence, 9th-graders were more likely to say that excluding someone from an activity on the basis of his or her crowd was all right. Students of all ages agreed that it was less acceptable to deny students resources because of crowd membership (which virtually all students viewed as immoral) than to exclude them from an activity (which was less often seen as a moral issue).

As we'll see in Chapter 9, this pattern of an increase and then a decline in the salience of peer crowds parallels developmental changes in adolescents' susceptibility to peer pressure. In other words, as crowds become more important between early and middle adolescence in defining the teenager's social world, the individual becomes more likely to accede to their influence. As crowds become less important, however, between middle and late adolescence, their influence over the individual's behavior weakens as well (B. Brown, 2004). Most probably, the interplay between changes in the importance of the crowd and changes in adolescent's susceptibility to peer influence is reciprocal.

Just as the changes in the structure of cliques play a role in the development of intimacy during adolescence, changes in the salience of crowds over the adolescent years play an important role in adolescent identity development. In Chapter 8, we'll see that adolescence is frequently a time for experimentation with different roles and identities. During the early adolescent years, before adolescents have "found" themselves, the crowd provides an important basis for self-definition (B. Newman & Newman, 2001). By locating themselves within the crowd structure of their school—through style of dress, language, or choice of hangouts—adolescents wear "badges" that say "This is who I am." At a time when adolescents may not actually know just who they are, associating with a crowd provides them with a rudimentary sense of identity.

As adolescents become more secure in their identity as individuals, the need for affiliation with a crowd diminishes. Indeed, by the time they have reached high school, older adolescents are likely to feel that remaining a part of a crowd stifles their sense of identity and self expression (Larkin, 1979). The breakup of the larger peer group in late adolescence may both foreshadow and reflect the emergence of each adolescent's unique and coherent sense of self (B. Brown & Larson, 2009).

FOOD FOR THOUGHT

Think back to your own high school experience. What were the major crowds in your school? What common characteristics did you share with the people who were in your clique?

RECAP

- As individuals move into adolescence, there is an increase in the amount of time they spend in the exclusive company of their peers, their peer groups function increasingly outside adult supervision, and they spend more time with other-sex peers.

- Social scientists distinguish between crowds and cliques. Cliques are small groups of friends; crowds, in contrast, are larger and more vaguely defined groups that are based on reputation.

- Cliques, which begin as same-sex groups of individuals, gradually merge to form larger, mixed-sex groups, as adolescents develop romantic relationships and start socializing with peers of the other sex. In late adolescence, these groups begin to break down, as adolescents' social lives start to revolve more around couple-based activities.

- Crowds, which peak in importance during mid-adolescence, become more differentiated and more permeable during high school, and their influence becomes less salient.

Adolescents and Their Crowds

THE SOCIAL MAP OF ADOLESCENCE

Although we often hear people talk about a monolithic "youth culture," most ethnographic studies of high schools indicate that the social world of adolescents is far more multifaceted than this. One helpful scheme for mapping the social world of adolescent crowds was suggested by Rigsby and McDill (1975) and later modified by Brown (1990).

According to this model, adolescents' crowds can be placed along two dimensions: how involved they are in the institutions controlled by adults, such as school and extracurricular activities, and how involved they are in the informal, peer culture (see Figure 5.4). "Jocks" and "populars," for example, are quite involved in the peer culture, but they are also very involved in the institutions valued by adults (sports and school organizations, for example). "Brains" and "nerds," in contrast, are also involved in adult-controlled organizations (in their case, academics), but they tend to be less involved in the peer culture. "Partyers" are on the opposite side of the map from "nerds": These adolescents are very involved in the peer culture but are not involved in adult institutions. "Toughs" and adolescents who are members of delinquent gangs are not involved in either the peer culture or adult institutions. Other crowds, such as "normals" or "druggies," fall somewhere between these extremes.

CROWDS AS REFERENCE GROUPS

Knowing where an adolescent fits into the social system of the school can often tell us a lot about the individual's behavior and values. This is because crowds contribute to the definition of norms and standards for such things as clothing, leisure, and tastes in music. Being a "jock" means more than simply being involved in athletics; it means wearing certain types of clothes, listening to certain types of music, spending Saturday nights in certain hangouts, and using a particular slang. These adolescents accept many of the values of the adults around them but also value many elements of the contemporary peer culture.

Another way of putting this is that adolescents' crowds serve as **reference groups.** They provide their members with an identity in the eyes of other adolescents. Adolescents judge one another on the basis of the

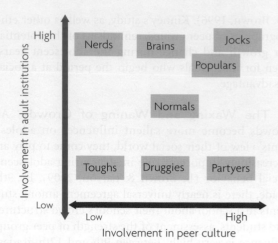

FIGURE 5.4   A model for mapping the social world of adolescent peer groups. (From Brown, 1990)

company they keep, and they become branded on the basis of whom they hang out with. Such labels as "jocks," "brains," "populars," "druggies," and "skaters" serve as shorthand notations—accurate or inaccurate—to describe what someone is like as a person and what he or she holds as important.

FOOD FOR THOUGHT

Think back on your own adolescent experience. What crowd were you in? Did you change crowds, or do you know someone who did? How was this accomplished? Do you know anyone who tried to change crowds but failed? Why did this happen?

▮ Crowd Membership and Adolescent Identity

Crowd membership is important not only because crowds are used by adolescents when talking about one another but also because membership in a crowd is often the basis for an adolescent's own identity (B. Brown & Larson, 2009). A girl who runs with the "preppies" identifies herself as such by wearing their "uniform," shopping in their stores, and speaking their language. After a while, preppiness becomes part of her own self-concept; she wouldn't think of dressing or talking any other way. Or consider the boys whose clique is held together by a dislike of school. Since this attitude toward school is continuously reinforced by the clique, each boy's feelings about school become strengthened, and not liking school becomes part of each boy's identity. Even if something very positive happens at school, it becomes difficult for someone in the clique to admit

reference groups   A group against which an individual compares him- or herself.

that it makes him feel good about himself. Doing well on a test or receiving a compliment from a teacher is likely to be dismissed as unimportant.

Because the adolescent's peer group plays such an important role as a reference group and a source of identity, the nature of the crowd with which an adolescent affiliates is likely to have an important influence on his or her behavior, activities, and self-conceptions (Prinstein & La Greca, 2002; Sussman et al., 1994). Although most adolescents feel pressure from their friends to behave in ways that are consistent with their crowd's values and goals, the specific nature of the pressure varies from one crowd to another. "Druggies" report much more peer pressure to misbehave, for example, than "jocks" (Clasen & Brown, 1985). Crowd membership can also affect the way adolescents feel about themselves. Adolescents' self-esteem is higher among students who are identified with peer groups that have relatively more status in their school. In one study of high schools, the "jocks" and "socies" were highest in status, and the "druggies" and "toughs" were lowest. Students who were identified with the higher-status groups had higher self-esteem than did those who were identified with the lower-status groups (B. Brown & Lohr, 1987). One recent study similarly found that over the course of adolescence, symptoms of psychological distress declined among the "populars" and "jocks" but increased among the "brains" (Prinstein & La Greca, 2002). Interestingly, adolescents whose peers identify them as members of low-status crowds fare better psychologically when they don't see themselves this way, but the opposite is true for adolescents whose peers label them as members of high-status crowds, where denying one's affiliation with the crowd is associated with worse mental health (B. Brown, Von Bank, & Steinberg, 2008). Of course, the longer-term consequences of crowd membership during adolescence are not necessarily the same as their immediate impact. One study that examined the young-adult outcomes of high school crowd membership found that both "brains" and "jocks" showed the most favorable patterns of psychological adjustment over time (Barber, Eccles, & Stone, 2001). Not surprisingly, individuals who had been members of antisocial peer groups fared the worst.

In multiethnic high schools, peer groups often divide along ethnic lines.

■ **Ethnicity and Crowd Membership**   Some research indicates that at least some of the basic distinctions among crowds that have been found in studies of predominantly White high schools (for example, academically oriented crowds, partying crowds, deviant crowds, trendy crowds) also exist among adolescents from ethnic minority groups (B. Brown & Mounts, 1989). There is evidence, however, that in multiethnic high schools adolescents may first divide across ethnic lines and then form into the more familiar adolescent crowds within ethnic groups. Thus, in a large multiethnic high school, there may be separate groups of Black "jocks" and White "jocks," of Hispanic "populars" and Black "populars," and so on (Steinberg et al., 1996). Interestingly, in multiethnic schools, adolescents from one ethnic group are less likely to see crowd distinctions within other ethnic groups than they are within their own group. Thus, to White students, all Asian adolescents are part of the "Asian" crowd, whereas the Asian students see themselves as divided into "brains," "populars," and other groups (B. Brown & Mounts, 1989).

There is also reason to believe that the meaning associated with belonging to different crowds may vary among ethnic and socioeconomic groups, although this varies considerably from school to school (Tyson, Darity, & Castellino, 2005). Although one widely cited study reported that high-achieving Black students are ostracized for "acting White" (Fordham & Ogbu, 1986), many studies do not find this to be typical (e.g., Horvat & Lewis, 2003; Tyson et al., 2005). In many schools, *all* students who are highly committed to school, regardless of their ethnicity, are teased or excluded for being "nerds" or "brains." Similarly, in some schools it may be admirable to be a "jock," while in others it may be frowned upon. Thus, the values we associate with being in one crowd as opposed to another may not be constant across all school contexts.

RECAP

- Although the specific crowd names may differ from one school to another, and from one ethnic group to the next, most high schools have relatively similar crowd structures, with some version of "jocks," "populars," "brains," "nerds," and "toughs."

- Adolescents' crowds can be mapped on two distinct dimensions: how involved they are in adult institutions, such as school, and how involved they are in the peer culture.

- Because they often serve as reference groups, crowds play an important role in the adolescent's identity development.

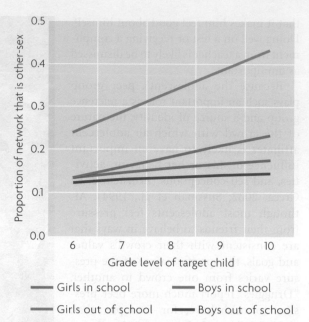

FIGURE 5.5   Over time, there is a dramatic increase in the number of boys from other schools who are members of girls' social networks. (Poulin & Pedersen, 2007)

Adolescents and Their Cliques

What draws adolescents into one clique and not another? Because cliques serve as a basis for adolescents' friendships and play an important role in their social development, many researchers have studied the determinants of clique composition.

SIMILARITY AMONG CLIQUE MEMBERS

The most important influence on the composition of cliques is similarity. Adolescents' cliques typically are composed of people who are of the same age and the same ethnicity, from the same socioeconomic background, and—at least during early and middle adolescence—the same sex (Ennett & Bauman, 1996).

▌ **Age Segregation**   Age grouping in junior and senior high schools makes it unlikely that an individual will have friends who are substantially older or younger. A 10th-grader who is enrolled in 10th-grade English, 10th-grade math, 10th-grade history, and 10th-grade science simply does not have many opportunities to meet adolescents who are in different grades. Age segregation in adolescents' cliques does, indeed, appear to result mostly from the structure of schools (Shrum, Cheek, & Hunter, 1988). When an adolescent's friends come from a different school, those friends are just as likely to be younger or older as to come from the same grade (Blyth, Hill, & Thiel, 1982). It is also the case that adolescents' online friends are less similar in age than the friends they make in school (Mesch & Talmud, 2007).

▌ **Sex Segregation**   During the early and middle adolescent years, cliques also tend to be composed of adolescents of the same sex (Ennett & Bauman, 1996). This sex cleavage begins in childhood and continues through most of adolescence, although it is stronger among White students than among Black students (Filardo, 1996; Sagar, Schofield, & Snyder, 1983), and it weakens later in adolescence (Shrum et al., 1988).

The causes of sex segregation in adolescents' cliques are more interesting than the causes of age segregation, because schools seldom separate boys and girls into different classes. Why, then, do adolescent males and females separate themselves into different cliques? Psychologist Eleanor Maccoby, an expert on gender and development, has suggested several reasons (Maccoby, 1990).

First, cliques are formed largely on the basis of shared activities and interests. Generally, preadolescent and early adolescent boys and girls are interested in different things. Not until adolescents begin dating do boys' cliques and girls' cliques mix, presumably because dating provides a basis for common activity. Consistent with this, a recent study of adolescents' social networks found that the proportion of other-sex friends more than doubles between 6th and 10th grades (Poulin & Pedersen, 2007). And, in keeping with the notion that this coincides with the onset of dating, the increase is especially notable among early-maturing girls, whose networks increasingly include somewhat older boys that they know outside of school (see Figure 5.5). Even so, by 10th grade, most adolescents' social networks are still dominated by same-sex friends, who make up about three quarters of the average teenager's network.

A second reason for the sex cleavage in adolescent peer groups concerns young adolescents' sensitivity about sex roles. Over the course of childhood, boys and girls become increasingly concerned about behaving in ways judged to be sex-appropriate. When boys show an interest in dolls, they are often told either explicitly (by parents, friends, and teachers) or implicitly (by television, books, and other mass media), "Little boys don't play with dolls—those are for girls." And when girls start wrestling or roughhousing, they are often similarly reprimanded.

As a consequence of these continual reminders that there are boys' activities and girls' activities, early adolescents—who are trying to establish a sense of identity—are very concerned about acting in sex-appropriate ways, although this is more true of boys than girls (Galambos, Berenbaum, & McHale, 2009). This makes it very difficult for an adolescent boy to be a part of a girls' clique, in which activities are likely to revolve around clothing, grooming, and talking about boys, or a girl to be part of a boys' clique, in which activities are likely to be dominated by athletics and other physical pursuits (Schofield, 1981). Adolescents who go against prevailing sex-role norms by forming friendships with members of the other sex may be teased about being "fags" or may be ostracized by their peers because they are "perverts." (Interestingly, gay male adolescents typically have more cross-sex friendships than same-sex friendships [Diamond & Dube, 2002].) Ironically, once dating becomes the norm, adolescents who *don't* have relationships with peers of the other sex become the objects of equally strong suspicion and social rejection.

▌ **Social Class Segregation**   One of the most important studies ever undertaken of adolescents' peer groups is *Elmtown's Youth* (Hollingshead, 1949/1975). In this study of adolescents in the Midwestern community of "Elmtown," sociologist August Hollingshead examined the relation between the social position of adolescents' families and the composition of teenagers' cliques. He was interested in determining whether adolescents' cliques were segregated along class lines.

Hollingshead found that adolescents associate chiefly with peers from the same social class. More than 60% of "close" friendships in Elmtown High School were between teenagers from the same background. Of the remaining clique relationships, the vast majority were between adolescents of adjacent social classes (for example, between middle-class and upper-middle-class adolescents). Almost never did adolescents from one social class associate with students from a class that was two ranks higher or lower. Hollingshead found similar patterns when he looked at adolescents' best friends and dating relationships: Rarely were social class lines crossed, and, when they were, it was virtually always between adolescents of adjacent classes. Moreover, adolescents became even more class conscious as they got older.

Adolescents are more likely to have friends from the same ethnic group than from the same socioeconomic background.

Several studies conducted since *Elmtown's Youth* have confirmed the enduring importance of social class in influencing adolescents' positions in the peer network of the high school. In the five-school study of cliques discussed earlier, for example, cliques were just as class segregated as they were found to be by Hollingshead many decades earlier. Within each clique, about 60% of adolescents came from the same social class, even though each school was considerably more diverse in its social class composition as a whole (Ennett & Bauman, 1996). Clique-based friendships between adolescents who were from very different social backgrounds were seldom observed.

▌ **Ethnic Segregation**   Ethnicity is not a strong determinant of clique composition during childhood, but like social class, it becomes increasingly powerful as youngsters get older, at least within the United States (Shrum et al., 1988). By middle and late adolescence, adolescents' peer groups typically are ethnically segregated, with very few ethnically mixed cliques present in most high schools (Ennett & Bauman, 1996). This appears to be the case, although somewhat less so, even within schools that have been desegregated. One study of a multiethnic New York City public high school found, for example, that nearly three quarters of the Latino students, two thirds of the Black students, and 85% of the Asian students had friends who were predominantly from the same ethnic group (Way & Chen, 2000). In fact, cross-ethnic friendships are less common in ethnically diverse schools than in schools where one ethnic group predominates (Moody, 2001; Quillian & Campbell, 2003).

A recent analysis of data from a large, nationally representative sample of adolescents found that ethnicity

FIGURE 5.6   Black students report increasingly more discrimination by other students over time, whereas it declines among Latino students. Asian American students report the highest level of peer discrimination. (Greene et al., 2006)

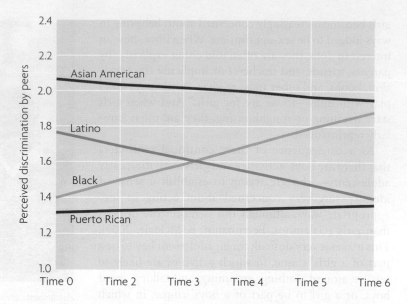

continues to be an enormously powerful determinant of friendship patterns—far more powerful than socioeconomic status (Quillian & Campbell, 2003). The rift between Black students and students from all other ethnic groups, especially Whites and Asians, is especially strong, and Black students' reports of being discriminated against by other students increase over time (although Asian students report the highest degree of discrimination by peers) (see Figure 5.6) (Greene, Way, & Pahl, 2006; Qin, Way, & Mukherjee, 2008). In fact, despite the social class segregation discussed earlier, adolescents are more likely to have friends of the same ethnicity who come from the opposite end of the socioeconomic spectrum than to have friends from the same social class but a different ethnic group. Studies of whether cross-ethnic friendships are more common among Asian and Hispanic adolescents who are American born than among their peers who are immigrants have found that immigrants are less likely to have cross-ethnic friendships, perhaps because of language barriers (Hamm, Brown, & Heck, 2005). But even among ethnic minority youth whose families have been in the United States for generations, there still exists a strong preference for same-ethnicity friends (Quillian & Campbell, 2003). Parents appear to influence this preference, as indicated by a recent study of Mexican American adolescents which found that adolescents were more likely to have non-Mexican friends when their parents were themselves more strongly oriented toward Anglo culture (Updegraff, McHale, Whiteman, Thayer, & Crouter, 2006). The social climate of the school likely matters as well: Feelings of discrimination often drive ethnic minority students into peer crowds that are defined by ethnicity (B. Brown, Herman, Hamm, & Heck, 2008).

It is difficult to know why such strong ethnic segregation persists in adolescents' friendship selection. We know that ethnic segregation in adolescents' cliques is only partly due to residential segregation (Mouw & Entwisle, 2006). One strong possibility is that some ethnic segregation in friendship patterns is due to differential levels of academic achievement of adolescents from different ethnic groups (Hamm et al., 2005). As you'll read in Chapter 12, on average, White and Asian adolescents earn significantly higher grades in school than do Black or Hispanic adolescents (Steinberg, Dornbusch, & Brown, 1992). Adolescents who are friends usually have similar attitudes toward school, similar educational aspirations, and similar school achievement levels (B. Brown, 2004). Ethnic differences in school achievement therefore may lead to ethnic separation in adolescent peer groups (Hallinan & Williams, 1989). Cross-ethnic friendships are more rare, for instance, in schools that frequently separate students into different academic tracks (Stearns, 2004).

A second reason for ethnically segregated peer groups—according to one study of adolescents in a recently desegregated school—is attitudinal. In this school, the White adolescents perceived their Black peers as aggressive, threatening, and hostile. The Black students, in turn, saw the White students as conceited, prejudiced, and unwilling to be friends with them. These perceptions, which fed on each other, made the formation of interracial peer groups unlikely. The more the White students believed that the Black students were hostile, the more the White students acted distant and kept to themselves. But the more the White students acted this way, the more likely the Black students were to feel rejected, and the more hostile they became. In general, White students are less apt to initiate contact with Black students and to select them as friends than vice versa (Quillian & Campbell, 2003). In many schools, adolescents' lack of familiarity with youngsters from other ethnic groups results in misperceptions of the others' attitudes and motives, and this misunderstanding limits cross-ethnic interaction (Schofield, 1981). This finding also has been reported in recent studies of Arab and Jewish students in Israel (Pitner, Astor, Benbenishty, Haj-Yahia, & Zeira, 2003).

One way out of this cycle of misunderstanding is to bring youngsters from different backgrounds together from an early age, before they have had time to build up prejudices and lock onto stereotypes. Interracial school busing, for example, has been far more successful in communities that began such programs during elementary school than in districts that implemented them for the first time at the high school level. If children grow up together from an early age, they are less likely to misunderstand each other and less likely to split off into separate peer groups purely on the basis of ethnicity.

FOOD FOR THOUGHT

As you now know, the ethnic composition of the American adolescent population is changing dramatically. What impact, if any, might this have on friendship patterns?

Indeed, one study of Canadian adolescents indicated that ethnic segregation in adolescent peer relationships is far less common in Canada than in the United States (Maharaj & Connolly, 1994). According to the researchers, one reason for this is that the broader cultural context in Canada is more supportive of multicultural tolerance and more aggressive in its approach to multicultural education and ethnic integration.

Of course, not all adolescents have especially strong preferences for friends from the same ethnic background. One comparison of two Chinese immigrant girls in a U.S. high school illustrates this point nicely (Shih, 1998). One of the girls, Christine, had a strong preference for friends who not only were Chinese but were Chinese immigrants as well. Although she initially was open-minded about having friends who were not Chinese, she came to feel psychologically distant from them—to feel that she had little in common with them and that they made fun of her speech and behavior. Denise, in contrast, was eager to become Americanized and went out of her way to acquire the slang, customs, and attitudes of mainstream adolescent culture. She saw having non-Chinese friends as a way of facilitating her Americanization and actively sought them for this reason.

COMMON INTERESTS AMONG FRIENDS

Thus far, we have seen that adolescents' cliques are usually composed of individuals who are the same age, in the same grade, from the same social class, and of the same ethnicity. But what about factors beyond these? Do adolescents who associate with one another also share certain interests and activities? Generally, they do. Three factors appear to be especially important in determining adolescent clique membership and friendship patterns: orientation toward school, orientation toward the teen culture, and involvement in antisocial activity (Crosnoe & Needham, 2004; Tolson, Halliday-Scher, & Mack, 1994).

■ **Orientation Toward School** Adolescents and their friends tend to be similar in their attitudes toward school, in their school achievement, and in their educational plans (Wentzel & Caldwell, 1997), although this tends to be more true among White and Asian adolescents than among Black adolescents (Hamm, 2000). Adolescents who earn high grades, study a great deal, and plan to go on to college usually have friends who share these characteristics and aspirations. One reason for this is that how much time students devote to schoolwork affects their involvement in other activities. Another is that students' friendships are often drawn from the peers with whom they have classes, and if schools track students on the basis of their academic achievement, their friends will be more likely to have similar records of school performance (Crosnoe, 2002). Someone who is always studying will not have many friends who stay out late partying, because the two activities conflict. By the same token, someone who wants to spend afternoons and evenings out having fun will find it difficult to remain friends with someone who prefers to stay home and study.

Students also may influence each other's academic performance. One analysis found, for instance, that girls' decisions about whether to take advanced math classes were significantly influenced by the course-taking decisions of their friends (K. A. Frank et al., 2008). Friends exert a similar influence on GPA: Given two students with similar records of past achievement, the student whose friends do better in school is likely to achieve more than the one whose friends do worse (J. Epstein, 1983). Similarly, adolescents whose friends are disruptive in school tend to become more disruptive over time (Berndt & Keefe, 1995). Indeed, of all the characteristics of friends that influence adolescents' behavior, their friends' school performance has the greatest impact, not only on their own academic achievement, but also on their involvement in problem behavior and drug use (T. Cook, Deng, & Morgano, 2007).

■ **Orientation Toward the Teen Culture** Adolescents and their friends generally listen to the same type of music, dress alike, spend their leisure time in similar types of activities, and share patterns of drug use (B. Brown & Larson, 2009). It would be very unlikely, for example, for a "jock" and a "druggie" to be part of the same clique, because their interests and attitudes are so different. In most high schools, it is fairly easy to see the split between cliques—in how people dress, where they eat lunch, how much they participate in the school's activities, and how they spend their time outside of school. Indeed, similarity in patterns of substance use is such a strong influence that it often serves as the basis for forming cross-ethnic group friendships, which, as we noted earlier, are not common (Hamm, 2000).

Involvement in Antisocial Activity A number of studies, involving both boys and girls from different ethnic groups, indicate that antisocial, aggressive adolescents may gravitate toward each other, forming deviant peer groups (Cairns, Cairns, Neckerman, Gest, & Gariepy, 1988; Dishion, Patterson, Stoolmiller, & Skinner, 1991; Espelage, Holt, & Henkel, 2003; Kiesner, Cadinu, Poulin, & Bucci, 2002; Kiesner & Pastore, 2005; Kreager, 2004). That is, contrary to the popular belief that antisocial adolescents do not have friends or that they are interpersonally inept, these youngsters do have friends, but their friends tend to be antisocial as well. Although adolescents with deviant friends show some of the same emotional problems as adolescents without friends, those with deviant friends, not surprisingly, are less lonely than their friendless peers (Brendgen, Vitaro, & Bukowski, 2000).

Although we would not necessarily want to call all of these peer groups "delinquent," since they are not always involved in criminal activity, understanding the processes through which antisocial peer groups are formed provides some insight into the development of delinquent peer groups, or gangs. **Gangs** are antisocial peer groups that can be identified by name (often denoting a neighborhood or part of the city) and common symbols ("colors," tattoos, hand signs, jewelry, etc.) (Branch, 1995; M. Harris, 1994; Winfree, Bäckström, & Mays, 1994). Adolescents who belong to gangs are at greater risk for many types of problems in addition to antisocial behavior, including elevated levels of psychological distress, exposure to violence, and violent victimization (X. Li et al., 2002; T. J. Taylor, Peterson, Esbensen, & Freng, 2007). This is also true for female adolescents who hang around with male gangs, which increases their involvement in high-risk sexual behavior, drug use, and crime. Here is one girl's description of another girl's rape, taken from a recent study of Mexican American females who associated with gang members in San Antonio:

> She was already drunk when she came to the party. I think she was 17, but I'm not too sure. She was a new girl. She didn't know nothing about the Brothers [male gang]. She didn't know nothing at all, nothing about gangs, drugs. All she knew about was drinking, and drinking, and drinking, and that's it.

The Brother, he just took her to a bedroom. He was telling her that he wanted to show her something. She went up to the room after he told her that he had a diamond ring for her. So she went upstairs. He put alcohol on some rag and covered her face. That's all I heard. My homeboy said just go home, and I went. He told me that he didn't want nothing to happen to me, and I just went home. (Cepeda & Valdez, 2003, p. 99).

Are adolescent gangs merely a peer group whose focus is on antisocial activity, or do they have unique characteristics? Research indicates that gangs both resemble and differ from other sorts of peer groups. On the one hand, as one study of Mexican American female gang members points out, adolescent gangs look much like other types of adolescent cliques, in that they are groups of adolescents who are similar in background and orientation, share common interests and activities, and use the group to derive a sense of identity (M. Harris, 1994). One study of Latino youth in Southern California found that it was especially important to differentiate between gangs, which were organized and had long histories of involvement in serious antisocial behavior, and "crews," which also engaged in fighting, tagging, and partying, but which did not engage in serious violence (Lopez, Wishard, Gallimore, & Rivera, 2006). This distinction has important legal ramifications, because anti-gang laws that mandate tougher penalties for crimes committed by gangs may be incorrectly applied to adolescents who commit delinquent acts with their friends (or crew) but who are not members of gangs.

It is also the case that the processes that lead adolescents to join gangs are not the same as those that lead to membership in crews and other sorts of peer groups. Gang members tend to be more isolated from their family, to have more emotional and behavioral problems, and to have poorer self-conceptions than other adolescents, including those who are involved in antisocial activity but who are not gang members (Dukes, Martinez, & Stein, 1997; Esbensen, Deschenes, & Winfree, 1999; Harper & Robinson, 1999). In addition, a study of Puerto Rican male adolescents from New York City suggests that the actual relationships that antisocial adolescents have with their cliquemates may be less satisfying than are those between other adolescents and their friends (Pabon, Rodriguez, & Gurin, 1992). Although these antisocial peers spent a great deal of time together, they did not describe their relationships as emotionally close or intimate. Rather, most of the boys felt estranged from each other. As the researchers point out, this finding has implications for the design of interventions aimed at controlling delinquency by involving antisocial peer groups in positive activities; in the absence of their shared interest in antisocial activities, delinquent peers may have little reason to maintain their friendship.

gangs   Organized peer groups of antisocial individuals.

▌ **The Role of Parents**   According to several studies (Dishion et al., 1991; Garnier & Stein, 2002; Scaramella, Conger, Spoth, & Simons, 2002; Tolan, Gorman-Smith, & Henry, 2003), the process of antisocial peer group formation in adolescence begins in the home, during childhood. Problematic parent–child relationships—ones that are coercive and hostile—lead to the development of an antisocial disposition in the child, and this disposition contributes, in elementary school, to both school failure and rejection by classmates (Dishion et al., 1991; Pardini, Loeber, & Stouthamer-Loeber, 2005). Rejected by the bulk of his classmates, the aggressive boy "shops" for friends and finds that he is accepted only by other aggressive boys. Once these friendships are formed, the boys, like any other clique, reward each other for participating in a shared activity—in this case, antisocial behavior. Interestingly, improvements in parenting during adolescence reduce teenagers' association with antisocial peers, which, in turn, reduces problematic behavior (R. Simons, Chao, Conger, & Elder, 2001).

The family and peer contexts are connected through other processes as well. As psychologist Nina Mounts has pointed out (2004, 2007), parents often "manage" their adolescent's friendships by monitoring the individuals their child spends time with, guiding their child toward peers they like, prohibiting contact with peers they dislike, and supporting friendships they approve of (Tilton-Weaver & Galambos, 2003). Parents also act as "consultants," helping their teenagers work out problems with their friends. Adolescents whose parents act as consultants in this way are less likely to be involved in drug use and delinquent activity and report more positive relationships with their friends (Mounts, 2004). Rather than viewing the family and peer contexts as separate worlds, it is important to keep in mind that what takes place in one setting often has an impact on what occurs in others.

The role of the family in friendship choice has also been described in studies of crowds (B. Brown, Mounts, Lamborn, & Steinberg, 1993; Curtner-Smith & MacKinnon-Lewis, 1994; C. Mason, Cauce, Gonzales, & Hiraga, 1996; Melby, 1995). One of the factors that influences the crowd an adolescent belongs to is her or his upbringing. Parents play a role in socializing certain traits in their children, and these orientations, whether toward aggression or academic achievement, predispose adolescents toward choosing certain friends or crowds with which to affiliate. Once in these cliques or crowds, adolescents are rewarded for the traits that led them there in the first place, and these traits are strengthened. One problem with accounts of adolescent development that posit the peer group as more important than the family (e.g., J. R. Harris, 1998) is that they fail to take into account the fact that the family has a strong effect on adolescents' choice of peers.

For example, a child who is raised to value academics will perform well in school and will likely select friends who share this orientation. Over time, these friends will reinforce the youngster's academic orientation and strengthen his or her school performance. By the same token, antisocial adolescents, who are drawn toward other antisocial peers, become more antisocial over time as a result (Vitaro, Tremblay, Kerr, Pagani, & Bukowski, 1997). Even when adolescents have relatively more antisocial friends, having better relationships at home and a stronger attachment to school will make them less susceptible to their friends' negative influence—even in the context of a gang (Crosnoe, Erickson, & Dornbusch, 2002; Vitaro, Brendgen, & Tremblay, 2000; Walker-Barnes & Mason, 2004).

The finding that adolescents become more antisocial when they spend time with antisocial peers has prompted some experts to question the wisdom of group-based interventions for adolescents with conduct problems (Dishion, McCord, & Poulin, 1999). Several studies of programs designed to diminish adolescents' delinquency or aggression, for example, have found that, instead of having the desired effect, the programs actually increased participants' problem behavior; that is, they had what scientists call iatrogenic effects (Mahoney, Stattin, & Lord, 2004). **Iatrogenic effects** are the undesirable consequences of well-intentioned treatments—for example, when the side effects of a medication are far worse than the problem it is intended to treat. When antisocial adolescents spend time with like-minded peers, they frequently teach each other how to be "more effective" delinquents and reward each other for misbehavior. One observational study of adolescent friends talking to each other on camera (Piehler & Dishion, 2007) found that individuals who had a history of involvement in antisocial behavior engaged in more spontaneous conversation about antisocial activities and rewarded each other in the way they responded (e.g., "We were so wasted last Friday." "Oh, yeah, that was great!" "Remember the time we stole that vodka?" "That was so awesome!"). Several writers have described this process as "deviancy training" (e.g., Capaldi, Dishion, Stoolmiller, & Yoerger, 2001; Dishion, Nelson, Winter, & Bullock, 2004). Knowing that group treatments for antisocial behavior have iatrogenic effects is obviously important for the design of programs for delinquent and aggressive youth.

SIMILARITY BETWEEN FRIENDS: SELECTION OR SOCIALIZATION?

Because antisocial activities seem to be such a strong determinant of clique composition, many adults have expressed concern over the influence of peers in the promotion of delinquent activity and drug and alcohol

iatrogenic effects   Unintended adverse consequences of a treatment or intervention.

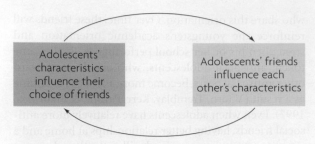

FIGURE 5.7 Adolescents' choice of friends both influences and is influenced by their traits and interests.

use. Parents often feel that if their youngster runs with the wrong crowd, he or she will acquire undesirable interests and attitudes. They express concern, for instance, when their child starts spending time with peers who seem to be less interested in school or more involved with drugs. But which comes first—joining a clique or being interested in a clique's activities? Do adolescents develop interests and attitudes because their friends influence them in this direction, or is it more the case that people with similar interests and tastes are likely to become friends?

This question has been examined in several large-scale studies that have tracked adolescents and their friendships over time (e.g., Curran, Stice, & Chassin, 1997; Dobkin, Tremblay, Mâsse, & Vitaro, 1995; Ennett & Bauman, 1994; Mounts & Steinberg, 1995; Poulin, Dishion, & Haas, 1999). By tracing patterns of attitudinal and behavioral change over time, and comparing these shifts with patterns of friendship formation and change, the researchers could determine whether adolescents are attracted to one another because of their initial similarity (what social scientists refer to as *selection*), whether they become similar because friends influence each other (what is referred to as *socialization*), or a combination of the two (Kandel, 1978).

In general, studies indicate that both selection and socialization are at work (see Figure 5.7) across a variety of attitudinal and behavioral domains, including school achievement, drug use, mental health, and delinquency (B. Brown & Larson, 2009), and in romantic relationships as well as friendships (Simon, Aikins, & Prinstein, 2008). Adolescents who use alcohol or tobacco, for example, are more likely to choose other alcohol or tobacco users as friends, especially when they attend schools with a large number of substance-using students (an example of selection). By the same token, spending time with friends who use these substances increases the adolescents' own use as well (an example of socialization) (Bryant & Zimmerman, 2002; H. Cleveland & Wiebe, 2003; Ennett et al., 2006; Urberg, Değirmencioğlu, & Pilgrim, 1997). The more substance-using friends an adolescent has, and the closer he or she feels to them, the more the adolescent is likely to use alcohol and drugs (Ennett et al., 2006; Hussong &

Hicks, 2003). Similarly, adolescents who report more depressive symptoms are likely to choose other depressed adolescents as friends, which, in turn, negatively affects their own mood and that of their friends (Baker, Milich, & Manolis, 1996; Hogue & Steinberg, 1995; E. A. Stevens & Prinstein, 2005). Adolescents who are bullies are more likely to have friends who themselves are bullies (Espelage, Holt, & Henkel, 2003). Conversely, antisocial adolescents who have few friends, and few aggressive friends in particular, are likely to become less antisocial over time (Adams, Bukowski, & Bagwell, 2005; Botvin & Vitaro, 1995), whereas those with antisocial friends who become even more antisocial themselves become more delinquent (Monahan, Steinberg, & Cauffman, 2009; Werner & Silbereisen, 2003).

How much of adolescents' similarity to their friends is due to selection and how much is due to socialization? The answer depends on what and who is being studied. Peer influence (socialization) is far stronger over day-to-day preferences in things like clothing or music than over many of the behaviors that adults worry about, such as binge drinking or risky sex (Jaccard, Blanton, & Dodge, 2005). Selection may be a somewhat stronger factor as far as delinquency and gang membership are concerned (Dobkin et al., 1995; R. A. Gordon et al., 2004; Haynie & Osgood, 2005; Selfhout, Branje, & Meeus, 2008), whereas selection and socialization are about equally influential when it comes to drug use (Curran et al., 1997; Dishion & Owen, 2002; Ennett & Bauman, 1994). Peer influence on antisocial behavior is generally stronger among White adolescents than in other cultural groups (C. S. Chen, Greenberger, Lester, Dong, & Guo, 1998).

One recent analysis of a data from a large, nationally representative sample of adolescents found that adolescents' friendship groups fall into one of four profiles: high functioning (a network of high-achieving friends who were involved in school-based extracurricular activities and who reported low use of alcohol and few symptoms of depression), maladjusted (friends showed the opposite pattern), disengaged (friends were not engaged in much of anything, including drinking), and engaged (friends were engaged in school, achieved decent grades, and neither abstained from nor abused alcohol) (Crosnoe & Needham, 2004). More importantly, an individual adolescent's behavior could be predicted on the basis of her or his friendship group's profile. Adolescents' socioeconomic background and family situation were strongly related to characteristics of their friendship network, with teenagers from more educated, two-parent families more likely to fall into the high-functioning and engaged groups.

Stability of Adolescent Friendships   How stable are adolescents' friendships over time? In general, adolescents' cliques show only moderate stability over the course of the school year—with some members staying in the clique, others leaving, and new ones joining—although cliques become more stable later in high school (Cairns, Leung, Buchanan, & Cairns, 1995; Değirmencioğlu, Tolson, & Urberg, 1993). Although the actual composition of adolescents' cliques may shift over time, the defining characteristics of their cliques or their best friends do not (Hogue & Steinberg, 1995; Luo, Urberg, & Rao, 1995; Neckerman, Cairns, & Cairns, 1993). That is, even though some members of an adolescent's clique may leave and be replaced by others, the new members are likely to have attitudes and values that are quite similar to the former members' (B. Brown, 2004). Even "best friendships" are likely to change during the school year. One study found that only about one third of students who were best friends in the fall of a school year named the same person as their best friend in the spring, although that person was typically listed as a friend (Değirmencioğlu et al., 1993; Değirmencioğlu, Urberg, Tolson, & Richard, 1998). Only half of all reciprocated best friendships (in which each person names the other as a best friend) that exist at the beginning of a school year exist at the end; surprisingly, remaining friends over the course of a school year has nothing to do with the quality of the friendship (Bowker, 2004).

RECAP

- Cliques are small groups of adolescents who are friends and who see each other regularly.
- Unlike crowds, cliques play an important role in the development of social skills and intimacy.
- Generally, adolescents form cliques with peers who are similar in family and ethnic background, in orientation toward school and the peer culture, and in their level of involvement in antisocial activities.
- Although clique members influence each other's behavior and values, research also shows that adolescents initially select their friends on the basis of similarity.
- Adolescents may change friends, but they rarely change the type of people they are friends with.

Popularity and Rejection in Adolescent Peer Groups

Thus far, our discussion has focused on how and why crowds and cliques serve as the basis for adolescents' social activities. But what about the internal structure of

peer groups? Within a clique or a crowd, what determines which adolescents are popular and which are not?

DETERMINANTS OF POPULARITY AND REJECTION

In recent years, psychologists have changed their thinking about what it is that leads to popularity during adolescence. Although it is widely agreed that popular adolescents are generally more socially skilled than their unpopular peers, there is surprising variability among popular teenagers with respect to other characteristics. One reason for this is that there are two forms of popularity, and they don't always go hand in hand (B. Brown & Larson, 2009). One form, **sociometric popularity,** refers to how well-liked someone is. The other form, **perceived popularity,** refers to how much status, or prestige, someone has (Cillessen & Rose, 2005). So, for example, a leader of the "preppie" crowd who is snobby might be very high in perceived popularity but not in sociometric popularity.

Whereas sociometric popularity is determined mainly by social skills, friendliness, sense of humor, and so forth, which are valued pretty much by people of all ages and backgrounds, the determinants of perceived popularity are highly variable. Having a boyfriend or girlfriend, for example, may have little to do with perceived popularity in fifth grade, but may be highly correlated with it in ninth grade. Because the determinants of status can easily differ between schools, or even among groups within the same school, it is hard to predict which adolescents will be popular without knowing what is valued in that adolescent's social context (Jonkmann, Trautwein, & Lüdtke, 2009; Kreager, 2007b). Although there is one main pathway to sociometric popularity (having good social skills), the determinants of perceived popularity are variable and ever changing. Within the very same school, some adolescents are highly regarded by their peers because they are good-looking and athletic (the conventional image of the popular teenager), whereas others are equally highly regarded because they are rebellious, delinquent, and aggressive (B. E. Becker & Luthar, 2007).

Predicting perceived popularity is further complicated by the fact that peer norms change, and socially competent adolescents are skilled at figuring them out, adjusting their behavior in response to them, and even influencing them. If, for instance, smoking marijuana becomes something that is valued by the peer group, popular adolescents will start getting high more regularly (Allen, Porter, McFarland, Marsh, & McElhaney,

sociometric popularity How well-liked an individual is.

perceived popularity How much status or prestige an individual has.

2005). And when popular adolescents start to engage in a particular behavior, that behavior often becomes more admired. Indeed, one of the reasons it is hard to persuade adolescents to "just say no" to drinking, smoking, and sex is that these activities are often associated with being popular (Mayeux, Sandstrom, & Cillessen, 2008). Even something like bullying, which most adolescents do not approve of, becomes more acceptable when popular adolescents start to bully others (Dijkstra, Lindenberg, & Veenstra, 2008). As you will read in a later chapter, in which we look at responses to peer pressure, adolescents are easily swayed by the opinions of high-status peers to endorse activities that they might otherwise reject and to run the other way from activities endorsed by low-status peers, even if they secretly enjoy them (G. L. Cohen & Prinstein, 2006).

▌ Popularity and Aggression Although psychologists used to believe that aggressive adolescents are likely to be rejected by their classmates, it turns out that some teenagers are both aggressive and popular. One study of preadolescent and young adolescent boys found two distinct types of popular boys (Rodkin, Farmer, Pearl, & Van Acker, 2000). One group, whom the researchers described as "model" boys, had the characteristics typically identified in studies of popular youth: They were physically and academically competent, friendly, and neither shy nor aggressive. A second group, however, whom the researchers described as "tough," were extremely aggressive, physically competent, and average or below average in friendliness, academic competence, and shyness. Similarly, a recent study of girls found two distinctly different groups of popular adolescents: girls who were prosocial and good students, and girls who were antisocial and anti-academic, some of whom actually were even bullies (de Bruyn & Cillessen, 2006).

How can we explain this? Evidently, it is not aggression alone, but the combination of aggression and poor emotion regulation or a lack of social skills, that leads to problems with peers (Farmer, Estell, Bishop, O'Neal, & Cairns, 2003; Pope & Bierman, 1999). Consistent with this, aggressive adolescents who use their aggression strategically—what is referred to as **instrumental aggression**—are much more popular than aggressive adolescents whose aggression is unplanned—what is referred to as **reactive aggression** (T. D. Little, Brauner, Jones, Nock, & Hawley, 2003; Prinstein & Cillessen, 2003).

Studies find that more than one third of American and European students report having been bullied during the past year.

▌ The Dynamics of Popularity Two ethnographic studies of early adolescent girls provide insight into the dynamics of popularity. Ethnographer Donna Eder (1985) spent two years in a middle school observing interactions among early adolescent girls in various extracurricular and informal settings (in the cafeteria, in the hallway, at school dances). In this school, the cheerleaders were considered the elite crowd, and girls who made the cheerleading squad were immediately accorded social status. Other girls then attempted to befriend the cheerleaders as a means of increasing their own status. This, in turn, increased the cheerleaders' popularity within the school, as they became the most sought-after friends. The girls who were successful in cultivating friendships with the cheerleaders then became a part of this high-status group and became more popular themselves. But because even popular adolescents can only maintain a finite number of friendships, they end up snubbing other classmates who want to be their friends. Ironically, this often leads to popular adolescents becoming disliked (Mayeux et al., 2008).

In another study, the researcher spent time observing and interviewing a group described by teachers as the "dirty dozen" (D. Merten, 1997). This group of girls, "considered 'cool,' 'popular,' and 'mean,'" were "a combination of cute, talented, affluent, conceited, and powerful" (1997, p. 178). The researcher was interested in understanding "why a clique of girls that was popular

---

instrumental aggression Aggressive behavior that is deliberate and planned.

reactive aggression Aggressive behavior that is unplanned and impulsive.

and socially sophisticated was also renowned for its meanness" (1997, p. 188). The answer, he discovered, was that meanness was one of the ways that the clique ensured that no one member became stuck-up as a result of her popularity in the eyes of her classmates. Thus, while it was important for clique members to maintain their popular image, if any clique member appeared to become too popular, the other members would turn on her, undermining her standing with other girls by gossiping, starting rumors, and deliberately attempting to disrupt her friendships. The following quote, from a girl whose friends turned on her, will sound all too familiar:

> Gretchen was starting to get really mad at me. I talked to her about it and I asked her what was wrong. She just said, "Oh, I heard something you said about me." But I didn't say anything about her. Sara was mad at me. I don't know why. She started being mad at me and then she started making things up that [she said] I said. Sara told Brenda and Gretchen so that they would get mad at me, too. So now I guess Gretchen has made up something and told Wellesley. They are all mad at me and laughing and everything. (D. Merten, 1997, p. 182)

Ironically, then, one of the potential costs of being popular in adolescence is that if you become too popular, you face the very real possibility of being the object of other classmates' meanness.

Although popularity clearly has some costs, the advantages of being popular far outweigh the disadvantages. Being popular is not the same as having close and intimate friendships (Asher, Parker, & Walker, 1996), but the two often go hand in hand (Franzoi, Davis, & Vasquez-Suson, 1994). Compared with their less popular age-mates, popular adolescents are more likely to have close and intimate friendships, participate in social activities with peers, take part in extracurricular activities, and receive more social recognition (such as being selected as leaders of school organizations) (Franzoi et al., 1994). Part of the overlap between popularity and friendship no doubt stems from the fact that many of the characteristics that make adolescents popular are the same ones that make them sought after as friends—chief among them, having good social skills.

Interestingly, adolescents who see themselves as well-liked and socially competent fare well over time, regardless of whether they are genuinely popular among their classmates (McElhaney, Antonishak, & Allen, 2008). One possible reason for this is that some adolescents who are not especially popular in school may have a well-developed network of friends outside of school. Because most research on adolescents' peer networks has been limited to school-based friendships, however, we know relatively little about the nature of nonschool friendships. We do know that many adolescents have a social life outside of school that is quite different from their life in school. Studies that examine the impact of

friends on adolescent development may miss important information if they do not include information about the number and characteristics of the adolescent's nonschool friends. One study of Italian middle school students found, for example, that having friends outside school buffered the harmful consequences of having few friends in school (Kiesner, Poulin, & Nicotra, 2003).

▌ **Rejected Adolescents**   Just as there are different reasons for being popular, there are also different reasons for being rejected. Social scientists have shown that it is important to distinguish among three types of disliked adolescents (Bierman & Wargo, 1995; Coie, Terry, Lenox, Lochman, & Hyman, 1995; D. French, Conrad, & Turner, 1995; Hatzichristou and Hopf, 1996; Hymel, Bowker, & Woody, 1993; Olweus, 1993; Parkhurst & Asher, 1992). As we have seen, one set of unpopular adolescents comprises teenagers who have trouble controlling their aggression. Withdrawn adolescents make up a second unpopular set; these adolescents are exceedingly shy, anxious, and inhibited and are frequently victims of bullying, especially when they are boys (Erath, Flanagan, & Bierman, 2007). A third group is both aggressive and withdrawn. These adolescents have problems controlling their hostility, but like other withdrawn children, they tend to be nervous about initiating friendships with other adolescents.

The origins of peer rejection in adolescence can often be traced to earlier periods of development. One recent study found that adolescents who were rejected by their peers also had experienced peer rejection during middle childhood and that this rejection, in turn, was the consequence of behavioral and emotional difficulties in early elementary school (Pedersen, Vitaro, Barker, & Borge, 2007).

RELATIONAL AGGRESSION

Most studies of the peer relations of aggressive children have focused on children who are overtly aggressive (either physically or verbally). This has led researchers to focus relatively more attention on the social relationships of aggressive boys than girls, because boys exhibit more overt aggression than girls (Card, Stucky, Sawalani, & Little, 2008). A series of studies by psychologist Nikki Crick, however, indicates that girls also act aggressively toward peers, but that their aggression is often social, not physical, in its expression (Crick, 1996; Crick, Bigbee, & Howes, 1996; Crick & Grotpeter, 1995). In particular, Crick has studied the use of **relational aggression**—aggression intended to harm other adolescents through deliberate

relational aggression   Acts intended to harm another through the manipulation of his or her relationships with others, as in malicious gossip.

Although boys are more physically aggressive than girls, girls often engage in what has been called relational aggression—an attempt to harm someone by ruining his or her reputation or disrupting his or her friendships.

manipulation of their social standing and relationships. Individuals who use relational aggression try to hurt others by excluding them from social activities, damaging their reputations with others, or withdrawing attention and friendship. Physical and relational aggression follow similar developmental trajectories during adolescence, increasing during early adolescence and then declining from mid-adolescence on, and are correlated (that is, individuals who are highly aggressive in one way are also aggressive in the other, and individuals who are frequent victims of physical aggression are also frequent victims of relational aggression) (Card et al., 2008; Karriker-Jaffe, Foshee, Ennett, & Suchindran, 2008; Nylund, Bellmore, Nishina, & Graham, 2007).

▎ **"Mean Girls"** Although relational aggression was first noticed in observations of girls, recent research suggests that both genders employ it, but that girls are more aware of and distressed by it (Card et al., 2008; D. French, Jansen, & Pidada, 2002; Paquette & Underwood, 1999; Sullivan, Farrell, & Kliewer, 2006). One recent study of adolescents' reasoning about excluding people from group activities found, for example, that girls are more likely than boys to say that it is morally wrong to exclude someone simply on the basis of the crowd to which he or she belongs (Horn, 2003). Although relational aggression is more covert than fighting or yelling, the use of relational aggression is nevertheless associated with rejection by peers (Crick, 1996; Rys & Bear, 1997). Interestingly, adolescents whose aggression is atypical for their gender (that is,

girls who are highly physically aggressive and boys who are highly relationally aggressive) show more maladjustment than their peers whose aggression is more gender-stereotypic (Crick, 1997).

Girls' use of relational aggression has attracted a great deal of popular attention, as reflected in the best-selling books *Odd Girl Out* (Simmons, 2003) and *Queen Bees and Wannabees* (Wiseman, 2003), which served as the basis for the movie *Mean Girls*. Perhaps in response, educators have expressed concerns about "meanness" in school environments, noting that teachers have devoted far more attention to preventing overt physical fighting than relational aggression—despite the fact that victims of relational aggression also suffer as a result. Some have called for educational programs designed to help teachers understand, assess, prevent, and respond to the problem when it arises in their classroom, as well as schoolwide programs designed to teach tolerance and acceptance and encourage students to disapprove of relational aggression when they see it. Changing students' attitudes about relational aggression—which many see as fine, even if they object to physical aggression—is important, because adolescents' attitudes about the acceptability of relational aggression (for example, agreeing with the statement "In general, it is OK to not let someone sit with your group of friends at the lunch table") predict their use of it (Werner & Nixon, 2005). In the opinion of most experts, middle schools ought to be the focus of such interventions (Yoon, Barton, & Taiarol, 2004).

FOOD FOR THOUGHT

Is relational aggression something that is more common in adolescence than adulthood? If so, why might this be? If not, is it expressed differently among adults?

As psychologist Amanda Rose has pointed out, however, preventing relational aggression is easier said than done (A. J. Rose, Swenson, & Waller, 2004). She has shown that adolescents who use relational aggression are more popular than their peers. In some ways, this is hardly surprising, because the whole *point* of using relational aggression is to enhance one's status and popularity, and because the same social skills that make one popular (learning how to "read" other people, being able to adjust one's behavior to maintain one's status, etc.) are useful when one is spreading rumors, gossiping, or trying to undermine someone else's reputation. In fact, Rose's findings suggest that the reason some physically aggressive boys are often more popular than their peers is that physical aggression and relational aggression may go hand in hand, and it is their relational aggression, not their physical aggression, that contributes to their popularity. One thing that adolescents are reluctant to do is to stop doing something that makes them popular, even if it is at the expense of someone else (A. J. Rose & Swenson, 2009).

■ **Consequences of Rejection**   Not surprisingly, being unpopular has negative consequences for adolescents' mental health and psychological development—peer rejection and friendlessness are associated with subsequent depression, behavior problems, and academic difficulties (D. French & Conrad, 2001; Kupersmidt, Burchinal, & Patterson, 1995; Morison & Masten, 1991; Olweus, 1993; Wentzel, 2003). But studies show that the specific consequences of peer rejection may differ for rejected youth who are aggressive versus those who are withdrawn. Aggressive individuals who are rejected are at risk for conduct problems and involvement in antisocial activity as adolescents, not just as a direct result of their rejection, but because the underlying causes of their aggression (for instance, poor self-control) also contribute to later conduct problems (S. Feldman, Rosenthal, Brown, & Canning, 1995; S. French et al., 1995; Laird, Pettit, Dodge, & Bates, 2005; Rubin, Chen, McDougall, Bowker, & McKinnon, 1995; Underwood, Kupersmidt, & Coie, 1996). In contrast, withdrawn children who are rejected are likely to feel exceedingly lonely and are at risk for low self-esteem, depression, and diminished social competence—again, both as a result of being rejected and in part because the underlying causes of their timidity (for instance, high anxiety) also contribute to later emotional problems (Card & Hodges, 2008; Hoza, Molina, Bukowski, & Sippola, 1995; Pedersen et al., 2007; Rubin et al., 1995). Rejection is especially likely to lead to depression in adolescents who place a lot of importance on their standing in the peer group and who believe that they, rather than the peers who reject them, are at fault (Prinstein & Aikins, 2004). Adolescents who are both aggressive and withdrawn are at the greatest risk of all (Parkhurst & Asher, 1992; Rubin, LeMare, & Lollis, 1990).

Many psychologists believe that unpopular youngsters lack some of the social skills and social understanding necessary to be popular with peers. According to findings from an extensive program of research by psychologist Kenneth Dodge and his colleagues, unpopular aggressive children are more likely than their peers to think that other children's behavior is deliberately hostile, even when it is not (Dodge, 1986; Dodge & Coie, 1987). When accidentally pushed while waiting in line, for instance, unpopular aggressive children are more likely than others to believe that the person who did the pushing did it on purpose and, consequently, to retaliate. Numerous studies have now confirmed that this so-called **hostile attributional bias** plays a central role in the aggressive behavior of rejected adolescents

(Astor, 1994; Courtney & Cohen, 1996; Crick & Dodge, 1994; C. Graham, 1993; S. Graham & Hudley, 1994; Waldman, 1996).

Not surprisingly, the inferences that adolescents draw from the behavior of others vary in part as a function of their ethnic and cultural backgrounds. Compared to Latino students, for instance, Black students are more likely to be described by other students as aggressive (S. Graham & Juvonen, 2002). In one fascinating study, the reactions of Black and Mexican American adolescents to videotapes of different social situations were compared (Rotheram-Borus & Phinney, 1990). In one situation, for example, a boy was rejected for a team. Whereas the Black adolescents said that in a similar situation they would get angry or leave, the Mexican American youngsters said that they would feel hurt but would not leave. In another vignette, two teenagers were working at a table on which the necessary supplies were closer to one adolescent than the other. The Mexican American adolescents were more likely to say simply that the adolescent who was closer to the supplies should hand them to the other teenager, whereas the Black adolescents were more likely to say that if they were the adolescent farther from the supplies, they would be upset and would reach over and get what they needed. These differences in social information processing likely reflect cultural differences in the emphases placed on group solidarity and cooperation—two qualities that tend to be highly valued in Mexican American families.

VICTIMIZATION AND HARASSMENT

What about unpopular withdrawn children? What are their social skills deficits? In general, research shows that unpopular withdrawn children are excessively anxious and uncertain around other children, often hovering around the group without knowing how to break into a conversation or activity (Rubin et al., 1990). Their hesitancy, low self-esteem, and lack of confidence make other children feel uncomfortable, and their submissiveness makes them easy targets for bullying (Olweus, 1993; Salmivalli, 1998). Many of these youngsters are especially sensitive to being rejected, a trait that may have its origins in early experiences with parents (Downey, Lebolt, Rincón, & Freitas, 1998). Unfortunately, the more these children are teased, rejected, and victimized, the more hesitant they feel, and the more they blame themselves for their victimization, which only compounds their problem—creating a sort of cycle of victimization (S. Graham & Juvonen, 1998; Hymel, Rubin, Rowden, & LeMare, 1990). Interestingly, children who are

hostile attributional bias   The tendency to interpret ambiguous interactions with others as deliberately hostile.

FIGURE 5.8 Being victimized in school can affect income in adulthood. (Macmillan & Hagan, 2004)

victimized but who have a best friend are less likely to be caught in this vicious cycle than those who are friendless (Hodges, Boivin, Vitaro, & Bukowski, 1999).

FOOD FOR THOUGHT

What can be done to reduce victimization in schools? If you were asked to design an intervention, what would it entail?

▌ **Victims and Bullies**   Young adolescents who are victimized by their peers typically develop problems that lead to further peer rejection and victimization (Hodges & Perry, 1999). One of the most pernicious effects of victimization is that it undermines feelings of academic competence, academic performance, and school engagement, which has cascading effects well beyond adolescence—even after taking into account background factors, victimization during adolescence is associated with lower educational attainment and, as a consequence, diminished earnings in adulthood (see Figure 5.8) (Macmillan & Hagan, 2004).

Peer harassment is something that students can be exposed to both directly (when they are the victims) or indirectly (when they witness harassment but aren't themselves victimized). According recent studies, these two different types of experience can have both similar and dissimilar effects (Janosz et al., 2008; Nishina & Juvonen, 2005). Being victimized or witnessing the harassment of others makes students anxious, but witnessing the harassment of others appears to buffer some of the harmful effects of being victimized. Adolescents who were victims of harassment but who did not see anyone else being victimized were more likely to feel humiliated and angry than those who were both victims and witnesses on the same day. Presumably, being singled out for harassment feels worse than being one of many who are picked on. For this reason, studies find that in ethnically diverse schools victimized students whose ethnic group is in the minority are not as harmed psychologically as are victimized students whose ethnic group is in the majority, who are less able to attribute

their victimization to their ethnicity and more likely to attribute it to their own shortcomings as individuals (Graham, Bellmore, Nishina, & Juvonen, 2009).

Although relationships between adolescents who dislike each other have not been studied extensively, such mutual antipathies are not uncommon among teenagers (Abecassis, Hartup, Haselager, Scholte, & Van Lieshout, 2002). These relationships frequently involve bullies and victims, often with an antisocial adolescent repeatedly harassing a withdrawn classmate (Güroglu, Haselager, van Lieshout, & Scholte, 2009). Studies of American and European youth indicate that about one third of students report having been bullied at some time during the past year, although in some studies, the percentage of students who report having been victimized has been considerably higher (Haynie et al., 2001; Nansel et al., 2001). Rates of victimization vary considerably from country, as Figure 5.9 indicates (Analitis et al., 2009).

Researchers are just now beginning to study **cyberbullying** (e.g., bullying that occurs over the Internet or via cell phones). Estimates of the prevalence of cyberbullying vary widely from study to study. For instance, one recent study found that only 10% of adolescents had engaged in electronic bullying, as compared with 40% who had physically bullied someone and 70% who had verbally bullied someone (K. Williams & Guerra, 2007). In contrast, in another study, conducted around the same time, nearly 75% of the sample reported having been the victim of harassment over the Internet (Juvonen & Gross, 2008). Other studies have arrived at an estimate between these two extremes (e.g., Raskauskas & Stoltz, 2007). At this point, it is difficult to say whether these very different estimates are due to differences in the way the survey questions are phrased (studies that ask adolescents if they had been perpetrators produce much lower estimates than those that ask if they had been victims), the samples (school-based surveys yield lower estimates than those polling users of particular websites), or the date of the study (there is some suggestion that cyberbullying has increased in recent years). One common finding, despite these disparities, is that adolescents who engage in traditional bullying also engage in cyberbullying; similarly, adolescents who are frequent victims of traditional bullying are also the victims of electronic harassment (Raskauskas & Stoltz, 2007). And contrary to popular belief, most Internet bullying is not anonymous (Juvonen & Gross, 2008).

cyberbullying   Bullying that occurs over the Internet or via cell phones.

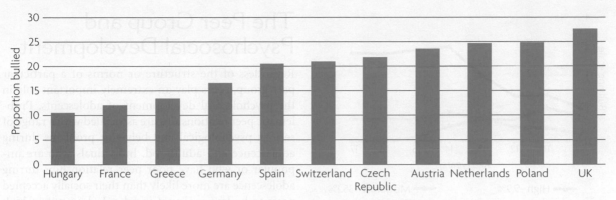

FIGURE 5.9   Rates of bullying vary considerably from country to country. (Analitis et al., 2009)

Students who are harassed by their classmates report a range of adjustment problems, including low self-esteem, depression, and academic difficulties, whereas those who report frequent bullying are more likely to show problems in social skills and in the control of aggression (Ando, Asakura, & Simons-Morton, 2005; Haynie et al., 2001; Juvonen, Nishina, & Graham, 2000). One recent study found that the effects of being harassed in middle school were still observed in high school (Rusby, Forrester, Biglan, & Metzer, 2005). One finding that has now been replicated in several different countries is that many of the same adolescents who report having been victimized also report bullying others and that these adolescents have the greatest adjustment problems, consistent with the finding discussed earlier, that children who are both aggressive and withdrawn are the most disturbed (Juvonen, Graham, & Schuster, 2003; Klomek, Marrocco, Kleinman, Schonfield, & Gould, 2007). One reason that bullying and victimization are often seen in the same children may be that certain elements of the broader context—the climate of the school, for instance—may increase the likelihood of aggression between classmates (Barboza et al., 2009; Bradshaw, Sawyer, & O'Brennan, 2009).

One recent longitudinal study by psychologist Debra Pepler, an expert on bullying, tracked a large sample of Toronto youth from age 10 to 17, in order to see how patterns of bullying changed over time (Pepler, Jiang, Craig, & Connolly, 2008). The researchers identified four different developmental trajectories (see Figure 5.10). About 40% of the sample never bullied anyone. Another 35% bullied other children occasionally when they were younger and continued to do so through adolescence. The remaining 25% fell into two groups—both groups were relatively frequent bullies when they were younger, but whereas one group (slightly less than 15% of the sample) curtailed this behavior over time, about 10% of the sample were persistent bullies. Not surprisingly, the persistent bullies had more troubled family relationships, peer relationships, and difficulties

controlling aggression. Interestingly, however, individuals who bullied other children when they were younger but who desisted over time were not dramatically different from those who never bullied at all. The researchers speculate that this group of individuals may be popular and socially skilled, using bullying strategically to establish their status in the peer group when they are younger. With age, as aggression becomes a less important contributor to status in the peer group, these adolescents are socially savvy enough to stop.

■ **Helping Unpopular Teens**   Can unpopular adolescents be helped? In recent years, several teams of psychologists have experimented with different sorts of interventions designed to improve the social skills of unpopular adolescents. These social competence training programs have focused on three different strategies. One type of program has been designed to teach social skills—self-expression, leadership, and how to converse (Repinski & Leffert, 1994). These programs have been shown to improve adolescents' abilities to get along with peers. A second approach has been to have unpopular adolescents participate in group activities with popular ones under the supervision of psychologists. Programs like this have been shown to improve adolescents' self-conceptions and their acceptance by others (Bierman & Furman, 1984). Finally, some social competence programs focus on a combination of behavioral and cognitive abilities, including social problem solving (e.g., Greenberg & Kusche, 1998; Weissberg, Caplan, & Harwood, 1991). Social-problem-solving programs, such as PATHS (Promoting Alternative Thinking Strategies), are designed to improve individuals' abilities to judge social situations and figure out acceptable ways of behaving. Adolescents are taught to calm down and think before they react, to decide what the problem is, to figure out what their goal is, and to think of positive approaches toward reaching that goal. Instead of lashing out at a classmate who grabbed the last basketball from a gym closet, for example, a hot-tempered

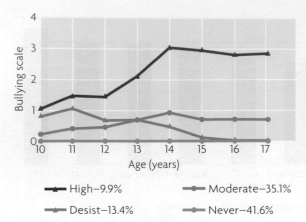

High—9.9%   Moderate—35.1%
Desist—13.4%   Never—41.6%

FIGURE 5.10   Trajectories of bullying over time. (Pepler et al., 2008)

boy who had been through this sort of program might calm himself down, tell himself that his goal is to play basketball rather than get into a fight, and approach another student to ask if he can get into a game. PATHS has been shown to effectively reduce behavioral problems among elementary school children (Conduct Problems Prevention Research Group, 1999).

RECAP

- It is important to distinguish between two types of popularity—sociometric (how well-liked someone is) and perceived (how much status someone has). Sociometric popularity is associated with being socially skilled, whereas the determinants of perceived popularity are different at different times and in different places.
- Unpopular adolescents tend to fall into three categories: aggressive adolescents who have difficulty controlling their emotions, withdrawn adolescents, and adolescents who are both aggressive and withdrawn.
- In general, adolescents who are rejected by their peers are at risk for a wide variety of psychological and behavioral problems, including academic failure, conduct problems, and depression.
- Victimization by peers, whether through physical bullying, relational aggression, or electronic harassment, have harmful and often enduring consequences for individuals' mental health.
- Numerous interventions have been designed to improve adolescents' social competence, including those that focus on improving unpopular adolescents' social skills and their social understanding.

The Peer Group and Psychosocial Development

Regardless of the structure or norms of a particular peer group, peers play an extremely important role in the psychological development of adolescents. Problematic peer relationships are associated with a range of serious psychological and behavior problems during adolescence and adulthood. Individuals who are unpopular or who have poor peer relationships during adolescence are more likely than their socially accepted peers to be low achievers in school, drop out of high school, show higher rates of delinquent behavior, and suffer from an array of emotional and mental health problems as adults (Savin-Williams & Berndt, 1990). Although it is likely that poorly adjusted individuals have difficulty making friends, good evidence also suggests that psychological problems result from—as well as cause—problems with peers (Bagwell, Newcomb, & Bukowski, 1998; Buhrmester & Yin, 1997; Coie et al., 1995; McCoy, 1996; J. Parker & Seal, 1996; Windle, 1994; Woodward & Ferguson, 1999).

Peers also play a crucial role in promoting healthy psychosocial development. In the realm of identity, for example, peers provide the sorts of models and feedback that adolescents cannot get from adults (B. Brown, 2004). In the context of the peer group, young people can try on different roles and personalities and can experiment with different identities with greater ease than at home. And, as we saw earlier, the peer group may serve as a way station in the development of identity as adolescents begin to establish a separate sense of self, one that is differentiated from the family (B. Brown & Larson, 2009). Experience in the peer group also can be an important influence on adolescents' self-image.

Spending time with peers also is vital for the development and expression of autonomy. The process of developing more mature and more independent relationships with parents is accompanied by the establishment of more mature relationships with peers. In addition, the peer group provides a context for adolescents to test out decision-making skills in an arena where there are no adults present to monitor and control their choices (W. A. Collins & Steinberg, 2006).

Intimacy and sexuality, of course, are much more common between peers than between adolescents and adults, for a variety of reasons. Perhaps most critical is that both intimacy and sexuality require interaction between two individuals who are relative equals. Moreover, sexual relationships and close intimacy within the family context would be likely to disrupt important functions of family relationships (Hartup, 1977). It is therefore the adolescent's peer group that generally plays the central role in socializing youngsters in appropriate sexual behavior and in developing the capacity for intimate friendship (H. S. Sullivan, 1953a).

Finally, peers are an important influence on adolescent achievement, especially in countries—like the United States, Spain, or Korea—where high schools tend not to be specialized or separated according to student ability. In countries like France, Germany, and Switzerland, in contrast, where students are assigned to different schools depending on their ability and aspirations (for example, vocational schools versus college prep schools), peers are a less important influence on achievement (Buchmann & Dalton, 2002). Although peers play a less prominent role than parents or teachers in influencing adolescents' long-term educational and occupational plans, adolescents' classmates are a significant influence on their day-to-day school behaviors and feelings, including how much they value school, how much effort they devote to their studies, and how well they perform in class (A. M. Ryan, 2001; Steinberg et al., 1996). Peers seem to be an especially important influence on the achievement of ethnic minority youth (Steinberg, Dornbusch, & Brown, 1992).

Adolescents consider the time they spend with their peers to be among the most enjoyable parts of the day (Csikszentmihalyi & Larson, 1984). One reason is that activities with friends are typically organized around having a good time, in contrast to activities with parents, which are more likely to be organized around

household chores and the enforcement of parental rules (Larson, 1983). Rather than being competing institutions, the family and peer group mainly provide contrasting opportunities for adolescent activities and behaviors. The family is organized around work and other tasks, and it may be important in the socialization of responsibility and achievement. The peer group provides more frequent opportunities for interaction and leisure, which contributes to the development of intimacy and enhances the adolescent's mood and psychological well-being.

RECAP

- Problematic peer relationships are associated with a range of serious psychological and behavior problems during adolescence and adulthood. These problems both cause, and result from, poor peer relationships.
- Peers play a crucial role in the development of identity, autonomy, intimacy, sexuality, and achievement in adolescence.
- Rather than being competing institutions, the family and peer group mainly provide contrasting opportunities for adolescent activities and behaviors.

Schools

BECAUSE OF THE IMPORTANT and multifaceted role it has come to play in modern society, the secondary educational system—**secondary education** refers to middle schools, junior high schools, and high schools—has been the target of a remarkable amount of criticism, scrutiny, and social science research.

Secondary school touches the lives of all adolescents in industrialized societies, as well as an increasingly larger proportion of the population in the developing world. Virtually all American adolescents under the age of 17 and nearly all 17- and 18-year-olds are enrolled in school. In most developing countries, attending high school is much more common among children of the wealthy, often because poor families need their adolescents to work. But even in the poorest parts of the world—sub-Saharan Africa, for example—close to two thirds of 10- to 14-year-olds and 40–50% of 15- to 19-year-olds are enrolled in school (National Research Council, 2005). And schooling is as time-consuming as it is pervasive. During most of the year, the typical American student spends more than one third of his or her waking hours each week in school or in school-related activities (Larson & Verma, 1999). One recent review estimates that between ages 11 and 18, the typical American student will spend about 7,000 hours in school—not even counting time on homework and school-related activities outside of school (Elmore, 2009).

Not only are schools the chief educational arena for adolescents, but they also play an extremely important role in defining the young person's social world and in shaping his or her psychosocial development. Naturally, the development of achievement—motivation, aspirations, and expectations—is profoundly affected by the adolescent's experiences in school. (Just think about the differences between going to a good school and going to a bad one.) But schools influence psychosocial development far beyond the domain of achievement. How adolescents do in school influences their academic self-conceptions and occupational choices—shaping their identity. The way in which a school is organized affects the adolescent's sense of independence, and the way a classroom is run affects the extent to which the adolescent learns to *think* independently. Schools often define adolescents' social networks, thereby influencing the development of interpersonal relationships. And the majority of adolescents, at least in the United States, learn about sexuality in school and are influenced by their classmates' norms for sexual behavior. You simply cannot understand adolescence as a developmental period without understanding the ways in which schools shape the adolescent experience.

In this chapter, we will examine the organization and workings of secondary schools at multiple levels of analysis. Perhaps your first inclination is to think about what takes place in the classroom. And while this is important, a thorough understanding of schooling and its impact on adolescent development requires an examination that goes beyond the classroom (Eccles & Roeser, 2009). What takes place in the classroom is influenced by the way in which the school is organized, and the way in which the school is organized, in turn, is influenced by the needs and demands of the community and of society. Unlike the family or peer group, whose structure is not under the direct or deliberate control of society, schools are environments created to serve specific purposes (Elmore, 2009). In many respects, the schools we have today—for all their strengths and weaknesses—are the schools we designed. This is abundantly clear when we look at the history of secondary education in America.

The Broader Context of U.S. Secondary Education

As Figure 6.1 shows, today, virtually all young people ages 14–17 are enrolled in school. In 1930, only about half of this age group were students, and at the turn of the 20th century, only 1 in 10 were (D. Tanner, 1972; William T. Grant Foundation, 1988).

Not only are there considerably more youngsters enrolled in school today than there were 50 years ago, but today's students also spend more days per year in school. In 1920, for example, the average school term was 162 days, and the average student attended for only 121 days, or 75% of the term. By 1968, however, the school term had been lengthened to nearly 180 days, which remains the national average, and the typical student today attends close to 90% of the term (National Center for Education Statistics, 2003).

Not only is the school year longer today than it was in the past, but adolescents also remain in school for

secondary education   The system of middle schools, junior high schools, and high schools.

more years now than they did in previous eras. In 1924, fewer than 33% of all youngsters entering the fifth grade eventually graduated from high school; today, more than 75% of all fifth-graders will eventually graduate on time, and a substantial number of those who do not graduate on schedule eventually get their diploma, either by completing high school at a later date or through equivalency programs or continuation schools.

THE ORIGINS OF COMPULSORY EDUCATION

The rise of secondary education in America was the result of several historical and social trends that converged at the turn of the 20th century. Most important were industrialization, urbanization, and immigration.

Following widespread industrialization during the late 19th century, the role of children and young adolescents in the workplace changed dramatically. As productivity became more dependent on workers' use of machines, employers recognized that they needed employees who were more skilled than youngsters ordinarily were. In addition, the few unskilled jobs that remained after industrialization required strength beyond the capacity of many youth (Church, 1976). Social reformers also expressed concerns about the dangers children faced working in factories, and labor unions—an increasingly powerful force in the early 1900s—sought to protect not only the welfare of children but also their own job security. In response, child labor laws narrowed and limited the employment of minors (Bakan, 1972). Together, these changes in the workplace kept many youngsters out of the labor force.

During this same period, the nature of life in American cities was changing markedly. Industrialization brought with it urbanization and, along with several waves of immigrants, new problems for urban centers. The effects of a rapidly expanding economy were seen in the tenements and slums of America's cities: poor housing, overcrowded neighborhoods, crime. Eager to improve living conditions for the urban masses, social reformers envisioned education as a means of improving the life circumstances of the poor and working classes. Many also saw compulsory secondary education as a means of social control. High schools would take many thousands of idle young people off the streets and place them in a social institution in which they could be supervised and kept out of trouble. In addition, anxious to see that foreign-born immigrants were well socialized to the American way of life, reformers presented universal secondary education as a necessary part of the process of Americanization (Church, 1976; D. Tanner, 1972). By 1915, the idea of universal compulsory education for adolescents had gained widespread acceptance.

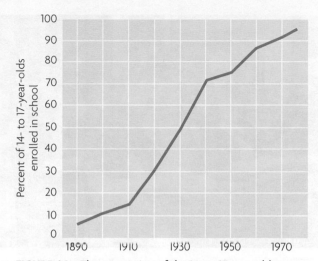

FIGURE 6.1   The proportion of the 14- to 17-year-old population enrolled in school increased dramatically between 1910 and 1940. Today, nearly 95 percent of individuals this age are in school. (D. Tanner, 1972; William T. Grant Foundation, 1988)

THE RISE OF THE COMPREHENSIVE HIGH SCHOOL

Prior to the early 20th century, high schools were for the elite. In curriculum, staff, and student composition, they were similar to the colleges of the day, with the emphasis mainly on classical liberal arts instruction (Church, 1976; D. Tanner, 1972).

By 1920, however, educators saw a need for curricular reform. Now that secondary education was aimed at the masses, schooling was seen not merely as a means of intellectual training but also as a way of preparing youth for life in modern society. It was argued that education should be more practical and include preparation for the roles of work and citizenship.

The 1920s marked the birth in the United States of what came to be known as the **comprehensive high school,** an educational institution that promised to meet the needs of a diverse and growing population of young people. Classes in general education, college preparation, and vocational education were all housed under one roof. As you saw in Figure 6.1, the proportion of high school–aged individuals enrolled in school jumped dramatically in the years between World War I and World War II—from 32% in 1920 to over 73% in 1940. This was also a time of tremendous change in the high school curriculum. During these years, new courses were added in music, art, family life, health, physical education, and other subjects designed to prepare adolescents for family and leisure as well as work roles.

comprehensive high school   An educational institution that evolved during the first half of the 20th century, offering a varied curriculum and designed to meet the needs of a diverse population of adolescents.

The proportion of American adolescents enrolled in high school grew dramatically between 1920 and 1940.

By the middle of the 20th century, the high school had come a long way from its exclusive focus at the turn of the century on the intellectual development of the socioeconomic elite. Its concern had broadened to include the social and intellectual development of all young people. And today, despite continuing questioning and criticism, the comprehensive high school remains the cornerstone of the American system of secondary education. It is, however, not the exemplar to which all countries aspire—few other countries attempt to educate such a diverse group of young people under one roof, choosing instead to separate the college-bound from the non-college-bound into separate schools. Indeed, the American "high school" is in many regards a distinctively American institution.

FOOD FOR THOUGHT

The comprehensive high school was invented within a specific historical context. Does it make sense within today's society? If not, what alternative or alternatives would you suggest?

SCHOOL REFORM: PAST AND PRESENT

Although we naturally think of schools as institutions whose primary goal is education, they are much more than this. Schools are also potentially important tools of social intervention, because it is through schools that the greatest number of young people can most easily be reached. For this reason, the study of schools is extremely important to social scientists and policymakers

social promotion   The practice of promoting students from one grade to the next automatically, regardless of their school performance.

who are interested in influencing adolescent development. In fact, one way to understand the ways in which adults want adolescents to change is to look at the ways that schools have been reformed over the years.

During the 1950s, for example, when politicians felt that the United States had lost its scientific edge to the former Soviet Union, schools were called upon to offer more courses in math and science (Conant, 1959). When social scientists felt that adolescents were growing up unfamiliar with the world of work—as they did in the 1970s—schools were asked to provide opportunities for work–study programs and classes in career education (President's Science Advisory Committee, 1974). In the 1990s, as society grappled with a broad array of social problems affecting and involving youth—problems such as violence, AIDS, and drug abuse—we once again looked to schools for assistance, asking schools to implement an array of preventive interventions (Dryfoos, 1993).

▌ **No Child Left Behind**   Toward the end of the 1990s, amidst growing concerns that our inner-city schools were not producing graduates who could compete for high-skills jobs, and in response to a public increasingly interested in alternatives to conventional public education, such as charter schools or home schooling, schools were called upon to raise standards for all students (e.g., Ravitch, 2001). In January 2002, President Bush signed into law the No Child Left Behind Act, a sweeping and controversial piece of legislation mandating that states ensure that all students, regardless of their economic circumstances, achieve academic proficiency (U.S. Department of Education, 2006). No Child Left Behind (NCLB) required that schools create and enforce academic standards by annually testing all students and by reporting the results of students' performance to the public. Underperforming schools—schools where students' test scores did not improve—initially would be given an opportunity to do a better job the following year, by providing additional instruction, tutoring, or special services for students who needed them. But schools that continued to fail eventually would have funding taken away and could even be forced to close.

On the face of it, NCLB sounds reasonable enough. As you'll read in Chapter 12, a huge proportion of American students do not meet even minimal standards for academic performance, and poor performance is disproportionately seen among disadvantaged, Black, Hispanic, and American Indian students. Many commentators had criticized the practice of **social promotion**—moving students from one grade to the next regardless of their academic performance—arguing that poor and ethnic minority youth especially were being cheated out of a good education and graduated without the skills necessary to succeed in college or in the labor force (Steinberg, 1996). Forcing schools to regularly assess student progress and publicize how their students were faring would give parents and the community the information they needed to put pressure on schools to do better. No one could disagree with the basic idea that all students—regardless of their background—deserve a high-quality public education (Borkowski & Sneed, 2006).

Although NCLB sounded good in principle, it was very problematic in practice and met with tremendous resistance (Darling-Hammond, 2006). States complained that they simply did not have the resources to conduct the mandated assessments or to respond to failing students' poor performance. Teachers and parents complained that the focus on standardized testing adversely affects what takes place in the classroom—if a school's financial future depends on its students' reading and math test scores, why should teachers do anything other than teach to the test? (Be honest—how much effort do *you* devote to learning material in your classes that you know you won't be tested on?) Many questions about the policy were raised: What happens to the teaching of subjects that will not appear on the test, like current events, or to the teaching of skills that are impossible to assess through standardized exams, such as **critical thinking?** Who determines how tough the tests are or what level of achievement on them is acceptable? And, with millions of dollars at stake, what was to stop schools from manipulating their average scores, by encouraging poor-performing students to be absent on testing days or by actually helping students cheat on the tests, which some schools evidently did (S. Levitt & Dubner, 2005)? Some critics of NCLB argued that it was having the opposite effect of what was intended, providing incentives for schools to push low-achieving students out of school (Darling-Hammond, 2006). Nevertheless, the movement toward performance-based accountability—holding teachers, schools, school districts, and states—accountable for the achievement of their students—has been the most important change in the world of American education in the past 20 years (Elmore, 2009).

It is difficult to forecast what the next wave of school reform proposals will bring. In 2009, President Obama's education secretary stressed the need to have high standards for all students and, just as important, a set of *common* standards across all 50 states (U.S. Department of Education, 2009). (One of the problems with NCLB is that it left standard setting up to individual states.) One thing we can be sure of is that as we move further into the 21st century, schools will continue to play a central role in the development and implementation of a wide range of social policies concerning young people. Whether this use of our educational system is proper or

misguided has been a matter of considerable debate for more than a century (Ravitch, 2000).

FOOD FOR THOUGHT

What do you think about mandating that all students pass a standardized examination before being promoted to the next grade or before being granted a diploma? What are the possible positive and negative effects of this policy?

WHAT SHOULD SCHOOLS TEACH?

Suppose you are asked to list the things you think young people need to know in order to function as competent, responsible, satisfied adults. Which items on your list should be the responsibility of high schools? Should high school curricula be limited to the traditional academic subjects, or should schools play a broader role in preparing young people for adulthood by providing instruction more directly relevant to work, family, leisure, and citizenship? Should students receive instruction only in English, mathematics, science, and social studies, or should they take courses as well in "general education"—in subjects such as art, home economics, health, sex education, driver education, and personal finance? Which courses should be required, and which should be left as electives?

▍ **Back to Basics**   The history of curricular reform in American has been one of frequent shifting between an emphasis on "rigor" and an emphasis on "relevance." For the past three decades, rigor has ruled. Critics of American education have been calling for a return to a curriculum that stresses the basics and that attempts to ensure that all students master them (Consortium on Productivity in the Schools, 1995; Consortium on Renewing Education, 1998; National Education Commission on Time and Learning, 1994; Ravitch, 1995). What has prompted this focus? The achievement test scores of American high school students had been falling. International comparisons of student achievement consistently found that American youngsters were faring poorly. Noting that America was losing its competitive edge in the world market, reformers called for more academic rigor in the schools as a means of preparing young people for the workplace of the future. On top of this, as budget crises forced schools to make tough decisions about what sorts of courses to eliminate in order to save money, schools began to drop parts of the curriculum that were not deemed essential.

critical thinking   Thinking that involves analyzing, evaluating, and interpreting information, rather than simply memorizing it.

Critical thinking is stimulated when students are encouraged to interpret, analyze, and evaluate information, rather than simply memorize it or use it in a routine way.

▌ **Standards-Based Reform** The return to basics has been accompanied by what is called **standards-based reform.** But although state after state began to implement standardized examinations to ensure that high school graduates actually knew what they were supposed to know, problems still arose. First, educators could not agree on the body of knowledge and skills that comprised what high school graduates should know and be able to do. Second, as states soon discovered, large numbers of students did not fully acquire the knowledge and capabilities assessed on standardized graduation examinations. It is all well and good to propose that all high school seniors must pass a graduation test in order to earn a diploma, but it is not at all clear what to do when one third or one half of a state's high school seniors fail the test.

Actually, many observers question whether the comprehensive public high school as it exists in America today should—or can—continue to play a central role in the education of adolescents. Most agree that schools for adolescents have grown too large and impersonal (Elmore, 2009). Others, like educational historian Diane Ravitch (2000), argue that the problem has been a lack of focus.

She notes that three beliefs, in particular, have interfered with successful educational reform: that the schools can solve any social or political problem (which has led to our diverting schools from their most important mission—academic instruction), that only a portion of youngsters are capable of benefiting from a high-quality education (which has led to our having vastly different standards for students from different backgrounds), and that imparting knowledge is relatively unimportant and that schools should focus on engaging students in activities and experiences (which has watered down the curriculum and led to an approach to instruction that is all process and no content).

Amid widespread disappointment over the state of public education in America, increasing numbers of parents have begun to look at other options—among them, **charter schools** (public schools that are given more freedom to set their own curricula), schools that are run by private corporations rather than local school boards, and government-subsidized **school vouchers** (which can be used for private school tuition). Although all of these alternatives gained popularity during the late 1990s, research on the costs and benefits of charter schools, privatization, and vouchers has been inconclusive (Loveless, 2002). As is the case with public schools, which vary tremendously in their quality and level of student achievement, there is considerable variability among charter, for-profit, and private schools. The bottom line is that what takes place within a school is probably more important than the nature of its funding and oversight. This idea has led many experts to argue that we should focus on the ways in which we train, certify, place, and compensate teachers (Darling-Hammond, 2006).

FOOD FOR THOUGHT

How do you feel about vouchers? About charter schools? What are the costs and benefits of each, to students and to society?

---

standards-based reform Policies designed to improve achievement by holding schools and students to a predetermined set of standards measured by achievement tests.

charter schools Public schools that have been given the autonomy to establish their own curricula and teaching practices.

school vouchers Government-subsidized vouchers that can be used for private school tuition.

EDUCATION IN THE INNER CITIES

Although concerns about the demise of American education raged during the late 1990s, some commentators argued that the problem of low student achievement was not an across-the-board problem, but one that was concentrated mainly among poor and minority youngsters living in inner cities (Berliner & Biddle, 1995).

Although other critics (e.g., Stedman, 1998; Steinberg, 1996) noted that poor achievement was a problem in all segments of American society, virtually all social scientists concur that the education crisis, and its implications for the future of the labor force, has become distressingly urgent within inner-city public schools. Indeed, the achievement gap between White and non-White youngsters, which had been closing for some time, grew wider during the 1990s, especially in large urban school districts. Although there are occasional success stories, such as the Harlem Children's Zone (Tough, 2008), inner-city schools in America continue to have tremendous problems. Just 12% of the high schools in the United States produce *half* of the country's dropouts, and nearly half the nation's Black and Latino students attend one of these schools (Balfanz, Legters, West, & Weber, 2007). In the District of Columbia, which serves a predominantly Black population, only 8% of all eighth-graders are judged proficient in math, and only 12% in reading. Similar gaps exist across the country. In California, eighth-grade White students who are proficient in math outnumber Latino youngsters by a ratio of 4 to 1. According to recent test results, in the nation's large inner-city public schools, which mainly serve minority youth, only one sixth of students are judged proficient in science, a fact that has enormous implications for these adolescents' chances at success in an increasingly high-tech economy (National Center for Education Statistics, 2006b).

Why has school reform failed in so many urban schools? Experts point to several reasons. First, the concentration of poverty in many inner-city communities has produced a population of students with an array of personal and situational problems—problems that few schools are equipped or able to address (Farrell et al., 2007). Recent surveys of American high school students indicate that so many are afraid of being victimized that 15% of boys and 8% of girls across the country carry a gun to school, with even higher percentages doing so in inner-city schools (Centers for Disease Control, 2006). Second, many urban school districts are burdened by huge administrative bureaucracies that often impede reform and hinder educational innovation. Third, students in urban schools report less of a sense of "belonging" to their school, which leads to disengagement and poor achievement (Anderman, 2002). Finally, the erosion of job opportunities in inner-city communities has left many students with little incentive to remain in school or to devote a great deal of effort to academic pursuits (Kantor & Brenzel, 1992). Many reformers now believe that to fix the problems of urban education, we must change the entire context in which inner-city children live, not merely what goes on in their schools (Garcia-Reid, 2007; Tough, 2008).

RECAP

- Schools play an extremely important role in structuring the nature of adolescence in modern society. In most of the industrialized world, virtually all 14- to 17-year-olds are enrolled in school, a pattern that is becoming increasingly prevalent in the developing world as well. In addition, school occupies an enormous amount of adolescents' time.

- A number of social forces combined to lead to the development of compulsory education for adolescents in America, including industrialization, immigration, and urbanization.

- During the 1920s, the high school as we know it in the United States today—the comprehensive high school—was born.

- Educators have long debated whether and how high schools should be reformed. The pendulum has swung back and forth between eras in which teaching basic academic skills was emphasized and those during which the emphasis was on making the school's curriculum relevant.

- At the turn of the 21st century, calls for the implementation and enforcement of rigorous academic standards became widespread, as the public grew increasingly worried about the competitiveness of American students in an international economy that is increasingly reliant on high-tech, high-skill jobs.

- There is broad consensus that inner-city public schools, which mainly serve disadvantaged ethnic minority adolescents, are in especially dire straits. Experts agree that to change this state of affairs, we need to transform the entire context in which poor urban youth live.

The Social Organization of Schools

In addition to debating curricular issues, social scientists interested in school reform have discussed the ways in which secondary schools should be organized. Because the organization of a school affects students' day-to-day experiences, variations in school organization can have profound effects on adolescents' development and behavior. In this section, we examine the research on five key aspects of school organization: (1) school and classroom size, (2) different approaches to age grouping and, in particular, how young adolescents should be grouped, (3) tracking, or the grouping of students in classes according to their academic abilities, (4) the ethnic composition of schools, and (5) public versus private schools.

Students and teachers are more satisfied in classes that combine a moderate degree of structure with high student involvement and high teacher support.

SCHOOL SIZE AND CLASS SIZE

As the idea of the comprehensive high school gained widespread acceptance, educators attempted to deliver a wider range of courses and services under a single roof. As a consequence, schools became larger and larger over the course of the 20th century. By the end of the 1990s, in many metropolitan areas, students attended enormous schools, with enrollments of several thousand students. One advantage enjoyed by larger schools is that they can offer a more varied curriculum—a large high school, for instance, may be able to offer many specialized courses that a small school would be unable to staff.

▌ **Is Bigger Better?**   When it comes to school size, however, is bigger necessarily better? Do students who attend larger schools reap any educational or psychological advantages as a result? A fair amount of research conducted over the past 40 years says, "No." Indeed, one of the most consistent conclusions to emerge from recent evaluations of school reform efforts is that student performance and interest in school improve when their schools are made less bureaucratic and more intimate. Numerous studies indicate that students achieve more when they attend smaller schools that create a cohesive sense of community (V. Lee, Smith, & Croninger,

1997; Ready, Lee, & Welner, 2004; Roeser, Midgley, & Urdan, 1996).

At the same time, however, there is no evidence that school size alone influences students' sense of belonging. School size may affect academic outcomes, but it does not necessarily affect students' emotional attachment to the institution (Anderman, 2002) or their mental health (T. T. Watt, 2003), perhaps because some large schools are able to maintain a more intimate climate by dividing students into smaller groups. Indeed, in recent years, many educators have recommended that large schools be broken down into **schools within schools,** and many districts have followed this recommendation. Although few such transformations have been studied systematically, the existing research indicates both advantages and disadvantages to this approach. On the positive side, creating schools within schools does lead to the development of a more positive social environment; on the negative side, though, if not done carefully, schools may inadvertently create "schools" within one school that vary considerably in their educational quality.

Although the move to reorganize large secondary schools into more personal institutions gained wider acceptance during the 1990s, researchers have been studying the pros and cons of large versus small high schools for nearly a half century (Barker & Gump, 1964; Elder & Conger, 2000). Actually, the most interesting findings of this research concern participation in extracurricular activities, not achievement in the classroom.

You might expect that, in addition to providing a more varied curriculum, large schools would be able to offer more diverse extracurricular activities to their students—and indeed they do. Large schools can support more athletic teams, after-school clubs, and student organizations. But because large schools also contain so many more students, actual rates of participation in different activities are only half as high in large schools as in smaller ones. As a result, in larger schools, students tend more often to be observers than participants in school activities. For instance, during the fall, a small school and a large school might each field teams in football, soccer, and cross-country running, together requiring a total of 100 students. An individual's chances of being 1 of those 100 students are greater in a school that has only 500 students than in a school with an enrollment of 4,000.

▌ **The Strengths of Small Schools**   Because students in small schools are more likely than students in large schools to be active in a wider range of activities, they are more likely to report doing things that help them develop their skills and abilities, allow them to work closely with others, and make them feel needed and important. In a small school, chances are, sooner or later, most students will find themselves on a team, in the student government, or in an extracurricular

schools within schools   Subdivisions of the student body within large schools created to foster feelings of belongingness.

organization. Students in small schools also are more likely to be placed in positions of leadership and responsibility, and they more often report having done things that made them feel confident and diligent. School size especially affects the participation of students whose grades are not very good. In large schools, academically marginal students often feel like outsiders and rarely get involved in school activities. In small schools, however, these students feel a sense of involvement and obligation equal to that of more academically successful students.

In short, although large schools may be able to offer more diverse curricula and provide greater material resources to their students, the toll that school size may take on student learning and engagement appears to exceed the benefits of size (V. Lee & Smith, 1995). Evidence also suggests that there is more inequality in students' educational experiences in larger schools, where students may be sorted into tracks of differing quality. In small schools, in contrast, it is more likely that all students are exposed to the same curriculum, if only because the school cannot afford to offer more than one. Experts now agree that the ideal size of a high school is between 600 and 900 students (V. Lee & Smith, 1997).

■ **Variations in Class Size** Unfortunately, policymakers do not always implement social science findings in ways that accurately reflect the research evidence. Encouraged by the results of research on smaller *schools*, many politicians began calling for smaller *classes*. However, in contrast to studies of schools, studies of classrooms indicate that variations within the typical range of classroom sizes—from 20 to 40 students—do not generally affect students' scholastic achievement once they have reached adolescence. Indeed, small classes may benefit young elementary school children (that is, up until third grade), who may need more individualized instruction (Finn, Gerber, & Boyd-Zaharias, 2005), but adolescents in classes with 40 students learn just as much as students in classes with 20 students (Mosteller, Light, & Sachs, 1996).

An important exception to this finding involves situations that call for highly individualized instruction or tutoring, in which case smaller classes do appear to be more effective. For example, in remedial education classes, where teachers must give a great deal of attention to each student, small classes are valuable. One implication of these findings is that it may be profitable for schools that maintain regular class sizes of 25–30 students to increase the sizes of these classes by a student or two in order to free instructors, and to trim the sizes of classes for students who need specialized, small-group instruction (Rutter, 1983).

■ **The Problem of Overcrowding** One certain impediment to delivering high-quality education, especially in large metropolitan school districts, is overcrowding (Ready et al., 2004). According to national surveys, nearly 15% of U.S. secondary schools are overcrowded—that is, the size of the student body is at least 6% larger than the school was designed to house—and an additional 8% are "severely overcrowded," with the student body 25% above capacity. Schools with more than 50% ethnic minority students are especially likely to be overcrowded. California, which has a very high proportion of ethnic minority students, has some of the most overcrowded schools in the country. Achievement is lower in overcrowded schools because of stress on both students and teachers, the use of facilities for instruction that were not designed to serve as classrooms (such as gyms), and inadequate resources.

Educators have attempted to reduce the adverse effects of overcrowding through a variety of measures—some successful, others not. Many school districts use temporary structures, such as trailers, to provide additional classroom space. Unfortunately, many such portable units, especially older ones, are constructed with materials that are harmful to students' physical health, and the tight quarters and poor ventilation common in these structures can create toxic environments (Ready et al., 2004). Other districts—most famously, Los Angeles—have created multitrack programs, whereby schools are used year round, and students are organized into groups, with one group on vacation at any given point in time. Evaluations of this approach have been mixed.

AGE GROUPING AND SCHOOL TRANSITIONS

A second issue that social scientists have examined in the study of school structure and organization concerns the ways in which schools group students of different ages and the frequency with which students are expected to change schools.

Early in the 20th century, most school districts separated youngsters into an elementary school (which had either six or eight grades) and a secondary school (which had either four or six grades). Students changed schools once (after either sixth or eighth grade). However, many educators felt that the two-school system was unable to meet the special needs of young adolescents, whose intellectual and emotional maturity was greater than that expected in elementary school, but not yet at the level necessary for high school. During the early years of compulsory secondary education, the establishment of separate schools for young adolescents began, and the **junior high school** (which contained the seventh, eighth, and sometimes ninth grades) was born (Hechinger, 1993). In more recent years, the

junior high school   An educational institution designed during the early era of public secondary education, in which young adolescents are schooled separately from older adolescents.

middle school—a three- or four-year school housing the seventh and eighth grades with one or more younger grades—gained in popularity, replacing the junior high school in many districts (Elmore, 2009). In more recent years, school districts have moved away from housing young adolescents separately and are returning to a two-school model (usually K–8 and 9–12), in light of many studies showing that students demonstrate higher achievement and fewer behavioral problems under this arrangement. It is important to note, however, that the particular grade configuration of a school is less important than the school's educational climate and quality of instruction (Elmore, 2009).

■ **The Transition Into Secondary School**   One of the most commonly reported findings is that students' academic motivation and school grades drop as they move from elementary into middle or junior high school (Eccles, 2004; Gentry, Gable, & Rizza, 2002; Gutman & Midgley, 2000; Murdock, Anderman, & Hodge, 2000). (Interestingly, scores on standardized achievement tests do not decline during this same time, suggesting that the decline in grades may be more a reflection of changes in grading practices and student motivation than in students' knowledge [Eccles, 2004]). One well-publicized report on this subject was issued by the Carnegie Corporation's Council on Adolescent Development (1989). Among its most important recommendations were to divide middle schools into units of 200–500 students in order to reduce students' feelings of anonymity, hire teachers who have special training in adolescent development, and strengthen ties between schools and the communities in which they are located.

FOOD FOR THOUGHT

When you were a young adolescent, did you go to school with older adolescents, with preadolescent children, or only with people your age? How do you think your experience was affected by this arrangement?

Researchers also have examined how changing schools affects student achievement and behavior. In many of these studies, researchers compared school arrangements in which students remain in elementary school until eighth grade—that is, where they have one school change—with arrangements in which they move from elementary school, to middle or junior high school, and then to high school—where they change

schools twice. In general, this research suggests that school transitions, whenever they occur, can disrupt the academic performance, behavior, and self-image of adolescents, although this effect may be stronger among White students than their ethnic minority peers (Kuperminc, Blatt, Shahar, Henrich, & Leadbeater, 2004). This disruption is generally temporary, however. Over time, most youngsters adapt successfully to changing schools, especially when other aspects of their life—family and peer relations, for example—remain stable and supportive and when the new school environment is well suited for adolescents (Anderman & Midgley, 1996; Gillock & Reyes, 1996; Lord, Eccles, & McCarthy, 1994; Seidman, Lambert, Allen, & Aber, 2003; Teachman, Paasch, & Carver, 1996).

Researchers do not agree about whether the drop in academic motivation and achievement that occurs after elementary school is due to the school transition itself (that is, students suffer *whenever* they have to change schools) or to the difference between elementary school, on the one hand, and middle or junior high school, on the other. Specifically, some experts believe that the poor showing of middle and junior high schools is due primarily to their failure to meet the particular developmental needs of young adolescents (Barber & Olsen, 2004; Eccles & Roeser, 2009). Between sixth and eighth grade, for example, students report declines in how supportive their teachers and classmates are, how much autonomy students have to make decisions, and how clear and fair school rules are (Way, Reddy, & Rhodes, 2007). Because adolescence is a time during which relationships with peers and nonfamilial adults become more important, independence becomes more desirable, and rules and regulations are increasingly scrutinized, these changes in school climate suggest that there is a substantial mismatch in early adolescence between what adolescents need and what schools provide (Eccles & Roeser, 2009).

HOW SECONDARY SCHOOLS DIFFER FROM ELEMENTARY SCHOOLS

Psychologist Jacquelynne Eccles and her colleagues have conducted the most comprehensive research to date on school transitions during the early adolescent years (Eccles et al., 1993; Eccles, Lord, & Roeser, 1996). Eccles has argued that the classroom environment in the typical middle school or junior high school is quite different from that in the typical elementary school. Not only are junior high schools larger and less personal, but middle and junior high school teachers also hold different beliefs about students than do elementary school teachers—even when they teach students of the same chronological age (Midgley, Berman, & Hicks, 1995). For example, teachers in junior high schools are less likely to trust their students and more likely to emphasize discipline, which creates a mismatch between what students at this age desire (more

middle school   An educational institution housing seventh- and eighth-grade students along with adolescents who are 1 or 2 years younger.

independence) and what their teachers provide (more control). Teachers in junior high schools also tend to be more likely to believe that students' abilities are fixed and not easily modified through instruction—a belief that interferes with their students' achievement. In addition, teachers who teach in junior high or middle schools are less likely than other teachers to feel confident about their teaching ability (Eccles & Roeser, 2009).

Eccles points out that it is hardly surprising that students experience a drop in achievement motivation when they enter middle or junior high school, given the change in environments they experience and the mismatch between what adolescents need developmentally and what the typical school context provides. The issue, according to Eccles, is not that the adolescents must make a transition; it is the *nature* of the transition they must make. Indeed, although students' self-esteem drops during the transition into middle or junior high school, it increases somewhat during the early high school years, suggesting that the initial decline reflects students' temporary difficulties in adapting to the new environment (Wigfield, Eccles, MacIver, Reuman, & Midgley, 1991). Consistent with this, middle school students attending more personal, less departmentalized schools do better than their peers in more rigid and more anonymous schools (V. Lee & Smith, 1993). Not surprisingly, changing schools is easier on students who move into small rather than large institutions (Russell, Elder, & Conger, 1997).

Why do junior high school teachers differ from those who teach elementary school? At this point, the answer is not clear-cut. The individuals who choose to become junior high teachers do not seem to differ all that much from those who choose to teach younger grades. Rather, Eccles has suggested that the organization and anonymity of junior high schools have a negative effect on the teachers who work in them, which, in turn, affects the way they interact with students. This is consistent with a large body of evidence that students are more engaged in school when their teachers themselves are more engaged in their work (Louis & Smith, 1992).

Cultural stereotypes about adolescence also may have a negative influence on junior high school teachers' beliefs. As we saw in the Introduction, many adults believe that adolescence is an inevitably difficult time—not only for teenagers themselves but also for those who work with them. To the extent that teachers come into the classroom with negative images of adolescence as a stage in the life cycle—that teenagers are inherently unruly, or unteachable, or perplexing—their preconceptions may interfere with their work as educators (Midgley, Feldlaufer, & Eccles, 1988). (Recall that this same sort of process affects parents who hold negative stereotypes about adolescence.) As we shall see in a later section, one of the most important influences on the adolescent's experience in school is the climate of his or her classroom.

■ **Individual Differences in the Extent of Transitional Problems** It is important to remember that although some aspects of the transition into secondary school may be difficult for students to negotiate, not all students experience the same degree of stress (Fenzel, 2001). Not surprisingly, students who have more academic and psychosocial problems before making a school transition cope less successfully with it (Berndt & Mekos, 1995; Carlson et al., 1999; S. A. Little & Garber, 2004; Murdock et al., 2000; Roeser, Eccles, & Freedman-Doen, 1999). Factors other than students' prior record may also influence the nature of their transition to middle or high school. Students who experience the transition earlier in adolescence have more difficulty with it than those who experience it later (Simmons & Blyth, 1987). And adolescents who have close friends before and during the transition adapt more successfully to the new school environment (Wentzel, Barry, & Caldwell, 2004), although the benefits of staying with their friends may accrue only to students who had been doing well previously; students who had been doing poorly actually adjust better if they enroll in a different school than their friends, perhaps because their friends were contributing to their poor performance (Schiller, 1999).

Evidently, then, the transition into secondary school is not the sort of stressor that has uniform effects on all students. More vulnerable adolescents, adolescents with fewer sources of social support, and adolescents moving into more impersonal schools may be more susceptible to the adverse consequences of this transition than their peers are. Not surprisingly, then, studies of poor, inner-city youngsters, who often are coping with problems associated with economic stress and neighborhood disadvantage, find especially significant negative effects of the school transition on these students' self-esteem, achievement, perceptions of the school environment, reports of social support, and participation in extracurricular activities (Eccles, 2004; Seidman, Aber, Allen, & French, 1996; Seidman, Allen, Aber, Mitchell, & Feinman, 1994). One study of Texas adolescents found that Black and, especially, Mexican American youngsters were more likely than their White peers to experience a variety of difficulties during the transition out of elementary school—including receiving poor grades, getting into trouble with teachers, and being hassled by other students (Munsch & Wampler, 1993). Another study found that, among Black and Latino students, transitioning to a school where the proportion of students from the same ethnic background is lower than it had been at their previous school is associated with greater disengagement from school, lower grades, and more frequent absences (see Figure 6.2) (Benner & Graham, 2009).

Low-income students' adjustment to middle school may be enhanced as a result of an intervention targeted at their parents, according to one study (Bronstein et al., 1998). The researchers had parents participate in an

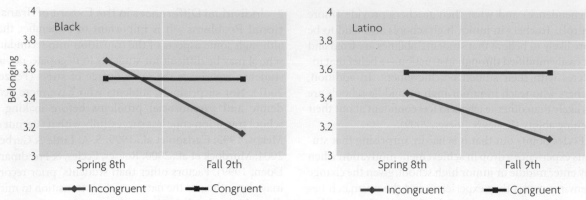

FIGURE 6.2 Transitioning into secondary school may lead to feelings of disengagement when there are fewer students of the same ethnic background. *Congruent* refers to whether the student's ethnicity is the same as that of the majority of students in the school. (Benner & Graham, 2009)

11-week program designed to increase their understanding of adolescent development and their effectiveness as parents. The children whose parents participated in the program were functioning better psychologically and behaviorally, both immediately after the program and one year later, than were their counterparts whose parents did not participate. Moreover, the children whose parents participated did not show the decline in functioning that often is associated with the transition into middle school. In general, parental support and involvement are associated with better adolescent adjustment during school transitions (Isakson & Jarvis, 1999). One study of low-income Black students found that students who fare best during the transition not only have parents who are involved in their education, but supportive teachers as well (Gutman & Midgley, 2000).

TRACKING

In some schools, students with different academic abilities and interests do not attend classes together. Some classes are designated as more challenging and more rigorous, and are reserved for students identified as especially capable. Other classes in the same subject area are designated as average classes and are taken by most students. Still others are designated as remedial classes and are reserved for students having academic difficulties. The process of separating students into different levels of classes within the same school is called ability grouping, or **tracking.** Not all high schools use tracking systems. In some schools, students with different abilities take all their classes together.

Even among schools that use tracking, there are important differences in the implementation of the tracking system (J. Jones, Vanfossen, & Ensminger, 1995). Some schools are more inclusive in their tracking,

permitting a relatively high proportion of students into the highest track (even, perhaps, some students whose abilities do not warrant such placement). Other schools are more exclusive, limiting the places in the highest track to a privileged few (even if this means placing some high-ability students in the lower tracks). And still other schools are "meritocratic," placing students in tracks that accurately match their abilities.

■ **Pros and Cons of Tracking** Educators have debated the pros and cons of tracking for years, but research provides no definitive answers about its overall effects (Eccles & Roeser, 2009). Proponents of tracking note that ability grouping allows teachers to design class lessons that are more finely tuned to students' abilities; tracking may be especially useful in high school, where students must master certain basic skills before they can learn such specialized subjects as science, math, or foreign languages. Critics of tracking point out, however, that students who are placed in the remedial track generally receive not just a different education, but a poorer-quality education, than those in the more advanced tracks (Darling-Hammond, 1997). Moreover, the effects of tracking are not limited to academic outcomes. Because schools play such an important role in influencing adolescents' friendships, when students are tracked, they tend to socialize only with peers from the same academic group. Tracking can thereby contribute to the polarization of the student body into different subcultures that are often hostile toward each other (Eccles & Roeser, 2009).

FOOD FOR THOUGHT

Tracking seems to have different effects on students in the more advanced and less advanced tracks. In view of this, should schools engage in ability grouping?

tracking   The grouping of students, according to ability, into different levels of classes within the same school grade.

Some critics of tracking also point out that decisions about track placements often discriminate against poor and ethnic minority students and may hinder rather than enhance their academic progress (Ayalon, 1994; Oakes, 1995; Wells & Serna, 1996). Some school counselors assume, for example, that ethnic minority or poor youngsters are not capable of handling the work in advanced classes and may automatically assign them to average or remedial classes, where less material is covered and the work is less challenging (Vanfossen, Jones, & Spade, 1987). One recent analysis of national data found, for instance, that Black students were especially more likely to be enrolled in lower-track math classes in schools in which Blacks are in the minority, even after taking into account students' qualifications (S. Kelly, 2009).

Not all research indicates that track placements are biased, however. Other studies have found that students' ability has a stronger influence than their background on initial track placement (Dauber, Alexander, & Entwisle, 1996), but that middle-class and White students initially placed in lower tracks are more likely to be moved into higher ones, in part because their parents frequently succeed in "lobbying" their child's school for a changed track placement (Hallinan, 1996; Oakes, 1995; Wells & Serna, 1996). It is also the case that adolescents from more well-off families more frequently consult with their parents about what courses to take than do less affluent adolescents, and this leads more affluent students to take more (and more advanced) math and science classes (Crosnoe & Huston, 2007).

One arena in which track assignments seem to be especially influenced by factors other than ability is in math, where boys are more likely than girls to be placed in more advanced classes. Although elementary school girls generally outscore boys on tests of math achievement, junior and senior high school boys are more likely to be enrolled in advanced math classes (Davenport et al., 1998). Studies also show that girls are less likely than boys to be moved from a lower math track into a higher one (Hallinan, 1996).

Tracking, Sexism, and Single-Sex Schools   Is this sort of sexism diminished in single-sex schools? According to one investigation involving 60 private schools—20 coeducational, 20 boys' schools, and 20 girls' schools—not necessarily (V. Lee, Marks, & Byrd, 1994). The researchers observed classes in these schools and carefully noted both subtle and blatant forms of sexism, such as a teacher's ignoring a young woman's interest in science or providing female students with less challenging math instruction than was warranted. Somewhat surprisingly, these sorts of practices existed even in girls' schools, despite the hope that girls might encounter less sexist instruction in a single-sex environment.

Although a number of academically demanding girls' schools were less sexist than the norm, there was considerable variation among the girls' schools studied. For example, the researchers observed teachers in girls' schools "talking down to girls, making academic activities more palatable by 'wrapping calculus in a nontechnical package,' setting up expectations that students would have difficulty with assignments by offering help before it was required or requested, or promulgating an attitude that 'trying hard is as important as succeeding' with difficult undertakings" (V. Lee et al., 1994, p. 114). In contrast, boys' schools were more likely to use an aggressive style of teaching that encouraged students to state their views assertively and to expect the intense scrutiny of their teachers and peers. Sexism was just as pronounced in coeducational schools, however, especially in science classes. For example, in one chemistry class, the female teacher responded positively to boys who spoke out without raising their hands but reprimanded girls for the exact same behavior. Another chemistry teacher at a different coeducational school told the researchers that he believed "girls are not suited to 'do' science" (V. Lee et al., 1994, p. 108).

The biased sorting of youngsters into math tracks has long-term implications for future course selection. An adolescent girl who is not assigned to a high-ability math class—despite her talent—may come to develop more negative attitudes toward math than she might have otherwise and may miss opportunities to pursue certain careers that require advanced mathematics training. Indeed, girls are less likely than boys to receive advice, encouragement, and counseling to take advanced courses in math or to prepare for careers that would require these courses (V. Lee et al., 1994).

On the Wrong Track   In many respects, then, early track placements set in motion an educational trajectory that is often difficult to change without the deliberate intervention of the student's parents (Dauber, Alexander, & Entwisle, 1996; Dornbusch, 1994; Hallinan, 1992, 1996; D. Stevenson, Schiller, & Schneider, 1994). And the ways in which students' schedules are arranged may lead students to be tracked in several different subject areas simply because they are tracked in one class, which makes the effects of tracking even more substantial (Heck, Price, & Thomas, 2004). If, for example, the only class period during which advanced math is offered is the same as the class period during which remedial English is taught, a student who is assigned to remedial English will not be able to take advanced math (Lucas & Berends, 2002).

Research on tracking in high schools indicates quite clearly that students in different tracks have markedly different opportunities to learn (Gamoran, 1996; D. Stevenson et al., 1994). Students in the more

Research on tracking suggests that it has positive effects on the achievement of students in the more advanced tracks but negative effects on students in the lower tracks.

advanced tracks receive more challenging instruction and better teaching, and they are more likely to engage in classroom activities that emphasize critical thinking rather than rote memorization (Darling-Hammond, 1997). Being placed in a more advanced track has a positive influence on school achievement (how much the student actually learns over time), on subsequent course selection (what curriculum the student is exposed to), and on ultimate educational attainment (how many years of schooling the student completes). To the extent that a student's family background influences his or her track placement, tracking has the effect of maintaining the status quo (Oakes, 2005).

In addition, because students are assigned to different tracks initially on the basis of test scores and other indicators of aptitude, and because students in the lower tracks receive an inferior education, the net effect of tracking over time is to increase preexisting differences among students. The students who need the most help are assigned to the tracks in which the quality of instruction is the poorest; not surprisingly, studies find that students in lower tracks exert less effort, which, in turn, limits their learning (Callahan, 2005; Carbanaro, 2005). In other words, in a school that uses tracking, the academically rich get richer, and the poor get poorer. Although students in the lower tracks usually get the short end of the educational stick, there are some exceptions— for example, schools in which classes in the lower tracks

gifted students Students who are unusually talented in some aspect of intellectual performance.

are taught by strong teachers who insist on maintaining high standards (Gamoran, 1993; Hallinan, 1996).

▮ The Effects of Tracking on Student Achievement
Literally hundreds of studies have been done on the impact of tracking on student achievement (Hallinan, 1996). Unfortunately, this research suggests both positive and negative effects and, more importantly, different effects among students in different tracks. More specifically, tracking has positive effects on the achievement of high-track students, negative effects on low-track students, and negligible effects on students in the middle (Fuligni, Eccles, & Barber, 1995; Hallinan, 1996). Because of this, decisions about whether to implement tracking in nontracked schools, or whether to "detrack" schools that use ability grouping, are typically quite controversial; not surprisingly, parents of students in the higher tracks favor the practice, while parents of students in the lower tracks oppose it (Wells & Serna, 1996).

Even in schools that do not have formal tracking, of course, teachers may group students within the same class into ability groups. In such an arrangement, students may have a wider range of peers with whom to compare themselves than they would in separate tracks, since their classes are more diverse in composition. The impact of this comparison process on both students and teachers is quite interesting. For high-ability students, within-classroom ability grouping raises their expectations for achievement and raises their teachers' evaluations of them; for low-ability students, the opposite is true: They have lowered expectations and get worse grades from their teachers (Reuman, 1989). Presumably, both adolescents and teachers make their evaluations based on unstated comparisons. In mixed classes with ability groups, the high-ability students look better, and the low-ability students look worse, than they would in a conventionally tracked school or in a school in which ability grouping is not used (H. Marsh, Chessor, Craven, & Roche, 1995). As is the case with tracking, within-classroom ability grouping also exposes students in different groups to different levels of educational quality, with students in the high-ability groups receiving more challenging instruction and more engaging learning experiences (Catsambis, 1992).

▮ Students at the Extremes
Related to the issue of tracking are questions concerning the placement of individuals who are considered **gifted students** and of

those who have a **learning disability.** Adolescents who score 130 or higher on an intelligence test are gifted. Adolescents with a learning disability are those whose actual performance is significantly poorer than their expected performance (based on intelligence tests and the like) and whose difficulty with academic tasks cannot be traced to an emotional problem, such as coping with a parental divorce, or sensory dysfunction, such as a visual or hearing impairment. Most learning disabilities are presumed to be neurological in origin (Lovitt, 1989).

Educators have debated whether gifted students and those with learning disabilities are best served by instruction in separate classes (for example, in enriched classes for gifted students or in special education classes for students with a learning disability) or by **main streaming,** the integration of all students with special needs into regular classrooms. Pros and cons of each approach have been identified. On the one hand, separate special education programs can be tailored to meet the specific needs of students and can target educational and professional resources in a cost-effective way. On the other hand, segregating students on the basis of academic ability may foster social isolation and stigmatization—either for being "stupid" or for being a "brainiac."

Generally, educators have tended to favor mainstreaming over separate classrooms for adolescents with special needs. (In the case of adolescents with disabilities, mainstreaming, whenever possible, is required by law.) Proponents of mainstreaming argue that the psychological costs of separating adolescents with special academic needs from their peers outweigh the potential academic benefits. Studies of gifted youngsters have found, for example, that those who were integrated into regular classrooms have more positive academic self-conceptions than did those assigned to special classes (H. Marsh et al., 1995) and that these effects persist even after graduating (H. Marsh, Trautwein, Lüdtke, Baumert, & Köller, 2007). One downside to being placed with students of high academic ability is that when other students compare themselves to their high-achieving classmates, they don't feel as competent as they would if their point of comparison were students who were not so smart. This phenomenon, called the **big fish–little pond effect,** has been documented around the world, most recently in an analysis of data from over 100,000 students attending schools in 26 different countries (H. Marsh & Hau, 2003). Being a big fish in a little pond is also helpful for admission to college. One recent study of some 45,000 applications to three elite universities found that applicants' chances of being accepted are greater when they come from high schools with a relatively lower proportion of other high-achieving students than when applicants with the same credentials come from high schools with many other high achievers (Espenshade, Hale, & Chung, 2005).

Whereas the big fish–little pond effect suggests that gifted students might not be better off psychologically in classes restricted to high-achieving students—and argues in favor of mainstreaming them—it poses a dilemma for those who favor mainstreaming students with learning disabilities. Low-achieving students, when mainstreamed, will end up comparing themselves to students whose performance is better than their own, and they may end up feeling worse about themselves than had they been separated into special classes with comparably achieving peers (H. Marsh & Hau, 2003). Perhaps because of this, studies find that, even with mainstreaming, adolescents who have learning disabilities may suffer psychological consequences related to their problems in school. Compared with average-achieving students, adolescents with learning disabilities report more social and behavioral difficulties and, not surprisingly, more problems in coping with school. They are also more likely than other adolescents to have poor peer relations, are less likely to participate in school-based extracurricular activities, and are more likely to drop out of school (Lovitt, 1989). Given the tremendous importance society places on school success, it is not difficult to see why students who have difficulties learning would suffer psychological as well as scholastic problems.

ETHNIC COMPOSITION

Following the landmark U.S. Supreme Court rulings in *Brown v. Board of Education of Topeka* (1954, 1955), in which the Court found that it was unconstitutional to maintain separate schools for children on the basis of race, many school districts adopted measures designed to make schools more diverse. They did this either by assigning students to schools in a way that would create ethnic diversity or by encouraging voluntary desegregation, through measures like having "magnet" schools that would create diversity by drawing students from different neighborhoods (for instance, by having city-wide schools specializing in the performing arts). Although the Supreme Court ruled in 2007 that school districts may no longer use race as a factor in deciding how to assign students to schools (R. Barnes, 2007), efforts to create ethnic and racial diversity through voluntary measures are still in use in many cities.

learning disability   A difficulty with academic tasks that cannot be traced to an emotional problem or sensory dysfunction.

mainstreaming   The integration of adolescents who have educational handicaps into regular classrooms.

big fish–little pond effect   The reason that individuals who attend high school with high-achieving peers feel worse about themselves than comparably successful individuals with lower-achieving peers.

■ **Effects of Desegregation** Does transforming the ethnic composition of a school make a big difference in student achievement? Studies of the short-term effects of desegregation on high school students have been mixed. On the one hand, research indicates that desegregation has surprisingly little impact on the achievement levels of either minority or White youngsters (Entwisle, 1990). In addition, some evidence suggests that minority youngsters' self-esteem is higher when they attend schools in which they are in the majority; in general, students fare better psychologically when the cultural environment of their neighborhood is consonant with the cultural environment of their school (Gray-Little & Carels, 1997; Goldsmith, 2004; Hudley, 1995; Nieto et al., 1996; Seaton & Yip, 2009). Consistent with this, students who have been bused to school out of their neighborhood report weaker feelings of attachment to their school than do students whose schools draw directly from the local community (Anderman, 2002). Students' attachment to school also is higher when they attend schools where relatively more of their classmates are from the same ethnic group; interestingly, ethnic composition affects students' emotional attachment to their school, but not their degree of participation in classroom activities (M. Johnston, Crosnoe, & Elder, 2001). Within multiethnic schools, however, students feel safer, less lonely, and less harassed in relatively more diverse schools (i.e., where the proportions of students from different ethnic groups are similar) than in schools that are less balanced (Juvonen, Nishina, & Graham, 2006). In general, though, research suggests that being in the minority in one's school is hard on students.

■ **Being in the Minority** The difficulties associated with attending school where one is in a distinct minority were tellingly illustrated in a study by Patricia Phelan and colleagues (Phelan, Yu, & Davidson, 1994). Consider these excerpts from the researchers' interviews with students:

Ivonne, Mexican American female: Well, I kind of feel uncomfortable. Not many Mexicans and Hispanics are in [my] classes. They [other students] probably think of me as weird, because they probably have this view that most Hispanics are dumb or something. They have that opinion, you know, [Hispanics] get bad grades. So, I don't know why I feel uncomfortable. I just . . . it means you're not really with any other . . . many people. Maybe by the end of the year they will realize that I belong. (Phelan et al., 1994, p. 425)

Trinh, Vietnamese American female: [Because I'm Vietnamese] I notice the little things more often than other people. Just like, I don't really get noticed by all the popular people. OK, everyone in the class, I know their names and everything. . . . Like being Vietnamese . . . like they have a lot of Americans in here. That there are more of

them, and when you're alone, you're nervous over little things. (Phelan et al., 1994, p. 425)

Sonia, Mexican American female: Yeah, it's weird, 'cause most teachers, you know—White teachers—some of them are kind of prejudiced. . . . It's probably the way they look at you, the way they talk, you know when they're talking about something—about something like when they talk about the people who are going to drop out, and they . . . look around, look around [at you].

And then Mr. Kula, when he's talking about teenage pregnancy or something like that. He turns around and he looks at us. It's like—he tries to look around the whole room, so we won't notice but like he mostly like tries to tell us, tries to get it through our heads, you know. Sometimes I think he's prejudiced. And sometimes I think he's trying to help us. (Phelan et al., 1994, p. 431)

ALTERNATIVES TO PUBLIC SCHOOLS

While the vast majority of students attending secondary school in America are enrolled in conventional public schools, a substantial minority attend private schools, either parochial (i.e., with a religious affiliation) or independent, or specially created public schools, like charter schools or magnet schools. In the past, researchers cared little about studying differences between public schools and their alternatives. But, as we noted earlier, during the late 1980s and 1990s, many education policymakers suggested that one way to improve

Although social scientists disagree over their interpretation, studies have shown that adolescents who attend parochial schools generally achieve at a higher rate than those attending public schools.

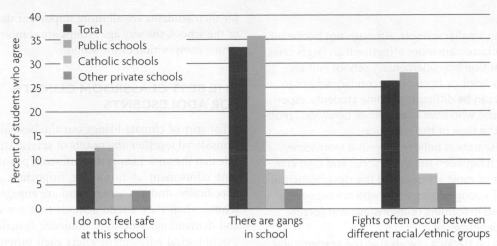

FIGURE 6.3   Students in private schools report more safety and less exposure to gangs and fighting than do students in public schools. (National Center for Education Statistics, 2002)

schools would be to give parents more of a choice in determining where their child was enrolled, in order to force schools to compete for the best students. There is some evidence to support this: When information about school test scores is provided to parents, parents choose to send their children to higher-performing schools, which in turn increases the students' achievement (Hastings & Weinstein, 2008).

One concrete suggestion in this spirit was that states provide parents with school vouchers that could be used to "purchase" education at a school of their choosing—private or public. Another suggestion was that states permit the development of charter schools—independent public schools that are freer to operate as they wish, without some of the constraints imposed by the state's education bureaucracy. In light of these suggestions, researchers became interested in whether some types of schools produced more high-achieving students than others.

Are alternatives to public schools better than public schools? Although students' test scores are higher in private schools (especially Catholic schools), this appears to be due more to the characteristics of the students who attend them than to the private schools themselves (Braun, Jenkins, & Grigg, 2006; Lubienski & Lubienski, 2006; Rumberger & Palardy, 2005), although some studies have found genuine advantages for Catholic school especially among poor, inner-city, minority youth (Jeynes, 2002). These studies, as well as a large body of research on the topic that we'll look at in Chapter 12, indicate that students' family background is a far more powerful influence on their achievement than is the quality of the school they attend. Similarly, evaluations of the impact of charter schools and voucher programs on student achievement, once students' background characteristics are taken into account, have not produced consistent results; at the very least, research

indicates that these are not likely to be "silver bullets" in the effort to raise American student achievement (Howell & Peterson, 2002; Loveless, 2002). This is also true in disadvantaged urban areas, where it had been hoped that charter schools might be the solution to the many problems that plague education in the inner city. One additional concern is that in urban areas, the availability of private schools contributes to racial segregation, because many White students who would otherwise attend their neighborhood public school attend private school instead (Saporito & Sohoni, 2006).

One thing we do know is that the climate of public and private schools, especially Catholic schools, is often very different. As many writers have pointed out, a Catholic school is a community in which parents, teachers, and students all share similar values and attitudes. Strong communities, whether based in neighborhoods or schools, generate what has been called **social capital**—interpersonal resources that, like financial capital, give "richer" students advantages over "poorer" ones. Students profit from the social capital associated with attending a Catholic school, for example, because the lessons taught in school are reinforced at home, at church, and in the neighborhood, and because the links between home and school are stronger (Teachman et al., 1996). In addition, private schools typically assign more homework and are more orderly and disciplined (as you will read, an important element of the climate in good schools) (Coleman, Hoffer, & Kilgore, 1982). As Figure 6.3 illustrates, for example, students who attend private schools (Catholic or otherwise) are substantially less likely to report feeling unsafe, being exposed to gangs, or witnessing fighting between ethnic groups (National Center for Education Statistics, 2002).

social capital   The interpersonal resources available to an adolescent or family.

RECAP

- Generally, smaller schools, although not necessarily smaller classes, are more effective than larger ones.
- The transition from elementary school into secondary school, or from one secondary school to another, can be difficult for some students, especially those who have academic or behavioral problems at the time of the transition.
- Many researchers believe there is a worrisome mismatch between the impersonal and rigid environment of most schools and the developmental needs of young adolescents, who are especially interested in forming relationships and forging their independence.
- Research on tracking reveals that the academically rich get richer and the poor get poorer. Students who are placed in the more advanced tracks or in high-ability groups in classrooms achieve more than those in lower tracks, in part because the quality of instruction in the higher tracks is superior.
- In general, the effects of changing the ethnic composition of a school on student achievement are very modest, although in general students are happier when their ethnic group is not in the minority.
- There appear to be advantages for students who attend Catholic schools, but these may be due more to student background characteristics than to the schools themselves. As a rule, what takes place within schools is more important than how they are funded or organized.

Classroom Climate

Thus far, we have seen that certain elements of the school's social organization—size, age grouping, tracking, and so forth—can affect students' motivation, behavior, and achievement. But these factors have relatively modest effects on students, and they are important mainly because they influence what takes place in classrooms and in other school settings. Indeed, most social scientists and educators now agree that the most important school-related influences on learning and psychosocial development during adolescence are those seen in the more immediate environment of the school and classroom.

Various aspects of the school climate have important effects on youngsters' learning and achievement (Eccles & Roeser, 2009). Specifically, how teachers interact with students, how classroom time is used, and what sorts of standards and expectations teachers hold

for their students are all more important than the size of the school, the way age groups are combined, or the ethnic composition of the school.

THE BEST CLASSROOM CLIMATE FOR ADOLESCENTS

What sort of climate brings out the best in students? Considered together, the results of several studies indicate that the same factors that influence positive adolescent adjustment at home are important at school. Specifically, students achieve and are engaged more in school when they attend schools that are responsive and demanding. Moreover, academic functioning and psychological adjustment affect each other, so that a positive school climate—where relationships between students and teachers are positive, and teachers are both supportive and demanding—enhances adolescents' psychological well-being as well as their achievement (Eccles, 2004; Gutierrez, 2000; Kalil & Ziol-Guest, 2008; Reddy, Rhodes, & Mulhall, 2003; Roeser, Eccles, & Sameroff, 1999).

Generally, both students and teachers are more satisfied in classes that combine a moderate degree of structure with high student involvement and high teacher support, a finding that has emerged in studies of both White and non-White students from various socioeconomic backgrounds (Langer, 2001; Vieno, Perkins, Smith, & Santinello, 2005; Way & Robinson, 2003; Wentzel, 2002). In these classes, teachers encourage their students' participation but do not let the class get out of control. Classes that are too task oriented—particularly those that also emphasize teacher control—tend to make students anxious, uninterested, and unhappy (Moos, 1978). Students do best when their teachers spend a high proportion of time on lessons (rather than on setting up equipment or dealing with discipline problems), begin and end lessons on time, provide clear feedback to students about what is expected of them and about their performance, and give ample praise to students when they perform well (Rutter, 1983).

Perhaps not surprisingly, one of the strongest influences on how much students enjoy going to school is the extent to which they feel their teachers respect and care about them (Hallinan, 2008). Students in schools in which teachers are supportive but firm and maintain high, well-defined standards for behavior and academic work have stronger bonds to their school and more positive achievement motives; these beliefs and emotions, in turn, lead to fewer problems, better attendance, lower rates of delinquency, more supportive friendships, and higher scores on tests of achievement (Eccles, 2004; Loukas, Suzuki, & Horton, 2006; A. M. Ryan & Patrick, 2001; Way & Pahl, 2001). Students also demonstrate higher achievement when the classroom climate promotes cooperation, rather than competition, between students (Roseth, Johnson, & Johnson, 2008).

Actually, there are many similarities between good teachers and good parents (Wentzel, 2002). If you think back to what you read in Chapter 4, you'll see that the pattern of classroom variables associated with positive student behavior and attitudes is reminiscent of the authoritative family environment (Pellerin, 2005). Similarly, an overemphasis on control in the classroom in the absence of support is reminiscent of the authoritarian family, whereas a lack of clarity and organization is reminiscent of both the indulgent family and the indifferent family—and these styles in the classroom appear to affect adolescents detrimentally, just as they do at home.

TEACHER EXPECTATIONS AND STUDENT PERFORMANCE

In addition to research on school climate, several studies also point to the importance of teachers' expectations. There is a strong correlation between teacher expectations and student performance. This is both because teachers' expectations are often accurate reflections of their students' ability and because teacher expectations actually create self-fulfilling prophecies that ultimately influence how their students behave (Jussim & Eccles & Madon, 1996).

Which pathway is more powerful—the impact of student performance on teacher expectations, or the impact of teacher expectations on student performance? It appears that about 80% of the connection between teacher expectations and student achievement results from teachers' having accurate perceptions, and about 20% is an effect of the self-fulfilling prophecy. (The self-fulfilling prophecy appears to be somewhat stronger for academically weaker students, whose performance is more tied to teacher expectations.) Even though the self-fulfilling prophecy effect is relatively small, it may be quite powerful when accumulated over years of schooling.

Because teachers' expectations influence students' performance, it is important to understand where these expectations come from. Unfortunately, research suggests that teachers are likely to base their expectations in part on students' ethnic and socioeconomic background. In much the same way that these factors sometimes influence tracking decisions, as we saw earlier, they may consciously and unconsciously shape teachers' expectations, which, in turn, affect students' learning. Thus, for example, teachers may call on poor or minority students less often than they call on affluent or White students—conveying a not-so-subtle message about whose responses the teacher believes are more worthy of class attention

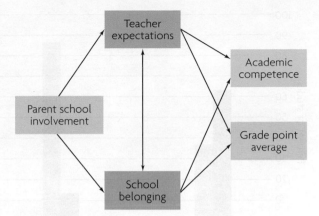

FIGURE 6.4   Parent involvement in school influences their high school children's achievement, both directly and indirectly, by raising teachers' expectations for their child's performance. (Kuperminc et al., 2008)

(T. Good & Brophy, 1984). Several studies report that Black and Latino students perceive their teachers as having low expectations and holding stereotypes about their likelihood of misbehaving (M. B. Spencer, 2005). Some evidence suggests that White teachers rate the misbehavior of Black students more harshly than do Black teachers (D. Downey & Pribesh, 2004), and, as you'll read later in this chapter, this leads to Black students receiving harsher discipline and more severe punishments than their peers receive for the same school infractions. It is not difficult to see how years of exposure to this sort of treatment can adversely affect students' self-concepts and interest in school. Indeed, teachers' biases against lower-class or minority adolescents may make it difficult for students from these groups to attain a level of academic accomplishment that permits upward mobility. In addition, biased treatment by teachers—having low expectations for some ethnic groups and high expectations for others—can contribute to feelings of hostility between students from different ethnicities (Rosenbloom & Way, 2004).

Parents also play an important role in the links between teacher expectations and student achievement. One recent study of Latino students found that how involved a student's parents were in school influenced their high school children's achievement directly (as in other studies, adolescents whose parents are involved in school perform better than their peers) but also affected teachers' expectations for their child's achievement, which, in turn, led to better student performance (see Figure 6.4) (Kuperminc, Darnell, & Alvarez-Jiminez, 2008). In addition, other research has found that one factor that helps protect low-income students against the impact of low teacher expectations is having high expectations for achievement from their parents (Benner & Mistry, 2007).

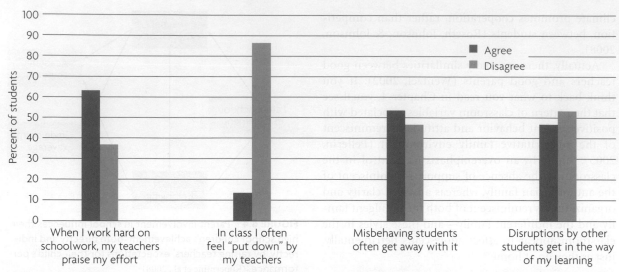

FIGURE 6.5   Students describe their teachers in positive terms but have less kind things to say about their peers' classroom behavior. (National Center for Education Statistics, 2002)

THE IMPORTANCE OF STUDENT ENGAGEMENT

It is important to keep in mind, of course, that students, as well as teachers, influence the classroom climate. In much the same way that the relationship between parents and adolescents is reciprocal—parents influence how their teenagers develop, but teenagers influence what their parents do—so is the relationship between teachers and their students. Effective teachers can engage and excite their students, and engaged and excited students can motivate their teachers to be more effective.

According to national surveys, however, levels of student engagement and excitement in American schools are not high. About half of all high school sophomores say that disruptive students get in the way of their learning and that students who misbehave are permitted to get away with it (see Figure 6.5) (National Center for Education Statistics, 2002). Studies also show that levels of student engagement in American high schools are very low, that many students are mainly going through the motions when they are in school, and that high school teachers often confront a roomful of students who are physically present but psychologically absent (Steinberg, 1996). Engaging students in school is also good for their overall mental health: Studies find that students who are disengaged from school are more likely to misbehave and engage in substance use (G. C. Patton, Bond, et al., 2006; Schmidt, 2003).

▮   **Boring Classes, Bored Students**   In view of this, several writers have suggested that if we want to

understand the impact of classroom climate on student achievement, we need to better understand how to enhance **student engagement**—the extent to which students are psychologically committed to learning and mastering the material rather than simply completing the assigned work (Newmann et al., 1996; Steinberg, 1996). Students frequently say they are bored while in school—especially high school students, who find school far more boring than do middle school students. As you can see in Figure 6.6, students are bored for most of the time on weekdays between 8:00 A.M. and 3:00 P.M., and the improvement in their mood seems to have more to do with the school day ending than with any special activity that takes place in the evening. Many experts believe that the make-work, routinized, rigid structure of most classrooms, in which teachers lecture at students rather than engage them in discussion, alienates most students from school and undermines their desire to achieve. Only about half of American sophomores agree with the statement "The subjects that I am taking are interesting and challenging," and one third say that they come to school because "I have nothing better to do" (see Figure 6.7) (National Center for Education Statistics, 2002). As one student explains:

> What do I like least about school? Basically, it's boring. Like English. What we do in there—we're supposed to read something, and then maybe do something in your notebook, when you could do everything at home. So I don't really have to show up. So, I'd say that class could be about 10 minutes long. (B. Brown, Lamborn, & Newmann, 1992)

The notion that many students feel disengaged from school—unchallenged and bored—has been borne out

student engagement   The extent to which students are psychologically committed to learning and mastering the material rather than simply completing the assigned work.

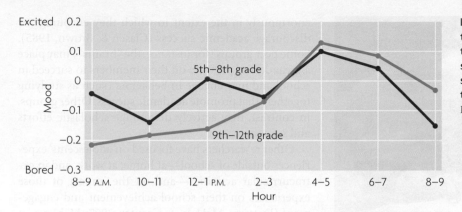

FIGURE 6.6 Studies of fluctuations in adolescents' mood over the course of the day show that students—especially high school students—feel bored most of the time they are in school. (Larson & Richards, 1998)

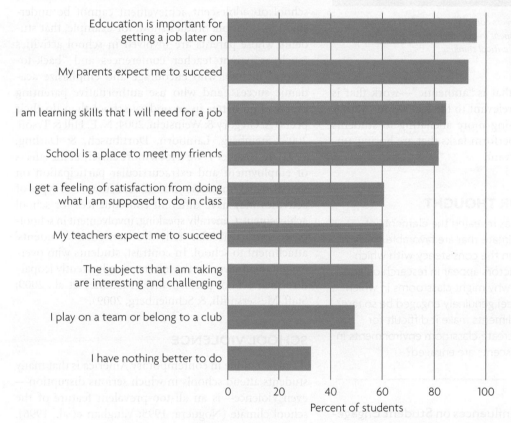

FIGURE 6.7 Students give a variety of reasons for attending school. (National Center for Education Statistics, 2002)

in numerous studies of contemporary American students (e.g., Owen, 1995; Steinberg, 1996). According to one study, titled *Getting By: What American Teenagers Really Think About Their Schools:*

> Students routinely admitted—some with bravado and some with chagrin—that they calibrate their efforts, often meticulously, to do only as much as it takes to get the grade they can live with. For youngsters aiming for private colleges or elite public universities, this concept of "getting by" implies a certain grade-point average.... Other youngsters ... seem satisfied with any passing grade.... Students from across the country repeatedly said that they could "earn" acceptable grades,

pass their courses, and receive a diploma, all while investing minimal effort in their school work.... Almost two-thirds of teens across the country (65%) say they could do better in school if they tried harder. (Public Agenda, 1997, p. 20)

Think back to your own high school experience. What distinguished the good classes from the tedious ones? Newmann (1992) suggests a number of specific factors that contribute to student engagement. First, teachers need to provide opportunities for students to genuinely display their competencies. Second, schools should try to facilitate students' feelings of belonging to their school. Finally, and most importantly, teachers

One reason so many teenagers complain of boredom in school is that few school hours are spent in activities that engage them intellectually or encourage critical thinking.

should assign work that is "authentic"—work that is interesting, fun, and relevant to the real world (Marks, 2000). There is nothing more alienating to students than being asked to perform tasks that are boring, uninteresting, and irrelevant.

FOOD FOR THOUGHT

Research has revealed the elements of school climate that are favorable to learning. Given the consistency with which these factors appear in research on good schools, why might classrooms in which students feel genuinely engaged be so rare? What impediments make it difficult for teachers to create classroom environments in which adolescents are engaged?

▌ **Out-of-School Influences on Student Engagement**   Teachers and school personnel, of course, are not the only influences on adolescents' behavior in school. Several writers have noted that the peer group's values and norms also exert an important influence, especially in high school (Bishop, 1999; Steinberg, 1996). High schools vary a great deal in the extent to which the prevailing peer culture emphasizes academic success as a route toward status and popularity. In schools in which academic success is not valued by the student body, students are less likely to achieve grades that are consonant with their tested ability. In other words, a bright student who attends a school in which getting good grades is frowned upon by other students will actually get lower grades than he or she would in a school in which scholastic success is generally admired. Even within the same school, cliques and crowds differ

enormously in the extent to which they encourage or discourage academic success (Clasen & Brown, 1985). Some peer groups (for instance, the "brains") may place a great deal of pressure on their members to succeed in school and may engage in behaviors (such as studying together) that promote academic success. Other groups, in contrast, may actively discourage scholastic efforts and success.

Other researchers have focused on adolescents' experiences outside of school—at home, at work, and in extracurricular activities—and on the impact of those experiences on their school achievement and engagement (Dotterer, McHale, & Crouter, 2007; Mahoney et al., 2009). This research demonstrates that the impact of school on adolescent achievement cannot be understood in isolation. Studies show, for example, that students whose parents are involved in school activities (such as parent–teacher conferences and "back-to-school" nights), who encourage and emphasize academic success, and who use authoritative parenting practices do better in secondary school than do their peers (A. Gregory & Weinstein, 2004; N. E. Hill & Tyson, 2009; Steinberg, Lamborn, Dornbusch, & Darling, 1992). In Chapter 7, we'll look more closely at the effects of employment and extracurricular participation on school achievement. As you will read, these two types of activities may have different consequences for school achievement. Generally speaking, involvement in school-based extracurricular activities strengthens students' attachment to school. In contrast, students who overextend themselves on the job may inadvertently jeopardize their school performance (Mahoney et al., 2009; Staff, Messersmith, & Schulenberg, 2009).

SCHOOL VIOLENCE

A sad fact of life in contemporary America is that many students attend schools in which serious disruption—even violence—is an all-too-prevalent feature of the school climate (Noguera, 1995; Vaughan et al., 1996). According to a national survey of secondary school students in American public schools, 1 out of every 4 students has been a victim of violence in or around school, and 1 out of 6 is worried about being physically attacked or hurt while in school. These problems are especially common in middle schools (Nolle, Guerino, & Dinkes, 2007). One recent study found that nearly half of all middle schoolers had been threatened at school (Flannery, Weseter, & Singer, 2004). In another study, of sixth-graders attending a multiethnic school in Los Angeles, half the students surveyed reported having been verbally harassed during the previous 2 weeks, and about one fifth said they had been physically victimized (Nishina & Juvonen, 2005). Violence is more common in overcrowded schools located in poor urban neighborhoods (Khoury-Kassabri, Benbenishty, Astor,

& Zeira, 2004). Fifty years ago, teachers expressed concerns about such disciplinary problems as students chewing gum, talking out of turn, or making noise; today, when teachers are surveyed about disciplinary problems in their schools, they list things like rape, robbery, and assault (Toch, 1993).

Interviews with students who live in communities where violence is common illuminate the ways in which these youngsters manage their day-to-day activities to avoid exposing themselves to harm (Irwin, 2004). Some make sure that they steer clear of students who have reputations for violent behavior and go out of their way to act friendly if they can't avoid them. Others learn which parts of town to avoid. Still others befriend peers who can serve as protectors, as this 16-year-old Latina did after someone at her school threatened to kill her:

> I got so scared. I didn't know what to do. I ran in the house and called my friend Daryl and I was really crying and [said] "I don't know what to do." And Daryl's all, "What's his number? What's his number?" And I gave it to him. Since that day, that same guy will leave me alone because Daryl went up to him and told him he better leave me alone or else something is going to happen to him and his family. (Irwin, 2004, pp. 467–468)

One study of violence in a multiethnic, urban high school found that Asian students were often the victims of violence and verbal harassment at the hands of their Black and Latino classmates, in part because of perceptions that teachers favored Asians and discriminated against their non-Asian classmates (Rosenbloom & Way, 2004). According to the researchers:

> Students reported random "slappings" by male and female peers as they walked through the hallways. Slappings are quick, pop shots, often to the head or body as students passed one another in the hall or anywhere else. Asian students described them as unnerving, randomly occurring, and humiliating violations that are particularly harrowing for the boys when girls slap them. . . . Along with the slappings, Asian American students were observed and reported being pushed, punched, teased, and mocked by their non–Asian American peers. The racial slur "chino" or "geek" was often heard as Asian American students passed by. (Rosenbloom & Way, p. 433)

Experts disagree about how best to respond to violence in schools. Some educators have suggested that schools should refer aggressive students to law enforcement, and many schools have police officers on duty to deter assaults and arrest students who cause trouble. But some writers contend that the new, get-tough approach to violence prevention in schools—referred to as **zero tolerance**—has not helped and that school violence is more effectively reduced through programs that attempt to create a more humane

Student performance influences, and is influenced by, teacher expectations.

climate (American Psychological Association [APA] Zero Tolerance Task Force, 2008). One unintended consequence of zero-tolerance policies is that many students end up with arrest records and contact with the justice system for acts that in the past would have been treated as disciplinary infractions by school officials (Casella, 2003). This has a disproportionate impact on Black students, who are more likely than other students to report that school rules are unfair and inconsistently enforced and to be suspended or expelled, even though they are no more likely to commit the sorts of acts that would warrant these responses (APA Zero Tolerance Task Force, 2008; Kupchik & Ellis, 2008). Among the many recommendations offered by a task force of the American Psychological Association, after a careful review of the research evidence, are that schools define infractions carefully and train all staff in how to respond appropriately to them, reserve suspension or expulsion for only the most serious disruptive behavior, require school police officers to have training in adolescent development, and implement preventive measures to improve school climate and increase students' attachment to school. Of course, one of the ways to do this would be to reduce the number of disruptive students, by intervening to change their behavior at an earlier age (LeBlanc, Swisher, Vitaro, & Tremblay, 2008).

■ **Lethal School Violence**   A series of widely publicized school shootings in the United States during the late 1990s—such as the school shootings at Columbine

zero tolerance   A get-tough approach to adolescent misbehavior that responds seriously or excessively to the first infraction.

High School—drew national attention to the problem of lethal school violence (M. Moore, Petrie, Braga, & McLaughlin, 2003). As with many topics that generate a great deal of attention in the media, much of what was asserted about school shootings has turned out not to be the case. Although violence in schools is indeed a significant problem, lethal school shootings are extremely rare events, especially when you consider the number of schools and students in the United States (there are about 50 million schoolchildren in the United States, and fewer than 20 students are killed in American schools each year) (M. Anderson et al., 2001). In fact, you may be surprised to learn that the number of school shootings has actually declined since the early 1990s; there has been an increase in the number of student deaths in schools, but this is due to the use of automatic weapons (which tends to leave more victims) and not to any increase in the number of shootings (M. Anderson et al., 2001).

Actually, far more children and adolescents are killed at home or in the community than in or around school; indeed, schools are among the *safest* places for adolescents to be (Mulvey & Cauffman, 2001). In fact, an American adolescent is 4 times more likely to be struck by lightning than to be shot in school (Steinberg, 2001)! In addition, although the school shootings that garnered public attention generally involved White youth, a disproportionate number of homicides in schools involve non-White youth, both as perpetrators and victims (M. Anderson et al., 2001). Perhaps most importantly, it is virtually impossible to predict which students will commit acts of lethal violence (Mulvey & Cauffman, 2001). Boys, students with mental health problems, and adolescents who have easy access to guns are more likely than others to be involved in school shootings (M. Moore et al., 2003), but identifying the specific students with these characteristics who will commit lethal crimes in school is a different matter altogether. Obviously, the vast majority of boys with mental health problems and access to guns never hurt anyone (Steinberg, 2000). Most experts believe that, in the absence of a proven means of identifying in advance adolescents who will commit acts of lethal violence in school, the most effective policy involves limiting adolescents' access to guns and identifying and treating young people with mental health problems (M. Moore et al., 2003).

RECAP

- Researchers agree that the climate of the school and its classrooms are more important influences on students' achievement, behavior, and psychological development than its organization or structure.
- Effective teachers are like authoritative parents— they are warm, firm, and fair, and they have high expectations for student performance.

- Several writers have suggested that if we want to understand the impact of the classroom environment on student achievement, we need to better understand how to enhance student engagement— the extent to which students are psychologically committed to learning and mastering the material. Unfortunately, many studies of American students indicate that they find school boring and undemanding.
- Students perform better in school when their parents are involved in their education, when their peers value academic achievement, and when their involvement in activities that compete with school is not excessively time-consuming.
- Many students attend schools in which serious disruption—even violence—is an all-too-prevalent feature of the school climate. Zero-tolerance policies, which harshly punish students for any act of violence, have been shown to have unintended and often harmful effects.

Beyond High School

THE COLLEGE-BOUND

The early 20th century was an important time in the development not only of secondary schools but also of postsecondary educational institutions in the United States. Although colleges and, to a lesser extent, universities had existed for some time previously, not until the latter part of the 19th century did diversity in institutions of higher education begin to develop. Early postsecondary institutions were typically small, private, liberal arts academies, often with a strong theological emphasis. But during a relatively brief period bridging the 19th and 20th centuries, these colleges were joined by a host of other types of institutions, including large private universities, technical colleges, professional schools, publicly financed state universities, land grant colleges, urban universities, and two-year community colleges (Brubacher & Rudy, 1976).

■ **The Growth of College Enrollment** Although postsecondary educational institutions multiplied and became more varied during the early 20th century, enrollment in college was still a privilege enjoyed by very few young people until the 1960s. In 1900, only 4% of the 18- to 21-year-old population was enrolled in college, and by 1930, the proportion had grown only to 12%. Even as recently as 1950, fewer than 1 in 5 young people were enrolled in college (Church, 1976). During the first half of the 20th century, then, colleges and

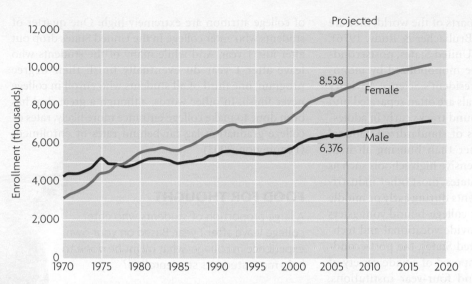

Projected

FIGURE 6.8 College enrollments in the United States continue to increase, especially among females. (National Center for Education Statistics, 2009)

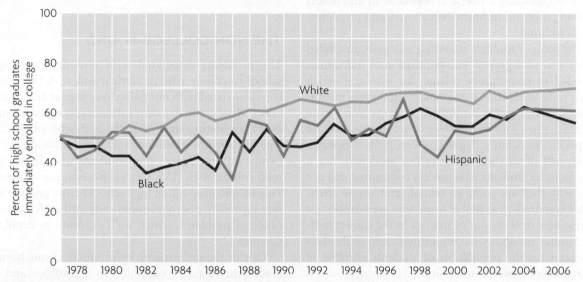

FIGURE 6.9 Today, nearly two thirds of all American high school graduates go immediately to college. (National Center for Education Statistics, 2009)

universities were not prominent in the lives of most American youth.

How different the state of affairs is today! Paralleling the rise of secondary education between 1920 and 1940, postsecondary education grew dramatically between 1950 and 1970. By 1960, one third of all young people were entering college directly from high school. Today, two thirds of high school graduates enroll in college immediately after graduation (National Center for Education Statistics, 2009). The increase in enrollments has been especially dramatic among women. In 1970, close to 70% of undergraduates were male; by the end of this decade, it is estimated that about 60% of all college students will be female (see Figure 6.8) (National Center for Education Statistics, 2009). Although there were large increases in the enrollment of

minority youth in higher education during the 1970s, the proportion fell during the early 1980s, primarily because of reductions in the availability of financial aid (Baker & Velez, 1996). Today, 70% of White high school graduates and about 60% of Black and Hispanic high school graduates go directly into college (see Figure 6.9). Youth from immigrant families, despite the fact that their parents typically did not attend American colleges themselves, and despite often having to support their family financially, are just as likely to enroll in and succeed in college as are American-born youth (Fuligni & Witkow, 2004).

▌ **American Postsecondary Education** If there are two dominant characteristics that distinguish the development of postsecondary education in contemporary

America from that in other parts of the world, they are diversity and accessibility (Brubacher & Rudy, 1976). In countries other than the United States, postsecondary education is likely to be monopolized by monolithic public universities (President's Science Advisory Committee, 1974). Individuals are often separated into college- and non-college-bound tracks early in adolescence, typically on the basis of standardized national examinations. In fact, rather than housing all high school students in comprehensive high schools such as those found in the United States, most other industrialized nations separate students during early or middle adolescence into schools for college-bound youngsters and schools designed to provide vocational and technical education. In the United States, the postsecondary education system is composed of a wide variety of public and private two- and four-year institutions, some emphasizing a liberal arts education and others focusing more on technical, vocational, and preprofessional training.

The goals of students attending college in the United States also vary greatly. The population of individuals enrolled in community college, for instance, which tends to be older than that attending four-year institutions, includes highly committed students who intend to transfer to a four-year college or are working toward a specific associate's degree or certificate (together, about half of all community college students). But it also includes students who are less committed and not sure why they are going to school (and whose attendance is sporadic), as well as some who are just taking a course here or there out of interest in the subject matter. Similar variability in commitment and goals likely characterizes the population of students enrolled in four-year colleges and universities.

▌ The Transition from High School to College

In some respects, the transition from high school to college parallels the transition from elementary to secondary school. For many students, going to college means entering an even larger, more formidable, and more impersonal environment. For some, the transition may coincide with other life changes, such as leaving home, breaking off or beginning an important romantic relationship, or having to manage their own residence or finances for the first time.

As a consequence of all these factors, although many more American adolescents enroll in college today than in previous years, a very large number do not graduate. Fewer than 60% of all students who enroll in a four-year college complete their degree within 6 years; at less selective schools, this figure is lower than 50% (American Enterprise Institute, 2009). Perhaps as a consequence of increasing accessibility, poor matching, and a lack of "consumer" knowledge among college applicants, rates of college attrition are extremely high: One quarter of students who enter college in the United States drop out after just 1 year. And while many of the students who leave after 1 year do eventually finish their degree program, one third of all students who enroll in college never finish. In other words, although a great deal has been done to make college entrance more likely, rates of college graduation lag far behind rates of enrollment (Pennington, 2003).

FOOD FOR THOUGHT

A large proportion of students who enter college leave after 1 year. Based on your own experience in college, what might be done to help more students stay enrolled?

THE NON-COLLEGE-BOUND

The problems associated with moving from high school to college pale in comparison with the problems associated with not going to college at all. In general, college graduates earn substantially more income over their lifetime than do individuals who attend college but do not graduate, and these individuals, in turn, earn much more than students who do not attend college at all (U.S. Census Bureau, 2009a). Individuals who drop out of high school before graduation fare especially poorly economically and suffer a wide range of problems, which we'll examine in detail in Chapter 12.

One of the unfortunate by-products of our having made postsecondary education so accessible—and so expected—is that we have turned our backs on individuals who do not go directly to college, even though they compose *one third* of the adolescent population. As many writers have noted, our secondary schools are geared almost exclusively toward college-bound youngsters (Krei & Rosenbaum, 2001).

We noted earlier that opportunities for learning and for critical thinking are much greater in college-prep classes than in the general or vocational tracks. In addition, students who are not headed for college—some by choice, others by unavoidable circumstance—find that their high schools have not prepared them at all for the world of work. Even those who complete school and earn a diploma—who have done what they were supposed to do as adolescents—may have a hard time finding employment and a nearly impossible time finding a satisfying, well-paying job. As a consequence, many individuals who do not go to college spend their early adult years floundering between periods of part-time work, underemployment (for example, working at a job that is less challenging than they would like), and unemployment. By the time they are 25 or so, most have found steady, if low-paying, employment. But they may have spent 6 or 7 years living very close to the edge, if not in genuine poverty. Rates of depression are significantly higher among young adults who are not in school than among those who are, and they are especially high among individuals who are neither in school nor steadily employed (Aseltine & Gore, 2005).

One important contributing factor to the continuing difficulties faced by adolescents who do not go to college has been the change in the world of work mentioned earlier in this chapter: As manufacturing jobs began to be replaced by minimum-wage service jobs, the chances of making a decent living without at least two years of college experience worsened appreciably. Today, young adults without college experience often must try to make ends meet on minimum-wage jobs— jobs that offer little in the way of promotion or advancement. The economic problems faced by non-college-bound youth have been compounded by the escalating costs of such essentials as housing and health care.

Given the high dropout rate already characteristic of most colleges, the answer to the problem does not seem to be simply to encourage more individuals to continue their education past high school. Obviously, for those who want a postsecondary education, we should make every attempt to see that they can obtain and afford it. But what about those adolescents who just are not interested in a college degree? How can these individuals be helped?

Experts believe that one potential answer involves strengthening the links between the worlds of school and work during high school, as discussed in Chapter 3 (S. Hamilton & Hamilton, 2009). In most other industrialized countries, non-college-bound youth begin apprenticeships during their last 2 years of compulsory school, so that by the time they have completed their formal schooling, they are well trained to take on skilled jobs (S. Hamilton & Hamilton, 2009). Instead of simply dumping such adolescents into the labor force at graduation, as we do in America, schools and communities provide training, career counseling, and job placement services throughout high school. In most contemporary American high schools, counseling is geared toward helping college-bound students continue their education. Billions of dollars, in the form of financial aid and subsidized public college tuition, are given to these students. Some critics have suggested that we should spend just as much time and money helping the other third of the adolescent population make their transition into adulthood as smooth as possible (Wald, 2005).

RECAP

- About two thirds of all American high school graduates go directly to some form of postsecondary education, but many college students drop out after their first year, probably because of a mismatch between their needs and the school environment, and only 60% graduate from college within 6 years of enrolling.
- High schools as they are presently structured do not serve non-college-bound adolescents very well. As a result, one third of the country's adolescents complete their formal education without adequate preparation for the world of work they hope to enter.
- Experts believe that one potential answer to the transition problems of students who do not go from high school to college involves strengthening the links between the worlds of school and work during high school.

Schools and Adolescent Development

CHARACTERISTICS OF GOOD SCHOOLS

Despite all the debate about how secondary schools ought to be organized and reformed, there is a fair degree of consensus among experts about the characteristics of good schools for adolescents (Eccles & Roeser, 2009), at least as far as student achievement is concerned (as you will read in Chapter 12, the characteristics of schools with high rates of student achievement are not the same as those with low rates of dropping out) (Rumberger & Palardy, 2005).

First and foremost, good schools emphasize intellectual activities (Ravitch, 1995, 2000). They create this atmosphere in different ways, depending on the nature and size of the student body, but in these good schools, a common purpose—quality education—is valued and shared by students, teachers, administrators, and parents (V. Lee, Smith, & Croninger, 1997). Learning is more important to students than athletics or extracurricular activities, and seeing that students learn is more important to teachers and administrators than seeing that they graduate. All students are expected to learn, and all students are taught by teachers who use proven instructional methods.

Second, good schools have teachers who are committed to their students and who are given a good deal of freedom and autonomy by administrators in the way that this commitment is expressed in the classroom

(V. Lee & Smith, 1996; V. Lee et al., 1997). In all schools, of course, teachers must have curricular requirements that they must fulfill. But in good schools, teachers are given relatively more authority to decide how their lessons are planned and how their classes are conducted. When teachers are given this sort of say in school governance, they may find it easier to commit to the shared values of the institution.

Third, good schools are well integrated into the communities they serve (Eccles & Roeser, 2009). Active attempts are made to involve parents in their youngsters' education, which is an important influence on student achievement and a deterrent against students dropping out (Rumberger & Palardy, 2005). Links are forged between the high school and local colleges and universities, so that advanced students may take more challenging and more stimulating courses for high school credit. Bridges are built between the high school and local employers, so that students begin to see the relevance of their high school education to their occupational futures.

Fourth, good schools are composed of good classrooms. In good classrooms, students are active participants in the process of education, not passive recipients of lecture material. The atmosphere should be orderly but not oppressive. Innovative projects replace rote memorization as a way of encouraging learning. Students are challenged to think critically and to debate important issues, rather than being asked simply to regurgitate yesterday's lessons (Newmann, Marks, & Gamoran, 1996).

Finally, good schools for adolescents are staffed by teachers who have received specific training in teaching adolescents (Eccles & Roeser, 2009).

FOOD FOR THOUGHT

Based on the criteria of good schools discussed in this chapter how would you rate the high school that you attended?

THE EFFECTS OF SCHOOL ON ADOLESCENT DEVELOPMENT

Whatever the shortcomings of schools, staying in school is preferable to dropping out, not only in terms of future earnings but in terms of cognitive development as well. One study contrasted the performance of dropouts and graduates on a battery of standardized tests of achievement administered during late adolescence (Alexander, Natriello, & Pallas, 1985). The study took into account differences in achievement levels that existed before the dropouts had left school (2 years before the assessment was conducted), because dropouts are more likely than graduates to show achievement problems early in their education. Compared with the dropouts, adolescents who stayed in school gained far more intellectually over the 2-year interval in a variety of content areas. More importantly, the results showed that the adverse effects of dropping out were most intense among socioeconomically disadvantaged youth. Paradoxically, then, those students who are most likely to leave school prior to graduation may be the most harmed by doing so.

One other way of assessing the contribution of schools to adolescents' intellectual development is by comparing early adolescents' intellectual gains during the school year with their gains during the summer. Several studies have done just this (e.g., H. Cooper, Charlton, Valentine, & Muhlenbruck, 2000). Using information about the academic progress of students measured at three points in time—the beginning of the school year, the end of the school year, and the beginning of the next year—researchers were able to see how the academic progress of students during the summer compared with their academic progress during the school session. Among students with higher socioeconomic status (SES), rates of academic progress during the school year and during the summer were comparable. Among disadvantaged students, however, the pattern was different. Although their rates of progress during the school year were more or less equal to those of higher-SES students, during the summer months, disadvantaged students' scores declined. In other words, if it were not for the effects of school on cognitive development, the discrepancy between affluent and poor youngsters' achievement scores would be much greater than it currently is. One benefit of summer school for disadvantaged students is that it diminishes the decline in achievement that would otherwise occur between the spring and fall semesters (H. Cooper et al., 2000).

Far less is known about the impact of schools on the psychosocial development of adolescents. Commentators have long noted that most schools are not structured to promote psychosocial development, given their excessive focus on conformity and obedience and their lack of encouragement for creativity, independence, and self-reliance (Friedenberg, 1967). This certainly comes through loud and clear when adolescents are asked about their classroom experiences. But there are many good schools in which students not only learn the academic material taught in classes but also learn about themselves, their relationships with others, and their society. Schools differ from each other, and it may be difficult to generalize about the impact of schools on adolescent development without knowing more about the particular school in question.

It is also important to recognize that despite adults' intentions and objectives, students do not view school solely in terms of its academic agenda. In one study, the researchers asked a sample of 7th- through 12th-graders to list the best and worst things about school. The best things? "Being with my friends" and "Meeting new people." The worst? Homework, tests, and the restrictive atmosphere of the school (B. Brown, Lamborn, & Newmann, 1992). Adults may evaluate schools in terms of their contribution to adolescents' cognitive and career development, but for the typical adolescent, school is a primary setting for socializing. A recent study of British 11- and 12-year-olds found that students' happiness in school was most influenced by their relationships with their peers (M. E. Booth & Sheehan, 2008). When we ask about the consequences of leaving school early, then, we must take into account the impact this may have on the individual's social, as well as cognitive, development.

Studies also show that students' experiences within a school can vary widely according to the track they are on, the peer group they belong to, and the extracurricular activities they participate in. It seems safe to say that academically talented and economically advantaged students have a more positive experience in school than their less capable or less affluent counterparts do—positive not only with respect to what they learn in class but also with respect to the impact of school on their feelings about themselves as individuals. They receive more attention from their teachers, are more likely to hold positions of leadership in extracurricular organizations, and are more likely to experience classes that are engaging and challenging. In other words, the structure of a school—its size, its tracking policy, its curricula—provides different intellectual and psychosocial opportunities for students who occupy different

places within that structure. The best answer to the question "How do schools affect adolescent development?" then, is another question: "Which schools, which adolescents, and in what ways?"

RECAP

- Good schools for adolescents have five characteristics: They emphasize intellectual activities, they have committed teachers who are given autonomy, they are well integrated into their community, they have a high proportion of classrooms in which students are active participants in their education, and they have teachers who have received specialized training in teaching adolescents.

- Evidence suggests that attending high school does, in fact, contribute to adolescents' intellectual development. However, critics of contemporary secondary schools have noted that most schools, with their focus on conformity and obedience and their lack of encouragement for creativity, independence, and self-reliance, are not structured to promote adolescents' psychosocial development.

- The ways in which adolescents are affected by school depend a great deal on the characteristics of the schools they attend. College-bound students in the more advanced tracks have markedly different experiences than do non-college-bound students in the lower tracks.

Work, Leisure, and Media

AS YOU KNOW, one of the hallmarks of teenage life in industrialized society is that adolescents have considerable amounts of time and money to devote to activities of their choosing. The scientific study of the ways in which work, leisure, and media influence adolescent development is not as well established as the study of other contexts (J. Mahoney, Vandell, Simpkins, & Zarrett, 2009; D. Roberts, Henriksen, & Foehr, 2009; Staff et al., 2009). But you may be surprised to know that today's teenagers spend more time in leisure activities than they do in the "productive" activities of school, more time alone than with members of their family, about 4 times the number of hours each week on a part-time job as on homework, and considerably more time "wired" to music, the Internet, or television than "tuned into" the classroom (D. Roberts et al., 2009; Staff, Messersmith, & Schulenberg, 2009). In this chapter, we look at these other important contexts of adolescence—the contexts of work, leisure, and the media, including the Internet.

Adolescents' Free Time in Contemporary Society

The abundance of free time in the lives of contemporary adolescents has several origins. Ironically, one of the most important contributors was the development of compulsory schooling. Prior to this, adolescents were expected to work full-time, and most maintained schedules comparable to those of adults, working long hours each week. With the spread of secondary schools during the early decades of the 20th century, however, adolescents were in effect barred from the labor force; the part-time jobs held by teenagers that are familiar to us today—working behind fast-food counters, for instance—simply did not exist in large numbers, making after-school employment opportunities rare.

One indirect effect of compulsory high school, then, was to increase the amount of free time available to young people—time that previously would have been occupied by work. Indeed, at the turn of the 20th century, adults were so worried about the free time available to adolescents that they began to organize various youth clubs and activities—such as the Boy Scouts and organized sports—in order to occupy their "idle hands" (Hine, 1999). In some respects, organized leisure became an institutionalized part of adolescence as a supplement to school and a replacement for full-time employment.

A second influence on the rise of free time for adolescents in contemporary society was the increased affluence of Americans following World War II. As noted in Chapter 3, the invention of the "teenager"—and, more importantly, the discovery of the teenager by those in advertising and marketing—changed the nature of adolescence in modern society. As adolescents gained more autonomy, they came to be recognized as consumers with plenty of discretionary income to spend on recreation, an accurate image that persists today (Osgerby, 2008). This week, notice the commercials and advertisements aimed at teenagers on television, in magazines, on the radio, or on the Internet. You'll see that much of the advertising targeted toward young people concerns leisure expenditures: music, movies, restaurants, electronic gadgets, cosmetics, athletic equipment, and so on.

FOOD FOR THOUGHT

Free time has not always played such an important role in the lives of teenagers. How do you think it has changed the nature of adolescence?

PATTERNS OF TIME USE IN CONTEMPORARY AMERICA

How much time do adolescents spend in various sorts of activities? In one study, early adolescents were asked to monitor their time use with electronic pagers (the adolescents were "beeped" periodically throughout the

One important feature of adolescence in contemporary society is the tremendous amount of time teenagers have for leisure activities.

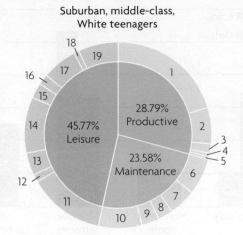

Suburban, middle-class, White teenagers

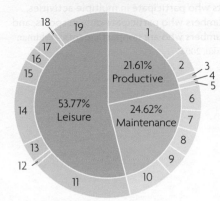

Urban, poor, Black teenagers

	Suburban	Urban
1	Classwork 19.92%	Classwork 14.74%
2	Homework 6.23%	Homework 4.48%
3	Extracurricular activities (includes school assemblies) 1.58%	Extracurricular activities (includes school assemblies) 1.13%
4	Working for pay (includes babysitting) 0.56%	Working for pay (includes babysitting) 0.27%
5	Religious activities 0.49%	Religious activities 0.99%
6	Eating 6.19%	Eating 4.53%
7	Transportation (includes walking) 4.63%	Transportation (includes walking) 3.76%
8	Resting 2.52%	Resting 4.46%
9	Chores and errands 2.92%	Chores and errands 3.99%
10	Personal maintenance 7.33%	Personal maintenance 7.89%
11	Television viewing 13.00%	Television viewing 17.53%
12	Music listening 1.27%	Music listening 0.83%
13	Creative activities 3.82%	Creative activities 3.34%
14	Talking 9.58%	Talking 11.12%
15	Playing 2.62%	Playing 3.97%
16	Playing games 1.83%	Playing games 2.55%
17	Playing sports (includes exercise, swimming, and other physical activities) 5.96%	Playing sports (includes exercise, swimming, and other physical activities) 3.73%
18	Public leisure (includes leisure shopping, attending a movie, outings) 0.89%	Public leisure (includes leisure shopping, attending a movie, outings) 0.77%
19	Idling (includes doing nothing, thinking, waiting) 6.79%	Idling (includes doing nothing, thinking, waiting) 9.94%

FIGURE 7.1 How suburban and urban adolescents spend their time. (Larson et al., 2001)

day and prompted to fill out questionnaires about what they were doing at the time). The results are presented in Figure 7.1 for two very different groups: suburban, middle-class, White teenagers, and urban, poor, Black teenagers. What is perhaps most striking about these data is how similar the groups' time allocation is, despite their very different backgrounds and living circumstances. In both groups, leisure activities, such as socializing, watching TV, and playing sports, account for about half their waking time; the balance is divided roughly evenly between productive activities, such as attending class and studying, and maintenance activities, such as grooming, eating, and running errands (Larson, Richards, Sims, & Dworkin, 2001) (see Figure 7.1).

Group averages can be deceptive, however, because there are wide variations even among teenagers from

similar socioeconomic and ethnic backgrounds in how they spend their free time. In one study, which tracked adolescents' time use over their high school years, the researchers identified several distinct groups of students (M. J. Shanahan & Flaherty, 2001). One especially busy group—about one third of the sample in all grades—spent considerable time in a wide range of activities, including extracurricular activities, paid work, schoolwork, time with friends, and household chores. A second group, about one fourth of the sample, was similarly busy but did not hold a paying job. A third group, whose numbers increased from about 12% in the 9th grade to 20% in the 12th grade, devoted substantial time to a paying job but spent little time on other activities. A fourth group spent no time in work or extracurricular activities, but a substantial amount of time hanging around with friends.

FIGURE 7.2   Studies of extracurricular participation generally find that there are large numbers of students who participate in multiple activities, large numbers who participate only in sports, and large numbers who are nonparticipants. (Feldman & Matjasko, 2007)

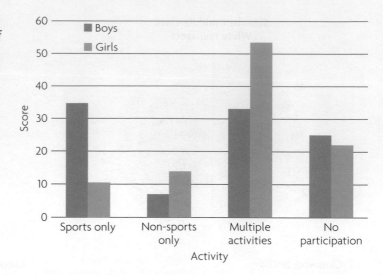

Although the study found that adolescents' time use patterns changed somewhat with age (not surprisingly, as adolescents got older, they were more likely to spend at least some of their free time working at a paid job), individuals who were busy ninth-graders were likely to be busy throughout high school. Overall, the results suggest that adolescents' free time is not best thought of as a "zero sum" phenomenon, whereby involvement in one activity necessarily displaces involvement in another. Rather, there appear to be well-rounded adolescents who have substantial time commitments across many different activities, adolescents who tend to focus on one type of activity (usually sports), and adolescents who are nonparticipants (see Figure 7.2) (A. F. Feldman & Matjasko, 2007). Generally, most studies, regardless of adolescents' socioeconomic or ethnic background, find that relatively busier adolescents are better adjusted and more achievement oriented than their classmates, but whether their better adjustment is caused by or results from their busy schedules is not clear (Bartko & Eccles, 2003). In one study of low-income minority youth, some forms of engagement—athletics, for example—were associated with positive outcomes when combined with a second type of engagement (for example, academics), but with negative outcomes if it was the only activity an adolescent was involved in (Pedersen et al., 2005).

PATTERNS OF TIME USE IN OTHER COUNTRIES

Patterns of time use differ considerably in different parts of the world. Generally, American adolescents spend far more time on leisure, and far less time in productive activities, than their counterparts in other countries. American students' use of their free time for school-related activities is especially low, and, as you would expect, it is particularly low among lower-achieving students (Witkow, 2009). For instance, the

average American high school student spends fewer than 5 hours per week on homework; in Asian countries such as India, Taiwan, and Japan, the average is between 4 and 5 hours *per day* (Larson & Verma, 1999). And European and Asian adolescents spend almost 3 times as many hours each week reading for pleasure as do American adolescents (Larson & Verma, 1999). In contrast, American teenagers spend relatively more time playing sports, socializing with friends, caring for their physical appearance, and working at after-school jobs (Alasker & Flammer, 1999; Flammer, Alasker, & Noack, 1999; Larson & Seepersad, 2003; Larson & Verma, 1999).

What is the effect of all this free time on adolescents' behavior and development? Are they learning about the real world from their part-time jobs? Are extracurricular activities beneficial? Are teenagers driven toward sex and violence by the mass media? Are they really affected by the lyrics of rock music, the images on MTV and BET, or the brutality of video games? Has the increase in time that they spend online adversely affected their ability to relate to others in person? Are concerns about adolescents' exposure to pornography and sexual predators on the Internet legitimate, or are they overstated? These are some of the questions we will address in this chapter. We begin by examining how teenagers are affected by after-school employment.

RECAP

- The rise of compulsory schooling and the increasing affluence of American society in the second half of the 20th century contributed to the increased importance of free time in the lives of contemporary adolescents.

- Today's American adolescents spend about half their time in leisure activities—far more than is the case in most other industrialized countries (where more time is devoted to school) and in developing nations (where more time is devoted to work).

- There is considerable variability in how individual adolescents spend their free time; some are very busy with structured extracurricular activities, while others' time is far more unstructured.

Adolescents and Work

Between 80% and 90% of today's high school students will have worked in an after-school job before graduating (Staff et al., 2009). Although working while attending high school may currently be the norm, only in the past 4 decades has part-time employment become widespread among American adolescents. As you will read, the employment of students in present-day America represents an important break from past eras, in which going to school and working were mutually exclusive activities.

SCHOOL AND WORK IN THE EARLY 20TH CENTURY

The place of paid work in the lives of teenagers has waxed and waned over the years. Prior to 1925—when continuing on in high school was the exception, not the rule—teenagers from all but the most affluent families left school between the ages of 12 and 15 and became full-time workers (Horan and Hargis, 1991; Modell, Furstenberg, & Hershberg, 1976). Depending on their social class, adolescents were either students or workers, but not both.

As secondary education became more widespread among different socioeconomic segments of American society, more youngsters remained in school well into middle and late adolescence, and fewer elected to work. Compulsory education laws were passed in most states that required individuals to remain in school until at least turning 16, part-time jobs were not plentiful, and a variety of child labor laws were enacted to restrict adolescents' employment (Kett, 1977). As a result of these social and legislative changes, the employment of American teenagers declined steadily during the first 4 decades of the 20th century. It's hard to imagine, given the presence of teenagers behind cash registers and fast-food counters today, but in 1940, only about 3% of high school students worked during the school year (U.S. Department of Commerce, 1940).

THE EMERGENCE OF THE STUDENT WORKER

The situation began to change during the second half of the 20th century, with the growth of the retail and

Many adolescents hold part-time jobs during the school year. Research has questioned whether working is good or bad for adolescent development.

service sectors of the economy. Employers needed workers who were willing to work part-time for relatively low wages and for short work shifts. Many businesses looked to teenagers to fill these jobs—and, in the mid-1970s, as you read in Chapter 5, teenagers were plentiful. The proportion of American high school students holding part-time jobs rose dramatically, and working during the school year became a way of life. Today, about 75% of seniors and 40% of sophomores work during the school year (Staff et al., 2009).

Not only are more high school students working today than ever before, but many students work fairly long hours. In 2006, for instance, about 30% of seniors worked between 1 and 15 hours each week, about 35% worked between 16 and 30 hours, and about 10% worked more than 30 hours weekly (Staff et al., 2009). Considering that the average school day runs for about 6 hours, many working adolescents are busy with school or work commitments for close to 50 hours a week, and this doesn't count time devoted to extracurricular activities or homework.

Although youngsters in contemporary America do not enter the formal labor force until age 15 or 16, many individuals will have worked on an informal basis during childhood, doing chores around the house or working for neighbors. This pattern is especially common in less industrialized societies and, among industrialized nations, more common in Western than Asian countries (Larson & Seepersad, 2003; Larson & Verma, 1999). In virtually all countries around the world, but especially in developing countries, household chores are more likely to be assigned to adolescent girls than boys, especially as they get older (National Research Council, 2005). Sex differences in time use are especially large among adolescents who are not students (Lloyd, Grant, & Ritchie, 2008). You might think of high schools as contributing to sex-role stereotypes, but without them, the differences between girls' and boys' lives would be even more severe.

TEENAGE EMPLOYMENT IN AMERICA AND IN OTHER NATIONS

The extent and nature of teenage employment vary considerably from country to country (Verma & Larson, 2003). In developing nations where industrialization is still in a relatively early stage and a large percentage of the population is poor, adolescents generally leave school early—at least by American standards. In many parts of the developing world, work obligations may take precedence over schooling. In these countries, most adolescents enter into full-time employment by age 15 or 16, in jobs similar to the ones they will hold as adults. Very often, adolescents work for their families. The pattern in these countries closely resembles that found in America 100 years ago: school for adolescents of the extremely affluent, and work for the rest (Larson & Verma, 1999). The trade-off between school and work is changing in the developing world. As more and more adolescents from developing nations are enrolled in school, the number of adolescents in these countries' labor force declines at about the same rate. In China, for example, where educational opportunities have expanded rapidly in recent decades, especially outside urban centers, about half of all 16-year-olds were employed in the late 1980s, but fewer than one quarter were employed just 10 years later (National Research Council, 2005).

What about student employment in other comparably industrialized countries, where social and economic conditions are more similar to those affecting American adolescents? In these nations, adolescents are far more likely than American teenagers to defer paid employment until their education is completed. Thus, whereas about two thirds of American high school juniors hold jobs during the school year, only one quarter of Japanese and Taiwanese juniors do (Larson & Verma, 1999). Paid employment during the school year is even rarer in most European countries and virtually nonexistent in many, such as France, Hungary, Russia, and Switzerland; in European countries where adolescents are employed during the school year, they tend to work very few hours each week and to be employed in more informal jobs, like babysitting (Flammer & Schaffner, 2003).

Why is student employment so much more common in the United States than in Europe or Asia? First, part-time employment opportunities are not as readily available elsewhere as they are in America. Fast-food restaurants, although increasingly popular in other coun-tries, are not seen on every major street. Second, the scheduling of part-time jobs in other countries is not well suited to the daily routines of students. In Europe, for example, the school day lasts well into the late after-noon, and relatively few shops are open in the evenings. In the United States, many adolescents leave school early in the afternoon and go straight to their part-time jobs, where they work until 9:00 or 10:00 P.M. Third, in most other industrialized countries, the employment of chil-dren is associated with being poor, and there is a strong stigma attached to having one's children work. Many middle-class parents do not feel that it is appropriate for their children to have jobs while attending school. Fi-nally, schools in countries other than the United States require much more out-of-school time for homework (Larson & Seepersad, 2003).

FOOD FOR THOUGHT

Student employment during the school year is far more common in the United States than elsewhere. How might this make the nature of adolescence differ-ent in the United States than in other parts of the world?

THE ADOLESCENT WORKPLACE TODAY

▍ **Common Adolescent Jobs**   Although opportu-nities for after-school work are generally plentiful in the United States (at least until the economic collapse of 2008–2009), the range of available jobs is very limited. The vast majority of teenagers are employed in the re-tail and service industries. In general, older students are more likely to hold formal jobs (for example, retail or restaurant work) than are younger students, who are more likely to hold informal jobs (such as babysitting or yard work) (see Figure 7.3) (Staff et al., 2009). As expected, working teenagers in rural areas are more likely to be employed in agricultural occupations than are their urban or suburban counterparts. Also, boys are more likely to work in manual labor than are girls, who are more likely than boys to work in service posi-tions (McNeal, 1997).

As you can see from Figure 7.3, a small number of jobs accounts for a very large proportion of today's stu-dent workers. About 60% of employed eighth-graders work in just one of two jobs: babysitting or yard work. Job opportunities are nearly as restricted for older teen-agers: Restaurant work (such as a counter worker in a fast-food restaurant) and retail sales work (such as a ca-shier in a clothing store) account for more than half of all working students' jobs. Very few teenagers are employed on farms or in factories anymore (Staff et al., 2009).

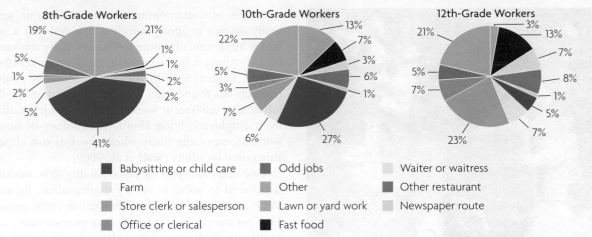

FIGURE 7.3   As adolescents age, they become less likely to work in informal jobs, like babysitting, and more likely to enter the formal labor force, mainly in retail stores and restaurants. (Staff et al., 2009)

■ **The Adolescent Work Environment** Unlike adolescents in traditional societies, whose work typically brings them into extensive contact with adults, contemporary adolescent workers spend as much time on the job interacting with other adolescents as they do with their elders. One study found that, in the typical fast-food restaurant, nearly all the workers were teenagers, the supervisor was usually not much older, and the customers were often young people, too. Few of the teenage workers surveyed reported having formed close relationships with adults at work. They were unlikely to see their adult supervisors or coworkers outside of work, felt reluctant to go to the adults at work with personal problems, and reported feeling less close to adults at work than to other people in their lives (Greenberger & Steinberg, 1986).

Studies indicate that most teenagers' jobs are fairly dreary. Few jobs permit adolescents to behave independently or make decisions; they receive little instruction from their supervisors, and they are rarely required to use the skills they have been taught in school (Greenberger & Steinberg, 1986). With occasional exceptions, most teenagers' jobs are repetitive, monotonous, and intellectually unstimulating. Some are even highly stressful, requiring that youngsters work under intense time pressure without much letup and exposing them to potential injury and accidents (National Research Council, 1998). Not all jobs are this tedious or dangerous, of course, and some researchers have argued that adolescents in better jobs—jobs in which they can learn genuinely useful skills, for example—benefit from employment as a result (Mortimer, Pimentel, Ryu, Nash, & Lee, 1996; Schulenberg & Bachman, 1993). While this may be true in theory, the fact is that the proportion of adolescents who hold good jobs—jobs in which there is ample opportunity to learn new or higher-level skills—is quite small.

FOOD FOR THOUGHT

Think back to your own work experiences as an adolescent, during either the summer or the school year. What were the best jobs you had? Which ones were the worst? Why?

This characterization of adolescents' jobs as dreary is not something that teenagers themselves report, however. The majority of adolescent workers describe their jobs in favorable terms, saying that they learned things, liked the people with whom they worked, had opportunities to exercise responsibility, and were satisfied with their pay. How can we explain this difference between adults' conceptions of adolescents' work environments and teenagers' own descriptions of their experiences? Perhaps compared to school, which is a context in which adolescents are frequently bored and seldom challenged, even the jobs that adults consider menial are comparatively satisfying to teenagers. And perhaps there is something about earning money and having some responsibility, regardless of how modest, that makes adolescents feel better about themselves and translates into a positive description of their work experience. As you will see in a later section of this chapter, when adolescents are placed in positions of responsibility, they come to feel more responsible.

EMPLOYMENT AND ADOLESCENT DEVELOPMENT

The impact of employment in the psychological development of adolescents has been the focus of numerous studies (Staff et al., 2009). Three broad questions have

Few adolescents who work save a large percentage of their earnings for their future education, and fewer still use their income to help their family with household expenses. Most working teenagers spend most of their earnings on clothing, cars, entertainment, and food.

been asked in this research: whether working helps adolescents develop a sense of responsibility and prepares them for the transition to adulthood; whether working interferes with other activities, such as school; and whether working promotes the development of undesirable behaviors, such as drug and alcohol use. As you will read, the answer to the question of how adolescents are affected by working depends on many factors, including the nature of the job, the number of hours worked each week, and the aspect of development studied.

▌ **The Development of Responsibility** Most people believe that working builds character, teaches adolescents about the real world, and helps them prepare for adulthood, but these assumptions are not generally supported by research. Indeed, studies indicate that the benefits of working during adolescence have probably been overstated and that intensive employment during the school year may even negatively affect young people's development and preparation for adult work.

Studies of contemporary youth, for example, generally do not support the view that holding a job makes adolescents become more personally responsible (Mortimer & Johnson, 1998; Steinberg et al., 1993; Wright, Cullen, & Williams, 1997). Moreover, some research has found high rates of misconduct on the job among adolescent workers (for example, stealing from employers, lying about the number of hours worked), especially those whose work is not closely supervised by adults (Staff et al., 2009).

One specific aspect of responsibility that working is believed to affect is money management. Because the average working high school senior earns around $500 per month, holding a job may provide many opportunities for learning how to budget, save, and spend money wisely. Research indicates, however, that few teenagers exercise a great deal of responsibility when it comes to managing their earnings. Most adolescent workers spend most of their earnings on personal expenses, like clothes or cars. Fewer than 10% of adolescents who work save most of their income for future education, and even fewer use their earnings to help their families with household expenses (National Center for Education Statistics, 2005). A fair proportion of adolescents' earnings are spent on drugs and alcohol (Greenberger & Steinberg, 1986). Many working teenagers may suffer from **premature affluence**—which results from getting used to having a relatively luxurious standard of living before one has any serious financial responsibilities, like rent, food, or utility bills. Perhaps as a consequence, adolescents who have earned (and spent) a lot from their jobs while in high school are less satisfied with their financial situations as young adults, because they had become accustomed to living in an unrealistic world, one in which they had a large amount of discretionary income and few obligations (Bachman, 1983). Ironically, then, the very experience that many adults believe builds character actually may teach adolescents undesirable lessons about the meaning of money.

Findings from studies that ask adolescents directly whether working has helped them become more responsible or mature suggest that adolescents' own perceptions differ from what objective assessments indicate, however (Mortimer, 2003). Many adults say that their jobs as teenagers helped them learn things like punctuality, ways to deal effectively with strangers, and even cope with work one didn't necessarily want to do. Here's how one adult put it, looking back on his job at a carwash:

> It was a brainless job. . . . The hardest part was fighting off the boredom, and we would get creative about how to do this, usually while getting high. But it was an important experience—I saw what it was like to work, got more independent, and made some friends I still know. The money helped me get my first car and first real girlfriend (Staff et al., 2009, p. 270).

premature affluence   Having more income than one can manage maturely, especially during adolescence.

We should not be surprised at discrepancies between what people say about an experience (as when people are interviewed about what they got out of their adolescent jobs) and what researchers conclude from objective assessments (as when adolescents fill out standardized questionnaires measuring their sense of responsibility), nor should we assume that the objective assessments are wrong simply because they differ from people's subjective appraisals or recollections (which may become distorted over time). Most studies of human behavior find that subjective reports and objective assessments are only modestly correlated (for instance, it is possible for you to believe that you have learned a great deal from a course but perform poorly on a test of what the course covered), and most social scientists believe that objective and subjective measures provide different, but nevertheless valid, information.

Perhaps the most reasonable conclusion we can draw about the impact of working on the development of maturity is that it depends largely on the nature of the job (Mortimer, 2003). In jobs in which adolescents are given genuine responsibility, make important decisions, and perform challenging tasks, they are more likely to come away feeling more mature, competent, and dependable. In jobs in which the work is repetitive, stressful, or unchallenging, however, they probably will gain very little from the experience. But given what we know about employment opportunities for teenagers, it seems reasonable to say that while it is *possible* for an adolescent to benefit psychologically from working, it is not *probable*, given the nature of most adolescents' jobs. According to one recent analysis, the most common adolescent jobs—in fast-food restaurants or retail stores, for example—ranked highest in stress and in interference with other parts of life, and lowest in their likelihood of providing skills or leading to a career (Staff et al., 2009).

■ **The Impact on Schooling** A second question that has received a fair amount of research attention concerns the impact of working on adolescents' involvement in other activities, most notably, schooling. Here, studies indicate that the issue is not whether a teenager works, but how much (Staff et al., 2009).

Many experts now believe that working more than 20 hours a week may jeopardize adolescents' school performance and engagement (National Research Council, 1998). Youngsters who work long hours are absent from school more often, are less likely to participate in extracurricular activities, report enjoying school less, spend less time on their homework, and earn slightly lower grades. These results occur both because teenagers who are less interested in school choose to work longer hours and because working long hours leads to disengagement from school (Monahan, Lee, & Steinberg, in press; Safron, Sy, & Schulenberg, 2003;

Schoenhals, Tienda, & Schneider, 1998; Warren, 2002). There is no evidence that summer employment, even for long hours, affects school performance, however, suggesting that the negative impact of working on school performance may be due to the time demands of having a job while going to school (Oettinger, 1999).

Intensive involvement in a part-time job may actually increase the likelihood of dropping out of school (Staff et al., 2009). Students who spend a lot of time on the job have less ambitious plans for further education (Carr, Wright, & Brody, 1996; H. Marsh & Kleitman, 2005), and they complete fewer years of college, partly because students with low aspirations for the future choose to work longer hours than their peers (Staff et al., 2009). It is important to stress, however, that working fewer than 20 hours per week does not appear to have these adverse effects (Staff et al., 2009). Indeed, some studies find that a large number of students are able to manage school and work effectively, as long as they keep their work hours in check, and that many may benefit from learning how to manage their time effectively (M. J. Shanahan & Flaherty, 2001). And although working long hours may constrain opportunities to participate in extracurricular activities (which, as you will read, usually have positive effects on adolescent development), it also may interfere with less desirable pastimes, like watching television (Osgood, 1999).

Although the impact of working on students' actual grades and achievement test scores is small (Staff et al., 2009), several studies indicate that extensive employment during the school year may take its toll on school performance in ways that are not revealed by looking only at grade point averages. Students who work a great deal, for example, report paying less attention in class, exerting less effort on their studies, and skipping class more frequently (Steinberg & Dornbusch, 1991). Additionally, when students work a great deal, they often develop strategies for protecting their grades. These strategies include taking easier courses, cutting corners on homework assignments, copying homework from friends, and cheating (Steinberg & Dornbusch, 1991). Teachers express concern about the excessive involvement of students in after-school jobs (Bills, Helms, & Ozcan, 1995), and some teachers may respond to an influx of students into the workplace by lowering classroom expectations, assigning less homework, and using class time for students to complete assignments that otherwise would be done outside of school (Bills et al., 1995). As a consequence, when large numbers of students in a school are employed, even nonworkers' schooling may be affected.

■ **The Promotion of Problem Behavior** Some studies have examined the belief that having a job deters youngsters from delinquent and criminal activity—that

Participation in extracurricular activities, such as performing in a school musical, is less common among students who work long hours at a part-time job.

keeping teenagers busy with work will keep them out of trouble. Contrary to popular belief, however, employment during adolescence does not deter delinquent activity (Steinberg & Cauffman, 1995). Indeed, several studies suggest that working long hours may actually be associated with *increases* in aggression, school misconduct, minor delinquency, and precocious sexual activity (Rich & Kim, 2002; Wright et al., 1997). However, at least one study reports that the higher rate of problem behavior among working adolescents is due to the fact that delinquent youth are simply more likely than their peers to choose to work long hours (Apel et al., 2007).

Many studies also have found that rates of smoking, drinking, and drug use are higher among teenage workers than nonworkers, especially among students who work long hours (Bachman & Schulenberg, 1993; Monahan et al., in press; Mortimer & Johnson, 1998; Ramchand, Ialongo, & Chilcoat, 2007; Wu, Schlenger, & Galvin, 2003). This is both because students who use alcohol and other drugs are more likely to want to work long hours and because increases in work hours tend to lead to increases in cigarette, drug, and alcohol use (Monahan et al., in press; Paschall, Flewelling, & Russell, 2004; Safron et al., 2003).

A variety of explanations have been proposed for the connection between working and smoking, drinking, and using drugs. The impact of extensive employment on adolescent drug and alcohol use probably reflects the fact that adolescents who work long hours have more discretionary income and, hence, greater opportunity to purchase drugs and alcohol. In addition, drug and alcohol use are more common among adolescents who work under conditions of high job stress than

among their peers who work for comparable amounts of time and money but under less stressful conditions—and many adolescents work in stressful work settings, like fast-food restaurants (Staff et al., 2009). It may also be the case that when adolescents work long hours, this disrupts their relationship with their parents, which, in turn, is associated with problem behavior (Longest & Shanahan, 2007; Roisman, 2002). Whatever the reason, the impact of school-year employment on drug and alcohol use persists over time; individuals who worked long hours as teenagers drink and use drugs more in their late 20s than their peers who worked less or not at all (Mihalic & Elliott, 1997).

■ **Possible Benefits for Poor Youth** One point of debate among researchers who study adolescent employment concerns the differential impact of working on middle-class versus poor youth. Some researchers have found that working, even in the sorts of minimum-wage jobs available to teenagers, may not lead to increased problem behavior and, in fact, may have special benefits for inner-city adolescents from poor families, with poor school records, or with prior involvement in delinquency (Apel et al., 2007; Bauermeister, Zimmerman, Barnett, & Caldwell, 2007; J. C. Lee & Staff, 2007; K. Newman, 1999; Staff & Mortimer, 2007; Sullivan, 1989). However, working during junior high school or the early high school years (as opposed to later in high school) may increase the chances that poor minority youth will drop out of school and engage in problem behavior (Entwisle, Alexander, & Olson, 2005; Olatunji, 2005; Roche, Ensminger, Chilcoat, & Storr, 2003). Why might this be? One possibility is that working in early adolescence may make school seem less important, whereas working in later adolescence, when making the transition to adult work roles is more imminent, may make school seem more so.

In sum, although teenagers generally enjoy working, there is little evidence that, with the exception of disadvantaged inner-city youth, doing so contributes in significant ways to their psychosocial development. Moreover, there is a fair amount of evidence that the psychological costs of working more than 20 hours a week may outweigh the benefits. Studies of work and adolescent development point to a complicated pattern of cause and effect that unfolds over time. In general, adolescents who are less attached and committed to school, and who are more involved in problem behavior, are more likely to choose to work long hours. Working long hours, in turn, leads to more disengagement from school and increased problem behavior. In other words, intensive employment during the school year most threatens the school performance and psychological well-being of those students who can least afford to suffer the consequences of overcommitment to a job.

FOOD FOR THOUGHT

How do you reconcile findings from research on the impact of adolescent employment, which do not indicate many positive effects on psychological development, and the reports of teenagers, who say they have benefited from their jobs?

YOUTH UNEMPLOYMENT

Although the employment of teenagers has become commonplace in contemporary America, some young people who wish to work are unable to find jobs. In general, however, except for summer months, youth unemployment is not very widespread, once the proportion of young people who are in school is taken into account. For example, in 2007, 84% of all 16- to 19-year-olds were enrolled in school (either in high school or college); of the remaining 16% who were not in school, more than half were employed (Morisi, 2008). Overall, then, only a small percentage of 16- to 19-year-olds—about 8%—were neither in school nor employed, and many of these were young parents who are at home full-time and not actively seeking work. Moreover, young people who are out of school and out of work are typically unemployed for only short periods of time. It won't surprise you to learn that the majority of unemployed youth are high school dropouts. Among 21-year-olds, for example, the unemployment rate is twice as high among high school dropouts as it is among high school graduates who are not enrolled in college (Bureau of Labor Statistics, 2009). Because dropout rates are higher among Black and Hispanic youth, they are far more likely to experience unemployment than are White youth. Whereas only 6% of White 16- to 19-year-olds were both out of school and out of work in 2007, nearly twice the percentage of Black and Hispanic youth were (Morisi, 2008).

Many different approaches have been taken over the years in trying to solve the youth unemployment problem. One set of proposals concerns the nearly one third of all adolescents who do not go on to college. As noted in Chapter 6, American secondary schools do little to prepare non-college-bound youngsters for the world of work. These youngsters, of course, are far more likely to experience unemployment during their late adolescent years. Many experts therefore believe that the youth unemployment problem is attributable mainly to the lack of clear linkages between school and work. They point out that there are so many "cracks" in the transition from school to work that it is easy for students who are not in school to fall into periods of unemployment.

Several suggestions have been made to combat this problem (Rosenbaum, 1996). Many commentators have argued that expanding opportunities for **community service** will help integrate adolescents into the community, enhance their feelings of confidence and responsibility, and put them in contact with adult role models. Studies of **service learning**—nonpaid programs, sometimes connected with school, that place adolescents in volunteer positions in the community—indicate that some volunteer experiences may enhance adolescents' self-esteem and feelings of efficacy, impart academic and career skills, enhance community involvement, improve mental health, and deter problem behavior. These positive results are most likely to occur in programs in which adolescents have good relationships with their supervisors, are given sufficient autonomy, are psychologically engaged in the activity, and have adequate time to reflect on and learn from their experience (Hansen, Larson, & Dworkin, 2003; Kahne & Sporte, 2008; McGuire & Gamble, 2006; Scales, Blyth, Berkas, & Kielsmeier, 2000; Stukas, Clary, & Snyder, 1999).

A second suggestion is that communities improve their employment and counseling services for young people and strengthen youth organizations. In Europe, for example, local communities provide much better employment services for youth—including job placement—than is the case in the United States. Such community programs might also help with career and college counseling, summer employment, and placement in volunteer activities. In most American high schools, guidance counselors are so busy counseling students for college that they rarely pay attention to the non-college-bound population.

Finally, it has been proposed that American schools experiment with apprenticeship programs modeled after those found in Europe (S. Hamilton & Hamilton, 2009). These programs would introduce young people to the world of work early in high school and would gradually move them from full-time school, into a mixture of school and work, and finally into full-time employment. Instead of working in the dead-end jobs of the adolescent workplace, teenagers would combine schooling and on-the-job training with employers likely to offer them full-time, career-oriented jobs after graduation.

What about the substantial proportion of adolescents who do not graduate from high school, who are at the greatest risk of experiencing unemployment? To date, many different types of interventions have been tried, but few have succeeded (T. Smith, 1993). Despite some 30 years of government programs designed to train unemployed youth and place them in the labor force, most evaluations of these efforts find that high school dropouts who participate in such programs are no more likely to find full-time employment than are dropouts who do

---

community service   The involvement of young people in activities that serve some social or economic need of society.

service learning   Structured educational experiences that involve volunteering in the community.

not participate in the programs (E. Foster, 1995). This is quite disconcerting, since the programs that have been evaluated have tried a wide array of approaches, including work experience, job training, job placement, and instruction in labor market skills (such as interviewing and job seeking). In light of this evidence, most experts believe that efforts should be redirected away from providing work experience programs and, instead, toward helping youngsters who are at risk for dropping out of school stay in school and graduate (E. Foster, 1995; Kantor, 1994). As the nature of the labor force has changed, completing more education has become far more important than acquiring job training.

RECAP

- The student worker emerged in the United States during the second half of the 20th century, as the need for cheap, part-time labor in the service and retail industries grew. Today, the majority of American teenagers hold part-time jobs during the school year, and many work more than 15–20 hours weekly.
- Part-time work during the school year is much less common in other parts of the world. In most other countries, students do not combine school and work, except in apprenticeship programs designed to help them find career-related jobs after they finish high school.
- Most employed U.S. adolescents work in retail stores or restaurants. Although studies suggest that the work they do is highly routine, uninteresting, and occasionally stressful, adolescents' own descriptions of their jobs are generally favorable.
- The impact of work on adolescent development depends on the nature of the job and the number of hours worked each week. Working generally has few effects on adolescents' psychological development, but working long hours may increase rates of delinquency and drug and alcohol use and take a toll on schooling.
- Many social commentators have worried about the high rate of youth unemployment, especially among poor, minority youth, many of whom are out of school as well as work. Among the suggestions offered for combating youth unemployment are increasing adolescents' opportunities to perform community service, strengthening counseling and career services for high school students, encouraging the development of apprenticeship programs, and, above all, encouraging all adolescents to complete high school.

Adolescents and Leisure

The average American middle-class teenager feels bored more than 25% of the time, and some complain of boredom more than 50% of the time (Larson & Richards, 1991). As one expert noted, "The litany of explanations for this boredom—'algebra sucks,' 'I'm always bored on Sunday,' 'there's nothing to do,' 'the *Odyssey* is boring'— reads like a script from Bart Simpson" (Larson, 2000, p. 170). Boredom is much more commonly reported by relatively more affluent students—in one study, more than one third of the middle-class respondents were chronically bored, compared with only one tenth of the students from poor families (Hunter & Csikszentmihalyi, 2003).

One context in which boredom is seldom reported by teenagers is leisure. In some regards, this is good news, because young people in the United States and other Western countries spend nearly half their waking hours in leisure activities (J. Mahoney, Larson, Eccles, & Lord, 2005). As noted earlier, leisure occupies more of the typical adolescent's waking hours than do school and work combined (Larson, 2000). Leisure activities include socializing with friends, playing sports and games, checking out people's personal websites, watching television and listening to music, browsing the Internet, playing video games, practicing a musical instrument, shopping, working on hobbies, hanging out with friends, and sometimes not doing anything at all.

One important difference between leisure and other activities is that adolescents choose their leisure activities, whereas their time at school and work is dictated by others (teachers, supervisors, etc.). Perhaps as a consequence, and not surprisingly, studies show that adolescents report being in a better mood during leisure activities than during school or work. Leisure activities that are both structured and voluntary—such as sports, hobbies, artistic activities, and clubs—seem to provide special psychological benefits (Larson, 2000).

ADOLESCENTS' FREE TIME AND THEIR MOODS

Studying adolescents' moods through the conventional methodologies of observational or questionnaire research is difficult. Questions concerning adolescents' emotional states, for instance, are especially tricky, because individuals' emotions change during the day and may not be, at the time of a researcher's assessment, reflective of their moods at other points in the day. Suppose a researcher wanted to know how adolescents' moods were affected by various activities—such as attending school, watching television, or having dinner with the family. Although it would be possible to interview respondents and ask them to recall their moods at

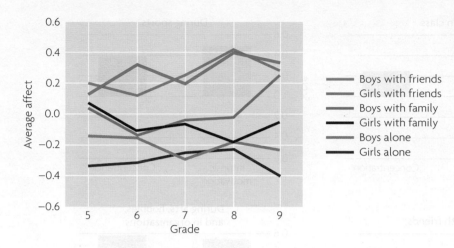

FIGURE 7.4 Average affect reported by girls and boys at different ages when alone, with friends, and with family. (Larson & Richards, 1991)

different points in the day, we cannot be sure whether their recollections would be entirely accurate.

▌ **The Experience Sampling Method** One of the most interesting innovations in the contemporary study of adolescence was designed to overcome this and other sorts of methodological problems. Using a technique called the **experience sampling method (ESM)**, researchers can collect much more detailed information about adolescents' experiences over the course of the day and thereby illuminate many different aspects of the adolescent experience. The ESM has been used to chart adolescents' moods, to monitor their social relationships, and to catalogue their activities in far greater detail than has been previously available.

The use of the ESM in the study of adolescent development was pioneered by psychologist Reed Larson and colleagues (Larson & Lampman-Petraitis, 1989; Larson & Richards, 1991). In studies using this method, adolescents carry electronic pagers and, when they are signaled, report on whom they are with, what they are doing, and how they are feeling (Larson & Richards, 1991); in the early days of ESM, adolescents filled out written questionnaires every time they were "beeped." Today, many researchers give adolescents personal digital assistants (PDAs), which can be programmed to allow the youngster to input data directly into the device every time he or she is signaled.

In one early ESM study, Larson had nearly 500 adolescents ages 9–15 carry pagers and booklets of self-report forms for one week and asked them to fill out a form each time they were signaled. The form contained a series of questions about companionship ("Who were you with [or talking to on the phone]?"), location ("Where were you?"), activity ("What were you doing?"), and mood (the adolescents used a checklist to report their feelings). The adolescents were beeped seven times each day, once within every two-hour block between 7:30 A.M. and 9:30 P.M. By examining the

adolescents' many reports, the researchers were able to chart changes in activities, companionship, and mood over the course of the week and to relate variations in activity, companionship, and mood to one another. Thus, the method permitted the researchers to ask how activities, companionship, and mood varied as a function of age; how mood varied as a function of what the adolescent was doing; and how both activity and mood varied as a function of whom the adolescent was with. One of the questions asked was how adolescents' moods varied as a function of whom they were with (parents, peers, or no one) and whether the connection between mood and companionship changed with age. The results are presented in Figure 7.4.

As you can see, adolescents' moods are generally most positive when they are with their friends and least positive when they are alone; their moods when with their family fall somewhere in between. More interesting, perhaps, is that between grades 5 and 9, adolescents' moods while with friends become more positive, whereas their moods while with their family follow a **curvilinear pattern** (a curvilinear pattern can be either U-shaped or can look like an inverted U). That is, their moods while with their family become more negative between elementary and middle school (between grades 5 and 7) and then rise between middle school and high school (between grades 8 and 9). As Larson and Richards point out, this dip parallels findings from other research on family relations (see Chapter 4) that point to early adolescence as a time of heightened strain in the parent–child relationship.

experience sampling method (ESM) A method of collecting data about adolescents' emotional states, in which individuals are paged and asked to report on their mood and activity.

curvilinear pattern In statistical analyses, a pattern of relations between two variables that resembles a U-shaped or an inverted U-shaped curve.

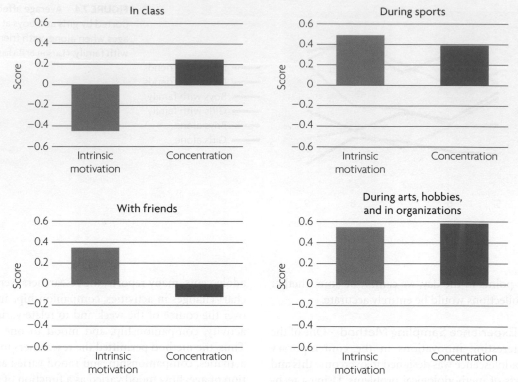

FIGURE 7.5 Adolescents' state of mind is more positive when they are in structured leisure activities than when they are in class or with friends. (Larson, 2000)

■ **Solitude** The data on adolescents' moods when they were alone are somewhat surprising. Given the fact that adolescents spend increasingly more time alone as they get older, you might expect that solitude would be associated with more positive—not more negative—affect. Although the researchers could not explain this finding easily, one hypothesis is that, when alone, adolescents spend a good deal of time thinking about themselves and working through the events of the day (Larson, 1990). Some of the time spent alone is spent listening to music, and some of the music adolescents listen to may have sad or depressing themes (unrequited love, broken relationships, etc.). Interestingly, other studies using the ESM (e.g., Csikszentmihalyi & Larson, 1984) have found that adolescents feel better after being alone and that, with age, solitude tends to become associated with more positive feelings (Larson, 1990, 1997). Together, these findings suggest that periods of solitude may be associated with negative mood in the short term but with positive mood in the long term.

Adolescents' moods are strongly influenced by where they are and whom they are with. When adolescents are in school, they report moderate levels of concentration but very low levels of motivation or interest in what they are doing, consistent with other studies indicating

that most American teenagers do not find high school engaging (e.g., Steinberg et al., 1996). When they are with friends, teenagers report moderate levels of motivation and interest but low levels of concentration. It is only when adolescents are playing sports or involved in the arts, a hobby, or an extracurricular organization that they report high levels of both concentration and interest (see Figure 7.5) (Bohnert, Richards, Kolmodin, & Lakin, 2008; Larson, 2000). This combination produces what some psychologists have referred to as a **flow experience** (Csikszentmihalyi, 1990). You've probably experienced this sensation at one time or another, when you were deeply involved in an activity that you found both enjoyable and absorbing.

One ESM study of after-school programs found that the positive combination of high motivation, concentration, and engagement was most commonly observed when young adolescents were involved in sports or arts enrichment (Shernoff & Vandell, 2007). While adolescents are in unstructured leisure activities, like watching TV, they tend to show the same pattern of moderate interest but low concentration as when they are socializing with friends. Moreover, participation in structured extracurricular activities, such as hobbies or sports, has been shown to be the most positive way for adolescents to spend free time, in terms of their current and future psychological development (McHale, Crouter, & Tucker, 2001; Zaff, Moore, Papillo, & Williams, 2003).

flow experience The experience of high levels of both concentration and interest at the same time.

STRUCTURED LEISURE ACTIVITIES

For many adolescents around the world, school-sponsored extracurricular activities provide the context for much of their leisure activity (J. Mahoney et al., 2009). According to recent surveys, about two thirds of American high school students participate in one or more extracurricular activities, although the participation rate varies greatly from school to school. The most popular extracurricular activity in the United States is athletics, in which about half of all adolescents participate; it is also the extracurricular activity that has been most extensively studied (Theokas, 2009). The other two main activities in which many adolescents participate are those related to music (such as band, chorus, orchestra, or glee club; about one fifth of all adolescent students participate in these) and those related to academic or occupational interests (such as science clubs, language clubs, or clubs oriented toward certain careers; about one fifth participate in these). The average American high school sophomore spends about five hours each week in extracurricular activities—about twice as much time as reading for pleasure and the same amount of time as doing homework, but only one third as much time as working for pay (National Center for Education Statistics, 2002b).

Participation in extracurricular activities is influenced by a number of factors, one of the most important of which is social class (A. F. Feldman & Matjasko, 2007; J. Mahoney et al., 2009; White & Gager, 2007). In general, participation is somewhat more prevalent among adolescents from more affluent families, among students who earn better grades, and among students from smaller schools and smaller, more rural communities, where school activities often play a relatively more central role in the lives of adults and adolescents alike (for example, where an entire community may turn out for a school's Friday night football or basketball game). Whereas boys are more likely than girls to participate in athletic activities, the reverse is true for nonathletic activities (Berk, 1992). Adolescents whose parents are themselves involved in the community or who reinforce their children's interests are also more likely to participate (Fletcher, Elder, & Mekos, 2000; Huebner & Mancini, 2003; Persson, Kerr, & Stattin, 2007).

▌ The Impact of Extracurricular Participation on Development

Although early research documenting a positive correlation between extracurricular participation and adolescents' well-being could not clearly show that participation *leads to* improved functioning (rather than the opposite), newer longitudinal studies indicate that participation in an extracurricular activity actually improves students' performance in school and reduces the likelihood of dropping out; deters delinquency, drug use, and other types of risk

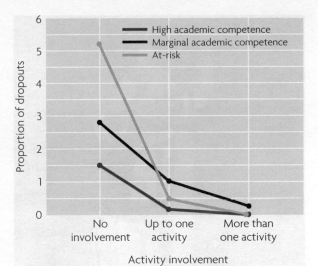

FIGURE 7.6   Participation in athletic extracurricular activities benefits less competent students more than their academically talented counterparts. (McNeal, 1995)

taking; and enhances students' psychological well-being and social status (Bohnert, Kane, & Garber, 2007; Boone & Leadbeater, 2006; Fauth, Roth, & Brooks-Gunn, 2007; Fredericks & Eccles, 2008; Guest & Schneider, 2003; J. Mahoney et al., 2009). The one exception to this uniformly positive picture is that some studies have found that involvement in team sports, which is associated with many psychological benefits, such as better mental health and higher school achievement, is also associated with increased alcohol use and delinquency. This latter consequence is seen especially among boys who have a strong "jock" identity and who participate in school-sponsored, male-dominated sports, like football (Gardner, Roth, & Brooks-Gunn, 2008; K. E. Miller, Melnick, Barnes, Sabo, & Farrell, 2007; M. J. Moore & Werch, 2005; Savage & Holcomb, 1999).

As Figure 7.6 illustrates, a positive link between athletic participation and academic performance—a so-called spillover effect—is found mainly among adolescents who are poorer students and in schools in poor communities (Guest & Schneider, 2003; J. Mahoney & Cairns, 1997). This is not the case for other types of extracurricular participation, which have similar effects across different types of students and schools. Extracurricular activities also may provide greater opportunities for cross-racial friendship than does the regular school day, and Black adolescents in integrated schools who participate in extracurricular activities show better mental health as a result. Extracurricular participation in high school also seems to be linked to extracurricular participation in college and to community involvement in adulthood—just as youngsters who are involved in extracurricular activities as ninth-graders are likely to be similarly busy throughout high school, "do-ers" as adolescents tend to remain so in young and middle

Participation in school-sponsored extracurricular activities, like athletics, leads to better school achievement.

adulthood. Along similar lines, individuals who participate in sports during adolescence are likely to continue athletic activities in adulthood (D. Perkins, Jacobs, Barber, & Eccles, 2003). One recent study found benefits of participating in structured extracurricular activities as many as 8 years after high school graduation, especially among individuals whose extracurricular participation lasted at least 2 years and participated for a relatively high number of hours each week, but only among individuals whose activities were school-sponsored (M. Gardner, Roth, & Brooks-Gunn, 2008). One reason for the special benefits of school-sponsored extracurricular participation is that it helps strengthen students' attachment to school, which in turn contributes to their future educational success. And despite concerns that the extracurricular overscheduling of affluent youth creates pressures that compromise adolescents' mental health, studies find no such effect (Luthar, Shoum, & Brown, 2006).

A recent study of a high school theater production also found that the experience contributed in important ways to adolescents' emotional development. Through the course of preparing for their performance, students learned how to better manage their emotions, better understand others' emotions, and learn how to deal more effectively with anger, frustration, and stress. Although these opportunities arise in

all sorts of situations, the atmosphere cultivated by the adults who advise and supervise adolescents appears to be especially important in making the experience a positive influence on the participants' development (Gaudreau, Amiot, & Vallerand, 2009; Larson & Brown, 2007). This interpretation is consistent with the idea that quality of relationships adolescents develop with the adults they encounter in extracurricular activities may be especially important (Scales, Benson, & Mannes, 2006).

Researchers speculate that extracurricular participation are generally positive in impact because these activities increase students' contact with teachers and other school personnel who may reinforce the value of school (as when a coach or advisor counsels a student about plans for college) and because participation itself may improve students' self-confidence and self-esteem. Some educators believe that extracurricular participation also helps bond students and parents to their school, especially in the case of adolescents who are not achieving academically; for many of them, their extracurricular activity is what keeps them coming to school each day (Broh, 2002; Dotterer, McHale, & Crouter, 2007; J. Mahoney et al., 2009; H. Marsh & Kleitman, 2002). Consistent with this, adolescents who combine participation in sports with other sorts of extracurricular activities, and who therefore have multiple points of "attachment" to their school, fare better than those who are solely involved in athletics (Linver, Roth & Brooks-Gunn, 2009; Zarrett et al., 2009).

Some of the positive effects of extracurricular participation may stem from the fact that these activities bring adolescents into contact with peers who influence them in beneficial ways (Simpkins, Eccles, & Becnel, 2008). When the activity strengthens membership in a peer group involved in prosocial activities that revolve around the school, participation can be beneficial to the adolescent's development and achievement (J. L. Mahoney, 2000). But not all activities revolve around prosocial endeavors, and as noted earlier, participation in certain sports can increase adolescents' involvement in problem behavior. For example, one study of male football players and wrestlers found that they were more likely than nonathletic males to get into serious fights (similar effects were not found for boys who played other sports) and that violence was most common among football players whose friends also played football (Kreager, 2007a). Another found similar effects of sports participation on delinquency—boys who participated in organized sports were more likely to spend their free time hanging out with their friends, and this led them to be involved in more antisocial (although not violent) behavior (Gardner et al., 2009). (As you will read in a moment, during adolescence, spending unstructured, unsupervised time with friends is often a recipe for trouble.)

Several cautions have been raised about adolescents' participation in athletics, however. As extracurricular sports have become more competitive, the number of young people injured during these activities has risen substantially. According to some estimates, around 25% of all adolescent athletes are injured while playing organized sports (Overbaugh & Allen, 1994). In addition, many adolescents feel anxious and tense within the competitive atmosphere that has come to dominate after-school sports in many communities. Thus, while competitive athletics are a source of considerable pleasure for some adolescents, they are a source of equally considerable stress for others (Larson, Hansen, & Moneta, 2006; Scanlan, Babkes, & Scanlan, 2005). This is why having a coach who understands and looks out for these potential problems is so important.

FOOD FOR THOUGHT

Why are the apparent effects of participation in extracurricular activities different from those associated with part-time employment? How might these two sets of experiences differ?

UNSTRUCTURED LEISURE TIME

One important distinction that is consistent with adults' preconceptions about leisure time and its impact on adolescent development is that between structured leisure activities, like school- or community-sponsored extracurricular activities, which are run and supervised by adults, and unstructured leisure activities, such as hanging out with friends without any organized activity in mind. Whereas participation in structured leisure activities tends to have positive effects on adolescent development, time spent in unstructured leisure activities does the reverse (Osgood, Anderson, & Shaffer, 2005).

▍ **Routine Activity Theory** Sociologist Wayne Osgood and colleagues (e.g., Osgood & Anderson, 2004) have argued that the combination of a lack of structure, socializing with peers, and the absence of adult supervision is a recipe for the encouragement of delinquency and other problem behaviors. Their view, called **routine activity theory,** is that "the less structured an activity, the more likely a person is to encounter opportunities for problem behavior in the simple sense that he or she is not occupied doing something else" (Osgood et al., 2005, p. 51). Because most adolescence is a time of heightened peer pressure and heightened susceptibility to peer influence (as you will read in Chapter 9), and because one of the strongest deterrents against problem behavior is the presence of

an adult, it is hardly surprising that unstructured peer activity without adult supervision is associated with all sorts of problems—delinquency, drug and alcohol use, and precocious sexual activity (A. Anderson & Hughes, 2009; Bratt, 2008).

Even something as positive sounding as attendance at a community recreation center can increase adolescents' problem behavior if their time there is unstructured and minimally supervised (J. Mahoney & Stattin, 2000; J. Mahoney, Stattin, & Lord, 2004). Hanging out with friends in the absence of adult supervision at night increases the likelihood of adolescents' engaging in problem behavior substantially; one study found that adolescents who spent 5 or more evenings out in an average week, for instance, were at least 4 times more likely than those who went out fewer than twice a week to be involved in antisocial activity (Gage, Overpeck, Nansel, & Kogan, 2005). As one team of writers succinctly put it, "Whether you like or dislike your father, it will be more convenient to smoke marijuana when he isn't around" (Osgood, Wilson, O'Malley, Bachman, & Johnston, 1996, p. 640).

▍ **Time After School** In 2006, nearly 75% of mothers with children between ages 6 and 17 were employed (J. Mahoney et al., 2009). As a consequence, one prime time for unstructured and unsupervised leisure is during the afternoon on school days—after school has let out but before parents have returned home from work. While some of these youngsters are involved in school- or community-based programs that provide adult supervision, others spend their after-school hours away from adults, in their homes, with friends, or simply hanging out in neighborhoods and shopping malls (Carnegie Council on Adolescent Development, 1992). Affluent, suburban, and White children are most likely to be home unsupervised, and poor, minority, and urban and rural children are least likely (J. Mahoney et al., 2009).

Psychologists have debated whether adolescents who take care of themselves after school profit from these opportunities for self-management or are at greater risk for problems because they are not supervised by adults. With regard to the first, in general, most studies show that children in self-care do not differ from their peers when it comes to psychological development, school achievement, and self-conceptions (J. Mahoney et al., 2009). These studies argue against the view that having to care for oneself contributes in positive ways to the development of self-reliance or personal responsibility—findings reminiscent of those reported in studies of part-time employment.

routine activity theory A perspective on adolescence that views unstructured, unsupervised time with peers as a main cause of misbehavior.

FIGURE 7.7 More arrests occur during school afternoons than at any other time, presumably because this is the time when adolescents are least likely to be supervised. (Osgood et al., 2005)

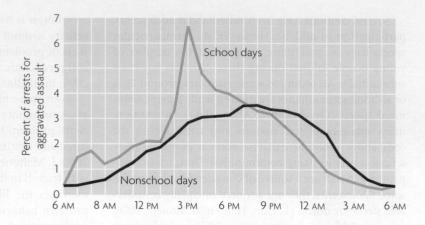

More importantly, perhaps, several studies, including a study of nearly 4,000 youngsters from a variety of ethnic backgrounds (J. Richardson, Radziszewska, Dent, & Flay, 1993), suggest that children in self-care are more socially isolated, more depressed, more likely to be involved in problem behavior, more likely to be sexually active at earlier ages, and likely to use more drugs and alcohol than young people who are supervised after school by adults (Carnegie Council on Adolescent Development, 1992; D. Cohen, Farley, Taylor, Martin, & Schuster, 2002; Richardson et al., 1993). Together, these studies seem to suggest that many self-care arrangements may have more costs than benefits. As Figure 7.7 indicates, for instance, delinquency is more common on weekday afternoons than at any other time (Osgood et al., 2005).

One limitation of studies of youth in self-care is that they typically lump together all children who take care of themselves after school, even though there are important differences within the self-care population and among after-school programs (J. Mahoney et al., 2009). Several studies have shown, for example, that the setting in which adolescents care for themselves makes a difference: Adolescents who go straight home after school are far less likely to engage in problem behavior than are their peers who go to a friend's house or who just hang out (Galambos & Maggs, 1991; Richardson et al., 1993; Steinberg, 1986). In addition, youngsters in self-care who are raised by authoritative parents and who are monitored by their parents from a distance— via telephone check-ins, for example—are no more susceptible to problem behavior than are children whose parents are home with them after school (Galambos & Maggs, 1991; Vandell & Ramanan, 1991). As noted earlier, one of the most consistent findings in studies of how adolescents spend their free time is that spending free time with peers in unstructured activities in the absence of adult supervision is associated with increased problem behavior (Mahoney, Schweder, & Stattin, 2002; McHale, Crouter, & Tucker, 2001; Osgood et al., 1996).

Several recent studies indicate that spending time after school with friends in unsupervised settings is more problematic under some circumstances than others. One study found, for example, that it was not simply spending unsupervised time with peers that increased an adolescent's likelihood of alcohol and drug use; it was the combination of lacking supervision, having friends who liked to party and use drugs, and being especially susceptible to peer pressure that was most damaging (L. Caldwell & Darling, 1999). A second study found that the harmful effects of low parental monitoring were especially bad in neighborhoods low in collective efficacy (discussed in Chapter 3), where other adults were unlikely to provide supervision if parents were not around (Coley, Morris, & Hernandez, 2004). In another study, the researchers examined rates of problem behavior among seventh-graders as a function of three factors: whether they spent their after-school time in unsupervised settings, whether they had parents who monitored their activities and whereabouts, and whether they lived in a neighborhood that was considered safe (Pettit, Bates, Dodge, & Meece, 1999). In all groups, being closely monitored by parents was a deterrent against problem behavior. And, not surprisingly, adolescents who reported spending a lot of after-school time with peers in unsupervised settings were more likely to show problem behavior one year later than were other teenagers. But the negative effects of low parental monitoring and unsupervised peer group activity were especially pronounced among teenagers living in unsafe neighborhoods. Indeed, in safe neighborhoods, adolescents who spent time in unsupervised peer activities were not at greater risk for developing problems, even if they were not monitored closely by their parents. This study serves as a reminder of the importance of looking at the broader context in which adolescents live in order to fully understand how they are affected by parents, peers, and other influences. Adolescents also differ in their susceptibility to the adverse effects of self-care—not surprisingly, teenagers with established behavior problems are more negatively

TABLE 7.1 The Five C's of positive youth development

Five C's	Definition
Competence	A positive view of one's actions in domain-specific areas, including social, academic, cognitive, and vocational. Social competence pertains to interpersonal skills (e.g., conflict resolution). Cognitive competence pertains to cognitive abilities (e.g., decision making). School grades, attendance, and test scores are part of academic competence. Vocational competence involves work habits and career choice explorations.
Confidence	An internal sense of overall positive self-worth and self-efficacy; one's global self-regard, as opposed to domain-specific beliefs.
Connection	Positive bonds with people and institutions that are reflected in bidirectional exchanges between the individual and peers, family, school, and community in which both parties contribute to the relationship.
Character	Respect for societal and cultural rules, possession of standards for correct behaviors, a sense of right and wrong (morality), and integrity.
Caring/compassion	A sense of sympathy and empathy for others.

Source: R. Lerner et al., 2005.

affected by being on their own than are their peers (Coley et al., 2004).

Taken together, these studies suggest that self-care after school probably does not hold great benefits for youngsters and, under some conditions, may cause problems if adolescents' parents do not promote the development of responsible behavior when they are with their child. What should parents who have no choice but to leave their youngsters in self-care do? Experts advise parents to provide clear instructions about the child's after-school activities and whereabouts, asking the child to check in with an adult as soon as he or she gets home, and teaching the child how to handle emergencies, should they arise (Steinberg, 2011).

FOOD FOR THOUGHT

Most studies link unstructured leisure time with adolescent problem behavior. But is there no value for adolescents in simply hanging out with friends, without having adults organizing their activities for them? Is all unstructured leisure time bad?

PROMOTING POSITIVE YOUTH DEVELOPMENT

In light of evidence that certain types of extracurricular activities appear to benefit adolescents, and in view of the potential dangers of leaving adolescents unsupervised after school, experts have called for better and more readily available after-school programming for adolescents. They argue that well-designed programs not only will deter problem behavior by providing adolescents with adult supervision but will also promote **positive youth development** (J. Lerner, Phelps, Forman, & Bowers, 2009; Small & Memmo, 2004). Although the label "positive youth development" is new, the concept is not. Indeed, the goals espoused by proponents of positive youth development programs today bear a striking resemblance to the stated goals of youth programs that have been around for ages, like the YMCA (founded in London in 1844 and transported to the United States in 1851), the Boys and Girls Clubs of America (with the first club founded in 1860), 4-H clubs (founded at the turn of the 20th century), and scouting (founded in 1910). Indeed, in 1866, the YMCA of New York City announced that its purpose was "the improvement of the spiritual, mental, social and physical condition of young men" (YMCA, 2006).

Experts' interest in helping young people develop strengths, rather than simply preventing them from getting into trouble, has burgeoned in recent years (e.g., Gano-Overway et al., 2009; Scales, Benson, Roehlkepartain, Sesma, Jr., & van Dulmen, 2006). There are many different models of positive youth development, but they all are very similar (J. Lerner et al., 2009; J. Mahoney et al., 2009). One of the most widely cited is that of psychologist Richard Lerner, who describes the Five C's of positive youth development: competence, confidence, connection, character, and caring compassion (see Table 7.1) (Lerner et al., 2005). These characteristics, in one form or another, are often the focus of contemporary community-based programming for youth, including programs emphasizing

positive youth development The goal of programs designed to facilitate healthy psychosocial development and not simply to deter problematic development.

community service, volunteer activity, mentoring, and skill building.

What makes a positive youth development program successful? One recent evaluation found that a key component to program success is the extent to which participants were placed in demanding roles, encouraged to meet high expectations, expected to take responsibility for their behavior, and helped to understand the consequences of failing to fulfill their obligations. As one girl explained:

> You have to carry your own. Mr. Baker and Mr. Jensen [the program advisors], they'll push you, they'll give you an encouragement, but they're not going to do it for you: no way, shape, or form (D. Wood, Larson, & Brown, 2009, p. 300).

This expectation, in turn, helped adolescents understand how important their behavior was to other members of the group. In contrast, in programs that were less successful in contributing to character development, program leaders "had lower expectations and more often let youth 'off the hook.' They filled in or covered up for weaker work. In several cases, when members . . . did not complete or backed out on doing a task, the leader reported doing the work himself" (Wood et al., 2009, p. 305). In other words, expecting adolescents to behave responsibly may help them develop a sense of responsibility (Coatsworth & Conroy, 2009). In some families, this may lead parents to see their adolescents as more self-reliant, which may increase parental autonomy-granting, further contributing to the development of adolescent independence (Larson, Pearce, Sullivan, & Jarrett, 2007).

RECAP

- In most industrialized countries, leisure occupies more time in adolescence than do school and work combined.
- It is important to distinguish between participation in structured leisure activities, such as school-sponsored extracurricular activities, and unstructured leisure, such as hanging out with friends in the absence of adult supervision.
- Adolescents' moods are better when they are engaged in structured leisure activities than at any other time. In addition, participation in school-sponsored extracurricular activities may enhance adolescents' well-being and strengthen their attachment to school.
- Having large amounts of unstructured leisure time increases adolescents' risk for engagement in problem behavior. Because many adolescents' parents work, self-care during the after-school hours can be problematic. The greatest risk for problem behavior after school is found among teenagers who live in

unsafe neighborhoods, spend a lot of time in unsupervised activity with peers, and are poorly monitored by their parents.

- Many experts have called for better and more readily available after-school programming that will not simply deter problem behavior but also promote positive youth development.

Adolescents, Media, and the Internet

PATTERNS OF MEDIA USE

In 2009, a Los Angeles high school teacher asked her 10th-grade class to unplug themselves for a week—to go entirely without electronics for that whole time (Lopez, 2009). Here's one student's report. It's very typical of what others wrote:

> For me, the hardest media to break away from for 7 days was the 46-inch TV in the living room, plus all of the other TVs in the house. I watch TV almost every day. When it is on, I cannot resist watching. I thought being without media was hard at the beginning, but while it went on, it got harder and harder, even in the same day. The first day was the hardest. I was left in silence, with everything gone and disconnected. I think that part was the hardest. Thinking about other things. Usually I like hearing my thoughts, but that day, they kind of got annoying. I didn't want to listen to myself any more.

As this young woman's account illustrates, electronic media have become so much a part of the typical adolescent's life that for many, staying "connected" starts to take on qualities of an addiction. Another young man in the study wrote, "Being without media was harder than I ever realized. I thought it was going to be a cake walk, but it turned into a hell. I found myself thinking that I should just give up, and I kept talking to myself." Many students reported sleeping much more than usual as a way of coping, in part because adolescents frequently use media to distract themselves from negative thoughts and emotions (Larson, 1995). At the end of the week, most said that the experience was interesting, in that it taught them how dependent on these media they were, but that they could not wait to return to their iPods, cell phones, and televisions.

During the past decade, there has been an explosion in adolescents' use of media, in part because access to electronic media has expanded so rapidly—adolescents not only access music and video content through the usual sources (stereos and televisions), but also access this material on computers and all sorts of portable devices, like cell phones—and because the sheer amount

Studies of adolescent media use now must take into account the fact that teenagers often use multiple forms of mass media at the same time.

of media content that is created and distributed is so vast. Although research has not kept up with this explosion (good research takes time, and the world of electronic media changes so rapidly that by the time a study is done and published, it may very well be outdated), three broad conclusions about adolescents' media exposure have emerged from recent large-scale surveys (D. Roberts et al., 2009).

▮ **Media Saturation**   First, the availability of media in young people's lives is remarkable—today's adolescents live in a world that is not simply "media-rich" but absolutely "media-saturated." Virtually all American households have at least one television, more than three quarters of all adolescents' homes have Internet access, and the majority of adolescents without home Internet have access to the Internet at school or at friends' houses. As you would expect, computers and Internet access are present in virtually all middle-class homes; even so, 80% of all poor households have a computer, and two thirds have Internet access. According to recent surveys, more than 90% of American teenagers use the Internet at least occasionally (A. Lenhart, Madden, Macgill, & Smith, 2007; Willoughby, 2008).

Second, adolescents' total media exposure—the amount of time they spend each day using one of the mass media—is extremely high. The average adolescent spends more than 6 hours each day using one or more media, and this includes time spent using different media simultaneously (that is, where 1 hour watching TV while on the Internet and talking on a cell phone would be recorded as only 1 hour of media use, even though it technically is 3 hours of exposure). When media multitasking is taken into account, the amount of time teenagers are *exposed* to media each day is between 8 and 9 hours (D. Roberts et al., 2009).

Third, there has been an enormous increase in the last decade in the amount of time adolescents spend on the computer (Greenfield & Yan, 2006). In 2006, about one third of teenagers reported being on the Internet at least 3 hours every day (Burst Media Corporation, 2006). Among teenagers, the most common online activities are playing video games (78% of teenagers, mainly boys), communicating with others via email (73%) or instant messaging (68%), using social networking sites (65%), getting news (63%), downloading music (59%), and watching videos (57%) (S. Jones & Fox, 2009). There is some research indicating that close to 10% of preadolescents and adolescents devote so much energy to playing video games that their behavior is "pathological" (see Table 7.2) (Gentile, 2009). Interestingly, moderate Internet use is associated with better academic performance than either high use or nonuse (Willoughby, 2008).

THEORIES OF MEDIA INFLUENCE AND USE

Given the considerable amount of time adolescents spend exposed to the mass media, not surprisingly, the impact of the media on teenagers' behavior and development has been the subject of much debate. Unfortunately, one tremendous problem in interpreting studies of media use and adolescent development is that it is extremely difficult to disentangle cause and effect, because adolescents choose which mass media they are exposed to (D. Roberts et al., 2009). (In Chapter 6 we saw that this is also a problem in identifying the "effects" of peers on adolescent behavior, because adolescents select their friends.) Although it has been speculated that violent film images and heavy metal music provoke aggression, for example, it is just as likely, if not more so, that aggressive adolescents are more prone to choose to watch violent images (Arnett, 1996; Roe, 1995). Similarly, sexual behavior may be correlated with listening to "sexy" music, but it is impossible to say which causes which. And, although a major study of media use (D. Roberts, Foehr, & Rideout, 2005) found that adolescents who listen to a lot of music or play a lot of video games were significantly more troubled (bored, unhappy, in trouble at home or school) than adolescents who used these media less often, it is not known whether large doses of mass media cause problems or, more plausibly, whether adolescents with more problems listen to more music and play more video games, perhaps as a way of distracting themselves from their troubles (Larson, 1995). It's probably a combination of both.

There are three basic schools of thought concerning the media's impact (or lack thereof) on adolescent development. One school of thought argues that adolescents are influenced by the content to which they are exposed, with respect to their knowledge about the

TABLE 7.2   Signs of pathological video game use

Symptom	Total Sample		"Yes" Responses Only	
	"Yes"	"Sometimes"	Boys	Girls
Over time, have you been spending much more time thinking about playing video games, learning about video-game playing, or planning the next opportunity to play?	21%	19%	29%	11%[b]
Do you need to spend more and more time and/or money on video games in order to feel the same amount of excitement?	8	9	12	3[b]
Have you tried to play video games less often or for shorter periods of time, but are unsuccessful?	2	22	2	3
Do you become restless or irritable when attempting to cut down or stop playing video games?	2	6	2	1
Have you played video games as a way of escaping from problems or bad feelings?	25	20	29	19[b]
Have you ever lied to family or friends about how much you play video games?	14	10	17	10[b]
Have you ever stolen a video game from a store or a friend, or have you ever stolen money in order to buy a video game?	2	2	3	1[a]
Do you sometimes skip household chores in order to spend more time playing video games?	33	21	40	24[b]
Do you sometimes skip doing homework in order to spend more time playing video games?	23	19	29	15[b]
Have you ever done poorly on a school assignment or test because you spent too much time playing video games?	20	12	26	11[b]
Have you ever needed friends or family to give you extra money because you spent too much money on video-game equipment, software, or game/Internet fees?	9	6	13	4[b]

Note: For each symptom, chi-square tests were used to compare prevalence among boys and girls. Overall, the number of symptoms reported was significantly different ($p < .001$) between boys ($M = 2.8$) and girls ($M = 1.3$). Also, the prevalence of pathological gaming (i.e., displaying at least 6 of the 11 symptoms) was significantly different ($p < .001$) between boys (12%) and girls (3%).

Source: Gentile, 2009.

[a] $p < .05$.   [b] $p < .001$.

world, their attitudes and values, and their behavior. You've no doubt heard contentions like these thousands of times: Playing violent video games makes adolescents aggressive, watching sexy movies makes adolescents sex-crazed, being exposed to Internet pornography affects the ways that adolescents think about gender roles, listening to rap lyrics encourages adolescents to engage in violence and crime, viewing beer commercials during the Super Bowl makes adolescents drink beer, and so on. According to this view, the media shape adolescents' interests, motives, and beliefs about the world—a view known as **cultivation theory** (Gerbner, Gross, Morgan, & Signorelli, 1994).

cultivation theory   A perspective on media use that emphasizes the impact media exposure has on individuals.

uses and gratification approach   A perspective on media use that emphasizes the active role users play in selecting the media to which they are exposed.

A second school of thought, called the **uses and gratifications approach** (E. Katz, Blumler, & Gurevitch, 1974), emphasizes the fact that adolescents choose the media to which they are exposed. According to this view, any correlation between what adolescents are exposed to and what they do or think is due not to the influence of the media, but to the fact that individuals with particular inclinations choose media that are consistent with their interests. According to this view, adolescents deliberately choose the media they use, either for entertainment, information, bonding with others, or developing a sense of identity. Thus, aggressive adolescents are more likely to purchase violent video games because they enjoy being aggressive; teenagers who are interested in sex are more likely to look for pornography on the Internet because they want to masturbate or feel sexually aroused; beer-drinking adolescents are more likely to watch football and to be exposed to beer commercials (which, after all, is why beer companies advertise during football games and not on the Animal Planet network); and adolescents who are involved with drugs like to listen to music that glorifies drug use. According to this view, adolescents' preexisting interests and motives shape their media choices.

According to the third school of thought, the links between adolescents' preferences, on the one hand, and their media exposure, on the other, are reciprocal (that is, they affect each other); moreover, adolescents not only choose what they are exposed to but *interpret* the media in ways that shape their impact. This view is referred to as the **media practice model** (Steele & Brown, 1995). Imagine two adolescents who accidentally stumble onto a sexually explicit website while on the Internet. One, a sexually experienced teenager who is curious about pornography, views the website with interest—perhaps it even makes him feel aroused. The other, who isn't interested in sex, sees the very same content and feels repulsed. Not only is the experience not arousing, but it also makes this adolescent even less interested in having sex than he was before landing on the site. One 13-year-old sees a beer commercial and thinks, "That's how I'm going to party when I'm old enough to drink." Another sees the exact same images and thinks, "What morons those people are—look how stupid beer makes you act." Two adolescents are flipping through television channels—one, who collects rap music, sees a flash of a music video that piques her interest and stops flipping channels to watch; the other, who is into country music, doesn't even notice the clip. According to this third view, the ways in which media do (or do not) affect adolescents depend on the ways in which the media are experienced and interpreted.

These problems in distinguishing among **correlation** (when two things go hand in hand), **causation** (when one thing actually causes another), **reverse causation** (when the correlation between two things is due not to the first thing causing the second, but to the reverse), and **spurious causation** (when the correlation between two things is due to the fact that each of them is correlated with some third factor) make it almost impossible to say for sure whether media exposure genuinely affects adolescent development (see Figure 7.8).

The only sure way to demonstrate cause and effect where media influence is concerned is to conduct an experiment in which people are randomly assigned to be (or not be) exposed to the medium of interest and see how it affects them. But experiments of this sort are rare, because they are difficult to do well. Even the most ardent believers in the power of media influence generally acknowledge that one exposure to a commercial, a movie, a song, or an Internet site is unlikely to change someone's behavior. But if the impact of media exposure is incremental and cumulative—perhaps taking years of exposure to have an effect—it may be quite powerful, but impossible to demonstrate in a brief experiment. All of this is to say that you should view any claims about the presence—or absence—

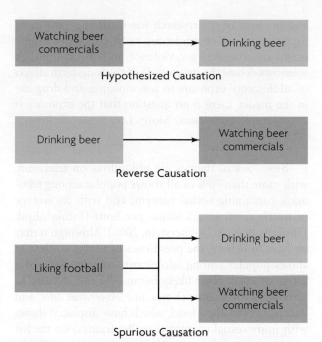

FIGURE 7.8 Two things can be correlated because the first causes the second (the hypothesized correlation), or some third factor causes both of them (spurious causation). Research on media "effects" on adolescent development has a hard time separating the three.

of media influence on adolescent development with tremendous caution.

THE IMPACT OF ADOLESCENTS' EXPOSURE TO CONTROVERSIAL MEDIA CONTENT

These chicken-and-egg problems notwithstanding, a few generalizations about media usage and adolescent development have enough supporting evidence, however indirect, to generate some consensus among experts in the area. Most of the relevant research has focused on television (as a consequence, we know very little about the impact of other media content on development),

media practice model   A perspective on media use that emphasizes the fact that adolescents not only choose what media they are exposed to but also interpret the media in ways that shape their impact.

correlation   The extent to which two things vary systematically with each other.

causation   The correlation between two things attributable to the effect one thing has on the other.

reverse causation   Relationship in which the correlation between two things is due not to the first thing causing the second, but to the second causing the first.

spurious causation   Relationship in which the correlation between two things is due to the fact that each of them is correlated with some third factor.

and the bulk of the research has focused on the three topics about which adults are most concerned (some might say obsessed): sex, violence, and drugs. Although scientists debate the magnitude of the long-term effects of adolescents' exposure to sex, violence, and drug use in the media, there is no question that the exposure is considerable (Jamieson, More, Lee, Busse, & Romer, 2008).

■ **Sex** Sexual themes are ubiquitous on television, with more than 70% of all shows popular among teenagers containing sexual content, and with an average of nearly seven sexual scenes per hour (Kunkel, Eyal, Finnerty, Biely, & Donnerstein, 2005). Although it may be hard to believe, the prevalence of sexual content in shows popular among adolescents actually declined a bit since 2000, most likely because of the increase in popularity of reality shows like *American Idol* and *America's Next Top Model*, which have displaced shows with more sexual content (usually dramas) on the list of programs most watched by teenagers. Generally, sex on TV is portrayed as pleasurable and carefree (L. M. Ward & Friedman, 2006). Most sexual content on prime-time TV is not composed of graphic images of individuals having sex, but instead is made up of humorous and suggestive comments. On daytime television, however, a lot of sexual imagery is of individuals engaging in passionate kissing and erotic touching. Sexual content is also very common in music videos (L. M. Ward, 2003).

The most common sexual messages concern men seeing women as sex objects ("Look at the body on that chick"; "In case she's a dog, I can fake a heart attack"), sex as a defining aspect of masculinity ("I slept with 10 girls last week"; "Oh, that's one afternoon for me"), sex as a competition ("You're supposed to be keeping score, not trying to score"), and sex as fun and exciting ("It's so romantic, all that passion, when you have to make love every minute of the day") (M. Ward, 1995). This message—that woman are sex objects—is one that teenagers seem especially susceptible to (L. M. Ward & Friedman, 2006). Similar messages are carried in most music videos, in which men are shown as aggressive and dominant, and women are seen as the subservient objects of men's sexual advances (D. Roberts et al., 2009). One issue that has concerned many sex educators is the relative absence of messages concerning the possible physical consequences of sex (for example, pregnancy, STDs), although these messages have become more common now than in the past, in part because the entertainment industry has tried to respond more responsibly to concerns about the way sex has been portrayed (Kunkel et al., 2005).

■ **Violence** Adolescents are also exposed to a great deal of violent imagery on television, in movies, in cer-

tain music genres, and in video games (D. Roberts et al., 2009). More than 60% of TV programming contains violence; as a consequence, young people see an estimated 10,000 acts of media violence each year, and more than one fourth of all violent incidents on TV involve guns. One analysis of MTV videos indicated that more than one fifth portrayed overt violence and one quarter showed weapons (Strasburger & Donnerstein, 1999).

Precise estimates of the amount of violent imagery in the most popular video games or other visual media are not available, but concerns also have been raised over the impact of violent video games on young people's behavior and attitudes (Ivory, 2008; Konijn, Nije, & Bushman, 2007). Studies have found that adolescents who spend a lot of time playing violent video games get into more fights and arguments than do their peers (e.g., Gentile, Lynch, Linder, & Walsh, 2004), but it is difficult to know whether playing such games makes adolescents more hostile or whether adolescents who are more aggressive to begin with are simply more likely to want to play these sorts of games. Experimental research on the effects of video games on adolescent behavior are inconclusive, with some studies finding small effects and others not (Ivory, 2008). Although controlled experiments have shown that exposure to the lyrics of violent songs increases individuals' aggressive thoughts (C. A. Anderson, Carnagey, & Eubanks, 2003), many experts doubt that playing violent video games or listening to music with violent lyrics causes adolescents to engage in the sorts of serious violent acts that alarmists have raised concerns about, such as lethal school shootings. As some have noted, given the millions of copies of violent games that have been sold, if playing video games had a significant impact on real-world violence, we'd likely be in the midst of a violence epidemic—yet juvenile violence has declined substantially since peaking in the early 1990s, despite the proliferation of violent video games (Reichhardt, 2003).

■ **Drugs** Finally, many analyses have shown that alcohol and tobacco use are ubiquitous in the mass media to which adolescents are exposed. Alcohol, tobacco, or illicit drugs are present in nearly three quarters of prime-time network dramatic programs, virtually all top-grossing movies, and half of all music videos. Nearly 10% of the commercials that young people see on TV are for beer or wine—and for every public service announcement discouraging alcohol use, teenagers will view 25–50 ads for alcoholic beverages. And alcohol and tobacco companies have an increasing presence on the Internet, sponsoring numerous websites and specially designed chat rooms (Strasburger & Donnerstein, 1999). Adolescents are also exposed to alcohol and tobacco through films, which frequently depict actors smoking and drinking. Teenagers are more likely to smoke if their favorite film star is a smoker (D. Roberts et al., 2009).

Importantly, the effects of seeing smoking in movies are strongest among adolescents who are initially less inclined to take up smoking, which argues against the notion that adolescents' desire to smoke leads to their exposure to smoking in movies and suggests instead that exposure to smoking in movies may actually influence adolescents to start smoking. As a consequence of this research, movie distributors are now putting anti-smoking ads on DVDs of movies that contain scenes with smoking (Heatherton & Sargent, 2009).

Studies that unequivocally demonstrate that exposure to messages about sex, violence, and drugs causes changes in adolescents' behavior are harder to find than simple documentation of exposure. The strongest evidence is in the area of violence, where numerous studies have shown that repeated exposure to violent imagery on television leads to aggressive behavior in children and youth, especially among those who have prior histories of aggression (Johnson, Cohen, Kotler, Kasen, & Brook, 2002) (see Figure 7.9). It is important to note, however, that other factors, such as experiences in the family or community, are likely far greater influences on adolescent violence than media exposure (Strasburger & Donnerstein, 1999). Nevertheless, it is now well established that exposure to TV violence in childhood is linked in adolescence and adulthood to aggressive behavior toward others, a heightened tolerance of violence, and greater desensitization to the effects of violence on others, although some of this effect is likely due to the tendency for people with aggressive tendencies to choose to watch violent programming (Huesmann, 2007; D. Roberts et al., 2009).

▌Misleading Media Messages Data linking exposure to messages about sex and drugs to actual sexual activity or drug use are less consistent than those concerning violence (Strasburger & Donnerstein, 1999). One recent study of whether frequent exposure to sexual content on television, in music, in movies, and in magazines increases adolescents' likelihood of engaging in sex found a significant effect among White but not among Black adolescents (J. D. Brown et al., 2006). Although questions remain about whether exposure to messages about sex alters adolescents' actual behavior, many studies demonstrate that repeated exposure affects adolescents' attitudes, beliefs, and intentions (L'Engle, Brown, & Kenneavy, 2006; D. Roberts et al., 2009; L. M. Ward, 2003). For example, adolescents who watch a lot of music videos have more tolerant attitudes toward sexual harassment and more sex-stereotyped attitudes about sexual relationships (Strouse, Goodwin, & Roscoe, 1994; L. M. Ward, Hansbrough, & Walker, 2005). Along similar lines, one study found that college students who frequently watched soap operas (which have a high sexual content) gave higher estimates than nonviewers did of the number of real-life extramarital affairs, children

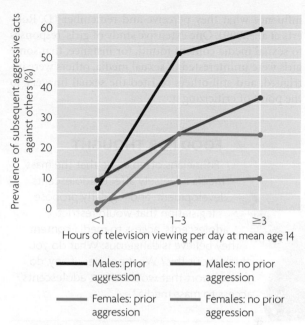

FIGURE 7.9 Exposure to violent television during adolescence is associated with increased aggression in young adulthood, especially among individuals who had a prior history of aggression. (Johnson et al., 2002)

born out of wedlock, and divorces. Another study found that high school students who believed that TV characters have highly satisfying sex were less likely themselves to feel that sex is satisfying, presumably because the images they saw on TV created false expectations (D. Roberts, 1993). Similarly, prolonged exposure to pornography leads to exaggerated beliefs about the extent of sexual activity in the real world (Zillman, 2000). Studies of exposure to ads for alcohol and tobacco, as well as antismoking commercial messages (such as those conveyed in the "Truth" campaign), have shown that they are effective in changing teenagers' attitudes about drinking and smoking and in developing brand recognition (Farrelly, Davis, Haviland, Healton, & Messeri, 2004; D. Roberts et al., 2009; Straub, Hills, Thompson, & Moscicki, 2003). There is some evidence showing that exposure to advertising may lead adolescents to begin using cigarettes or alcohol, but the evidence is far less compelling.

It is important to note that discussions of media effects often fail to distinguish between what adolescents actually perceive and remember and what adults believe adolescents see and remember. After all, media are not simply viewed or heard—they are interpreted. Studies of "violent" video games, for example, find that adolescents, college students, and parents rate the same games very differently (Funk, Flores, Buchman, & Germann, 1999). Adolescents are not exposed to the mass media as blank slates; rather, they bring preexisting values, beliefs, and expectations to the experience of watching or listening, and these preexisting states influence what they perceive and remember (D. Roberts et al., 2009). One extensive study of girls' responses to sexual media content found, for instance, that some girls were uninterested in sexual media, others were intrigued, and still others resisted the sexual imagery to the point of criticizing it.

FOOD FOR THOUGHT

Politicians often argue that the mass media adversely affects adolescents' development, and regularly propose legislation that would restrict adolescents' access to media content they believe is dangerous. What do you think about this? What policies, if any, do you support that would affect adolescents' access to mass media?

ELECTRONIC MEDIA AND ADOLESCENT DEVELOPMENT

Can you decipher the following exchange?

wru

wmao

wuu2

h/w, hbu

boomm f2t?

nn pir

cml8r

K

In case you need help with the translation, the preceding conversation went as follows:

"Where are you?"

"Working my ass off."

"What are you up to?"

"Homework. How about you?"

"Bored out of my mind. Can you talk?"

"Not now. My parents are in the room."

"Call me later."

"Okay."

There is no question that the increased availability of electronic communication has influenced the way that adolescents socialize. Indeed, among the most popular websites visited by adolescents are those designed for communication, such as social networking sites like Facebook or MySpace, which permit individuals to create their own web pages with personal information and photographs that can be viewed by others. In keeping with the general notion that the main purposes of adolescents' media use, in addition to commu-

nication, are entertainment and information seeking, other sites that draw many teenage visitors are YouTube (for entertainment) and Google (for information).

The impact of Internet socializing on adolescents' behavior and development is interesting, poorly understood, and controversial. Among the main concerns that have been raised are whether communicating with friends and acquaintances electronically rather than in person is adversely affecting adolescents' development and whether strangers who might wish to harm young people, such as sexual predators, could use publicly posted information to establish relationships and initiate sexual contact with them.

◼ Adolescent Development and the Internet

Many parents are concerned that the large amount of time that teenagers spend on the Internet has had a negative effect on their social development and relationships. Some worry that electronic interactions have replaced face-to-face interactions, to the detriment of the development of social skills. Still others worry that adolescents are forming relationships with strangers and that these may take time away from intimacy with "real" friends. And, of course, many simply worry that the sheer amount of time adolescents spend online is unhealthy because it has displaced other, more valuable activities. Has adolescents' extensive use of the Internet affected their development and mental health? Research on this question suggests that the answer is complicated, and many unanswered questions remain, but it looks as if the effects of Internet use—whether positive or negative—are much smaller than its proponents or detractors have claimed (Jackson, 2008).

We can safely assume that, to the extent that time on the Internet is displacing time spent in physical activity, it is having a detrimental impact on adolescents' physical health. On average, the typical American 15-year-old spends at least 6 hours each day sitting in front of one sort of screen or another, but less than an hour in moderate physical activity (Nader, Bradley, Houts, McRitchie, & O'Brien, 2008; D. Roberts et al., 2009). The amount of time adolescents spend watching TV and playing video games is inversely linked to the amount of time they spend in physical activity (Motl, McAuley, Birnbaum, & Lytle, 2006). Most experts believe that the high rate of obesity among American teenagers is due, in part, to the large amount of time—estimated in 2005 to be close to 50 hours a week, and rising steadily—young people spend sitting in front of one screen or another, whether watching TV, playing video games, or using the computer. Studies have found that some time adolescents spend on the Internet displaces physical activity but that a fair amount simply replaces time that would have been spent watching television (Jackson, 2008).

Researchers have also asked whether adolescents use the Internet to acquire information that can improve their health or understanding of the world. To the extent that the Internet is used by adolescents to acquire accurate information, it can be a positive force. This may be especially true with respect to educating adolescents about healthy behavior, such as safe sex, in developing countries, where it is often difficult to reach a large audience of adolescents through classrooms (Borzekowski, Fobil, & Asante, 2006). But the ultimate value of the Internet as an educational tool depends on the quality and content of the information conveyed, as two recent studies of eating disorders illustrate. Whereas one study found that an Internet-based intervention was effective in reducing binge eating (M. Jones et al., 2008) another found that many adolescents with eating disorders visit websites that actually promote disordered eating (J. L. Wilson, Peebles, Hardy, & Litt, 2006). Similarly, whereas some message boards on the Internet devoted to self-injurious behavior, like cutting, can provide valuable social support to adolescents who compulsively injure themselves, others may promote the behavior and provide instructions on various techniques (Whitlock, Powers, & Eckenrode, 2006). One study of race-related exchanges among adolescents on the Internet found plenty of examples of both hostile, racist comments and civil discussions of racial tolerance (Tynes, 2007).

Whether spending time online is harmful to teenagers' psychological development and social relationships is equally complicated. A lot depends on what adolescents are doing when they are online. Studies find that more frequent online communication with friends brings friends closer, perhaps because online communication facilitates self-disclosure between friends, and communicating online with friends may be especially important for socially anxious adolescents, who may find it easier to interact online than in person (Blais, Craig, Pepler, & Connolly, 2008; Valkenburg & Peter, 2007, 2009). However, these same studies find that spending a lot of time in other online activities, like visiting chat rooms or interacting with strangers, leads to *lower* quality relationships with one's close friends. Another factor appears to be where individuals meet the people they communicate with online; if their online friends are people they know from school or from the neighborhood, their relationships tend to be closer than those with people they met over the Internet (Mesch & Talmud, 2007). It seems, then, that the Internet can help strengthen adolescents' close relationships if it is used to communicate with one's existing friends (and in this sense, using the Internet to stay in touch is probably not all that different from spending time with one's friends on the phone), but has the potential to weaken friendships if it occupies the adolescent in activities that aren't shared. Frequent instant messaging, especially with acquaintances who are not close friends, can become compulsive and lead to feelings of depres-

Although many adults worry that the increased use of electronic communication has had an adverse impact on adolescents' social development, this does not seem to be the case.

sion (van den Eijnden, Meerkerk, Vermulst, Spijkerman, & Engels, 2008).

As with other research in media "effects," studies of the Internet have difficulty separating cause and effect, and these problems are compounded when the research is conducted over the Internet, since the samples in these studies are bound to be individuals who are online more frequently. Some evidence suggests that adolescents with relatively more psychological problems and poorer family relationships are more likely than their peers to form close online relationships with strangers, but we do not know whether having these sorts of online relationships leads to or follows from maladjustment (Wolak, Mitchell, & Finkelhor, 2003; Ybarra, Alexander, & Mitchell, 2005). That is, it is quite plausible that adolescents who have problems simply are more likely to seek out relationships with people over the Internet (M. Gould, Munfakh, Lubell, Kleinman, & Parker, 2002). Despite the considerable media attention given to the topic, rates of Internet addiction are very low, and the evidence linking psychological problems to excessive Internet use is inconsistent, with some studies linking Internet addiction to insomnia, depression, social isolation, and missed school, but others finding no such effects (Jackson, 2008).

Some parents are anxious about the ways in which the anonymity of the Internet may expose their teenagers to individuals who wish to harm them in some way, like sexual predators and cyberbullies. As you read in Chapter 5, however, despite the attention devoted to it in the popular media, electronic bullying is a far less prevalent problem than is face-to-face bullying (Raskauskas & Stolz, 2007; K. Williams & Guerra, 2007), and most cyberbullying is very mild, taking the form of ignoring or disrespecting the victim (Jackson,

2008). Is the same true for sexual predators on the Internet? Has this problem been exaggerated by media coverage as well?

■ **Sexual Predators**   According to the Youth Internet Safety Survey, conducted by the U.S. Department of Justice in 2005, about 13% of young people receive an unwanted sexual solicitation online each year (a decline since the previous survey, a few years earlier), and 4% reported that the online solicitation was followed by an attempt to contact them through some means other than the computer; these attempts were almost never successful, and no one in the survey was actually assaulted (Mitchell, Wolak, & Finkelhor, 2007; Wolak, Mitchell, & Finkelhor, 2006). Most at risk for unwanted solicitation were adolescent high school–aged girls who were frequent Internet users, were often in chat rooms, and reported higher-than-average rates of depression or life stress; boys who identify themselves over the Internet as gay or who ask questions about their sexual orientation are also relatively more likely to be victimized online. And despite media hype about the dangers of posting personal information on MySpace, Facebook, and other social networking sites, systematic studies find that doing so does not increase the risk of receiving unwanted sexual communication from strangers. It seems clear that what adolescents *do* when online (for instance, whether they engage in sexy communication with others) is what places teenagers at risk, not merely having a personal website (Wolak, Finkelhor, Mitchell, & Ybarra, 2008). Rather than forbid adolescents from having personal websites, a better strategy for parents and educators is to teach adolescents about how, and how not, to interact with others over the Internet.

Although adults often express concerns about adolescents' using the Internet to view pornography, much of the pornographic material on the Internet to which adolescents are exposed is unwanted rather than actively sought; in 2005, one third of all adolescents reported receiving unwanted sexual material, although less than 10% of adolescents said that they had received material that upset them (Wolak et al., 2006). One study of teen chat rooms found that only 5% of users' comments contained sexual content, and only 3% contained obscenity (Subrahmanyam, Smahel, & Greenfield, 2006). Adolescents are far more likely to visit entertainment websites (for example, disneychannel.com) or sports (espn.com) than pornographic ones. Indeed, many of the most popular websites among teenagers are the ones also visited frequently by adults.

■ **The Internet and Cognitive Development**
Very few studies have looked at the impact of Internet use on cognitive development, despite hopes that adolescents will benefit from having increased access to a world of information and fears that the Internet will distract teenagers from more stimulating pursuits, like reading (an odd fear, given the fact that even before computers were so widespread, reading outside of school had been pretty much displaced by television). To date, research suggests that both the hopes and the fears are probably exaggerated. There is no evidence that adolescents' school performance is either helped or harmed by Internet use. A few studies show that video-game playing may enhance visual skills, reaction time, and hand-eye coordination, however (Ivory, 2008; Jackson, 2008).

FOOD FOR THOUGHT

Based on the current scientific literature on the impact of Internet use on adolescent development, what advice would you give parents about the extent to which they should regulate their teenagers' Internet use? Would you place restrictions on the number of hours they are allowed to spend online? On the sites they are allowed to visit?

MASS MEDIA AND ADOLESCENT GIRLS' BODY IMAGE

Several commentators have raised concerns about the messages to which young women are exposed in mass media aimed at adolescent girls, especially in light of evidence (discussed in Chapter 1) of widespread body dissatisfaction among adolescent females (Brumberg, 1997; van Hoeken, Lucas, & Hoek, 1998). The majority of articles in these magazines focus on dating and heterosexual relationships, and most emphasize the importance of physical attractiveness and thinness, in particular, for young women. According to researchers, the articles and advertisements contained in such magazines convey a clear message that attracting males by being physically beautiful is the road to true happiness for women. Interestingly, adolescent girls who frequently read fashion magazines are more dissatisfied with their body than are girls who do not, and controlled experiments have indicated that showing girls images of thin models increases their body dissatisfaction (M. Levine & Harrison, 2004; D. Roberts et al., 2009). Moreover, frequent reading of magazine articles about dieting or weight loss leads to increases in unhealthy weight control behaviors, such as intentional vomiting and inappropriate use of laxatives (van der Berg, Neumark-Sztainer, Hannan, & Haines, 2007).

Similar results are reported in studies of girls' responses to appearance-related commercials on television, which, like ads in fashion magazines, typically feature thin models (Harrison & Hefner, 2008). In a fascinating study of the impact of TV on adolescent girls' body image, the researchers examined girls' self-image and eating habits before and after the introduction of TV to the Fiji islands (A. Becker, Burwell, Herzog, Hamburg, & Gilman, 2002). Within 3 years of the introduction of TV, self-induced vomiting to control weight, which had been nonexistent, was practiced by 11% of adolescent girls, and the proportion of girls showing signs of disordered eating doubled. Prior to having access to TV, adolescent girls in Fiji endorsed cultural norms that valued having a large appetite and body; after TV was introduced, three quarters of the adolescent girls reported feeling "too big or fat," and close to 70% said that they had dieted to lose weight. The actual content of the televised programs matters, however. A more recent study of Latina adolescents in the United States found that frequent exposure to mainstream television led to the development of a more negative body image, whereas exposure to Black-oriented television led to greater body satisfaction (Schooler, 2008).

THE ADOLESCENT CONSUMER

A final, and very important, aspect of adolescent media use is economic. The size of the adolescent population, the prevalence of student employment, and the fact that adolescents save less than any other age group make young people an attractive target for a variety of businesses (Osgerby, 2008). The amount of money spent by and for adolescents between 12 and 17 is projected to exceed $200 billion in 2011; the spending by preadolescents (called **tweens** by market researchers) and youth between 18 and 24 is also huge (Packaged Facts, 2007). The average adolescent has about $400 per month in spending money—and spends nearly all of it. Not surprisingly, much of adolescents' money is spent on discretionary purchases related to leisure activities. Girls spend their money on clothes, food, and cosmetics, in that order; boys use their money for food and clothes, and they also save for big-ticket items, like cars and stereo equipment (Meyer, 1994). And, unfortunately, many adolescents spend money on alcohol and cigarettes—according to one estimate, underage drinkers account for about one sixth of the $100 billion dollars spent each year on alcohol (Horner, Jamieson, & Romer, 2008).

We can certainly debate the merits of cultivating such strong consumer urges among the young and impressionable. Some critics contend that advertising aimed at teenagers takes advantage of the fact that they are more impulsive and self-conscious than adults (see Pechmann, Levine, Loughlin, & Leslie, 2005). On the other hand, America's economy is driven by consumer spending, and the segments of our economy that are devoted to leisure and recreation depend on the adolescent market. Among the most important industries are those connected with movies, music, sports, and television. Teenagers make up a large, and therefore influential, segment of the consumers of these products—as a glance at the local movie or TV listings or a trip through a music store will readily attest. And, of course, the jobs held by millions of adults who work in these sectors of the economy depend on adolescents' purchases.

Supporters of adolescent consumerism also have been quick to point out the strong influence that teenagers have on each other when it comes to purchases—and new ways of tapping into this influence that take advantage of the Internet and other new technologies, referred to as **viral marketing,** have been exploited by businesses wishing to expand their share of the teen consumer market. "Viral marketing" refers to a strategy that encourages people to pass on a marketing message to others, "creating the potential for exponential growth in the message's exposure and influence": "Like viruses, such strategies take advantage of rapid multiplication to explode the message to thousands, to millions" (R. Wilson, 2005). Because adolescents are likely to use technologies that can easily and instantly connect them to thousands of other teenagers, using young people to spread the word about new products is a highly effective marketing strategy. (Think of how quickly Gmail, an Internet mail service, went from a new, unknown service to one of the largest email services in the world—this is a classic example of viral marketing.)

The influence of the adolescent market extends well beyond the youth cohort, however—as evidenced by the uncanny predictability with which adult tastes in clothing and music often follow those of teenagers, albeit in a toned-down fashion. Teenagers often have considerable influence over their parents' purchases, which gives added incentive for advertisers to market products with young people's tastes in mind (Zollo, 2004).

FOOD FOR THOUGHT

Have you been the recipient of viral marketing? What product was marketed, and how did you find out about it? In what ways might viral marketing be more effective than conventional advertising when attempting to target teenage consumers?

---

tweens A term used by marketing experts to refer to preadolescents.

viral marketing A way of promoting products or services by encouraging individuals to pass information on to others.

RECAP

- Today's adolescents live in a media-saturated environment, with the average adolescent exposed to the mass media more than 6 hours each day. If media multitasking is factored into the equation, daily exposure is somewhere between 8 and 9 hours.

- One of the most significant changes in recent years has been in the amount of time adolescents spend each day on the computer. The most frequent computer activities reported by teenagers are playing games and communicating with friends, via email, instant messaging, or social networking websites.

- Theories of media influence and use examine three different processes: the influence of the media on adolescents' attitudes, knowledge, and behavior; the fact that adolescents choose the media that they are exposed to; and the fact that adolescents interpret the media that they are exposed to.

- Many observers of the adolescent scene are concerned about the high level of adolescents' exposure to messages about sex, violence, and drug use through the mass media. Some studies have shown that exposure to media violence does in fact lead to more aggressive behavior (although not to serious violence) and that exposure to images of drug and alcohol use and sex affects adolescents' attitudes and beliefs about these matters.

- Adolescents' use of the Internet has increased substantially in recent years, for communication, entertainment, and information. Many claims in the popular press about the toll the Internet is taking on teenagers' lives have not been supported by scientific study. Rates of sexual predation by strangers and Internet addiction are very low. Moreover, the notion that socializing over the Internet is taking time away from "real" relationships does not seem to be true. Most communication that takes place electronically is between adolescents who are already established friends, and the Internet is better viewed as another means of communication between them rather than a substitute for face-to-face interaction.

- Adolescents wield enormous power as consumers, both because they have a great deal of discretionary income of their own and because they influence how their families spend money.

Free Time and Adolescent Development

Adults have mixed feelings about adolescents' activities outside of school. On the positive side, adults take pride in watching their children's sports teams and creative activities, and they believe that these productive uses of leisure time help build character and teach important skills, such as teamwork and perseverance. (Think about all the movies you have seen about the character-building benefits of team sports.) Similarly, most adults view holding a part-time job as a worthwhile activity that provides opportunities for learning and for the development of a sense of responsibility.

On the other hand, adults view many adolescent leisure activities as wasted time or, worse, as preludes to trouble: They worry about groups of teenagers cruising the mall; they poke fun at groups of girls sequestered in front of a mirror trying on an array of cosmetics; they cringe at images of adolescents plugged into their MP3 players, mindlessly staring off into space; and they worry about adolescents' exposure to sex and violence on television, in film, in music, and on the Internet. Although we might wish for the "good old days" before the advent of cell phones, email, iPods, satellite television, DVD players, and personal computers, those good old days are long gone. And keep in mind that even during those supposed good old days, adults worried about how adolescents spent their idle time and about the corrupting influence of such evils as rock 'n' roll, dime-store romances, and comic books.

This mixed view of adolescents' free time reflects an interesting paradox about the nature of adolescence in modern society. Because industrialized society has "given" adolescents a good deal of free time, adults expect them to use it productively. But by definition, free time is supposed to be time that can be used for purposes other than being productive. As you will read in the next chapter, some theorists of adolescence believe that the existence of large blocks of uncommitted time is one feature of adolescence in modern society that has the potential to contribute in positive ways to young people's development; one potential benefit of participation in leisure activities is that this may help adolescents explore different sides of themselves (Barber, Stone, Hunt, & Eccles, 2005).

Nevertheless, many misconceptions about the pros and cons of various uses of free time abound. Most adults view participation in structured extracurricular activities as a good thing, and this seems to be the case. But most people are equally sure that working is good for teenagers, even though studies show that the costs of intensive involvement in part-time work during the school year may outweigh the benefits. And, although adults believe that the mass media have a negative effect on adolescents' behavior, studies show that it is more likely that adolescents' interests affect their media use than the reverse.

The impact of the mass media on adolescent development has become especially controversial as the role of technology in adolescents' lives has expanded. Most adults, especially parents, are absolutely certain that nothing good comes from adolescents' exposure to television, movies, video games, popular music, or the Internet, and they often blame the mass media for a wide array of adolescents' problems—despite the fact that parents themselves exert a far greater influence on adolescent development than do any of the media about which they are often so alarmed. Moreover, as you now know, because adolescents choose the media to which they are exposed, it has been very difficult to demonstrate that adolescents are actually affected by what they see and hear. This is not to say that the media have no impact on adolescents' behavior and well-being, but it is to suggest that we should be careful not to confuse cause and effect. It is also important to keep in mind that the mass media can be used to promote positive behavior and healthy development, to provide information about a rapidly changing world, and to facilitate communication with others.

By valuing adolescents' free time only when it is used productively, adults may misunderstand the important functions that leisure time serves in the psychosocial development of young people. For example, studies show that a moderate amount of solitude (during which daydreaming is a central activity) is positively related to high school students' psychological well-being (Csikszentmihalyi & Larson, 1984; Larson, 1997). Free time plays an important role in helping young people develop a sense of themselves, explore their relationships with each other, and learn about the society around them (Coatsworth et al., 2005). And, for better or for worse, the mass media are globalizing adolescence, contributing to the development of a common culture that gives adolescents all over the world much to share.

RECAP

- Adults' ambivalence about adolescents' free time reflects an interesting paradox about the nature of adolescence in modern society. Because industrialized society has "given" adolescents a good deal of free time, adults expect them to use it productively. But by definition, free time is supposed to be time that can be used for purposes other than being productive.

- Many misconceptions about the pros and cons of various uses of free time abound. Some of the activities that adults believe are uniformly good for adolescents, like employment, have more costs than benefits. Other activities that adults believe can be a waste of time, or even bad for adolescents' development, like watching television, playing video games, and browsing the Internet, are probably not as bad for teenagers as they are often assumed to be.

- Leisure plays an important role in helping young people develop a sense of themselves, explore their relationships with each other, and learn about the society around them.

Psychosocial Development During Adolescence

Identity

AS YOU MAY RECALL from your own adolescence, there are few experiences as trying—or as exhilarating—as questioning who you really are and, more important, who you would like to be. Some, but not all, adolescents share the feelings of self-consciousness and confusion expressed in the statement below. For these young people, adolescence is a time of identity crisis. For other adolescents, though, this period is one of more gradual and more subtle changes. Here's how a 15-year-old girl responded when asked to describe herself:

> What am I like as a person? You're probably not going to understand. I'm complicated! With my really close friends, I am very tolerant. I mean, I'm understanding and caring. With a group of friends, I'm rowdier. I'm also usually friendly and cheerful but I can get pretty obnoxious and intolerant if I don't like how they're acting. I'd like to be friendly and tolerant all of the time, that's the kind of person I want to be, and I'm disappointed when I'm not. At school, I'm serious, even studious every now and then, but on the other hand I'm a goof-off too, because if you're too studious, you won't be popular. So I go back and forth, which means I don't do all that well in terms of my grades. But that causes problems at home, where I'm pretty anxious when I'm around my parents. They expect me to get all A's, and get pretty annoyed with me when report cards come out. I care what they think about me, and so then I get down on myself, but it's not fair! I mean, I worry about how I probably should get better grades, but I'd be mortified in the eyes of my friends if I did too well. So I'm usually pretty stressed out at home, or sarcastic, since my parents are always on my case. But I really don't understand how I can switch so fast. I mean, how can I be cheerful with my friends, then coming home and feeling anxious, and then getting frustrated and sarcastic with my parents. Which one is the real me? I have the same question when I'm around boys. Sometimes I feel phony. Say I think some guy might be interested in asking

me out. I try to act different, like Madonna. I'll be a real extrovert, fun loving and even flirtatious, and think I am really good-looking. And then everybody, I mean everybody else is looking at me like they think I'm totally weird! They don't act like they think I'm attractive, so I end up thinking I look terrible. I just hate myself when that happens. Because it gets worse! Then I get self-conscious and embarrassed and become radically introverted, and I don't know who I really am! Am I just acting like an extrovert, am I just trying to impress them, when really I'm an introvert? But I don't really care what they think anyway. I mean, I don't want to care, that is. I just want to know what my close friends think. I can be my true self with my close friends. I can't be my real self with my parents. They don't understand me. What do they know about what it's like to be a teenager? They treat me like I'm still a kid. At least at school people treat you more like you're an adult. That gets confusing, though. I mean, which am I, a kid or an adult? . . . I have a part-time job and the people there treat me like an adult. I want to make them approve of me, so I'm very responsible at work. . . . But then I go out with my friends and I get pretty crazy and irresponsible. So which am I, responsible or irresponsible? How can the same person be both? . . . So I think a lot about who is the real me, and sometimes I try to figure it out when I write in my diary, but I can't resolve it. There are days when I wish I could just become immune to myself! (Harter, 1999, pp. 67–68)

Because changes—whether gradual or abrupt—take place during adolescence in the ways young people view and feel about themselves, the study of identity development has been a major focus of research and theory on adolescents (Côté, 2009). In this chapter, we examine why adolescence is a time of major changes in identity and how the course of adolescent identity development is shaped by the nature of life in contemporary society.

Identity as an Adolescent Issue

Changes in the way we view and feel about ourselves occur throughout the life cycle. You have probably heard and read about the so-called midlife crisis, for example—an identity crisis thought to occur during middle age. And certainly, important changes in self-conceptions and in self-image take place throughout childhood. When a group of 4-year-olds and a group of 10-year-olds are asked to describe themselves, the older children provide a far more complex self-portrait. Whereas young children restrict their descriptions to

lists of what they own or what they like to do, older children are more likely to tell you about their personality as well.

If changes in identity occur throughout the life cycle, why have researchers who are interested in identity development paid so much attention to adolescence? One reason is that the changes in identity that take place during adolescence involve the first substantial reorganization and restructuring of the individual's sense of self at a time when he or she has the intellectual capability to appreciate fully just how significant the changes are. Although important changes in identity certainly occur during childhood, the adolescent is far more self-conscious about these changes and feels them much more acutely.

▌ Puberty and Identity Development   Another reason for the attention that researchers and theorists have given the study of identity development during adolescence concerns the fundamental biological, cognitive, and social changes characteristic of the period. Puberty, as we saw in Chapter 1, brings with it dramatic changes in physical appearance and alters the adolescent's self-conceptions and relationships with others. It is not hard to see why puberty plays an important role in provoking identity development during adolescence. When you change the way you look—for example, when you have your hair colored or cut in a different way, lose a great deal of weight, or dramatically change your style of dress—you sometimes feel as though your personality has changed, too. During puberty, when adolescents are changing so dramatically on the outside, they understandably have questions about changes that are taking place on the inside. For the adolescent, undergoing the physical changes of puberty may prompt fluctuations in self-image and a reevaluation of who he or she really is.

▌ Cognitive Change and Identity Development
Just as the broadening of intellectual capabilities during early adolescence provides new ways of thinking about problems, values, and interpersonal relationships, it also permits adolescents to think about themselves in new ways. We saw in Chapter 2 that it is not until adolescence that the young person is able to think in systematic ways about hypothetical and future events. This is manifested in two specific ways that have implications for identity development. First, adolescents become much more able to imagine their **possible selves**—the various alternative identities that they may adopt (Markus & Nurius, 1986). This may be related to heightened self-consciousness characteristic of early adolescence discussed in Chapter 2. Indeed, recent brain-imaging studies find that patterns of brain activity during tasks in which individuals were asked to think about themselves differed significantly between adolescents and adults (Sebastian, Burnett, & Blakemore, 2008).

Second is an impressive increase in **future orientation**—the ability and tendency to consider the long-term consequences of one's decisions and imagine what one's life might be like in the years to come (Nurmi, 2004; Steinberg et al., 2009). For this reason, it is not until adolescence that individuals typically begin to wonder "Who will I become?" or "What am I really like?" Because the preadolescent child's thinking is concrete, it is difficult for him or her to think seriously about being a different person. But the changes in thinking that take place during adolescence open up a whole new world of alternatives.

Adolescence is often a time when individuals ask questions about who they are and where they are headed. Concerns with physical appearance often intensify.

▌ Social Roles and Identity Development   Finally, as we saw in Chapter 3, the changes in social roles that occur at adolescence open up a new array of choices and decisions for the young person that were not concerns previously. In contemporary society, adolescence is a time of important decisions about work, marriage, and the future. Facing these decisions about their place in society does more than provoke adolescents to ask questions about who they are and where they are headed—it *necessitates* the questions. At this point in the life cycle, young people must make important choices about their careers and their commitments to other people, and thinking about these questions prompts them to ask more questions about themselves: "What do I really want out of life?" "What things are important to me?" "What kind of person would I really like to be?" Questions about the future, which inevitably arise as the adolescent prepares for adulthood, raise questions about identity (Côté, 2009).

Identity development is complex and multifaceted. Actually, it is better understood as a series of interrelated developments—rather than one single development—that all involve changes in the way we view ourselves in relation to others and in relation to the broader society in which we live. Generally, researchers and theorists have taken three different approaches to the question of how the individual's sense of identity changes over the course of adolescence.

possible selves   The various identities an adolescent might imagine for him- or herself.

future orientation   The extent to which an individual is able and inclined to think about the potential consequences of decisions and choices.

The first approach emphasizes changes in **self-conceptions**—the ideas that individuals have of themselves with regard to various traits and attributes. An entirely different approach focuses on adolescents' **self-esteem,** or self-image—how positively or negatively they feel about themselves. Finally, a third approach emphasizes changes in the **sense of identity**—the sense of who one is, where one has come from, and where one is going.

RECAP

- Although changes in the way we see and feel about ourselves occur throughout the life cycle, the study of identity development has been a prominent issue in the field of adolescent development in particular.

- One reason for this attention concerns the impact that the biological, cognitive, and social role changes of adolescence have on the young person's ability to engage in self-examination and on his or her interest in doing so.

- Researchers have traditionally distinguished among three aspects of identity development in adolescence: changes in self-conceptions, changes in self-esteem, and changes in the sense of identity.

Changes in Self-Conceptions

As individuals mature intellectually and undergo the sorts of cognitive changes described in Chapter 2, they come to conceive of themselves in more sophisticated and more differentiated ways. As we saw in that chapter, adolescents are much more capable than children of thinking about abstract concepts and considerably more proficient in processing large amounts of information. These intellectual capabilities affect the way in which individuals characterize themselves. Compared with children, who tend to describe themselves in relatively simple, concrete terms, adolescents are more likely to employ complex, abstract, and psychological self-characterizations (Harter, 1999). In addition, with development comes greater consistency between how

self-conceptions   The collection of traits and attributes that individuals use to describe or characterize themselves.

self-esteem   The degree to which individuals feel positively or negatively about themselves.

sense of identity   The extent to which individuals feel secure about who they are and who they are becoming.

individuals describe themselves and how they actually behave (Davis-Kean et al., 2008). There is also evidence that adolescents' ideas about the sort of person they would like to be (their "ideal self") become more stable over time (Zentner & Renaud, 2007).

CHANGES IN THE CONTENT AND STRUCTURE OF SELF-CONCEPTIONS

Self-conceptions change in structure and content during the transition from childhood into and through adolescence. Structurally, self-conceptions become more differentiated and better organized (Byrne & Shavelson, 1996). Let's first consider the idea that self-conceptions become more differentiated.

▌ Differentiation of the Self-Concept In answer to the question "Who am I?" adolescents are more likely than children to link traits and attributes that describe themselves to specific situations, rather than using them as global characterizations. Whereas a preadolescent might say "I am nice" or "I am friendly," but not specify when or under what conditions, an adolescent is more likely to say "I am nice if I am in a good mood" or "I am friendly when I am with people I have met before." The realization that their personality is expressed in different ways in different situations is one example of the increased differentiation that characterizes the self-conceptions of youngsters as they mature toward adulthood.

There is another way in which self-conceptions become more highly differentiated at adolescence. As opposed to characterizations provided by children, adolescents' self-descriptions take into account who is doing the describing (Harter, 1999). Teenagers differentiate between their own opinions of themselves and the views of others. Suppose you ask a group of youngsters to describe how they behave when they are with other people. Instead of saying, "I am shy" or "I am outgoing," an adolescent is more likely to say "People think I'm not at all shy, but most of the time, I'm really nervous about meeting other kids for the first time." Adolescents also recognize that they may come across differently to different people, another type of differentiation in self-conceptions that does not appear until this point in time—for example, "My parents think I'm quiet, but my friends know I really like to party a lot."

▌ Organization and Integration of the Self-Concept With this shift toward increased differentiation in self-conceptions comes better organization and integration (Harter, 1999). When children are asked to describe themselves, the traits and attributes they list remain somewhat disorganized, like items haphazardly placed on a grocery list. Adolescents, in contrast, are likely to organize and integrate different

Despite the stereotype of adolescence as a time of psychological difficulty, most adolescents have positive self-conceptions.

aspects of their self-concept into a more logical, coherent whole. Whereas a younger child may list a sequence of several traits that appear to be contradictory ("I am friendly, and I am shy"), an adolescent will attempt to organize apparently discrepant bits of information into more highly organized statements ("I am shy when I first meet people, but after I get to know them, I'm usually pretty friendly").

Although it does not appear that self-conceptions become even more differentiated after early adolescence (H. Marsh, 1989), the movement toward more abstract and more psychological self-conceptions continues well into the high school years. The increased abstraction and psychological complexity of self-conceptions may present some difficulties for middle adolescents, though, who may be able to recognize—but not yet quite understand or reconcile—inconsistencies and contradictions in their personality. The proportion of adolescents who give opposite traits in self-descriptions, who feel conflicts over such discrepancies, and who feel confused over such discrepancies increases markedly between seventh and ninth grades and then declines somewhat (Harter & Monsour, 1992). In one study, when asked to reflect on contradictions in their personalities, early, middle, and late adolescents responded in very different ways, as in the following examples (Harter, 1990, p. 358):

> I guess I just think about one thing about myself at a time and don't think about the other until the next day. (11–12 years old)

> I really think I am a happy person and I want to be that way with everyone, but I get depressed with my family

and it really bugs me because that's not what I want to be like. (14–15 years old)

> You can be shy on a date, and then outgoing with friends because you are just different with different people; you can't always be the same person and probably shouldn't be. (17–18 years old)

Although the recognition that one's personality is multifaceted—even contradictory—may initially cause some distress, in the long run, it probably has a number of advantages. Indeed, some psychologists have suggested that the development of a more complicated view of the self is one way that individuals cope with the recognition of their faults and weaknesses, a recognition that comes with the increased self-awareness of adolescence ("I'm not really a nasty person, I just act mean when people tease me"). Consistent with this, adolescents who have more complex self-conceptions are less likely to be depressed (D. Evans, 1993; A. Jordan & Cole, 1996).

One additional advantage of having a more differentiated self-concept is that the adolescent is now able to distinguish among his or her actual self (who the adolescent really is), ideal self (who the adolescent would like to be), and feared self (who the adolescent most dreads becoming). According to one view, being able to make these distinctions provides a motive for adolescents to improve—either to bring their actual self more into line with the ideal self or to strive to become their ideal self and avoid becoming their feared self (Markus & Nurius, 1986). An important aspect of having a healthy self-concept is having an ideal self to balance a feared self. One study found, for example, that delinquent adolescents were less likely than nondelinquent youth to have this sort of balanced view; although delinquent adolescents might dread becoming criminals, for instance, they may not have a positive ideal self (for example, being successfully employed) to balance this fear (Oyserman & Markus, 1990).

❚ **False-Self Behavior** Another interesting consequence of adolescents' recognition that they are not always consistent in their personality concerns their ability to distinguish between their true and false selves (that is, their authentic and inauthentic selves). Adolescents are most likely to behave inauthentically in romantic and dating situations and with classmates, and they are least likely to put on a false front with close friends. Interestingly, **false-self behavior**—acting in a way that one knows is inauthentic—occurs less often with parents than with dates, but more often with parents than with close friends (Harter, 1990). Although

false-self behavior Behavior that intentionally presents a false impression to others.

adolescents sometimes say that they dislike false-self behavior, they also say that sometimes it is acceptable, such as when trying to impress another person or hide an aspect of their personality that others do not like. You can easily imagine how the ability to put on a false front would come in handy on a date, at school, or with your parents.

Adolescents differ in the degree to which they present false fronts and in their reasons for doing so. In general, adolescents who report less emotional support from parents and peers, those who have low self-esteem, and those who are relatively more depressed and hopeless than their peers are more likely to engage in false-self behavior (Impett, Sorsoli, Schooler, Henson, & Tolman, 2008). Whereas some adolescents engage in false-self behavior because they are low in self-esteem, others experience a drop in self-esteem because they knowingly put on a false front. Depression and hopelessness are highest among adolescents who engage in false-self behavior because they genuinely devalue their true self, in contrast to those who put on a false front because they want to please others or because they are experimenting with different personalities (Harter, Marold, Whitesell, & Cobbs, 1996).

FOOD FOR THOUGHT

There have been relatively few studies of false-self behavior among adults. When was the last time you put on a false self? What was your motivation? How did you feel afterward?

Understanding how self-conceptions change during adolescence helps to explain why issues of identity begin to take on so much importance at this stage in the life span. As self-conceptions become more abstract, and as young people become more able to see themselves in psychological terms, they become more interested in understanding their own personalities and why they behave the way they do. The distress caused by recognizing one's inconsistencies may spur identity development. You may recall having wondered as a teenager about your personality development, the influences that shaped your character, and how your personality had changed over time: "Am I more like my father or like my mother? Why do my sister and I seem so different? Will I always be so shy?" Although these sorts of questions may seem commonplace to you now,

in all likelihood, you did not think about these things until adolescence, when your own self-conceptions became more abstract and more sophisticated.

DIMENSIONS OF PERSONALITY IN ADOLESCENCE

While many researchers have studied adolescent personality development by examining young people's self-conceptions, others have administered standardized inventories designed to assess the most important aspects of personality. Most researchers now approach the study of personality using the **five-factor model** (McCrae & John, 1992). This model is based on the observation that there are five critical personality dimensions, often referred to as the "big five": extraversion (how outgoing and energetic someone is), agreeableness (how kind or sympathetic), conscientiousness (how responsible and organized), neuroticism (how anxious or tense), and openness to experience (how curious and imaginative). Although the five-factor model was developed through research on adults, it has been successfully applied to adolescents as well (Caspi, 1997; McCrae et al., 2002). For example, delinquent adolescents are more likely than their peers to score high in extraversion and low in agreeableness and conscientiousness, whereas adolescents who are high achievers in school score high in conscientiousness and openness (John, Caspi, Robins, Moffitt, & Stouthamer-Loeber, 1994). In general, the structure of personality appears comparable across groups of adolescents from different ethnic backgrounds (Markstrom-Adams & Adams, 1995; Rowe, Vazsonyi, & Flannery, 1994).

Researchers point to both genetic and environmental influences on individual differences in personality. Individuals may inherit temperamental predispositions (such as a high activity level or an inclination to be sociable), which are observable early in life, and these predispositions may "harden" and become organized into personality traits partially in response to the environment (Caspi, 2000; Gest, 1997; John et al., 1994). Thus, an active and sociable child who enjoys interacting with others may be rewarded for doing so and, over time, become extraverted. Longitudinal studies show that both temperament and personality become increasingly stable as we grow older, in part because we tend to spend time in environments that reward and reinforce the traits that draw us to these settings (B. Roberts & DelVecchio, 2000). As a result, we become more like ourselves every day! There is also evidence that, between adolescence and young adulthood, individuals on average become more extraverted, more conscientious, more agreeable, and more emotionally stable (Huntsinger & Jose, 2006; B. Roberts, Walton, & Viechtbauer, 2006). There also is evidence that girls mature earlier than boys, but that boys catch up over time, so that by the

---

five-factor model   The theory that there are five basic dimensions to personality: extraversion, agreeableness, conscientiousness, neuroticism, and openness to experience.

end of adolescence, there are no gender differences in maturity (Klimstra, Hale, Raaijmakers, Branje, & Meeus, 2009).

In sum, a good deal of evidence indicates that many core personality traits, such as impulsivity or timidity, are quite stable between childhood and adolescence and between adolescence and young adulthood (McCrae et al., 2002; B. Roberts, Caspi, & Moffitt, 2001). Extraversion appears to be especially stable over time (Hampson & Goldberg, 2006). Although the external manifestations of these traits may change with age (for example, anxiety may appear as bed-wetting in early childhood but as nervous talkativeness in adolescence), our basic, underlying traits turn out to be remarkably stable. For example, individuals who displayed relatively higher levels of aggression in preadolescence, temper tantrums during childhood, or negative emotions during infancy are more likely to behave aggressively as adolescents (Caspi, Henry, McGee, Moffitt, & Silva, 1995; Hart, Hofman, Edelstein, & Keller, 1997). Similarly, individuals who had difficulty controlling their impulses as preschoolers are more likely to be impulsive, aggressive, and danger seeking as adolescents and young adults, while individuals who were inhibited as young children tend to be relatively more timid, anxious, and shy as teenagers. Not surprisingly, then, individuals who are judged to be well adjusted in early and middle childhood tend to be resilient and competent in adolescence (Caspi & Silva, 1995; Gest, 1997; Gjerde, 1995; Hart et al., 1997; Shiner, Masten, & Tellegen, 2002). Despite popular stereotypes about adolescence as a time of "rebirth," research has not supported the view that adolescence is a time of tumultuous upheaval in personality. Far from it. Indeed, as one team of researchers put it, "The person who enters adolescence is basically the same as that who exits it" (Dusek & Flaherty, 1981, p. 39).

FOOD FOR THOUGHT

Why is there continuity in personality over childhood and adolescence? Do you see elements of yourself that have always been present in your personality? Thinking about yourself, would you agree with the statement "The person who enters adolescence is basically the same as that who exits it"?

RECAP

- During the transition into adolescence, self-conceptions become increasingly complex, abstract, and psychological.
- Adolescents' self-conceptions are more differentiated and better organized than those of children.

- Although having more complex self-conceptions may be unsettling to adolescents initially, it ultimately provides for a more sophisticated and more accurate view of themselves.
- Adolescents are able to distinguish between their actual and their imagined selves and between their authentic and false selves.
- There are five basic personality dimensions in adolescence and adulthood, often referred to as the big five: extraversion, agreeableness, conscientiousness, neuroticism, and openness to experience.
- Longitudinal studies show strong links between early temperament and adolescent personality, and stability in basic personality traits over time.

Changes in Self-Esteem

One of the manifestations assumed to result from the "storm and stress" of adolescence involves problems in adolescents' self-esteem—how they evaluate themselves. As you will read, although there is no dramatic drop in self-esteem in adolescence, research indicates that adolescents' feelings about themselves fluctuate from day to day, particularly during the early adolescent years. From about eighth grade on, however, self-esteem remains highly stable. And, despite commentary in the popular press about the excessively high self-esteem characteristic of today's teenagers, careful statistical analyses show that there has been no appreciable increase in American adolescents' self-esteem during the past several decades (Trzesniewski & Donnellan, 2009).

STABILITY AND CHANGES IN SELF-ESTEEM

As you read in Chapter 2, the stability of a trait (like intelligence or self-esteem) has nothing to do with the degree to which people change with age, because stability merely refers to the extent to which individuals' relative standing stays more or less the same over time. Height, for instance, is a stable trait (tall children tend to become tall adults) that nevertheless changes a great deal with age (individuals grow taller between childhood and adulthood). Asking whether self-esteem changes during adolescence (that is, whether on average people's view of themselves becomes more positive or negative) is not the same as asking whether self-esteem is stable during this period (that is, whether individuals with high self-esteem as children are likely to have high self-esteem as adolescents). In general, self-esteem tends to become increasingly more stable between childhood and early adulthood, suggesting

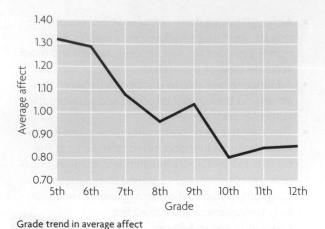

Grade trend in average affect

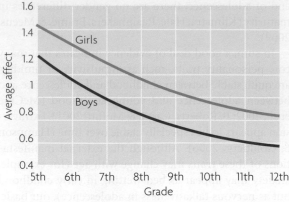

Estimated time trends of mean affect across grades for girls and boys

FIGURE 8.1 On average, individuals become less positive in their mood between 5th and 9th grades. Around 10th grade, however, this decline in mood starts to level off. (Larson et al., 2002)

that adolescents' feelings about themselves gradually consolidate over time, becoming less likely to fluctuate in response to different experiences (Alasker & Olweus, 1992; Trzesniewski, Donnellan, & Robins, 2003). Along similar lines, day-to-day fluctuations in mood tend to become smaller between early adolescence and late adolescence (Larson, Moneta, Richards, & Wilson, 2002).

Studies of changes in self-esteem as individuals move through adolescence have not yielded consistent findings, partly because researchers have focused on different aspects of individuals' self-image. As a consequence, some studies find that individuals' feelings about themselves decline over the course of adolescence (e.g., Jacobs, Lanza, Osgood, Eccles, & Wigfield, 2002), but others find that they increase (D. Cole et al., 2001). In general, however, *changes* in self-perceptions (whether positive or negative) are greater during early adolescence than during middle or late adolescence; from middle adolescence through young adulthood, self-esteem either remains at about the same level or increases (Côté, 2009). Interestingly, although there is a general trend for individuals' average mood to become less positive over the course of adolescence (that is, on average, children are usually in a more positive mood than young adolescents, who are generally in a better mood than older adolescents), this trend begins to level off around 10th grade, around the time that self-esteem seems to stop changing as well (Larson et al., 2002) (see Figure 8.1).

Although adolescence is not a time of storm and stress, some evidence suggests that for a brief period during early adolescence, minor problems in self-image may arise. To fully understand this pattern, it is necessary to distinguish among three aspects of adolescents' self-image: their self-esteem (how positively or negatively they feel about themselves), their **self-consciousness** (how much they worry about their self-image), and their **self-image stability** (how much they feel that their self-image changes from day to day) (Simmons, Rosenberg, & Rosenberg, 1973).

Fluctuations in adolescents' self-image are most likely to occur between the ages of 12 and 14. Compared with older adolescents (15 years and older) and with preadolescents (8–11 years old), early adolescents have lower self-esteem, are more self-conscious, and have a more unstable self-image than do other youngsters. Younger adolescents are also more prone to feel ashamed than older individuals, which may result from and contribute to their heightened self-consciousness (Reimer, 1996). Generally, the small but reliable differences between preadolescents and early adolescents are greater than those between younger and older adolescents, which indicates that the most marked fluctuations in self-image occur during the transition into adolescence, rather than over the course of adolescence itself (Simmons et. al., 1973). Consistent with this, a recent study of poor, urban students in New York City, Baltimore, and Washington, DC, found that the transition from elementary into junior high school was more likely to disrupt adolescents' self-esteem than was the transition into high school (Seidman & French, 2004).

FOOD FOR THOUGHT

What do you think makes self-esteem more volatile in some individuals than others? Do you think it is possible for someone to have both high and volatile self-esteem?

self-consciousness   The degree to which an individual is preoccupied with his or her self-image.

self-image stability   The degree to which an individual feels that his or her self-image changes from day to day.

Oddly enough, the extent to which an individual's self-esteem is volatile is itself a fairly stable trait; that is, young adolescents whose self-image fluctuates a lot from moment to moment are likely to develop into older adolescents who experience the same thing (Savin-Williams & Demo, 1983). Young adolescents with the most volatile self-image report the highest levels of anxiety, tension, psychosomatic symptoms, and irritability (Rosenberg, 1986). This is especially likely among adolescents who have a great deal of stress in their day-to-day lives (Tevendale, DuBois, Lopez, & Prindiville, 1997). In other words, having a volatile self-image may make individuals especially vulnerable to the effects of stress.

Fluctuations in self-image during early adolescence probably are due to several interrelated factors. First, the sort of egocentrism common in early adolescence, discussed in Chapter 2, may make young adolescents painfully aware of others' reactions to their behavior. Second, as individuals become more socially active, they begin to learn that people play games when they interact, and consequently they learn that it is not always possible to tell what people are thinking on the basis of how they act or what they say. This ambiguity may leave young adolescents—who are relatively unskilled at this sort of "impression management"—puzzled and uncomfortable about how they are really viewed by others. Finally, because of the increased importance of peers in early adolescence, young adolescents are especially interested in their peers' opinions of them. For the first time, they may have to come to terms with contradictions between the messages they get from their parents ("I think that new hairstyle makes you even prettier") and the messages they get from their peers ("You'd better wear a hat until your hair grows back!"). Hearing contradictory messages probably generates a certain degree of uncertainty about themselves (Rosenberg, 1986).

▌ The Wrong Question?

Some researchers have argued that the question of whether self-esteem is stable during adolescence is a poor one, because averages often hide substantial differences between people. According to several studies, some adolescents show very high stability in self-esteem over time, whereas others do not (Diehl, Vicary, & Deike, 1997; Hirsch & DuBois, 1991; M. Zimmerman, Copeland, Shope, & Dielman, 1997). In one study, the researchers identified four dramatically different patterns of self-esteem over time that were followed by youngsters during the transition into junior high school. Approximately one third of the adolescents were classified as consistently high in self-esteem, and approximately one sixth were classified as chronically low. Half the sample, however, showed impressive patterns of change over just a 2-year period: About one fifth were categorized as steeply declining,

Early adolescent girls' self-esteem is lower, their degree of self-consciousness is higher, and their self-image is shakier than is the case for boys.

and nearly one third showed a small but significant increase in self-esteem. Boys may be disproportionately overrepresented in the group of adolescents whose self-esteem increases, whereas girls may be overrepresented in the group whose self-esteem declines—even though the majority of boys and girls show stability rather than dramatic change in self-esteem during adolescence (Block & Robins, 1993; Koenig, 1995; M. Zimmerman et al., 1997). Not surprisingly, adolescents with better family and peer relationships are more likely than their peers to maintain positive self-esteem or develop enhanced self-esteem over time (Diehl et al., 1997).

Some critics of studies of the stability of self-esteem in adolescence also question the validity of examining self-esteem in such a general sense. Although most research on adolescent self-esteem has focused on teenagers' overall feelings about themselves, most researchers today believe that young people evaluate themselves both globally (which may be a good indicator of general psychological well-being) and along several distinct dimensions, such as academics, athletics, appearance, social relationships, and moral conduct (which may indicate specific areas of strength and weakness) (Côté, 2009). As a consequence, it is possible for an adolescent to have, say, high self-esteem when it comes to academic abilities, low self-esteem when it comes to athletics, and moderate self-esteem when it comes to physical appearance, social relationships, or moral conduct. The following comments, spoken by the adolescent girl whose remarks opened the chapter, are fairly typical:

How much do I like the kind of person I am? Well, I like some things about me, but I don't like others. I'm glad that I'm popular since it's really important to me to have friends. But in school I don't do as well as the really smart

FIGURE 8.2   Sex differences in various domains of self-esteem. (Harter, 1999)

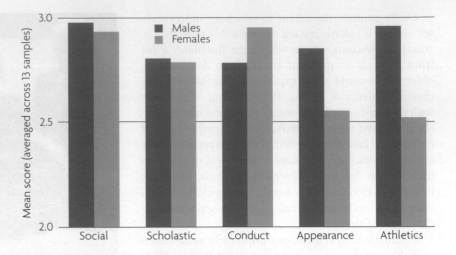

kids. That's OK, because if you're too smart you'll lose your friends. So being smart is just not that important. Except to my parents. I feel like I'm letting them down when I don't do as well as they want. But what's really important to me is how I look. If I like the way I look, then I really like the kind of person I am. (Harter, 1990, p. 364)

■ **Components of Self-Esteem**   Even within the broad domains of self-esteem mentioned previously (for example, academics, athletics, social relationships), adolescents may have quite differentiated views of themselves. Studies show, for example, that adolescents' evaluations of their social competence within the context of their relationships with their parents may be very different from the way they see themselves in the context of their relationships with teachers, which in turn may differ from their evaluations of themselves in the context of their friendships with peers (Harter, Waters, & Whitesell, 1998). And within the realm of peer relationships, adolescents' social self-esteem may vary depending on whether they are thinking about their friendships or their romantic relationships (Connolly & Konarski, 1994). Therefore, it may be misleading to characterize an adolescent's social self-esteem as low or high without specifying the context of the relationship. The same goes for academic self-esteem: Because students evaluate their abilities in specific subject areas both in comparison to other students ("I am terrible at math compared to everyone else in this class") and relative to their abilities in other subject areas ("I am so much better at math than I am at history"), making sweeping statements about an adolescent's overall academic self-image is often unwise (Marsh & Hau, 2004). Much depends on the basis of comparison.

Do some aspects of self-esteem contribute more to an adolescent's overall self-image than others? Yes, they do. In general, adolescents' physical self-esteem—how they feel about their appearance—is the most important predictor of overall self-esteem, followed by self-esteem

about relationships with peers (Harter, 1999). Less important are self-esteem about academic ability, athletic ability, or moral conduct. Interestingly, although researchers find that adolescents' physical self-esteem is the best predictor of their overall self-esteem, adolescents, when asked, say that their physical appearance is one of the least important contributors to how they feel about themselves. In other words, adolescents may be unaware of the degree to which their self-worth is based on their feelings about their appearance (DuBois, Tevendale, Burk-Braxton, Swenson, & Hardesty, 2000). It is important to note both that physical self-esteem is a more important influence on overall self-esteem among girls than among boys (Harter, 1990; Usmiani & Daniluk, 1997) and that girls' physical self-esteem is on average lower than boys' (D. Cole et al., 2001; Harter, 1999) (see Figure 8.2). Taken together, these findings help to explain why there are sex differences in the extent to which adolescents' experience self-image difficulties and, as we'll see in Chapter 13, depression.

GROUP DIFFERENCES IN SELF-ESTEEM

■ **Sex Differences**   Several studies have shown that early adolescent girls are more vulnerable to disturbances in the self-image than any other group of youngsters. Specifically, early adolescent girls' self-esteem is lower, their degree of self-consciousness is higher, and their self-image is shakier than is the case for boys. As a consequence, girls also are more likely than boys to say negative things about themselves, to feel insecure about their abilities, and to worry about whether other people like being with them. Sex differences in adolescents' self-perceptions become smaller over the course of adolescence (Fredricks & Eccles, 2002).

Although sex differences in self-esteem are most pronounced among White adolescents, similar patterns have been found among Puerto Rican adolescents but not, for the most part, among Black adolescents (Erkut,

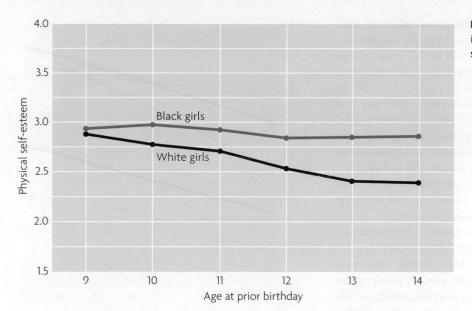

FIGURE 8.3   Race differences in patterns of change in physical self-esteem. (Brown et al., 1998)

Szalacha, Garcia Coll, & Alarcon, 2000; Harter, 1999; K. Kling, Hyde, Showers, & Buswell, 1999). Studies of Black girls do not find the same sort of self-esteem vulnerability as is found in studies of White girls, in part because Black girls do not experience the same drop in body image during puberty (K. Brown et al., 1998) (see Figure 8.3).

Why would girls have greater self-esteem problems during early adolescence than boys? The answer may be related to the special significance of physical appearance and acceptance by peers in determining self-esteem, as discussed earlier. Compared with other youngsters, young girls worry a great deal about their looks and about dating and being popular in school. Yet they are also worried about doing well academically. Other adolescents care about these things, of course, but they have a more casual attitude.

Young adolescent girls may feel caught in a bind between pressures to do well academically and pressures to do well socially, especially as they move into secondary school. As we saw in Chapter 5, getting good grades in school is at the bottom of the list of attributes that adolescent girls feel are important for being accepted into the leading crowd. Several studies have shown that adolescents who worry a lot about being popular are most likely to feel self-conscious and to have unstable views of themselves (Simmons & Rosenberg, 1975). Because young girls appear to be more concerned than boys about physical attractiveness, dating, and peer acceptance, they may experience a greater number of self-image problems. Because Black girls do not feel as negatively about their appearance as White or Hispanic girls, they have higher overall self-esteem and show less of a decline in self-esteem over adolescence (Gray-Little & Hafdahl, 2000; Malanchuk & Eccles, 1999; Prosser & Carlson, 1999).

■ **Ethnic Differences**   Most research indicates that Black adolescents have higher self-esteem than White adolescents, who, in turn, tend to have higher self-esteem than Hispanic, Asian, or Native American youth (Biro, Striegel-Moore, et al., 2006; Gray-Little & Hafdahl, 2000; Twenge & Crocker, 2002). Several studies indicate that Asian American adolescents have particularly low self-esteem relative to their peers (e.g., Herman, 2004), a finding that some researchers have attributed to higher rates of peer rejection (recall the discussion of peer discrimination in Chapter 5) (Greene & Way, 2005).

A number of researchers have asked why Black adolescents have such high self-esteem, given the prevalence of prejudice in American society and the generally disadvantaged position of Black individuals in the workplace and school, two institutions where individuals' performance influences their self-image. Three main explanations for the relatively high self-esteem of Black adolescents have been offered.

First, some writers have argued that, despite their encounters with racism and prejudice, Black teenagers benefit from the support and positive feedback of adults in the Black community, especially in the family (Gaylord-Harden, Ragsdale, Mandara, Richards, & Petersen, 2007). This is not surprising, given the wealth of research showing that the approval of significant others is an especially powerful influence on adolescents' self-esteem—much more so than the opinion of the broader society (e.g., Gray-Little & Hafdahl, 2000; Robinson, 1995; Whitesell, Mitchell, Kaufman, Spicer, 2006).

Second, other researchers suggest that all teenagers—minority and otherwise—tend to shift their priorities over time so that they come to value those activities at which they excel. In doing so, adolescents are able to protect their self-esteem by focusing on areas of strength instead of weakness. For example, a boy who is an outstanding student but who feels physically unattractive and does not do well in sports will likely derive positive self-esteem from his school achievement and not restrict his self-evaluation to his looks or performance on the playing field (Luster & McAdoo, 1995). One way that Black adolescents may respond to their relatively poorer school performance is to change their feelings about the importance of doing well in school, which weakens the connection between academic success and self-esteem.

Finally, several writers have suggested that the very strong sense of ethnic identity (which we look at later in this chapter) among Black adolescents serves to enhance their overall self-esteem (DuBois, Burk-Braxton, Swenson, Tevendale, & Hardesty, 2002; Gaylord-Harden et al., 2007; Gray-Little & Hafdahl, 2000). One study found that Black adolescents who identify with popular Black characters on television (such as Darrell, on *The Hughleys*) report higher self-esteem than Black adolescents who identify with popular White characters (for example, Chandler, on *Friends*) (L. M. Ward, 2003). Interestingly, ethnic differences in self-esteem, favoring Black adolescents, have increased over the past 25 years (perhaps because ethnic identity has become a more relevant issue in society) and are greater during adolescence than childhood (perhaps because, as we shall see, ethnic identity is a more salient issue during adolescence than before) (Twenge & Crocker, 2002).

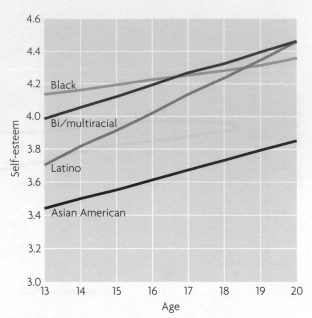

FIGURE 8.4   Ethnic differences in patterns of self-esteem over time. (Greene & Way, 2005)

FOOD FOR THOUGHT

Studies of ethnic differences in self-esteem, indicating relatively higher self-esteem among Black adolescents and lower self-esteem among Asian adolescents, have almost all been conducted in the United States. Do you think similar patterns would emerge in research conducted in other countries that have ethnically diverse populations?

Ethnic differences also exist in patterns of change in self-esteem during adolescence. In one recent study of Black, Latino, and Asian urban adolescents, the researchers found that Black students and biracial students (mainly Black/Latino) had higher self-esteem in early adolescence, and this remained high throughout the adolescent years. In contrast, Latino students had relatively lower self-esteem early in adolescence, but caught up with their Black peers by the end of high school. Asian students began with the lowest self-esteem, and it remained lower than that of other groups over time (see Figure 8.4). Interestingly, and in contrast to studies of White adolescents, there were no sex

differences in levels or patterns of change in self-esteem in this sample of ethnic minority adolescents.

The ethnic diversity of the context in which adolescents develop has a substantial impact on their self-image, however. Some research indicates, for example, that high school students who live in a social environment or go to a school in which their ethnic or socioeconomic group is in the minority are more likely to have self-image problems than those who are in the majority (Rosenberg, 1975). This seems to be true with regard to religion, socioeconomic status, ethnicity, and household composition. Black teenagers, for example, have a higher opinion of themselves when they go to schools in which Black students are a majority than when they attend predominantly White schools, where they may feel out of place and under pressure to play down their cultural heritage. By the same token, Jewish adolescents have higher self-esteem in schools in which there are many other Jewish students than in schools in which Jews compose a small minority of the student body. Similarly, levels of maladjustment are higher among both Hispanic and non–Hispanic youngsters when they are in the minority in their school (Kaufman, Gregory, & Stephan, 1990). As you will read later in this chapter, adolescents' psychological well-being, including their self-esteem, is adversely affected by discrimination and prejudice. Adolescents who report frequent experiences of being insulted, excluded, and teased about their race or ethnicity have relatively more psychological problems than do their peers who face no discrimination (C. H. Caldwell, Kohn-Wood, Schmeelk-Cone, Chavous, & Zimmerman, 2004; DuBois, Burk-Braxton, et al., 2002; Sellers, Copeland-Linder, Martin, & Lewis, 2006).

ANTECEDENTS AND CONSEQUENCES OF HIGH SELF-ESTEEM

Several researchers have examined the link between self-esteem and adolescent behavior, in an attempt to see whether certain sorts of experiences contribute—either positively or negatively—to adolescents' feelings about themselves. Others have posed the question in reverse: Does having high (or low) self-esteem lead adolescents to behave in particular ways?

▍ Influences on Self-Esteem Regarding the first question, studies find that self-esteem is enhanced by having the approval of others, especially of parents and peers, and by succeeding in school (DuBois, Burk Braxton, et al., 2002; Luster & McAdoo, 1995; Ojanen & Perry, 2007; A. Roberts et al., 2000; R. B. Wilkinson, 2004). These correlates of high self-esteem have been found in virtually all ethnic and cultural groups, although the self-esteem of Asian youngsters seems especially influenced by their academic success (e.g., Szesulski, Martinez, & Reyes, 1994). Thus, even though there are ethnic differences in average levels of self-esteem, the correlates of self-esteem are similar in different ethnic groups (Rowe et al., 1994).

Adolescents whose self-esteem is too wrapped up in the approval of others—especially the approval of peers—may be at risk for developing self image problems, since peer acceptance may fluctuate over time, leading to temporary drops in self-esteem (Harter, Stocker, & Robinson, 1996). Consistent with this, adolescents who tend to derive their self-esteem relatively more from peers than from teachers or parents show more behavioral problems and poorer school achievement (DuBois, Felner, Brand, & George, 1999; DuBois, Bull, Sherman, & Roberts, 1998; DuBois, Burk-Braxton, et al., 2002). In fact, one explanation for the increase in problem behavior that takes place over the course of adolescence is that adolescents tend to look relatively more to their peers for social support as they get older (DuBois, Burk-Braxton, et al., 2002).

▍ Consequences of High Self-Esteem How does having high self-esteem influence adolescents' adjustment and behavior? Although it once was believed that enhanced self-esteem leads to school success, there actually is little evidence for this, and a good deal of evidence for the opposite (e.g., X. Liu, Kaplan, & Rosser, 1992; J. Schmidt & Padilla, 2003). That is, academic success leads to improvements in how adolescents feel about themselves, not the other way around. These findings cast doubt on the logic behind programs designed to raise teenagers' school performance by increasing their self-esteem. High self-esteem during adolescence does enhance adolescents' well-being, however, whereas low self-esteem may lead to involvement in deviant ac-

Adolescents who attend schools in which they are in the ethnic minority may suffer greater self-esteem problems than their peers who attend schools in which they are in the majority. Although desegregation may have a positive impact on minority adolescents' academic achievement, this benefit may be counterbalanced by the apparently negative impact of desegregation on minority students' self-image.

tivity, psychological distress, and victimization, both in the short run (Andrews, Alpert, Hops, & Davis, 1996; DuBois & Tevendale, 1999; Egan & Perry, 1998; X. Liu et al., 1992) and well into adulthood (Trzesniewski et al., 2006), although this may be due to the fact that many of the same factors that contribute to high self-esteem in adolescence (such as doing well in school) are themselves stable over time (Boden, Fergusson, & Horwood, 2008).

The relationship between low self-esteem and emotional and behavioral problems is complicated (D. Cole, Peeke, Dolezal, Murray, & Canzoniero, 1999; Gerard & Buehler, 2004; Tram & Cole, 2000). Low self-esteem is one of several symptoms of depression, but it is not clear whether depression leads to low self-esteem, or vice versa. The answer, it seems, depends on the individual. For about half of all adolescents, depression leads to low self-esteem. For the other half, however, the reverse is true—having low self-esteem leads to depression and other forms of emotional distress (Harter, 1999). One reason that low self-esteem may lead to depression is that adolescents with negative feelings about themselves are less likely to seek positive feedback from others (Cassidy, Ziv, Mehta, & Feeney, 2003).

The link between self-esteem and behavior problems (as opposed to emotional problems) is even less clear. Although low self-esteem initially may impel some adolescents toward delinquency, involvement with delinquent peers actually may lead to an increase in self-esteem, perhaps because involvement in delinquency earns teenagers approval from certain peers (Dishion, Andrews, & Crosby, 1995; Jang & Thornberry, 1998; W. Mason, 2001). Furthermore, adolescents with high self-esteem are more likely to experiment with alcohol than are those with low self-esteem (Scheier, Botvin, Griffin, & Diaz, 2000), most probably because high self-esteem is associated with being in the more popular social crowds, in which drinking is more common.

RECAP

- Researchers have differed in their approach to the study of self-esteem. While some have studied adolescents' general, or global, feelings about themselves, others have stressed the multidimensional nature of self-esteem.

- Adolescence is a time of gradual rather than tumultuous change in individuals' self-image. For most individuals, global self-esteem is quite stable during adolescence and, contrary to popular belief, increases slightly.

- During early adolescence, individuals may experience periods of heightened self-consciousness, and their self-image may fluctuate more than during other periods.

- Generally, males and Black adolescents have higher self-esteem than females or adolescents from other ethnic groups, although sex differences in self-esteem are much more pronounced among White teenagers. Asian adolescents have especially low self-esteem relative to their peers.

- Across all demographic groups, high self-esteem is related to parental approval, peer support, and success in school. Although it is difficult to disentangle cause and effect, high self-esteem is associated with better mental health, whereas low self-esteem is correlated with a number of emotional problems.

identity versus identity diffusion   According to Erikson, the normative crisis characteristic of the fifth stage of psychosocial development, predominant during adolescence.

The Adolescent Identity Crisis

Many of literature's most important novels, from classics like *Jane Eyre*, *Portrait of the Artist as a Young Man*, and *The Catcher in the Rye* to more contemporary stories like *The Secret Life of Bees*, *The House on Mango Street*, *The God of Animals*, and *Everything Is Illuminated*, revolve around an adolescent's identity crisis. Indeed, the coming-of-age novel is a classic literary genre.

If you were asked to write a novel about your own identity development, what sorts of things would you mention? Perhaps you would talk about the development of a sense of purpose, or the clarification of your long-term plans and values, or the growing feeling of knowing who you really are and where you are headed. If these are the sorts of things that come to mind when you think about identity development in adolescence, you are thinking about an aspect of development that psychologists refer to as the sense of identity. The dominant view in the study of adolescent identity development emphasizes precisely these aspects of psychosocial development, and the theorist whose work has been most influential in this area is Erik Erikson.

ERIKSON'S THEORETICAL FRAMEWORK

Erikson's (1959, 1963, 1968) theory developed out of his clinical and cross-cultural observations of young people at various stages of development. He viewed the developing person as moving through a series of eight psychosocial crises over the course of the life span. Each crisis, although present in one form or another at all ages, takes on special significance at a given period of the life cycle because biological and social forces interact to bring the crisis into prominence. Erikson believed that the establishment of a coherent sense of identity—what he called the crisis of **identity versus identity diffusion**—is the chief psychosocial crisis of adolescence.

IDENTITY VERSUS IDENTITY DIFFUSION

Prior to adolescence, the child's identity is like patches of fabric that have not yet been sewn together. But by the end of adolescence, these patches will be woven into a patchwork quilt that is unique to the individual. The maturational and social forces that converge at adolescence force young people to reflect on their place in society, on the ways that others view them, and on their options for the future. As Erikson described it, "From among all possible and imaginable relations, [the young person] must make a series of ever-narrowing selections of personal, occupational, sexual, and ideological commitments" (1968, p. 245).

Achieving a balanced and coherent sense of identity is an intellectually and emotionally taxing process. In fact, according to Erikson, it is not until adolescence that one even has the mental or emotional capacity to tackle this task. The key to resolving the crisis of identity versus identity diffusion, argued Erikson, lies in the adolescent's interactions with others. By responding to the reactions of people who matter, the adolescent selects and chooses from among the many elements that could conceivably become a part of his or her adult identity. The other people with whom the young person interacts serve as a mirror that reflects back to the adolescent information about who he or she is and ought to be. As such, the responses of these significant others shape and influence the adolescent's developing sense of identity. Through others' reactions, adolescents learn whether they are competent or clumsy, attractive or ugly, socially adept or tactless. Perhaps more importantly—especially during periods when their sense of identity is still forming—they learn from others what they do that they ought to keep doing and what they do that they ought to stop doing.

One process through which this occurs is via the sharing of important memories with others. But the way children talk about their life is very different from how adolescents do. A recent study of Danish youngsters found, for instance, that when asked to tell their "life story," children usually talked about single events ("I got lost from my mum and dad on the beach. And they had to ask other people to help search for me. And then they finally found me down on the beach, and then we had to go home."), whereas adolescents were more likely to weave together a coherent, fuller narrative (Bohn & Berntsen, 2008, p. 1135).

When we tell stories to friends or family members about our previous experiences, we do so for a variety of reasons, one of which is to help ourselves understand who we are and how we were changed by the experience. In one recent study of college undergraduates (McLean, 2005), students were asked to describe occasions in the past year in which they shared an important memory with another person. One participant described the following event, which took place when he was in high school:

> I was at my friend's house one night with my main group of friends. They were all smoking marijuana and drinking. I did not feel comfortable with trying marijuana. They tried hard to get me to try it, but I chose not to. One of my friends (my best) supported my choice. *I learned who my real friends were. But more important, I learned that I can be strong with my decisions if I choose to, regardless of the outside influence.*

He then described telling his college friends about the event:

> The subject of drugs came up and so I explained the above story to them. They seemed to enjoy the story and

applauded me on my resiliency. Now, my friends here [at college] will ask me if I want to do anything and they will not harass me about it, regardless of my answer. *It pays to be strong when you want to.* (McLean, 2005, p. 687)

In other words, developing an identity is a social as well as mental process. Erikson placed a great deal of weight on the role of society (and, especially, on those individuals who have influence over the adolescent) in shaping the adolescent's sense of self. The adolescent's identity is the result of a mutual recognition between the young person and society: The adolescent forges an identity, but, at the same time, society identifies the adolescent.

THE SOCIAL CONTEXT OF IDENTITY DEVELOPMENT

The social context in which the adolescent attempts to establish a sense of identity exerts a tremendous impact on the nature and outcome of the process. Clearly, if adolescents' identities are forged out of a recognition on the part of society, society will play an important role in determining which sorts of identities are possible alternatives; and of those identities that are genuine options, society will influence which are desirable and which are not.

As a consequence, the course of identity development will vary in different cultures, among different subcultures within the same society, and over different historical eras (Kroger, 1993). For example, the career options open to women in contemporary American society have changed dramatically in the past 40 years and, consequently, so has the nature of adolescent girls' identity development. In the past, most young women assumed that their adult identity would be exclusively tied to marriage and family life. But today, many more alternative identities are open to women. As a result, the process of choosing among different alternatives has become more complicated than it once was.

The social context in which an adolescent develops also determines to a large extent whether the youngster's search for self-definition will take the form of a full-blown crisis or whether it will be a more manageable challenge. Generally, the more alternatives available to the young person, and the more arenas in which decisions must be made, the more difficult establishing a sense of identity will be. Growing up in contemporary America, where adolescents have a range of careers to decide among, for example, is far more likely to provoke an occupational identity crisis than is growing up in a small agrarian community in which each young person continues farming the family's land.

The rapid rate of social change in most of the industrialized world has raised new and more complex sets of questions for young people to consider—questions not only about occupational plans but also about

Role experimentation during adolescence often involves trying on different looks, images, and patterns of behavior. According to theorists such as Erik Erikson, having the time and freedom to experiment with different roles is an important prelude to establishing a coherent sense of identity.

values, lifestyles, and commitments to other people. Today, adolescents must ask themselves if they want to remain single, live with someone, or marry; if and when they want to have children; and how they plan to incorporate these choices into their career plans. Consequently, the likelihood of going through a prolonged and difficult identity crisis is probably greater today than it has ever been.

▮ The Psychosocial Moratorium

According to Erikson, the complications inherent in identity development in modern society have created the need for a **psychosocial moratorium**—a "time out" during adolescence from the sorts of excessive responsibilities and obligations that might restrict the young person's pursuit of self-discovery. Adolescents in contemporary America are given a moratorium of sorts by being encouraged to remain in school for a long time, where they can think seriously about their plans for the future without making irrevocable decisions.

During the psychosocial moratorium, the adolescent can experiment with different roles and identi-

ties in a context that permits and encourages this sort of exploration. The experimentation involves trying on different postures, personalities, and ways of behaving—sometimes to the consternation of the adolescent's parents, who may wonder why their child's personality seems so changeable. One week, an adolescent girl will spend hours putting on makeup; the next week, she will insist to her parents that she is tired of caring so much about the way she looks. An adolescent boy will come home one day with a shaved head and piercings, and a few weeks later he will discard this image for that of a preppie. Many parents worry about their teenage children going through these sorts of phases. Much of this behavior, however, is actually normal experimentation with roles and personalities.

Having the time to experiment with roles is an important prelude to establishing a coherent sense of identity. But role experimentation can take place only in an environment that allows and encourages it (Côté, 2009). Without a moratorium, a full and thorough exploration of the options and available alternatives cannot occur, and identity development will be somewhat impeded. In other words, according to Erikson, adolescents must grow into an adult identity, rather than be forced into one prematurely.

It is clear, however, that the sort of moratorium Erikson described is an ideal; indeed, some might even consider it to be a luxury of the affluent. Many young people—perhaps even most—do not have the economic freedom to enjoy a long delay before taking on the responsibilities of adult life. For many youngsters, alternatives do not exist in any realistic sense, and introspection only interferes with the more pressing task of survival. Does the 17-year-old who must drop out of school to work a full-time factory job go through life without a sense of identity? Do youngsters who cannot afford a psychosocial moratorium fail to resolve the identity crisis?

Certainly not. But from an Eriksonian point of view, the absence of a psychosocial moratorium in some adolescents' lives—either because of restrictions they place on themselves, restrictions placed on them by others, or their life circumstances—is truly regrettable. The price these youngsters pay is not the failure to develop a sense of identity but lost potential. You may know people whose parents forced them into prematurely choosing a certain career or who had to drop out of college and take a job they really did not want because of financial pressures. According to Erikson, without a chance to explore, to experiment, and to choose among options for the future, these young people may not realize all that they are capable of becoming. It is easy to see how the broader context in which adolescents grow up affects this. Think, for example, of how individuals' plans for the future may have had to change once the economic downturn of 2008–2009 occurred.

---

psychosocial moratorium   A period during which individuals are free from excessive obligations and responsibilities and can therefore experiment with different roles and personalities.

RESOLVING THE IDENTITY CRISIS

Is establishing a sense of identity something that is conscious? According to Erikson, it is. It is experienced as a sense of well-being, a feeling of "being at home in one's body," a sense of knowing where one is going, and an inner assuredness of recognition from those who count. It is a sense of sameness through time—a feeling of continuity between the past and the future.

FOOD FOR THOUGHT

Have you experienced the sort of identity crisis described by Erikson? If so, when did it happen, and what did it feel like? Was it triggered by anything in particular? How, if at all, were you changed by the experience?

Establishing a coherent sense of identity is a lengthy process. Most writers on adolescence and youth believe that identity exploration continues well into young adulthood. But rather than thinking of the adolescent as going through a single identity crisis, it probably makes more sense to view the phenomenon as a series of crises that may concern different aspects of the young person's identity and that may surface—and resurface—at different points in time throughout the adolescent and young-adult years. Indeed, during adolescence, the feeling of well-being associated with establishing a sense of identity is often fleeting. Ultimately, however, the identity crisis of adolescence, when successfully resolved, culminates in a series of basic life commitments: occupational, ideological, social, religious, ethical, and sexual (Côté, 2009).

PROBLEMS IN IDENTITY DEVELOPMENT

Given the wide variations in developmental histories that individuals bring to adolescence and the wide variations in the environments in which they develop, it is not surprising to find differences in the ways in which individuals approach and resolve the crisis of identity versus identity diffusion. Problems in identity development can result when an individual has not successfully resolved earlier crises or when the adolescent is in an environment that does not provide the necessary period of moratorium. Three sorts of problems received special attention from Erikson: identity diffusion, identity foreclosure, and negative identity.

▌ **Identity Diffusion** **Identity diffusion** is characterized by an incoherent, disjointed, incomplete sense of self. Identity diffusion can vary in degree from a mild

state of not quite knowing who one is while in the midst of an identity crisis to a more severe, psychopathological condition that persists beyond a normal period of exploration. It is marked by disruptions in the individual's sense of time (some things seem to happen much faster than they really do, while others seem to take forever); excessive self-consciousness, to the point that it is difficult to make decisions; problems in work and school; difficulties in forming intimate relationships with others; and concerns over sexuality. In other words, identity diffusion is reflected not only in problems of identity but also in the areas of autonomy, intimacy, sexuality, and achievement.

A classic example of an adolescent in the throes of identity diffusion is Holden Caulfield in the 1951 novel *The Catcher in the Rye*. He has flunked out of several prep schools, has severed most of his friendships, and has no sense of where he is headed. At one point in the book, for example, walking up Fifth Avenue in New York City, Holden says, "Every time I came to the end of a block and stepped off the goddam curb, I had this feeling that I'd never get to the other side of the street. I thought I'd just go down, down, down, and nobody'd ever see me again. Boy, did it scare me" (Salinger, 1951/1964, pp. 197–198).

▌ **Identity Foreclosure** Some young people bypass—either willingly or unwillingly—the period of exploration and experimentation that precedes the establishment of a healthy sense of identity. Instead of considering a range of alternatives, these adolescents prematurely commit themselves to a role, or series of roles, and settle upon a certain identification as a final identity. In essence, these individuals are not given—or do not take advantage of—a psychosocial moratorium. For example, a college freshman who made up her mind about becoming a doctor at the age of 13 may enroll in a rigid premed curriculum without considering other career possibilities. The circumvention of the identity crisis is called **identity foreclosure.**

Typically, the roles adopted in the process of identity foreclosure revolve around the goals set for the young person by parents or other authority figures. The adolescent may be led into these roles directly or may be forced into them indirectly by being denied a true psychosocial moratorium. Perhaps the parents of the would-be doctor have arranged their child's school schedule and summer vacations so that all of her spare time is spent taking extra science courses. No time is left for role experimentation or introspection.

identity diffusion   The incoherent, disjointed, incomplete sense of self characteristic of not having resolved the crisis of identity.

identity foreclosure   The premature establishment of a sense of identity, before sufficient role experimentation has occurred.

Individuals who have bypassed the identity crisis have made commitments, but they have not gone through a period of experimentation before making them. Identity foreclosure is an interruption of the identity development process, an interruption that interferes with the individual's discovery of his or her full range of potentials.

■ **Negative Identity** Occasionally, adolescents appear to select identities that are obviously undesirable to their parents and their community. The examples are familiar: the daughter of the local police chief who repeatedly gets into trouble with the law, the son of prestigious and successful parents who refuses to go to college, or the child of a devoutly religious family who insists that he or she is a confirmed atheist. Because the establishment of a healthy sense of identity is so intimately tied to the recognition of the adolescent by those who count in her or his life, the adoption of a so-called **negative identity** is a sign that problems in identity development have arisen. The adolescent who adopts a negative identity is recognized by those around him or her, but not in a way that fosters healthy development.

Usually, selecting a negative identity represents an attempt to forge some sense of self-definition in an environment that has made it difficult to establish an acceptable identity. This appears to be especially likely when, after repeatedly trying and failing to receive positive recognition from those who are important in their lives, adolescents turn to a different, perhaps more successful, route to being noticed—adopting a negative identity. Consider this example: The son of successful parents is a good student but not quite good enough to please his excessively demanding parents. He feels he is a nobody in his parents' eyes, so he drops out of school to play guitar in a band—something his parents vehemently oppose. As Erikson pointed out, most adolescents would rather be somebody "bad" than nobody at all.

FOOD FOR THOUGHT

The broader context in which adolescents develop affects the nature of their identity development. Are there any aspects of today's environment that might make the resolution of the identity crisis especially difficult?

RECAP

- According to Erikson, the major psychosocial issue of adolescence revolves around the identity crisis—coming to terms with who one is and where one is headed.
- To resolve the identity crisis, the young person needs some time out from excessive responsibilities—a psychosocial moratorium—in order to engage in identity exploration and experimentation.
- Some adolescents have trouble resolving the identity crisis. The three most common problems described by Erikson are identity diffusion, identity foreclosure, and negative identity.
- Problems in identity development can result when the individual has not resolved earlier crises or when the adolescent is in an environment that does not provide the necessary period of psychosocial moratorium.

Research on Identity Development

DETERMINING AN ADOLESCENT'S IDENTITY STATUS

The term *identity status* refers to the point in the identity development process that characterizes an adolescent at a given time. In order to determine an individual's identity status, most researchers have used an approach developed by James Marcia (1966), which focuses on identity exploration in three areas—occupation, ideology (values and beliefs), and interpersonal relations. Based on responses to an interview or questionnaire, individuals are rated on two dimensions: (1) the degree to which they have made commitments and (2) the degree to which they engaged in a sustained search in the process (see Figure 8.5). On the basis of these ratings, the researchers assign young people to one of four categories: (1) identity achievement (the individual has established a coherent sense of identity—that is, has made commitments after a period of crisis and experimentation), (2) moratorium (the individual is in the midst of a period of crisis and experimentation), (3) identity foreclosure (the individual has made commitments but without a period of crisis or experimentation), or (4) identity diffusion (the individual does not have firm commitments and is not currently trying to make them). Within each of these categories, it is also possible to draw somewhat finer distinctions—for example, between foreclosed individuals whose foreclosure seems temporary and those whose foreclosure appears "firm" (Kroger, 1995).

---

negative identity   The selection of an identity that is obviously undesirable in the eyes of significant others and the broader community.

	Commitment	
	Present	Absent
Exploration Present	Identity achievement	Moratorium
Absent	Identity foreclosure	Identity diffusion

FIGURE 8.5   Identity status categories derived from Marcia's (1966) measure.

Generally, research employing this approach has supported many aspects of Erikson's theory (Côté, 2009). The strongest support for the theory comes from studies that show a pattern of correlations between various traits and the different identity statuses that are consistent with predictions based on Erikson's model. As you might expect, for example, identity achievers are psychologically healthier than other individuals on a variety of measures: They score highest on measures of achievement motivation, moral reasoning, intimacy with peers, reflectiveness, and career maturity. Individuals in the moratorium category score highest on measures of anxiety, show the highest levels of conflict over issues of authority, and are themselves the least rigid and least authoritarian. Individuals classified as being in the foreclosure group have been shown to be the most authoritarian and most prejudiced and to have the highest need for social approval, the lowest level of autonomy, and the greatest closeness to their parents. Individuals in a state of identity diffusion display the highest level of psychological and interpersonal problems: They are the most socially withdrawn and show the lowest level of intimacy with peers (Adams, Gullotta, & Montemayor, 1992; Fulton, 1997; Meeus, 1996; Wallace-Broscious, Serafica, & Osipow, 1994).

■ **Ways of Resolving the Identity Crisis**   Several researchers have also described the ways in which different individuals approach the resolution of the identity crisis (e.g., Berzonsky, 2004). According to this framework, it is possible to differentiate among individuals who tend to actively seek information and approach identity-related decisions with an open mind (described as having an "informational" orientation), those who attempt to conform to family and other social expectations and try to get identity-related decisions over as quickly as possible (a "normative" orientation), and those who tend to procrastinate and avoid making identity-related decisions (a "diffuse/avoidant" orientation). Not surprisingly, the informational orientation is more characteristic of identity achievers, the normative orientation is more characteristic of individuals who are identity foreclosed, and the diffuse/

avoidant orientation is more characteristic of individuals who exhibit identity diffusion.

More evidence of this sort comes from a study that attempted to link classifications based on a measure of identity development with scores on the personality dimensions tapped within the five-factor model of personality discussed earlier (Clancy & Dollinger, 1993). As expected, adolescents who were classified as identity achievers were higher in extraversion and less neurotic than other adolescents; foreclosed adolescents were less open; and diffused adolescents were more neurotic, less open, and less agreeable. It was not clear from this study whether different personality constellations led to different patterns of identity development or, alternatively, whether different patterns of identity development influenced subsequent personality. Given what we know about the childhood antecedents of personality traits, however, the former explanation (that personality affects identity development) seems more likely than the latter.

One of the defining characteristics of individuals who have achieved a coherent sense of identity, at least in contemporary American society, is that they approach life's decisions with a strong sense of **agency**—they take responsibility for themselves, they feel in control of their decisions, and they have confidence that they will be able to overcome obstacles along the way (Côté, 2000). In recent studies of college students from different ethnic groups, psychologist James Côté and colleagues have shown that a strong sense of personal agency is predictive of identity achievement across ethnic and socioeconomic groups (e.g., Schwartz, Côté, & Arnett, 2005). Being "in charge" of one's life may be especially important in contemporary industrialized society, where the transition to adulthood is prolonged and where individuals are faced with a tremendous number of identity-related decisions. Consistent with this, individuals in their late teens or early 20s who, when asked whether they are adolescents or adults, say they are not sure, are less likely to have achieved a sense of identity than are those who are certain that they have reached adulthood (L. J. Nelson & Barry, 2005). It is not clear whether having a coherent sense of identity leads one to think of oneself as an adult or, instead, whether seeing oneself as an adult leads one to have a more coherent sense of identity. But it does seem that becoming an adult, at least in industrialized society, is a psychological transition as well as one characterized by entering the formal roles of adulthood.

What sorts of parenting practices are associated with different identity statuses? Generally, individuals whose identity development is healthy are more likely to come from authoritative homes characterized by warm, but not excessively constraining, relations, a finding that

agency   The sense that one has an impact on one's world.

Most research indicates that the chief period for identity development is in late adolescence, when many individuals are enrolled in college.

although self-examination may take place throughout adolescence, the consolidation of a coherent sense of identity does not begin until very late in the period (Côté, 2009; Kroger, 2003). The late teens and early 20s appear to be the critical times for the crystallization of a sense of identity (Nurmi, 2004; Schwartz, Côté, & Arnett, 2005). Interestingly, although individuals engage in more of this sophisticated self-reflection as they mature through adolescence, attempts to speed up this process, by training individuals to think more about how specific life events had played a role in their development, are not effective (Habermas & de Silveira, 2008).

Given the fact that college provides a sort of psychosocial moratorium for many people, researchers have asked whether college attendance facilitates identity development (Côté, 2009). This has proven to a difficult question to answer. While studies have found that the proportion of college students who are classified as identity achieved increases from around 20% during freshman year to as many as 40% by senior year, whether this development can be attributed to the college experience is hard to say, since this increase might have taken place just as a result of maturation (Pascarella & Terenzini, 2005). Although in theory one could test this by comparing identity development among college students with late adolescents who are not enrolled in college, in practice this is not easy to do. One problem (in addition to the difficulty researchers find in recruiting samples of non-college individuals to participate in research studies) is that people are not randomly assigned to go to college or not. Thus, even if one were to find that college students showed relatively greater identity development, this could be due to factors that differentiate people who go to college from those who do not. As you probably figured out, this is the same "selection versus socialization" problem we have encountered many times.

has been replicated in both White and Latino samples (Berzonsky, 2004; W. Beyers & Goossens, 2008; Perosa, Perosa, & Tam, 1996; Schwartz, Pantin, Prado, Sullivan, & Szapocznik, 2005). As we saw in Chapter 4, individuals who grow up in these environments are encouraged to assert their individuality but remain connected to their families at the same time. Typically, the absence of parental warmth is associated with problems in making commitments—the most extreme case being identity diffusion—whereas the absence of parental encouragement of individuality is associated with problems in engaging in extensive exploration (Côté, 2009).

STUDYING IDENTITY DEVELOPMENT OVER TIME

In order to examine the development of a sense of identity, researchers have done both cross-sectional studies (comparing individuals of different ages) and longitudinal studies (following the same individuals over a period of time). Many of these studies have raised questions about the accuracy of the identity status model (Côté, 2009). Perhaps the most significant finding to emerge from this research is that a coherent sense of identity generally is not established before age 18, let alone earlier in adolescence, as originally hypothesized (Côté, 2009). In general, when comparisons are made among groups of youngsters of different ages over the span from 12 to 24, differences in identity status are most frequently observed between groups in the 18- to 21-year-old range. Few consistent differences emerge in comparisons of teenagers in the middle adolescent years, suggesting that,

SHIFTS IN IDENTITY STATUS

As you will recall, Erikson theorized that the sense of identity that is developed during adolescence is constantly lost and regained, that the identity challenge is not resolved once and for all at one point in time. If, according to Erikson's model, identity crises surface and resurface throughout the life cycle, we ought to find that individuals move from one identity status to another, particularly during the adolescent and young-adult years.

This appears to be precisely the case. In a longitudinal study of Dutch youth ages 12–14, for example, nearly 60% of the individuals classified as diffused with respect to their educational and occupational identity were no longer classified that way 4 years later, and nearly 75% of individuals who were in the midst of a moratorium at the beginning of the study were no longer in this category at the later assessment (Meeus, Iedema, & Volleburg,1999). Nearly 67% of individuals who had apparently foreclosed the identity development process were in the midst of an identity crisis 4 years later, suggesting that foreclosure may be a temporary stage, at least for some adolescents. Other longitudinal studies of adolescents have revealed similar findings (Côté, 2009).

FOOD FOR THOUGHT

Erikson developed his ideas about identity development in the 1950s. Do you think that this accounts for findings that most identity development occurs in late adolescence or early adulthood, rather than in early or middle adolescence, as he proposed?

Much of this shifting is understandable and perfectly consistent with Erikson's view of adolescent identity development. But how can we account for the fact that in these same longitudinal studies, a large proportion of the identity achievement group also shifted status over the course of the study? In the Dutch study, for example, half of the adolescents who were classified as identity-achieved at the first assessment were not classified this way 4 years later. How could some individuals who at one point had apparently resolved their identity crisis actually not have resolved it—at least, not in any final sense? According to some writers, these sorts of regressions to a less mature identity status are part of the normal process through which individuals ultimately establish a coherent sense of self (Kroger, 2003). That is, we should not view the achievement of a sense of identity in adolescence as a final state, but rather as a step on a long route toward the establishment of a mature sense of self.

Because little research has focused on the processes through which identity development occurs, the factors associated with changing from one identity status to another are not well understood (Kroger & Green, 1996; LaVoie, 1994). Indeed, it is fair to say that psychologists have been much better at describing the various stages that adolescents move through over the course of their identity development than at explaining why or how individuals' sense of identity changes when it does. The little research that has been done on this subject indicates that turning points in the development of a sense of identity

are provoked both by internal factors—discontent with one's life, for example—and by specific life events or changes in life circumstances, such as making the transition into or out of high school (Kalakoski & Nurmi, 1998; Kroger & Green, 1996). Individuals are able to "make meaning" out of these turning points, by using the event to come to a better understanding of oneself (McLean & Pratt, 2006).

One recent attempt to extend the model of identity formation in a way that focuses somewhat more on the underlying process has led researchers to propose that there are actually two different processes going on simultaneously, one in which individuals explore various identities before making commitments, and one in which individuals explore their commitments in depth after having made them, perhaps resulting in a reevaluation and questioning of their initial commitments (Luyckx et al., 2006). According to this view, which actually is closer to Erikson's belief that identity development is an ongoing process, rather than one that leads an individual to an identity that never changes, identity development doesn't follow a straight line, with a steady increase in commitments, but rather is a process characterized by alternating periods of increasing commitment and exploration. On average, people's identity strengthens over time, but at any given moment, an individual may be in a period of uncertainty and reevaluation.

RECAP

- The predominant influence on the study of identity development in adolescence was Erik Erikson, who suggested that the major psychosocial issue of adolescence revolves around the identity crisis—coming to terms with who one is and where one is headed.
- To resolve this crisis successfully, young people need some time out from excessive responsibilities—a psychosocial moratorium—in order to engage in identity exploration and experimentation.
- Some adolescents have difficulty in successfully resolving the identity crisis. Among the three most common problems described by Erikson are identity diffusion, identity foreclosure, and negative identity.
- Research on identity development from Erikson's theoretical perspective, which has been heavily influenced by the work of James Marcia, has generally supported his model.
- Most studies indicate that the major developments in identity occur in late adolescence and young adulthood, rather than earlier during the adolescent decade.

The Development of Ethnic Identity

For all individuals who are not part of the majority culture, integrating a sense of **ethnic identity** into their overall sense of personal identity is likely to be an important task of late adolescence, perhaps as important as establishing a coherent occupational, ideological, or interpersonal identity (Fuligni, Hughes, & Way, 2009; Phinney & Rosenthal, 1992). Over the past two decades, an extensive literature has been amassed on the process through which ethnic identity develops and on the implications of having a strong versus weak sense of ethnic identity for adolescent adjustment and behavior. Ethnic identity has been studied in samples of Black, Hispanic, Native American, Asian, and White youth (M. D. Jones & Galliher, 2007; Marshall, 1995; D. L. Newman, 2005; Phinney & Devich-Navarro, 1997; H. Stevenson, 1995; Vega, Khoury, Zimmerman, Gil, & Warheit, 1995). In America, White youth generally have a weaker sense of ethnic identity than their non-White peers, but many White adolescents, especially those from more working-class backgrounds, identify strongly with a particular ethnic group (such as German, Irish, Italian, Jewish) and derive part of their overall sense of self from this identification (J. M. Grossman & Charmaraman, 2009; R. Martinez & Dukes, 1997; R. Roberts, Phinney, et al., 1999). Nevertheless, if given a list of labels to identify their own ethnic background, White adolescents in America are less likely than ethnic minority adolescents to choose labels based on their specific heritage (for example, "German," "Italian American") and more likely to use generic "panethnic" labels (for example, "White") or simply to identify themselves as "American" (Fuligni, Witkow, & Garcia, 2005). Among immigrant adolescents, there is considerable vacillation between identifying oneself as a member of a broad ethnic category (e.g., Latino, Asian) and identifying oneself as a member of a group defined by one's country of origin (e.g., Mexican, Chinese) (Fuligni, Kiang, Witkow, & Baldelomar, 2008).

THE PROCESS OF ETHNIC IDENTITY DEVELOPMENT

The process of ethnic identity development follows the process of identity development in general, with an unquestioning view of oneself often being displaced or upset by a crisis. Often, but not always, the precipitating

event involves an experience during which the individual encounters prejudice (46%), becomes aware of his or her group's underrepresentation in some activity or setting (25%), or suddenly feels different from adolescents from other backgrounds (12%) (Syed & Azmitia, 2006). Here's how one Asian American woman described her "awakening":

> I was on the computer chatting with my friend, and he was telling me he has plans to go to Japan to visit for vacation. Then I told him I would like to visit China, and he said to me, "China sounds so shady, but you dirty chink would totally fit in anyway." I told him immediately I was offended by his comment, but he thought I was joking about my emotions. I told him to take that comment back because I didn't find it funny. I felt very offended; I was thinking to myself, "Is that how others view Chinese people?" (Syed & Azmitia, 2006, p. 1019).

Following the crisis, individuals engage in a period of exploration, during which they may immerse themselves in learning about their ethnic heritage. (Increasingly, a good deal of this exploration occurs online [Tynes, 2007]). This process of exploration leads to increases in self-esteem (Umaña-Taylor, Gonzales-Backen, & Guimond, 2009). Eventually, as the value of having a strong ethnic identity becomes clear, the individual establishes a more coherent sense of personal identity that includes this ethnic identity (Seaton, Yip, & Sellers, 2009; Whitehead, Ainsworth, Wittig, & Gadino, 2009). Consistent with this, a recent study of ethnic identity development among students attending urban public schools found that adolescents' feelings about their own ethnic group became more positive during both early and middle adolescence (when ethnic identity first becomes salient and individuals become immersed in their own culture), but that actual identity exploration did not really begin until middle adolescence, perhaps because it was at that point that students began to prepare to make the transition from relatively homogeneous schools into much more diverse ones (S. E. French, Seidman, Allen, & Aber, 2006). Between middle and late adolescence, exploration declines, as individuals begin to develop a more consolidated identity (Pahl & Way, 2006). As is the case with identity development more generally, individuals with a strong sense of ethnic identity have better mental health than their peers whose sense of ethnic identity is more diffuse (Seaton, Scottham, & Sellers, 2006; Yip, Seaton, & Sellers, 2006).

Some research indicates that moving through the early stages of ethnic identity development may be speeded up somewhat when parents take a more deliberate approach to racial, or ethnic, socialization (McHale et al., 2006; Quintana, Castaneda-English, & Ybarra, 1999; Umaña-Taylor, Bhanot, & Shin, 2006; Umaña-Taylor, Alfaro, Bamaca, & Guimond, 2009). **Racial socialization** refers to the process parents use to

---

ethnic identity   The aspect of individuals' sense of identity concerning ancestry or racial group membership.

racial socialization   The process through which individuals develop an understanding of their racial or ethnic background.

For individuals who are not part of the majority culture, integrating a sense of ethnic identity into their overall sense of personal identity is likely to be an important task.

attempt to teach their children about their ethnic identity and about the special experiences they may encounter within the broader society as a result of their ethnic background. Ethnic socialization in minority families focuses on three themes: understanding and valuing one's culture, dealing with racism, and succeeding in mainstream society (Lesane-Brown, 2006). However, although racial socialization by parents may speed up the process of ethnic identity development and encourage adolescents to think about their ethnic heritage, it does not appear to lead adolescents to an ultimately stronger sense of ethnic identity (DeBerry, Scarr, & Weinberg, 1996; Marshall, 1995; Phinney & Chavira, 1995; Supple, Ghazarian, Frabutt, Plunkett, & Sands, 2006). Nor is more racial socialization necessarily better; in one study, the best-adjusted Black adolescents came from homes in which their mothers provided a moderate number of racial socialization messages, rather than many or few (Frabutt, Walker, & MacKinnon-Lewis, 2002). Another found that less frequent communication of highly positive messages may be most effective (Neblett, Smalls, Ford, Nguyên, & Sellers, 2009). Racial socialization also occurs indirectly, for example, when parents stress the importance of family obligations (Kiang & Fuligni, 2009). Interestingly, having

positive attitudes about one's own ethnic group is correlated with having positive attitudes about adolescents from other ethnic groups, suggesting that racial socialization may enhance, rather than upset, interracial relations (Phinney, Ferguson, & Tate, 1997). In fact, many adolescents with a strong ethnic identity are members of peer crowds for which ethnicity is *not* a defining feature; a better predictor of whether an adolescent is a member of an ethnically defined crowd is the proportion of that adolescent's friends who are from the same ethnic group (B. Brown, Herman, Hamm, & Heck, 2008).

Having a strong ethnic identity is consistently associated with higher self-esteem, stronger self-efficacy, and better mental health among minority youngsters, whereas the link between ethnic identity and mental health is weaker among White youth (DeBerry et al., 1996; Deyhle, 1995; DuBois, Burk-Braxton, et al., 2002; R. Martinez & Dukes, 1997; McCreary, Slavin, and Berry, 1996; McMahon & Watts, 2002; Reviere & Bakeman, 1992; E. Smith, 1996; Verkuyten, 1995). One study of drug use found, for instance, that ethnic pride was associated with less use among Black, Mexican American, and biracial adolescents, but with more use among White adolescents (Marsiglia, Kulis, & Hecht, 2001). It would seem, therefore, that establishing a sense of ethnic identity is more important for individuals who are part of an ethnic minority than for those who are part of a majority (Gray-Little & Hafdahl, 2000).

The mental health of ethnic minority youth is also affected by their orientation to the mainstream culture. In general, positive mental health among ethnic minority adolescents is associated with what might be described as "savvy biculturalism"—having a strong, positive ethnic identity and a healthy awareness of the potential for discrimination, but not with outright rejection of the mainstream culture (Gil, Vega, & Dimas, 1994; Juang, Nguyen, & Lin, 2006; Phinney, Devich-Navarro, DuPont, Estrada, & Onwughala, 1994; Pillay, 2005; A. Smith & Lalonde, 2003; Umaña-Taylor, 2004; Yasui, Dorham, & Dishion, 2004). For example, among ethnic minority youth, academic achievement is highest when adolescents feel connected to their ethnic group, are aware of racism, and believe that it is important to the people in their life to be academically successful within mainstream society (Altschul, Oyserman, & Bybee, 2006). Being aware of potential racism and mistrusting others are not the same thing, however; awareness of racism is associated with better achievement, but mistrust is associated with doing more poorly in school (Huynh & Fuligni, 2008).

FOOD FOR THOUGHT

How strong is your own sense of ethnic identity? Have there been points in your life when it was especially important? How has it changed as you've gotten older?

■ **Recent Immigrants** Several researchers have focused on the special situation of ethnic minority youth who are recent immigrants to a new culture (e.g., Fuligni, Hughes, & Way, 2009; Phinney, Romero, Nava, & Huang, 2001; Rumbaut & Cornelius, 1995). Interestingly, foreign-born ethnic minority adolescents tend to express more positive feelings about mainstream American ideals than do their counterparts whose families have been in the United States longer, and foreign-born ethnic minority youth perform better in school and are less likely to be involved in delinquent behavior or have physical, emotional, and behavioral problems than are their more acculturated peers (Kulis, Marsiglia, & Hurdle, 2003; Rumbaut, 1997; Vega et al., 1995). One interpretation of this is that ethnic minority immigrants arrive in America idealistic about the "melting pot" society, only to discover that they are objects of prejudice and discrimination. This realization may prompt a strengthening of ethnic identity, a desire for separatism, cynicism

about endorsing mainstream American values, and increased conflict within the family (Phinney et al., 1994; Samaniego & Gonzales, 1999). Another explanation for the higher achievement and better mental health of immigrant adolescents is that newly arrived immigrant parents provide relatively closer supervision of their children (Harker, 2001).

The process of identity development among adolescents from recent immigrant families also depends on the context in which the family lives, as a recent study of Vietnamese adolescents from Southern California illustrates (Vo-Jutabha, Dinh, McHale, & Valsiner, 2009). In this study, the researchers compared the identity development of adolescents living in a Vietnamese enclave ("Little Saigon") with those who lived nearby, but in a more diverse community. For adolescents living inside the enclave, pressures on them to adopt a strong Vietnamese identity had both helped focus their identity development but also constrained it, frustrating those teenagers whose behavior conflicted with the expectations of adults in the community. As one girl from Little Saigon noted,

> You want to do what makes you feel happy or comfortable but they put you in this little ethnicity box. Especially here. Going to church you wear *ao dai* [traditional Vietnamese dress]. I'm not rebelling but I don't want to be another Asian girl in an American crowd. I want to be myself. I'm not going against my parents or tradition. I want to make my own morals and traditions and it makes me happy. (p. 682)

Adolescents living outside the enclave had more opportunities to explore a wider range of alternatives, but were more passive in their identity exploration and often actively fought attempts by their parents to encourage a strong Vietnamese identity. As one boy put it,

> My parents expect me to speak Vietnamese consistently. Every now and then they just say that I forgot it and that I don't know how to speak it anymore. . . . Of course, I understand it and my parents expect me to be in a Viet Club or something. But I mean c'mon, really c'mon. (pp. 683–684)

As many writers have noted, the task of developing a coherent sense of identity is much more complicated for minority adolescents than for their majority counterparts (Gray-Little & Hafdahl, 2000; H. Stevenson, Reed, Bodison, & Bishop, 1997). Because identity development is profoundly influenced by the social context in which the adolescent lives, the development of minority adolescents must be understood in relation to the specific context that they face in contemporary society (Garcia Coll et al., 1996). All too often, this context includes racial stereotypes, discrimination, and mixed messages about the costs and benefits of identifying too closely with the majority culture (see Figure 8.6).

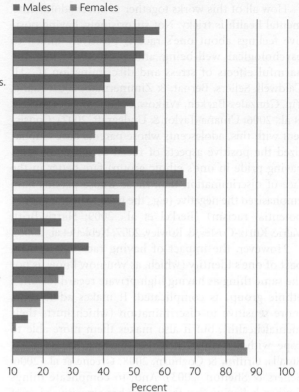

FIGURE 8.6   The experience of discrimination is common among Black adolescents. (Seaton, Caldwell, Sellers, & Jackson, 2008)

DISCRIMINATION AND ITS EFFECTS

It is well established that individuals—from any group—who report experiencing high levels of discrimination suffer psychologically as a result. Studies of both Black and Latino youth have found that feeling discriminated against is predictive of subsequent conduct problems, depression, and lower achievement in school (Brody, Chen, Murry, Ge, Simons, et al., 2006; DeGarmo & Martinez, Jr., 2006; Romero, Carvajal, Valle, & Orduña, 2007; Seaton, Caldwell, Sellers, & Jackson, 2008; Seaton & Yip, 2009). There are all sorts of reasons that feeling discriminated against may be harmful to one's mental health, but one important process derives from the effect of discrimination on adolescents' feelings of control: Adolescents who feel discriminated against in school report feeling less control over their academic achievement, which leads to feelings of depression (Lambert, Herman, Bynum, & Ialongo, 2009).

Individuals vary both in the extent to which they feel discriminated against and in the extent to which they are adversely affected by it, and it appears that ethnic identity is an important factor (Greene, Way, & Pahl, 2006; Oppedal, Røysamb, & Sam, 2004; Sellers et al., 2006). Psychologist Robert Sellers and colleagues developed the **multidimensional model of racial identity** to help make sense out of a complex web of findings

(Sellers et al., 2006). According to this model, we need to take into account three different aspects of racial identity: racial centrality (how important race is in defining individuals' identity), private regard (how individuals feel about being a member of their race), and public regard (how individuals think others view their race).

Not surprisingly, Black adolescents who have experienced discrimination firsthand are more likely to believe that the public has low regard for African Americans (Seaton et al., 2009). However, Black individuals who believe that the public has low regard for African Americans are more sensitive to racial cues, which, in turn, may heighten their experience of discrimination. This is not to say that individuals with heightened sensitivity to discrimination are simply imagining it; rather, individuals with heightened sensitivity may be better at perceiving more subtle signs of genuine racial bias.

multidimensional model of racial identity (MMRI)   Sellers's perspective on ethnic identity, which emphasizes three different phenomena: racial centrality (how important race is in defining individuals' identity), private regard (how individuals feel about being a member of their race), and public regard (how individuals think others feel about their race).

How all of this works together to affect adolescents' mental health is tricky. Not surprisingly, having positive feelings about one's race is positively linked to psychological well-being and protects against the harmful effects of stress and discrimination (C. H. Caldwell, Sellers, Bernat, & Zimmerman, 2004; Kiang, Yip, Gonzales-Backen, Witkow, & Fuligni, 2006; Sellers et al., 2006; Umaña-Taylor & Updegraff, 2007). Consistent with this, adolescents whose parents have emphasized the positive aspects of racial socialization (e.g., having pride in one's ethnic group) fare better in the face of discrimination than those whose parents have emphasized the negative (e.g., the need to be wary about potential racism) (Berkel et al., 2009; Harris-Britt, Valrie, Kurtz-Costes, & Rowley, 2007; Neblettet al., 2008).

However, the impact of having race as a central part of one's identity (which, as you now know, is not the same thing as having high private regard for one's ethnic group) is complicated: It makes adolescents more sensitive to discrimination (which hurts their mental health), but it also makes them more able to cope with it (which helps) (Chavous, Rivas-Drake, Smalls, Griffin, & Cogburn, 2008; Greene et al., 2006; Sellers & Shelton, 2003). And, to complicate things further, believing that the public has a positive view of one's race (which is generally beneficial) intensifies the effects of discrimination—perhaps because people feel especially wounded when they don't expect to encounter it (Sellers, Copeland-Linder, Martin, & Lewis, 2006).

A recent study of ethnic identity and academic achievement illustrates how racial centrality, private regard, and public regard work together to influence Black adolescents' school performance and motivation (Chavous et al., 2003). The researchers identified four distinct clusters within their sample of 600 students: buffering/defensive (high centrality, high private regard, low public regard; 29% of the sample), low connectedness/high affinity (low centrality, high private regard, low public regard; 21%), idealized (high on all three dimensions; 31%), and alienated (low on all three dimensions; 19%) (see Figure 8.7). Alienated students were the most disengaged from school and most likely to drop out, while idealized students were more likely to hold positive beliefs about school. But it was members of the buffering/defensive group who were the least likely to drop out and the most likely to be enrolled in college two years after graduation. The researchers speculated that the success of this group was due to the combination of strong feelings of group pride and a realistic expectation of facing discrimination. Sadly, as

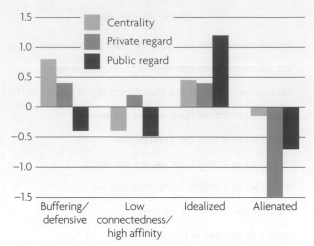

FIGURE 8.7   Racial identity groups among Black adolescents, as indicated by feelings of centrality, private regard, and public regard. (Chavous et al., 2003)

long as discrimination persists in American society, adolescents who are its victims will need to protect themselves against its pernicious effects.

MULTIETHNIC ADOLESCENTS

One understudied group of adolescents for whom developing a sense of ethnic identity may be especially challenging consists of **biracial** youth—adolescents whose parents are not from the same ethnic or racial group. Understanding psychological development among biracial adolescents has taken on increased importance as their numbers have grown. In the 1970s, for example, 1 out of every 100 children was born to parents of different races; by 2000, this had increased to 1 out of 20 (Herman, 2004). No one doubts that this proportion will be even higher when the 2010 Census is tallied.

You've probably filled out many forms and applications asking you to indicate your racial or ethnic background, and for the majority of individuals, this is not an especially challenging task. But what about individuals who are of mixed heritage? Today, when questionnaires ask individuals to provide information on their ethnic background, they typically provide respondents with the opportunity to indicate that they are multiracial, by permitting them to select more than one answer. Prior to 2000, however, even the U.S. Census forced people to choose an identification from one of several broad categories (for example, Asian, Black, Latino, White, Other). The problem, of course, is that a forced choice of this sort demands that multiracial individuals either select one of the ethnic groups or use the category "Other," neither of which allows them to be identified as multiracial. Moreover, each ethnic category will include individuals with two parents from that group as well as multiracial individuals who

biracial   Having two parents of different ethnic or racial backgrounds.

TABLE 8.1   Percentage of multiracial respondents who self-identify in each monoracial category and counts of multiracial respondents using alternative categorization methods

	% Black	% White	% Asian	% Hispanic	% Other	% No Choice	Precise *N*	Parsimonious *N*
Black-Asian	57	15	7	7	7	7	60	30
Black-Hispanic	56	7	1	25	7	4	70	52
Other-Asian	11	14	23	15	37	1	89	27
Asian-Hispanic	13	15	15	40	12	5	101	55
Other-Hispanic	9	9	2	46	33	0	117	46
Other-Black	61	11	3	4	20	1	159	91
Black-White	68	16	1	2	4	9	160	160
White-Asian	4	33	43	6	10	4	298	250
Other-White	5	62	1	8	25	0	450	324
White-Hispanic	3	38	1	52	1	5	485	461
Total							1,989	1,496

Note: Precise counts each respondent in as many race categories as befit his or her parentage; parsimonious counts each respondent in only one category according to norms of hypodescent.

Source: Herman, 2004.

have an especially strong identification with one of their parents' ethnic heritage. It is little wonder that we know so little about multiracial adolescents, given the fact that in many studies they are impossible to identify.

A recent study by sociologist Melissa Herman took advantage of a unique opportunity to examine what biracial adolescents do when forced to choose an ethnic identity and whether biracial adolescents who choose one ethnicity to describe themselves differ from adolescents with parents of the same two ethnic backgrounds who choose the other ethnicity for self-description (Herman, 2004). In a survey that I conducted many years ago with Sanford Dornbusch and Bradford Brown, we accidentally asked adolescents about their ethnic background twice: once when we asked them to tell us the ethnic background of each of their parents, and once when we asked them to identify their own ethnic background but did not permit them to choose more than one category. (To be honest, this was a mistake that we overlooked when developing the questionnaire, but the truth is that researchers' mistakes often lead to more interesting discoveries than their deliberate choices.)

Capitalizing on our error, Herman was able to identify biracial adolescents (based on their descriptions of each of their parents) and examine how they described themselves. For instance, some adolescents with a White father and a Hispanic mother, when forced to choose, described themselves as White, others said they were Hispanic, and a third group chose neither. Table 8.1 shows the results; the leftmost column gives the parental combination (such as Black-Asian), and the remaining columns indicate the proportion of adolescents with that combination who chose a specific ethnic group for

self-identification. For instance, the top row of the table indicates that 57% of adolescents with one Black and one Asian parent identified themselves as Black, whereas only 7% identified themselves as Asian. (Adolescents who did not choose either of their parents' ethnicity usually did so because one of their parents was multiethnic.) Two patterns in the table are noteworthy. First, individuals with one Black parent were significantly more likely to identify themselves as Black than as a member of the second group. Second, individuals with one White and one ethnic minority parent were more likely to identify themselves as a member of the ethnic minority group, regardless of the ethnicity.

Herman then asked whether certain factors, beyond the ethnicities of his or her parents, predicted which ethnic group an adolescent chose. Although few variables operated the same across all ethnic groups, two that did were the adolescent's physical appearance (based on ratings of a yearbook photo) and the ethnic background of the adolescent's friends. Biracial adolescents who appeared White to the yearbook raters were more likely to identify themselves as White, and biracial adolescents who reported that the majority of their friends were from an ethnic minority group were less likely to identify themselves as White. Individuals with one or two Black parents reported the highest levels of discrimination (these groups did not differ from each other), and those with two White parents reported the lowest.

Actually, many biracial adolescents change their racial identity over time, switching between adolescence and young adulthood from being biracial to being "monoracial" (identifying oneself with just one ethnic group), or the reverse (Hitlin, Brown, & Elder, Jr., 2006). Although this switching was observed in all ethnic groups, it was especially common among adolescents who identified as Native Americans, either exclusively or in combination with a White self-identification. The majority of individuals who identified themselves as both White and Native American when they were adolescents identified themselves only as White when they were young adults. However, a large number of adolescents who identified themselves only as White identified themselves as both White and Native American several years later. Similar patterns of change were seen among other multiracial individuals, but not nearly as often.

RECAP

- Many researchers have studied the process through which ethnic identity develops and the implications of having a strong versus weak sense of ethnic identity for adolescent adjustment and behavior.

- The process of ethnic identity development follows the process of identity development in general, with an unquestioning view of the self being displaced or upset by an event or experience that provokes a period of exploration. Over time, a more coherent sense of ethnic identity emerges.

- Racial socialization is the process through which parents attempt to teach their children about their ethnic identity and about the special experiences they may encounter within the broader society as a result of their ethnic background.

- Positive mental health among ethnic minority adolescents is associated with having a strong, positive ethnic identity and an awareness of the potential for discrimination, but not with outright rejection of the mainstream culture.

- Adolescents who report experiencing high levels of discrimination suffer psychologically as a result, but individuals vary both in the extent to which they feel discriminated against and in the extent to which they are adversely affected by it.

- One understudied group of adolescents for whom developing a sense of ethnic identity may be especially challenging are biracial youth—adolescents whose parents are not from the same ethnic or racial group.

androgyny   The combination of both highly masculine and highly feminine traits.

gender intensification hypothesis   The idea that pressures to behave in sex-appropriate ways intensify during adolescence.

Gender-Role Development

Like ethnicity, gender is a critical component of individuals' identity. From birth, boys and girls are socialized to behave in "sex-appropriate" ways—that is, to conform to society's standards for acceptable masculine and acceptable feminine behavior. In American society, strong gender-role stereotypes prevail among children, adolescents, and adults. Traits such as logic, independence, ambition, and aggressiveness are considered masculine; and traits such as gentleness, sociability, empathy, and tenderness are considered feminine (Broverman, Vogel, Broverman, Clarkson, & Rosenkrantz, 1972).

Individuals vary in their degrees of masculinity and femininity. Some are decidedly more masculine than feminine, and others are decidedly more feminine than masculine. But some people have a high degree of both masculinity and femininity. For instance, some people are both highly ambitious (a trait usually considered masculine) and highly sensitive (a trait usually considered feminine). Individuals who are both highly masculine and highly feminine are said to be high in **androgyny** (S. Bem, 1975).

Many researchers have been interested in the relation between gender-role stereotypes and adolescent identity development. Are teenagers, for example, pressured more than children to behave in stereotypically masculine or feminine ways? If so, to what extent does a person's compliance with prevailing gender-role stereotypes affect his or her self-image?

GENDER-ROLE SOCIALIZATION DURING ADOLESCENCE

Pressures to behave in sex-appropriate ways may temporarily intensify during middle adolescence (Crouter, Manke, & McHale, 1995; Galambos, Berenbaum, & McHale, 2009; Lobel, Nov-Krispin, Schiller, Lobel, & Feldman, 2004). The **gender intensification hypothesis** (J. P. Hill & Lynch, 1983) holds that many of the sex differences observed between adolescent boys and girls result from an acceleration in their socialization to act in stereotypically masculine and feminine ways. Even though individuals' beliefs about gender roles may become more flexible as they move through adolescence, largely as a result of the cognitive changes of the period, social pressures may drive teenagers toward more gender-stereotypic behavior; indeed, the impact of environmental factors on gender-role behavior is much stronger than the impact of the hormonal changes of puberty (Galambos et al., 2009). As teenagers begin to date, for example, it may become more important for them to act in ways that are

Pressures to behave in sex-stereotypic ways may temporarily intensify during middle adolescence.

consistent with gender-role expectations and that meet with approval in the peer group. Boys who do not act masculine enough and girls who do not act feminine enough may be less popular with and less accepted by their same- and opposite-sex peers (T. E. Smith & Leaper, 2005).

However, not all studies find an increase in gender-stereotyped behavior in middle adolescence (e.g., Jacobs et al., 2002; McHale, Kim, Whiteman, & Crouter, 2004). One reason for discrepancies between studies is that the extent to which gender-stereotypic behavior becomes more pronounced in early adolescence likely depends on the realm of behavior studied, the developmental history of the adolescent, and the broader context in which the adolescent lives (Galambos, Berenbaum, & McHale, 2009; McHale, Shanahan, Updegraff, Crouter, & Booth, 2004; H. M. Watt, 2004). For instance, although individuals become more traditional in their attitudes about gender roles between early and middle adolescence, this pattern is not universal. One recent study of changes in gender role attitudes broke the sample down by sex, birth order, and the sorts of attitudes the parents had. The findings illustrate how

much context matters: Whereas firstborn boys with brothers and parents with traditional attitudes about gender become more traditional in their own attitudes over time, second-born girls with brothers and less traditional parents did not (Crouter, Whiteman, McHale, & Osgood, 2007).

FOOD FOR THOUGHT

The gender intensification hypothesis was developed more than 25 years ago. Based on your recollection of adolescence, does it still ring true?

MASCULINITY, FEMININITY, AND ANDROGYNY

If gender-role socialization becomes more intense during adolescence, we would expect to find that conformity to gender-role expectations is an important influence on

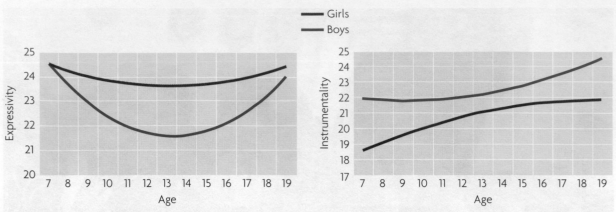

FIGURE 8.8   During adolescence, boys increasingly avoid displaying stereotypically feminine traits, but comparable pressure on girls to avoid stereotypically masculine traits is much milder. As a consequence, boys show a drop in emotional expressiveness, but girls do not show a similar decline in instrumentality. (McHale et al., 2009)

adolescents' self-image. Do more feminine girls and more masculine boys feel better about themselves than do their peers, or are boys and girls both better off when they show a mix of typically masculine and typically feminine traits?

Recent research suggests that the answer to this question may differ for males and females (Galambos et al., 2009). Although boys and girls who behave in gender-typical ways are more accepted than their peers whose behavior does not conform with gender-role stereotypes—and feel better about themselves as a result of this peer acceptance—the costs of being gender-atypical are greater for boys than girls (T. E. Smith & Leaper, 2005). Put another way, the relative benefits of androgyny to youngsters' self-image are greater for girls than for boys. This is because it is specifically the masculine component of androgyny that is associated with better mental health in adolescence (Markstrom-Adams, 1989). Interestingly, this is not the case during childhood, when aspects of both masculinity and femininity are linked to well-being for both sexes (Allgood-Merten & Stockard, 1991), or during young adulthood, when both femininity and masculinity are predictive of well-being among young women (J. Stein, Newcomb, & Bentler, 1992). It is not surprising, therefore, to find that during adolescence boys are likely to cut back on the display of traditionally feminine traits, such as being emotionally expressive, whereas neither boys nor girls reduce the display of traditionally masculine traits, such as instrumentality (McHale, Kim, Dotterer, Crouter, & Booth, 2009) (see Figure 8.8).

Although masculinity is predictive of mental health among both adolescent males and females, androgynous girls feel better about themselves than either very masculine or very feminine girls, whereas masculine boys—not androgynous boys—show the highest lev-

els of self-acceptance, a finding that has emerged in studies of both Western and non-Western youth (Frome & Eccles, 1996; E. Orr & Ben-Eliahu, 1993). These findings suggest that it is easier for girls to behave sometimes in masculine ways during adolescence than it is for boys to act occasionally in feminine ways. Consistent with research on younger children, during adolescence—at least in contemporary American society—males who do not conform to traditionally masculine gender-role norms are judged more deviant than are females whose behavior departs from exclusively feminine roles. Interestingly, however, boys who have a more traditionally masculine orientation, while higher in self-acceptance than other boys, are more likely to be involved in various types of problem behavior—perhaps because part of being masculine in contemporary society involves being "macho" enough to experiment with delinquency, drugs and alcohol, and unprotected sex (Kulis, Marsiglia, & Hurdle, 2003; Pleck, Sonenstein, & Ku, 1994), or because boys who live in difficult environments, where problem behavior is prevalent, adopt a more "macho" posture to survive in the community (Cunningham, 1999). Conversely, girls who have a more traditionally feminine gender-role orientation are more likely to develop more traditionally feminine sorts of psychological problems, such as disordered eating (McHale, Corneal, Crouter, & Birch, 2001).

Given that pressures to conform with gender-role norms affect both girls and boys during adolescence, why is it that boys suffer greater self-image problems when they deviate from what is viewed as appropriate behavior for their sex? The answer is that although girls may be pressured to adopt (or maintain) certain feminine traits during adolescence, they are not necessarily pressured to relinquish all elements of masculinity. In contrast, boys are socialized from a very early age not to adopt feminine traits and are judged deviant if they show signs of femininity. Consistent with this, boys are more likely to see themselves as "typical males" than girls are to see themselves as "typical females," more likely to be content to be male than girls are to be female, and more pressured to act in stereotypically male ways than girls are to act in stereotypically female ways (Egan & Perry, 2001).

In other words, girls can be highly pressured during adolescence to behave in feminine ways without necessarily being punished or labeled deviant for exhibiting some masculine traits at the same time; thus, for girls, androgyny is a viable alternative to exclusive femininity. Girls may feel increasingly pressured to dress nicely and to wear makeup when they reach adolescence, but they are not pressured to give up athletics or other typically masculine interests. Boys, however, from childhood on, are pressured not to behave in feminine ways—even if the femininity is in the context of androgyny. Their gender-role socialization does not intensify during adolescence as much as it does for girls because it is so intense to begin with.

RECAP

- An important aspect of adolescent identity involves gender-role development.
- Although individuals grow more flexible during adolescence in the way that they think about gender roles, adolescents may feel especially strong pressure to adhere to stereotypical gender roles.
- The extent to which individuals' gender-role behavior changes during adolescence is influence by many factors, including birth order, the presence and sex of older or younger siblings, and their parents' attitudes.
- In general, among both males and females, many traits traditionally labeled as masculine are associated in adolescence with better adjustment and greater peer acceptance. As a result, androgynous females and masculine males report higher self-esteem than their peers do.

Autonomy

When I got my driver's license, I looked at it as freedom, getting out from my parents, going places you couldn't get to before because you had to have your parent's permission . . . not having to be worried about being dropped off and being picked up. Going to the library even or a dance club or a party and not having to worry about, I don't know, your parents having to come pick you up. Not necessarily, it wasn't embarrassment for me, it was more, just like okay, I make my own choices I can leave when I want to you know, I made this decision to come here you know I'll drop you off. I felt more like an adult but um, I don't know, I went to the beach, to people's houses, friends' houses, the movies. (Best, 2006, p. 63)

FOR MOST ADOLESCENTS, like the teenager quoted above, establishing a sense of autonomy is as important a part of becoming an adult as is establishing a sense of identity. Becoming an autonomous person—a self-governing person—is one of the fundamental developmental tasks of adolescence.

Although we often use the words *autonomy* and *independence* interchangeably, in the study of adolescence, they mean slightly different things. Independence generally refers to individuals' capacity to behave on their own. The growth of independence is surely a part of becoming autonomous during adolescence, but, as you will see in this chapter, autonomy has emotional and cognitive as well as behavioral components. In other words, autonomy is not just about acting independently—it is also about feeling independent and thinking independently.

During adolescence, there is a movement away from the dependency typical of childhood and toward the autonomy typical of adulthood. But the growth of autonomy during adolescence is frequently misunderstood. Autonomy is often confused with rebellion, and becoming an independent person is often equated with breaking away from the family. This perspective on autonomy goes hand in hand with the idea that adolescence is inevitably a time of stress and turmoil. But as we have seen in previous chapters, the view that adolescence is a period of storm and stress has been questioned repeatedly by scientific research. The same sort of rethinking has taken place with regard to the development of autonomy. Rather than viewing adolescence as a time of rebellion, researchers now see the growth of autonomy during adolescence as gradual, progressive, and—although

important—relatively undramatic (McElhaney, Allen, Stephenson, & Hare, 2009).

Because today's adolescents spend so much time away from the direct supervision of adults, either by themselves or with their peers, learning how to govern their own behavior in a responsible fashion is a crucial task. As we saw in previous chapters, with increasing numbers of single-parent and two-career households, more young people are expected to supervise themselves for a good part of the day. Many young people feel pressured—by parents, by friends, and by the media—to grow up quickly and to act like adults at an earlier age. Many adolescents who grow up in poverty feel a different sort of pressure to grow up—they are expected to take on adult responsibilities to assist their families during times of need (Burton, 2007).

There is a curious paradox in all of this, however. At the same time that adolescents have been asked to become more autonomous psychologically and socially, they have become less autonomous economically. Because of the extension of schooling well into the young-adult years for most individuals, financial independence may not come until long after psychological independence has been established. Many young people who are emotionally independent find it frustrating to discover that they have to abide by their parents' rules as long as they are being supported economically. They may believe that the ability to make their own decisions has nothing to do with financial dependence. A 16-year-old who drives, has a part-time job, and has a serious relationship with his girlfriend, for example, may be independent in these respects, but he is nonetheless still dependent on his parents for food and shelter. His parents may feel that as long as their son lives in their home, they should decide how late he can stay out at night. But the adolescent may feel that his parents have no right to tell him when he can come and go. This sort of difference of opinion can be a real source of problems and confusion for teenagers and their parents, particularly when they have difficulty agreeing on a level of independence for the adolescent. Disagreements over autonomy-related concerns are at the top of the list of things that provoke quarrels between adolescents and parents (Laursen & Collins, 2009; Holmbeck & O'Donnell, 1991; Steinberg, 2001).

Autonomy as an Adolescent Issue

Like identity, autonomy is a psychosocial concern that surfaces and resurfaces during the entire life cycle. The development of independent behavior begins long before puberty. Toddlers try to establish an initial sense of autonomy when they begin to explore their surroundings on their own and assert their desire to do as they please—a stage of development so frustrating to parents that it is often called "the terrible twos." The toddler who insists on saying "No!" and the young adolescent who insists on keeping her whereabouts secret are both demonstrating their growing sense of independence and autonomy. And just as psychologists see toddlers' oppositional behavior as normal, they also see adolescents' interest in privacy as normal, too—however frustrating *that* might be to *their* parents (McElhaney et al., 2009).

Although childhood and adolescence are important periods for the development of autonomy, it is a mistake to suggest that issues of autonomy are resolved once and for all upon reaching young adulthood. Questions about their ability to function independently arise whenever individuals find themselves in positions that demand a new degree of self-reliance. Following a divorce, for example, someone who has depended on a spouse over the years for economic support, guidance, or nurturance must find a way to function more autonomously and more independently. During late adulthood, autonomy may become a significant concern of the person who suddenly finds it necessary to depend on others for assistance and support.

If establishing and maintaining a healthy sense of autonomy is a lifelong concern, why has it attracted so much attention among scholars interested in adolescence? When we look at the development of autonomy in relation to the biological, cognitive, and social changes of adolescence, it is easy to see why.

▎ **Puberty and the Development of Autonomy** Consider first the impact of puberty. Some theorists, like Anna Freud (1958), have suggested that the physical changes of early adolescence trigger changes in the young person's emotional relationships at home (Laursen & Collins, 2009; Holmbeck, 1996). Adolescents' interest in turning away from their parents and toward their peers for emotional support—a development that is part of establishing adult independence—may be sparked by their emerging interest in sexual relationships and by their concerns over such things as dating and intimate friendships. In some senses, then, puberty drives the adolescent away from exclusive emotional dependence on the family. Furthermore, the changes in stature and physical appearance occurring

Being able to drive greatly increases adolescents' autonomy from parental control.

at puberty may provoke changes in how much autonomy the young person is granted by parents and teachers. Youngsters who simply look more mature may be given more responsibility by the adults around them.

▎ **Cognitive Change and the Development of Autonomy** The cognitive changes of adolescence also play an important role in the development of autonomy. Part of being autonomous involves being able to make independent decisions. When individuals turn to others for advice, they often receive conflicting opinions. For example, if you are trying to decide between staying home to study for an exam and going out to a party, your professor and the person throwing the party will probably give you different advice. As an adult, you are able to see that each individual's perspective influences his or her advice. The ability to see this, however, calls for a level of intellectual abstraction that is not available until adolescence. Being able to take other people's perspectives into account, to reason in more sophisticated ways, and to foresee the future consequences of alternative courses of action all help the young person to weigh the opinions and suggestions of others more effectively and to reach his or her independent decisions. The cognitive changes of adolescence also provide the logical foundation for changes in the young person's thinking about social, moral, and ethical problems. These changes in thinking are important prerequisites to the development of a system of values based on the individual's own sense of right and wrong, and not merely on rules and regulations handed down by parents or other authority figures (N. Eisenberg et al., 2009; Smetana & Villalobos, 2009).

▌ **Social Roles and the Development of Autonomy**   Finally, changes in social roles and activities during adolescence are bound to raise concerns related to independence, as the adolescent moves into new positions that demand increasing degrees of responsibility and self-reliance (Coatsworth & Conroy, 2009; Larson, Pearce, Sullivan, & Jarrett, 2007). Becoming involved in new roles and taking on new responsibilities, such as having a job or a driver's license, place the adolescent in situations that require and stimulate the development of independent decision making. A teenager might not really think much about the responsibilities associated with taking a job, for example, until she actually ends up in one (D. Wood, Larson, & Brown, 2009). Choosing whether to drink does not become an important question until the adolescent begins to approach the legal drinking age. And deciding what his political beliefs are becomes a more pressing concern when the young person realizes that he will soon have the right to vote.

FOOD FOR THOUGHT

Many psychologists contend that the two periods of life during which autonomy is an especially salient issue are early adolescence and toddlerhood. What do these periods share in common that might account for the importance of autonomy during each?

▌ **Three Types of Autonomy**   We have talked a great deal thus far about the need to develop a sense of autonomy during adolescence. But what does it really mean to be an autonomous or independent person? Psychologists have described autonomy in three ways (McElhaney et al., 2009). The first characterization involves **emotional autonomy**—that aspect of independence related to changes in the individual's close relationships, especially with parents. The second is **behavioral autonomy**—the capacity to make independent decisions and follow through on them. And the third is referred to as **cognitive autonomy** (sometimes called "value autonomy"), which involves having independent values, opinions, and beliefs.

emotional autonomy   The establishment of more adultlike and less childish close relationships with family members and peers.

behavioral autonomy   The capacity to make independent decisions and to follow through with them.

cognitive autonomy   The establishment of an independent set of values, opinions, and beliefs.

RECAP

- Although the development of autonomy is an important psychosocial issue throughout the life span, it is especially salient during adolescence because of the physical, cognitive, and social changes of the period.
- Emotional autonomy (feeling independent) refers to emotional independence in relationships with others, especially parents.
- Behavioral autonomy (acting independently) refers to the development of independent decision-making abilities.
- Cognitive autonomy (thinking independently) concerns the development of independent values, opinions, and beliefs.

The Development of Emotional Autonomy

The relationship between children and their parents changes repeatedly over the course of the life cycle. Changes in the expression of affection, the distribution of power, and patterns of verbal interaction, to give a few examples, are likely to occur whenever important transformations take place in the child's or parents' competencies, concerns, and social roles.

By the end of adolescence, individuals are far less emotionally dependent on their parents than they were as children. We can see this in several ways. First, older adolescents do not generally rush to their parents when they are upset, worried, or in need of assistance. Second, they do not see their parents as all-knowing or all-powerful. Third, they often have a great deal of emotional energy wrapped up in relationships outside the family; in fact, they may feel more attached to a boyfriend or a girlfriend than to their parents. And finally, older adolescents are able to see and interact with their parents as people—not just as their parents. Many parents find, for example, that they can confide in their adolescent children, something that was not possible when their children were younger, or that their adolescent children can easily sympathize with them when they have had a hard day at work. These sorts of changes in the adolescent–parent relationship all reflect the development of emotional autonomy (McElhaney et al., 2009).

EMOTIONAL AUTONOMY AND DETACHMENT

▌ **Psychoanalytic Theory and Detachment**   Early writings about emotional autonomy were influenced by psychoanalytic thinkers such as Anna Freud

(1958), who argued that the physical changes of puberty cause substantial disruption and conflict inside the family system. The reason, Freud believed, is that intrapsychic conflicts that have been repressed since early childhood are reawakened at early adolescence by resurgent sexual impulses. (These conflicts revolve around the young child's unconscious attraction toward the parent of the other sex and ambivalent feelings toward the parent of the same sex.) The reawakened conflicts are expressed as increased tension among family members, an increase in arguments, and a certain degree of discomfort around the house. As a consequence of this tension, early adolescents are driven to separate themselves, at least emotionally, from their parents, and they turn their emotional energies to relationships with peers—in particular, peers of the opposite sex. Psychoanalytic theorists call this process of separation **detachment,** because to them it appears as though the early adolescent is attempting to sever the attachments that have been formed during infancy and strengthened throughout childhood.

Freud and her followers viewed detachment, and the accompanying storm and stress inside the family, as normal, healthy, and inevitable aspects of emotional development during adolescence. In fact, Freud believed that the absence of conflict between an adolescent and his or her parents signified that the young person was having problems growing up.

■ **Research on Detachment**　Studies of adolescents' family relationships have not supported Freud's view, however. In contrast to predictions that high levels of adolescent–parent tension are the norm, that adolescents detach themselves from relationships with their parents, and that adolescents are driven out of the household by unbearable levels of family conflict, every major study done to date of teenagers' relations with their parents has shown that most families get along quite well during the adolescent years (McElhaney et al., 2009). Although parents and adolescents may bicker more often than they did during earlier periods of development, there is no evidence that this bickering significantly diminishes closeness between them in any lasting way (W. A. Collins & Steinberg, 2006; Laursen & Collins, 2009). Most individuals report becoming closer to their parents in late adolescence, especially after they have made the transition into college (Lefkowitz, 2005; McElhaney et al., 2009).

In other words, although teenagers and their parents undoubtedly modify their relationships during adolescence, their emotional bonds are by no means severed. This is an important distinction, for it means that emotional autonomy during adolescence involves a *transformation,* not a breaking off, of family relationships (Guisinger & Blatt, 1994; Laursen & Collins, 2009). In other words, adolescents can become emotionally

In contrast to the view that tension between adolescents and their parents is the norm, every major study done to date of family relations in adolescence has shown that most teenagers and their parents get along quite well.

autonomous from their parents without becoming detached from them (McElhaney et al., 2009). Interestingly, adolescents who are better able to balance autonomy and connectedness in their relationships with their parents are also better able to balance autonomy and intimacy in their romantic relationships (Taradash, Connolly, Pepler, Craig, & Costa, 2002).

EMOTIONAL AUTONOMY AND INDIVIDUATION

As an alternative to the classic psychoanalytic perspective on adolescent detachment, some theorists have suggested that the development of emotional autonomy be looked at in terms of the adolescent's developing sense of **individuation** (Blos, 1967). The process of individuation, which begins during infancy and continues into late adolescence, involves a gradual, progressive sharpening of the young person's sense of self as

detachment　In psychoanalytic theory, the process through which adolescents sever emotional attachments to their parents or other authority figures.

individuation　The progressive sharpening of an individual's sense of being an autonomous, independent person.

autonomous, competent, and separate from her or his parents. Individuation, therefore, has a great deal to do with the development of a sense of identity, in that it involves changes in how adolescents come to see and feel about themselves.

Individuation does not involve stress and turmoil, however. Rather, individuation entails relinquishing childish dependencies on parents in favor of a more mature, more responsible, and less dependent relationship (McElhaney et al., 2009). Adolescents who establish a sense of individuation can accept responsibility for their choices and actions instead of looking to their parents to do it for them. For example, rather than rebelling against her parents' midnight curfew by deliberately staying out later, a girl who has a healthy sense of individuation might take her parents aside before going out and say, "This party tonight may last longer than midnight. If it does, I'd like to stay a bit longer. Suppose I call you at eleven o'clock and let you know when I'll be home?"

RESEARCH ON EMOTIONAL AUTONOMY

Studies that the development of emotional autonomy is a long process, beginning early in adolescence and continuing into young adulthood (McElhaney et al., 2009). In one study (Steinberg & Silverberg, 1986), a questionnaire measuring four aspects of emotional autonomy was administered to a sample of 10- to 15-year-olds. The four components were (1) the extent to which adolescents de-idealized their parents ("My parents sometimes make mistakes"), (2) the extent to which adolescents were able to see their parents as people ("My parents act differently with their own friends than they do with me"), (3) nondependency, or the degree to which adolescents depended on themselves, rather than on their parents, for assistance ("When I've done something wrong, I don't always depend on my parents to straighten things out"), and (4) the degree to which adolescents felt individuated within the relationship with their parents ("There are some things about me that my parents do not know"). As you can see in Figure 9.1, scores on three of the four scales—all except "parents as people"—increased over the age period studied.

Other research has yielded similar findings. In one study, for example, the researchers found that as adolescents aged the number of their friends whom their parents knew declined significantly, reflecting greater individuation and privacy (Feiring & Lewis, 1993). Other studies show that, with age, adolescents become less likely to say that they have the same opinions as their parents or that they always agree with them (McElhaney et al., 2009; Zhang & Fuligni, 2006). This, in turn, is associated with changes in adolescents' beliefs about their parents' authority over them; as you read in

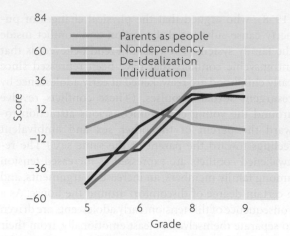

FIGURE 9.1 Age differences in four aspects of emotional autonomy. (Steinberg & Silverberg, 1986)

Chapter 2, adolescents become increasingly likely to draw distinctions between aspects of their life that their parents have the right to regulate and those that they think are not really their parents' business (Darling, Cumsille, & Martinez, 2008; S. A. Perkins & Turiel, 2007).

Important changes in adolescents' emotional relationship with their parents occur as well. For example, one study, which examined adolescent boys' reports of homesickness during summer camp, found that homesickness—which was experienced by youngsters as anxiety and depression—became less prevalent during middle adolescence than it had been in early adolescence or preadolescence (Thurber, 1995). And adolescents' willingness to express negative emotions in front of their parents—for example, anger and sadness—is lower during early adolescence than before or after, perhaps because keeping some emotional distance from one's parents is a part of the individuation process (Zeman & Shipman, 1997).

■ **De-Idealization** Psychologists believe that the de-idealization of parents may be one of the first aspects of emotional autonomy to develop, because adolescents may shed their childish images of their parents before replacing them with more mature ones. Yet, although middle adolescents are less likely than young adolescents to hold onto idealized pictures of their parents, when it comes to seeing their parents as individuals, 15-year-olds are no more emotionally autonomous than are 10-year-olds. In other words, de-idealization is the beginning, not the end, of a long process that gradually leads adolescents to adopt more realistic views of their parents. Even during the high school years, adolescents appear to have some difficulty in seeing their parents as individuals beyond their roles as parents. This aspect of emotional autonomy may not develop until much later—perhaps not until young adulthood (Smollar & Youniss, 1985). Seeing one's parents as

As adolescents develop emotional autonomy, they often begin to question and challenge their parents more frequently.

people also appears to develop later in adolescents' relations with their fathers than with their mothers, because fathers seem to interact less often with their adolescents in ways that permit them to be seen as individuals (Smollar & Youniss, 1985).

FOOD FOR THOUGHT

Why does it take relatively longer for individuals to develop more sophisticated views of their parents as people than it does to develop other types of emotional autonomy?

■ **The Importance of Maintaining the Connection** Interestingly, and in contrast to the old view that adolescents needed to sever their ties with their parents in order to grow up healthily, a number of studies find that the development of emotional autonomy, and individuation in particular, may have different psychological effects on adolescents depending on whether the parent–child relationship is a close one. Adolescents who become emotionally autonomous, but who also feel distant or detached from their parents, score poorly on measures of psychological adjustment, whereas

adolescents who demonstrate the same degree of emotional autonomy, but who still feel close and attached to their parents, are psychologically healthier than their peers (J. Allen, Porter, McFarland, McElhaney, & Marsh, 2007; Lamborn & Steinberg, 1993; Mahoney, Schweder, & Stattin, 2002; R. Ryan & Lynch, 1989).

In one study of Black, Mexican American, and White adolescents, for example, young people from all ethnic groups who reported greater feelings of separation from their parents and higher levels of family conflict (a combination indicative of detachment) also showed increases in alcohol use over time, whereas alcohol use declined among those who reported higher levels of individuation and family cohesion (Bray, Adams, Getz, & Baer, 2001). Taken together, these studies remind us that it is important to distinguish between separating from one's parents in a way that nevertheless maintains emotional closeness in the relationship (which is healthy) and breaking away from one's parents in a fashion that involves alienation, conflict, and hostility (which is unhealthy) (W. Beyers, Goossens, Vansant, & Moors, 2003). Consistent with this, lying to one's parents and concealing undesirable things from them, which may be more an indicator of detachment than of healthy individuation, is associated with psychological problems (Finkenauer, Engels, & Meeus, 2002; Frijns, Finkenauer, Vermulst, & Engels, 2005). Not surprisingly, as individuals make the transition from adolescence into adulthood and work through much of the individuation process, they increasingly see lying to their parents as unacceptable (Jensen, Arnett, Feldman, & Cauffman, 2004).

■ **What Triggers Individuation?** What triggers the process of individuation? Two different models have been suggested (Laursen & Collins, 2009). According to several researchers, puberty is the main catalyst (e.g., Holmbeck, 1996; Steinberg, 2000). Changes in the adolescent's physical appearance provoke changes in the way that adolescents are viewed— by themselves and by their parents—which, in turn, provoke changes in parent–child interaction. As we saw in Chapter 4, shortly after puberty, most families experience an increase in bickering and squabbling. Some writers have suggested that this increase in conflict helps adolescents see their parents in a different light and develop a sense of individuation (Holmbeck & Hill, 1991; Steinberg, 1990). Consistent with this, adolescents' feelings of connectedness to their parents may decline in early adolescence, when bickering is more frequent, but increase in late adolescence after this temporary period of heightened squabbling is over (Pinquart & Silbereisen, 2002).

Other authors believe that adolescents' movement toward higher levels of individuation is stimulated by their social-cognitive development (W. A. Collins, 1990;

Smetana, 1995a). As you read in Chapter 2, social cognition refers to the thinking we do about ourselves and our relationships with others. The development of emotional autonomy in adolescence may be provoked by young people's development of more sophisticated understandings of themselves and their parents. Prior to adolescence, individuals accept their parents' views of themselves as accurate ("My parents think I am a good girl, so I must be"). But as individuals develop more differentiated self-conceptions in early and middle adolescence (as you read in Chapter 8), they come to see that their parents' view is but one of many—and one that may not be entirely accurate ("My parents think I am a good girl, but they don't know what I am really like"). By late adolescence, individuals are able to see that these apparent discrepancies between their self-conceptions and their parents' views are perfectly understandable ("There are sides of me that my parents know and sides of me that they don't") (see Mazor & Enright, 1988).

This is not to suggest that the process of individuation is always a smooth one. Some writers have suggested that as adolescents de-idealize their parents, they may begin to feel both more autonomous and more insecure—what one research team labeled a "double-edged sword" (S. Frank, Pirsch, & Wright, 1990). That is, even though their childish images of their parents as being all-knowing and all-powerful may be inaccurate, the images still provide a degree of emotional comfort. Leaving such images behind can be both liberating and frightening, for parents as well as teenagers. Indeed, some researchers have found that the development of emotional autonomy is associated not only with insecurity among adolescents but also with increased feelings of anxiety and rejection among parents (Hock, Eberly, Bartle-Haring, Ellwanger, & Widaman, 2001; R. Ryan & Lynch, 1989; Steinberg & Steinberg, 1994). Difficulties in the process of individuation may also arise when adolescents push for independence at an earlier age than parents are willing to grant it. One recent study found, for example, that adolescents believe that individuals should be granted autonomy earlier than parents do (Ruck, Peterson-Badali, & Day, 2002).

Several writers have explored the ways in which the process of developing autonomy may differ for adolescents whose parents have divorced (S. Feldman & Quatman, 1988; Sessa & Steinberg, 1991). These writers argue that having divorced parents prompts adolescents to grow up faster—to de-idealize parents at an earlier age, because observing their parents during the process of divorce may reveal their flaws and failings. To the extent that de-idealization of their parents is the first step in the individuation process, adolescents from divorced homes may take that step somewhat earlier than their peers.

EMOTIONAL AUTONOMY AND PARENTING PRACTICES

Whether provoked by puberty or by the development of more advanced cognitive skills, and whether approached with confidence or with trepidation, one fact is certain: Healthy individuation and positive mental health are fostered by close, not distant, family relationships (J. Allen, Hauser, Eickholt, Bell, & O'Connor, 1994; Bomar & Sabatelli, 1996; L. Foster & Ritter, 1995; McElhaney et al., 2009). Tense family relationships during adolescence indicate problems, not positive development (Fuhrman & Holmbeck, 1995). Researchers have found, for example, that adolescents who feel the most autonomous—that is, those who are most likely to feel that they have been granted enough freedom by their parents—are not the ones who have severed relationships at home. In fact, just the opposite is true: Autonomous adolescents report that they are close to their parents, enjoy doing things with their families, have few conflicts with their mothers and fathers, feel free to turn to them for advice, and say they would like to be like their parents (McElhaney et al., 2009). Rebellion, negativism, and excessive involvement in the peer group are more common among psychologically immature adolescents than among mature ones (Steinberg, 1990). Even during college, students who live away from home (which is in its own way a type of autonomy)—as opposed to remaining in their parents' home and commuting to school—report more affection for their parents, better communication, and higher levels of satisfaction in the relationship (Holmbeck, Durbin, & Kung, 1995). In other words, strained family relationships appear to be associated with a *lack* of autonomy during adolescence, rather than with its presence (Bomar & Sabatelli, 1996).

At the same time, adolescents whose parents are emotionally close to the point of being intrusive or overprotective—parents who use a lot of **psychological control**—may have difficulty individuating from them, which may lead to depression, anxiety, and diminished social competence (J. Allen & McElhaney, 2000; Bean, Bush, McKenry, & Wilson, 2003; Holmbeck et al., 2000; Soenens et al., 2007). Adolescents whose parents impede the individuation process are more likely to show signs of anxiety, depression, and other forms of psychological distress (Barber, 1996; Steinberg, 1990; Q. Wang, Pomerantz, & Chen, 2007). Overprotectiveness may be especially harmful for adolescents who are less competent to begin with (Thompson & Zuroff, 1999). As a consequence, the impact of parental psychological control is even more harmful when it is accompanied

psychological control   Parenting that attempts to control the adolescent's emotions and opinions.

by negative self-evaluations by the adolescent; adolescents who do not feel good about themselves and who have very intrusive parents are especially vulnerable to depression (Pomerantz, 2001).

FOOD FOR THOUGHT

Studies show that parents' behavior can help or impede the development of emotional autonomy. Based on what you've read, what advice would you give the parents of a preadolescent in this regard?

▌ Individuation in the Context of Closeness

Psychologists now know that emotional autonomy develops best under conditions that encourage both individuation and emotional closeness. The need for parents to strike the right balance can be seen quite clearly in the work of Joseph Allen, who has studied videotapes of parents and adolescents in discussions and has examined whether certain types of interaction are more or less facilitative of healthy adolescent development (J. Allen & McElhaney, 2000; J. Allen, Hauser, Bell, & O'Connor, 1994; J. Allen, Hauser, O'Connor, Bell, & Eickholt, 1996). In this research, the tapes were coded for two specific types of behavior: "enabling" and "constraining." Parents who use a lot of enabling accept their adolescent and at the same time help the teenager to develop and state his or her own ideas through questions, explanations, and the tolerance of differences of opinion. In contrast, parents high in constraining have difficulty accepting their child's individuality and react to expressions of independent thinking with remarks that are distracting, judgmental, or devaluing. After hearing an adolescent's opinion that differs from his own, for example, an enabling father might ask for more clarification or might genuinely probe the adolescent's logic, whereas a constraining father might cut off further discussion by saying that the adolescent is wrong or ignorant.

Not surprisingly, adolescents whose parents use a great deal of enabling and relatively little constraining are more likely to develop in healthy ways: They are more individuated and score higher on measures of identity development and psychosocial competence. This is in line with other research showing that adolescents fare best when their relationships at home strike the right balance between autonomy and connectedness (L. G. Bell & Bell, 2005; Hodges, Finnegan, & Perry, 1999). Adolescents who grow up in families that inhibit individuation are more likely to report feeling anxious and depressed, while adolescents from families with low levels of closeness are more likely to display behav-

ioral problems, such as poor impulse control (J. Allen et al., 1994; Pavlidis & McCauley, 1995). One study that followed individuals between ages 16 and 25 found that the negative effects of having parents who constrain the development of autonomy during adolescence even persist into young adulthood—adolescents whose parents were overly intrusive were relatively more hostile and angry as young adults (J. Allen, Hauser, O'Connor, & Bell, 2002).

▌ Emotional Autonomy and Parenting Style

As we saw in Chapter 4, adolescents' development is affected differently by different styles of parenting. In particular, independence, responsibility, and self-esteem are all fostered by parents who are authoritative (friendly, fair, and firm) rather than authoritarian (excessively harsh), indulgent (excessively lenient), or indifferent (aloof to the point of being neglectful). At least some of these differences may be related to the development of emotional autonomy in different types of households.

In authoritative families, guidelines are established for the adolescent's behavior, and standards are upheld, but they are flexible and open to discussion. Although parents may have the final say when it comes to their child's behavior, the decision that is reached usually comes after consultation and discussion—with the child included. In discussing an adolescent's curfew, for example, authoritative parents will sit down with their child and explain how they arrived at their decision and why they picked the hour they did. They will also ask the adolescent for his or her suggestions and consider them carefully in making a final decision.

It is not difficult to see why the sort of give-and-take that is found in authoritative families is well suited to the healthy development of emotional autonomy. Because standards and guidelines are flexible and adequately explained, it is not hard for the family to adjust and modify them as the child matures, physically, emotionally, and intellectually (Smetana & Asquith, 1994). Gradual changes in family relations that permit the young person more independence and encourage more responsibility but that do not threaten the emotional bond between parent and child—in other words, changes that promote increasing emotional autonomy—are relatively easy to make for the family that has been flexible and has been making these sorts of modifications in family relationships all along (Vuchinich, Angeletti, & Gatherum, 1996).

In authoritarian households, where rules are rigidly enforced and seldom explained to the child, adjusting to adolescence is more difficult for the family. Authoritarian parents may see the child's increasing emotional independence as rebellious or disrespectful, and they may resist their adolescent's growing need for independence rather than accepting it. For example, authoritarian parents, on seeing that their daughter is becoming interested in boys, may implement a rigid curfew in order to restrict her social life. Instead of encouraging autonomy, authoritarian parents may inadvertently maintain the dependencies of childhood by failing to give their child sufficient practice in making decisions and being responsible for his or her actions. In essence, authoritarian parenting may interfere with adolescent individuation.

When closeness, as well as support for autonomy, is absent, the problems are compounded. In families in which excessive parental control is accompanied by extreme coldness and punitiveness, the adolescent may rebel against parents' standards explicitly, in an attempt to assert her or his independence in a visible and demonstrable fashion. Accordingly, adolescents whose parents refuse to set reasonable curfews are the ones who typically stay out the latest. Such rebellion is not indicative of genuine emotional autonomy, though; it is more likely a demonstration of the adolescent's frustration with his or her parents' rigidity and lack of understanding. And, as noted earlier, when adolescents attempt to establish emotional autonomy within the context of a cold or hostile family, the effect on their mental health is likely to be negative (Lamborn & Steinberg, 1993). In fact, adolescents from hostile or stressful family environments may do best when they actively detach themselves from their parents (Fuhrman & Holmbeck, 1995).

In both indulgent families and indifferent families, a different sort of problem arises. These parents do not provide sufficient guidance for their children, and as a result, the youngsters do not acquire adequate standards for behavior. In the absence of parental guidance and rules, permissively reared teenagers often turn to their peers for advice and emotional support—a practice that can be problematic when the peers are themselves still relatively young and inexperienced. Not surprisingly, adolescents whose parents have failed to provide sufficient guidance are likely to become psychologically dependent on their friends—emotionally detached from their parents, perhaps, but not genuinely autonomous (Steinberg, 1990). The problems of parental permissiveness are exacerbated by a lack of closeness, as is the case in indifferent families.

Some parents who have raised their children permissively until adolescence are caught off guard by the consequences of not having been stricter earlier on. The greater orientation toward the peer group of permissively raised adolescents may involve the young person in behavior that his or her parents disapprove of. As a consequence, some parents who have been permissive throughout a youngster's childhood shift gears when he or she enters adolescence, becoming autocratic in an attempt to control a youngster over whom they feel they have lost control. For instance, parents who have never placed any restrictions on their daughter's afternoon activities during elementary school may suddenly begin monitoring her social life once she enters junior high school. Shifts like these can be extremely hard on adolescents—just at the time when they are seeking greater autonomy, their parents become more restrictive. Having become accustomed to relative leniency, adolescents whose parents change the rules in the middle of the game may find it difficult to accept standards that are being strictly enforced for the first time.

RECAP

- Although adolescence historically has been viewed as a time during which individuals need to break away from and rebel against their parents, research indicates that the growth of emotional autonomy is typically smoother and less tumultuous than stereotypes suggest.
- Instead of emphasizing the young person's need for detachment, contemporary psychologists stress the more gradual process of individuation, which may be triggered by the physical and cognitive changes of early adolescence.
- One of the first signs of individuation may be the adolescent's de-idealization of his or her parents.
- Healthy individuation is fostered by close, not distant, family relationships, with adolescents encouraged to develop and assert their individuality.
- Adolescents who are raised in authoritative homes in which their parents are both accepting and tolerant of the young person's individuality enjoy many psychological advantages over their peers, including a more fully developed sense of emotional autonomy.

The Development of Behavioral Autonomy

Whereas the development of emotional autonomy is played out mainly in adolescents' relationships with their parents, the development of behavioral autonomy—the ability to act independently—is seen both inside and outside the family, in relationships with peers as well as parents. Broadly speaking, behavioral autonomy refers to the capacity for independent decision making. More specifically, researchers who have studied behavioral autonomy have looked at changes in *decision-making abilities*, in *susceptibility to the influence of others*, and in *feelings of self-reliance*.

CHANGES IN DECISION-MAKING ABILITIES

As you read in Chapter 2, the more sophisticated reasoning processes employed by adolescents permit them to hold multiple viewpoints in mind simultaneously, allowing comparisons among the viewpoints to be drawn—an ability that is crucial for weighing the opinions and advice of others. In addition, because adolescents are better able than children to think in hypothetical terms, they are more likely to consider the possible long-term consequences of choosing one course of action over another. And the enhanced role-taking capabilities of adolescence permit teenagers to consider another person's opinion while taking into account that person's perspective. This is important in determining whether someone who gives advice has special areas of expertise, particular biases, or vested interests that the young person should keep in mind. Taken together, these cognitive changes result in improved decision-making skills and, consequently, in the individual's greater ability to behave independently.

Many studies have documented that important improvements in decision-making abilities occur during middle and late adolescence.

■ **Improvements in Decision-Making Abilities** Many studies have documented that important improvements in decision-making abilities occur during middle and late adolescence. With age, adolescents become more likely to consider both the risks and benefits associated with the decisions they make and more likely to weigh the long-term consequences of their choices (Crone & van der Molen, 2007; Halpern-Felsher & Cauffman, 2001; Steinberg, Graham, et al., 2009). These improvements appear to be due to two separate, but related developments.

First, there is a decline over the course of adolescence in the extent to which decisions are influenced by their potential to produce an immediate reward. Most situations in which we have to decide among alternative choices (Should I stay home and study or go out with my friends? Should we sneak into the movie theater or stand in line and pay for tickets? Should I sleep with my girlfriend right now or wait until tomorrow night, when I'll make sure to have a condom?) present a combination of potential rewards and potential costs, and what we decide to do is often the result of how strong those rewards and costs are. You can imagine that someone who is just thinking about having fun with his friends, the prospect of seeing the movie for free, or how good sex is going to feel would act very differently than someone who is thinking about the grade he might get on a test he didn't study for, what would happen if he got caught, or the possibility of getting his girlfriend pregnant.

Recent research has revealed that the ways in which rewards and costs influence decisions change over the course of adolescence. During early adolescence, individuals are much more drawn to the potential benefits

of a decision than the potential costs. As they mature, the relative balance of reward and cost changes, so that by late adolescence, these factors are weighed about evenly (Cauffman et al., 2010). Psychologists have now mapped this development onto changes in patterns of brain activation, showing that the regions of the brain that are especially sensitive to reward are more intensely activated during early and middle adolescence than adulthood (Galvan et al., 2006). In fact, some of the heightened "reward sensitivity" seen among adolescents may not even be conscious (Cauffman et al., 2010). Adolescents are just as consciously aware as adults of the potential rewards and costs of a decision—they are just affected by them differently (Van Leijenhorst, Westenberg, & Crone, 2008).

Not only are younger adolescents more drawn to rewards than are adults, but they also seem especially drawn to *immediate* rewards (Steinberg, 2008). Consider the following question: Would you rather have $200 tomorrow or $1,000 a year from now? How about $600 tomorrow versus $1,000 a year from now? This is a good way to assess how important it is for someone to get a reward immediately, because individuals who are willing to settle for a smaller amount in order to get it sooner are more drawn to immediate rewards. Figure 9.2 shows the amount of money individuals of different ages would settle for if they received it tomorrow rather than waiting a year (Steinberg, Graham, et al., 2009). As you can see, preadolescents and early adolescents are much more willing to settle for less, as long as they can get it sooner.

A second influence on changes in decision making concerns individuals' ability to control their impulses (Steinberg, Albert, et al., 2008). As you know from Chapter 2, regions of the brain that are important for

FIGURE 9.2 Younger adolescents are especially drawn to immediate rewards. This graph shows age differences in the amount of money individuals would settle for if they could have it immediately, versus waiting 1 year for $1,000. (Steinberg, Graham, et al., 2009)

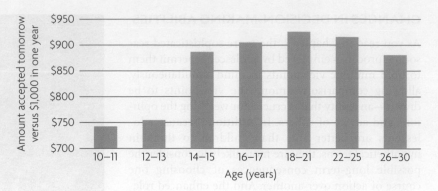

FIGURE 9.3 Age differences in how individuals believe one should respond to a police interrogation when one has committed a crime. (Grisso et al., 2003)

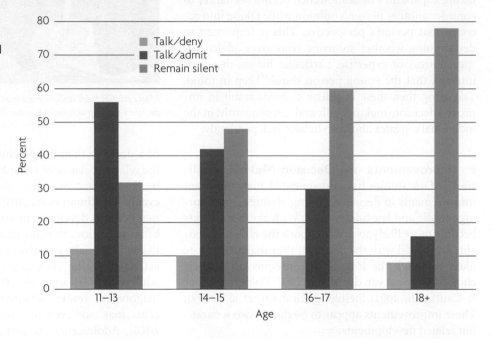

self-regulation are still developing during adolescence and early adulthood. This has important implications for decision making, because it means that, with age, individuals are better at thinking ahead, imagining and analyzing the consequences of their decision, seeking and evaluating the advice of others, and making decisions that are not hasty or excessively influenced by their emotions.

▌ **Legal Decision Making**   One interesting line of research on changes in decision-making abilities has examined adolescents' legal decision making (Grisso et al., 2003; M. G. Schmidt, Reppucci, & Woolard, 2003). In the typical study, adolescents and adults are presented with vignettes involving an individual who had gotten into trouble with the law and asked how the individual should handle different situations—being interrogated by the police, consulting with an attorney, deciding whether to plead guilty in return for a lesser sentence versus going to trial, or taking her or his chances on the outcome. Researchers find that adolescents are less likely than adults to think about the

long-term implications of their decisions, more likely to focus on the immediate consequences, and less able to understand the ways in which other people's positions might bias their interests. For example, when asked what a guilty individual should do when being interrogated by the police, younger adolescents are more likely than adults to say that they should confess (which is not what most attorneys would recommend) rather than remain silent (which most attorneys would say is the most advisable thing to do). The younger adolescents are thinking about the immediate consequences of their actions ("If I tell the police the truth, they'll let me go home"), and not the longer-term implications ("If I confess, this information can be used against me in court) (see Figure 9.3).

WHEN DO ADOLESCENTS MAKE DECISIONS AS WELL AS ADULTS?

The recognition that individuals' decision-making skills improve over the course of adolescence has prompted numerous debates about young people's abilities to make decisions in the real world—for example, with regard to having access to medical care without their parents' approval or functioning as competent defendants in court. Many such debates revolve around where we should draw the legal boundary between adolescence and adulthood (Fagan & Zimring, 2000; Gittler, Quigley-Rick, & Saks, 1990; Steinberg, 2009).

Part of the difficulty in making decisions about where to draw lines between adolescents and adults is that mature decision making is the product of both cognitive abilities (such as being able to reason logically) and psychosocial factors (such as being able to control one's impulses), and these aspects of development appear to proceed along somewhat different timetables (Steinberg, Cauffman, et al., 2009). For example, as you read in Chapter 2, the maturation of basic cognitive abilities is complete at around age 16. On the basis of this, youth advocates have argued that older adolescents should have the right to seek health care services (including abortions and contraception) without parental knowledge or consent (Blum, Resnick, & Stark, 1990; Melton, 1990; Scherer & Gardner, 1990). At the same time, because there are improvements in things like impulse control, planning ahead, and risk assessment well into early adulthood, there is a period during which adolescents may *think* like adults but *behave* in a much more immature way. Individuals who are opposed to trying juvenile offenders as adults use *this* evidence to argue in favor of treating juveniles who have committed crimes less harshly than adults because of their immature judgment (C. S. Fried & Reppucci, 2001; Modecki, 2008; Owen-Kostelnik, Reppucci, & Meyer, 2006; E. Scott & Steinberg, 2008).

One way of resolving this problem is to make sure our treatment of adolescents under the law is aligned with what we know about adolescent development in ways that are specific to the legal matters in question (Steinberg, Cauffman, et al. 2009). In other words, if the skills necessary for one type of decision mature earlier than those necessary for another, it would make sense to have a different age boundary for each.

FOOD FOR THOUGHT

Based on what you have read about changes in decision-making abilities in adolescence, should adolescents be treated like adults under the law? If you were a lawmaker, where would you draw the line for issues concerning access to health care? For issues concerning criminal activity?

Peers have a powerful influence over adolescents' tastes in clothes, hairstyles, and other day-to-day decisions.

CHANGES IN SUSCEPTIBILITY TO INFLUENCE

As adolescents come to spend more time outside the family, the opinions and advice of others—not only peers but adults as well—become more important. For example, at a certain point, adolescents seek the advice of friends rather than their parents concerning how to dress. They may turn to a teacher or guidance counselor for advice about what courses to take in school, instead of bringing such questions home. Understandably, a variety of situations arise in which adolescents may feel that their parents' advice may be less valid than the opinions of others.

There also are issues that might be talked over with more than one person. For example, a teenage girl who is trying to decide whether to take a part-time job after school might discuss the pros and cons with her parents but also ask friends for their advice. When friends and parents disagree, adolescents must reconcile the differences of opinion and reach their own independent conclusions.

In situations in which parents and peers give conflicting advice, do teenagers tend to follow one group more often than the other? Adolescents are often portrayed as being extremely susceptible to the influence of peer pressure—more so than children or young adults—and as being stubbornly resistant to the influence of their parents. But is peer pressure really more potent during adolescence than during other times in the life cycle?

In general, most studies using the question of whether conformity to peers is higher during middle adolescence...

■ **The Influence of Parents and Peers** Researchers have studied conformity and peer pressure during adolescence by putting adolescents in situations in which they must choose either between the wishes of their parents and those of their peers or between their own wishes and those of others—typically, parents or friends. For example, an adolescent might be told to imagine that he and his friends discover the answer sheet to an upcoming test on the floor outside the teachers' lounge. His friends tell him that they should keep it a secret. But the adolescent tells his mother about it, and she advises him to tell the teacher. He then would be asked by the researcher to say what he would do.

In general, studies that contrast parents' and peers' influences indicate that in some situations, peers' opinions are more influential, but that in other situations, parents' opinions are more powerful. Specifically, adolescents are more likely to conform to their peers' opinions when it comes to short-term, day-to-day, and social matters—styles of dress, tastes in music, choices among leisure activities, and so on. This is particularly true during the junior high school and early high school years. When it comes to long-term questions concerning educational or occupational plans, however, or to issues concerning values, religious beliefs, or ethics, teenagers are primarily influenced by their parents (W. A. Collins & Steinberg, 2006). In general, when adolescents' problems center on a relationship with a friend, they turn to a peer, a preference that becomes stronger with age. But adolescents' willingness to turn to an adult for advice with problems—especially those that involve adolescents and their parents—remains very strong and increases as individuals move toward late adolescence. This suggests that older adolescents are quite willing to turn to adult experts whose advice they value (Morrison, Laughlin, Miguel, Smith, & Widaman, 1997; Wintre, Hicks, McVey, & Fox, 1988). In short, adolescents turn for advice to different people in different situations (Finken & Jacobs, 1996).

■ **Responding to Peer Pressure**   Studies that contrast the influence of peers and adults do not really reveal all there is to know about peer pressure, however, because most peer pressure operates when adults are absent—when adolescents are at a party, driving home from school, or hanging out with their friends before dinner. To get closer to this issue, researchers have studied how adolescents respond when they must choose between the pressure of their friends and their own opinions of what to do. For example, an adolescent boy might be asked whether he would go along with his friends' pressure to vandalize some property even though he did not want to do so (e.g., Bámaca & Umana-Taylor, 2006).

In general, most studies using this approach show that conformity to peers is higher during middle adolescence than later adolescence (Steinberg & Monahan, 2007). Some studies find that conformity to peers increases between early and middle adolescence, peaking

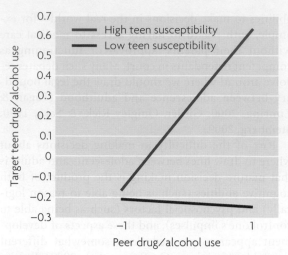

FIGURE 9.4   The consequence of being susceptible to peer pressure depends on the peers one might be influenced by. (Allen et al., 2006)

around age 14, whereas others find no change during this time (T. Sim & Koh, 2003). The heightened susceptibility to peer pressure around age 14 is most often seen when the behavior in question is antisocial—such as cheating, stealing, or trespassing—especially in studies of boys (Erickson, Crosnoe, & Dornbusch, 2000). These findings are in line with studies of delinquent acts, which are often committed by boys in groups, during middle adolescence (Farrington, 2009). Several studies indicate that, compared with their more autonomous friends, adolescents who are more susceptible to peer pressure to engage in delinquent activity actually are more likely to misbehave (Allen, Porter, & McFarland, 2006; Monahan, Steinberg, et al., 2009). Susceptibility to antisocial peer pressure is also higher among relatively more acculturated Latino adolescents than their less acculturated peers, and higher among Latino adolescents who were born in the United States than those who were born abroad, consistent with research showing higher rates of delinquency among more acculturated adolescents (Bámaca & Umaña-Taylor, 2006 Umaña-Taylor & Bámaca-Gómez, 2003; Wall, Power, & Arbiona, 1993). As you would expect, the consequences of being especially susceptible to one's peers depend on who those peers are. For instance, whereas high susceptibility to peer influence predicts adolescents' substance use if their friends are substance users, the same level of susceptibility is not predictive of substance use if their friends are not (J. Allen et al., 2006) (Figure 9.4).

One interesting application of research on adolescents' susceptibility to social pressure concerns adolescents' false confessions to police officers. In several well-publicized cases involving adolescents who had confessed to crimes—such as the case of the Central Park jogger, in which a group of adolescents confessed to assaulting a woman who was running through the

New York City park—it was subsequently discovered that the juveniles had given false confessions to the police (Kassin, 2008). Although most of us find it hard to understand why someone would confess to a crime that he or she did not commit, studies that simulate police interrogations have found that it is not at all unusual for adolescents to do so when questioned under pressure. In one such study (Redlich & Goodman, 2003), subjects of different ages participated in an experiment that involved typing letters on a computer as they were read by the experimenter. Before beginning the experiment, subjects were instructed not to touch the ALT key, because doing so would crash the computer and ruin the experiment. The experiment was rigged, however, so that the computer would crash after a set amount of time, even without the subject's touching the ALT key. After the computer crashed, the experimenter questioned the subjects about whether they had hit the ALT key. When subjects denied doing so, the experimenter presented false evidence "proving" that the ALT key had been pressed. The subjects were then questioned once again about what they had done. In the face of false evidence, significantly more young adolescents (ages 12–16) than young adults confessed to having hit the ALT key, even when they actually had not (see Figure 9.5).

Although we know that conformity to peer pressure is greater during early adolescence than before or after, it is not clear why this is so. One interpretation is that adolescents are more susceptible to peer influence during this time because of their heightened orientation toward the peer group. Because they care more about what their friends think of them, they are more likely to go along with the crowd to avoid being rejected (W. A. Collins & Steinberg, 2006). Consistent with this, in a recent experimental study, adolescents who were led to believe they were interacting in a chat room with either high-status or low-status peers (manipulated by the experimenters in the way the peers' interests were described) about the acceptability of various illegal or risky behaviors were more influenced by the opinions of high-status peers (G. L. Cohen & Prinstein, 2006). This heightened conformity to peer pressure during early adolescence may be a sign of a sort of emotional "way station" between becoming emotionally autonomous from parents and becoming a genuinely autonomous person (Steinberg & Silverberg, 1986). In other words, these adolescents may become emotionally autonomous from their parents before they are emotionally ready for this degree of independence and may turn to peers to fill this void.

A different version of the same story focuses on changes in the sheer strength of peer pressure. For instance, individuals' susceptibility to peer pressure may remain constant over adolescence even as the peer pressure itself strengthens and then weakens over the

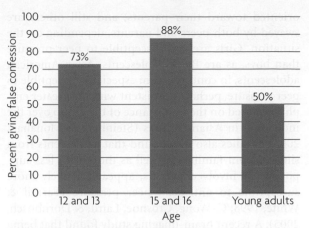

FIGURE 9.5 In a controlled experiment, adolescents were more likely than adults to provide false confessions when confronted with fake "evidence" that they had made a computer crash when they actually had not. (Redlich & Goodman, 2003)

period. Early adolescent peer groups may exert more pressure on their members to conform than do groups of younger or older individuals, and the pressure may be strong enough to make even the most autonomous teenagers comply. Although this is an attractive alternative explanation—particularly to adolescents who appeal to their parents by saying, "No one will talk to me if I don't do it!"—studies have not borne it out. In fact, peer pressure to misbehave seems to increase steadily throughout adolescence, beyond the age at which it would be expected to diminish (Brown et al., 1986).

When we put together the research about peer pressure, peer conformity, and parental conformity, the following picture emerges: During childhood, boys and girls are highly oriented toward their parents and far less oriented toward their peers, and peer pressure is not especially strong. As they approach adolescence, children become somewhat less oriented toward their parents and more oriented toward their peers, and peer pressure begins to escalate. As a result, during preadolescence, there is little net gain in behavioral autonomy—overall levels of conformity do not change, but the source of influence shifts. During early adolescence, conformity to parents continues to decline, and peer pressure continues to rise. It is not until middle adolescence that genuine increases in behavioral autonomy occur, for it is during this time (between the 9th and 12th grades) that conformity both to parents and to peers declines even though peer pressure continues to increase.

■ **Individual Differences in Susceptibility to Peer Influence** Within a group of teenagers of the same age, of course, some are highly autonomous, others are easily influenced by their peers, others are oriented toward their parents, and still others are swayed by both peers and parents, depending on the situation. Girls are less susceptible to peer pressure than boys, as are Black adolescents. Asian American adolescents, in contrast, seem especially susceptible to peer pressure, perhaps consistent with the greater emphasis placed on the importance of the group over the individual in Asian cultures (Steinberg & Monahan, 2007). Studies also have found that adolescents from single-parent families, as well as those with less supportive or involved parents, appear relatively more susceptible to antisocial peer pressure (Farrell & White, 1998; C. Wong, Crosnoe, Laird, & Dornbusch, 2003). A recent brain-imaging study found that being able to resist peer pressure is associated with stronger connections between regions of the brain active during decision making and other brain regions, suggesting, perhaps, that individuals who are more likely to stand up to their friends may be able to better control the sort of impulsive, emotional decision making that often occurs in the peer group (Grosbras et al., 2007; Paus, Toro, et al., 2008). This is consistent with the idea that a key aspect of positive development in adolescence involves the development of self-regulation (Gestdóttir & Lerner, 2007; Monahan, Steinberg, Cauffman, & Mulvey, 2009).

Like emotional autonomy, behavioral autonomy appears to be associated with authoritative rather than permissive, authoritarian, or neglectful parenting (W. A. Collins & Steinberg, 2006). Consistent with this, the sexual behavior of adolescents who have discussed sex with their parents is less influenced by peer pressure than is the behavior of adolescents who have not done so (Whitaker & Miller, 2000), and adolescents whose parents strongly disapprove of smoking are less likely to be influenced by their friends' smoking than are adolescents whose parents do not voice their disapproval (Sargent & Dalton, 2001).

The situation may be somewhat more complicated than this, however. It turns out that the impact of having authoritative parents on adolescents' susceptibility to peer pressure depends on the nature of the peer pressure in question. Adolescents from authoritative homes are less susceptible to antisocial peer pressure, but they may be *more* susceptible to the influence of positive peers. Adolescents from authoritative homes, for example, are less likely than other teenagers to be influenced by having drug-using friends, but they are more likely than their peers to be influenced by having friends who perform well in school (Mounts & Steinberg, 1995). It is also important to distinguish between adolescents who are excessively dependent on their peers (and who forgo their parents' rules and pay less attention to their schoolwork for the sake of being popular with peers) and those who turn to peers for counsel but do not ignore their parents' guidance (Fuligni, Eccles,

Barber, & Clements, 2001). Substituting peers for parents leads to problem behavior; adding peers to the list of persons to whom the adolescent turns for advice, so long as that list includes parents, does not. In other words, it is detachment from parents, rather than attachment to peers, that is potentially harmful.

The ways in which parents and adolescents negotiate changes in behavioral autonomy have implications for adolescents' adjustment, according to several studies (e.g., Fuligni & Eccles, 1993; S. Goldstein, Davis-Kean, & Eccles, 2005; T. Sim, 2000). Not surprisingly, adolescents who have less positive relationships with their parents are more likely to be especially peer oriented, to affiliate with negative peers, and to spend time with friends in unsupervised settings, all of which heighten adolescents' risk for problem behavior. But studies also show that parents need to maintain a healthy balance between asserting control and granting autonomy. Generally, granting too much autonomy before adolescents are ready for it *or* granting too little autonomy once adolescents are mature enough to handle it creates adolescents who are the most strongly peer oriented. Adolescents whose parents become more authoritarian (that is, stricter and less likely to permit the adolescent to make decisions) over time are the most peer oriented of all. Although many parents clamp down on their teenagers' independence out of fear that not doing so will allow the youngsters to fall under the "evil" influence of the peer group, this strategy often backfires. Evidently, having parents limit their autonomy at just the time when more independence is desired and expected makes adolescents turn away from the family and toward their friends.

ETHNIC AND CULTURAL DIFFERENCES IN EXPECTATIONS FOR AUTONOMY

The development of behavioral autonomy varies across cultures because of differences in the age expectations that adolescents and parents have for independent behavior. Psychologist Shirley Feldman and colleagues have examined this issue by asking parents and adolescents from both Asian and White backgrounds to fill out a "teen timetable"—a questionnaire that asks at what age adolescents should be permitted to engage in various behaviors that signal autonomy (for example, "spend money however you want," "go out on dates," "go to rock concerts with friends") (S. Feldman & Wood, 1994). In general, White adolescents and their parents living in America, Australia, or Hong Kong have earlier expectations for adolescent autonomy than do Asian adolescents and parents from these same countries (S. Feldman & Quatman, 1988; Rosenthal & Feldman, 1990). Because of this, adolescents from Asian families may be less likely to seek autonomy from their parents than their White counterparts. And perhaps because of this, whereas individuation tends to be associated with higher self-esteem among American youth, it is associated with lower self-esteem among Asian adolescents (Chun & MacDermid, 1997). In general, though, adolescents' mental health is best when their desire for autonomy matches their expectations for what their parents are willing to grant (Juang, Lerner, McKinney, & von Eye, 1999).

Surprisingly, in these studies of expectations for behavioral autonomy, there were neither sex nor birth order differences in age expectations—contrary to the popular beliefs that boys expect more autonomy than girls and that later-born adolescents are granted earlier freedom because their older siblings have paved the way. There are sex and birth order differences in the extent to which parents grant autonomy, but the pattern varies depending on the particular constellation of sons and daughters in the household and on the parents' attitudes toward sex roles. Although it is generally thought that parents are more controlling of daughters than sons, this is more likely to be the case in households where parents have traditional views of gender roles (Bumpus, Crouter, & McHale, 2001). Sex differences in the extent to which adolescents are granted independence appear to be especially pronounced within Black households, where, compared to other ethnic groups, boys are given relatively more freedom but girls are given less (Bulcroft, Carmody, & Bulcroft, 1996; Daddis & Smetana, 2005). And, contrary to expectations, parents grant more autonomy to firstborns than to second-borns, especially when the firstborn is a girl and the second-born is a boy (Bumpus et al., 2001). In addition, adolescents who feel older seek more independence than their same-aged peers who feel younger (Galambos, Kolaric, & Maggs, 1994).

Interestingly, the autonomy-granting timetable of families that have emigrated from a culture relatively slower to grant adolescents autonomy to a culture in which autonomy is granted sooner falls somewhere between the two extremes; this has been found in studies of Chinese immigrants in both America and Australia (Rosenthal & Feldman, 1990) and of East German immigrants in the former West Germany (Silbereisen & Schmitt-Rodermund, 1995). One problem facing many families that have immigrated to a new culture is that parents and adolescents may have very different expectations for what an appropriate timetable is with respect to granting autonomy—although this will depend, of course, on the degree of discrepancy in timetables in the initial and new contexts. But, as a rule, because adolescents generally acculturate more quickly to a new culture than do parents, a family that has moved from a culture in which it is normal to grant autonomy relatively later in adolescence (as in most Asian countries) to one in which it is normal to grant autonomy rela-

tively earlier (as in the United States) may experience conflict as a result of differences in the expectations of adolescents and parents (Kwak, 2003).

FOOD FOR THOUGHT

Suppose you were writing a book for parents of teenagers. What special advice would you give to parents who have recently moved to the United States about coping with peer pressure?

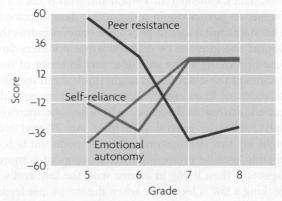

CHANGES IN FEELINGS OF SELF-RELIANCE

A third approach to the study of behavioral autonomy focuses on adolescents' own judgments of how autonomous they are. When adolescents of different ages are asked to complete standardized tests of self-reliance, for example, the results show that subjective feelings of autonomy increase steadily over the adolescent years and that adolescent girls report feeling more self-reliant than do adolescent boys (W. A. Collins & Steinberg, 2006); girls also are better able to resist peer pressure, consistent with the idea that girls mature psychosocially earlier than boys in general (Steinberg & Monahan, 2007). This is especially interesting in light of the findings concerning susceptibility to peer pressure, discussed earlier, since it indicates that adolescents may describe themselves as gaining in self-reliance during a period when their susceptibility to peer pressure may be increasing (see Figure 9.6). Although adults may view adolescents' giving in to peer pressure as a sign of diminished autonomy, adolescents may not see their own behavior in this light. Not surprisingly, adolescents who have a stronger sense of self-reliance report higher self-esteem and fewer behavior problems (Owens, Mortimer, & Finch, 1996; S. Wolfe & Truxillo, 1996).

FIGURE 9.6   Age differences in three types of autonomy. (Steinberg & Silverberg, 1986)

RECAP

- As individuals mature, they become better able to seek out and weigh the advice of individuals with different degrees of expertise and to use this information in making independent decisions.
- One controversy involves whether adolescents' decision-making abilities are mature enough to warrant their treatment as adults under the law.
- Although adolescence is a time of advances in decision-making abilities, during early adolescence, youngsters are particularly susceptible to peer pressure, especially on issues concerning day-to-day activities.
- Susceptibility to peer pressure is high during early adolescence but decreases over the high school years.
- Adolescents whose parents are extremely authoritarian or extremely permissive are the most easily influenced by their friends, especially in antisocial contexts.
- Adolescents do not experience this increased susceptibility to peer pressure as a decline in self-reliance. In fact, self-reports of self-reliance increase steadily throughout adolescence.

The Development of Cognitive Autonomy

The development of cognitive autonomy entails changes in the adolescent's beliefs, opinions, and values and has been studied mainly by looking at how adolescents think about moral, political, and religious issues. Three trends in the development of cognitive autonomy during adolescence are especially noteworthy. First, adolescents become increasingly abstract in the way they think about moral, political, and religious issues. Consider an 18-year-old who is deciding whether to participate in a disruptive demonstration in his state capital against policies he believes indirectly support the interests of environmental polluters. Instead of looking at the situation only in terms of the specifics of the situation, he might think about the implications of knowingly violating the law in general. Second, during adolescence, beliefs become increasingly rooted in general principles. An 18-year-old might say that demonstrating against pollution is acceptable because protecting the environment is more important than living in accord with the law, and so breaking a law is legitimate when the status quo leads to environmental degradation. Finally, beliefs become increasingly founded in the young person's own values,

and not merely in a system of values passed on by parents or other authority figures. Thus, an 18-year-old may look at the issue of environmental protection in terms of what he himself believes, rather than in terms of what his parents have told him to think.

Much of the growth in cognitive autonomy can be traced to the cognitive changes characteristic of the period. With adolescents' enhanced reasoning capabilities and the further development of hypothetical thinking come a heightened interest in ideological and philosophical matters and a more sophisticated way of looking at them. The ability to consider alternate possibilities and to engage in thinking about thinking allows for the exploration of differing value systems, political ideologies, personal ethics, and religious beliefs.

But the growth of cognitive autonomy is encouraged by the development of emotional and behavioral independence as well. As we shall see, some evidence suggests that the development of cognitive autonomy occurs later (between ages 18 and 20) than does the development of emotional or behavioral autonomy, which take place during early and middle adolescence (W. A. Collins & Steinberg, 2006). The establishment of emotional autonomy provides adolescents with the ability to look at their parents' views more objectively. When young people no longer see their parents as omnipotent and infallible authorities, they may seriously reevaluate the ideas and values that they accepted without question as children. Not surprisingly, individuals with a stronger sense of cognitive autonomy show more maturity in other psychological domains as well, such as in the realms of identity development and self-awareness (Hart & Chmeil, 1992; Hart & Fegley, 1995).

As adolescents begin to test the waters of independence behaviorally, they may experience a variety of cognitive conflicts caused by having to compare the advice of parents and friends and having to deal with competing pressures to behave in different ways. These conflicts may prompt young people to consider in more serious and thoughtful terms what they really believe. For example, during adolescence, individuals become increasingly likely to say that it is permissible to lie to one's parents about disobeying them when they think their parents' advice is immoral (for instance, if the parents had forbidden their teenager to date someone from another race) (S. A. Perkins & Turiel, 2007). This struggle to clarify values, provoked in part by the exercise of behavioral autonomy, is a key component of the process of developing a sense of cognitive autonomy.

MORAL DEVELOPMENT DURING ADOLESCENCE

Moral development has been the most widely studied aspect of cognitive autonomy during adolescence. The study of moral development involves both reasoning (how individuals think about moral dilemmas) and behavior (how they behave in situations that call for moral judgments). Related to this is the study of **prosocial behavior,** the behaviors individuals engage in to help others.

▌ **Assessing Moral Reasoning**   The dominant theoretical viewpoint in the study of moral reasoning has been a perspective grounded in Piaget's theory of cognitive development. As you will recall from the discussion in Chapter 2 of changes in thinking processes during adolescence, the emphasis within the Piagetian view, or cognitive-developmental perspective, is on changes in the structure and organization of thought, rather than on changes in its content. Theories of morality that stem from the cognitive-developmental viewpoint similarly emphasize shifts in the type of reasoning that individuals use in making moral decisions, rather than changes in the content of the decisions they reach or the actions they take as a result. Although the initial formulation of the cognitive-developmental perspective on morality was presented by Piaget himself, the theory was subsequently expanded by Lawrence Kohlberg, and it is Kohlberg's work that is more relevant to the study of moral development during adolescence (N. Eisenberg et al., 2009; Smetana & Villalobos, 2009).

Researchers assess individuals' levels of moral reasoning by examining their responses to hypothetical moral dilemmas about difficult, real-world situations. These dilemmas are presented either in an interview, in which case the adolescents' responses are recorded, transcribed, and coded (Gibbs, Basinger, Grime, & Snarney, 2007), or in a questionnaire, in which adolescents respond to the dilemmas in a multiple-choice format (Rest, Narvaez, Bebeau, & Thoma, 1999). Here are examples of the sorts of dilemmas researchers have used:

> Judy was a 12-year-old girl. Her mother promised her that she could go to a special rock concert coming to their town if she saved up from babysitting and lunch money to buy a ticket to the concert. She managed to save up the $15 the ticket cost plus another $5. But then her mother changed her mind and told Judy that she had to spend the money on new clothes for school. Judy was disappointed and decided to go to the concert anyway. She bought a ticket and told her mother that she had only been able to save $5. That Saturday she went to the performance and told her mother that she was spending the day with a friend. A week passed without her mother finding out. Judy then told her older sister, Louise, that she had gone to the performance and had lied to her mother about it. Louise wonders whether to tell their mother what Judy did.
>
> Should Louise, the older sister, tell their mother that Judy lied about the money, or should she keep quiet?

Two young men, brothers, had got into serious trouble. They were secretly leaving town in a hurry and needed money. Karl, the older one, broke into a store and stole $1,000. Bob, the younger one, went to a retired old man who was known to help people in town. He told the man that he was very sick and that he needed $1,000 to pay for an operation. Bob asked the old man to lend him the money and promised that he would pay him back when he recovered. Really, Bob wasn't sick at all, and he had no intention of paying the man back. Although the old man didn't know Bob very well, he lent him the money. So Bob and Karl skipped town, each with $1,000.

> Which is worse, stealing like Karl or cheating like Bob?

Perhaps Kohlberg's best-known dilemma involved a man who had to choose between stealing a drug to save his wife or letting his wife remain mortally ill:

> In Europe, a woman was near death from a very bad disease, a special kind of cancer. There was one drug that the doctors thought might save her. It was a form of radium that a druggist in the same town had recently discovered. The drug was expensive to make, but the druggist was charging 10 times what the drug cost him to make. He paid $200 for the radium and charged $2,000 for a small dose of the drug. The sick woman's husband, Heinz, went to everyone he knew to borrow the money, but he could only get together about $1,000, which was half of what it cost. He told the druggist that his wife was dying, and asked him to sell it cheaper or let him pay later. But the druggist said, "No, I discovered the drug and I'm going to make money from it." Heinz got desperate and broke into the man's store to steal the drug for his wife. Should the husband have done that? Was it right or wrong?

▌ **Stages of Moral Reasoning**   According to Kohlberg, whether or not you think that Heinz should have stolen the drug, or that Louise should tell her mother, or that cheating someone is worse than stealing from a store is less important than the reasoning behind your answers. Kohlberg theorized that individuals' reasoning about moral issues becomes more sophisticated with development. Specifically, Kohlberg suggested that there are three levels of moral reasoning: **preconventional moral reasoning,** which is dominant during most of childhood; **conventional moral reasoning,** which is usually dominant during late childhood and early

prosocial behavior   Behaviors intended to help others.

preconventional moral reasoning   According to Kohlberg, the first level of moral reasoning, which is typical of children and is characterized by reasoning that is based on rewards and punishments associated with different courses of action.

conventional moral reasoning   According to Kohlberg, the second level of moral development, which occurs during late childhood and early adolescence and is characterized by reasoning that is based on the rules and conventions of society.

The ways in which individuals think about moral dilemmas change during adolescence.

adolescence; and **postconventional moral reasoning** (sometimes called principled moral reasoning), which emerges sometime during the adolescent or young adult years.

Preconventional thinking is characterized by reference to external and physical events. Preconventional moral decisions are not based on society's standards, rules, or conventions (hence the label *pre*conventional). Children at this stage approach moral dilemmas in ways that focus on the rewards and punishments associated with different courses of action. One preconventional child might say that Heinz should not have stolen the drug because he could have been caught and sent to jail. Another might say that Heinz was right to steal the drug because people would have been angry with him if he had let his wife die. In either case, the chief concern to the preconventional thinker is what would happen to Heinz as a result of his choice.

Conventional thinking about moral issues focuses not so much on tangible rewards and punishments as

on how an individual will be judged by others for behaving in a certain way. In conventional moral reasoning, special importance is given to the roles people are expected to play and to society's rules, institutions, and conventions. Individuals behave properly because, in so doing, they receive the approval of others and help to maintain the social order. The correctness of society's rules is not questioned, however—individuals do their duty by upholding and respecting the social order. A conventional thinker might say that Heinz should not have stolen the drug because stealing is against the law. But another might counter that Heinz was right to steal the drug because it is what a good husband is expected to do. According to most studies of moral reasoning, the majority of adolescents and adults think primarily in conventional terms—they evaluate moral decisions in terms of a set of rules that people are supposed to abide by.

Postconventional reasoning is relatively rare. At this level of reasoning, society's rules and conventions are seen as relative and subjective rather than as absolute and definitive. Individuals may have a moral duty to abide by society's standards for behavior—but only insofar as those standards support and serve moral ends. Thus, occasions arise in which conventions ought to be questioned and when more important principles—such as justice, fairness, or the sanctity of human life—take precedence over established social norms. For instance, a postconventional response might be that Heinz should not have stolen the drug because in doing so he violated an implicit agreement among members of society—an agreement that gives each person the freedom to pursue his or her livelihood. However, another principled thinker might respond that Heinz was right to steal the drug because someone's life was at stake and because preserving human life is more important than respecting individual freedoms. Whereas conventional thinking is oriented toward society's rules, postconventional thinking is founded on more broadly based abstract principles. For this reason, the development of postconventional reasoning is especially relevant to the discussion of cognitive autonomy.

Studies have confirmed Kohlberg's suggestion that moral reasoning becomes more principled over the course of childhood and adolescence and that modal development appears to proceed through the sequence described in Kohlberg's theory (N. Eisenberg et al., 2009). Preconventional reasoning dominates the responses of children; conventional responses begin to appear during preadolescence and continue into middle adolescence; and postconventional reasoning does not appear until late adolescence, if at all. According to Kohlberg's theory, movement into higher stages of moral reasoning occurs when the adolescent is developmentally "ready"—when his or her reasoning is predominantly at one stage but partially at the next higher

postconventional moral reasoning   In Kohlberg's theory, the stage of moral development during which society's rules and conventions are seen as relative and subjective rather than as authoritative; also called principled moral reasoning.

one—and when he or she is exposed to the more advanced type of reasoning by other people, such as parents or peers (N. Eisenberg et al., 2009). The development of moral reasoning tends to follow a pattern in which individuals move from periods of consolidation (in which their reasoning is consistently at a particular stage of development), into periods of transition (in which there is more variability in their stages of reasoning), into new periods of consolidation (in which their reasoning is consistent, but at a higher stage than during the previous period of consolidation) (L. Walker, Gustafson, & Hennig, 2001).

As is the case with formal operations, the most advanced stage of thinking described by Piaget (see Chapter 2), not all individuals develop the capacity to engage in postconventional moral reasoning. Advanced levels of moral reasoning are more common among children raised in authoritative families in which parents encourage their child to participate in family discussions, in which the level of conflict in family discussions is neither extremely low nor extremely high, and in which parents expose the adolescent to moral arguments that are fashioned at a higher stage than her or his own (N. Eisenberg et al., 2009). There is also some evidence that the development of advanced moral reasoning among Black youth is facilitated by commitment to traditional African values of spirituality and community (Woods & Jagers, 2003).

Although not all individuals enter a stage of postconventional thinking during adolescence, many begin to place greater emphasis on abstract values and moral principles (Rest et al., 1999). Moreover, if individuals of different ages are presented with other peoples' moral arguments, older individuals are more often persuaded by arguments that in Kohlberg's framework are more advanced. Thus, the appeal of postconventional moral reasoning increases over the course of adolescence, while the appeals of preconventional and of conventional reasoning both decline. Interestingly, the appeal of postconventional thinking appears to increase both with age and with schooling; most adults reach a plateau in moral reasoning after completing their formal education. Although for many years psychologists debated whether there were sex differences in the way that individuals approach moral problems, and many popular books were based on the idea that men and women think differently about ethical issues, studies have not supported this (Smetana & Villalobos, 2009).

Moral Reasoning and Moral Behavior   It is one thing to reason about hypothetical moral problems in an advanced way; it is quite another to behave in strict accordance with one's reasoning. After all, it is common for people to say one thing (for example, cheating on a test is immoral) but do another (for example, sneak a peek at a classmate's test when running out of time during an exam). Some critics have argued that although Kohlberg's theory may provide a window on how people think about abstract and hypothetical dilemmas, or about life-and-death situations, as in the Heinz story, it does not tell us very much about the ways people reason about day-to-day problems or behave when they find themselves in situations that might evoke moral considerations.

As it turns out, research on Kohlberg's theory has answered these criticisms fairly well. As for the first of these concerns, for example, research indicates that people reason about life-and-death dilemmas in ways that parallel their reasoning about the moral dilemmas they actually encounter in everyday life (N. Eisenberg et al., 2009). And as for the second of these concerns, many studies indicate that individuals' behavior is related to the ways in which they reason about hypothetical moral dilemmas. Although individuals do not always behave in ways that are absolutely consistent with their moral reasoning, on average, individuals who reason at higher stages behave in more moral ways. For example, individuals who are capable of reasoning at higher stages of moral thought are less likely to commit antisocial acts, less likely to cheat, and less likely to bow to the pressures of others, as well as being more tolerant, more likely to engage in political protests, more likely to engage in volunteer activities, and more likely to assist others in need of help. They are also more likely to be influential over their friends in group decisions about moral problems (Gummerum, Keller, Takezawa, & Mata, 2008). Conversely, those who reason at lower stages of moral thought are more aggressive, delinquent, accepting of violence, and tolerant of others' misbehavior (N. Eisenberg et al., 2009; Stams et al., 2006).

FOOD FOR THOUGHT

Should schools attempt to facilitate adolescents' moral development as a part of their curriculum? If so, what sorts of activities would be most useful?

Of course, moral behavior and moral reasoning do not always go hand in hand. Most of us have found ourselves in situations in which we behaved less morally than we would have liked to. Accordingly, we should not expect moral behavior to follow exactly from moral reasoning, because other factors complicate moral decision making. In tests measuring moral reasoning, assessments are made in a social vacuum, but such vacuums rarely exist in the real world. For example, you probably realize in the abstract that complying with highway speed limits is important because such limits prevent accidents, and you may obey these limits most of the time. But you may have found yourself in a situation in which you weighed your need to get somewhere in a hurry (perhaps you were late for an important job interview) against your moral belief in the importance of obeying speeding laws, and you decided that in this instance you would behave in a way inconsistent with your belief. Situational factors influence moral choices, and they also influence moral reasoning. When individuals perceive that they will be severely hurt by behaving in a morally advanced way (for example, if standing up for someone will lead to severe punishment), they are less likely to reason at a higher moral level (Sobesky, 1983). Moral reasoning is an important influence on moral behavior, but it cannot be considered out of context.

The correlation between adolescents' moral reasoning and their moral behavior is especially likely to break down when they define issues as personal choices rather than ethical dilemmas (for instance, when using drugs is seen as a personal matter rather than a moral issue). This observation turns out to be especially important for understanding why adolescents' moral reasoning and risk taking are for the most part unrelated (N. Eisenberg et al., 2009). If individuals consider various risky behaviors (for example, experimenting with drugs, having unprotected sex) to be personal decisions rather than moral choices, their moral reasoning will be relatively unimportant in predicting how they will act. In other words, individuals are more likely to engage in risky behavior (even if it is unethical) when they see the behavior as a matter of personal taste rather than a question of right and wrong. It is not clear, however, whether viewing risk taking as a personal choice is likely to lead to more risk taking, or whether individuals, once they've engaged in a risky activity, are likely to redefine the issue as a personal rather than moral one, as a way of justifying their behavior after the fact. In either case, this suggests that interventions designed to stimulate moral reasoning will have little impact on adolescents' risk taking if they fail to convince adolescents that the behavior in question involves a moral and not just a personal choice. Delinquency and aggression are also more common among adolescents who score higher on measures of **moral disengagement** (the tendency to rationalize immoral behavior as legitimate, as when one justifies stealing from someone as a way of retaliating) (Paciello, Fida, Tramontano, Lupinetti, & Caprara, 2008).

PROSOCIAL REASONING, PROSOCIAL BEHAVIOR, AND VOLUNTEERISM

▌ **Changes in Prosocial Reasoning** Although most research on the development of morality has focused on what adolescents do under circumstances in

which a law might be broken or a rule violated, researchers have increasingly turned their attention to the study of reasoning and behavior in prosocial situations. In general, the ways in which individuals think about prosocial phenomena, such as honesty or kindness, become more sophisticated during late adolescence (N. Eisenberg et al., 2009; Killen & Turiel, 1998). Over the course of adolescence, for example, individuals come to devalue prosocial acts that are done for self-serving reasons (for example, receiving a reward, returning a favor, or improving their image) and value those that are done out of genuine empathy for others, a pattern that has been observed across a variety of cultures (N. Eisenberg et al., 2009). During late adolescence, prosocial reasoning becomes increasingly advanced, leveling off sometime in the early 20s (N. Eisenberg, Cumberland, Guthrie, Murphy, & Shepard, 2005).

Several researchers have asked whether moral and prosocial reasoning is facilitated by certain types of parenting. Generally, the same type of parenting that facilitates the growth of healthy emotional autonomy, discussed earlier, also contributes to the development of prosocial reasoning. Adolescents whose parents engage them in discussion, elicit their point of view, and practice authoritative parenting display more advanced reasoning than their peers (N. Eisenberg et al., 2009).

▌ **Prosocial Reasoning and Prosocial Behavior** Adolescents who show more advanced reasoning behave in ways that are consistent with this. For example, exemplary youth—adolescents who have volunteered considerable amounts of time in service activities—score higher on measures of moral reasoning than do their peers, are more committed to the betterment of society, and, as children, were made aware of the suffering of those who are less fortunate (Hart & Fegley, 1995; Matsuba & Walker, 2005; Yates & Youniss, 1996). Individuals who score high on measures of prosocial moral reasoning also have been shown to be more sympathetic and empathic (N. Eisenberg, Carlo, Murphy, & Van Court, 1995), to engage in more prosocial behavior (N. Eisenberg, Zhou, & Koller, 2001), and to be less likely to behave violently after having witnessed violence themselves (Brookmeyer, Henrich, & Schwab-Stone, 2005). In general, female adolescents score higher on measures of prosocial moral reasoning than do male adolescents, as do both males and females who are relatively more feminine (Carlo, Koller, Eisenberg, Da Silva, & Frohlick, 1996; N. Eisenberg et al., 1995, 2001).

Although, as noted earlier, prosocial reasoning becomes more advanced over the course of adolescence, research on changes in prosocial *behavior* during adolescence is not as consistent. Some studies find that individuals become more empathic, sympathetic, and helpful as they move into and through adolescence, but

moral disengagement Rationalizing immoral behavior as legitimate, as a way of justifying one's own bad acts.

many do not (N. Eisenberg et al., 2009), and some have found that adolescents become *less* helpful toward others over the high school years (Carlo, Crockett, Randall, & Roesch, 2007). More consistent are research findings indicating that prosocial behavior is fairly stable over time and that individuals who are relatively more prosocial tend to behave this way across different contexts (that is, adolescents who are helpful to classmates in school are more likely than their less prosocial peers to also be helpful to strangers in the mall). Also, girls are more caring and prosocial than boys, perhaps because parents emphasize prosocial development more in raising daughters than sons (N. Eisenberg et al., 2009). And individuals with prosocial friends tend to behave more prosocially themselves (Barry & Wentzel, 2006).

■ **Volunteerism**   One of the most obvious ways in which adolescents can demonstrate prosocial behavior is through volunteerism (Flanagan, 2004). Volunteering in community service activities is more common in the United States than in most other countries and, in fact, is now required by many school districts. Researchers have been interested in both the antecedents of volunteering (that is, what leads adolescents to become involved in volunteer activities) and its consequences (that is, how adolescents are affected by volunteering). Several conclusions have emerged from this work. First, apart from attending a school in which some sort of community service is required, the best predictors of volunteerism in adolescence are being actively involved in religion (most probably because many volunteer activities are organized through religious institutions) and having parents who are active as volunteers in the community. Volunteers also tend to be female, more socially mature, more extraverted, and, not surprisingly, more altruistic (N. Eisenberg et al., 2009).

It has been more difficult to document the effects of volunteering on adolescent development because individuals who choose to volunteer are different to begin with from their peers who do not (Atkins, Hart, & Donnelly, 2005). Nevertheless, studies of volunteering that follow adolescents over time indicate that engaging in community service leads to short-term gains in social responsibility, increases in the importance individuals place on helping others, and increased commitment to tolerance, equal opportunity, and cultural diversity (N. Eisenberg et al., 2009; Flanagan, 2004; Lawford, Pratt, Hunsburger, & Pancer, 2005; Reinders & Youniss, 2006). There also is some evidence that volunteering in adolescence predicts volunteering in adulthood (Hart, Donnelly, Youniss, & Atkins, 2007). The extent to which these effects persist over time depends, in part, on how long the volunteer activity lasts; the shorter the activity, the more short-lived the results of participation.

During the past several decades, many school districts began requiring, or considering requiring, community service of all students. This suggestion was met with both praise and criticism. Proponents argued that service activities would help develop concern for the community and facilitate adolescents' prosocial development. Opponents argued that forcing adolescents to do something they did not want to do would make them even *more* negative about community service and less likely to volunteer at later points in their development. Some even suggested that turning an activity that some adolescents wanted to do into a school requirement would make the activity less intrinsically rewarding.

In order to inform this issue, several studies have been conducted that have compared students who have volunteered for community service with those who have had it forced on them. It does not seem that requiring community service makes students develop negative attitudes about volunteering, regardless of whether they had been volunteers previously. But the evidence is mixed with regard to whether the effects are different between adolescents who willingly participate and those who do it only because it is a requirement. Whereas some studies find that participating in community service activities has positive effects regardless of whether the participation is voluntary or required by the adolescent's school (Hart et al., 2007; J. Schmidt, Shumow, & Kackar, 2007), another found that participation had little effect in either group (Henderson, Brown, Pancer, & Ellis-Hale, 2007). One important difference, however, between students who are forced into community service and those who volunteer is that volunteers are more likely to continue their service work after graduation, suggesting that, whatever the positive effects of participation, they are not enough to turn adolescents who aren't especially interested in community work into adults who are (Planty, Bozick, & Regnier, 2006). Perhaps the most reasonable conclusion one can draw from these studies is that the potential benefits to the recipients of the adolescents' service (the children they tutor, the elderly they visit, or the neighborhoods whose parks they clean up) may be greater than the effects on the participants themselves.

POLITICAL THINKING DURING ADOLESCENCE

Less is known about the development of political thinking during adolescence than about moral development, but research on this topic is generally consistent with the view that beliefs become more principled, more abstract, and more independent during the adolescent years. This pattern is linked in part to the general cognitive developments of adolescence and in part to the growth of specific expertise, as the adolescent is exposed to more political information and ideas (Flanagan, 2004; Torney-Purta, 1990).

■ **Changes in Political Thinking**   Political think-ing changes during adolescence in several important ways (Flanagan, 2004; Torney-Purta, 1990). First, it be-comes more abstract. In response to the question "What is the purpose of laws?" for example, 12- and 13-year-olds are likely to reply with concrete answers—"So peo-ple don't kill or steal," "So people don't get hurt," and so on. Older adolescents, in contrast, are likely to respond with more abstract and more general statements—"To ensure safety and enforce the government" or "They are basically guidelines for people. I mean, like this is wrong and this is right and to help them under-stand" (Adelson, 1972, p. 108). Individuals' understand-ing of various rights—for example, their beliefs about whether children and adolescents have the right to have some control over their lives—becomes more abstract with age, as well (Ruck, Abramovitch, & Keating, 1998). Additionally, with age, individuals are more likely to judge the appropriateness of having certain rights (for example, freedom of speech) in light of char-acteristics of the individual (for example, whether the individual is mature enough to act responsibly) and the context within which the right is expressed (for exam-ple, whether the authority who is regulating speech is a parent or a government official) (Helwig, 1997). Never-theless, there is strong support among adolescents for fundamental democratic principles such as representa-tion and majority rule, even among adolescents grow-ing up in countries whose governments do not operate on these principles (Helwig, Arnold, Tan, & Boyd, 2007; Smetana & Villalobos, 2009).

Second, political thinking during adolescence be-comes less authoritarian and less rigid (Flanagan & Galay, 1995). Young adolescents are inclined toward obedience, authority, and an uncritical, trusting, and acquiescent stance toward government. For example, when asked what might be done in response to a law that is not working out as planned, the young adoles-cent will "propose that it be enforced more rigorously." An older teenager may suggest, instead, that the law needs to be reexamined and perhaps amended. In con-trast to older adolescents, younger adolescents are "more likely to favor one-man rule as [opposed to] rep-resentative democracy," show "little sensitivity to indi-vidual or minority rights"; and are "indifferent to the claims of personal freedom" (Adelson, 1972, p. 108).

Of special significance is the development during late adolescence of a roughly coherent and consistent set of attitudes—a sort of ideology—that does not ap-pear before this point. This ideology is "more or less organized in reference to a more encompassing . . . set of political principles" (Adelson, 1972, p. 121). These principles may concern a wide range of issues, includ-ing civil liberties, freedom of speech, and social equal-ity (Flanagan & Galay, 1995; Helwig, 1995). As is the case among adults, adolescents' views about political matters—the causes of unemployment, poverty, or homelessness, for example—are strongly linked to their social upbringing. Adolescents from higher so-cial classes tend to attribute unemployment, poverty, and homelessness to societal factors ("People are un-employed because companies are moving a lot of jobs to Mexico"), whereas adolescents from lower-class backgrounds are more likely to attribute these prob-lems to individual factors ("People are poor because they have problems managing money") (Flanagan & Tucker, 1999).

Shifts in all three of these directions—increasing ab-straction, decreasing authoritarianism, and increasing use of principles—are similar to the shifts observed in studies of moral development, and they support the idea that cognitive autonomy begins to emerge during late adolescence. The movement away from authori-tarianism, obedience, and unquestioning acceptance of the rulings of authority is especially interesting because it suggests further that an important psychological con-cern for adolescents involves questioning the values and beliefs emanating from parents and other authority fig-ures and trying to establish their own priorities.

■ **Political Thinking and Political Behavior**   As is the case with moral development, there may be gaps between adolescents' political thinking in hypothetical situations and their actual political attitudes and be-havior. In general, the most important influences on the political behavior of young people tends to be the social context in which they come of age (Flanagan, 2004; Torney-Purta, 1990). This context includes both the immediate community and the larger social and historical environment. Thus, minority adolescents, es-pecially those living in environments in which there are limited economic opportunities, tend to be more cyn-ical about politics than their White counterparts. Similarly, a study of German youth indicates that ado-lescents are more likely to develop right-wing (exces-sively authoritarian) attitudes when they are raised by authoritarian parents within a broader context that promotes antiforeigner and antidemocratic attitudes (Noack, Kracke, & Hofer, 1994).

RELIGIOUS BELIEFS DURING ADOLESCENCE

Despite the fact that religion plays an important role in the lives of many adolescents, the development of reli-gious beliefs has been very much neglected by social scientists (P. King & Roeser, 2009).

Religious beliefs, like moral and political beliefs, become more abstract, more principled, and more independent during the adolescent years. Specifically, adolescents' beliefs become more oriented toward spiri-tual and ideological matters and less oriented toward rituals, practices, and the strict observance of religious customs. For example, although close to 90% of all adolescents pray, and 95% believe in God, a substantial proportion of young people feel that organized religion does not play a very important role in their lives (Gallup & Bezilla, 1992; Holder et al., 2000; Wallace, Forman, Caldwell, & Willis, 2003). Compared with children, adolescents place more emphasis on the internal aspects of religious commitment (such as what an individual believes) and less on the external manifestations (such as whether an individual goes to church). Adolescence is an important time for "spiritual questioning, doubting, and creating" (P. King & Roeser, 2009, p. 447).

Studies of the development of religious beliefs during adolescence indicate many parallels with the development of moral and political reasoning. During late adolescence, individuals enter into a stage in which they begin to form a system of personal religious beliefs, rather than relying solely on the teachings of their parents (P. King & Roeser, 2009). This is reminiscent, of course, of adolescents' transition to principled moral reasoning or to the development in middle to late adolescence of a coherent political ideology. In all likelihood, developments in all three domains—moral, political, and religious—probably reflect the underlying growth of cognitive abilities and the shift from concrete to abstract reasoning that characterizes the adolescent transition. As you now know, this fundamental shift in cognitive ability affects adolescents' thinking across a wide variety of topics.

The development of religious beliefs is multifaceted, but in many ways we can think of religious development as having two main components: **religiosity** (which refers to the religious practices one engages in) and **spirituality** (which refers to one's personal quest for answers to questions about God and the meaning of life) (P. King & Roeser, 2009). Although both can be part of the process of psychosocial development, religiosity may be more important for identity development, since it involves the identification of oneself with a particular religious group and its practices and beliefs (not unlike identifying oneself with a particular ethnic group), whereas spirituality may be more closely linked to the development of cognitive autonomy, since it involves the development of a personal meaning system, self-awareness, and certain values. For most religious adolescents, religiosity and spirituality are deeply interconnected, as they are among many Muslim youth (D. C. French, Eisenberg, Vaughan, Purwono, & Suryanti, 2008). But there are substantial numbers of adolescents who practice religion without giving much thought to its spiritual aspects (for instance, adolescents who attend religious services each week or celebrate religious holidays mainly because their parents expect them to or because they enjoy the familiarity and routine of regular observance) and substantial numbers who de-

During adolescence, religious beliefs become more oriented toward spiritual and ideological matters and less oriented toward rituals, practices, and the strict observance of religious customs.

vote a great deal of time and energy to thinking about spiritual matters but who don't identify with an organized religion or practice customary religious rituals.

Patterns of Religious Involvement Generally, the stated importance of religion—and especially religiosity—declines somewhat during the adolescent years (Koenig, McGue, & Iacono, 2008). Compared with older adolescents, younger ones are more likely to attend church regularly and to state that religion is important to them (Wallace et al., 2003) (see Figure 9.7). In addition, church attendance and religious observation are more common among rural youth, especially those from farm families (V. King, Elder, & Whitbeck, 1997). The early years of college appear to be a time when some individuals reexamine and reevaluate many of the beliefs and values they grew up with. For many, this involves a decline in regular participation in organized religious activities (perhaps because the college environment doesn't encourage this) but an increase in

religiosity   The degree to which one engages in religious practices, like attending services.

spirituality   The degree to which one places importance on the quest for answers to questions about God and the meaning of life.

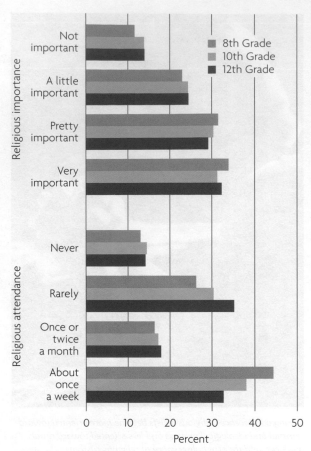

FIGURE 9.7   Age differences in religious activity. (Wallace et al., 2003)

spirituality and religious faith (Lefkowitz, 2005). The religious context of the college environment plays an important role; religious commitment may become stronger among students who attend a college with a religious orientation (Barry & Nelson, 2005).

Although some parents may interpret this decline in religiosity as indicating a sort of rebellion against the family's values, the development of religious thinking during late adolescence might be better understood as part of the overall development of cognitive autonomy. As the adolescent develops a stronger sense of independence, he or she may leave behind the unquestioning conventionality of earlier religious behavior as a first step toward finding a truly personal faith. The adolescent who continues to comply with her or his parents' religious beliefs without ever questioning them may actually be showing signs of immature conformity or identity foreclosure, and not spiritual maturity.

Individual Differences in Religiosity   Although individuals generally become less involved in formal religion during adolescence, there are differences among adolescents in their degree of religiosity. According to U.S. surveys (and bearing in mind that the United States is one of the most religious countries in the world),

about half of all American adolescents say that formal religious participation is important in their life (P. King & Roeser, 2009). Approximately 38% of adolescents report weekly attendance at religious services, 17% attend once or twice per month, and about 45% rarely or never attend services; regular attendance at religious services drops over the course of high school. Adolescent religious attendance declined gradually during the 1980s and 1990s but has changed very little since then. The vast majority of adolescents in the United States (more than 85%) report having a religious affiliation, with about half identifying themselves as Protestant (and close to half of Protestants identifying themselves as conservative Christians), and about one fifth as Catholic. Adolescent girls are slightly more likely to be religious than adolescent boys (this sex difference is found among adults, too). In general, Black and Latino adolescents are more religious than youth from other ethnic backgrounds, as are adolescents who live in the South or Midwest (P. King & Roeser, 2009; C. Smith & Denton, 2005; Wallace et al., 2003).

The Impact of Religious Involvement on Development   A growing body of research suggests that religious adolescents are less depressed than other adolescents, less likely to engage in premarital sexual intercourse, less likely to use drugs, and less likely to engage in delinquent behavior (C. Y. Chen, Dormitzer, Bejarano, & Anthony, 2004; Holder et al., 2000; P. King & Roeser, 2009; Litchfield, Thomas, & Li, 1997; A. M. Meier, 2003; L. Miller, Davies, & Greenwald, 2000; Sinha, Cnaan, & Gelles, 2007). Although some of the apparent positive effects of religious involvement are due to the fact that adolescents who are involved in religion often have other positive influences in their life that on their own promote positive development and prevent problem behavior (for example, supportive parents, prosocial peers, adults who care about them) (P. E. King & Furrow, 2004), being religious in and of itself appears to deter problem behavior and delay the onset of sexual activity (Hardy & Raffaelli, 2003; R. K. Jones, Darroch, & Singh, 2005; McCree, Wingood, DiClemente, Davies, & Harrington, 2003; Steinman & Zimmerman, 2004). As you read in Chapter 3, religious involvement may play an especially important role in buffering inner-city Black adolescents against the harmful effects of neighborhood disorganization and exposure to violence (Aceves & Cookston, 2007; Benhorin & McMahon, 2008; Brookmeyer et al., 2005; Fowler et al., 2008; Kliewer et al., 2006; S. T. Li, Nussbaum, & Richards, 2007; Rosario et al., 2008). There is more consistent evidence for the role that religion plays in preventing problem behavior than for its role in promoting positive development. Although studies show that religious adolescents are more involved in the community, more altruistic, and more prosocial, other research finds that rates of identity foreclosure (see Chapter 8) are higher among religious adolescents (P. King & Roeser, 2009).

FOOD FOR THOUGHT

A great deal of research indicates that adolescents who report high levels of religious involvement also report better mental health and lower levels of problem behavior. Given this, some writers advocate more religious participation in adolescence. Do you agree? Why or why not?

Some clues into the reasons that religious involvement may protect against involvement in problem behavior comes from the finding that religiosity rather than spirituality is the stronger predictor of staying out of trouble (M. Good & Willoughby, 2006). Moreover, it does not appear to be attending religious services that matters—it is being a part of a community of individuals who share similar values and engage in similar activities. In one study of churchgoing rural youth, the adolescents frequently mentioned participating in youth groups and the relationships they formed with youth group leaders as important influences on their behavior and development (M. Good & Willoughby, 2007). Seen in this light, the connection between religious participation and lower problem behavior is not surprising, since, as you know from Chapter 5 (and will see again in later chapters), among the strongest predictors of adolescents' involvement in sex, drugs, and delinquency are the behavior and attitudes of their peers.

RECAP

- According to Kohlberg's theory, which is the dominant perspective on the development of moral reasoning, late adolescence is a time of potential shifting from a morality that defines right and wrong in terms of society's rules to one that defines right and wrong on the basis of one's own basic moral principles.
- Adolescents' moral behavior does not always match their moral reasoning, in part because contextual factors influence how they act when they face moral dilemmas in the real world.
- The ways in which individuals think about prosocial phenomena, such as honesty or kindness, become more sophisticated during adolescence, although there is no consistent evidence that individuals become more helpful or kind as they move through adolescence.
- Studies of volunteerism find that involvement in community service leads to gains in social responsibility, tolerance, and the importance individuals place on helping others.
- Changes in the domains of political and religious thinking during adolescence also reflect the individual's growing sense of cognitive autonomy. As with moral reasoning, political and religious thinking become more abstract, more principled, and more independent, especially during late adolescence.
- Religious involvement during adolescence lowers the risk for problem behavior, primarily because it helps situate adolescents in peer groups of other well-behaved adolescents.

Intimacy

My boyfriend and I fell asleep together one night at my house [when I was 15]. We were curled up facing each other. I fell asleep looking at his face. I had a dream that night where I was falling. . . . I looked into his eyes and I knew that we were having the same dream. We immediately hugged each other and we both knew what had happened simply by looking in each other's eyes. (A 21-year-old's response when asked to recall "a vivid, highly memorable, personally important memory that 'conveys powerfully how you have come to be the person you currently are.'") (McLean & Thorne, 2003, p. 641).

ONE OF THE MOST REMARKABLE things about adolescence is the ways in which close relationships change during these years. Think about the friendships you had as a child, and compare them with those you had as a teenager. Think about the boyfriends or girlfriends that children have and the boyfriends or girlfriends adolescents have. And think about relationships between parents and their children and about how these relationships change during adolescence. In all three cases, adolescents' relationships are closer, more personal, more involved, and more emotionally charged than children's. During adolescence, in short, relationships become more intimate. In this chapter, we examine how and why this occurs.

At the outset, we need to draw a distinction between intimacy and sexuality. The concept of **intimacy**—at least as it is used in the study of adolescence—does not have a sexual or physical connotation. Rather, an intimate relationship is an emotional attachment between two people that is characterized by concern for each other's well-being; a willingness to disclose private, and occasionally sensitive, topics; and a sharing of common interests and activities. (An easy way to remember this is "caring," "daring," and "sharing.") Two individuals can therefore have an intimate relationship without having a sexual one. And, by the same token, two people can have a sexual relationship without being especially intimate.

Although the development of intimacy during adolescence is almost always studied in relation to friendships and romantic relationships with peers, adolescents' intimate relationships are by no means limited to other teenagers. Parents often have intimate relationships with their adolescent children, especially when the children have reached a sufficient level of maturity. Siblings, even with many years between them, are often close confidants. Sometimes, young people even form intimate relationships with adults who are not in their immediate family.

Obviously, one of the central issues in the study of intimacy during adolescence is the onset of dating. Although the young person's initiation into romantic relationships is undoubtedly important, it is not the only noteworthy change that occurs in close relationships during adolescence. Adolescence is also an important time for changes in what individuals look for in friends, in their capacity to be intimate with people of both sexes, and in the way they express their closeness with friends.

Intimacy as an Adolescent Issue

Intimacy is an important concern throughout most of the life span. Friends and confidants provide support in times of emotional vulnerability, assistance when needed, and companionship in a variety of activities and contexts (Weiss, 1974). During childhood, not having friends is associated with a wide range of psychological and social problems (Hartup, 1992). And during adulthood, having at least one intimate friendship is beneficial to an individual's health: People who have others to turn to for emotional support are less likely to suffer from psychological and physical disorders (Myers, Lindentthal, & Pepper, 1975). Without question, close relationships are extremely important to people of all ages. Why, then, is the development of intimacy especially important during adolescence?

One reason is that it is not until adolescence that truly intimate relationships—relationships characterized by openness, honesty, self-disclosure, and trust—emerge. Although children certainly have important friendships, their relationships are different from those formed during adolescence. Children's friendships are activity oriented; they are built around games and shared pastimes. To a child, a friend is someone who likes to do the same things he or she does. But teenagers' close friendships are more likely to have a strong emotional foundation; they are built on the sorts of bonds that form between people who care about and know and understand each other in a special way (Newcomb & Bagwell, 1995).

intimacy   The psychosocial domain concerning the formation, maintenance, and termination of close relationships.

FOOD FOR THOUGHT

In your experience, what are the defining features of an intimate relationship? What things have been special about the relationships in your life that you consider to be intimate? Do you agree with the assertion that genuine intimacy in relationships does not appear before adolescence?

Another reason for the importance of intimacy during adolescence concerns the changing nature of the adolescent's social world—during early adolescence, the increasing importance of peers in general, and during middle and late adolescence, the increasing importance of other-sex peers in particular (Furman, Brown, & Feiring, 1999). In Chapter 9, we looked at the young person's growing orientation toward peers as part of the development of emotional autonomy. In this chapter, we look at changes in adolescent peer relations again, but in a different light—as part of the development of intimacy.

Puberty and the Development of Intimacy
Why do such important changes take place in close relationships during adolescence? Several theorists point to significant links between the development of intimacy during adolescence and the biological, cognitive, and social changes of the period (Savin-Williams & Berndt, 1990). Naturally, changes in sexual impulses at puberty provoke interest in sexual relationships, and although sexual relationships are not necessarily emotionally intimate, they frequently are. In addition, with puberty and sexuality come new issues and concerns requiring serious, intimate discussions. Some young people feel hesitant to discuss sex and dating with their parents and turn instead to relationships outside the family. And some of the most intimate conversations adolescents have with their friends concern their feelings about and relationships with romantic partners.

Cognitive Change and the Development of Intimacy
Advances in thinking—especially in the realm of social cognition—are also related to the development of intimacy during adolescence (Smetana & Villalobos, 2009). As we saw in Chapter 2, the growth of social cognition during adolescence is reflected in the young person's more sophisticated conceptions of social relationships and in improvements in interpersonal understanding and communication. These changes permit adolescents to establish and maintain far more mature relationships that are characterized by higher levels of empathy, self-disclosure, and responsiveness to each other's thoughts and feelings. The limitations in pre-adolescents' ability to look at things from another person's point of view may make intimate interpersonal relationships a cognitive impossibility, because it is hard to be an intimate friend to someone when you are unable to empathize with her or him. Improvements in social competence and gains in intimacy during adolescence, therefore, are partly attributable to improvements in social cognition (Smetana & Villalobos, 2009).

Changes in Social Roles and the Development of Intimacy
We can also point to changes in the adolescent's social roles as potentially affecting the development of intimacy. Perhaps most simply, the behavioral independence that often accompanies the transition from childhood into adolescence provides greater opportunities for adolescents to be alone with their friends, engaged in intimate discussion. Adolescents spend more time in conversation with their friends than in any other activity (Csikszentmihalyi & Larson, 1984). Moreover, the recognition of adolescents as "near adults" may prompt their parents and other adults to confide in them and turn to them for support. Shared experiences such as working, as well as the development of emotional autonomy, may help give young people and their parents more of a basis for friendship and communication (Youniss & Smollar, 1985). Finally, changes in the structure of schools during early adolescence—often giving younger teenagers more contact with older ones—may promote new types of peer relationships (Eccles & Roeser, 2009).

During the course of preadolescence and adolescence, relationships are gradually transformed from the friendly but activity-oriented friendships of childhood to the more self-conscious, more analytical, and more intimate relationships of adulthood. In the next section, we examine why and how this transformation occurs.

RECAP

- In adolescence, the development of intimacy refers to the development of relationships that are characterized by self-disclosure, trust, and concern.
- The changes of puberty, which draw young people together around common concerns and which stimulate interest in romantic relationships, contribute to the development of intimacy.
- The development of intimacy is also stimulated by the cognitive changes of the period, which allow for a more sophisticated understanding of relationships.
- Intimate relationships are facilitated by the social changes of the period, which provide for more opportunities for adolescents to be alone with each other and for them to acquire experiences that bring them closer to adults.

Theoretical Perspectives on Adolescent Intimacy

The most important theoretical perspectives on the development of intimacy during adolescence are those of Harry Stack Sullivan (1953a), Erik Erikson (1968), and various writers who have studied attachment relationships in adolescence (McElhaney, Allen, Stephenson, & Hare, 2009). Let's look at each of these views in turn.

SULLIVAN'S THEORY OF INTERPERSONAL DEVELOPMENT

Like Erikson, whose theory of adolescent identity development was discussed at length in Chapter 8, Sullivan took a far less biological view of development than other psychoanalytic thinkers, such as Anna Freud. Instead, Sullivan emphasized the social aspects of growth, suggesting that psychological development can be best understood when looked at in interpersonal terms. Specifically, Sullivan's theory focuses on transformations in the adolescent's relationships with others. In particular, the challenges of adolescence (and indeed, according to Sullivan, of the entire life cycle) revolve around trying to satisfy changing interpersonal needs (Buhrmester, 1996). Although Sullivan's theoretical work is not especially popular today, it has had a profound influence on many contemporary researchers, and much of what Sullivan hypothesized about the development of intimacy has been confirmed in empirical studies.

■ **Stages of Interpersonal Needs** Sullivan's perspective starts from the premise that, as children develop, different interpersonal needs surface that lead to either feelings of security (when the needs are satisfied) or feelings of anxiety (when the needs are frustrated). Sullivan charted a developmental progression of needs, beginning in infancy and continuing through adolescence (see Table 10.1): the needs for contact and for tenderness (infancy), the need for adult participation (early childhood), the need for peers and for peer acceptance (middle childhood), the need for intimacy (preadolescence), the need for sexual contact and the need for intimacy with a peer of the other sex (early adolescence), and the need for integration into adult society (late adolescence) (Sullivan, 1953b). These changing interpersonal needs define the course of interpersonal development through different phases of the life span. During middle childhood, for example, youngsters need to be accepted into peer groups, or else they feel rejected and ostracized.

In Sullivan's view, the security that is derived from having satisfying relationships with others is the glue that holds one's sense of self together. Identity and self-esteem are gradually built up through interpersonal relationships. Like Erikson, Sullivan viewed psychosocial development as cumulative: The frustrations and satisfactions individuals experience during earlier periods affect their later relationships and developing sense of identity. For instance, the child who as an infant has her need for contact or tenderness frustrated will approach interpersonal relationships in subsequent eras with greater anxiety, a more intense need for security, and a shakier sense of self. In contrast, the infant who has his interpersonal needs met will approach later relationships with confidence and optimism.

When important interpersonal transitions arise (for example, during childhood, when the social world is broadened to include significant relationships with peers), having a solid foundation of security in past relationships aids in the successful negotiation of the transition. An individual who is very anxious about forming relationships with others is likely to have trouble forming new types of relationships, because they threaten an already shaky sense of security. A child who does not have a strong sense of security may have many friends in elementary school but be too afraid to form intimate friendships upon reaching preadolescence. She or he may try to maintain friendships like those of childhood—friendships that focus on playing games, for example, rather than talking—long after friends have outgrown getting together to "play." As a result, that youngster may be rejected by peers and may feel lonely and isolated.

TABLE 10.1 Interpersonal needs associated with different developmental eras: Sullivan's theory

Developmental Epochs	Interpersonal Needs
Infancy (0 to 2–3 yrs)	Need for contact with people, need for tenderness from mothering one
Early childhood (2–3 to 6–7 yrs)	Need for adult participation in child's play
Middle childhood (6–7 to 8–10 yrs)	Need for peer playmates, need for acceptance into peer society groups
Preadolescence (8–10 to 12–14 yrs)	Need for intimacy and consensual validation in same-sex chumships
Early adolescence (12–14 to 17–18 yrs)	Need for sexual contact, need for intimacy with other-sex partner
Late adolescence (17–18 yrs to adult)	Need for integration into adult society

Source: H. S. Sullivan, 1953a.

INTERPERSONAL DEVELOPMENT DURING ADOLESCENCE

Looking back at the progression of interpersonal needs that Sullivan mapped out, we can see that he distinguished between intimacy and sexuality; perhaps more importantly, he suggested that the need for intimacy—which surfaces during preadolescence—precedes the development of romantic or sexual relationships, which do not emerge until adolescence. In other words, Sullivan believed that the capacity for intimacy first develops prior to adolescence and in the context of same-sex, not other-sex, relationships. This turns out to be one of the most important observations in Sullivan's work, because as you will read, the quality of individuals' same-sex friendships is predictive of the quality of their later romantic relationships. One of the main challenges of adolescence, according to Sullivan, is making the transition from the nonsexual, intimate, same-sex friendships of preadolescence to the sexual, intimate, other-sex friendships of late adolescence.

Sullivan divided the years between childhood and adulthood into three periods: preadolescence, early adolescence, and late adolescence. During preadolescence, children begin to focus their attention on relationships with a few close friends, generally of the same sex. It is through these friendships that the need for intimacy is first satisfied. With these close friends, the young person learns to disclose and receive intimate, private information and to build caring, mutual friendships based on honesty, loyalty, and trust. Sullivan believed that these relationships could even have a corrective influence, helping to repair interpersonal problems that might have developed during childhood. A good preadolescent friend, for example, can help someone overcome feelings of insecurity that have developed as a result of poor family relationships.

Not all youngsters feel secure enough as preadolescents, however, to forge these more mature, intimate friendships. The feelings of insecurity are so strong for some individuals that anxiety holds them back. As a result, some youngsters never fully develop the capacity to be intimate with others, a limitation that takes its toll on relationships throughout adolescence and adulthood. In other words, Sullivan felt that forming intimate friendships during preadolescence is a necessary precondition to forming close relationships as an adolescent or young adult.

FOOD FOR THOUGHT

According to Sullivan, intimacy first develops in same-sex friendships. Given the differences in the ways that males and females are socialized, how might we expect male and female versions of intimacy to differ?

As adolescents' needs for intimacy increase, so might the emphasis they place on intimacy as an important component of friendship.

According to Sullivan, the preadolescent era comes to an end with the onset of puberty. Early adolescence is marked by the emergence of sexuality, in the form of a powerful, biologically based sex drive. As a consequence of this development, a change in the preferred "target" of the adolescent's need for intimacy takes place. He or she must begin to make the shift from intimate relationships with members of the same sex to intimate relationships with members of the other sex. It is important to note that during the historical epoch when Sullivan was writing, homosexuality was considered abnormal, and like other writers of his era, Sullivan equated normal sexual development with the development of heterosexual relationships. Social scientists no longer hold this view, however, and most would say that the crucial interpersonal challenge for the young adolescent is not the movement from same-sex to other-sex friendships, but the transition from nonromantic to romantic relationships.

Like all interpersonal transitions, the movement from nonromantic to romantic relationships can be fraught with anxiety. For adolescents who do not have a healthy sense of security, it can be scary to leave the safety of nonsexual friendships and venture into the world of dating and sexuality.

The overarching challenge of adolescence, according to Sullivan, is to integrate the individual's established need for intimacy with the emerging need for sexual contact in a way that does not lead to excessive anxiety. Just as Erikson viewed adolescence as a time of experimentation with different identities, Sullivan saw adolescence as a time of experimentation with different types of interpersonal relationships. Some adolescents choose to date many different people to try to find out what they are looking for in a relationship. Others get involved very deeply with a boyfriend or girlfriend in a relationship that lasts throughout their entire adolescence. Others may have a series of serious relationships. Still others keep intimacy and sexuality separate. They may develop close **platonic relationships** (nonsexual relationships) with other-sex peers, for example, or they may have sexual relationships without getting very intimate with their sex partners. And just as Erikson viewed role experimentation as a healthy part of the adolescent's search for identity, Sullivan viewed the adolescent's experimentation with different types of relationships as a normal way of handling new feelings, new fears, and new interpersonal needs. For many young people, experimentation with sex and intimacy continues well into late adolescence.

If the interpersonal tasks of adolescence have been negotiated successfully, the young person enters late adolescence able to be intimate, able to enjoy sex, and, most critically, able to experience intimacy and sexuality in the same relationship. This accomplished, the adolescent turns to the interpersonal needs of late adolescence: carving a niche in adult society. This latter task, in some senses, is reminiscent of the adolescent identity crisis described by Erikson.

FOOD FOR THOUGHT

A central proposition in Sullivan's theory is that we first learn how to be intimate within same-sex friendships and that later this capacity for intimacy is used in romantic relationships. If this is true, would you expect to see differences in the ways in which males and females express intimacy with romantic partners?

platonic relationships   Nonsexual relationships with individuals who might otherwise be romantic partners.

attachment   The strong affectional bond that develops between an infant and a caregiver.

secure attachment   A healthy attachment between infant and caregiver, characterized by trust.

anxious-avoidant attachment   An insecure attachment between infant and caregiver, characterized by indifference on the part of the infant toward the caregiver.

anxious-resistant attachment   An insecure attachment between infant and caregiver, characterized by distress at separation and anger at reunion.

internal working model   The implicit model of interpersonal relationships that an individual employs throughout life, believed to be shaped by early attachment experiences.

ATTACHMENT IN ADOLESCENCE

In recent decades, a different theoretical perspective has greatly influenced the study of intimate relationships in adolescence, one that draws on theories of the development of the attachment relationship during infancy (e.g., Ainsworth, Blehar, Waters, & Wall, 1978; Bowlby, 1969; Sroufe, 1979). In many ways, the basic ideas developed by Sullivan (namely, that early relationships set the stage for later ones) were maintained, but a different perspective and vocabulary have come to dominate theory and research on adolescents' intimate relationships. In order to understand how attachment theory is applied to the study of adolescence, we need to look first at how this construct has been used to understand development in infancy.

❚ **Attachment in Infancy**   In writings on infant development, an **attachment** is defined as a strong and enduring emotional bond. Virtually all infants form attachment relationships with their mothers (and most do so with their fathers and other caregivers as well), but not all infants have attachment relationships of the same quality. Psychologists differentiate among three types of infant attachment: secure, anxious-avoidant, and anxious-resistant. A **secure attachment** between infant and caregiver is characterized by trust; an **anxious-avoidant attachment** is characterized by indifference on the part of the infant toward the caregiver; and an **anxious-resistant attachment** is characterized by ambivalence. The security of the early attachment relationship is important, because studies show that infants who have had a secure attachment are more likely to grow into psychologically and socially skilled children (Matas, Arend, & Sroufe, 1978).

Attachment theory has given rise to two different, but related, questions about adolescent development. First, is there a link between the quality of attachment formed in infancy and mental health or behavior in adolescence? And, second, can the same three-category framework used to characterize interpersonal relationships in infancy—secure, anxious-avoidant, anxious-resistant—be used to characterize interpersonal relationships in adolescence?

❚ **Does Infant Attachment Predict Adolescent Intimacy?**   With respect to the first question, many theorists who study adolescent development believe that the nature of individuals' attachment to caregivers during infancy continues to have an influence on their capacity to form satisfying intimate relationships during adolescence and adulthood, for two reasons (McElhaney et al., 2009). First, some theorists have argued that the initial attachment relationship forms the basis for a more general model of interpersonal relationships employed throughout life. This so-called **internal working model** determines to a large measure whether individuals feel trusting or apprehensive in relationships with others and whether they see themselves as worthy of others' affection. We might think of an internal working model as a set of beliefs and expectations people draw on in forming close relationships with others—whether they go into relationships expecting acceptance or anticipating rejection. According to the theory, individuals who enjoyed a secure attachment relationship during infancy will have a more positive and healthy internal working model of relationships during adolescence, whereas individuals who were anxiously attached as infants will have a less positive model (McElhaney et al., 2009).

In support of this view, several studies have found that adolescents' working models for their relationships with parents are similar to their working models of relationships with friends, and adolescents' working models of relationships with friends are similar to their working models of relationships with romantic partners (e.g., Furman, Simon, Shaffer, & Bouchey, 2002). In addition, a number of writers have suggested that individuals who emerge from infancy with an insecure attachment relationship are more sensitive to being rejected by others in later romantic encounters, a trait that psychologists have called **rejection sensitivity** (N. L. Collins & Feeney, 2004; G. Downey, Bonica, & Rincón, 1999). Although studies that compare adolescents' working models of their relationships with parents, peers, and romantic partners do not directly tell us whether emotional attachments in adolescence are influenced by attachments formed during infancy (since these working models could all have been revised or formed during adolescence), they do support the contention that our beliefs and expectations about relationships are similar across different interpersonal domains.

FOOD FOR THOUGHT

Think about your own internal working model of relationships. Are there consistencies in the ways in which you approach close relationships with different people? Would you say that you are high or low in "rejection sensitivity"?

A second reason for the continued importance of early attachment relationships during adolescence is that interpersonal development is cumulative: What happens during infancy affects what happens in early childhood, which affects what happens in middle childhood, and so on (Kerns, 1996). In other words, individuals who leave infancy with a secure attachment may be on a different interpersonal trajectory than those who leave infancy insecure. (Here's where you can see similarities between this perspective and Sullivan's.) The only way to examine

this proposition is to follow individuals over time and trace their interpersonal development.

Numerous studies that have done this show that insecure infants are more likely to develop psychological and social problems during childhood and adolescence, including poor peer relationships (e.g., M. Lewis, Feiring, McGuffog, & Jaskir, 1984; Renken, Egeland, Marvinney, Mangelsdorf, & Sroufe, 1989; Weinfield, Ogawa, & Sroufe, 1997). It has been hypothesized that these problems in peer relations during childhood affect the development of social competence during adolescence—in essence, forming a link between early experience and later social relations (Jaffari-Bimmel, Juffer, Van IJzendoorn, Bakermans-Kranenburg, & Mooijaart, 2006). Additionally, several studies indicate that the benefits of positive relations with peers extend beyond adolescence: Individuals who establish healthy intimate relationships with age-mates during adolescence are psychologically healthier and more satisfied with their lives as middle-aged adults (Hightower, 1990).

Of course, it is possible for interpersonal development to be cumulative without the root cause of this continuity being the individual's internal working model. Individuals who have positive peer relationships in childhood may simply learn how to get along better with others, and this may lead to more positive peer relationships in adolescence, which, in turn, may lead to better relationships in adulthood. For instance, one study that followed individuals from birth through midlife found a cascade of interpersonal connections over time: low-quality parent–child relationships were linked to low-quality parent–adolescent relationships, which predicted low quality romantic relationships in young adulthood and, later, dissatisfaction with life in middle age (Overbeck, Stattin, Vermulst, Ha, & Engels, 2007). Similarly, other research finds that individuals with more negative views of themselves disengage from peers, which may lead to poorer-quality peer relationships and peer rejection, thereby intensifying their negative self-image (M. S. Caldwell, Rudolph, Troop-Gordon, & Kim, 2004).

How strong is the *specific* link between infant attachment and the quality of interpersonal relationships in adolescence and young adulthood? Do individuals who were securely attached as infants have more positive working models of relationships as adolescents or young adults? Studies that have followed individuals from infancy all the way through adolescence and beyond have yielded conflicting results. Some have shown considerable continuity from infancy through adolescence (e.g., C. Hamilton, 2000; Waters, Merrick, Treboux, Crowell, & Albersheim, 2000), but others have shown no continuity whatsoever (M. Lewis, Feiring, & Rosenthal, 2000; Weinfield, Sroufe, & Egelund, 2000).

rejection sensitivity　Heightened vulnerability to being rejected by others.

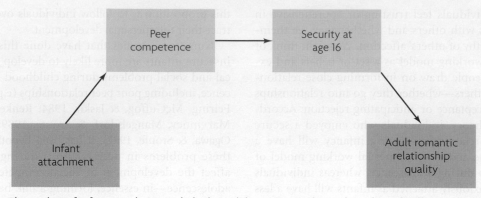

FIGURE 10.1   The quality of infant attachment is linked to adult romantic relationships through effects on social development in childhood and adolescence. (Simpson et al., 2007)

Some researchers have suggested that individuals' security of attachment remains stable only in the absence of major life events that could upset the course of interpersonal development (such as the loss of a parent or parental divorce) and that the lack of continuity observed in some studies is due to the importance of intervening events (Beckwith, Cohen, & Hamilton, 1999; Waters et al., 2000; Weinfield et al., 2000). Others, however, argue that the significance of early attachment for later relationships is far outweighed by the importance of the experiences the individual has in childhood and the context in which he or she lives as an adolescent (M. Lewis et al., 2000).

■ **Attachment in Adolescence**   In addition to employing the three-way attachment classification scheme to study the links among infancy, childhood, and adolescence, attachment theorists have applied similar classifications to the study of adolescents' attachments to others (e.g., McElhaney et al., 2009), as well as to adolescents' internal working models (e.g., Kobak, Cole, Ferenz-Gillies, Fleming, & Gamble, 1993). In some of these studies, adolescents' current relationships with parents and peers are assessed; in others, adolescents are asked to recount their childhood experiences through the use of a procedure called the **Adult Attachment Interview.** The Adult Attachment Interview, developed by psychologist Mary Main and her colleagues (Main, Kaplan, & Cassidy, 1985), is designed to yield insight into an individual's internal working model. The interview focuses on individuals' recollections of their early attachment experiences and obtains information on the ways in which the individual has come to terms with his or her childhood history. A variety of schemes for coding responses to the interview have been devised, but most categorize individuals as "secure," "dismissing," or "preoccupied."

Many researchers have found that adolescents in different attachment categories differ in predictable ways (McElhaney et al., 2009). Compared with dismissing or preoccupied adolescents, for example, secure adolescents interact with their mothers with less unhealthy anger and more appropriate assertiveness, suggesting that they may experience fewer difficulties in establishing emotional autonomy (Kobak et al., 1993). Individuals with dismissive or preoccupied attachment profiles are more likely to show a range of emotional and behavior problems in adolescence, including depression, maladaptive coping, anxiety, eating disorders, conduct problems, and delinquency (e.g., J. Allen, Porter, McFarland, McElhaney, & Marsh, 2007; Kobak & Cole, 1994; Kobak, Sudler, & Gamble, 1992; Lieberman, Doyle, & Markiewicz, 1999; Seiffge-Krenke & Beyers, 2005; P. Zimmermann & Becker-Stoll, 2002). Adolescents with a secure attachment to their mother perceive her as supportive while maintaining an objective, deidealized appraisal of her; when they disagree, they are able to discuss their differences in a way that allows for both individuation and connectedness (J. Allen et al., 2003). Not surprisingly, individuals who are judged to be secure have more stable romantic relationships than their insecure counterparts (K. Davis & Kirkpatrick, 1994).

Numerous studies also have looked at the quality of adolescents' current attachments to parents and peers as well as their early attachments (McElhaney et al., 2009). In general, individuals who have secure attachments during adolescence are more socially competent, more successful in school, and better adjusted than their insecure peers (J. Allen et al., 2007; K. Black & McCartney, 1997; M. L. Cooper, Shaver, & Collins, 1998; Mayseless & Scharf, 2007). One recent study linked security of attachment in infancy with social competence in childhood, security of attachment to close friends in adolescence, and positive romantic relationships in adulthood (Simpson, Collins, Tran, & Haydon, 2007) (Figure 10.1). Of course, it is hard to say whether social competence leads to healthier

Adult Attachment Interview   A structured interview used to assess an individual's past attachment history and "internal working model" of relationships.

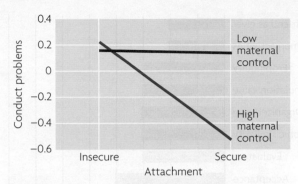

FIGURE 10.2 Maternal control has different effects on adolescent behavior depending on the security of the adolescent's working model. (Allen et al., 2002)

attachments or vice versa (most probably, both are true). There is also some evidence that attachments to different people (mothers, fathers, best friends, romantic partners) may serve different purposes at different points in adolescence, although adolescents' attachment to their mother seems to be important, and attachment to father less important, over the entire adolescent period (Markiewicz, Lawford, Doyle, & Haggart, 2006).

Because interpersonal development is cumulative—i.e., influenced both by early and by later experiences—the quality of an adolescent's attachments to peers is affected not only by early experience but also by her or his close relationships in childhood and early adolescence. For example, secure adolescents are more likely to come from homes with authoritative parents, whereas avoidant adolescents are more likely to come from homes where parents are neglectful (Karavasilis, Doyle, & Markiewicz, 2003). Security of attachment is also related to whether and at what age adolescents "leave the nest": Insecurely attached adolescents are more likely to delay moving out or to return to their parents' home than their more securely attached peers (Seiffge-Krenke, 2006). Keep in mind, however, that while attachment security is generally highly stable over the adolescent years, it can change if adolescents are living in dysfunctional family situations or under high amounts of stress (J. Allen, McElhaney, Kuperminc, & Jodl, 2004). In other words, early attachment security is not an "inoculation" that protects individuals from psychological problems forever, but rather a psychological advantage that increases the probability of developing in healthy ways.

By the same token, the degree of security in an adolescent's attachment style interacts with other experiences to shape mental health and behavior: Positive experiences (like having an authoritative parent) have even more positive effects among adolescents with a secure style, and negative experiences are not as harmful (J. Allen et al., 2002). Similarly, among adolescents with an insecure attachment style, negative experiences

(like having excessively intrusive parents) have an even worse effect than they would otherwise (P. Marsh, McFarland, & Allen, 2003). As Figure 10.2 indicates, for example, maternal control and supervision seem to deter conduct problems among adolescents who are securely (but not insecurely) attached.

RECAP

- According to Sullivan, the need for intimacy emerges in preadolescence and is typically satisfied through same-sex friendships.

- In Sullivan's view, the main challenge of adolescence is to integrate an already established need for intimacy with the emerging need for sexual contact in a way that does not engender excessive anxiety.

- Attachment theory now dominates the study of intimate relationships in adolescence. Individuals who enjoyed a secure attachment to their caregiver during infancy develop a healthier or more secure internal working model of relationships, which is thought to permit more satisfying intimate relationships during adolescence and adulthood.

- There is also evidence that interpersonal development is cumulative: Positive experiences in early family relationships contribute to social competence, which facilitates the development of intimate relationships with peers and romantic partners.

The Development of Intimacy in Adolescence

CHANGES IN THE NATURE OF FRIENDSHIP

Changes in Definitions of Friendship Not until early adolescence are such features as self-disclosure and loyalty mentioned as important dimensions of friendship. A classic study of age differences in children's conceptions of friendship revealed that not until seventh grade did individuals mention intimacy, common interests, or similar attitudes and values (Bigelow & LaGaipa, 1975) (see Figure 10.3). Responses mentioning prosocial behavior and common activities were high at all age levels. In other words, it may be important to differentiate between defining friendship in terms of companionship, which appears much before adolescence, and intimacy, which may not emerge until considerably later (Buhrmester & Furman, 1987).

That conceptions of friendship come to place greater weight on such dimensions as intimacy, loyalty, and shared values and attitudes during early adolescence is

FIGURE 10.3 Children and adolescents have different conceptions of "friendship." Some sorts of conceptions do not appear until the fifth or sixth grade.
(Derived from Bigelow & LaGaipa, 1975)

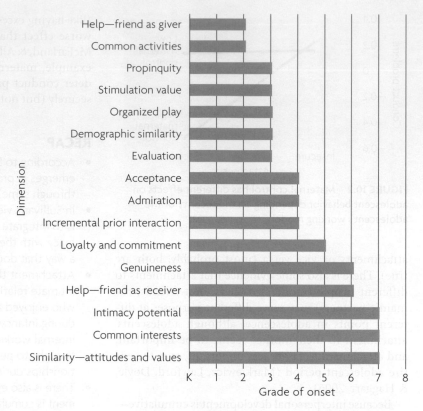

consistent with Sullivan's theory (Savin-Williams & Berndt, 1990). As adolescents' needs for intimacy increase, so might the emphasis they place on intimacy as an important component of friendship. The findings are also consistent with what we know about other cognitive changes characteristic of early adolescence. As we saw in Chapter 2, adolescents have greater facility than children in thinking about abstract concepts such as intimacy and loyalty. And as you know, adolescents' judgments of others are more sophisticated, more psychological, and less tied to concrete attributes than are those of children.

▌ **Jealousy** Several studies indicate that the importance of intimacy as a defining feature of close friendship continues to increase throughout early and middle adolescence (Berndt & Perry, 1990; McNelles & Connolly, 1999; Phillipsen, 1999). But an interesting pattern of change occurs around age 14. During middle adolescence (between ages 13 and 15), particularly among girls, concerns about loyalty and anxieties over rejection become more pronounced and may temporarily overshadow concerns about intimate self-disclosure (Berndt & Perry, 1990). Consistent with this, the sorts of conflicts adolescents have with their friends change during this time; whereas older adolescents' conflicts are typically over private matters, younger adolescents' conflicts are often over perceived public disrespect (Shulman & Laursen, 2002).

Girls, in particular, show a pronounced increase in jealousy over their friends' friends during early adoles-

cence (J. Parker, Low, Walker, & Gamm, 2005; J. Parker, Low, & Wargo, 1999). Girls who have low self-esteem and are high in rejection sensitivity are especially likely to become jealous of their friends' relationships with other girls. In some senses, intimate friendship is a mixed blessing for young adolescent girls—they get the benefits of having confidantes with whom they can easily talk about their problems, but their friendships are more fragile and more easily disrupted by feelings of betrayal. As a consequence, girls' friendships on average do not last as long as boys' do (Benenson & Christakos, 2003).

How might Sullivan have explained this pattern? Why might loyalty become such a pressing concern for girls during the middle adolescent years? One possibility is that at this age, girls may start to feel more nervous about their relationships with friends because they are beginning to make the transition into other-sex relationships. These transitions, as Sullivan noted, can make individuals feel insecure. Perhaps it is anxiety over dating and heightened feelings of insecurity that cause adolescent girls to temporarily place a great deal of emphasis on the trust and loyalty of their close friends. Indeed, close friends who have highly intimate and exclusive relationships with each other often behave more aggressively with friends than they do toward peers who are not their close friends (Grotpeter & Crick, 1996).

Adolescents' close friendships also are distinguished from their casual friendships in the types of conflicts they have and in the ways in which their conflicts are resolved (Laursen, 1995, 1996; Raffaelli, 1997; Whitesell & Harter, 1996). Although conflicts between adolescents and their close friends are less frequent than they are between adolescents and other peers, arguments with close friends are more emotional (that is, lots of anger and hurt feelings). More importantly, though, conflict between close friends is more likely to provoke efforts to restore the relationship than is conflict between casual friends.

CHANGES IN THE DISPLAY OF INTIMACY

In addition to placing greater emphasis on intimacy and loyalty in defining friendship than children do, teenagers are also more likely actually to display intimacy in their relationships, with respect to what they know about their friends, how responsive they are, how empathic they are, and how they resolve disagreements.

▌ **Knowing Who Their Friends Are** As individuals move into and through adolescence, they gain knowledge about more intimate aspects of their friends' lives. For example, although preadolescents and adolescents have comparable degrees of knowledge about characteristics of their best friends that are not especially personal (such as the friend's telephone number or birth date), adolescents know significantly more things about their friends that might be classified as intimate (such as what their friends worry about or what they are proud of) (Savin-Williams & Berndt, 1990). Along similar lines, between the 5th and 11th grades, increasingly more adolescents agree with such statements as "I know how [my friend] feels about things without his [or her] telling me" and "I feel free to talk to [my friend] about almost everything" (Sharabany, Gershoni, & Hofman, 1981). Over the course of adolescence, adolescents' reports of friendship quality increase steadily, a pattern observed in all ethnic groups. Although there are ethnic differences in average levels of friendship quality—Asian American adolescents report more dissatisfaction with their friendships than do other adolescents—the rate of improvement in friendship quality over time is the same (Way & Greene, 2006). Consistent with Sullivan's viewpoint, then, during preadolescence and early adolescence, youngsters' friendships become more personal.

FOOD FOR THOUGHT

Do you remember your first intimate friendship? What made the relationship different from other friendships that you had previously had?

▌ **Caring and Concern** Individuals also become more responsive to close friends, less controlling, and more tolerant of their friends' individuality during adolescence (Berndt & Perry, 1990; Estrada, 1995; Keller, Edelstein, Schmid, Fang, & Fang, 1998; Newcomb & Bagwell, 1995; Shulman, Laursen, Kalman, & Karpovsky, 1997). This can be interpreted as another indicator of their increased capacity for intimacy. Before preadolescence, for example, children are actually less likely to help and share with their friends than with other classmates (perhaps because children are more competitive with their friends than with other youngsters and do not want to feel inferior). By about fourth grade, children treat their friends and other classmates similarly when it comes to sharing and cooperation. But by the time they have reached eighth grade, friends are more helpful and generous toward each other than toward other classmates. Interestingly, adolescents are also physically and physiologically responsive to their friends: Studies show that the behaviors and emotional states of pairs of friends are more frequently synchronized, or "on the same wavelength," than are those of acquaintances, even when the friends and acquaintances are engaged in the same task (Field et al., 1992).

Perhaps because of this, adolescents are more interpersonally sensitive than children—they show greater levels of empathy and social understanding—in situations in which they are helping or comforting others. Compared with children, adolescents are more likely to understand and acknowledge how their friends feel when those friends are having problems. Indeed, over the course of adolescence, individuals' attempts to help their friends with personal problems of all sorts become more centered on providing support for the troubled friend and less aimed at mere distraction (Denton & Zarbatany, 1996).

▌ **Conflict Resolution** The ways in which close friends resolve conflict also change over the course of adolescence. According to a comprehensive review of research on this topic by psychologist Brett Laursen and his colleagues (Laursen, Finkelstein, & Betts, 2001), as individuals move from childhood into adolescence, and from adolescence into young adulthood, they become more likely to end their disagreements by negotiation (trying to compromise or find a solution that is acceptable to both friends) or disengagement (walking away from the situation) and less likely to end them with one person coercing or overpowering the other and getting his or her way. Negotiation is also more common between romantic partners than between friends and more common between close friends than between acquaintances.

SEX DIFFERENCES IN INTIMACY

▌ **How Females Are More Intimate** There are striking sex differences in intimacy during adolescence.

By virtually any measure, girls display more intimacy in their friendships than do boys.

When asked to name the people who are most important to them, adolescent girls—particularly in the middle adolescent years—list more friends than boys do, and girls are more likely to mention intimacy as a defining aspect of close friendship. In interviews, adolescent girls express greater interest in their close friendships, talk more frequently about their intimate conversations with friends, express greater concern about their friends' faithfulness and greater anxiety over rejection, and place greater emphasis on emotional closeness in their evaluation of romantic partners (Feiring, 1999; Feiring & Lewis, 1991; J. Parker, Low, Walker, Gamm, 2005). Girls are more likely than boys to make distinctions in the way they treat intimate and nonintimate friends and to fight about relationships; girls prefer to keep their friendships more exclusive and are less willing to include other classmates in their cliques' activities (Bukowski, Sippola, Gauze, Hoza, & Newcomb, 1993; Raffaelli, 1997). In conversations, girls are more collaborative, whereas boys are more controlling (Strough & Berg, 2000).

When self-disclosure is used as the measure of intimacy, boys' friendships with other boys do not approach girls' friendships with other girls until late in

adolescence, if at all (McNelles & Connolly, 1999; Radmacher & Azmitia, 2006; Savin-Williams & Berndt, 1990; Shulman et al., 1997). And girls appear to be more sensitive and empathic than boys, especially when comforting friends who are distressed and in knowing when their friends are depressed (N. Eisenberg, Miller, Shell, McNalley, & Shea, 1991; Swenson & Rose, 2003). In these very numerous—and very important—respects, the expression of intimacy certainly appears to be more advanced among adolescent girls than among boys (Buhrmester, 1996).

Although this carries many advantages for girls, it also carries some liabilities: Girls are more likely than boys to spend excessive time discussing each other's problems—a phenomenon that has been called **co-rumination** (A. J. Rose, 2002). Co-rumination, often done in the context of discussing problems in romantic relationships, turns out to be a double-edged sword, at least for girls—it brings friends closer, but it also contributes to girls' depression and anxiety (Starr & Davila, 2009). Interestingly, among boys, co-rumination also improves friendships, but does not increase depression or anxiety (as you will read in Chapter 13, adolescent girls are much more susceptible to depression than are boys) (A. J. Rose, Carlson, & Waller, 2007). Adolescents have to be careful, however, not to engage in too much "negative feedback seeking" (asking other people to verify their flaws, as in, "My voice is so annoying, right?"); too much of this leads to rejection by others, which then only makes people feel even worse (Borelli & Prinstein, 2006).

There are also interesting sex differences in the nature of conflicts between close friends during adolescence that are consistent with other sex differences in the expression of intimacy. Boys' conflicts with their friends are briefer, typically over issues of power and control (such as whose turn it is in a game); more likely to escalate into physical aggression; and usually resolved without any explicit effort to do so, often by just "letting things slide." Girls' conflicts, in contrast, are longer, typically about some form of betrayal in the relationship (such as breaking a confidence or ignoring the other person), and only resolved when one of the friends apologizes (Noakes & Rinaldi, 2006; Raffaelli, 1997).

▌ **And How They Aren't** On some measures of friendship, however, adolescent boys and girls show similar degrees of intimacy. Although girls are more likely to mention self-disclosure when asked to define close friendship and report more self-disclosure in their friendships, boys and girls have equivalent degrees of intimate knowledge about their best friends (McNelles & Connolly, 1999; Shulman et al., 1997). When boys are with their friends, they are just as likely as girls to share each other's emotional state (McNelles & Connolly, 1999). And although girls are generally more

co-rumination Excessive talking with another about problems.

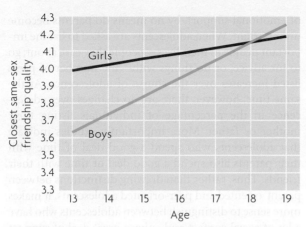

FIGURE 10.4 Changes in friendship quality over time. (Way & Greene, 2006)

considerate, sex differences in helpfulness are very small (N. Eisenberg et al., 2009).

It seems safe to say that, at the very least, intimacy is a more conscious concern for adolescent girls than for boys. But this does not mean that intimacy is absent from boys' relationships. Rather, they express intimacy in different ways. In general, boys' friendships are more oriented toward shared activities than toward the explicit satisfaction of emotional needs—as is often the case in girls' friendships; and the development of intimacy between adolescent males may be a more subtle phenomenon and one that is reflected more in shared activities than in self-disclosure, even in young adulthood (McNelles & Connolly, 1999; Radmacher & Azmitia, 2006) and even in online communication (Valkenberg & Peter, 2007). Another possibility is that the development of close friendships among males starts at a later age than it does among females. One recent study found, for instance, that there are substantial sex differences in friendship quality at age 13, but that by age 18 these are gone (see Figure 10.4) (Way & Greene, 2006). Once again we see the same old story: during early and middle adolescence, girls are more emotionally and socially mature than boys, but by late adolescence, boys have caught up.

■ **Origins of Sex Differences** Many theorists have suggested that sex differences in intimacy are the result of different patterns of socialization, with females being more strongly encouraged to develop and express intimacy—especially verbal intimacy—than males. Consistent with this, research shows that an individual's sex role (how masculine, feminine, or androgynous he or she is) is a better predictor of the person's capacity for intimate friendship than his or her sex (D. Jones & Costin, 1993). For instance, androgynous males (males who display both masculine and feminine traits) report levels of intimacy in their friendships that are comparable to females' levels of intimacy.

Other factors could be at work, however, that lead to the greater expression of certain types of intimacy between females than between males. Social pressures on males and females during adolescence are quite different and may lead to differences in expressions of intimacy in certain types of relationships. As we noted in Chapter 8, boys are punished much more for acting in feminine ways than girls are for acting in masculine ways. This is especially so within ethnic groups that stress the importance of machismo (a strong and sometimes exaggerated sense of masculinity), as is often the case among Mexican Americans (Stanton-Salazar & Spina, 2005). One reason that adolescent males may not be as intimate in their friendships as adolescent females may be that boys are nervous that expressions of intimacy will be taken as a sign of their lack of masculinity.

FOOD FOR THOUGHT

Some sex differences in friendship quality predate adolescence—girls are more verbal than boys at an early age, for example—but others, such as differences in conflict resolution or in feelings of jealousy do not seem to emerge until this developmental period. What aspects of the transition into adolescence differ for girls and boys that might account for sex differences in intimacy?

Although much research to date has concluded that girls experience more intimacy in their relationships than boys do (Buhrmester, 1996; Maccoby, 1990), it is important to bear in mind that these studies have been based mainly on samples of White youngsters. Several recent studies of non-White youth suggest that there may *not* be similar patterns of sex differences in intimacy in some ethnic groups (DuBois & Hirsch, 1990; D. Jones, Costin, & Ricard, 1994). Indeed, one study of Black, Asian American, and Latino adolescents found no sex differences in support between friends among African American teenagers; slight sex differences among Latino teenagers, with girls reporting more friendship support than boys; and large sex differences among Asian American teenagers, with boys reporting more support than girls (Way & Chen, 2000). Sanctions against intimate disclosure may be especially strong among White males, but they may be far less so among their minority counterparts.

CHANGES IN THE TARGETS OF INTIMACY

According to Sullivan, adolescence is a time of noteworthy changes in the "targets" of intimate behavior.

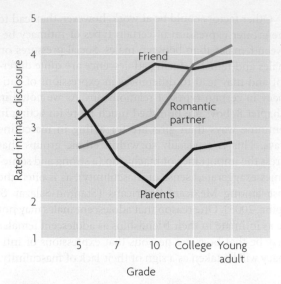

FIGURE 10.5 Age differences in self-disclosure to parents, friends, and romantic partners. (Buhrmester, 1996)

During preadolescence and early adolescence, intimacy with peers is hypothesized to replace intimacy with parents, and during late adolescence, intimacy with peers of the other sex is thought to take the place of intimacy with same-sex friends. Actually, this view appears to be only somewhat accurate. As we'll see, new targets of intimacy do not *replace* old ones. Rather, new targets are *added to* old ones.

▎ **Parents and Peers as Targets of Intimacy** Two conclusions emerge repeatedly in studies of adolescents' intimacy with parents and peers, at least in the contemporary United States. First, from early adolescence on, teenagers describe their relationships with their best friends and romantic partners as more intimate than those with their mother or father (Beaumont, 1996; K. Rice & Mulkeen, 1995). Second, although there may be a slight drop in intimacy between adolescents and parents sometime during adolescence, the decline reverses as young people move toward young adulthood.

Consider, for example, the results of one study of age differences in intimate self-disclosure with parents, friends, and romantic partners over the course of childhood and young adulthood (Buhrmester, 1996). As Figure 10.5 indicates, intimacy between individuals and their parents declines between the 5th and 10th grades, but increases between 10th grade and young adulthood. Intimacy with friends increases steadily throughout adolescence, although most dramatically during the early adolescent years. Intimacy with romantic partners also increases steadily throughout adolescence, but in this case, the most dramatic increase takes place during the late high school years.

In other words, while peers become relatively more important during adolescence as confidants and sources of emotional support, by no means do parents become unimportant. When adolescents are asked to list the important people in their lives—people they care about, go to for advice, or do things with—the number of peers listed increases over the course of adolescence. At the same time, however, there are no changes over adolescence in the percentage of individuals listing their mother or father. More importantly, studies indicate that adolescents who spend a good deal of time with their parents also spend a good deal of time with their friends. Thus, rather than drawing distinctions between parent-oriented and peer-oriented adolescents, it makes more sense to distinguish between adolescents who have a lot of social contact and enjoy a great deal of support from others (both family and friends) and those who are socially isolated or lonely (Fallon & Bowles, 1997; Scholte, van Lieshout, & van Aken, 2001).

Indeed, one of the most consistent findings to emerge from studies of adolescents' peer and family relationships is that the qualities of these relationships are closely linked (C. Cooper, Carlson, Keller, Koch, & Spradling, 1993). In other words, we can see features of adolescents' relationships with their parents and their parents' relationships with each other—how close they are, how much they tolerate independence, how they deal with conflict, how much control they assert over their children's friends, and so forth—in their relationships with their friends and romantic partners (Connolly & McIssac, 2009; Taradash, Connolly, Pepler, Craig, & Costa, 2001; Updegraff et al., 2004). This link between the quality of peer relationships and of family relationships has been found across ethnic groups (Way & Chen, 2000). On a theoretical level, this provides support for both social learning and attachment-based views of adolescent intimacy, in that it suggests that the lessons young people learn in close relationships at home provide a template for the close relationships they form with others—in both good and bad ways. One recent study of Black adolescents found that teenagers whose relationships with parents were emotionally close but not very individuated tended to stay longer in romantic relationships, even though the relationships may not have been very good, suggesting that difficulties in establishing healthy autonomy at home may carry over to romantic relationships (Smetana & Gettmen, 2006). On a practical level, these findings suggest that one approach to improving the peer relationships of adolescents who are having difficulties might be to focus on improving the quality of their relationships at home (Updegraff, Madden-Derdich, Estrada, Sales, & Leonard, 2002).

Studies of adolescents' preferences for social support similarly show that the likelihood of turning to a peer during a time of trouble increases during adolescence, but that the likelihood of turning to a parent remains constant. In a study of Black, Hispanic American, and

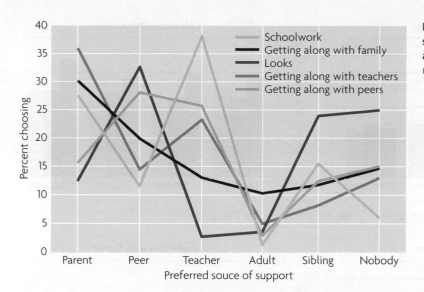

FIGURE 10.6 Preferred sources of social support among Hispanic students vary as a function of their area of concern. (Morrison et al., 1997)

White youth, the researchers found that between ages 7 and 14, the amount of support received from the immediate family remained fairly constant, while the amount of support received from friends increased—a pattern seen in all three ethnic groups (M. Levitt, Guacci-Franci, & Levitt, 1993). In other words, even though adolescents begin to see their friends as increasingly important sources of emotional support, they do not cease needing or using their parents for the same purpose. What seems to occur, instead, is that adolescents develop preferences for social support that vary as a function of the specific issue (see Figure 10.6).

Interestingly, adolescents may feel freer to express anger during arguments with family members than during arguments with friends, presumably because anger may lead to the end of a friendship but not to the end of a family relationship (Laursen, 1993). Perhaps because of this, adolescents report more angry feelings after conflicts with their parents than after conflicts with their friends (Adams & Laursen, 2001). And when asked to recall key events in their past that contributed to their sense of identity, college students' reminiscences of their relationships with their parents more often emphasize conflict and separation, whereas their recollections of their relationships with their friends more often emphasize closeness (McLean & Thorne, 2003).

Cultural Differences in Patterns of Intimacy

Patterns of adolescents' relationships with parents and peers vary across cultures, however, and it may be misleading to generalize results of studies of U.S. or Canadian teenagers to other countries. A comparison of American and Indonesian youth found, for instance, that Indonesian adolescents ranked parents higher in social support and ranked friends lower than was the case for the American adolescents (D. French, Rianasari, Pidada, Nelwan, & Buhrmester, 2001). Similarly, a comparison of adolescents from Canada, Belgium, and Italy found that Italian adolescents were closer to their family, whereas Canadian adolescents were closer to their friends (Claes, 1998). It may be wrong to automatically assume that American youngsters are more peer-oriented than their counterparts in *all* other cultures, however. In fact, one study found that Japanese adolescents (and Japanese boys, in particular) were less likely than American adolescents to list their parents—and more likely to list their peers—as significant others (Darling, Hamilton, & Matsuda, 1990). Another study, of Dutch youth, found that parent–adolescent relationships were least positive during late adolescence, not early adolescence, as has been found in U.S. samples (van Wel, 1994).

Whereas there are substantial differences among ethnic groups *within* the United States with respect to patterns of parental discipline (discussed in Chapter 4) and ethnic socialization (discussed in Chapter 8), differences between ethnic groups in the expression of intimacy between adolescents and parents are fairly modest (Fuligni, Hughes, & Way, 2009). Ethnic minority American adolescents are more likely to say that it is important to respect, assist, and support their family than are White adolescents (Fuligni, Tseng, & Lam, 1999), but ethnic differences in adolescents' beliefs and expectations appear to be more substantial than ethnic differences in how adolescents and their parents actually interact. Indeed, with the exception of families who are very recent immigrants to the United States, relations between American adolescents and their parents look surprisingly similar across ethnic groups (Fuligni, 1998).

There are important differences between adolescents' relationships with mothers versus fathers, however. In general, adolescents interact much more often with, are closer to, and argue more with their mother than with their father, a pattern seen among males as

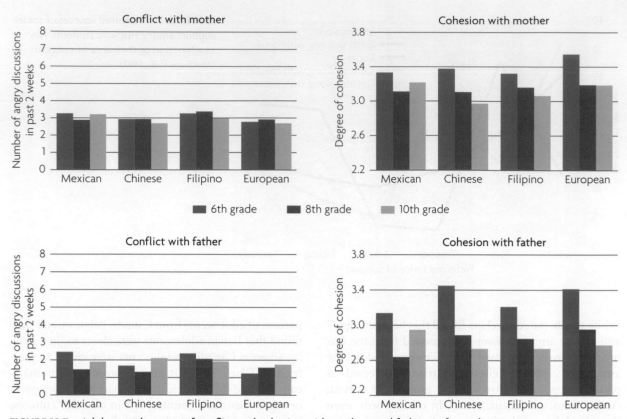

FIGURE 10.7 Adolescents' reports of conflict and cohesion with mothers and fathers in four ethnic groups. (Fuligni, 1998)

well as females and across a variety of cultures (Claes, 1998; C. Cooper, 1994; Fuligni, 1998). Of their two parents, adolescents see their mother as being more understanding, more accepting, and more willing to negotiate, and as less judgmental, less guarded, and less defensive (see Figure 10.7). The difference between perceptions of mothers and fathers is especially large among girls: As a rule, the mother–daughter relationship tends to be the closest, and the father–daughter relationship the least intimate, with mother–son and father–son relationships falling in between (Monck, 1991; Noller & Callan, 1990; K. Rice & Mulkeen, 1995).

All in all, then, an important transition in intimate relationships appears to take place sometime between the fifth and eighth grades. During this period, peers become the most important source of companionship and intimate self-disclosure—surpassing parents and, interestingly, other family members such as siblings (Buhrmester & Furman, 1987; Larson & Richards, 1991). Peers may become increasingly important as targets of intimacy not simply because they are similar in age but also because they do not share the same family with the adolescent. As adolescents begin the process of individuation, they may need to seek intimacy outside the family as a means of establishing an identity beyond their family role. Although this shift in intimacy is normative, a shift in primary attachment figures at this age is not: Adolescents who report that

their strongest attachment is to a friend or romantic partner are more likely to have insecure attachments with their parents (Freeman & Brown, 2001).

■ **The Different Roles of Parents and Peers** Adolescents also have very different sorts of intimate relationships with parents and peers, and these differences point to different ways in which mothers, fathers, and friends may contribute to their social development. Even in close families, parent–adolescent relations are characterized by an imbalance of power, with parents as nurturers, advice givers, and explainers whom adolescents turn to for their experience and expertise. Adolescents' interactions with their friends, in contrast, are more mutual, more balanced, and more likely to provide them with opportunities to express alternative views and engage in an equal exchange of feelings and beliefs. Consistent with this, conflicts between adolescents and their parents are relatively more likely to end with a "winner" and a "loser," whereas conflicts between adolescents and their friends are relatively more likely to end in compromise or, at least, equal outcomes (Adams & Laursen, 2001).

Rather than viewing one type of relationship as more or less intimate than the other, it seems wiser to say that both types of intimacy are important, for each influences a different aspect of the adolescent's developing character in important ways. Intimacy with parents provides opportunities to learn from those older and wiser; intimacy with friends provides opportunities to share experiences with individuals who have a similar perspective and degree of expertise. Consistent with this view, studies find that adolescents who have strong attachments to both parents and peers are better adjusted than those who have strong attachments in one type of relationship but not in the other (Laible, Carlo, & Raffaelli, 2000). In addition, the positive impact of having supportive friends in adolescence is greater when an adolescent also has supportive parents (Helsen, Vollebergh, & Meeus, 2000).

The different functions of intimacy with parents and peers are nicely illustrated in a study of social support during a transition into a new school (S. Dunn, Putallaz, Sheppard, & Lindstrom, 1987). As you will recall from Chapter 6, changing schools during adolescence can sometimes be stressful, and **social support**—emotional or instrumental assistance from others—can help buffer adolescents against the potential negative effects of stress (Hauser & Bowlds, 1990). The study found that support from family members was more predictive of adaptation to the demands of the new school, as indexed by grades and attendance, but that support from peers was more predictive of psychological well-being, as indexed by low levels of depression and anxiety. The absence of peer support was especially critical for boys, perhaps because girls are more likely than boys to seek out other sources of support when their peers do not provide it. Although more research on the nature and effects of social support among minority adolescents is needed, at least one study indicates that parental support is more strongly related to self-esteem among White than Black adolescents (M. Levitt et al., 1993).

Studies show that a lack of support from parents or from friends in school is associated with low self-worth and poorer social adjustment in early adolescence. Social support from one source (such as the family) can be especially important when other sources of support (such as friends) are lacking (Ohannessian, Lerner, Lerner, & von Eye, 1994). A supportive family is more important for the healthy adjustment of adolescents who do not have a close friend, whereas support from friends is more crucial among adolescents whose family relationships are strained (Gauze, Bukowski, Aquan-Assee, & Sippola, 1996). Having support from parents, siblings, or nonschool friends does not fully compensate for a lack of support from classmates, though, and having support from siblings, classmates, or others does not fully compensate for a lack of support from parents (East & Rook, 1992; Gore & Aseltine, 1995). In other words, optimal social development during adolescence may require healthy relationships with *both* parents and peers (Barber & Olsen, 1997; Eccles, Early, Frasier,

Belansky, & McCarthy, 1997; Young, Berenson, Cohen, & Garcia, 2005). Family relationships and peer relationships influence, rather than compete with, each other (Fallon & Bowles, 1997; Gavin & Furman, 1996).

A study of the differential uses of parents and peers as sources of support indicates that whom adolescents turn to is likely to be highly dependent upon the specific issue at hand, which explains, in part, why adolescents may need support from both parents and peers (Boldero & Fallon, 1995; Morrison et al., 1997). This particular study asked adolescents whom they would turn to if they had a substance abuse problem; the respondents could name as many different people as desired (Windle, Miller-Tutzauer, & Barnes, 1991). Among the early adolescents surveyed, only 43% listed their parents among people they would turn to for help, whereas 60% listed friends; among the middle adolescents, the proportions were 39% and 70%, respectively. More interestingly, 10% of all early adolescents and almost that proportion of middle adolescents said that they would turn to no one at all—a far more common response among boys than girls. There also were interesting ethnic differences in adolescents' responses, with Black and Hispanic American youngsters twice as likely as White adolescents to report being socially isolated (that is, having *no one* to turn to). An absence of social support may be especially problematic for poor youth, who often rely on peers to provide emotional support in the face of stress and other difficulties inherent in living in high-risk environments (Stanton-Salazar & Spina, 2005).

In general, then, the results of research on changes in intimacy with parents and peers as an individual ages are similar to the findings discussed in Chapter 9 regarding autonomy: Although the importance of peer relationships undoubtedly increases during adolescence, the significance of family relationships does not decline so much as it narrows in focus. Parents do not cease to be important sources of influence or, as we see here, targets of intimacy. Throughout adolescence, parents and adolescents remain close, parents (especially mothers) remain important confidants, and both mothers and fathers continue to be significant influences on the young person's behavior and decisions. Indeed, even in adolescence, being close to one's parents has a more positive impact on psychological health than being close to one's friends (Greenberg, Siegel, & Leitch, 1983). That said, peers take on an increasingly important role in the individual's social life over the course of adolescence (B. Brown & Larson, 2009). Although peers do not replace parents, they clearly contribute to the adolescent's social development in a unique and influential way.

social support   The extent to which an individual receives emotional or instrumental assistance from his or her social network.

▌ Other Individuals as Targets of Intimacy Intimacy in sibling relationships is a complicated matter and often includes a mix of affection and rivalry (East, 2009). Generally, adolescents say they are less intimate with siblings than with parents or friends (Buhrmester & Furman, 1987). Adolescents fight more with brothers and sisters than they do with close friends, and their arguments with siblings tend to be resolved less by giving in or by letting things slide than through the intervention of others, presumably parents (Raffaelli, 1997). Over the course of adolescence, conflict between siblings decreases, but this may be due to the fact that siblings spend less time together in adolescence than they did in childhood as they become involved in romantic relationships and extracurricular activities; a better way to think about it is that sibling relationships become less intense. Nevertheless, although overt conflict between siblings declines during adolescence, so do warmth and closeness; early adolescence appears to be the low point in sibling relationships, but even college students report ambivalent feelings about their siblings (Stocker, Lanthier, & Furman, 1997).

Comparatively little is known about intimacy with members of adolescents' extended family or with nonfamilial adults like teachers or coaches. Actual contact with extended family is infrequent for many adolescents, however, because those family members often live outside the adolescent's immediate area (Feiring & Lewis, 1991). There appears to be a slight increase in intimacy with extended family members during childhood but an especially steep drop-off in intimacy with grandparents and other extended family members between childhood and adolescence (Buhrmester & Furman, 1987; Creasey & Kaliher, 1994; M. Levitt et al., 1993).

Although a decline in intimacy with grandparents is often observed during adolescence, this may not be as common among adolescents who are living with a single, divorced mother (Clingempeel, Colyar, Brand, & Hetherington, 1992; Hirsch, Mickus, & Boerger, 2002). Divorce may be associated with increased contact between adolescents and their grandparents, especially between the adolescent and his or her maternal grandfather. Ties to grandmothers are especially strong among Black adolescents, particularly among girls from divorced households (Hirsch et al., 2002). Interestingly, puberty seems to increase the intimacy between adolescent boys from divorced homes and their grandfathers (perhaps to compensate for diminished contact with their father), whereas it seems to distance adolescent girls from their grandfathers (perhaps because of discomfort with the girl's sexuality).

Researchers also have asked whether relationships between adolescents and nonfamilial adults in schools, workplaces, or neighborhoods can play a significant role in teenagers' lives (Greenberger, Chen, & Beam, 1998; Munsch, Liang, & DeSecottier, 1996). Indeed, recent studies suggest that the development of relationships with nonfamilial adults is a normative part of adolescence, not a sign of difficulties at home (Beam, Chen, & Greenberger, 2002; Rhodes & Lowe, 2009). Close friendships may develop naturally between adolescents and their teachers or work supervisors or can be cultivated through community organizations, such as Big Brothers/Big Sisters, or similar programs designed to pair young people—especially those under stress—with supportive and caring adults. Indeed, linking an adolescent with a mentor is one of the most important components of successful youth programs (Theokas & Lerner, 2006). The benefits of having a Big Brother or Big Sister may be especially significant among adolescents with more difficulties at home, such as those living in foster care (Rhodes, Haight, & Briggs, 1999). Not all close relationships with nonparental adults benefit adolescents' development, however: Adolescent boys who have close friendships with young adult men are more likely to engage in antisocial behavior when they perceive their older friends as likely to condone or commit antisocial acts themselves (Greenberger et al., 1998).

FRIENDSHIPS WITH THE OTHER SEX

Not until late adolescence do intimate friendships with other-sex peers begin to be important. Consistent with Sullivan's theory, studies of preadolescents and young teenagers point to very strong sex segregation in adolescents' friendships, with boys rarely reporting friendships with girls, and girls rarely reporting friendships with boys, at least until middle adolescence (Galambos, Berenbaum, & McHale, 2009).

▌ Origins of the "Sex Cleavage" The schism between boys and girls during early adolescence results from various factors. First, despite whatever changes may have taken place in American society with regard to sex-role socialization during the past 40 years, it is still the case that preadolescent and early adolescent boys and girls have different interests, engage in different sorts of peer activities, and perceive themselves to be different from each other (Galambos et al., 2009). The sex cleavage in adolescent friendships results more from adolescents' preferring members of the same sex—and the activities they engage in—than from their actually disliking members of the other sex, although boys express more positive feelings about their female classmates than vice versa (Bukowski, Gauze, Hoza, & Newcomb, 1993; Bukowski, Sippola, & Hoza, 1999).

The transitional period—between same-sex nonsexual relationships and other-sex sexual ones—can be a trying time for adolescents. This period usually coincides with the peer group's shift from same-sex cliques to mixed-sex crowds, which we examined in Chapter 5.

The interpersonal strains and anxieties inherent in the transition show up in the high levels of teasing, joking around, and overt discomfort that young adolescents so often display in situations that are a little too close to being romantic or sexual. One reason for the mutual physical playfulness that boys and girls engage in is that it is ambiguous enough to be denied as motivated by genuine sexual interest. Whereas rough play—play fighting—between boys is typically done to show who is dominant, the same behavior between boys and girls is often semisexual in nature—what some have labeled "poke and push courtship" (Pellegrini, 2003).

These observations support Sullivan's claim that intimacy between adolescent boys and girls is relatively slow to develop and generally is tinged with an air of sexuality. Contrary to his notion that cross-sex intimacy comes to replace intimacy with peers of the same sex, however, researchers have found that intimate relationships between adolescents of the same sex continue to develop throughout adolescence. They clearly are not displaced by the eventual emergence of intimacy between adolescent males and females (Connolly & Johnson, 1993). Although researchers find that the likelihood of other-sex peers appearing on adolescents' lists of people who are important to them increases during early and middle adolescence, and although the amount of time adolescents spend with other-sex peers increases as well, the number of same-sex peers listed also increases or remains constant, and time spent with same-sex peers does not decline (Feiring & Lewis, 1991; Richards, Crowe, Larson, & Swarr, 1998; Zimmer-Gembeck, 1999). However, there are substantial individual differences in patterns of time allocation to same- and other-sex relationships; some adolescents shift their energy from same-sex friends to other sex relationships early and abruptly, others do so gradually over the course of high school, and still others do not shift their focus at all (Zimmer-Gembeck, 1999).

Although intimacy between the sexes increases during early adolescence (Buhrmester & Furman, 1987), many adolescents do not list a single other-sex peer as a significant person in their lives. In middle school, only 8% of adolescents' friendships are with members of the other sex; by high school, this figure has risen only to 13% (Degirmencioglu & Urberg, 1994). One exception to this general trend is seen among gay male adolescents, who tend to have more female than male friends (Diamond & Dube, 2002).

When females do include other-sex peers on their list of important people, the boys they mention are often older and often from another school; when boys list girls as important friends, they generally are of the same age or younger (Poulin & Pedersen, 2007). Consistent with this, the increase in time spent with other-sex peers that occurs in adolescence takes place much earlier among girls than boys—by the time they are in

As cross-sex relationships begin to develop, adolescents may mask their anxieties by teasing and joking around with members of the other sex.

11th grade, girls are spending 10 hours each week alone with a boy, compared to only 5 hours per week spent by boys alone with a girl. Young adolescents of both sexes spend a lot of time thinking about the other sex, but relatively little time with them. Interestingly, as adolescents get older, the time they spend thinking about the other sex tends to be increasingly associated with negative mood states, perhaps because the fantasies about the other sex experienced in early adolescence come to be replaced by more realistic longings for romantic companionship (Richards et al., 1998).

Some Functions of Other-Sex Friendships

Although the emergence of close other-sex friendships in early adolescence is not explicitly in the context of romance, it likely sets the stage for later romantic experiences (Connolly & McIssac, 2009). The pattern of age differences in other-sex friendships, for example, is consistent with what we know about age differences between dating partners in early and middle adolescence, with boys generally older than their girlfriends, rather than the reverse (Montgomery & Sorell, 1998). In addition, adolescents who have more other-sex friends than their peers early in adolescence tend to enter into romantic relationships at an earlier age and tend to have longer romantic relationships as well (Feiring, 1999). This could be due to many factors, including the adolescent's use of the pool of other-sex friends to "rehearse" for later romantic relationships or to develop a social network that is used to meet potential dates later on (Connolly, Furman, & Konarski, 2000; Connolly

& Goldberg, 1999; Darling, Dowdy, Van Horn, & Caldwell, 1999). In any case, clearly, even preadolescents as young as 9 differentiate between cross-sex relationships that are platonic and those that are romantic (Connolly, Craig, Goldberg, & Pepler, 1999).

Not all relationships between males and females in adolescence are romantic, of course, and having close, other-sex friendships is a common experience among contemporary youth (Connolly & McIssac, 2009; Kuttler, La Greca, & Prinstein, 1999; Stanton-Salazar & Spina, 2005). Two very different types of adolescents appear to have close other-sex friends—adolescents who are socially competent and highly popular with same-sex peers, and adolescents who are socially incompetent and highly unpopular with same-sex peers (Bukowski, Sippola, & Hoza, 1999; Değirmencioğlu & Urberg, 1994; Feiring & Lewis, 1991). Among boys, having an other-sex friend serves as a "backup system" for those who do not have same-sex friends, leading to more positive mental health than is seen among boys without any friends at all. Among girls, however, the results are mixed. Although some studies have found that "there is no advantage, or perhaps there is even a disadvantage, to having a friendship with a boy" (Bukowski et al., 1999, p. 457), others have found that, among less sexually advanced girls, having platonic friendships with boys is associated with a more positive body image—perhaps because these friendships permit girls to feel that boys like them for themselves, without the added cost of feeling pressured to have sex (Compian, Gowen, & Hayward, 2004). Having male friends, however, increases girls' likelihood of being involved in antisocial behavior (Arndorfer & Stormshak, 2008), especially if their male friends are antisocial (Cauffman, Farruggia, & Goldweber, 2008), which makes sense, given that boys are more likely to be antisocial and that adolescents' behavior often mimics that of their friends.

FOOD FOR THOUGHT

Anecdotal evidence suggests that nonsexual friendships between males and females have become more common in recent decades. Why do you think this might be?

In general, though, the overall picture suggests that boys have more to gain from friendships with girls than vice versa. Having an intimate relationship with an other-sex peer is more strongly related to boys' general level of interpersonal intimacy than it is to girls' (Buhrmester & Furman, 1987); and whereas boys report that their friendships with girls are more rewarding than their friendships with other boys, girls do not

describe their friendships with boys as more rewarding than their friendships with other girls (J. Thomas & Daubman, 2001). These findings are not surprising, given that adolescents' friendships with girls (regardless of whether they themselves are male or female) tend to be more intimate and supportive than their friendships with boys (Kuttler et al., 1999).

A recent study of peer networks among low-income Mexican American adolescents in San Diego illustrates how important platonic friendships with girls can be for adolescent boys in the development of more mature relationships. Many boys likened their nonsexual friendships with girls to relationships with sisters, emphasizing the ease with which they could explicitly ask for emotional support, something that many adolescent males find difficult to request from their same-sex friends:

> Le tengo un cariño así con ella como si fuera también mi hermana [I have such love for her, as if she were my sister].... We always support each other, it doesn't matter what it is; if she asks me, I help her, and if I ask her, she helps me, with anything. (Stanton-Salazar & Spina, 2005, pp. 397–398)

Some boys also discussed the important role their female friends played in helping them manage their tempers:

> You know, I'm the kind of guy that can go around and like, you know, get mad and you know . . . siento como que quiero cingar a alguien [I feel like I wanna fuck somebody up (i.e., to hit and seriously injure someone)]. She's the person that when she looks at me, you know [giggles], all those mad feelings go to, like, Oh God!, you know. Like she can control me, like she's holding me back, just by looking at me [laughs]. (pp. 399–400)

As in studies of non-Latino youth, this study of Mexican American adolescents indicates that the benefits of cross-sex friendships are less evident for females than for males. Many such friendships draw females into traditional caregiving roles, reinforcing traditional sex-role stereotypes.

RECAP

- With development, adolescents place more emphasis on trust and loyalty as defining features of friendship, become more self-disclosing in their relationships, and become more responsive and sensitive to their friends' needs.
- Sex differences in the expression of intimacy in adolescents' friendships are striking, with girls' relationships being more intimate than boys' across many different indicators. Boys' friendships do not lack intimacy, but intimacy is a much more conscious concern for girls than it is for boys, in part because of sex differences in the way they are socialized.

- New types of relationships are added to the adolescent's social world without replacing previous ones. Beginning in preadolescence, the network of intimate relationships widens to include peers as well as family members and, sometimes, non-familial adults.
- Many adolescents have platonic friendships with other-sex peers. Other-sex friendships help to set the stage for the emergence of romantic relationships later on.
- Boys may profit psychologically from other-sex friendships more than girls.

Dating and Romantic Relationships

Dating plays a very different role in adolescent lives today than it did in previous times (Conn̄̄̄ 2009). In earlier eras, dating during adolescence was not so much a recreational activity (as it part of the process of courtship and m

Individuals would date in order to ready themselves for marriage, and unmarried individuals would play the field—under the watchful eyes of chaperones—for a relatively long period before settling down (Montgomery, 1996). You may be surprised to learn that, at the turn of the 20th century, most individuals did not marry until their mid-20s (U.S. Census Bureau, 2009b). The first half of this century saw a gradual decline in the average age of marriage, however, and as a result, individuals began dating more seriously at an earlier age. By the mid-1950s, the average age at first marriage in the United States had fallen to 20 among women and 22 among men—which means that substantial numbers of individuals were courting during high school and marrying during their late adolescent years.

The function of adolescent dating changed, however, as individuals began to marry later and later—a trend that began in the mid-1950s and continues today (see Figure 10.8). Now, the average age at which people marry is considerably later than it was 40 years ago—about age 26 for women and 27 for men (U.S. Census ... this, of course, gives high school dating ... meaning, because today it is clearly ... function in mate selection. Adults ... and monitor adolescent dating in ... sh or impulsive commitments to

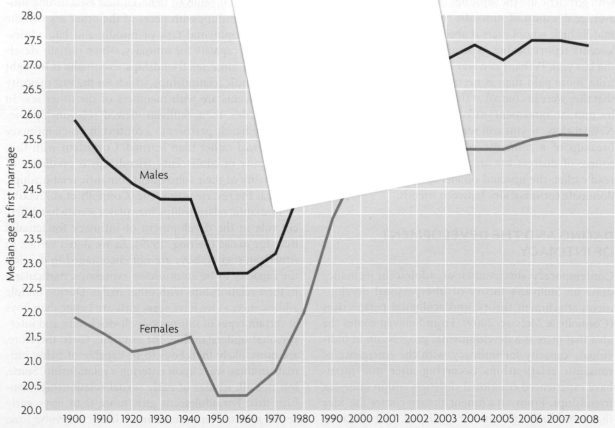

FIGURE 10.8   The median age at marriage in the United States declined from 1900 through the mid-1950s but rose markedly during the second half of the 20th century. (U.S. Census Bureau, 2009)

early marriage (Laursen & Jensen-Campbell, 1999), but in the minds of most young people, high school dating has little to do with courtship or marriage. Nor do today's adolescents see cohabitation (living together) as a substitute for marriage (Manning, Longmore, & Giordano, 2007).

Only recently have social scientists begun writing systematically about adolescents' romantic relationships (W. A. Collins, 2003; Connolly & McIssac, 2009; Furman et al., 1999). However, recent studies of adolescent romance indicate that romantic relationships are very common: One fourth of American 12-year-olds, one half of 15-year-olds, and more than two thirds of 18-year-olds report having had a romantic relationship in the past 18 months. The average American adolescent begins dating around age 13 or 14, although nearly half of all adolescents have at least one date before they turn 12. By age 16, more than 90% of adolescents of both sexes have had at least one date, and during the later years of high school, more than half of all students average one or more dates weekly. Only 15% of high school students date less than once a month (Feiring, 1993). By age 18, virtually all adolescents have dated once, and three fourths have had at least one steady relationship (Neemann, Hubbard, & Masten, 1995).

Girls tend to become involved with boys who are slightly older, whereas boys tend to become involved with girls who are the same age or younger. Because the average duration of romantic relationships during the middle high school years is about 6 months, most adolescents report having experienced a breakup during the last year. Perhaps as a way of protecting themselves from more pain than is necessary, most teenagers say that they were in control of the breakup (either alone or by mutual agreement) (Connolly & McIssac, 2009). Nevertheless, as you will read later in this chapter, the breakup of a romantic relationship is a significant source of distress for many adolescents, and, as you read earlier, the ups and downs of romantic life often dominate conversations between friends.

DATING AND THE DEVELOPMENT OF INTIMACY

Contemporary discussions of adolescent romance draw on Sullivan's theory of interpersonal development, attachment theory, and ecological perspectives (Connolly & McIssac, 2009). From Sullivan comes the idea that there is a developmental progression in individuals' capacity for intimacy, with the emergence of romantic relationships occurring after individuals have experienced emotional closeness within same-sex friendships. From attachment theory comes the idea that individuals differ in the quality of their romantic relationships and that these differences are paralleled by differences in the relationships individuals have with

One of the fundamental developmental tasks of adolescence is to begin to develop the capacity for intimate, romantic relationships.

parents and peers. And from the ecological perspective comes the idea that romantic relationships, like all relationships, need to be viewed within the social context in which they occur.

The Nature and Significance of Romance As you may recall, Sullivan believed that establishing intimate relationships with peers of the other sex was the chief developmental task of middle and late adolescence. The capacity for intimacy, which initially develops out of same-sex friendships, eventually is brought into romantic relationships, which for the vast majority of adolescents are with members of the other sex. In some senses, then, Sullivan viewed relationships between romantic partners as a context in which intimacy is *expressed* rather than learned. Consistent with this, the quality of adolescents' friendships is predictive of the quality of their subsequent romantic relationships, whereas the reverse is not true (Connolly et al., 2000).

Romantic relationships may play a somewhat different role in the development of intimacy for females than for males (Feiring, 1999). As we noted earlier, in American society, boys are not encouraged to develop the capacity to be emotionally expressive, particularly in their relationships with other males. During middle adolescence, as we have seen, girls are better than boys at certain types of intimacy—self-disclosure and interpersonal understanding, for example. Girls, therefore, are more likely than boys to be capable of being intimate in these ways upon entering a relationship. Some, but not all, studies of early sexual relationships confirm this: For adolescent girls more than boys, early sexual relationships are far more likely to involve love, emotional involvement, and intimacy (Montgomery, 2005; Shulman & Scharf, 2000). In other words, whereas for girls cross-sex relationships may provide a context for further *expression* of intimacy, for boys they may provide a context for the further *development* of intimacy. This notion is consistent with the finding, discussed earlier, that other-sex relationships may play a more important role in the development of intimacy among boys than among girls, who, on average, develop and experience intimacy earlier with same-sex friends than boys do (Buhrmester & Furman, 1987). One recent study found that the way a girl interacts with her boyfriend is more strongly related to the girl's internal working model of relationship than the boy's, perhaps because girls' greater prior experience with intimacy has led them to better align how they behave with how they really feel (Furman & Simon, 2006).

Although boys' capacity for intimacy may lag behind girls', it is important not to confuse ability with aspiration. In the past, much was made of the different meanings of romantic relationships to adolescent males and females, but today it appears that the sexes are more similar than different in how their romantic relationships develop (Connolly & McIssac, 2009). The stereotype of the emotionally stunted but swaggering boy who enters into a romantic relationship purely for sex and uses his power and influence to get it no longer appears accurate. Indeed, research shows that boys are often more awkward and less confident than the girls they are dating and just as eager to be emotionally close. In one study, in which boys were interviewed about their relationships, they frequently responded with answers that contradict the macho stereotype. Here's a 17-year-old talking about his girlfriend:

> She kept insisting I wasn't going to work out and I kept insisting I wanted to try it and one night, and like I said I couldn't sleep, and I wrote her a letter, front and back, crying the whole time and then I handed the letter to her the next morning. . . . It was really emotional, like how she hurt me and how it wasn't right. (Giordano, Longmore, & Manning, 2006, p. 277)

Or how about this 18-year-old:

> I guess she was more mature than I was and I guess I wasn't on her level you know because she wanted to do it [have sex] more than I did. . . . she said that I wasn't mature enough and you know all that stuff. . . . I was too young, I was scared, I didn't know what I was doing I wasn't ready for it. I think I felt like I was too young. . . . she was my girlfriend and that's what she wanted. (Giordano et al., 2006, p. 281)

■ **The Role of Context** The age at which dating begins is influenced by the norms and expectations in the adolescent's community. Romantic relationships are more common at a younger age in other industrialized countries than in North America, but by late adolescence, rates of dating are similar. Within the United States and in Canada, Asian adolescents are less likely than other adolescents to date, whereas the prevalence of dating is very similar among Black, Hispanic, American Indian, and White adolescents, although some studies find that Hispanic girls start dating at a later age than either Black or White girls (Connolly & McIssac, 2009).

Although early maturers begin dating somewhat earlier than late maturers (Lam, Shi, Ho, Stewart, & Fan, 2002; Neemann et al., 1995), age norms within the adolescent's school and peer group are more important in determining the age at which dating begins than is the adolescent's level of physical development. In other words, a physically immature 14-year-old who goes to school where it is expected that 14-year-olds will date is more likely to date than is a physically mature 14-year-old who lives in a community where dating is typically delayed until age 16. Early maturers whose peers are dating are especially likely to date early (Friedlander, Connolly, Pepler, & Craig, 2007). Sexual activity, however, as we'll see in Chapter 11, is more strongly influenced by biological development (Udry, Billy, Morris, Gruff, & Raj, 1985). Dating also begins earlier among adolescents who have older siblings, among adolescents whose parents do not monitor them well, and among those with single mothers, especially if the mother is sexually active herself (Longmore, Manning, & Giordano, 2001; Neeman et al., 1995). Family instability (changes in parents' marital status through divorce or remarriage) is associated with dating, especially among boys, with adolescents from more unstable families more likely to date and more likely to have multiple romantic partners. Whether this is due to less vigilant parental monitoring, a desire on the part of the adolescent to escape a difficult home environment, or both is not known (Cavanaugh, Crissey, & Raley, 2008).

The influence of context on expectations for dating is vividly illustrated in the sorts of letters that adolescents write to the advice columns in teen magazines (van Roosmalen, 2000, p. 207):

> All my friends have boyfriends and I don't (I'm 12). It makes me so depressed because I feel like I'll never have one. I'm afraid of what everyone will think.
> *Bummed out*

> Every kid in my class has either a boyfriend or a girlfriend. I don't have a boyfriend, so I use the excuse that boys don't look good yet. But how long can I hold out with the same excuse?
> *Boyfriendless*

> I'm just entering junior high school and all around me there are couples kissing, holding hands, and hugging. . . . It really hurts to see everyone with a boyfriend and then me just all alone.
> *Heartbroken*

FIGURE 10.9 Participation in various romantic activities in early adolescence. (Connolly et al., 2004)

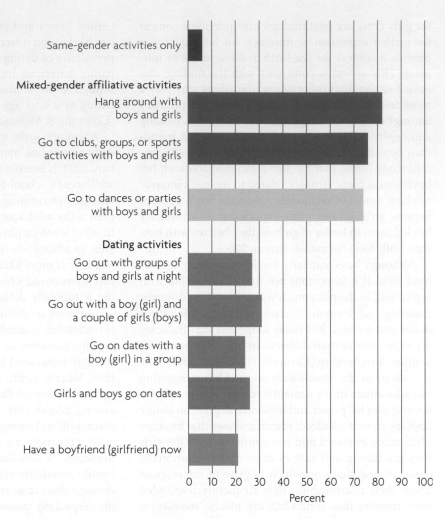

Same-gender activities only

Mixed-gender affiliative activities

Hang around with boys and girls

Go to clubs, groups, or sports activities with boys and girls

Go to dances or parties with boys and girls

Dating activities

Go out with groups of boys and girls at night

Go out with a boy (girl) and a couple of girls (boys)

Go on dates with a boy (girl) in a group

Girls and boys go on dates

Have a boyfriend (girlfriend) now

0   10   20   30   40   50   60   70   80   90   100
Percent

■ **Patterns of Dating**   "Dating" can mean a variety of different things, of course, from group activities that bring males and females together (without much actual contact between the sexes), to group dates in which a group of boys and girls go out jointly (and spend part of the time in couples and part of the time in the larger group), to casual dating in couples, to serious involvement with a steady boyfriend or girlfriend. Generally, casual socializing with other-sex peers and experiences in a mixed-sex social network occur before the development of romantic relationships (Connolly & McIssac, 2009). As a consequence, more adolescents have experience in mixed-sex group activities like parties or dances than in dating, and more have experience in dating than in having a serious boyfriend or girlfriend or a sexual relationship (see Figure 10.9) (Connolly, Craig, Goldberg, & Pepler, 2004; O'Sullivan, Cheng, Harris, & Brooks-Gunn, 2007). Involvement in one-on-one romantic relationships does not replace same-sex or mixed-sex group activities—like other aspects of intimacy in adolescence, new forms of relationships are added to the adolescent's repertoire while old ones are retained. The sequence of transitioning into romantic relationships

follows similar patterns across ethnic groups, although Asian American youth appear to make this transition at a somewhat later stage than their peers from other backgrounds, consistent with other findings on ethnic differences in beliefs about the appropriate age at which adolescents should begin dating and engaging in other adultlike activities (Connolly et al., 2004) (see Chapter 9).

Even for adolescents with a history of intimate friendships with same- and other-sex peers, the transition into romantic relationships can be difficult. In one study, in which adolescents were asked to discuss social situations they thought were difficult, themes having to do with communicating with the other sex were mentioned frequently. Many adolescents discussed difficulty in initiating or maintaining conversations, in person ("He will think I am an idiot," "Sometimes you don't know, if you're like sitting with a guy and you're watching a basketball game or something, you don't know if you should start talking or if you should just sit there") and on the phone ("I think it is hard to call. After it's done with, you don't know how to get off the phone"). Others mentioned problems in asking people out ("Asking a girl out on a first date—complete panic!") or in turning people down ("How about if you go on a date and you're really not interested, but he keeps calling?"). Still others noted problems in making or ending romantic commitments ("You don't know if you are going out with someone or if you are just seeing them," "It is hard to say, 'so, are we gonna make a commitment?'" "I avoided [breaking up] for two weeks because I was trying to think of what to say") (Grover & Nangle, 2003, pp. 133–134).

THE DEVELOPMENT OF DATING RELATIONSHIPS

Dating serves many purposes in adolescence, only one of which is the development of intimacy. Indeed, it is not until late adolescence that dating relationships begin to be characterized by a level of emotional depth and maturity that can be described as intimate, and it is not until late adolescence that individuals develop genuinely deep attachments to individuals other than their parents (Furman & Simon, 1999; Hazan, 1994; Montgomery, 2005). One recent study comparing the way adolescents interacted with their mother, a close friend, and a romantic partner found that interactions with romantic partners were characterized by more conflict and fewer positive interactions than with friends, and more off-task behavior than with mothers (Furman & Shomaker, 2008). Over the course of adolescence, the importance of a romantic partner—relative to other relationships—increases, and by college, individuals typically name their romantic partner first on a list of significant others (up from fourth in grade 7 and third in grade 10) (Buhrmester, 1996; Furman & Wehner, 1994).

The ways in which adolescents interact with romantic partners also changes with development, with increasing willingness to acknowledge, analyze, and work through disagreements. (The major sources of conflict between boyfriends and girlfriends are issues related to how the dyad is functioning, such as jealousy, neglect, betrayal, and trust [McIsaac, Connolly, McKenney, Pepler, & Craig, 2008].) One study of Israeli couples' conflict resolution found that whereas 70% of the adolescent couples either denied or dismissed the conflict as insignificant, only 20% of the young adults did. Interestingly, the adolescents whose conversations looked more like those of the young adults were less likely to break up (Shulman, Tuval-Mashiach, Levran, & Anbar, 2006).

▌ **Reasons for Dating**   Prior to middle or late adolescence, dating may be less important for the development of intimacy than it is for other purposes, including establishing emotional and behavioral autonomy from parents (Dowdy & Kliewer, 1999; Gray & Steinberg,

1999), furthering the development of gender identity (Feiring, 1999), learning about oneself as a romantic partner (Furman & Simon, 1999), and establishing and maintaining status and popularity in the peer group (B. Brown, 1999). For these reasons, younger adolescents' choice of dating partners may have more to do with how they will be seen by others (for example, as "grown up," "macho," or "popular") than with the actual quality of the relationship itself. Consistent with this, between elementary school and middle school, there is an increase in girls' attraction to aggressive boys who stand out in the peer group (Bukowski, Sippola, & Newcomb, 2000).

▌ **Phases of Romance**   The development of intimacy and more sophisticated social cognitive abilities is paralleled by changes in the ways adolescents think about and behave within romantic relationships. Several stage theories of romantic relationships have been advanced (Connolly & McIssac, 2009). The evolution of romance in the adolescent's life proceeds through three distinct phases. During the first phase (roughly between 11 and 13), adolescents first discover an interest in socializing with potential romantic and sexual partners. The focus of activity during this phase is primarily on learning about themselves, as adolescents broaden their self-conceptions to include seeing themselves as a potential romantic partner to someone else. Actual romantic relationships tend to be short-lived (the average romantic relationship at this age lasts only a few weeks) and are frequently based on superficial infatuations. Indeed, the main purpose of romantic activity at this age involves establishing, improving, or maintaining peer group status. Success in socializing with the other sex becomes an important determinant of status in the peer group, and high-status adolescents generally start dating before their lower-status peers (Connolly & McIssac, 2009).

During the second phase (from about 14 to 16), adolescents slowly move toward more meaningful dyadic relationships. During this period, dating is very casual and often occurs in a group context in which peer networks start to include couples who have a special relationship. Although adolescents are still learning about themselves as romantic and sexual partners and are still aware of the way their peers view their romantic relationships, they are now sufficiently involved in the emotional side of romance for this to completely overshadow the personal and status concerns that dominated the earlier phases of romantic involvement. Relationships become a source of passion and preoccupation—recalling the themes expressed in popular love songs that appeal to teenagers. Although relationships are more enduring at this age than they were during early adolescence, the average romance still lasts only about six months (Connolly & McIssac, 2009). One reason for this is that "dating the 'wrong' person or conducting romantic relationships in the 'wrong' way can seriously damage one's standing in the group. . . . This makes it difficult to sustain relationships that are too heavily focused inward, on the quality of the interaction or needs of the couple" (B. Brown, 1999, p. 297).

Finally, toward the later years of high school (around 17 or 18), concerns about commitment begin to move to the forefront, as adolescents begin to think about the long-term survival and growth of their romantic attachments. Often during this stage, there are tensions between partners' needs for intimacy (which draw them together) and their needs for autonomy (which distance them). As conceptions of romance develop, adolescents come to value commitment and caring as features of relationships that are as important as passion and pleasure, if not more so (B. Brown, 1999; Seiffge-Krenke, 2003). Relationships begin to look more like those seen among young adults, and couples increasingly spend time by themselves, rather than in the larger peer group. The average romantic relationship at age 18 lasts more than a year (Connolly & McIssac, 2009).

Although the progression through the different phases of dating and romance may characterize the development of most adolescents, a number of writers interested in the experiences of gay, lesbian, and bisexual adolescents have pointed out that this picture may be less applicable to **sexual-minority youth**— adolescents who are not exclusively heterosexual (Diamond, 2000; Diamond, Savin-Williams, & Dubé, 1999). Although great strides have been made in increasing the public's tolerance and understanding of homosexuality, stigmas and stereotypes still make the development of intimate relationships—whether nonsexual friendships, dating relationships, or sexual relationships—far more complicated among sexual-minority youth than among their straight peers. For example, because few sexual-minority youth have the freedom to publicly express their romantic and sexual interests in members of the same sex, they often find it difficult, if not impossible, to engage in many of the social and interpersonal activities that their heterosexual friends are permitted to enjoy. Thus, many sexual-minority youth end up pursuing sexual activity *outside* the context of a dating relationship, because the prejudices and harassment of others may preclude any public display of romantic intimacy with a same-sex partner. At the same time, for sexual-minority youth who are even somewhat open about their sexual identity, the development of close, nonsexual friendships with same-sex peers may be hampered by the suspicions and homophobia of others. As one group of writers explains the special predicament faced by sexual-minority adolescents, "A sexual-minority adolescent may already be privately plagued by the sense that he or she is profoundly different from other youths. To have this differentness acknowledged and perhaps ridiculed by peers may prove intolerable" (Diamond, Savin-Williams, & Dubé, 1999).

■ **Sex Differences in Partner Preferences**   There are both age and sex differences in what adolescents look for in romantic partners, and these differences parallel what is known about age and sex differences in romantic relationships. During middle adolescence, boys are more likely to mention physical attractiveness and girls are more likely to mention interpersonal qualities, such as support or intimacy. By late adolescence, however, both sexes emphasize interpersonal qualities, and the ingredients of a satisfying relationship are very similar for males and females (and quite similar to those mentioned by adults): passion, communication, commitment, emotional support, and togetherness (W. A. Collins, 2003; Connolly, Craig, Goldberg, & Pepler, 1999; Feiring, 1996; Levesque, 1993). Interestingly, however, adolescents' satisfaction with their romantic relationships are not as negatively affected by such qualities as conflict or possessiveness as are adults' (Levesque, 1993).

FOOD FOR THOUGHT

Traditional, one-on-one dating is far less common today than in past generations, and relatively more interaction between males and females, even those who are romantically interested in each other, occurs in groups than in couples. What implications does it have for the development of intimacy? For preparation for marriage?

THE IMPACT OF DATING ON ADOLESCENT DEVELOPMENT

When considering the impact of dating on adolescents' development and mental health, it is important to differentiate between group and couple activities. Participating in mixed-sex activity in group situations—going to parties or dances, for example—has a positive impact on the psychological well-being of adolescents, perhaps because at this stage of development, participating in these activities is status enhancing. The impact of more serious dating is complicated and, as we shall see, may depend a great deal on the adolescent's age. Early starters (those who enter into dating relationships well before their peers) and late bloomers (those who do not have a romantic relationship until young adulthood) may both be at risk, although for different

sexual-minority youth   Gay, lesbian, and bisexual youth.

reasons and with different consequences. This is not to say that dating is not a valuable interpersonal experience for the adolescent, just that its benefits may only accrue among teenagers who wait until they are a certain age (Neemann et al., 1995).

▌ **Early Starters** There is considerable evidence that entering into a serious romantic relationship before it is normative (say, before age 15) is associated with a wide range of negative correlates (Connolly & McIssac, 2009). This is probably true for both sexes, but researchers have focused primarily on girls because boys are less likely to begin serious dating quite so early. Even so, the few studies that have looked at early dating among boys do not show consistent effects.

Compared with their peers, girls who begin serious dating early are worse off psychologically than their peers—less mature socially, less imaginative, less oriented toward achievement, less happy with who they are and how they look, more depressed, more likely to engage in disordered eating, less likely to do well in school, and more likely to be involved in delinquency, substance use, and risky behavior (Connolly & McIssac, 2009). The links between early dating and poorer mental health have been reported consistently for at least 50 years. Early dating seems to have especially negative implications among White girls (Compian et al., 2004), girls whose family relationships are more strained (Doyle et al., 2003), and girls who are either early maturers (Natsuaki, Biehl, & Ge, 2009). Adolescents who are unpopular with same-sex peers are especially harmed by early serious dating, perhaps because having few same-sex friends makes the dating relationships excessively important (Brendgen, Vitaro, Doyle, Markiewicz, & Bukowski, 2002). Research also shows that adolescents who begin dating early and who have multiple dating partners experience a drop in the quality of their relationships over time (W. A. Collins, 2003).

A variety of explanations for the link between early dating and psychological problems have been offered, but before we get ahead of ourselves, let's keep in mind the difficulty in distinguishing between selection and socialization (Zimmer-Gembeck, Siebenbrunner, & Collins, 2001). (I know you are probably tired of hearing this, but even experienced researchers often forget it.) There are all sorts of reasons to believe that girls with psychological problems are more likely to get involved in dating relationships at a younger age, and because we cannot randomly assign some teenagers to date and others to remain single, we cannot be sure that early dating actually *causes* problems. Moreover, early dating may be part of a larger profile that includes precocious involvement in many adultlike activities, often because their dating partners are older than they are, and there is a good deal of evidence that this sort of

The impact of dating on adolescent development depends on the age of the adolescent and the intensity of the relationship. Early, serious dating may have a negative impact on psychological development.

"pseudomaturity" is associated with a range of psychological problems (Connolly & McIssac, 2009). Because this profile is itself associated with many factors known to place adolescents at risk (poor parenting, early puberty, or family instability, for example), it is hard to pinpoint early dating as the culprit.

That said, it has been suggested that the link between early dating and poor mental health may have something to do with pressures on girls to engage in sexual activity before they are willing or psychologically ready. (Early daters are more likely to be sexually active at a younger age [Marin, Kirby, Hudes, Coyle, & Gomez, 2006].) Sexual coercion and date rape are common during the high school years (B. Brown, 2004; McMaster, Connolly, & Craig, 1997; W. Patton & Mannison, 1995). Although boys may feel peer pressure to become sexually active, this may be a very different sort of pressure—with very different consequences—from what girls feel. Because boys generally begin dating at a later age than girls—and date people who are younger rather than older—beginning to date in couples may be less anxiety-provoking for boys, who have the advantage of a few additional years of "maturity."

FOOD FOR THOUGHT

In addition to the possibility that the negative impact of early dating on girls' mental health is due to pressures to have sex, what other explanations occur to you?

To Date, or Not to Date? About 10% of late adolescents report having had no serious romantic relationships, and another 15% have not been in a relationship that lasted more than a few months (Connolly & McIssac, 2009). In looking at the effects of being a "late bloomer," it is important to distinguish between adolescents who delay dating because it is culturally normative to do so (as is the case in many Asian American communities) and those who delay because they are shy, unattractive, or unpopular (Connolly & McIssac, 2009). Although one would think that it is the latter group whose development is most at risk, not enough research has been done on late bloomers to draw definitive conclusions.

In general, adolescents who do not date at all show signs of retarded social development and feelings of insecurity (Connolly & McIssac, 2009), while adolescents who date and go to parties regularly are more popular, have a stronger self-image, and report greater acceptance by their friends (Connolly & Johnson, 1993). Conversely, stopping or cutting back on dating after having dated heavily is associated with a drop in self-image and an increase in symptoms of depression (Davies & Windle, 2000).

It is not clear, of course, whether age-appropriate dating leads to better social development or whether more socially advanced adolescents are simply more likely to date; both are probably true. But it does seem safe to conclude that a moderate degree of dating—and a delay in serious involvement until age 15 or so—appears to be the most potentially valuable pattern.

This conclusion must be tempered by recent research indicating that, as with the case of peer relationships in general, characteristics of the romantic partner play a role in shaping the impact of dating on psychological development. Adolescents who are not all that popular to begin with, but who date popular peers, gain in popularity over time, and adolescents with problems who date peers whose mental health is good show improvements in their psychological functioning over time (Simon, Aikins, & Prinstein, 2008). It is also the case, just as in the selection of friends, that adolescents tend to select romantic partners with whom they share certain attributes. (Generally speaking, research suggests that the saying, "birds of a feather flock together" is more often true than "opposites attract.")

Regardless of the impact that dating does or doesn't have on adolescents' psychosocial development, studies show that romance has a powerful impact on their emotional state. According to several studies, adolescents' real and fantasized relationships trigger more of their strong emotional feelings during the course of a day (one third of girls' strong feelings and one quarter of boys') than do family, school, or friends. Not surprisingly, the proportion of strong emotions attributed to romantic relationships increases dramatically between preadolescence and early adolescence, and between early and middle adolescence as well. And although the majority of adolescents' feelings about their romantic relationships are positive, a substantial minority of their feelings—more than 40%, in fact—are negative, involving anxiety, anger, jealousy, and depression (Larson, Clore, & Wood, 1999). Consistent with this, adolescents who have entered into a romantic relationship in the past year report more symptoms of depression than do those who have not (Joyner & Udry, 2000). One reason for this may be that many adolescents who are involved romantically also experience breakups during the same time period (W. A. Collins, 2003), and the breakup of a romantic relationship is the single most common trigger of the first episode of major depression (Monroe, Rohde, Seeley, & Lewinsohn, 1999). As you would expect, negative emotions associated with being in a relationship are more common among adolescents who are high in rejection sensitivity (G. Downey et al., 1999) or who have an insecure working model, especially those who form preoccupied attachments to romantic partners (because they are unable to fully trust their partner or see themselves as worthy of their partner's affection) (Davila, 2008).

Breaking up does not have severe effects on all adolescents, of course. Those who are most vulnerable to the potential negative consequences of ending a relationship are adolescents high in rejection sensitivity, those who have experienced a series of breakups, those who have other sorts of problems (such as binge drinking or involvement in delinquency), and, not surprisingly, those who identify themselves as the one who was broken up with (rather than the breaker-upper) (Connolly & McIssac, 2009).

Violence in Dating Relationships Unfortunately many romantic relationships in adolescence are characterized by hostility, aggression, and abuse (B. Brown, 2004), and dating violence becomes more common with age (Halpern, Oslak, Young, Martin, & Kupper, 2001). Estimates vary from study to study, but between one fifth and two thirds of American adolescents may have been the victim of violence within the context of a romantic relationship at one time or another (Feiring, Deblinger, Hoch-Espada, & Haworth, 2002; Gorman-Smith, Tolan, Sheidow, & Henry, 2001; Linder & Collins, 2005; Silverman, Raj, Mucci, & Hathaway, 2001). (One reason for the wide range of estimates is that studies vary considerably in how violence is defined—for example, some may include threats of violence while others may be limited to violence that actually causes physical harm.) Male and female adolescents are equally likely to be the victims of violence in dating relationships (Halpern et al., 2001; J. Miller & White, 2003; O'Leary, Slep, Avery-Leaf, & Cascardi, 2008), and violence is often associated with drinking (Buzy et al., 2004). Dating violence is more common in rural areas than in suburban or urban communities (G. A. Spencer & Bryant, 2000) and is common among both sexual-minority adolescents and heterosexual youth (Freedner, Freed, Yang, & Austin, 2002; Halpern, Young, Waler, Martin, & Kupper, 2004). Individuals who are aggressive in romantic relationships are more likely to have had problems with aggression earlier in life (L. O'Donnell, Stueve, et al., 2006). Adolescents who have been the victims of violence within the context of a romantic relationship are more likely to be depressed, contemplate suicide, use illegal drugs, become pregnant during adolescence, and drop out of school (Hagan & Foster, 2001; Kim & Capaldi, 2004; Silverman et al., 2001). They are also more likely to be victimized again in the future (P. H. Smith, White, & Holland, 2003).

We also know that adolescents behave in a variety of ways within dating relationships that are shaped by "scripts" for how males and females are expected to behave—scripts that are learned at home and from the mass media (Feiring, 1999; Gray & Steinberg, 1999; Larson, Clore, & Wood, 1999). In general, adolescents' ways of dealing with conflict in their romantic relationships are linked to the models they had been exposed to at home. For example, adolescents who have witnessed a great deal of conflict between their parents (either physical or verbal) report higher levels of verbal aggression, physical aggression, and relationship difficulties with their romantic partners, both as perpetrators and victims (Kinsfogel & Grych, 2004; Martin, 1990; Tschann et al., 2009). Other studies have found that adolescents who are either perpetrators or victims of violence in dating relationships are more likely to have had parents who were harsh or behaved inappropriately toward them (Lavoie et al., 2002; Linder & Collins, 2005). These studies, along with those discussed earlier about adolescent attachments, suggest that variations in adolescents' romantic relationships may have their origins—at least in part—in adolescents' family experiences.

The main point to keep in mind is that the qualities of adolescents' relationships with others—whether with parents, siblings, friends, or romantic partners—are correlated across different types of relationships (B. Brown, 2004). Adolescents who have supportive and satisfying relationships at home are more likely to have high-quality friendships, and adolescents who have high-quality friendships are more likely to have high-quality romantic relationships. Thus, individuals' early experiences in the family, in interaction with their cumulative experiences with peers during childhood and preadolescence, affect the nature and quality of their romantic relationships in adolescence (B. Brown, 2004; W. A. Collins, 2003; W. A. Collins & Sroufe, 1999), and the quality of adolescents' family relationships affect the quality of the romantic relationships they have in young adulthood (R. Conger, Cui, Bryant, & Elder, 2000; Donnellan, Larsen-Rife, & Conger, 2005).

RECAP

- In general, social activities with the other sex begin in early adolescence as group activities that bring males and females together, proceed to casual dating in couples, and later in adolescence progress to serious involvement with a steady romantic partner.

- Paralleling these changes in the context of dating are changes in the nature and function of dating. As adolescents develop, dating shifts from a focus on infatuation and status, to intimacy, and, finally to bonding.

- Although early intense dating appears to have adverse effects on adolescents' mental health and behavior, a moderate degree of dating after age 15 or so is associated with better mental health and well-being than no dating at all.

- Adolescents who have supportive and satisfying relationships at home are more likely to have high-quality friendships, and adolescents who have high-quality friendships are more likely to have high-quality romantic relationships. Conversely, adolescents who have been exposed to high levels of conflict or violence in their family, are more likely to experience violence in their own dating relationships.

Intimacy and Psychosocial Development

Intimate relationships during adolescence, whether with peers or adults, inside or outside the family, or sexual or nonsexual, play an important role in young people's overall psychological development (Hartup & Stevens, 1997). Close friends serve as a sounding board for adolescents' fantasies and questions about the future. Adolescents often talk to their friends about the careers they hope to have, the people they hope to get involved with, and the life they expect to lead after they leave home. Friends provide advice on a range of identity-related matters—from how to act in different situations to what sorts of occupational and educational paths to pursue. At least one study finds that having an intimate friendship is more central to adolescents' mental health than it is to children's (Buhrmester, 1990). It also has been found that intimacy with same-sex friends and intimacy with romantic partners make distinct contributions to adolescents' self-esteem (Connolly & Konarski, 1994). Not surprisingly, adolescents who report having at least one close friendship also report higher levels of self-esteem than their peers who do not, although we do not know whether intimacy enhances mental health, mental health facilitates intimacy, or, most likely, both (B. Brown, 2004).

FOOD FOR THOUGHT

Do you think changes in family life—divorce, remarriage, parental employment, and so on—have affected the nature of the development of intimacy in adolescence?

Keep in mind, however, that the effects of having an intimate friendship with someone depend on who that someone is and what takes place in the relationship. Being popular is less important than genuinely having friends, and having friends is less important than having *good* friendships (Asher, Parker, & Walker, 1996; Berndt, 1996; Hartup & Stevens, 1997; Hussong, 2000; Keefe & Berndt, 1996). Not all friendships are consistently good friendships, however; friendships often provide for positive things like self-disclosure, intimacy, and companionship, but they also may give rise to insecurity, conflict, jealousy, and mistrust (J. Parker, Low, Walker, & Gamm, 2005). And, as you know, adolescents who are close to peers or romantic partners who have antisocial values or habits are themselves more likely to develop similar patterns of behavior (Cauffman et al.,

2008; Haynie, Giordano, Manning, & Longmore, 2005; Hussong & Hicks, 2003). It is easy to forget, but it goes without saying, that not all close relationships foster positive developmental outcomes.

Nevertheless, studies consistently show that individuals with satisfying close friendships fare better than those without them, not only in adolescence but in adulthood as well. Adolescence is an especially important time in the development of close relationships because many of the capacities and capabilities that permit intimacy in adult relationships make their debut in adolescence.

RECAP

- Adolescents who have intimate friendships typically have better mental health than their peers who do not, although we do not know which comes first, intimacy or psychological health.
- Experts agree that close peer relationships are an essential part of healthy social development during adolescence.
- Any discussion of the impact of close friends on development must take into account the characteristics of these friends.
- Being popular is less important than genuinely having friends, and having friends is less important than having good friendships.

Sexuality

AMERICAN ADULTS HAVE an ambivalent attitude toward adolescent sexuality. On the one hand, they are fascinated by it—it is nearly impossible to turn on the television and avoid seeing sexual imagery that either depicts or is directed at adolescents (Roberts et al., 2009). On the other hand, adults deplore it—most adults (80%, in fact) say that teenage sex is always or almost always wrong (Diamond & Savin-Williams, 2009). Adults look, and then they look the other way. Talk about a love–hate relationship!

This same ambivalence is reflected in the way that social scientists have studied adolescent sexuality. Sex has always been a popular subject among adolescence researchers. But rather than try to understand it, most research focuses simply on enumerating it—counting how many people have done which things how often, at what age, and with whom. When studies probe more deeply than this, they almost always start from the premise that sex between teenagers is wrong—that only troubled teenagers do it or that doing it will get normal teenagers into trouble. As a result, the problematic aspects of adolescent sexuality—precocious sex, promiscuous sex, unsafe sex, unwanted sex, casual sex, and so forth—have received far more attention than its normative aspects (Diamond & Savin-Williams, 2009). This is not to make light of these problems, which for many adolescents are very real. But it is worth pointing out that the study of other aspects of adolescent psychosocial development is not similarly dominated by research on what can go wrong. Imagine if researchers interested in identity, autonomy, or intimacy studied only negative self-conceptions, angry rebellion, or failed friendships. As you will read, and in contrast to adults' concerns, most of the time, sex during adolescence is not associated with problems.

Sexuality as an Adolescent Issue

Like other aspects of psychosocial development, sexuality is not an entirely new issue that surfaces for the first time during adolescence. Young children are curious about their sex organs and at a very early age derive pleasure (if not what adults would label orgasm) from genital stimulation—as both Sigmund Freud and the famous sex researcher Alfred Kinsey pointed out long ago (Kinsey, Pomeroy, & Martin, 1948). And, of course, sexual activity and sexual development continue long after adolescence. Although sexual development may be more dramatic and more obvious prior to adulthood, it by no means ceases at the end of adolescence. Nonetheless, most of us would agree that adolescence is a fundamentally important time—if not the most important time in the life cycle—for the development of sexuality. There are several reasons for this.

▌ **Puberty and Adolescent Sexuality** Perhaps most obvious is the link between adolescent sexuality and puberty (Diamond & Savin-Williams, 2009; Susman & Dorn, 2009). A substantial increase in the sex drive in early adolescence is clearly the result of hormonal changes. Moreover, not until puberty do individuals become capable of sexual reproduction. Before puberty, children are certainly capable of kissing, fondling, masturbating, and even having sexual intercourse, and erotic feelings are reported by individuals prior to adolescence; sexual feelings do not suddenly switch on at puberty (Herdt & McClintock, 2000; McClintock & Herdt, 1996). But not until puberty can males ejaculate semen or can females begin to ovulate, and the fact that pregnancy is a possible outcome of sexual activity changes the nature and meaning of sexual behavior markedly—for the adolescent and for others. What had previously been innocuous sex play becomes serious business when pregnancy is a genuine possibility. Finally, as we saw in Chapter 1, not until puberty do individuals develop the secondary sex

Most individuals' first experiences in sexual relationships occur during adolescence.

characteristics that serve as a basis for sexual attraction and as dramatic indicators that the young person is no longer physically a child.

Cognitive Change and Adolescent Sexuality

The increased importance of sexuality at adolescence is not solely a result of puberty. The cognitive changes of adolescence play a part in the changed nature of sexuality as well. One obvious difference between the sex play of children and the sexual activity of adolescents is that children are not especially introspective or reflective about sexual behavior. In contrast, sex during adolescence is the subject of sometimes painful conjecture ("Will she or won't she?"), decision making ("Should I or shouldn't I?"), hypothetical thinking ("What if he wants to do it tonight?"), and self-conscious concern ("Am I good-looking enough?"). As we saw in Chapter 10, one of the chief tasks of adolescence is to figure out how to deal with sexual desires and how to incorporate sex successfully and appropriately into social relationships. Much of this task is cognitive in nature, and much of it is made possible by the expansion of intellectual abilities that takes place during the period.

Social Roles and Adolescent Sexuality

In addition to how the physical changes of puberty and the growth of sophisticated thinking capabilities influence sexuality during adolescence, the new social meaning given to sexual and dating behavior at this time in the life cycle makes sexuality an especially important psychosocial concern. Adolescence is a turning point in the development of sexuality because it marks the onset of deliberate sexually motivated behavior that is recognized, both by oneself and by others, as primarily and explicitly sexual in nature. Sexual activity in adolescence is motivated by more than hormones. For many adolescents (especially girls, but boys as well), sex is motivated by love and the desire for the sort of serious emotional relationship that begins to take on features of adult romance. For many adolescents (especially boys, but girls as well), sex is motivated by a desire to enhance their status with peers (Diamond & Savin-Williams, 2009).

Positive Sexual Development

Although the history of research on adolescent sexuality has emphasized its problematic aspects, in recent years, there has been increased interest (if not much actual research) in the factors that lead to positive sexual development (Diamond & Savin-Williams, 2009). There are four distinct aspects to positive sexuality in adolescence that can serve as the basis for how parents and educators discuss sex with teenagers (Brooks-Gunn & Paikoff, 1993). First, the adolescent needs to come to feel comfortable with his or her maturing body—its shape, size, and attractiveness. Second, the adolescent should

accept having feelings of sexual arousal as normal and appropriate. Third, the adolescent needs to feel comfortable about choosing to engage in—or not to engage in—various sexual activities; that is, healthy sexual development involves understanding that sex is a *voluntary* activity for oneself and for one's partner. Finally, the adolescent (at least, one who is sexually active) must understand and practice safe sex—sex that avoids pregnancy and sexually transmitted infections.

FOOD FOR THOUGHT

What role, if any, should school-based sex education play in the promotion of healthy sexuality? Should the focus of sex education be on preventing sexual activity during adolescence or on promoting positive sexual development?

RECAP

- Adolescence is a fundamentally important time in the life cycle for the development of sexuality.
- The physical and hormonal changes of puberty increase sex drive, change the adolescent's appearance, and permit reproduction, all of which affect the development of sexuality.
- The cognitive changes of adolescence result in the increased capacity of the individual to understand and think about sexual feelings.
- The transition of the individual into new social roles gives new meaning to sexual behavior in the eyes of individuals, society, and social institutions and provides new motives for establishing sexual relationships.
- Four aspects of positive sexual development in adolescence are accepting one's changing body, accepting one's feelings of sexual arousal, understanding that sexual activity is voluntary, and practicing safe sex.

How Sexually Permissive Is Contemporary Society?

It is impossible to understand sexuality as a psychosocial phenomenon without taking into account the social milieu in which adolescents learn about and first experience sex. Although we tend to think of sex as

In restrictive societies, sexual activity before marriage is explicitly discouraged.

youngsters to refrain from sexual activity until they either have undergone a formal rite of passage into adulthood or have married. Of course, this doesn't necessarily stop adolescents from having sex, and in many restrictive societies, adolescents pursue sex in secrecy. Within the broad category of restrictive societies, there are wide variations in the degree of restrictiveness and in the methods used to discourage sexual activity before marriage. For example, in some societies, the sexual activity of young people is controlled by separating the sexes throughout childhood and adolescence. Boys and girls are not permitted to play together, and they never associate with each other before marriage in the absence of chaperones. In other societies, sexual activity before the attainment of adult status is restricted through the physical punishment and public shaming of sexually active youngsters (C. Ford & Beach, 1951).

something that adolescents are inevitably anxious or concerned about, it is no more true to suggest that sexuality is always riddled with problems during adolescence than it is to say that all adolescents have problems in establishing a sense of identity or in developing a sense of autonomy. Like any other aspect of psychosocial growth, the development of sexuality is determined largely by its context. Of particular importance is the way in which adolescents and children are exposed to and educated about sexuality—a process called **sexual socialization.** Anthropologists have found that cultures vary considerably in the ways in which they handle sexual socialization. Generally speaking, societies fall into one of three groups: restrictive, semirestrictive, and permissive (C. Ford & Beach, 1951).

SEXUAL SOCIALIZATION IN RESTRICTIVE SOCIETIES

In **restrictive societies,** the adolescent's transition into adult sexual activity is highly discontinuous, in the sense that there is little advance preparation for adult sexuality during childhood. Pressure is exerted on

SEXUAL SOCIALIZATION IN SEMIRESTRICTIVE SOCIETIES

In **semirestrictive societies,** adults frown upon sexual activity among adolescents but do not consistently enforce prohibitions against it. For example, sexual activity among youngsters may be formally prohibited, but children playing together may imitate the sexual behavior of their elders, and unless this play is brought explicitly to the attention of adults, little is done about it. In other semirestrictive societies, "Premarital promiscuity is common, and the parents do not object as long as the love affairs are kept secret" (C. Ford & Beach, 1951, p. 187). It is premarital pregnancy, rather than premarital sex, that is objectionable, and unmarried adolescents whose sexual activity has resulted in pregnancy are often forced to marry.

We are frequently told that contemporary America is excessively permissive when it comes to sex, but by world standards, the sexual socialization of children and adolescents in contemporary America is semirestrictive. For most American children, masturbation, sexual exploration, and explicit sex play are frowned upon. Adults rarely mention sexual matters in the presence of children, and there are regulations prohibiting children from being exposed to sexual activity on television (by restricting the broadcasting of programs with sexual content to later in the evening) or in the movies (by having a ratings system that makes some movies off-limits to children). Adults openly try to discourage young people—especially young women—from becoming sexually active by lecturing to them about the virtues of virginity or by telling them that

sexual socialization   The process through which adolescents are exposed to and educated about sexuality.

restrictive societies   Societies in which adolescents are pressured to refrain from sexual activity until they have married or undergone a formal rite of passage into adulthood.

semirestrictive societies   Societies in which pressures against adolescent sexual activity exist but are not vigilantly enforced.

females do not need sex as much as males do (Diamond & Savin-Williams, 2009). At the same time, however, adolescent boys and girls are not typically segregated, and they usually date without chaperones present. In fact, adolescents are *encouraged* to date, even though adults know that dating provides a context for sexual activity. Of course, adults are well aware that young people are sexually active, but for the most part, they prefer to look the other way rather than restrict adolescents' activities.

SEXUAL SOCIALIZATION IN PERMISSIVE SOCIETIES

In **permissive societies,** the transition of young people into adult sexual activity is highly continuous and usually begins in childhood. Although religious conservatives bemoan the lack of morals among the young in contemporary society, by no stretch of the imagination is America a sexually permissive culture—at least in comparison with many of the cultures described by anthropologists. Consider, for example, these descriptions of sexual socialization in some of the societies that were categorized as permissive:

- Among the Pukapukans of Polynesia, where parents simply ignore the sexual activities of young children, boys and girls masturbate freely and openly in public.

- Lesu children playing on the beach give imitations of adult sexual intercourse, and adults in this society regard this to be a natural and normal game.

- In the absence of adult control, typical forms of amusement for Trobriand girls and boys include manual and oral stimulation of the genitals and simulated coitus. Sexual life begins in earnest among the Trobrianders at six to eight years for girls, ten to twelve for boys. Both sexes receive explicit instruction from older companions whom they imitate in sex activities. . . . At any time a couple may retire to the bush, the bachelor's hut, an isolated yam house, or any other convenient place and there engage in prolonged sexual play with full approval of their parents. (C. Ford & Beach, 1951, pp. 188–191)

FOOD FOR THOUGHT

Just as we can categorize societies as restrictive, semirestrictive, or permissive when it comes to sexual socialization, we can also sort families and communities into these same categories. In light of what you've read, how would you characterize the context in which you grew up?

RECAP

- Cultures vary in their approach to sexual socialization—the way in which children and adolescents are taught about sex. Societies generally fall into one of three categories: restrictive, semirestrictive, or permissive.

- Although many people think of contemporary industrialized society as being sexually permissive, many societies around the world are far more lenient about sex.

- By most indications, Americans' attitudes toward adolescent sex are neither restrictive nor permissive—but semirestrictive.

Sexual Activity During Adolescence

Given the field's historical focus on problematic aspects of adolescent sexuality, such as precocious sex (having sex at too young an age), promiscuous sex (having sex with too many partners), unwanted sex (having sex against one's will), or unsafe sex (having sex than can result in pregnancy or a sexually transmitted disease [STD]), most of the research conducted into the sexual behavior of adolescents has focused on sexual intercourse (Diamond & Savin-Williams, 2009). With the possible exception of oral sex, adults have tended not to worry about sexual behavior other than intercourse, and worries about oral sex have surfaced only in recent years, as exaggerated media reports about teenagers reporting giving or receiving oral sex promiscuously have risen; in fact, although national surveys show that slightly more teenagers have had oral sex than intercourse, they also indicate that the vast majority of teenagers who engage in oral sex also engage in sexual intercourse and that promiscuity is not the norm for either behavior (L. Lindberg, Jones, & Santelli, 2008).

Although adolescents' involvement in sexual intercourse is undoubtedly an important topic, it is also wise to remember that a good deal of the sexual activity of adolescents—even sexually experienced adolescents—involves activities other than sexual intercourse, such as kissing and touching parts of each other's body (broadly referred to as "noncoital activity"). Moreover, because most individuals do not begin their sexual experiences with intercourse but progress toward it through stages of gradually increasing intimacy, it is important to view

permissive societies Societies in which sexual activity during childhood and adolescence is not greatly restrained.

Although most research on adolescent sexuality has focused on sexual intercourse, adolescents' initial forays into the world of sex typically begin with less intimate sexual activity and gradually build toward intercourse.

intercourse as one activity in a long progression, rather than as an isolated behavior (Diamond & Savin-Williams, 2009).

STAGES OF SEXUAL ACTIVITY

Before we turn to statistics on adolescent sexual activity, a word of caution is in order. Reports of sexual behavior vary markedly as a function of the ways in which questions are worded and data are collected. When former president Clinton, referring to his affair with Monica Lewinsky, infamously said "I did not have sexual relations with that woman," what he meant (we assume) is that he did not have vaginal intercourse

autoerotic behavior   Sexual behavior that is experienced alone, such as masturbation or sexual fantasizing.

with her. Whether the fact that they engaged in oral sex makes his statement false depends on what one takes the expression "sexual relations" to mean. Similarly, when adolescents respond to questions asking whether they have "had sex," have been "sexually active," or were "still a virgin," it is not clear how they interpret the question. Is genital touching "sex"? Are you a "virgin" if you have engaged in anal sex but not vaginal intercourse? Adolescents, like adults, don't always agree. And to make things even more complicated, adolescents distinguish between acts that culminate in orgasm (which are more likely to be viewed as leading to a loss of virginity) and those that don't (Bersamin, Fisher, Walker, Hill, & Grube, 2007). Moreover, adolescents who have engaged in a specific behavior are more likely to say that the behavior doesn't "count" in their definition of losing one's virginity, which means that adolescents' responses to surveys about sex are biased by their actual experience. So bear in mind that all figures to follow are necessarily approximate.

Most adolescents' first experience with sex falls into the category of **autoerotic behavior**—sexual behavior that is experienced alone. The most common autoerotic activities reported by adolescents are having erotic fantasies (about three quarters of all teenagers report having sexual fantasies, mainly about TV or movie stars) and masturbation (different surveys yield different estimates, depending on the age of the respondents and the wording of the questions, but about half of all adolescent boys and about one fourth of all adolescent girls masturbate prior to age 18) (Diamond & Savin-Williams, 2009).

By the time most adolescents reach high school, they have made the transition from autoerotic behavior to sexual activity that involves another person (for lack of a more technical term, this is often referred to as "fooling around"). By the time individuals have turned 16, about 80% have engaged in some type of noncoital activity with another person. Interestingly, the developmental progression of sexual behaviors, from less intimate to more intimate, has not changed very much over the past 50 years, and the sequence in which males and females engage in various sexual activities is remarkably similar. According to recent, large-scale studies of American adolescents, holding hands comes first, followed (in this order) by kissing, making out (kissing for a long time), feeling breasts through clothes, feeling breasts under clothes, feeling a penis through clothes, feeling a penis under clothes or while naked, feeling a vagina through clothes, feeling a vagina under clothes or while naked, and intercourse or oral sex. Some studies find that adolescents' first experience with oral sex generally precedes their first experience with intercourse, whereas others find the reverse (Diamond & Savin-Williams, 2009). One worrisome finding is that most adolescents report talking about contraception *after* they first have intercourse, rather than before (O'Sullivan, Cheng, Harris, & Brooks-Gunn, 2007). For most adolescents, this sequence of increasingly advanced behaviors unfolds gradually over time, but for a significant minority, it is compressed into a shorter interval (de Graaf, Vanwesenbeeck, Meijer, Woertman, & Meeus, 2009). The expected timetable for progressive sexual activities is faster among adolescents who expect a relatively faster timetable for achieving autonomy from parents and experimenting with drugs and alcohol, suggesting that earlier involvement in sex may be part of a larger pattern of earlier involvement in "adult" activities (Rosenthal & Smith, 1997).

SEXUAL INTERCOURSE DURING ADOLESCENCE

▌ **Prevalence of Sexual Intercourse**   Estimates of the prevalence of sexual intercourse among contemporary adolescents vary from study to study, depending on the nature of the sample surveyed, the year and region in which the study was undertaken, the reliability of the data gathered, and, of course, the wording of the questions (Santelli, Lindberg, Abma, McNeely, & Resnick, 2000). Some studies suggest that adolescents do not always report their sexual activity honestly or accurately, with males tending to overstate their level of activity and females tending to understate it (Alexander, Somerfield, Ensminger, Johnson, & Kim, 1993). The following paragraphs summarize what social scientists have concluded from recent surveys with these caveats in mind.

Although regional and ethnic variations make it difficult—if not misleading—to generalize about the average age at which American adolescents initiate sexual intercourse, national surveys indicate that more adolescents are sexually active at an earlier age today than several decades ago; however, there has been a slight decrease in the proportion of sexually experienced teenagers since the mid-1990s—in other words, slightly fewer adolescents are having sexual intercourse, but those who are do so at a somewhat earlier age (Diamond & Savin-Williams, 2009). The best estimates we have are that, by the end of their sophomore year in high school, more than 40% of American adolescents have had heterosexual vaginal intercourse (these estimates, which are based on large national surveys, do not include same-sex intercourse or other types of sex, like oral or anal sex). By age 18, this number has risen to about two thirds (see Figure 11.1) (Centers for Disease Control and Prevention, 2008). Whatever we might think about these figures, one conclusion is inescapable: Sexual intercourse during high school is now a part of the normative experience of adolescence in America.

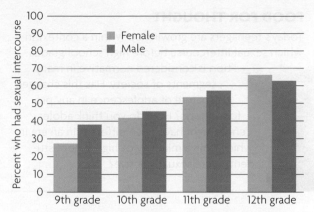

FIGURE 11.1   About one third of American ninth-graders have had sexual intercourse. By senior year, about two thirds have. (Centers for Disease Control and Prevention, 2008)

▌ **Ethnic Differences in Age of Sexual Initiation** There are substantial ethnic differences in age of sexual initiation, especially among males (Centers for Disease Control and Prevention, 2008). Among Black males, the average age of first intercourse is 15; among White and Hispanic males, it is 16.5; and among Asian American males, it is 18 (Upchurch, Levy-Storms, Sucoff, & Aneshensel, 1998). Ethnic differences in the age of sexual initiation are far smaller among females, although Hispanic and Asian American females generally have their first sexual intercourse at a later age than is the case among their Black and White counterparts (Grunbaum, Lowry, Kann, & Pateman, 2000). One reason for the relatively high rate of early sexual activity among Black males is the higher proportion of Black youth who grow up in single-parent homes and in poor neighborhoods, both of which, as you will read later in this chapter, are risk factors for early sexual activity (Brewster, 1994; Lauritsen, 1994). In general, Mexican American youngsters who were born in Mexico are less likely to be sexually active at an early age than are Mexican Americans who are American-born, reflecting differences in norms between the two countries (Aneshensel, Becerra, Fielder, & Schuler, 1990). Consistent with this, Americanized Latino adolescents are more likely than their less acculturated peers to have sex at a younger age, to have multiple sex partners, and to become pregnant (Kaplan, Erickson, & Juarez-Reyes, 2002; Upchurch, Aneshensel, Mudgal, & McNeely, 2001), and more acculturated Asian American girls are more likely to be sexually active than their less Americanized peers (Hahm, Lahiff, & Barreto, 2006). Studies also indicate that, among all ethnic groups, rates of sexual activity are higher among economically disadvantaged youth, although the gap in rates of sexual activity between rich and poor is substantially narrower now than it was a decade ago, again pointing to the increasingly normative nature of sexual intercourse among American teenagers (Singh & Darroch, 1999).

FOOD FOR THOUGHT

Today's teenagers are growing up within a context in which sexual intercourse before high school graduation is considered normative in many segments of society. Has this changed the nature of adolescence in any profound ways? How do you think adolescence might have been different in an era in which only a minority of high school students were sexually active?

It is important to note that for many girls, their first sexual experience is forced (Diamond & Savin-Williams, 2009). Involuntary sex is especially frequent among girls who have sex for the first time when they are 13 or younger; one fourth of younger adolescents report that their first intercourse was against their will, in contrast to 10% of women whose first intercourse was after age 18. Moreover, many other young women who report that they had sex voluntarily the first time nevertheless report that they did not really *want* to have sex. Young girls whose first partner was 7 or more years older were twice as likely as others to report having had voluntary but unwanted intercourse (Abma, Driscoll, & Moore, 1998). Young adolescents with a significantly older romantic partner are far more likely to have sexual intercourse than those whose boyfriend is the same age (Kaestle, Morisky, & Wiley, 2002; Leitenberg & Saltzman, 2000).

■ **Timing of Sexual Initiation** Adolescents are more likely to lose their virginity during certain times of the year than during others. There are two seasonal peaks in the timing of first intercourse: June and December (Levin, Xu, & Bartkowski, 2002) (see Figure 11.2). June and, to a lesser extent, May and July are common months for first intercourse regardless of whether the adolescents were romantically involved; December, however, is a peak time only among adolescents who are

with a serious boyfriend or girlfriend, and particularly so among girls. Several explanations for these seasonal trends have been offered, including the general tendency for people to be more sexually active when the weather is very hot or very cold and the fact that adolescents have more unsupervised time when they are on summer or winter vacation. As for what has been called "the holiday effect" (the rise in sexual debuts among romantic partners in December)—well, perhaps you can figure that out for yourself.

CHANGES IN SEXUAL ACTIVITY OVER TIME

Attitudes toward premarital intercourse during adolescence became more liberal beginning in the mid-1960s and, especially, during the early 1970s. Not surprisingly, accompanying this shift in attitudes was an equally noteworthy shift in sexual behavior (Alan Guttmacher Institute, 1994).

■ **Recent Historical Trends** Three trends are of special interest. First, the overall percentage of American adolescents who had engaged in premarital sex accelerated markedly during the early 1970s and again during the late 1980s, and then declined between 1995 and 2001; it has remained flat, at a little less than 50%, since then (see Figure 11.3) (Centers for Disease Control and Prevention, 2008; Santelli et al., 2000, 2004; Diamond & Savin-Williams, 2009). Interestingly, the recent decline in the proportion of adolescents who have had sexual intercourse is not paralleled by a decline in the proportion of adolescents who are having other types of sex—in fact, today's teenagers are far more "active" sexually than were previous generations (Diamond & Savin-Williams, 2009). It is likely that the threat of AIDS and other sexually transmitted diseases has led many adolescents to substitute a safer type of sex (such as oral sex, which, although safer than vaginal or anal intercourse, still carries some

FIGURE 11.2 Adolescents are most likely to have intercourse for the first time during early summer or in December. (Levin et al., 2002)

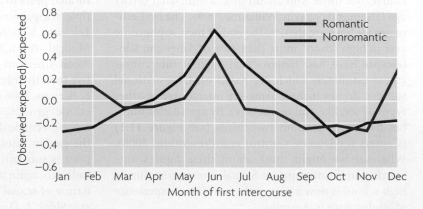

risk) for intercourse, with what appear to be the desired results: Adolescents who engage in oral sex, but not sexual intercourse, are less likely to feel guilty or used and less likely to contract a sexually transmitted infection (Brady & Halpern-Felsher, 2007).

Second, the proportion of individuals who have sexual intercourse *early* in adolescence is substantial. Although the median age at which adolescents first engage in intercourse has remained somewhere between 16 and 17 for quite some time, today, one third of all contemporary American adolescents have had intercourse by the time they are ninth-graders, and more than 7% have had intercourse by age 13 (Centers for Disease Control and Prevention, 2008). Among adolescents who have not had sex, fears of pregnancy and disease (including HIV/AIDS) are the most common reasons for abstaining (Blinn-Pike, 1999; Loewensen, Ireland, & Resnick, 2004). As we'll see later, these figures on sexual activity among younger adolescents are noteworthy, because the younger individuals are when they have sex, the more likely they are to have unprotected sex, exposing themselves to the risks of pregnancy and STDs (Diamond & Savin-Williams, 2009; Dittus, Jaccard, & Gordon, 1997; Kaestle, Halpern, Miller, & Ford, 2005). (Because Black males initiate sex at an earlier age, they are also more likely than other adolescents to engage in risky sex [Fergus, Zimmerman, & Caldwell, 2007].) The fact that a large number of adolescents are sexually active before high school is also an important factor in discussions of sex education, because programs that do not begin until students' later years of high school are probably too late for a substantial number of young people.

Finally, the greatest increase in the prevalence of intercourse among adolescents, and the greatest decline in the age at first intercourse, has been among females (Diamond & Savin-Williams, 2009). Before 1965, there were substantial gaps between the proportions of sexually active boys and girls. Since about 1965, the proportion of sexually experienced high school males has nearly tripled, but the proportion of sexually experienced high school females is about 5 times higher today. Sex differences in rates of sexual intercourse today are negligible (Centers for Disease Control and Prevention, 2008).

The bottom line: Whether adults approve or not, sexual activity has become a normative part of the American teenager's life. And while many parents, educators, and other adults are alarmed by sexual activity among the young, for most adolescents, sexual involvement is accompanied by affection, emotional involvement, and commitment to a relationship. Although many high school students are sexually active on a regular basis, promiscuity is not the norm (Singh & Darroch, 1999). According to recent data, 80% of sexually active high

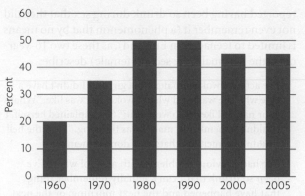

FIGURE 11.3 The proportion of American high school students who had sexual intercourse rose substantially between 1960 and 1980, but declined between 1990 and 2000. It has remained stable since then.

school girls, and 67% of sexually active high school boys, had intercourse with only one partner during the past 3 months, and the proportion of adolescents who have had multiple sex partners has decreased substantially over the past decade, although it is still substantial today—15% of contemporary high school students have had intercourse with four or more persons (Centers for Disease Control and Prevention, 2008).

About one third of sexually active adolescents have had intercourse with someone they are not in a romantic relationship with (Manning, Longmore, & Giordano, 2005). Although many adults have expressed concern about adolescents having sex with someone outside the context of a dating relationship, or "hooking up," these encounters are usually with someone the adolescent knows well, like a friend or ex-partner (sometimes referred to as "friends with benefits"). And in one third of these "nonromantic" encounters, one of the persons was hoping that the friendship would turn into (or return to) a romantic relationship (Manning, Giordana, & Longmore, 2006). In other words, the broad category of "casual sex" includes a wide range of behavior, from one-night stands to sex with a desired (but not yet committed) romantic partner.

▌ **Sex and Alcohol** One particular cause for concern is that the percentage of adolescents who use alcohol or other drugs prior to having sex has increased in recent years—in one national survey, about one fourth of American adolescents said they drank or used drugs before the last time they had sex, a behavior that is relatively more common among White and Hispanic adolescents (Centers for Disease Control and Prevention, 2008). Not surprisingly, sexual risk taking is more likely when alcohol is involved, mainly because of impaired judgment and loss of control. One study of British adolescents found that one fourth of those interviewed reported having been so drunk during sex that they did not even remember it (a phenomenon that by no means is limited to teenagers in England), as these two 16-year-olds (the first male, the second female) describe:

> I've actually woken up next to a girl and I didn't have a clue who she was. And when I woke up I was like, "What's your name? Like, Who were you?" She explained herself, I couldn't remember it, man. I was thinking, "How the hell couldn't I remember that?". . . I don't remember.

> I've had previous problems with alcohol where I've been so drunk that I can't actually remember things that have happened and the next morning, or the next couple of weeks, I get told about things and then it [having sex with someone] suddenly comes back and I think, oh my God, what have I done? (L. M. Coleman & Cater, 2005, p. 656)

Although it is interesting to speculate on the causes of these changes in adolescents' sexual behavior—the increased availability of contraception, the overall liberalization of social attitudes, and the earlier age of puberty have all been suggested—the more pressing issue is how society ought to react to the changed nature of sex during adolescence. Sexual intercourse during adolescence is not limited to males, to minority youngsters, or to individuals with emotional problems. It is a part of life for the *average* teenager. Many experts contend that the longer we ignore this—by failing to provide adequate sex education, by limiting the accessibility of effective contraception methods, and by not dealing with the issue squarely—the more difficulties society in general, and young people in particular, will face.

RECAP

- Important changes in attitudes toward adolescent premarital sex occurred during the 1970s and have persisted since that time. Most teenagers today believe that it is acceptable to have intercourse before marriage as long as it takes place within the context of a loving, intimate relationship.
- Sexual intercourse, once delayed until early adulthood, is clearly now a part of the typical adolescent's experience, regardless of her or his ethnic or socioeconomic background.
- One third of all American 14-year-olds and two thirds of all American 18-year-olds have had sexual intercourse.
- The proportion of individuals who have had sexual intercourse before entering high school has risen significantly in recent decades.
- The most substantial change in recent decades has been in the sexual activity of females.

The Sexually Active Adolescent

PSYCHOLOGICAL AND SOCIAL CHARACTERISTICS OF SEXUALLY ACTIVE ADOLESCENTS

For many years, researchers studied the psychological and social characteristics of sexually active adolescents on the assumption that these teenagers were more troubled than their peers (either before or as a consequence of becoming sexually active). This view has been replaced as sexual activity has become more prevalent among "normal" adolescents.

■ **Sexual Activity and Psychological Development** Numerous studies show that sexual activity during adolescence is decidedly *not* associated with psychological disturbance (Diamond & Savin-Williams, 2009). Adolescents who become sexually active earlier than their peers have levels of self-esteem and life satisfaction similar to those of other adolescents (Goodson, Buhi, & Dunsmore, 2006). Losing one's virginity does not have negative psychological repercussions, either in the short or long term (Bingham & Crockett, 1996; Langer, Zimmerman, & Katz, 1995), even when one's sexual debut is outside the context of a romantic relationship (Monahan & Lee, 2008). Thus, both the prejudice that only "troubled" adolescents have sex and the belief that sexual activity during adolescence leads to later psychological disturbance are false (Goodson, Buhi, & Dunsmore, 2006; A. M. Meier, 2007; Spriggs & Halpern, 2008). It is important, however, to distinguish between predictors of being sexually active and predictors of engaging in *risky sex* (unprotected sex, sex with multiple partners, etc.), which is associated with the same sorts of psychological and behavioral problems correlated with other forms of risk taking (L. K. Brown et al., 2006; Camenga, Klein, & Roy, 2006; Crockett, Raffaelli, & Shen, 2006; Ethier et al., 2006).

However, *early* sexual activity (that is, having intercourse before age 16) is associated with a more general attitudinal and behavioral profile that includes more permissive attitudes toward sex, experimentation with drugs and alcohol, minor delinquency, low levels of religious involvement, lower interest in academic achievement, and a stronger orientation toward independence (Armour & Haynie, 2007; Lohman & Billings, 2008; Zimmer-Gembeck & Helfand, 2008). One study that measured adolescents' likelihood of losing their virginity found that individuals who fit the profile in seventh or eighth grade were *25 times more likely* to lose their virginity within the next 2 years than those who did not (L'Engle & Jackson, 2008; L'Engle, Jackson, & Brown, 2006) (see Figure 11.4). In contrast, studies of adolescents who become sexually active at *age 16 or later* do

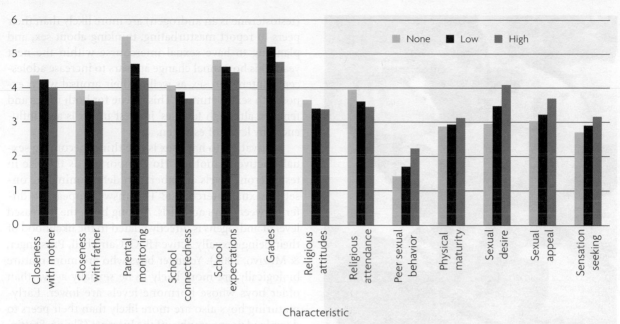

FIGURE 11.4 Characteristics that distinguish adolescents who are low, moderate, or high in their likelihood of becoming sexually active. (L'Engle et al., 2006)

not find major differences between these youth and their virginal counterparts. Less is known about characteristics of individuals who do not have sex at any time in adolescence, but the most consistent correlate of abstaining from sex until after age 18 is strong religious commitment (Zimmer-Gembeck & Helfand, 2008).

FOOD FOR THOUGHT

Why do you think the psychological correlates of early sexual intercourse are different from the correlates of sexual intercourse when it is delayed until the last years of high school? Would you be in favor of sex education courses whose focus was on persuading adolescents to wait until they were 16 before having intercourse?

Causation or Correlation? Although many studies have found a link between early sexual activity and small-scale deviance, the nature of the causal chain is not entirely clear (Diamond & Savin-Williams, 2009; Zimmer-Gembeck, Siebenbrunner, & Collins, 2004). Several studies show that involvement in deviance (especially alcohol and drug use, but aggression as well) precedes early involvement with sex (Capaldi, Crosby, & Stoolmiller, 1996; Miller-Johnson et al., 1996; C. Mitchell, Whitesell, Spicer, Beals, & Kaufman, 2007; Schofield et al., 2008; Underwood, Kupersmidt,

& Coie, 1996; T. Williams, Connolly, & Cribbie, 2008), whereas others suggest that experimentation with deviant activity and early sex occur simultaneously and may reflect some common underlying factor, such as the propensity to take risks (e.g., Bingham & Crockett, 1996; Dorius, Heaton, & Steffen, 1993; Harden, Mendle, Hill, Turkheimer, & Emery, 2008; D. Orr, Beiter, & Ingersoll, 1991). (In contrast, there is virtually no support for the notion that early sex leads to other types of risky or antisocial activity.) As you'll read in Chapter 13, many experts believe that a general inclination toward problem behavior and lack of impulse control is behind an overarching pattern that includes minor delinquency, precocious or promiscuous sex, disengagement from school, and drug and alcohol use (Costa, Jessor, Donovan, & Fortenberry, 1995; Crockett et al., 2006; Rosenthal, Smith, & de Visser, 1999; Valois, Oeltmann, Waller, & Hussey, 1999).

Another factor that affects adolescents' sexual activity is the extent to which they are supervised by their parents or other adults. In contrast to stereotypes of adolescent couples having sex in the backseat of their car on a Friday or Saturday night, most sexual activity between teenagers takes place in one of the two individuals' homes—most often, the boy's. (The third most popular setting is at the home of a friend.) And the most common time for adolescents to have sex is not on the weekend, but on weekdays, after school. Not surprisingly, then, adolescents who are unsupervised after school and who do not participate in after-school programs are more likely to be sexually active, more likely to have multiple sexual partners, and more likely to

Research shows that adolescents who are sexually active are no more likely to have psychological problems than their nonactive peers. However, engaging in risky sexual activity is associated with involvement in other forms of reckless behavior.

contract an STD (Buhi & Goodson, 2007; D. Cohen, Farley, Taylor, Martin, & Schuster, 2002).

HORMONAL AND CONTEXTUAL INFLUENCES ON SEXUAL ACTIVITY

One factor that is consistently related to the age at which adolescents initiate sex is physical maturation; adolescents who mature earlier are also likely to have sex earlier (Diamond & Savin-Williams, 2009; Lam et al., 2002; B. Miller, Norton, Fan, & Christopherson, 1998). Increased interest in sex at adolescence is likely to have social as well as biological causes, however. Specifically, adolescents are thought to become interested in sex in part because of increases in sex hormones at puberty and in part because sexual activity becomes accepted—even encouraged—in their peer group. A fuller understanding of adolescent sexual behavior necessitates looking at biological and social influences in interaction with each other, rather than at either set of influences alone (Halpern, 2003; Udry, 1987). Moreover, the story line is somewhat different for males than females.

▌ **Hormonal Influences** Boys' and girls' initial interest in sex is influenced primarily by the surge in certain hormones—**testosterone,** to be specific—at puberty. Adolescents with higher levels of androgens

(testosterone is an androgen) are more likely than their peers to report masturbating, thinking about sex, and planning to have sexual intercourse within the next year. This hormonal change appears to increase adolescents' interest in sex as well as their arousal when exposed to sexual stimuli. This is true for both males and females, although females' interest in sex is also influenced by levels of estrogen.

Motivation to have sex is one thing; becoming sexually active is another. How important is the rise in testosterone levels at puberty in determining the onset of sexual intercourse? The answer appears to differ between boys and girls. Among boys, the increased level of androgens is directly related to the likelihood of their being sexually active (B. C. Campbell, Prossinger, & Mbzivo, 2005). Younger boys who are more mature biologically are more likely to be sexually active than older boys whose hormone levels are lower. Early-maturing boys also are more likely than their peers to download pornography off the Internet (Skoog, Stattin, & Kerr, 2009).

Boys' sexual activity is not entirely dependent on their hormone levels, however, because whether they are sexually active also depends on how receptive girls are to them. Not surprisingly, boys who are more popular with girls in their school are more likely to initiate sex early than are boys who are less popular with girls. As you know from Chapter 1, androgens, including testosterone, do not just contribute to increases in boys' sex drive—they also affect height, strength, and the development of secondary sex characteristics, like facial hair. (Remember that one role of secondary sex characteristics is to signal to others that the individual is ready for sex.) In other words, increases in androgens lead to boys' increased sexual activity both because they increase their sex drive (which may make boys with higher testosterone levels want to have sex more) and because they change their physical appearance (which may make them more attractive to girls).

These factors are easier to separate in girls. Although androgens are responsible for increases in girls' sex drive, a different set of hormones—estrogens—is primarily responsible for changes in their appearance, including breast development. Because of this, it is possible to study whether increased sexual activity among girls after puberty is more biologically influenced by increases in their sex drive or by changes in their physical appearance (both of which, presumably, influence their sexual attractiveness to boys). It turns out that differences in adolescent girls' sexual activity have little to do with differences in their testosterone levels but is correlated with differences in their estrogen levels. Although it was once believed that estrogen played an important role in influencing girls' receptivity to boys' advances, it turns out that this is not the case

testosterone One of the sex hormones secreted by the gonads, found in both sexes but in higher levels among males than females.

(Diamond & Savin-Williams, 2009). Estrogen influences girls' sexual activity mainly through its impact on their attractiveness to boys.

Of course, girls' involvement in sex is not solely determined by whether boys want them as sexual partners. Girls' own interest in sex and their receptivity to boys' interest in them are also crucial. But in girls, it turns out, these factors are much more determined by context than by biology.

■ **The Role of Context**   Numerous studies show that social factors are far more important in influencing girls' involvement in sexual intercourse than boys' (Crockett, Bingham, Chopak, & Vicary, 1996; D. B. Henry, Schoeny, Deptula, & Slavick, 2007). Although increases in androgens lead to increased interest in sex among girls, and although increases in estrogens lead to increased attractiveness to boys, whether this interest and attractiveness are translated into behavior depends largely on the social environment (Diamond & Savin-Williams, 2009). Among girls with high levels of androgens, for example, those who have sexually permissive attitudes and whose friends are sexually active are more likely to engage in intercourse. But girls whose social environment is less encouraging of sex—even those with high levels of androgens—are unlikely to be sexually active. In other words, whereas hormones seem to have a direct and powerful effect on the sexual behavior of boys, the impact of hormones on the sexual behavior of girls seems to depend on the social context.

Why might this be? One explanation is that boys develop in an environment that is more uniformly tolerant and encouraging of sexual behavior than girls do. All that boys need to become sexually active is the biological jolt from the increase in androgens at puberty—there is nothing in the environment to hold them back. For girls, however, the environment is more varied. Some girls develop within a context that permits and even encourages sexual activity; others do not. Although the increase in androgens also provides a jolt to the sex drive of the adolescent girl, and although the increase in estrogens makes her more attractive to boys, if she develops within a context that places strong social controls on sexual activity, this hormonal awakening will not be translated into sexual activity. Among the most important forces in this context are parents and peers.

PARENTAL AND PEER INFLUENCES ON SEXUAL ACTIVITY

Many researchers have asked whether adolescents who become sexually active earlier than their peers have different sorts of relationships with their parents or their peers. The answer is clear: Not surprisingly,

given the correlation between early sexual activity and other forms of problem behavior, most studies have found that adolescents from authoritative homes—that is, homes where parents are warm, are involved in their adolescent's life, and monitor their adolescent's behavior—are less likely to become sexually active at an early age and less likely to engage in risky sexual activity, such as having sex without protection against pregnancy or STDs (Capaldi, Stoolmiller, Clark, & Owen, 2002; Frisco, 2005; Huebner & Howell, 2003; Manlove, Logan, Moore, & Ikramullah, 2008). Parent–adolescent conflict is also associated with early sexual activity, especially among adolescents who are relatively more mature physically (McBride, Paikoff, & Holmbeck, 2003). These strong and consistent links between effective parenting and safer sexual behavior have been found across ethnic groups (Meschke, Bartholomae, & Zentall, 2000; B. Miller, Benson, & Galbraith, 2001).

■ **Parent–Adolescent Communication**   A great deal of attention has been devoted by researchers to the study of parent–adolescent communication about sex, although it is quite clear from this research that any conclusions you might draw about the nature and impact of these conversations depends entirely on whom you ask. Many more parents report communicating with their adolescent about sex than vice versa. In addition, parents often say that they have communicated about a particular topic (such as AIDS) when their teenager says they have not (K. Miller, Kotchick, Dorsey, Forehand, & Ham, 1998). Other discrepancies abound as well. For instance, parents underestimate their adolescents' sexual activity and unrealistically assume that if they disapprove of sexual activity, the adolescents are not likely to be sexually active; on the other hand, sexually active adolescents underestimate their parents' disapproval of sexual activity (Jaccard, Dittus, & Gordon, 1998). Generally, teenagers are more likely to talk about sex with mothers than fathers, and they rate their mothers as better sex educators (DiIorio, Kelley, & Hockenberry-Eaton, 1999; S. Feldman & Rosenthal, 2000; Raffaelli & Green, 2003). Adolescents also are likely to be more receptive to having multiple conversations over a period of time about sex than to having one "big talk" (Martino, Elliott, Corona, Kanouse, & Schuster, 2008).

Most discussions about sex between parents and teenagers focus on issues of safety (AIDS, condom use) rather than issues of sexual behavior or relationships (DiIorio et al., 1999; K. Miller et al., 1998). And, despite the progressive image of countries like the Netherlands, studies indicate that parent–adolescent communication about sex is no more open in Europe than in the United States (Arnett, 2002). Across cultures, however, adolescents are more likely to be well educated about sex when their conversations with their parents are genuinely interactive, rather than dominated by the parents (Lefkowitz, Romo, Corona, Au, & Sigman, 2000). This is important because conversations between mothers and daughters about sex tend to be more interactive than conversations between mothers and sons (Lefkowitz, Boone, Sigman, & Kit-fong Au, 2002). Perhaps because of this, parent–adolescent communication about sex is more predictive of daughters' behavior than of sons' (McNeely et al., 2002). Although there is not a great deal of research on ethnic differences in parent–adolescent communication about sex, it does appear as if conversations about sex are very infrequent in Asian American homes (J. L. Kim & Ward, 2007).

Although one would assume that it is beneficial for adolescents to discuss sex with their parents, the effect of parent–child communication on adolescents' sexual behavior depends on who is doing the communicating and what is being communicated. Overall, most studies find that the impact of parent–adolescent communication on the likelihood of an adolescent being sexually active is very small (Casper, 1990; B. Miller et al., 2001; Paikoff et al., 1997), although parent–child communication about contraception in particular does appear to lower the rate of *risky* sex (Aspy et al., 2007; Hutchinson, Jemmott, Jemmott, Braverman, & Fong, 2003; K. Miller & Whitaker, 2001; K. Rodgers, 1999), especially if the discussions take place before the adolescent becomes sexually active (K. Miller, Levin, Whitaker, & Xu, 1998). Communication with older siblings about safe sex is also effective (Kowal & Blinn-Pike, 2004).

A growing body of research suggests that what is most important are the attitudes and values communicated by parents during discussions of sex and, of course, the ways in which these attitudes and values are interpreted by the adolescent (Bersamin, Walker, Waiters, Fisher, & Grube, 2005; Jaccard, Dodge, & Dittus, 2003b; B. Miller et al., 2001). Among girls with liberal parents, for instance, talking about sex is associated with *more* sexual activity; this is not true among girls with parents who disapprove of premarital sex, however (Dittus & Jaccard, 2000; Fingerson, 2005; T. Fisher, 1989; Hovell et al., 1994; Usher-Seriki, Bynum, & Callands, 2008). In Hispanic families, in which parental attitudes about sex tend to be relatively more conservative, communication with adolescents about values and beliefs concerning sex is associated with less sexual activity, but the degree to which parents directly caution their teenagers against sex does not seem to make a difference (Romo, Lefkowitz, Sigman, & Au, 2002). In addition, adolescents who speak regularly with their parents about sex are more likely to turn down unwanted sex when they are pressured by others

(Sionéan et al., 2002). Moreover, studies find that it is important for parents to maintain a close relationship with their teenager after the adolescent has become sexually active and to resist the temptation to pull away in anger over the teenager's behavior (G. Ream & Savin-Williams, 2005).

It is important to note that parent–adolescent communication about sex is more effective in deterring *risky* sexual activity than in promoting abstinence, and even here, the effect that parents have is small. (This principle holds true for school-based sex education as well.) Thus, despite some parents' beliefs that they can prevent their adolescent's sexual activity by talking about it, and despite other parents' fears that talking about sex will have the unintended effect of encouraging their teenager's sexual behavior, studies show that parent–adolescent communication about sex has surprisingly little impact on whether adolescents are sexually active, one way or the other. While it is possible to teach parents how to talk more effectively to their teenagers about sex, it is not clear that doing so leads to dramatic changes in teenagers' knowledge, attitudes, or behavior (Lefkowitz, Sigman, & Au, 2000). Adolescents' opportunity to have sex (for example, whether they are in a steady relationship or date frequently), their having sexually active friends, and their use of alcohol and drugs are far better predictors of early sexual initiation than is parent–adolescent communication (M. Black, Ricardo, & Stanton, 1997; B. Miller, Norton et al., 1997; Whitbeck, Yoder, Hoyt, & Conger, 1999).

Sexual Activity and Household Composition

One family factor that does predict adolescent sexual involvement, however—especially among girls—is household composition. Researchers consistently find that adolescents whose parents are in the process of divorcing as well as girls who live in single-parent households—regardless of when (or if) a divorce took place—are more likely to be sexually active earlier than their peers (Crockett et al., 1996; Ellis et al., 2003; Hogan, Sun, & Cornwell, 2000; Lammers, Ireland, Resnick, & Blum, 2000; B. Miller, Norton et al., 1997; Wu & Thomson, 2001). One hypothesis, consistent with what we know about divorce and parent–adolescent relationships, is that parental divorce temporarily disrupts the parent–child relationship, leading the adolescent into early involvement with drugs, alcohol, and minor delinquency, which, according to some studies, increases the likelihood of sex. In other words, it is not family structure per se, but the quality of family relationships in divorced homes, that helps explain why girls from single-parent homes are more sexually active at an earlier age (E. Davis & Friel, 2001).

But why should growing up in a single-parent home affect *girls'* sexual behavior more than boys'? At least four possibilities exist. One, as noted earlier, is that social influences on girls' sexual behavior are stronger and more varied than are the influences on boys' behavior (Whitbeck, Simons, & Kao, 1994). Boys' parents simply may not attempt to exert much control over their sexual activity, regardless of whether the household has one parent or two, and as a result, boys from single- and two-parent homes may be equally likely to be sexually active. Girls' sexual behavior, in contrast, may be more subject to parental controls. Single-parent homes are typically more permissive than two-parent homes (Laursen & Collins, 2009), and this difference in control may be enough to make a difference in girls' sexual activity.

A second possibility is that many single-parent mothers are likely to be dating and, in so doing, may inadvertently be role models of sexual activity to their adolescents (B. Miller & Moore, 1990; Whitbeck et al., 1994). Other research shows, for example, that adolescents whose mothers had been sexually active at an early age are themselves more likely to begin having sex early (Mott et al., 1996). To the extent that this modeling effect is stronger between parents and children of the same sex, we would expect to find a more powerful effect of growing up in a single-parent home on the sexual behavior of daughters than sons.

Yet a third possibility is that girls are more likely than boys to respond to problems at home by going outside the family for alternative sources of warmth and support; if their family environment is not satisfying, girls (whether in divorced homes or not) may be more likely than boys to seek the attention of a romantic partner (Whitbeck, Hoyt, Miller, & Kao, 1992). During or immediately following their parents' divorce, girls may seek the support of individuals with whom they become sexually involved.

Finally, some researchers suggest that the link between growing up in a single-parent household and earlier involvement in sex is genetic. They have shown that the same gene that makes men more likely to leave their family may, when passed on to daughters, make adolescent girls more likely to go through puberty early and become sexually active at an earlier age (Comings, Muhleman, Johnson, & MacMurray, 2002).

■ **Influences Other Than Parents** Additional studies have examined the influence of forces other than parents on adolescents' sexual behavior. Generally, adolescents are more likely to be sexually active when their peers are (and more likely to engage in risky sex when their peers do) (DiBlasio & Benda, 1992; East, Felice, & Morgan, 1993; D. B. Henry et al., 2007); when they *believe* that their friends are sexually active, whether or not their friends actually are (Babalola, 2004; Brooks-Gunn & Furstenberg, 1989; DiIorio et al., 2001; Prinstein, Meade, & Cohen, 2003); and when they have older siblings who model more sexually ad-

Talking to teenagers about sex does not increase their likelihood of becoming sexually active, but may encourage adolescents to practice safe sex.

vanced behavior (East, 2009). Consistent with this, although religious involvement deters adolescents' sexual activity, regular church attendance is associated with delayed sexual activity only among adolescents whose friends attend the same church (Mott, Fondell, Hu, Kowaleski-Jones, & Menaghan, 1996). Importantly, adolescents whose parents discuss sex with them in an open and understanding way are less influenced by having sexually active peers (Fasula & Miller, 2006; Whitaker & Miller, 2000).

Peer influences on adolescents' sexual activity appear to operate in two different, but compatible, ways. First, when an adolescent's peers are sexually active, they establish a normative standard that having sex is acceptable (Gillmore et al., 2002; Sieving, Eisenberg, Pettingell, & Skay, 2006; Stack, 1994). One of the reasons that minor drug use is associated with earlier involvement in sexual activity is that drug use may lead an adolescent to form friendships with a different group of friends, a group that is sexually more permissive (D. French & Dishion, 2003; Whitbeck, Conger, Simons, & Kao, 1993). Consistent with this, adolescents' initiation of sexual activity varies from neighborhood to neighborhood, with earlier sexual activity more likely in relatively more disorganized neighborhoods, where adults have little control over teenagers and where peer groups are relatively more powerful

Over the past two decades, several million American adolescents have taken a virginity pledge, promising to abstain from sex until they are married. Research has found, however, that high school students who have pledged to remain virgins are just as likely to have sex as those who haven't made such pledges.

(T. Leventhal, Dupéré, & Brooks-Gunn, 2009; Upchurch, Aneshensel, Sucoff, & Levy-Storms, 1999). Generally, the more individual **risk factors** there are in an adolescent's life for involvement in early sexual activity (for example, drug and alcohol use, poor parental monitoring, sexually active friends, antisocial peers, disengagement from school, a disadvantaged neighborhood), the more likely the adolescent is to be sexually active (Small & Luster, 1994). The factors that place adolescents at risk for early sexual activity are the same across ethnic groups (D. Perkins, Luster, Villarruel, & Small, 1998).

Peers also influence each other's sexual behavior directly, either through communication among friends ("You haven't done it yet! What's the matter with you?" "You're thinking of doing what?") or, more commonly, between potential sex partners. Several studies show that sexual activity spreads within a community of adolescents much like an epidemic, with sexually experienced adolescents initiating their less experienced partners into increasingly more advanced sex (J. Rodgers & Rowe, 1993). Once they become sexually experienced, previously inexperienced adolescents then "infect" other adolescents. Over time, the percentage of sexually experienced adolescents within a community grows and grows.

▎ **Virginity Pledges** Studies of "virginity pledges" also shed light on the way in which the social context

can influence adolescent sexual activity (Bearman & Brückner, 2001; Rosenbaum, 2009). Over the past two decades, several million American adolescents have taken a virginity pledge, promising to abstain from sex until they are married. How effective is this? Research finds that virginity pledges work only for younger adolescents—they have no effect on high school students. Among high school students, "pledgers" are just as likely to have sex (including intercourse, oral sex, and anal sex) as "nonpledgers." And longitudinal studies show that after having sex, adolescents who had taken a virginity pledge frequently deny having made one (Hollander, 2006; Rosenbaum, 2006). Ironically, one way in which those who take a virginity pledge differ from their nonpledging peers is that those who take the pledge are less likely to use contraception, suggesting that encouraging abstinence may actually promote unsafe sex (Rosenbaum, 2009). Perhaps more interestingly, the impact of pledging varies as a function of how many other adolescents in the same school have taken the pledge. Pledging has little effect in schools in which few students take virginity pledges (presumably because there is little social support for abstinence) or in schools in which nearly everyone pledges (because one of the ways in which pledging works is by allowing those who pledge to make a statement about their values). By the way, it turns out that making a promise to *oneself* to delay becoming sexually active is more effective than making a formal, public pledge (Bersamin, Walker, Waiters, Fisher, & Grube, 2005).

Finally, several studies have examined the role of the broader environment in influencing adolescent sexual behavior. Adolescents growing up in poor neighborhoods, for example, are more likely to engage in early sexual activity than adolescents from more affluent communities (Dupéré, Lacourse, Willms, Leventhal, & Tremblay, 2008; T. Leventhal et al., 2009). When adolescents grow up in poverty, they may see little hope for the future, and they therefore may be more likely to risk their occupational and economic future by becoming sexually active (Benda & Corwyn, 1998). To a young person who believes that the chances of getting a good job are slim, an early pregnancy does not seem as costly as it might to someone who hopes to complete high school, attend college, and secure a good job. Adolescents' sexual behavior is more strongly influenced by the values and attitudes of their schoolmates than the characteristics of their neighborhood, however (Teitler & Weiss, 2000).

SEX DIFFERENCES IN THE MEANING OF SEX

Any discussion of the psychosocial significance of sexual experience during adolescence must be sensitive to the very substantial sex differences in how early sexual

risk factors Factors that increase the likelihood of some behavior or condition.

activity is experienced. Despite the convergence of males' and females' rates of sexual activity in recent decades, the early sexual experiences of adolescent boys and girls are still very different and, as a consequence, are imbued with very different *meanings* (Diamond & Savin-Williams, 2009). In other words, the sexual behavior of males and females may be similar, but the sexual socialization of males and females is quite different.

▌ **The Way Boys Feel** The typical boy's first sexual experience is masturbation in early adolescence (Diamond & Savin-Williams, 2009). At the outset, then, the sexual socialization of males typically places sex outside of an interpersonal context. Before adolescent boys begin dating, they have generally already experienced orgasm and know how to arouse themselves sexually. For males, the development of sexuality during adolescence revolves around efforts to integrate the capacity to form close relationships into an already-existing sense of sexual capability.

Perhaps because of this, at the time of first intercourse, boys are likely to keep matters of sex and intimacy separate. Boys often have as their first partner someone they just met or describe as a casual date, and it is generally the male partner of a couple who is likely to initiate sex (Diamond & Savin-Williams, 2009). These findings suggest that the early sexual experiences of males are often interpreted not in terms of intimacy and emotional involvement, but in terms of recreation (Hendrick & Hendrick, 1994). Consistent with this, boys are more likely than girls to mention sexual arousal (rather than emotional factors) as a reason for having sex (Eyre & Millstein, 1999). And males typically report that the people to whom they describe their first sexual liaison—most probably, male peers—are overwhelmingly approving. Not surprisingly, the most common immediate reactions among adolescent males to having intercourse for the first time are excitement, satisfaction, exhilaration, and happiness (Oswald, Bahne, & Feder, 1994; Diamond & Savin-Williams, 2009).

▌ **The Way Girls Feel** The typical girl's first experience and feelings afterward are likely to be very different. Masturbation is far less prevalent among girls than boys, and it is far less regularly practiced (Diamond & Savin-Williams, 2009). As a consequence, the typical adolescent girl, in contrast to the typical boy, is more likely to experience sex for the first time with another person. For girls, unlike boys, the development of sexuality involves the integration of sexual activity into an already existing capacity for intimacy and emotional involvement. As a consequence, the girl's sexual script is one that, from the outset, tinges sex with romance, love, friendship, and intimacy. Girls are more likely

than boys to engage in sex in order to enhance an emotional connection (Hendrick & Hendrick, 1994; Diamond & Savin-Williams, 2009).

Boys and girls also encounter very different social attitudes about sex. Because of the possibility of pregnancy, the potential adverse consequences of sexual activity are far more serious for girls than for boys. For this reason, society monitors the sexual activity of girls more carefully, and girls are more likely to be encouraged to approach sex cautiously (Rosenthal, 1994). Girls' feelings of sexual desire are "tempered by their knowledge that girls are not supposed to be sexual or that if they are, they will be marked as bad and unlovable" (Tolman, 1993, p. 4). Perhaps because of this, girls have an easier time saying no to unwanted sex than boys do (R. Zimmerman, Sprecher, Langer, & Holloway, 1995).

Not surprisingly, then, at the time of first intercourse, the adolescent girl's sexual partner is likely to be someone she says she was in love with at the time (Diamond & Savin-Williams, 2009). After having intercourse for the first time, she is more likely to encounter disapproval or mixed feelings on the part of others in whom she confides (generally, peers) than is the typical boy (Diamond & Savin-Williams, 2009). And although the majority of girls report more positive than negative feelings about their first sexual experience, girls are more likely than boys to report feeling afraid, guilty, and worried as well as happy or excited about the experience (Oswald et al., 1994; Diamond & Savin-Williams, 2009).

It is important to keep in mind that differences between males and females in the meaning of sex are neither inevitable nor consistent across cultures or historical time. Nor is it the case that all adolescent boys follow the male "script" and all adolescent girls follow the female "script." As Lisa Diamond and Ritch Savin-Williams, two experts on adolescent sexuality, recently noted, "Girls are more sexually oriented and boys more romantically oriented than previous research might suggest" (Diamond & Savin-Williams, 2009, p. 514). Moreover, as they mature, adolescent boys and girls become more similar in their motives to have sex (males increasingly emphasize the place of sex in an emotional relationship and place less importance on the role of sex in elevating their social status, whereas females become less likely to justify their interest in sex solely in terms of their intimate relationships).

FOOD FOR THOUGHT

Can you think of any evolutionary explanations for the different ways in which males and females react to their first sexual experiences?

HOMOSEXUALITY DURING ADOLESCENCE

▌ Prevalence of Homosexuality   It is not uncommon for young adolescents to engage in sex play with members of the same sex, to have sexual fantasies about people of the same sex, or to have questions about the nature of their feelings for same-sex peers (Diamond & Savin-Williams, 2009). According to the national (and confidential) Add Health survey, about 6% of boys and 13% of girls reported having had same-sex attractions, a nonheterosexual orientation, or engaging in same-sex activity during adolescence. A smaller number of adolescents—between 2% and 5%—identify themselves as gay, lesbian, or bisexual, and this number increases to about 8% among adults (Michael, Laumann, & Kolata, 1994; Diamond & Savin-Williams, 2009). Researchers have not found consistent predictors that distinguish individuals who experiment with same-sex relations in adolescence and who later identify themselves as gay, lesbian, or bisexual from those whose experimentation during adolescence is passing and who later identify themselves as exclusively heterosexual. By the same token, the majority of gay, lesbian, and bisexual adults engaged in heterosexual activity during adolescence. As Diamond and Savin-Williams note, "contrary to the widespread notion that desire, behavior, and identity coalesce neatly in adolescence and young adulthood to signal an unambiguously heterosexual or homosexual orientation, the reality is much more complicated" (2009, p. 505).

It is important to distinguish between homosexuality as an exclusive preference and homosexuality as an interest that may exist simultaneously with strong heterosexual interests (Diamond & Savin-Williams, 2009). Many people mistakenly view sexual orientation as an "either-or" attribute, with individuals being either exclusively heterosexual or exclusively homosexual. In fact, however, of the individuals who do not develop an exclusive preference for heterosexual relationships, only one third are exclusively homosexual in their orientation. Nearly twice as many describe themselves as bisexual—having both heterosexual and homosexual interests. About 3% of adult males and 1% of adult females are exclusively homosexual (Michael et al., 1994).

The development of sexual orientation follows different patterns among sexual minority males and females. Males are more likely to have had same-sex relations before identifying themselves as gay or bisexual, whereas the reverse sequence is more characteristic among females. And whereas more lesbian and bisexual females had heterosexual experiences before their first same-sex sexual activity, the opposite is true for males. In addition, females who have had same-sex contact during adolescence almost always pursue same-sex contact in adulthood (whereas the same is not true for males (about 60% do) (Diamond & Savin-Williams, 2009).

A great deal of confusion about homosexuality results because people tend to confuse **sexual orientation** (the extent to which someone is oriented toward heterosexual activity, homosexual activity, or both), **sex-role behavior** (the extent to which an individual behaves in traditionally masculine or feminine ways), and **gender identity** (the gender an individual believes he or she is psychologically). There is no connection between an adolescent's sexual orientation and his or her sex-role behavior. Individuals with strong, or even exclusive, preferences for homosexual relationships exhibit the same range of masculine and feminine behaviors seen among individuals with strong or exclusive heterosexual interests. In other words, exclusively gay men (like exclusively heterosexual men) may act in very masculine, very feminine, or both masculine and feminine ways, and the same holds true for exclusively lesbian and exclusively heterosexual women, as it does for bisexual individuals. Along similar lines, individuals with homosexual interests are generally not confused about their gender identity—or, at least, they are no more confused than are individuals with heterosexual interests.

▌ Origins of Homosexuality   Studies of the antecedents of homosexuality generally have focused on two sets of factors: biological influences, such as hormones, and social influences, such as the parent–child relationship. More is known about the development of homosexuality among men than among women, but the weight of the evidence thus far suggests that an adolescent's sexual orientation is likely to be shaped by a complex interaction of social and biological influences (D. Bem, 1996; Paul, 1993; Savin-Williams, 2006).

Support for the contention that homosexuality is determined at least partly by biological factors comes from two sources. You may recall that in Chapter 1 we distinguished between the organizational and the activational roles of hormones on behavior. The hormonal changes of puberty activate sexual behavior, but the particular pattern of sexual behavior that is activated may depend on the way in which hormonal pathways in the brain were organized early in life. There is suggestive evidence that gay and lesbian adults may have been exposed prenatally to certain hormones that, in theory, could affect sexual orientation through their effects on early brain

---

sexual orientation   An individual's orientation toward same- or other-sex sex partners.

sex-role behavior   Behavior that is consistent with prevailing expectations for how individuals of a given sex are to behave.

gender identity   The gender an individual identifies with.

Sexual orientation is influenced by a complex interplay of biological and contextual factors.

organization (Meyer-Bahlburg et al., 1995). Second, some evidence indicates that homosexuality has a strong genetic component, since sexual orientation is more likely to be similar among close relatives than distant relatives and between identical twins than fraternal twins (Savin-Williams, 2006). Although environmental explanations for this similarity cannot be ruled out, chances are that at least some of the predisposition to develop a homosexual orientation is inherited.

Several studies suggest as well that a higher proportion of homosexuals than heterosexuals report having had problems in their early family relationships—specifically, in their relationship with their father. The stereotype of the homosexual's father as cold and distant once was rejected as an artifact of popular stereotype and poor research designs. But more carefully designed studies have offered at least partial confirmation of this notion. Both bisexual and homosexual adolescents are more likely than heterosexuals to describe their fathers as distant and rejecting (Bos, Sandfort, de Bruyn, & Hakvoort, 2008; Busseri, Willoughby, Chalmers, & Bogaert, 2008). Whereas gay men are more likely than heterosexuals to report having had close and generally positive relationships with their mothers, lesbians are more likely than heterosexuals to describe their

mothers as cold and unpleasant (A. Bell, Weinberg, & Hammersmith, 1981). However, gay and lesbian adolescents are no more likely than heterosexual youth to have had gay or lesbian parents—in fact, studies of adolescents with same-sex parents find few differences between them and their peers with opposite-sex parents (Wainwright, Russell, & Patterson, 2004).

Although these studies point to certain factors that appear more often than not in the early histories of homosexuals, they hardly indicate that all individuals who show patterns of gender nonconformity or who have distant relations with their fathers inevitably become homosexual (Golombock & Tasker, 1996). Nor does research show that all homosexuals have identical developmental histories. For example, although, on average, homosexuals are more likely than heterosexuals to describe their parents in negative terms, not all gay and lesbian individuals feel this way. Indeed, only about half do, suggesting that a large number of gay and lesbian individuals had quite positive family relationships growing up. And, of course, many heterosexuals describe their parents in exceedingly negative terms. Similarly, although the majority of boys with persistently feminine behavior preferences may grow up to be gay, a substantial number of feminine boys do not.

▌ Development of Sexual Identity   Several writers have described the process through which gay, lesbian, and bisexual individuals discover, come to terms with, and disclose their sexual-minority identity (Diamond, 2008; Dubé & Savin-Williams, 1999). Although the traditional model of this progression—feeling different as a child, engaging in gender-atypical behavior, being attracted to members of the same sex and uninterested in those of the other sex, realizing one's sexual attraction to others of the same sex, and consciously questioning one's sexual identity—describes the experience of many sexual-minority adolescents, it by no means is universal. Indeed, some writers have suggested that this may be more applicable to the development of White gay men than to lesbians, bisexual adolescents, or ethnic minority gay men (Diamond, 1998; Dubé & Savin-Williams, 1999). For example, there is evidence that females' sexual orientation may be more fluid than males', with many bisexual or lesbian late adolescents changing sexual orientation during young adulthood (Diamond, 2008).

FOOD FOR THOUGHT

Should social scientists be interested in the antecedents of homosexuality? Is it important to know whether homosexuality is biologically or contextually determined? Why or why not?

Society's prejudice and ignorance about homosexuality likely cause significant psychological distress for gay and lesbian adolescents, especially if they encounter hostility from those around them (T. E. Smith & Leaper, 2006). As you know by now, the developmental tasks in the domains of identity, intimacy, and sexuality present formidable challenges for many teenagers. These challenges may be exacerbated for sexual-minority adolescents, who are forced to resolve these issues without the same degree of social support as their heterosexual peers (Diamond & Lucas, 2004). (Interestingly, adolescents are more intolerant about peers behaving in gender-atypical ways than they are about sexual orientation [Horn, 2007]). Indeed, many studies have found that a substantial number of gay, lesbian, and bisexual adolescents had been harassed, physically abused, or verbally abused by peers or adults while growing up (Hershberger & D'Augelli, 1995; Pilkington & D'Augelli, 1995; Russell, Franz, & Driscoll, 2001; Russell & Joyner, 2001; Savin-Williams, 1994). Abuse of this sort, as well more distant family relationships, may account for the relatively higher rates of depression, suicide, substance abuse, running away from home, and school difficulties reported by gay, lesbian, and bisexual adolescents (Bontempo & D'Augelli, 2002; Bos et al., 2008; Busseri et al., 2008; Cochran, Stewart, Ginzler, & Cauce, 2002; Galliher, Rostosky, & Hughes, 2004).

SEXUAL HARASSMENT, RAPE, AND SEXUAL ABUSE DURING ADOLESCENCE

▌ Sexual Harassment and Date Rape   Although most research on adolescent sexual activity has focused on voluntary sexual behavior between consenting individuals, there is growing public awareness that a large proportion of teenagers are sexually harassed and that a significant minority are forced to have sex against their will (V. Lee, Croninger, Linn, & Chen, 1996; T. Lewin, 1997; N. Stein, 1995; Vicary, Klingaman, & Harkness, 1995). This latter group includes adolescents who have been the victims of forcible rape by a stranger, sexual abuse within the family, or **date rape**—when a young person, typically a woman, is forced by a date to have sex when she does not want to. Sexual coercion and sex under the influence of alcohol or drugs are more likely to occur when there is a large age difference (3 years or more) between a girl and her partner (Gowen, Feldman, Diaz, & Yisrael, 2004).

For all the concern that is expressed about the sexual harassment of teenagers over the Internet, adolescents are far more at risk at school than online. Recent studies indicate that sexual harassment—both cross-gender and between members of the same sex—is widespread within American public schools (Leaper & Brown, 2008; V. Lee et al., 1996; Loredo, Reid, & Deaux, 1995; McMaster, Connolly, Pepler, & Craig, 2002; N. Stein, 1995). According to one study of a nationally representative sample of middle and secondary school students, more than 80% of girls and 60% of boys reported having received unwanted sexual attention while in school (V. Lee at al., 1996) (see Figure 11.5). Sexual harassment is especially distressing to early-maturing girls, whose physical maturity already makes them stand apart from their peers (S. M. Lindberg, Grabe, & Hyde, 2007).

Because the majority of those who had been sexually harassed had themselves harassed others and because many incidents occurred within full view of teachers and other school personnel—indeed, a significant percentage of students report having been sexually harassed by their *teachers*—numerous experts have suggested the need for wholesale changes in the moral and ethical climate of secondary schools (V. Lee et al., 1996; N. Stein, 1995; Timmerman, 2002). This is easier said than done, however; one evaluation of a school-based program called Safe Dates found significant reductions in psychological abuse and sexual violence

date rape   Being forced by a date to have sex against one's will.

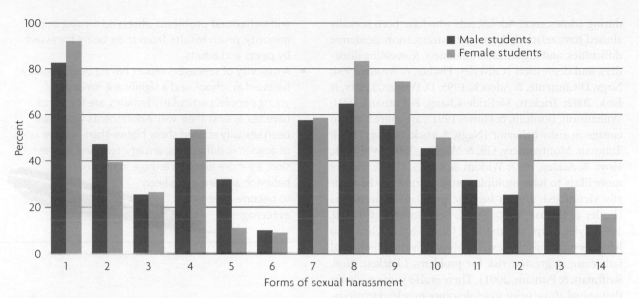

FIGURE 11.5   The percentage of male and female students having ever experienced different forms of sexual harassment.
(Lee et al., 1996)

1. Made sexual comments, jokes, gestures, or looks
2. Showed you sexual pictures, photographs, messages, etc.
3. Wrote sexual messages about you on bathroom walls, etc.
4. Spread sexual rumors about you
5. Said you were gay or lesbian
6. Spied on you as you dressed or showered at school
7. Flashed or mooned you

8. Touched, grabbed, or pinched you in a sexual way
9. Intentionally brushed up against you in a sexual way
10. Pulled at your clothing in a sexual way
11. Pulled your clothing off or down
12. Blocked your way or cornered you in a sexual way
13. Forced you to kiss him/her
14. Forced you to do something sexual, other than kissing

1 month after the program was implemented, but these effects had disappeared within 1 year (Foshee et al., 2000). Other research, on the histories of individuals who commit dating violence, indicates that perpetrators themselves were likely to have been exposed to physical punishment and abuse at home (Basile et al., 2006; Capaldi & Clark, 1998; R. Simons, Lin, & Gordon, 1998; D. Wolfe, Wekerle, Reitzel-Jaffe, & Lefebvre, 1998).

FOOD FOR THOUGHT

If you were asked to devise a sexual harassment policy for a high school, what would be the main elements of your policy? Should policies governing adolescents' conduct in school be the same as those governing adults in the workplace?

▮ **Sexual Abuse**   Because both perpetrators and victims of sexual assaults are often reluctant to admit their experiences, it is difficult to obtain accurate estimates of the numbers of adolescents who have been sexually victimized. We do know that adolescent

victims of sexual abuse are disproportionately female and poor (Cappelleri, Eckenrode, & Powers, 1993). According to several studies, between 7% and 18% of adolescents report having had nonvoluntary sexual intercourse before age 18; reports by females are substantially higher than those by males, but it is not known how much of this is due to different prevalence rates and how much to different willingness on the part of females and males to report having been raped (Diamond & Savin-Williams, 2009). (These figures on sexual abuse do not include adolescents who have been physically forced to engage in sexual activity other than intercourse and, as such, clearly underestimate the proportion of teenagers who have been sexually abused.) Women who were most likely to have been raped during adolescence were those who lived apart from their parents before age 16; who were physically, emotionally, or mentally impaired; who were raised at or below the poverty level; or whose parents abused alcohol or used other drugs. Indeed, two thirds of all women who had three or more of these risk factors were raped as adolescents. In contrast to popular perception, adolescents are abused (sexually, physically, and emotionally) and neglected at a higher rate than are younger children (Cappelleri et al., 1993).

Several studies have examined the psychological consequences of having been the victim of sexual abuse during adolescence. Adolescents who have been sexually abused have relatively lower self-esteem, more academic difficulties, and higher rates of anxiety, fear, eating disorders, and depression (Calverley, Fischer, & Ayoub, 1994; Nagy, DiClimente, & Adcock, 1995; D. Perkins, Luster, & Jank, 2002; Trickett, McBride-Chang, & Putnam, 1994; Williamson, Borduin, & Howe, 1991); are more likely to engage in risky behavior (Nagy, Adcock, & Nagy, 1994; Tubman, Montgomery, Gil, & Wagner, 2004; Whitbeck, Hoyt, & Ackley, 1997; Widom & Kuhns, 1996); and are more likely to have multiple sexual partners, to be sexually victimized, and to become pregnant as teenagers (Butler & Burton, 1990; Stock, Bell, Boyer, & Connell, 1997; Tyler, Hoyt, Whitbeck, & Cauce, 2001). Girls who have been chronically sexually abused by their biological father are at greatest risk for problems (Trickett, Noll, Reiffman, & Putnam, 2001). There is also some evidence that sexual abuse prior to adolescence may lead to precocious (that is, very early) puberty (J. Brown, Cohen, Chen, Smailes, & Johnson, 2004).

At the same time, it is worth noting that there are substantial differences among individuals in the extent to which they show problems as a result of having been sexually abused and in the form those problems take (Bauserman & Rind, 1997). Generally, individuals who have been both sexually and physically abused fare worse than those who experience sexual abuse alone. But adolescents who have been sexually abused fare better psychologically when they have parents (presumably not the perpetrators of the abuse) who are authoritative (firm and supportive) and when they are successful in school (Luster & Small, 1997).

RECAP

- In general, sexual activity during adolescence does not carry the psychological risks that many adults associate with it. Adolescents who are sexually active have psychological profiles that are similar to, rather than different from, their nonactive peers.
- Some evidence suggests that early sexual activity (having intercourse before age 16) is more common among teenagers growing up in single-parent households and is associated with higher rates of problem behaviors, such as drug and alcohol use.
- Any discussion of the psychological aspects of adolescent sexuality must differentiate between the experiences of males and females. Early sexuality for males is tinged with elements of recreation, whereas for females it is more linked to feelings of intimacy and love.
- About 6% of boys and 13% of girls report having had same-sex attractions, a nonheterosexual orientation, or engaging in same-sex activity during adolescence. The higher rate of psychological

and behavioral problems observed among sexual minority youth results from their being harassed by peers and adults.

- A majority of teenagers report having been sexually harassed in school, and a significant minority of young people, particularly females, are forced to have sex against their will. Adolescents who have been sexually abused show higher-than-average rates of academic difficulties, anxiety, fear, and depression; are more likely to engage in risky behavior; and are more likely to become pregnant as teenagers.

Risky Sex and Its Prevention

CONTRACEPTIVE USE

One reason for the great concern among adults over the sexual activity of adolescents is the failure of many sexually active young people to use contraception regularly. Among sexually active high school students, nearly 40% report not having used a condom the last time they had sex. Adolescents' condom use increased significantly during the 1990s (from less than half to close to 60%), but has not changed since 2003. Surprisingly, condom use is higher among sexually active 9th-graders than sexually active 12th-graders, most likely because more than twice as many 12th-grade girls than 9th-grade girls are on the birth control pill. Of course, using the pill prevents pregnancy but provides no protection against sexually transmitted diseases. Condom use is higher among Black adolescents than White or Hispanic adolescents (Centers for Disease Control and Prevention, 2008).

Among adolescents who do use contraception, the most popular method by far is using a condom, the method used by close to 60% of sexually active teenage couples, followed by the birth control pill, which is used by about one fifth of couples; this is a significant change from previous generations of adolescents, who were far more likely to depend on the birth control pill than on condoms (Everett et al., 2000). (About 20% of girls who are on the pill report that their partner uses a condom as well [Santelli et al., 1997].) Withdrawal, a highly ineffective method of preventing pregnancy, unfortunately is still used by a large number of teenagers, as is the rhythm method—a method of birth control that requires more regular menstrual cycling than many teenagers have and more careful monitoring of menstrual cycling than most teenagers are capable of. Researchers estimate that the risk of teen pregnancy is about half due to the absence of

One of the reasons for adults' concern about adolescent sexual activity is the failure of many sexually active teenagers to use contraception regularly.

contraceptive use and about half due to failed contraceptive use (Santelli, Morrow, Anderson, & Lindberg, 2006). A large proportion of condom users do not use condoms correctly, for example (e.g., not putting the condom on before first entry or not holding onto the condom while withdrawing) (Oakley & Bogue, 1995), and many adolescents who might benefit from using emergency contraception (the "morning after pill," or "Plan B") do not know how to use it properly (Mollen et al., 2008). The rate of adolescent pregnancy is substantially higher in the United States than in other industrialized countries—despite the fact that the rate of teenage sexual activity in the United States is comparable to that in other countries (Darroch, Singh, & Frost, 2001).

▌ Adolescents' Reasons for Not Using Contraception

Why do so few adolescents use contraception regularly and effectively? Social scientists point to three broad factors: lack of planning, lack of access, and lack of knowledge.

By far the most important reason many adolescents fail to use birth control is that their sexual activity is unplanned (D. Kirby, 2007). This absence of planning may reflect adolescents' resistance to admitting that they are choosing to be sexually active, which may explain why adolescents who have taken virginity pledges are less likely to use contraception when they break their pledge and have sex (Brückner & Bearman, 2005; Rosenbaum, 2009) and why conservatively religious adolescents are less likely to be sexually active but also are less likely to use birth control if they do have sex (L. Miller & Gur, 2002; Studer & Thornton, 1987). Or adolescents' failure to use contraceptives may just reflect the fact that adolescents are less likely to plan ahead and think about the future consequences of their behavior than adults (Steinberg et al., 2009). In either case, going on the pill or purchasing a condom requires an adolescent to acknowledge that he or she is having or is going to have sexual relations.

Consistent with this, studies show that one of the best predictors of condom use is the individual's intent to use a condom and willingness to communicate about it with his or her partner (Sheeran et al., 1999; Tschann & Adler, 1997; Widman, Welsh, McNulty, & Little, 2006). Interventions designed to strengthen adolescents' intentions and their ability to communicate with their partner about contraception, and not just increase their knowledge, have been shown to be effective in promoting condom use, even within high-risk populations (DiClemente et al., 2004; Jemmott, Jemmott, Fong, & McCaffree, 1999).

A second reason for adolescents' failure to use contraception, although a far less important one, is that some adolescents can't afford birth control or don't know where to obtain it (D. Kirby, 2007). Lack of access (or perceived lack of access) is an especially important barrier among younger adolescents, who may feel uncomfortable discussing their sexual activity with parents or other adults whose help or consent may be necessary in order to obtain birth control. Having ready access to a free, confidential family planning service that does not require parents' consent is a strong predictor of whether adolescents will use contraceptives at all or will use them consistently (Averett, Rees, & Argys, 2002; Blake et al., 2003; S. Ryan, Franzetta, & Manlove, 2007). One study found that teen pregnancies and childbearing rose after the imposition of a requirement that adolescents get their parents' consent in order to obtain contraception (Zavodny, 2004), and surveys of sexually active teenagers who use contraceptives indicate that one fifth of them would stop using them if they had to notify their parents in order to get them (R. K. Jones, Purcell, Singh, & Finer, 2005).

FOOD FOR THOUGHT

Think back to your own sexual experience as an adolescent. If you were sexually active, what factors influenced your use (or lack of use) of contraception? Given the fact that many adolescents' sexual experiences are unplanned, what steps might society take to increase safe sex?

Finally, many young people are insufficiently educated about sex, contraception, and pregnancy, which may leave them misinformed about when and how to use contraception (D. Kirby, 2007; S. Ryan et al., 2007). For example, although it is important for adolescents to understand the need to use contraception every time they have sex, a very large proportion of teenagers who have had sex with contraception have also had sex *without* contraception (Arnett & Balle-Jensen, 1993; Gillmore, Morrison, Lowery, & Baker, 1994). That said, knowledge alone does not seem to be sufficient to promote contraceptive use; individuals must be *motivated* to use contraception as well as know why they need to (Sheeran, Abraham, & Orbell, 1999).

Given all these reasons—lack of planning, lack of access, and lack of knowledge—it is not surprising that one of the best predictors of contraceptive use is the adolescent's age: Older teenagers are better at thinking ahead, less guilty about having sex, more likely to be able to discuss contraception with their partner, and better able to grasp the potential negative consequences of an unwanted pregnancy (Sheeran et al., 1999). Relatively younger women are even less likely to use contraception if their partner is older and more likely, as a result, to contract an STD (Glei, 1999; K. Miller, Clark, & Moore, 1997; S. Ryan, Franzetta, Manlove, & Schelar, 2008).

■ **Improving Contraceptive Behavior**   Taken together, research suggests that there is a great deal that adults can do to improve the contraceptive behavior of adolescents. First, adults can see that contraceptives are made accessible to the young people who feel they need them. Second, parents and schools should provide sex education at an early enough age to instruct young people in the fundamentals of contraceptive use before, rather than after, adolescents have become sexually active; such education should be aimed at strengthening adolescents' intentions to use contraception and not just their contraceptive knowledge. Third, parents can be more open and responsive in the ways in which they communicate with their teenagers about sex, and about safe sex in particular, so that when adolescents become sexually active, they find it easier to plan ahead without feeling guilty. Finally, it is important that adolescents be encouraged to consider the potential future consequences of an unplanned pregnancy or a sexually transmitted disease. One way to do this is to engage adolescents in school, which may improve their aspirations for the future (D. Kirby, 2007). Adolescents who do not believe that a pregnancy will be an impediment to their future goals are less likely to take steps to avoid getting pregnant (Jumping-Eagle, Sheeder, Kelly, & Stevens-Simon, 2008).

AIDS AND OTHER SEXUALLY TRANSMITTED DISEASES

Helping youngsters understand sex, pregnancy, and contraception is an important goal of sex education programs for adolescents. Helping them avoid the risks of **sexually transmitted diseases (STDs)** is another. STDs are caused by viruses, bacteria, or parasites that are transmitted through sexual contact (Slap & Jablow, 1994). About 3 million adolescents are diagnosed with a sexually transmitted infection each year (Ozer & Irwin, 2009). Some of the most common STDs among adolescents are **gonorrhea** and **chlamydia** (both caused by a bacterium), and **herpes** and **human papillomavirus** (both caused by a virus) (Slap & Jablow, 1994). These infections pose a significant health risk to young people, because they are associated with increased rates of cancer and infertility. They also place a tremendous financial burden on taxpayers—in 2000, the treatment of new cases of STDs among young Americans cost taxpayers $6.5 billion (Chesson, Blandford, Gift, Tao, & Irwin, 2004). Countries vary considerably in rates of STD infection, with the United States having one of the highest rates in the world (Panchaud, Singh, Feivelson, & Darroch, 2000).

■ **HIV/AIDS**   During the 1980s, a new and far more serious STD commanded the world's attention: **AIDS,** or **acquired immune deficiency syndrome.** The virus that causes AIDS, **human immunodeficiency virus (HIV),** is transmitted through bodily fluids, especially semen, during sex, or blood when drug users share needles. AIDS itself has no symptoms, but HIV attacks the body's immune system, interfering with the body's ability to defend itself against life-threatening diseases like pneumonia or cancer. Because there is a long period of time between HIV infection and the actual manifestation of illness, however—sometimes as long as 10 years—adolescents are likely to be asymptomatic carriers of the HIV virus who may develop AIDS in young adulthood; indeed, during the last decade, cases of AIDS increased by 7% among adolescents, but by 47% among 20- to 24-year-olds (Ozer & Irwin, 2009).

Although the incidence of AIDS in the United States was initially concentrated within two groups, gay men and drug users who use needles, surveys indicate that

sexually transmitted disease (STD)   Any of a group of infections—including gonorrhea, herpes, chlamydia, and AIDS—passed on through sexual contact.

gonorrhea   A sexually transmitted infection caused by a bacterium.

chlamydia   A sexually transmitted infection caused by a bacterium.

herpes   A sexually transmitted infection caused by a virus.

human papillomavirus   One of several viruses that causes a sexually transmitted disease.

AIDS (acquired immune deficiency syndrome)   A disease, caused by a virus transmitted by means of bodily fluids, that devastates the immune system.

HIV (human immunodeficiency virus)   The virus associated with AIDS.

the transmission of AIDS through heterosexual activity is a clear danger to male and female adolescents and is especially prevalent among inner-city minority youngsters (Andrinopoulos, Kerrigan, & Ellen, 2006; Rangel, Gavin, Reed, Fowler, & Lee, 2006). Nor is HIV infection limited to poor, inner-city adolescents (Gayle et al., 1990). Given what we know about adolescents' sporadic condom use, straight, bisexual, and gay youth are *all* at high risk for HIV (Rotheram-Borus, Marelich, & Srinivasan, 1999).

The chances of contracting HIV are greatest among individuals who use drugs, have unprotected sex, have many sexual partners, and already have another STD (such as gonorrhea) (Hein, Dell, Futterman, Rotheram-Borus, & Shaffer, 1995; Lowry et al., 1994). Because these risk factors are more common among young people than adults, the risk of HIV infection among adolescents is substantial. Accordingly, in recent years, efforts have been made to develop AIDS education programs specifically aimed at teenagers (e.g., DiClemente et al., 2004, Fang, Stanton, Feigelman, & Baldwin, 1998; Jemmott et al., 1999).

▌ **Protecting Against STDs** Adults often forget that adolescents' sexual behavior is as much, if not more, influenced by their perceptions of benefits (for example, the fun of having different partners or the physical sensation of unprotected intercourse) as it is by their perceptions of costs (for example, the risks of contracting an STD) (R. Levinson, Jaccard, & Beamer, 1995). Adolescents have sex because they want intimacy with their partner, status with their peers, and, of course, physical pleasure (Ott, Millstein, Offner, & Halpern-Felsher, 2006). Even adolescents who know they are vulnerable to infection are less likely to protect themselves when they feel negatively about using condoms, when they are positively inclined toward risk taking, and when their friends are actively engaged in risky sex (Romer et al., 1994; Serovich & Greene, 1997; Shoop & Davidson, 1994; St. Lawrence, Brasfield, Jefferson, Allyene, & Shirley, 1994).

Short of abstinence, the best way for teenagers to protect themselves against contracting HIV and many other STDs is by using condoms during sex; adolescents who consistently use condoms are half as likely as those who do not to contract an STD (Crosby, DiClemente, Wingood, Lang, & Harrington, 2003). Educating young people about the risk factors associated with AIDS is also important, because studies show that adolescents who believe that they are at risk for HIV infection and who are motivated to avoid the risk are more likely to take precautions during intercourse (DiClemente et al., 1992; Hausser & Michaud, 1994; Jemmott et al., 1999; D. Orr & Langefeld, 1993; Rotheram-Borus & Koopman, 1991). Increasing adolescents' perceptions of vulnerability to HIV infection

Each year, about 750,000 American adolescents become pregnant—giving the United States the highest rate of teen pregnancy in the industrialized world.

is not sufficient to motivate them to use condoms, however (Gerrard, Gibbons, & Bushman, 1996).

TEEN PREGNANCY

Given the high rate of sexual activity and poor record of contraceptive use among contemporary adolescents, it comes as little surprise to learn that many young women become pregnant before the end of adolescence. Each year, about 750,000 American adolescents become pregnant—giving the United States the highest rate of teen pregnancy in the industrialized world (Ventura, Abma, Mosher, & Henshaw, 2008).

▌ **Prevalence of Teen Pregnancy** Recent statistics indicate that nearly one third of American young women become pregnant at least once by age 20, although rates of teen pregnancy vary considerably by ethnicity: The rate is twice as high among Black youth as among White youth, and the rate among Hispanic teenagers is 3 times as high as among White youth; the lowest rate of teen pregnancy is among Asian adolescents (B. Hamilton, Martin, & Ventura, 2007). These rates are lower than they were in the past several decades, in part because of increased contraceptive use and in part because fewer younger teenagers are sexually active, although the rate of teen pregnancy has risen very slightly in recent years (Kaye, 2009; Santelli,

Lindberg, Finer, & Singh, 2007). Whether this is a temporary blip in the curve or the beginning of a reversal of the long-standing downward trend is not known.

Keep in mind that not all adolescent pregnancies result in childbirth. The proportion of teen pregnancies that are aborted differs from country to country, from a low of about 20% in Ireland to a high of close to 70% in Sweden (Singh & Darroch, 2000). In the United States, about one third of all teenage pregnancies are aborted, and slightly more than 15% end in miscarriage (Ventura et al., 2008). Thus, approximately half of teenage pregnancies in the United States end in abortion or miscarriage, and about half result in the birth of an infant who will be raised by his or her mother (with or without the help of a partner or other family members). Among American adolescents who carry their pregnancy full term, very few put the baby up for adoption.

■ **Abortion** There are important differences between pregnant teenagers who do and do not seek abortion. Although studies show that teenagers can make well-reasoned decisions about abortion (Adler, Ozer, & Tschann, 2003), this option is not chosen equally often within all segments of the adolescent population. Unplanned pregnancies are much more likely to be terminated by abortion among young women who are academically successful and ambitious, who come from middle- or upper-class families, whose parents are well educated, who live in wealthier neighborhoods, whose significant others support the decision to terminate the pregnancy, and who are more inclined to seek psychological counseling (P. K. Coleman, 2006; C. Hayes, 1987; B. Miller & Moore, 1990; South & Baumer, 2001). An important factor accounting for the racial and socioeconomic differences in adolescent childbearing, therefore, is that White and middle-class adolescent women perceive themselves as having more to lose—economically and in terms of their careers—by having a child so early in life than do their minority and poor counterparts.

Several studies have examined whether teenagers who choose to abort an unwanted pregnancy are harmed psychologically by the experience. The consensus among experts is that they are not (Adler, Ozer, & Tschann, 2003). Indeed, several studies indicate that pregnant teenage women who abort their pregnancy are significantly better off, psychologically as well as socially and economically, than comparable women who choose to give birth to their child, both in the United States (Zabin, Hirsch, & Emerson, 1989) and abroad (Bailey et al., 2001). Among the most important differences between pregnant adolescents who abort their pregnancy and those who do not is that young women who terminate their pregnancy by abortion are less likely over the next 2 years to experience a subsequent pregnancy and more likely to practice contraception.

Given the apparent psychological and economic benefits of terminating an unwanted adolescent pregnancy, it is easy to understand why many social scientists have questioned the wisdom of court decisions designed to restrict adolescents' access to abortion services (Blum, Resnick, & Stark, 1990). While some studies show that laws requiring parental notification or limiting access to legal abortion do, in fact, result in fewer terminated pregnancies among adolescents (Joyce & Mocan, 1990; J. Rogers, Boruch, Stoms, & DeMoya, 1991), not all studies reach the same conclusion (e.g., Henshaw, 1995). A recent analysis of the parental notification law in Texas found that it was associated with a overall decrease in abortion, but an increase in late-term abortion (Joyce, Kaestner, & Colman, 2006). One possible reason for these inconsistent findings is that states requiring parental notification also tend to have high levels of religious involvement, both of which are associated with a lower teen abortion rate (Tomal, 2001).

■ **Causes of Teen Pregnancy** Many myths permeate discussions of the causes of adolescent pregnancy and complicate what is actually a fairly simple matter. The most important differences between young women who do and do not become pregnant during adolescence are in their sexual activity and contraceptive use. As you have read, sexual activity among American young people is high while contraceptive use is sporadic and inadequate. Although some evidence indicates that Black and Hispanic teenagers are more likely than White teenagers to say they intend to have a baby at an early age, the large racial difference in teenage childbearing is due mainly to racial differences in *unintended* pregnancies (Mosher & Bachrach, 1996; Trent & Crowder, 1997).

Deep down inside, though, do adolescents who become pregnant actually want to have a baby? This has been an extremely difficult question for social scientists to answer. According to national surveys, 85% of births to women ages 15–19 are unintended, a figure suggesting that the vast majority of adolescent mothers did not become pregnant intentionally. Yet, studies that plumb the issue a bit deeper find that many young women who say they do not want to become pregnant are actually ambivalent, and not unequivocally negative, about the prospect of having a child (Jaccard, Dodge, & Dittus, 2003a). More importantly, those who are ambivalent about childbearing or who believe that having a child will be a positive experience are less likely to use contraception effectively (Unger, Molina, & Teran, 2000; Zabin, Astone, & Emerson, 1993). Thus, while the vast majority of sexually active teenagers do not actively wish to become pregnant, a significant minority feel less troubled by the prospect of early parenthood than do their peers, and these youngsters are more likely to risk pregnancy by having unprotected sex. As one team of authors wrote, "Adolescent childbearing is more an unintended result of risky behaviors than a result of rational choice" (Trent & Crowder, 1997, p. 532). Research also indicates that the younger sisters of adolescent mothers may be more likely to become adolescent parents themselves, in part because the older sisters may communicate some acceptance of early motherhood (East, 2009).

■ **The Role of the Father** A number of studies have focused on the male partners of pregnant adolescents. In general, research indicates that these males share a number of distinguishing characteristics that differentiate them from their peers who have not gotten a teenager pregnant. Most important is the fact that they are relatively more likely to have problems with self-esteem, school, work, aggression, drugs and alcohol, and the law, and to have fathered a child previously (Dearden, Hale, & Woolley, 1995; Fagot, Pears, Capaldi, Crosby, & Leve, 1998; Males & Chew, 1996; Miller-Johnson, Winn, Coie, Malone, & Lochman, 2004; Thornberry, Smith, & Howard, 1997). Much has been made in the popular media about the age gap between teenage mothers and the men who have fathered their children, but the proportion of teenage births fathered by adult men (that is, age 20 or older) actually has declined over the past 40 years, and the age difference between teenage mothers (most of whom are 18 or 19) and their sexual partners is generally about 2 or 3 years—a gap not substantially different from the age gap between husbands and wives in the general population (Elo, King, & Furstenberg, 1999). Moreover, girls who choose to get involved with older partners have more psychological problems than girls who do not, well before the relationship begins (Young & D'Arcy, 2005). Nevertheless, adolescent girls who have sex for the first time before 16 with a man who is more than 3 years older are less likely to use contraception and more likely to bear a child (Manlove, Terr-Humen, & Ikramullah, 2006). Regardless of the age difference between mother and father, however, the higher rates of problem behavior among the male partners of pregnant adolescents help to explain why marriage may not be the best response to pregnancy for teenage women, as we'll see shortly.

Although many of their problems precede the pregnancy, young men's educational development and mental health are adversely affected by fathering a child early in life, even if they do not marry the child's mother (Furstenberg, Brooks-Gunn, & Chase-Lansdale, 1989; Nock, 1998; Sigler-Rushton, 2005; Vera Institute of Justice, 1990). Men who impregnate adolescent women are more likely to drop out of school and to report feeling anxious and depressed as young adults than their peers. The adverse effects of teenage fatherhood appear to be

Because adolescent mothers are more likely than adult mothers to be both unmarried and poor, their children are at greater risk of developing a variety of psychological and social problems.

greater among White and Hispanic men than among Black men, however, perhaps because teenage fatherhood is more disruptive and is seen as less acceptable within the White and Hispanic communities (M. Buchanan & Robbins, 1990). In general, however, teenage fathers receive little in the way of supportive services or assistance in becoming responsible parents (Kiselica & Sturmer, 1993).

ADOLESCENT PARENTHOOD

It is important to distinguish between pregnancies and actual births—a distinction that often is lost in debates over the consequences of teenage pregnancy. Because of the many pregnant adolescents choosing abortion, the birthrate among teenage women is far lower than it would otherwise be, and it may surprise you to learn that the birthrate among adolescent women today is considerably lower than it was in previous eras. Contrary to the popular idea that teenage childbearing has reached epidemic proportions in this country, relatively more women gave birth to an infant before reaching adulthood in previous decades than do so today—and by a large margin.

Nevertheless, the rate of teenage births in the United States continues to be more than twice as high as in Canada; 3 times greater than in Ireland; 5 times greater than in France; 10 times greater than in Japan; and 17 times greater than in Korea (UNICEF, 2001). All sorts of explanations for the astoundingly high rate of teenage childbearing in the United States have been offered (often, the finger is pointed at the mass media, which are blamed for pretty much everything adolescents do that adults disapprove of), but the answer can probably be found in Figure 11.6, which shows teenage childbearing rates in different industrialized countries alongside rates of income equality and educational attainment. Generally speaking, the greater the gap between rich and poor, and the lower the rate of school attendance among young people, the higher the rate of teen childbearing. Given the fact that the United States leads the list in income inequality and comes in 25th (out of 28) in school enrollment, it is little surprise that we lead the industrialized world in teen childbearing (UNICEF, 2001).

Rates of teenage childbearing vary markedly across ethnic and socioeconomic groups. Middle-class women are far more likely to abort their pregnancies than are poor women, and as a consequence, the problem of teenage childbearing is densely concentrated among economically disadvantaged youth (Russell, 1994). Because minority adolescents are more likely to grow up poor, teenage childbearing is especially prevalent in non-White communities.

Part of the controversy surrounding teenage childbearing is linked to the public's concern about the large number of teenage mothers who spend extended periods of time on welfare—more than half of all welfare funding in the United States is spent on families resulting from teenage births (Coley & Chase-Lansdale, 1998). Among White adolescents, nearly two thirds of all births occur outside of marriage, but a large proportion of these births occur within the context of cohabitation; among Black adolescents, virtually all childbirths are out of wedlock, and relatively few of these occur even among cohabiting couples (Manning & Landale, 1996; Schellenbach, Whitman, & Borkowski, 1992). The rate for Hispanic teenagers falls somewhere in between; interestingly, young Mexican American women are more likely to bear their first child within marriage, whereas young Puerto Rican women are more likely to bear children out of wedlock but within the context of cohabitation. This suggests that cultural attitudes toward marriage and cohabitation influence the context of childbearing in important ways (East & Blaustein, 1995; Manning & Landale, 1996; Milan et al., 2006).

Because minority youth are more likely to experience problems such as school failure or unemployment, early childbearing is likely to take place in the context

	Teenage birthrate	Income inequality index	15- to 19-year-olds not in education (%)
Korea	2.0		21.4
Japan	4.6		
Switzerland	5.5	35.5	15.9
Netherlands	6.2	30.2	14.0
Sweden	6.5	25.3	13.9
Italy	6.6	35.9	30.2
Spain	7.9	32.4	23.5
Denmark	8.1	24.6	19.9
Finland	9.2	24.8	17.9
France	9.3	32.4	12.2
Luxembourg	9.7	26.9	
Belgium	9.9	27.7	13.9
Greece	11.8	35.6	22.4
Norway	12.4	25.7	13.6
Germany	13.1	30.0	11.7
Austria	14.0	30.4	23.8
Czech Republic	16.4	25.8	25.1
Australia	18.4	33.7	18.4
Ireland	18.7	34.6	19.3
Poland	18.7	35.8	18.6
Canada	20.2	31.7	22.0
Portugal	21.2	38.2	23.8
Iceland	24.7		20.3
Hungary	26.5	25.0	24.6
Slovak Republic	26.9	26.2	
New Zealand	29.8	37.0	28.3
UK	30.8	36.6	30.5
USA	52.1	40.6	25.8

FIGURE 11.6 Countries characterized by greater income inequality and lower school enrollment have higher teen birthrates. (UNICEF, 2001)

of limited social and economic resources. Indeed, the main reason for the high rate of nonmarital childbearing among Black teenagers is the higher proportion of adolescents growing up in single-parent homes (Bumpass & McLanahan, 1987), which experience more economic stress. In addition, many poor, young, Black women believe that it is perfectly normal to become a mother while still a teenager and to become a grandmother before turning 40 (Perez-Febles, Allison, & Burton, 1999), norms that may be handed down from one generation to the next (Hardy, Astone, Brooks-Gunn, Shapiro, & Miller, 1998).

Because teenage childbearing tends to go hand in hand with a variety of other problems—the most critical of which is poverty—it is extremely difficult to know whether any problems of teenage mothers or their children result from the mother's young age or from other, correlated factors. Separating the effects of early childbearing from poverty is a matter of more than theoretical importance: If early childbearing is, in fact, a problem in and of itself, it becomes important to direct preventive programs at deterring adolescent pregnancy (either by discouraging sexual activity or by encouraging effective contraceptive use) and childbearing (by encouraging adoption and abortion). But if poverty, not the mother's age, is the key, an entirely different set of strategies is called for, aimed not at youngsters' sexual behavior but at all individuals' economic circumstances. It is extremely important, therefore, to ask whether and in what ways a mother's age at the time she gives birth affects her and her child's well-being.

▌ **Children of Teen Mothers** We now know that many of the problems that plague children born to adolescent mothers result primarily from the environment of poverty and single parenthood in which these children are raised and from other qualities that often characterize young women who become teen parents (such as poor school achievement), rather than from the mother's youth (e.g., Kalil & Kunz, 2002; J. A. Levine, Emery, & Pollack, 2007; Pittard, Laditka, & Laditka, 2008). In other words, infants born to middle-class adolescents differ little from their counterparts born to older middle-class mothers, and infants born to poor adolescents are similar to children born to equally poor adults.

One important exception to this general similarity between the children of adolescent and adult mothers is that adolescent mothers—even of similar socioeconomic status—may perceive their babies as being especially difficult and may interact with their infants less often in ways that are known to be beneficial to the child's cognitive and social development (Coley & Chase-Lansdale, 1998; B. Miller & Moore, 1990; Schellenbach et al., 1992; Sommer et al., 1993). To what extent this directly jeopardizes the child's development is not known, although studies suggest that children born to

adolescent mothers are more likely to have school problems, more likely to be involved in misbehavior and delinquent activity, more likely themselves to be sexually active at an early age, and more likely to become an adolescent parent (Campa & Eckenrode, 2006; Coley & Chase-Lansdale, 1998; Conseur, Rivara, Barnoski, & Emanuel, 1997; Hofferth & Reid, 2002; Wakschlag et al., 2000). In general, and for reasons that are not known, the cognitive and psychosocial problems of children born to adolescent mothers grow increasingly more apparent with age (that is, the differences between children born to teen versus adult mothers are more evident in adolescence than infancy). Again, though, studies show that the adverse outcomes of being born to an adolescent mother—even outcomes not visible until the children have reached young adulthood—are attributable both to characteristics of young women who are likely to become teen parents (for example, the adverse effects of being raised by someone who is poorly educated) and to the circumstances that characterize the family environments of young mothers (for example, the adverse effects of growing up in poverty) (Jaffee, Caspi, Moffitt, Belsky, & Silva, 2001; Pogarsky, Lizotte, & Thornberry, 2003). Not surprisingly, then, adolescent mothers who were relatively more intelligent and better adjusted *before* the birth of their infant have greater parenting skills later (Mylod, Whitman, & Borkowski, 1997; O'Callaghan, Borkowski, Whitman, Maxwell, & Keogh, 1999), and children whose adolescent mothers are better educated, married, and better off financially do better in school than those whose mothers are less accomplished and single (Luster, Bates, Fitzgerald, Vandenbelt, & Key, 2000).

Because adolescent mothers are more likely than adult mothers to be both unmarried and poor, their children are at greater risk of developing a variety of psychological and social problems. Indeed, many of the problem behaviors seen among children of adolescent mothers are prevalent among poor children growing up in single-parent homes generally. In other words, the greater incidence of problems among offspring of adolescent mothers may reflect the overall environment in which their children grow up, rather than the ways in which they are raised. Although in theory we can separate the effects of poverty on children from the effects of adolescent childbearing, in reality, the two usually go together, and the end result is that children born to adolescent mothers are more likely than other children to suffer the effects both of malnutrition—in the womb as well as in the world— and of environmental deprivation.

▌ **Consequences for Teen Mothers** Studies of the long-term consequences of adolescent parenthood indicate that the problems associated with it may actually be greater for the mothers than for their children. In general, women who bear children early suffer disruptions in their educational and occupational careers (Fergusson & Woodward, 2000; Hofferth, Reid, & Mott, 2001; Klepinger, Lundberg, & Plotnick, 1995; Otterblad Olausson, Haglund, Ringback Weitoft, & Cnattingius, 2001). Not only are adolescent mothers more likely to come from a poor background and to have a history of academic difficulties, but they are also more likely to remain poor than their equally disadvantaged peers who delay childbearing until after their schooling is completed (S. Hoffman, Foster, & Furstenberg, Jr., 1993; Mollborn, 2007; K. Moore et al., 1993; R. Richardson, 1996). It is important to bear in mind, however, that many adolescent mothers were poor students *before* becoming pregnant, and the limited educational attainment of teenage mothers is at least partly due to factors that were in play long before the pregnancy, perhaps even during early childhood (Fergusson & Woodward, 2000; Frisco, 2008; Miller-Johnson et al., 1999; Roenkae & Pulkkinen, 1998; Russell, 2002; Shearer et al., 2002). In short, poverty and low achievement are both causes *and* consequences of early childbearing.

Having a child early in life does not inevitably cast in concrete a life of poverty and misery for the mother and her youngster, however. Studies show that there is considerable diversity among teenage mothers in the routes that their adult lives take (Ahn, 1994; Coley & Chase-Lansdale, 1998; Oxford, Gilchrist, Gillmore, & Lohr, 2006). One recent study identified three distinct groups: a problem-prone group (15% of the sample), who had chronic problems in many areas of life, including antisocial behavior; a psychologically vulnerable group (42%), who had relatively high rates of mental health problems but who were able to transition into adult roles with some degree of success; and a normative group (43%), who defied common stereotypes of adolescent mothers as doomed to failure and poverty and who were able to make a successful transition to adulthood (Oxford et al., 2005). Some research also suggests that the long-term consequences of early childbearing may not be as negative among African Americans as among Whites or Hispanics, especially among African Americans living in communities in which early childbearing is accepted as normative (K. Moore et al., 1993; E. Smith & Zabin, 1993).

In general, young mothers who remain in, or return to, high school and delay subsequent childbearing fare a great deal better over the long run—as do their children—than their counterparts who drop out of school or have more children relatively early on (Furstenberg et al., 1987; Leadbeater, 1996; Upchurch & McCarthy, 1990). Indeed, remaining in school and living at home with one's parents significantly diminishes the chances of a second unwanted pregnancy (Manlove, Mariner, &

Papillo, 2000). Marriage, in contrast, tends to be a high-risk strategy (Furstenberg et al., 1987). In some cases, when a stable relationship is formed and economic resources are available, marriage improves the mother's and the child's chances for life success; this seems to be especially true for women who marry somewhat later. In other cases, however, a hasty decision to marry in the absence of a stable relationship and economic security actually exacerbates many other problems (Teti & Lamb, 1989).

■ **After the Baby Is Born** Research on the consequences of adolescent childbearing also suggests that many of the negative effects of having children early can be prevented or at least minimized by lessening the disruptive economic impact of teenage parenthood on young women's lives (Sandfort & Hill, 1996). What do we know about the factors that work toward this end? First, it is clear that marrying the father of the child may place the adolescent mother at greater risk if the father is not capable of supporting himself economically, much less his family. Studies show, in contrast, that if the father is able to find a good job and remain employed, he can be an important source of psychological and economic support and a healthy influence on the mother and child. Given the characteristic problems of male partners of adolescent mothers that we discussed earlier, however, it is all too likely that marriage may diminish, rather than enhance, an adolescent mother's economic circumstances. In addition, marriage places the adolescent mother at greater risk of having another child relatively soon, which further jeopardizes her already precarious economic situation and is one of the factors most likely to worsen her other problems (Apfel & Seitz, 1997; Furstenberg et al., 1987; Kalmuss & Namerow, 1994). Moreover, teenage marriage is very likely to end in divorce, which itself is an additional stressor on the mother and child.

Adolescent mothers therefore cannot always look to the father of the child to help break the cycle of poverty that afflicts many young parents. However, they can, in many cases, look to their own parents for support, and this may be an effective strategy for some (J. Stevens, 1988). Teenage mothers who move in with their own family *for a short time*—a practice far more common among African Americans than among Hispanics or White adolescents—are more likely to enjoy educational and occupational success than their counterparts who live on their own, because the family's help allows the young mother to return to school or find employment (B. Miller & Moore, 1990; Roye & Balk, 1996; Trent & Harlan, 1994). Without this help, many young mothers must drop out of school and find and pay for child care, which often is more costly than the income their low-paying jobs generate. Without a high school diploma, these women have little chance of improving their economic situation and, consequently, of improving the opportunities for their child.

Although having the support of her own family is important for the adolescent mother's development and well-being, living with the family of origin for an extended period after having a baby is not uniformly beneficial, as several studies of three-generational Black families show. On the negative side, when the adolescent mother lives with her own mother, the living arrangement may undermine the development of her own parenting skills and increase the risk of getting pregnant again (Chase-Lansdale, Brooks-Gunn, & Zamsky, 1994; Gillmore, Lewis, Lohr, Spencer, & White, 1997; Spieker & Bensley, 1994), and problems in the relationship between the adolescent and her mother can adversely affect the teen parent's mental health (A. Davis & Rhodes, 1994; Fast & Felice, 1996; Musick, 1994). On the positive side, living with one's mother is associated with continued schooling, which confers long-term economic advantages (Spieker & Bensley, 1994). Interestingly, several studies have found that support from the adolescent's father, in addition to that of her mother, may be especially beneficial (A. Davis, Rhodes, & Hamilton-Leaks, 1997; Oyserman, Radin, & Benn, 1993).

FOOD FOR THOUGHT

Based on what you've read in this section, what advice would you give a 17-year-old young woman who was pregnant and unsure about what she should do?

One fact is certain, though: Adolescent mothers who receive social support fare better, are better parents, and have healthier children than do adolescent mothers who lack support (Barratt, Roach, Morgan, & Colbert, 1996; Leadbeater & Bishop, 1994; Riggs, Holmbeck, Paikoff, & Bryant, 2004; Turner, Sorenson, & Turner, 2000). Studies suggest that a lack of support is an especially dire problem among poor Hispanic adolescent mothers (Wasserman, Rauh, Brunelli, Garcia-Castro, & Necos, 1990). Taken together, these and other studies suggest that the best arrangement for a teenage mother may be to live independently from her own parents but rely on them for emotional support and child care (Coley & Chase-Lansdale, 1998).

Because it is so important for young mothers to have an adequate income and the chance for adequate employment, many policymakers have called for changes in the ways that schools and other social institutions treat pregnant students and changes in the provision of day care (Sandfort & Hill, 1996; Seitz & Apfel, 1993, 1994). Among the most important are adaptations in school schedules and the development of school-based child care centers so that pregnant students can remain in school after the birth of their child; the expansion of subsidized child care for young mothers who are out of school so that the economic benefits of having a job are not outweighed by the costs of child care; and the expansion of family planning services to adolescent mothers so that they can prevent yet another pregnancy. Unfortunately, evaluations of programs aimed at enhancing teen mothers' employability, decreasing their reliance on welfare, or preventing their subsequent pregnancies have been largely disappointing (Coley & Chase-Lansdale, 1998), although occasional successes have been reported in the literature (e.g., Solomon & Liefeld, 1998).

Although there are stories of young women whose lives are not devastated by early childbearing, in general, studies suggest that the successes are young women who have avoided poverty, rather than achieving great economic success. Although the picture of adolescent parenthood appears less uniformly dire than typically painted in the media, there is still consensus among experts that it is important to try to prevent teenage pregnancy and childbearing.

SEX EDUCATION

Each year, millions of dollars are spent attempting to prevent teen pregnancy and the spread of sexually transmitted diseases. Many adolescents receive some sort of classroom instruction about sex—whether through high school health classes, biology classes, classes designated exclusively for the purpose of sex education, or educational programs administered through youth or religious organizations. Do these programs do any good?

The answer to this question is complicated and depends on the nature of the program and the outcome it is trying to achieve. Most evaluations of formal sex education programs administered through schools have shown them to have no effect on whether adolescents are sexually active but some effect on whether they use contraception (Franklin, Grant, Corcoran, Miller, & Bultman, 1997). That is, *effective* sex education (and "effective" is the key word here, because not all programs work) can reduce adolescents' likelihood of having unsafe sex, but it does not reduce their likelihood of having sex.

Experts now agree that carefully constructed educational interventions can reduce rates of risky sexual activity among adolescents (D. Kirby, 2007). But they also agree that successful interventions must do more than provide information about contraception, STDs, and pregnancy. They must also teach adolescents how to refuse unwanted sex and avoid unintended sex, increase adolescents' motivation to engage in safe sex, and change perceptions about peer norms and attitudes. These approaches, collectively, are referred to as **comprehensive sex education.** Although many adults understandably have been concerned that teaching adolescents how to engage in safe sex sends a message encouraging more teenagers to become sexually active, evaluations of effective comprehensive sex education programs (even those that distribute condoms to teenagers) show that this is not the case (D. Kirby, Laris, & Rolleri, 2007). Evaluations of school-based clinics, which make contraceptive services more accessible to adolescents, do not appear to increase sexual activity (a concern of many parents), but neither do they have the hoped-for effect on contraceptive use.

We also know a fair amount about what *doesn't* work. Programs designed to increase safe sex (which includes both abstinence as well as condom use) are far more effective than those that emphasize abstinence alone. Indeed, careful evaluations of **abstinence-only sex education** programs have shown unequivocally that they are not successful, either in changing adolescents' sexual behavior or in reducing rates of pregnancy or STDs (D. Kirby, 2007; P. K. Kohler, Manhart, & Lafferty, 2008). Programs that attempt to reduce sexual risk taking by reducing other forms of risky behavior (such as delinquency or substance use) also are not effective, consistent with the notion that sexual risk taking, while correlated with other types of risk taking, may have some unique causes (Santelli, Carter, Orr, & Dittus, 2009). The evidence on other types of programs designed to reduce unsafe sex, such as those designed to encourage safe sex indirectly, by facilitating positive youth development, is inconclusive (D. Kirby, 2007).

RECAP

- Most experts agree that the primary reason so few adolescents use contraceptives regularly is that using contraception requires the sort of long-term planning that many young people are reluctant or unable to engage in. In addition, some adolescents are insufficiently educated about pregnancy and contraception, and they seldom anticipate having intercourse until they become sexually active on a regular basis.

- Because of their erratic use of condoms, several million sexually active adolescents contract a sexually transmitted disease each year. Cases of HIV infection, the most serious sexually transmitted disease, have been increasing among adolescents and young adults.

- The United States has the highest rate of teen childbearing in the industrialized world. About 750,000 American teenagers become pregnant annually. Experts believe that adolescent pregnancy is more likely to be an unintended result of risky sexual behavior than the result of a rational choice to become pregnant.

- About half of all teenage pregnancies result in the birth of a child who is raised by the teen parent; the majority of other pregnancies are aborted. Teenagers are not harmed psychologically by aborting their pregnancy, but studies of the consequences of teenage childbearing indicate that both short- and long-term problems for the teenage mother may be considerable.

- While there are occasional success stories, teenage parents are more likely than their peers to experience disruptions in their educational and occupational development. Adolescent mothers who have social support from family or friends and who are able to complete high school fare far better than those who do not.

- Careful evaluations of sex education programs find that comprehensive sex education, which combines information about how to practice safe sex with practical instruction in how to avoid unwanted and unplanned sex, can be effective. In contrast, abstinence-only education has been shown to be entirely ineffective.

---

comprehensive sex education Programs that not only provide information about contraception, STDs, and pregnancy but also teach adolescents how to refuse unwanted sex and avoid unintended sex, increase their motivation to engage in safe sex, and change perceptions about peer norms and attitudes.

abstinence-only sex education Programs that encourage adolescents to avoid sexual activity but that do not provide information about safe sex.

Achievement

BECAUSE ADOLESCENCE IS typically a time of preparation for the roles of adulthood, considerable attention has been paid to the development and expression of achievement during these years. Broadly defined, **achievement** concerns the development of motives, capabilities, interests, and behavior that have to do with performance in evaluative situations. More specifically, the study of achievement during adolescence has focused on young people's performance in educational settings and on their hopes and plans for future scholastic and occupational careers. Since most young people form their first realistic educational and vocational plans during adolescence, researchers have long been interested in the factors that play the greatest role in influencing individuals' futures.

Achievement is a particularly important consideration in the study of adolescence in contemporary society. Industrialized societies place an extraordinary emphasis on achievement, competition, and success. During childhood and adolescence, youngsters are continually tested to determine how they stand scholastically in relation to their peers. In most industrialized societies, the amount of education a person has completed and the job he or she holds—two of the most important indicators of achievement—provide a basis for the individual's self-conceptions and his or her image in the eyes of others.

A second reason for the importance of the concept of achievement in the study of adolescence in contemporary society concerns the range and rapidly changing nature of the choices faced by today's young people. Unlike youth in most traditional cultures, adolescents in modern societies are confronted with an array of difficult occupational and educational decisions before they turn 25. Beyond such fundamental questions as what type of career to follow and whether to continue with schooling after high school, adolescents must think about what specific sorts of jobs should be pursued within a particular career path, what kind of educational preparation would be most appropriate, and how their entry into the labor force is best negotiated. For the college student contemplating a career in business, for instance, is it better to major in business administration or to follow a liberal arts course of study? How early is it necessary to decide which aspects of business to specialize in? Is it necessary to go to graduate school, or do employers prefer applicants with work experience in place of an advanced degree? These are all difficult questions to answer. And they are made more difficult because the nature of work, and the preparation one needs for specific careers, changes so rapidly in contemporary society.

Finally, achievement is a particularly important issue in the study of adolescence in contemporary society because of the wide variation in levels of educational and occupational success. By the end of high school, many adolescents demonstrate a high enough level of academic achievement to enter selective colleges and universities; at the other extreme are a sizable number of their peers who enter adulthood unable even to read a newspaper or understand a bus schedule. Although three quarters of adolescents in the United States today complete high school and go on to college, 10% leave high school before graduating. Similar disparities exist in the world of work: Most youth make the transition from school to work without a great deal of difficulty, but a significant number experience frustrating unemployment. Even within the population of young people who enter the labor force, there is considerable variation in earnings and in occupational status. Many important questions in the study of adolescent achievement, therefore, concern factors that distinguish between young people who are successful—however success is defined—and those who are not.

Achievement as an Adolescent Issue

Development in the realm of achievement neither begins nor ends during adolescence, of course. Educational institutions—even for young children—stress performance, competition, and success on tests of knowledge and ability. Concerns over achievement continue throughout adulthood as well. Like their younger counterparts, adults for the most part place a premium on success, and in American society, what one does for a living is an important part of one's identity.

Achievement during the adolescent years, though, merits special attention for several reasons (Masten et al., 1995). First, the fact that adolescence is a time of preparation for adult work roles raises questions about

achievement The psychosocial domain concerning behaviors and feelings in evaluative situations.

the nature of the preparation young people receive and the processes through which they sort themselves (or are sorted) into the occupational roles that may influence the remainder of their lives. Many of the factors that narrow an individual's educational options and vocational alternatives are prominent during the high school and college years, and it is important to ask how such options are defined and at what age educational and occupational decisions are made.

FOOD FOR THOUGHT

Adults disagree about the extent to which achievement is, and should be, made an especially salient issue among adolescents. Some contend that we place too much pressure on teenagers to succeed in school. Others argue that we do not place enough. What's your view?

Second, although differences in school performance and achievement are apparent as early as the first grade, not until adolescence do individuals begin to fully appreciate the implications of these differences for immediate and future success. Children's occupational plans are to a large extent made on the basis of fantasy and passing interests, without any realistic assessment of their practicality or feasibility. Not until adolescence do individuals begin to evaluate their occupational choices in light of their talents, abilities, opportunities, and the performance of those around them. For example, high-achieving students who attend schools in which average achievement levels are high do not feel as good about themselves as their high-achieving counterparts in schools with lower average achievement levels (H. Marsh, Kong, & Hau, 2000).

Third, the educational and occupational decisions made during adolescence are more numerous, and the consequences of such decisions more serious, than the decisions characteristic of childhood. For example, in most elementary schools, although children may be grouped by ability—groupings that have implications for subsequent achievement—they generally are all exposed to fairly similar curricula and have few opportunities to veer from the educational program established by their school system. In high school, however, students can select how much science and math they want to take, whether they wish to study a foreign language, whether they want to pursue an academic or vocational track— even whether they want to remain in school once they have reached the legal age for leaving school. Moreover, it is during adolescence that most individuals decide whether they want to pursue postsecondary education or enter a full-time job directly from high school. All these

decisions have important implications for the sort of choices and plans the adolescent will make in the future, which, in turn, will influence his or her earnings, lifestyle, identity, and subsequent psychosocial development.

How might the biological, cognitive, and social changes of adolescence affect the ways in which individuals respond in achievement-related situations?

■ Puberty and Achievement   Although the biological changes of puberty are less obvious influences on achievement than are the cognitive and social transitions of the period, they may nevertheless affect the development of achievement in important ways. As you will read, the transition into secondary school is usually marked by a temporary drop in individuals' motivation to achieve, and some of this may be related to puberty, because it introduces new issues (like dating and sex) into the adolescent's mix of concerns. To the extent that puberty changes what's important for maintaining status in the peer group, it may lead some adolescents to worry about whether trying too hard to do well will make them less attractive to their classmates. In addition, puberty intensifies differences between males and females, and one impact of this is to make individuals think about what is "appropriate" achievement-related behavior for each of the sexes.

■ Cognitive Change and Achievement   The intellectual changes of the period are important influences on achievement as well. Not until adolescence are individuals cognitively capable of seeing the long-term consequences of educational and occupational choices or of realistically considering the range of scholastic and work possibilities open to them. Thus, a second reason for the prominence of achievement-related issues during adolescence relates to the advent of more sophisticated forms of thinking. The ability to think in hypothetical terms, for example, raises new achievement concerns for the individual ("Should I go to college after I graduate, or should I work for a while?"); it also permits the young person to think through such questions in a logical and systematic fashion ("If I decide to go to college, then . . .").

■ Social Roles and Achievement   The main reason that many achievement-related issues take on new significance during adolescence, however, involves the social transition of the period. In virtually all societies, adolescence is the period when important educational and occupational decisions are made, and society has structured its educational and work institutions accordingly. In most industrialized societies it is not until adolescence that individuals attain the status necessary to decide whether they will continue or end their formal education. Similarly, it is not until adolescence that individuals are allowed to enter the labor force in an official capacity, since child labor regulations typically prohibit the formal employment of youngsters under the age of 14 or so. In other words, the transition from school to work—one of the central issues in the study of achievement during adolescence—is a socially defined transition, a passage that society has determined will be negotiated during adolescence.

In this chapter, we look at the nature of achievement during the adolescent years. As you will see, the extent to which an adolescent is successful in school and in preparing for work is influenced by a complex array of personal and environmental factors. We begin with a look at one set of factors that reliably differentiates adolescents who are successful from their peers who are not: how motivated they are to achieve and their beliefs about the causes of their successes and failures.

RECAP

- Achievement is an important issue during adolescence because society typically designates adolescence as a time for preparation for adult work roles, because individuals now can understand the long-term implications of their educational and career decisions and because during adolescence schools begin making distinctions among individuals that potentially have profound effects on their long-term occupational development.
- The fundamental changes of adolescence affect the development of achievement in several ways. Puberty may affect the development of achievement by introducing new psychological and interpersonal concerns, which may affect the adolescents' priorities and behavior in school.
- The cognitive changes of adolescence allow individuals to engage in longer-term, hypothetical thinking and planning about their educational and occupational futures.
- The transition into new social roles is probably the most important influence on achievement in adolescence. Society has structured the worlds of school and work so that major decisions about school and work take place in adolescence.

need for achievement A need that influences the extent to which an individual strives for success in evaluative situations.

Achievement Motives and Beliefs

ACHIEVEMENT MOTIVATION

There is no question that success is partly determined by sheer ability. But as many writers have pointed out, it takes more than talent to succeed—it takes desire and determination as well. Individuals differ in the extent to which they strive for success, and this differential striving—which can be measured independently of ability—helps to account for different degrees of actual achievement. Two students may both score equally on an intelligence or aptitude test, but if one student simply tries much harder than the other to do well in school, their actual grades will probably differ. As someone who has been advising undergraduate and graduate students for more than three decades, I can assure you that the difference between those who are successful and those who are not usually has much more to do with their drive and capacity for self-direction than with their intelligence.

The extent to which an individual strives for success is referred to as his or her **need for achievement** (McClelland, Atkinson, Clark, & Lowell, 1953). Need for achievement is an intrinsically motivated desire to perform well that operates even in the absence of external rewards for success. A student who works very hard on an assignment that is not going to be graded probably has a very strong need for achievement. All other factors being equal, a student who tries hard to succeed in school is, in fact, more likely to succeed than one who tries less. Motivation becomes a more and more important determinant of success during adolescence, as individuals increasingly are expected to take charge of their own educational careers. In fact, by the time one enters college, doing well is influenced as much by conscientiousness as it is by intelligence (Poropat, 2009).

Where does a strong motive to succeed come from? More than half a century ago, psychologists discovered that adolescents who have a strong need for achievement come from families in which parents have set high performance standards, have rewarded achievement success during childhood, and have encouraged autonomy and independence (Rosen & D'Andrade, 1959; Winterbottom, 1958). Equally important, however, is the fact that this training for achievement and independence generally takes place in the context of a warm parent–child relationship in which the child forms close identifications with his or her parents (M. Shaw & White, 1965). Put most succinctly, authoritative parenting, coupled with parents' encouragement of success, is probably the most important contributor to strong need for achievement.

Individuals who are intrinsically motivated strive to achieve because of the pleasure they get out of learning and mastering the material. Generally speaking, they perform better in school than students who are extrinsically motivated.

Fear of Failure Need for achievement is only part of the story, however. One psychological factor that interacts with an adolescent's need for achievement is a related, and in some senses complementary, motive—**fear of failure.** Fear of failure, which is often manifested in feelings of anxiety during tests or in other evaluative situations, can interfere with successful performance. Generally, when the achievement situation involves an easy task, and when a little anxiety helps to focus attention (if, for example, the task is boring), a moderate amount of fear of failure may improve performance by increasing one's concentration. The anxiety generated by a *strong* fear of failure interferes with successful performance, however. This is often the case in situations in which the task involves learning something new or solving a complex problem—like many tasks faced by adolescents in school settings. Individuals with a high fear of failure often come from family environments in which parents have set unrealistically high standards for their children's achievement and react very negatively to failure (rather than simply reacting positively to success) (Spielberger, 1966). Recent studies of adolescents from affluent backgrounds who are under strong pressure to do well in school find that it isn't so much parents' pressure to do well that creates mental health problems, but rather, parents' criticism when expectations are not achieved (Luthar, Shoum, & Brown, 2006).

An adolescent's need for achievement and her or his fear of failure work together to pull the individual toward (or repel the individual from) achievement situations. Individuals with a relatively strong need for achievement and a relatively weak fear of failure are more likely to actively approach challenging achievement situations—by taking more difficult classes, for example—and to look forward to them. In contrast, those whose fear of failure is relatively intense and whose need for achievement is relatively weak will dread challenging situations and do what they can to avoid them. Many students who have trouble persisting at tasks and who fear failure become **underachievers**—their grades are far lower than one would expect based on their intellectual ability.

Self-Handicapping Distinguishing between students whose underachievement is due mainly to anxiety and those who underperform for other reasons is important (Midgley, Arunkumar, & Urdan, 1996; Midgley & Urdan, 1995). Some students, for example, want to appear uninterested in school because in some contexts this presentation may garner more respect and admiration from peers than academic success. Others want to make sure that they have an excuse for poor performance other than a lack of ability (Nurmi, Onatsu, & Haavisto, 1995). Still others may downplay the importance of academics as a response to their poor performance (Gibbons, Benbow, & Gerrard, 1994). These students may use various **self-handicapping** strategies—such as joking around in class, waiting until the last minute to study for a test, turning in incomplete homework, or partying excessively the night before a big exam—as a way of self-protection ("I failed the test because I didn't try hard, not because I'm stupid") or as a means of enhancing their self-presentation ("I'm too cool to care about doing well in school"). Although self-handicapping is common among both males and females, there are sex differences in the ways in which adolescent girls and boys undermine their own success in school: Boys who self-handicap tend to attribute their poor performance to a lack of effort, whereas girls are more likely to mention emotional problems (Warner & Moore, 2004). A number of writers have drawn special attention to the use of self-handicapping strategies among ethnic minority youth, who may disengage from school because they perceive their long-term prospects as being limited by discrimination and

fear of failure Fear of the consequences of failing in achievement situations.

underachievers Individuals whose actual school performance is lower than what would be expected on the basis of objective measures of their aptitude or intelligence.

self-handicapping Deliberately behaving in ways that will likely interfere with doing well, in order to have an excuse for failing.

prejudice (Mickelson, 1990; R. Taylor, Casten, Flickinger, Roberts, & Fulmore, 1994).

■ **Two Types of Motivation**   Two individuals can be equally motivated to succeed, but for very different reasons. Psychologists draw a distinction between **intrinsic motivation** (sometimes referred to as "mastery motivation") and **extrinsic motivation** (sometimes referred to as "performance motivation"). Individuals who are intrinsically motivated strive to achieve because of the pleasure they get out of learning and mastering the material. Individuals who are extrinsically motivated strive to achieve because of the rewards they get for performing well and the punishments they receive for performing poorly. Generally speaking, individuals whose motivation is mainly intrinsic perform better than those whose motivation is mainly extrinsic, because intrinsically motivated individuals are more confident about their ability and more likely to persist in the face of failure (Pintrich, Roeser, & De Groot, 1994).

You read earlier that adults—parents and teachers, for instance—can affect adolescents' degree of achievement motivation. Adults can also affect the extent to which an adolescent's achievement motives are intrinsic or extrinsic. When adults attempt to control an adolescent's achievement behavior by rewarding good grades (such as by giving prizes or money), punishing bad grades (such as by restricting privileges), or excessively supervising their performance (such as by constantly checking up on their homework), adolescents are more likely to develop an extrinsic orientation and, as a result, are less likely to do well in school. In contrast, adolescents whose parents encourage their autonomy, provide a cognitively stimulating home environment, and are supportive of school success (without rewarding it concretely) are more likely to develop a strong intrinsic motivation to succeed and tend to perform better in school as a consequence (Ginsburg & Bronstein, 1993; Gottfried, Fleming, & Gottfried, 1998).

THE IMPORTANCE OF BELIEFS

How we behave in achievement situations is also influenced by our beliefs about our abilities and our chances for success and failure. You may have a very strong need for achievement, but if you are put into a situation in which you see little likelihood of succeeding, you will behave very differently than if you are in a situation in which you think your odds of doing well are good. For this reason, researchers have studied adolescents' beliefs about achievement, and not simply their motives.

Many studies show that adolescents make judgments about their likelihood of succeeding or failing and exert different degrees of effort accordingly (Dweck, 2002). For example, adolescents' choices of what classes to take in school are influenced by their beliefs about their abilities. Students who believe that they are good at math, for instance, will take more, and more difficult, math courses than their peers. But because course selection influences subsequent achievement (students who take more challenging math classes perform better on math tests), and achievement, in turn, influences students' beliefs about their abilities (students who do well on math tests come to see themselves as better math students), a cycle is set in motion in which students' beliefs, abilities, and actual achievement have a reciprocal influence on each other (H. Marsh & Yeung, 1997). One of the most interesting applications of this idea involves what psychologists call stereotype threat.

■ **Stereotype Threat**   Students' beliefs about their abilities and, as a consequence, their performance can also be affected by situational factors operating when they take an exam. Psychologist Claude Steele (1997) has demonstrated that when students are told that members of their ethnic group usually perform poorly on a particular test (for example, before the test is administered, students are told that previous studies have shown that members of their ethnic group do not score as well as other students), their performance actually suffers, whereas the reverse is true when students are told that members of their ethnic group usually perform better than others. This **stereotype threat** effect has also been demonstrated to depress females' performance when they are told before taking a test that males usually outperform females (Keller, 2002). To the extent that adolescents believe widely held stereotypes about ethnic or sex differences in ability (for example, that boys are just better at math than girls or that Asians are more intelligent than individuals from other ethnic groups), their achievement may be enhanced or depressed, depending on how they think they are expected to perform. For instance, biracial students who identify themselves as Black or Hispanic (groups often stereotyped as poor achievers) achieve lower grades in school than those with identical backgrounds who identify themselves as White or Asian (groups often stereotyped as high achievers) (Herman, 2009).

Because stereotypes can change over time, the strength of the stereotype threat effect should vary as well. One recent study found, for instance, that the impact of stereotype threat on Black students' performance weakened considerably both after Barack

---

intrinsic motivation   Motivation based on the pleasure one will experience from mastering a task.

extrinsic motivation   Motivation based on the rewards one will receive for successful performance.

stereotype threat   The harmful effect that exposure to stereotypes about ethnic or sex differences in ability has on student performance.

Obama received the Democratic presidential nomination and after he became the first Black president in U.S. history, presumably because the worldwide attention devoted to his accomplishments weakened the stereotype of Blacks as less capable (Marx, Ko, & Friedman, 2009).

Although it is too early to know whether the "Obama effect" is real—not all studies have found it (Aronson, Jannone, McGlone, & Johnson-Campbell, 2009)—there is reason to think that changing views of male and female intellectual ability have affected adolescent girls' test performance. For many years experts expressed special concern about the achievement motives and beliefs of adolescent girls, particularly with regard to performance in math and science, but more recent studies have shown that many previously observed sex differences have gotten much smaller or have disappeared (Vermeer, Boekaerts, & Seegers, 2000). One possible reason for this is that stereotypes about sex differences in cognitive ability have weakened considerably. Indeed, in contrast to several decades ago, when raters in experiments judged successful females as less likable, less attractive, and less likely to be happy, similar experiments conducted more recently show the opposite effect, perhaps because we have become that much more accustomed to seeing successful girls and women in a variety of settings and endeavors (Quatman, Sokolik, & Smith, 2000).

With improvements in girls' achievement across all subject areas—the achievement gap between males and females is closing, even in subjects that traditionally have been dominated by males. When sex differences in math and science achievement are reported today, they are very slight, especially in the United States (E. Evans, Schweingruber, & Stevenson, 2002; Leahy, 2001). Indeed, observations that boys are not doing as well in school as girls, that boys are disciplined more in school than girls, and that boys are more likely to perceive their schools and teachers as unfair (Nichols & Good, 1998; Pomerantz, Altermatt, & Saxon, 2002) have prompted numerous writers to express concern about the achievement problems of boys (H. Marsh & Yeung, 1997; Sommers, 2000). Sex differences in educational attainment have grown in recent years, with females far outnumbering males on American college campuses (T. Lewin, 2006). Sex differences in educational attainment, favoring females, are especially great among Black adolescents (J. King, 2006; Saunders, Davis, Williams, & Williams, 2004).

■ **Beliefs About Intelligence**   Other studies suggest that the way in which adolescents think about intelligence in general (in addition to how they view their own capability) also enters into the achievement equation; what's especially crucial is whether intelligence is thought of as something that is fixed or as something that is changeable (Stipek & Gralinski, 1996). These

Although there are many exceptions, on average, Asian American adolescents outperform their peers from other ethnic groups.

studies show that three factors interact to predict students' behavior in school: whether the student believes that intelligence is fixed or malleable, whether the student is oriented more toward extrinsic rewards (performance) or intrinsic rewards (mastery), and whether the student is confident about his or her abilities, or, as some theorists have put it, has a strong sense of **self-efficacy** (Bandura, Barbaranelli, Caprara, & Pastorelli, 1996). The way in which these factors are combined has a significant impact on actual achievement.

Students who believe that intelligence is fixed tend to be oriented toward their performance and to be greatly affected by their degree of confidence (Stipek & Gralinski, 1996). If they are confident about their abilities, they tend to work hard and to seek out challenges. If they are insecure, however, they tend to give up easily and to feel helpless. In other words, if you believe that intelligence is fixed, it's important to have confidence in your own abilities.

In contrast, students who believe that intelligence is malleable approach achievement situations from a different perspective. These students are more likely to be intrinsically than extrinsically motivated; for them, satisfaction comes from mastering the material, not simply from gaining a good evaluation. They are also far less affected by their level of confidence, because they are less concerned about their performance. Whether assured or insecure, these students exert extra effort and seek out challenges, because they are motivated by learning rather than by performing (Purdie, Hattie, & Douglas, 1996).

These newer models of the psychological aspects of achievement during adolescence illustrate how students' beliefs (about the nature of ability in general and

self-efficacy   The sense that an individual has some control over his or her life.

the nature of their own ability in particular) influence their motivation, which, in turn, influences their performance (Bandura et al., 1996; Bassi, Steca, Delle Fave, & Caprara, 2007; K. Gordon, 1995; Legault, Green-Demers, & Pelletier, 2006; Simpkins, Davis-Kean, & Eccles, 2006). Understanding how these forces work together has important implications for teachers, because, as you will read, adolescents' motives and beliefs are influenced by the context in which they are educated. In other words, there are specific steps teachers can take that will help bring out the best in their students.

▌ The Importance of Context

Although students' orientation toward mastery versus performance is determined in part by psychological factors, the educational context matters as well. When classroom conditions change so that performance becomes more important than learning, students' motives and beliefs change as a result. You have probably experienced this when you enrolled in a course in which the instructor stressed grades rather than mastery of the material. This sort of emphasis brings out the worst in students—literally. Under some circumstances, performance goals make students more extrinsically motivated, more insecure about their abilities, more hesitant to challenge themselves, and less likely to ask for help to improve their performance (R. Newman & Schwager, 1995). This is especially likely when students are motivated mainly by trying to avoid looking stupid (which diminishes their performance) rather than by trying to compete with and outperform their classmates (which enhances their performance) (Pintrich, 2000). In classrooms in which teachers are very performance-oriented (rather than mastery-oriented), students, on average, feel more alienated from school, have lower feelings of self-efficacy, and are more likely to engage in self-handicapping behavior (Kalil & Ziol-Guest, 2008; Urdan, 2004).

Students' feelings of self-efficacy influence, and are influenced by, their experiences, the messages they receive from teachers and parents, and the ways in which they compare themselves to their classmates (Usher, 2009). Here is how Jamaal, an eighth-grade student who is high in self-efficacy, described his reaction to the performance of a high-achieving classmate:

> I was real mad when Stacey had got a 100. I wasn't really mad, but I was kind of jealous. Like I envied it. Like I wished I was that one that got 100. I mean sometimes, now that, *that's* one of the things that give me the extra drive. That gives me the extra determination to work harder in math to get good grades like everyone else. (Usher, 2009, p. 295)

When he felt challenged by a math problem, Jamaal would give himself pep talks:

> I'll be like, "Come on." I'll be thinking about different ways to solve problems and stuff like that. I'll be saying, "Come on, Jamaal, you can do this," and stuff like that. . . . I don't know what it does, but it's just like extra comfort to me. (p. 295).

Compare this sentiment to that expressed by Tanisha, a classmate of Jamaal's who is low in self-efficacy:

> Some of my friends tell me about [algebra], and, you know, some of their tests that they told me about, they said it was hard. But, you know, that's kind of what makes me feel like I'm not going to do good in it. Because, like, if they can't do it, then I probably can't do it. (p. 297)

▌ Attributions for Success and Failure

How students interpret their successes and failures is also important. Researchers who are interested in what are called **achievement attributions** have studied how the explanations that individuals give for their success or failure influence their performance (Dweck, 2002). According to these theorists, individuals attribute their performance to a combination of four factors: ability, effort, task difficulty, and luck. When individuals succeed and attribute their success to internal causes such as their ability or effort, they are more likely to approach future tasks confidently and with self-assurance. If, however, they attribute their success to external factors outside their control, such as luck or an easy task, they are more likely to remain unsure of their abilities. Not surprisingly, scholastically successful individuals, who tend to be high in achievement motivation, are likely to attribute their successes to internal causes (Carr, Borkowski, & Maxwell, 1991; Durik, Vida, & Eccles, 2006; Randel, Stevenson, & Witruk, 2000; Vispoel, 1995).

FOOD FOR THOUGHT

When you succeed in school, to what do you attribute your success? When you fail, how do you explain your failure? Have you had teachers who influenced your beliefs about your own abilities?

How adolescents interpret their failures is also important in influencing their subsequent behavior. Some youngsters try harder in the face of failure, whereas others withdraw and exert less effort. According to psychologist Carol Dweck (Dweck, 2002), when individuals attribute their failures to a lack of effort, they are more likely to try harder on future tasks. But individuals who attribute their failure to factors that they feel cannot be changed (such as bad luck, lack of intelligence, or

achievement attributions The beliefs an individual holds about the causes of her or his successes and failures.

task difficulty) are more likely to feel helpless and to exert less effort in subsequent situations.

Suppose, for instance, a student takes the SAT and receives a combined score of 1000. He then is told by his guidance counselor that the SAT is a measure of intelligence, that intelligence is fixed, and that his score reflects how smart he is. The counselor tells the student that he can retake the test if he wants to but that he should not expect to score much higher than 1000. Now imagine a different student, who also scores 1000 on the test. She is told by her guidance counselor that effort has a great deal to do with scores on the SAT and that she can raise her score by trying harder. In all likelihood, the next time these students take the test, the first student will not try as hard as the second student, because he is more likely to feel helpless.

Students who are led to believe that their efforts do not make a difference—by being told, for example, that they are stupid or that the work is too difficult for them—develop what psychologists call **learned helplessness:** the belief that failure is inevitable (Dweck, 2002). As a result of learned helplessness, some students try less hard than their peers, and they do not do as well as they might. Students who suffer from learned helplessness and who use a lot of self-handicapping strategies tend not only to perform worse in school but also to have more overall adjustment problems than their peers (Määta, Nurmi, & Stattin, 2007; Määta, Stattin, & Nurmi, 2002). Research on adolescents' attributions for success and failure suggests that, instead of dismissing low-achieving students as having "low needs for achievement" or "low intelligence," teachers and other school personnel can help students achieve more by helping them learn to attribute their performance to factors that are under their own control (Blackwell et al., 2007; Hudley, 1997; Usher, 2007).

■   **The Drop in Motivation During the Transition Into Secondary School**   One of the most interesting applications of research on achievement-related beliefs has been in studies of changes in adolescents' academic motivation during the transition from elementary school to junior high school (Eccles et al., 1993). As you read in Chapter 6, studies find that students' motivation and school performance decline when they move into secondary school (Eccles & Rosser, 2009; Elmen, 1991; Yoon, Eccles, Wigfield, & Barber, 1996). Why might this be? Among the other important changes that take place during this school transition is a shift on the part of teachers toward a more performance-oriented style of instruction and evaluation. Elementary school teachers tend to stress the importance of mastering the material. During secondary school, however, students discover that more of an emphasis is placed on grades. This shift in emphasis undermines many students' intrinsic motivation and their self-

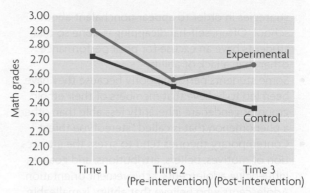

FIGURE 12.1   A recent experiment found that teaching adolescents that intelligence is malleable can head off the decline in school performance often seen during the transition into secondary school. (Blackwell et al., 2007)

confidence, which, in turn, diminishes their performance. Indeed, during the early years of high school, there is a general decline in adolescents' feelings of self-efficacy and in their mastery motivation, and an increase in their use of self-handicapping strategies (Gottfried, Fleming, & Gottfried, 2001; Pintrich, 2000). In addition, studies find that individuals' beliefs about intelligence change as they move into and through adolescence, with older students more likely to view intelligence as stable (Ablard & Mills, 1996).

One recent experiment demonstrated that this decline does not have to be inevitable (Blackwell, Trzesniewski, & Dweck, 2007). The researchers randomly assigned students enrolled in seventh-grade math classes to one of two groups: an experimental group, which received two class sessions on how it is possible to "grow your intelligence" and on how experience can actually affect brain development, and a control group, which was taught strategies to improve memory. Figure 12.1 shows the effects of the intervention. As you can see, while both groups showed a comparable drop in math grades initially, after the intervention, the group that was taught that intelligence is malleable improved, whereas the control group continued to decline.

RECAP

- Adolescents' need for achievement and their fear of failure work together to pull them toward or repel them from achievement situations. A strong need for achievement is facilitated by parenting that combines the basic elements of authoritativeness with high expectations for success.
- Although some students underachieve because they have an intense fear of failure, which makes them anxious, others engage in "self-handicapping"

learned helplessness   The acquired belief that an individual is not able to influence events through his or her own efforts or actions.

strategies in order to appear nonchalant about school. Often, self-handicapping is done so that students have an excuse for poor performance other than a lack of ability.

- Some students perform poorly because they have been led to believe that members of their ethnic group or gender are inherently less able than others, a phenomenon that is called "stereotype threat."
- Contemporary theories tend to stress the interaction of motives, beliefs, attributions, and goals as influencing adolescents' achievement orientation. Adolescents who believe that ability is malleable, who are motivated by intrinsic rather than extrinsic rewards, who are confident about their abilities, and who attribute their successes and failures to effort rather than to things they can't control achieve more in school than their peers.
- Teachers can help improve their students' achievement by creating environments that stress mastery over performance, by helping students attribute their successes and failures to how hard they work, and by stressing that intelligence is malleable rather than fixed.

Environmental Influences on Achievement

Ability, beliefs, and motivation may play a large role in influencing individual performance, but opportunity and situational factors also have a great deal to do with achievement (Eccles & Roeser, 2009). Many of the differences in academic or occupational achievement that are observed among adolescents result not from differences in their abilities, motives, or beliefs but from differences in the schools and classrooms where their abilities and motives are expressed.

School environments differ markedly—in physical facilities, in opportunities for pursuing academically enriched programs, and in classroom atmospheres. For example, students are more engaged and achieve more in schools that are more personal, less departmentalized, and less rigidly tracked, and in which team teaching is used more frequently (Gamoran, 1992; V. Lee & Smith, 1993). Unfortunately, many school districts, plagued with shrinking tax bases, are characterized by decaying school buildings, outdated equipment, and textbook and teacher shortages. In some schools, problems of crime and discipline have become so overwhelming that attention to these matters has taken precedence over learning and instruction. In short, many young people who genuinely want to succeed are impeded not by a

lack of talent or motivation but by a school environment that makes their academic success virtually impossible. Students who attend schools with a high concentration of poor, minority students are especially disadvantaged, as are students who attend schools with a high proportion of students from single-parent families (Bankston & Caldas, 1996, 1998; Pong, 1997, 1998).

THE INFLUENCE OF THE HOME ENVIRONMENT

The school, of course, is not the only environment that makes a difference in adolescents' achievement, and few would argue that schools should accept full responsibility for adolescents who do not succeed at a level consonant with their abilities. If anything, the evidence suggests that important aspects of the home environment are better predictors of adolescents' academic achievement than are features of the school environment (J. Coleman et al., 1966; Steinberg, 1996). Researchers have studied three ways in which the adolescent's home may influence his or her level of achievement (see Figure 12.2).

Parental Values and Expectations Adolescents' achievement is directly related to their parents' values and expectations (Jodl, Michael, Malanchuk, Eccles, & Sameroff, 2001). Parental encouragement of academic success may be manifested in a number of ways, all of which have been shown to be beneficial to adolescents' school performance. First, parents who encourage school success set higher standards for their child's school performance and homework, and they have higher aspirations for their child, which, in turn, contribute to school success (Luthar et al., 2006; Patrikakou, 1996; P. Wilson & Wilson, 1992).

Second, parents who encourage school success also have values that are consistent with doing well in school, and they structure the home environment to support academic pursuits so that the messages children receive from their teachers are echoed at home (Benner, Graham, & Mistry, 2008; Jodl et al., 2001; Sui-Chu & Willms, 1996). Studies show that even high school students profit from having parents who help them learn more effective time management strategies and healthier work habits (Xu, 2004).

Finally, parents who encourage success are likely to be more involved in their child's education—more likely to attend school programs, to help in course selection, to maintain interest in school activities and assignments, and the like—all of which contribute to students' success (Benner et al., 2008; Bogenschneider, 1997; N. E. Hill et al., 2004; Hoover-Dempsey & Sandler, 1995; Muller, 1998; Shumow & Miller, 2001). Parental involvement in schooling may make academics seem both more important and more conquerable to the

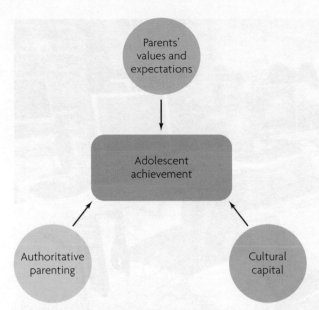

FIGURE 12.2   Parents influence adolescent achievement through three mechanisms: their values and expectations, the way they parent, and the cultural capital they provide in the home environment

adolescent, which may enhance the young person's academic self-conceptions (Grolnick & Slowiaczek, 1994; Ibañez, Kuperminc, Jurkovic, & Perilla, 2004); it may also send an important message to teachers (Kuperminc, Darnell, & Alvarez-Jiminez, 2008). In contrast, parental disengagement from school may make students themselves more likely to disengage and do poorly (Roeser, Lord, & Eccles, 1994). Parental involvement seems to be an especially strong influence on the achievement of Mexican American youth, perhaps because of the importance of the family in Mexican culture (Trusty, Plata, & Salazar, 2003). The way in which parents are involved matters, however: Studies show that encouraging and expecting achievement in school, and being involved in school-based activities, are both effective forms of parental involvement, whereas helping with homework is not (N. E. Hill & Tyson, 2009). Interestingly, parental involvement in schooling has a more substantial effect when the adolescent attends a school in which a large proportion of other students' parents are involved as well (Darling & Steinberg, 1997; Pong, 1998).

▌ **Authoritative Parenting**   A second way in which parents influence student achievement is more indirect—through their general approach to parenting. Numerous studies have shown that authoritative parenting—parenting that is warm, firm, and fair—is linked to school success during adolescence, as indexed by better performance, better attendance, higher expectations, more positive academic self-conceptions, and stronger engagement in the classroom (Bronstein

et al., 1996; Corville-Smith, Ryan, Adams, & Dalicandro, 1998; Sirin & Rogers-Sirin, 2004; Steinberg, Lamborn, Darling, Mounts, & Dornbusch, 1994; Wentzel, 1998). In contrast, parenting that is especially punitive, harsh, overcontrolling, or inept is associated with lower school engagement and diminished achievement (R. Clark, Dogan, & Akbar, 2003; DeBaryshe, Patterson, & Capaldi, 1993; Eamon, 2005; Melby & Conger, 1996; Q. Wang, Pomerantz, & Chen, 2007). Interestingly, extreme parental permissiveness, not authoritarianism, is associated with higher rates of dropping out of school (Rumberger, Ghatak, Poulos, Ritter, & Dornbusch, 1990). Authoritative parenting has also been shown to help adolescents adjust to middle school (Bronstein et al., 1998) and help poorly performing early adolescents turn their academic performance around in high school (Catterall, 1998).

Why do adolescents achieve more in school when they come from authoritative homes? One reason is that authoritative parenting promotes the development of a healthy achievement orientation—including an emphasis on intrinsic motivation and a healthier attributional style—which, in turn, enhances adolescent school performance (Aunola, Stattin, & Nurmi, 2000; Bronstein, Ginsburg, & Herrera-Leavitt, 2000; DeBaryshe et al., 1993; Glasgow, Dornbusch, Ritter, Troyer, & Steinberg, 1997). This is in part because authoritative parents are more likely themselves to hold healthier beliefs about their child's achievement and less likely to be overly controlling—two factors that strengthen adolescents' work ethic and intrinsic motivation (Arbeton, Eccles, & Harold, 1994; Grolnick & Slowiaczek, 1994). Having a strong work orientation enhances achievement both directly, as we saw earlier, and indirectly, through the positive impression it makes on teachers (Farkas, Grobe, & Shuan, 1990).

In general, these findings are in line with a good deal of research suggesting that consistent, authoritative parenting is associated with a wide array of benefits to the adolescent, including higher achievement motivation, greater self-esteem, and enhanced competence (Steinberg, 2001; Wentzel, 1994). Authoritative parents also tend to have more involvement in school activities, which is associated with scholastic success, although parents' involvement both affects and is affected by adolescents' achievement (Crosnoe, 2001; Juang & Silbereisen, 2002; Paulson, 1994; Steinberg, Dornbusch, & Brown, 1992). Students also perform better when the values and expectations they encounter at home are consistent with those they encounter in school (Arunkumar, Midgley, & Urdan, 1999).

▌ **The Quality of the Home Environment**   A third mechanism of familial influence is through the quality of the home environment provided. Studies have shown that the quality of an adolescent's home

Schools in the United States vary considerably in the resources their students have access to.

environment—as measured simply in terms of the presence of such items as a television, dictionary, encyclopedia, newspaper, vacuum cleaner, and other indicators of family income—is more strongly correlated with youngsters' level of academic achievement than is the quality of the physical facility of the school they attend, the background and training of their teachers, or the level of teachers' salaries paid by the school district (Armor, 1972). A number of researchers have also shown that the extent to which the adolescent's parents provide the youngster with what is called **cultural capital**—by exposing the adolescent to art, music, literature, and so forth—exerts a positive impact on achievement above and beyond the effects of the parents' own level of education (Buechel & Duncan, 1998; DiMaggio, 1982; Roscigno & Ainsworth-Darnell, 1999).

Several researchers have asked whether adolescents' school achievement is affected by genetic factors. Interestingly, evidence on the heritability of school achievement suggests that while intelligence and cognitive

achievement both have strong genetic components (and influence grades through this mechanism), school performance is highly influenced by environmental factors, both inside and outside the family (W. Johnson, McGue, & Iacono, 2006; Teachman, 1997). With this in mind, it is important to point out that a disheartening number of young people in this country live in overcrowded, inadequate housing and come from families that are under severe economic and social stress—so much so that parental encouragement and involvement are often undermined by neighborhood conditions (Gonzales, Cauce, Friedman, & Mason, 1996). It is extremely difficult for a parent to provide a supportive home environment when he or she is under severe economic stress. Stress at home, in turn, spills over into the adolescent's school life, leading to academic problems and diminished achievement (Flook & Fuligni, 2008).

Put succinctly, many American youngsters do not grow up in an atmosphere that is conducive to academic achievement. Many communities lack what social scientists sometimes call **social capital**—the support, encouragement, and involvement of adults necessary to facilitate youngsters' success in school (J. Coleman & Hoffer, 1987). Social capital, which is strengthened when families have strong ties to other families in the community, has been shown to be an important contributor

cultural capital   The resources provided within a family through the exposure of the adolescent to art, music, literature, and other elements of "high culture."

social capital   The interpersonal resources available to an adolescent or family.

to success in school, above and beyond the contribution of adolescents' family income, their parents' education, or their household composition (Pong, 1997, 1998). Not surprisingly, students whose families lack social capital are more likely to have difficulty in school (Teachman, Paasch, & Carver, 1997).

FOOD FOR THOUGHT

What sorts of programs for parents existed in the district in which you attended high school? In view of what we know about the home environments of high-achieving students, how likely are these sorts of activities to succeed? What do you think would motivate parents to become more involved in their adolescent's schooling?

THE INFLUENCE OF FRIENDS

There is also evidence that friends influence adolescents' achievement. Indeed, some studies suggest that friends are the most salient influences on adolescents' day-to-day school behaviors, such as doing homework and exerting effort in class (Kurdek, Fine, & Sinclair, 1995; Midgley & Urdan, 1995; Steinberg et al., 1996). That is, although parents are stronger influences on long-range educational plans, what adolescents do in school on a daily basis is more affected by their friends. Indeed, one of the main reasons that adolescents growing up in poor neighborhoods achieve less is that they are often surrounded by peers who are disengaged from school (South, Baumer, & Lutz, 2003).

When most of us think about the influence of adolescents' peers on achievement, we tend immediately to think of the ways in which peers undermine academic success. But contrary to the notion that the influence of the peer group is always negative, studies suggest that the impact of friends on adolescents' school performance depends on the academic orientation of the peer group. Having friends who earn high grades and aspire to further education can enhance adolescents' achievement, whereas having friends who earn low grades or disparage school success may interfere with it (Steinberg et al., 1996). Students whose friends are more engaged in school are themselves more engaged and less likely to drop out (R. Ream & Rumberger, 2008). Friends also influence course selection and appear to play an especially important role in girls' decisions to take math and science classes (Riegle-Crumb, Farkas, & Muller, 2006).

Students' grades change over time in relation to the grades of their friends (Mounts & Steinberg, 1995). Students with best friends who achieve high grades in school are more likely to show improvements in their own grades than are students who begin at similar levels of achievement but whose friends are not high achievers. Peers also exert a small but significant influence on each other's college plans. Among low-achieving adolescents, for example, those with high-achieving friends are more likely to plan to continue their education than are those with low-achieving friends.

Although peers can influence achievement for better or for worse, many observers have noted that in the contemporary United States, the influence of the peer culture on academic achievement is far more negative than positive (Bishop, Bishop, Gelbwasser, Green, & Zuckerman, 2003; Steinberg et al., 1996). Perhaps because of this, adolescents with an extremely high orientation toward peers tend to perform worse in school (Fuligni & Eccles, 1993). Conversely, adolescents who are neglected by their peers often have a stronger academic orientation than relatively more popular students (Luthar & McMahon, 1996; Wentzel & Asher, 1995). As they move into middle school, adolescents become increasingly worried about their friends' reactions to success in school; one study found, for example, that by eighth grade students did not want their classmates to know that they worked hard in school, even though they knew that it would be helpful to convey this impression to their teachers (Juvonen & Murdock, 1995).

Doing well in school does not have to come at the cost of having a decent social life, however. A recent study in which adolescents maintained daily diaries of their time use sheds interesting light on the differences between high- and low-achieving students in how they spend their time (Witkow, 2009). Not surprisingly, students who earn higher grades than their peers spend more time studying, both on weekdays and on weekends. But as Figure 12.3 shows, a key difference between the groups is in how much—and when—they spend time with their friends. As you can see, high-achieving students spend less time with their friends than do low-achieving students on weekdays, but not on weekends. This suggests that high-achieving students are able to maintain an active social life by allocating their time more judiciously during the week. As you read in Chapter 5, adolescents tend to have friends whose orientation toward school is similar. In all likelihood, one reason that high-achieving students spend less time with friends on weekdays is that their friends are also busy studying.

A number of researchers have studied how the influences of parents and peers operate together to affect adolescents' achievement (B. Brown, Mounts, Lamborn, & Steinberg, 1993; Fletcher, Darling, Steinberg, & Dornbusch, 1995; Gonzales, Cauce, Friedman, & Mason, 1996; Kurdek et al., 1995; Steinberg et al., 1996). These studies show that the family environment has an effect on adolescents' choice of friends, and this, in turn, can

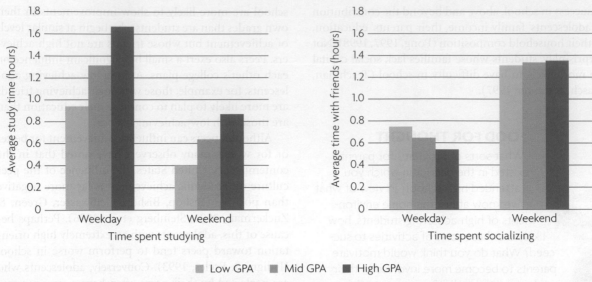

FIGURE 12.3 High- and low-achieving students allocate their time spent studying and socializing differently. (Witkow, 2009)

influence school achievement (B. Brown et al., 1993). In addition, having friends who value school can positively affect academic achievement, even among teenagers who do not come from nonauthoritative homes; having academically oriented peers is especially beneficial to adolescents from single-parent homes, where parental involvement in schooling is typically lower (Garg, Melanson, & Levin, 2007). By the same token, having friends who disparage school success may offset the benefits of authoritative parenting (Steinberg et al., 1996). Rather than asking whether family or friends influence adolescents' school performance, then, it may make more sense to ask how these two forces—along with the influence of the school itself—work together.

A recent study examining the influence of peers and parents on school achievement in 12 different countries shows that the broader context in which schooling takes place can affect the degree to which peers and parents influence adolescents' achievement. Peers and parents more strongly influence student achievement in countries where schools serve more heterogeneous groups of students, as in the United States. In countries where students with different long-term educational aspirations attend different schools (that is, in countries like Germany, where there are separate schools for adolescents who are planning to go to college versus those who are not), peers and parents are less influential (Buchmann & Dalton, 2002).

In sum, although psychological factors play a key role in determining occupational and scholastic success, it is important to take into account the broader environment in which individuals pursue their educational and occupational careers (Gonzales, Cauce, Friedman, & Mason, 1996; Steinberg et al., 1996). Moreover, distinguishing between motivational and environmental factors is hard, because they typically go hand in hand. Living in an envi-

ronment that offers few opportunities for success induces feelings of learned helplessness, which, in turn, leads individuals to feel that exerting any effort to succeed is futile. Attending school in an environment in which achievement is not encouraged engenders attitudes and beliefs inconsistent with striving to do well. Rather than viewing achievement during adolescence as being determined by one single factor, such as ability or motivation, it is more accurate to say that patterns of achievement are the result of a cumulative process that includes a long history of experience and socialization in school, in the family, in the peer group, and in the community.

RECAP

- In addition to the influence of beliefs, motives, attributions, and goals, individuals' levels of achievement are affected by the social context in which they develop.
- Adolescents perform better and are more engaged in school when they come from homes in which their parents value and expect scholastic success, practice authoritative parenting, and provide a home environment that is high in cultural capital.
- In addition, adolescents whose friends support academic achievement perform better in school than do peers whose friends disparage doing well in school.
- Researchers now understand that patterns of achievement are the result of a cumulative process that includes a long history of experience and socialization in school, in the family, in the peer group, and in the community.

Educational Achievement

Educational achievement is usually defined in one of three ways: **school performance** (the grades students earn in school), **academic achievement** (their performance on standardized tests), or **educational attainment** (the number of years of schooling they complete). These different measures of educational achievement are, not surprisingly, interrelated, but they are less tied to each other than you might expect.

No single factor adequately accounts for differences in adolescents' levels of educational achievement. Generally, intellectual ability—as assessed by IQ tests—is highly correlated with performance on achievement tests (hardly a surprise, since IQ tests and achievement tests are designed to tap similar abilities). But grades in school—and to an even greater extent, educational attainment—are influenced by a wider range of factors than simply the adolescent's intellectual abilities. Grades, for example, are influenced by teachers' judgments of students' mastery of the material, and these judgments may be influenced by teachers' evaluations of students' efforts and behaviors in the classroom (Farkas, Grobe, & Shuan, 1990). How many years of school an adolescent completes is likely to be influenced by his or her family background and living circumstances, as well as by school performance. Two adolescents may have similar grade point averages, but if one comes from a poor family and cannot afford to go to college, the two will have different levels of educational attainment. Even as early as elementary school, for example, many inner-city youth have very limited occupational expectations, and these low expectations affect their educational achievement and attainment (T. Cook et al., 1996).

Regardless of what influences it, educational attainment has important implications for subsequent earnings (Ceci & Williams, 1999). The gap in earnings between high school graduates and college graduates is considerable, and this is true across all ethnic groups. When they enter the labor force, individuals with a college degree earn twice as much per year as do individuals with only a high school diploma (U.S. Census Bureau, 2009a).

THE IMPORTANCE OF SOCIOECONOMIC STATUS

▌ **A Head Start for the More Affluent** One of the most powerful influences on educational achievement is the socioeconomic status of the adolescent's family. Five decades of studies have shown over and over that middle-class adolescents score higher on basic tests of academic skills, earn higher grades, and complete more years of schooling than their working-class and lower-class peers (Muller, Stage, & Kinzie, 2001; Schoon, Parsons, & Sacker, 2004). Adolescents who come from

lower socioeconomic levels are more likely to score lower than their more advantaged peers on standardized tests of achievement (Sackett, Kuncel, Arneson, Cooper, & Waters, 2009). Although some of the socioeconomic gaps in school achievement have narrowed, disparities in achievement between the social classes remain strong, and the importance of socioeconomic status in determining educational achievement remains substantial across all ethnic groups (Goyette & Xie, 1999; S. Hanson, 1994; Kao & Tienda, 1998; Lucas, 1996; Teachman & Paasch, 1998). Socioeconomic status also influences adolescent achievement through neighborhood processes. Poor Black students who live in neighborhoods with a relatively higher proportion of middle-class neighbors place more value on education and try harder in school than comparably poor students who live in disadvantaged neighborhoods (Ceballo, McLoyd, & Toyokawa, 2004; E. B. Stewart, Stewart, & Simons, 2007).

Socioeconomic status, therefore, influences both educational achievement and attainment and, as a consequence, influences occupational achievement as well. However, keep in mind that variations within socioeconomic categories are often as substantial as differences between categories. Not all youngsters from affluent backgrounds go further in school than adolescents from poorer families, and many youngsters from economically disadvantaged households go on to earn college and postgraduate degrees.

One big reason that family background is related to educational achievement is that children from lower socioeconomic levels are more likely to enter elementary school scoring low on tests of basic academic competence (Rouse, Brooks-Gunn, & McLanahan, 2005). These initial differences reflect both genetic and environmental factors. Middle-class adults generally have higher IQs than lower-class adults, and this advantage is passed on to their children—both through inheritance and through the benefit that middle-class youngsters receive from growing up under more favorable environmental conditions (C. S. Chen, Lee, & Stevenson, 1996; Teachman, 1996). Affluent youngsters receive better health care and better nutrition, for example, both of which contribute to their higher performance on IQ tests. The disadvantages of poorer youngsters in achievement test scores persist—and may even increase—throughout elementary and secondary school (Rouse,

school performance   A measure of achievement based on an individual's grades in school.

academic achievement   Achievement that is measured by standardized tests of scholastic ability or knowledge.

educational attainment   The number of years of schooling completed by an individual.

Brooks-Gunn, & McLanahan, 2005). Because progress in high school depends so heavily on having a solid foundation of basic academic competence, adolescents who enter secondary school without having mastered basic academic skills quickly fall behind, and some leave high school before graduating.

▌ **Early Intervention** One bit of encouraging news on this front comes from long-term evaluations of interventions designed to improve the academic achievement of very poor youngsters who, by virtue of their poverty, are at high risk for academic failure (F. Campbell & Ramey, 1995; A. Reynolds & Temple, 1998). In these evaluations, researchers compared groups of adolescents who had participated in an intensive educational program during their preschool and elementary school years with matched samples of adolescents who had had the preschool intervention only, the elementary school intervention only, or no educational intervention at all. The interventions were targeted at improving the children's school skills and at strengthening the links between parents and their child's school.

Long-term evaluations show that individuals who participated in preschool interventions (with or without participation in elementary school interventions) perform significantly better in school during adolescence than those who did not (F. Campbell & Ramey, 1995). In one study, participating in both the preschool and the elementary school programs provided additional advantages over the preschool program alone (A. Reynolds, Temple, Robertson, & Mann, 2001). Interestingly, however, adolescents who had been in the elementary school program but not the preschool program had no advantages over those who had been in no intervention at all (F. Campbell & Ramey, 1995). These findings suggest that intervening prior to entering first grade may be extremely important in preventing long-term academic problems among impoverished adolescents and that extended participation in educational programs may be better than short-term participation. Consistent with this, longitudinal research shows that school difficulties as early as kindergarten are predictive of poor school performance in adolescence (Hamre & Pianta, 2001).

One reason for the relatively poorer school performance of disadvantaged youth, therefore, is that these youngsters begin school at a distinct academic disadvantage. A second reason for the disparity is stress, however—both before and during adolescence. Adolescents who come from lower-class backgrounds experience more stressful life events, report more daily hassles, and attend schools with more negative climates (DuBois, Felner, Meares, & Krier, 1994; Felner et al., 1995; Gillock & Reyes, 1999; Pungello, Kupersmidt, Burchinal, & Patterson, 1996). Stress has been shown to

adversely affect adolescents' mental health, well-being, and school performance (DuBois, Felner, Brand, Adan, & Evans, 1992; Felner et al., 1995).

▌ **Parental Involvement** Some studies also suggest that parents from higher social classes are more likely to be involved in their adolescent's education, especially through formal parent–teacher organizations, like the PTA or PTO (Shumow & Miller, 2001). Middle- and upper-middle-class parents are also more likely to have information about their child's school, to be responsive to their child's school problems, and to help select more rigorous courses for their child to take (Crosnoe & Huston, 2007). Because adolescents whose parents are involved in their schooling perform better than those whose parents are not involved, youngsters from higher social classes may achieve more in school than their less advantaged peers in part because of their parents' more active involvement (V. Lee & Croninger, 1994). In addition, parents with greater economic resources are able to provide their children with more cultural capital, which, as we have seen, is an important contributor to school success (Roscigno & Ainsworth-Darnell, 1999).

FOOD FOR THOUGHT

In light of the profound impact that socioeconomic status has on student achievement, what would you suggest as policies or practices to raise the achievement of poor youth? Think about people you know who overcame economic disadvantage and were highly successful in school (perhaps *you* are in this category). To what would you attribute this success?

Socioeconomic differences in school achievement obviously reflect the cumulative and combined effects of a variety of influences, and it is simplistic to explain social class differences in achievement without considering these factors simultaneously. What is perhaps more interesting—and more worthy of scientific study—is the question of what it is about the many youngsters from economically disadvantaged backgrounds who are successful that accounts for their overcoming the tremendous odds against them. Put concretely, the successful college student who comes from an environment of severe economic disadvantage has had to overcome incredible barriers.

Although more research on successful students from poor backgrounds is sorely needed, several findings suggest that what might be most important is social support for academic achievement: the presence of warm and encouraging parents who raise their children authoritatively, take an interest in their children's academic progress, and hold high aspirations for their children's educational attainment, as well as the availability of peers who support and encourage academic success (Brody, Stoneman, & Flor, 1995; L. Gregory, 1995; Melby, Conger, Fang, Wickrama, & Conger, 2008; Steinberg et al., 1996; Sui-Chu & Willms, 1996). In other words, positive relations at home and the encouragement of significant others can in some circumstances overcome the negative influence of socioeconomic disadvantage.

ETHNIC DIFFERENCES IN EDUCATIONAL ACHIEVEMENT

Among the most controversial—and intriguing—findings in research on adolescents' achievement are those concerning ethnic differences in school success. On average, the educational achievement of Black and Hispanic students—virtually however indexed—lags behind that of White students, and all three groups achieve less in school than do Asian students. Although some of these differences can be attributed to socioeconomic differences among these ethnic groups, the group disparities persist even after socioeconomic factors are taken into account (Fuligni, Hughes, & Way, 2009). The academic superiority of Asian students tends to emerge during the transition into junior high school—when most other students' grades typically decline—and it persists through high school and into college (Fuligni, 1994; Fuligni & Witkow, 2004). What has been most intriguing to social scientists is the observation that Black and Hispanic students have educational aspirations and attitudes that are similar to those of Asian and White students but significantly poorer academic skills, habits, and behavior (Ainsworth-Darnell & Downey, 1998). If Black and Hispanic students ostensibly have the same long-term goals as other students, why do they not behave in similar ways?

▌ False Optimism Rather Than Realistic Pessimism   Several theories have been advanced to explain this finding. One set of theories involves the perceptions that adolescents have about the likely payoff of hard work in school. Some writers, for instance, have argued that even though they have high aspirations in the abstract, many minority youth do not believe that educational success will have substantial occupational payoff for them, because discrimination and prejudice will limit their actual opportunities (Mickelson, 1990). Although intuitively appealing, this theory has not received convincing empirical support (Fuligni et al.,

Adolescents whose parents are involved in their schooling perform better than adolescents whose parents are not. One reason that students from higher social classes do better in school is that their parents tend to be more involved.

2009). It is true that adolescents who believe they have been victims of discrimination, or who believe that their opportunities for occupational success are unfairly constrained by society, achieve less in school and report more emotional distress than do peers who do not hold these beliefs (C. Fisher, Wallace, & Fenton, 2000; R. Taylor et al., 1994; P. Wood & Clay, 1996). It is also true that students who are more confident about and oriented to the future do better in school (W. T. Brown & Jones, 2004; Oyserman, Bybee, & Terry, 2006). It is not true, however, that Black or Hispanic youngsters are more likely than other adolescents to believe that their opportunities for success are blocked (Ainsworth-Darnell & Downey, 1998; D. Downey & Ainsworth-Darnell, 2002; Kao & Tienda, 1998; Steinberg et al., 1992). Indeed, several studies indicate that Black and Hispanic youth have more optimistic beliefs and positive feelings about school than other students (e.g., Ainsworth-Darnell & Downey, 1998; D. Downey, Ainsworth, & Qian, 2009; Shernoff & Schmidt, 2008; Voelkl, 1997). Actually, some research suggests that beliefs about the likelihood of future discrimination may motivate adolescents to perform better in school (perhaps because they feel that they will need to be even better prepared than others to overcome prejudicial treatment), but that feeling discriminated against in the present, by classmates or teachers, hinders academic achievement (perhaps by causing psychological distress or hopelessness) (Eccles & Roeser, 2009; Mattison & Aber, 2007). All in all, however, adolescents' hopes and aspirations for the future are very similar across ethnic groups (Chang, Chen, Greenberger, Dooley, & Heckhausen, 2006).

If anything, it may be adolescents' fear of failure, rather than their desire (or lack of desire) to succeed, that matters most (Steinberg et al., 1992). Asian youngsters not only believe in the value of school success but also are very anxious about the possible negative repercussions of not doing well in school, in terms of both occupational success and their parents' disappointment (Eaton & Dembo, 1997; Herman, 2009; Steinberg et al., 1996). Moreover, many Asian youth believe that the only way they can succeed in mainstream American society is through educational achievement (Sue & Okazaki, 1990). Interestingly, Asian students' sense of obligation to their parents—a factor frequently suggested as a reason for their high rates of school success—does not seem to play a very important role in predicting school achievement. If anything, being expected to assist the family by performing household chores and other family work—something that is especially salient in Asian and Hispanic households—has a negative impact on school performance (Fuligni, Tseng, & Lam, 1999; Telzer & Fuligni, 2009).

▋ The Burden of "Acting White"

Another popular explanation for ethnic differences in achievement is that some ethnic minority students underperform in school because they are stigmatized for "acting White" if they try to do well and, as a consequence, develop an "oppositional" identity that is hostile to doing well in school (Fordham & Ogbu, 1986). This view has not held up, however, perhaps because the extent of this negative peer pressure varies from school to school and from peer group to peer group (e.g., Akom, 2003; D. Downey & Ainsworth-Darnell, 2002; Farkas, Lleras, & Maczuga, 2002; Horvat & Lewis, 2003; Tyson, Darity, & Castellino, 2005). Black peer groups are not all the same, and while some may disparage academic achievement, many admire it. Here's how one academically successful Black student replied when asked if students from different peer groups treated her differently:

> I think, yes. The black people who, say, aren't as smart as me or Renée or whoever else they say, "Oh, you act white" because we're in high classes or whatever, and that really upsets me. They say we talk white. I don't even have like proper English or whatever, but they say we talk white because we use all these big words and everything. To me, that's total ignorance.

When asked to describe her own friends, however, she said:

> They're always, "I'm so proud of you. You have a job, you're still in school, and you're not pregnant." All this other good stuff. But it makes me feel good. (Horvat & Lewis, 2003, pp. 270–272)

Another successful student from the same school noted that even her friends who had dropped out of school in the eighth or ninth grade were supportive of her achievement:

> They just treat me as one of them. School's not a subject that really comes up as far as my neighborhood is concerned. They'll say, "How was your day at school?" "Fine." They accept me for what I am and what I do. If I am smart, I am smart. It seems they really congratulated me, if anything, especially now. So many of my friends have told me, "I'm so proud of you." Basically pushing me on. (Horvat & Lewis, 2003, p. 272)

▋ Ethnic Differences in Beliefs

An alternative account of ethnic differences in achievement stresses differences in ethnic groups' beliefs about ability. We noted earlier that adolescents who believe that intelligence is malleable are more likely to be intrinsically motivated and, as a consequence, academically successful. It is therefore interesting to note that Asian cultures tend to place more emphasis on effort than on ability in explaining school success and are more likely to believe that all students have the capacity to succeed (H. Stevenson & Stigler, 1992). By and large, students from Asian backgrounds tend to be more invested in mastering the material than in simply performing well—an orientation that, as we saw earlier, contributes to school success (J. Li, 2006). It is also important to note that Asian students—both in the United States and in Asia—spend significantly more time each week on homework and other school-related activities, and significantly less time socializing and watching television, than do other youth (Asakawa & Csikszentmihalyi, 2000; Caplan, Choy, & Whitmore, 1992; Fuligni & Stevenson, 1995; Steinberg et al., 1996).

You may be interested to know that, contrary to popular belief, Asian students do not pay a price for their superior achievement in terms of increased anxiety, depression, stress, or social competence; the suicide rate among American teenagers is substantially higher than it is among Japanese youth, for example (X. Chen, Rubin, & Li, 1997; Crystal et al., 1994; C. King, Akiyama, & Elling, 1996). However, there is some evidence that the long hours of studying that Korean high school seniors must endure while in "examination hell"—the period of preparation for that country's college entrance exam—may take its toll on adolescents' mental health (M. Lee & Larson, 2000). During regular periods of school in the United States, however, Asian students' moods while studying are significantly more positive than those of other students (Asakawa & Csikszentmihalyi, 1998), and the links between academic motivation and various indices of happiness and adjustment are stronger among Asian adolescents than other youth (Asakawa & Csikszentmihalyi, 2000). Among Asian students more than their peers from other ethnic groups, then, engagement in academics is linked to positive emotion and well-being.

■ **The Success of Immigrants** Of course, as is the case with research on socioeconomic differences in educational achievement, research on ethnic differences indicates that there are large and important variations within as well as between ethnic groups. First, there are differences in educational achievement among youngsters from different countries of origin who may be classified together by researchers into the same larger ethnic group for purposes of statistical comparison. For example, although both groups are classified as Asian, Chinese American adolescents have much higher academic achievement than Filipino Americans; similarly, there are large differences in academic achievement among Puerto Rican, Cuban American, and Mexican American adolescents, all of whom are classified as Hispanic (Fuligni et al., 2009).

Second, studies of ethnic minority youngsters show that foreign-born adolescents, as well as those who are children of immigrants, tend to achieve more in school than do minority youngsters who are second- or third-generation Americans, a finding that has now emerged in many studies of Asian, Latino, and Caribbean youth (Fuligni et al., 2009; Kao, 1999; Kao & Tienda, 1995; Rong & Brown, 2001; Steinberg et al., 1996). One explanation for this has been that part of becoming acculturated to American society—at least among teenagers—may be learning to devalue academic success. There is also some evidence that the higher school achievement of immigrant youth—at least among adolescents who have immigrated from Mexico—may be due to the higher quality of the schooling they receive before coming to the United States (Padilla & Gonzalez, 2001). As psychologist Andrew Fuligni has pointed out, the exceptional achievement of immigrant youth is all the more remarkable in light of the fact that these adolescents typically have much greater family obligations—providing financial support to their parents, for instance—than their American-born peers (Fuligni & Witkow, 2004).

FOOD FOR THOUGHT

Many immigrant adolescents in the United States achieve more in school than their counterparts from the same ethnic group who were born in America—despite the fact that adolescents who are immigrants often arrive without proficiency in English or familiarity with American culture. How do you account for this?

Third, and most important, studies indicate that within all ethnic groups, students achieve more when they feel a sense of belonging to their school, when they see the connection between academic accomplishment and future success, when their friends and parents value and support educational achievement, and when their parents are effective monitors of their children's behavior and schooling (Alva, 1993; C. S. Chen et al., 1996; Conchas, 2001; Connell, Spencer, & Aber, 1994; D. Ford and Harris, 1996; Luthar, 1994; Murdock, 1994; Reyes & Jason, 1993; Steinberg et al., 1996). There is also some evidence that having a positive role model who is the same sex and from the same ethnic group can help facilitate adolescents' academic success (Zirkel, 2002).

CHANGES IN EDUCATIONAL ACHIEVEMENT OVER TIME

As we noted in Chapter 6, more students are going on to postsecondary education today than ever before. Today, three fourths of high school graduates enroll in college, two thirds of them immediately after graduation (National Center for Education Statistics, 2009). Although ethnic differences in educational attainment have narrowed over the past 40 years, there remain substantial gaps in attainment between White and non-White individuals, and especially between White and Hispanic individuals. Thus, whereas about 30% of all White adults ages 25 and over, and 53% of all Asian adults of this age, are college graduates, only 20% of Black adults and only 13% of Hispanic adults are (U.S. Census Bureau, 2009a). (There is considerable variation within the Hispanic population in rates of college graduation, however—only 9% of Mexican American adults ages 25 and older are college graduates, compared with 16% of Puerto Rican adults and 27% of Cuban American adults.) Discrepancies in rates of high school graduation between Hispanic and non–Hispanic Americans are also substantial—86% of White adults have completed high school, compared with 82% of Blacks and 88% of Asian Americans, but only 60% of Hispanic adults have (U.S. Census Bureau, 2010). In light of the rapidly increasing size of the Latino population in the United States, the gap in educational attainment between Latinos and non-Latinos is one of the most important challenges facing American educational institutions.

■ **More Schooling, But Less Learning** Trends in academic achievement (what students know) have not paralleled trends in educational attainment (how many years of schooling they have completed), however. In other words, although more students are staying in school longer, they are not necessarily learning more. For example, as Figure 12.4 indicates, between 1970 and 1980, average scores on the Scholastic Assessment Test (SAT) declined by about 35 points on the verbal portion and 20 points on the math. Scores remained more or less flat between 1980 and 1990, when math

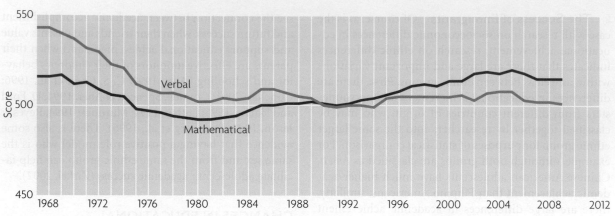

FIGURE 12.4   Changes in SAT scores over time. (College Board, 2009)

(but not verbal) scores began to rise; in fact, verbal scores dropped between 2004 and 2006. Moreover, the gap in SAT scores between Black and Hispanic students on the one hand, and Asian and White students on the other, remains substantial (Berends, Lucas, & Penaloza, 2008; College Board, 2009).

The relatively poor showing of American adolescents on standardized tests of achievement has been carefully documented in a series of reports based on the **National Assessment of Educational Progress (NAEP).** This national assessment of student achievement is conducted by the federal government in order to track trends in educational achievement over time. Because the NAEP tests have been administered regularly for nearly 40 years, it is possible to compare the achievement levels of today's adolescents with their counterparts 4 decades ago.

FOOD FOR THOUGHT

Why do you think it has been so difficult to improve the educational achievement of American youth?

According to recent NAEP reports, adolescent achievement in reading, writing, math, and science has improved only slightly among 13-year-olds and not at all among 17-year-olds over the past 40 years, despite massive national efforts at education reform. Contemporary 17-year-olds, for example, score no better than their counterparts did in the early 1970s in reading or math, and *worse* than their counterparts did in science.

National Assessment of Educational Progress (NAEP)   A periodic testing of American 4th-, 8th-, and 12th-graders by the federal government, used to track achievement.

Among 13-year-olds, reading scores in 2008 were marginally better than they had been in the 1970s, and science scores showed no improvement between 1970 and 2000. In fact, science scores actually declined in the late 1990s and have remained flat since then. The only bit of good news has been in math scores among 13-year-olds, with scores improving steadily since the 1970s (Grigg, Lauko, & Brockway, 2006; Rampey, Dion, & Donahue, 2009).

Perhaps more importantly, most analyses of the NAEP data indicate that the modest gains in achievement that have occurred during recent years have been in relatively simple skills. In reading and writing, for example, although more than half of all American 13-year-olds today can read well enough to be able to search for specific information and can make generalizations from reading material, only 10% can understand and summarize relatively complicated information. Only one third are able to read or write at their grade level, and fewer than one third are able to write a persuasive essay. The news is even more dismal with regard to 12th-graders: 25% cannot even write the simplest of essays, and only 25% can write at their grade level (the other 50% fall somewhere between these two points). Only about one third of high school seniors can read at grade level or better.

Levels of achievement in math and science show a similarly worrisome pattern. The picture is rosier among 13-year-olds than 17-year-olds, but, as the saying goes, everything is relative. For example, much has been made of the improved math performance of 13-year-olds, and while this is technically true, the fact remains that fewer than one third of eighth-graders are performing at grade level (J. Lee, Grigg, & Dion, 2007). The data are even more depressing with respect to older students. Thus, while virtually all 17-year-olds can add, subtract, multiply, and divide using whole numbers, only half can perform computations with decimals, fractions, and percentages and solve simple equations, and only

6% can do basic algebra. And according to the latest NAEP data, the low level of science achievement among American students is equally alarming: Fewer than one third of 8th-graders, and fewer than one fifth of 12th-graders, score at grade level. The last time the science test was administered, more than 40% of 8th-graders and nearly half of all seniors scored in the lowest possible category (Grigg, Lauko, & Brockway, 2006).

As is the case in rates of high school graduation and SAT scores, the gap in achievement test performance among ethnic groups narrowed during the 1970s, but a wide disparity still exists. The achievement gap did not shrink at all during the 1980s, widened a bit during the 1990s, and has not changed since then (Rampey, Dion, & Donahue, 2009). About 3 times as many White and Asian students score in the proficient range in writing, for example, as do Black students, and nearly twice as many White and Asian students score in the proficient range as do Hispanic students. The gaps are even larger in math—about 8 times as many White and Asian students are competent in algebra as are Black or Hispanic students (National Center for Education Statistics, 2006b). Obviously, this gap has important implications for the labor market success of adolescents from different ethnic groups.

■ **International Competitions** Although the poor achievement test performance of Black and Latino students is certainly cause for concern, there is no reason to be sanguine about the performance of White high school students. Since the 1970s, their achievement test scores have remained more or less stagnant, and U.S. scores on standardized tests of math and science are mediocre in comparison with scores of other industrialized countries. More interestingly, the gap between American students' performance and that of students from other countries widens as they move from elementary to middle to high school. That is, when elementary school students from around the world are compared, American students fare just about as well as students from other countries. When middle school students are compared, Americans perform more poorly than their counterparts from most industrialized Asian countries, but at a level comparable to young adolescents from most western European countries, and considerably better than adolescents from less developed nations (National Center for Education Statistics, 2009). But when the comparison focuses on high school students, the gap between the United States and other countries becomes substantial (J. Schmidt, 2003).

The relatively poor performance of American high school students in international competitions persists despite the fact that spending on education in the United States is among the world's highest (Walberg, 1998). Despite how much is spent, nearly one third of entering college freshmen in the United States require some sort of remedial education in order to do college-level work; the figure is even higher at community colleges. As a result, employers and postsecondary educational institutions alike today devote vast amounts of money to remedial education—colleges and universities spend an estimated $2.5 billion annually covering subject matter that students should have mastered before graduating from high school. And, as astounding as it may sound, more than 80% of college students enrolled in remedial education graduated from high school with a GPA of 3.0 or better (Strong American Schools, 2008).

If more American students are remaining in high school, and so many are going on to college, why are their achievement test scores so low according to absolute, historical, and international standards? Experts suggest several reasons: that teachers are not spending enough time on basic instruction in the classroom; that there has been a pervasive decline in the difficulty of textbooks; that parents are not encouraging academic pursuits at home; that students are not spending sufficient time on their studies outside of school; that students are permitted to choose what courses they take; and that students know that, thanks to "grade inflation," they can earn good grades without working very hard (D. Hayes, Wolfer, & Wolfe, 1996; Owen, 1995; Public Agenda, 1997; J. Schmidt, 2003; Steinberg, 2003).

DROPPING OUT OF HIGH SCHOOL

There was a time when leaving high school before graduating did not have the dire consequences that it does today. With changes in the labor force, however, have come changes in the educational requirements for entry into the world of work. Today, educational attainment is a powerful predictor of adult occupational success and earnings. Not surprisingly, high school dropouts are far more likely than graduates to live at or near the poverty level, to experience unemployment, to depend on government-subsidized income maintenance programs, to become pregnant while still a teenager, and to be involved in delinquent and criminal activity (Manlove, 1998; Rumberger, 1995).

Because there are different ways of counting dropouts, different studies often report very different figures. For example, many students drop out of school temporarily but return in their early 20s and obtain a diploma or GED—so while these students would be classified as dropouts at the age of 17, they would be classified as graduates if they were surveyed just a few years later. Based on the definition used by the U.S. Department of Education—the proportion of individuals aged 16 to 24 who are not enrolled in school and who have not earned a high school diploma or GED—the dropout rate has declined steadily over the past half century, to about 9% (National Center for Education Statistics, 2009). There are huge variations in

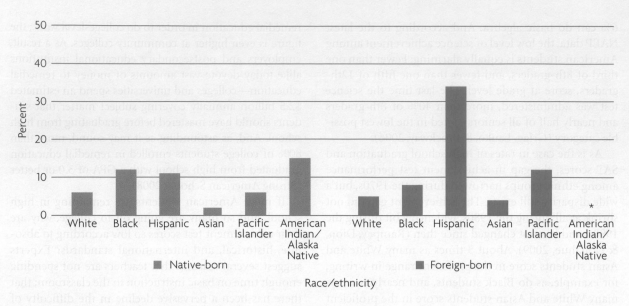

*Reporting standards not met (too few cases).

FIGURE 12.5 Dropout rates vary as a function of ethnicity and place of birth. (National Center for Education Statistics, 2009)

dropout rates from region to region, however; indeed, in some urban districts, well over 50% of students leave school prematurely (Alexander, Entwisle, & Kabbani, 2001). Black and American-born Hispanic youngsters drop out of high school at twice the rate of White youngsters, and 6 times more frequently than Asian youngsters, but foreign-born Hispanic youngsters drop out at more than 3 times the rate of American-born Hispanic youth (see Figure 12.5) (National Center for Education Statistics, 2009). One reason for this is the large proportion of foreign-born Hispanic youth who are not English-speaking; among these youth, a lack of proficiency in English is a major determinant of dropping out (Singh & Hernandez-Gantes, 1996; Stanton-Salazar & Dornbusch, 1995).

■ **Correlates of Dropping Out** Given the findings on educational achievement discussed earlier, the other correlates of dropping out come as no surprise. In addition to the higher prevalence of dropping out among foreign-born Hispanic youngsters, adolescents who leave high school before graduating are more likely to come from lower socioeconomic levels, poor communities, large families, single-parent families, permissive or disengaged families, and households where little reading material is available. In short, adolescents who drop out of school are more likely to come from backgrounds with limited financial, social, and cultural capital (Alexander et al., 2001; L. E. Davis, Ajzen, Saunders, & Williams, 2002; Pong & Ju, 2000; Rumberger, 1995).

Coupled with this disadvantage in background, adolescents who drop out of high school also are more

likely to have a history of poor school performance, low school involvement, multiple changes of schools, poor performance on standardized tests of achievement and intelligence, negative school experiences, and a variety of behavioral problems, some of which contribute to academic failure and some of which result from it (Battin-Pearson et al., 2000; Crosnoe, 2006; W. Jordan, Lara, & McPartland, 1996; Kasen, Cohen, & Brook, 1998; Rumberger & Larson, 1998). Many high school dropouts had to repeat one or more grades in elementary school; indeed, having been held back is one of the strongest predictors of dropping out (Janosz, LeBlanc, Boulerice, & Tremblay, 1997; Roderick, 1994; Rumberger, 1995).

In other words, dropping out of high school is not so much a discrete decision made during the adolescent years as it is the culmination of a long process (Alexander et al., 2001; Garnier, Stein, & Jacobs, 1997; Sweeten, Bushway, & Paternoster, 2009). Specific factors may instigate a student's final decision to leave school—a suspension for misbehavior, a failed course, an unintended pregnancy, the lure of a job—but by and large, dropping out is a process characterized by a history of repeated academic failure and increasing alienation from school (W. Jordan et al., 1996). While programs designed to enhance adolescents' academic skills have been largely unsuccessful in preventing dropping out, one approach that has met with success has focused on involving at-risk adolescents in service learning and in guided discussions of their life options, which may help them see how important it is to graduate from high school (J. Allen, Philliber, Herrling, & Kuperminc, 1997).

In some urban school districts, well over 50 percent of students drop out of high school.

Although adolescents who drop out of school often share certain characteristics in common (for example, a history of poor school performance), there is nevertheless diversity within this population. According to one extensive study of Canadian students (Janosz, LeBlanc, Boulerice, & Tremblay, 2000), there are at least four distinct groups of dropouts: (1) quiet dropouts (whose histories and personal characteristics actually look very similar to those of students who do not drop out of school, but who appear somewhat withdrawn—they almost seem to "fade out" rather than drop out, perhaps as a result of depression), (2) disengaged dropouts (whose dropping out appears mainly to be the result of low commitment to school and poor academic motivation), (3) low-achiever dropouts (whose dropping out is primarily the result of very poor school performance), and (4) maladjusted dropouts (whose dropping out is part of a larger constellation of behavioral and psychological problems). The idea that different developmental histories lead to dropping out is important to the design of preventive interventions, because it suggests that different sorts of programs may work for different sorts of students. For instance, dropping out early in high school is more likely to be the result of disciplinary problems at school, whereas dropping out later in high school is more likely to be driven by the desire to work (Stearns & Glennie, 2006). Other studies indicate that it

is important to distinguish between students who temporarily drop out of school but return at some later point and obtain their GED—as do between one third and one half of all dropouts—and those who leave and never return (Entwisle, Alexander, & Olson, 2004).

FOOD FOR THOUGHT

Based on what we know about the causes and consequences of dropping out, what steps should be taken to reduce the dropout rate?

School Factors Although most research on the causes of dropping out has focused on characteristics of adolescents who leave school prematurely, some studies have focused on the schools that dropouts leave (Rumberger & Palardy, 2005). In general, dropping out is less likely from schools where the environment is orderly, where academic pursuits are emphasized, and where the faculty is supportive and committed (V. Lee & Burkam, 2003). Students who are at particularly high risk of dropping out (low-achieving, economically disadvantaged youth) are helped especially by having teachers who are sources of social support and guidance (Croninger & Lee, 2001). Dropout rates are also higher in larger schools that group students according to ability and that fail a relatively high proportion of students in the early years of high school (Bryk & Thum, 1989; Roderick & Camburn, 1999). Consistent with this, some research suggests that dropout rates may be reduced in some cases by permitting students who are having educational difficulties to change schools, rather than leaving school altogether (V. Lee & Burkham, 1992). Although some educators have expressed concern about the recent trend toward toughening graduation requirements and ending **social promotion**—the practice of promoting students from one grade to the next on the basis of age rather than actual achievement—evaluations of policies such as the use of high school exit examinations to determine whether students can graduate show that they do not increase the rate of dropping out or differentially affect minority and White students (Bishop, 2001; Hoffer, 1997; Warren, Grodsky, & Lee, 2008; Warren & Jenkins, 2005).

RECAP

- Socioeconomic status is an extremely powerful influence on educational achievement. Generally, adolescents from higher social classes perform better in school and complete more years of schooling than do their less advantaged counterparts.
- Studies also indicate that there are ethnic differences in educational achievement above and beyond those attributable to socioeconomic status. In the United States, Asian adolescents outperform White students, who, in turn, do better than Black, Hispanic, or American Indian students. One reason for the superior performance of Asian students is that they are more likely to hold the sorts of beliefs about achievement that are predictive of success in school in all ethnic groups.
- The low level of educational achievement among American youth in general has been a concern for several decades. Although some gains in scores on standardized tests of achievement were reported during the mid-1980s, with the exception of early adolescents' math scores, achievement by and large has not improved since then, and American high school students continue to fare poorly in international comparisons.
- Dropouts are more likely than their peers to be foreign-born Hispanic youth, to come from economically disadvantaged backgrounds, to come from

single-parent homes, and to have had a poor record of educational achievement throughout their school years. Dropping out is not so much a decision that is made during adolescence as it is the culmination of a long process that begins early on.

Occupational Achievement

School, rather than work, is the setting in which achievement is most often studied by contemporary scholars interested in adolescence. Although many individuals in previous generations began their occupational careers during adolescence (and researchers devoted considerable attention to the study of career development in adolescence), this is very rare today in most industrialized societies, where the majority of individuals pursue some form of postsecondary education before entering into full-time work. With the exception of apprenticeships, which, as we noted in earlier chapters, are popular in only a handful of European countries, the work individuals perform during adolescence is rarely relevant to their future careers; as we saw in Chapter 7, it is mainly a means of earning spending money. Work experiences in adolescence, in general, have little or no impact on adolescents' plans or aspirations for adult work, especially among students from nonpoor families (Entwisle, Alexander, & Olson, 2005; M. Johnson, 2002), although it is possible that the small minority of adolescents who hold "good" jobs may learn something about their career interests from them. According to one recent analysis, fast-food, restaurant, and retail jobs provide the fewest opportunities to build career-related skills, whereas office and clerical jobs are among the best (Staff, Messersmith, & Schulenberg, 2009).

Although we often think of school and work as separate domains, achievement is one aspect of psychosocial development during adolescence that links them together. The number of years of schooling an individual completes is the single best indicator of his or her eventual occupational success (Arum & Hout, 1998). It is not simply that adolescents benefit in the labor force by having a high school diploma or a college degree. Although these credentials matter, research shows that each year of education—even without graduating—adds significantly to occupational success. In other words, individuals who have completed three years of college earn more money, on average, than individuals who have completed only one year, even though neither group has a college degree in hand.

Researchers who are interested in occupational achievement during adolescence have examined several

---

social promotion　The practice of promoting students from one grade to the next automatically, regardless of their school performance.

issues, including the ways in which young people make decisions about their careers and the influences on their occupational aspirations and expectations. We begin with a look at the development of adolescents' occupational plans.

THE DEVELOPMENT OF OCCUPATIONAL PLANS

The development of occupational plans during adolescence can be viewed in many respects as paralleling, or even as part of, the identity development process (Skorikov & Vondracek, 2007; Staff et al., 2009). As with developing a coherent sense of identity, the development of occupational plans follows a sequence that involves an examination of one's traits, abilities, and interests; a period of experimentation with different work roles; and an integration of influences from one's past (primarily, identification with familial role models) with one's hopes for the future. And as is also the case with identity development, the development of an occupational identity is profoundly influenced by the social environment in which it takes place.

According to many theories of occupational development, occupational plans form in stages, with late adolescence being an important time for the crystallization of plans that are more realistic, less based on fantasy, and more grounded in the adolescent's assessment of his or her talents. According to one influential theory (Super, 1967), between ages 14 and 18, individuals first begin to crystallize a vocational preference. During this period of **crystallization,** they begin to formulate ideas about appropriate work and begin to develop occupational self-conceptions that will guide subsequent educational decisions. They may also make decisions about what sort of work they *don't* want to do.

Although adolescents may not settle on a particular career at this point, they do begin to narrow their choices according to their interests, values, and abilities. One adolescent may decide that she wants a career in which she works with people. Another may decide that he wants a career in which he can earn a great deal of money. A third may think about a career in science. A fourth is not sure what she wants to do, but knows that she doesn't want to be cooped up in an office. During this period, the adolescent begins to seek out information on her or his tentative choice and make plans for the future. The process is reminiscent of the sort of role experimentation described by Erikson in his theory of adolescent identity development, which we discussed in Chapter 8. In both cases, during middle adolescence, alternative identities are considered and evaluated on the basis of exploration, experimentation, and self-examination (Staff et al., 2009).

Following the period of crystallization is a period of **specification,** occurring roughly between the ages of 18 and 21, or during the college years. During this period, the young person recognizes the need to specify his or her vocational interests and begins to seek appropriate information to accomplish this. In many regards, a similar process is followed during the stage of specification as during the stage of crystallization: Alternatives are considered, information is sought, decisions are made, and preferences are consolidated. The chief difference, however, is that during the period of specification, more narrowly defined career pursuits within a general career category are considered (rather than general career categories themselves). For example, during the period of crystallization, an adolescent may decide to pursue a career in the field of mental health, without being able to specify a vocational preference within this general category. During the specification stage, he or she might begin to consider and compare a variety of careers within the mental health profession—social work, educational counseling, clinical psychology, psychiatry, and so on—and make choices among them.

Changes in the broader environment in which adolescents develop—in this case, changes in the need for and accessibility of higher education—have exerted a powerful influence on the developmental course of occupational planning. Although many theories of occupational plans originally focused on adolescence, changes in the labor force, requiring individuals to complete more and more education before beginning their careers, have made young adulthood a far more important phase than adolescence for the development of occupational plans. For many individuals, the crystallization of occupational plans may not take place until the final years of college, and the specification process may not even begin until after college graduation. As we saw in Chapter 3, many developmental challenges that in the past were faced during the teenage years are now delayed until the 20s.

INFLUENCES ON OCCUPATIONAL CHOICES

What makes one individual choose to become an attorney and another decide to be a teacher? Why do some students pursue careers in psychology while others major in information technology? Researchers have long been interested in the reasons that individuals end up in certain careers.

crystallization According to Super, the stage during which individuals, typically ages 14–18, first begin to formulate their ideas about appropriate occupations.

specification According to Super, the stage during which individuals, typically ages 18–21, first begin to consider narrowly defined occupational pursuits.

TABLE 12.1   People look for different things in a job. Which types of rewards are most important to you?

Type of Reward	Example
Extrinsic	Earning a good income
Security	Enjoying job stability
Intrinsic	Having opportunities for creativity
Influence	Wielding power over others
Altruistic	Helping others
Social	Enjoying one's coworkers
Leisure	Having opportunities for vacation or time off

■ **Work Values** Recent researchers interested in why people enter different occupational fields have examined the role of work values in the process of career selection. **Work values** refer to the sorts of rewards individuals seek from their jobs (e.g., M. Johnson, 2002). When you think about your future work, what will you look for in a job? For example, are you most interested in making a lot of money, in having a secure job, or in having a job that permits you to have a lot of vacation time? According to most theories of work values, seven basic types of work rewards define individuals' work values: extrinsic rewards (earning a high income), security (enjoying job stability), intrinsic rewards (being able to be creative or to learn things from work), influence (having authority over others or power over decision making), altruistic rewards (helping others), social rewards (working with people you like), and leisure (having an opportunity for free time or vacation). Individuals choose jobs based on the relative importance of these various work rewards to them (see Table 12.1).

Several writers have noted that many contemporary adolescents have unrealistic and overly ambitious ideas about the rewards they will derive from their future work. One set of authors noted that a very large proportion of adolescents aspire to levels of work rewards that they are highly unlikely to attain (Schneider & Stevenson, 1999). One specific problem is that adolescents tend to rate almost all work rewards very highly, optimistically believing that they can find jobs that satisfy multiple rewards simultaneously. When they actually enter their first full-time adult jobs, though, they soon discover that it is difficult, if not impossible, to have a career in which, say, one makes a lot of money, is creative, helps other people, enjoys job security, and has a lot of free time. Over the course of young adulthood, then, one of the most important changes that occurs in

the domain of occupational development is that individuals become both somewhat disillusioned and more focused on what they want from a job, abandoning the unrealistic notion that one can "have it all" (B. Roberts, O'Donnell, & Robins, 2004). As adolescents move into young adulthood, the degrees to which they value the extrinsic, altruistic, and social rewards of jobs, which are all strongly valued when individuals are seniors in high school, decline most dramatically, whereas the values they place on intrinsic rewards and job security, which are also strong at the end of high school, remain strong (M. Johnson, 2002) (see Figure 12.6).

There are important limitations to theories of career choice that are based solely on reward preferences assessed in adolescence, however. First, interests and abilities are not fixed during adolescence, but continue to develop and change during the adult years (M. Johnson, 2002). Indeed, one of the most important influences on personality development during adulthood is work itself. Thus, through working in a job that emphasizes certain personality characteristics, requires certain abilities, or provides certain types of rewards, individuals begin to change their personality, skills, and values. Consequently, a job that seems like a bad match during early adulthood may, over time, become a good match, as the individual grows and changes in response to the work environment. For example, someone may not be especially interested in a job that involves a lot of social interaction but may, because of a tight job market, end up in a teaching position after graduating from college. Over time, the more he interacts with students, the more appealing the interpersonal aspects of the job may become. Eventually, he may come to feel that having opportunities for social interaction on the job is very important.

A second problem with theories of career choice that emphasize adolescents' work values is that they may underestimate the importance of other factors that influence and shape vocational decisions, most importantly, the social context in which adolescents make career decisions (Staff et al., 2009). Many career decisions are influenced more by individuals' beliefs about what sorts of jobs are accessible or "appropriate" for them than by their interests and preferences (M. Johnson, 2002). It is all well and good, for example, for an adolescent to discover that he is well suited for a career in medicine, but the realization is of little value if his family cannot afford the cost of college or medical school. Or an adolescent girl may discover through taking a vocational preference test that she is well suited for work in the area of construction or building, but she may find that her parents, peers, teachers, and potential employers all discourage her from following this avenue of employment because they think it is not appropriate for women. One recent study found that early adolescent Mexican American girls, in particular, were more likely

work values   The particular sorts of rewards an individual looks for in a job (extrinsic, intrinsic, social, altruistic, security, influence, leisure).

than Black or White girls to have stereotypically female career goals (N. E. Hill, Ramirez, & Dumka, 2003).

Put most simply, career choices are not made solely on the basis of individual preference; they are the result of an interaction among individual preferences, social influences, and important forces in the broader social environment. It is to these influences and forces that we now turn.

■ The Influence of Parents and Peers

No influence on occupational choice is stronger than socioeconomic status, and as a result, adolescents' occupational ambitions and achievements are highly correlated with the ambitions and achievements of those around them (Dubow, Huesmann, Boxer, Pulkkinen, & Kokko, 2006). Youngsters from middle-class families are more likely than their less advantaged peers to aspire to and enter middle-class occupations. Socioeconomic status also influences work values, with individuals from higher classes more likely to value intrinsic rewards and influence and less likely to value extrinsic rewards and security. The importance of social class as a determinant of what people look for in their jobs is strong and constant throughout adolescence and young adulthood (M. Johnson, 2002).

A variety of explanations have been offered for the fit between adolescents' ambitions and the socioeconomic status of those around them. First, and perhaps most important, **occupational attainment**—the prestige or status an individual achieves in the world of work—depends strongly on educational attainment (Elmore, 2009). As we saw earlier, educational attainment is greatly influenced by socioeconomic status. Thus, because middle-class adolescents are likely to complete more years of schooling than their lower-class peers, economically advantaged adolescents are more likely to seek and enter higher-status occupations.

Second, middle-class parents, as noted earlier, are more likely to raise their children in ways that foster the development of strong achievement orientation and career exploration (Kracke, 2002). The development of achievement motivation, which has an impact on school performance, also has an impact on youngsters' occupational ambitions—both directly (in that individuals with strong needs for achievement will express these needs by aspiring to occupations that provide opportunities to achieve status or wealth) and indirectly, through the effects of achievement motivation on academic achievement (in that youngsters who are successful in school are likely to be encouraged to seek higher-status occupations and engage in identity exploration). Indeed, parents influence their adolescents' career aspirations mainly by influencing their educational achievement (Jodl et al., 2001).

Third, the same opportunities that favor economically advantaged youngsters in the world of education—

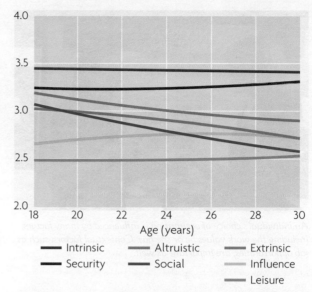

FIGURE 12.6 As adolescents move into young adulthood, the value they place on the extrinsic, altruistic, and social rewards of a job declines, whereas the value they place on intrinsic job rewards and job security remains strong. (Johnson, 2002)

better facilities, more opportunities for enrichment, greater accessibility of higher education—also favor middle-class youngsters in the world of work. Because their parents, for example, are more likely to work in positions of power and leadership, middle-class youngsters often have important family connections and sources of information about the world of work that are less available to youngsters from poorer families. In addition, coming from a family that is economically well off may provide an adolescent with more time to explore career options and to wait for an especially desirable position, rather than having to take the first job that becomes available out of economic necessity.

Fourth, parents, siblings, and other important sources of influence serve as models for adolescents' occupational choices (Barber & Eccles, 1992). Although some young people establish career choices through the explicit rejection of their parents' careers, the weight of the evidence suggests that adolescents' and parents' vocations are more similar than different, particularly when the adolescent's family relationships have been warm and close and when strong identifications have formed between the adolescent and his or her parents.

Finally, parents—and, to a lesser extent, peers—influence adolescents' occupational plans by establishing a value context in which certain occupational

occupational attainment A measure of achievement based on the status or prestige of the job an individual holds.

An individual's choice of occupation is influenced by many factors, including the work values he or she has. Contextual factors, such as job opportunities, are important as well.

choices are encouraged and others are discouraged (Kohn, 1977). Middle-class families and middle-class schools encourage children to value autonomy, self-direction, and independence—three features that are more likely to be found in middle-class than in working-class jobs. The children are told, implicitly and explicitly, how important it is to have freedom, power, and status. Adolescents who have been raised to value attributes that are characteristic of middle-class jobs, not surprisingly, will seek those attributes when they plan their careers. They will look for jobs that offer independence and power. In working-class families, in contrast, children are more likely to be raised to value obedience and conformity—two characteristics that are highly valued in most working-class jobs. For youngsters from this socioeconomic background, jobs that appeal to these values will be relatively more attractive. They will have been raised to value such things as job security and not having to worry too much about making high-pressured decisions. Indeed, to many working-class youngsters, the high-stress world of the business executive is not at all an attractive career possibility.

▌ **The Broader Context of Occupational Choice** Adolescents' occupational choices are made, of course, within a broader social context that profoundly influences the nature of their plans (Staff et al., 2009). Whereas in the past, for example, female adolescents had lower educational and occupational expectations than males, the reverse is true today (Mello, 2008). At different times, different employment opportunities arise, and young people—particularly by the time they reach the end of their formal schooling—are often very aware of the prospects for employment in different fields. Indeed, one study of inner-city youngsters found that many had developed ideas about their future

job prospects by the time they were in second grade (T. Cook et al., 1996). Understandably, young people often tailor their plans in response to what they perceive as the future needs and demands of the labor market and the acceptability of given occupational choices within their community. In addition, whether an adolescent's occupational expectations are actually realized depends on many factors that are not in his or her control (as anyone graduating during the economic downturn of 2008–2009 could certainly attest).

FOOD FOR THOUGHT

Think about your own occupational development. What factors have most influenced your choices? How did your occupational plans change during adolescence? How similar are they now to the ones you had when you were just entering high school?

Unfortunately, adolescents also tailor their plans based on their beliefs regarding which jobs society says are "acceptable" for individuals of particular social class, ethnicity, or sex (M. Johnson, 2002). Despite the substantial liberalization in sex-role stereotypes that has occurred during the past 40 years, for example, adolescent girls' vocational choices still tend to be concentrated among jobs that have historically been occupied by women, such as secretarial work, teaching, and nursing, and they are more oriented toward occupations that involve working with people and that allow the expression of compassion and altruism (Beutel & Marini, 1995; Marini, Fan, Finley, & Beutel, 1996). In contrast, relatively fewer adolescent girls plan to enter jobs in which the main tasks involve working with things, rather than people, as is the case in science or engineering (Jozefowicz, Barber, Eccles, & Mollasis, 1994). Girls are more likely than boys to value the intrinsic, altruistic, and social rewards of work, whereas boys are more likely to value influence and leisure; sex differences in the value placed on extrinsic rewards are small (M. Johnson, 2002). Moreover, many more adolescent girls than boys express concern about having to balance family and work demands in adulthood, and this further affects their occupational decision making, since they may be reluctant to pursue careers that they believe will interfere with family life (Cinamon & Rich, 2002). Perhaps because of this, adolescent boys' occupational expectations are predictive of what they actually end up doing as adults, whereas this is not the case for adolescent girls (Mello, 2008).

One problem faced by all young people in making career plans is obtaining accurate information about the labor market needs of the future and the appropriate means of pursuing positions in various fields. The majority of young people do not have educational plans that are consistent with the educational requirements of the jobs they hope to enter, and many adolescents are overly optimistic about their chances for success (Chang et al., 2006; Schneider & Stevenson, 1999). One goal of career educators is to help adolescents make more informed and more realistic choices about their careers and to free them from stereotypes that constrain their choices. Career counselors, especially on college campuses, have come to play an increasingly important role in individuals' career decision making, because the rapid pace at which the labor market changes has made it less likely that adolescents will be able to obtain accurate information from their family (Staff et al., 2009).

RECAP

- The development of occupational plans follows a process that is similar to the process of identity development, with a period of experimentation and exploration leading to increasingly more specific plans.
- Adolescents' career choices are influenced by a number of factors, including their work values, their social background, and their perceptions of the labor market and their potential place within it.
- As is the case with educational achievement, occupational attainment is strongly influenced by socioeconomic status.
- Occupational plans are also influenced by the broader context, including adolescents' perceptions of what occupations are "appropriate" for them given their sex, ethnicity, and social background.

Psychosocial Problems in Adolescence

ALTHOUGH THE VAST MAJORITY of young people move through the adolescent years without experiencing major difficulty, some encounter serious psychological and behavioral problems that disrupt not only their lives but also the lives of those around them. Problems such as substance abuse, delinquency, and depression—while certainly not the norm during adolescence—do affect a worrisome number of teenagers. Moreover, these problems indirectly touch the lives of all of us, either directly, through the personal contact we may have with a troubled young person, or indirectly, through increased taxes for community services or heightened anxiety about the safety of our neighborhoods. In this final chapter, we look at some of the more serious psychological problems we typically associate with adolescence.

Although the stereotype of adolescence is one of a developmental period riddled with difficulty, as you now know, this is not an accurate portrayal. We should not gloss over the fact that many healthy adolescents at one time or another experience self-doubt, family squabbles, academic setbacks, or broken hearts, of course. But it is important to keep in mind as we look at psychosocial problems during adolescence that there is an important distinction between the normative, and usually transitory, difficulties encountered by many young people—and by many adults, for that matter—and the serious psychosocial problems experienced by a relatively small minority of youth.

Some General Principles About Problems in Adolescence

The mass media like nothing more than to paint extreme pictures of the world in which we live. This exaggerated worldview is obvious in the presentation of teenage problem behavior. Rarely are popular portrayals of behavioral disorders, psychological distress, or drug use accurate: A breakup with a boyfriend is followed that evening by a suicide attempt. An after-school prank develops into a life of crime. A weekend of heavy drinking fades into a commercial, and when the program returns, the adolescent is on his way to a life of addiction, delinquency, and school failure. Those of you for whom adolescence was not that long ago know that these "facts" about adolescent problem behavior are rarely true. But we are so often bombarded with images of young people in trouble that it is easy to be fooled into believing that "adolescence" equals "problems."

One of the purposes of this chapter is to put these problems in perspective. It is therefore helpful, before we look at several specific sorts of problems in detail, to lay out some general principles about adolescent psychosocial problems that apply to a range of issues.

▌ Most Problems Reflect Transitory Experimentation First, we need to distinguish between occasional experimentation and enduring patterns of dangerous or troublesome behavior. Research shows that rates of occasional, usually harmless, experimentation far exceed rates of enduring problems. For example, the majority of adolescents experiment with alcohol sometime before high school graduation, and the majority will have been drunk at least once; but, as we'll

see, relatively few teenagers develop drinking problems or permit alcohol to adversely affect their school or personal relationships. Similarly, although the vast majority of teenagers do something during adolescence that is against the law, very few of these young people go on to have criminal careers. In a period of development during which it is normal, even expected, that individuals will seek independence and explore themselves and their relationships with others, it is hardly surprising that some of the experimentation in which individuals engage is risky (A. Siegel & Scovill, 2000). In fact, adolescents who experiment occasionally with risky behavior report a quality of life that is more similar to that reported by adolescents who abstain from risk taking entirely than it is to the quality of life reported by frequent risk takers (Topolski et al., 2001).

FOOD FOR THOUGHT

Why do you think stereotypes of problem behavior in adolescence differ from reality? What are some dangers of holding on to the stereotypic view?

▌ Not All Problems Begin in Adolescence Second, we need to distinguish between problems that have their origins and onset during adolescence, and those that have their roots during earlier periods of development. It is true, for example, that some teenagers fall into patterns of criminal or delinquent behavior during adolescence, and for this reason, we tend to associate delinquency with the adolescent years. But most teenagers who have recurrent problems with the law had problems at home and at school from an early age;

It is important to differentiate between occasional experimentation with risky or unhealthful activities and enduring patterns of troublesome behavior.

in some samples of delinquents, the problems were evident as early as preschool (Farrington, 2009). Many individuals who develop depression during adolescence suffered from other types of psychological distress, such as excessive anxiety, as children (Graber & Sontag, 2009). In other words, simply because a problem may be displayed *during* adolescence does not mean that it is a problem *of* adolescence.

Most Problems Do Not Persist Into Adulthood

Third, it is important to remember that many, although not all, of the problems experienced by adolescents are relatively transitory in nature and are resolved by the beginning of adulthood, with few long-term repercussions in most cases. Substance abuse, delinquency, and eating disorders are three good examples of problems that tend to follow this pattern: Rates of drug and alcohol use, delinquency, and disordered eating are all higher within the adolescent population than in the adult population, but most individuals who abused drugs and alcohol, committed delinquent acts, or were bulimic as teenagers grow up to be sober, law-abiding adults without eating disorders. Individuals for whom problem behavior persists into adulthood are likely to have had a problematic childhood as well as a problem-

atic adolescence. The fact that some of the problems of adolescence seem to fade away with time does not make their prevalence during adolescence any less significant, but it should be kept in mind when rhetoric about the inevitable decline of civilization at the hands of contemporary youth is bandied about.

Problems During Adolescence Are Not Caused by Adolescence

Finally, problem behavior during adolescence is virtually never a direct consequence of the normative changes of adolescence itself. Popular theories about "raging hormones" causing oppositional or deviant behavior have no scientific support whatsoever, for example, nor do the widely held beliefs that problem behaviors are manifestations of an inherent need to rebel against authority or that bizarre behavior results from an identity crisis. As you learned in previous chapters, the hormonal changes of puberty have only a modest direct effect on adolescent behavior; rebellion during adolescence is atypical, not normal; and few adolescents experience a tumultuous identity crisis. When a young person exhibits a serious psychosocial problem, such as depression, the worst possible interpretation is that it is a normal part of growing up. It is more likely a sign that something is wrong.

RECAP

- The vast majority of individuals do not develop serious psychological or social problems during the adolescent years, but a significant minority do.
- It is important to distinguish between experimentation and enduring patterns of behavior, between problems that have their origins during adolescence and those that do not, and between problems that are transitory and those that persist into adulthood.
- Serious problem behavior during adolescence is almost never a direct consequence of the normative changes of adolescence itself.

Psychosocial Problems: Their Nature and Covariation

Clinical practitioners (psychologists, psychiatrists, social workers, and counselors) and other experts on the development and treatment of psychosocial problems during adolescence typically distinguish among three broad categories of problems: substance abuse, internalizing disorders, and externalizing disorders (Achenbach & Edelbrock, 1987). **Substance abuse** refers to the maladaptive use of drugs, including legal drugs like alcohol or nicotine; illegal drugs like marijuana, cocaine, and ecstasy; and prescription drugs such as stimulants or sedatives. **Internalizing disorders** are those in which the young person's problems are turned inward and are manifested in emotional and cognitive distress, such as depression, anxiety, or phobia. **Externalizing disorders** are those in which the young person's problems are turned outward and are manifested in behavioral problems (some writers use the expression "acting out" to refer to this set of problems). Common externalizing problems during adolescence are delinquency, antisocial aggression, and truancy. Some adolescents also have problems that do not fit neatly into one of these three categories, such as academic problems (for example, low motivation, poor attention) or peer problems (for example, low popularity, poor social skills) (Wångby, Bergman, & Magnusson, 1999).

Although we often think of adolescent substance abuse as an externalizing disorder, research indicates that it is just as likely to accompany depression and other internalizing disorders as it is to be a part of "acting out" behavior. We are simply more likely to be aware of substance abuse problems when they are seen among adolescents who are antisocial (such as a rowdy group of drunk delinquent youth) than when they occur in the context of internalizing problems (such as a depressed teenager who drinks herself to sleep each night). Because substance abuse problems co-occur, or are **comorbid,** with both externalizing and internalizing problems, and because many adolescents who experiment with drugs have neither internalizing nor externalizing problems, we look at substance abuse as a separate category of problem behavior.

While the distinction between internalizing disorders and externalizing disorders is useful for organizing information about psychosocial problems during adolescence, it is important to bear in mind that some adolescents experience problems in both domains simultaneously. That is, some adolescents who engage in

delinquency or show other behavior problems also suffer from depression (J. M. Beyers & Loeber, 2003; Capaldi, 1992; Garnefski & Diekstra, 1997; Hinden, Compas, Howell, & Achenbach, 1997; Kiesner, 2002; Sheidow et al., 2008). And, as noted earlier, many depressed or anxious adolescents as well as many antisocial adolescents also abuse drugs and alcohol (Armstrong & Costello, 2002; Garnefski & Diekstra, 1997; Flisher et al., 2000; B. Henry et al., 1993; Repetto, Zimmerman, & Caldwell, 2008). Many researchers believe that it is important to distinguish among adolescents who exhibit one specific problem without any others (for example, depressed adolescents who do not have other internalizing or externalizing problems), adolescents who exhibit more than one problem within the same general category (for example, violent delinquent youth or anxious-depressed youth), and adolescents who exhibit both internalizing and externalizing problems (for example, depressed delinquents). These adolescents may have followed very different pathways to deviance and may require very different types of treatment. In general, studies show that multiproblem teenagers have had far worse family experiences than those with one problem (Aseltine, Gore, & Colten, 1998; Capaldi, 1992; Ge, Best, Conger, & Simons, 1996). Co-occurring internalizing and externalizing problems are more often seen among females than among males (Ritakallio et al., 2008). One explanation for this is that conduct problems mean different things when they are displayed by boys and girls. Among boys, conduct problems are, in some senses, an extreme version of behavior that is considered "normal" among males (who are expected to be more aggressive and unruly). In contrast, for a girl to be diagnosed with a conduct problem, she has to depart in a very significant way from the norm. Accordingly, girls who have externalizing problems are usually much more disturbed in a wide variety of ways, including being depressed or anxious. In contrast, many boys with conduct problems are "normal" in other respects (Wiesner & Kim, 2006).

COMORBIDITY OF EXTERNALIZING PROBLEMS

One of the reasons it is helpful to differentiate between internalizing and externalizing disorders is that the specific problems within each broad category are often highly intercorrelated. Delinquency, for example, is often associated with problems such as truancy, defiance, sexual promiscuity, academic difficulties, and violence (Farrington, 2009). All these problems are different sorts of manifestations of a lack of impulse control, and adolescents who engage in these behaviors are often described as "undercontrolled" (Robins, John, Caspi, Moffitt, & Stouthamer-Loeber, 1996; Young et al., 2009).

---

substance abuse   The misuse of alcohol or other drugs to a degree that causes problems in the individual's life.

internalizing disorders   Psychosocial problems that are manifested in a turning of the symptoms inward, as in depression or anxiety.

externalizing disorders   Psychosocial problems that are manifested in a turning of the symptoms outward, as in aggression or delinquency.

comorbid   Co-occurring, as when an individual has more than one problem at the same time.

FOOD FOR THOUGHT

How might the recognition that there is considerable comorbidity of problems in adolescence change our approaches to prevention and intervention?

▌ **Problem Behavior Syndrome**   Researchers have devoted a great deal of attention to studying the covariation among externalizing problems during adolescence in general, and a number of theories about the origins of what some experts call **problem behavior syndrome** have been proposed. The most widely cited perspective, now more than 30 years old, comes from the work of social psychologist Richard Jessor and his colleagues (Jessor & Jessor, 1977). According to Jessor, the underlying cause of externalizing problems during adolescence is unconventionality in both the adolescent's personality and the social environment (Donovan & Jessor, 1985; Menard & Huizinga, 1994). Unconventional individuals are tolerant of deviance in general, are not highly connected to educational or religious institutions, and are very liberal in their views. Unconventional environments are those in which a large number of individuals share these same attitudes. Unconventional individuals in unconventional environments are more likely to engage in a wide variety of risk-taking behavior, including experimentation with illegal drugs, risky sex, delinquent activity, and even risky driving (Brack, Brack, & Orr, 1996; M. L. Cooper, Wood, Orcutt, & Albino, 2003; Fergusson & Lynskey, 1996; Jakobsen, Rise, Aas, & Anderssen, 1997; Spingarn & DuRant, 1996). A recent comparison of adolescents in the United States and China found that the same factors heighten or diminish adolescents' risk for problem behavior in both countries (Jessor et al., 2003).

Although Jessor's theory does not specifically hypothesize about the origins of unconventionality, a number of possibilities have been proposed. One set of theories emphasizes the biological underpinnings of risk taking or unconventionality and argues that a predisposition toward deviance may actually be inherited (e.g., Mednick, Gabrielli, & Hitchings, 1987; Rowe, Rodgers, Meseck-Bushey, & St. John, 1989). A second view stresses biologically based differences (either inherited or acquired through experience) among individuals in arousal, sensation seeking, and fearlessness (e.g., Ortiz & Raine, 2004; Zuckerman, 1983). Yet a third view emphasizes the early family context in which deviance-prone children are reared and frames problem behavior as a sort of adaptive response to a hostile environment (Belsky, Steinberg, & Draper, 1991).

▌ **Problem Clusters**   An alternative to the view that an underlying trait drives all problem behavior has

been proposed by sociologist Denise Kandel. She and her associates argue that different types of deviance have distinctly different origins, but that involvement in a given problem behavior may itself lead to involvement in a second one. Thus, problem behaviors may cluster together not because of a common underlying trait like unconventionality, but because involvement in some problematic activities (such as drug and alcohol use) leads to involvement in others (such as delinquency) (Bingham & Shope, 2004; Hussong, Curran, & Moffitt, 2004; Malone, Taylor, & Marmorstein, 2004; W. Mason & Windle, 2002; Ridenour et al., 2002; Rohde, Lewinsohn, Kahler, Seeley, & Brown, 2001). Some writers have talked about "cascading" effects, where one sort of problem leads to another, which leads to a third (Burrell & Roosa, 2009; Ingoldsby et al., 2006; Mun, Windle, & Schainker, 2008; Siebenbruner, Englund, Egeland, & Hudson, 2006). For example, one recent analysis of individuals followed from preadolescence into adulthood found that externalizing problems in childhood led to academic difficulties in adolescence, which, in turn, led to internalizing problems in adulthood (see Figure 13.1) (Masten et al., 2005). Similarly, a longitudinal study of Black youth found that problems in school led to drug and alcohol use, which led to dropping out (M. Zimmerman & Schmeelk-Cone, 2003).

▌ **Social Control Theory**   According to a third view, **social control theory** (Gottfredson & Hirschi, 1990), individuals who do not have strong bonds to society's institutions—such as the family, school, or workplace—will be likely to deviate and behave unconventionally in a variety of ways. This view suggests that the apparent clustering of different problem behaviors may stem not from a problem "in" the person (such as inherent unconventionality or a biological predisposition toward risky behavior), but from an underlying weakness in the attachment of certain youngsters to society. This underlying problem leads to the development of an unconventional attitude, to membership in an unconventional peer group, or to involvement in one or several problem behaviors that may set a chain of problem activities in motion. Social control theory helps to explain why behavior problems are not just clustered together but are far more prevalent among poor, inner-city, minority youngsters.

▌ **Overstating the Case?**   Finally, a number of researchers stress that we should be careful about

---

problem behavior syndrome   The covariation among various types of externalizing disorders believed to result from an underlying trait of unconventionality.

social control theory   A theory of delinquency that links deviance with the absence of bonds to society's main institutions.

FIGURE 13.1 One explanation for comorbidity is that problems in one domain can create problems in another. (Masten et al., 2005)

| Externalizing problems in childhood | → | Academic problems in adolescence | → | Internalizing problems in adulthood |

overstating the case for a single problem behavior "syndrome" (Farrell, Sullivan, Esposito, Meyer, & Valois, 2005; Resnicow, Ross-Gaddy, & Vaughan, 1995; Willoughby, Chalmers, & Busseri, 2004). They note that although engaging in one type of problem behavior increases the likelihood of engaging in another, the overlap among behavior problems is far from perfect. Indeed, in one study, it was found that the vast majority of delinquents are *not* serious drug users (D. Elliott, Huizinga, & Menard, 1989). Other studies suggest that it is important to differentiate between problem behavior that adults disapprove of but that many adolescents consider normative (such as smoking, drinking, having sex) versus problem behavior that both adults and adolescents view as serious (such as violent crime) (Basen-Engquist, Edmundson, & Parcel, 1996; Willoughby et al., 2004; Zweig, Lindberg, & McGinley, 2001). Like other types of behavior, problem behavior has multiple and complex causes that vary from one individual to the next. It may be just as erroneous to generalize about the troubled adolescent as it is to generalize about young people overall.

It is also true that the clustering of different problem behaviors is seen more often in some populations than others and more often in studies of adolescents than in studies of either children or young adults (Gillmore et al., 1991; McGee & Newcomb, 1992). For instance, some studies find that two factors that often are correlated with externalizing problems such as delinquency—disengagement from school and early sexual intercourse—may not be part of a problematic syndrome among inner-city Black youth or American Indians (C. Mitchell & O'Nell, 1998; Neumark-Sztainer et al., 1996; Resnicow et al., 1995; Rotheram-Borus, Rosario, Van Rossem, Reid, & Gillis, 1995; Stanton et al., 1993). It therefore may be erroneous to view certain behaviors, such as precocious sexual activity, as indicative of underlying problems in certain communities.

COMORBIDITY OF INTERNALIZING PROBLEMS

Although covariation among internalizing problems has been less extensively studied than covariation

among externalizing problems, there is also a good deal of comorbidity in internalizing disorders, which tend to have in common the subjective state of distress. For example, depressed adolescents are more likely than their peers to experience anxiety, panic, phobia, obsessional thinking, suicidal ideation, eating disorders, and various psychosomatic disturbances (that is, physical problems that have psychological causes) (Gerhardt, Compas, Connor, & Achenbach, 1999; Graber & Sontag, 2009; J. G. Johnson, Cohen, Kotler, Kasen, & Brook, 2002; Masi et al., 2004; Measelle, Stice, & Hogansen, 2006; Skitch & Abela, 2008; Zaider, Johnson, & Cockell, 2003). Some experts question whether it even makes sense to consider some of these problems as separate entities when speaking about children or adolescents (for example, to draw a distinction between anxiety and depression) because rates of comorbidity are so high (Graber & Sontag, 2009).

Just as different externalizing problems are hypothesized to reflect an underlying antisocial syndrome, various indicators of internalizing problems may be thought of as different manifestations of a common underlying factor. This factor is referred to as **negative affectivity** (Lonigan, Carey, & Finch, Jr., 1994). Individuals who are high in negative affectivity—who become distressed easily—are at greater risk for depression, anxiety disorders, and a range of internalizing problems. As is the case with the underpinnings of externalizing problems, the underpinnings of internalizing problems are believed to have both biological and environmental origins, including high levels of biological reactivity to stress (Katainen, Raeikkoenen, & Keltikangas-Jaervinen, 1998; Susman, Dorn, Inoff-Germain, Nottelmann, & Chrousos, 1997). These common underpinnings contribute to stability in predispositions toward internalizing problems over time (Bardone, Moffitt, Caspi, Dickson, & Silva, 1996).

In this chapter, we examine the nature, prevalence, consequences, and amelioration of the three sets of problems often seen during adolescence: substance abuse, antisocial behavior and other externalizing problems, and depression and other internalizing problems. In each case, we ask four central questions: (1) What is the nature of this sort of problem in adolescence? (2) How many, and which, young people have these problems? (3) What do we know about factors that contribute to these problems? and, (4) What approaches to prevention and intervention appear to have the most promise?

negative affectivity The presumed underlying cause of internalizing disorders, characterized by high levels of subjective distress.

RECAP

- Experts distinguish among three categories of problems in adolescence: substance abuse, internalizing problems, and externalizing problems.
- There is a great deal of covariation, or "comorbidity," among different psychosocial problems during adolescence within and across these broad categories.
- Adolescents who engage in delinquency are more likely than their peers to be truant, to engage in precocious sexual behavior, and to commit acts of aggression—a pattern that has been termed problem behavior syndrome.
- Adolescents who are high in negative affectivity are more likely to suffer from depression, feel anxious, and report other symptoms of distress.

Substance Use and Abuse

Our society sends young people mixed messages about drugs and alcohol. Television programs aimed at preadolescents urge viewers to "Just Say No!" but the football games and sitcoms that many of these same viewers watch tell them, no less subtly, that having a good time with friends is virtually impossible without something alcoholic to drink. Many celebrities who are idolized by teenagers speak out against cocaine and marijuana, but many equally famous stars admit to using these same drugs. Tobacco companies spend enormous amounts of money marketing cigarettes to teenagers, and research shows that adolescents are especially drawn to cigarette advertisements that appear to be aimed at teenagers (Arnett, 2001; Biener & Siegel, 2000). On music videos, tobacco and alcohol use is common and often linked to sex, and more often than not, the lead performer is the individual doing the drinking, smoking, and lovemaking (DuRant et al., 1997). Although there is not conclusive evidence that exposure to alcohol or cigarette advertising *causes* adolescents to start drinking or smoking—advertising is mainly effective in increasing brand recognition (National Research Council, 2004)—the messages these ads communicate is that these are pleasurable activities (hardly a surprise, since the ads are designed to get people to buy the products).

The mixed signals sent to young people about drugs reflect, no doubt, the inconsistent way that we view these substances as a society: Some drugs (like alcohol or Adderall) are fine, as long as they are not abused, but

Alcohol and marijuana remain the main drugs of choice among American adolescents.

others (like cocaine or ecstasy) are not; some drinking (enough to relax at a party) is socially appropriate, but too much (enough to impair an automobile driver) is not; some people (those over 21) are old enough to handle drugs, but others (those under 21) are not. It is easy to see why teenagers do not follow the dictates of their elders when it comes to alcohol and other drugs. How, then, should we view substance use and abuse among teenagers, when our backdrop is a society that much of the time tolerates, if not actively encourages, adults who use these same substances?

As with most of the problem behaviors that are common during adolescence, discussions of teenage substance use are often filled more with rhetoric than reality. The popular stereotype of contemporary young people is that they use and abuse a wide range of drugs more than their counterparts did previously, that the main reason adolescents use drugs is peer pressure, and that the "epidemic" level of substance use among American teenagers is behind many of the other problems associated with this age group—including academic underachievement, early pregnancy, suicide, and crime. The simplicity of these assertions is certainly tempting—after all, what could be more reassuring than to identify the "real" culprit (drugs) and the "real" causes (peers) of all the maladies of young people? And what could be even more comforting than the belief that, if we simply teach young people to "say no" to their peers, these problems will disappear?

Unfortunately, what we might like to believe about adolescent substance use is not necessarily correct. As we shall see, although there are grains of truth to many of the popular claims about the causes, nature, and consequences of teenage substance use and abuse, there are many widely held misconceptions about the subject, too.

PREVALENCE OF SUBSTANCE USE AND ABUSE

Each year since 1975, a group of researchers from the University of Michigan has surveyed a nationally representative sample of about 15,000 American high school seniors on several aspects of their lifestyle and values, including their use and abuse of a variety of drugs. Beginning in 1991, comparable samples of 8th- and 10th-graders were added to the annual survey. Because of the size and representativeness of the sample of respondents, this survey, called **Monitoring the Future** (L. D. Johnston, O'Malley, Bachman, & Schulenberg, 2009), is an excellent source of information about

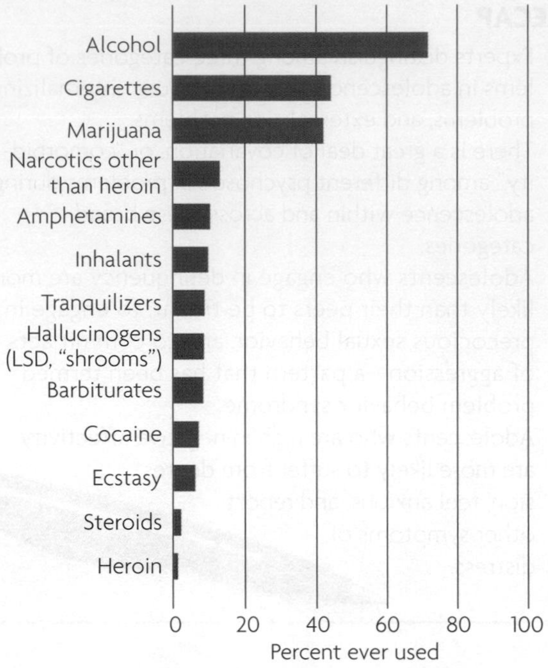

FIGURE 13.2 Percentages of American high school seniors who have ever used various drugs. (Johnston et al., 2009)

patterns of adolescent drug and alcohol use, at least among young people who have not dropped out of school. (The latest survey results can be accessed at www.monitoringthefuture.org.)

Drugs of Choice The surveys consistently indicate that the two major legal drugs—alcohol and nicotine—are by far the most commonly used and abused substances, in terms of both prevalence (the percentage of teenagers who have ever used the drug) and recency of use (the percentage of teenagers who have used the drug within the last month). By the time they are seniors in high school, three fourths of teenagers have tried alcohol and 45% have smoked cigarettes. Experimentation with marijuana is also common: 43% of all seniors have tried marijuana, 32% have smoked marijuana at least once within the last year, and 19% have done so within the past 30 days. After marijuana, however, the percentage of young people who have tried various other drugs drops precipitously, and only about 9% of teenagers have used an illicit drug other than marijuana within the last month (L. D. Johnston et al., 2009) (see Figure 13.2). And, notwithstanding all the media attention given in recent years to fears that adolescents will mimic the steroid use of professional athletes, many fewer high school seniors have ever used steroids than have tried smokeless tobacco (16%) or prescription opioids, like Percocet or Vicodin, whose recreational use is on the rise (J. A. Ford, 2009; Wu, Ringwalt, Mannelli, & Patkar, 2008). Although alcohol and tobacco use among adolescents in most other

Monitoring the Future An annual survey of a nationwide sample of American 8th-, 10th-, and 12th-graders, mainly known for its data on adolescent substance use.

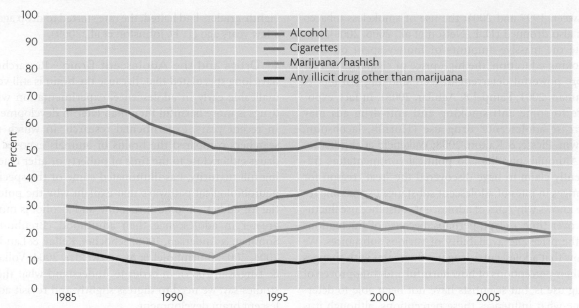

FIGURE 13.3   Over-time trends in the proportion of high school seniors who report having used various drugs in the 30 days preceding the survey. (Monitoring the Future, 2009)

industrialized countries is comparable to that in the United States, illicit drug use by adolescents is less prevalent abroad than in America (Arnett, 2002).

Prevalence statistics, especially those that tap whether an individual has ever tried the substance in question, tell us little about the nature and extent of drug use from the standpoint of adolescents' health and well-being. It is one thing to have tried alcohol or marijuana; it is something else to use either of these substances so often that one's life and behavior are markedly affected.

One of the best ways to examine this issue is to look at the percentage of young people who report using various substances daily or nearly daily. It turns out that cigarettes are the only substances used by a substantial number of high school seniors daily (about 10% smoke daily), and of the remaining drugs, only alcohol and marijuana are used daily by even a modest percentage of teenagers (alcohol is used daily by about 3% of seniors, and marijuana by about 5%). Although daily use of alcohol is relatively infrequent among adolescents, about 25% of all seniors, 15% of all 10th-graders, and 10% of all 8th-graders report having abused alcohol (had more than five drinks in a row, sometimes called **binge drinking**) at least once during the past 2 weeks (L. D. Johnston et al., 2009).

Taken together, the findings from these surveys cast doubt on some of the most fervently held stereotypes about adolescent drug use. Many adolescents who drink do so to excess—more than a quarter of all seniors have been drunk at least once in the last month (L. D. Johnston et al., 2009). But only a very small proportion of young people have serious drug dependency problems (which would lead to daily use) or use hard

drugs at all. Moreover, it is very unlikely that drug and alcohol use lurks behind the wide assortment of adolescent problems for which it is so frequently blamed. Rather, the pattern suggests that most adolescents have experimented with alcohol and marijuana, that many have used one or both of these drugs regularly, that alcohol is clearly the drug of choice among teenagers (a substantial minority of whom drink to excess), and that most teenagers have not experimented with other drugs. From a health and safety standpoint, therefore, education about alcohol use and abuse is more urgently needed and may potentially affect a larger percentage of young people than education about any other drug type.

■ **Changes in Substance Use Over Time**   The Monitoring the Future study has also been used to chart changes over time in adolescent substance use, and recent administrations of the survey have given experts both cause for relief and cause for concern (see Figure 13.3). Marijuana use, which had been on a steady decline since the late 1970s, rose quite sharply during the mid-1990s and has not declined to its former levels (L. D. Johnston et al., 2009). Alcohol use, which declined steadily during the 1980s (from more than 70% of seniors drinking monthly to about 50%), has declined much more slowly since then. One bit of very good news is that cigarette use by teenagers, which increased during the 1990s, has dropped by nearly 50% since 1997—probably because there was a 70% increase in the price of cigarettes

binge drinking   Consuming five or more drinks in a row on one occasion, an indicator of alcohol abuse.

between 1997 and 2001; the use of smokeless tobacco has also dropped (D. E. Nelson et al., 2006, 2008). Despite the massive amounts of money spent on anti-smoking education, the high price of cigarettes is a far more powerful deterrent to teen smoking (Gruber & Zinman, 2001; Pampel & Aguilar, 2008). In fact, exposure to some anti-smoking and anti-drug ads may *increase* adolescents' drug use (Hornik, Jacobsohn, Orwin, Piesse, & Kalton, 2008; Wakefield et al., 2006).

Although pundits and political commentators frequently claim to have discovered the "real" reason for changes in rates of adolescent substance use, no one really knows why rates of adolescent substance use fluctuate over time, except, perhaps, because of fluctuations in the price and availability of various substances. We know that adolescents' drug use fluctuates with changes in their perceptions of how harmful and disapproved of drug use is, but scientists have not been able to determine what influences these perceptions, although it is likely that the messages teenagers receive about drugs—from parents, teachers, and mass media—are important (Bachman, Johnston, & O'Malley, 1998). What is clear, however, is that cohorts of U.S. adolescents born after World War II use more legal and illegal drugs at an earlier age than did their counterparts who were born in the first half of the century (R. Johnson & Gerstein, 1998). Interestingly, the once-existent gender gap in drug use, with males more likely to use and abuse drugs, has all but disappeared for alcohol, marijuana, and cigarettes and has narrowed substantially for other drugs as well (R. Johnson & Gerstein, 1998).

Perhaps the most worrisome finding to emerge in recent surveys is that experimentation with drugs begins at an earlier age now than previously, so that the most pressing problem may not be the prevalence of drug use among high school seniors but early experimentation with drugs among younger teenagers. Nearly 1 in 6 of all eighth-graders drink alcohol regularly, and nearly 7% smoke cigarettes at least once a month. One sixth of eighth-graders have tried inhalants, one sixth have tried marijuana, and nearly 20% have been drunk at least once (L. D. Johnston et al., 2009).

Rates of substance use among eighth-graders are important to watch, because evidence strongly suggests that the chances of becoming addicted to alcohol or nicotine are dramatically increased when substance use begins prior to age 15 (G. C. Patton, Coffey, Carlin, Sawyer, & Wakefield, 2006). Because the typical adolescent who smokes cigarettes begins around the seventh or eighth grade, looking at changes in the number of eighth-graders who smoke is a good way of forecasting rates of smoking among adults in the future. Fortunately, although the decline in rate of smoking among

eighth-graders had halted, the rate started to drop again a few years ago (L. D. Johnston et al., 2009).

■ **Drugs and the Adolescent Brain**   Researchers have long speculated that, because the brain is still very malleable early in adolescence, experimentation with drugs is more harmful then than later in development. In recent years, experimental research, in which researchers compared the brains of animals exposed to drugs either close to the time of puberty or after reaching full maturity, has illuminated some of the specific neurobiological pathways that explain why the potential for addiction to both nicotine and alcohol is much greater in adolescence than adulthood (Brenhouse, Sonntag, & Andersen, 2008; Schochet, Kelley, & Landry, 2004, 2005; Sturmhöfel & Swartzwelder, 2004; Volkow & Ting-Kai, 2005). In order to understand what these studies say, we need to digress slightly and revisit adolescent brain development.

As you read in Chapter 2, changes in the limbic system that take place during adolescence affect receptors for **dopamine,** one of the neurotransmitters that influence our experience of pleasure. We experience things like great sex or fabulous food as enjoyable because they result in higher levels of dopamine in the brain; these higher levels permit more electrical activity through the synapses that connect the circuits in the brain that regulate feelings of pleasure. Keep in mind, though, that levels of dopamine are monitored and regulated so that feelings of pleasure stay within a normal range; when they get too high, dopamine levels are diminished, and when they get too low, they are increased.

Certain drugs make users feel good primarily because they affect the same receptors that are sensitive to the dopamine that is in the brain naturally. In fact, the molecules of addictive drugs are so similar to dopamine molecules that the dopamine receptors act in the same way in their presence as they do in the presence of actual dopamine. As a result, when drugs enter the brain (which is where they go whether they enter the body through the mouth, nose, or blood vessels), they are "read" by dopamine receptors as the real thing. On the positive side, this makes the user feel good (the same way that natural dopamine does)—which, of course, is why people take drugs. The problem, though, is that frequent drug use signals the brain to reduce levels of natural dopamine, in order to maintain the proper level, because the dopamine receptors can't tell the difference between the drug molecules and dopamine molecules. As a result, the more you use drugs, the less natural dopamine circulates in your brain.

This would not be a problem if it were easily reversed—if, say, as soon as you stopped using a drug, your brain upped its production of dopamine to compensate. But the animal studies referred to earlier have shown that experiences in early adolescence, when the

dopamine   A neurotransmitter especially important in the brain circuits that regulate the experience of pleasure.

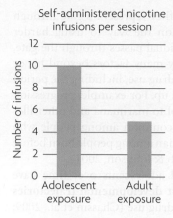

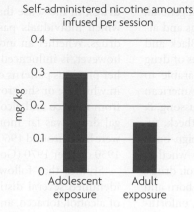

FIGURE 13.4 Animal studies show that first exposure to nicotine during adolescence is more likely to lead to addiction than first exposure in adulthood. (Zickler, 2004)

limbic system is changing naturally, can *permanently* affect the way the dopamine system functions. (As you know, various brain systems and regions change during different periods of development, and it is during periods of change that these brain systems are most easily and irreversibly affected by outside influences.) Repeated exposure to drugs during this period of heightened malleability in the limbic system can affect the brain in ways that make it *necessary* to use drugs in order to experience normal amounts of pleasure. Over time, the brain's ability to produce natural dopamine is permanently hampered, and in order to experience pleasurable feelings, it is necessary to "supplement" the low levels of natural dopamine in the brain with drugs.

How many exposures to a drug does it take to permanently alter the adolescent brain's dopamine system? No one knows for sure, and the answer varies from person to person, largely because of genetic factors (this is why some people are more likely to develop addictions than others) (Laucht et al., 2008). What we now know, though, is that this permanent alteration in the dopamine system is more likely to happen in adolescence, when the limbic system is still malleable, than in adulthood, when it is less changeable.

If this is true, we should expect to find that exposure to drugs during adolescence is more likely to lead to addiction than is exposure during adulthood. And, in fact, studies show that, compared with individuals who delay drinking until they are 21, people who begin drinking in early adolescence (before age 14) are *7 times* more likely to binge drink as teenagers and *5 times* more likely to develop a substance abuse or dependence disorder at some point in their life (Hingson, Heeren, & Winter, 2006). Similar evidence suggests that individuals who begin smoking regularly before age 14 are at greater risk for nicotine dependence as adults than are those who start in late adolescence (Orlando, Tucker, Ellickson, & Klein, 2004), and, as well, that early use of inhalants is associated with higher rates of abuse and dependence (Wu, Pilowsky, & Schlenger, 2004). Experimental studies comparing the consequences of drug

exposure during adolescence and adulthood have confirmed this pattern (see Figure 13.4).

The increased vulnerability of the adolescent brain to the addicting effects of alcohol is compounded by the fact that adolescents don't feel the negative consequences of drinking as profoundly as adults do (this can only be studied in animals, because researchers are not allowed to give teenagers alcohol) (Spear, 2009). Studies comparing juvenile rodents with adult rodents find that juveniles can drink more than adults before they become tired or have their reflexes slow, and the consequences of drinking too much (otherwise known as a hangover) are less intense among juveniles than adults. To make matters worse, juveniles feel the positive effects of alcohol more intensely than adults—alcohol makes juvenile rodents want to socialize, for instance, but it makes adults want to be left alone.

Although the short-term effects of alcohol are less severe in adolescents than adults, there is solid evidence that the lasting effects of alcohol on brain functioning are worse in adolescence than in adulthood—again, because the brain is more vulnerable to influences during periods of plasticity. One area of the adolescent brain that appears especially vulnerable to the harmful effects of alcohol is the hippocampus, which is important for memory and, along with the prefrontal cortex, for "putting the brakes" on impulsive behavior (Squeglia, Jacobus, & Tapert, 2009; Sturmhöfel & Swartzwelder, 2004; E. Walker et al., 2004). Evidence also indicates that alcohol has harmful effects on the development of regions of the brain involved in higher-order cognitive abilities, such as planning, and in the regulation of impulses (Butler, 2006). Although there is some evidence that the harmful neurobiological consequences of drinking in early adolescence can be reversed, the fact that early exposure is more likely to lead to addiction and long-term use indicates that interventions designed to prevent substance abuse should begin prior to adolescence.

■ Ethnic Differences in Substance Use Several national surveys have examined ethnic differences in rates of adolescent substance use and abuse. In general, White adolescents are more likely to use drugs and alcohol than minority youngsters, especially Black and Asian youth (L. D. Johnston et al., 2009). Rates of drug use among Hispanic adolescents are comparable to those of White youngsters, and use among American Indian adolescents is the highest (Chassin, Hussong, & Beltran, 2009; L. D. Johnston et al., 2009; Whitbeck, Yu, Johnson, Hoyt, & Walls, 2008). In general, foreign-born and less Americanized minority youngsters—whether Asian or Hispanic in background—use alcohol, drugs, and tobacco at a lower rate than do American-born and more acculturated minority youth, suggesting, unfortunately, that part of becoming an "American" teenager means experimenting with drugs (Delva et al., 2005; Georgiades, Boyle, Duku, & Racine, 2006; Gfroerer & Tan, 2003; Hahm, Lahiff, & Guterman, 2004). Indeed, the rate of drug use among immigrant adolescents is *half* the rate of use among adolescents from the same ethnic group who were born in the United States (K. Harris, 1999).

■ **Does Substance Use Follow a Particular Progression?**   Researchers have also been interested in the sequence through which adolescents experiment with different drugs. In general, young people experiment with beer and wine before trying cigarettes or hard liquor, which precedes marijuana use, which, in turn, precedes the use of other illicit drugs (Kandel, 1980). However, although experimentation may follow this sequence, this does not mean that alcohol use invariably leads to marijuana use, or that marijuana use necessarily leads to experimentation with harder drugs. In fact, there is little evidence to support the idea that marijuana is an inevitable stepping-stone to hard-drug use (much appears to depend on how frequently marijuana is used) (Treaster, 1994).

The fact that there is a fairly standard sequence of drug use, however, suggests that virtually all users of hard drugs have also tried alcohol, cigarettes, and marijuana and, moreover, that one way to prevent adolescents from experimenting with more serious drugs is to stop them from experimenting with alcohol and marijuana. In fact, studies show that adolescents who have not experimented with alcohol or marijuana by the time they are in their 20s are unlikely ever to use these or any other drugs (Chen & Kandel, 1996). For this reason, alcohol and marijuana are considered **gateway**

drugs, in the sense that they represent a gate through which individuals pass on the way to using harder drugs. Whether an individual passes through the gate, however, is influenced by many factors beyond his or her previous patterns of drug use, including the period in which he or she grows up. For example, progression from tobacco and alcohol to marijuana and other illegal drugs was far more common among people who were born around 1960 than among people born before 1950 or after 1970 (Golub & Johnson, 2001).

Studies that followed adolescents over time have identified several distinct **developmental trajectories** of alcohol, tobacco, and drug use (Chassin et al., 2009; Flory, Lynam, & Milich, 2004; Sher, Gotham, & Watson, 2004; Windle & Wiesner, 2004). In one study, six distinct groups were identified. Nonusers (who made up one third of the sample) rarely experimented with substances at any point in adolescence. Alcohol experimenters (25% of the sample) first tried alcohol early in adolescence and continued to drink occasionally, but did not try other drugs and did not increase their drinking over time. Low escalators (5% of the sample) began using substances early in adolescence and increased their use slowly but steadily over time. Early starters (6% of the sample) showed very high substance use in early adolescence and escalated gradually over time, so that by the end of high school they were smoking and drinking frequently and experimenting with drugs. Late starters (20% of the sample) used substances infrequently during early adolescence but increased their use rapidly during high school—so much so that by the end of high school their substance use was similar to that of the early starters. Finally, high escalators (8% of the sample) showed moderate use in early adolescence, escalated rapidly between early and middle adolescence, and continued to increase their use throughout high school (Zapert, Snow, & Tebes, 2002).

CAUSES AND CONSEQUENCES OF SUBSTANCE USE AND ABUSE

In looking at the causes and consequences of substance use and abuse in adolescence, it is especially important to keep in mind the distinction between occasional experimentation and problematic use. Psychologists distinguish between two levels of severity of pathological substance use: **substance abuse,** whereby the use causes problems (see Table 13.1), and **substance dependence,** whereby the individual is physically addicted. All individuals who are substance dependent by definition are substance abusers, but the reverse is not true.

■ **Users, Abusers, and Abstainers**   Because the majority of adolescents have experimented with alcohol and marijuana, we can speculate that occasional alcohol and marijuana use has become normative

gateway drugs   Drugs that, when used over time, lead to the use of other, more dangerous substances.

developmental trajectories   Patterns of change over time.

substance abuse   The misuse of alcohol or other drugs to a degree that causes problems in the individual's life.

substance dependence   The misuse of alcohol or other drugs to a degree that causes physical addiction.

TABLE 13.1 DSM-IV diagnostic criteria for substance abuse

A maladaptive pattern of substance use leading to clinically significant impairment or distress as manifested by one (or more) of the following, occurring within a 12-month period:

1. Recurrent substance use resulting in a failure to fulfill major role obligations at work, school, or home (such as repeated absences or poor work performance related to substance use; substance-related absences, suspensions, or expulsions from school; or neglect of children or household)

2. Recurrent substance use in situations in which it is physically hazardous (such as driving an automobile or operating a machine when impaired by substance use)

3. Recurrent substance-related legal problems (such as arrests for substance-related disorderly conduct)

4. Continued substance use despite having persistent or recurrent social or interpersonal problems caused or exacerbated by the effects of the substance (for example, arguments with spouse about consequences of intoxication and physical fights)

among American high school students and, consequently, that there are plenty of normal, healthy young people who have used these drugs at least once. In fact, several studies indicate that adolescents who experiment with alcohol and marijuana are no worse adjusted than their peers who abstain from alcohol and marijuana (Scheier & Botvin, 1998; Shedler & Block, 1990; J. S. Tucker, Ellickson, Collins, & Klein, 2006). This substantial body of research shows quite clearly that it is important to differentiate among four groups of adolescents: frequent drug users (for example, at least once a week); hard-drug users (that is, drugs other than alcohol, tobacco, or marijuana); those who experiment with marijuana and alcohol but who do not use them frequently (that is, no more than once a month); and those who abstain (Hughes, Power, & Francis, 1992; C. Mitchell et al., 1996; Wills, McNamara, Vacaro, & Hirky, 1996). Experimenters and abstainers score higher on measures of psychological adjustment than frequent users. Longer-term follow-up studies also show that moderate alcohol use during adolescence does not have negative long-term effects (Paschall, Freisthler, & Lipton, 2005). Indeed, cigarette use during adolescence has more harmful long-term health consequences than does experimentation with alcohol or marijuana, partly because nicotine is a more addictive drug, and its use is more likely to persist into middle adulthood (K. Chen & Kandel, 1996; Elders, Perry, Eriksen, & Giovino, 1994; Pierce & Gilpin, 1996).

These results do not mean that occasional experimentation with drugs during adolescence *leads* to better adjustment, of course. In fact, research shows that the psychological advantages observed among adoles-

cents who experiment with alcohol and marijuana were evident when these individuals were younger children (Shedler & Block, 1990). Taken together, though, the studies suggest that moderate alcohol and marijuana use has become normative among adolescents in contemporary society (however troublesome some adults may find this), that these substances are typically used in social situations, and that better-adjusted and more interpersonally competent young people are likely to participate in social activities in which alcohol and other drugs are present (Ludden & Eccles, 2007; Scheier & Botvin, 1998; Shedler & Block, 1990). Relative to experimenters, abstainers—and "irrational" abstainers, in particular—tend to be over-controlled, narrow in their interests, anxious, and inhibited (Shedler & Block, 1990).

■ **Predictors and Consequences of Substance Abuse** Substance abuse (using drugs in a way that causes significant problems at home, school, work, or with the law) is a different matter. Adolescents who are frequent users of alcohol, tobacco, and other drugs score lower on measures of psychological adjustment as teenagers and were more likely to be maladjusted as children (Shedler & Block, 1990). Indeed, a team of researchers who followed a sample of individuals from preschool into young adulthood report that, at age 7, individuals who would later become frequent drug users as adolescents were described as "not getting along well with other children, not showing concern for moral issues . . . not planful or likely to think ahead, not trustworthy or dependable . . . [and] not self-reliant or confident" (Shedler & Block, 1990, p. 618). As 11-year-olds, these individuals were described as deviant, emotionally labile (unstable), stubborn, and inattentive. In other words, drug and alcohol abuse during adolescence is often a symptom of prior psychological disturbance.

Substance abuse during adolescence, whatever its antecedents, is associated with a host of other problems. Young people who abuse alcohol, tobacco, and other drugs are more likely to experience problems at school; suffer from psychological distress and depression; become involved in dangerous or deviant activities, including crime, delinquency, and truancy; and engage in unprotected sexual activity: As adults, they are more likely to have physical health problems, experience unemployment and out-of-wedlock childbearing, and develop substance abuse problems (Chassin et al., 2009; Green & Ensminger, 2006; Holmen, Barrett-Connor, Holmen, & Bjermer, 2000; Kandel, Johnson, Bird, & Canino, 1997; Stuart & Green, 2008; Wu & Anthony, 1999). These problems are especially severe among adolescents who are involved in drug dealing (Centers & Weist, 1998). Alcohol and other drugs are often implicated in adolescent automobile crashes, the leading cause of death and disability among American teenagers (Lang, Waller, & Shope, 1996; O'Malley & Johnston, 1999), and in other fatal and nonfatal accidents, such as drownings, falls, and burns (Irwin, 1986; Wintemute, Kraus, Teret, & Wright, 1987). Adolescent substance abusers also expose themselves to the long-term health risks of excessive drug use that stem from addiction or dependency; in the case of cigarettes, alcohol, and marijuana, these risks are substantial and well documented—among them, cancer, heart disease, and kidney and liver damage. It is also now well established that heavy cigarette smoking during adolescence can exacerbate feelings of emotional distress and lead to depression and anxiety disorders (Chassin et al., 2009).

■ **Risk Factors for Substance Abuse**   Which adolescents are most likely to become substance abusers? Generally, four sets of risk factors—psychological, familial, social, and contextual—for substance abuse have been identified, and the more risk factors that are present for an individual, the more likely she or he is to use and abuse drugs (J. Hawkins, Catalano, & Miller, 1992; Ostaszewski & Zimmerman, 2006; Petraitis, Flay, & Miller, 1995). These same risk factors have been found across a variety of studies and in samples of adolescents from a wide range of ethnic and socioeconomic backgrounds, although there is some evidence that family factors may be more influential in early adolescence and peer factors more so in middle adolescence (M. J. Cleveland, Feinberg, Bontempo, & Greenberg, 2008). In other words, the factors that place an adolescent at risk for substance abuse are more or less the same regardless of the adolescent's sex, social class, or ethnicity (Choi, Harachi, Gillmore, & Catalano, 2005). As one team of researchers points out, this is good news, because it suggests that preventive interventions do not need to be specifically tailored to different subgroups of adolescents (Hu, Davies, & Kandel, 2006).

The first set of risk factors is psychological. Individuals with certain personality characteristics—which typically are present prior to adolescence—are more likely to develop drug and alcohol problems than their peers. These characteristics include anger, impulsivity, and inattentiveness (Chassin et al., 2009; Tapert, Baratta, Abrantes, & Brown, 2002; Wills, Sandy, Yaeger, & Shinar, 2001; M. Wong et al., 2006). In addition, individuals who have more tolerant attitudes about drug use (and about deviance in general) are at greater risk for drug abuse (Schulenberg, Wadsworth, O'Malley, Bachman, & Johnston, 1996; Petraitis et al., 1995), as are those who expect alcohol or other drugs to improve their social relationships (Griffin, Epstein, Botvin, & Spoth, 2001; G. Smith, Goldman, Greenbaum, & Christiansen, 1995). Even as children, for example, individuals who eventually become heavy drinkers as adolescents expect alcohol to have positive effects on them (M. Dunn & Goldman, 1998).

Second, individuals with distant, hostile, or conflicted family relationships are more likely to develop substance abuse problems than are their peers who grow up in close, nurturing families (Dishion, Capaldi, & Yoerger, 1999; J. A. Ford, 2009; Kilpatrick et al., 2000; Sale et al., 2005). Drug-abusing youngsters are also more likely than their peers to have parents who are excessively permissive, uninvolved, neglectful, or rejecting (Chassin et al., 2009); one explanation for high rates of substance use among affluent suburban teenagers is that their parents often are tolerant of this behavior (Luthar & Goldstein, 2008). In addition, they are more likely to come from homes where one or more other family members (parents or siblings) smoke, drink, or use drugs; there are both genetic and family environmental influences on adolescent alcohol and drug use (Chassin et al., 2009; Gilman et al., 2009; K. G. Hill, Hawkins, Catalano, Abbott, & Guo, 2005; Nofziger & Lee, 2006).

Third, individuals with substance abuse problems are more likely to have friends who use and tolerate the use of drugs, both because they are influenced by these friends and because they are drawn to them (G. M. Barnes et al., 2006; Bray, Adams, Getz, & McQueen, 2003; Ennett et al., 2006; J. Hill, Emery, Harden, Mendle, & Turkheimer, 2008; I. J. Kim, Zane, & Hong, 2002; Parsai, Voisine, Marsiglia, Kulis, & Nieri, 2009). As you read in Chapter 5, whether and how often adolescents use drugs is an important defining characteristic of peer groups—abstainers tend to have other abstainers as friends, and users tend to be friends with other users. Drug-using adolescents seek drug-using peers, and drug-using peers encourage even more drug use among their friends (Chassin, Presson, Todd, Rose, & Sherman, 1998; Schulenberg et al., 1999). Indeed, the most common setting in which adolescents use alcohol and drugs is in a friend's home (Hussong, 2000). Substance-using adolescents who have many substance-using friends may also overestimate how common substance use is because they are so much more likely to see other people engaged in it (Unger & Rohrbach, 2002).

Finally, adolescents who become substance abusers are more likely to live in a social context that makes drug use easier (Chassin et al., 2009). Important contextual factors are the availability of drugs, the community's norms regarding drug use, the degree to which drug laws are enforced, and the ways in which drug use is presented via the mass media (K. Allison et al., 1999; X. Li, Stanton, & Feigelman, 1996; Petraitis et al., 1995). A recent New Zealand study found, for example, that lowering the minimum purchasing age for alcohol significantly increased the rate of alcohol-related car crashes among younger drivers (Kypri et al., 2006). All other factors being equal, adolescents who have easy access to drugs, who believe that there are ample opportunities to use drugs, and who are exposed to messages that tolerate or even encourage drug use are more likely to use and abuse drugs. Binge drinking and drinking while driving are higher among adolescents who live in neighborhoods with relatively more retail outlets for alcohol (Truong & Sturm, 2009), and smoking is more common among adolescents who live in neighborhoods with relatively more stores that sell tobacco (Novak, Reardon, Raudenbush, & Buka, 2006).

Researchers have also identified important **protective factors** that decrease the likelihood of adolescents' engaging in substance abuse (Jessor, Van Den Bos, Vanderryn, Costa, & Turbin, 1995). Among the most important protective factors are positive mental health (including high self-esteem and the absence of depressive symptoms), high academic achievement, engagement in school, close family relationships, and involvement in religious activities (Albers & Biener, 2003; Bahr, Maughan, Marcos, & Li, 1998; Bryant, Schulenberg, O'Malley, Bachman, & Johnston, 2003; Jessor, Turbin, & Costa, 1998; L. C. Jordan & Lewis, 2005). These protective factors appear to operate over and above the effects of the risk factors discussed previously. As with the factors that place adolescents at risk for substance abuse, the protective factors identified operate similarly among adolescents from different ethnic groups and explain why some groups of adolescents use drugs more than others do (G. Barnes & Farrell, 1992; Ennett et al., 2008; Flannery, Vazsonyi, & Rowe, 1996). One of the reasons for the lower rate of drinking among Black youth, for example, is that their parents are less likely to drink or to tolerate adolescent drinking (Peterson, Hawkins, Abbott, & Catalano, 1994).

PREVENTION AND TREATMENT OF SUBSTANCE USE AND ABUSE

Efforts to prevent substance use and abuse among teenagers focus on one of three factors: the supply of drugs, the environment in which teenagers may be exposed to drugs, and characteristics of the potential drug user (Newcomb & Bentler, 1989). Although a good deal of government spending and media attention have been devoted to the first of these approaches—attempts to control or limit the availability of drugs—the consensus among experts is that it is more realistic to try to change adolescents' motivation to use drugs and the environment in which they live, since it has proven virtually impossible to remove drugs totally from society. Indeed, the two most commonly used and abused drugs—cigarettes and alcohol—are both legal and widely available, and laws prohibiting the sale of these substances to minors are not well enforced (Centers for Disease Control and Prevention, 2006). Research does show, however, that raising the price of alcohol and cigarettes does reduce adolescents' use of them (M. Grossman, Chaloupka, Saffer, & Laixuthai, 1994;

Gruber & Zinman, 2001). Attempts to enforce laws governing the purchase of cigarettes are less effective, in part because many adolescents obtain cigarettes through means other than purchasing them from stores (for example, bumming them from older friends, stealing them from parents) (Fichtenberg & Glantz, 2002; Pokorny, Jason, & Schoeny, 2006).

Many different types of drug abuse prevention interventions have been tried, either alone or in combination. In programs designed to change some characteristic of the adolescent, drug use is targeted indirectly either by attempting to enhance adolescents' psychological development in general or by helping adolescents develop other interests and participate in other activities that will make drug use less likely. The idea behind these sorts of efforts is that adolescents who have high self-esteem, for example, or who are gainfully employed will be less likely to use drugs. In other programs, the intervention is directly focused on preventing drug use. These programs include information-based efforts (in which adolescents are educated about the dangers of drugs), social skills training (in which adolescents are taught how to turn down drugs), and some combination of informational and general psychological intervention (in which adolescents are educated about drug abuse and exposed to a program designed to enhance their self-esteem, for instance) (Newcomb & Bentler, 1989).

FOOD FOR THOUGHT

Why do you think that interventions designed to change individuals' knowledge about drug use and its consequences have been such failures? How do you explain the fact that many individuals continue to engage in behaviors that they know are dangerous or unhealthy, such as smoking?

Generally, the results of research designed to evaluate these sorts of individual-focused approaches have not been especially encouraging (Dielman, 1994; H. Leventhal & Keeshan, 1993). Careful evaluations of Project DARE, for example—the most widely implemented drug education program in the United States— show that the program is largely ineffective (Ennett, Tobler, Ringwall, & Flewelling, 1994). Experts are now fairly confident that drug education alone, whether based on rational information or scare tactics, does not prevent drug use. This is reminiscent of research on sex education, which, as we saw in Chapter 11, has shown that informational programs are simply not effective on

protective factors Factors that limit individual vulnerability to harm.

their own. As a rule, educational programs may change individuals' knowledge, but they rarely affect their behavior. In addition, a recent large-scale study of drug testing in schools found that the practice has no effect on adolescents' drug use (Yamaguchi, Johnston, & O'Malley, 2003).

The most encouraging results have been found in programs that do not focus only on the individual adolescent but rather combine some sort of social competence training with a communitywide intervention aimed not only at adolescents but also at their peers, parents, and teachers (Fletcher, Bonell, & Hargreaves, 2008; J. D. Hawkins et al., 2008; Liddle, Rowe, Henderson, Dakoff, & Greenbaum, 2009; M. Siegel & Biener, 2000). These multifaceted efforts have been shown to be effective in reducing adolescents' use of alcohol, cigarettes, and other drugs, especially if the programs begin when youngsters are preadolescents and continue well into high school (Bruvold, 1993; Dielman, 1994; Ellickson, Bell, & McGuigan, 1993; Flynn et al., 1994; Perry et al., 1996). Overall, most experts agree that efforts designed simply to change the potential adolescent drug user without transforming the environment in which the adolescent lives are not likely to succeed. Despite their intuitive appeal, efforts to help adolescents "Just Say No" have been remarkably unsuccessful.

One of the problems with all prevention programs is that they often do not distinguish between drug *use* (which is not always problematic) and drug *abuse* (which is). Trying to stop teenagers from *ever* using alcohol, for instance, is both unlikely to succeed and probably not a very wise allocation of resources, whereas preventing binge drinking or drunk driving is a far more important—and attainable—goal.

Distinguishing between use and abuse is also important in treatment. Some experts worry that adolescents who are mistakenly enrolled in treatment programs (because their parents have overreacted to the adolescent's normative and probably harmless experimentation with drugs) may end up more alienated and more distressed—and more likely to become drug abusers— as a result of the "treatment." Evaluations of treatment programs for adolescents who are genuine drug abusers suggest that efforts that involve the adolescent's family, and not just the teenager, are more likely to be successful (Dielman, 1994; Dishion & Andrews, 1995; St. Pierre, Mark, Kaltreider, & Aikin, 1997; Zavela et al., 1997).

conduct disorder   A repetitive and persistent pattern of antisocial behavior that results in problems at school or work, or in relationships with others.

oppositional-defiant disorder   A disorder of childhood and adolescence characterized by excessive anger, spite, and stubbornness.

RECAP

- Among contemporary adolescents, alcohol and cigarettes are still the drugs of choice, although a substantial number of young people have experimented with marijuana as well.
- Experts have expressed particular concern about the use of substances early in adolescence, especially in light of new brain research indicating that the potential for addiction and for other harmful physical consequences is significantly greater when the first use of substances occurs before age 14.
- Research indicates a clear need to distinguish between experimentation with alcohol and marijuana (which has not been shown to be harmful) and regular or heavy use (which has).
- Adolescents who abuse alcohol and other drugs are more likely to come from hostile family environments, to have friends who use drugs, and to have other problems in school as well as in interpersonal relationships.
- The most promising interventions for substance abuse problems in adolescence are those that target the adolescent's social environment as well as the individual.

Externalizing Problems

Generally, experts distinguish among three main categories of externalizing problems in adolescence: conduct disorder, aggression, and delinquency. Although these three classes of problems are highly interrelated, their definitions differ.

CATEGORIES OF EXTERNALIZING PROBLEMS

▌ **Conduct Disorder**   The first category of externalizing problems is **conduct disorder,** which is a clinical diagnosis that refers to a repetitive and persistent pattern of antisocial behavior in which the rights of others or age-appropriate societal norms are violated and where, as a result of this behavior, the individual has problems in social relationships, school, or the workplace (see Table 13.2) (Farrington, 2009). (A related, but less serious, diagnosis is **oppositional-defiant disorder,** which refers to behavior that is spiteful, angry, and argumentative, but not necessarily aggressive.) An estimated 6%–16% of adolescent males and 2%–9% of adolescent females have conduct disorder (Farrington, 2009), although these estimates vary considerably from sample to sample. Estimates of the prevalence of conduct disorder have been increasing in recent years,

TABLE 13.2   DSM-IV diagnostic criteria for conduct disorder

A repetitive and persistent pattern of behavior in which the basic rights of others or major age-appropriate societal norms or rules are violated, as manifested by the presence of three (or more) of the following criteria in the past 12 months, with at least one criterion present in the past 6 months, and where the behavior causes impairment in school, work, or relationships:

1. Often bullies, threatens, or intimidates others
2. Often initiates physical fights
3. Has used a weapon that can cause serious physical harm to others (e.g., a bat, brick, broken bottle, knife, gun)
4. Has been physically cruel to people
5. Has been physically cruel to animals
6. Has stolen while confronting a victim (e.g., mugging, purse snatching, extortion, armed robbery)
7. Has forced someone into sexual activity
8. Has deliberately engaged in fire setting with the intention of causing serious damage
9. Has deliberately destroyed others' property (other than by fire setting)
10. Has broken into someone else's house, building, or car
11. Often lies to obtain goods or favors or to avoid obligations (i.e., "cons" others)
12. Has stolen items of nontrivial value without confronting a victim (e.g., shoplifting, but without breaking and entering; forgery)
13. Often stays out at night despite parental prohibitions, beginning before age 13 years
14. Has run away from home overnight at least twice while living in parental or parental surrogate home (or once without returning for a lengthy period)
15. Is often truant from school, beginning before age 13 years

although it is hard to know whether this is due to increases in the numbers of children who genuinely have the disorder or to increases in the number of badly behaving children who are diagnosed. Conduct disorder is very stable between childhood and adolescence—about half of all individuals who are diagnosed with it as children are also diagnosed with it as teenagers, and many had oppositional-defiant disorder when they were younger.

Individuals who have been diagnosed with conduct disorder and who persist in their antisocial behavior after age 18 may subsequently be diagnosed with **antisocial personality disorder,** which is characterized by a lack of regard for the moral or legal standards of the community and a marked inability to get along with others or abide by societal rules. Some individuals with antisocial personality disorder are called **psychopaths,** which refers to individuals who are not only antisocial in their behavior but manipulative, superficially charming, impulsive, and indifferent to the feelings of others (Hare, 1991). Because the terms "antisocial personality disorder" and "psychopath" imply a deep-seated personality problem that is unlikely to change, experts advise against applying them to people younger than 18, because, as you will read, most individuals who engage in antisocial behavior as teenagers do not continue to do so after their mid-20s. Moreover, studies show that juvenile offenders who are labeled as "psychopaths" are more likely to receive harsh sentences than those who have committed similar crimes but who have not

received the same label (Boccaccini, Murrie, Clark, & Cornell, 2008; S. Jones & Cauffman, 2008). Social scientists disagree about whether it is possible to identify "juvenile psychopaths" or "fledgling psychopaths"—individuals who, despite their youth, exhibit many of the same characteristics as adult psychopaths. Some contend that it is possible to do so (e.g., M. A. Campbell, Porter, & Santor, 2004; Frick, Kotov, Loney, & Vasey, 2005; Lynam, Caspi, Moffitt, Loeber, & Stouthamer-Loeber, 2007; Salekin, 2008), while others note that some of the distinguishing features of adult psychopaths that are considered pathological (impulsivity, irresponsibility, instability in romantic relationships) may be transient characteristics that are normative during adolescence and that reflect immaturity, not pathology (Edens, Skeem, Cruise, & Cauffman, 2000; Skeem & Cauffman, 2003; Vincent, Vitacco, Grisso, & Corrado, 2003).

▌ **Aggression**   A second category of externalizing problems is **aggression,** which is behavior that is done to intentionally hurt someone. "Aggression" is a

antisocial personality disorder   A disorder of adulthood characterized by antisocial behavior and persistent disregard for the rules of society and the rights of others.

psychopaths   Individuals who are not only antisocial but also manipulative, superficially charming, impulsive, and indifferent to the feelings of others.

aggression   Acts done to be intentionally harmful.

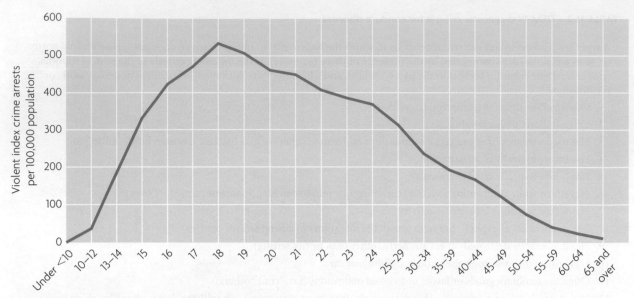

FIGURE 13.5   Age differences in violent criminal activity. (Federal Bureau of Investigation, 2009)

very broad term that includes physical fighting, relational aggression, and intimidation, and it can be either instrumental (planned) or reactive (unplanned). It is very difficult to estimate the prevalence of aggression during adolescence, because the category is so far-reaching. Virtually everyone has done *something* aggressive at one time or another. Most psychologists are concerned with adolescents whose aggression is persistent and causes serious injury to others. Aggressive behavior actually declines over the course of childhood and adolescence—in sheer quantity, the most aggressive period of development is the preschool years, when children frequently hit, kick, or bite each other—although aggression committed by adolescents is generally more serious than that committed by children (Bongers, Koot, van der Ende, & Verhulst, 2004). Like conduct disorder, aggression is also very stable over time, although much more so in boys than girls (Broidy et al., 2003). One likely reason for this sex difference is that aggressive little girls are more often forced to curtail their bad behavior than

aggressive little boys are, which will make girls' aggression less stable over time.

■ **Juvenile Offending**   The third main category of externalizing problems is **juvenile offending,** which includes **delinquency** (crimes committed by minors that are dealt with in the juvenile justice system) and **criminal behavior** (crimes that are dealt with in the criminal justice system, regardless of the age of the offender). **Status offenses,** a special category of delinquent acts, are behaviors that are not against the law for adults but that nevertheless violate established codes of conduct for juveniles, like truancy or running away from home (Woolard & Scott, 2009). Unlike conduct disorder or aggression, which are defined in terms of behavior, juvenile offending is defined legally. A large proportion of juvenile offenders have conduct disorder, and most are aggressive, but not all adolescents who have conduct disorder or who are aggressive are juvenile offenders, because that depends entirely on whether they have broken the law.

Both violent crimes (such as assault, rape, robbery, and murder) and property crimes (such as burglary, theft, and arson) increase in frequency between the preadolescent and adolescent years, peak during the late high school years (slightly earlier for property than for violent crimes), and decline during young adulthood. The so-called **age–crime curve** has been remarkably stable over time and is consistently seen around the world (Piquero, Farrington, & Blumstein, 2003). In the United States, almost one third of arrests for serious crimes involve a suspect under 18, and individuals under 18 account for one sixth of all violent crimes (Federal Bureau of Investigation, 2008) (see Figure 13.5). About 10% of serious delinquency is committed by children who are younger than 13

juvenile offending   An externalizing problem that includes delinquency and criminal behavior.

delinquency   Juvenile offending that is processed within the juvenile justice system.

criminal behavior   Crimes that are dealt with in the criminal justice system, regardless of the age of the offender.

status offenses   Violations of the law that pertain to minors but not adults.

age–crime curve   The relationship between chronological age and offending, showing that the prevalence of offending peaks in late adolescence.

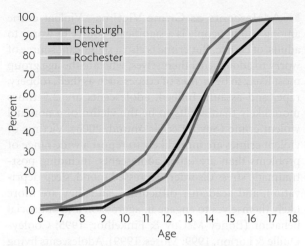

FIGURE 13.6 Cumulative onset of persistent serious and violent delinquency in three inner-city samples. Most serious delinquency begins between the ages of 13 and 16. (Loeber & Farrington, 2000)

(Loeber & Farrington, 2000). The onset of serious delinquency generally begins between the ages of 13 and 16 (Farrington, 2009) (see Figure 13.6).

DEVELOPMENTAL PROGRESSION OF ANTISOCIAL BEHAVIOR

Antisocial behavior can take different forms. **authority conflicts** (such as truancy or running away from home), **covert antisocial behavior** (such as stealing), and **overt antisocial behavior** (such as attacking someone with a weapon). Within these broad categories, there are some fairly predictable progressions (Farrington, 2009). Authority conflicts usually first appear as stubborn behavior, which escalates into defiance and disobedience, and then progresses to more serious signs of problems with authority, such as truancy and running away from home. Covert antisocial behavior typically begins with acts like lying and shoplifting; progresses to property damage, such as vandalism; and then to more serious property crimes, such as burglary. Overt antisocial behavior generally first presents itself as fighting or bullying, which escalates to things like gang fighting and, ultimately, to violent criminal activity.

This is not to say that all bullies grow up to be violent criminals or that all stubborn preschoolers end up running away from home as teenagers. But the reverse is almost always true: Virtually all violent juveniles have a history of escalating aggressive behavior; most adolescents who commit serious property crimes started with less serious forms of overt behavior; and most chronically rebellious teenagers were oppositional children. Of course, some juveniles commit all three types of acts; generally, the more serious an adolescent's behavior is in one category, the more likely he or she is to have displayed the others. That is, most adolescents who

commit violent crimes have also engaged in covert and authority-related antisocial behavior, but not all adolescents who have conflicts with authority or who engage in covert antisocial behavior are necessarily aggressive. The authority conflict pathway almost always starts in childhood (contrary to the stereotype, few people suddenly develop serious authority problems for the first time as teenagers). The covert and overt pathways, in contrast, can begin either in childhood or in adolescence—and, as you will read, individuals whose antisocial behavior begins in childhood are very different from those whose antisocial behavior doesn't start until adolescence (Moffitt, 2006).

CHANGES IN JUVENILE OFFENDING OVER TIME

When social scientists track changes in antisocial behavior over time, they generally look at juvenile offending, because statistics are kept on the numbers of juveniles arrested each year and the crimes with which they have been charged. Between 1965 and 1988, and especially after 1984, arrests for the most serious violent crimes— murder, rape, armed robbery, and aggravated assault— increased substantially among young people. After 1993, violent crime among young people declined dramatically; it began to rise very slightly in the mid-2000s (Federal Bureau of Investigation, 2008). In addition, the average age at which individuals are arrested has fallen during the past several decades, as criminal behavior has become increasingly prevalent among younger boys and girls (Snyder & Sickmund, 2006)—not unlike, and probably related to, the drop in age of initiation into drug and alcohol use discussed earlier in this chapter.

▌ **Bad Girls**   Much recent attention has been devoted to what appears to be a substantial reduction in the gender gap in serious offenses over the past several decades (Federal Bureau of Investigation, 2008). Although antisocial behavior is still far more common among males than females, the male-to-female ratio in juvenile arrests today (about 2.5 to 1) is about one third what it was in 1980. The male-to-female ratio in juvenile arrests for violent crime changed dramatically during the 1990s (Federal Bureau of Investigation, 2008). However, it is not clear whether this change is mainly due to changes in actual offending or to changes in

authority conflicts   A type of antisocial behavior characterized by stubbornness and rebelliousness.

covert antisocial behavior   A type of antisocial behavior characterized by misdeeds that are not always detected by others, such as lying or stealing.

overt antisocial behavior   A type of antisocial behavior characterized by aggression toward others.

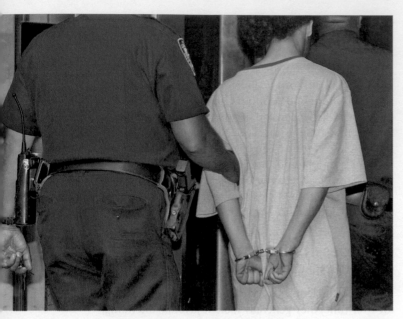

In the United States, almost one third of arrests for serious crimes involve a suspect under 18.

arrest practices. We need to be careful not to make the same mistake about the growing numbers of violent girls that was made about the coming wave of "superpredators" a decade ago. Changes in arrest rates can occur without there being any changes in actual offending (if, for example, the police crack down on crime, more people will be arrested, even if more people are not offending), and studies that rely on official statistics often reach conclusions different from those that rely on police or court records (Farrington et al., 2003). In fact, a recent analysis of data on actual offending found that there has *not* been an increase in violent acts committed by adolescent girls; rather, girls are simply being arrested more frequently for the same things they did in the past but were not arrested for (Steffensmeier, Schwartz, Zhong, & Ackerman, 2005).

It also appears that the ratio of males to females who have been arrested has changed not because of an increase in female offending, but because the drop in juvenile offending since 1993 was steeper for males than females (Cauffman, 2008). If female offending increased just a little since then, but male offending dropped by more than 50%, the ratio of male-to-female offending would be cut in half. Regardless of the size or causes of the gender gap in arrests, there is good evidence that violent females have significantly more mental health problems than do violent males, consistent with the notion that gender-inappropriate displays of aggression may be indicative of greater maladjustment (Cauffman, 2008). There is also good evidence that girls' antisocial behavior may be especially influenced by the boys who are their friends and boyfriends (Arndorfer & Stormshak, 2008; Cauffman, Farruggia, & Goldweber, 2008).

█ Adolescents as Crime Victims   Violent crime among young people is a significant source of worry to adults, of course. But crime is also a significant source of worry to adolescents themselves, who are the age group most likely to be *victims* of crimes such as theft, robbery, rape, and assault. Indeed, adolescents are 2.5 times more likely than adults to be the victim of a nonfatal violent crime (Snyder & Sickmund, 2006). Victims of violent crimes are more likely to report a wide range of problems than are other adolescents, including post-traumatic stress disorder, depressed mood, sleep deprivation, and academic difficulties, and they are more likely themselves to engage in aggression and antisocial behavior (Boney-McCoy & Finkelhor, 1995; Cooley-Quille & Lorion, 1999; Moses, 1999). Adolescents living in single-parent homes in the inner city are disproportionately likely to be the victims of violent crime; although Black and Hispanic adolescents are more likely to be victimized than White adolescents, this is due to the higher proportion of non-White adolescents living in single-parent homes in poor neighborhoods (Snyder & Sickmund, 2006). Indeed, for many adolescents growing up in the inner city, gang violence and victimization are chronic problems. Among 15- to 19-year-olds, for example, homicide accounts for 40% of all deaths among Blacks and 23% of all deaths among Hispanic Americans, but 4% of White deaths (National Center for Health Statistics, 2008).

Most researchers agree that violence and aggression among youth are strongly linked to poverty for a number of reasons. First, when families live in impoverished neighborhoods, parents are less effective in nurturing and monitoring their children, and this diminished effectiveness leads to increased aggression and crime (Snyder & Sickmund, 2006). One study of an American Indian community before and after it had benefited from the added income generated by the opening of a casino on the reservation found a substantial drop in adolescents' behavioral problems as a result of the increase in parental monitoring (Costello, Compton, Keeler, & Angold, 2003). Second, concentrated poverty upsets the social fabric of a neighborhood, making it more difficult for adults and social institutions to provide the guidance and supervision that adolescents need (Sampson, 1992). Third, in many inner-city communities devastated by unemployment, aggression is used by males to demonstrate their standing and power—characteristics that are typically demonstrated in middle-class communities through occupational success (M. Wilson & Daly, 1985). Finally, the widespread prevalence of guns in inner-city neighborhoods changes the sorts of interactions that take place when adolescents fight, transforming what might have been aggressive disputes into lethal exchanges (P. J. Cook & Ludwig, 2004; D. Wilkinson & Fagan, 1996). The significance of neighborhood influences on violence was confirmed in a recent experiment, in which poor families with adolescents were randomly selected to be relocated into better neighborhoods: After their relocation, rates of violent behavior among the juveniles dropped significantly (J. R. Kling, Ludwig, & Katz, 2005).

■ **Official Statistics Versus Adolescents' Reports**
Official figures about adolescent crime both underreport and selectively report rates of juvenile offending (Farrington, Loeber, & Stouthamer-Loeber, 2003). Underreporting results from the fact that many adolescents commit offenses that are undetected by authorities or that are handled outside official reporting procedures—for example, when an adolescent who is caught shoplifting is reprimanded by the storekeeper instead of being referred to the police. Selective reporting results from the fact that poor and minority youngsters are more likely to be arrested and, if convicted, to be treated more harshly than other youngsters who commit similar offenses, so that official statistics may artificially inflate the proportion of crimes committed by poor, minority youth (Bridges & Steen, 1998; Farrington et al., 2003). One recent experiment found that people hold such strong negative stereotypes about Black males that when provided with information about a crime and asked to evaluate the perpetrator, individuals who were unconsciously led to believe that the offender was Black were significantly more likely than those who were not to rate him as likely to reoffend in the future and as deserving of harsh punishment, an effect that was consistent regardless of the race of the rater (S. Graham & Lowery, 2004). Racial bias is especially strong in the processing of relatively more *minor* crimes; when a very serious crime, like armed robbery, is committed, juveniles of different ethnic backgrounds are likely to receive similar treatment (Cauffman, Piquero, Kimonis, Steinberg, & Chassin, 2007).

An alternative to relying on official records is to go to adolescents directly and ask them about their involvement in various criminal or status offenses. Several researchers have done this, promising the respondents anonymity and confidentiality. The results of these surveys do not necessarily provide a more accurate picture of juvenile crime, but they certainly suggest a different one. Two conclusions are especially interesting.

First, a very large proportion of adolescents—between 60% and 80%, depending on the survey sample—report having engaged in delinquent behavior at one time or another; nearly one third of American 17-year-old boys have committed a violent crime in the past year, and nearly half of all males report being responsible for an assault sometime during adolescence (Farrington, 2009; Zimring, 1998). Second, ethnic differences in the prevalence of actual offending are smaller than what you might think based on official records (Farrington et al., 2003). More minority than

White youth admit to having committed a serious crime, but ethnic differences in self-reported offending are far smaller than ethnic differences in rates of arrest. There also are social class and neighborhood differences in rates of serious criminal activity, and because minority youth are overrepresented among the poor, they are also overrepresented among those who commit crimes (McNulty & Bellair, 2003). Delinquency is by no means limited to poor adolescents, however. One third of adolescents in affluent neighborhoods report involvement in violent and serious delinquency (J. M. Beyers, Loeber, Wikström, & Stouthamer-Loeber, 2001).

FOOD FOR THOUGHT

Why do you think antisocial behavior follows the developmental course reflected in the age–crime curve? How do you explain the fact that this pattern is seen around the world?

Although studies indicate that most adolescents—regardless of their social backgrounds—do something that violates the law at one time or another, the vast majority of teenagers who violate the law do so only once, and not violently. In fact, a relatively small number of adolescents—between 5% and 10%, depending on the study—account for most serious criminal activity (Piquero et al., 2003). It is important, therefore, in thinking about the causes of delinquent behavior, to distinguish between delinquent behavior that is serious and chronic and delinquent behavior that is less worrisome. As you will see momentarily, these two sets of delinquent behavior have very different antecedents (Moffitt, 2006).

CAUSES OF ANTISOCIAL BEHAVIOR

In general, the earlier an adolescent's "criminal career" begins—in particular, if it begins before adolescence—the more likely he or she is to become a chronic offender, to commit serious and violent crimes, and to continue committing crimes as an adult (Farrington, 2009). Conversely, the older an adolescent is when the delinquent activity first appears, the less worrisome his or her behavior is likely to become. For purposes of discussion, therefore, it is helpful to distinguish between youngsters who begin misbehaving before adolescence and those whose delinquent activity first appears during adolescence.

■ **Two Types of Offenders** One of the most influential ways of characterizing these two groups of delinquents has been suggested by psychologist Terrie

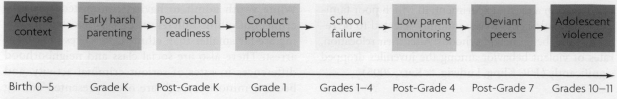

FIGURE 13.7   Adolescent violence is often the long-term consequence of a process that begins early in life. (Dodge et al., 2008)

Moffitt (2006), who distinguishes between **life-course-persistent offenders** and **adolescence-limited offenders.** The first group demonstrates antisocial behavior before adolescence, is involved in delinquency during adolescence, and is at great risk for continuing criminal activity in adulthood. The second group engages in antisocial behavior *only* during adolescence; some adolescence-limited offenders become involved in crime relatively early in adolescence, whereas others begin during mid-adolescence (Fergusson & Horwood, 2002). Some researchers have suggested that there are other groups of offenders as well (for example, individuals who do not start offending until adolescence but who continue on into adulthood, and those who display antisocial behavior as children but desist before adulthood) (Piquero et al., 2003), and others have pointed out that virtually everybody desists from crime by midlife, so that there really is no such thing as "life-course-persistent" offending (Sampson & Laub, 2003). Nevertheless, experts agree that the causes and consequences of delinquent behavior that begins during childhood or preadolescence are quite different from those of delinquency that begins—and typically ends—during adolescence or young adulthood (e.g., Moffitt, 2006; van der Geest, Blokland, & Bijleveld, 2009). Although many more males than females are life-course-persistent offenders, the risk factors for early-onset antisocial behavior are similar for the sexes (Fergusson & Horwood, 2002; Storvoll & Wichtström, 2002).

One important ramification of Moffitt's theory is that it is extremely difficult to predict which antisocial adolescents will persist in their bad behavior solely on the basis of their behavior during adolescence. Indeed, social scientists who have attempted to assess juvenile offenders' risk for future reoffending based solely on their adolescent characteristics have a remarkably poor track record (Mulvey et al., 2004). According to Moffitt's model, it is necessary to have information on the juvenile's behavior and history *before* adolescence in order to predict whether her or his offending is likely to be adolescence-limited or life-course-persistent, because the best predictor of continued offending in adulthood is the presence of serious antisocial behavior in childhood.

Life-Course-Persistent Offenders Many studies indicate that youngsters whose problems with the law begin before adolescence are often psychologically troubled. Most of these delinquents are male, many are poor, and a disproportionate number come from homes in which divorce has occurred (Farrington, 2009). More importantly, a large and consistent body of research shows that chronic delinquents typically come from disorganized families with hostile, inept, or neglectful parents who have mistreated their children and failed to instill in them proper standards of behavior or the psychological foundations of self-control (Compton, Snyder, & Schrepferman, 2003; Dogan, Conger, Kim, & Masyn, 2007; Patterson, DeGarmo, & Knutson, 2000). There is some evidence that exposure to harsh parenting may adversely affect the developing child's brain chemistry—in particular, the activity of serotonin receptors—which may increase the risk of antisocial behavior (Pine et al., 1996).

As Figure 13.7 illustrates, serious adolescent violence is typically the result of a cascade that begins early in life (Dodge, Greenberg, Malone, & Conduct Problems Prevention Research Group, 2008). You have already read about many components of this chain in previous chapters on family and peer relationships. Early economic disadvantage in the home leads to harsh and inconsistent parenting, which leads to cognitive and social deficits. This style, in turn, leads to conduct problems, which contribute to peer rejection and academic failure in elementary school and, over time, a reduction in parental supervision and monitoring. Once poorly monitored, adolescents tend to drift into antisocial peer groups, which heightens their involvement in violence.

The idea that family factors may underlie chronic delinquency—because of genetic factors, environmental influences, or both—is supported by observations that preadolescent delinquency tends to run in families (Farrington, 2009; Thornberry, Freeman-Gallant, Lizotte, Krohn, & Smith, 2003). Many adolescents who have been in trouble with the law from an early age have siblings and parents who have had similar

life-course-persistent offenders   Individuals who begin demonstrating antisocial or aggressive behavior during childhood and continue their antisocial behavior throughout adolescence and into adulthood.

adolescence-limited offenders   Antisocial adolescents whose delinquent or violent behavior begins and ends during adolescence.

problems (Farrington, 2009; Rowe, Rodgers, & Meseck-Bushey, 1992). Although studies have identified genetic influences on all types of antisocial behavior, aggression is especially heritable (Deater-Deckard & Plomin, 1999; Eley, Lichtenstein, & Stevenson, 1999).

There is also considerable evidence that, apart from family factors, certain characteristics distinguish persistently delinquent youngsters from their peers at a relatively early age. First and most importantly, children who become delinquent—especially those who engage in violence—have histories of aggressive and antisocial behavior that were identifiable as early as age 8 (Broidy et al., 2003; Farrington, 2009; Kokko, Pulkkinen, Huesmann, Dubow, & Boxer, 2009; Patterson, Forgatch, Yoerger, & Stoolmiller, 1998). Although this has been confirmed in hundreds of studies, it is important to keep in mind that the majority of children who have histories of aggressive behavior problems do *not* grow up to be delinquent. (If this seems confusing, think about it this way: The majority of delinquents probably have eaten in fast-food restaurants at some point in their childhood, but the majority of children who eat in fast-food restaurants do not grow up to be delinquent.)

Second, studies show that many children who become persistent offenders have problems in self-regulation—they are more impulsive, less able to control their anger, and more likely than their peers to suffer from hyperactivity, or as it is technically known, **attention deficit/hyperactivity disorder (ADHD)** (A. Carroll et al., 2006; B. Henry, Caspi, Moffitt, Harrington, & Silva, 1999; Patterson, DeGarmo, & Knutson, 2000; Sourander et al., 2006). ADHD is believed to be primarily biological in origin and is characterized by impulsivity, inattentiveness, restlessness, and inappropriately high levels of activity, especially in learning situations. Although ADHD does not directly cause antisocial behavior, it does elevate the risk for other family and academic problems, which, in turn, increase the likelihood of an adolescent developing externalizing problems (Nagin & Tremblay, 1999; Patterson et al., 2000). The current thinking is that chronically conduct-disordered adolescents are born with strong biological predispositions toward antisocial behavior, some of which are genetic in origin, including low levels of serotonin (which diminish their ability to delay gratification), an emotional system that is easily aroused and difficult to regulate, and a temperament that makes them hard to control (Dodge & Pettit, 2003; Guo, Roettger, & Cai, 2008; Vloet, Konrad, Huebner, Herpetz, & Herpetz-Dahlmann, 2008). Poor self-regulation is an especially potent risk factor for continued antisocial behavior (T. Gardner, Dishion, & Connell, 2008; Monahan, Steinberg, Cauffman, & Mulvey, 2009). There is also evidence that antisocial adolescents have a significantly lower resting heart rate than other youth, which may indicate a biologically inherited tendency toward fearlessness (Bimmel,

van IJzendoorn, Bakersman-Kranenburg, Juffer, & De Geus, 2008; Ortiz & Raine, 2004).

Third, and probably as a result of these biological inclinations, children who become chronically delinquent are more likely than their peers to score low in standardized tests of intelligence and neuropsychological functioning and to perform poorly in school (Cauffman, Steinberg, & Piquero, 2005; B. Henry et al., 1999; Pajer et al., 2008; Raine et al., 2005). Some of this is due to genetic factors, but some is also due to conditions surrounding their birth and prenatal care. A disproportionate number of persistently violent adolescents were born to poor mothers who abused drugs during pregnancy and had medical complications during delivery that likely affected their baby's neuropsychological and intellectual development (Arseneault, Tremblay, Boulerice, & Saucier, 2002; Brennan, Hall, Bor, Najman, & Williams, 2003; J. Liu, Raine, Wuerker, Venables, & Mednick, 2009; Piquero & Chung, 2001).

Finally, as you read in Chapter 5, aggressive adolescents often have a prior history of poor relations with peers (Agnew & Brezina, 1997; L. Lewin, Davis, & Hops, 1999; Loeber & Farrington, 2000). The combination of early aggression and peer rejection is especially devastating. As you may recall from Chapter 5, however, not all aggressive children are unpopular (Rodkin et al, 2000).

Research by psychologist Kenneth Dodge and his colleagues into the cognitive aspects of antisocial behavior indicates that especially aggressive youngsters are likely to suffer from a tendency toward what has been called a **hostile attributional bias** (Dodge & Pettit, 2003; Fontaine, Yang, Dodge, Bates, & Pettit, 2008; Lansford et al., 2006; Lochman & Dodge, 1998). Individuals with a hostile attributional bias are more likely than their peers to interpret ambiguous interactions with other children as deliberately hostile and to react aggressively. What might be viewed by the average adolescent as an innocent and accidental bump on the basketball court may be interpreted as an intentional shove by someone with a biased viewpoint, and it may lead to a fight. Such problematic information processing has been linked to aggression among White, Black, and Hispanic youngsters alike (S. Graham, Hudley, & Williams, 1992). Adolescents who have this sort of attributional bias are also likely to interpret teachers' behavior as hostile when it is not (Wyatt & Haskett, 2001). There is also evidence that some adolescents have more positive views about using aggression as a means to solve problems and that this inclination, in combination with a hostile attributional bias, leads to aggressive behavior that is

attention deficit/hyperactivity disorder (ADHD) A biologically based psychological disorder characterized by impulsivity, inattentiveness, and restlessness, often in school situations.

hostile attributional bias The tendency to interpret ambiguous interactions with others as deliberately hostile.

Some aggressive adolescents are prone to having a "hostile attributional bias"—they are more likely to interpret ambiguous interactions with others as intentionally hostile.

almost automatic (Griffith Fontaine, Salzer Burks, & Dodge, 2002).

Because aggressiveness, impulsivity, hyperactivity, and intelligence are relatively stable traits over childhood, there is a great deal of continuity in problem behaviors over time. Studies that have followed individuals from childhood through adolescence and into adulthood find very high correlations between behavior problems at one point in time and antisocial behavior later in life (Farrington, 2009; Fergusson, Lynskey, & Horwood, 1996; B. Henry, Caspi, Moffitt, & Silva, 1996; Lahey et al., 1995; Rönkä & Pulkkinen, 1995). As noted earlier, this does not mean that all individuals who show antisocial behavior early invariably show it later—in fact, the majority do not. Nevertheless, many chronically antisocial adolescents grow up to be adults who persist in their antisocial behavior and who are at increased risk for other problems as well, such as substance abuse and depression (Wiesner, Kim, & Capaldi, 2005; Wiesner & Windle, 2006).

▌ Adolescence-Limited Offenders In contrast to youngsters who begin their delinquent behaviors

prior to adolescence (and who often continue their antisocial behavior into adulthood), those who begin during adolescence do not ordinarily show signs of psychological abnormality or severe family pathology (Moffitt, 2006; Van Lier, Wanner, & Vitaro, 2007). Typically, the offenses committed by these youngsters do not develop into serious criminality, and these individuals do not commit serious violations of the law after adolescence, although they may be more likely to have subsequent problems with drugs and alcohol (Nagin, Farrington, & Moffitt, 1995). In general, individuals who are involved in adolescence-limited antisocial activities have learned the norms and standards of society and are far better socialized than life-course-persistent antisocial individuals. Nor do adolescence-limited offenders show the sorts of temperamental difficulties and neuropsychological problems seen among life-course-persistent offenders (Moffitt, Caspi, Harrington, & Milne, 2002). Interestingly, in contrast to the greatly disproportionate number of males who make up the life-course-persistent population (10 times more of these offenders are males than females), the ratio of males to females whose delinquency begins in adolescence is much smaller (about 1.5 to 1) (Moffitt & Caspi, 2001).

Although adolescence-limited offenders do not show the same degree of pathology as life-course-persistent offenders, they do have more problems both during adolescence and in early adulthood than youth who are not at all delinquent (Aguilar, Sroufe, Egeland, & Carlson, 2000). Indeed, a long-term follow-up of individuals who had earlier been classified as life-course-persistent offenders, adolescence-limited offenders, or neither found that as young adults the adolescence-limited offenders had more mental health, substance abuse, and financial problems than individuals who had not been delinquent at all as teenagers (Moffitt et al., 2002). It would be incorrect, therefore, to assume that just because an adolescent's antisocial behavior is limited to adolescence that he or she is not troubled. These individuals' serious offending may be limited to adolescence, but their other problems may persist into early adulthood.

The main risk factors for adolescence-limited offending are well established: poor parenting (especially poor monitoring) and affiliation with antisocial peers (Goodnight, Bates, Newman, Dodge, & Pettit, 2006; D. J. Jones, Forehand, Brody, & Armistead, 2002; Lacourse, Nagin, & Tremblay, 2003; McCabe, Hough, Wood, & Yeh, 2001; Monahan, Steinberg, & Cauffman, 2009). The first of these (poor parenting) usually leads to the second (hanging around with antisocial peers) (Dishion, Patterson, Stoolmiller, & Skinner, 1991; Laird, Criss, Pettit, Dodge, & Bates, 2008). Influences on adolescence-limited offending are virtually identical for males and females and among adolescents from different ethnic groups (Choi, Harachi, Gillmore, & Catalano,

2005; Dekovi, Buist, & Reitz, 2004; Fergusson & Horwood, 2002; Sameroff, Peck, & Eccles, 2004).

The role of the peer group in adolescence-limited offending is extremely important, especially in industrialized countries, where peer influence tends to be relatively strong (Cheung, 1997; Dishion, Andrews, & Crosby, 1995; Heimer & Matsueda, 1994; Keenan, Loeber, Zhang, Stouthamer-Loeber, & Van Kammen, 1995; Tremblay, Mâsse, Vitaro, & Dobkin, 1995). As you read in Chapter 7, one of the strongest predictors of delinquency and other forms of problem behavior is the extent to which the adolescent spends unsupervised time in unstructured activities with peers—activities like hanging out, cruising around, and going to parties (Osgood, Wilson, O'Malley, Bachman, & Johnston, 1996). Arrest statistics show that most delinquent activity occurs in group situations in which adolescents are pressured by their friends to go along with the group (Zimring, 1998). It is not coincidental that the peak years of susceptibility to peer pressure overlap with the peak years for this sort of delinquency. Indeed, one of the central tenets of Moffit's theory is that adolescence-limited offending is largely done in an effort to impress other adolescents with one's bravado and independence from adult authority; nondelinquent youth may mimic antisocial peers to increase their status and popularity (Moffitt, 2006; Rebellon, 2006).

PREVENTION AND TREATMENT OF EXTERNALIZING PROBLEMS

Given the important differences between the causes of life-course-persistent and adolescence-limited antisocial behavior, it makes sense that these two groups of adolescents would be best served by different sorts of preventive and after-the-fact interventions. In order to lower the rate of chronic antisocial behavior, experts argue that we need mainly to prevent disruption in early family relationships and to head off early academic problems through a combination of family support and preschool intervention (Loeber & Farrington, 2000; Tolan & Gorman-Smith, 2002; Tremblay, Pagani-Kurtz, Mâsse, Vitaro, & Pihl, 1995; Yoshikawa, 1994). There is also some evidence that interventions designed to improve the transition into school and work roles in young adulthood may prove helpful (Roisman, Aguilar, & Egeland, 2004; Stouthamer-Loeber, Wei, & Loeber, 2004).

These sorts of preventive strategies are easier proposed than done, however. Our society is hesitant to intervene to prevent family problems, and we typically wait until we see a sign of trouble in a family before acting. Unfortunately, research shows that the outlook for delinquents who have begun criminal careers early is not very good, although recent evaluations of a variety of interventions that follow **evidence-based practices** (that is, programs that have a strong scientific basis)

have been encouraging (Lipsey, 2009). This is the case for treatment approaches that employ individual psychotherapy, family-based interventions, and diversion programs designed to remove delinquents from the juvenile justice system and provide them with alternative opportunities for productive behavior. One recent evaluation of a family-based prevention program found the strongest effects among adolescents who had a genetic predisposition for problem behavior (Brody, Beach, Philibert, Chen, & Murry, 2009). In contrast, interventions that group antisocial youth together tend to be less effective, because they may inadvertently foster friendships among delinquent peers, and more antisocial adolescents may teach less antisocial ones some of the "tricks of the trade" (Mager, Milich, Harris, & Howard, 2005).

The prognosis for delinquents whose antisocial behavior is adolescence-limited is considerably better. Because they have internalized a basic foundation of norms and moral standards, it is easier to help these youngsters control their own behavior and stop misbehaving. Four types of strategies have been proposed. First, we can help youngsters by teaching them how to learn to resist peer pressure and to settle conflicts without resorting to aggression (Conduct Problems Prevention Research Group, 1999). Second, by training parents to monitor their children more effectively, we can minimize the number of opportunities adolescents have to engage in peer-oriented misbehavior (Forgatch, Patterson, Degarmo, & Beldavs, 2009). Third, by intervening within classrooms, schools, and neighborhoods, we may be able to alter the broader climate in ways that discourage antisocial behavior and encourage prosocial behavior (Kellam, Ling, Merisca, Brown, & Ialongo, 1998). Finally, by treating delinquency seriously when it occurs—by making sure that an adolescent knows that misbehavior has definite consequences—we can deter her or him from doing the same thing again in the future (E. Scott & Steinberg, 2008).

RECAP

- Experts distinguish among three broad categories of externalizing problems in adolescence: conduct disorder, aggression, and juvenile offending. Although there is considerable overlap among them, they have different definitions.
- Antisocial behavior takes three forms: authority-related conflicts, covert antisocial behavior, and overt antisocial behavior. Within each of these types, there are predictable patterns of progression from less serious to more serious forms.
- Although the juvenile crime rate has declined considerably from its peak in the early 1990s, adolescents

evidence-based practices   Programs and practices that have a proven scientific basis.

still account for a disproportionately high number of crimes, including violent crimes.

- It is important to distinguish between life-course-persistent offenders, whose antisocial behavior begins before adolescence and continues into adulthood, and adolescence-limited offenders, whose antisocial behavior typically begins and ends during the teenage years.
- Life-course-persistent offenders typically have histories of early family problems, childhood aggression, and neuropsychological deficits, as well as strong biological predispositions toward antisocial behavior.
- Adolescence-limited offenders, in contrast, are normal adolescents whose problems usually stem from poor parental monitoring and affiliation with antisocial peers.
- Recent evaluations suggest that evidence-based programs can be effective in treating delinquency.

Internalizing Problems

Most individuals emerge from adolescence confident, with a healthy sense of who they are and where they are headed. But in some instances, the changes and demands of adolescence may leave a teenager feeling helpless, confused, and pessimistic about the future. Although minor fluctuations in self-esteem during early adolescence are commonplace—as you read in Chapter 8—it is not normal for adolescents (or adults, for that matter) to feel a prolonged or intense sense of hopelessness or frustration. Such young people are likely to be psychologically depressed and in need of professional help. Depression is by far the most significant internalizing problem in adolescence.

THE NATURE AND PREVALENCE OF DEPRESSION

In its mild form, **depression** is the most common psychological disturbance among adolescents (Graber & Sontag, 2009). Although we typically associate depression with feelings of sadness, there are other symptoms that are important signs of the disturbance, and sadness alone without any other symptoms may not indicate depression in the clinical sense of the term. Depression has emotional symptoms, including dejection, decreased enjoyment of pleasurable activities, and low

depression A psychological disturbance characterized by low self-esteem, decreased motivation, sadness, and difficulty in finding pleasure in formerly pleasurable activities.

TABLE 13.3   DSM-IV diagnostic criteria for mild depressive disorder (dysthymic disorder)

1. Depressed or irritable mood for most of the day, for more days than not, for at least one year.
2. The presence, while depressed, of at least two of the following:
   a. Poor appetite or overeating
   b. Insomnia or hypersomnia (sleeping too much)
   c. Low energy or fatigue
   d. Low self-esteem
   e. Poor concentration or difficulty making decisions
   f. Feelings of hopelessness
3. The symptoms cause clinically significant distress or impairment in social, school, or other important areas of functioning.

self-esteem. It has cognitive symptoms, such as pessimism and hopelessness. It has motivational symptoms, including apathy and boredom. Finally, it usually has physical symptoms, such as a loss of appetite, difficulty sleeping, and loss of energy. The symptoms of major depression are the same in adolescence as in adulthood and among males and females, although, as you'll read, there are sex differences in the prevalence of the illness (Lewinsohn, Pettit, Joiner, & Seeley, 2003).

Mood, Syndromes, and Disorder   Many people use the term *depression* imprecisely, to refer to a wide range of affective problems. Psychologists believe that it is important to distinguish among depressed mood (feeling sad), depressive syndromes (having multiple symptoms of depression), and depressive disorder (having enough symptoms to be diagnosed with the illness) (Graber & Sontag, 2009). All individuals experience periods of sadness or depressed mood at one time or another. According to one large-scale survey, nearly one third of all adolescents feel so sad and hopeless so often that they stop engaging in their usual activities (Centers for Disease Control and Prevention, 2008). According to other surveys, about 25% of adolescents regularly feel depressed (Avenevoli & Steinberg, 2001).

Fewer individuals report a pattern of depressive symptoms that includes a wider range of symptoms than sadness alone. At any one point in time, somewhat fewer than 10% of American teenagers report moderate or severe symptoms of depression—about 5% have the symptoms of a depressive syndrome, and approximately 3% meet the DSM-IV diagnostic criteria for depressive disorder (see Table 13.3) (Compas, Ey, & Grant, 1993; Lewinsohn, Hops, Roberts, Seeley, & Andrews, 1993; Rushton, Forcier, & Schectman, 2002). Some studies estimate that as many as 25% of individuals will experience at least one bout of depression by the end of adolescence (Forbes & Dahl, 2005).

One reason the incidence of depression is greater among adolescent girls than boys is that girls are more likely to react to stress by ruminating about the problem and feeling helpless.

Depressed mood, depressive syndrome, and depressive disorder all become more common over adolescence, in part because of the increasing prevalence of stressful events during the adolescent years (Graber & Sontag, 2009) and in part because the cognitive changes of adolescence permit the introspection and rumination that often accompany depression (Avenevoli & Steinberg, 2001). There is also a significant decline in positive mood over the adolescent years (Weinstein, Mermelstein, Hankin, Hedeker, & Flay, 2007).

There is an especially dramatic increase in the prevalence of depressive feelings around the time of puberty; depression is one third as common during childhood as it is during adolescence (Graber & Sontag, 2009). One intriguing idea links the increase in depression to the same changes in the brain's dopamine system that increase the vulnerability to alcohol and other drugs (Davey, Yücel, & Allen, 2008). According to this view, the coincidence of increased reward seeking caused by this brain change with changes in the adolescent's social world leads to an intensification in adolescents' desire for the rewards of intimate friendships and romantic relationships. When these rewards don't materialize, adolescents may become frustrated and depressed. Symptoms of depression increase steadily throughout adolescence and then start to decline—making late adolescence the period of the life span with

the highest risk for the disorder (Wight, Sepúlveda, & Aneshensel, 2004). One reason that depression declines in late adolescence is that individuals report a significant decline in stress during this period (J. S. Brown, Meadows, & Elder, Jr., 2007; Seiffge-Krenke, Aunola, & Nurmi, 2009).

Some studies also indicate that there have been historical increases in the prevalence of depression and other signs of internalized distress, especially among adolescents, with the rates increasing in each generation (Lewinsohn, Rohde, Seeley, & Fischer, 1993). Indeed, one analysis found that the *average* American child in the 1980s reported feeling more anxious than child *psychiatric patients* did in the 1950s; increases in stressors such as divorce and crime seem to have played a major role (Twenge, 2000). Several recent studies have also indicated that there may be ethnic differences in the prevalence of depression during adolescence, with significantly more Hispanic teenagers reporting depressive symptoms than their White, Black, or Asian peers, especially within samples of girls (Roberts, Roberts, & Chen, 1997; J. Siegel, Aneshensel, Taub, Cantwell, & Driscoll, 1998).

▌ **Problems in Diagnosing Depression in Adolescence** Diagnosing and studying depression among adolescents has been a tricky business for three very

FIGURE 13.8   Depressed mood among males and females as a function of age. (Wichstrøm, 1999)

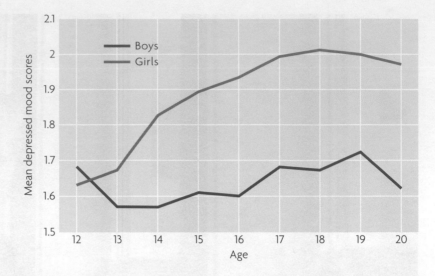

different reasons. First, depression during adolescence is often accompanied by other psychosocial or behavioral problems, including anxiety, phobias, psychosomatic complaints, and substance abuse (Graber & Sontag, 2009). Low-income urban adolescents who are depressed are especially likely to report psychosomatic symptoms such as headaches and stomachaches, rather than the symptoms we more automatically associate with depression, like apathy or sadness (L. K. Reynolds, O'Koon, Papademetriou, Szczygiel, & Grant, 2001).

Second, many professionals have been tempted to attribute nearly all observable difficulties in adolescence to unseen depression. In the past, for example, behaviors such as school phobia, running away from home, and anorexia nervosa were thought to hide the "real" problem—depression. Now, however, it is widely recognized that not all adolescents with behavior problems are "really" depressed; rather, as we saw earlier, depression and other problems are often comorbid (Compas et al., 1993; Graber & Sontag, 2009). In cases in which the main problem seems not to be depression, a careful clinician would certainly want to probe to see whether depressive symptoms were present but would not necessarily jump to the conclusion that depression and behavior problems always go hand in hand.

Third, the popular stereotype of adolescents as normally disturbed leads many parents and teachers to fail to recognize genuine psychological problems when they appear. You can probably imagine a parent's description of an adolescent daughter who is critical of herself (which can be an emotional manifestation of depression), unduly negative (a possible cognitive manifestation), bored with everything (a possible motivational manifestation), and uninterested in eating (a possible physical manifestation). It would be easy for this parent to overlook a potentially very real problem and dismiss the daughter's mood and behavior as normal. Obviously, not all instances of self-criticism or apathy reflect

psychological disturbance. But a good rule of thumb is that an individual who displays three or more of the signs of depression (see Table 13.3) for 2 weeks should probably consult a professional.

SEX DIFFERENCES IN DEPRESSION

One of the most consistent findings in the study of adolescent depression involves the emergence of a very large sex difference in rates of depression in early adolescence. As Figure 13.8 indicates, before adolescence, boys are somewhat more likely to exhibit depressive symptoms than girls, but after puberty, the sex difference in prevalence of depression reverses. From early adolescence until very late in adulthood, twice as many females as males suffer from depressive disorder, and females are somewhat more likely than males to report depressed mood (Compas et al., 1997; Holsen, Kraft, & Vitterso, 2000; Twenge & Nolen-Hoeksema, 2002; Wade, Cairney, & Pevalin, 2002). The increased risk for depression among girls emerges during puberty, rather than at a particular age or grade in school (Angold, Costello, & Worthman, 1998; G. C. Patton et al., 2008). Although sex differences in major depression persist beyond adolescence, reports of depressive symptoms tend to diminish somewhat in early adulthood; both sexes report less stress and less depression in their mid-20s than late teens, but the decline is steeper among females, perhaps because they experience a greater drop in stress as they leave adolescence behind (Galambos, Barker, & Krahn, 2006; Ge, Natsuaki, & Conger, 2006; Meadows, Brown, & Elder, Jr., 2006; Stoolmiller, Kim, & Capaldi, 2005).

Psychologists do not have a definitive explanation for the emergence of sex differences in depressive disorder at adolescence. Some evidence indicates that females are more susceptible than males to genetic influences on depression, such that even when males and females inherit the same genetic predisposition toward depression from their parents, that predisposition is more likely to be manifested among girls (Jacobson & Rowe, 1999), but it is not known why this is the case. More likely, changes in social relationships around the time of puberty may leave girls more vulnerable than boys to some forms of psychological distress (with some individuals inheriting a stronger predisposition than others), and depression may be a stereotypically feminine way of manifesting it.

■ **Gender Roles**   More specifically, social scientists speculate that the emergence of sex differences in depression has something to do with the social role that the adolescent girl may find herself in as she enters the world of boy–girl relationships (Petersen et al., 1993; Wichstrøm, 1999). As you read in previous chapters, this role may bring heightened self-consciousness over her physical appearance and increased concern over popularity with peers. Since many of these feelings may provoke helplessness, hopelessness, and anxiety, adolescent girls may be more susceptible to depressive feelings. To make matters worse, pressures on young women to behave in sex-stereotyped ways, which intensify during adolescence (see Chapter 8), may lead girls to adopt some behaviors and dispositions—passivity, dependency, and fragility, for example—that they have been socialized to believe are part of the feminine role and that may contribute to their depressed mood. Consistent with this, studies show that depression in girls is significantly correlated with having a poor body image and being low in masculinity (Bearman & Stice, 2008; Eberhart, Shih, Hammen, & Brennan, 2006; Obeidallah, McHale, & Silbereisen, 1996; Seiffge-Krenke & Stemmler, 2002; Wichstrøm, 1999).

The gender-role intensification hypothesis is only one explanation for sex differences in the prevalence of depression during adolescence. Three other accounts focus on sex differences in the degree to which adolescence is stressful, in the ways of coping with stress, and in vulnerability to different types of stress (Cyranowski & Frank, 2000; Leadbeater, Blatt, & Quinlan, 1995; Nolen-Hoeksema & Girgus, 1994; Rudolph & Hammen, 1999).

■ **Stress, Rumination, and Sensitivity to Others**
With respect to the first of these explanations, it is important to note that the link between stress and depression during adolescence is well documented among both males and females; individuals who experience more stress are more vulnerable to depression and other internalizing problems (Petersen et al., 1993). Of interest, then, is evidence that early adolescence is generally a more stressful time for girls than boys (Allgood-Merten, Lewisohn, & Hops, 1990; Petersen, Sarigiani, & Kennedy, 1991; Rudolph & Hammen, 1999). This is because the bodily changes of puberty, especially when

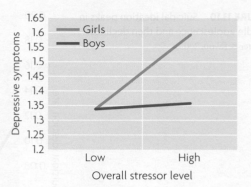

FIGURE 13.9   Adolescent girls are more likely than boys to become depressed when exposed to the same level of stress. (Hankin et al., 2007)

they occur early in adolescence, are more likely to be stressful for girls than boys; because girls are more likely than boys to experience multiple stressors at the same time (for example, going through puberty while making the transition into junior high school); and because girls are likely to experience more stressful life events than boys (Graber & Sontag, 2009).

Second, there is evidence that girls are more likely than boys to react to stress by turning their feelings inward—for instance, by ruminating about the problem and feeling helpless—whereas boys are more likely to respond either by distracting themselves or by turning their feelings outward, in aggressive behavior or in drug and alcohol abuse (Calvete & Cardeñoso, 2005; Grant et al., 2004; Jose & Brown, 2008; Nolen-Hoeksema & Girgus, 1994; Papadakis, Prince, Jones, & Strauman, 2006). As a result, even when exposed to the same degree of stress, girls are more likely to respond to the stressors by becoming depressed (Angold et al., 1996; Hankin, Mermelstein, & Roesch, 2007; Rudolph & Hammen, 1999) (see Figure 13.9). This difference in the ways that boys and girls react to stress helps explain why the prevalence of externalizing disorders is higher in boys, while the prevalence of internalizing disorders is higher in girls. Girls who are more able to tolerate conflicts in their relationships are less likely to develop internalizing symptoms (Gunlicks-Stoessel & Powers, 2008).

The third explanation emphasizes girls' generally greater orientation toward and sensitivity to interpersonal relations (Cyranowski & Frank, 2000; Guyer, McClure-Tone, Shiffrin, Pine, & Nelson, 2009). Sex differences in levels of the hormone **oxytocin** may both encourage females to invest more in their close relationships and make them more vulnerable to the adverse consequences of relational disruptions and interpersonal difficulties. Consistent with this, research indicates that girls are much more likely than boys to develop

oxytocin   A hormone known to influence emotional bonding to others.

FIGURE 13.10 Suicidal ideation peaks in middle adolescence and then declines. (Rueter & Kwon, 2005)

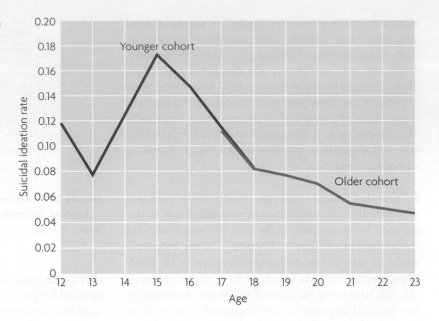

emotional problems as a result of family discord or problems with peers (Crawford, Cohen, Midlarsky, & Brook, 2001; Leadbeater, Kuperminc, Blatt, & Hertzog, 1999; Seiffge-Krenke & Stemmler, 2002; Washburn-Ormachea, Hillman, & Sawilowsky, 2004). Because adolescence is a time of many changes in relationships—in the family, with friends, and with romantic partners—the capacity of females to invest heavily in their relationships with others may be both a strength and a source of vulnerability.

FOOD FOR THOUGHT

In light of what we know about the likely causes of sex differences in depression, what preventive interventions should be targeted at young adolescent girls?

SUICIDE

▌ **Prevalence of Suicide** According to recent national surveys, in any given year, close to 10% of American female high school students and about 5% of males attempt suicide; nearly one third of these attempts are serious enough to require treatment by a physician or nurse. Twice as many adolescents (about 20% of girls and 10% of boys) think about killing themselves—referred to as **suicidal ideation**—and the majority of these have gone so far as to make a plan (Centers for Disease Control and Prevention, 2008). Suicidal ideation increases during early adolescence, peaks around

age 15, and then declines (see Figure 13.10) (Rueter & Kwon, 2005). Adolescents who attempt to kill themselves usually have made appeals for help and have tried but failed to get emotional support from family or friends. They report feeling trapped, lonely, worthless, and hopeless (Kidd, 2004).

The adolescent suicide rate among 15- to 19-year-olds increased alarmingly between 1950 and 1990, fueled by the increased use of drugs and alcohol and the increased availability of firearms (Judge & Billick, 2004). The rate peaked and declined somewhat during the 1990s, as new forms of antidepressant medication were more widely prescribed to adolescents (Zametkin, Alter, & Yemini, 2001; Zito et al., 2002). You may have read that suicide is a leading cause of death among young people, but this is primarily because very few young people die from other causes, such as disease. Although the rate of suicide rises rapidly during the middle adolescent years, it continues to rise throughout adulthood, and suicide is a much more common cause of death among adults than it is among young people, largely because very few suicide attempts by adolescents are successful. The most common method of suicide among adolescents is with a firearm, followed by hanging. Drug overdoses and carbon monoxide poisoning are also common (Judge & Billick, 2004). The suicide rate is highest among American Indian and Alaskan Native adolescents and lowest among Black and White adolescents; rates among Hispanic, and Asian adolescents fall in between these extremes (Goldston et al., 2008).

▌ **Risk Factors for Suicide** Systematic studies have identified four established sets of risk factors for attempting suicide during adolescence, and they are similar for males and females and among Black, Hispanic, and White adolescents: having a psychiatric problem,

suicidal ideation Thinking about ending one's life.

especially depression or substance abuse; having a history of suicide in the family; being under stress, especially in the areas of achievement and sexuality; and experiencing parental rejection, family disruption, or extensive family conflict (Judge & Billick, 2004; Schilling, Aseltine, Glanovsky, James, & Jacons, 2009; Swahn, Bossarte, & Sullivent, 2008). Adolescents who have one of these risk factors are significantly more likely to attempt suicide than their peers, and adolescents who have more than one risk factor are dramatically more likely to try to kill themselves. Adolescents who have attempted suicide once are at risk for attempting it again (Lewinsohn, Rohde, & Seely, 1994). Adolescents are also more likely to attempt suicide if one of their friends or someone else in their community has committed suicide (Bearman & Moody, 2004; R. X. Liu, 2006).

CAUSES OF DEPRESSION AND INTERNALIZING DISORDERS

A variety of theories have been proposed to account for the onset of depression and other types of internalizing problems during adolescence, and the current consensus is that internalizing problems are likely to result from interacting environmental conditions and individual predispositions rather than either set of factors alone. Today, most experts endorse a **diathesis–stress model** of depression, which suggests that depression may occur when individuals who are predisposed toward internalizing problems (the term "diathesis" refers to this predisposition) are exposed to chronic or acute stressors that precipitate a depressive reaction (Hilsman & Garber, 1995; Lewinsohn, Joiner, & Rohde, 2001). Individuals without the diathesis—who are not predisposed toward depression—are able to withstand a great deal of stress, for instance, without developing any psychological problems. In contrast, individuals who have strong predispositions toward the disorder may become depressed in the face of stressful circumstances that most of us would consider to be quite normal. Research has focused on both the diathesis and the stress—on identifying individual predispositions toward depression and on identifying the environmental circumstances likely to precipitate the disorder.

▌ **The Diathesis** Two categories of predispositions have received the most attention. First, because depression has been found to have a strong genetic component, it is believed that at least some of the diathesis is biological and may be related to problematic patterns of neuroendocrine functioning (**neuroendocrine** refers to hormonal activity in the brain and nervous system). In particular, researchers have focused on the predisposition toward intense problems in regulation of activity in one or more of the hypothalamic-pituitary axes, including those involving the adrenal, thyroid, gonadal,

and somatotropic axes (Graber & Sontag, 2009). This biological predisposition may make it difficult for individuals to regulate their emotions, which, in turn, may make them susceptible to depression and other psychological problems (Silk et al., 2007). Individuals who are prone to intense activation of the hypothalamic-pituitary-adrenocortical (HPA) axis, in particular, are more biologically reactive to stress than others, and they are more prone to depression and other internalizing disorders. Scientists have recently discovered that abnormalities in one of several genes, in particular, may make some individuals more likely to develop depression in the face of stress (Caspi et al., 2003; Cicchetti, Rogosh, & Sturge-Apple, 2007). Not surprisingly, then, given the role that genes play in the development of depression, vulnerability to depression tends to run in families—adolescents with a depressed parent are 3 times as likely to develop depression as are other youth (Graber & Sontag, 2009).

Other researchers have focused more on the cognitive style of depressed individuals, suggesting that people with tendencies toward hopelessness, pessimism, and self-blame are more likely to interpret events in their lives in ways that lead to the development of depression (Clements, Aber, & Seidman, 2008; Kaslow, Adamson, & Collins, 2000; Prinstein & Aikins, 2004). These sorts of cognitive sets, which may be linked to the ways in which children think they are viewed first by parents and later by peers, develop during childhood and are thought to play a role in the onset of depression during adolescence (D. Cole & Jordan, 1995; D. Cole, Martin, & Powers, 1997; Garber, Weiss, & Shanley, 1993; Nolen-Hoeksema, Girgus, & Seligman, 1992). As with the case of stress-reactivity, there is some evidence that individuals' cognitive style is moderately heritable (Lau & Eley, 2008).

▌ **The Stress** Researchers who have been more concerned with the stress component of the diathesis–stress model—that is, with environmental influences on depression—have focused on three broad sets of stressors (Aseltine, Gore, & Colten, 1994; Lewinsohn, Roberts et al., 1994; Lewinsohn, Gotlib, & Seeley, 1997). By and large, these factors have been found to be linked to depression among adolescents from very different cultures (Greenberger, Chen, Tally, & Dong, 2000; S. Kim & Ge, 2000; Xia & Qian, 2001). First, depression is more common among adolescents from families

diathesis–stress model A perspective on disorder that posits that problems are the result of an interaction between a preexisting condition (the diathesis) and exposure to a stressful event or condition.

neuroendocrine Hormonal activity in the brain and nervous system.

Contrary to myth, suicide attempts by adolescents are rarely impulsive reactions to specific events. Rather, adolescents who attempt to kill themselves typically have had a history of depression and have not been able to find emotional support from family or friends.

characterized by high conflict and low cohesion, and it is higher among adolescents from divorced homes (Graber & Sontag, 2009). Second, depression is more prevalent among adolescents who are unpopular or who have poor peer relations (Conley & Rudolph, 2009). Third, depressed adolescents report more chronic and acute stress than nondepressed adolescents do (Graber & Sontag, 2009). These psychosocial factors may both contribute to and exacerbate the development of negative cognitive sets (Garber, Robinson, & Valentiner, 1997). There is also evidence that academic difficulties are correlated with depression, especially among adolescents from Asian cultures, in which relatively more stress may be placed on achievement (Chan, 1997; Greenberger, Chen, Tally, & Dong, 2000). Similar findings on the connection between academic pressure and depression have emerged from studies of affluent suburban youth (Luthar & Becker, 2002). Although all sorts of stressors have been linked to the onset of psychological problems (Steinberg & Avenevoli, 2000), the single most common trigger of the

first episode of major depression in adolescence is the breakup of a romantic relationship (Monroe, Rohde, Seeley, & Lewinsohn, 1999).

You read earlier that the prevalence of depression rises during adolescence. Can diathesis–stress models of depression account for this increase? For the most part, they can. Biological theorists can point to the hormonal changes of puberty, which are likely to have implications for neuroendocrine activity; as you read in Chapter 1, one of the effects of pubertal hormones is to make individuals more sensitive to stress (E. Walker, Sabuwalla, & Huot, 2004). Depression and negative affect among both boys and girls are correlated with various hormones known to change at puberty (Angold, Costello, Erkanli, & Worthman, 1999; Graber & Sontag, 2009). Many studies show that the increase in depression in adolescence is more closely linked to puberty than age (Hayward, Gotlib, Schraedley, & Litt, 1999), although it is difficult to pinpoint puberty as the cause of the problem, since many other changes typically occur around the same time (such as the transition out of elementary school). Cognitive theorists can point to the onset of hypothetical thinking at adolescence, which may result in new (and perhaps potentially more depressing) ways of viewing the world (Kuhn, 2009). And theorists who emphasize environmental factors draw attention to the new environmental demands of adolescence, such as changing schools, beginning to date, or coping with transformations in family relationships—all of which may lead to heightened stress (Graber & Sontag, 2009). Thus, there are many good reasons to expect that the prevalence of depression would increase as individuals pass from childhood into adolescence. It is also important to note that individuals who develop internalizing disorders such as depression and anxiety in adolescence are at elevated risk to suffer from these problems as adults (Lewinsohn, Rohde, Seeley, Klein, & Gotlib, 2003; Pine, Cohen, Gurley, Brook, & Ma, 1998).

TREATMENT AND PREVENTION OF INTERNALIZING PROBLEMS

The treatment of depression during adolescence is very similar to its treatment at other points in the life span. Clinicians use a wide range of approaches, including biological therapies employing antidepressant medication (these address the neuroendocrine problem, if one exists); psychotherapies designed to help depressed adolescents understand the roots of their depression, to increase the degree to which they experience reinforcement in their daily activities, or to change the nature of their cognitive set; and family therapy, which focuses on changing patterns of family relationships that may be contributing to the adolescent's symptoms. A recent comprehensive review found that psychotherapy with depressed and anxious adolescents has a significant, but modest, effect; although most of the treatment studies employed cognitive-behavioral therapy, the review found that other evidence-based practices (e.g., interpersonal therapy) were equally effective (Weisz, McCarty, & Valeri, 2006). Importantly, however, the researchers found that evidence-based approaches are superior to approaches that do not have a scientific basis, which, unfortunately, are widely used (Weisz, Jensen-Doss, & Hawley, 2006). With regard to antidepressants, research has confirmed the effectiveness of a class of drugs called **selective serotonin reuptake inhibitors (SSRIs),** such as Prozac, in the treatment of depression in adolescence (Graber & Sontag, 2009). These medications are also effective in treating other types of internalizing problems, such as anxiety disorders and social phobias, especially when used in conjunction with cognitive behavioral therapy (Brent et al., 2008; Vitiello et al., 2006; Walkup et al., 2008).

RECAP

- Depression is the most common internalizing disorder of adolescence, afflicting as many as 25% of individuals by the time they enter adulthood.
- Significant sex differences in depression emerge in early adolescence that are maintained throughout adulthood. Females are more likely to be depressed than males, although experts disagree about why this is the case.
- Nearly 10% of adolescent girls and 5% of boys have attempted suicide, and twice this number have seriously thought about killing themselves.
- Depression is the result of an interacting set of environmental conditions (especially stress) and individual predispositions, or diatheses (including biological and cognitive predispositions).
- Depression during adolescence can be successfully treated through medication and psychotherapy, which are especially effective if combined.

Stress and Coping

Nearly half of all adolescents report difficulty in coping with stressful situations at home or at school (Gans, 1990). These stressors include major life changes (such as going through parental divorce, changing schools, or having someone in the family suddenly become seriously ill), chronically stressful conditions (such as poverty, a disabling illness, or constant family conflict),

and day-to-day hassles (such as school exams, fights with friends, and arguments with siblings and parents) (Compas & Reeslund, 2009).

Research indicates that stress can affect individuals in different ways (Steinberg & Avenevoli, 2000). For some teenagers, stress can lead to internalized disorders, such as anxiety, depression, headaches, and indigestion—even compromised immune system functioning (Birmaher et al., 1994). For others, the consequences of stress are externalized, in behavior and conduct problems. For still others, the impact of stress is manifested in drug and alcohol abuse. These links between stress and psychosocial problems have been documented in studies of youngsters from all ethnic groups and family backgrounds and among youth exposed to both relatively common stressors (such as breaking up with a romantic partner) and relatively severe ones (such as exposure to war trauma) (Macksoud & Aber, 1996; Sack & Clarke, 1996).

Yet, for some adolescents, the very same sources and levels of stress do not seem to be associated with psychological or physical upset at all. Thus, although we tend to think of stress as having negative effects on our well-being, the connection between stress and dysfunction is not clear-cut. Some adolescents show enormous **resilience** in the face of enormous adversity (Compas & Reeslund, 2009; Luthar, Cicchetti, & Becker, 2000; Masten, 2001). What makes some adolescents more vulnerable to the effects of stress than others? Psychologists point to three sets of factors.

First, the effect of any one stressor is exacerbated if it is accompanied by other stressors. Studies show that stress tends to have a multiplicative effect: An adolescent who faces two stressors at the same time (parental divorce and school change, for example) is more than twice as likely to experience psychological problems as someone who has experienced only one of the two stressors (Compas & Reeslund, 2009; Forehand, Biggar, & Kotchick, 1998).

Second, adolescents who have other resources—either internal resources, such as high self-esteem, healthy identity development, high intelligence, or strong feelings of competence, or external resources, such as social support from others—are less likely to be adversely affected by stress than their peers (Compas & Reeslund, 2009; Luthar, 1991; Masten et al., 1999; Steinberg et al., 2006). Adolescents with close friends and good social skills seem to be better able to handle stressors such as parental divorce or starting junior high

selective serotonin reuptake inhibitors (SSRIs)   A class of antidepressant medications that has proven to be effective with adolescents suffering from internalizing problems, such as depression.

resilience   The ability of an individual to continue to function competently in the face of adversity or stress.

school than are teenagers who lack close friendships or have fewer interpersonal resources. Most importantly, teenagers who have warm and close family relationships are less likely to be distressed by a stressful experience than are teenagers without such familial support (Weist, Freedman, Paskewitz, Proescher, & Flaherty, 1995). Indeed, studies consistently show that the presence of a close parent–adolescent relationship is probably the single most important factor in protecting adolescents from psychological harm (Resnick et al., 1997). The importance of social support as a buffer against the adverse effects of stress has been documented in studies of adolescents around the world.

Finally, some adolescents use more effective coping strategies than do others. Specialists who study coping strategies distinguish between strategies that involve taking steps to change the source of the stress, called **primary control strategies,** and those that involve efforts to adapt to the problem, called **secondary control strategies** (Compas & Reeslund, 2009). For instance, if you are very worried about an upcoming exam in this course, a primary control strategy might be to form a study group with other students in order to review the material, whereas a secondary control strategy might be to go out to a movie or for a run in order to relax yourself.

In some situations, secondary control strategies are quite effective. These tend to be stressful situations that are clearly uncontrollable, such as being diagnosed with a serious illness or learning that one's parents are getting a divorce (Hall, Chipperfield, Perry, Ruthig, & Goetz, 2006). In these instances, trying to distract and calm oneself may help alleviate some of the stress, and trying to exert control over an uncontrollable situation may only make matters worse (Jaser et al., 2007). But, in general, research shows that adolescents who employ primary control strategies are less vulnerable to the detrimental health consequences of stress, especially if the source of the stress is controllable (Clarke, 2006). Studies of a wide range of male and female adolescents from different ethnic groups show that individuals who use primary or secondary control strategies are better adjusted, less depressed, and less likely to have behavioral problems than those who react to stress through disengagement or avoidance (Compas & Reeslund, 2009; Dumont & Provost, 1999; Herman-Stahl, Stemmler, & Petersen, 1995; L. D. Scott & House, 2005; Seiffge-Krenke & Klessinger, 2000; Tolan, Gorman-Smith, Henry, Chung, & Hunt, 2002).

FOOD FOR THOUGHT

How do you cope with stress? Are you more likely to use primary or secondary control strategies?

RECAP

- For some adolescents, exposure to chronic or severe stress can result in psychological or physical difficulties, but for others, the very same sources and levels of stress do not seem to be associated with upset at all.
- In general, the effect of stress is exacerbated if it is accompanied by other stressors, if the adolescent lacks sufficient internal or external resources, or if the adolescent has poorly developed coping skills.
- Coping with stress by trying to change the source of stress (if it is controllable) or to adapt to the problem (if it is not) is generally more effective than coping through distraction or avoidance.

primary control strategies Coping strategies in which an individual attempts to change the stressor.

secondary control strategies Coping strategies that involve attempts by the individual to adapt to the stressor.

Glossary

A

abstinence-only sex education   Programs that encourage adolescents to avoid sexual activity but that do not provide information about safe sex.

academic achievement   Achievement that is measured by standardized tests of scholastic ability or knowledge.

achievement   The psychosocial domain concerning behaviors and feelings in evaluative situations.

achievement attributions   The beliefs an individual holds about the causes of her or his successes and failures.

activational role (of hormones)   The process through which changes in hormone levels, especially at puberty, stimulate changes in the adolescent's behavior, appearance, or growth.

adolescence   The second decade of life.

adolescence-limited offenders   Antisocial adolescents whose delinquent or violent behavior begins and ends during adolescence.

adolescent growth spurt   The dramatic increase in height and weight that occurs during puberty.

adolescent health care   A field of study and health care devoted to understanding the health care needs of individuals during the second decade of life.

adrenarche   The maturation of the adrenal glands that takes place during adolescence.

Adult Attachment Interview   A structured interview used to assess an individual's past attachment history and "internal working model" of relationships.

age–crime curve   The relationship between chronological age and offending, showing that the prevalence of offending peaks in late adolescence.

age grading   The process of grouping individuals within social institutions on the basis of age.

age of majority   The designated age at which an individual is recognized as an adult.

agency   The sense that one has an impact on one's world.

aggression   Acts done to be intentionally harmful.

AIDS (acquired immune deficiency syndrome)   A disease, caused by a virus transmitted by means of bodily fluids, that devastates the immune system.

androgens   A class of sex hormones secreted by the gonads, found in both sexes, but in higher levels among males than females following puberty.

androgyny   The combination of both highly masculine and highly feminine traits.

anorexia nervosa   An eating disorder found chiefly among young women, characterized by dramatic and severe self-induced weight loss.

antisocial personality disorder   A disorder of adulthood characterized by antisocial behavior and persistent disregard for the rules of society and the rights of others.

anxious-avoidant attachment   An insecure attachment between infant and caregiver, characterized by indifference on the part of the infant toward the caregiver.

anxious-resistant attachment   An insecure attachment between infant and caregiver, characterized by distress at separation and anger at reunion.

attachment   The strong affectional bond that develops between an infant and a caregiver.

attention deficit/hyperactivity disorder (ADHD)   A biologically based psychological disorder characterized by impulsivity, inattentiveness, and restlessness, often in school situations.

authoritarian parents   Parents who use punitive, absolute, and forceful discipline, and who place a premium on obedience and conformity.

authoritative parents   Parents who use warmth, firm control, and rational, issue-oriented discipline, in which emphasis is placed on the development of self-direction.

authority conflicts   A type of antisocial behavior characterized by stubbornness and rebelliousness.

autoerotic behavior   Sexual behavior that is experienced alone, such as masturbation or sexual fantasizing.

autonomy   The psychosocial domain concerning the development and expression of identity.

B

baby boom   The period following World War II, during which the number of infants born was extremely large.

Bar (Bas) Mitzvah   In Judaism, the religious ceremony marking the young person's transition to adulthood.

basal metabolism rate   The minimal amount of energy used by the body during a resting state.

behavioral autonomy   The capacity to make independent decisions and to follow through with them.

behavioral decision theory   An approach to understanding adolescent risk taking, in which behaviors are seen as the outcome of systematic decision-making processes.

behavioral genetics   The scientific study of genetic influences on behavior.

big fish–little pond effect   The reason that individuals who attend high school with high-achieving peers feel worse about themselves than comparably successful individuals with lower-achieving peers.

binge drinking   Consuming five or more drinks in a row on one occasion, an indicator of alcohol abuse.

biracial   Having two parents of different ethnic or racial backgrounds.

body mass index (BMI)   A measure of an individual's body fat, the ratio of weight to height; used to gauge overweight and obesity.

brain function   Patterns of brain activity.

brain structure   The physical form or shape of the brain.

bulimia   An eating disorder found primarily among young women, characterized by a pattern of binge eating and self-induced vomiting.

C

causation   The correlation between two things attributable to the effect one thing has on the other.

charter schools   Public schools that have been given the autonomy to establish their own curricula and teaching practices.

child protectionists   Individuals who argued, early in the 20th century, that adolescents needed to be kept out of the labor force in order to protect them from the hazards of the workplace.

chlamydia   A sexually transmitted infection caused by a bacterium.

circumcision   A procedure in which some part of the genitals is cut and permanently altered.

cliques   Small, tightly knit groups of between 2 and 12 friends, generally of the same sex and age.

cognitive autonomy   The establishment of an independent set of values, opinions, and beliefs.

cognitive-developmental view   A perspective on development, based on the work of Piaget, that takes a qualitative, stage-theory approach.

cohort   A group of individuals born during the same general historical era.

collective efficacy   A community's social capital, derived from its members' common values and goals.

community service   The involvement of young people in activities that serve some social or economic need of society.

comorbid   Co-occurring, as when an individual has more than one problem at the same time.

comprehensive high school   An educational institution that evolved during the first half of the 20th century, offering a varied curriculum and designed to meet the needs of a diverse population of adolescents.

comprehensive sex education   Programs that not only provide information about contraception, STDs, and pregnancy but also teach adolescents how to refuse unwanted sex and avoid unintended sex, increase their motivation to engage in safe sex, and change perceptions about peer norms and attitudes.

concrete operations   The third stage of cognitive development, according to Piaget, spanning the period roughly between age 6 and early adolescence.

conduct disorder   A repetitive and persistent pattern of antisocial behavior that results in problems at school or work, or in relationships with others.

continuous transitions   Passages into adulthood in which adult roles and statuses are entered into gradually.

conventional moral reasoning   According to Kohlberg, the second level of moral development, which occurs during late childhood and early adolescence and is characterized by reasoning that is based on the rules and conventions of society.

correlation   The extent to which two things vary systematically with each other.

cortisol   A hormone produced when a person is exposed to stress.

co-rumination   Excessive talking with another about problems.

covert antisocial behavior   A type of antisocial behavior characterized by misdeeds that are not always detected by others, such as lying or stealing.

criminal behavior   Crimes that are dealt with in the criminal justice system, regardless of the age of the offender.

criminal justice system   The system of courts and related institutions developed to handle adult crime.

critical thinking   Thinking that involves analyzing, evaluating, and interpreting information, rather than simply memorizing it.

cross-sectional study   A study that compares two or more groups of individuals at one point in time.

crowds   Large, loosely organized groups of young people, composed of several cliques and typically organized around a common shared activity.

crystallization   According to Super, the stage during which individuals, typically ages 14–18, first begin to formulate their ideas about appropriate occupations.

cultivation theory   A perspective on media use that emphasizes the impact media exposure has on individuals.

cultural capital   The resources provided within a family through the exposure of the adolescent to art, music, literature, and other elements of "high culture."

culture-fair tests   Standardized tests that do not, by virtue of their construction, favor one cultural or ethnic group over another.

curvilinear pattern   In statistical analyses, a pattern of relations between two variables that resembles a U-shaped or an inverted U-shaped curve.

cyberbullying   Bullying that occurs over the Internet or via cell phones.

D

date rape   Being forced by a date to have sex against one's will.

deductive reasoning   A type of logical reasoning in which one draws logically necessary conclusions from a general set of promises, or givens.

delayed phase preference   A pattern of sleep characterized by later sleep and wake times, which usually emerges during puberty.

delinquency   Juvenile offending that is processed within the juvenile justice system.

depression   A psychological disturbance characterized by low self-esteem, decreased motivation, sadness, and difficulty in finding pleasure in formerly pleasurable activities.

detachment   In psychoanalytic theory, the process through which adolescents sever emotional attachments to their parents or other authority figures.

developmental trajectories   Patterns of change over time.

diathesis–stress model   A perspective on disorder that posits that problems are the result of an interaction between a preexisting condition (the diathesis) and exposure to a stressful event or condition.

diffusion tensor imaging (DTI)   A technique used to produce images of the brain that shows connections among different regions.

discontinuous transitions Passages into adulthood in which adult roles and statuses are entered into abruptly.

disordered eating Mild, moderate, or severe disturbance in eating habits and attitudes.

divided attention The process of paying attention to two or more stimuli at the same time.

dopamine A neurotransmitter especially important in the brain circuits that regulate the experience of reward.

dorsolateral prefrontal cortex The outer and upper areas of the front of the brain, important for skills such as planning ahead and controlling impulses.

E

early adolescence The period spanning roughly ages 10–13, corresponding roughly to the junior or middle high school years.

ecological perspective on human development A perspective on development that emphasizes the broad context in which development occurs.

educational attainment The number of years of schooling completed by an individual.

electroencephalography (EEG) A technique for measuring electrical activity at different locations on the scalp.

emerging adulthood The period spanning roughly ages 18–25, during which individuals make the transition from adolescence to adulthood.

emotional autonomy The establishment of more adultlike and less childish close relationships with family members and peers.

endocrine system The system of the body that produces, circulates, and regulates hormones.

ephebephobia The irrational fear of adolescents.

epiphysis The closing of the ends of the bones, which terminates growth after the adolescent growth spurt has been completed.

estrogens A class of sex hormones secreted by the gonads, found in both sexes, but in higher levels among females than males following puberty.

ethnic identity The aspect of individuals' sense of identity concerning ancestry or racial group membership.

ethnography A type of research in which individuals are observed in their natural settings.

event-related potentials (ERP) Changes in electrical activity in areas of the brain in response to specific stimuli or events.

evidence-based practices Programs and practices that have a proven scientific basis.

exo-system In the ecological perspective on human development, the layer of the environment that does not directly contain the developing person but that affects the setting in which the person lives.

experience sampling method (ESM) A method of collecting data about adolescents' emotional states, in which individuals are paged and asked to report on their mood and activity.

externalizing disorders Psychosocial problems that are manifested in a turning of the symptoms outward, as in aggression or delinquency.

extrinsic motivation Motivation based on the rewards one will receive for successful performance.

extrusion The practice of separating children from their parents and requiring them to sleep in other households, part of the process of social redefinition at adolescence in many societies.

F

false-self behavior Behavior that intentionally presents a false impression to others.

family systems theory A perspective on family functioning that emphasizes interconnections among different family relationships (such as marital, parent–child, sibling).

fear of failure Fear of the consequences of failing in achievement situations.

feedback loop A cycle through which two or more bodily functions respond to and regulate each other, such as that formed by the hypothalamus, the pituitary gland, and the gonads.

five-factor model The theory that there are five basic dimensions to personality: extraversion, agreeableness, conscientiousness, neuroticism, and openness to experience.

flow experience The experience of high levels of both concentration and interest at the same time.

formal operations The fourth stage of cognitive development, according to Piaget, spanning the period from early adolescence through adulthood.

functional magnetic resonance imaging (fMRI) A technique used to produce images of the brain, often while the subject is performing some sort of mental task.

future orientation The extent to which an individual is able and inclined to think about the potential consequences of decisions and choices.

G

gangs Organized peer groups of antisocial individuals.

gateway drugs Drugs that, when used over time, lead to the use of other, more dangerous substances.

gender identity The gender an individual identifies with.

gender intensification hypothesis The idea that pressures to behave in sex-appropriate ways intensify during adolescence.

generation gap The popular phrase for the alleged conflict between young people and adults over values and attitudes.

generational dissonance Divergence of views between adolescents and parents that is common in families of immigrant parents and American-born adolescents.

gifted students Students who are unusually talented in some aspect of intellectual performance.

glands Organs that stimulate particular parts of the body to respond in specific ways to particular hormones.

gonadotropin-releasing hormone (GnRH) neurons Specialized neurons that are activated by certain pubertal hormones.

gonads The glands that secrete sex hormones; in males, the testes; in females, the ovaries.

gonorrhea A sexually transmitted infection caused by a bacterium.

H

herpes   A sexually transmitted infection caused by a virus.

HIV (human immunodeficiency virus)   The virus associated with AIDS.

hormones   Highly specialized substances secreted by one or more endocrine glands.

hostile attributional bias   The tendency to interpret ambiguous interactions with others as deliberately hostile

HPG (hypothalamic-pituitary-gonadal) axis   The neurophysiological pathway that involves the hypothalamus, the pituitary gland, and the gonads.

human papillomavirus   One of several viruses that causes a sexually transmitted disease.

hypothalamus   A part of the brain that controls the functioning of the pituitary gland.

I

iatrogenic effects   Unintended adverse consequences of a treatment or intervention.

identity   The domain of psychosocial development involving self-conceptions, self-esteem, and the sense of who one is.

identity diffusion   The incoherent, disjointed, incomplete sense of self characteristic of not having resolved the crisis of identity.

identity foreclosure   The premature establishment of a sense of identity, before sufficient role experimentation has occurred.

identity versus identity diffusion   According to Erikson, the normative crisis characteristic of the fifth stage of psychosocial development, predominant during adolescence.

imaginary audience   The belief, often brought on by the heightened self-consciousness of early adolescence, that everyone is watching and evaluating one's behavior.

indifferent parents   Parents who are characterized by low levels of both responsiveness and demandingness.

individuation   The progressive sharpening of an individual's sense of being an autonomous, independent person.

inductive reasoning   Reasoning that involves drawing an inference from the evidence that one has.

indulgent parents   Parents who are characterized by responsiveness but low demandingness, and who are mainly concerned with the child's happiness.

information-processing perspective   A perspective on cognition that derives from the study of artificial intelligence and attempts to explain cognitive development in terms of the growth of specific components of the thinking process (such as memory).

initiation ceremony   The formal induction of a young person into adulthood.

instrumental aggression   Aggressive behavior that is deliberate and planned.

internal working model   The implicit model of interpersonal relationships that an individual employs throughout life, believed to be shaped by early attachment experiences.

internalizing disorders   Psychosocial problems that are manifested in a turning of the symptoms inward, as in depression or anxiety.

intimacy   The psychosocial domain concerning the formation, maintenance, and termination of close relationships.

intrinsic motivation   Motivation based on the pleasure one will experience from mastering a task.

inventionists   Theorists who argue that the period of adolescence is mainly a social invention.

J

junior high school   An educational institution designed during the early era of public secondary education, in which young adolescents are schooled separately from older adolescents.

juvenile justice system   A separate system of courts and related institutions developed to handle juvenile crime and delinquency.

juvenile offending   An externalizing problem that includes delinquency and criminal behavior.

L

late adolescence   The period spanning roughly ages 18–21, corresponding approximately to the college years.

learned helplessness   The acquired belief that an individual is not able to influence events through his or her own efforts or actions.

learning disability   A difficulty with academic tasks that cannot be traced to an emotional problem or sensory dysfunction.

leptin   A protein produced by the fat cells that may play a role in the onset of puberty.

life-course-persistent offenders   Individuals who begin demonstrating antisocial or aggressive behavior during childhood and continue their antisocial behavior throughout adolescence and into adulthood.

limbic system   An area of the brain that plays an important role in the processing of emotional experience, social information, and reward and punishment.

longitudinal study   A study that follows the same group of individuals over time.

long-term memory   The ability to recall something from a long time ago.

M

macro-system   In the ecological perspective on human development, the outermost layer of the environment, containing forces such as history and culture.

mainstreaming   The integration of adolescents who have educational handicaps into regular classrooms.

media practice model   A perspective on media use that emphasizes the fact that adolescents not only choose what media they are exposed to but also interpret the media in ways that shape their impact.

melatonin   A hormone secreted by the brain that contributes to sleepiness.

menarche   The time of first menstruation, one of the most important changes to occur among females during puberty.

meso-system   In the ecological perspective on human development, the layer of the environment formed by two or more immediate settings, as in the home–school linkage.

metacognition   The process of thinking about thinking itself.

micro-systems In the ecological perspective on human development, the immediate settings in which adolescents develop, such as the family or the peer group.

middle adolescence The period spanning roughly ages 14–17, corresponding to the high school years.

middle school An educational institution housing seventh- and eighth-grade students along with adolescents who are 1 or 2 years older.

midlife crisis A psychological crisis over identity believed to occur between the ages of 35 and 45, the age range of most adolescents' parents.

Monitoring the Future An annual survey of a nationwide sample of American 8th-, 10th-, and 12th-graders, mainly known for its data on adolescent substance use.

moral disengagement Rationalizing immoral behavior as legitimate, as a way of justifying one's own bad acts

multidimensional model of racial identity (MMRI) Sellers's perspective on ethnic identity, which emphasizes three different phenomena: racial centrality (how important race is in defining individuals' identity), private regard (how individuals feel about being a member of their race), public regard (how individuals think others feel about their race).

mutual role taking In Selman's theory, the stage of social perspective taking during which the young adolescent can be an objective third party and can see how the thoughts or actions of one person can affect those of another.

myelination The process through which brain circuits are insulated with myelin, which improves the efficiency of information processing.

N

National Assessment of Educational Progress (NAEP) A periodic testing of American 4th-, 8th-, and 12th-graders by the federal government, used to track achievement.

need for achievement A need that influences the extent to which an individual strives for success in evaluative situations.

negative affectivity The presumed underlying cause of internalizing disorders, characterized by high levels of subjective distress.

negative identity The selection of an identity that is obviously undesirable in the eyes of significant others and the broader community.

neuroendocrine Hormonal activity in the brain and nervous system.

neurons Nerve cells.

neurotransmitters Specialized chemicals that carry electrical impulses between neurons.

nonshared environmental influences The nongenetic influences in individuals' lives that make them different from people they live with.

O

occupational attainment A measure of achievement based on the status or prestige of the job an individual holds.

oppositional-defiant disorder A disorder of childhood and adolescence characterized by excessive anger, spite, and stubbornness.

orbitofrontal cortex The region of the brain located directly behind the eyes, important for the evaluation of risk and reward.

organizational role (of hormones) The process through which early exposure to hormones, especially prenatally, organizes the brain or other organs in anticipation of later changes in behavior or patterns of growth.

ovaries The female gonads.

overt antisocial behavior A type of antisocial behavior characterized by aggression toward others.

oxytocin A hormone known to influence emotional bonding to others.

P

parental demandingness One of two important dimensions of parenting; demandingness refers to the degree to which the parent expects and insists on mature, responsible behavior from the child.

parental responsiveness One of the two important dimensions of parenting; responsiveness refers to the degree to which the parent responds to the child's needs in an accepting, supportive manner.

participant observation A research technique in which the researcher "infiltrates" a group of individuals in order to study their behavior and relationships.

particularistic norms Guidelines for behavior that vary from one individual to another; more commonly found in less industrialized societies.

peak height velocity The point at which the adolescent is growing most rapidly.

peer groups Groups of individuals of approximately the same age.

perceived popularity How much status or prestige an individual has.

permissive societies Societies in which sexual activity during childhood and adolescence is not greatly restrained.

personal fable An adolescent's belief that he or she is unique and therefore not subject to the rules that govern other people's behavior.

pheromones A class of chemicals secreted by animals that stimulate certain behaviors in other members of the species.

pituitary gland One of the chief glands responsible for regulating levels of hormones in the body.

platonic relationships Nonsexual relationships with individuals who might otherwise be romantic partners.

positive youth development The goal of programs designed to facilitate healthy psychosocial development and not simply to deter problematic development.

possible selves The various identities an adolescent might imagine for him- or herself.

postconventional moral reasoning In Kohlberg's theory, the stage of moral development during which society's rules and conventions are seen as relative and subjective rather than as authoritative; also called principled moral reasoning.

preconventional moral reasoning According to Kohlberg, the first level of moral reasoning, which is typical of children and is characterized by reasoning that is based on rewards and punishments associated with different courses of action.

prefrontal cortex The region of the brain most important for sophisticated thinking abilities, such as planning, thinking ahead, weighing risks and rewards, and controlling impulses.

premature affluence Having more income than one can manage maturely, especially during adolescence.

preoperational period The second stage of cognitive development, according to Piaget, spanning roughly ages 2–5.

primary control strategies Coping strategies in which an individual attempts to change the stressor.

problem behavior syndrome The covariation among various types of externalizing disorders believed to result from an underlying trait of unconventionality.

prosocial behavior Behaviors intended to help others.

protective factors Factors that limit individual vulnerability to harm.

psychological control Parenting that attempts to control the adolescent's emotions and opinions.

psychopaths Individuals who are not only antisocial but also manipulative, superficially charming, impulsive, and indifferent to the feelings of others.

psychosocial Referring to aspects of development that are both psychological and social in nature, such as developing a sense of identity or sexuality.

psychosocial moratorium A period during which individuals are free from excessive obligations and responsibilities and can therefore experiment with different roles and personalities.

puberty The biological changes of adolescence.

Q

quinceañera An elaborate sort of "coming-out" celebration for adolescent girls that is practiced in many Latino communities.

R

racial socialization The process through which individuals develop an understanding of their racial or ethnic background.

reactive aggression Aggressive behavior that is unplanned and impulsive.

reference groups A group against which an individual compares him- or herself.

rejection sensitivity Heightened vulnerability to being rejected by others.

relational aggression Acts intended to harm another through the manipulation of his or her relationships with others, as in malicious gossip.

religiosity The degree to which one engages in religious practices, like attending services.

resilience The ability of an individual to continue to function competently in the face of adversity or stress.

restrictive societies Societies in which adolescents are pressured to refrain from sexual activity until they have married or undergone a formal rite of passage into adulthood.

reverse causation Relationship in which the correlation between two things is due not to the first thing causing the second, but to the second causing the first.

risk factors Factors that increase the likelihood of some behavior or condition.

rite of passage A ceremony or ritual marking an individual's transition from one social status to another, especially marking the young person's transition to adulthood.

routine activity theory A perspective on adolescence that views unstructured, unsupervised time with peers as a main cause of misbehavior.

S

scaffolding Structuring a learning situation so that it is just within the reach of the student.

scarification The intentional creation of scars on some part or parts of the body, often done as part of an initiation ceremony.

school performance A measure of achievement based on an individual's grades in school.

school vouchers Government-subsidized vouchers that can be used for private school tuition.

schools within schools Subdivisions of the student body within large schools created to foster feelings of belongingness.

secondary control strategies Coping strategies that involve attempts by the individual to adapt to the stressor.

secondary education The system of middle schools, junior high schools, and high schools.

secondary sex characteristics The manifestations of sexual maturity at puberty, including the development of breasts, the growth of facial and body hair, and changes in the voice.

secular trend The tendency, over the past two centuries, for individuals to be larger in stature and to reach puberty earlier, primarily because of improvements in health and nutrition.

secure attachment A healthy attachment between infant and caregiver, characterized by trust.

selective attention The process by which we focus on one stimulus while tuning out another.

selective serotonin reuptake inhibitors (SSRIs) A class of antidepressant medications that have proven to be effective with adolescents suffering from internalizing problems, such as depression.

self-conceptions The collection of traits and attributes that individuals use to describe or characterize themselves.

self-consciousness The degree to which an individual is preoccupied with his or her self-image.

self-efficacy The sense that an individual has some control over his or her life.

self-esteem The degree to which individuals feel positively or negatively about themselves.

self-fulfilling prophecy The idea that individuals' behavior is influenced by others' expectations for them.

self-handicapping Deliberately behaving in ways that will likely interfere with doing well, in order to have an excuse for failing.

self-image stability The degree to which an individual feels that his or her self-image changes from day to day.

semirestrictive societies Societies in which pressures against adolescent sexual activity exist but are not vigilantly enforced.

sensation seeking The enjoyment of novel and intense experiences.

sense of identity The extent to which individuals feel secure about who they are and who they are becoming.

sensorimotor period The first stage of cognitive development, according to Piaget, spanning the period roughly between birth and age 2.

serotonin A neurotransmitter that is especially important for the experience of different moods.

service learning Structured educational experiences that involve volunteering in the community.

set point A physiological level or setting (e.g., of a specific hormone) that the body attempts to maintain through a self-regulating system.

sex cleavage The separation of boys and girls into different cliques, common during late childhood and early adolescence.

sex-role behavior Behavior that is consistent with prevailing expectations for how individuals of a given sex are to behave.

sexual-minority youth Gay, lesbian, bisexual, and transgender youth.

sexual orientation An individual's orientation toward same- or opposite-sex sex partners.

sexual socialization The process through which adolescents are exposed to and educated about sexuality.

sexuality The psychosocial domain concerning the development and expression of sexual feelings.

sexually transmitted disease (STD) Any of a group of infections—including gonorrhea, herpes, chlamydia, and AIDS—passed on through sexual contact.

shared environmental influences Nongenetic influences that make individuals living in the same family similar to each other.

sibling deidentification The process through which siblings deliberately try to be different from each other.

sibling rivalry Competition between siblings, often for parental attention.

social capital The interpersonal resources available to an adolescent or family.

social cognition The aspect of cognition that concerns thinking about other people, about interpersonal relations, and about social institutions.

social control theory A theory of delinquency that links deviance with the absence of bonds to society's main institutions.

social conventions The norms that govern everyday behavior in social situations.

social perspective taking The ability to view events from the perspective of others.

social promotion The practice of promoting students from one grade to the next automatically, regardless of their school performance.

social redefinition The process through which an individual's position or status is redefined by society.

social support The extent to which an individual receives emotional or instrumental assistance from his or her social network.

sociometric popularity How well-liked an individual is.

specification According to Super, the stage during which individuals, typically ages 18–21, first begin to consider narrowly defined occupational pursuits.

spirituality The degree to which one places importance on the quest for answers to questions about God and the meaning of life.

spurious causation When the correlation between two things is due to the fact that each of them is correlated with some third factor.

standards-based reform Policies designed to improve achievement by holding schools and students to a predetermined set of standards measured by achievement tests.

status offense A violation of the law that pertains to minors but not adults.

stereotype threat The harmful effect that exposure to stereotypes about ethnic or sex differences in ability has on student performance.

student engagement The extent to which students are psychologically committed to learning and mastering the material rather than simply completing the assigned work.

substance abuse The misuse of alcohol or other drugs to a degree that causes problems in the individual's life.

substance dependence The misuse of alcohol or other drugs to a degree that causes physical addiction.

suicidal ideation Thinking about ending one's life.

synapse The gap in space between neurons, across which neurotransmitters carry electrical impulses.

synaptic pruning The process through which unnecessary connections between neurons are eliminated, improving the efficiency of information processing.

T

Tanner stages A widely used system used to describe the five stages of pubertal development.

teenager A term popularized about 50 years ago to refer to young people; it connoted a more frivolous and lighthearted image than did "adolescent."

testes The male gonads.

testosterone One of the sex hormones secreted by the gonads, found in both sexes but in higher levels among males than females.

theory of mind The ability to understand that others have beliefs, intentions, and knowledge that may be different from one's own.

tracking The grouping of students, according to ability, into different levels of classes within the same school grade.

tweens A term used by marketing experts to refer to preadolescents.

U

underachievers Individuals whose actual school performance is lower than what would be expected on the basis of objective measures of their aptitude or intelligence.

universalistic norms Guidelines for behavior that apply to all members of a community; more common in industrialized societies.

uses and gratification approach A perspective on media use that emphasizes the active role users play in selecting the media to which they are exposed.

V

ventromedial prefrontal cortex The lower and central area at the front of the brain, important for gut-level decision making.

viral marketing A way of promoting products or services by encouraging individuals to pass information on to others.

W

work values The particular sorts of rewards an individual looks for in a job (extrinsic, intrinsic, social, altruistic, security, influence, leisure).

working memory That aspect of memory in which information is held for a short time while a problem is being solved.

Y

youth Today, a term used to refer to individuals ages 18–22; it once referred to individuals ages 12–24.

youth apprenticeship A structured, work-based learning experience that places an adolescent under the supervision of a skilled adult.

Z

zero tolerance A get-tough approach to adolescent misbehavior that responds seriously or excessively to the first infraction.

zone of proximal development In Vygotsky's theory, the level of challenge that is still within the individual's reach but that forces an individual to develop more advanced skills.

References

Abbott-Chapman, J., Denholm, C., & Wyld, C. (2008). Gender differences in adolescent risk taking: Are they diminishing?: An Australian intergenerational study. *Youth and Society, 40*, 131–154.

Abecassis, M., Hartup, W. W., Haselager, G. T., Scholte, R. J., & Van Lieshout, C. M. (2002). Mutual antipathies and their significance in middle childhood and adolescence. *Child Development, 73*, 1543 1556.

Ablard, K., & Mills, C. (1996). Implicit theories of intelligence and self-perceptions of academically talented adolescents and children. *Journal of Youth and Adolescence, 25*, 137–148.

Abma, J., Driscoll, A., & Moore, K. (1998). Young women's degree of control over first intercourse: An exploratory analysis. *Family Planning Perspectives, 30*, 12–18.

Abrahamson, A., Baker, L. A., & Caspi, A. (2002). Rebellious teens? Genetic and environmental influences on the social attitudes of adolescents. *Journal of Personality and Social Psychology, 83*, 1392–1408.

Aceves, M. J., & Cookston, J. T. (2007). Violent victimization, aggression, and parent–adolescent relations: Quality parenting as a buffer for violently victimized youth. *Journal of Youth and Adolescence, 36*, 635–647.

Achenbach, T., & Edelbrock, C. (1987). *The manual for the Youth Self-Report and Profile.* Burlington: University of Vermont.

Adalbjarnardottir, S., & Hafsteinsson, L. G. (2001). Adolescents' perceived parenting styles and their substance use: Concurrent and longitudinal analyses. *Journal of Research on Adolescence, 11*, 401–423.

Adam, E., & Chase-Lansdale, P. (2002). Home sweet home(s): Parental separations, residential moves, and adjustment problems in low-income adolescent girls. *Developmental Psychology, 38*, 792–805.

Adamczyk-Robinette, S. L., Fletcher, A. C., & Wright, K. (2002). Understanding the authoritative parenting–early adolescent tobacco use link: The mediating role of peer tobacco use. *Journal of Youth and Adolescence, 31*, 311–318.

Adams, G., Gullotta, T., & Montemayor, R. (Eds.). (1992). *Adolescent identity formation.* Newbury Park, CA: Sage.

Adams, R., & Laursen, B. (2001). The organization and dynamics of adolescent conflict with parents and friends. *Journal of Marriage and the Family, 63*, 97–110.

Adams, R. E., Bukowski, W. M., & Bagwell, C. (2005). Stability of aggression during early adolescence as moderated by reciprocated friendship status and friend's aggression. *International Journal of Behavioral Development, 29*, 139.

Adegoke, A. (1993). The experience of spermarche (the age of onset of sperm emission) among selected adolescent boys in Nigeria. *Journal of Youth and Adolescence, 22*, 201–209.

Adelson, J. (1972). The political imagination of the young adolescent. In J. Kagan & R. Coles (Eds.), *Twelve to sixteen: Early adolescence.* New York: Norton.

Adler, N., Boyce, T., Chesney, M., Cohen, S., Folkman, S., Kahn, R., et al. (1994). Socioeconomic status and health: The challenge of the gradient. *American Psychologist, 49*, 15–24.

Adler, N. E., Ozer, E. J., & Tschann, J. (2003). Abortion among adolescents. *American Psychologist, 58*, 211–217.

Agnew, R., & Brezina, T. (1997). Relational problems with peers, gender, and delinquency. *Youth and Society, 29*, 84–111.

Agras, W. S., Schneider, J., Arnow, B., Raeburn, S., and Telch, C. (1989). Cognitive-behavioral and response-prevention treatments for bulimia nervosa. *Journal of Consulting and Clinical Psychology, 57*, 215–221.

Aguilar, B., Sroufe, L. A., Egeland, B., & Carlson, E. (2000). Distinguishing the early onset/persistent and adolescence-onset antisocial behavior types: From birth to 16 years. *Development and Psychopathology, 12*, 109–132.

Ahn, N. (1994). Teenage childbearing and high school completion: Accounting for individual heterogeneity. *Family Planning Perspectives, 26*, 17–21.

Ainsworth, J. W. (2002). Why does it take a village? The mediation of neighborhood effects on educational achievement. *Social Forces, 81*, 117–152.

Ainsworth, M., Blehar, M., Waters, E., & Wall, S. (1978). *Patterns of attachment.* Hillsdale, NJ: Erlbaum.

Ainsworth-Darnell, J., & Downey, D. (1998). Assessing the oppositional culture explanation for racial/ethnic differences in school performance. *American Sociological Review, 63*, 536–553.

Akom, A. A. (2003). Reexamining resistance as oppositional behavior: The nation of Islam and the creation of a Black achievement ideology. *Sociology of Education, 76*, 305–325.

Alan Guttmacher Institute. (1994). *Sex and America's teenagers.* New York: Author.

Alasker, F., & Flammer, A. (1999). Time use by adolescents in an international perspective. II: The case of necessary activities. In F. Alasker & A. Flammer (Eds.), *The adolescent experience: European and American adolescents in the 1990s* (pp. 61–83). Hillsdale, NJ: Erlbaum.

Alasker, F., & Olweus, D. (1992). Stability of global self-evaluations in early adolescence: A cohort longitudinal study. *Journal of Research on Adolescence, 1*, 123–145.

Albers, A. B., & Biener, L. (2003). Adolescent participation in tobacco promotions: The role of psychosocial factors. *Pediatrics, 111*, 402–406.

Alberts, A., Elkind, D., & Ginsberg, S. (2007). The personal fable and risk-taking in early adolescence. *Journal of Youth and Adolescence, 36*, 71–76.

Albrecht, A. K., Galambos, N. L., & Jansson, S. M. (2007). Adolescents' internalizing and aggressive behaviors and perceptions of parents' psychological control: A panel study examining direction of effects. *Journal of Youth and Adolescence, 36*, 673–684.

Albrecht, C., & Teachman, J. D. (2003). Childhood living arrangements and the risk of premarital intercourse. *Journal of Family Influence, 24*, 867–894.

Alexander, C., Somerfield, M., Ensminger, M., Johnson, K., & Kim, Y. (1993). Consistency of adolescents' self-report of sexual behavior in a longitudinal study. *Journal of Youth and Adolescence, 22*, 455–471.

Alexander, K., Natriello, G., & Pallas, A. (1985). For whom the cognitive bell tolls: The impact of dropping out on cognitive performance. *American Sociological Review, 50*, 409–420.

Alexander, K. L., Entwisle, D. R., & Kabbani, N. S. (2001). The dropout process in life course perspective: Early risk factors at home and school. *Teachers College Record, 103*, 760–822.

Allen, J. (2008). The attachment system in adolescence. In J. Cassidy & P. R. Shaver (Eds.), *Handbook of attachment theory and research* (2nd ed.). New York: Guilford.

Allen, J., Hauser, S., Bell, K., & O'Connor, T. (1994). Longitudinal assessment of autonomy and relatedness in adolescent–family interactions as predictors of adolescent ego development and self-esteem. *Child Development, 65*, 179–194.

Allen, J., Hauser, S., Eickholt, C., Bell, K., & O'Connor, T. (1994). Autonomy and relatedness in family interactions as predictors of expressions of negative adolescent affect. *Journal of Research on Adolescence, 4*, 535–552.

Allen, J., Hauser, S., O'Connor, T., & Bell, K. (2002). Prediction of peer-rated adult hostility from autonomy struggles in adolescent–family interactions. *Development and Psychopathology, 14*, 123–137.

Allen, J., Hauser, S., O'Connor, T., Bell, K., & Eickholt, C. (1996). The connection of observed hostile family conflict to adolescents' developing autonomy and relatedness with parents. *Development and Psychopathology, 8*, 425–442.

Allen, J., & McElhaney, K. (March, 2000). *Autonomy in discussions vs. autonomy in decision-making as predictors of developing close friendship competence.* Paper presented at the biennial meetings of the Society for Research on Adolescence, Chicago.

Allen, J., McElhaney, K., Kuperminc, G., & Jodl, K. (2004). Stability and change in attachment security across adolescence. *Child Development, 75,* 1792–1805.

Allen, J., McElhaney, K., Land, D., Kuperminc, G., Moore, C., O'Beime-Kelly, H., et al. (2003). A secure base in adolescence: Markers of attachment security in the mother–adolescent relationship. *Child Development, 74,* 292–307.

Allen, J., Philliber, S., Herrling, S., & Kuperminc, G. (1997). Preventing teen pregnancy and academic failure: Experimental evaluation of a developmentally based approach. *Child Development, 64,* 729–742.

Allen, J., Porter, M. R., & McFarland, F. C. (2006). Leaders and followers in adolescent close friendships: Susceptibility to peer influence as a predictor of risky behavior, friendship instability, and depression. *Development and Psychopathology, 18,* 155–172.

Allen, J., Porter, M., McFarland, F., Marsh, P., & McElhaney, K. (2005). The two faces of adolescents' success with peers: Adolescent popularity, social adaptation, and deviant behavior. *Child Development, 76,* 747–760.

Allen, J., Porter, M., McFarland, C., McElhaney, K. B., & Marsh, P. (2007). The relation of attachment security to adolescents' paternal and peer relationships, depression, and externalizing behavior. *Child Development, 78,* 1222–1239.

Allen, M. L., Elliott, M. N., Morales, L. S., Diamant, A. L., Hambarsoomian, K., & Schuster, M. A. (2007). Adolescent participation in preventive health behaviors, physical activity, and nutrition: Differences across immigrant generations for Asians and Latinos compared with Whites. *American Journal of Public Health, 97,* 337–343.

Allen, R., & Mirabell, J. (1990, May). *Shorter subjective sleep of high school students from early compared to late starting schools.* Paper presented at the second meeting of the Society for Research on Biological Rhythms, Jacksonville, FL.

Allgood-Merten, B., Lewinsohn, P., & Hops, H. (1990). Sex differences and adolescent depression. *Journal of Abnormal Psychology, 99,* 55–63.

Allgood-Merten, B., & Stockard, J. (1991). Sex role identity and self-esteem: A comparison of children and adolescents. *Sex Roles, 25,* 129–140.

Allison, K., Crawford, I., Leone, P., Trickett, E., Perez-Febles, A., Burton, L., et al. (1999). Adolescent substance use: Preliminary examinations of school and neighborhood context. *American Journal of Community Psychology, 27,* 111–141.

Allison, P., & Furstenberg, F., Jr. (1989). How marital dissolution affects children: Variations by age and sex. *Developmental Psychology, 25,* 540–549.

Allwood, M., & Bell, D. (2008). A preliminary examination of emotional and cognitive mediators in the relations between violence exposure and violent behaviors in youth. *Journal of Community Psychology, 36,* 989–1007.

Althaus, F. (1997). Female circumcision: Rite of passage or violation of rights? *International Family Planning Perspectives, 23,* 130–133.

Altschul, I., Oyserman, D., & Bybee, D. (2006). Racial-ethnic identity in mid-adolescence: Content and change as predictors of academic achievement. *Child Development, 77,* 1155–1169.

Alva, S. (1993). Differential patterns of achievement among Asian-American adolescents. *Journal of Youth and Adolescence, 22,* 407–423.

Amato, P., & Booth, A. (1996). A prospective study of divorce and parent–child relationships. *Journal of Marriage and the Family, 58,* 356–365.

Amato, P., & Keith, B. (1991a). Parental divorce and the well-being of children: A meta-analysis. *Psychological Bulletin, 110,* 26–46.

Amato, P., & Keith, B. (1991b). Separation from a parent during childhood and adult socioeconomic attainment. *Social Forces, 70,* 187–206.

Amato, P., & Rezac, S. (1994). Contact with non-residential parents, interparental conflict, and children's behavior. *Journal of Family Issues, 15,* 191–207.

Amato, P. R., & Fowler, F. (2002). Parenting practices, child adjustment, and family diversity. *Journal of Marriage and the Family, 64,* 703–716.

Amato, P. R., & Sobolewski, J. M. (2001). The effects of divorce and marital discord on adult children's psychological well being. *American Sociological Review, 66,* 900–921.

American Psychiatric Association. (1994). *Diagnostic and statistical manual of the American Psychiatric Association (DSM-IV).* Washington, DC: Author.

American Psychological Association Zero Tolerance Task Force. (2008). Are zero tolerance policies effective in the schools?: An evidentiary review and recommendations. *American Psychologist, 63,* 852–862.

Analitis, F., Velderman, M. K., Ravens-Sieberer, U., Detmar, S., Erhart, M., Herdman, M., et al. (2009). Being bullied: Associated factors in children and adolescents 8 to 18 years old in 11 European countries. *Pediatrics, 123,* 569–577.

Anastasi, A. (1988). *Psychological testing* (6th ed.). New York: Macmillan.

Anderman, E. (2002). School effects on psychological outcomes during adolescence. *Journal of Educational Psychology, 94,* 795–809.

Anderman, E., & Midgley, C. (1996, March). *Changes in achievement goal orientations*

after the transition to middle school. Paper presented at the biennial meetings of the Society for Research on Adolescence, Boston.

Anderson, A. L., & Hughes, L. A. (2009). Exposure to situations conducive to delinquent behavior: The effects of time use, income, and transportation. *Journal of Research in Crime and Delinquency, 46,* 5–34.

Anderson, C. A., Carnagey, N. L., & Eubanks, J. (2003). Exposure to violent media: The effects of songs with violent lyrics on aggressive thoughts and feelings. *Journal of Personality and Social Psychology, 84,* 960–971.

Anderson, E. (1992, March). *Consistency of parenting in stepfather families.* Paper presented at the biennial meetings of the Society for Research on Adolescence, Washington, DC.

Anderson, E., Hetherington, E. M., & Clingempeel, W. (1989). Transformations in family relations at puberty: Effects of family context. *Journal of Early Adolescence, 9,* 310–334.

Anderson, E., Hetherington, E. M., Reiss, D., & Howe, G. (1994). Parents' nonshared treatment of siblings and the development of social competence during adolescence. *Journal of Family Psychology, 8,* 303–320.

Anderson, M., Kaufman, J., Simon, T. R., Barrios, L., Paulozzi, L., Ryan, G., et al. (2001). School-associated violent deaths in the United States, 1994–1999. *Journal of the American Medical Association, 286,* 2695–2702.

Anderson, S. E., Dallal, G. E., & Must, A. (2003). Relative weight and race influence average age at menarche: Results from two nationally representative surveys of U.S. girls studied 25 years apart. *Pediatrics, 111,* 844–891.

Andersson, T., & Magnusson, D. (1990). Biological maturation in adolescence and the development of drinking habits and alcohol abuse among young males: A prospective longitudinal study. *Journal of Youth and Adolescence, 19,* 33–42.

Ando, M., Asakura, T., & Simons-Morton, B. (2005). Psychosocial influences on physical, verbal, and indirect bullying among Japanese early adolescents. *Journal of Early Adolescence, 25,* 268–297.

Andrews, J., Alpert, A., Hops, H., & Davis, B. (1996, March). *The relation of competence in middle adolescence to depression and antisocial behavior: A multi-method assessment.* Paper presented at the biennial meetings of the Society for Research on Adolescence, Boston.

Andrinopoulos, K., Kerrigan, D., & Ellen, J. M. (2006). Understanding sex partner selection from the perspective of inner-city Black adolescents. *Perspectives on Sexual and Reproductive Health, 38,* 132–138.

Aneshensel, C., Becerra, R., Fielder, E., & Schuler, R. (1990). Onset of fertility-related events during adolescence: A prospective comparison of Mexican American and Non-Hispanic White females. *American Journal of Public Health, 80,* 959–963.

Angold, A., Costello, E. J., Erkanli, A., & Worthman, C. M. (1999). Pubertal changes in hormone levels and depression in girls. *Psychological Medicine, 29,* 1043–1053.

Angold, A., Costello, E. J., & Worthman, C. (1998). Puberty and depression: The roles of age, pubertal status, and pubertal timing. *Psychological Medicine, 28,* 51–61.

Angold, A., Worthman, C., Costello, E., Stangl, D., Messer, S., & Tweed, D. (1996, March). *Puberty and depression.* Paper presented at the Society for Research on Adolescence, Boston.

Apel, R., Bushway, S., Brame, R., Haviland, A. M., Nagin, D. S., & Paternoster, R. (2007). Unpacking the relationship between adolescent employment and antisocial behavior: A matched samples comparison. *Criminology, 45,* 67–97.

Apel, R., & Kaukinen, C. (2008). On the relationship between family structure and antisocial behavior: Parental cohabitation and blended households. *Criminology: An Interdisciplinary Journal, 46,* 35–69.

Apfel, N., & Seitz, V. (1997). The firstborn sons of African American teen mothers: Perspectives on risk and resilience. In S. Luthar, J. Burack, D. Cicchetti, & J. Weisz (Eds.), *Developmental psychopathology: Perspectives on risk and disorder* (pp. 484–506). New York: Cambridge University Press.

Apter, T. (1990). *Altered loves: Mothers and daughters during adolescence.* New York: St. Martin's Press.

Aquilino, W. (1991). Family structure and home-leaving: A further specification of the relationship. *Journal of Marriage and the Family, 53,* 999–1010.

Aquilino, W. S. (2005). Impact of family structure on parental attitudes toward the economic support of adult children over the transition to adulthood. *Journal of Family Influence, 26,* 143–167.

Aquilino, W. S., & Supple, A. J. (2001). Long-term effects of parenting practices during adolescence on well-being: Outcomes in young adulthood. *Journal of Family Issues, 22,* 289–308.

Arbeton, A., Eccles, J., & Harold, R. (1994, February). *Parents' perceptions of their children's competence: The role of parent attributions.* Paper presented at the biennial meetings of the Society for Research on Adolescence, San Diego.

Archibald, A., Graber, J., & Brooks-Gunn, J. (1999). Associations among parent–adolescent relationships, pubertal growth, dieting, and body image in young adolescent girls: A short-term longitudinal study. *Journal of Research on Adolescence, 9,* 395–415.

Archibald, A., Linver, M., Graber, J., & Brooks-Gunn, J. (2002). Parent–adolescent relationships and girls' unhealthy eating: Testing reciprocal effects. *Journal of Research on Adolescence, 12,* 451–461.

Ardelt, M., & Day, L. (2002). Parents, siblings, and peers: Close social relationships and adolescent deviance. *Journal of Early Adolescence, 22,* 310–349.

Arias, D. F., & Hernández, A. M. (2007). Emerging adulthood in Mexican and Spanish youth: Theories and realities. *Journal of Adolescent Research, 22,* 476–503.

Armor, D. (1972). School and family effects on Black and White achievement: A reexamination of the USOE data. In F. Mosteller & D. Moynihan (Eds.), *On equality of educational opportunity.* New York: Random House.

Armour, S., & Haynie, D. L. (2007). Adolescent sexual debut and later delinquency. *Journal of Youth and Adolescence, 36,* 141–152.

Armstrong, T. D., & Costello, E. (2002). Community studies on adolescent substance use, abuse, or dependence and psychiatric comorbidity. *Journal of Consulting and Clinical Psychology, 70,* 1224–1239.

Arndorfer, C. L., & Stormshak, E. A. (2008). Same-sex versus other-sex best friendship in early adolescence: Longitudinal predictors of antisocial behavior throughout adolescence. *Journal of Youth and Adolescence, 37,* 1059–1070.

Arnett, J. (1994). Are college students adults? Their conceptions of the transition to adulthood. *Journal of Adult Development, 1,* 213–224.

Arnett, J. (1996). *Metalheads.* Boulder, CO: Westview Press.

Arnett, J. (1998). Learning to stand alone: The contemporary American transition to adulthood in cultural and historical context. *Human Development, 41,* 295–315.

Arnett, J. (2000). Emerging adulthood: A theory of development from the late teens through the twenties. *American Psychologist, 55,* 469–480.

Arnett, J. (2001). Adolescents' responses to cigarette advertisements for five "youth brands" and one "adult brand." *Journal of Research on Adolescence, 11,* 425–443.

Arnett, J. (2002). Adolescents in Western countries on the threshold of the 21st century. In B. Brown, R. Larson, & T. Saraswathi (Eds.), *The world's youth: Adolescence in eight regions of the globe.* New York: Cambridge University Press.

Arnett, J. (2004). *Emerging adulthood: The winding road from the late teens through the twenties.* New York: Oxford University Press.

Arnett, J. (2007). Suffering, selfish, slackers? Myths and reality about emerging adults. *Journal of Youth and Adolescence, 36,* 23–29.

Arnett, J., & Balle-Jensen, L. (1993). Cultural bases of risk behavior: Danish adolescents. *Child Development, 64,* 1842–1855.

Aronson, J., Jannone, S., McGlone, M., & Johnson-Campbell, T. (2009). The Obama effect: An experimental test. *Journal of Experimental Social Psychology, 45,* 957–960.

Arseneault, L., Tremblay, R. E., Boulerice, B., & Saucier, J. (2002). Obstetrical complications and violent delinquency: Testing two developmental pathways. *Child Development, 73,* 496–508.

Arum, R., & Hout, M. (1998). The early returns: The transition from school to work in the United States. In Y. Shavit & W. Mueller (Eds.), *From school to work: A comparative study of educational qualifications and occupational destinations* (pp. 471–510). Oxford: Clarendon Press.

Arunkumar, R., Midgley, C., & Urdan, T. (1999). Perceiving high or low home–school dissonance: Longitudinal effects on adolescent emotional and academic well-being. *Journal of Research on Adolescence, 9,* 441–466.

Asakawa, K., & Csikszentmihalyi, M. (1998). The quality of experience of Asian American adolescents in academic activities: An exploration of educational achievement. *Journal of Research on Adolescence, 8,* 241–262.

Asakawa, K., & Csikszentmihalyi, M. (2000). Feelings of connectedness and internalization of values in Asian American adolescents. *Journal of Youth and Adolescence, 29,* 121–145.

Aseltine, R., & Gore, S. (2005). Work, post-secondary education, and psychosocial functioning following the transition from high school. *Journal of Adolescent Research, 20,* 615–639.

Aseltine, R., Gore, S., & Colten, M. (1994). Depression and the social developmental context of adolescence. *Journal of Personality and Social Psychology, 67,* 252–263.

Aseltine, R., Jr., Gore, S., & Colten, M. (1998). The co-occurrence of depression and substance abuse in late adolescence. *Development & Psychopathology, 10,* 549–570.

Asher, S., Parker, J., & Walker, D. (1996). Distinguishing friendship from acceptance: Implications for intervention and assessment. In W. Bukowski, A. Newcomb, & W. Hartup (Eds.), *The company they keep: Friendship in childhood and adolescence* (pp. 366–405). New York: Cambridge University Press.

Asmussen, L., & Larson, R. (1991). The quality of family time among young adolescents in single-parent and married-parent families. *Journal of Marriage and the Family, 53,* 1021–1030.

Aspy, C. B., Vesely, S. K., Oman, R. F., Rodine, S., Marshall, L., & McLeroy, K. (2007). Parental communication and youth sexual behaviour. *Journal of Adolescence, 30,* 449–466.

Astor, R. (1994). Children's moral reasoning about family and peer violence: The role of provocation and retribution. *Child Development, 65,* 1054–1067.

Atkins, R., Hart, D., & Donnelly, T. M. (2005). The association of childhood personality type with volunteering during adolescence. *Merrill-Palmer Quarterly, 2,* 145–162.

Attie, I., & Brooks-Gunn, J. (1989). The development of eating problems in adolescent girls: A longitudinal study. *Developmental Psychology, 25,* 70–79.

Aunola, K., Stattin, H., & Nurmi, J.-E. (2000). Parenting styles and adolescents' achievement strategies. *Journal of Adolescence, 23,* 205–222.

Austin, S. B., & Gortmaker, S. L. (2001). Dieting and smoking initiation in early adolescent girls and boys: A prospective study. *American Journal of Public Health, 91,* 446–450.

Avenevoli, S., & Steinberg, L. (2001). The continuity of depression across the adolescent transition. In H. Reese & R. Kail (Eds.), *Advances in child development and behavior* (Vol. 28, pp. 139–173). New York: Academic Press.

Averett, S. L., Rees, D. I., & Argys, L. M. (2002). The impact of government policies and neighborhood characteristics on teenage sexual activity and contraceptive use. *American Journal of Public Health, 92,* 1773–1778.

Ayalon, H. (1994). *Monopolizing knowledge? The ethnic composition and curriculum of Israeli high schools.* Paper presented at the biennial meetings of the Society for Research on Adolescence, Boston. *Sociology of Education, 67,* 264–278.

Babalola, S. (2004). Perceived peer behavior and the timing of sexual debut in Rwanda: A survival analysis of youth data. *Journal of Youth and Adolescence, 33,* 353–363.

Bachman, J. (1983, Summer). Premature affluence: Do high school students earn too much? *Economic Outlook USA,* 64–67.

Bachman, J., Johnston, L., & O'Malley, P. (1998). Explaining recent increases in students' marijuana use: Impacts of perceived risks and disapproval, 1976 through 1996. *American Journal of Public Health, 88,* 887–892.

Bachman, J., & Schulenberg, J. (1993). How part-time work intensity relates to drug use, problem behavior, time use, and satisfaction among high school seniors: Are these consequences or merely correlates? *Developmental Psychology, 29,* 220–235.

Baer, J. (2002). Is family cohesion a risk or protective factor during adolescent development? *Journal of Marriage and the Family, 64,* 668–675.

Baer, J., & Schmitz, M. F. (2007). Ethnic differences in trajectories of family cohesion for Mexican American and non-Hispanic White adolescents. *Journal of Youth and Adolescence, 36,* 583–592.

Bagwell, C., Newcomb, A., & Bukowski, W. (1998). Preadolescent friendship and peer rejection as predictors of adult adjustment. *Child Development, 69,* 140–153.

Bahr, S., Maughan, S., Marcos, A., & Li, B. (1998). Family, religiosity, and the risk of adolescent drug use. *Journal of Marriage and the Family, 60,* 979–992.

Bailey, P. E., Bruno, Z. V., Bezerra, M. F., Queiroz, I., Oliveira, C. M., & Chen-Mok, M. (2001). Adolescent pregnancy 1 year later: The effects of abortion vs. motherhood in Northeast Brazil. *Journal of Adolescent Health, 29,* 223–232.

Bakan, D. (1972). Adolescence in America: From idea to social fact. In J. Kagan & R. Coles (Eds.), *Twelve to sixteen: Early adolescence.* New York: Norton.

Baker, M., Milich, R., & Manolis, M. (1996). Peer interactions of dysphoric adolescents. *Journal of Abnormal Child Psychology, 24,* 241–255.

Baker, T., & Velez, W. (1996). Access to and opportunity in postsecondary education in the United States: A review. *Sociology of Education, Extra Issue, 69,* 82–101.

Balfanz, R., Legters, N., West, T. C., & Weber, L. M. (2007). Are NCLB's measures, incentives, and improvement strategies the right ones for the nation's low-performing high schools? *American Education Research Journal, 44,* 559–593.

Bámaca, M. Y., & Umaña-Taylor, A. J. (2006). Testing a model of resistance to peer pressure among Mexican-origin adolescents. *Journal of Youth and Adolescence, 35,* 631–645.

Bandura, A., Barbaranelli, C., Caprara, G., & Pastorelli, C. (1996). Multifaceted impact of self-efficacy beliefs on adcademic functioning. *Child Development, 67,* 1206–1222.

Bandura, A., & Walters, R. (1959). *Adolescent aggression.* New York: Ronald Press.

Bank, L., Burraston, B., & Snyder, J. (2004). Sibling conflict and ineffective parenting as predictors of adolescent boys' antisocial behavior and peer difficulties: Additive and interactional effects. *Journal of Research on Adolescence, 14,* 99–125.

Bank, L., Reid, J., & Greenley, K. (1994, February). *Middle childhood predictors of adolescent and early adult aggression.* Paper presented at the biennial meetings of the Society for Research on Adolescence, San Diego.

Bankston, C., III., & Caldas, S. (1996). Majority African American schools and social injustice: The influence of de facto segregation on academic achievement. *Social Forces, 75,* 535–555.

Bankston, C. L., III, & Caldas, S. (1998). Family structure, schoolmates, and racial inequalities in school achievement. *Journal of Marriage & the Family, 60,* 715–723.

Barber, B. (1994). Cultural, family, and personal contexts of parent-adolescent conflict. *Journal of Marriage and the Family, 56,* 375–386.

Barber, B. (1996). Parental psychological control: Revisiting a neglected construct. *Child Development, 67,* 3296–3319.

Barber, B., & Eccles, J. (1992). Long-term influence of divorce and single parenting on adolescent family- and work-related values, behaviors, and aspirations. *Psychological Bulletin, 111,* 108–126.

Barber, B., Eccles, J., & Stone, M. (2001). Whatever happened to the jock, the brain, and the princess? Young adult pathways linked to adolescent activity involvement and social identity. *Journal of Adolescent Research, 16,* 429–455.

Barber, B., & Olsen, J. (1997). Socialization in context: Connection, regulation, and autonomy in the family, school, neighborhood, and with peers. *Journal of Adolescent Research, 12,* 287–315.

Barber, B., & Olsen, J. (2004). Assessing the transitions to middle and high school. *Journal of Adolescent Research, 19,* 3–30.

Barber, B., Stone, M., Hunt, J., & Eccles, J. (2005). Benefits of activity participation: The roles of identity affirmation and peer norm sharing. In J. Mahoney, R. Larson, & J. Eccles (Eds.), *Organized activities as contexts of development* (pp. 185–210). Hillsdale, NJ: Erlbaum.

Barboza, G. E., Schiamberg, L. B., Oehmke, J., Korzeniewski, S. J., Post, L. A., & Heraux, C. G. (2009). Individual characteristics and the multiple contexts of adolescent bullying: An ecological perspective. *Journal of Youth and Adolescence, 38,* 101–121.

Bardone, A., Moffitt, T., Caspi, A., Dickson, N., & Silva, P. (1996). Adult mental health and social outcomes of adolescent girls with depression and conduct disorder. *Development and Psychopathology, 8,* 811–829.

Barker, R., & Gump, P. (1964). *Big school, small school: High school size and student behavior.* Stanford, CA: Stanford University Press.

Barnes, G., & Farrell, M. (1992). Parental support and control as predictors of adolescent drinking, delinquency, and related problem behaviors. *Journal of Marriage and the Family, 54,* 763–776.

Barnes, G. M., Hoffman, J. H., Welte, J. W., Farrell, M. P., & Dintcheff, B. A. (2006). Effects of parental monitoring and peer deviance on substance use and delinquency. *Journal of Marriage and Family, 68,* 1084–1104.

Barnes, R. (2007, June 29). Divided court limits use of race by school districts. *Washington Post,* p. A01.

Barratt, M., Roach, M., Morgan, K., & Colbert, K. (1996). Adjustment to motherhood by single adolescents. *Family Relations, 45,* 209–215.

Barrera, M., Jr., Li, S., & Chassin, L. (1995). Effects of parental alcoholism and life stress on Hispanic and non-Hispanic Caucasian adolescents: A prospective study. *American Journal of Community Psychology, 23,* 479–507.

Barrera, M., Jr., Prelow, H. M., Dumka, L. E., Gonzales, N. A., Knight, G. P., Michaels, M., et al. (2002). Pathways from family economic conditions to adolescents' distress: Supportive parenting, stressors outside the family, and deviant peers. *Journal of Community Psychology, 30,* 135–152.

Barrett-Singer, A. T., & Weinstein, R. S. (2000). Differential parent treatment predicts achievement and self-perceptions in two cultural contexts. *Journal of Family Psychology, 14,* 491–509.

Barry, C. M., & Nelson, L. J. (2005). The role of religion in the transition to adulthood for young emerging adults. *Journal of Youth and Adolescence 34,* 245–255.

Barry, C. M., & Wentzel, K. R. (2006). Friend influence on prosocial behavior: The role of motivational factors and friendship characteristics. *Developmental Psychology, 42,* 153–163.

Bartko, W. T., & Eccles, J. (2003). Adolescent participation in structured and unstructured activities: A person-oriented analysis. *Journal of Youth and Adolescence, 32,* 233–241.

Basen-Enquist, K., Edmundson, E., & Parcel, G. (1996). Structure of health risk behavior among high school students. *Journal of Consulting and Clinical Psychology, 64,* 764–775.

Basile, K. C., Black, M. C., Simon, T. R., Arias, I., Brener, N. D., & Saltzman, L. E. (2006). The association between self-reported lifetime history of forced sexual intercourse and recent health-risk behaviors: Findings from the 2003 national youth risk behavior survey. *Journal of Adolescent Health, 39,* e1–e7.

Bassi, M., Steca, P., Delle Fave, A., & Caprara, G. V. (2007). Academic self-efficacy beliefs and quality of experience in learning. *Journal of Youth and Adolescence, 36,* 301–312.

Battin-Pearson, S., Newcomb, M. D., Abbott, R. D., Hill, K. G., Catalano, R. F., & Hawkins, J. (2000). Predictors of early high school dropout: A test of five theories. *Journal of Educational Psychology, 92,* 568–582.

Bauermeister, J. A., Zimmerman, M. A., Barnett, T. E., & Caldwell, C. H. (2007). Working in high school and adaptation in the transition to young adulthood among African American youth. *Journal of Youth and Adolescence, 36,* 877–890.

Baumer, E. P., & South, S. J. (2001). Community effects on youth sexual activity. *Journal of Marriage and the Family, 63,* 540–554.

Baumrind, D. (1978). Parental disciplinary patterns and social competence in children. *Youth and Society, 9,* 239–276.

Bauserman, R., & Rind, B. (1997). Psychological correlates of male child and adolescent sexual experiences with adults: A review of the nonclinical literature. *Archives of Sexual Behavior, 26,* 105–141.

Beam, M. R., Chen, C., & Greenberger, E. (2002). The nature of adolescents' relationship with their "very important" nonparental adults. *American Journal of Community Psychology, 30,* 305–325.

Bean, R. A., Barber, B. K., & Crane, D. R. (2006). Parental support, behavioral control, and psychological control among African American youth: The relationships to academic grades, delinquency, and depression. *Journal of Family Issues, 27,* 1335–1355.

Bean, R. A., Bush, K. R., McKenry, P. C., & Wilson, S. M. (2003). The impact of parental support, behavioral control, and psychological control on the academic achievement and self-esteem of African American and European American adolescents. *Journal of Adolescent Research, 18,* 523–541.

Bearman, P., & Moody, J. (2004). Suicide and friendships among American adolescents. *American Journal of Public Health, 94,* 89–96.

Bearman, P. S., & Brückner, H. (2001). Promising the future: Virginity pledges and first intercourse. *American Journal of Sociology, 106,* 859–912.

Bearman, S. K., & Stice, E. (2008). Testing a gender additive model: The role of body image in adolescent depression. *Journal of Abnormal Child Psychology, 36,* 1251–1263.

Beaumont, S. (1996). Adolescent girls' perceptions of conversations with mothers and friends. *Journal of Adolescent Research, 11,* 325–346.

Beaver, K. M., DeLisi, M., Wright, J. P., & Vaughn, M. G. (2009). Gene-environmental interplay and delinquent involvement: Evidence of direct, indirect, and interactive effects. *Journal of Adolescent Research, 24,* 147–168.

Beaver, K. M., & Wright, J. P. (2007). A child effects explanation for the association between family risk and involvement in an antisocial lifestyle. *Journal of Adolescent Research, 22,* 640–664.

Bechara, A. (2005). Decision making, impulse control and loss of willpower to resist drugs: A neurocognitive perspective. *Nature Neuroscience, 8,* 1458–1463.

Becker, A., Burwell, R., Herzog, D., Hamburg, P., & Gilman, S. (2002). Eating behaviors and attitudes following prolonged exposure to television among ethnic Fijian adolescent girls. *British Journal of Psychiatry, 180,* 509–514.

Becker, B. E., & Luthar, S. S. (2007). Peer-perceived admiration and social preference: Contextual correlates of positive peer regard among suburban and urban adolescents. *Journal of Research on Adolescence, 17,* 117–144.

Beckwith, L., Cohen, S., & Hamilton, C. (1999). Maternal sensitivity during infancy and subsequent life events relate to attachment representation at early adulthood. *Developmental Psychology, 35,* 693–700.

Bell, A., Weinberg, M., & Hammersmith, S. (1981). *Sexual preference: Its development in men and women.* Bloomington: Indiana University Press.

Bell, J., & Bromnick, R. (2000, March). *A grounded approach to understanding modern dilemmas of individuality.* Paper presented at the eighth biennial meeting of the Society for Research on Adolescence, Chicago.

Bell, L. G., & Bell., D. C. (2005). Family dynamics in adolescence affect midlife well-being. *Journal of Family Psychology, 19,* 198–207.

Belsky, J., Steinberg, L., & Draper, P. (1991). Childhood experience, interpersonal development, and reproductive strategy: An evolutionary theory of socialization. *Child Development, 62,* 647–670.

Belsky, J., Steinberg, L., Houts, R., Friedman, S., DeHart, G., Cauffman, E., et al. (2007). Family rearing antecedents of pubertal timing. *Child Development, 78,* 1302–1321.

BeLue, R., Francis, L. A., Colaco, B. (2009). Mental health problems and overweight in a nationally representative sample of adolescents: Effects of race and ethnicity. *Pediatrics, 123,* 697–702.

Bem, D. (1996). Exotic becomes erotic: A developmental theory of sexual orientation. *Psychological Review, 103,* 320–335.

Bem, S. (1975). Sex-role adaptability: One consequence of psychological androgyny. *Journal of Personality and Social Psychology, 31,* 634–643.

Ben-Zur, H., & Reshef-Kfir, Y. (2003). Risk taking and coping strategies among Israeli adolescents. *Journal of Adolescence, 26,* 255–265.

Benda, B., & Corwyn, R. (1998). Race and gender differences in theories of sexual behavior among rural adolescents residing in AFDC families. *Youth and Society, 30,* 59–88.

Bender, H., Allen, J., McElhaney, K., Antonishak, J., Moore, C., Kelly, H., et al. (2007). Use of harsh physical discipline and developmental outcomes in adolescence. *Development and Psychopathology, 19,* 227–242.

Benenson, J. F., & Christakos, A. (2003). The greater fragility of females' versus males' closest same-sex friendships. *Child Development, 74,* 1123–1129.

Benhorin, S., & McMahon, S. (2008). Exposure to violence and aggression: Protective roles of social support among urban African American youth. *Journal of Community Psychology, 36,* 723–743.

Benjet, C., & Hernandez-Guzman, L. (2002). A short-term longitudinal study of pubertal change, gender, and psychological well being of Mexican early adolescents. *Journal of Youth and Adolescence, 31,* 429–442.

Benner, A. D., & Graham, S. (2007). Navigating the transition to multi-ethnic urban high schools: Changing ethnic congruence and adolescents' school-related affect. *Journal of Research on Adolescence, 17,* 207–220.

Benner, A. D., & Graham, S. (2009). The transition to high school as a developmental process among multiethnic urban youth. *Child Development, 80,* 356–376.

Benner, A. D., Graham, S., & Mistry, R. S. (2008). Discerning direct and mediated effects of ecological structures and processes on adolescents' educational outcomes. *Developmental Psychology, 44,* 840–854.

Benner, A. D., & Mistry, R. S. (2007). Congruence of mother and teacher educational expectations and low-income youth's academic competence. *Journal of Educational Psychology, 99,* 140–153.

Berends, M., Lucas, S. R., & Penaloza, R. V. (2008). How changes in families and schools are related to trends in Black-White test scores. *Sociology of Education, 81,* 313–344.

Berk, L. (1992). The extracurriculum. In P. Jackson (Ed.), *Handbook of research on curriculum.* New York: Macmillan.

Berkel, C., Murry, V. M., Hurt, T. R., Chen, Y., Brody, G. H., Simons, R. L., et al. (2009). It takes a village: Protecting rural African American youth in the context of racism. *Journal of Youth and Adolescence, 38,* 175–188.

Berkowitz, R. I., Wadden, T. A., Tershakovec, A. M., & Cronquist, J. L. (2003). Behavior therapy and sibutramine for the treatment of adolescent obesity. *Journal of the American Medical Association, 289,* 1805–1812.

Berliner, D., & Biddle, B. (1995). *The manufactured crisis: Myths, fraud, and attack on America's public schools.* Reading, MA: Addison-Wesley.

Berndt, T. (1996). Exploring the effects of friendship quality on social development. In W. Bukowski, A. Newcomb, & W. Hartup, W. (Eds.), *The company they keep: Friendship in childhood and adolescence* (pp. 346–365). New York: Cambridge University Press.

Berndt, T., & Keefe, K. (1995). Friends' influence on adolescents' adjustment to school. *Child Development, 66,* 1312–1329.

Berndt, T., & Mekos, D. (1995). Adolescents' perceptions of the stressful and desirable aspects of the transition to junior high. *Journal of Research on Adolescence, 5,* 123–142.

Berndt, T., & Perry, T. (1990). Distinctive features and effects of early adolescent friendships. In R. Montemayor, G. Adams, & T. Gullota (Eds.), *Advances in adolescence research* (Vol. 2, pp. 269–287). Beverly Hills, CA: Sage.

Bersamin, M., Fisher, D., Walker, S., Hill, D., & Grube, J. (2007). Defining virginity and abstinence: Adolescents' interpretations of sexual behaviors. *Journal of Adolescent Health, 41,* 182–188.

Bersamin, M., Walker, S., Waiters, E., Fisher, D., & Grube, J. (2005). Promising to wait: Virginity pledges and adolescent sexual behavior. *Journal of Adolescent Health, 36,* 428–436.

Berzonsky, M. (2004). Identity style, parental authority, and identity commitment. *Journal of Youth and Adolescence, 33,* 213–220.

Best, A. L. (2006). Freedom, constraint, and family responsibility: Teens and parents collaboratively negotiate around the car, class, gender, and culture. *Journal of Family Issues, 27,* 55–84.

Bettis, P. (1996). Urban students, liminality, and the postindustrial context. *Sociology of Education, 69,* 105–125.

Beutel, A., & Marini, M. (1995). Gender and values. *American Sociological Review, 60,* 436–448.

Beyers, J. M., Bates, J. E., Pettit, G. S., & Dodge, K. A. (2003). Neighborhood structure, parenting processes, and the development of youths' externalizing behaviors: A multilevel analysis. *American Journal of Community Psychology, 31,* 35–53.

Beyers, J. M., & Loeber, R. (2003). Untangling developmental relations between depressed mood and delinquency in male adolescents. *Journal of Abnormal Child Psychology, 31,* 247–266.

Beyers, J. M., Loeber, R., Wikstrom, P. H., & Stouthamer-Loeber, M. (2001). What predicts adolescent violence in better-off neighborhoods? *Journal of Abnormal Psychology, 29,* 369–381.

Beyers, W., & Goossens, L. (2008). Dynamics of perceived parenting and identity formation in late adolescence. *Journal of Adolescence, 31,* 165–184.

Beyers, W., Goossens, L., Vasant, I., & Moors, E. (2003). A structural model of autonomy in middle and late adolescence; Connectedness, separation, detachment, and agency. *Journal of Youth and Adolescence, 32,* 351–365.

Beyth-Marom, R., Austin, L., Fischoff, B., Palmgren, C., & Jacobs-Quadrel, M. (1993). Perceived consequences of risky behaviors: Adults and adolescents. *Developmental Psychology, 29,* 549–563.

Biehl, M., & Halpern-Felsher, B. L. (2001). Adolescents' and adults' understanding of probability expressions. *Journal of Adolescent Health, 28,* 30–35.

Biehl, M. C., Natsuaki, M. N., & Ge, X. (2007). The influence of pubertal timing on alcohol use and heavy drinking trajectories. *Journal of Youth and Adolescence, 36,* 153–167.

Biener, L., & Siegel, M. (2000). Tobacco marketing and adolescent smoking: More support for a causal inference. *American Journal of Public Health, 90,* 407–411.

Bierman, K., Coie, J., Dodge, K., Foster, E., Greenberg, M., Lochman, J., et al. (2007). Fast track randomized controlled trial to prevent externalizing psychiatric disorders: Findings from grades 3 to 9. *Journal of the American Academy of Child & Adolescent Psychiatry, 46,* 1250–1262.

Bierman, K., & Furman, W. (1984). The effects of social skills training and peer involvement on the social adjustment of preadolescents. *Child Development, 55,* 151–162.

Bierman, K., & Wargo, J. (1995). Predicting the longitudinal course associated with aggressive-rejected, aggressive-nonrejected, and rejected non-aggressive status. *Development and Psychopathology, 7,* 669–682.

Bigelow, B., & LaGaipa, J. (1975). Children's written descriptions of friendship. *Developmental Psychology, 11,* 857–858.

Bills, D., Helms, L., & Ozcan, M. (1995). The impact of student employment on teachers' attitudes and behaviors toward working students. *Youth and Society, 27,* 169–193.

Bimmel, N., van IJzendoorn, M. H., Bakermans-Kranenburg, M., Juffer, F., & De Geus, E. (2008). Problem behavior and heart rate reactivity in adopted adolescents: Longitudinal and concurrent relations. *Journal of Research on Adolescence, 18,* 201–214.

Bingenheimer, J. B. (2005). Firearm violence exposure and serious violent behavior. *Science, 308,* 1323–1326.

Bingham, C., & Crockett, L. (1996). Longitudinal adjustment patterns of boys and girls experiencing early, middle, and late sexual intercourse. *Developmental Psychology, 32,* 647–658.

Bingham, C., & Shope, J. T. (2004). Adolescent problem behavior and problem driving in young adulthood. *Journal of Adolescent Research, 19,* 205–223.

Birmaher, B., Rabin, B., Garcia, M., Jain, U., Whiteside, T., Williamson, D., et al. (1994). Cellular immunity in depressed, conduct disorder, and normal adolescents: Role of adverse life events. *Journal of the American Academy of Child and Adolescent Psychiatry, 33,* 671–678.

Biro F., Huang, B., Crawford, P., Lucky, A., Striegel-Moore, R., Barton, B., et al. (2006). Pubertal correlates in Black and White girls. *Journal of Pediatrics, 148,* 234–240.

Biro, F. M., Striegel-Moore, R., Franko, D. L., Padgett, J., & Bean, J. A. (2006). Self-esteem in adolescent females. *Journal of Adolescent Health, 39,* 501–507.

Bishop, D., Hardiman, M., Uwer, R., & von Suchodoletz, W. (2007). Maturation of the long-latency auditory ERP: Step function changes at start and end of adolescence. *Developmental Science, 10,* 565–575.

Bishop, J. (1999) Nerd harrassment, incentives, school priorities and learning. In S. Mayer & P. Peterson (Eds.), *Earning and learning.* Washington, DC: Brookings Institution.

Bishop, J. (2001). The role of end-of-course exams and minimum competency exams in standards-based reforms. In D. Ravitch (Ed.), *Brookings papers on educational policy.* Washington, DC: Brookings Institution.

Bishop, J., Bishop, M., Gelbwasser, L., Green, S., & Zuckerman, A. (2003). Why do we harass nerds and freaks?: Towards a theory of student culture and norms. In D. Ravitch (Ed.), *Brookings papers on education policy.* Washington, DC: Brookings Institution.

Bjorklund, D. (1997). In search of a metatheory for cognitive development (or, Piaget is dead and I don't feel so good myself). *Child Development, 68,* 144–148.

Black, K., & McCartney, K. (1997). Adolescent females' security with parents predicts the quality of peer interactions. *Social Development, 6,* 91–110.

Black, M., Ricardo, I., & Stanton, B. (1997). Social and psychological factors associated with AIDS risk behaviors among low-income, urban, African American adolescents. *Journal of Research on Adolescence, 7,* 173–195.

Blackwell, L. S., Trzesniewski, K. H., & Dweck, C. S. (2007). Implicit theories of intelligence predict achievement across an adolescent transition: A longitudinal study and an intervention. *Child Development, 78,* 246–263.

Blais, J. J., Craig, W. M., Pepler, D., & Connolly, J. (2008). Adolescents online: The importance of Internet activity choices to salient relationships. *Journal of Youth and Adolescence, 37,* 522–536.

Blake, S. M., Ledsky, R., Goodenow, C., Sawyer, R., Lohrmann, D., & Windsor, R. (2003). Condom availability programs in Massachusetts high schools: Relationships with condom use and sexual behavior. *American Journal of Public Health, 93,* 955–962.

Blinn-Pike, L. (1999). Why abstinent adolescents report they have not had sex: Understanding sexually resilient youth. *Family Relations, 48,* 295–301.

Block, J., & Robins, R. (1993). A longitudinal study of consistency and change in self-esteem from early adolescence to early adulthood. *Child Development, 64,* 909–923.

Blos, P. (1967). The second individuation process of adolescence. In R. S. Eissler et al. (Eds.), *Psychoanalytic study of the child* (Vol. 15). New York: International Universities Press.

Blos, P. (1979). *The adolescent passage.* New York: International Universities Press.

Blum, R., Beuhring, T., Wunderlich, M., & Resnick, M. (1996). Don't ask, they won't tell: The quality of adolescent health screening in five practice settings. *American Journal of Public Health, 86,* 1767–1772.

Blum, R., Resnick, M., & Stark, T. (1990). Factors associated with the use of court bypass by minors to obtain abortions. *Family Planning Perspectives, 22,* 158–160.

Blum, R., & Rinehart, P. (2000). *Reducing the risk: Connections that make a difference in the lives of youth.* Minneapolis: Division of General Pediatrics and Adolescent Health, University of Minnesota.

Blum, R. W., & Nelson-Mmari, K. (2004). The health of young people in a global context. *Journal of Adolescent Health, 35,* 402–418.

Blyth, D., Hill, J., & Thiel, K. (1982). Early adolescents' significant others: Grade and gender differences in perceived relationships with familial and non-familial adults and young people. *Journal of Youth and Adolescence, 11,* 425–450.

Blyth, D., Simmons, R., & Zakin, D. (1985). Satisfaction with body image for early adolescent females: The impact of pubertal timing within different school environments. *Journal of Youth and Adolescence, 14,* 227–236.

Boccaccini, M. T., Murrie, D. C., Clark, J. W., & Cornell, D. G. (2008). Describing, diagnosing, and naming psychopathy: How do youth psychopathy labels influence jurors? *Behavioral Sciences and the Law, 25,* 487–510.

Boden, J. M., Fergusson, D. M., & Horwood, L. J. (2008). Does adolescent self-esteem predict later life outcomes? A test of the causal role of self-esteem. *Development and Psychopathology, 20,* 319–339.

Bogenschneider, K. (1997). Parental involvement in adolescent schooling: A proximal process with transcontextual validity. *Journal of Marriage and the Family, 59,* 1–16.

Bogenschneider, K., Small, S., & Tsay, J. (1997). Child, parent, and contextual influences on perceived parenting competence among parents of adolescents. *Journal of Marriage and the Family, 59,* 345–362.

Bohn, A., & Berntsen, D. (2008). Life story development in childhood: The development of life story abilities and the acquisition of cultural life scripts from late middle childhood to adolescence. *Developmental Psychology, 44,* 1135–1147.

Bohnert, A. M., Kane, P., & Garber, J. (2008). Organized activity participation and internalizing and externalizing symptoms: Reciprocal relations during adolescence. *Journal of Youth and Adolescence, 37,* 239–250.

Bohnert, A. M., Richards, M. H., Kolmodin, K. E., & Lakin, B. L. (2008). Young urban African American adolescents' experience of discretionary time activities. *Journal of Research on Adolescence, 18,* 517–539.

Boldero, J., & Fallon, B. (1995). Adolescent help-seeking: What do they get help for and from whom? *Journal of Adolescence, 18,* 193–209.

Bolland, J. M., Lian, B. E., & Formichella, C. M. (2005). The origins of hopelessness among inner-city African American adolescents. *American Journal of Community Psychology, 36,* 293–305.

Bomar, J., & Sabatelli, R. (1996). Family system dynamics, gender, and psychosocial maturity in late adolescence. *Journal of Adolescent Research, 11,* 421–439.

Boney-McCoy, S., & Finkelhor, D. (1995). The psychosocial impact of violent victimization in a national sample. *Journal of Consulting and Clinical Psychology, 63,* 726–736.

Bongers, I. L., Koot, H. M., van der Ende, J., & Verhulst, F. C. (2004). Developmental trajectories of externalizing behaviors in childhood and adolescence. *Child Development, 75,* 1523–1537.

Bontempo, D. E., & D'Augelli, A. R. (2002). Effects of at-school victimization and sexual orientation on lesbian, gay, or bisexual youths' health risk behavior. *Journal of Adolescent Health, 30,* 364–374.

Boone, E., & Leadbeater, B. (2006). Game on: Diminishing risks for depressive symptoms in early adolescence through positive involvement in team sports. *Journal of Research on Adolescence, 16,* 79–90.

Booth, A., Johnson, D., Granger, D., Crouter, A., & McHale, S. (2003). Testosterone and child and adolescent adjustment: The moderating role of parent–child relationships. *Developmental Psychology, 39,* 85–98.

Booth, M. Z., & Sheehan, H. C. (2008). Perceptions of people and place: Young adolescents' interpretation of their schools in the United States and the United Kingdom. *Journal of Adolescent Research, 23,* 722–744.

Borelli, J. L., & Prinstein, M. J. (2006). Reciprocal, longitudinal associations among adolescents' negative feedback-seeking, depressive symptoms, and peer relations. *Journal of Abnormal Child Psychology, 34,* 159–169.

Borkowski, J., & Sneed, M. (2006). Will NCLB improve or harm public education? *Harvard Educational Review, 76,* 503–525.

Borzekowski, D., Fobil, J., & Asante, K. (2006). Online access by adolescents in Accra: Ghanaian teens' use of the Internet for health information. *Developmental Psychology, 42,* 450–458.

Bos, H., Sandfort, T., de Bruyn, E., & Hakvoort, E. (2008). Same-sex attraction, social relationships, psychosocial functioning, and school performance in early adolescence. *Developmental Psychology, 44,* 59–68.

Botstein, L. (1997). *Jefferson's children: Education and the promise of American culture.* New York: Doubleday.

Botticello, A. L. (2009). School contextual influences and the risk for adolescent alcohol misuse. *American Journal of Community Psychology, 43,* 85–97.

Botvin, M., & Vitaro, F. (1995). The impact of peer relationships on aggression in childhood: Inhibition through coercion or promotion through peer support. In J. McCord (Ed.), *Coercion and punishment in long-term perspectives* (pp. 183–197). New York: Cambridge University Press.

Bowen, N. K., & Bowen, G. L. (2002). Neighborhood social disorganization, families, and the educational behavior of adolescents. *Journal of Adolescent Research, 17,* 468–490.

Bowker, A. (2004). Predicting friendship stability during early adolescence. *Journal of Early Adolescence, 24,* 85–112.

Bowlby, J. (1969). *Attachment and loss:* Vol. 1. *Attachment.* New York: Basic Books.

Boyer, T. W. (2006). The development of risk-taking: A multi-perspective review. *Developmental Review, 26,* 291–345.

Boyle, M. H., Georgiades, K., Racine, Y., & Mustard, C. (2007). Neighborhood and family influences on educational attainment: Results from the Ontario Child Health Study follow-up 2001. *Child Development, 78,* 168–189.

Brack, C., Brack, G., & Orr, D. (1996). Adolescent health promotion: Testing a model using multidimensional scaling. *Journal of Research on Adolescence, 6,* 139–149.

Bradford, K., Vaughn, L. B., & Barber, B. K. (2008). When there is conflict: Interparental conflict, parent–child conflict, and youth problem behaviors. *Journal of Family Issues, 29,* 780–805.

Bradley, R. H., Corwyn, R. F., Pipes McAdoo, H., & Garcia-Coll, C. (2001). The home environments of children in the United States, part 1: Variations by age, ethnicity, and poverty status. *Child Development, 72,* 1844–1867.

Bradshaw, C. P., Sawyer, A. L., & O'Brennan, L. M. (2009). A social disorganization perspective on bullying-related attitudes and behaviors: The influences of school context. *American Journal of Community Psychology, 43,* 204–220.

Brady, S., & Halpern-Felsher, B. (2007). Adolescents' reported consequences of having oral sex versus vaginal sex. *Pediatrics, 119,* 229–236.

Brahmbhatt, S. B., McAuley, T., & Barch, D. M. (2008). Functional developmental similarities and differences in the neural correlates of verbal and nonverbal working memory tasks. *Neuropsychologia, 46,* 1020–1031.

Branch, C. (1995, August). *Gang bangers: Ethnic variations.* Paper presented at the American Psychological Association, New York.

Bratt, C. (2008). Guardians to counter adolescent drug use? Limitations of a routine activities approach. *Youth and Society, 39,* 385–405.

Braun, H., Jenkins, F., & Grigg, W. (2006). *Comparing private schools and public schools using hierarchical linear modeling.* U.S. Department of Education, National Center for Education Statistics. Washington, DC: U.S. Government Printing Office.

Bray, J., Adams, J., Getz, J., & Baer, P. E. (2001). Developmental, family, and ethnic in influences on adolescent alcohol usage: A growth curve approach. *Journal of Family Psychology, 15,* 301–314.

Bray, J., Adams, G., Getz, J., & McQueen, A. (2003). Individuation, peers, and adolescent alcohol use: A latent growth analysis. *Journal of Consulting and Clinical Psychology, 71,* 553–564.

Bray, J., Berger, S., Tiuch, G., & Boethel, C. (1993, March). *Nonresidential parent–child relationships following divorce and remarriage: A longitudinal perspective.* Paper presented at the biennial meetings of the Society for Research in Child Development, New Orleans.

Brendgen, M., Vitaro, F., & Bukowski, W. (2000). Deviant friends and early adolescents' emotional and behavioral adjustment. *Journal of Research on Adolescence, 10,* 173–189.

Brendgen, M., Vitaro, F., Doyle, A., Markiewicz, D., & Bukowski, W. (2002). Same-sex peer relations and romantic relationships during early adolescence: Interactive links to emotional, behavioral, and academic adjustment. *Merrill-Palmer Quarterly, 48,* 77–103.

Brenhouse, H. C., Sonntag, K. C., & Andersen, S. L. (2008). Transient D-sub-1 dopamine receptor expression on prefrontal cortex projection neurons: Relationship to enhanced motivational salience of drug cues in adolescence. *Journal of Neuroscience, 28,* 2375–2382.

Brennan, P. A., Hall, J., Bor, W., Najman, J. M., & Williams, G. (2003). Integrating biological and social processes in relation to early-onset persistent aggression in boys and girls. *Developmental Psychology, 39,* 309–323.

Brent, D., Emslie, G., Clarke, G., Wagner, K. D., Asarnow, J. R., Keller, M., et al. (2008). Switching to another SSRI or to venlafaxine with or without cognitive behavioral therapy for adolescents with SSRI-resistant depression: The TORDIA randomized controlled trial. *JAMA: Journal of the American Medical Association, 299,* 901–913.

Brewster, K. (1994). Race differences in sexual activity among adolescent women: The role of neighborhood characteristics. *American Sociological Review, 59,* 408–424.

Bridges, G., & Steen, S. (1998). Racial disparities in official assessments of juvenile offenders: Attributional stereotypes as mediating mechanisms. *American Sociological Review, 63,* 554–570.

Brody, G., Beach, S., Philibert, R., Chen, Y., & Murry, V. (2009). Prevention effects moderate the association of 5-httlpr and youth risk behavior initiation: G×E hypotheses tested via a randomized prevention design. *Child Development, 80,* 645–661.

Brody, G., Chen, Y., Murry, V., Ge, X., Simons, R., Gibbons, F., et al. (2006). Perceived discrimination and the adjustment of African American youths: A five-year longitudinal analysis with contextual moderation effects. *Child Development, 77,* 1170–1189.

Brody, G., Ge, X., Yeong, K., McBride, M., Simons, R., Gibbons, F., et al. (2003). Neighborhood disadvantage moderates associations of parenting and older sibling problem attitudes and behavior with conduct disorders in African American children. *Journal of Consulting and Clinical Psychology, 71,* 211–222.

Brody, G., Moore, K., & Glei, D. (1994). Family processes during adolescence as predictors of parent–young adult attitude similarity: A six-year longitudinal analysis. *Family Relations, 43,* 369–373.

Brody, G., Murry, V., Kogan, S., Gerrard, M., Gibbons, F., Molgaard, V., et al. (2006). The strong African American families program: A cluster-randomized prevention trial of long-term effects and a mediational model. *Journal of Consulting and Clinical Psychology, 74,* 356–366.

Brody, G., Stoneman, Z., & Burke, M. (1987). Child temperaments, maternal differential treatment, and sibling relationships. *Developmental Psychology, 23,* 354–362.

Brody, G., Stoneman, Z., & Flor, D. (1995). Linking family processes and academic competence among rural African American youths. *Journal of Marriage and the Family, 57,* 567–579.

Brody, G., Stoneman, Z., & Flor, D. (1996). Parental religiosity, family processes, and youth competence in rural, two-parent African-American families. *Developmental Psychology, 32,* 696–706.

Brody, G., Stoneman, Z., Flor, D., & McCrary, C. (1994). Religion's role in organizing family relationships: Family process in rural, two-parent African American families. *Journal of Marriage and the Family, 56,* 878–888.

Brody, G., Stoneman, Z., & McCoy, J. (1994). Forecasting sibling relationships in early adolescence from child temperaments and family processes in middle childhood. *Child Development, 65,* 771–784.

Broh, B. A. (2002). Linking extracurricular programming to academic achievement: Who benefits and why? *Sociology of Education, 75,* 69–95.

Broidy, L., Nagin, D., Tremblay, R., Bates, J., Brame, B., Dodge, K., et al. (2003). Developmental trajectories of childhood disruptive behaviors and adolescent delinquency: A six-site, cross-national study. *Developmental Psychology, 39,* 222–245.

Bronfenbrenner, U. (1974). The origins of alienation. *Scientific American, 231,* 53–61.

Bronfenbrenner, U. (1979). *The ecology of human development.* Cambridge, MA: Harvard University Press.

Bronstein, P., Duncan, P., Clauson, J., Abrams, C. L., Yannett, N., Ginsburg, G., et al. (1998). Preventing middle school adjustment problems for children from lower-income families: A program for aware parenting. *Journal of Applied Developmental Psychology, 19,* 129–152.

Bronstein, P., Duncan, P., D'Ari, A., Pieniadz, J., Fitzgerald, M., Abrams, C., et al. (1996). Family and parenting behaviors predicting middle school adjustment: A longitudinal study. *Family Relations, 45,* 415–426.

Bronstein, P., Ginsburg, G., & Herrera-Leavitt, I. (2000). *Parental predictors of motivational orientation and academic performance in early adolescence: A longitudinal study.* Unpublished manuscript. Burlington, VT: Department of Psychology, University of Vermont.

Brookmeyer, K. A., Henrich, & Schwab-Stone, M. (2005). Adolescents who witness community violence: Can parent support and prosocial cognitions protect them from committing violence? *Child Development, 76,* 917–929.

Brooks-Gunn, J., & Donahue, E. (Eds.) (2008). Children and electronic media. *The Future of Children, 18.*

Brooks-Gunn, J., & Furstenberg, F., Jr. (1989). Adolescent sexual behavior. *American Psychologist, 44,* 249–257.

Brooks-Gunn, J., Graber, J., & Paikoff, R. (1994). Studying links between hormones and negative affect: Models and measures. *Journal of Research on Adolescence, 4,* 469–486.

Brooks-Gunn, J., Newman, D., Holderness, C., & Warren, M. (1994). The experience of breast development and girls' stories about the purchase of a bra. *Journal of Youth and Adolescence, 23,* 539–565.

Brooks-Gunn, J., & Paikoff, R. (1993). "Sex is a gamble, kissing is a game": Adolescent sexuality and health promotion. In S. Millstein, A. Petersen, & E. Nightingale (Eds.), *Promoting the health of adolescents: New directions for the twenty-first century* (pp. 180–208). New York: Oxford University Press.

Brooks-Gunn, J., & Reiter, E. (1990). The role of pubertal processes. In S. Feldman & G. Elliott (Eds.), *At the threshold: The developing adolescent* (pp. 16–23). Cambridge, MA: Harvard University Press.

Brooks-Gunn, J., & Warren, M. (1985). The effects of delayed menarche in different contexts: Dance and nondance students. *Journal of Youth and Adolescence, 14,* 285–300.

Broverman, I., Vogel, S., Broverman, D., Clarkson, F., & Rosenkrantz, P. (1972). Sex-role stereotypes: A current appraisal. *Journal of Social Issues, 28,* 59–78.

Brown, A. (1975). The development of memory: Knowing, knowing about knowing, and knowing how to know. In H. Reese (Ed.), *Advances in child development and behavior* (Vol. 10). New York: Academic Press.

Brown, B. (1990). Peer groups. In S. Feldman & G. Elliott (Eds.), *At the threshold: The developing adolescent* (pp. 171–196). Cambridge, MA: Harvard University Press.

Brown, B. (1996). Visibility, vulnerability, development, and context: Ingredients for a fuller understanding of peer rejection in adolescence. *Journal of Early Adolescence, 16,* 27–36.

Brown, B. (1999). "You're going out with who?": Peer group influences on adolescent romantic relationships. In W. Furman, B. Brown, & C. Feiring (Eds.), *Contemporary perspectives on adolescent romantic relationships* (pp. 291–329). New York: Cambridge University Press.

Brown, B. (2004). Adolescents' relationships with peers. In R. Lerner & L. Steinberg (Eds.), *Handbook of adolescent psychology.* New York: Wiley.

Brown, B., Clasen, D., & Eicher, S. (1986). Perceptions of peer pressure, peer conformity dispositions, and self-reported behavior among adolescents. *Developmental Psychology, 22,* 521–530.

Brown, B., Dolcini, M., & Leventhal, A. (1995, March). *The emergence of peer crowds: Friend or foe to adolescent health?* Paper presented at the biennial meetings of the Society for Research in Child Development, Indianapolis.

Brown, B., Freeman, H., Huang, B., & Mounts, N. (1992, March). *"Crowd hopping": Incidence, correlates and consequences of change in crowd affiliation during adolescence.* Paper presented at the biennial meetings of the Society for Research on Adolescence, Washington, DC.

Brown, B., Herman, M., Hamm, J. V., & Heck, D. (2008). Ethnicity and image: Correlates of minority adolescents' affiliation with individual-based versus ethnically defined peer crowds. *Child Development, 79,* 529–546.

Brown, B., Lamborn, S., & Newmann, F. (1992). "You live and you learn": The place of school engagement in the lives of teenagers. In F. Newmann (Ed.), *Student engagement and achievement in American high schools.* New York: Teachers College Press.

Brown, B., & Larson, J. (2009). Peer relationships in adolescence. In R. Lerner & L. Steinberg (Eds.), *Handbook of adolescent psychology* (3rd ed., Vol. 2, pp. 74–103). New York: Wiley.

Brown, B., & Lohr, M. J. (1987). Peer group affiliation and adolescent self-esteem: An integration of ego-identity and symbolic interaction theories. *Journal of Personality and Social Psychology, 52,* 47–55.

Brown, B., Mory, M., & Kinney, D. (1994). Casting crowds in a relational perspective: Caricature, channel, and context. In R. Montemayor, G. Adams, & T. Gullotta (Eds.), *Advances in adolescent development: Vol. 5. Personal relationships during adolescence.* Newbury Park, CA: Sage.

Brown, B., & Mounts, N. (1989, April). *Peer group structures in single versus multiethnic high schools.* Paper presented at the biennial meetings of the Society for Research in Child Development, Kansas City.

Brown, B., Mounts, N., Lamborn, S., & Steinberg, L. (1993). Parenting practices and peer group affiliation in adolescence. *Child Development, 64,* 467–482.

Brown, B., Von Bank, H., & Steinberg, L. (2008). Smoke in the looking glass: Effects of discordance between self- and peer rated crowd affiliation on adolescent anxiety, depression and self-feelings. *Journal of Youth and Adolescence, 37,* 1163–1177.

Brown, J., Cohen, P., Chen, H., Smailes, E., & Johnson, J. (2004). Sexual trajectories of abused and neglected youths. *Journal of Developmental & Behavioral Pediatrics, 25,* 77–82.

Brown, J. D., L'Engle, K. L., Pardun, C. J., Guo, G., Kenneavy, K., & Jackson, C. (2006). Sexy media matter: Exposure to sexual content in music, movies, television, and magazines predicts Black and white adolescents' sexual behavior. *Pediatrics, 117,* 1018–1027.

Brown, J. S., Meadows, S. O., & Elder, G. H., Jr. (2007). Race-ethnic inequality and psychological distress: Depressive symptoms from adolescence to young adulthood. *Developmental Psychology, 43,* 1295–1311.

Brown, K., McMahon, R., Biro, F., Crawford, P., Schreiber, G., Similo, et al. (1998). Changes in self-esteem in Black and White girls between the ages of 9 and 14 years: The NHLBI Growth and Health Study. *Journal of Adolescent Health, 23,* 7–19.

Brown, L. K., Tolou-Shams, M., Lescano, C., Houck, C., Zeidman, J., Pugatch, D., et al. (2006). Depressive symptoms as a predictor of sexual risk among African American adolescents and young adults. *Journal of Adolescent Health, 39,* e1–e8.

Brown, W. T., & Jones, J. M. (2003). The substance of things hoped for: A study of the future orientation, minority status perceptions, academic engagement, and academic performance of Black high school students. *Journal of Black Psychology, 30,* 248–273.

Browning, C. R., Leventhal, T., & Brooks-Gunn, J. (2005). Sexual initiation in early adolescence: The nexus of parental and community control. *American Sociological Review, 70,* 758–778.

Brubacher, J., & Rudy, W. (1976). *Higher education in transition* (3rd ed). New York: Harper & Row.

Brückner, H., & Bearman, P. (2005). After the promise: The STD consequences of adolescent virginity pledges. *Journal of Adolescent Health, 36,* 271–278.

Brumberg, J. (1997). *The body project: An intimate history of American girls.* New York: Random House.

Bruvold, W. (1993). A meta-analysis of adolescent smoking prevention programs. *American Journal of Public Health, 83,* 872–880.

Bryant, A., Schulenberg, J., O'Malley, P., Bachman, J., & Johnston, L. (2003). How academic achievement, attitudes, and behaviors relate to the course of substance use during adolescence: A 60-year, multiwave national longitudinal study. *Journal of Research on Adolescence, 13,* 361–397.

Bryant, A., & Zimmerman, M. A. (2002). Examining the effects of academic beliefs and behaviors on changes in substance use among urban adolescents. *Journal of Educational Psychology, 94,* 621–637.

Bryant, A., & Zimmerman, M. (2003). Role models and psychosocial outcomes among African American adolescents. *Journal of Adolescent Research, 18,* 36–67.

Bryk, A., & Thum, Y. (1989). The effects of high school organization on dropping out: An exploratory investigation. *American Educational Research Journal, 26,* 353–383.

Buchanan, C. (2003). Mother's generalized beliefs about adolescents: Links to expectations for a specific child. *Journal of Early Adolescence, 23,* 29–50.

Buchanan, C., Eccles, J., & Becker, J. (1992). Are adolescents the victims of raging hormones? Evidence for activational effects of hormones on moods and behavior at adolescence. *Psychological Bulletin, 111,* 62–107.

Buchanan, C., & Holmbeck, G. (1998). Measuring beliefs about adolescent personality and behavior. *Journal of Youth and Adolescence, 27,* 607–627.

Buchanan, C., & Maccoby, E. (1993, March). *Relationships between adolescents and their nonresidential parents: A comparison of nonresidential mothers and fathers.* Paper presented at the biennial meetings of the Society for Research in Child Development, New Orleans.

Buchanan, C., Maccoby, E., & Dornbusch, S. (1996). *Adolescents after divorce.* Cambridge, MA: Harvard University Press.

Buchanan, M., & Robbins, C. (1990). Early adult psychological consequences for males of adolescent pregnancy and its resolution. *Journal of Youth and Adolescence, 19,* 413–424.

Buchmann, C., & Dalton, B. (2002). Interpersonal influences and educational aspirations in 12 countries: The importance of institutional context. *Sociology of Education, 75,* 99–122.

Buechel, F., & Duncan, G. (1998). Do parents' social activities promote children's school attainments? Evidence from the German Socioeconomic Panel. *Journal of Marriage and the Family, 60,* 95–108.

Buehler, C. (2006). Parents and peers in relation to early adolescent problem behavior. *Journal of Marriage and Family, 68,* 109–124.

Buehler, C., Benson, M., & Gerard, J. (2006). Interpersonal hostility and early adolescent problem behavior: The mediating role of specific aspects of parenting. *Journal of Research on Adolescence, 16,* 265–292.

Buehler, C., Krishnakumar, A., Stone, G., Anthony, C., Pemberton, S., Gerard, J., & Barber, B. (1998). Interparental conflict styles and youth problem behaviors: A two-sample replication study. *Journal of Marriage and the Family, 60,* 119–132.

Buehler, C., Lange, G., & Franck, K. L. (2007). Adolescents' cognitive and emotional responses to marital hostility. *Child Development, 78,* 775–789.

Buehler, C., & Welsh, D. P. (2009). A process model of adolescents' triangulation into parents' marital conflict: The role of emotional reactivity. Journal of Family Psychology, 23, 167–180.

Buhi, E. R., & Goodson, P. (2007). Predictors of adolescent sexual behavior and intention: A theory-guided systematic review. *Journal of Adolescent Health, 40,* 4–21.

Buhrmester, D. (1990). Intimacy of friendship, interpersonal competence, and adjustment during preadolescence and adolescence. *Child Development, 61,* 1101–1111.

Buhrmester, D. (1996). Need fulfillment, interpersonal competence, and the developmental contexts of early adolescent friendship. In W. Bukowski, A. Newcomb, & W. Hartup, W. (Eds.), *The company they keep: Friendship in childhood and adolescence* (pp. 158–185). New York: Cambridge University Press.

Buhrmester, D., & Furman, W. (1987). The development of companionship and intimacy. *Child Development, 58,* 1101–1113.

Buhrmester, D., & Furman, W. (1990). Perceptions of sibling relationships during middle childhood and adolescence. *Child Development, 61,* 1387–1396.

Buhrmester, D., & Yin, J. (1997, April). *A longitudinal study of friends' influence on adolescents' adjustment.* Paper presented at the biennial meetings of the Society for Research in Child Development, Washington, DC.

Bukowski, W., Gauze, C., Hoza, B., & Newcomb, A. (1993). Differences and consistency between same-sex and other-sex peer relationships during early adolescence. *Developmental Psychology, 29,* 255–263.

Bukowski, W., Sippola, L., Gauze, C., Hoza, B., & Newcomb, A. (1993, March). *On which aspects of friendship are there differences between boys and girls?* Paper presented at the biennial meetings of the Society for Research in Child Development, New Orleans.

Bukowski, W., Sippola, L., & Hoza, B. (1999). Same and other: Interdependency between participation in same- and other-sex friendships. *Journal of Youth and Adolescence, 28,* 439–459.

Bukowski, W., Sippola, L., & Newcomb, A. F. (2000). Variations in patterns of attraction of same- and other-sex peers during early adolescence. *Developmental Psychology, 36,* 147–154.

Bulcroft, R., Carmody, D., & Bulcroft, K. (1996). Patterns of parental independence giving to adolescents: Variations by race, age, and gender of child. *Journal of Marriage and the Family, 58,* 866–883.

Bullock, B., & Dishion, T. J. (2002). Sibling collusion and problem behavior in early adolescence: Toward a process model for family mutuality. *Journal of Abnormal Child Psychology, 30,* 143–153.

Bumpass, L., & McLanahan, S. (1987, April). *Unmarried motherhood: A note on recent trends, composition and Black-White differences.* Paper presented at the annual meeting of the Population Association of America, Chicago.

Bumpus, M. F., Crouter, A., & McHale, S. (2001). Parental autonomy granting during adolescence: Exploring gender differences in context. *Developmental Psychology, 37,* 163–173.

Bureau of Labor Statistics. (2009a). *America's youth at 21.* Washington: Author.

Bureau of Labor Statistics. (2009b). *College enrollment and work activity of 2008 high school graduates.* Retrieved from http://www.bls.gov/news.release/hsgec.nr0.htm

Burke, J. D., Pardini, D. A., & Loeber, R. (2008). Reciprocal relationships between parenting behavior and disruptive psychopathology from childhood through adolescence. *Journal of Abnormal Child Psychology, 36,* 679–692.

Burrell, G. L., & Roosa, M. W. (2009). Mothers' economic hardship and behavior problems in their early adolescents. *Journal of Family Issues, 30,* 511–531.

Burst Media Corporation. (2006). *Online Insights, 4,* 1.

Burt, K., Obradović, J., Long, J., & Masten, A. (2008). The interplay of social competence and psychopathology over 20 years: Testing transactional and cascade models. *Child Development, 79,* 359–374.

Burt, S. A., Barnes, A. R., McGue, M., & Iacono, W. G. (2008). Parental divorce and adolescent delinquency: Ruling out the impact of common genes. *Developmental Psychology, 44,* 1668–1677.

Burt, S. A., McGue, M., Krueger, R. F., & Iacono, W. G. (2007). Environmental contributions to adolescent delinquency: A fresh look at the shared environment. *Journal of Abnormal Child Psychology, 35,* 787–800.

Burton, L. (2007). Childhood adultification in economically disadvantaged families: A conceptual model. *Family Relations, 56,* 329–345.

Busseri, M. A., Willoughby, T., Chalmers, H., & Bogaert, A. F. (2008). On the association between sexual attraction and adolescent risk behavior involvement: Examining mediation and moderation. *Developmental Psychology, 44,* 69–80.

Butler, J., & Burton, L. (1990). Rethinking teenage childbearing: Is sexual abuse a missing link? *Family Relations, 39,* 73–80.

Butler, K. (2006, July 4). The grim neurology of teenage drinking. *The New York Times.* Conger, R., Conger, K. Elder, G. Jr., Lornez, F., Simons, R., Whitbeck, L. (1993). Family economic stress and adjustment of early adolescent girls. *Developmental Psychology, 29,* 206–219.

Buzy, W. M., McDonald, R., Jouriles, E. N., Swank, P. R., Rosenfield, D., Shimek, J. S., et al. (2004). Adolescent girls' alcohol use as a risk factor for relationship violence. *Journal of Research on Adolescence, 14,* 449–470.

Byrne, B., & Shavelson, R. (1996). On the structure of social self-concept for pre-, early, and late adolescents: A test of the Shavelson, Hubner, and Stanton (1976) model. *Journal of Personality and Social Psychology, 70,* 599–613.

Byrnes, J. (1997). *The nature and development of decision-making: A self-regulation model.* Hillsdale, NJ: Erlbaum.

Byrnes, J., Miller, D., & Schafer, W. (1999). Gender differences in risk taking: A meta-analysis. *Psychological Bulletin, 125,* 367–383.

Cairns, R., Cairns, B., Neckerman, H., Gest, S., & Gariepy, J. L. (1988). Social networks and aggressive behavior: Peer support or peer rejection? *Developmental Psychology, 24,* 815–823.

Cairns, R., Leung, M., Buchanan, L., & Cairns, B. (1995). Friendships and social networks in childhood and adolescence: Fluidity, reliability, and interrelations. *Child Development, 66,* 1330–1345.

Caldwell, C. H., Kohn-Wood, L. P., Schmeelk-Cone, K. H., Chavous, T. M., & Zimmerman, M. A. (2004). Racial discrimination and racial identity as risk or protective factors for violent behaviors in African American young adults. *American Journal of Community Psychology, 33,* 91–105.

Caldwell, C. H., Sellers, R. M., Bernat, D. H., & Zimmerman, M. A. (2004). Racial identity, parental support, and alcohol use in a sample of academically at-risk African American high school students. *American Journal of Community Psychology, 34,* 71–82.

Caldwell, L., & Darling, N. (1999). Leisure context, parental control, and resistance to peer pressure as predictors of adolescent partying and substance use: An ecological perspective. *Journal of Leisure Research, 31,* 57–77.

Caldwell, M. S., Rudolph, K. D., Troop-Gordon, W., & Kim, D. Y. (2004). Reciprocal influence among relational self-views, social disengagement, and peer stress during early adolescence. *Child Development, 75,* 1140–1154.

Call, K. T., Riedel, A. A., Hein, K., McLoyd, V., Petersen, A., & Kipke, M. (2002). Adolescent health and well-being in the twenty-first century: A global perspective. *Journal of Research on Adolescence, 12,* 69–98.

Callahan, R. (2005). Tracking and English learners: Limiting opportunity to learn. *American Educational Research Journal, 42,* 305–328.

Calverley, R., Fischer, K., & Ayoub, C. (1994). Complex splitting of self-representations in sexually abused adolescent girls. *Development and Psychopathology, 6,* 195–213.

Calvete, E., & Cardeñoso, O. (2005). Gender differences in cognitive vulnerability to depression and behavior problems in adolescents. *Journal of Abnormal Child Psychology, 33,* 179–192.

Camenga, D. R., Klein, J. D., & Roy, J. (2006). The changing risk profile of the American adolescent smoker: Implications for prevention programs and tobacco interventions. *Journal of Adolescent Health, 39,* e1–e10.

Campa, M. I., & Eckenrode, J. J. (2006). Pathways to intergenerational adolescent childbearing in a high-risk sample. *Journal of Marriage and Family, 68,* 558–572.

Campbell, B. C., Prossinger, H., & Mbzivo, M. (2005). Timing of pubertal maturation and the onset of sexual behavior among Zimbabwe school boys. *Archives of Sexual Behavior, 34,* 505–516.

Campbell, F., Pungello, E., Miller-Johnson, S., Burchinal, M., & Ramey, C. (2001). The development of cognitive and academic abilities: Growth curves from an early childhood educational experiment. *Developmental Psychology, 37,* 231–242.

Campbell, F., & Ramey, C. (1995). Cognitive and school outcomes for high-risk African-American students at middle adolescence: Positive effects of early intervention. *American Educational Research Journal, 32,* 743–772.

Campbell, M. A., Porter, S., & Santor, D. (2004). Psychopathic traits in adolescent offenders: An evaluation of criminal history, clinical, and psychosocial correlates. *Behavioral Sciences and the Law, 22,* 23–47.

Campione-Barr, N., & Smetana, J. G. (2004). In the eye of the beholder: Subjective and observer ratings of middle-class African American mother–adolescent interactions. *Developmental Psychology, 40,* 927–934.

Cantillon, D. (2006). Community social organization, parents, and peers as mediators of perceived neighborhood block characteristics on delinquent and prosocial activities. *American Journal of Community Psychology, 37,* 111–127.

Capaldi, D. (1992). Co-occurrence of conduct problems and depressed mood in early adolescent boys, II: A two-year follow-up at grade 8. *Development and Psychopathology, 4,* 125–144.

Capaldi, D., & Clark, S. (1998). Prospective family predictors of aggression toward female partners for at-risk young men. *Developmental Psychology, 34,* 1175–1188.

Capaldi, D., Crosby, L., & Stoolmiller, M. (1996). Predicting the timing of first sexual intercourse for at-risk adolescent males. *Child Development, 67,* 344–359.

Capaldi, D., Dishion, T., Stoolmiller, M., & Yoerger, K. (2001). Aggression toward female partners by at-risk young men: The contribution of male adolescent friendships. *Developmental Psychology, 37,* 61–73.

Capaldi, D., Stoolmiller, M., Clark, S., & Owen, L. (2002). Heterosexual risk behaviors in at-risk young men from early adolescence to young adulthood: Prevalence, prediction, and association with STD contraction. *Developmental Psychology, 38,* 394–406.

Caplan, N., Choy, M., & Whitmore, J. (1992, February). Indochinese refugee families and academic achievement. *Scientific American,* pp. 36–42.

Cappelleri, J., Eckenrode, J., & Powers, J. (1993). The epidemiology of child abuse: Findings from the Second National Incidence and Prevalence Study of Child Abuse and Neglect. *American Journal of Public Health, 83,* 1622–1624.

Carbonaro, W. (2005). Tracking, students' effort, and academic achievement. *Sociology of Education, 78,* 27–49.

Card, N. A., & Hodges, E. V. E. (2008). Peer victimization among schoolchildren: Correlations, causes, consequences, and consideration in assessment and intervention. *School Psychology Quarterly, 23,* 451–461.

Card, N. A., Stucky, B. D., Sawalani, G. M., & Little, T. D. (2008). Direct and indirect aggression during childhood and adolescence: A meta-analytic review of gender differences, intercorrelations, and relations to maladjustment. *Child Development, 79,* 1185–1229.

Carlo, G., Crockett, L. J., Randall, B. A., & Roesch, S. C. (2007). A latent growth curve analysis of prosocial behavior among rural adolescents. *Journal of Research on Adolescence, 17,* 301–324.

Carlo, G., Koller, S., Eisenberg, N., Da Silva, M., & Frohlich, C. (1996). A cross-national study of the relations among prosocial moral reasoning, gender role orientations, and prosocial behaviors. *Developmental Psychology, 32,* 231–240.

Carlson, E., Sroufe, L. A., Collins, W. A., Jimerson, S., Weinfield, N., Henninghausen, K., et al. (1999). Early environmental support and elementary school adjustment as predictors of school adjustment in middle adolescence. *Journal of Adolescent Research, 14,* 72–94.

Carlson Jones, D. (2004). Body image among adolescent girls and boys: A longitudinal study. *Developmental Psychology, 40,* 823–835.

Carnegie Council on Adolescent Development. (1989). *Turning points: Preparing youth for the 21st century.* New York: Carnegie Corporation of New York.

Carnegie Council on Adolescent Development. (1992). *A matter of time: Risk and opportunity in the after-school hours.* Washington, DC: Author.

Carr, M., Borkowski, J., & Maxwell, S. (1991). Motivational components of underachievement. *Developmental Psychology, 27,* 108–118.

Carr, R., Wright, J., & Brody, C. (1996). Effects of high school work experience a decade later: Evidence from the National Longitudinal Survey. *Sociology of Education, 69,* 66–81.

Carroll, A., Hemingway, F., Bower, J., Ashman, A., Houghton, S., & Durkin, K. (2006). Impulsivity in juvenile delinquency: Differences among early-onset, late-onset, and non-offenders. *Journal of Youth and Adolescence, 35,* 519–529.

Carroll, J. S., Willoughby, B., Badger, S., Nelson, L. J., Barry, C. M., & Madsen, S. D. (2007). So close, yet so far away: The impact of varying marital horizons on emerging adulthood. *Journal of Adolescent Research, 22,* 219–247.

Carskadon, M., & Acebo, C. (2002). Regulation of sleepiness in adolescence: Update, insights, and speculation. *Sleep, 25,* 606–616.

Carskadon, M., Acebo, C., Richardson, G., Tate, B., & Seifer, R. (1997). Long nights protocol: Access to circadian parameters in adolescents. *Journal of Biological Rhythms, 12,* 278–289.

Carson, D., Chowdhury, A., Perry, C., & Pati, C. (1999). Family characteristics and adolescent competence in India: Investigation of youth in southern Orissa. *Journal of Youth and Adolescence, 28,* 211–233.

Casella, R. (2003). Zero tolerance policy in schools: Rationale, consequences, and alternatives. *Teachers College Review, 105,* 872–892.

Casey, B. J., Getz, S., & Galvan, A. (2008). The adolescent brain. *Developmental Review, 28,* 62–77.

Casey, B. J., Tottenham, N., Liston, C., & Durston, S. (2005). Imaging the developing brain: What have we learned about cognitive development? *Trends in Cognitive Science, 9,* 104–110.

Cash, T. F., Morrow, J., Hrabosky, J. I., & Perry, A. A. (2004). How has body image changed? A cross-sectional investigation of college women and men from 1983 to 2001. *Journal of Consulting and Clinical Psychology, 72,* 1081–1089.

Casper, L. (1990). Does family interaction prevent adolescent pregnancy? *Family Planning Perspectives, 22,* 109–114.

Caspi, A. (1997). Personality development across the life course. In W. Damon (Ser. ed.) & N. Eisenberg (Vol. Ed.), *Handbook of child psychology:* Vol. 3. *Social, emotional and personality development* (5th ed.). New York, NY: Wiley.

Caspi, A. (2000). The child is father of the man: Personality continuities from childhood to adulthood. *Journal of Personality and Social Psychology, 78,* 158–172.

Caspi, A., Henry, B., McGee, R. O., Moffitt, T. E., & Silva, P. A. (1995). Temperamental origins of child and adolescent behavior problems: From age 3 to age 15. *Child Development, 66,* 55–68.

Caspi, A., Lynam, D., Moffitt, T., & Silva, P. (1993). Unraveling girls' delinquency: Biological, dispositional, and contextual contributions to adolescent misbehavior. *Developmental Psychology, 29,* 19–30.

Caspi, A., & Moffitt, T. (1991). Individual differences and personal transitions: The sample case of girls at puberty. *Journal of Personality and Social Psychology, 61,* 157–168.

Caspi, A., & Silva, P. (1995). Temperamental qualities at age three predict personality traits in young adulthood: Longitudinal evidence from a birth cohort. *Child Development, 66,* 486–498.

Caspi, A., Sugden, K., Moffitt, T., Taylor, A., Craig, I., Harrington, H., et al. (2003). Influence of life stress on depression: Moderation by a polymorphism in the 5-HTT gene. *Science, 301,* 386–389.

Cassidy, J., Ziv, Y., Mehta, T. G., & Feeney, B. C. (2003). Feedback seeking in children and adolescents: Associations with self-perceptions, attachment representations, and depression. *Child Development, 74,* 612–628.

Casteel, M. (1993). Effects of inference necessity and reading goal on children's inferential generation. *Developmental Psychology, 29,* 346–357.

Catsambis, S. (1992, March). *The many faces of tracking in middle school grades: Between- and within-school differentiation of students and resources.* Paper presented at the biennial meetings of the Society for Research on Adolescence, Washington, DC.

Catterall, J. (1998). Risk and resilience in student transitions to high school. *American Journal of Education, 106,* 302–333.

Cauffman, E. (2008). Understanding the female offender. *Future of Children, 18,* 119–142.

Cauffman, E., Farruggia, S. P., & Goldweber, A. (2008). Bad boys or poor parents: Relations to female juvenile delinquency. *Journal of Research on Adolescence, 18,* 699–712.

Cauffman, E., Piquero, A., Kimonis, E., Steinberg, L., & Chassin, L. (2007). Legal, individual, and contextual predictors of court disposition. *Law and Human Behavior, 31,* 519–535.

Cauffman, E., Shulman, E., Steinberg, L., Claus, E., Banich, M., Graham, S., et al. (2010). Age differences in affective decision making as indexed by performance on the Iowa Gambling Task. *Developmental Psychology, 46,* 193–207.

Cauffman, E., & Steinberg, L. (1996). Effects of menarche, dating, and heterosocial involvement on dieting behavior in early adolescence. *Developmental Psychology, 32,* 631–635.

Cauffman, E., Steinberg, L., & Piquero, A. R. (2005). Psychological, neuropsychological and physiological correlates of serious antisocial behavior in adolescence: The role of self-control. *Criminology, 43,* 133–175.

Cavanagh, S. E., Crissey, S. R., & Raley, R. K. (2008). Family structure history and adolescent romance. *Journal of Marriage and Family, 70,* 698–714.

Ceballo, R., McLoyd, V. C., & Toyokawa, T. (2004). The influence of neighborhood quality on adolescents' educational values and school effort. *Journal of Adolescent Research, 19,* 716–739.

Ceci, S., & Williams, W. (1999). Schooling, intelligence, and income. *American Psychologist, 52,* 1051–1058.

Centers for Disease Control and Prevention. (2006). Youth behavior surveillance—United States, 2005. *Morbidity and Mortality Weekly Report, 55,* SS-5.

Centers for Disease Control and Prevention. (2008). Youth risk behavior surveillance—United States, 2007. *Morbidity and Mortality Weekly Report, 57,* SS4.

Centers, N., & Weist, M. (1998). Inner city youth and drug dealing: A review of the problem. *Journal of Youth and Adolescence, 27,* 395–411.

Cepeda, A., & Valdez, A. (2003). Risk behaviors among young Mexican American gang-associated females: Sexual relations, partying, substance abuse, and crime. *Journal of Adolescent Research, 18,* 90–106.

Chalmers, D., & Lawrence, J. (1993). Investigating the effects of planning aids on adults' and adolescents' organisation of a complex task. *International Journal of Behavioural Development, 16,* 191–214.

Chan, D. (1997). Depressive symptoms and perceived competence among Chinese secondary school students in Hong Kong. *Journal of Youth and Adolescence, 26,* 303–319.

Chandler, M. (1987). The Othello effect: Essay on the emergence and eclipse of skeptical doubt. *Human Development, 30,* 137–159.

Chang, E. S., Chen, C., Greenberger, E., Dooley, D., & Heckhausen, J. (2006). What do they want in life?: The life goals of a multi-ethnic, multi-generational sample of high school seniors. *Journal of Youth and Adolescence, 35,* 321–332.

Chanoine, J., Hampl, S., Jensen, C., Boldrin, M., & Hauptman, J. (2005). Effect of orlistat on weight and body composition in obese adolescents: A randomized controlled trial. *Journal of the American Medical Association, 293,* 1873–1883.

Chao, R. (1994). Beyond parental control and authoritarian parenting style: Understanding Chinese parenting through the cultural notion of training. *Child Development, 65,* 1111–1119.

Chao, R. (2001). Extending research on the consequences of parenting style for Chinese Americans and European Americans. *Child Development, 72,* 1832–1843.

Chase-Landsdale, P. L., Brooks-Gunn, J., & Zamsky, E. (1994). Young African-American multigenerational families in poverty: Quality of mothering and grandmothering. *Child Development, 65,* 373–393.

Chase-Landsdale, P. L., Moffit, R. A., Lohman, B. J., Cherlin, A. J., Coley, R. L., Pittman, L. D., et al. (2003). Mothers' transitions from welfare to work and the well-being of preschooler and adolescents. *Science, 299,* 15–28.

Chassin, L., Hussong, A., & Beltran, I. (2009). Adolescent substance use. In R. Lerner & L. Steinberg (Eds.), *Handbook of adolescent psychology* (3rd ed., Vol. 1, pp. 723–764). New York: Wiley.

Chassin, L., Presson, C., Todd, M., Rose, J., & Sherman, S. (1998). Maternal socialization of adolescent smoking: The intergenerational transmission of parenting and smoking. *Developmental Psychology, 34,* 1189–1201.

Chavous, T., Bernat, D., Schmeelk-Cone, K., Caldwell, C., Kohn-Wood, L., & Zimmerman, M. (2003). Racial identity and academic attainment among African American adolescents. *Child Development, 74,* 1076–1090.

Chavous, T., Rivas-Drake, D., Smalls, C., Griffin, T., & Cogburn, C. (2008). Gender matters, too: The influences of school racial discrimination and racial identity on academic engagement outcomes among African American adolescents. *Developmental Psychology, 44,* 637–654.

Chen, C. S., Greenberger, E., Lester, J., Dong, Q., & Guo, M. (1998). A cross-cultural study of family and peer correlates of adolescent misconduct. *Developmental Psychology, 34,* 770–781.

Chen, C. S., Lee, S. Y., & Stevenson, H. W. (1996). Academic achievement and motivation of Chinese students: A cross-national perspective. In S. Lau (Ed.), *Growing up the Chinese way: Chinese child and adolescent development.* Hong Kong: Chinese University Press.

Chen, C. Y., Dormitzer, C. M., Bejarno, J., & Anthony, J. C. (2004). Religiosity and the earliest stages of adolescent drug involvement in seven countries of Latin America. *American Journal of Epidemiology, 159,* 1180–1188.

Chen, E., Langer, D. A., Raphaelson, Y. E., & Matthews, K. (2004). Socioeconomic status and health in adolescents: The role of stress interpretations. *Child Development, 75,* 1039–1052.

Chen, K., & Kandel, D. (1996). The natural history of drug use from adolescence to the mid-thirties in a general population sample. *American Journal of Public Health, 85,* 41–47.

Chen, X., Rubin, K., & Li, D. (1997). Relation between academic achievement and social adjustment: Evidence from Chinese children. *Developmental Psychology, 33,* 518–525.

Cherlin, A., Chase-Lansdale, P., & McRae, C. (1998). Effects of parental divorce on mental health throughout the life course. *American Sociological Review, 63,* 239–249.

Cherney, I. D., & Shing, Y. L. (2008). Children's nurturance and self-determination rights: A cross-cultural perspective. *Journal of Social Issues, 64,* 835–856.

Chesson, H. W., Blandford, J. M., Gift, T. L., Tao, G., & Irwin, K. L. (2004). The estimated direct medical cost of sexually transmitted diseases among American youth. *Perspectives on Sexual and Reproductive Health, 36,* 11–19.

Cheung, Y. (1997). Family, school, peer, and media predictors of adolescent deviant behavior in Hong Kong. *Journal of Youth and Adolescence, 26,* 569–596.

Children's Defense Fund. (1989). *Service opportunities for youths.* Washington, DC: Author.

Chisholm, L., & Hurrelmann, K. (1995). Adolescence in modern Europe: Pluralized transition patterns and their implications for personal and social risks. *Journal of Adolescence, 18,* 129–158.

Choi, Y., Harachi, T. W., Gillmore, M. R., & Catalano, R. F. (2005). Applicability of the social development model to urban ethnic minority youth: Examining the relationship between external constraints, family socialization, and problem behaviors. *Journal of Research on Adolescence, 15,* 505–534.

Choi, Y., He, M., & Harachi, T. W. (2008). Intergenerational cultural dissonance, parent–child conflict and bonding, and youth problem behaviors among Vietnamese and Cambodian immigrant families. *Journal of Youth and Adolescence, 37,* 85–96.

Choudhury, S., Blakemore, S., & Charman, T. (2006). Social cognitive development during adolescence. *Social Cognitive and Affective Neuroscience, 3,* 165–174.

Chumlea, W., Schubert, C., Roche, A., Kulin, H., Lee, P., Himes, J., et al. (2003). Age at menarche and racial comparisons in U.S. girls. *Pediatrics, 111,* 110–113.

Chun, Y.-J., & MacDermid, S. M. (1997). Perceptions of family differentiation, individuation, and self-esteem among Korean adolescents. *Journal of Marriage and the Family, 59,* 451–462.

Chung, H. L., & Steinberg, L. (2006). Relations between neighborhood factors, parenting behaviors, peer deviance, and delinquency among serious juvenile offenders. *Developmental Psychology, 42,* 319–331.

Church, R. (1976). *Education in the United States.* New York: Free Press.

Cicchetti, D., Rogosch, F. A., & Sturge-Apple, M. (2007). Interactions of child maltreatment and serotonin transporter and monoamine oxidase A polymorphisms: Depressive symptomatology among adolescents from low socioeconomic status backgrounds. *Development and Psychopathology, 19,* 1161–1180.

Cillessen, A. H. N., & Rose, A. J. (2005). Understanding popularity in the peer system. *Current Directions in Psychological Science, 14,* 102–105.

Cinamon, R. G., & Rich, Y. (2002). Gender difference in the importance of work and family roles: Implications for work–family conflict. *Sex Roles, 47,* 531–541.

Claes, M. (1998). Adolescents' closeness with parents, siblings, and friends in three countries: Canada, Belgium, and Italy. *Journal of Youth and Adolescence, 27,* 165–184.

Clancy, S., & Dollinger, S. (1993). Identity, self, and personality, I: Identity status and the five-factor model of personality. *Journal of Research on Adolescence, 3,* 227–246.

Clark, J., & Barber, B. (1994). Adolescents in postdivorce and always-married families: Self-esteem and perceptions of fathers' interest. *Journal of Marriage and the Family, 56,* 608–614.

Clark, R., & Delia, J. (1976). The development of functional persuasive skills in childhood and early adolescence. *Child Development, 47,* 1008–1014.

Clark, R., Dogan, R. R., & Akbar, N. J. (2003). Youth and parental correlates of externalizing symptoms, adaptive functioning, and academic performance: An exploratory study in preadolescent Blacks. *Journal of Black Psychology, 29,* 210–229.

Clark, R., Novak, J. D., & Dupree, D. (2002). Relationship of perceived parenting practices to anger regulation and coping strategies in African American adolescents. *Journal of Adolescence, 25,* 373–384.

Clarke, A. T. (2006). Coping with interpersonal stress and psychosocial health among children and adolescents: A meta-analysis. *Journal of Youth and Adolescence, 35,* 11–24.

Clasen, D., & Brown, B. (1985). The multidimensionality of peer pressure in adolescence. *Journal of Youth and Adolescence, 14,* 451–468.

Clements, M., Aber, J. L., & Seidman, E. (2008). The dynamics of life stressors and depressive symptoms in early adolescence: A test of six theoretical models. *Child Development, 79,* 1168–1182.

Cleveland, H. (2003). The influence of female and male risk on the occurrence of sexual intercourse within adolescent relationships. *Journal of Research on Adolescence, 13,* 81–112.

Cleveland, H., & Wiebe, R. P. (2003). The moderation of adolescent-to-peer similarity in tobacco and alcohol use by school levels of substance use. *Child Development, 74,* 279–291.

Cleveland, M. J., Feinberg, M. E., Bontempo, D. E., & Greenberg, M. T. (2008). The role of risk and protective factors in substance use across adolescence. *Journal of Adolescent Health, 43,* 157–164.

Cleveland, M. J., Gibbons, F., Gerrard, M., Pomery, E., & Brody, G. (2005). The impact of parenting on risk cognitions and risk behavior: A study of mediation and moderation in a panel of African American adolescents. *Child Development, 76,* 900–916.

Clingempeel, W., Colyar, J., Brand, E., & Hetherington, E. (1992). Children's relationships with maternal grandparents: A longitudinal study of family structure and pubertal status effects. *Child Development, 63,* 1404–1422.

Coatsworth, J. D., & Conroy, D. E. (2009). The effects of autonomy-supportive coaching, need satisfaction, and self-perceptions on initiative and identity in youth swimmers. *Developmental Psychology, 45,* 320–328.

Coatsworth, J. D., Sharp, E. H., Palen, L., Darling, N., Cumsille, P., & Marta, E. (2005). Exploring adolescent self-defining leisure activities and identity experiences across three countries. *International Journal of Behavioral Development, 29,* 361–370.

Cochran, B. N., Stewart, A. J., Ginzler, J. A., & Cauce, A. (2002). Challenges faced by homeless sexual minorities: Comparison of gay, lesbian, bisexual, and transgender homeless adolescents with their heterosexual counterparts. *American Journal of Public Health, 92,* 773–777.

Coe, C., Hayashi, K., & Levine, S. (1988). Hormones and behavior at puberty: Activation or concatenation. In M. Gunnar & W. A. Collins (Eds.), *The Minnesota Symposia on Child Psychology* (Vol. 21, pp. 17–41). Hillsdale, NJ: Erlbaum.

Cohen, D., Farley, T., Taylor, S., Martin, D., & Schuster, M. (2002). When and where do youths have sex? The potential role of adult supervision. *Pediatrics, 110,* E66.

Cohen, G. L., & Prinstein, M. J. (2006). Peer contagion of aggression and health risk behavior among adolescent males: An experimental investigation of effects on public conduct and private attitudes. *Child Development, 77,* 967–983.

Cohen, P. K., Chen, H., Hartmark, C., & Gordon, K. (2003). Variations in patterns of developmental transmissions in the emerging adulthood period. *Developmental Psychology, 39,* 657–669.

Cohen, Y. (1964). *The transition from childhood to adolescence.* Chicago: Aldine.

Coie, J., Terry, R., Lenox, K., Lochman, J., & Hyman, C. (1995). Childhood peer rejection and aggression as predictors of stable patterns of adolescent disorder. *Development and Psychopathology, 7,* 697–713.

Coiro, M., & Emery, R. (1996, March). *Adolescents' adjustment as a function of their involvement in post-divorce conflict.* Paper presented at the biennial meetings of the Society for Research on Adolescence, Boston.

Cole, A., & Kerns, K. A. (2001). Perceptions of sibling qualities and activities of early adolescents. *Journal of Early Adolescence, 21,* 204–226.

Cole, D., & Jordan, A. (1995). Competence and memory: Integrating psychosocial and cognitive correlates of child depression. *Child Development, 66,* 459–473.

Cole, D., Martin, J., & Powers, B. (1997). A competency-based model of child depression: A longitudinal study of peer, parent, teacher, and self-evaluations. *Journal of Child Psychology and Psychiatry and Allied Disciplines, 38,* 505–514.

Cole, D., Maxwell, S., Martin, J., Peeke, L., Seroczynski, A., Tram, J., et al. (2001). The development of multiple domains of child and adolescent self-concept: A cohort sequential longitudinal design. *Child Development, 72,* 1723–1746.

Cole, D., Peeke, L., Dolezal, S., Murray, N., & Canzoniero, A. (1999). A longitudinal study of negative affect and self-perceived competence in young adolescents. *Journal of Personality and Social Psychology, 77,* 851–862.

Coleman, J. (1961). *The adolescent society.* Glencoe, IL: Free Press.

Coleman, J., Campbell, E., Hobson, C., McPartland, J., Mood, A., Weinfeld, F., & York, R. (1966). *Equality of educational opportunity.* Washington, DC: U.S. Government Printing Office.

Coleman, J., & Hoffer, T. (1987). *Public and private high schools: The impact of communities.* New York: Basic Books.

Coleman, J., Hoffer, T., & Kilgore, S. (1982). *High school achievement: Public, Catholic and other private schools compared.* New York: Basic Books.

Coleman, L. M., & Cater, S. M. (2005). A qualitative study of the relationship between alcohol consumption and risky sex in adolescents. *Archives of Sexual Behavior, 34,* 649–661.

Coleman, P. K. (2006). Resolution of unwanted pregnancy during adolescence through abortion versus childbirth: Individual and family predictors and psychological consequences. *Journal of Youth and Adolescence, 35,* 903–911.

Coley, R. L., & Chase-Lansdale, P. L. (1998). Adolescent pregnancy and parenthood: Recent evidence and future directions. *American Psychologist, 53,* 152–166.

Coley, R. L., & Medeiros, B. L. (2007). Reciprocal longitudinal relations between nonresident father involvement and adolescent delinquency. *Child Development, 78,* 132–147.

Coley, R. L., Medeiros, B. L., & Schindler, H. S. (2008). Using sibling differences to estimate effects of parenting on adolescent sexual risk behaviors. *Journal of Adolescent Health, 43,* 133–140.

Coley, R. L., Morris, J. E., & Hernandez, D. (2004). Out-of-school care and problem behavior trajectories among low-income adolescents: Individual, family, and neighborhood characteristics as added risks. *Child Development, 75,* 948–965.

Coley, R. L., Votruba-Drzal, E., & Schindler, H. S. (2008). Trajectories of parenting processes and adolescent substance use: Reciprocal

effects. *Journal of Abnormal Child Psychology, 36,* 613–625.

Collaer, M., & Hines, M. (1995). Human behavioral sex differences: A role for gonadal hormones during early development? *Psychological Bulletin, 118,* 55–107.

College Board (2009). 2009 college-bound seniors. New York: Author.

Collins, N. L., & Feeney, B. C. (2004). Working models of attachment shape perceptions of social support: Evidence from experimental and observational studies. *Journal of Personality and Social Psychology, 87,* 363–383.

Collins, W. A. (1990). Parent–child relationships in the transition to adolescence: Continuity and change in interaction, affect, and cognition. In R. Montemayor, G. Adams, & T. Gullotta (Eds.), *Advances in adolescent development:* Vol. 2. *The transition from childhood to adolescence* (pp. 85–106). Beverly Hills, CA: Sage.

Collins, W. A. (2003). More than a myth: The developmental significance of romantic relationships during adolescence. *Journal of Research on Adolescents, 13,* 1–24.

Collins, W. A., Maccoby, E., Steinberg, L., Hetherington, E. M., & Bornstein, M. (2000). Contemporary research on parenting: The case for nature and nurture. *American Psychologist, 55,* 218–232.

Collins, W. A., & Sroufe, L. A. (1999). Capacity for intimate relationships: A developmental construction. In W. Furman, B. Brown, & C. Feiring (Eds.). *Contemporary perspectives on adolescent romantic relationships,* pp. 125–147. New York: Cambridge University Press.

Collins, W. A., & Steinberg, L. (2006). Adolescent development in interpersonal context. In W. Damon and R. Lerner (Ser. Eds.) & N. Eisenberg (Vol. Ed.),. *Handbook of child psychology:* Vol. 3. *Social, emotional, and personality development* (6th ed., pp. 1003–1067). New York: Wiley.

Comings, D. E., Muhleman, D., Johnson, J. P., & MacMurray, J. P. (2002). Parent–daughter transmission of the androgen receptor gene as an explanation of the effect of father absence on age of menarche. *Child Development, 73,* 1046–1051.

Compas, B., Ey, S., & Grant, K. (1993). Taxonomy, assessment, and diagnosis of depression during adolescence. *Psychological Bulletin, 114,* 323–344.

Compas, B., Oppedisano, G., Connor, J., Gerhardt, C., Hinden, B., Achenbach, T., et al. (1997). Gender differences in depressive symptoms in adolescence: Comparison of national samples of clinically referred and nonreferred youths. *Journal of Consulting and Clinical Psychology, 65,* 617–626.

Compas, B., & Reeslund, K. (2009). Processes of risk and resilience during adolescence. In R. Lerner & L. Steinberg (Eds.), *Handbook of adolescent psychology* (3rd ed., Vol. 1, pp. 561–588). New York: Wiley.

Compian, L., Gowen, L., & Hayward, C. (2004). Peripubertal girls' romantic and platonic involvement with boys: Associations with body image and depression symptoms. *Journal of Research on Adolescence, 14,* 23–47.

Compton, K., Snyder, J., & Schrepferman, L. (2003). The contribution of parents and siblings to antisocial and depressive behavior in adolescents: A double jeopardy coercion model. *Development and Psychopathology, 15,* 163–182.

Conant, J. (1959). *The American high school today.* New York: McGraw-Hill.

Conchas, G. Q. (2001). Structuring failure and success: Understanding the variability in Latino school engagement. *Harvard Educational Review, 71,* 475–504.

Condit, V. (1990). Anorexia nervosa: Levels of causation. *Human Nature, 1,* 391–413.

Conduct Problems Prevention Research Group (1999). Initial impact of the Fast Track Prevention Trial for Conduct Problems, II: Classroom effects. *Journal of Consulting and Clinical Psychology, 67,* 648–657.

Conger, K., & Conger, R. (1994). Differential parenting and change in sibling differences in delinquency. *Journal of Family Psychology, 8,* 287–302.

Conger, K., Conger, R., & Elder, G., Jr. (1994). Sibling relationships during hard times. In R. Conger & G. Elder, Jr. (Eds.), *Families in troubled times: Adapting to change in rural America,* pp. 235–252. New York: Aldine.

Conger, R., Conger, K., Matthews, L., & Elder, G. H., Jr. (1999). Pathways of economic influence on adolescent adjustment. *American Journal of Community Psychology, 27,* 519–541.

Conger, K., Conger, R., & Scaramella, L. (1997). Parents, siblings, psychological control, and adolescent adjustment. *Journal of Adolescent Research, 12,* 113–138.

Conger, R., Cui, M., Bryant, C. M., & Elder, G. H., Jr. (2000). Competence in early adult romantic relationships: A developmental perspective on family influences. *Journal of Personality and Social Psychology, 79,* 224–237.

Conger, R., Ge, X., Elder, G., Jr., Lorenz, F., & Simons, R. (1994). Economic stress, coercive family process, and developmental problems of adolescents. *Child Development, 65,* 541–561.

Conger, R., Patterson, G., & Ge, X. (1995). It takes two to replicate: A mediational model for the impact of parents' stress on adolescent adjustment. *Child Development, 66,* 80–97.

Conklin, H. M., Luciana, M., Hooper, C. J., & Yarger, R. S. (2007). Working memory performance in typically developing children and adolescents: Behavioral evidence of protracted frontal lobe development. *Developmental Neuropsychology, 31,* 103–128.

Conley, C. S., & Rudolph, K. D. (2009). The emerging sex differences in adolescent depression: Interacting contributions of puberty and peer stress. *Development and Psychopathology, 21,* 593–620.

Connell, A. M., & Dishion, T. J. (2008). Reducing depression among at-risk early adolescents: Three-year effects of a family-centered intervention embedded within schools. *Journal of Family Psychology, 22,* 574–585.

Connell, J., Spencer, M., & Aber, J. (1994). Educational risk and resilience in African-American youth: Context, self, action, and outcomes in school. *Child Development, 65,* 493–506.

Connolly, J., Craig, W., Goldberg, A., & Pepler, D. (1999). Conceptions of cross-sex friendships and romantic relationships in early adolescence. *Journal of Youth and Adolescence, 28,* 481–494.

Connolly, J., Craig, W., Goldberg, A., & Pepler, D. (2004). Mixed-gender groups, dating, and romantic relationships in early adolescence. *Journal of Research on Adolescence, 14,* 185–207.

Connolly, J., Furman, W., & Konarski, R. (2000). The role of peers in the emergence of heterosexual romantic relationships in adolescence. *Child Development, 71,* 1395–1408.

Connolly, J., & Goldberg, A. (1999). Romantic relationships in adolescence: The role of friends and peers in their emergence and development. In W. Furman, B. Brown, & C. Feiring (Eds.), *Contemporary perspectives on adolescent romantic relationships* (pp. 266–290). New York: Cambridge University Press.

Connolly, J., & Johnson, A. (1993, March). *The psychosocial context of romantic relationships in adolescence.* Paper presented at the biennial meetings of the Society for Research in Child Development, New Orleans.

Connolly, J., & Konarski, R. (1994). Peer self-concept in adolescence: Analysis of factor structure and of associations with peer experience. *Journal of Research on Adolescence, 4,* 385–403.

Connolly, J., & McIsaac, C. (2009). Romantic relationships in adolescence. In R. Lerner & L. Steinberg (Eds.), *Handbook of adolescent psychology* (3rd ed., Vol. 2, pp. 104–151). New York: Wiley.

Conseur, A., Rivara, F., Barnoski, R., & Emanuel, I. (1997). Maternal and perinatal risk factors for later delinquency. *Pediatrics, 99,* 785–790.

Consortium on Productivity in the Schools. (1995). *Using what we have to get the schools we need: A productivity focus for American education.* New York: Institute on Education and the Economy, Teachers College, Columbia University.

Consortium on Renewing Education. (1998). *20/20 vision: A strategy for doubling America's academic achievement by the year 2020.* Nashville, TN: Peabody Center for Education Policy, Vanderbilt University.

Cook, P. J., & Ludwig, J. (2004). Does gun prevalence affect teen gun carrying after all? *Criminology, 42,* 27–54.

Cook, T., Church, M., Ajanaku, S., Shadish, W., Jr., Kim, J., & Cohen, R. (1996). The development of occupational aspirations and expectations among inner-city boys. *Child Development, 67,* 3368–3385.

Cook, T., Deng, Y., & Morgano, E. (2007). Friendship influences during early adolescence: The special role of friends' grade point average. *Journal of Research on Adolescence, 17,* 325–356.

Cook, T., Herman, M., Phillips, M., & Settersten, R., Jr. (2002). Some ways in which neighborhoods, nuclear families, friendship groups, and schools jointly affect changes in early adolescent development. *Child Development, 73,* 1283–1309.

Cook, W. L. (2001). Interpersonal influence in family systems: A social relations model analysis. *Child Development, 72,* 1179–1197.

Cooksey, E. C., Mott, F. L., & Neubauer, S. A. (2002). Friendships and early relationships: Links to sexual initiation among American adolescents born to young mothers. *Perspectives on Sexual and Reproductive Health, 34,* 118–126.

Cooley-Quille, M., & Lorion, R. (1999). Adolescents' exposure to community violence: Sleep and psychophysiological functioning. *Journal of Community Psychology, 27,* 367–375.

Cooper, C. (1994). Cultural perspectives on continuity and change in adolescents' relationships. In R. Montemayor, G. Adams, & T. Gullotta (Eds.), *Personal relationships during adolescence.* Thousand Oaks, CA: Sage.

Cooper, C., Carlson, C., Keller, J., Koch, P., & Spradling, V. (1993, March). *Conflict negotiation in early adolescence: Links between family and peer relational patterns.* Paper presented at the biennial meetings of the Society for Research in Child Development, New Orleans.

Cooper, H., Charlton, K., Valentine, J., & Muhlenbruck, L. (2000). Making the most of summer school: A meta-analytic and narrative review. *Monographs of the Society for Research in Child Development, 65,* Serial No. 260.

Cooper, M. L., Shaver, P. R., & Collins, N. L. (1998). Attachment styles, emotion regulation, and adjustment in adolescence. *Journal of Personality and Social Psychology, 74,* 1380–1397.

Cooper, M., L., Wood, P. K., Orcutt, H. K., & Albino, A. (2003). Personality and the predisposition to engage in risky or problem behaviors during adolescence. *Journal of Personality and Social Psychology, 84,* 390–410.

Cornwell, G., Eggebeen, D., & Meschke, L. (1996). The changing family context of early adolescence. *Journal of Early Adolescence, 16,* 141–156.

Corville-Smith, J., Ryan, B., Adams, G., & Dalicandro, T. (1998). Distinguishing absentee students from regular attenders: The combined influence of personal, family, and

school factors. *Journal of Youth and Adolescence, 27,* 629–640.

Costa, F., Jessor, R., Donovan, J., & Fortenberry, J. (1995). Early initiation of sexual intercourse: The influence of psychosocial unconventionality. *Journal of Research on Adolescence, 5,* 93–121.

Costello, E. J., Compton, S. N., Keeler, G., & Angold, A. (2003). Relationships between poverty and psychopathology. *Journal of the American Medical Association, 290,* 2023–2029.

Cota-Robles, S., Neiss, M., & Rowe, D. C. (2002). The role of puberty in violent and nonviolent delinquency among Anglo American, Mexican American, and African American boys. *Journal of Adolescent Research, 17,* 364–376.

Côté, J. (2000). *Arrested adulthood: The changing nature of maturity and identity.* New York: New York University Press.

Côté, J. (2009). Identity formation and self development in adolescence. In R. Lerner & L. Steinberg (Eds.), *Handbook of adolescent psychology* (3rd ed., Vol. 1, pp. 266–304). New York: Wiley.

Côté, J., & Bynner, J. (2008). Changes in the transition to adulthood in the UK and Canada: The role of structure and agency in emerging adulthood. *Journal of Youth Studies, 11,* 251–268.

Couperus, J. W., & Nelson, C. A. (2006). Early brain development and plasticity. In K. McCartney & D. Phillips (Eds.), *Blackwell handbook of early childhood development* (pp. 85–105). Malden, MA: Blackwell Publishing.

Courtney, M., & Cohen, R. (1996). Behavior segmentation by boys as a function of aggressiveness and prior information. *Child Development, 67,* 1034–1047.

Crandall, C. (1988). Social contagion of binge eating. *Journal of Personality and Social Psychology, 55,* 588–598.

Crane, D. R., So Wa, N., Larson, J. H., & Hafen, M., Jr. (2005). The influence of family functioning and parent–adolescent acculturation on North American Chinese adolescent outcomes. *Family Relations, 54,* 400–410.

Crane, J. (1991). The epidemic theory of ghettos and neighborhood effects on dropping out and teenage childbearing. *American Journal of Sociology, 96,* 1226–1259.

Crawford, T. N., Cohen, P., Midlarsky, E., & Brook, J. S. (2001). Internalizing symptoms in adolescents: Gender differences in vulnerability to parental distress and discord. *Journal of Research on Adolescence, 11,* 95–118.

Creasey, G., & Kaliher, G. (1994). Age differences in grandchildren's perceptions of relations with grandparents. *Journal of Adolescence, 17,* 411–426.

Crick, N. (1996). The role of overt aggression, relational aggression, and prosocial behavior in the prediction of children's future social adjustment. *Child Development, 67,* 2317–2327.

Crick, N. (1997). Engagement in gender normative versus nonnormative forms of aggression: Links to social-psychological adjustment. *Developmental Psychology, 33*, 610–617.

Crick, N., Bigbee, M., & Howes, C. (1996). Gender differences in children's normative beliefs about aggression: How do I hurt thee? Let me count the ways. *Child Development, 67*, 1003–1014.

Crick, N., & Dodge, K. (1994). A review and reformulation of social information-processing mechanisms in children's social adjustment. *Psychological Bulletin, 115*, 74–101.

Crick, N., & Grotpeter, K. (1995). Relational aggression, gender, and social-psychological adjustment. *Child Development, 66*, 710–722.

Criss, M. M., & Shaw, D. (2005). Sibling relationships as contexts for delinquency training in low-income families. *Journal of Family Psychology, 19*, 592–600.

Crockett, L., & Bingham, C. (2000). Anticipating adulthood: Expected timing of work and family transitions among rural youth. *Journal of Research on Adolescence, 10*, 151–172.

Crockett, L., Bingham, C., Chopak, J., & Vicary, J. (1996). Timing of first sexual intercourse: The role of social control, social learning and problem behavior. *Journal of Youth and Adolescence, 25*, 89–111.

Crockett, L., Brown, J., Russell, S. T., & Shen, Y. (2007). The meaning of good parent–child relationships for Mexican American adolescents. *Journal of Research on Adolescence, 17*, 639–668.

Crockett, L., Raffaelli, M., & Shen, Y. (2006). Linking self-regulation and risk proneness to risky sexual behavior: Pathways through peer pressure and early substance use. *Journal of Research on Adolescence, 16*, 503–525.

Croll, J., Neumark-Sztainer, D., Story, M., & Ireland, M. (2002). Prevalence and risk and protective factors related to disordered eating behaviors among adolescents: Relationship to gender and ethnicity. *Journal of Adolescent Health, 31*, 166–175.

Crone, E., Somsen, R., Zanolie, K., & Van der Molen, M. (2006). A heart rate analysis of developmental change in feedback processing and rule shifting from childhood to early adulthood. *Journal of Experimental Child Psychology, 95*, 99–116.

Crone, E. A., & van der Molen, M. W. (2007). Development of decision making in school-aged children and adolescents: Evidence from heart rate and skin conductance analysis. *Child Development, 78*, 1288–1301.

Croninger, R. G., & Lee, V. E. (2001). Social capital and dropping out of school: Benefits to at-risk students of teachers' support and guidance. *Teachers College Record, 103*, 548–581.

Crosbie-Burnett, M., & Giles-Sims, J. (1994). Adolescent adjustment and stepparenting styles. *Family Relations, 43*, 394–399.

Crosby, R. A., DiClemente, R. J., Wingood, G. M., Lang, D., & Harrington, K. F. (2003). Value of consistent condom use: A study of sexually transmitted disease prevention among African American adolescent females. *American Journal of Public Health, 93*, 901–902.

Crosnoe, R. (2001). Academic orientation and parental involvement in education during high school. *Sociology of Education, 74*, 210–230.

Crosnoe, R. (2002). High school curriculum track and adolescent association with delinquent friends. *Journal of Adolescent Research, 17*, 143–167.

Crosnoe, R. (2006). The connection between academic failure and adolescent drinking in secondary school. *Sociology of Education, 79*, 44–60.

Crosnoe, R. (2007). Gender, obesity, and education. *Sociology of Education, 80*, 241–260.

Crosnoe, R., Erickson, K., & Dornbusch, S. M. (2002). Protective functions of family relationships and school factors on the deviant behavior of adolescent boys and girls: Reducing the impact of risky friendships. *Youth and Society, 33*, 515–544.

Crosnoe, R., & Huston, A. C. (2007). Socioeconomic status, schooling, and the developmental trajectories of adolescents. *Developmental Psychology, 43*, 1097–1110.

Crosnoe, R., Mistry, R. S., & Elder, G. H., Jr. (2002). Economic disadvantage, family dynamics, and adolescent enrollment in higher education. *Journal of Marriage and the Family, 64*, 690–702.

Crosnoe, R., & Needham, B. (2004). Holism, contextual variability, and the study of friendships in adolescent development. *Child Development, 75*, 264–279.

Crouter, A., Bumpus, M., Davis, K., & McHale, S. (2005). How do parents learn about adolescents' experiences? Implications for parental knowledge and adolescent risky behavior. *Child Development, 76*, 869–882.

Crouter, A., Manke, B., & McHale, S. (1995). The family context of gender intensification in early adolescence. *Child Development, 66*, 317–329.

Crouter, A., Whiteman, S., McHale, S., & Osgood, D. (2007). Development of gender attitude traditionality across middle childhood and adolescence. *Child Development, 78*, 911–926.

Crow, S., Eisenberg, M. E., Story, M., & Neumark-Sztainer, D. (2006). Psychosocial and behavioral correlates of dieting among overweight and non-overweight adolescents. *Journal of Adolescent Health, 38*, 569–574.

Crystal, D., Chen, C., Fuligni, A., Stevenson, H., Hsu, C., Ko, H., et al. (1994). Psychological maladjustment and academic achievement: A cross-cultural study of Japanese, Chinese, and American high school students. *Child Development, 65*, 738–753.

Csikszentmihalyi, M. (1990). *Flow: The psychology of optimal experience*. New York: Harper and Row.

Csikszentmihalyi, M., & Larson, R. (1984). *Being adolescent*. New York: Basic Books.

Cubbin, C., Santelli, J., Brindis, C. D., & Braveman, P. (2005). Neighborhood context and sexual behaviors among adolescents: Findings from the National Longitudinal Study of Adolescent Health. *Perspectives on Sexual and Reproductive Health, 37*, 125–134.

Cui, M., & Conger, R. (2008). Parenting behavior as mediator and moderator of the association between marital problems and adolescent maladjustment. *Journal of Research on Adolescence, 18*, 261–284.

Cui, M., Conger, R., Bryant, C., & Elder, G. H. (2002). Parental behavior and the quality of adolescent friendships: A social contextual perspective. *Journal of Marriage and the Family, 64*, 676–689.

Cui, M., Conger, R., & Lorenz, F. O. (2005). Predicting change in adolescent adjustment from change in marital problems. *Developmental Psychology, 41*, 812–823.

Cui, M., Donnellan, M. B., & Conger, R. (2007). Reciprocal influences between parents' marital problems and adolescent internalizing and externalizing behavior. *Developmental Psychology, 43*, 1544–1552.

Cummings, E., Ballard, M., El-Sheikh, M., & Lake, M. (1991). Resolution and children's responses to interadult anger. *Developmental Psychology, 27*, 462–470.

Cumsille, P., Darling, N., Flaherty, B., & Martinez, M. (2009). Heterogeneity and change in the patterning of adolescents' perceptions of the legitimacy of parental authority: A latent transition model. *Child Development, 80*, 418–432.

Cunningham, M. (1999). African-American adolescent males' perceptions of their community resources and constraints: A longitudinal analysis. *Journal of Community Psychology, 27*, 569–588.

Curran, P., Stice, E., & Chassin, L. (1997). The relation between adolescent alcohol use and peer alcohol use: A longitudinal random coefficients model. *Journal of Consulting and Clinical Psychology, 65*, 130–140.

Curtner-Smith, M., & MacKinnon-Lewis, C. (1994). Family process effects on adolescent males' susceptibility to antisocial peer pressure. *Family Relations, 43*, 462–468.

Cusick, P. A. (1973). *Inside high school*. New York: Holt, Rinehart & Winston.

Cvijanovich, N. Z., Cook, L. J., Mann, N. C., & Dean, J. M. (2001). A population-based study of crashes involving 16- and 17-year-old drivers: The potential benefit of graduated driver licensing restrictions. *Pediatrics, 107*, 632–637.

Cyranowski, J., & Frank, E. (2000). Adolescent onset of the gender difference in lifetime rates of major depression. *Archives of General Psychiatry, 57*, 21–27.

Daddis, C., & Smetana, J. (2005). Middle-class African American families' expectations for adolescents' behavioral autonomy. *International Journal of Behavioral Development, 29,* 371–381.

Dahl, R. (2008). Biological, developmental, and neurobehavioral factors relevant to adolescent driving risks, *American Journal of Preventive Medicine, 35,* S278–S284.

Dahl, R., & Hariri, A. (2005). Lessons from G. Stanley Hall: Connecting new research in biological science to the study of adolescent development. *Journal of Research on Adolescence 15,* 367–382.

Daniel, D. B., & Klaczynski, P. A. (2006). Developmental and individual differences in conditional reasoning: Effects of logic instructions and alternative antecedents. *Child Development, 77,* 339–354.

Daniels, D., Dunn, J., Furstenberg, F., Jr., & Plomin, R. (1985). Environmental differences within the family and adjustment differences within pairs of adolescent siblings. *Child Development, 56,* 764–774.

Darling, N., Cumsille, P., & Martínez, M. L. (2007). Adolescents as active agents in the socialization process: Legitimacy of parental authority and obligation to obey as predictors of obedience. *Journal of Adolescence, 30,* 297–311.

Darling, N., Cumsille, P., & Martinez, M. (2008). Individual differences in adolescents' beliefs about the legitimacy of parental authority and obligation to obey: A longitudinal investigation. *Child Development, 79,* 1103–1118.

Darling, N., Dowdy, B. B., Van Horn, M. L., & Caldwell, L. L. (1999). Mixed-sex settings and the perception of competence. *Journal of Youth and Adolescence, 28,* 461–480.

Darling, N., Hamilton, S., & Matsuda, S. (1990, March). *Functional roles and social roles: Adolescents' significant others in the United States and Japan.* Paper presented at the biennial meetings of the Society for Research on Adolescence, Atlanta.

Darling, N., & Steinberg, L. (1993). Parenting style as context: An integrative model. *Psychological Bulletin, 113,* 487–496.

Darling, N., & Steinberg, L. (1997). Community influences on adolescent achievement and deviance. In J. Brooks-Gunn, G. Duncan, & L. Aber (Eds.), *Neighborhood poverty: Context and consequences for children:* Vol. 2. *Conceptual, methodological, and policy approaches to studying neighborhoods* (pp 120–131). New York: Russell Sage Foundation.

Darling-Hammond, L. (1997). *The right to learn.* San Francisco: Jossey-Bass.

Darling-Hammond, L. (2006). No child left behind and high school reform. *Harvard Educational Review, 76,* 642–667.

Darroch, J. E., Singh, S., & Frost, J. J. (2001). Differences in teenage pregnancy rates among five developed countries: The roles of sexual activity and contraceptive use. *Family Planning Perspectives, 33,* 244–250.

Dauber, S., Alexander, K., & Entwisle, D. (1996). Tracking and transitions through the middle grades: Channeling educational trajectories. *Sociology of Education, 69,* 290–307.

Davenport, E., Davison, M., Kuang, H., Ding, S., Kim, S., & Kwak, N. (1998). High school mathematics course-taking by gender and ethnicity. *American Educational Research Journal, 35,* 497–514.

Davey, C. G., Yücel, M., & Allen, N. B. (2008). The emergence of depression in adolescence: Development of the prefrontal cortex and the representation of reward. *Neuroscience & Biobehavioral Reviews, 32,* 1–19.

Davies, P., & Cummings, M. (1994). Marital conflict and child adjustment: An emotional security hypothesis. *Psychological Bulletin, 116,* 387–411.

Davies, P., & Lindsay, L. (2004). Interparental conflict and adolescent adjustment: Why does gender moderate early adolescent vulnerability? *Journal of Family Psychology, 18,* 160–170.

Davies, P., & Windle, M. (1997). Gender-specific pathways between maternal depressive symptoms, family discord, and adolescent adjustment. *Developmental Psychology, 33,* 657–668.

Davies, P., & Windle, M. (2001). Interparental discord and adolescent adjustment trajectories: The potentiating and protective role of intrapersonal attributes. *Child Development, 72,* 1163–1178.

Davies, P. T., & Windle, M. (2000). Middle adolescents' dating pathways and psychosocial adjustment. *Merrill-Palmer Quarterly, 46,* 90–118.

Davila, J. (2008). Depressive symptoms and adolescent romance: Theory, research, and implications. *Child Development Perspectives, 2,* 26–31.

Davis, A., & Rhodes, J. (1994). African-American teenage mothers and their mothers: An analysis of supportive and problematic interactions. *Journal of Community Psychology, 22,* 12–19.

Davis, A., Rhodes, J., & Hamilton-Leaks, J. (1997). When both parents may be a source of support and problems: An analysis of pregnant and parenting female African American adolescents' relationships with their mothers and fathers. *Journal of Research on Adolescence, 7,* 331–348.

Davis, B., & Carpenter, C. (2009). Proximity of fast-food restaurants to schools and adolescent obesity. *American Journal of Public Health, 99,* 505–510.

Davis, E., & Friel, L. V. (2001). Adolescent sexuality: Disentangling the effects of family structure and family context. *Journal of Marriage and the Family, 63,* 669–681.

Davis, K., & Kirkpatrick, L. (1994). Attachment style, gender, and relationship stability: A longitudinal analysis. *Journal of Personality and Social Psychology, 66,* 502–512.

Davis, L. E., Ajzen, I., Saunders, J., & Williams, T. (2002). The decision of African American students to complete high school: An application of the theory of planned behavior. *Journal of Educational Psychology, 94,* 810–819.

Davis-Kean, P., Huesmann, L. R., Jager, J., Collins, W. A., Bates, J. E., & Lansford, J. E. (2008). Changes in the relation of self-efficacy beliefs and behaviors across development. *Child Development, 79,* 1257–1269.

de Bruyn, E. H., & Cillessen, A. H. N. (2006). Heterogeneity of girls' consensual popularity: Academic and interpersonal behavioral profiles. *Journal of Youth and Adolescence, 35,* 435–445.

de Graaf, H., Vanwesenbeeck, I., Meijer, S., Meeus, W., & Woertman, L. (2009). Sexual trajectories during adolescence: Relation to demographic characteristics and sexual risk. *Archives of Sexual Behavior, 38,* 276–282.

Dearden, K., Hale, C., & Woolley, T. (1995). The antecedents of teen fatherhood: A retrospective case-control study of Great Britain youth. *American Journal of Public Health, 85,* 551–554.

Deardorff, J., Gonzales, N. A., Christopher, F. S., Roosa, M. W., & Millsap, R. E. (2005). Early puberty and adolescent pregnancy: The influence of alcohol use. *Pediatrics 116,* 1451–1456.

Deater-Deckard, K., & Plomin, R. (1999). An adoption study of etiology of teacher and parent reports of externalizing behavior problems in middle childhood. *Child Development, 70,* 144–154.

DeBaryshe, K., Patterson, G., & Capaldi, D. (1993). A performance model for academic achievement in early adolescent boys. *Developmental Psychology, 29,* 795–804.

DeBerry, K., Scarr, S., & Weinberg, R. (1996). Family racial socialization and ecological competence: Longitudinal assessments of African-American transracial adoptees. *Child Development, 67,* 2375–2399.

Dee, T., & Evans, W. (2001). Teens and traffic safety. In J. Gruber (Ed.). *Risky behavior among youths: An economic analysis* (pp. 121–165). Chicago: University of Chicago Press.

DeGarmo, D. S., & Martinez, C. R. J. (2006). A culturally informed model of academic well-being for Latino youth: The importance of discriminatory experiences and social support. *Family Relations, 55,* 267–278.

Değirmencioğlu, S., Tolson, J., & Urberg, K. (1993, March). *Stability of adolescent social networks over the school year.* Paper presented at the biennial meetings of the Society for Research in Child Development, New Orleans.

Değirmencioğlu, S., & Urberg, K. (1994, February). *Cross-gender friendships in adolescence: Who chooses the "other"?* Paper presented at the biennial meetings of the Society for Research on Adolescence, San Diego.

Değirmencioğlu, S., Urberg, K., Tolson, J., & Richard, P. (1998). Adolescent friendship networks: Continuity and change over the school year. *Merrill-Palmer Quarterly, 44,* 313–337.

Dekovi, M., Buist, K. L., & Reitz, E. (2004). Stability and changes in problem behavior during adolescence: Latent growth analysis. *Journal of Youth and Adolescence, 33,* 1–12.

Del Giudice, M., Angeleri, R., & Manera, V. (2009). The juvenile transition: A developmental switch point in human life history. *Developmental Review, 29,* 1–31.

Delsing, M. J. M. H., ter Bogt, Tom F. M., Engels, R. C. M. E., & Meeus, W. H. J. (2007). Adolescents' peer crowd identification in the Netherlands: Structure and associations with problem behaviors. *Journal of Research on Adolescence, 17,* 467–480.

Delva, J., O'Malley, P. M., & Johnston, L. D. (2006). Racial/ethnic and socioeconomic status differences in overweight and health-related behaviors among American students: National trends 1986–2003. *Journal of Adolescent Health, 39,* 536–545.

Delva, J., Wallace, J. M., Jr., O'Malley, P. M., Bachman, J. G., Johnston, L. D., & Schulenberg, J. E. (2005). The epidemiology of alcohol, marijuana, and cocaine use among Mexican American, Puerto Rican, Cuban American, and other Latin American eighth-grade students in the United States: 1991–2002. *American Journal of Public Health, 95,* 696–702.

Demetriou, A., Christou, C., Spanoudis, G., & Platsidou, M. (2002). The development of mental processing: Efficiency, working memory, and thinking. *Monographs of the Society for Research in Child Development, 67,* Serial No. 268.

Demo, D., & Acock, A. (1996). Family structure, family process, and adolescent well-being. *Journal of Research on Adolescence, 6,* 457–488.

Demorest, A., Meyer, C., Phelps, E., Gardner, H., & Winner, E. (1984). Words speak louder than actions: Understanding deliberately false remarks. *Child Development, 55,* 1527–1534.

Denton, K., & Zarbatany, L. (1996). Age differences in support processes in conversations between friends. *Child Development, 67,* 1360–1373.

Deyhle, D. (1995). Navajo youth and Anglo racism: Cultural integrity and resistance. *Harvard Educational Review, 65,* 403–444.

Diamond, L. (1998). Development of sexual orientation among adolescent and young adult women. *Developmental Psychology, 34,* 1085–1095.

Diamond, L. (2000). Passionate friendships among adolescent sexual-minority women. *Journal of Research on Adolescence, 10,* 191–209.

Diamond, L. (2008). Female bisexuality from adolescence to adulthood: Results from a 10-year longitudinal study. *Developmental Psychology, 44,* 5–14.

Diamond, L., & Dubé, E. M. (2002). Friendship and attachment among heterosexual and sexual-minority youths: Does the gender of your friend matter? *Journal of Youth and Adolescence, 31,* 155–166.

Diamond, L., & Lucas, S. (2004). Sexual-minority and heterosexual youths' peer relationships: Experiences, expectations, and implications for well-being. *Journal of Research of Adolescence, 14,* 313–340.

Diamond, L., & Savin-Williams, R. (2009). Adolescent sexuality. In R. Lerner & L. Steinberg (Eds.), *Handbook of adolescent psychology* (3rd ed., Vol. 1, pp. 479–523). New York: Wiley.

Diamond, L., Savin-Williams, R., & Dubé, E. (1999). Sex, dating, passionate friendships, and romance: Intimate peer relations among lesbian, gay, and bisexual adolescents. In W. Furman, B. Brown, & C. Feiring (Eds.), *Contemporary perspectives on adolescent romantic relationships* (pp. 175–210). New York: Cambridge University Press.

DiBlasio, F., & Benda, B. (1992). Gender differences in theories of adolescent sexual activity. *Sex Roles, 27,* 221–240.

Dick, D., Rose, R., Pulkkinen, L., & Kaprio, J. (2001). Measuring puberty and understanding its impact: A longitudinal study of adolescent twins. *Journal of Youth and Adolescence, 30,* 385–400.

Dick, D., Rose, R. J., Viken, R. J., & Kaprio, J. (2000). Pubertal timing and substance use: Associations between and within families across late adolescence. *Developmental Psychology, 36,* 180–189.

Dick, D., Viken, R., Purcell, S., Kaprio, J., Pulkkinen, L., & Rose, R. J. (2007). Parental monitoring moderates the importance of genetic and environmental influences on adolescent smoking. *Journal of Abnormal Psychology, 116,* 213–218.

DiClemente, R., Durbin, M., Siegel, D., Krasnovsky, F., Lazarus, N., & Comacho, T. (1992). Determinants of condom use among junior high school students in a minority, inner-city school district. *Pediatrics, 89,* 197–202.

DiClemente, R., Wingood, G., Harrington, K., Lang, D., Davies, S., Hook, E., et al. (2004). Efficacy of an HIV prevention intervention for African American adolescent girls: A randomized controlled trial. *Journal of the American Medical Association, 292,* 171–179.

Diehl, L., Vicary, J., & Deike, R. (1997). Longitudinal trajectories of self-esteem from early to middle adolescence and related psychosocial variables among rural adolescents. *Journal of Research on Adolescence, 7,* 393–411.

Dielman, T. (1994). School-based research on the prevention of adolescent alcohol use and misuse: Methodological issues and advances. *Journal of Research on Adolescence, 4,* 271–293.

DiIorio, C., Dudley, W. N., Kelly, M., Soet, J. E., Mbwara, J., & Sharpe Potter, J. (2001). Social cognitive correlates of sexual experience and condom use among 13- through 15-year-old adolescents. *Journal of Adolescent Health, 29,* 208–216.

DiIorio, C., Kelley, M., & Hockenberry-Eaton, M. (1999). Communication about sexual issues: Mothers, fathers, and friends. *Journal of Adolescent Health, 24,* 181–189.

Dijkstra, J. K., Lindenberg, S., & Veenstra, R. (2008). Beyond the class norm: Bullying behavior of popular adolescents and its relation to peer acceptance and rejection. *Journal of Abnormal Child Psychology, 36,* 1289–1299.

DiMaggio, P. (1982). Cultural capital and school success: The impact of status culture participation on the grades of U.S. high school students. *American Sociological Review, 47,* 189–201.

Dishion, T., & Andrews, D. (1995). Preventing escalation in problem behaviors with high-risk young adolescents: Immediate and 1-year outcomes. *Journal of Consulting and Clinical Psychology, 63,* 538–548.

Dishion, T., Andrews, D., & Crosby, L. (1995). Antisocial boys and their friends in early adolescence: Relationship characteristics, quality, and interactional process. *Child Development, 66,* 139–151.

Dishion, T., Capaldi, D., & Yoerger, K. (1999). Middle childhood antecedents to progressions in male adolescent substance use: An ecological analysis of risk and protection. *Journal of Adolescent Research, 14,* 175–205.

Dishion, T., McCord, J., & Poulin, F. (1999). When interventions harm: Peer groups and problem behavior. *American Psychologist, 54,* 755–764.

Dishion, T., Nelson, S., & Bullock, B. (2004). Premature adolescent autonomy: Parent disengagement and deviant peer process in the amplification of problem behavior. *Journal of Adolescence, 27,* 515–530.

Dishion, T., Nelson, S., Winter, C., & Bullock, B. (2004). Adolescent friendship as a dynamic system: Entropy and deviance in the etiology and course of male antisocial behavior. *Journal of Abnormal Child Psychology, 32,* 651–663.

Dishion, T., & Owen, L. (2002). A longitudinal analysis of friendships and substance use: Bidirectional influence from adolescence to adulthood. *Developmental Psychology, 38,* 480–491.

Dishion, T., Patterson, G., Stoolmiller, M., & Skinner, M. (1991). Family, school, and behavioral antecedents to early adolescent involvement with antisocial peers. *Developmental Psychology, 27,* 172–180.

Dittus, P. J., & Jaccard, J. (2000). Adolescents' perceptions of maternal disapproval of sex:

Relationship to sexual outcomes. *Journal of Adolescent Health, 26,* 268–278.

Dittus, P., Jaccard, J., & Gordon, V. (1997). The impact of African American fathers on adolescent sexual behavior. *Journal of Youth and Adolescence, 26,* 445–465.

Dmitrieva, J., Chen, C., Greenberger, E., & Gil-Rivas, V. (2004). Family relationships and adolescent psychosocial outcomes: Converging findings from Eastern and Western cultures. *Journal of Research on Adolescence, 14,* 425–447.

Dobkin, P., Tremblay, R., Mâsse, L., & Vitaro, F. (1995). Individual and peer characteristics in predicting boys' early onset of substance abuse: A seven-year longitudinal study. *Child Development, 66,* 1198–1214.

Dobkin, P., Tremblay, R., & Sacchitelle, C. (1997). Predicting boys' early onset substance abuse from father's alcoholism, son's disruptiveness, and mother's parenting behavior. *Journal of Consulting and Clinical Psychology, 65,* 86–92.

Dodge, K. (1986). A social information-processing model of social competence in children. In M. Perlmutter (Ed.), *Minnesota Symposium on Child Psychology,* (Vol. 18, pp. 77–125). Hillsdale, NJ: Erlbaum.

Dodge, K., & Coie, J. (1987). Social information-processing factors in reactive and proactive aggression in children's peer groups. *Journal of Personality and Social Psychology, 53,* 1146–1158.

Dodge, K., Coie, J., & Lynam, D. (2006). Aggression and antisocial behavior in youth. In W. Damon and R. Lerner (Ser. Eds.) & N. Eisenberg (Vol. Ed.), *Handbook of child psychology:* Vol. 3. *Social, emotional, and personality development* (6th ed., pp. 719–788). New York: Wiley.

Dodge, K., Greenberg, M., Malone, P., & Conduct Problems Prevention Research Group. (2008). Testing an idealized dynamic cascade model of the development of serious violence in adolescence. *Child Development, 79,* 1907–1927.

Dodge, K., & Pettit, G. (2003). A biopsychosocial model of the development of chronic conduct problems in adolescence. *Developmental Psychology, 39,* 349–371.

Dogan, S., Conger, R., Kim, K., & Masyn, K. (2007). Cognitive and parenting pathways in the transmission of antisocial behavior from parents to adolescents. *Child Development, 78,* 335–349.

Donnellan, M., Larsen-Rife, D., & Conger, R. (2005). Personality, family history, and competence in early adult romantic relationship. *Journal of Personality and Social Psychology, 88,* 562–576.

Donnelly, D., & Finkelhor, D. (1992). Does equality in custody arrangement improve the parent–child relationship? *Journal of Marriage and the Family, 54,* 837–845.

D'Onofrio, B. M., Turkheimer, E., Emery, R. E., Slutske, W. S., Heath, A. C., Madden, P. A., et al. (2006). A genetically informed study of the processes underlying the association between parental marital instability and offspring adjustment. *Developmental Psychology, 42,* 486–499.

Donovan, J., & Jessor, R. (1985). Structure of problem behavior in adolescence and young adulthood. *Journal of Consulting and Clinical Psychology, 53,* 890–904.

Dorfman, L., Woodruff, K., Chavez, V., & Wallack, L. (1997). Youth and violence on local television news in California. *American Journal of Public Health, 87,* 1311–1316.

Dorius, G., Heaton, T., & Steffen, P. (1993). Adolescent life events and their association with the onset of sexual intercourse. *Youth and Society, 25,* 3–23.

Dorn, L., Dahl, R., Woodward, H., & Biro, F. (2006). Defining the boundaries of early adolescence: A user's guide to assessing pubertal status and pubertal timing in research with adolescents. *Applied Developmental Science, 1,* 30–56.

Dorn, L. D., Nottelmann, E. D., Susman, E. J., Inoff-Germain, G., Cutler, G. B., Jr., & Chrousos, G. P. (1999). Variability in hormone concentrations and self-reported menstrual histories in young adolescents: Menarche as an integral part of a developmental process. *Journal of Youth and Adolescence, 28,* 283–304.

Dornbusch, S. (1994, February). *Off the track.* Presidential address to the Society for Research on Adolescence, San Diego.

Dornbusch, S., Carlsmith, J., Bushwall, S., Ritter, P., Leiderman, P., Hastorf, A., et al. (1985). Single parents, extended households, and the control of adolescents. *Child Development, 56,* 326–341.

Dornbusch, S., Carlsmith, J., Gross, R., Martin, J., Jennings, D., Rosenberg, A., et al. (1981). Sexual development, age, and dating: A comparison of biological and social influences upon one set of behaviors. *Child Development, 52,* 179–185.

Dornbusch, S., Erickson, K., Laird, J., & Wong, C. (2001). The relation of family and school attachment to adolescent deviance in diverse groups and communities. *Journal of Adolescent Research, 16,* 396–422.

Dornbusch, S., Ritter, P., Liederman, P., Roberts, D., & Fraleigh, M. (1987). The relation of parenting style to adolescent school performance. *Child Development, 58,* 1244–1257.

Dotterer, A., McHale, S., & Crouter, A. (2007). Implications of out-of-school activities for school engagement in African American adolescents. *Journal of Youth and Adolescence, 36,* 391–401.

Dowdy, B. B., & Kliewer, W. (1998). Dating, parent–adolescent conflict, and behavioral autonomy. *Journal of Youth and Adolescence, 27,* 473–492.

Downey, D. (1995). Understanding academic achievement among children in stephouseholds: The role of parental resources, sex of stepparent, and sex of child. *Social Forces, 73,* 875–894.

Downey, D., & Ainsworth-Darnell, J. W. (2002). The search for oppositional culture among Black students. *American Sociological Review, 67,* 156–164.

Downey, D., Ainsworth-Darnell, J., & Dufur, M. (1998). Sex of parent and children's well-being in single-parent households. *Journal of Marriage and the Family, 60,* 878–893.

Downey, D., Ainsworth, J. W., & Qian, Z. (2009). Rethinking the attitude-achievement paradox among Blacks. *Sociology of Education, 82,* 1–19.

Downey, D., & Pribesh, S. (2004). When race matters: Teachers' evaluations of students' classroom behavior. *Sociology of Education, 77,* 267–282.

Downey, G., Bonica, C., & Rincón, C. (1999). Rejection sensitivity and adolescent romantic relationships. In W. Furman, B. Brown, & C. Feiring (Eds.), *Contemporary perspectives on adolescent romantic relationships* (pp. 148–174). New York: Cambridge University Press.

Downey, G., Lebolt, A., Rincón, C., & Freitas, A. (1998). Rejection sensitivity and children's interpersonal difficulties. *Child Development, 69,* 1074–1091.

Doyle, A., Brendgen, M., Markiewicz, D., & Kamkar, K. (2003). Family relationships as moderators of the association between romantic relationships and adjustment in early adolescence. *Journal of Early Adolescence, 23,* 316–340.

Doyle, A. B., & Markiewicz, D. (2005). Parenting, marital conflict, and adjustment from early to mid-adolescence: Mediated by adolescent attachment style? *Journal of Youth and Adolescence, 34,* 97–110.

Drapela, L. A., Gebelt, J. L., & McRee, N. (2006). Pubertal development, choice of friends, and smoking initiation among adolescent males. *Journal of Youth and Adolescence, 35,* 717–727.

Driscoll, A., Russell, S., & Crockett, L. (2008). Parenting styles and youth well-being across immigrant generations. *Journal of Family Issues, 29,* 185–209.

Drumm, P., & Jackson, D. (1996). Developmental changes in questioning strategies during adolescence. *Journal of Adolescent Research, 11,* 285–305.

Dryfoos, J. (1990). *Adolescents at risk: Prevalence and prevention.* New York: Oxford University Press.

Dryfoos, J. (1993). Schools as places for health, mental health, and social services. *Teachers College Record, 94,* 540–567.

Dubas, J., Graber, J., & Petersen, A. (1991). A longitudinal investigation of adolescents' changing perceptions of pubertal timing. *Developmental Psychology, 27,* 580–586.

Dubé, E., & Savin-Williams, R. (1999). Sexual identity development among ethnic sexual-minority male youths. *Developmental Psychology, 35,* 1389–1398.

Dube, S. R., Felitti, V. J., Dong, M., Chapman, D. P., Giles, W. H., & Anda, R. F. (2003). Childhood abuse, neglect, and household dysfunction and the risk of illicit drug use: The adverse childhood experiences study. *Pediatrics, 111,* 564–572.

DuBois, D., Bull, C., Sherman, M., & Roberts, M. (1998). Self-esteem and adjustment in early adolescence: A social-contextual perspective. *Journal of Youth and Adolescence, 27,* 557–583.

DuBois, D., Burk-Braxton, C., Swenson, L. P., Tevendale, H. D., & Hardesty, J. L. (2002). Race and gender influences on adjustment in early adolescence: Investigation of an integrative model. *Child Development, 73,* 1573–1592.

DuBois, D., Felner, R., Brand, S., Adan, A., & Evans, E. (1992). A prospective study of life stress, social support, and adaptation in early adolescence. *Child Development, 63,* 542–557.

DuBois, D., Felner, R., Brand, S., & George, G. (1999). Profiles of self-esteem in early adolescence: Identification and investigation of adaptive correlates. *American Journal of Community Psychology, 27,* 899–932.

DuBois, D., Felner, R., Meares, H., & Krier, M. (1994). Prospective investigation of the effects of socioeconomic disadvantage, life stress, and social support on early adolescent adjustment. *Journal of Abnormal Psychology, 103,* 511–522.

DuBois, D., & Hirsch, B. (1990). School and neighborhood friendship patterns of Blacks and Whites in early adolescence. *Child Development, 61,* 524–536.

DuBois, D., Holloway, B., Valentine, J., & Cooper, H. (2002). Effectiveness of mentoring programs for youth: A meta-analytic review. *American Journal of Community Psychology, 30,* 157–197.

DuBois, D., & Silverthorn, N. (2005). Natural mentoring relationships and adolescent health: Evidence from a national study. *American Journal of Public Health, 95,* 518–524.

DuBois, D., & Tevendale, H. (1999). Self-esteem in childhood and adolescence: Vaccine or epiphenomenon. *Applied and Preventive Psychology, 8,* 103–117.

DuBois, D., Tevendale, H., Burk-Braxton, C., Swenson, L., & Hardesty, J. (2000). Self-system influences during early adolescence: Investigation of an integrative model. *Journal of Early Adolescence, 20,* 12–43.

Dubow, E. F., Huesmann, L. R., Boxer, P., Pulkkinen, L., & Kokko, K. (2006). Middle childhood and adolescent contextual and personal predictors of adult educational and occupational outcomes: A mediational model in two countries. *Developmental Psychology, 42,* 937–949.

Dukes, R., Martinez, R., & Stein, J. (1997). Precursors and consequences of membership in youth gangs. *Youth and Society, 29,* 139–165.

Dumont, M., & Provost, M. (1999). Resilience in adolescents: Protective role of social support, coping strategies, self-esteem, and social activities on experience of stress and depression. *Journal of Youth and Adolescence, 28,* 343–363.

Duncan, G. (1994). Families and neighbors as sources of disadvantage in the schooling decisions of White and Black adolescents. *American Journal of Education, 103,* 20–53.

Dunn, J., Slomkowski, C., & Beardsall, L. (1994). Sibling relationships from the preschool period through middle childhood and early adolescence. *Developmental Psychology, 30,* 315–324.

Dunn, M., & Goldman, M. (1998). Age and drinking-related differences in the memory organization of alcohol expectances in 3rd-, 6th-, 9th-, and 12th-grade children. *Journal of Consulting & Clinical Psychology, 66,* 579–585.

Dunn, S., Putallaz, M., Sheppard, B., & Lindstrom, R. (1987). Social support and adjustment in gifted adolescents. *Journal of Educational Psychology, 79,* 467–473.

Dunphy, D. (1969). *Cliques, crowds, and gangs.* Melbourne: Cheshire.

Dupéré, V., Lacourse, E., Willms, D., Leventhal, T., & Tremblay, R. (2008). Neighborhood poverty and early transition to sexual activity in young adolescents: A developmental ecological approach. *Child Development, 79,* 1463–1476.

Dupéré, V., Lacourse, É., Willms, J. D., Vitaro, F., & Tremblay, R. E. (2007). Affiliation to youth gangs during adolescence: The interaction between childhood psychopathic tendencies and neighborhood disadvantage. *Journal of Abnormal Child Psychology, 35,* 1035–1045.

DuRant, R., Rome, E., Rich, M., Allred, E., Emans, S., & Woods, E. (1997). Tobacco and alcohol use behaviors portrayed in music videos: A content analysis. *American Journal of Public Health, 87,* 1131–1135.

Durik, A. M., Vida, M., & Eccles, J. (2006). Task values and ability beliefs as predictors of high school literacy choices: A developmental analysis. *Journal of Educational Psychology, 98,* 382–393.

Dusek, J., & Flaherty, J. (1981). The development of the self-concept during the adolescent years. *Monographs of the Society for Research in Child Development, 46,* Serial No. 191.

Dweck, C. S. (2002). The development of ability conceptions. In A. Wigfield & J. Eccles (Eds.), *The development of achievement motivation* (pp. 57–88). New York: Academic Press.

Dyer, G., & Tiggemann, M. (1996). The effects of school environment on body concerns in adolescent women. *Sex Roles, 34,* 127–138.

Eamon, M. K. (2005). Social-demographic, school, neighborhood, and parenting influences on the academic achievement of Latino young adolescents. *Journal of Youth and Adolescence, 34,* 163–174.

Earls, F., Cairns, R., & Mercy, J. (1993). The control of violence and the promotion of nonviolence in adolescents. In S. Millstein, A. Petersen, & E. Nightingale (Eds.), *Promoting the health of adolescents: New directions for the twenty-first century* (pp. 285–304). New York: Oxford University Press.

Early, D., & Eccles, J. (1994, February). *Predicting parenting behavior: The role of SES, neighborhood risk, and parental values.* Paper presented at the biennial meetings of the Society for Research on Adolescence, San Diego.

East, P. (2009). Adolescents' relationships with siblings. In R. Lerner & L. Steinberg (Eds.), *Handbook of adolescent psychology* (3rd ed., Vol. 2, pp. 43–73). New York: Wiley.

East, P., & Blaustein, E. (1995, March). *Perceived timing of life-course transitions: Race differences in early adolescent girls' sexual, marriage, and childbearing expectations.* Paper presented at the biennial meetings of the Society for Research in Child Development, Indianapolis.

East, P., & Felice, M. (1992). Pregnancy risk among the younger sisters of pregnant and childbearing adolescents. *Developmental and Behavioral Pediatrics, 13,* 128–136.

East, P., & Felice, M. (1996). *Adolescent pregnancy and parenting: Findings from a racially diverse sample.* Mahwah, NJ: Erlbaum.

East, P., Felice, M., & Morgan, M. (1993). Sisters' and girlfriends' sexual and childbearing behavior: Effects on early adolescent girls' sexual outcomes. *Journal of Marriage and the Family, 55,* 953–963.

East, P., & Jacobson, L. (2003). Mothers' differential treatment of their adolescent childbearing and nonchildbearing children: Contrasts between and within families. *Journal of Family Psychology, 19,* 384–396.

East, P., & Khoo, S. (2005). Longitudinal pathways linking family factors and sibling relationship qualities to adolescent substance use and sexual risk behaviors. *Journal of Family Psychology, 19,* 571–580.

East, P., Reyes, B. T., & Horn, E. J. (2007). Association between adolescent pregnancy and a family history of teenage births. *Perspectives on Sexual and Reproductive Health, 39,* 108–115.

East, P., & Rook, K. (1992). Compensatory patterns of support among children's peer relationships: A test using school friends, nonschool friends, and siblings. *Developmental Psychology, 28,* 163–172.

Eaton, M. J., & Dembo, M. H. (1997). Differences in the motivational beliefs of Asian American and non-Asian students. *Journal of Educational Psychology, 89,* 433–440.

Eberhart, N. K., Shih, J. H., Hammen, C. L., & Brennan, P. A. (2006). Understanding the sex difference in vulnerability to adolescent depression: An examination of child and parent characteristics. *Journal of Abnormal Child Psychology, 34,* 495–508.

Ebin, V. J., Sneed, C. D., Morisky, D. E., Rotherman-Borus, M., Magnusson, A. M., & Malotte, C. (2001). Acculturation and interrelationships between problem and health-promoting behaviors among Latino adolescents. *Journal of Adolescent Health, 28,* 62–72.

Eccles, J. (2004). Schools, academic motivation, and stage-environment fit. In R. Lerner & L. Steinberg (Eds.), *Handbook of adolescent psychology.* New York: Wiley.

Eccles, J., Early, D., Frasier, K., Belansky, E., & McCarthy, K. (1997). The relation of connection, regulation, and support for autonomy to adolescents' functioning. *Journal of Adolescent Research, 12,* 263–286.

Eccles, J., Lord, S. E., Roeser, R. (1996). Round holes, square pegs, rocky roads, and sore feet: The impact of stage/environment fit on young adolescents' experiences in schools and families. In S. L. Toth D. Cicchetti (Eds.), *Adolescence: Opportunities and challenges,* (Vol. 7, pp. 49–93). Rochester, NY: University of Rochester Press.

Eccles, J., Midgley, C., Wigfield, A., Buchanan, C., Reuman, D., Flanagan, C., et al. (1993). Development during adolescence: The impact of stage-environment fit on young adolescents' experiences in schools and families. *American Psychologist, 48,* 90–101.

Eccles, J., & Roeser, R. (2009). Schools, academic motivation, and stage-environment fit. In R. Lerner & L. Steinberg (Eds.), *Handbook of adolescent psychology* (3rd ed., Vol. 1, pp. 404–434). New York: Wiley.

Edens, J., Skeem, J., Cruise, K., & Cauffman, E. (2000). The assessment of juvenile psychopathy and its association with violence: A critical review. *Behavioral Sciences and the Law, 18,* 53–80.

Eder, D. (1985). The cycle of popularity: Interpersonal relations among female adolescence. *Sociology of Education, 58,* 154–165.

Egan, S., & Perry, D. (1998). Does low self-regard invite victimization? *Developmental Psychology, 34,* 299–309.

Egan, S., & Perry, D. (2001). Gender identity: A multidimensional analysis with implications for psychosocial adjustment. *Developmental Psychology, 37,* 451–463.

Eisenberg, M. E., Neumark-Sztainer, D., Haines, J., & Wall, M. (2006). Weight-teasing and emotional well-being in adolescents: Longitudinal findings from project EAT. *Journal of Adolescent Health, 38,* 675–683.

Eisenberg, N., Carlo, G., Murphy, B., & Van Court, P. (1995). Prosocial development in late adolescence: A longitudinal study. *Child Development, 66,* 1179–1197.

Eisenberg, N., Cumberland, A., Guthrie, I. K., Murphy, B. C., & Shepard, S. A (2005). Age changes in prosocial responding and moral reasoning in adolescence and early adulthood. *Journal of Research on Adolescence, 15,* 235–260.

Eisenberg, N., Miller, P., Shell, R., McNalley, S., & Shea, C. (1991). Prosocial development in adolescence: A longitudinal study. *Developmental Psychology, 27,* 849–857.

Eisenberg, N., Morris, A., McDaniel, B., & Spinrad, T. (2009). Moral cognitions and prosocial responding in adolescence. In R. Lerner & L. Steinberg (Eds.), *Handbook of adolescent psychology* (3rd ed., Vol. 1, pp. 229–265). New York: Wiley.

Eisenberg, N., Zhou, Q., & Koller, S. (2001). Brazilian adolescents' prosocial moral judgment and behavior: Relations to sympathy, perspective taking, gender-role orientation, and demographic characteristics. *Child Development, 72,* 518–534.

Eisenstadt, S. (1956). *From generation to generation.* Glencoe, IL: Free Press.

Elder, G. H., Jr. (1974). *Children of the Great Depression.* Chicago: University of Chicago Press.

Elder, G. H., Jr. (1980). Adolescence in historical perspective. In J. Adelson (Ed.), *Handbook of adolescent psychology.* New York: Wiley.

Elder, G. H., Jr., & Ardelt, M. (1992, March). *Families adapting to economic pressure: Some consequences for parents and adolescents.* Paper presented at the biennial meetings of the Society for Research on Adolescence, Washington, DC.

Elder, G. H., Jr., & Conger, R. (2000). *Children of the land.* Chicago: University of Chicago Press.

Elder, G. H., Jr., Conger, R., Foster, E., & Ardelt, M. (1992). Families under economic pressure. *Journal of Family Issues, 13,* 5–37.

Elder, G. H., Jr., van Nguyen, T., & Caspi, A. (1985). Linking family hardship to children's lives. *Child Development, 56,* 361–375.

Elders, M., Perry, C., Eriksen, M., & Giovino, G. (1994). The report of the Surgeon General: Preventing tobacco use among young people. *American Journal of Public Health, 84,* 543–547.

Eley, T., Lichenstein, P., & Stevenson, J. (1999). Sex differences in the etiology of aggressive and nonaggressive antisocial behavior: Results from two twin studies. *Child Development, 70,* 155–168.

Elkind, D. (1967). Egocentrism in adolescence. *Child Development, 38,* 1025–1034.

Ellickson, P., Bell, R., & McGuigan, K. (1993). Preventing adolescent drug use: Long-term results of a junior high program. *American Journal of Public Health, 83,* 856–861.

Elliott, B., & Richards, M. (1991, July). *Children and divorce: Educational performance and behaviour before and after parental separation.*

Paper presented at the meetings of the International Society for the Study of Behavioural Development, Minneapolis.

Elliott, D., Huizinga, D., & Menard, S. (1989). *Multiple problem youth: Delinquency, substance abuse, and mental health problems.* New York: Springer-Verlag.

Ellis, B. (2004). Timing of pubertal maturation in girls: An integrated life history approach. *Psychological Bulletin, 130,* 920–958.

Ellis, B., Bates, J., Dodge, K., Fergusson, D., Horwood, L., Pettit, G., et al. (2003). Does father absence place daughters at special risk for early sexual activity and teenage pregnancy? *Child Development, 74,* 801–821.

Elmen, J. (1991). Achievement orientation in early adolescence: Developmental patterns and social correlates. *Journal of Early Adolescence, 11,* 125–151.

Elmore, R. (2009). Schooling adolescents. In R. Lerner & L. Steinberg (Eds.), *Handbook of adolescent psychology* (3rd ed., Vol. 2, pp. 193–227). New York: Wiley.

Elo, I., King, R., & Furstenberg, F., Jr. (1999). Adolescent females: Their sexual partners and the fathers of their children. *Journal of Marriage and the Family, 61,* 74–84.

Ennett, S., & Bauman, K. (1994). The contribution of influence and selection to adolescent peer group homogeneity: The case of adolescent cigarette smoking. *Journal of Personality and Social Psychology, 67,* 653–663.

Ennett, S., & Bauman, K. (1996). Adolescent social networks: School, demographic, and longitudinal considerations. *Journal of Adolescent Research, 11,* 194–215.

Ennett, S., Bauman, K., Hussong, A., Faris, R., Foshee, V., Cai, L., & DuRant, R. (2006). The peer context of adolescent substance use: Findings from social network analysis. *Journal of Research on Adolescence, 16,* 159–186.

Ennett, S., Foshee, V. A., Bauman, K. E., Hussong, A., Cai, L., Luz, H., et al. (2008). The social ecology of adolescent alcohol misuse. *Child Development, 79,* 1777–1791.

Ennett, S., Tobler, N., Ringwalt, C., & Flewelling, R. (1994). How effective is drug abuse resistance education? A meta-analysis of Project DARE outcome evaluations. *American Journal of Public Health, 84,* 1394–1401.

Enright, R., Levy, V., Harris, D., & Lapsley, D. (1987). Do economic conditions influence how theorists view adolescents? *Journal of Youth and Adolescence, 16,* 541–560.

Ensminger, M., Lamkin, R., & Jacobson, N. (1996). School leaving: A longitudinal perspective including neighborhood effects. *Child Development, 67,* 2400–2416.

Entwisle, D. (1990). Schools and the adolescent. In S. Feldman and G. Elliott (Eds.), *At the threshold: The developing adolescent* (pp. 197–224). Cambridge, MA: Harvard University Press.

Entwisle, D., Alexander, K., & Olson, L. (2004). Temporary as compared to permanent high school dropout. *Social Forces, 82,* 1181–1205.

Entwisle, D., Alexander, K., & Olson, L. (2005). Urban teenagers work and dropout. *Youth and Society, 37,* 3–32.

Epstein, J. (1983). Selecting friends in contrasting secondary school environments. In J. Epstein & N. Karweit (Eds.), *Friends in school.* New York: Academic Press.

Epstein, R. (2007). *The case against adolescence: Rediscovering the adult in every teen.* Sanger, CA: Quill Driver Books.

Erath, S. A., Flanagan, K. S., & Bierman, K. L. (2007). Social anxiety and peer relations in early adolescence: Behavioral and cognitive factors. *Journal of Abnormal Child Psychology, 35,* 405–416.

Erel, O., & Burman, B. (1995). Interrelatedness of marital relations and parent–child relations: A meta-analytic review. *Psychological Bulletin, 118,* 108–132.

Erickson, K., Crosnoe, R., & Dornbusch, S. M. (2000). A social process model of adolescent deviance: Combining social control and differential association perspectives. *Journal of Youth and Adolescence, 29,* 395–425.

Erikson, E. (1959). Identity and the life cycle. *Psychological Issues, 1,* 1–171.

Erikson, E. (1963). *Childhood and society.* New York: Norton.

Erikson, E. (1968). *Identity: Youth and crisis.* New York: Norton.

Erkut, S., Szalacha, L. A., Garcia Coll, C., & Alarcon, O. (2000). Puerto Rican early adolescents' self-esteem patterns. *Journal of Research on Adolescence, 10,* 339–364.

Ernst, M., Nelson, E., Jazbec, S., McClure, E., Monk, C., Leibenluft, E., et al. (2005). Amygdala and nucleus accumbens in response to receipt and omission of gains in adults and adolescents. *Neuroimage, 25,* 1279–1291.

Esbensen, F., Deschenes, E., & Winfree, L., Jr. (1999). Differences between gang girls and gang boys: Results from a multisite survey. *Youth and Society, 31,* 27–53.

Eshel, N., Nelson, E. E., Blair, R. J., Pine, D. S., & Ernst, M. (2007). Neural substrates of choice selection in adults and adolescents: Development of the ventrolateral prefrontal and anterior cingulate cortices. *Neuropsychologia, 45,* 1270–1279.

Espelage, D. L., Holt, M. K., & Henkel, R. R. (2003). Examination of peer-group contextual effects on aggression during early adolescence. *Child Development, 74,* 205–220.

Espenshade, T. J., Hale, L. E., & Chung, C. Y. (2005). The frog pond revisited: High school academic context, class rank, and elite college admission. *Sociology of Education, 78,* 269–293.

Estrada, P. (1995). Adolescents' self-reports of prosocial responses to friends and acquaintances: The role of sympathy-related cognitive, affective, and motivational processes. *Journal of Research on Adolescence, 5,* 173–200.

Ethier, K. A., Kershaw, T. S., Lewis, J. B., Milan, S., Niccolai, L. M., & Ickovics, J. R. (2006). Self-esteem, emotional distress and sexual behavior among adolescent females: Interrelationships and temporal effects. *Journal of Adolescent Health, 38,* 268–274.

Euling, S., Herman-Giddens, M., Lee, P., Selevan, S., Juul, A., Sørensen, T., et al. (2008). Examination of US puberty-timing data from 1940 to 1994 for secular trends: Panel findings. *Pediatrics,121,* S172-91.

Evans, D. (1993, March). *A model of structural self-complexity: Its relation to age, symptomatology and self-perception.* Paper presented at the biennial meetings of the Society for Research in Child Development, New Orleans.

Evans, E., Schweingruber, H., & Stevenson, H. W. (2002). Gender differences in interest and knowledge acquisition: The United States, Taiwan, and Japan. *Sex Roles, 47,* 153–167.

Eveleth, P., & Tanner, J. (1990). *Worldwide variation in human growth* (2nd ed.). New York: Cambridge University Press.

Everett, S. A., Warren, C. W., Santelli, J. S., Kann, L., Collins, J. L., & Kolbe, L. J. (2000). Use of birth control pills, condoms, and withdrawal among U.S. high school students. *Journal of Adolescent Health, 27,* 112–118.

Eyre, S., & Millstein, S. (1999). What leads to sex? Adolescent preferred partners and reasons for sex. *Journal of Research on Adolescence, 9,* 277–307.

Fagan., J, & Zimring, F. (Eds.). (2000). *The changing borders of juvenile justice: Transfer of adolescents to the criminal court.* Chicago: University of Chicago Press.

Fagot, B., Pears, K., Capaldi, D., Crosby, L., & Leve, C. (1998). Becoming an adolescent father: Precursors and parenting. *Developmental Psychology, 34,* 1209–1219.

Falk, R., & Wilkening, F. (1998). Children's construction of fair chances: Adjusting probabilities. *Developmental Psychology, 34,* 1340–1357.

Fallon, B. J., & Bowles, T. V. (1997). The effect of family structure and family functioning on adolescents' perceptions of intimate time spent with parents, siblings, and peers. *Journal of Youth and Adolescence, 26,* 25–43.

Fang, X., Stanton, B., Li, X., Feigelman, S., & Baldwin, R. (1998). Similarities in sexual activity and condom use among friends within groups before and after a risk-reduction intervention. *Youth and Society, 29,* 431–450.

Farkas, G., Grobe, R., & Shuan, Y. (1990). Cultural resources and school success: Gender, ethnicity, and poverty groups within an urban school district. *American Sociological Review, 55,* 127–142.

Farkas, G., Lleras, C., & Maczuga, S. (2002). Does oppositional culture exist in minority and poverty peer groups? *American Sociological Review, 67,* 148–155.

Farmer, T. W., Estell, D. B., Bishop, J. L., O'Neal, K. K., & Cairns, B. D. (2003). Rejected bullies or popular leaders? The social relations of aggressive subtypes of rural African American early adolescents. *Developmental Psychology, 39,* 992–1004.

Farrell, A. D., Erwin, E. H., Allison, K. W., Meyer, A., Sullivan, T., Camou, S., et al. (2007). Problematic situations in the lives of urban African American middle school students: A qualitative study. *Journal of Research on Adolescence, 17,* 413–454.

Farrell, A. D., & Sullivan, T. (2004). Impact of witnessing violence on growth curves for problem behaviors among early adolescents in urban and rural settings. *Journal of Community Psychology, 32,* 505–525.

Farrell, A. D., Sullivan, T. N., Esposito, L. E., Meyer, A. L., & Valois, R. F. (2005). A latent growth curve analysis of the structure of aggression, drug use, and delinquent behaviors and their interrelations over time in urban and rural adolescents. *Journal of Research on Adolescence, 15,* 179–203.

Farrell, A. D., & White, K. S. (1998). Peer influences and drug use among urban adolescents: Family structure and parent–adolescent relationship as protective factors. *Journal of Consulting and Clinical Psychology, 66,* 248–258.

Farrelly, M. C., Davis, K. C., Haviland, M. L., Healton, C. G., & Messeri, P. (2005). Evidence of a dose-response relationship between "truth" antismoking ads and youth smoking prevalence. *American Journal of Public Health, 95,* 425–431.

Farrington, D. (2009). Conduct disorder, aggression, and delinquency. In R. Lerner & L. Steinberg (Eds.), *Handbook of adolescent psychology* (3rd ed., Vol. 1, pp. 683–722). New York: Wiley.

Farrington, D., Loeber, R., & Stouthamer-Loeber, M. (2003). How can the relationship between race and violence be explained? In D. Hawkins (Ed.), *Violent crimes: Assessing race and ethnic differences* (pp. 213–237). New York: Cambridge University Press.

Fasick, F. (1994). On the "invention" of adolescence. *Journal of Early Adolescence, 14,* 6–23.

Fasula, A. M., & Miller, K. S. (2006). African-American and Hispanic adolescents' intentions to delay first intercourse: Parental communication as a buffer for sexually active peers. *Journal of Adolescent Health, 38,* 193–200.

Fauth, R. C., Leventhal, T., & Brooks-Gunn, J. (2007). Welcome to the neighborhood? Long-term impacts of moving to low-poverty neighborhoods on poor children's and adolescents' outcomes. *Journal of Research on Adolescence, 17,* 249–284.

Fauth, R. C., Roth, J. L., & Brooks-Gunn, J. (2007). Does the neighborhood context alter the link between youth's after-school time activities and developmental outcomes? A multilevel analysis. *Developmental Psychology, 43,* 760–777.

Federal Bureau of Investigation. (2008). *Crime in the United States, 2007.* Washington, DC: Author.

Feinberg, M. E., & Hetherington, E. (2000). Sibling differentiation in adolescence: Implications for behavioral genetic theory. *Child Development, 71,* 1512–1524.

Feinberg, M. E., Howe, G. W., Reiss, D., & Hetherington, E. (2000). Relationship between perceptual differences of parenting and adolescent antisocial behavior and depressive symptoms. *Journal of Family Psychology, 14,* 531–555.

Feinberg, M., McHale, S., Crouter, A., & Cumsille, P. (2003). Sibling differentation: Sibling and parent relationship trajectories in adolescence. *Child Development, 74,* 1261–1274.

Feinberg, M., Neiderhiser, J., Simmens, S., Reiss, D., & Hetherington, E. (2000). Sibling comparison of differential parental treatment in adolescence: Gender, self-esteem, and emotionality as mediators of the parenting-adjustment association. *Child Development, 71,* 1611–1628.

Feiring, C. (1993, March). *Developing concepts of romance from 15 to 18 years.* Paper presented at the biennial meetings of the Society for Research in Child Development, New Orleans.

Feiring, C. (1996). Concepts of romance in 15 year-old adolescents. *Journal of Research on Adolescence, 6,* 181–200.

Feiring, C. (1999). Gender identity and the development of romantic relationships in adolescence. In W. Furman, B. Brown, & C. Feiring (Eds.), *Contemporary perspectives on adolescent romantic relationships* (pp. 211–232). New York: Cambridge University Press.

Feiring, C., Deblinger, E., Hoch-Espada, A., & Haworth, T. (2002). Romantic relationship aggression and attitudes in high school students: The role of gender, grade, and attachment and emotional styles. *Journal of Youth and Adolescence, 31,* 373–385.

Feiring, C., & Lewis, M. (1991). The transition from middle childhood to early adolescence: Sex differences in the social network and perceived self-competence. *Sex Roles, 24,* 489–510.

Feiring, C., & Lewis, M. (1993). Do mothers know their teenagers' friends? Implications for individuation in early adolescence. *Journal of Youth and Adolescence, 22,* 337–354.

Feldman, A. F., & Matjasko, J. L. (2007). Profiles and portfolios of adolescent school-based extracurricular activity participation. *Journal of Adolescence, 30,* 313–332.

Feldman, S., & Fisher, L. (1997). The effect of parents' marital satisfaction on young adults' adaptation: A longitudinal study. *Journal of Research on Adolescence, 7,* 55–80.

Feldman, S., & Gehring, T. (1988). Changing perceptions of family cohesion and power across adolescence. *Child Development, 59,* 1034–1045.

Feldman, S., & Quatman, T. (1988). Factors influencing age expectations for adolescent autonomy: A study of early adolescents and parents. *Journal of Early Adolescence, 8,* 325–343.

Feldman, S., & Rosenthal, D. (2000). The effect of communication characteristics on family members' perceptions of parents as sex educators. *Journal of Research on Adolescence, 10,* 119–150.

Feldman, S., Rosenthal, D., Brown, N., & Canning, R. (1995). Predicting sexual experience in adolescent boys from peer rejection and acceptance during childhood. *Journal of Research on Adolescence, 5,* 387–411.

Feldman, S., & Wentzel, K. (1995). Relations of marital satisfaction to peer outcomes in adolescent boys: A longitudinal study. *Journal of Early Adolescence, 15,* 220–237.

Feldman, S., & Wood, D. (1994). Parents' expectations for preadolescent sons' behavioral autonomy: A longitudinal study of correlates and outcomes. *Journal of Research on Adolescence, 4,* 45–70.

Felner, R., Brand, S., DuBois, D., Adan, A., Mulhall, P., & Evans, E. (1995). Socioeconomic disadvantage, proximal environmental experiences, and socioemotional and academic adjustment in early adolescence: Investigation of a mediated effects model. *Child Development, 66,* 774–792.

Fenzel, L. (2001). Prospective study of changes in global self-worth and strain during the transition to middle school. *Journal of Early Adolescence, 20,* 93–116.

Fergus, S., Zimmerman, M. A., & Caldwell, C. H. (2007). Growth trajectories of sexual risk behavior in adolescence and young adulthood. *American Journal of Public Health, 97,* 1096–1101.

Fergusson, D., & Horwood, L. (2002). Male and female offending trajectories. *Development and Psychopathology, 14,* 159–177.

Fergusson, D., & Lynskey, M. (1996). Alcohol misuse and adolescent sexual behaviors and risk taking. *Pediatrics, 98,* 91–96.

Fergusson, D., Lynskey, M., & Horwood, L. (1996). Factors associated with continuity and changes in disruptive behavior patterns between childhood and adolescence. *Journal of Abnormal Child Psychology, 24,* 533–553.

Fergusson, D., & Woodward, L. (2000). Teenage pregnancy and female educational underachievement: A prospective study of a New Zealand birth cohort. *Journal of Marriage and the Family, 62,* 147–161.

Fichtenberg, C. M., & Glantz, S. A. (2002). Youth access interventions do not affect youth smoking. *Pediatrics, 109,* 1088–1092.

Field, T., Greenwald, P., Morrow, C., Healy, B., Foster, T., Guthertz, M., et al. (1992). Behavior state matching during interactions of preadolescent friends versus acquaintances. *Developmental Psychology, 28,* 242–250.

Fields, J. (2003). *Children's living arrangements and characteristics: March 2002.* Current Population Reports P20-547. Washington, DC: U.S. Census Bureau.

Filardo, E. (1996). Gender patterns in African American and White adolescents' social interactions in same-race, mixed-gender groups. *Journal of Personality and Social Psychology, 71,* 71–82.

Fincham, F. (1994). Understanding the association between marital conflict and child adjustment: Overview. *Journal of Family Psychology, 8,* 123–127.

Fingerson, L. (2005). Do mother's opinions matter in teens' sexual activity? *Journal of Family Influence, 26,* 947–974.

Finken, L., & Jacobs, J. (1996). Consultant choice across decision contexts: Are abortion decisions different? *Journal of Adolescent Research, 11,* 235–260.

Finkenauer, C., Engles, R., & Meeus, W. (2002). Keeping secrets from parents: Advantages and disadvantages of secrecy in adolescence. *Journal of Youth and Adolescence, 31,* 123–136.

Finn, J., Gerber, S. B., & Boyd-Zaharias, J. (2005). Small classes in the early grades, academic achievement, and graduating from high school. *Journal of Educational Psychology, 97,* 214–223.

Fischhoff, B. (2008). Assessing adolescent decision-making competence. *Developmental Review, 28,* 12–28.

Fischhoff, B., & Quadrel, M. (1995). Adolescent alcohol decisions. In G. Boyd, J. Howard, & R. Zucker (Eds.), *Alcohol problems among adolescents: Current directions in prevention research* (pp. 59–84). Hillsdale, NJ: Erlbaum.

Fisher, C., Wallace, S. A., & Fenton, R. E. (2000). Discrimination distress during adolescence. *Journal of Youth and Adolescence, 29,* 679–695.

Fisher, M., Golden, N., Katzman, D., Kriepe, R., Rees, J., Schebendach, J., Sigman, G., Ammerman, S., & Hoberman, H. (1995). Eating disorders in adolescents: A background paper. *Journal of Adolescent Health, 16,* 420–437.

Fisher, T. (1989). An extension of the findings of Moore, Peterson, & Furstenberg [1986] regarding family sexual communication and adolescent sexual behavior. *Journal of Marriage and the Family, 51,* 637–639.

Flammer, A., Alasker, F., & Noack, P. (1999). Time use by adolescents in an international perspective, I: The case of leisure activities. In F. Alasker & A. Flammer (Eds.), *The adolescent experience: European and American adolescents in the 1990s* (pp. 33–60). Hillsdale, NJ: Erlbaum.

Flammer, A., & Schaffner, B. (2003). Adolescent leisure across European nations. *New Directions for Child and Adolescent Development, 99,* 65–78.

Flanagan, C. (1990). Change in family work status: Effects on parent–adolescent decision making. *Child Development, 61,* 163–177.

Flanagan, C. (2004). Volunteerism, leadership, political socialization, and civic engagement. In R. Lerner & L. Steinberg (Eds.), *Handbook of adolescent psychology.* New York: Wiley.

Flanagan, C., & Galay, L. (1995). Reframing the meaning of "political" in research with adolescents. *Perspectives on Political Science, 24,* 34–41.

Flanagan, C., & Tucker, C. (1999). Adolescents' explanations for political issues: Concordance with their views of self and society. *Developmental Psychology, 35,* 1198–1209.

Flannery, D., Torquati, J., & Lindemeier, L. (1994). The method and meaning of emotional expression and experience during adolescence. *Journal of Adolescent Research, 9,* 8–27.

Flannery, D., Vazsonyi, A., & Rowe, D. (1996). Caucasian and Hispanic early adolescent substance use: Parenting, personality, and school adjustment. *Journal of Early Adolescence, 16,* 71–89.

Flannery, D., Weseter, K., & Singer, M. (2004). Impact of exposure to violence in school on child and adolescent mental health and behavior. *Journal of Community Psychology, 32,* 559–573.

Flavell, J., Green, F., & Flavell, E. (1998). The mind has a mind of its own: Developing knowledge about mental uncontrollability. *Cognitive Development, 13,* 127–138.

Fletcher, A., Bonell, C., & Hargreaves, J. (2008). School effects on young people's drug use: A systematic review of intervention and observational studies. *Journal of Adolescent Health, 42,* 209–220.

Fletcher, A., Darling, N., Steinberg, L., & Dornbusch, S. (1995). The company they keep: Relation of adolescents' adjustment and behavior to their friends' perceptions of authoritative parenting in the social network. *Developmental Psychology, 31,* 300–310.

Fletcher, A., Elder, G., Jr., & Mekos, D. (2000). Parental influences on adolescent involvement in community activities. *Journal of Research on Adolescence, 10,* 29–48.

Fletcher, A., Steinberg, L., & Sellers, E. (1999). Adolescents' well-being as a function of perceived inter-parental consistency. *Journal of Marriage and the Family, 61,* 599–610.

Fletcher, A., Steinberg, L., & Williams-Wheeler, M. (2004). Parental influences on adolescent problem-behavior: Revisiting Stattin and Kerr. *Child Development, 75,* 781–796.

Flieller, A. (1999). Comparison of the development of formal thought in adolescent cohorts aged 10 to 15 years (1967–1996 and 1972–1993). *Developmental Psychology, 35,* 1048–1058.

Flisher, A. J., Kramer, R. A., Hoven, C. W., King, R. A., Bird, H. R., Davies, M., et al. (2000). Risk behavior in a community sample of children and adolescents. *Journal of the American Academy of Child and Adolescent Psychiatry, 39,* 881–887.

Flook, L., & Fuligni, A. J. (2008). Family and school spillover in adolescents' daily lives. *Child Development, 79,* 776–787.

Flory, K., Lynam, D., & Milich, R. (2004). Early adolescent through young adult alcohol and marijuana use trajectories: Early predictors, young adult outcomes, and predictive utility. *Development and Psychopathology, 16,* 193–213.

Flynn, B., Worden, J., Secker-Walker, R., Pirie, P., Badger, G., Carpenter, J., et al. (1994). Mass media and school interventions for cigarette smoking prevention: Effects 2 years after completion. *American Journal of Public Health, 84,* 1148–1150.

Fontaine, R., Yang, C., Dodge, K., Bates, J., & Pettit, G. (2008). Testing an individual systems model of response evaluation and decision (RED) and antisocial behavior across adolescence. *Child Development, 79,* 462–475.

Forbes, E., & Dahl, R. (2005). Neural systems of positive affect: Relevance to understanding child and adolescent depression? *Development and Psychopathology, 17,* 827–850.

Ford, C., & Beach, F. (1951). *Patterns of sexual behavior.* New York: Harper & Row.

Ford, D., & Harris, J. I. (1996). Perceptions and attitudes of Black students toward school, achievement, and other educational variables. *Child Development, 67,* 1141–1152.

Ford, J. A. (2009). Nonmedical prescription drug use among adolescents: The influence of bonds to family and school. *Youth and Society, 40,* 336–352.

Fordham, C., & Ogbu, J. (1986). Black students' school success: Coping with the burden of "acting White." *Urban Review, 18,* 176–206.

Forehand, R., Armistead, L., & David, C. (1997). Is adolescent adjustment following parental divorce a function of predivorce adjustment? *Journal of Abnormal Child Psychology, 25,* 157–164.

Forehand, R., Biggar, H., & Kotchick, B. (1998). Cumulative risk across family stressors: Short- and long-term effects for adolescents. *Journal of Abnormal Child Psychology, 26,* 119–128.

Forehand, R., Neighbors, B., Devine, D., & Armistead, L. (1994). Interparental conflict and parental divorce: The individual, relative, and interactive effects on adolescents across four years. *Family Relations, 43,* 387–393.

Forehand, R., Thomas, A. M., Wierson, M., Brody, G., & Fauber, R. (1990). Role of maternal functioning and parenting skills in adolescent functioning following parental divorce. *Journal of Abnormal Psychology, 99,* 278–283.

Forehand, R., Wierson, M., Thomas, A., Fauber, R., Armistead, L., Kemptom, T., & Long, N. (1991). A short-term longitudinal examination of young adolescent functioning following divorce: The role of family factors. *Journal of Abnormal Child Psychology, 19,* 97–111.

Forgatch, M., DeGarmo, D., & Knutson, N. (1994, February). *Transitions within transitions: The impact of adolescence and family structure on boys' antisocial behavior.* Paper presented at the biennial meetings of the Society for Research on Adolescence, San Diego.

Forgatch, M., Patterson, G. R., Degarmo, D. S., & Beldavs, Z. G. (2009). Testing the Oregon delinquency model with 9-year follow-up of the Oregon Divorce Study. *Development and Psychopathology, 21,* 637–660.

Formoso, D., Ruiz, S., & Gonzales, N. (1997, March). *Parent–adolescent conflict: Resolution strategies reported with African-American, Mexican-American, and Anglo-American families.* Paper presented at the Society for Research in Child Development, Washington, DC.

Fortner, M., Crouter, A., & McHale, S. (2004). Is parents' work involvement responsive to the quality of relationships with adolescent offspring? *Journal of Family Psychology, 19,* 530–538.

Foshee, V., Bauman, K., Greene, W., Koch, G., Linder, G., & MacDougall, J. (2000). The safe dates program: 1-year follow-up results. *American Journal of Public Health, 90,* 1619–1622.

Foss, R. D., Feaganes, J. R., & Rodgman, E. A. (2001). Initial effects of graduated driver licensing on 16-year-old driver crashes in North Carolina. *Journal of the American Medical Association, 286,* 1588–1592.

Foster, E. (1995). Why teens do not benefit from work experience programs: Evidence from brother comparisons. *Journal of Policy Analysis and Management, 14,* 393–414.

Foster, L., & Ritter, J. (1995, March). *Independence from parents as a predictor of happiness and life satisfaction.* Paper presented at the Society for Research in Child Development, Indianapolis.

Fowler, P., Ahmed, S., Tompsett, C., Jozefowicz-Simbeni, D., & Toro, P. (2008). Community violence and externalizing problems: Moderating effects of race and religiosity in emerging adulthood. *Journal of Community Psychology, 36,* 835–850.

Frabutt, J. M., Walker, A. M., & MacKinnon-Lewis, C. (2002). Racial socialization messages and the quality of mother/child interactions in African American families. *Journal of Early Adolescence, 22,* 200–217.

Frank, K. A., Muller, C., Schiller, K. S., Riegle-Crumb, C., Mueller, A. S., Crosnoe, R., et al. (2008). The social dynamics of mathematics coursetaking in high school. *American Journal of Sociology, 113,* 1645–1696.

Frank, S., & Jackson, S. (1996). Family experiences as moderators of the relationship between eating symptoms and personality disturbance. *Journal of Youth and Adolescence, 25,* 55–72.

Frank, S., Pirsch, L., & Wright, V. (1990). Late adolescents' perceptions of their relationships with their parents: Relationships among deidealization, autonomy, relatedness, and insecurity and implications for adolescent adjustment and ego identity status. *Journal of Youth and Adolescence, 19,* 571–588.

Frankenberger, K. D. (2000). Adolescent egocentrism: A comparison among adolescents and adults. *Journal of Adolescence, 23,* 343–354.

Franklin, C., Grant, D., Corcoran, J., Miller, P., & Bultman, L. (1997). Effectiveness of prevention programs for adolescent pregnancy: A meta-analysis. *Journal of Marriage and the Family, 59,* 551–567.

Franzoi, S., Davis, M., & Vasquez-Suson, K. (1994). Two social worlds: Social correlates and stability of adolescent status groups. *Journal of Personality and Social Psychology, 67,* 462–473.

Fredricks, J. A., & Eccles, J. (2002). Children's competence and value beliefs from childhood through adolescence: Growth trajectories in two male-sex-typed domains. *Developmental Psychology, 38,* 519–533.

Fredricks, J. A., & Eccles, J. (2006). Is extracurricular participation associated with beneficial outcomes? concurrent and longitudinal relations. *Developmental Psychology, 42,* 698–713.

Fredricks, J. A., & Eccles, J. (2008). Participation in extracurricular activities in the middle school years: Are there developmental benefits for African American and European American youth? *Journal of Youth and Adolescence, 37,* 1029–1043.

Fredriksen, K., Rhodes, J., Reddy, R., & Way, N. (2004). Sleepless in Chicago: Tracking the effects of adolescent sleep loss during the middle school years. *Child Development, 75,* 84–95.

Freedle, R. O. (2003). Correcting the SAT's ethnic and social-class bias: A method for reestimating SAT scores. *Harvard Educational Review, 73,* 1–43.

Freedner, N., Freed, L. H., Yang, Y., & Austin, S. (2002). Dating violence among gay, lesbian, and bisexual adolescents: Results from a community survey. *Journal of Adolescent Health, 31,* 469–474.

Freeman, H., & Brown, B. (2001). Primary attachment to parents and peers during adolescence: Differences by attachment style. *Journal of Youth and Adolescence, 30,* 653–674.

French, D., & Conrad, J. (2001). School dropout as predicted by peer rejection and antisocial behavior. *Journal of Research on Adolescence, 11,* 225–244.

French, D., Conrad, J., & Turner, T. (1995). Adjustment of antisocial and nonantisocial rejected adolescents. *Development and Psychopathology, 7,* 857–874.

French, D., & Dishion, T. (2003). Predictors of early initiation of sexual intercourse among high-risk adolescents. *Journal of Early Adolescence, 23,* 295–315.

French, D., Jansen, E., & Pidada, S. (2002). United States and Indonesian children's and adolescents' reports of relational aggression by disliked peers. *Child Development, 73,* 1143–1150.

French, D., Rianasari, M., Pidada, S., Nelwan, P., & Buhrmester, D. (2001). Social support of Indonesian and U.S. children and adolescents by family members and friends. *Merrill-Palmer Quarterly, 47,* 377–394.

French, D. C., Eisenberg, N., Vaughan, J., Purwono, U., & Suryanti, T. A. (2008). Religious involvement and the social competence and adjustment of Indonesian Muslim adolescents. *Developmental Psychology, 44,* 597–611.

French, S., Story, M., Downes, B., Resnick, M., & Blum, R. (1995). Frequent dieting among adolescents: Psychosocial and health behavior correlates. *American Journal of Public Health, 85,* 695–701.

French, S. E., Seidman, E., Allen, L., & Aber, J. L. (2006). The development of ethnic identity during adolescence. *Developmental Psychology, 42,* 1–10.

Freud, A. (1958). Adolescence. *Psychoanalytic Study of the Child, 13,* 255–278.

Freud, S. (1938). *An outline of psychoanalysis.* London: Hogarth Press.

Frick, P., Kotov, R., Loney, B., & Vasey, M. (2005). The latent structure of psychopathy in youth: A taxometric investigation. *Journal of Abnormal Child Psychology, 33.*

Fried, C. S., & Reppucci, N. (2001). Criminal decision-making: The development of adolescent judgment, criminal responsibility, and culpability. *Law and Human Behavior, 25,* 45–61.

Fried, M., & Fried, M. (1980). *Transitions: Four rituals in eight cultures.* New York: Norton.

Friedenberg, E. (1959). *The vanishing adolescent.* Boston: Beacon Press.

Friedenberg, E. (1967). *Coming of age in America.* New York: Vintage Books.

Friedlander, L. J., Connolly, J. A., Pepler, D. J., & Craig, W. M. (2007). Biological, familial, and peer influences on dating in early adolescence. *Archives of Sexual Behavior, 36,* 821–830.

Frijns, T., Finkenauer, C., Vermulst, A. A., & Engels, R. (2005). Keeping secrets from parents: Longitudinal associations of secrecy in adolescence. *Journal of Youth and Adolescence, 34,* 137–148.

Frisch, R. (1983). Fatness, puberty, and fertility: The effects of nutrition and physical training on menarche and ovulation. In J. Brooks-Gunn & A. Petersen (Eds.), *Girls at puberty.* New York: Plenum.

Frisco, M. L. (2005). Parental involvement and young women's contraceptive use. *Journal of Marriage and the Family, 67,* 110.

Frisco, M. L. (2008). Adolescents' sexual behavior and academic attainment. *Sociology of Education, 81,* 284–311.

Frisco, M. L., Muller, C., & Frank, K. (2007). Parents' union dissolution and adolescents' school performance: Comparing methodological approaches. *Journal of Marriage and Family, 69,* 721–741.

Frome, P., & Eccles, J. (1996, March). *Gender-role identity and self-esteem.* Paper presented at the biennial meetings of the Society for Research on Adolescence, Boston.

Fromme, K., Corbin, W. R., & Kruse, M. I. (2008). Behavioral risks during the transition from high school to college. *Developmental Psychology, 44,* 1497–1504.

Fuhrman, T., & Holmbeck, G. (1995). A contextual-moderator analysis of emotional autonomy and adjustment in adolescence. *Child Development, 66,* 793–811.

Fuligni, A. (1994, February). *Academic achievement and motivation among Asian-American and European-American early adolescents.* Paper presented at the biennial meetings of the Society for Research on Adolescence, San Diego.

Fuligni, A. (1998). Authority, autonomy, and parent–adolescent conflict and cohesion: A study of adolescents from Mexican, Chinese, Filipino, and European backgrounds. *Developmental Psychology, 34,* 782–792.

Fuligni, A., & Eccles, J. (1993). Perceived parent–child relationships and early adolescents' orientation toward peers. *Developmental Psychology, 29,* 622–632.

Fuligni, A., Eccles, J., &, Barber, B. (1995). The long-term effects of seventh grade ability grouping in mathematics. *Journal of Early Adolescence, 15,* 58–89.

Fuligni, A., Eccles, J., Barber, B., & Clements, P. (2001). Early adolescent peer orientation and adjustment during high school. *Developmental Psychology, 37,* 28–36.

Fuligni, A., & Hardway, C. (2006). Daily variation in adolescents' sleep, activities, and psychological well-being. *Journal of Research on Adolescence, 16,* 353–378.

Fuligni, A., Hughes, D., & Way, N. (2009). Ethnicity and immigration. In R. Lerner & L. Steinberg (Eds.), *Handbook of adolescent psychology* (3rd ed., Vol. 2, pp. 527–569). New York: Wiley.

Fuligni, A., Kiang, L., Witkow, M., & Baldelomar, O. (2008). Stability and change in ethnic labeling among adolescents from Asian and Latin American immigrant families. *Child Development, 79,* 944–956.

Fuligni, A., & Pedersen, S. (2002). Family obligation and the transition to young adulthood. *Developmental Psychology, 38,* 856–868.

Fuligni, A., & Stevenson, H. (1995). Time-use and mathematics achievement among American, Chinese, and Japanese high school students. *Child Development, 66,* 830–842.

Fuligni, A., Tseng, V., & Lam, M. (1999). Attitudes toward family obligations among American adolescents from Asian, Latin American, and European backgrounds. *Child Development, 70,* 1030–1044.

Fuligni, A., & Witkow, M. (2004). The postsecondary educational progress of youth from immigrant families. *Journal of Research on Adolescence, 14,* 159–183.

Fuligni, A., Witkow, M., & Garcia, C. (2005). Ethnic identity and the academic adjustment of adolescents from Mexican, Chinese and European backgrounds. *Developmental Psychology, 41,* 799–811.

Fuligni, A., Yip, T., & Tseng, V. (2002). The impact of family obligation on the daily activities and psychological well-being of Chinese American adolescents. *Child Development, 73,* 302–314.

Fuligni, A., & Zhang, W. (2004). Attitudes toward family obligation among adolescents in contemporary urban and rural China. *Child Development, 75,* 180–192.

Fulkerson, J. A., & French, S. A. (2003). Cigarette smoking for weight loss or control among adolescents: Gender and racial/ethnic differences. *Journal of Adolescent Health, 32,* 306–313.

Fulton, A. (1997). Identity status, religious orientation, and prejudice. *Journal of Youth and Adolescence, 26,* 1–11.

Funk, J., Flores, G., Buchman, D., & Germann, J. (1999). Rating electronic games: Violence is in the eye of the beholder. *Youth and Society, 30,* 283–312.

Furbey, M., & Beyth-Marom, R. (1992). Risktaking in adolescence: A decision-making perspective. *Developmental Review, 12,* 1–44.

Furman, W., & Buhrmester, D. (1985). Children's perceptions of the personal relationships in their social networks. *Developmental Psychology, 21,* 1016–1024.

Furman, W., & Shomaker, L. B. (2008). Patterns of interaction in adolescent romantic relationships: Distinct features and links to other close relationships. *Journal of Adolescence, 31,* 771–788.

Furman, W., Brown, B., & Feiring, C. (Eds.). (1999). *Contemporary perspectives on adolescent romantic relationships.* New York: Cambridge University Press.

Furman, W., & Simon, V. (1999). Cognitive representations of adolescent romantic relationships. In W. Furman, B. Brown, & C. Feiring (Eds.), *Contemporary perspectives on adolescent romantic relationships* (pp. 75–98). New York: Cambridge University Press.

Furman, W., & Simon, V. A. (2006). Actor and partner effects of adolescents' romantic working models and styles on interactions with romantic partners. *Child Development, 77,* 588–604.

Furman, W., Simon, V. A., Shaffer, L., & Bouchey, H. A. (2002). Adolescents' working models and styles for relationships with parents, friends, and romantic partners. *Child Development, 73,* 241–255.

Furman, W., & Wehner, E. (1994). Romantic views: Toward a theory of adolescent romantic relationships. In R. Montemayor (Ed.), *Advances in adolescent development: Vol. 3. Relationships in adolescence* (pp. 168–195). Newbury Park, CA: Sage.

Furstenberg, F., Jr. (1990). Coming of age in a changing family system. In S. Feldman & G. Elliott (Eds.), *At the threshold: The developing adolescent* (pp. 147–170). Cambridge, MA: Harvard University Press.

Furstenberg, F., Jr. (1996). *Family management of adolescent success in inner-city Philadelphia.* Paper presented at the biennial meetings of the Society for Research on Adolescence, Boston.

Furstenberg, F., Jr. (2000). The sociology of adolescence and youth in the 1990s: A critical commentary. *Journal of Marriage and Family, 62,* 896–910.

Furstenberg, F., Jr. (2006, March). *Diverging development: The not-so-invisible hand of social class in the United States.* Invited address, Society for Research on Adolescence, San Francisco.

Furstenberg, F., Jr., Brooks-Gunn, J., & Chase-Lansdale, P. L. (1989). Teenaged pregnancy and childbearing. *American Psychologist, 44,* 313–320.

Furstenberg, F., Jr., Cook, T., Eccles, J., Elder, G., Jr., & Sameroff, A. (1999). *Managing to make it: Urban families and adolescent success.* Chicago: University of Chicago Press.

Furstenberg, F., Jr., et al. (1987). Race differences in the timing of adolescent intercourse. *American Sociological Review, 52,* 511–518.

Furstenberg, F., Jr., Morgan, S. P., & Allison, P. (1987). Paternal participation and children's well-being after marital dissolution. *American Sociological Review, 52,* 695–701.

Fussell, M., & Greene, M. (2002). Demographic trends affecting youth around the world. In B. Brown, R. Larson, & T. Saraswathi (Eds.), *The world's youth: Adolescence in eight regions of the globe.* New York: Cambridge University Press.

Gaddis, A., & Brooks-Gunn, J. (1985). The male experience of pubertal change. *Journal of Youth and Adolescence, 14,* 61–70.

Gage, J. C., Overpeck, M. D., Nansel, T. R., & Kogan, M. D. (2005). Peer activity in the evenings and participation in aggressive and problem behaviors. *Journal of Adolescent Health, 37,* 517.e7–517.e14.

Galambos, N., Barker, E., & Almeida, D. (2003). Parents do matter: Trajectories of change in externalizing and internalizing problems in adolescence. *Child Development, 74,* 578–594.

Galambos, N., Barker, E., & Krahn, H. (2006). Depression, self-esteem, and anger in emerging adulthood: Seven-year trajectories. *Developmental Psychology, 42,* 350–365.

Galambos, N., Barker, E., & Tilton-Weaver, L. (2003). Who gets caught at maturity gap? A study of pseudomature, immature, and mature adolescents. *International Journal of Behavioral Development, 27,* 253–263.

Galambos, N., Berenbaum, S., & McHale, S. (2009). Gender development in adolescence. In R. Lerner & L. Steinberg (Eds.), *Handbook of adolescent psychology* (3rd ed., Vol. 1, pp. 305–357). New York: Wiley.

Galambos, N., Kolaric, G., & Maggs, J. (1994, February). *Adolescents' subjective age: An indicator of phenomenological maturity.* Paper presented at the biennial meetings of the Society for Research on Adolescence, San Diego.

Galambos, N., Kolaric, G., Sears, H., & Maggs, J. (1999). Adolescents' subjective age: An indicator of perceived maturity. *Journal of Research on Adolescence, 9,* 309–337.

Galambos, N., & Maggs, J. (1991). Out-of-school care of young adolescents and self-reported behavior. *Developmental Psychology, 27,* 644–655.

Galambos, N., & Silbereisen, R. (1987). Income change, parental life outlook, and adolescent expectations for job success. *Journal of Marriage and the Family, 49,* 141–149.

Galambos, N., Turner, P., & Tilton-Weaver, L. (2005). Chronological and subjective age in emerging adulthood: The crossover effect. *Journal of Adolescent Research, 20,* 538–556.

Galliher, R. V., Rostosky, S. S., & Hughes, H. K. (2004). School belonging, self-esteem, and depressive symptoms in adolescents: An examination of sex, sexual attraction status, and urbanicity. *Journal of Youth and Adolescence, 33,* 235–245.

Gallup, G., & Bezilla, R. (1992). *The religious life of young Americans.* Princeton, NJ: Gallup Institute.

Galotti, K., Komatsu, L., & Voelz, S. (1997). Children's differential performance on deductive and inductive syllogisms. *Developmental Psychology, 33,* 70–78.

Galvan, A., Hare, T. A., Parra, C. E., Penn, J., Voss, K., Glover, G., et al. (2006). Earlier development of the accumbens relative to orbitofrontal cortex might underlie risktaking behavior in adolescents. Journal of Neuroscience, 26, 6885–6892.

Galvan, A., Hare, T., Voss, H., Glover, G., & Casey, B. J. (2007). Risk-taking and the adolescent brain: Who is at risk? *Developmental Science, 10,* f8–f14.

Gamoran, A. (1992). The variable effects of high school tracking. *American Sociological Review, 57,* 812–828.

Gamoran, A. (1993). Alternative uses of ability grouping in secondary schools: Can we bring high-quality instruction to low-ability classes? *American Journal of Education, 102,* 1–22.

Gamoran, A. (1996). Curriculum standardization and equality of opportunity in Scottish secondary education: 1984–90. *Sociology of Education, 69,* 1–21.

Gano-Overway, L., Newton, M., Magyar, T. M., Fry, M. D., Kim, M., & Guivernau, M. R. (2009). Influence of caring youth sport contexts on efficacy-related beliefs and social behaviors. *Developmental Psychology, 45,* 329–340.

Gans, J. (1990). *America's adolescents: How healthy are they?* Chicago: American Medical Association.

Garbarino, J., Burston, N., Raber, S., Russell, R., & Crouter, A. (1978). The social maps of children approaching adolescence: Studying the ecology of youth development. *Journal of Youth and Adolescence, 7,* 417–428.

Garber, J., Robinson, N., & Valentiner, D. (1997). The relation between parenting and adolescent depression: Self-worth as a mediator. *Journal of Adolescent Research, 12,* 12–33.

Garber, J., Weiss, B., & Shanley, N. (1993). Cognitions, depressive symptoms, and development in adolescents. *Journal of Abnormal Psychology, 102,* 47–57.

Garcia Coll, C., Lamberty, G., Jenkins, R., McAdoo, H., Crnic, K., Wasik, B., et al. (1996). An integrative model for the study of developmental competencies in minority children. *Child Development, 67,* 1891–1914.

Garcia-Reid, P. (2007). Examining social capital as a mechanism for improving school engagement among low income Hispanic girls. *Youth and Society, 39,* 164–181.

Gardner, H. (1983). *Frames of mind.* New York: Basic Books.

Gardner, M., & Brooks-Gunn, J. (2009). Adolescents' exposure to community violence: Are neighborhood youth organizations protective? *Journal of Community Psychology, 37,* 505–525.

Gardner, M., Roth, J., & Brooks-Gunn, J. (2008). Adolescents' participation in organized activities and developmental success 2 and 8 years after high school: Do sponsorship, duration, and intensity matter? *Developmental Psychology, 44,* 814–830.

Gardner, M., & Steinberg, L. (2005). Peer influence on risk taking, risk preference, and risky decision making in adolescence and adulthood: An experimental study. *Developmental Psychology, 41,* 625–635.

Gardner, T. W., Dishion, T. J., & Connell, A. M. (2008). Adolescent self-regulation as re-silience: Resistance to antisocial behavior within the deviant peer context. *Journal of Abnormal Child Psychology, 36,* 273–284.

Garg, R., Melanson, S., & Levin, E. (2007). Educational aspirations of male and female adolescents from single-parent and two biological parent families: A comparison of influential factors. *Journal of Youth and Adolescence, 36,* 1010–1023.

Gargiulo, J., Attie, I., Brooks-Gunn, J., & Warren, M. (1987). Girls' dating behavior as a function of social context and maturation. *Developmental Psychology, 23,* 730–737.

Garnefski, N. (2000). Age differences in depressive symptoms, antisocial behavior, and negative perceptions of family, school, and peers among adolescents. *Journal of the American Academy of Child and Adolescent Psychiatry, 39,* 1175–1181.

Garnefski, N., & Diekstra, R. (1997). "Comorbidity" of behavioral, emotional, and cognitive problems in adolescence. *Journal of Youth and Adolescence, 26,* 321–338.

Garner, R., Bootcheck, J., Lorr, M., & Rauch, K. (2006). The adolescent society revisited: Cultures, crowds, climates, and status structures in seven secondary schools. *Journal of Youth and Adolescence, 35,* 1023–1035.

Garnier, H., & Stein, J. (2002). An 18-year model of family and peer effects on adolescent drug use and delinquency. *Journal of Youth and Adolescence, 31,* 45–56.

Garnier, H., Stein, J., & Jacobs, J. (1997). The process of dropping out of high school: A 19-year perspective. *American Educational Research Journal, 34,* 395–419.

Gathercole, S. E., Pickering, S. J., Ambridge, B., & Wearing, H. (2004). The structure of working memory from 4 to 15 years of age. *Developmental Psychology, 40,* 177–190.

Gau, S. S., Soong, W., & Merikangas, K. R. (2004). Correlates of sleep-wake patterns among children and young adolescents in Taiwan. *Sleep, 27,* 512–519.

Gaudreau, P., Amiot, C. E., & Vallerand, R. J. (2009). Trajectories of affective states in adolescent hockey players: Turning point and motivational antecedents. *Developmental Psychology, 45,* 307–319.

Gauze, C., Bukowski, W., Aquan-Assee, J., & Sippola, L. (1996). Interactions between family environment and friendship and associations with self-perceived well-being during early adolescence. *Child Development, 67,* 2201–2216.

Gavin, L., & Furman, W. (1996). Adolescent girls' relationships with mothers and best friends. *Child Development, 67,* 375–386.

Gayle, H., Keeling, R., Garcia-Tunon, M., Kilbourne, B., Narkunas, J., Ingram, F., Rogers, M., & Curran, J. (1990). Prevalence of the human immunodeficiency virus among university students. *New England Journal of Medicine, 323,* 1538–1541.

Gaylord-Harden, N., Ragsdale, B. L., Mandara, J., Richards, M. H., & Petersen, A. C. (2007). Perceived support and internalizing symptoms in African American adolescents: Self-esteem and ethnic identity as mediators. *Journal of Youth and Adolescence, 36,* 77–88.

Ge, X., Best, K., Conger, R., & Simons, R. (1996). Parenting behaviors and the occurrence and co-occurrence of adolescent depressive symptoms and conduct problems. *Developmental Psychology, 32,* 717–731.

Ge, X., Brody, G., Conger, R., Simons, R., & Murry, V. (2002). Contextual amplification of pubertal transition effects on deviant peer affiliation and externalizing behavior among African American children. *Developmental Psychology, 38,* 42–54.

Ge, X., & Conger, R. (1995, March). *Parents' depressive symptoms, hostile behaviors, and adolescent depressive symptoms.* Paper presented at the Society for Research in Child Development, Indianapolis.

Ge, X., Conger, R., & Elder, G. H., Jr. (2001). The relation between puberty and psychological distress in adolescent boys. *Journal of Research on Adolescence, 11,* 49–70.

Ge, X., Conger, R., Lorenz, F., Shanahan, M., & Elder, G., Jr. (1995). Mutual influences in parent and adolescent psychological distress. *Developmental Psychology, 31,* 406–419.

Ge, X., Kim, I. J., Brody, G., Conger, R., Simons, R., Gibbons, F., & Cutrona, C. (2003). It's about timing and change: Pubertal transition effects on symptoms of major depression among African American youths. *Developmental Psychology, 39,* 430–439.

Ge, X., Natsuaki, M., & Conger, R. (2006). Trajectories of depressive symptoms and stressful life events among male and female adolescents in divorced and nondivorced families. *Development and Psychopathology, 18,* 253–273.

Ge, X., Natsuaki, M., Neiderhiser, J., & Reiss, D. (2007). Genetic and environmental influences on pubertal timing: Results from two national sibling studies. *Journal of Research on Adolescence, 17,* 767–788.

Gecas, V., & Seff, M. (1990). Families and adolescents: A review of the 1980s. *Journal of Marriage and the Family, 52,* 941–958.

Gennetian, L. A., Duncan, G., Knox, V., Vargas, W., Clark-Kauffman, E., & London, A. S. (2004). How welfare policies affect adolescents' school outcomes: A synthesis of evidence from experimental studies. *Journal of Research on Adolescence, 14,* 399–423.

Gentile, D. A. (2009). Pathological video game use among youth 8 to 18: A national study. *Psychological Science, 20,* 594–602.

Gentile, D. A., Lynch, P. J., Linder, J. R., & Walsh, D. A. (2004). The effects of violent video game habits on adolescent hostility, aggressive behaviors, and school performance. *Journal of Adolescence, 27,* 5–22.

Gentry, M., Gable, R. K., & Rizza, M. G. (2002). Students' perceptions of classroom activities: Are there grade-level and gender differences? *Journal of Educational Psychology, 94,* 539–544.

Georgiades, K., Boyle, M. H., Duku, E., & Racine, Y. (2006). Tobacco use among immigrant and nonimmigrant adolescents: Individual and family level influences. *Journal of Adolescent Health, 38,* 443.e1–443.e7.

Gerard, J. M., & Buehler, C. (2004). Cumulative environmental risk and youth maladjustment: The role of youth attributes. *Child Development, 75,* 1832–1849.

Gerbner, G., Gross, L., Morgan, M., & Signorelli, N. (1994). Growing up with television: The cultivation perspective. In J. Bryant & D. Zillman (Eds.), *Media effects: Advances in theory and research* (pp. 17–41). Hillsdale, NJ: Erlbaum.

Gerhardt, C., Compas, B., Connor, J., & Achenbach, T. (1999). Association of a mixed anxiety-depression syndrome and symptoms of major depressive disorder during adolescence. *Journal of Youth and Adolescence, 28,* 305–323.

Gerrard, M., Gibbons, F., & Bushman, B. (1996). Relation between perceived vulnerability to HIV and precautionary sexual behavior. *Psychological Bulletin, 119,* 390–409.

Gest, S. (1997). Behavioral inhibition: Stability and associations with adaptation from childhood to early adulthood. *Journal of Personality and Social Psychology, 72,* 467–475.

Gestsdóttir, S., & Lerner, R. M. (2007). Intentional self-regulation and positive youth development in early adolescence: Findings from the 4-H study of positive youth development. *Developmental Psychology, 43,* 508–521.

Gfroerer, J. C., & Tan, L. L. (2003). Substance use among foreign-born youths in the United States: Does the length of residence matter? *American Journal of Public Health, 93,* 1892–1895.

Gibbons, F., Benbow, C., & Gerrard, M. (1994). From top dog to bottom half: Social comparison strategies in response to poor performance. *Journal of Personality and Social Psychology, 67,* 638–652.

Gibbs, J., Basinger, K. S., Grime, R., & Snarney, J. (2007). Moral judgment development across cultures: Revisiting Kohlberg's universality claims. *Developmental Review, 27,* 443–500.

Giedd, J. N. (2008). The teen brain: Insights from neuroimaging. *Journal of Adolescent Health, 42,* 335–343.

Gil, A., Vega, W., & Dimas, J. (1994). Acculturative stress and personal adjustment among Hispanic adolescent boys. *Journal of Community Psychology, 22,* 43–54.

Gilliam, F., & Bales, S. (2001). Strategic frame analysis: Reframing America's youth. *SRCD Social Policy Report, 15.*

Gillmore, M., Archibald, M. E., Morrison, D. M., Wilsdon, A., Wells, E. A., Hoppe, M. J., et al.

(2002). Teen sexual behavior: Applicability of the theory of reasoned action. *Journal of Marriage and the Family, 64,* 885–897.

Gillmore, M., Hawkins, J., Catalano, R., Jr., Day, L., Moore, M., & Abbott, R. (1991). Structure of problem behaviors in preadolescence. *Journal of Consulting and Clinical Psychology, 59,* 499–506.

Gillmore, M., Lewis, S., Lohr, M., Spencer, M., & White, R. (1997). Repeat pregnancies among adolescent mothers. *Journal of Marriage and the Family, 59,* 536–550.

Gillmore, M., Morrison, D., Lowery, C., & Baker, S. (1994). Beliefs about condoms and their association with intentions to use condoms among youths in detention. *Journal of Adolescent Health, 15,* 228–237.

Gillock, K., & Reyes, O. (1996). High school transition-related changes in urban minority students' academic performance and perceptions of self and school environment. *Journal of Community Psychology, 24,* 245–261.

Gillock, K., & Reyes, O. (1999). Stress, support, and academic performance of urban, low-income, Mexican-American adolescents. *Journal of Youth and Adolescence, 28,* 259–282.

Gilman, S. E., Rende, R., Boergers, J., Abrams, D. B., Buka, S. L., Clark, M. A., et al. (2009). Parental smoking and adolescent smoking initiation: An intergeneration perspective on tobacco control. *Pediatrics, 123,* 274–281.

Ginsburg, G., & Bronstein, P. (1993). Family factors related to children's intrinsic/extrinsic motivational orientation and academic performance. *Child Development, 64,* 1461–1474.

Giordano, P. C., Longmore, M. A., & Manning, W. D. (2006). Gender and the meanings of adolescent romantic relationships: A focus on boys. *American Sociological Review, 71,* 260–287.

Gittler, J., Quigley-Rick, M., & Saks, M. (1990). *Adolescent health care decision making: The law and public policy.* Washington, DC: Carnegie Council on Adolescent Development.

Gjerde, P. (1995, March). A typological analysis of girls' personality: A longitudinal study of developmental pathways. Paper presented at the Society for Research in Child Development, Indianapolis.

Glaberson, W. (2007, June 7). A legal debate in Guantánamo on boy fighters. *The New York Times,* p. A1.

Glasgow, K., Dornbusch, S., Ritter, P., Troyer, L., & Steinberg, L. (1997). Parenting styles, dysfunctional attributions, and adolescent outcomes in diverse groups. *Child Development, 67,* 507–529.

Glei, D. (1999). Measuring contraceptive use patterns among teenage and adult women. *Family Planning Perspectives, 31,* 73–80.

Goede, I., Branje, S., & Meeus, W. (2009). Developmental changes in adolescents' perceptions of relationships with their parents. *Journal of Youth and Adolescence, 38,* 75–88.

Goldsmith, P. A. (2004). Schools' racial mix, students' optimism, and the Black-White and Latino-White achievement gaps. *Sociology of Education, 77,* 121–147.

Goldstein, B. (1976). *Introduction to human sexuality.* Belmont, CA: Star.

Goldstein, S., Davis-Kean, P., & Eccles, J. (2005). Parents, peers, and problem behavior: A longitudinal investigation of the impact of relationship perceptions and characteristics on the development of adolescent problem behavior. *Developmental Psychology, 41,* 401–413.

Goldston, D., Molock, S., Whitbeck, L., Murakami, J., Zayas, L., & Hall, G. (2008). Cultural considerations in adolescent suicide prevention and psychosocial treatment. *American Psychologist, 63,* 14–31.

Goleman, D. (1995). *Emotional intelligence.* New York: Bantam Books.

Golombok, S., & Tasker, F. (1996). Do parents influence the sexual orientation of their children? Findings from a longitudinal study of lesbian families. *Developmental Psychology, 32,* 3–11.

Golub, A., & Johnson, B. D. (2001). Variation in youthful risks of progression from alcohol and tobacco to marijuana and to hard drugs across generations. *American Journal of Public Health, 91,* 225–232.

Gonzales, N., Cauce, A., Friedman, R., & Mason, C. (1996). Family, peer, and neighborhood influences on academic achievement among African-American adolescents: One-year prospective effects. *American Journal of Community Psychology, 24,* 365–387.

Gonzales, N., Cauce, A., & Mason, C. (1996). Interobserver agreement in the assessment of parental behavior and parent–adolescent conflict: African American mothers, daughters, and independent observers. *Child Development, 67,* 1483–1498.

Gonzales, N. A., Deardorff, J., Formoso, D., Barr, A., & Barrera, M. Jr. (2006). Family mediators of the relation between acculturation and adolescent mental health. *Family Relations, 55,* 318–330.

Good, M., & Willoughby, T. (2006). The role of spirituality versus religiosity in adolescent psychosocial adjustment. *Journal of Youth and Adolescence, 35,* 41–55.

Good, M., & Willoughby, T. (2007). The identity formation experiences of church-attending rural adolescents. *Journal of Adolescent Research, 22,* 387–412.

Good, T., & Brophy, J. (1948). *Looking in classrooms.* New York: Harper & Row.

Goodnight, J. A., Bates, J. E., Newman, J. P., Dodge, K. A., & Pettit, G. S. (2006). The interactive influences of friend deviance and reward dominance on the development of externalizing behavior during middle adolescence. *Journal of Abnormal Child Psychology, 34,* 573–583.

Goodson, P., Buhi, E. R., & Dunsmore, S. C. (2006). Self-esteem and adolescent sexual behaviors, attitudes, and intentions: A systematic review. *Journal of Adolescent Health, 38,* 310–319.

Goosby, B. J. (2007). Poverty duration, maternal psychological resources, and adolescent socioemotional outcomes. *Journal of Family Issues, 28,* 1113–1134.

Goossens, L., Seiffge-Krenke, I., & Marcoen, A. (1992, March). *The many faces of adolescent egocentrism: Two European replications.* Paper presented at the biennial meetings of the Society for Research on Adolescence, Washington, DC.

Goran, M., et al. (1998). Developmental changes in energy expenditure and physical activity in children: Evidence for a decline in physical activity in girls before puberty. *Pediatrics, 101,* 887–891.

Gordis, E., Margolin, G., & St. John, R. (1997). Marital aggression, observed parental hostility, and child behavior during triadic family interaction. *Journal of Family Psychology, 11,* 76–89.

Gordon, K. (1995). Self-concept and motivational patterns of resilient African American high school students. *Journal of Black Psychology, 21,* 239–255.

Gordon, R. A., Lahey, B. B., Kawai, E., Loeber, R., Stouthamer-Loeber, M., & Farrington, D. P. (2004). Antisocial behavior and youth gang membership. *Criminology, 42,* 55–87.

Gore, S., & Aseltine, R., Jr. (1995). Protective processes in adolescence: Matching stressors with social resources. *American Journal of Community Psychology, 23,* 301–327.

Gorman-Smith, D., & Tolan, P. (1998). The role of exposure to community violence and developmental problems among inner city youth. *Development and Psychopathology, 10,* 101–116.

Gorman-Smith, D., Tolan, P., Sheidow, A., & Henry, D. (2001). Partner violence and street violence among urban adolescents: Do the same family factors relate? *Journal of Research on Adolescence, 11,* 273–295.

Gottfredson, M., & Hirschi, T. (1990). *A general theory of crime.* Stanford, CA: Stanford University Press.

Gottfried, A., Fleming, J., & Gottfried, A. (1998). Role of cognitively stimulating home environment in children's academic intrinsic motivation: A longitudinal study. *Child Development, 69,* 1448–1460.

Gottfried, A., Fleming, J. S., & Gottfried, A. W. (2001). Continuity of academic intrinsic motivation from childhood through late adolescence: A longitudinal study. *Journal of Educational Psychology, 93,* 3–13.

Gottlieb, B. H., Still, E., & Newby-Clark, I. (2007). Types and precipitants of growth and decline in emerging adulthood. *Journal of Adolescent Research, 22,* 132–155.

Gould, M., Munfakh, J., Lubell, K., Kleinman, M., & Parker, S. (2002). Seeking help from the Internet during adolescence. *Journal of the American Academy of Child and Adolescent Psychiatry, 41,* 1182–1189.

Gould, R. (1972). The phases of adult life. *American Journal of Psychiatry, 129,* 521–531.

Gowen, L., Hayward, C., Killen, J., Robinson, T., & Taylor, C. (1999). Acculturation and eating disorder symptoms in adolescent girls. *Journal of Research on Adolescence, 9,* 67–83.

Gowen, L. K., Feldman, S. S., Diaz, R., & Yisrael, D. S. (2004). A comparison of the sexual behaviors and attitudes of adolescent girls with older vs. similar-aged boyfriends. *Journal of Youth and Adolescence, 33,* 167–175.

Goyette, K., & Xie, Y. (1999). Educational expectations of Asian American youths: Determinants and ethnic differences. *Sociology of Education, 72,* 22–36.

Graber, J., Brooks-Gunn, J., & Warren, M. P. (2006). Pubertal effects on adjustment in girls: Moving from demonstrating effects to identifying pathways. *Journal of Youth and Adolescence, 35,* 391–401.

Graber, J., Brooks-Gunn, J., Paikoff, R., & Warren, M. (1994). Prediction of eating problems: An 8-year study of adolescent girls. *Developmental Psychology, 30,* 823–834.

Graber, J., Lewinsohn, P., Seeley, J., & Brooks-Gunn, J. (1997). Is psychopathology associated with the timing of pubertal development? *Journal of the American Academy of Child and Adolescent Psychiatry, 36,* 1768–1776.

Graber, J., Seeley, J., Brooks-Gunn, J., & Lewinsohn, P. (2004). Is pubertal timing associated with psychopathology in young adulthood? *Journal of the American Academy of Child and Adolescent Psychiatry, 43,* 718–726.

Graber, J., & Sontag, L. (2009). Internalizing problems during adolescence. In R. Lerner & L. Steinberg (Eds.), *Handbook of adolescent psychology* (3rd ed., Vol. 1, pp. 642–682). New York: Wiley.

Graham, C. (1991). Menstrual synchrony: An update and review. *Human Nature, 2,* 293–311.

Graham, S. (1993, March). *Peer-directed aggression in African-American youth from an attributional perspective.* Paper presented at the biennial meetings of the Society for Research in Child Development, New Orleans.

Graham, S., Bellmore, Nishina, & Juvonen, J. (2009). "It must be 'me'": Ethnic diversity and attributions for peer victimization in middle school. *Journal of Youth and Adolescence, 38,* 487–499.

Graham, S., & Hudley, C. (1994). Attributions of aggressive and nonaggressive African-American male early adolescents: A study of construct accessibility. *Developmental Psychology, 30,* 365–373.

Graham, S., Hudley, C., & Williams, E. (1992). Attributional and emotional determinants of aggression among African-American and Latino young adolescents. *Developmental Psychology, 28,* 731–740.

Graham, S., & Juvonen, J. (1998). Self-blame and peer victimization in middle school: An attributional analysis. *Developmental Psychology, 34,* 587–599.

Graham, S., & Juvonen, J. (2002). Ethnicity, peer harassment, and adjustment in middle school: An exploratory study. *Journal of Early Adolescence, 22,* 173–199.

Graham, S., & Lowery, B. (2004). Priming unconscious racial stereotypes about adolescent offenders. *Law and Human Behavior, 28,* 483–504.

Granic, I., Hollenstein, T., Dishion, T. K., & Patterson, G. R. (2003). Longitudinal analysis of flexibility and reorganization in early adolescence: A dynamic systems study of family interactions. *Developmental Psychology, 39,* 606–617.

Grant, K., Lyons, A., Finkelstein, J., Conway, K., Reynolds, L., O'Koon, J., et al. (2004). Gender differences in rates of depressive symptoms among low-income, urban, African American youth: A test of two mediational hypotheses. *Journal of Youth and Adolescence, 33,* 523–533.

Gray-Little, B., & Carels, R. (1997). The effect of racial dissonance on academic achievement in elementary, junior high, and high school students. *Journal of Research on Adolescence, 7,* 109–131.

Gray-Little, B., & Hafdahl, A. (2000). Factors influencing racial comparisons of self-esteem: A quantitative review. *Psychological Bulletin, 126,* 26–54.

Gray, M., & Steinberg, L. (1999). Adolescent romance and the parent–child relationship: A contextual perspective. In W. Furman, B. Brown, & C. Feiring (Eds.), *Contemporary perspectives on adolescent romantic relationships* (pp. 235–265). New York: Cambridge University Press.

Green, K. M., & Ensminger, M. E. (2006). Adult social behavioral effects of heavy adolescent marijuana use among African Americans. *Developmental Psychology, 42,* 1168–1178.

Greenberg, M., & Kusche, C. (1998). *Promoting alternative thinking strategies.* Boulder: Institute of Behavioral Sciences, University of Colorado.

Greenberg, M., Siegel, J., & Leitch, C. (1983). The nature and importance of attachment relationships to parents and peers during adolescence. *Journal of Youth and Adolescence, 12,* 373–386.

Greenberger, E., & Chen, C. (1996). Perceived family relationships and depressed mood in early and late adolescence: A comparison of European and Asian Americans. *Developmental Psychology, 32,* 707–716.

Greenberger, E., Chen, C., & Beam, M. R. (1998). The role of "very important" nonparental adults in adolescent development. *Journal of Youth and Adolescence, 27*, 321–343.

Greenberger, E., Chen, C., Beam, M., Whang, S., & Dong, Q. (2000). The perceived social contexts of adolescents' misconduct: A comparative study of youths in three cultures. *Journal of Research on Adolescence, 10*, 365–388.

Greenberger, E., Chen, C., Tally, S., & Dong, Q. (2000). Family, peer, and individual correlates of depressive symptomatology among U.S. and Chinese adolescents. *Journal of Consulting and Clinical Psychology, 68*, 209–219.

Greenberger, E., & Steinberg, L. (1986). *When teenagers work: The psychological and social costs of adolescent employment.* New York: Basic Books.

Greene, M. L., & Way, N. (2005). Self-esteem trajectories among ethnic minority adolescents: A growth curve analysis of the patterns and predictors of change. *Journal of Research on Adolescence, 15*, 151–177.

Greene, M. L., Way, N., & Pahl, K. (2006). Trajectories of perceived adult and peer discrimination among Black, Latino, and Asian American adolescents: Patterns and psychological correlates. *Developmental Psychology, 42*, 218–236.

Greenfield, P., & Yan, Z. (2006). Children, adolescents, and the Internet: A new field of inquiry in developmental psychology. *Developmental Psychology, 42*, 391–394.

Gregory, A., & Weinstein, R. S. (2004). Connection and regulation at home and in school: Predicting growth in achievement for adolescents. *Journal of Adolescent Research, 19*, 405–427.

Gregory, L. (1995). The "turnaround" process: Factors influencing the school success of urban youth. *Journal of Adolescent Research, 10*, 136–154.

Griffin, K. W., Epstein, J. A., Botvin, G. J., & Spoth, R. L. (2001). Social competence and substance use among rural youth: Mediating role of social benefit expectancies of use. *Journal of Youth and Adolescence, 30*, 485–498.

Griffith Fontaine, R., Salzer Burks, V., & Dodge, K. (2002). Response decision processes and externalizing behavior problems in adolescents. *Development and Psychopathology, 14*, 107–122.

Grigg, W. S., Lauko, M. A., & Brockway, D. M. (2006). *The nation's report card: Science 2005.* National Center for Education Statistics. Washington, DC: U.S. Government Printing Office.

Grisso, T., Steinberg, L., Woolard, J., Cauffman, E., Scott, E., Graham, S., et al. (2003). Juveniles' competence to stand trial: A comparison of adolescents' and adults' capacities as trial defendants. *Law and Human Behavior, 27*, 333–363.

Grolnick, W., Kurowski, C. O., Dunlap, K. G., & Hevey, C. (2000). Parental resources and the transition to junior high. *Journal of Research on Adolescence, 10*, 465–488.

Grolnick, W., & Slowiaczek, M. (1994). Parents' involvement in children's schooling: A multidimensional conceptualization and motivational model. *Child Development, 65*, 237–252.

Grosbras, M., Jansen, M., Leonard, G., McIntosh, A., Osswald, K., Poulsen, C., et al. (2007). Neural mechanisms of resistance to peer influence in early adolescence. *Journal of Neuroscience, 27*, 8040–8045.

Grossman, J. M., & Charmaraman, L. (2009). Race, context, and privilege: White adolescents' explanations of racial-ethnic centrality. *Journal of Youth and Adolescence, 38*, 139–152.

Grossman, M., Chaloupka, F., Saffer, H., & Laixuthai, A. (1994). Effects of alcohol price policy on youth: A summary of economic research. *Journal of Research on Adolescence, 4*, 347–364.

Grotevant, H. (1997). Adolescent development in family contexts. In N. Eisenberg (Ed.), *Handbook of child psychology:* Vol. 3. *Social, emotional, and personality development* (5th ed., pp. 1097–1149). New York: Wiley.

Grotpeter, J., & Crick, N. (1996). Relational aggression, overt aggression, and friendship. *Child Development, 67*, 2328–2338.

Grover, R. L., & Nangle, D. W. (2003). Adolescent perceptions of problematic heterosocial situations: A focus group study. *Journal of Youth and Adolescence, 32*, 129–139.

Gruber, J. (Ed.). (2001). *Risky behavior among youths: An economic analysis.* Chicago: University of Chicago Press.

Gruber, J., & Zinman, J. (2001). Youth smoking in the United States. In J. Gruber (Ed.), *Risky behavior among youths: An economic analysis* (pp. 69–120). Chicago: University of Chicago Press.

Grumbach, M., Roth, J., Kaplan, S., & Kelch, R. (1974). Hypothalamic-pituitary regulation of puberty in man: Evidence and concepts derived from clinical research. In M. Grumbach, G. Grave, & F. Mayer (Eds.), *Control of the onset of puberty.* Lippincott Williams & Wilkins.

Grunbaum, J., Lowry, R., Kann, L., & Pateman, B. (2000). Prevalence of health risk behaviors among Asian American/Pacific Islander high school students. *Journal of Adolescent Health, 27*, 322–330.

Grych, J. H., Raynor, S. R., & Fosco, G. M. (2004). Family processes that shape the impact of interparental conflict on adolescents. *Development and Psychopathology, 16*, 649–665.

Guberman, S. (1996). The development of everyday mathematics in Brazilian children with limited formal education. *Child Development, 67*, 1609–1623.

Guest, A., & Schneider, B. (2003). Adolescents' extracurricular participation in context: The mediating effects of schools, communities, and identity. *Sociology of Education, 76*, 89–109.

Guillen, E., & Barr, S. (1994). Nutrition, dieting, and fitness messages in a magazine for adolescent women, 1970–1990. *Journal of Adolescent Health, 15*, 464–472.

Guisinger, S., & Blatt, S. (1994). Individuality and relatedness: Evolution of a fundamental dialectic. *American Psychologist, 49*, 104–111.

Guldi, M., Page, M., & Stevens, A. (2007). Family background and children's transition to adulthood over time. In S. Danziger & C. Rouse (Eds.), *The price of independence: The economics of early adulthood.* New York: Russell Sage Foundation.

Gummerum, M., Keller, M., Takezawa, M., & Mata, J. (2008). To give or not to give: Children's and adolescents' sharing and moral negotiations in economic decision situations. *Child Development, 79*, 562–576.

Gunlicks-Stoessel, M., & Powers, S. I. (2008). Adolescents' emotional experiences of mother-adolescent conflict predict internalizing and externalizing symptoms. *Journal of Research on Adolescence, 18*, 621–642.

Gunnar, M., Wewerka, S., Frenn, K., Long, J., & Griggs, C. (2009). Developmental changes in hypothalamus–pituitary–adrenal activity over the transition to adolescence: Normative changes and associations with puberty. *Development and Psychopathology, 21*, 69–85.

Gunnoe, M. (1994, February). *Noncustodial mothers' and fathers' contributions to the adjustment of adolescents in stepfamilies.* Paper presented at the biennial meetings of the Society for Research on Adolescence, San Diego.

Gunnoe, M., Hetherington, E. M., & Reiss, D. (1999). Parental religiosity, parenting style, and adolescent social responsibility. *Journal of Early Adolescence, 19*, 199–225.

Guo, G., Roettger, M. E., & Cai, T. (2008). The integration of genetic propensities into social-control models of delinquency and violence among male youths. *American Sociological Review, 73*, 543–568.

Guo, G., Tong, Y., & Cai, T. (2008). Gene by social context interactions for number of sexual partners among White male youths: Genetics informed sociology. *American Journal of Sociology, 114*, 36–66.

Güroğlu, B., Haselager, G. J. T., van Lieshout, Cornelis F. M., & Scholte, R. H. J. (2009). Antagonists in mutual antipathies: A person-oriented approach. *Journal of Research on Adolescence, 19*, 35–46.

Gutierrez, R. (2000). Advancing African American, urban youth in mathematics: Unpacking the success of one math department. *American Journal of Education, 109*, 63–111.

Gutman, L., & Midgley, C. (2000). The role of protective factors in supporting the academic achievement of poor African American students during the middle school transition. *Journal of Youth and Adolescence, 29*, 223–248.

Gutman, L., McLoyd, V., & Tokoyawa, T. (2005). Financial strain, neighborhood stress, parenting behaviors, and adolescent adjustment in urban African American families. *Journal of Research on Adolescence, 15*, 425–449.

Gutman, L. M., & Eccles, J. (2007). Stage-environment fit during adolescence: Trajectories of family relations and adolescent outcomes. *Developmental Psychology, 43,* 522–537.

Guyer, A., McClure-Tone, E., Shiffrin, N., Pine, D., & Nelson, E. (2009). Probing the neural correlates of anticipated peer evaluation in adolescence. *Child Development, 80,* 1000–1015.

Habermas, T., & de Silveira, C. (2008). The development of global coherence in life narratives across adolescence: Temporal, causal, and thematic aspects. *Developmental Psychology, 44,* 707–721.

Hacker, D. (1994). An existential view of adolescence. *Journal of Early Adolescence, 14,* 300–327.

Hafetz, E. (1976). Parameters of sexual maturity in man. In E. Hafetz (Ed.), *Perspectives in human reproduction:* Vol. 3. *Sexual maturity: Physiological and clinical parameters.* Ann Arbor, MI: Ann Arbor Science Publishers.

Hagan, J., & Foster, H. (2001). Youth violence and the end of adolescence. *American Sociological Review, 66,* 874–899.

Hahm, C. H., Lahiff, M., & Barreto, R. M. (2006). Asian American adolescents' first sexual intercourse: Gender and acculturation differences. *Perspectives on Sexual and Reproductive Health, 38,* 28–36.

Hahm, H., Lahiff, M., & Guterman, N. (2003). Acculturation and parental attachment in Asian-American adolescents' alcohol use. *Journal of Adolescent Health, 33,* 119–129.

Hahm, H., Lahiff, M., & Guterman, N. (2004). Asian American adolescents' acculturation, binge drinking, and alcohol- and tobacco-using peers. *Journal of Community Psychology, 32,* 295–308.

Haines, J., Neumark-Sztainer, D., Eisenberg, M., & Hannan, P. (2006). Weight teasing and disordered eating behaviors in adolescents: Longitudinal findings from Project EAT (Eating Among Teens). *Pediatrics, 117,* e209–15.

Hair, E. C., Moore, K. A., Garrett, S. B., Ling, T., & Cleveland, K. (2008). The continued importance of quality parent–adolescent relationships during late adolescence. *Journal of Research on Adolescence, 18,* 187–200.

Haj-Yahia, M. M., Musleh, K., & Haj-Yahia, Y. (2002). The incidence of adolescent maltreatment in Arab society and some of its psychological effects. *Journal of Family Issues, 23,* 1032–1064.

Hale, S. (1990). A global developmental trend in cognitive processing speed. *Child Development, 61,* 653–663.

Hale, S., Bronik, M., & Fry, A. (1997). Verbal and spatial working memory in school-age children: Developmental differences in susceptibility to interference. *Developmental Psychology, 33,* 364–371.

Hall, G. S. (1904). *Adolescence.* New York: Appleton.

Hall, N. C., Chipperfield, J. G., Perry, R. P., Ruthig, J. C., & Goetz, T. (2006). Primary and secondary control in academic development: Gender-specific implications for stress and health in college students. *Anxiety, Stress & Coping: An International Journal, 19,* 189–210.

Hallinan, M. (1992). The organization of students for instruction in the middle school. *Sociology of Education, 65,* 114–127.

Hallinan, M. (1996). Track mobility in secondary school. *Social Forces, 74,* 983–1002.

Hallinan, M. (2008). Teacher influences on students' attachment to school. *Sociology of Education, 81,* 271–283.

Hallinan, M., & Williams, R. (1989). Interracial friendship choices in secondary schools. *American Sociological Review, 54,* 67–78.

Halpern, C., King, R., Oslak, S., & Udry, J. (2005). Body mass index, dieting, romance, and sexual activity in adolescent girls: Relationships over time. *Journal of Research on Adolescence, 15,* 535–559.

Halpern, C., Oslak, S., Young, M., Martin, S., & Kupper, L. (2001). Partner violence among adolescents in opposite-sex romantic relationships: Findings from the National Longitudinal Study of Adolescent Health. *American Journal of Public Health, 91,* 1679–1685.

Halpern, C., & Udry, J. (1994, February). *Pubertal increases in body fat and implications for dieting, dating, and sexual behavior among Black and White females.* Paper presented at the biennial meetings of the Society for Research on Adolescence, San Diego.

Halpern, C., Udry, J., Campbell, B., & Suchindran, C. (1999). Effects of body fat on weight concerns, dating, and sexual activity: A longitudinal analysis of Black and White adolescent girls. *Developmental Psychology, 35,* 721–736.

Halpern, C., Udry, J., & Suchindran, C. (1996, March). *Monthly measures of salivary testosterone predict sexual activity in adolescent males.* Paper presented at the biennial meetings of the Society for Research on Adolescence, Boston.

Halpern, C., Young, M., Waller, M., Martin, S., & Kupper, L. (2004). Prevalence of partner violence in same-sex romantic and sexual relationships in a national sample of adolescents. *Journal of Adolescent Health, 35,* 124–131.

Halpern, C. T. (2003). Biological influences on adolescent romantic and sexual behavior. In P. Florsheim (Ed.), *Adolescent romantic relations and sexual behavior: Theory, research, and practical implications* (pp. 57–84). Mahwah, NJ: Lawrence Erlbaum.

Halpern-Felsher, B., & Cauffman, E. (2001). Costs and benefits of a decision: Decision-making competence in adolescents and adults. *Journal of Applied Developmental Psychology, 22,* 257–273.

Halpern-Meekin, S., & Tach, L. (2008). Heterogeneity in two-parent families and adolescent well-being. *Journal of Marriage and Family, 70,* 435–451.

Hamill, S. (1994). Parent–adolescent communication in sandwich generation families. *Journal of Adolescent Research, 9,* 458–482.

Hamilton, B., Martin, J., & Ventura, S. (2007). Births: Preliminary data for 2006. *National Vital Statistics Reports, 56,* Number 7.

Hamilton, C. (2000). Continuity and discontinuity of attachment from infancy through adolescence. *Child Development, 71,* 690–694.

Hamilton, S., & Hamilton, M. (2009). The transition to adulthood: Challenges of poverty and structural lag. In R. Lerner & L. Steinberg (Eds.), *Handbook of adolescent psychology* (3rd ed., Vol. 2, pp. 492–526). New York: Wiley.

Hamm, J. (2000). Do birds of a feather flock together? The variable bases for African American, Asian American, and European American adolescents' selection of similar friends. *Developmental Psychology, 36,* 209–219.

Hamm, J., Brown, B., & Heck, D. (2005). Bridging the ethnic divide. Student and school characteristics in African American, Asian-descent, Latino, and White adolescents' cross-ethnic friend nominations. *Journal of Research on Adolescence, 15,* 21–46.

Hampson, S. E., & Goldberg, L. R. (2006). A first large cohort study of personality trait stability over the 40 years between elementary school and midlife. *Journal of Personality and Social Psychology, 91,* 763–779.

Hamre, B. K., & Pianta, R. C. (2001). Early teacher–child relationships and the trajectory of children's school outcomes through eighth grade. *Child Development, 72,* 625–638.

Hankin, B. L., Mermelstein, R., & Roesch, L. (2007). Sex differences in adolescent depression: Stress exposure and reactivity models. *Child Development, 78,* 279–295.

Hansen, D. M., Janssen, I., Schiff, A., Zee, P. C., & Dubocovich, M. L. (2005). The impact of school daily schedule on adolescent sleep. *Pediatrics, 115,* 1555–1561.

Hansen, D. M., Larson, R. W., & Dworkin, J. B. (2003). What adolescents learn in organized youth activities: A survey of self-reported developmental experiences. *Journal of Research on Adolescence, 13,* 25–55.

Hanson, S. (1994). Lost talent: Unrealized educational aspirations and expectations among U.S. youths. *Sociology of Education, 67,* 159–183.

Hanson, T., McLanahan, S., & Thomson, E. (1996). Double jeopardy: Parental conflict and stepfamily outcomes for children. *Journal of Marriage and the Family, 58,* 141–154.

Harden, K. P., Mendle, J., Hill, J. E., Turkheimer, E., & Emery, R. E. (2008). Rethinking timing of first sex and delinquency. *Journal of Youth and Adolescence, 37,* 373–385.

Harding, D. J. (2003). Counterfactual models of neighborhood effects: The effect of neighborhood poverty on dropping out and teenage pregnancy. *American Journal of Sociology, 109,* 676–719.

Hardway, C., & Fuligni, A. (2006). Dimensions of family connectedness among adolescents with Mexican, Chinese, and European backgrounds. *Developmental Psychology, 42,* 1246–1258.

Hardy, D., Astone, N., Brooks-Gunn, J., Shapiro, X., & Miller, X. (1998). Like mother, like child: Intergenerational patterns of age at first birth and associations with childhood and adolescent characteristics and adult outcomes in the second generation. *Developmental Psychology, 34,* 1220–1232.

Hardy, S. A., & Raffaelli, M. (2003). Adolescent religiosity and sexuality: An investigation of reciprocal influences. *Journal of Adolescence, 26,* 731–739.

Hare, R. (1991). *The Hare Psychopathy Checklist–Revised.* Toronto, Ontario: Multi-Health Systems.

Hargreaves, D., & Tiggemann, M. (2003). The effect of thin ideal television commercials on body dissatisfaction and schema activation during early adolescence. *Journal of Youth and Adolescence, 32,* 367–373.

Harker, K. (2001). Immigrant generation, assimilation and adolescent psychological well-being. *Social Forces, 79,* 969–1004.

Harold, G., & Conger, R. (1997). Marital conflict and adolescent distress: The role of adolescent awareness. *Child Development, 68,* 333–350.

Harper, G., & Robinson, W. L. (1999). Pathways to risk among inner-city African-American adolescent females: The influence of gang membership. *American Journal of Community Psychology, 27,* 383–404.

Harre, N. (2000). Risk evaluation, driving, and adolescents: A typology. *Developmental Review, 20,* 206–226.

Harris, J. (1995). Where is the child's environment? A group socialization theory of development. *Psychological Bulletin, 102,* 458–489.

Harris, J. R. (1998). *The nurture assumption: Why children turn out the way they do.* New York: Free Press.

Harris, K. (1999). The health status and risk behavior of adolescents in immigrant families. In D. Hernandez (Ed.), *Children of immigrants: Health, adjustment, and public assistance* (pp. 286–347). Washington, DC: National Academy Press.

Harris, M. (1994). Cholas, Mexican-American girls, and gangs. *Sex Roles, 30,* 289–301.

Harris-Britt, A., Valrie, C. R., Kurtz-Costes, B., & Rowley, S. J. (2007). Perceived racial discrimination and self-esteem in African American youth: Racial socialization as a protective factor. *Journal of Research on Adolescence, 17,* 669–682.

Harrison, K., & Heffner, V. (2008). Media, body image, and eating disorders. In S. L. Calvert & B. J. Wilson (Eds.), *The handbook of children, media, and development* (pp. 381–406). Oxford: Wiley-Blackwell.

Hart, D., & Chmiel, S. (1992). Influence of defense mechanisms on moral judgment development: A longitudinal study. *Developmental Psychology, 28,* 722–730.

Hart, D., Donnelly, T. M., Youniss, J., & Atkins, R. (2007). High school community service as a predictor of adult voting and volunteering. *American Educational Research Journal, 44,* 197–219.

Hart, D., & Fegley, S. (1995). Prosocial behavior and caring in adolescence: Relations to self-understanding and social judgment. *Child Development, 66,* 1346–1359.

Hart, D., Hofmann, V., Edelstein, W., & Keller, M. (1997). The relation of childhood personality types to adolescent behavior and development: A longitudinal study of Icelandic children. *Developmental Psychology, 33,* 195–205.

Harter, S. (1990). Identity and self development. In S. Feldman & G. Elliott (Eds.), *At the threshold: The developing adolescent* (pp. 352–387). Cambridge, MA: Harvard University Press.

Harter, S. (1999). *The construction of the self.* New York: Guilford Press.

Harter, S., Marold, D., Whitesell, N., & Cobbs, G. (1996). A model of the effects of parent and peer support on adolescent false self behavior. *Child Development, 67,* 360–374.

Harter, S., & Monsour, A. (1992). Developmental analysis of conflict caused by opposing attributes in the adolescent self-portrait. *Developmental Psychology, 28,* 251–260.

Harter, S., Stocker, C., & Robinson, N. (1996). The perceived directionality of the link between approval and self-worth: The liabilities of a looking glass self orientation among young adolescents. *Journal of Research on Adolescence, 6,* 285–308.

Harter, S., Waters, P., & Whitesell, N. (1998). Relational self-worth: Differences in perceived worth as a person across interpersonal contexts among adolescents. *Child Development, 69,* 756–766.

Hartney, C. (2006). *Youth under 18 in the criminal justice system.* Oakland: National Council on Crime and Delinquency.

Hartup, W. (1977). Adolescent peer relations: A look to the future. In J. Hill & F. Monks (Eds.), *Adolescence and youth in prospect.* Guildford, England: IPC Press.

Hartup, W. (1992). Friendships and their developmental significance. In H. McGurk (Ed.), *Contemporary issues in childhood social development* (pp. 175–205). London: Routledge.

Hartup, W., & Stevens, N. (1997). Friendships and adaptation in the life course. *Psychological Bulletin, 121,* 335–370.

Hasebe, Y., Nucci, L., & Nucci, M. S. (2004). Parental control of the personal domain and adolescent symptoms of psychopathology: A cross-national study in the United States and Japan. *Child Development, 75,* 815–828.

Hastings, J. S., & Weinstein, J. M. (2008). Information, school choices, and academic achievement: Evidence from two experiments. *Quarterly Journal of Economics, 123,* 1373–1414.

Hatzichristou, C., & Hopf, D. (1996). A multiperspective comparison of peer sociometric status groups in childhood and adolescence. *Child Development, 67,* 1085–1102.

Hauser, S., & Bowlds, M. (1990). Stress, coping, and adaptation. In S. Feldman & G. Elliott (Eds.), *At the threshold: The developing adolescent* (pp. 388–413). Cambridge, MA: Harvard University Press.

Hausser, D., & Michaud, P. (1994). Does a condom-promoting strategy (the Swiss STOP-AIDS campaign) modify sexual behavior among adolescents? *Pediatrics, 93,* 580–585.

Havighurst, R. (1952). *Developmental tasks and education.* New York: McKay.

Hawkins, D. N., Amato, P. R., & King, V. (2006). Parent–adolescent involvement: The relative influence of parent gender and residence. *Journal of Marriage and Family, 68,* 125–136.

Hawkins, D. N., Amato, P. R., & King, V. (2007). Nonresident father involvement and adolescent well-being: Father effects or child effects? *American Sociological Review, 72,* 990–1010.

Hawkins, J., Catalano, R., & Miller, J. (1992). Risk and protective factors for alcohol and other drug problems in adolescence and early adulthood: Implications for substance abuse prevention. *Psychological Bulletin, 112,* 64–105.

Hawkins, J. D., Brown, E. C., Oesterle, S., Arthur, M. W., Abbott, R. D., & Catalano, R. F. (2008). Early effects of communities that care on targeted risks and initiation of delinquent behavior and substance use. *Journal of Adolescent Health, 43,* 15–22.

Hay, C., Fortson, E. N., Hollist, D. R., Altheimer, I., & Schaible, L. M. (2007). Compounded risk: The implications for delinquency of coming from a poor family that lives in a poor community. *Journal of Youth and Adolescence, 36,* 593–605.

Hayes, C. (Ed.). (1987). *Risking the future: Adolescent sexuality, pregnancy, and childbearing* (Vol. 1). Washington, DC: National Academy Press.

Hayes, D., Wolfer, L., & Wolfe, M. (1996). Schoolbook simplification and its relation to the decline in SAT-Verbal scores. *American Educational Research Journal, 33,* 489–508.

Hayford, S. R., & Furstenberg, F. F. J. (2008). Delayed adulthood, delayed desistance? Trends in the age distribution of problem behaviors. *Journal of Research on Adolescence, 18,* 285–304.

Haynie, D. L. (2003). Contexts of risk? Explaining the link between girls' pubertal development and their delinquency involvement. *Social Forces, 82,* 355–397.

Haynie, D. L., Giordano, P. C., Manning, W. D., & Longmore, M. A. (2005). Adolescent romantic relationships and delinquency involvement. *Criminology, 43,* 177–210.

Haynie, D. L., & McHugh, S. (2003). Sibling deviance in the shadows of mutual and unique friendship effects? *Criminology, 41,* 355–391.

Haynie, D. L., Nansel, T., Eitel, P., Crump, A., Saylor, K., Yu, K., et al. (2001). Bullies, victims, and bully/victims: Distinct groups of at-risk youth. *Journal of Early Adolescence, 21,* 29–49.

Haynie, D. L., & Osgood, D. W. (2005). Reconsidering peers and delinquency: How do peers matter? *Social Forces, 84,* 1109–1130.

Hayward, C., Gotlib, I., Schraedley, P., & Litt, I. (1999). Ethnic differences in the association between pubertal status and symptoms of depression in adolescent girls. *Journal of Adolescent Health, 25,* 143–149.

Hazan, C. (1994, February). *The role of sexuality in peer attachment formation.* Paper presented at the biennial meetings of the Society for Research on Adolescence, San Diego.

Heard, H. E. (2007). The family structure trajectory and adolescent school performance: Differential effects by race and ethnicity. *Journal of Family Issues, 28,* 319–354.

Heatherton, T. F., & Sargent, J. D. (2009). Does watching smoking in movies promote teenage smoking? *Current Directions in Psychological Science, 18,* 63–67.

Hechinger, F. (1993). Schools for teenagers: A historic dilemma. *Teachers College Record, 94,* 522–539.

Heck, R. H., Price, C. L., & Thomas, S. L. (2004). Tracks as emergent structures: A network analysis of student differentiation in a high school. *American Journal of Education, 110,* 321–353.

Heimer, K., & Matsueda, R. (1994). Role-taking, role commitment, and delinquency: A theory of differential social control. *American Sociological Review, 59,* 365–390.

Hein, K. (1988). *Issues in adolescent health: An overview.* Washington, DC: Carnegie Council on Adolescent Development.

Hein, K., Dell, R., Futterman, D., Rotheram-Borus, M., & Shaffer, N. (1995). Comparison of HIV+ and HIV− adolescents: Risk factors and psychosocial determinants. *Pediatrics, 95,* 96–104.

Helsen, M., Vollebergh, W., & Meeus, W. (2000). Social support from parents and friends and emotional problems in adolescence. *Journal of Youth and Adolescence, 29,* 319–335.

Helwig, C. (1995). Adolescents' and young adults' conceptions of civil liberties: Freedom of speech and religion. *Child Development, 66,* 152–166.

Helwig, C. (1997). The role of agent and social context in judgments of freedom of speech and religion. *Child Development, 68,* 484–495.

Helwig, C. C., Arnold, M. L., Tan, D., & Boyd, D. (2007). Mainland Chinese and Canadian adolescents' judgments and reasoning about the fairness of democratic and other forms of government. *Cognitive Development, 22,* 96–109.

Henderson, A., Brown, S. D., Pancer, S. M., & Ellis-Hale, K. (2007). Mandated community service in high school and subsequent civic engagement: The case of the "double cohort" in Ontario, Canada. *Journal of Youth and Adolescence, 36,* 849–860.

Hendrick, S., & Hendrick, C. (1994, February). *Gender, sexuality, and close relationships.* Paper presented at the biennial meetings of the Society for Research on Adolescence, San Diego.

Henry, B., Caspi, A., Moffitt, T., Harrington, H., & Silva, P. (1999). Staying in school protects boys with poor self-regulation in childhood from later crime: A longitudinal study. *International Journal of Behavioral Development, 23,* 1049–1073.

Henry, B., Caspi, A., Moffitt, T., & Silva, P. (1996). Temperamental and familial predictors of violent and nonviolent criminal convictions: Age 3 to age 18. *Developmental Psychology, 32,* 614–623.

Henry, B., Feehan, M., McGee, R., Stanton, W., Moffitt, T., & Silva, P. (1993). The importance of conduct problems and depressive symptoms in predicting adolescent substance use. *Journal of Abnormal Child Psychology, 21,* 469–480.

Henry, C., & Lovelace, S. (1995). Family resources and adolescent life satisfaction in remarried households. *Journal of Family Issues, 16,* 765–786.

Henry, D. B., Schoeny, M. E., Deptula, D. P., & Slavick, J. T. (2007). Peer selection and socialization effects on adolescent intercourse without a condom and attitudes about the costs of sex. *Child Development, 78,* 825–838.

Henshaw, S. (1995). The impact of requirements for parental consent on minors' abortions in Mississippi. *Family Planning Perspectives, 27,* 120–122.

Herdt, G., & McClintock, M. (2000). The magical age of 10. *Archives of Sexual Behavior, 29,* 587–606.

Herman, M. (2004). Forced to choose: Some determinants of racial identification in multiracial adolescents. *Child Development, 75,* 730–748.

Herman, M. (2009). The Black-White-other achievement gap: Testing theories of academic performance among multiracial and monoracial adolescents. *Sociology of Education, 82,* 20–46.

Herman-Giddens, M., Slora, E., Wasserman, R., Bourdony, C., Bhapkar, M., Koch, G., et al. (1997). Secondary sexual characteristics and menses in young girls seen in office practice: A study from the Pediatric Research in Office Settings Network. *Pediatrics, 88,* 505–512.

Herman-Stahl, M., Stemmler, M., & Petersen, A. (1995). Approach and avoidant coping: Implications for adolescent mental health. *Journal of Youth and Adolescence, 24,* 649–665.

Hernandez, D. (1997). Child development and the social demography of childhood. *Child Development, 68,* 149–169.

Herrenkohl, T. I., Hill, K. G., Hawkins, J. D., Chung, I., & Nagin, D. (2006). Developmental trajectories of family management and

risk for violent behavior in adolescence. *Journal of Adolescent Health, 39,* 206–213.

Herrenkohl, T. I., Kosterman, R., Hawkins, J. D., & Mason, W. A. (2009). Effects of growth in family conflict in adolescence on adult depressive symptoms: Mediating and moderation effects of stress and school bonding. *Journal of Adolescent Health, 44,* 146–152.

Herrenkohl, T. I., Maguin, E., Hill, K. G., Hawkins, J., Abbott, R. D., & Catalano, R. F. (2000). Developmental risk factors for youth violence. *Journal of Adolescent Health, 26,* 176–186.

Hershberger, S., & D'Augelli, A. (1995). The impact of victimization on the mental health and suicidality of lesbian, gay, and bisexual youths. *Developmental Psychology, 31,* 65–74.

Hess, F., Schneider, M., Carey, K., & Kelly, A. (2009). *Diplomas and dropouts: Which colleges actually graduate their students (and which don't).* Washington: American Enterprise Institute.

Hetherington, E. M. (1991). The role of individual differences and family relationships in children's coping with divorce and remarriage. In P. Cowan & E. M. Hetherington (Eds.), *Advances in family research: Vol. 2. Family transitions.* Hillsdale, NJ: Erlbaum.

Hetherington, E. M. (1993). An overview of the Virginia longitudinal study of divorce and remarriage with a focus on early adolescence. *Journal of Family Psychology, 7,* 39–56.

Hetherington, E. M., Bridges, M., & Insabella, G. (1998). What matters? What does not? Five perspectives on the association between marital transitions and children's adjustment. *American Psychologist, 53,* 167–184.

Hetherington, E. M., Clingempeel, W., Anderson, E., Deal, J., Hagan, M., Hollier, E., & Lindner, M. (1992). Coping with marital transitions: A family systems perspective. *Monographs of the Society for Research in Child Development,* Serial No. 227.

Hetherington, E. M., Henderson, S., & Reiss, D. (1999). Adolescent siblings in stepfamilies: Family functioning and adolescent adjustment. *Monographs of the Society for Research in Child Development, 64,* Serial No. 259.

Hetherington, E. M., Reiss, D., & Plomin, R. (Eds.). (1994). *Separate social worlds of siblings: The impact of nonshared environment on development.* Hillsdale, NJ: Erlbaum.

Hetherington, E. M., & Stanley-Hagan, M. (1995). Parenting in divorced and remarried families. In M. Bornstein (Ed.), *Handbook of parenting:* Vol. 3. *Status and social conditions of parenting* (pp. 233–254). Mahwah, NJ: Erlbaum.

Higgins, A., & Turnure, J. (1984). Distractibility and concentration of attention in children's development. *Child Development, 44,* 1799–1810.

Hightower, E. (1990). Adolescent interpersonal and familial predictors of positive mental health at midlife. *Journal of Youth and Adolescence, 19,* 257–276.

Hill, C., & Holzer, H. (2007). Labor market experiences and the transition to adulthood. In S. Danziger & C. Rouse (Eds.), *The price of independence: The economics of early adulthood*. New York: Russell Sage Foundation.

Hill, J., Emery, R. E., Harden, K. P., Mendle, J., & Turkheimer, E. (2008). Alcohol use in adolescent twins and affiliation with substance using peers. *Journal of Abnormal Child Psychology, 36*, 81–94.

Hill, J. P. (1983). Early adolescence: A framework. *Journal of Early Adolescence, 3*, 1–21.

Hill, J. P., & Lynch, M. (1983). The intensification of gender-related role expectations during early adolescence. In J. Brooks-Gunn & A. Petersen (Eds.), *Girls at puberty* (pp. 201–228). New York: Plenum.

Hill, K. G., Hawkins, J. D., Catalano, R. F., Abbott, R. D., & Guo, J. (2005). Family influences on the risk of daily smoking initiation. *Journal of Adolescent Health, 37*, 202–210.

Hill, N. E., Castellino, D. R., Lansford, J. E., Nowlin, P., Dodge, K. A., Bates, J. E., & Pettit, G. S. (2004). Parent academic involvement as related to school behavior, achievement, and aspirations: Demographic variations across adolescence. *Child Development, 75*, 1491–1509.

Hill, N. E., Ramirez, C., & Dumka, L. E. (2003). Early adolescents' career aspirations: A qualitative study of perceived barriers and family support among low-income, ethnically diverse adolescents. *Journal of Family Issues, 24*, 934–959.

Hill, N. E., & Tyson, D. (2009). Parental involvement in middle school: A meta-analytic assessment of the strategies that promote achievement. *Developmental Psychology, 45*, 740–763.

Hilsman, R., & Garber, J. (1995). A test of the cognitive diathesis–stress model of depression in children: Academic stressors, attributional style, perceived competence, and control. *Journal of Personality and Social Psychology, 69*, 370–380.

Hinden, B., Compas, B., Howell, D., & Achenbach, T. (1997). Covariation of the anxious-depressed syndrome during adolescence: Separating fact from artifact. *Journal of Consulting and Clinical Psychology, 65*, 6–14.

Hinduja, S., & Patchin, J. W. (2008). Personal information of adolescents on the Internet: A quantitative content analysis of MySpace. *Journal of Adolescence, 31*, 125–146.

Hine, T. (1999). *The rise and fall of the American teenager*. New York: Bard Books.

Hines, A. (1997). Divorce-related transitions, adolescent development, and the role of the parent–child relationship: A review of the literature. *Journal of Marriage and the Family, 59*, 375–388.

Hingson, R., Heeren, T, & Winter, M. (2006). Age at drinking onset and alcohol dependence: Age at onset, duration, and severity. *Archives of Pediatric and Adolescent Medicine, 160*, 739–746.

Hirsch, B., & DuBois, D. (1991). Self-esteem in early adolescence: The identification and prediction of contrasting longitudinal trajectories. *Journal of Youth and Adolescence, 20*, 53–72.

Hirsch, B., Mickus, M., & Boerger, R. (2002). Ties to influential adults among Black and White adolescents: Culture, social class, and family networks. *American Journal of Community Psychology, 30*, 289–303.

Hitlin, S., Brown, J. S., & Elder, G. H. J. (2006). Racial self-categorization in adolescence: Multiracial development and social pathways. *Child Development, 77*, 1298–1308.

Hock, E., Eberly, M., Bartle-Haring, S., Ellwanger, P., & Widaman, K. F. (2001). Separation anxiety in parents of adolescents: Theoretical significance and scale development. *Child Development, 72*, 284–298.

Hodges, E., Boivin, M., Vitaro, F., & Bukowski, W. (1998). The power of friendship: Protection against an escalating cycle of peer victimization. *Developmental Psychology, 35*, 94–101.

Hodges, E., Finnegan, R., & Perry, D. (1999). Skewed autonomy-relatedness in preadolescents' conceptions of their relationships with mother, father, and best friend. *Developmental Psychology, 35*, 737–748.

Hodges, E., & Perry, D. (1999). Personal and interpersonal antecedents and consequences of victimization by peers. *Journal of Personality and Social Psychology, 76*, 677–685.

Hoeve, M., Blokland, A., Dubas, J. S., Loeber, R., Gerris, J., & van der Laan, P. (2008). Trajectories of delinquency and parenting styles. *Journal of Abnormal Child Psychology, 36*, 223–235.

Hoffer, T. (1997). High school graduation requirements: Effects on dropping out and student achievement. *Teachers College Record, 98*, 584–607.

Hofferth, S. L., & Reid, L. (2002). Early childbearing and children's achievement and behavior over time. *Perspectives on Sexual and Reproductive Health, 34*, 41–49.

Hofferth, S. L., Reid, L., & Mott, F. L. (2001). The effects of early childbearing on schooling over time. *Family Planning Perspective, 33*, 259–267.

Hoffman, J. P. (2002). The community context of family structure and adolescent drug use. *Journal of Marriage and the Family, 64*, 314–330.

Hoffman, J. P. (2003). A contextual analysis of differential association, social control, and strain theories of delinquency. *Social Forces, 81*, 753–785.

Hoffman, K. L., Kiecolt, J., & Edwards, J. N. (2005). Physical violence between siblings: A theoretical and empirical analysis. *Journal of Family Issues, 26*, 1103–1130.

Hoffman, S., Foster, E., & Furstenberg, F., Jr. (1993). Reevaluating the costs of teenage childbearing. *Demography, 30*, 1–13.

Hogan, D., Sun, R., & Cornwell, G. (2000). Sexual and fertility behaviors of American females aged 15–19 years: 1985, 1990, and 1995. *American Journal of Public Health, 90*, 1421–1425.

Hogue, A., & Steinberg, L. (1995). Homophily of internalized distress in adolescent peer groups. *Developmental Psychology, 31*, 897–906.

Holder, D. W., DuRant, R. H., Harris, T. L., Henderson Daniel, J., Obeidallah, D., & Goodman, E. (2000). The association between adolescent spirituality and voluntary sexual activity. *Journal of Adolescent Health, 26*, 295–302.

Hollander, D. (2006). Many teenagers who say they have taken a virginity pledge retract that statement after having intercourse. *Perspectives on Sexual and Reproductive Health, 38*, 168.

Hollingshead, A. (1975). *Elmtown's youth and Elmtown revisited*. New York: Wiley. (Original work published 1949)

Holmbeck, G. (1996). A model of family relational transformations during the transition to adolescence: Parent–adolescent conflict and adaptation. In J. Graber, J. Brooks-Gunn, & A. Petersen (Eds.), *Transitions through adolescence: Interpersonal domains and context* (pp. 167–199). Mahwah, NJ: Erlbaum.

Holmbeck, G., Durbin, D., & Kung, E. (1995, March). *Attachment, autonomy, and adjustment before and after leaving home: Sullivan and Sullivan revisited*. Paper presented at the Society for Research in Child Development, Indianapolis.

Holmbeck, G., & Hill, J. P. (1991). Conflictive engagement, positive affect, and menarche in families with seventh-grade girls. *Child Development, 62*, 1030–1048.

Holmbeck, G., & O'Donnell, K. (1991). Longitudinal study of discrepancies between maternal and adolescent perceptions of decision-making and desired behavioral autonomy. In R. Paikoff & W. A. Collins (Eds.), *New directions for child development: Shared views of the family during adolescence* (pp. 51–69). San Francisco: Jossey-Bass.

Holmbeck, G., Shapera, W., Westhoven, V., Johnson, S., Millstein, R., & Hommeyer, J. (2000, March). *A longitudinal study of observed and perceived parenting behaviors and autonomy development in families of young adolescents with spina bifida*. Paper presented at the biennial meetings of the Society for Research on Adolescence, Chicago.

Holmen, T., Barrett-Connor, E., Holmen, J., & Bjerner, L. (2000). Health problems in teenage daily smokers versus nonsmokers, Norway, 1995–1997. *American Journal of Epidemiology, 151*, 148–155.

Holsen, I., Kraft, P., & Vitterso, J. (2000). Stability in depressed mood in adolescence: Results from a 6-year longitudinal panel study. *Journal of Youth and Adolescence, 29,* 61–78.

Hooper, C. J., Luciana, M., Conklin, H. M., & Yarger, R. S. (2004). Adolescents' performance on the Iowa gambling task: Implications for the development of decision making and ventromedial prefrontal cortex. *Developmental Psychology, 40,* 1148–1158.

Hoover-Dempsey, K., & Sandler, H. (1995). Parental involvement in children's education: Why does it make a difference? *Teachers College Record, 97,* 310–331.

Horan, P., & Hargis, P. (1991). Children's work and schooling in the late nineteenth-century family economy. *American Sociological Review, 56,* 583–596.

Horn, S. S. (2003). Adolescents' reasoning about exclusion from social groups. *Developmental Psychology, 39,* 71–84.

Horn, S. S. (2007). Adolescents' acceptance of same-sex peers based on sexual orientation and gender expression. *Journal of Youth and Adolescence, 36,* 363–371.

Horner, J., Jamieson, P., & Romer, D. (2008). The changing portrayal of alcohol use in television. In P. Jamieson & D. Romer (Eds.), *The changing portrayal of adolescents in the media since 1950* (pp. 284–312). New York: Oxford University Press.

Hornik, R., Jacobsohn, L., Orwin, R., Piesse, A., & Kalton, G. (2008). Effects of the national youth anti-drug media campaign on youths. *American Journal of Public Health, 98,* 2229–2236.

Horvat, E. M., & Lewis, K. S. (2003). Reassessing the "burden of 'acting White'": The importance of peer group in managing academic success. *Sociology of Education, 76,* 265–280.

Hovell, M., Sipan, C., Blumberg, E., Atkins, C., Hofsterrer, C., & Kreitner, S. (1994). Family influences on Latino and Anglo adolescents' sexual behavior. *Journal of Marriage and the Family, 56,* 973–986.

Howell, W., & Peterson, P. (2002). *The education gap: Vouchers and urban schools.* Washington, DC: Brookings Institution.

Hoza, B., Molina, B., Bukowski, W., & Sippola, L. (1995). Peer variables as predictors of later childhood adjustment. *Development and Psychopathology, 7,* 787–802.

Hu, M., Davies, M., & Kandel, D. (2006). Epidemiology and correlates of daily smoking and nicotine dependence among young adults in the United States. *American Journal of Public Health, 96,* 299–308.

Hudley, C. (1995). Assessing the impact of separate schooling for African American male adolescents. *Journal of Early Adolescence, 15,* 38–57.

Hudley, C. (1997). Supporting achievement beliefs among ethnic minority adolescents: Two case examples. *Journal of Research on Adolescence, 7,* 133–152.

Huebner, A. J., & Howell, L. W. (2003). Examining the relationship between adolescent sexual risk-taking and perceptions of monitoring, communication, and parenting styles. *Journal of Adolescent Health, 33,* 71–78.

Huebner, A. J., & Mancini, J. A. (2003). Shaping structured out-of-school time use among youth: The effects of self, family, and friend systems. *Journal of Youth and Adolescence, 32,* 453–463.

Huesmann, L. R. (2007). The impact of electronic media violence: Scientific theory and research. *Journal of Adolescent Health, 41,* S6–S13.

Hughes, S., Power, T., & Francis, D. (1992). Defining patterns of drinking in adolescence: A cluster analytic approach. *Journal of Studies on Alcohol, 53,* 40–47.

Huh, D., Tristan, J., Wade, E., & Stice, E. (2006). Does problem behavior elicit poor parenting?: A prospective study of adolescent girls. *Journal of Adolescent Research, 21,* 185–204.

Huizenga, H., Crone, E., & Jansen, B. (2007). Decision-making in healthy children, adolescent and adults explained by the use of increasingly complex proportional reasoning rules. *Developmental Science, 10,* 814–825.

Hunter, J., & Csikszentmihalyi, M. (2003). The positive psychology of interested adolescents. *Journal of Youth and Adolescence, 32,* 27–35.

Huntsinger, C. S., & Jose, P. E. (2006). A longitudinal investigation of personality and social adjustment among Chinese American and European American adolescents. *Child Development, 77,* 1309–1324.

Hurley, D. (2005, April 19). Divorce rate: It's not as high as you think. *The New York Times.*

Hussong, A. M. (2000). Perceived peer context and adolescent adjustment. *Journal of Research on Adolescence, 10,* 391–415.

Hussong, A. M., & Hicks, R. E. (2003). Affect and peer context interactively impact adolescent substance use. *Journal of Abnormal Child Psychology, 31,* 413–426.

Hussong, A. M., Curran, P. J., & Moffitt, T. E. (2004). Substance abuse hinders desistance in young adults' antisocial behavior. *Development and Psychopathology, 16,* 1029–1046.

Hutchinson, M. K., Jemmott, J. B., III, Jemmott, L. S., Braverman, P., & Fong, G. T. (2003). The role of mother–daughter sexual risk communication in reducing sexual risk behaviors among urban adolescent females: A prospective study. *Journal of Adolescent Health, 33,* 98–107.

Huynh, V. W., & Fuligni, A. (2008). Ethnic socialization and the academic adjustment of adolescents from Mexican, Chinese, and European backgrounds. *Developmental Psychology, 44,* 1202–1208.

Hymel, S., Bowker, A., & Woody, E. (1993). Aggressive versus withdrawn unpopular children: Variations in peer and self-perceptions in multiple domains. *Child Development, 64,* 879–896.

Hymel, S., Rubin, K., Rowden, L., & LeMare, L. (1990). Children's peer relationships: Longitudinal prediction of internalizing and externalizing problems from middle to late childhood. *Child Development, 61,* 2004–2021.

Ibañez, G. E., Kuperminc, G. P., Jurkovic, G., & Perilla, J. (2004). Cultural attributes and adaptations linked to achievement motivation among Latino adolescents. *Journal of Youth and Adolescence, 33,* 559–568.

Iglowstein, I., Jenni, O., Molinari, L., & Largo, R. (2003). Sleep duration from infancy to adolescence: Reference values and generational trends. *Pediatrics, 111,* 302–307.

Impett, E. A., Sorsoli, L., Schooler, D., Henson, J. M., & Tolman, D. L. (2008). Girls' relationship authenticity and self-esteem across adolescence. *Developmental Psychology, 44,* 722–733.

Impett, E. A., & Tolman, D. L. (2006). Late adolescent girls' sexual experiences and sexual satisfaction. *Journal of Adolescent Research, 21,* 628–646.

Ingoldsby, E. M., Kohl, G. O., McMahon, R. J., & Lengua, L. (2006). Conduct problems, depressive symptomatology and their co-occurring presentation in childhood as predictors of adjustment in early adolescence. *Journal of Abnormal Child Psychology, 34,* 603–621.

Inhelder, B., & Piaget, J. (1958). *The growth of logical thinking from childhood to adolescence.* New York: Basic Books.

Institute of Medicine (2006). *Food marketing to children and youth: Threat or opportunity?* Washington, DC: National Academies Press.

Irwin, C., Jr. (1986). Biopsychosocial correlates of risk-taking behavior during adolescence: Can the physician intervene? *Journal of Adolescent Health Care, 7,* 82–96.

Irwin, K. (2004). The violence of adolescent life experiencing and managing everyday threats. *Youth and Society, 35,* 452–479.

Isakson, K., & Jarvis, P. (1999). The adjustment of adolescents during the transition into high school: A short term longitudinal study. *Journal of Youth and Adolescence, 28,* 1–26.

Ivory, J. (2008). The games, they are a-changin': Technological advancements in video games and implications for effects on youth. In P. Jamieson & D. Romer (Eds.), *The changing portrayal of adolescents in the media since 1950* (pp. 347–376). New York: Oxford University Press.

Jaccard, J., Blanton, H., & Dodge, T. (2005). Peer influences on risk behavior: An analysis of the effects of a close friend. *Developmental Psychology, 41,* 135–147.

Jaccard, J., Dittus, P., & Gordon, V. (1998). Parent–adolescent congruency in reports of adolescent sexual behavior and in communications about sexual behavior. *Child Development, 69,* 247–261.

Jaccard, J., Dodge, T., & Dittus, P. (2003a). Do adolescents want to avoid pregnancy? Attitudes toward pregnancy as predictors of pregnancy. *Journal of Adolescent Health, 33,* 79–83.

Jaccard, J., Dodge, T., & Dittus, P. (2003b). Maternal discussion about pregnancy and adolescents' attitudes towards pregnancy. *Journal of Adolescent Health, 33,* 84–87.

Jacklin, C. (1989). Female and male: Issues of gender. *American Psychologist, 44,* 127–133.

Jackson, C. (2002). Perceived legitimacy of parental authority and tobacco and alcohol use during early adolescence. *Journal of Adolescent Health, 31,* 425–432.

Jackson, L. (2008). Adolescents and the Internet. In P. Jamieson & D. Romer (Eds.), *The changing portrayal of adolescents in the media since 1950* (pp. 377–411). New York: Oxford University Press.

Jackson-Newsom, J., Buchanan, C. M., & McDonald, R. M. (2008). Parenting and perceived maternal warmth in European American and African American adolescents. *Journal of Marriage and Family, 70,* 62–75.

Jacobi, C., Hayward, C., de Zwaan, M., Kraemer, H. C., & Agras, W. S. (2004). Coming to terms with risk factors for eating disorders: Application of risk terminology and suggestions for a general taxonomy. *Psychological Bulletin, 130,* 19–65.

Jacobs, J. E., Chin, C. S., & Shaver, K. (2005). Longitudinal links between perceptions of adolescence and the social beliefs of adolescents: Are parents' stereotypes related to beliefs held about and by their children? *Journal of Youth and Adolescence, 34,* 61–72.

Jacobs, J. E., Lanza, S., Osgood, D., Eccles, J., & Wigfield, A. (2002). Changes in children's self-competence and values: Gender and domain differences across grades one through twelve. *Child Development, 73,* 509–527.

Jacobs, J. E., & Portenza, M. (1991). The use of judgment heuristics to make social and object decisions: A developmental perspective. *Child Development, 62,* 166–178.

Jacobsen, T., Edelstein, W., & Hofmann, V. (1994). A longitudinal study of the relation between representations of attachment in childhood and cognitive functioning in childhood and adolescence. *Developmental Psychology, 30,* 112–124.

Jacobson, K., & Rowe, D. (1999). Genetic and environmental influences on the relationships between family connectedness, school connectedness, and adolescent depressed mood: Sex differences. *Developmental Psychology, 35,* 926–939.

Jaffari-Bimmel, N., Juffer, F., van IJzendoorn, M. H., Bakermans-Kranenburg, M., & Mooijaart, A. (2006). Social development from infancy to adolescence: Longitudinal and concurrent factors in an adoption sample. *Developmental Psychology, 42,* 1143–1153.

Jaffee, S., Caspi, A., Moffitt, T. E., Belsky, J., & Silva, P. (2001). Why are children born to teen mothers at risk for adverse outcomes in young adulthood? Results from a 20-year longitudinal study. *Development and Psychopathology, 13,* 377–397.

Jakobsen, R., Rise, J., Aas, H., & Anderssen, N. (1997). Noncoital sexual interactions and problem behaviour among young adolescents: The Norwegian Longitudinal Health Behaviour Study. *Journal of Adolescence, 20,* 71–83.

Jamieson, P., More, E., Lee, S., Busse, P., & Romer, D. (2008). It matters what young people watch: Health risk behaviors portrayed in top-grossing movies since 1950. In P. Jamieson & D. Romer (Eds.), *The changing portrayal of adolescents in the media since 1950* (pp. 105–131). New York: Oxford University Press.

Jang, S., & Thornberry, T. (1998). Self-esteem, delinquent peers, and delinquency: A test of the self-enhancement thesis. *American Sociological Review, 63,* 586–598.

Janosz, M., Archambault, I., Pagani, L. S., Pascal, S., Morin, A. J. S., & Bowen, F. (2008). Are there detrimental effects of witnessing school violence in early adolescence? *Journal of Adolescent Health, 43,* 600–608.

Janosz, M., LeBlanc, M., Boulerice, B., & Tremblay, R. E. (1997). Disentangling the weight of school dropout predictors: A test on two longitudinal samples. *Journal of Youth & Adolescence, 26,* 733–762.

Janosz, M., LeBlanc, M., Boulerice, B., & Tremblay, R. E. (2000). Predicting different types of school dropouts: A typological approach with two longitudinal samples. *Journal of Educational Psychology, 92,* 171–190.

Jarrett, R. (1995). Growing up poor: The family experiences of socially mobile youth in low-income African American neighborhoods. *Journal of Adolescent Research, 10,* 111–135.

Jaser, S. S., Champion, J. E., Reeslund, K. L., Keller, G., Merchant, M. J., Benson, M., et al. (2007). Cross-situational coping with peer and family stressors in adolescent offspring of depressed parents. *Journal of Adolescence, 30,* 917–932.

Jemmott, J., III, Jemmott, L., Fong, G., & McCaffree, K. (1999). Reducing HIV risk-associated sexual behavior among African American adolescents: Testing the generality of intervention effects. *American Journal of Community Psychology, 27,* 161–187.

Jensen, L. A., Arnett, J. J., Feldman, S. S., & Cauffman, E. (2004). The right to do wrong: Lying to parents among adolescents and emerging adults. *Journal of Youth and Adolescence, 33,* 101–112.

Jessor, R., & Jessor, S. (1977). Problem behavior and psychosocial development: A longitudinal study of youth. New York: Academic Press.

Jessor, R., Turbin, M., & Costa, F. (1998). Protective factors in adolescent health behavior. *Journal of Personality and Social Psychology, 75,* 788–800.

Jessor, R., Turbin, M. S., Costa, F. M., Dong, Q., Zhang, H., & Wang, C. (2003). Adolescent problem behavior in China and the United States: A cross-national study of psychosocial protective factors. *Journal of Research on Adolescence, 13,* 329–360.

Jessor, R., Van Den Bos, J., Vanderryn, J., Costa, F., & Turbin, M. (1995). Protective factors in adolescent problem behavior: Moderator effects and developmental change. *Developmental Psychology, 31,* 923–933.

Jeynes, W. (1999). Effects of remarriage following divorce on the academic achievement of children. *Journal of Youth and Adolescence, 28,* 385–393.

Jeynes, W. (2001). The effects of recent parental divorce on their children's consumption of alcohol. *Journal of Youth and Adolescence, 30,* 305–319.

Jeynes, W. (2002). A meta-analysis of the effects of attending religious schools and religiosity on Black and Hispanic academic achievement. *Education and Urban Society, 35,* 27–49.

Jodl, K. M., Michael, A., Malanchuk, O., Eccles, J., & Sameroff, A. (2001). Parents' roles in shaping early adolescents' occupational aspirations. *Child Development, 72,* 1247–1265.

John, O., Caspi, A., Robins, R., Moffitt, T., & Stouthamer-Loeber, M. (1994). The "Little Five": Exploring the nomological network of the five-factor model of personality in adolescent boys. *Child Development, 65,* 160–178.

Johnson, C. A., Xiao, L., Palmer, P., Sun, P., Wang, Q., Wei, Y., et al. (2008). Affective decision-making deficits, linked to a dysfunctional ventromedial prefrontal cortex, revealed in 10th grade Chinese adolescent binge drinkers. *Neuropsychologia, 46,* 714–726.

Johnson, E., Roth, T., Schultz, L., & Breslau, N. (2006). Epidemiology of DSM-IV insomnia in adolescence: Lifetime prevalence, chronicity, and emergent gender difference. *Pediatrics, 117,* 247–256.

Johnson, J. G., Cohen, P., Kotler, L., Kasen, S., & Brook, J. S. (2002). Psychiatric disorders associated with risk for the development of eating disorders during adolescence and early adulthood. *Journal of Consulting and Clinical Psychology, 70,* 1119–1128.

Johnson, M. (2002). Social origins, adolescent experiences, and work value trajectories during the transition to adulthood. *Social Forces, 80,* 1307–1341.

Johnson, M., Elder, G., & Stern, M. (2005). Attachments to family and community and the young adult transition of rural youth. *Journal of Research on Adolescence, 15,* 99–125.

Johnson, R., & Gerstein, D. (1998). Initiation of use of alcohol, cigarettes, marijuana, cocaine, and other substances in U.S. birth cohorts since 1919. *American Journal of Public Health, 88,* 27–33.

Johnson, R., Johnson, D., Wang, M., Smiciklas-Wright, H., & Guthrie, H. (1994). Characterizing nutrient intakes of adolescents by sociodemographic factors. *Journal of Adolescent Health, 15,* 149–154.

Johnson, W., McGue, M., & Iacono, W. G. (2006). Genetic and environmental influences on academic achievement trajectories during adolescence. *Developmental Psychology, 42,* 514–532.

Johnston, L. D., O'Malley, P., Bachman, J., & Schulenberg, J. (2009). *Monitoring the Future national results on adolescent drug use: Overview of key findings, 2008.* Bethesda, MD: National Institute on Drug Abuse.

Johnston, M., Crosnoe, R., & Elder, G. H., Jr. (2001). Students' attachment and academic engagement: The role of race and ethnicity. *Sociology of Education, 74,* 318–340.

Jones, D., & Costin, S. (1993, March). *Helping orientations, sex role characteristics, and friendship satisfaction during preadolescence and adolescence.* Paper presented at the biennial meetings of the Society for Research in Child Development, New Orleans.

Jones, D., Costin, S., & Ricard, R. (1994, February). *Ethnic and sex differences in best friendship characteristics among African-American, Mexican-American, and European-American adolescents.* Paper presented at the biennial meetings of the Society for Research on Adolescence, San Diego.

Jones, D. C., Vigfusdottir, T. II., & Lee, Y. (2004). Body image and the appearance culture among adolescent girls and boys: An examination of friend conversations, peer criticism, appearance magazines, and the internalization of appearance ideals. *Journal of Adolescent Research, 19,* 323–339.

Jones, D. J., Forehand, R., Brody, G., & Armistead, L. (2002). Psychosocial adjustment of African American children in single-mother families: A test of three risk models. *Journal of Marriage and the Family, 64,* 105–115.

Jones, J., Vanfossen, B., & Ensminger, M. (1995). Individual and organizational predictors of track placement. *Sociology of Education, 68,* 287–300.

Jones, M., Luce, K. H., Osborne, M. I., Taylor, K., Cunning, D., Doyle, A. C., et al. (2008). Randomized, controlled trial of an Internet-facilitated intervention for reducing binge eating and overweight in adolescents. *Pediatrics, 121,* 453–462.

Jones, M. C., & Bayley, N. (1950). Physical maturing among boys as related to behavior. *Journal of Educational Psychology, 41,* 129–148.

Jones, M. D., & Galliher, R. V. (2007). Ethnic identity and psychosocial functioning in Navajo adolescents. *Journal of Research on Adolescence, 17,* 683–696.

Jones, N., Pieper, C., & Robertson, L. (1992). The effect of legal drinking age on fatal injuries of adolescents and young adults. *American Journal of Public Health, 82,* 112–115.

Jones, R. K., Darroch, J. E., & Singh, S. (2005). Religious differentials in the sexual and reproductive behaviors of young women in the United States. *Journal of Adolescent Health, 36,* 279–288.

Jones, R. K., Purcell, A., Singh, S., & Finer, L. B. (2005). Adolescents' reports of parental knowledge of adolescents' use of sexual health services and their reactions to mandated parental notification for prescription contraception. *Journal of the American Medical Association, 293,* 340–348.

Jones, S., & Cauffman, E. (2008). Juvenile psychopathy and judicial decision making: An empirical analysis of an ethical dilemma. *Behavioral Sciences & the Law, 26,* 151–165.

Jones, S., & Fox, S. (2009). *Generations online in 2009.* Washington: Pew Internet & American Life Project.

Jonkmann, K., Trautwein, U., & Ludtke, O. (2009). Social dominance in adolescence: The moderation role of the classroom context and behavioral heterogeneity. *Child Development, 80,* 338–355.

Jordan, A., & Cole, D. (1996). Relation of depressive symptoms to the structure of self-knowledge in childhood. *Journal of Abnormal Psychology, 105,* 530–540.

Jordan, L. C., & Lewis, M. L. (2005). Paternal relationship quality as a protective factor: Preventing alcohol use among African American adolescents. *Journal of Black Psychology, 31,* 152–171.

Jordan, W., Lara, J., & McPartland, J. (1996). Exploring the causes of early dropout among race-ethnic and gender groups. *Youth and Society, 28,* 62–94.

Jose, P. E., & Brown, I. (2008). When does the gender difference in rumination begin? Gender and age differences in the use of rumination by adolescents. *Journal of Youth and Adolescence, 37,* 180–192.

Joyce T., Kaestner, R., & Colman, S. (2006). Changes in abortions and births and the Texas parental notification law. *New England Journal of Medicine, 354,* 1031–1038.

Joyce, T., & Mocan, N. (1990). The impact of legalized abortion on adolescent childbearing in New York City. *American Journal of Public Health, 80,* 273–278.

Joyner, K., & Udry, J. R. (2000). You don't bring me anything but down: Adolescent romance and depression. *Journal of Health and Social Behavior, 41,* 369–391.

Jozefowicz, D., Barber, B., Eccles, J., & Mollasis, C. (1994, February). *Relations between maternal and adolescent values and beliefs: Gender differences and implications for occupational choice.* Paper presented at the biennial meetings of the Society for Research on Adolescence, San Diego.

Juang, L., Lerner, J., McKinney, J., & von Eye, A. (1999). The goodness of fit in autonomy timetable expectations between Asian-Americans late adolescents and their parents. *International Journal of Behavioral Development, 23,* 1023–1048.

Juang, L., Nguyen, H. H., & Lin, Y. (2006). The ethnic identity, other-group attitudes, and psychosocial functioning of Asian American emerging adults from two contexts. *Journal of Adolescent Research, 21,* 542–568.

Juang, L., & Silbereisen, R. K. (2002). The relationship between adolescent academic capability beliefs, parenting and school grades. *Journal of Adolescence, 25,* 3–18.

Judge, B., & Billick, S. B. (2004). Suicidality in adolescence: Review and legal considerations. *Behavioral Sciences and the Law, 22,* 681–695.

Jumping-Eagle, S., Sheeder, J., Kelly, L. S., & Stevens-Simon, C. (2008). Association of conventional goals and perceptions of pregnancy with female teenagers' pregnancy avoidance behavior and attitudes. *Perspectives on Sexual and Reproductive Health, 40,* 74–80.

Jussim, L., Eccles, J., & Madon, S. (1996). Social perception, social stereotypes, and teacher expectations: Accuracy and the quest for the powerful self-fulfilling prophecy. *Advances in Experimental Social Psychology, 28,* 281–388.

Juvonen, J., Graham, S., & Schuster, M., A. (2003). Bullying among young adolescents: The strong, the weak, and the troubled. *Pediatrics, 112,* 1231–1237.

Juvonen, J., & Gross, E. F. (2008). Extending the school grounds? Bullying experiences in cyberspace. *Journal of School Health, 78,* 496–505.

Juvonen, J., & Murdock, T. (1995). Grade-level differences in the social value of effort: Implications for self-presentation tactics of early adolescents. *Child Development, 66,* 1694–1705.

Juvonen, J., Nishina, A., & Graham, S. (2000). Peer harassment, psychological adjustment, and school functioning in early adolescence. *Journal of Educational Psychology, 92,* 349–359.

Juvonen, J., Nishina, A., & Graham, S. (2006). Ethnic diversity and perceptions of safety in urban middle schools. *Psychological Science, 17,* 393–400.

Kaestle, C. E., Halpern, C. T., Miller, W. C., & Ford, C. A. (2005). Young age at first sexual intercourse and sexually transmitted infections in adolescents and young adults. *American Journal of Epidemiology, 161,* 774–780.

Kaestle, C. E., Morisky, D. E., & Wiley, D. J. (2002). Sexual intercourse and the age difference between adolescent females and their romantic partners. *Perspectives on Sexual and Reproductive Health, 34,* 304–305.

Kahne, J. E., & Sporte, S. E. (2008). Developing citizens: The impact of civic learning opportunities on students' commitment to civic participation. *American Educational Research Journal, 45,* 738–766.

Kahneman, D., Slovic, P., & Tversky, A. (Eds.). (1982). *Judgment under uncertainty: Heuristics and biases.* New York: Cambridge University Press.

Kail, R. V., & Ferrer, E. (2007). Processing speed in childhood and adolescence: Longitudinal models for examining developmental change. *Child Development, 78,* 1760–1770.

Kalakoski, V., & Nurmi, J.-E. (1998). Identity and educational transitions: Age differences in adolescent exploration and commitment related to education, occupation, and family. *Journal of Research on Adolescence, 8,* 29–47.

Kalil, A., & Eccles, J. (1998). Does welfare affect family processes and adolescent adjustment? *Child Development, 69,* 1597–1613.

Kalil, A., & Kunz, J. (2002). Teenage childbearing, marital status, and depressive symptoms in later life. *Child Development, 73,* 1748–1760.

Kalil, A., & Ziol-Guest, K. (2008). Teacher support, school goal structures, and teenage mothers' school engagement. *Youth and Society, 39,* 524–548.

Kalmuss, D., & Namerow, P. (1994). Subsequent childbearing among teenage mothers: The determinants of a closely spaced second birth. *Family Planning Perspectives, 26,* 149–153, 159.

Kamenetz, A. (2006, May 30). Take this internship and shove it. *The New York Times,* p. A19.

Kandel, D. (1978). Homophily, selection, and socialization in adolescent friendships. *American Journal of Sociology, 84,* 427–436.

Kandel, D. (1980). Drug and drinking behavior among youth. *Annual Review of Sociology, 6,* 235–285.

Kandel, D., Johnson, J., Bird, H., & Canino, G. (1997). Psychiatric disorders associated with substance use among children and adolescents: Findings from the Methods for the Epidemiology of Child and Adolescent Mental Disorders (MECA) Study. *Journal of Abnormal Child Psychology, 25,* 121–132.

Kantor, H. (1994). Managing the transition from school to work: The false promise of youth apprenticeship. *Teachers College Record, 95,* 442–461.

Kantor, H., & Brenzel, B. (1992). Urban education and the "truly disadvantaged": The historical roots of the contemporary crisis, 1945–1990. *Teachers College Record, 94,* 278–314.

Kao, G. (1999). Psychological well-being and educational achievement among immigrant youth. In D. Hernandez (Ed.), *Children of immigrants: Health, adjustment, and public assistance* (pp. 410–477). Washington, DC: National Academy Press.

Kao, G., & Tienda, M. (1995). Optimism and achievement: The educational performance of immigrant youth. *Social Science Quarterly, 76,* 1–19.

Kao, G., & Tienda, M. (1998). Educational aspirations of minority youth. *American Journal of Education, 106,* 349–384.

Kaplan, C., Erickson, P., & Juarez-Reyes, M. (2002). Acculturation, gender role orientation, and reproductive risk-taking behavior among Latina adolescent family planning. *Journal of Adolescent Research, 17,* 103–121.

Karavasilis, L., Doyle, A. B., & Markiewicz, D. (2003). Associations between parenting style and attachment to mother in middle childhood and adolescence. *International Journal of Behavioral Development, 27,* 153–164.

Karpati, A. M., Rubin, C. H., Kieszak, S. M., Marcus, M., & Troiano, R. P. (2002). Stature and pubertal stage assessment in American boys: The 1988–1994 Third National Health and Nutrition Examination Survey. *Journal of Adolescent Health, 30,* 205–212.

Karriker-Jaffe, K., Foshee, V. A., Ennett, S. T., & Suchindran, C. (2008). The development of aggression during adolescence: Sex differences in trajectories of physical and social aggression among youth in rural areas. *Journal of Abnormal Child Psychology, 36,* 1227–1236.

Karriker-Jaffe, K., Foshee, V. A., Ennett, S. T., & Suchindran, C. (2009). Sex differences in the effects of neighborhood socioeconomic disadvantage and social organization on rural adolescents' aggression trajectories. *American Journal of Community Psychology, 43,* 189–203.

Kasen, S., Cohen, P., & Brook, J. (1998). Adolescent school experiences and dropout, adolescent pregnancy, and young adult deviant behavior. *Journal of Adolescent Research, 13,* 49–72.

Kaslow, N. J., Adamson, L. B., & Collins, M. H. (2000). A developmental psychopathology perspective on the cognitive components of child and adolescent depression. In A. J. Sameroff, M. Lewis, & S. M. Miller (Eds.), *Handbook of developmental psychopathology* (2nd ed., pp. 491–510). New York: Plenum.

Kassin, S. (2008). The psychology of confessions. *Annual Review of Law and Social Science, 4,* 193–217.

Katainen, S., Raeikkoenen, K., & Keltikangas-Jaervinen, L. (1998). Development of temperament: Childhood temperament and the mother's childrearing attitudes as predictors of adolescent temperament in a 9-year follow-up study. *Journal of Research on Adolescence, 8,* 485–509.

Katz, E., Blumler, J., & Gurevitch, M. (1974). Uses and gratifications research. *Public Opinion Quarterly, 37,* 509–523.

Katz, M. (1975). *The people of Hamilton, Canada West: Family and class in a mid-nineteenth-century city.* Cambridge, MA: Harvard University Press.

Kaufman, K., Gregory, W., & Stephan, W. (1990). Maladjustment in statistical minorities within ethnically unbalanced classrooms. *American Journal of Community Psychology, 18,* 757–762.

Kaye, K. (2009). *Changes in the teen birth rate from 1991 to 2005 and 2005 to 2006: Assessing the role of changes in the teen population.* Washington, DC: National Campaign to Prevent Teen and Unplanned Pregnancy.

Kazis, R. (1993). *Improving the transition from school to work in the United States.* Washington, DC: American Youth Policy Forum, Competitiveness Policy Council, and Jobs for the Future.

Keating, D. (1995). Habits of mind: Developmental diversity in competence and coping. In D. Detterman (Ed.), *Current topics in human intelligence: The role of the environment* (pp. 31–44). Norwood, NJ: Ablex.

Keating, D. (2004). Cognitive and brain development. In R. Lerner & L. Steinberg (Eds.), *Handbook of adolescent psychology* (2nd ed.). New York: Wiley.

Keating, D., & Hertzman, C. (Eds.). (2000). *Developmental health and the wealth of nations: Social, biological, and educational dynamics.* New York: Guilford Press.

Keefe, K., & Berndt, T. (1996). Relations of friendship quality to self-esteem in early adolescence. *Journal of Early Adolescence, 16,* 110–129.

Keel, P. K., & Klump, K. L. (2003). Are eating disorders culture-bound syndromes? Implications for conceptualizing their etiology. *Psychological Bulletin, 129,* 747–769.

Keenan, K., Loeber, R., Zhang, Q., Stouthamer-Loeber, M., & Van Kammen, W. (1995). The influence of deviant peers on the development of boys' disruptive and delinquent behavior: A temporal analysis. *Development and Psychopathology, 7,* 715–726.

Kellam, S., Ling, X., Merisca, R., Brown, C., & Ialongo, N. (1998). The effect of the level of aggression in the first grade classroom on the course and malleability of aggressive behavior into middle school. *Development and Psychopathology, 10,* 165–185.

Keller, J. (2002). Blatant stereotype threat and women's math performances: Self-handicapping as a strategic means to cope with obtrusive negative performance expectations. *Sex Roles, 47,* 193–198.

Keller, M., Edelstein, W., Schmid, C., Fang, F., & Fang, G. (1998). Reasoning about responsibilities and obligations in close relationships: A comparison across two cultures. *Developmental Psychology, 34,* 731–741.

Kelly, A., Wall, M., Eisenberg, M., Story, M., & Neumark-Sztainer, D. (2005). Adolescent girls with high body satisfaction: Who are they and what can they teach us? *Journal of Adolescent Health, 37,* 391–396.

Kelly, S. (2009). The Black-White gap in mathematics course taking. *Sociology of Education, 82,* 47–69.

Keniston, K. (1970). Youth: A "new" stage of life. *American Scholar, 39,* 631–641.

Kenyon, D. B., Rankin, L. A., Koerner, S. S., & Dennison, R. P. (2007). What makes an adult? Examining descriptions from adolescents of divorce. *Journal of Youth and Adolescence, 36*, 813–823.

Kerns, K. (1996). Individual differences in friendship quality: Links to child–mother attachment. In W. Bukowski, A. Newcomb, & W. Hartup, W. (Eds.), *The company they keep: Friendship in childhood and adolescence* (pp. 137–157). New York: Cambridge University Press.

Kerr, M., & Stattin, H. (2000). What parents know, how they know it, and several forms of adolescent adjustment: Further support for a reinterpretation of monitoring. *Developmental Psychology, 36*, 366–380.

Kett, J. (1977). *Rites of passage: Adolescence in America, 1790 to the present.* New York: Basic Books.

Khoury-Kassibri, M., Benbensihty, R., Astor, R. A., & Zeira, A. (2004). The contributions of community, family, and school variables to student victimization. *American Journal of Community Psychology, 34*, 187–204.

Kiang, L., & Fuligni, A. J. (2009). Ethnic identity and family processes among adolescents from Latin American, Asian, and European backgrounds. *Journal of Youth and Adolescence, 38*, 228–241.

Kiang, L., Yip, T., Gonzales-Backen, M., Witkow, M., & Fuligni, A. J. (2006). Ethnic identity and the daily psychological well-being of adolescents from Mexican and Chinese backgrounds. *Child Development, 77*, 1338–1350.

Kidd, S. A. (2004). "The walls were closing in, and we were trapped": A qualitative analysis of street youth suicide. *Youth and Society, 36*, 30–55.

Kiesner, J. (2002). Depressive symptoms in early adolescence: Their relations with classroom problem behavior and peer status. *Journal of Research on Adolescence, 12*, 463–478.

Kiesner, J., Cadinu, M., Poulin, F., & Bucci, M. (2002). Group identification in early adolescence: Its relation with peer adjustment and its moderator effect on peer influence. *Child Development, 73*, 196–208.

Kiesner, J., & Pastore, M. (2005). Differences in the relations between antisocial behavior and peer acceptance across contexts and across adolescence. *Child Development, 76*, 1278–1293.

Kiesner, J., Poulin, F., & Nicotra, E. (2003). Peer relations across contexts: Individual–network homophily and network inclusion in and after school. *Child Development, 74*, 1328–1343.

Kilborn, P. (1996, November 27). Shifts in families reach a plateau, study says. *The New York Times*, p. A16.

Killen, M., Henning, A., Kelly, M. C., Crystal, D., & Ruck, M. (2007). Evaluations of interracial peer encounters by majority and minority U.S. children and adolescents. *International Journal of Behavioral Development, 31*, 491–500.

Killen, M., & Turiel, E. (1998). Adolescents' and young adults' evaluations of helping and sacrificing for others. *Journal of Research on Adolescence, 8*, 355–375.

Killian, K. (1994). Fearing fat: A literature review of family systems understandings and treatments of anorexia and bulimia. *Family Relations, 43*, 311–318.

Kilpatrick, D., Acierno, R., Saunders, B., Resnick, H., Best, C., & Schnurr, P. (2000). Risk factors for adolescent substance abuse and dependence: Data from a national sample. *Journal of Consulting and Clinical Psychology, 68*, 19–30.

Kim, C. R., & Free, C. (2008). Recent evaluations of the peer-led approach in adolescent sexual health education: A systematic review. *Perspectives on Sexual and Reproductive Health, 40*, 144–151.

Kim, H. K., & Capaldi, D. M. (2004). The association of antisocial behavior and depressive symptoms between partners and risk for aggression in romantic relationships. *Journal of Family Psychology 18*, 82–96.

Kim, H. K., Capaldi, D. M., & Stoolmiller, M. (2003). Depressive symptoms across adolescence and young adulthood in men: Predictions from parental and contextual risk factors. *Development and Psychopathology, 15*, 469–495.

Kim, I. J., Zane, N., & Hong, S. (2002). Protective factors against substance use among Asian American youth: A test of the peer cluster theory. *Journal of Community Psychology, 30*, 565–584.

Kim, J., Hetherington, E. M., & Reiss, D. (1999). Associations among family relationships, antisocial peers, and adolescents' externalizing behaviors: Gender and family type differences. *Child Development, 70*, 1209–1230.

Kim, J., McHale, S. M., Crouter, A. C., & Osgood, D. W. (2007). Longitudinal linkages between sibling relationships and adjustment from middle childhood through adolescence. *Developmental Psychology, 43*, 960–973.

Kim, J., McHale, S. M., Osgood, D. W., & Crouter, A. C. (2006). Longitudinal course and family correlates of sibling relationships from childhood through adolescence. *Child Development, 77*, 1746–1761.

Kim, J. L., & Ward, L. M. (2007). Silence speaks volumes: Parental sexual communication among Asian American emerging adults. *Journal of Adolescent Research, 22*, 3–31.

Kim, K., Conger, R. D., Elder, G. H., Jr., & Lorenz, F. O. (2003). Reciprocal influences between stressful life events and adolescent internalizing and externalizing problems. *Child Development, 74*, 127–143.

Kim, K., Conger, R. D., Lorenz, F. O., & Elder, G. H., Jr. (2001). Parent–adolescent reciprocity in negative affect and its relation to early adult social development. *Developmental Psychology, 37*, 775–790.

Kim, S., & Brody, G. H. (2005). Longitudinal pathways to psychological adjustment among Black youth living in single-parent households. *Journal of Family Psychology, 19*, 305–313.

Kim, S., & Ge, X. (2000). Parenting practices and adolescent depressive symptoms in Chinese American families. *Journal of Family Psychology, 14*, 420–435.

King, C., Akiyama, M., & Elling, K. (1996). Self-perceived competencies and depression among middle school students in Japan and the United States. *Journal of Early Adolescence, 16*, 192–210.

King, J. (2006). *Gender equity in higher education, 2006.* Washington: American Council on Education.

King, P., & Roeser, R. (2009). Religion and spirituality in adolescent development. In R. Lerner & L. Steinberg (Eds.), *Handbook of adolescent psychology* (3rd ed., Vol. 1, pp. 435–478). New York: Wiley.

King, P. E., & Furrow, J. L. (2004). Religion as a resource for positive youth development: Religion, social capital, and moral outcomes. *Developmental Psychology, 40*, 703–713.

King, V. (2006). The antecedents and consequences of adolescents' relationships with stepfathers and nonresident fathers. *Journal of Marriage and Family, 68*, 910–928.

King, V., Elder, G. H., Jr., & Whitbeck, L. B. (1997). Religious involvement among rural youth: An ecological and life-course perspective. *Journal of Research on Adolescence, 7*, 431–456.

King, V., & Sobolewski, J. M. (2006). Nonresident fathers' contributions to adolescent well-being. *Journal of Marriage and Family, 68*, 537–557.

Kinney, D. (1993). From nerds to normals: The recovery of identity among adolescents from middle school to high school. *Sociology of Education, 66*, 21–40.

Kinsey, A., Pomeroy, W., & Martin, C. (1948). *Sexual behavior in the human male.* Philadelphia: Saunders.

Kinsfogel, K. M., & Grynch, J. H. (2004). Interparental conflict and adolescent dating relationships: Integrating cognitive, emotional, and peer influences. *Journal of Family Psychology, 18*, 505–515.

Kirby, D. (2007). *Emerging answers 2007: Research findings on programs to reduce teen pregnancy and sexually transmitted diseases.* Washington, DC: National Campaign to Prevent Teen and Unplanned Pregnancy.

Kirby, D., Coyle, K., & Gould, J. B. (2001). Manifestations of poverty and birthrates among young teenagers in California zip code areas. *Family Planning Perspectives, 33*, 63–69.

Kirby, D., Laris, B. A., & Rolleri, L. A. (2007). Sex and HIV education programs: Their impact on sexual behaviors of young people throughout the world. *Journal of Adolescent Health, 40,* 206–217.

Kirby, J. B. (2006). From single-parent families to stepfamilies: Is the transition associated with adolescent alcohol initiation? *Journal of Family Issues, 27,* 685–711.

Kiselica, M., & Sturmer, P. (1993). Is society giving teenage fathers a mixed message? *Youth and Society, 24,* 487–501.

Klaczynski, P. (2000). Motivated scientific reasoning biases, epistemological beliefs, and theory polarization: A two-process approach to adolescent cognition. *Child Development, 71,* 1347–1366.

Klaczynski, P. (2001). Analytic and heuristic processing influences on adolescent reasoning and decision making. *Child Development, 72,* 844–861.

Klaczynski, P., & Narasimham, G. (1998). Development of scientific reasoning biases: Cognitive versus ego-protective explanations. *Developmental Psychology, 34,* 175–187.

Klepinger, D., Lundberg, S., & Plotnick, R. (1995). Adolescent fertility and the educational attainment of young women. *Family Planning Perspectives, 27,* 23–28.

Klerman, L. (1993). The influence of economic factors on health-related behaviors in adolescents. In S. Millstein, A. Petersen, & E. Nightingale (Eds.), *Promoting the health of adolescents: New directions for the twenty-first century* (pp. 38–57). New York: Oxford University Press.

Kliewer, W., Murrelle, L., Prom, E., Ramirez, M., Obando, P., Sandi, L., et al. (2006). Violence exposure and drug use in Central American youth: Family cohesion and parental monitoring as protective factors. *Journal of Research on Adolescence, 16,* 455–478.

Klimstra, T. A., Hale, W. W. I., II, Raaijmakers, Q. A. W., Branje, S. J. T., & Meeus, W. H. J. (2009). Maturation of personality in adolescence. *Journal of Personality and Social Psychology, 96,* 898–912.

Kling, J. R., Ludwig, J., & Katz, L. F. (2005). Neighborhood effects on crime for female and male youth: Evidence from a randomized housing voucher experiment. *Quarterly Journal of Economics, 120,* 87–130.

Kling, K., Hyde, J., Showers, C., & Buswell, B. (1999). Gender differences in self-esteem: A meta-analysis. *Psychological Bulletin, 125,* 470–500.

Klingberg, T. (2006). Development of a superior frontal-intraparietal network for visuospatial working memory. *Neuropsychologia, 44,* 2171–2177.

Kloep, M. (1995). Concurrent and predictive correlates of girls' depression and antisocial behaviour under conditions of economic crisis and value change: The case of Albania. *Journal of Adolescence, 18,* 445–458.

Klomek, A. B., Marrocco, F., Kleinman, M., Schonfeld, I. S., & Gould, M. S. (2007).

Bullying, depression, and suicidality in adolescents. *Journal of the American Academy of Child & Adolescent Psychiatry, 46,* 40–49.

Knafo, A., & Schwartz, S. H. (2003). Parenting and adolescents' accuracy in perceiving parental values. *Child Development, 74,* 595–611.

Knight, G., Virdin, L., & Roosa, M. (1994). Socialization and family correlates of mental health outcomes among Hispanic and Anglo American children: Consideration of cross-ethnic scalar equivalence. *Child Development, 65,* 212–224.

Knoester, C., & Haynie, D. L. (2005). Community context, social integration into family, and youth violence. *Journal of Marriage and the Family, 67,* 767.

Knoester, C., Haynie, D. L., & Stephens, C. M. (2006). Parenting practices and adolescents' friendship networks. *Journal of Marriage and Family, 68,* 1247–1260.

Kobak, R., & Cole, H. (1994). Attachment and meta-monitoring: Implications for adolescent autonomy and psychopathology. In D. Cicchetti & S. Toth (Eds.), *Rochester symposium on developmental psychopathology:* Vol. 5. *Disorders and dysfunctions of the self* (pp. 267–297). Rochester, NY: University of Rochester Press.

Kobak, R., Cole, H., Ferenz-Gillies, R., Fleming, W., & Gamble, W. (1993). Attachment and emotion regulation during mother–teen problem-solving: A control theory analysis. *Child Development, 64,* 231–245.

Kobak, R., Sudler, N., & Gamble, W. (1992). Attachment and depressive symptoms during adolescence: A developmental pathways analysis. *Development and Psychopathology, 3,* 461–474.

Koenig, L. (1995, March). *Change in self-esteem from 8th to 10th grade: Effects of gender and disruptive life events.* Paper presented at the biennial meetings of the Society for Research in Child Development, Indianapolis.

Koenig, L. B., McGue, M., & Iacono, W. G. (2008). Stability and change in religiousness during emerging adulthood. *Developmental Psychology, 44,* 532–543.

Koerner, S., Jacobs, S., & Raymond, M. (2000). When mothers turn to their adolescent daughters: Predicting daughters' vulnerability to negative adjustment outcomes. *Family Relations, 49,* 301–309.

Koerner, S. S., Wallace, S. R., Lehman, S. J., Lee, S., & Escalante, K. A. (2004). Sensitive mother-to-adolescent disclosures after divorce: Is the experience of sons different from that of daughters? *Journal of Family Psychology, 18,* 46–57.

Koff, E., & Rierdan, J. (1996). Premenarcheal expectations and postmenarcheal experiences of positive and negative menstrual related changes. *Journal of Adolescent Health, 18,* 286–291.

Kohler, J. K., Grotevant, H. D., & McRoy, R. G. (2002). Adopted adolescents' preoccupation with adoption: The impact on adoptive family relationships. *Journal of Marriage and Family, 64,* 93–104.

Kohler, P. K., Manhart, L. E., & Lafferty, W. E. (2008). Abstinence-only and comprehensive sex education and the initiation of sexual activity and teen pregnancy. *Journal of Adolescent Health, 42,* 344–351.

Kohn, M. (1977). *Class and conformity* (2nd ed.). Chicago: University of Chicago Press.

Kokko, K., Pulkkinen, L., Huesmann, L. R., Dubow, E. F., & Boxer, P. (2009). Intensity of aggression in childhood as a predictor of different forms of adult aggression: A two-country (Finland and the United States) analysis. *Journal of Research on Adolescence, 19,* 9–34.

Kowal, A., & Blinn-Pike, L. (2004). Sibling influences on adolescents' attitudes toward safe sex practices. *Family Relations, 53,* 377–384.

Konijn, E. A., Nije Bijvank, M., & Bushman, B. J. (2007). I wish I were a warrior: The role of wishful identification in the effects of violent video games on aggression in adolescent boys. *Developmental Psychology, 43,* 1038–1044.

Kowal, A., & Kramer, L. (1997). Children's understanding of parental differential treatment. *Child Development, 68,* 113–126.

Kowaleski-Jones, L. (2000). Staying out of trouble: Community resources and problem behavior among high-risk adolescents. *Journal of Marriage and the Family, 62,* 449–464.

Kowaleski-Jones, L., & Dunifon, R. (2006). Family structure and community context: Evaluating influences on adolescent outcomes. *Youth and Society, 38,* 110–130.

Kracke, B. (2002). The role of personality, parents and peers in adolescents career exploration. *Journal of Adolescence, 25,* 19–30.

Kramer, L., & Kowal, A. K. (2005). Sibling relationship quality from birth to adolescence: The enduring contributions of friends. *Journal of Family Psychology, 19,* 503–511.

Kreager, D. A. (2004). Strangers in the halls: Isolation and delinquency in social networks. *Social Forces, 83,* 351–390.

Kreager, D. A. (2007a). Unnecessary roughness? School sports, peer networks, and male adolescent violence. *American Sociological Review, 72,* 705–724.

Kreager, D. A. (2007b). When it's good to be "bad": Violence and adolescent peer acceptance. *Criminology: An Interdisciplinary Journal, 45,* 893–923.

Krei, M., & Rosenbaum, J. E. (2001). Career and college advice to the forgotten half: What do counselors and vocational teachers advise? *Teachers College Record, 103,* 823–842.

Krevans, J., & Gibbs, J. (1996). Parents' use of inductive discipline: Relations to children's empathy and prosocial behavior. *Child Development, 67,* 3263–3277.

Krishnakumar, A., & Buehler, C. (1996, March). *Interparental conflict styles and youth problem behaviors: The mediational role of parental behavioral control.* Paper presented at the biennial meetings of the Society for Research on Adolescence, Boston.

Kroger, J. (1993). The role of historical context in the identity formation process of late adolescence. *Youth and Society, 24,* 363–376.

Kroger, J. (1995). The differentiation of "firm" and "developmental" foreclosure identity statuses: A longitudinal study. *Journal of Adolescent Research, 10,* 317–337.

Kroger, J. (2003). Identity development during adolescence. In G. R. Adams, & M. D. Berzonsky (Eds.), *Blackwell Handbook of Adolescence* (pp. 205–226). Malden, MA: Blackwell.

Kroger, J., & Green, K. (1996). Events associated with identity status change. *Journal of Adolescence, 19,* 477–490.

Kuhn, D. (2009). Adolescent thinking. In R. Lerner & L. Steinberg (Eds.), *Handbook of adolescent psychology* (3rd ed., Vol. 1, pp. 152–186). New York: Wiley.

Kuhn, D., Garcia-Mila, M., Zohar, A., & Andersen, C. (1995). Strategies of knowledge acquisition. *Monographs of the Society for Research in Child Development, 60* (Serial No. 245).

Kulis, S., Marsiglia, F., & Hurdle, D. (2003). Gender identity, ethnicity, acculturation, and drug use: Exploring differences among adolescents in the Southwest. *Journal of Community Psychology, 31,* 167–188.

Kumpfer, K. L., & Alvarado, R. (2003). Family-strengthening approaches for the prevention of youth problem behaviors. *American Psychologist, 58,* 457–465.

Kunkel, D., Eyal, E., Finnerty, K., Biely, E., & Donnerstein, E. (2005). *Sex on TV.* Menlo Park, CA: Kaiser Family Foundation.

Kupchik, A., & Ellis, N. (2008). School discipline and security: Fair for all students? *Youth and Society, 39,* 549–574.

Kuperminc, G., Blatt, S., Shahar, B., Henrich, C., & Leadbeater, B. (2004). Cultural equivalence and cultural variance in longitudinal associations of young adolescents' self-definition and interpersonal relatedness to psychological and school adjustment. *Journal of Youth and Adolescence, 33,* 13–30.

Kuperminc, G., Darnell, A., & Alvarez-Jimenez, A. (2008). Parent involvement in the academic adjustment of Latino middle and high school youth: Teacher expectations and school belonging as mediators. *Journal of Adolescence, 31,* 469–483.

Kupersmidt, J., Burchinal, M., & Patterson, C. (1995). Developmental patterns of childhood peer relations as predictors of externalizing behavior problems. *Development and Psychopathology, 7,* 825–843.

Kurdek, L., & Fine, M. (1993). The relation between family structure and young adolescents' appraisals of family climate and parenting behavior. *Journal of Family Issues, 14,* 279–290.

Kurdek, L., Fine, M., & Sinclair, R. (1995). School adjustment in sixth graders: Parenting transitions, family climate, and peer norm effects. *Child Development, 66,* 430–445.

Kurlychek, M. C., & Johnson, B. D. (2004). The juvenile penalty: A comparison of juvenile and young adult sentencing outcomes in criminal court. *Criminology, 42,* 485–517.

Kuttler, A. F., & La Greca, A. M. (2004). Linkages among adolescent girls' romantic relationships, best friendships, and peer networks. *Journal of Adolescence, 27,* 395–414.

Kuttler, A. F., La Greca, A. M., & Prinstein, M. J. (1999). Friendship qualities and social-emotional functioning of adolescents with close, cross-sex friendships. *Journal of Research on Adolescence, 9,* 339–366.

Kwak, K. (2003). Adolescents and their parents: A review of intergenerational family relations for immigrant and non-immigrant families. *Human Development, 46,* 115–136.

Kypri, K., Voas, R. B., Langley, J. D., Stephenson, S. C. R., Begg, D. J., Tippetts, A. S., et al. (2006). Minimum purchasing age for alcohol and traffic crash injuries among 15- to 19-year-olds in New Zealand. *American Journal of Public Health, 96,* 126–131.

L'Engle, K. L., & Jackson, C. (2008). Socialization influences on early adolescents' cognitive susceptibility and transition to sexual intercourse. *Journal of Research on Adolescence, 18,* 353–378.

L'Engle, K. L., Brown, J. D., & Kenneavy, K. (2006). The mass media are an important context for adolescents' sexual behavior. *Journal of Adolescent Health, 38,* 186–192.

L'Engle, K. L., Jackson, C., & Brown, J. D. (2006). Early adolescents' cognitive susceptibility to initiating sexual intercourse. *Perspectives on Sexual and Reproductive Health, 38,* 97–105.

Lacourse, R., Nagin, D., & Tremblay, R. E. (2003). Developmental trajectories of boys' delinquent group membership and facilitation of violent behaviors during adolescence. *Development and Psychopathology, 15,* 183–197.

Ladouceur, C. D., Dahl, R. E., & Carter, C. S. (2007). Development of action monitoring through adolescence into adulthood: ERP and source localization. *Developmental Science, 10,* 874–891.

Lahey, B., Loeber, R., Hart, E., Frick, P., Applegate, B., Zhang, Q., Green, S., & Russo, M. (1995). Four-year longitudinal study of conduct disorder in boys: Patterns and predictors of persistence. *Journal of Abnormal Psychology, 104,* 83–93.

Lahey, B., Van Hulle, C. A., D'Onofrio, B. M., Rodgers, J. L., & Waldman, I. D. (2008). Is parental knowledge of their adolescent offspring's whereabouts and peer associations spuriously associated with offspring delinquency? *Journal of Abnormal Child Psychology, 36,* 807–823.

Laible, D., Carlo, G., & Raffaelli, M. (2000). The differential relations of parent and peer attachment to adolescent adjustment. *Journal of Youth and Adolescence, 29,* 45–59.

Laird, R., Criss, M., Pettit, G., Dodge, K., & Bates, J. (2008). Parents' monitoring knowledge attenuates the link between antisocial friends and adolescent delinquent behavior. *Journal of Abnormal Child Psychology, 36,* 299–310.

Laird, R., Pettit, G., Bates, J., & Dodge, K. (2003). Parents' monitoring-relevant knowledge and adolescents' delinquent behavior: Evidence of correlated developmental changes and reciprocal influences. *Child Development, 74,* 752–768.

Laird, R., Pettit, G., Dodge, K., & Bates, J. (2005). Peer relationship antecedents of delinquent behavior in late adolescence: Is there evidence of demographic group differences in developmental processes? *Development and Psychopathology, 17,* 127–144.

Lam, L. T., & Yang, L. (2007). Overweight/obesity and attention deficit and hyperactivity disorder tendency among adolescents in China. *International Journal of Obesity, 31,* 584–590.

Lam, T., Shi, H., Ho, L., Stewart, S. M., & Fan, S. (2002). Timing of pubertal maturation and heterosexual behavior among Hong Kong Chinese adolescents. *Archives of Sexual Behavior, 31,* 359–366.

Lambert, S. F., Herman, K. C., Bynum, M. S., & Ialongo, N. S. (2009). Perceptions of racism and depressive symptoms in African American adolescents: The role of perceived academic and social control. *Journal of Youth and Adolescence, 38,* 519–531.

Lamborn, S., & Nguyen, D. T. (2004). African American adolescents' perceptions of family interactions: Kinship support, parent–child relationships, and teen adjustment. *Journal of Youth and Adolescence, 33,* 547–558.

Lamborn, S., & Steinberg, L. (1993). Emotional autonomy redux: Revisiting Ryan and Lynch. *Child Development, 64,* 483–499.

Lamborn, S., Dornbusch, S., & Steinberg, L. (1996). Ethnicity and community context as moderators of the relation between family decision-making and adolescent adjustment. *Child Development, 66,* 283–301.

Lammers, C., Ireland, M., Resnick, M., & Blum, R. (2000). Influences on adolescents' decision to postpone onset of sexual intercourse: A survival analysis of virginity among youths aged 13 to 18 years. *Journal of Adolescent Health, 26,* 42–48.

Lang, S., Waller, P., & Shope, J. (1996). Adolescent driving: Characteristics associated with single-vehicle and injury crashes. *Journal of Safety Research, 27,* 241–257.

Langer, J. A. (2001). Beating the odds: Teaching middle and high school students to read and write well. *American Educational Research Journal, 38,* 837–880.

Langer, L., Zimmerman, R., & Katz, J. (1995). Virgins' expectations and nonvirgins' reports: How adolescents feel about themselves. *Journal of Adolescent Research, 10,* 291–306.

Langhout, R. D., Rhodes, J. E., & Osborne, L. N. (2004). An exploratory study of youth mentoring in an urban context: Adolescents' perceptions of relational styles. *Journal of Youth and Adolescence, 33,* 293–306.

Lansford, J. E., Malone, P. S., Dodge, K. A., Crozier, J. C., Pettit, G. S., & Bates, J. E. (2006). A 12-year prospective study of patterns of social information processing problems and externalizing behaviors. *Journal of Abnormal Child Psychology, 34,* 715–724.

Lanz, M., Scabini, E., Vermulst, A. A., & Gerris, J. M. (2001). Congruence on child rearing in families with early adolescent and middle adolescent children. *International Journal of Behavioral Development, 25,* 133–139.

Lapsley, D., Enright, R., & Serlin, R. (1985). Toward a theoretical perspective on the legislation of adolescence. *Journal of Early Adolescence, 5,* 441–466.

Larkin, R. W. (1979). *Suburban youth in cultural crisis.* New York: Oxford.

Larson, R. (1983). Adolescents' daily experience with family and friends: Contrasting opportunity systems. *Journal of Marriage and the Family, 11,* 739–750.

Larson, R. (1990). The solitary side of life: An examination of the time people spend alone from childhood to old age. *Developmental Review, 10,* 155–183.

Larson, R. (1995). Secrets in the bedroom: Adolescents' private use of media. *Journal of Youth and Adolescence, 24,* 535–550.

Larson, R. (1997). The emergence of solitude as a constructive domain of experience in early adolescence. *Child Development, 68,* 80–93.

Larson, R. (2000). Toward a psychology of positive youth development. *American Psychologist, 55,* 170–183.

Larson, R., & Brown, J. R. (2007). Emotional development in adolescence: What can be learned from a high school theater program? *Child Development, 78,* 1083–1099.

Larson, R., Clore, G., & Wood, G. (1999). The emotions of romantic relationships: Do they wreak havoc on adolescents? In W. Furman, B. Brown, & C. Feiring (Eds.), *Contemporary perspectives on adolescent romantic relationships* (pp. 19–49). New York: Cambridge University Press.

Larson, R., & Gillman, S. (1996, March). *Daily processes in single parent families.* Paper presented at the biennial meetings of the Society for Research on Adolescence, Boston.

Larson, R., Hansen, D. M., & Moneta, G. (2006). Differing profiles of developmental experiences across types of organized youth activities. *Developmental Psychology, 42,* 849–863.

Larson, R., & Lampman-Petraitis, C. (1989). Daily emotional states as reported by children and adolescents. *Child Development, 60,* 1250–1260.

Larson, R., Moneta, G., Richards, M. H., & Wilson, S. (2002). Continuity, stability, and change in daily emotional experience across adolescence. *Child Development, 73,* 1151–1165.

Larson, R., Pearce, N., Sullivan, P., & Jarrett, R. (2007). Participation in youth programs as a catalyst for negotiation of family autonomy with connection. *Journal of Youth and Adolescence, 36,* 31–45.

Larson, R., & Richards, M. (1991). Daily companionship in late childhood and early adolescence: Changing developmental contexts. *Child Development, 62,* 284–300.

Larson, R., & Richards, M. (1994). Family emotions: Do young adolescents and their parents experience the same states? *Journal of Research on Adolescence, 4,* 567–583.

Larson, R., & Richards, M. (1998). Waiting for the weekend: Friday and Saturday night as the emotional climax of the week. *New Directions for Child and Adolescent Development, Winter,* 37–51.

Larson, R., Richards, M., Moneta, G., Holmbeck, G., & Duckett, E. (1996). Changes in adolescents' daily interactions with their families from ages 10 to 18: Disengagement and transformation. *Developmental Psychology, 32,* 744–754.

Larson, R., Richards, M., Sims, B., & Dworkin, J. (2001). How urban African American young adolescents spend their time: Time budgets for locations, activities, and companionship. *American Journal of Community Psychology, 29,* 565–597.

Larson, R., & Seepersad, S. (2003). Adolescents' leisure time in the United States: Partying, sports, and the American experiment. *New Directions for Child and Adolescent Development, 99,* 53–64.

Larson, R., & Verma, S. (1999). How children and adolescents spend time across the world: Work, play, and developmental opportunities. *Psychological Bulletin, 125,* 701–736.

Larson, R., Wilson, S., & Rickman, A. (2009). Globalization, societal change, and adolescence across the world. In R. Lerner & L. Steinberg (Eds.), *Handbook of adolescent psychology* (3rd ed., Vol. 2, pp. 590–622). New York: Wiley.

Lau, J. Y. F., & Eley, T. C. (2008). Attributional style as a risk marker of genetic effects for adolescent depressive symptoms. *Journal of Abnormal Psychology, 117,* 849–859.

Laucht, M., Becker, K., Frank, J., Schmidt, M. H., Esser, G., Treutlein, J., et al. (2008). Genetic variation in dopamine pathways differentially associated with smoking progression in adolescence. *Journal of the American Academy of Child & Adolescent Psychiatry, 47,* 673–681.

Lauritsen, J. (1994). Explaining race and gender differences in adolescent sexual behavior. *Social Forces, 72,* 859–884.

Laursen, B. (1993). The perceived impact of conflict on adolescent relationships. *Merrill-Palmer Quarterly, 39,* 535–550.

Laursen, B. (1995). Conflict and social interaction in adolescent relationships. *Journal of Research on Adolescence, 5,* 55–70.

Laursen, B. (1996). Closeness and conflict in adolescent peer relationships: Interdependence with friends and romantic partners. In W. Bukowski, A. Newcomb, & W. Hartup (Eds.), *The company they keep: Friendship in childhood and adolescence* (pp. 186–210). New York: Cambridge University Press.

Laursen, B., & Collins, W. A. (2009). Parent–child relationships during adolescence. In R. Lerner & L. Steinberg (Eds.), *Handbook of adolescent psychology* (3rd ed., Vol. 2, pp. 3–42). New York: Wiley.

Laursen, B., & Collins, W. (1994). Interpersonal conflict during adolescence. *Psychological Bulletin, 115,* 197–209.

Laursen, B., Coy, K., & Collins, W. A. (1998). Reconsidering changes in parent–child conflict across adolescence: A meta-analysis. *Child Development, 69,* 817–832.

Laursen, B., Finkelstein, B. D., & Townsend Betts, N. (2001). A developmental meta-analysis of peer conflict resolution. *Developmental Review, 21,* 423–449.

Laursen, B., & Jensen-Campbell, L. (1999). The nature and functions of social exchange in adolescent romantic relationships. In W. Furman, B. Brown, & C. Feiring (Eds.), *Contemporary perspectives on adolescent romantic relationships* (pp. 50–74). New York: Cambridge University Press.

Lavoie, F., Hebert, M., Tremblay, R., Vitaro, F., Vezina, L., & McDuff, P. (2002). History of family dysfunction and perpetration of dating violence by adolescent boys: A longitudinal study. *Journal of Adolescent Health, 30,* 375–383.

LaVoie, J. (1994). Identity in adolescence: Issues of theory, structure, and transition. *Journal of Adolescence, 17,* 17–28.

Lawford, H., Pratt, M. W., Hunsberger, B., & Pancer, S. M. (2005). Adolescent generativity: A longitudinal study of two possible contexts for learning concern for future generations. *Journal of Research on Adolescence, 15,* 261–273.

Leadbeater, B. (1996). School outcomes for minority-group adolescent mothers at 28 to 36 months postpartum: A longitudinal follow-up. *Journal of Research on Adolescence, 6,* 629–648.

Leadbeater, B., & Bishop, S. (1994). Predictors of behavior problems in preschool children of inner-city Afro-American and Puerto Rican adolescent mothers. *Child Development, 65,* 638–648.

Leadbeater, B., Blatt, S., & Quinlan, D. (1995). Gender-linked vulnerabilities to depressive symptoms, stress, and problem behaviors in adolescents. *Journal of Research on Adolescence, 5*, 1–29.

Leadbeater, B., Kuperminc, G., Blatt, S., & Hertzog, C. (1999). A multivariate model of gender differences in adolescents' internalizing and externalizing problems. *Developmental Psychology, 35*, 1268–1282.

Leahy, E. (2001). Gender differences in mathematical trajectories. *Social Forces, 80*, 713–732.

Leaper, C., & Brown, C. S. (2008). Perceived experiences with sexism among adolescent girls. *Child Development, 79*, 685–704.

LeBlanc, A. (2003). *Random family: Love, drugs, trouble, and coming of age in the Bronx.* New York: Scribner.

Leblanc, L., Swisher, R., Vitaro, F., & Tremblay, R. E. (2008). High school social climate and antisocial behavior: A 10 year longitudinal and multilevel study. *Journal of Research on Adolescence, 18*, 395–419.

Lee, J. (2008). "A Kotex and a Smile": Mothers and daughters at menarche. *Journal of Family Issues, 29*, 1325–1347.

Lee, J., Grigg, W., & Dion, G. (2007). *The Nation's Report Card: Mathematics 2007.* Washington, DC: National Center for Education Statistics.

Lee, J. C., & Staff, J. (2007). When work matters: The varying impact of work intensity on high school dropout. *Sociology of Education, 80*, 158–178.

Lee, M., & Larson, R. (2000). The Korean "examination hell": Long hours of studying, distress, and depression. *Journal of Youth and Adolescence, 29*, 249–271.

Lee, S. (2001). More than "model minorities" or "delinquents": A look at Hmong American high school students. *Harvard Educational Review, 71*, 505–528.

Lee, V., & Burkam, D. (1992). Transferring high schools: An alternative to dropping out? *American Journal of Education, 100*, 420–453.

Lee, V., & Burkam, D. (2003). Dropping out of high school: The role of school organization and structure. *American Educational Research Journal, 40*, 353–393.

Lee, V., Burkam, D., Zimiles, H., & Ladewski, B. (1994). Family structure and its effect on behavioral and emotional problems in young adolescents. *Journal of Research on Adolescence, 4*, 405–437.

Lee, V., & Croninger, R. (1994). The relative importance of home and school in the development of literacy skills for middle-grade students. *American Journal of Education, 102*, 286–329.

Lee, V., Croninger, R., Linn, E., & Chen, X. (1996). The culture of sexual harassment in secondary schools. *American Educational Research Journal, 33*, 383–417.

Lee, V., Marks, H., & Byrd, T. (1994). Sexism in single-sex and coeducational independent secondary school classrooms. *Sociology of Education, 67*, 92–120.

Lee, V., & Smith, J. (1993). Effects of school restructuring on the achievement and engagement of middle-grade students. *Sociology of Education, 66*, 164–187.

Lee, V., & Smith, J. (1995). Effects of high school restructuring and size in early gains in achievement and engagement. *Sociology of Education, 68*, 241–270.

Lee, V., & Smith, J. (1996). Collective responsibility for learning and its effects on gains in achievement for early secondary school students. *American Journal of Education, 104*, 103–147.

Lee, V., & Smith, J. (1997). High school size: Which works best, and for whom? *Educational Evaluation and Policy Analysis, 19*, 205–227.

Lee, V., Smith, J., & Croninger, R. (1997). How high school organization influences the equitable distribution of learning in mathematics and science. *Sociology of Education, 70*, 128–150.

Leets, L., & Sunwolf. (2005). Adolescent rules for social exclusion: When is it fair to exclude someone else? *Journal of Moral Education, 34*, 343–362.

Lefkowitz, E. (2005). "Things have gotten better": Developmental changes among emerging adults after the transition to university. *Journal of Adolescent Research, 20*, 40–63.

Lefkowitz, E., Boone, T. L., Sigman, M., & Kitfong Au, T. (2002). He said, she said: Gender differences in mother-adolescent conversations about sexuality. *Journal of Research on Adolescence, 12*(2), 217–242.

Lefkowitz, E., Romo, L., Corona, R., Au, T., & Sigman, M. (2000). How Latino American and European American adolescents discuss conflicts, sexuality, and AIDS with their mothers. *Developmental Psychology, 36*, 315–325.

Lefkowitz, E., Sigman, M., & Au, T. (2000). Helping mothers discuss sexuality and AIDS with adolescents. *Child Development, 71*, 1383–1394.

Legault, L., Green-Demers, I., & Pelletier, L. (2006). Why do high school students lack motivation in the classroom? Toward an understanding of academic amotivation and the role of social support. *Journal of Educational Psychology, 98*, 567–582.

Leitenberg, H., & Saltzman, H. (2000). A statewide survey of age at first intercourse for adolescent females and age of their male partners: Relation to other risk behaviors and statutory rape implications. *Archives of Sexual Behavior, 29*, 203–215.

Lempers, J., & Clark-Lempers, D. (1992). Young, middle, and late adolescents' comparisons of the functional importance of five significant relationships. *Journal of Youth and Adolescence, 21*, 53–96.

Lengua, L. J. (2006). Growth in temperament and parenting as predictors of adjustment during children's transition to adolescence. *Developmental Psychology, 42*, 819–832.

Lenhart, A., Madden, M., Macgill, A. R., & Smith, A. (2007). *Teens and social media.* Washington, DC: Pew Internet & American Life Project.

Lenhart, L., & Rabiner, D. (1995). An integrative approach to the study of social competence in adolescence. *Development and Psychopathology, 7*, 543–561.

Lenroot, R. K., & Giedd, J. N. (2008). The changing impact of genes and environment on brain development during childhood and adolescence: Initial findings from a neuroimaging study of pediatric twins. *Development and Psychopathology, 20*, 1161–1175.

Leon, G., Fulkerson, J. A., Perry, C. L., Keel, P. K., & Klump, K. L. (1999). Three to four year prospective evaluation of personality and behavioral risk factors for later disordered eating in adolescent girls and boys. *Journal of Youth and Adolescence, 28*, 181–196.

Lerner, J., Castellino, D., & Perkins, D. (1994, February). *The influence of adolescent behavioral and psychosocial characteristics on maternal behaviors and satisfaction.* Paper presented at the biennial meetings of the Society for Research on Adolescence, San Diego.

Lerner, R., Lerner, J. V., Almerigi, J. B., Theokas, C., Phelps, E., Gestsdottir, S., et al. (2005). Positive youth development, participation in community youth development programs, and community contributions of fifth-grade adolescents findings from the first wave of the 4-H study of positive youth development. *Journal of Early Adolescence, 25*, 17–71.

Lerner, J., Phelps, E., Forman, Y., & Bowers, E. (2009). Positive youth development. In R. Lerner & L. Steinberg (Eds.), *Handbook of adolescent psychology* (3rd ed., Vol. 1, pp. 524–558). New York: Wiley.

Lerner, R., & Steinberg, L. (Eds.) (2009). *Handbook of adolescent psychology* (3rd ed.). New York: Wiley.

Lesane-Brown, C. (2006). A review of race socialization within Black families. *Developmental Review, 26*, 400–426.

Lesko, N. (1996). Denaturalizing adolescence: The politics of contemporary representations. *Youth and Society, 28*, 139–161.

Lesthaeghe, R., & Neidert, L. (2006). *The "Second Demographic Transition" in the U.S.: Spatial patterns and correlates.* PSC Research Report No. 06-592. Ann Arbor: Institute for Social Research, University of Michigan.

Leventhal, H., & Keeshan, P. (1993). Promoting healthy alternatives to substance abuse. In S. Millstein, A. Petersen, & E. Nightingale (Eds.), *Promoting the health of adolescents: New directions for the twenty-first century*, (pp. 260–284). New York: Oxford University Press.

Leventhal, T., & Brooks-Gunn, J. (2004). Diversity in developmental trajectories across adolescence: Neighborhood influences. In R. Lerner & L. Steinberg (Eds.), *Handbook of adolescent psychology.* New York: Wiley.

Leventhal, T., Dupéré, V., & Brooks-Gunn, J. (2009). Neighborhood influences on adolescent development. In R. Lerner & L. Steinberg (Eds.), *Handbook of adolescent psychology* (3rd ed., Vol. 2, pp. 411–443). New York: Wiley.

Leventhal, T., Fauth, R. C., & Brooks-Gunn, J. (2005). Neighborhood poverty and public policy: A 5-year follow-up of children's educational outcomes in the New York City Moving to Opportunity demonstration. *Developmental Psychology, 41,* 933–952.

Levesque, R. (1993). The romantic experience of adolescents in satisfying love relationships. *Journal of Youth and Adolescence, 22,* 219–251.

Levin, M., Xu, X., & Bartkowski, J. (2002). Seasonality of sexual debut. *Journal of Marriage and the Family, 64,* 871–884.

Levine, J. A., Emery, C. R., & Pollack, H. (2007). The well-being of children born to teen mothers. *Journal of Marriage and Family, 69,* 105–122.

Levine, M., & Harrison, K. (2004). Media's role in the perpetuation and prevention of negative body image and disordered eating. In J. K. Thompson (Ed.), *Handbook of eating disorders and obesity* (pp. 695–717). New York: John Wiley.

Levine, M., Smolak, L., & Hayden, H. (1994). The relation of sociocultural factors to eating attitudes and behaviors among middle school girls. *Journal of Early Adolescence, 14,* 471–490.

Levine, P. (2001). The sexual activity and birth control use of American teenagers. In J. Gruber (Ed.), *Risky behavior among youths: An economic analysis* (pp. 167–218). Chicago: University of Chicago Press.

Levinson, D. (1978). *The seasons of a man's life.* New York: Knopf.

Levinson, R., Jaccard, J., & Beamer, L. (1995). Older adolescents' engagement in casual sex: Impact of risk perception and psychosocial motivations. *Journal of Youth and Adolescence, 24,* 349–364.

Levitt, M., Guacci-Franci, N., & Levitt, J. (1993). Convoys of social support in childhood and early adolescence: Structure and function. *Developmental Psychology, 29,* 811–818.

Levitt, S., & Dubner, S. (2005). *Freakonomics.* New York: William Morrow.

Lewin, K. (1951). *Field theory and social science.* New York: Harper & Row.

Lewin, L., Davis, B., & Hops, H. (1999). Childhood social predictors of adolescent antisocial behavior: Gender differences in predictive accuracy and efficacy. *Journal of Abnormal Child Psychology, 27,* 277–292.

Lewin, T. (1997, October 1). Sexual abuse tied to 1 in 4 girls in teens. *New York Times,* p. A24.

Lewin, T. (July 9, 2006). At colleges, women are leaving men in the dust. *New York Times,* pp. 1ff.

Lewinsohn, P., Gotlib, I., & Seeley, J. (1997). Depression-related psychosocial variables: Are they specific to depression in adolescents? *Journal of Abnormal Psychology, 106,* 365–375.

Lewinsohn, P., Hops, H., Roberts, R., Seeley, J., & Andrews, J. (1993). Adolescent psychopathology, I: Prevalence and incidence of depression and other DSM-III-R disorders in high school students. *Journal of Abnormal Psychology, 102,* 133–144.

Lewinsohn, P., Joiner, T. E., Jr., & Rohde, P. (2001). Evaluation of cognitive diathesis–stress models in predicting major depressive disorder in adolescents. *Journal of Abnormal Psychology, 110,* 203–215.

Lewinsohn, P., Pettit, J., Joiner, T., Jr., & Seeley, J. (2003). The symptomatic expression of major depressive disorder in adolescents and young adults. *Journal of Abnormal Psychology, 112,* 244–252.

Lewinsohn, P., Roberts, R., Seeley, J., Rohde, P., Gotlib, I., & Hops, H. (1994). Adolescent psychopathology, II: Psychosocial risk factors for depression. *Journal of Abnormal Psychology, 103,* 302–325.

Lewinsohn, P., Rohde, P., & Seeley, J. (1994). Psychosocial risk factors for future adolescent suicide attempts. *Journal of Consulting and Clinical Psychology, 62,* 297–305.

Lewinsohn, P., Rohde, P., Seeley, J., & Fischer, S. (1993). Age-cohort changes in the lifetime occurrence of depression and other mental disorders. *Journal of Abnormal Psychology, 102,* 110–120.

Lewinsohn, P., Rohde, P., Seeley, J., Klein, D., & Gotlib, I. (2003). Psychosocial functioning of young adults who have experienced and recovered from major depressive disorder during adolescence. *Journal of Abnormal Psychology, 112,* 353–363.

Lewis, C. (1987). Minors' competence to consent to abortion. *American Psychologist, 41,* 84–88.

Lewis, M., Feiring, C., & Rosenthal, S. (2000). Attachment over time. *Child Development, 71,* 707–720.

Lewis, M., Feiring, C., McGuffog, C., & Jaskir, J. (1984). Predicting psychopathology in six-year-olds from early social relations. *Child Development, 55,* 123–136.

Li, J. (2006). Self in learning: Chinese adolescents' goals and sense of agency. *Child Development, 77,* 482–501.

Li, S. T., Nussbaum, K. M., & Richards, M. H. (2007). Risk and protective factors for urban African American youth. *American Journal of Community Psychology, 39,* 21–35.

Li, X., Stanton, B., & Feigelman, S. (2000). Impact of perceived parental monitoring on adolescent risk behavior over 4 years. *Journal of Adolescent Health, 27,* 49–56.

Li, X., Stanton, B., Pack, R., Harris, C., Cottrell, L., & Burns, J. (2002). Risk and protective factors associated with gang involvement among urban African American adolescents. *Youth and Society, 34,* 172–194.

Liddle, H. A., Rowe, C. L., Dakof, G. A., Henderson, C. E., & Greenbaum, P. E. (2009). Multidimensional family therapy for young adolescent substance abuse: Twelve-month outcomes of a randomized controlled trial. *Journal of Consulting and Clinical Psychology, 77,* 12–25.

Lieberman, M., Doyle, A., & Markiewicz, D. (1999). Developmental patterns in security of attachment to mother and father in late childhood and early adolescence: Associations with peer relations. *Child Development, 70,* 202–213.

Lindberg, L., Jones, R., Santelli, J. (2008). Non-coital sexual activities among adolescents. *Journal of Adolescent Health, 43,* 231–238.

Lindberg, S. M., Grabe, S., & Hyde, J. S. (2007). Gender, pubertal development, and peer sexual harassment predict objectified body consciousness in early adolescence. *Journal of Research on Adolescence, 17,* 723–742.

Linder, J. R., & Collins, W. A. (2005). Parent and peer predictors of physical aggression and conflict management in romantic relationships in early adulthood. *Journal of Family Psychology, 19,* 252–262.

Lindfors, K., Elovainio, M., Wickman, S., Vuorinen, R., Sinkkonen, J., Dunkel, L., et al. (2007). Brief report: The role of ego development in psychosocial adjustment among boys with delayed puberty. *Journal of Research on Adolescence, 17,* 601–612.

Linver, M. R., Roth, J. L., & Brooks-Gunn, J. (2009). Patterns of adolescents' participation in organized activities: Are sports best when combined with other activities? *Developmental Psychology, 45,* 354–367.

Lipsey, M. (2009). The primary factors that characterize effective interventions with juvenile offenders: A meta-analytic overview. *Victims and Offenders, 4,* 124–147.

Litchfield, A., Thomas, D., & Li, B. (1997). Dimensions of religiosity as mediators of the relations between parenting and adolescent deviant behavior. *Journal of Adolescent Research, 12,* 199–226.

Little, S. A., & Garber, J. (2004). Interpersonal and achievement orientations and specific stressors predict depressive and aggressive symptoms. *Journal of Adolescent Research, 19,* 63–84.

Little, T. D., Brauner, J., Jones, S. M., Nock, M. K., & Hawley, P. H. (2003). Rethinking aggression: A typological examination of the functions of aggression. *Merrill-Palmer Quarterly, 49,* 343–369.

Liu, J., Raine, A., Wuerker, A., Venables, P. H., & Mednick, S. (2009). The association of birth complications and externalizing behavior in early adolescents: Direct and mediating effects. *Journal of Research on Adolescence, 19,* 93–111.

Liu, R. X. (2006). Vulnerability to friends' suicide influence: The moderating effects of gender and adolescent depression. *Journal of Youth and Adolescence, 35,* 479–489.

Liu, X., Kaplan, H., & Risser, W. (1992). Decomposing the reciprocal relationships between academic achievement and general self-esteem. *Youth and Society, 24,* 123–148.

Livson, N., & Peskin, H. (1980). Perspectives on adolescence from longitudinal research. In J. Adelson (Ed.), *Handbook of adolescent psychology* (pp. 47–98). New York: Wiley.

Lloyd, C. B., Grant, M., & Ritchie, A. (2008). Gender differences in time use among adolescents in developing countries: Implications of rising school enrollment rates. *Journal of Research on Adolescence, 18,* 99–120.

Lobel, T. E., Nov-Crispin, N., Schiller, D., Lobel, O., & Feldman, A. (2004). Gender discriminatory behavior during adolescence and young adulthood: A developmental analysis. *Journal of Youth and Adolescence, 33,* 535–546.

Lochman, J., & Dodge, K. (1998). Distorted perceptions in dyadic interactions of aggressive and nonaggressive boys: Effects of prior expectations, context, and boys' age. *Development and Psychopathology, 10,* 495–512.

Loeber, R., & Farrington, D. P. (2000). Young children who commit crime: Epidemiology, developmental origins, risk factors, early interventions, and policy implications. *Development and Psychopathology, 12,* 737–762.

Loehlin, J. C., Neiderhiser, J. M., & Reiss, D. (2005). Genetic and environmental components of adolescent adjustment and parental behavior: A multivariate analysis. *Child Development, 76,* 1104–1115.

Loewenson, P. R., Ireland, M., & Resnick, M. D. (2004). Primary and secondary sexual abstinence in high school students. *Journal of Adolescent Health, 34,* 209–215.

Lohman, B. J., & Billings, A. (2008). Protective and risk factors associated with adolescent boy's early sexual debut and risky sexual behaviors. *Journal of Youth and Adolescence, 37,* 723–735.

Longest, K. C., & Shanahan, M. J. (2007). Adolescent work intensity and substance use: The mediational and moderational roles of parenting. *Journal of Marriage and Family, 69,* 703–720.

Longmore, M. A., Manning, W. D., & Giordano, P. C. (2001). Preadolescent parenting strategies and teens' dating and sexual initiation: A longitudinal analysis. *Journal of Marriage and the Family, 63,* 322–335.

Lonigan, C., Carey, M., & Finch, A., Jr. (1994). Anxiety and depression in children and adolescents: Negative affectivity and the utility of self-reports. *Journal of Consulting and Clinical Psychology, 62,* 1000–1008.

Lopez, E. M., Wishard, A., Gallimore, R., & Rivera, W. (2006). Latino high school students? Perceptions of gangs and crews. *Journal of Adolescent Research, 21,* 299–318.

Lopez, S. (2009). The rigors of life unplugged. *Los Angeles Times,* May 6.

Lord, S., Eccles, J., & McCarthy, K. (1994). Surviving the junior high transition: Family processes and self-perceptions as protective and risk factors. *Journal of Early Adolescence, 14,* 162–199.

Loredo, C., Reid, A., & Deaux, K. (1995). Judgments and definitions of sexual harassment by high school students. *Sex Roles, 32,* 29–45.

Louis, K., & Smith, B. (1992). Breaking the iron law of social class: The renewal of teachers' professional status and engagement. In F. Newmann (Ed.), *Student engagement and achievement in American high schools.* New York: Teachers College Press.

Loukas, A., Suzuki, R., & Horton, K. D. (2006). Examining school connectedness as a mediator of school climate effects. *Journal of Research on Adolescence, 16,* 491–502.

Lourenco, O., & Machado, A. (1996). In defense of Piaget's theory: A reply to 10 common criticisms. *Psychological Review, 103,* 143–164.

Loveless, T. (2002). *How well are American students learning? The 2002 Brown Center Report on American Education.* Washington, DC: Brookings Institution.

Lovitt, T. (1989). *Introduction to learning disabilities.* Boston: Allyn & Bacon.

Lowry, R., Holtzman, D., Truman, B., Kann, L., Collins, J., & Kolbe, L. (1994). Substance use and HIV related sexual behaviors among US high school students: Are they related? *American Journal of Public Health, 84,* 1116–1120.

Lubienski, S. T., & Lubienski, C. (2006). School sector and academic achievement: A multilevel analysis of NAEP mathematics data. *American Education Research Journal, 43,* 651–698.

Lucas, S. (1996). Selective attrition in a newly hostile regime: The case of 1980 sophomores. *Social Forces, 75,* 511–533.

Lucas, S. R., & Berends, M. (2002). Sociodemographic diversity, correlated achievement, and de facto tracking. *Sociology of Education, 75,* 328–348.

Luciana, M., Conklin, H. M., Hooper, C. J., & Yarger, R. S. (2005). The development of nonverbal working memory and executive control processes in adolescents. *Child Development, 76,* 697.

Ludden, A. B., & Eccles, J. (2007). Psychosocial, motivational, and contextual profiles of youth reporting different patterns of substance use during adolescence. *Journal of Research on Adolescence, 17,* 51–88.

Ludwig, J., Duncan, G., & Hirschfield, P. (2001). Urban poverty and juvenile crime: Evidence from a randomized housing-mobility experiment. *Quarterly Journal of Economics, 116,* 665–679.

Luna B., Garver K., Urban, T., Lazar, N., & Sweeney, J. (2004). Maturation of cognitive processes from late childhood to adulthood. *Child Development, 75,* 1357–1372.

Luna, B., Thulborn, K. R., Munoz, D. P., Merriam, E. P., Garver, K. E., Minshew, N. J., et al. (2001). Maturation of widely distributed brain function subserves cognitive development. *Neuroimage, 13,* 786–793.

Luo, Q., Urberg, K., & Rao, P. (1995, March). *Selection of best friends among Chinese adolescents.* Paper presented at the biennial meetings of the Society for Research in Child Development, Indianapolis.

Luster, T., Bates, L., Fitzgerald, H., Vandenbelt, M., & Key, J. (2000). Factors related to successful outcomes among preschool children born to low-income adolescent mothers. *Journal of Marriage and the Family, 62,* 133–146.

Luster, T., & McAdoo, H. (1995). Factors related to self-esteem among African American youths: A secondary analysis of the High/Scope Perry Preschool data. *Journal of Research on Adolescence, 5,* 451–467.

Luster, T., & Small, S. (1997). Sexual abuse history and problems in adolescence: Exploring the effects of moderating variables. *Journal of Marriage and the Family, 59,* 131–142.

Luthar, S. (1991). Vulnerability and resilience: A study of high-risk adolescents. *Child Development, 62,* 600–616.

Luthar, S. (1994, February). *Social competence of inner-city adolescents: A six-month prospective study.* Paper presented at the biennial meetings of the Society for Research on Adolescence, San Diego.

Luthar, S., & Becker, B. (2002). Privileged but pressured? A study of affluent youth. *Child Development, 73,* 1593–1610.

Luthar, S., Cicchetti, D., & Becker, B. (2000). The construct of resilience: A critical evaluation and guidelines for future work. *Child Development, 71,* 543–562.

Luthar, S., & Goldstein, A. S. (2008). Substance use and related behaviors among suburban late adolescents: The importance of perceived parent containment. *Development and Psychopathology, 20,* 591–614.

Luthar, S., & Latendresse, S. (2005). Comparable "risks" at the socioeconomic status extremes: Preadolescents' perceptions of parenting. *Development and Psychopathology, 17,* 207–230.

Luthar, S., & McMahon, T. (1996). Peer reputation among inner-city adolescents: Structure and correlates. *Journal of Research on Adolescence, 6,* 581–603.

Luthar, S., Shoum, K. A., & Brown, P. J. (2006). Extracurricular involvement among affluent youth: A scapegoat for "ubiquitous achievement pressures"? *Developmental Psychology, 42,* 583–597.

Luyckx, K., Goossens, L., & Soenens, B. (2006). A developmental contextual perspective on identity construction in emerging adulthood: Change dynamics in commitment formation and commitment evaluation. *Developmental Psychology, 42,* 366–380.

Lynam, D. R., Caspi, A., Moffitt, T. E., Loeber, R., & Stouthamer-Loeber, M. (2007). Longitudinal evidence that psychopathy scores in early adolescence predict adult psychopathy. *Journal of Abnormal Psychology, 116,* 155–165.

Lynam, D. R., Caspi, A., Moffitt, T. E., Wikstroem, P. O., Loeber, R., & Novak, S. (2000). The interaction between impulsivity and neighborhood context on offending: The effects of impulsivity are stronger in poorer neighborhoods. *Journal of Abnormal Psychology, 109,* 563–574.

Määttä, S., Nurmi, J., & Stattin, H. (2007). Achievement orientations, school adjustment, and well-being: A longitudinal study. *Journal of Research on Adolescence, 17,* 789–812.

Määttä, S., Stattin, H., & Nurmi, J. E. (2002). Achievement strategies at school: Types and correlates. *Journal of Adolescence, 25,* 31–46.

Maccoby, E. (1990). Gender and relationships: A developmental account. *American Psychologist, 45,* 513–520.

Maccoby, E., & Martin, J. (1983). Socialization in the context of the family: Parent–child interaction. In E. M. Hetherington (Ed.), *Handbook of child psychology: Vol. 4. Socialization, personality, and social development* (pp. 1–101). New York: Wiley.

MacDonald, W., & DeMaris, A. (1995). Remarriage, stepchildren, and marital conflict: Challenges to the incomplete institutionalization hypothesis. *Journal of Marriage and the Family, 57,* 387–398.

Mackey, E. R., & La Greca, A. M. (2008). Does this make me look fat? Peer crowd and peer contributions to adolescent girls' weight control behaviors. *Journal of Youth and Adolescence, 37,* 1097–1110.

Mackey, K., Arnold, M. L., & Pratt, M. W. (2001). Adolescents' stories of decision making in more and less authoritative families: Representing the voices of parents in narrative. *Journal of Adolescent Research, 16,* 243–268.

Macksoud, M., & Aber, J. (1996). The war experiences and psychosocial development of children in Lebanon. *Child Development, 67,* 70–88.

Macmillan, R., & Hagan, J. (2004). Violence in the transition to adulthood: Adolescent victimization, education, and socioeconomic attainment in later life. *Journal of Research on Adolescence, 14,* 127–158.

Madon, S., Willard, J., Guyll, M., Trudeau, L., & Spoth, R. (2006). Self-fulfilling prophecy effects of mothers' beliefs on children's alcohol use: Accumulation, dissipation, and stability over time. *Journal of Personality and Social Psychology, 90,* 911–926.

Mager, W., Milich, R., Harris, M. J., & Howard, A. (2005). Intervention groups for adolescents with conduct problems: Is aggregation harmful or helpful? *Journal of Abnormal Child Psychology, 33,* 349–362.

Magnusson, D., Stattin, H., & Allen, V. (1986). Differential maturation among girls and its relation to social adjustment in a longitudinal perspective. In P. Baltes, D. Featherman, & R. Lerner (Eds.), *Life span development and behavior* (Vol. 7). Hillsdale, NJ: Erlbaum.

Maharaj, S., & Connolly, J. (1994). Peer network composition of acculturated and ethnoculturally-affiliated adolescents in a multicultural setting. *Journal of Adolescent Research, 9,* 218–240.

Mahoney, A., Donelly, W. O., Boxer, P., & Lewis, T. (2003). Marital and severe parent-to-adolescent physical aggression in clinic-referred families: Mother and adolescent reports on co-occurrence and links to child behavior problems. *Journal of Family Psychology, 17,* 3–19.

Mahoney, J., & Cairns, R. (1997). Do extracurricular activities protect against early school dropout? *Developmental Psychology, 33,* 241–253.

Mahoney, J., Larson, R., Eccles, J., & Lord, H. (2005). Organized activities as developmental contexts for children and adolescents. In J. Mahoney, R. Larson, & J. Eccles (Eds.), *Organized activities as contexts of development* (pp. 3–22). Hillsdale, NJ: Erlbaum.

Mahoney, J., Schweder, A. E., & Stattin, H. (2002). Structured after-school activities as a moderator of depressed mood for adolescents with detached relations to their parents. *Journal of Community Psychology, 30,* 69–86.

Mahoney, J., & Stattin, H. (2000). Leisure activities and adolescent antisocial behavior: The role of structure and social context. *Journal of Adolescence, 23,* 113–127.

Mahoney, J., Stattin, H., & Lord, H. (2004). Unstructured youth recreation centre participation and antisocial behaviour development: Selective influences and the moderating role of antisocial peers. *International Journal of Behavioral Development, 28,* 553–560.

Mahoney, J., Vandell, D., Simpkins, S., & Zarrett, N. (2009). Adolescent out-of-school activities. In R. Lerner & L. Steinberg (Eds.), *Handbook of adolescent psychology* (3rd ed., Vol. 2, pp. 228–269). New York: Wiley.

Mahoney, J. L. (2000). School extracurricular activity participation as a moderator in the development of antisocial patterns. *Child Development, 71,* 502–516.

Main, M., Kaplan, N., & Cassidy, J. (1985). Security in infancy, childhood and adulthood: A move to the level of representation. In I. Bretherton and E. Waters (Eds.), *Growing points of attachment theory and research, Monographs of the Society for Research on Child Development, 50*(1–2), Serial No. 209, pp. 66–106.

Malanchuk, O., & Eccles, J. (April, 1999). *Determinants of self-esteem in African-American and White adolescent girls.* Paper presented at the biennial meetings of the Society for Research on Child Development, Albuquerque.

Males, M. (1998). *Framing youth: 10 myths about the next generation.* Monroe, ME: Common Courage Press.

Males, M., & Chew, K. (1996). The ages of fathers in California adolescent births. *American Journal of Public Health, 86,* 565–568.

Malone, S. M., Taylor, J., & Marmorstein, N. R. (2004). Genetic and environmental influences on antisocial behavior and alcohol dependence from adolescence to early adulthood. *Development and Psychopathology, 16,* 943–966.

Mandara, J., & Murray, C. B. (2000). Effects of parental marital status, income, and family functioning on African American adolescent self-esteem. *Journal of Family Psychology, 14,* 475–490.

Manlove, J. (1998). The influence of high school dropout and school disengagement on the risk of school-age pregnancy. *Journal of Research on Adolescence, 8,* 187–220.

Manlove, J., Logan, C., Moore, K. A., & Ikramullah, E. (2008). Pathways from family religiosity to adolescent sexual activity and contraceptive use. *Perspectives on Sexual and Reproductive Health, 40,* 105–117.

Manlove, J., Mariner, C., & Papillo, A. (2000). Subsequent fertility among teen mothers: Longitudinal analyses of recent national data. *Journal of Marriage and the Family, 62,* 430–448.

Manlove, J., Terry-Humen, E., & Ikramullah, E. (2006). Young teenagers and older sexual partners: Correlates and consequences for males and females. *Perspectives on Sexual and Reproductive Health, 38,* 197–207.

Mannheim, K. (1952). The problem of generations. In K. Mannheim (Ed.), *Essays on the sociology of knowledge.* London: Routledge & Kegan Paul.

Manning, W. D., Giordano, P. C., & Longmore, M. A. (2006). Hooking up: The relationship contexts of 'nonrelationship' sex. *Journal of Adolescent Research, 21,* 459–483.

Manning, W., & Lamb, K. (2003). Adolescent well-being in cohabiting, married, and single-parent families. *Journal of Marriage and Family, 65,* 876–893.

Manning, W., & Landale, N. (1996). Racial and ethnic differences in the role of cohabitation in premarital childbearing. *Journal of Marriage and the Family, 58,* 63–77.

Manning, W. D., Longmore, M. A., & Giordano, P. (2007). The changing institution of marriage: Adolescents' expectations to cohabit and to marry. *Journal of Marriage and Family, 69,* 559–575.

Manning, W., Longmore, M., & Giordano, P. (2005). Adolescents' involvement in nonromantic sexual activity. *Social Science Research, 34,* 384–407.

Marcia, J. (1966). Development and validation of ego identity status. *Journal of Personality and Social Psychology, 3,* 551–558.

Marin, B. V., Kirby, D. B., Hudes, E. S., Coyle, K. K., & Gomez, C. A. (2006). Boyfriends, girlfriends and teenagers' risk of sexual involvement. *Perspectives on Sexual and Reproductive Health, 38,* 76–83.

Marini, M., Fan, P., Finley, E., & Beutel, A. (1996). Gender and job values. *Sociology of Education, 69,* 49–65.

Markiewicz, D., Lawford, H., Doyle, A. B., & Haggart, N. (2006). Developmental differences in adolescents' and young adults' use of mothers, fathers, best friends, and romantic partners to fulfill attachment needs. *Journal of Youth and Adolescence, 35,* 127–140.

Markovits, H., & Valchon, R. (1989). Reasoning with contrary-to-fact propositions. *Journal of Experimental Child Psychology, 47,* 398–412.

Markovits, H., & Valchon, R. (1990). Conditional reasoning, representation, and level of abstraction. *Developmental Psychology, 26,* 942–951.

Markovits, H., Venet, M., Janveau-Brennan, G., Malfait, N., Pion, N., & Vadeboncoeur, I. (1996). Reasoning in young children: Fantasy and information retrieval. *Child Development, 67,* 2857–2872.

Marks, H. M. (2000). Student engagement in instructional activity: Patterns in the elementary, middle, and high school years. *American Educational Research Journal, 37,* 153–184.

Markstrom-Adams, C. (1989). Androgyny and its relation to adolescent psychological well-being: A review of the literature. *Sex Roles, 21,* 469–473.

Markstrom-Adams, C., & Adams, G. (1995). Gender, ethnic group, and grade differences in psychosocial functioning during middle adolescence? *Journal of Youth and Adolescence, 24,* 397–417.

Markstrom, C. A., & Iborra, A. (2003). Adolescent identity formation and rites of passage: The Navajo kinaalda ceremony for girls. *Journal of Research on Adolescence, 13,* 399–426.

Markus, H., & Nurius, P. (1986). Possible selves. *American Psychologist, 41,* 954–969.

Marsh, H. (1989). Age and sex effects in multiple dimensions of self-concept: Preadolescence to early adulthood. *Journal of Educational Psychology, 81,* 417–430.

Marsh, H., Chessor, D., Craven, R., & Roche, L. (1995). The effects of gifted and talented programs on academic self-concept: The big fish strikes again. *American Educational Research Journal, 32,* 285–319.

Marsh, H., & Hau, K. (2003). Big-fish–little-pond effect on academic self-concept: A cross-cultural (26-country) test of the negative effects of academically selective schools. *American Psychologist, 58,* 364–376.

Marsh, H., & Hau, K. (2004). Explaining paradoxical relationship between academic self-concepts and achievements: Cross-cultural generalizability of the internal/external frame of reference predictions across 26 countries. *Journal of Educational Psychology 96,* 56–67.

Marsh, H., & Kleitman, S. (2002). Extracurricular school activities: The good, the bad, and the nonlinear. *Harvard Educational Review, 72,* 464–514.

Marsh, H., & Kleitman, S. (2005). Consequences of employment during high school: Character building, subversion of academic goals, or a threshold? *American Educational Research Journal, 42,* 331–369.

Marsh, H., Kong, C., & Hau, K. (2000). Longitudinal multilevel models of the big-fish–little-pond effect on academic self-concept: Counterbalancing contrast and reflected-glory effects in Hong Kong schools. *Journal of Personality and Social Psychology, 78,* 337–349.

Marsh, H., Trautwein, U., Ludtke, O., Baumert, J., & Koller, O. (2007). The big-fish–little-pond effect: Persistent negative effects of selective high schools on self-concept after graduation. *American Education Research Journal, 44,* 631–669.

Marsh, H., & Yeung, A. (1997). Coursework selection: Relations to academic self-concept and achievement. *American Educational Research Journal, 34,* 691–720.

Marsh, H., & Yeung, A. S. (1998). Longitudinal structural equation models of academic self-concept and achievement: Gender differences in the development of math and English constructs. *American Educational Research Journal, 35,* 705–738.

Marsh, P., McFarland, F. C., & Allen, J. P. (2003). Attachment, autonomy, and multifinality in adolescent internalizing and risky behavioral symptoms. *Development and Psychopathology, 15,* 451–467.

Marshall, S. (1995). Ethnic socialization of African American children: Implications for parenting, identity development, and academic achievement. *Journal of Youth and Adolescence, 24,* 377–396.

Marshall, W., & Tanner, J. (1969). Variations in the pattern of pubertal change in girls. *Archive of Diseases of Childhood, 44,* 130.

Marsiglia, F., Kulis, S., & Hecht, M. L. (2001). Ethnic labels and ethnic identity as predictors of drug use among middle school students in the Southwest. *Journal of Research on Adolescence, 11,* 21–48.

Martin, B. (1990). The transmission of relationship difficulties from one generation to the next. *Journal of Youth and Adolescence, 19,* 181–200.

Martinez, C. R. J. (2006). Effects of differential family acculturation on Latino adolescent substance use. *Family Relations, 55,* 306–317.

Martinez, R., & Dukes, R. (1997). The effects of ethnic identity, ethnicity, and gender on adolescent well-being. *Journal of Youth and Adolescence, 26,* 503–516.

Martino, S. C., Elliott, M. N., Corona, R., Kanouse, D. E., & Schuster, M. A. (2008). Beyond the "big talk": The roles of breadth and repetition in parent–adolescent communication about sexual topics. *Pediatrics, 121,* 612–618.

Marx, D., Ko, S., & Friedman, R. (2009). The "Obama Effect": How a salient role model reduces race-based performance differences. *Journal of Experimental Social Psychology, 45,* 953–956.

Masi, G., Millepiedi, S., Mucci, M., Poll, P., Bertini, N., & Milantoni, L. (2004). Generalized anxiety disorder in referred children and adolescents. *Journal of the American Academy of Child and Adolescent Psychiatry, 43,* 752–760.

Mason, C., Cauce, A., Gonzales, N., & Hiraga, Y. (1994). Adolescent problem behavior: The effect of peers and the moderating role of father absence and the mother–child relationship. *American Journal of Community Psychology, 22,* 723–743.

Mason, C., Cauce, A., Gonzales, N., & Hiraga, Y. (1996). Neither too sweet nor too sour: Problem peers, maternal control, and problem behavior in African American adolescents. *Child Development, 67,* 2115–2130.

Mason, C., Cauce, A., Gonzales, N., Hiraga, Y., & Grove, K. (1994). An ecological model of externalizing behaviors in African-American adolescents: No family is an island. *Journal of Research on Adolescence, 4,* 639–655.

Mason, W. (2001). Self-esteem and delinquency revisited (again): A test of Kaplan's self-derogation theory of delinquency using latent growth curve modeling. *Journal of Youth and Adolescence, 30,* 83–102.

Mason, W., & Windle, M. (2002). Reciprocal relations between adolescent substance use and delinquency: A longitudinal latent variable analysis. *Journal of Abnormal Psychology, 111,* 63–76.

Masten, A. (2001). Ordinary magic: Resilience processes in development. *American Psychologist, 56,* 227–238.

Masten, A., Burt, K. B., & Roisman, G. I. (2004). Resources and resilience in the transition to adulthood: Continuity and change. *Development and Psychopathology, 16,* 1071–1094.

Masten, A., Coatsworth, J., Neemann, J., Gest, S., Tellegen, A., & Garmezy, N. (1995). The structure and coherence of competence from childhood through adolescence. *Child Development, 66,* 1635–1659.

Masten, A., Hubbard, J., Gest, S., Tellegen, A., Garmezy, N., & Ramirez, M. (1999). Competence in the context of adversity: Pathways to resilience and maladaptation from childhood to late adolescence. *Development and Psychopathology, 11,* 143–169.

Masten, A., Miliotis, D., Graham-Bermann, S., Ramirez, M., & Neemann, J. (1993). Children in homeless families: Risks to mental health and development. *Journal of Consulting and Clinical Psychology, 61,* 335–343.

Masten, A., Roisman, G. I., Long, J. D., Burt, K. B., Obradovic, J., Riley, J. R., et al. (2005). Developmental cascades: Linking academic achievement and externalizing and internalizing symptoms over 20 years. *Developmental Psychology, 41,* 733–746.

Matas, L., Arend, R., & Sroufe, L. (1978). Continuity in adaptation in the second year: The relationship between quality of attachment and later competence. *Child Development, 49,* 547–556.

Matsuba, M. K., & Walker, L. J. (2005). Young adult moral exemplars: The making of self through stories. *Journal of Research on Adolescence, 15,* 275–297.

Matsueda, R. L., Kreager, D. A., & Huizinga, D. (2006). Deterring delinquents: A rational choice model of theft and violence. *American Sociological Review, 71,* 95–122.

Matthews, D., & Keating, D. (1995). Domain specificity and habits of mind: An investigation of patterns of high-level development. *Journal of Early Adolescence, 15,* 319–343.

Matthews, L. S., & Conger, R. D. (2004). "He did it on purpose!" Family correlates of negative attributions about an adolescent sibling. *Journal of Research on Adolescence, 14,* 257–284.

Mattison, E., & Aber, M. S. (2007). Closing the achievement gap: The association of racial climate with achievement and behavioral outcomes. *American Journal of Community Psychology, 40,* 1–12.

Matza, L. S., Kupersmidt, J. B., & Glenn, D. (2001). Adolescents' perceptions and standards of their parents as a function of sociometric status. *Journal of Research on Adolescence, 11,* 245–272.

Mayeux, L., Sandstrom, M. J., & Cillessen, A. H. N. (2008). Is being popular a risky proposition? *Journal of Research on Adolescence, 18,* 49–74.

Mayseless, O., & Scharf, M. (2007). Adolescents' attachment representations and their capacity for intimacy in close relationships. *Journal of Research on Adolescence, 17,* 23–50.

Mayseless, O., Scharf, M., & Sholt, M. (2003). From authoritative parenting practices to an authoritarian context: Exploring the person–environment fit. *Journal of Research on Adolescence, 13,* 427–457.

Mazor, A., & Enright, R. (1988). The development of the individuation process from a social-cognitive perspective. *Journal of Adolescence, 11,* 29–47.

McBride, C. K., Paikoff, R. L., & Holmbeck, G. N. (2003). Individual and familial influences on the onset of sexual intercourse among urban African American adolescents. *Journal of Consulting and Clinical Psychology, 71,* 159–167.

McCabe, K. (1997, April). *Early adolescents at risk: Familial factors that mediate and moderate the effect of risk on child adjustment.* Paper presented at the biennial meetings of the Society for Research in Child Development.

McCabe, K., Hough, R., Wood, P. A., & Yeh, M. (2001). Childhood and adolescent onset conduct disorder: A test of the developmental taxonomy. *Journal of Abnormal Child Psychology, 29,* 305–316.

McCarthy, K., Lord, S., Eccles, J., Kalil, A., & Furstenberg, F., Jr. (1992, March). *The impact of family management strategies on adolescents in high risk environments.* Paper presented at the biennial meetings of the Society for Research on Adolescence, Washington.

McClelland, D., Atkinson, J., Clark, R., & Lowell, E. (1953). *The achievement motive.* New York: Appleton-Century-Crofts.

McClintock, M. (1980). Major gaps in menstrual cycle research: Behavioral and physiological controls in a biological context. In P. Komenich, M. McSweeney, J. Noack, & N. Elder (Eds.), *The menstrual cycle* (Vol. 2, pp. 7–23). New York: Springer.

McClintock, M., & Herdt, G. (1996). Rethinking puberty: The development of sexual attraction. *Psychological Sciences, 5,* 178–183.

McCoy, J. (1996, March). *Parents' involvement in youths' peer relationships as a predictor of youths' later psychological well-being.* Paper presented at the biennial meetings of the Society for Research on Adolescence, Boston.

McCoy, J., Brody, G., & Stoneman, Z. (1994). A longitudinal analysis of sibling relationships as mediators of the link between family processes and youths' best friendships. *Family Relations, 43,* 400–408.

McCrae, R., Costa, P. T., Jr., Terracciano, A., Parker, W. D., Mills, C. J., De Fruyt, F., et al. (2002). Personality trait development from age 12 to age 18: Longitudinal, cross-sectional and cross-cultural analyses. *Journal of Personality and Social Psychology, 83,* 1456–1468.

McCrae, R., & John, O. (1992). An introduction to the five-factor model and its applications. *Journal of Personality, 60,* 175–215.

McCreary, M., Slavin, L., & Berry, E. (1996). Predicting problem behavior and self-esteem among African American adolescents. *Journal of Adolescent Research, 11,* 216–234.

McCree, D. J., Wingood, G. M., DiClemente, R., Davies, S., & Harrington, K. F. (2003). Religiosity and risky sexual behavior in African-American adolescent females. *Journal of Adolescent Health, 33,* 2–8.

McElhaney, K., Allen, J., Stephenson, J., & Hare, A. (2009). Attachment and autonomy during adolescence. In R. Lerner & L. Steinberg (Eds.), *Handbook of adolescent psychology* (3rd ed., Vol. 1, pp. 358–403). New York: Wiley.

McElhaney, K. B., Antonishak, J., & Allen, J. P. (2008). "They like me, they like me not": Popularity and adolescents' perceptions of acceptance predicting social functioning over time. *Child Development, 79,* 720–731.

McGee, L., & Newcomb, M. (1992). General deviance syndrome: Expanded hierarchical evaluations at four ages from early adolescence to adulthood. *Journal of Consulting and Clinical Psychology, 60,* 766–776.

McGue, M., Elkins, I., Walden, B., & Iacono, W. G. (2005). Perceptions of the parent–adolescent relationship: A longitudinal investigation. *Developmental Psychology, 41,* 971–984.

McGue, M., Sharma, A., & Benson, P. (1996). The effects of common rearing on adolescent adjustment: Evidence from a U.S. adoption cohort. *Developmental Psychology, 32,* 604–613.

McGuire, J. K., & Gamble, W. C. (2006). Community service for youth: The value of psychological engagement over number of hours spent. *Journal of Adolescence, 29,* 289–298.

McGuire, S., Manke, B., Saudino, K., Reiss, D., Hetherington, E. M., & Plomin R. (1999). Perceived competence and self-worth during adolescence: A longitudinal behavioral genetic study. *Child Development, 70,* 1283–1296.

McGuire, S., Neiderhiser, J., Reiss, D., Hetherington, E. M., & Plomin, R. (1994). Genetic and environmental influences on perceptions of self-worth and competence in adolescence: A study of twins, full siblings, and step-siblings. *Child Development, 65,* 785–799.

McHale, S., Corneal, D., Crouter, A., & Birch, L. (2001). Gender and weight concerns in early and middle adolescence: Links with well-being and family characteristics. *Journal of Clinical Child Psychology, 30,* 338–348.

McHale, S., Crouter, A., Kim, J., Burton, L., Davis, K., Dotterer, A., et al. (2006). Mothers' and fathers' racial socialization in African American families: Implications for youth. *Child Development, 77,* 1387–1402.

McHale, S., Crouter, A., & Tucker, C. (2001). Free time activities in middle childhood: Links with adjustment in early adolescence. *Child Development, 72,* 1764–1778.

McHale, S., Shanahan, L., Updegraff, K. A., Crouter, A., & Booth, A. (2004). Developmental and individual differences in girls' sex-typed activities in middle childhood and adolescence. *Child Development, 75,* 1575–1593.

McHale, S. M., Kim, J., Dotterer, A., Crouter, A., & Booth, A. (2009). The development of gendered interests and personality qualities from middle childhood through adolescence: A biosocial analysis. *Child Development, 80,* 482–495.

McHale, S. M., Kim, J., Whiteman, S., & Crouter, A. C. (2004). Links between sex-typed time use in middle childhood and gender development in early adolescence. *Developmental Psychology, 40,* 868–881.

McIsaac, C., Connolly, J., McKenney, K., Pepler, D., & Craig, W. (2008). Conflict negotiation and autonomy processes in adolescent romantic relationships: An observational study of interdependency in boyfriend and girlfriend effects. *Journal of Adolescence, 31,* 691–707.

McKeown, R., Garrison, C., Jackson, K., Cuffe, S., Addy, C., & Waller, J. (1997). Family structure and cohesion, and depressive symptoms in adolescents. *Journal of Research on Adolescence, 7,* 267–281.

McKinney, C., & Renk, K. (2008). Differential parenting between mothers and fathers: Implications for late adolescents. *Journal of Family Issues, 29,* 806–827.

McLanahan, S., & Bumpass, L. (1988). Intergenerational consequences of family disruption. *American Journal of Sociology, 94,* 130–152.

McLean, K. (2005). Late adolescent identity development: Narrative meaning making and memory telling. *Developmental Psychology, 41,* 683–691.

McLean, K., & Pratt, M. (2006). Life's little (and big) lessons: Identity statuses and meaning-making in the turning point narratives of emerging adults. *Developmental Psychology, 42,* 714–722.

McLean, K., & Thorne, A. (2003). Late adolescents' self-defining memories about relationships. *Developmental Psychology, 39,* 635–645.

McLellan, J. A., & Youniss, J. (2003). Two systems of youth service: Determinants of voluntary and required youth community service. *Journal of Youth and Adolescence, 32,* 47–58.

McLoyd, V. (1990). The impact of economic hardship on Black families and children: Psychological distress, parenting, and socioemotional development. *Child Development, 61,* 311–346.

McLoyd, V., Kaplan, R., Purtell, K., Bagley, E., Hardaway, C., & Smalls, C. (2009). Poverty and socioeconomic disadvantage in adolescence. In R. Lerner & L. Steinberg (Eds.), *Handbook of adolescent psychology* (3rd ed., Vol. 2, pp. 444–491). New York: Wiley.

McMahon, S. D., & Watts, R. J. (2002). Ethnic identity in urban African American youth: Exploring links with self-worth, aggression, and other psychosocial variables. *Journal of Community Psychology, 30,* 411–431.

McMaster, L., Connolly, J., & Craig, W. (1997, March). *Sexual harassment and dating violence among early adolescents.* Paper presented at the biennial meetings of the Society for Research in Child Development, Washington, DC.

McMaster, L., Connolly, J., Pepler, D., & Craig, W. (2002). Peer to peer sexual harassment in early adolescence: A developmental perspective. *Development and Psychopathology, 14,* 91–105.

McNeal, R., Jr. (1997). Are students being pulled out of high school? The effect of adolescent employment on dropping out. *Sociology of Education, 70,* 206–220.

McNeely, C., Shew, M. L., Beurhing, T., Sieving, R., Miller, B. C., & Blum, R. (2002). Mothers' influence on the timing of first sex among 14- and 15-year olds. *Journal of Adolescent Health, 31,* 256–265.

McNelles, L., & Connolly, J. (1999). Intimacy between adolescent friends: Age and gender differences in intimate affect and intimate behaviors. *Journal of Research on Adolescence, 9,* 143–159.

McNulty, T., & Bellair, P. (2003). Explaining racial and ethnic differences in serious adolescent violent behavior. *Criminology, 41,* 709–748.

McQueen, A., Getz, J., & Bray, J. (2003). Acculturation, substance use, and deviant behavior: Examining separation and family conflict as mediators. *Child Development, 74,* 1737–1750.

Mead, M. (1978). *Coming of age in Samoa.* New York: Morrow. (Original work published 1928)

Meadows, S. O., Brown, J. S., & Elder, G. H. J. (2006). Depressive symptoms, stress, and support: Gendered trajectories from adolescence to young adulthood. *Journal of Youth and Adolescence, 35,* 93–103.

Measelle, J. R., Stice, E., & Hogansen, J. M. (2006). Developmental trajectories of co-occurring depressive, eating, antisocial, and substance abuse problems in female adolescents. *Journal of Abnormal Psychology, 115,* 524–538.

Mednick, S., Gabrielli, W., & Hitchings, B. (1987). Genetic factors in the etiology of criminal behavior. In S. Mednick, T. Moffitt, & S. Stack (Eds.), *The causes of crime: New biological approaches* (pp. 74–91). Cambridge: Cambridge University Press.

Meeus, W. (1996). Studies on identity development in adolescence: An overview of research and some new data. *Journal of Youth and Adolescence, 25,* 569–598.

Meeus, W., Iedema, J., & Vollebergh, W. (1999). Rejoinder: Identity formation re-revisited: A rejoinder to Waterman in developmental and cross-cultural issues. *Developmental Review, 19,* 480–496.

Meier, A. M. (2003). Adolescents' transition to first intercourse, religiosity, and attitudes about sex. *Social Forces, 81,* 1031–1052.

Meier, A. M. (2007). Adolescent first sex and subsequent mental health. *American Journal of Sociology, 112,* 1811–1847.

Meier, M., Slutske, W., Arndt, S., & Cadoret, R. (2008). Impulsive and callous traits are more strongly associated with delinquent behavior in higher risk neighborhoods among boys and girls. *Journal of Abnormal Psychology, 117,* 377–385.

Mekos, D., Hetherington, E. M., & Reiss, D. (1996). Sibling differences in problem behavior and parental treatment in non-divorced and remarried families. *Child Development, 67,* 2148–2165.

Melby, J. (1995, March). *Early family and peer predictors of later adolescent tobacco use.* Paper presented at the biennial meetings of the Society for Research in Child Development, Indianapolis.

Melby, J., & Conger, R. (1996). Parental behaviors and adolescent academic performance: A longitudinal analysis. *Journal of Research on Adolescence, 6,* 113–137.

Melby, J. N., Conger, R. D., Fang, S., Wickrama, K. A. S., & Conger, K. J. (2008). Adolescent family experiences and educational attainment during early adulthood. *Developmental Psychology, 44,* 1519–1536.

Mello, Z. R. (2008). Gender variation in developmental trajectories of educational and occupational expectations and attainment from adolescence to adulthood. *Developmental Psychology, 44,* 1069–1080.

Melton, G. (1990). Knowing what we do know: APA and adolescent abortion. *American Psychologist, 45,* 1171–1173.

Menard, S., & Huizinga, D. (1994). Changes in conventional attitudes and delinquent behavior in adolescence. *Youth and Society, 26,* 23–53.

Mendle, J., Turkheimer, E., & Emery, R. E. (2007). Detrimental psychological outcomes associated with early pubertal timing in adolescent girls. *Developmental Review, 27,* 151–171.

Menning, C. L. (2002). Absent parents are more than money: The joint effect of activities and financial support on youths' educational attainment. *Journal of Family Issues, 23,* 648–671.

Merskin, D. (1999). Adolescence, advertising, and the ideology of menstruation. *Sex Roles, 40,* 941–957.

Merten, D. (1997). The meaning of meanness: Popularity, competition and conflict among junior high school girls. *Sociology of Education, 70,* 175–191.

Merten, M., Wickrama, K., & Williams, A. (2008). Adolescent obesity and young adult psychosocial outcomes: Gender and racial differences. *Journal of Youth and Adolescence, 37,* 1111–1122.

Mesch, G. S., & Talmud, I. (2007). Similarity and the quality of online and offline social relationships among adolescents in Israel. *Journal of Research on Adolescence, 17,* 455–466.

Meschke, L. L., Bartholomae, S., & Zentall, S. R. (2000). Adolescent sexuality and parent–adolescent processes: Promoting healthy teen choices. *Family Relations: Interdisciplinary Journal of Applied Family Studies, 49,* 143–154.

Meyer, L. (1994). *Teenspeak.* Princeton, NJ: Peterson.

Meyer-Bahlburg, H., Ehrhardt, A., Rosen, L., Gruen, R., Veridiano, N., Vann, F., & Neuwalder, H. (1995). Prenatal estrogens and the development of homosexual orientation. *Developmental Psychology, 31,* 12–21.

Michael, R., Laumann, E., & Kolata, G. (1994). *Sex in America.* Boston: Little, Brown.

Mickelson, R. (1990). The attitude–achievement paradox among Black adolescents. *Sociology of Education, 63,* 44–61.

Midgley, C., Arunkumar, R., & Urban T. (1996). If I don't do well tomorrow, there's a reason: Predictors of adolescents' use of academic self-handicapping strategies. *Journal of Educational Psychology, 88,* 423–434.

Midgley, C., Berman, E., & Hicks, L. (1995). Differences between elementary and middle school teachers and students: A goal theory approach. *Journal of Early Adolescence, 15,* 90–113.

Midgley, C., Feldlaufer, H., & Eccles, J. (1988). The transition to junior high school: Beliefs of pre- and posttransition teachers. *Journal of Youth and Adolescence, 17,* 543–562.

Midgley, C., & Urdan, T. (1995). Predictors of middle school students' use of self-handicapping strategies. *Journal of Early Adolescence, 15,* 389–411.

Miech, R. A., Kumanyika, S. K., Stettler, N., Link, B. G., Phelan, J. C., & Chang, V. W. (2006). Trends in the association of poverty with overweight among US adolescents, 1971–2004. *JAMA: Journal of the American Medical Association, 295,* 2385–2393.

Mihalic, S., & Elliot, D. (1997). Short- and long-term consequences of adolescent work. *Youth and Society, 28,* 464–498.

Milan, S., Ethier, K., Lewis, J., Kershaw, T., Niccolai, L., & Ickovics, J. (2006). Reproductive health of urban adolescents: Differences in the behaviors, cognitions, and social context of African-American and Puerto Rican females. *Journal of Youth and Adolescence, 35,* 959–967.

Miller-Johnson, S., Winn, D., Coie, J., Hyman, C., Terry, R., Lochman, J., & Maumary-Gremaud, A. (1996, March). *Parenthood during the teen years: A developmental perspective on risk factors for childbearing.* Paper presented at the biennial meetings of the Society for Research on Adolescence, Boston.

Miller-Johnson, S., Winn, D., Coie, J., Maumary-Gremaud, A., Hyman, C., Retty, R., et al. (1999). Motherhood during the teen years: A developmental perspective on risk factors for childbearing. *Development and Psychopathology, 11,* 85–100.

Miller-Johnson, S., Winn, D. C., Coie, J. D., Malone, P. S., & Lochman, J. (2004). Risk factors for adolescent pregnancy reports among African American males. *Journal of Research on Adolescence 14,* 471–495.

Miller-Jones, D. (1989). Culture and testing. *American Psychologist, 44,* 360–366.

Miller, B., Benson, B., & Galbraith, K. A. (2001). Family relationships and adolescent pregnancy risk: A research synthesis. *Developmental Review, 21,* 1–38.

Miller, B., Fan, X., Christensen, M., Grotevant, H. D., & van Dulmen, M. (2000). Comparisons of adopted and nonadopted adolescents in a large, nationally represented sample. *Child Development, 71,* 1458–1473.

Miller, B., & Moore, K. (1990). Adolescent sexual behavior, pregnancy, and parenting: Research through the 1980s. *Journal of Marriage and the Family, 52,* 1025–1044.

Miller, B., Norton, M., Curtis, T., Hill, E., Schvaneveldt, P., & Young, M. (1997). The timing of sexual intercourse among adolescents: Family, peer, and other antecedents. *Youth and Society, 29,* 54–83.

Miller, B., Norton, M., Fan, X., & Christopherson, C. (1998). Pubertal development, parental communication, and sexual values in relation to adolescent sexual behaviors. *Journal of Early Adolescence, 18,* 27–52.

Miller, D., & Byrnes, J. (1997). The role of contextual and personal factors in children's risk taking. *Developmental Psychology, 33,* 814–823.

Miller, J., & White, N. (2003). Gender and adolescent relationship violence: A contextual examination. *Criminology, 41,* 1207–1248.

Miller, K., Clark, L., & Moore, J. (1997). Sexual initiation with older male partners and subsequent HIV risk behavior among female adolescents. *Family Planning Perspectives, 29,* 212–214.

Miller, K., Kotchick, B., Dorsey, S., Forehand, R., & Ham, A. (1998). Family communication about sex: What are parents saying and are their adolescents listening? *Family Planning Perspectives, 30,* 218–222, 235.

Miller, K., Levin, M., Whitaker, D., & Xu, X. (1998). Patterns of condom use among adolescents: The impact of mother–adolescent communication. *American Journal of Public Health, 88,* 1542–1544.

Miller, K., & Whitaker, D. (2001). Predictors of mother–adolescent discussions about condoms: Implications for providers who serve youth. *Pediatrics, 108,* E28.

Miller, K. E., Melnick, M. J., Barnes, G. M., Sabo, D., & Farrell, M. P. (2007). Athletic involvement and adolescent delinquency. *Journal of Youth and Adolescence, 36,* 711–723.

Miller, L., Davies, M., & Greenwald, S. (2000). Religiosity and substance use and abuse among adolescents in the National Comorbidity Survey. *Journal of the American Academy of Child and Adolescent Psychiatry, 39,* 1190–1197.

Miller, L., & Gur, M. (2002). Religiousness and sexual responsibility in adolescent girls. *Journal of Adolescent Health, 31,* 401–406.

Miller, N. (1928). *The child in primitive society.* New York: Brentano's.

Mills, B., Reyna, V., & Estrada, S. (2008). Explaining contradictory relations between risk perception and risk taking. *Psychological Science, 19,* 429–433.

Millstein, S. G., & Halpern-Felsher, B. L. (2002). Judgments about risk and perceived invulnerability in adolescents and young adults. *Journal of Research on Adolescence, 12,* 399–422.

Milnitsky-Sapiro, C., Turiel, E., & Nucci, L. (2006). Brazilian adolescents' conceptions of autonomy and parental authority. *Cognitive Development, 21,* 317–331.

Minuchin, S., Rosman, B., & Baker, L. (1978). *Psychosomatic families: Anorexia nervosa in context.* Cambridge, MA: Harvard University Press.

Mitchell, B., Wister, A., & Burch, T. (1989). The family environment and leaving the parental home. *Journal of Marriage and the Family, 51,* 605–613.

Mitchell, C., & O'Nell, T. (1998). Problem and conventional behavior among American Indian adolescents: Structure and validity. *Journal of Research on Adolescence, 8,* 97–122.

Mitchell, C., O'Nell, T., Beals, J., Dick, R., Keane, E., & Manson, S. (1996). Dimensionality of alcohol use among American Indian adolescents: Latent structure, construct validity, and implications for developmental research. *Journal of Research on Adolescence, 6,* 151–180.

Mitchell, C. M., Whitesell, N. R., Spicer, P., Beals, J., & Kaufman, C. E. (2007). Cumulative risk for early sexual initiation among American Indian youth: A discrete-time survival analysis. *Journal of Research on Adolescence, 17,* 387–412.

Mitchell, E. (Ed.). (1985). *Anorexia nervosa and bulimia: Diagnosis and treatment.* Minneapolis: University of Minnesota Press.

Mitchell, K. J., Wolak, J., & Finkelhor, D. (2007). Trends in youth reports of sexual solicitations, harassment and unwanted exposure to pornography on the Internet. *Journal of Adolescent Health, 40,* 116–126.

Mitru, G., Millrood, D. L., & Mateika, J. H. (2002). The impact of sleep on learning and behavior in adolescents. *Teachers College Record, 104,* 704–726.

Modecki, K. L. (2008). Addressing gaps in the maturity of judgment literature: Age differences and delinquency. *Law and Human Behavior, 32,* 78–91.

Modell, J., & Goodman, M. (1990). Historical perspectives. In S. Feldman & G. Elliott (Eds.), *At the threshold: The developing adolescent* (pp. 93–122). Cambridge, MA: Harvard University Press.

Modell, J., Furstenberg, F., Jr., & Hershberg, T. (1976). Social change and transitions to adulthood in historical perspective. *Journal of Family History, 1,* 7–32.

Moffitt, T. (2006). Life-course persistent versus adolescence-limited antisocial behavior. In D. Cicchetti & D. Cohen (Eds.), *Developmental psychopathology* (2nd ed.). New York: Wiley.

Moffitt, T., & Caspi, A. (2001). Childhood predictors differentiate life-course persistent and adolescence-limited antisocial pathways among males and females. *Development and Psychopathology, 13,* 355–375.

Moffitt, T., Caspi, A., Harkness, A., & Silva, P. (1993). The natural history of change in intellectual performance: Who changes? How much? Is it meaningful? *Journal of Child Psychology and Psychiatry, 34,* 455–506.

Moffitt, T., Caspi, A., Harrington, H., & Milne, B. J. (2002). Males on the life-course-persistent and adolescence-limited antisocial pathways: Follow-up at age 26 years. *Development and Psychopathology, 14,* 179–207.

Molina, B., & Chassin, L. (1996). The parent–adolescent relationship at puberty: Hispanic ethnicity and parent alcoholism as moderators. *Developmental Psychology, 32,* 675–686.

Mollborn S. (2007). Making the best of a bad situation: Material resources and teenage parenthood. *Journal of Marriage and Family, 69,* 92–104.

Mollen, C. J., Barg, F. K., Hayes, K. L., Gotcsik, M., Blades, N. M., & Schwarz, D. F. (2008). Assessing attitudes about emergency contraception among urban, minority adolescent girls: An in-depth interview study. *Pediatrics, 122,* 395–401.

Molnar, B. E., Cerda, M., Roberts, A. L., & Buka, S. L. (2008). Effects of neighborhood resources on aggressive and delinquent behaviors among urban youths. *American Journal of Public Health, 98,* 1086–1093.

Monahan, K., & Lee, J. (2008). Adolescent sexual activity: Links between relational context and depressive symptoms. *Journal of Youth and Adolescence, 37,* 917–927.

Monahan, K., Lee, J., & Steinberg, L. (in press). Revisiting the negative impact of part-time work on adolescent adjustment: Distinguishing between selection and socialization using propensity score matching. *Child Development.*

Monahan, K., Steinberg, L., & Cauffman, E. (2009). Affiliation with antisocial peers, susceptibility to peer influence, and desistance from antisocial behavior during the transition to adulthood. *Developmental Psychology, 45,* 1520–1530.

Monahan, K., Steinberg, L., Cauffman, E., & Mulvey, E. (2009). Trajectories of antisocial behavior and psychosocial maturity from adolescence to young adulthood. *Developmental Psychology, 45,* 1654–1668.

Monck, E. (1991). Patterns of confiding relationships among adolescent girls. *Journal of Child Psychology and Psychiatry, 32,* 333–345.

Monroe, S. M., Rohde, P., Seeley, J. R., & Lewinsohn, P. M. (1999). Life events and depression in adolescence: Relationship loss as a prospective risk factor for first onset of major depressive disorder. *Journal of Abnormal Psychology, 108,* 606–614.

Montgomery, M. (1996). "The fruit that hangs highest": Courtship and chaperonage in New York high society, 1880–1920. *Journal of Family History, 21,* 172–191.

Montgomery, M. J. (2005). Psychosocial intimacy and identity: From early adolescence to emerging adulthood. *Journal of Adolescent Research, 20,* 346–374.

Montgomery, M. J., & Sorell, G. T. (1998). Love and dating experience in early and middle adolescence: Grade and gender comparisons. *Journal of Adolescence, 21,* 677–689.

Moody, J. (2001). Race, school integration, and friendship segregation in America. American Journal of Sociology, 107, 679–716.

Moore, K., Myers, D., Morrison, D., Nord, C., Brown, B., & Edmonston, B. (1993). Age at first childbirth and later poverty. *Journal of Research on Adolescence, 3,* 393–422.

Moore, M., Petrie, C., Braga, A., & McLaughlin, B. (2003). *Deadly lessons: Understanding lethal school violence.* Washington, DC: National Academies Press.

Moore, M. J., & Werch, C. E. (2005). Sport and physical activity participation and substance use among adolescents. *Journal of Adolescent Health, 36,* 486–493.

Moore, M. R., & Chase-Lansdale, P. L. (2001). Sexual intercourse and pregnancy among African American girls in high-poverty neighborhoods: The role of family and perceived community environment. *Journal of Marriage and the Family, 63,* 1146–1157.

Moore, S. (1995). Girls' understanding and social construction of menarche. *Journal of Adolescence, 18,* 87–104.

Moore, S., & Gullone, E. (1996). Predicting adolescent risk behavior using a personalized cost-benefit analysis. *Journal of Youth and Adolescence, 25,* 343–359.

Moos, R. (1978). A typology of junior high and high school classrooms. *American Educational Research Journal, 15,* 53–66.

Morabia, A. Costanza, M., & World Health Organization Collaborative Study of Neoplasia and Steroid Contraceptives. (1998). International variability in ages at menarche, first livebirth, and menopause. *American Journal of Epidemiology, 148,* 1195–1205.

Morisi, T. (2008). Youth enrollment and employment during the school year. *Monthly Labor Review, 131,* 51–63.

Morison, P., & Masten, A. (1991). Peer reputation in middle childhood as a predictor of adaptation in adolescence: A seven-year follow-up. *Child Development, 62,* 991–1007.

Morris, A., & Sloutsky, V. (1998). Understanding of logical necessity: Developmental antecedents and cognitive consequences. *Child Development, 69,* 721–741.

Morris, B., & Sloutsky, V. (2001). Children's solutions of logical versus empirical problems: What's missing and what develops? *Cognitive Development, 16,* 907–928.

Morris, N., Udry, J. (1980). Validation of a self-administered instrument to assess stage of adolescent development. *Journal of Youth and Adolescence, 9,* 271–280.

Morrison, G. M., Laughlin, J., Miguel, S. S., Smith, D. C., & Widaman, K. (1997). Sources of support for school-related issues: Choices of Hispanic adolescents varying in migrant status. *Journal of Youth and Adolescence, 26,* 233–252.

Morrison Gutman, L., Sameroff, A. J., & Eccles, J. (2002). The academic achievement of African American students during early adolescence: An examination of multiple risk, promotive, and protective factors. *American Journal of Community Psychology, 30,* 367–399.

Mortimer, J. (2003). *Working and growing up in America.* Cambridge, MA: Harvard University Press.

Mortimer, J., & Johnson, M. (1998). New perspectives on adolescent work and the transition to adulthood. In R. Jessor & M. Chase (Eds.), *New perspectives on adolescent risk behavior.* New York: Cambridge University Press.

Mortimer, J., & Larson, R. (2002). Adolescence in the 21st century: A worldwide perspective. Introduction: Macro societal trends and the changing experiences of adolescence. In J. Mortimer & R. Larson (Eds.), *The future of adolescent experience: Societal trends and the transition to adulthood.* New York: Cambridge University Press.

Mortimer, J., Pimentel, E., Ryu, S., Nash, K., & Lee, C. (1996). Part-time work and occupational value formation in adolescence. *Social Forces, 74,* 1405–1418.

Mory, M. (1992, March). *"Love the ones you're with": Conflict and consensus in adolescent peer group stereotypes.* Paper presented at the biennial meetings of the Society for Research on Adolescence, Washington, DC.

Mory, M. (1994, February). *When people form or perceive sets, they tend to be fuzzy: The case of adolescent crowds.* Paper presented at the biennial meetings of the Society for Research on Adolescence, San Diego.

Moses, A. (1999). Exposure to violence, depression, and hostility in a sample of inner city high school youth. *Journal of Adolescence, 22,* 21–32.

Mosher, W., & Bachrach, C. (1996). Understanding U.S. fertility: Continuity and change in the National Survey of Family Growth, 1988–1995. *Family Planning Perspectives, 28,* 4–12.

Moshman, D. (1993). Adolescent reasoning and adolescent rights. *Human Development, 36,* 27–40.

Mosteller, F., Light, R., & Sachs, J. (1996). Sustained inquiry in education: Lessons from skill grouping and class size. *Harvard Educational Review, 66,* 797–842.

Motl, R. W., McAuley, E., Birnbaum, A. S., & Lytle, L. A. (2006). Naturally occurring changes in time spent watching television are inversely related to frequency of physical activity during early adolescence. *Journal of Adolescence, 29,* 19–32.

Mott, F., Fondell, M., Hu, P., Kowaleski-Jones, P., & Menaghan, E. (1996). The determinants of first sex by age 14 in a high-risk adolescent population. *Family Planning Perspectives, 28,* 13–18.

Mounts, N. (2002). Parental management of adolescent peer relationships in context: The role of parenting style. *Journal of Family Psychology, 16,* 58–69.

Mounts, N. (2004). Adolescents' perceptions of parental management of peer relationships in an ethnically diverse sample. *Journal of Adolescent Research, 19,* 446–467.

Mounts, N. (2007). Adolescents' and their mothers' perceptions of parental management of peer relationships. *Journal of Research on Adolescence, 17,* 169–178.

Mounts, N., & Steinberg, L. (1995). An ecological analysis of peer influence on adolescent grade point average and drug use. *Developmental Psychology, 31,* 915–922.

Mouw, T., & Entwisle, B. (2006). Residential segregation and interracial friendship in schools. *American Journal of Sociology, 112,* 394–441.

Muise, A. M., Stein, D. G., & Arbess, G. (2003). Eating disorders in adolescent boys: A review of the adolescent and young adult literature. *Journal of Adolescent Health, 33,* 427–435.

Mukai, T. (1996). Mothers, peers, and perceived pressure to diet among Japanese adolescent girls. *Journal of Research on Adolescence, 6,* 309–324.

Muller, C. (1998). Gender differences in parental involvement and adolescents' mathematics achievement. *Sociology of Education, 71,* 336–356.

Muller, P. A., Stage, F. K., & Kinzie, J. (2001). Science achievement growth trajectories: Understanding factors related to gender and racial-ethnic differences in precollege science achievement. *American Educational Research, 3,* 981–1012.

Mulvey, E., & Cauffman, E. (2001). The inherent limits of predicting school violence. *American Psychologist, 56,* 797–802.

Mulvey, E., Steinberg, L., Fagan, J., Cauffman, E., Piquero, A., Chassin, L., et al. (2004). Theory and research on desistance from antisocial activity among serious adolescent offenders. *Youth Violence and Juvenile Justice, 2,* 213–236.

Mun, E. Y., Windle, M., & Schainker, L. M. (2008). A model-based cluster analysis approach to adolescent problem behaviors and young adult outcomes. *Development and Psychopathology, 20,* 291–318.

Munsch, J., Liang, S., & DeSecottier, L. (1996, March). *Natural mentors: Who they are and the roles they fill. A gender and ethnic comparison.* Paper presented at the biennial meetings of the Society for Research on Adolescence, Boston.

Munsch, J., & Wampler, R. (1993). Ethnic differences in early adolescents' coping with school stress. *American Journal of Orthopsychiatry, 63,* 633–646.

Murdock, T. (1994, February). *Who are you and how do you treat me? Student withdrawal as motivated alienation.* Paper presented at the biennial meetings of the Society for Research on Adolescence, San Diego.

Murdock, T. B., Anderman, L. H., & Hodge, S. A. (2000). Middle-grade predictors of students' motivation and behavior in high school. *Journal of Adolescent Research, 15,* 327–351.

Musick, J. (1994). Grandmothers and grandmothers-to-be: Effects on adolescent mothers and adolescent mothering. *Infancy and Young Children, 6,* 1–9.

Mustanski, B. S., Viken, R. J., Kaprio, J., Pulkkinen, L., & Rose, R. J. (2004). Genetic and environmental influences on pubertal development: Longitudinal data from Finnish twins at ages 11 and 14. *Developmental Psychology, 40,* 1188–1198.

Myers, J., Lindentthal, J., & Pepper, M. (1975). Life events, social integration, and psychiatric symptomatology. *Journal of Health and Social Behavior, 16,* 421–429.

Mylod, D., Whitman, T., & Borkowski, J. (1997). Predicting adolescent mothers' transition to adulthood. *Journal of Research on Adolescence, 7,* 457–478.

Nadeem, E., & Graham, S. (2005). Early puberty, peer victimization, and internalizing symptoms in ethnic minority adolescents. *Journal of Early Adolescence, 25,* 197–222.

Nader, P. R., Bradley, R. H., Houts, R. M., McRitchie, S. L., & O'Brien, M. (2008). Moderate-to-vigorous physical activity from ages 9 to 15 years. *Journal of the American Medical Association, 300,* 295–305.

Nagin, D., Farrington, D., & Moffitt, T. (1995). Life-course trajectories of different types of offenders. *Criminology, 33,* 111–139.

Nagin, D., & Tremblay, R. (1999). Trajectories of boys' physical aggression, opposition, and hyperactivity on the path to physically violent and nonviolent juvenile delinquency. *Child Development, 70,* 1181–1196.

Nagy, S., Adcock, A., & Nagy, C. (1994). A comparison of risky health behaviors of sexually active, sexually abused, and abstaining adolescents. *Pediatrics, 93,* 570–575.

Nagy, S., DiClimente, R., & Adcock, A. (1995). Adverse factors associated with forced sex among Southern adolescent girls. *Pediatrics, 96,* 944–946.

Nansel, T. R., Overpeck, M., Pilla, R. S., Ruan, W., Simons-Morton, B., & Scheidt, P. (2001). Bullying behaviors among U.S. youth. *Journal of the American Medical Association, 285,* 2094–2100.

Nation, M., Crusto, C., Wandersman, A., Kumpfer, K. L., Seybolt, D., Morrissey-Kane, E., et al. (2003). What works in prevention: Principles of effective prevention programs. *American Psychologist, 58,* 449–456.

National Center for Children in Poverty. (2002). *Early childhood poverty: A statistical profile.* New York: Author.

National Center for Education Statistics (2002a). *Educational Longitudinal Study of 2002.* Washington, DC: Author.

National Center for Education Statistics. (2002b). *Digest of education statistics, 2001.* Washington, DC: Author.

National Center for Education Statistics. (2003). *Digest of educational statistics, 2002.* Washington, DC: Author.

National Center for Education Statistics. (2005). *Youth indicators, 2005.* Washington, DC: Author.

National Center for Education Statistics. (2006a). *Comparing private schools and public schools using Hierarchical Linear Modeling.* Washington, DC: Author.

National Center for Education Statistics (2006b). *The nation's report card: Science 2005 Trial Urban District Assessment.* Washington: Author.

National Center for Education Statistics (2006c). *Annual expenditures on public and private institutions per student and as a percentage of gross domestic product (GDP) in OECD countries, by level of education: 2002.* Washington, DC: Author.

National Center for Education Statistics. (2009). *The condition of education 2009.* Washington: Author.

National Center for Health Statistics (2008). *Leading causes of death, 2005.* Retrieved from http://www.cdc.gov/nchs/data/dvs/LCWK4_2005.pdf

National Education Commission on Time and Learning. (1994). *Prisoners of time.* Washington, DC: U.S. Government Printing Office.

National Heart, Lung, and Blood Institute Growth and Health Study Research Group. (1992). Obesity and cardiovascular disease risk factors in Black and White girls: The NHLBI Growth and Health Study. *American Journal of Public Health, 82,* 1613–1620.

National Research Council. (1993). *Losing generations.* Washington, DC: National Academy Press.

National Research Council. (1998). *Protecting youth at work.* Washington, DC: National Academy Press.

National Research Council. (2004). *Reducing underage drinking: A collective responsibility.* Washington, DC: National Academies Press.

National Research Council. (2005). *Growing up global.* Washington, DC: National Academies Press.

National Research Council and Institute of Medicine. (2009). *Adolescent health services: Missing opportunities.* Washington: The National Academies Press.

Natsuaki, M. N., Biehl, M. C., & Ge, X. (2009). Trajectories of depressed mood from early adolescence to young adulthood: The effects of pubertal timing and adolescent dating. *Journal of Research on Adolescence, 19,* 47–74.

Neblett, E., Smalls, C., Ford, K., Nguyên, H., & Sellers, R. (2009). Racial socialization and racial identity: African American parents' messages about race as precursors to identity. *Journal of Youth and Adolescence, 38,* 189–203.

Neblett, E., White, R., Ford, K., Philip, C., Nguyên, H., & Sellers, R. M. (2008). Patterns of racial socialization and psychological adjustment: Can parental communications about race reduce the impact of racial discrimination? *Journal of Research on Adolescence, 18,* 477–515.

Neckerman, H., Cairns, B., & Cairns, R. (1993, March). *Peers and families: Developmental changes, constraints, and continuities.* Paper presented at the biennial meetings of the Society for Research on Child Development, New Orleans.

Needle, R., Su, S., & Doherty, W. (1990). Divorce, remarriage, and adolescent substance use: A prospective longitudinal study. *Journal of Marriage and the Family, 52,* 157–169.

Neemann, J., Hubbard, J., & Masten, A. (1995). The changing importance of romantic relationship involvement to competence from late childhood to late adolescence. *Development and Psychopathology, 7,* 727–750.

Neiderhiser, J. M., Reiss, D., Pedersen, N. L., Lictenstein, P., Spotts, F. L., Hansson, K., et al. (2004). Genetic and environmental influences on mothering of adolescents: A comparison of two samples. *Developmental Psychology, 40,* 335–351.

Nelson, C., Bloom, F., Cameron, J., Amaral, D., Dahl, R., & Pine, D. (2002). An integrative, multidisciplinary approach to the study of brain–behavior relations in the context of typical and atypical development. *Development and Psychopathology, 14,* 499–520.

Nelson, D. E., Mowery, P., Asman, K., Pederson, L. L., O'Malley, P. M., Malarcher, A., et al. (2008). Long-term trends in adolescent and young adult smoking in the United States: Metapatterns and implications. *American Journal of Public Health, 98,* 905–915.

Nelson, D. E., Mowery, P., Tomar, S., Marcus, S., Giovino, G., & Zhao, L. (2006). Trends in smokeless tobacco use among adults and adolescents in the United States. *American Journal of Public Health, 96,* 897–905.

Nelson, E., Leibenluft, E., McClure, E., & Pine, D. (2005). The social re-orientation of adolescence: A neuroscience perspective on the process and its relation to psychopathology. *Psychological Medicine, 35,* 163–174.

Nelson, E., McClure, E., Parrish, J., Leibenluft, E., Ernst, M., Fox, N., et al. (2007). *Brain systems underlying peer social acceptance in adolescents.* Unpublished paper, Development and Anxiety Neuroscience Section, Mood and Activity Disorders Program, National Institute of Mental Health, Washington, DC.

Nelson, L. J., Badger, S., & Bo, W. (2004). The influence of culture in emerging adulthood: Perspectives of Chinese college students. *International Journal of Behavioral Development, 28,* 26–36.

Nelson, L. J., & Barry, C. M. (2005). Distinguishing features of emerging adulthood. *Journal of Adolescent Research, 20,* 242–262.

Nelson, L. J., Padilla-Walker, L., Carroll, J. S., Madsen, S. D., Barry, C. M., & Badger, S. (2007). "If you want me to treat you like an adult, start acting like one!" Comparing the criteria that emerging adults and their parents have for adulthood. *Journal of Family Psychology, 21,* 665–674.

Neugarten, B., & Datan, N. (1974). The middle years. In S. Arieti (Ed.), *American handbook of psychiatry* (2nd ed., Vol. 1, Part 3). New York: Basic Books.

Neumark-Sztainer, D., Paxton, S. J., Hannan, P. J., Haines, J., & Story, M. (2006). Does body satisfaction matter? Five-year longitudinal associations between body satisfaction and health behaviors in adolescent females and males. *Journal of Adolescent Health, 39,* 244–251.

Neumark-Sztainer, D., Story, M., Dixon, L., & Murray, D. (1998). Adolescents engaging in unhealthy weight control behaviors: Are they at risk for other health-compromising behaviors? *American Journal of Public Health, 88,* 952–955.

Neumark-Sztainer, D., Story, M., French, S., Cassuto, N., Jacobs, J. D., & Resnick, M. (1996). Patterns of health-compromising behaviors among Minnesota adolescents: Sociodemographic variations. *American Journal of Public Health, 86,* 1599–1606.

Newcomb, A., & Bagwell, C. (1995). Children's friendship relations: A meta-analytic review. *Psychological Review, 117,* 306–347.

Newcomb, M., & Bentler, P. (1988). Impact of adolescent drug use and social support on problems of young adults: A longitudinal study. *Journal of Abnormal Psychology, 97,* 64–75.

Newman, B., & Newman, P. (2001). Group identity and alienation: Giving the we its due. *Journal of Youth and Adolescence, 30,* 515–538.

Newman, D. L. (2005). Ego development and ethnic identity formation in rural American Indian adolescents. *Child Development, 76,* 734–746.

Newman, K. (1999). *No shame in my game.* New York: Knopf.

Newman, R., & Schwager, M. (1995). Students' help seeking during problem solving: Effects of grade, goal, and prior achievement. *American Educational Research Journal, 32,* 352–376.

Newmann, F. (1992). Higher order thinking and prospects for classroom thoughtfulness. In F. Newmann (Ed.), *Student engagement and achievement in American high schools.* New York: Teachers College Press.

Newmann, F., Marks, H., & Gamoran, A. (1996). Authentic pedagogy and student performance. *American Journal of Education, 104,* 280–312.

Nichols, S., & Good, T. (1998). Students' perceptions of fairness in school settings: A gender analysis. *Teachers College Record, 100,* 369–401.

Nieto, M., Lambert, S., Briggs, E., McCoy, J., Brunson, L., & Aber, M. (1996, March). *Untangling the relationship between ethnic composition of neighborhood and school adjustment.* Paper presented at the biennial meetings of the Society for Research on Adolescence, Boston.

Nightingale, E., & Wolverton, L. (1993). Adolescent rolelessness in modern society. *Teachers College Record, 94,* 472–486.

Nishina, A., Ammon, N. Y., Bellmore, A. D., & Graham, S. (2006). Body dissatisfaction and physical development among ethnic minority adolescents. *Journal of Youth and Adolescence, 35,* 189–201.

Nishina, A., & Juvonen, J. (2005). Daily reports of witnessing and experience peer harassment in middle school. *Child Development, 76,* 435–450.

Noack, P., Kracke, B., & Hofer, M. (1994, February). *The family context of rightist attitudes among adolescents in East and West Germany.* Paper presented at the biennial meetings of the Society for Research on Adolescence, San Diego.

Noakes, M. A., & Rinaldi, C. M. (2006). Age and gender differences in peer conflict. *Journal of Youth and Adolescence, 35,* 881–891.

Nock, S. (1998). The consequences of premarital fatherhood. *American Sociological Review, 63,* 250–263.

Nofziger, S., & Lee, H. (2006). Differential associations and daily smoking of adolescents: The importance of same-sex models. *Youth and Society, 37,* 453–478.

Noguera, P. (1995). Preventing and producing violence: A critical analysis of responses to school violence. *Harvard Educational Review, 65,* 189–212.

Nolen-Hoeksema, S., & Girgus, J. (1994). The emergence of gender differences in depression during adolescence. *Psychological Bulletin, 115,* 424–443.

Nolen-Hoeksema, S., Girgus, J., & Seligman, M. (1992). Predictors and consequences of childhood depressive symptoms: A 5-year longitudinal study. *Journal of Abnormal Psychology, 101,* 405–422.

Nolle, K., Guerino, P., & Dinkes, R. (2007). *Crime, violence, discipline, and safety in U.S. public schools: Findings from the School Survey on Crime and Safety: 2005–06.* National Center for Education Statistics, Institute of Education Sciences, U.S. Department of Education. Washington, DC.

Noller, P., & Callan, V. (1990). Adolescents' perceptions of the nature of their communication with parents. *Journal of Youth and Adolescence, 19,* 349–362.

Novak, S. P., Reardon, S. F., Raudenbush, S. W., & Buka, S. L. (2006). Retail tobacco outlet density and youth cigarette smoking: A propensity-modeling approach. *American Journal of Public Health, 96,* 670–676.

Nurmi, J. (1993). Adolescent development in an age-graded context: The role of personal beliefs, goals, and strategies in the tackling of developmental tasks and standards. *International Journal of Behavioural Development, 16,* 169–189.

Nurmi, J. (2004). Socialization and self-development: Channeling, selection, adjustment, and reflection. In R. Lerner & L. Steinberg (Eds.), *Handbook of adolescent psychology.* New York: Wiley.

Nurmi, J., Onatsu, T., & Haavisto, T. (1995). Underachievers' cognitive and behavioral strategies: Self-handicapping at school. *Contemporary Educational Psychology, 20,* 188–200.

Nylund, K., Bellmore, A., Nishina, A., & Graham, S. (2007). Subtypes, severity, and structural stability of peer victimization: What does latent class analysis say? *Child Development, 78,* 1706–1722.

O'Donnell, D., Schwab-Stone, M., & Ruchkin, V. (2006). The mediating role of alienation in the development of maladjustment in youth exposed to community violence. *Development and Psychopathology, 18,* 215–232.

O'Donnell, L., Stueve, A., Myint-U, A., Duran, R., Agronick, G., & Wilson-Simmons, R. (2006). Middle school aggression and subsequent intimate partner physical violence. *Journal of Youth and Adolescence, 35,* 693–703.

O'Leary, K. D., Slep, A. M. S., Avery-Leaf, S., & Cascardi, M. (2008). Gender differences in dating aggression among multiethnic high school students. *Journal of Adolescent Health, 42,* 473–479.

O'Brien, S., & Bierman, K. (1988). Conceptions and perceived influence of peer groups: Interviews with preadolescents and adolescents. *Child Development, 59,* 1360–1365.

O'Callaghan, M., Borkowski, J., Whitman, T., Maxwell, S., & Keogh, D. (1999). A model of adolescent parenting: The role of cognitive readiness to parent. *Journal of Research on Adolescence, 9,* 203–225.

O'Connor, T., Caspi, A., DeFries, J., & Plomin, R. (2000). Are associations between parental divorce and children's adjustment genetically mediated? An adoption study. *Developmental Psychology, 36,* 429–437.

O'Connor, T., Deater-Deckard, K., Fulker, D., Rutter, M., & Plomin, R. (1998). Genotype-environment correlations in late childhood and early adolescence: Antisocial behavioral problems and coercive parenting. *Developmental Psychology, 34,* 970–981.

O'Connor, T., Hetherington, E. M., Reiss, D., & Plomin, R. (1995). A twin-sibling study of observed parent–adolescent interactions. *Child Development, 66,* 812–829.

O'Hare, E. D., Lu, L. H., Houston, S. M., Bookheimer, S. Y., & Sowell, E. R. (2008). Neurodevelopmental changes in verbal working memory load-dependency: An fMRI investigation. *Neuroimage, 42,* 1678–1685.

O'Malley, P., & Johnston, L. (1999). Drinking and driving among U.S. high school seniors, 1984–1997. *American Journal of Public Health, 89,* 678–684.

O'Sullivan, L. F., Cheng, M. M., Harris, K. M., & Brooks-Gunn, J. (2007). I wanna hold your hand: The progression of social, romantic and sexual events in adolescent relationships. *Perspectives on Sexual and Reproductive Health, 39,* 100–107.

Oakes, J. (1995). Two cities' tracking and within-school segregation. *Teachers College Record, 96,* 681–690.

Oakes, J. (2005) *Keeping track: How schools structure inequality.* New Haven: Yale University Press.

Oakley, D., & Bogue, E. (1995). Quality of condom use as reported by female clients of a family planning clinic. *American Journal of Public Health, 85,* 1526–1530.

Obeidallah, D., Brennan, R. T., Brooks-Gunn, J., & Earls, F. (2004). Links between pubertal timing and neighborhood contexts: Implications for girls' violent behavior. *Journal of the American Academy of Child and Adolescent Psychiatry, 43,* 1460–1468.

Obeidallah, D., McHale, S., & Silbereisen, R. (1996). Gender role socialization and adolescents' reports of depression: Why some girls and not others? *Journal of Youth and Adolescence, 25,* 775–786.

Oettinger, G. (1999). Does high school employment affect high school academic performance? *Industrial and Labor Relations Review, 53,* 136–151.

Ogden, C. L., Carroll, M. D., & Flegal, K. M. (2008). High body mass index for age among US children and adolescents, 2003–2006. *JAMA: Journal of the American Medical Association, 299,* 2401–2405.

Ogle, J. P., & Damhorst, M. L. (2003). Mothers' and daughters' interpersonal approaches to body and dieting. *Journal of Family Influence, 24,* 448–487.

Ogletree, M. D., Jones, R. M., & Coyl, D. D. (2002). Fathers and their adolescent sons: Pubertal development and paternal involvement. *Journal of Adolescent Research, 17,* 418–424.

Ohannessian, C., Lerner, R., Lerner, J., & von Eye, A. (1994). A longitudinal study of perceived family adjustment and emotional adjustment in early adolescence. *Journal of Early Adolescence, 14,* 371–390.

Ohida, T., Osaki, Y., Doi, Y., Tanihata, T., Minowa, M., Suzuki, K., et al. (2004). An epidemiologic study of self-reported sleep problems among Japanese adolescents. *Sleep, 27,* 978–985.

Ojanen, T., & Perry, D. G. (2007). Relational schemas and the developing self: Perceptions of mother and of self as joint predictors of early adolescents' self-esteem. *Developmental Psychology, 43,* 1474–1483.

Olatunji, A. N. (2005). Dropping out of high school among Mexican-origin youths: Is early work experience a factor? *Harvard Educational Review, 75,* 286–305.

Olweus, D. (1993). Victimization by peers: Antecedents and long-term outcomes. In K. Rubin & J. Asendorf (Eds.), *Social withdrawal, inhibition, and shyness in childhood.* Hillsdale, NJ: Erlbaum.

Oppedal, B., Røysamb, E., & Sam, D. L. (2004). The effect of acculturation and social support on change in mental health among young immigrants. *International Journal of Behavioral Development, 28,* 481–494.

Orlando, M., Tucker, J. S., Ellickson, P., & Klein, D. (2004). Developmental trajectories of cigarette smoking and their correlates from early adolescence to young adulthood. *Journal of Consulting and Clinical Psychology, 72,* 400–410.

Orr, D., Beiter, M., & Ingersoll, G. (1991). Premature sexual activity as an indicator of psychosocial risk. *Pediatrics, 87,* 141–147.

Orr, D., & Langefeld, C. (1993). Factors associated with condom use by sexually active male adolescents at risk for sexually transmitted disease. *Pediatrics, 91,* 873–879.

Orr, E., & Ben-Eliahu, E. (1993). Gender differences in idiosyncratic sex-typed self-images and self-esteem. *Sex Roles, 29,* 271–296.

Ortiz, J., & Raine, A. (2004). Heart rate level and antisocial behavior in children and adolescents. *Journal of the American Academy of Child and Adolescent Psychiatry, 43,* 154–162.

Osgerby, B. (2008). Understanding the "Jackpot Market": Media, marketing, and the rise of the American teenager. In P. Jamieson & D. Romer (Eds.), *The changing portrayal of adolescents in the media since 1950* (pp. 27–58). New York: Oxford University Press.

Osgood, D. W. (1999). Having the time of their lives: All work and no play? In A. Booth, A. Crouter, & M. Shanahan (Eds.), *Transitions to adulthood in a changing economy: No work, no family, no future* (pp. 176–186). Westport, CT: Praeger.

Osgood, D. W., & Anderson, A. (2004). Unstructured socializing and rates of delinquency. *Criminology, 42,* 519–549.

Osgood, D. W., Anderson, A., & Shaffer, J. (2005). Unstructured leisure in the after-school hours. In J. Mahoney, R. Larson, & J. Eccles (Eds.), *Organized activities as contexts of development* (pp. 45–64). Hillsdale, NJ: Erlbaum.

Osgood, D. W., Ruth, G., Eccles, J., Jacobs, J., & Barber, B. (2005). Six paths to adulthood. In R. Settersten, R., Furstenberg, F., Jr., & R. Rumbaut (Eds.), *On the frontier of adulthood* (pp. 340–355). Chicago: University of Chicago Press.

Osgood, D. W., Wilson, J., O'Malley, P., Bachman, J., & Johnston, L. (1996). Routine activities and individual deviant behavior. *American Sociological Review, 61,* 635–655.

Osofsky, J. (1995). The effects of exposure to violence on young children. *American Psychologist, 50*, 782–788.

Ostaszewski, K., & Zimmerman, M. A. (2006). The effects of cumulative risks and promotive factors on urban adolescent alcohol and other drug use: A longitudinal study of resiliency. *American Journal of Community Psychology, 38*, 237–249.

Oswald, H., Bahne, J., & Feder, M. (1994, February). *Love and sexuality in adolescence: Gender-specific differences in East and West Berlin*. Paper presented at the biennial meetings of the Society for Research on Adolescence, San Diego.

Ott, M. A., Millstein, S. G., Ofner, S., & Halpern-Felsher, B. L. (2006). Greater expectations: Adolescents' positive motivations for sex. *Perspectives on Sexual and Reproductive Health, 38*, 84–89.

Otterblad Olausson, P., Haglund, B., Ringback Weitoft, G., & Cnattingius, S. (2001). Teenage childbearing and long-term socioeconomic consequences: A case study in Sweden. *Family Planning Perspectives, 33*, 70–74.

Overbaugh, K., & Allen, J. (1994). The adolescent athlete, II: Injury patterns and prevention. *Journal of Pediatric Health Care, 8*, 203–211.

Overbeek, G., Stattin, H., Vermulst, A., Ha, T., & Engels, R. (2007). Parent-child relationships, partner relationships, and emotional adjustment: A birth-to-maturity prospective study. *Developmental Psychology, 43*, 429–437.

Overton, W. (1990). Competence and procedures: Constraints on the development of logical reasoning. In W. Overton (Ed.), *Reasoning, necessity, and logic: Developmental perspectives* (pp. 1–32). Hillsdale, NJ: Erlbaum.

Owen, J. (1995). *Why our kids don't study*. Baltimore: Johns Hopkins University Press.

Owen-Kostelnik, J., Reppucci, N. D., & Meyer, J. R. (2006). Testimony and interrogation of minors: Assumptions about maturity and morality. *American Psychologist, 61*, 286–304.

Owens, T., Mortimer, J., & Finch, M. (1996). Self-determination as a source of self-esteem in adolescence. *Social Forces, 74*, 1377–1404.

Oxford, M. L., Gilchrist, L. D., Gillmore, M. R., & Lohr, M. J. (2006). Predicting variation in the life course of adolescent mothers as they enter adulthood. *Journal of Adolescent Health, 39*, 20–26.

Oxford, M. L., Gilchrist, L. D., Lohr, M. J., Gillmore, M. R., Morrison, D. M., & Spieker, S. J. (2005). Life course heterogeneity in the transition from adolescence to adulthood among adolescent mothers. *Journal of Research on Adolescence, 15*, 479–504.

Oyserman, D., Bybee, D., & Terry, K. (2006). Possible selves and academic outcomes: How and when possible selves impel action. *Journal of Personality and Social Psychology, 91*, 188–204.

Oyserman, D., & Markus, H. (1990). Possible selves and delinquency. *Journal of Personality and Social Psychology, 59*, 112–125.

Oyserman, D., Radin, N., & Benn, R. (1993). Dynamics in a three-generational family: Teens, grandparents, and babies. *Developmental Psychology, 29*, 564–572.

Ozer, E., & Irwin, C. (2009). Adolescent and young adult health: From basic health status to clinical interventions. In R. Lerner & L. Steinberg (Eds.), *Handbook of adolescent psychology* (3rd ed., Vol. 1, pp. 618–641). New York: Wiley.

Pabon, E., Rodriguez, O., & Gurin, G. (1992). Clarifying peer relations and delinquency. *Youth and Society, 24*, 149–165.

Paciello, M., Fida, R., Tramontano, C., Lupinetti, C., & Caprara, G. V. (2008). Stability and change of moral disengagement and its impact on aggression and violence in late adolescence. *Child Development, 79*, 1288–1309.

Packaged Facts. (2007). *The teens market in the U.S.* New York: Market Research Group.

Padilla, A. M., & Gonzalez, R. (2001). Academic performance of immigrant and U.S.-born Mexican heritage students: Effects of schooling in Mexico and bilingual/English language instruction. *American Educational Research Journal, 38*, 727–742.

Padilla-Walker, L. (2008). Domain-appropriateness of maternal discipline as a predictor of adolescents' positive and negative outcomes. *Journal of Family Psychology, 22*, 456–464.

Pahl, K., & Way, N. (2006). Longitudinal trajectories of ethnic identity among urban Black and Latino adolescents. *Child Development, 77*, 1403–1415.

Paikoff, R., & Brooks-Gunn, J. (1991). Do parent–child relationships change during puberty? *Psychological Bulletin, 110*, 47–66.

Paikoff, R., Parfenoff, S., Williams, S., McCormick, A., Greenwood, G., & Holmbeck, G. (1997). Parenting, parent–child relationships, and sexual possibility situations among urban African American preadolescents: Preliminary findings and implications for HIV prevention. *Journal of Family Psychology, 11*, 11–22.

Pajer, K., Chung, J., Leininger, L., Wang, W., Gardner, W., & Yeates, K. (2008). Neuropsychological function in adolescent girls with conduct disorder. *Journal of the American Academy of Child & Adolescent Psychiatry, 47*, 416–425.

Paley, B., Conger, R., & Harold, G. (2000). Parents' affect, adolescent cognitive representations, and adolescent social development. *Journal of Marriage and the Family, 62*, 761–776.

Palladino, G. (1996). *Teenagers: An American history*. New York: Basic Books.

Pallock, L., & Lamborn, S. (2006). Beyond parenting practices: Extended kinship support and the academic adjustment of African-American and European-American teens. *Journal of Adolescence, 29*, 813–828.

Pampel, F. C., & Aguilar, J. (2008). Changes in youth smoking, 1976–2002: A time-series analysis. *Youth and Society, 39*, 453–479.

Panchaud, C., Singh, S., Feivelson, D., & Darroch, J. E. (2000). Sexually transmitted diseases among adolescents in developed countries. *Family Planning Perspectives, 32*, 24–32, 45.

Papadakis, A. A., Prince, R. P., Jones, N. P., & Strauman, T. J. (2006). Self-regulation, rumination, and vulnerability to depression in adolescent girls. *Development and Psychopathology, 18*, 815–829.

Paquette, J., & Underwood, M. (1999). Gender differences in young adolescents' experiences of peer victimization: Social and physical aggression. *Merrill-Palmer Quarterly, 45*, 242–266.

Pardini, D. A., Loeber, R., & Stouthamer-Loeber, M. (2005). Developmental shifts in parent and peer influences on boys' beliefs about delinquent behavior. *Journal of Research on Adolescence 15*, 299–323.

Parke, R. (1988). Families in life-span perspective: A multilevel developmental approach. In E. M. Hetherington & M. Perlmutter (Eds.), *Child development in life-span perspective*, pp. 159–190. Hillsdale, NJ: Erlbaum.

Parke, R., & Buriel, R. (1998). Socialization in the family: Ethnic and ecological perspectives. In W. Damon (Series Ed.) & N. Eisenberg (Vol. Ed.), *Handbook of child psychology* (5th ed., pp. 463–552). New York: Wiley.

Parker, J., Low, C., & Wargo, J. (1999, April). *Children's jealousy over their friends' friends: Personal and relational correlates in preadolescent and adolescent boys and girls*. Paper presented at the biennial meetings of the Society for Research in Child Development, Albuquerque.

Parker, J., Low, C., Walker, A. R., & Gamm, B. K. (2005). Friendship jealousy in young adolescents: Individual differences and links to sex, self-esteem, aggression, and social adjustment. *Developmental Psychology, 41*, 235–250.

Parker, J., & Seal, J. (1996). Forming, losing, renewing, and replacing friendships: Applying temporal parameters to the assessment of children's friendship experiences. *Child Development, 67*, 2248–2268.

Parker, K. F., & Reckdenwald, A. (2008). Concentrated disadvantage, traditional male role models, and African-American juvenile violence. *Criminology, 46*, 711–735.

Parkhurst, J., & Asher, S. (1992). Peer rejection in middle school: Subgroup differences in behavior, loneliness, and interpersonal concerns. *Developmental Psychology, 28*, 231–241.

Parsai, M., Voisine, S., Marsiglia, F. F., Kulis, S., & Nieri, T. (2009). The protective and risk effects of parents and peers on substance use, attitudes, and behaviors of Mexican and Mexican American female and male adolescents. *Youth and Society, 40*, 353–376.

Pascarella, E., & Terenzini, P. (2005). *How college affects students: Vol. 2. A third decade of research*. San Francisco: Jossey-Bass.

Paschall, M. J., Flewelling, R. L., & Russell, T. (2004). Why is work intensity associated with heavy alcohol use among adolescents? *Journal of Adolescent Health, 34*, 79–87.

Paschall, M. J., Freisthler, B., & Lipton, R. I. (2005). Moderate alcohol use and depression in young adults: Findings from a national longitudinal study. *American Journal of Public Health, 95*, 453–457.

Pasley, K., & Gecas, V. (1984). Stresses and satisfactions of the parental role. *Personnel and Guidance Journal, 2*, 400–404.

Pasupathi, M., Staudinger, U. M., & Baltes, P. B. (2001). Seeds of wisdom: Adolescents' knowledge and judgment about difficult life problems. *Developmental Psychology, 37*, 351–361.

Patrikakou, E. (1996). Investigating the academic achievement of adolescents with learning disabilities: A structural modeling approach. *Journal of Education Psychology, 88*, 435–450.

Patten, C. A., Choi, W. S., Gillin, C. J., & Pierce, J. P. (2000). Depressive symptoms and cigarette smoking predict development and persistence of sleep problems in U.S. adolescents. *Pediatrics, 106*, Article e23.

Patterson, G., DeGarmo, D., & Knutson, M. (2000). Hyperactive and antisocial behaviors: Comorbid or two points in the same process? *Development and Psychopathology, 12*, 91–106.

Patterson, G., Forgatch, M., Yoerger, K., & Stoolmiller, M. (1998). Variables that initiate and maintain an early-onset trajectory for juvenile offending. *Development and Psychopathology, 10*, 531–547.

Patton, G. C., Bond, L., Carlin, J. B., Thomas, L., Butler, H., Glover, S., et al. (2006). Promoting social inclusion in schools: A group-randomized trial of effects on student health risk behavior and well-being. *American Journal of Public Health, 96*, 1582–1587.

Patton, G. C., Coffey, C., Carlin, J. B., Sawyer, S. M., & Wakefield, M. (2006). Teen smokers reach their mid twenties. *Journal of Adolescent Health, 39*, 214–220.

Patton, G. C., Olsson, C., Bond, L., Toumbourou, J. W., Carlin, J. B., Hemphill, S. A., et al. (2008). Predicting female depression across puberty: A two-nation longitudinal study. *Journal of the American Academy of Child & Adolescent Psychiatry, 47*, 1424–1432.

Patton, W., & Mannison, M. (1995). Sexual coercion in high school dating. *Sex Roles, 33*, 447–457.

Paul, J. (1993). Childhood cross-gender behavior and adult homosexuality: The resurgence of biological models of sexuality. *Journal of Homosexuality, 24*, 41–54.

Paulson, S. (1994). Relations of parenting style and parental involvement with ninth-grade students' achievement. *Journal of Early Adolescence, 14*, 250–267.

Paus, T. (2009). Brain development. In R. Lerner & L. Steinberg (Eds.), *Handbook of adolescent psychology* (3rd ed., Vol. 1, pp. 95–115). New York: Wiley.

Paus, T., Keshavan, B., & Giedd, J. (2008). Why do so many psychiatric disorders emerge during adolescence? *Nature Reviews Neuroscience, 9*, 947–957.

Paus, T., Toro, R., Leonard, G., Lerner, J., Lerner, R., Perron, M., et al. (2008). Morphological properties of the action-observation cortical network in adolescents with low and high resistance to peer influence. *Social Neuroscience, 3*, 303–316.

Pavlidis, K., & McCauley, E. (1995, March). *Autonomy and relatedness in family interactions with depressed adolescents*. Paper presented at the biennial meetings of the Society for Research in Child Development, Indianapolis.

Paxton, S., Wertheim, E., Gibbons, K., Szmukler, G., Hillier, L., & Petrovich, J. (1991). Body image satisfaction, dieting beliefs, and weight loss behaviors in adolescent girls and boys. *Journal of Youth and Adolescence, 20*, 361–380.

Paxton, S. J., Eisenberg, M. E., & Neumark-Sztainer, D. (2006). Prospective predictors of body dissatisfaction in adolescent girls and boys: A five-year longitudinal study. *Developmental Psychology, 42*, 888–899.

Pearce, M. J., Jones, S. M., Schwab-Stone, M. E., & Ruchkin, V. (2003). The protective effects of religiousness and parent involvement on the development of conduct problems among youth exposed to violence. *Child Development, 74*, 1682–1696.

Pearce, R. R. (2006). Effects of cultural and social structural factors on the achievement of White and Chinese American students at school transition points. *American Educational Research Journal, 43*, 75–101.

Pechmann, C., Levine, L., Loughlin, S., & Leslie, F. (2005). Impulsive and self-conscious: Adolescents' vulnerability to advertising and promotion. *Journal of Public Policy and Marketing, 24*, 202–221.

Pedersen, S., Seidman, E., Yoshikawa, H., Rivera, A. C., Allen, L., & Aber, J. L. (2005). Contextual competence: Multiple manifestations among urban adolescents. *American Journal of Community Psychology, 35*, 65–82.

Pedersen, S., Vitaro, F., Barker, E. D., & Borge, A. I. H. (2007). The timing of middle-childhood peer rejection and friendship: Linking early behavior to early-adolescent adjustment. *Child Development, 78*, 1037–1051.

Pellegrini, A. D. (2003). Perceptions and functions of play and real fighting in early adolescence. *Child Development, 74*, 1522–1533.

Pellegrini, A. D., & Long, J. D. (2007). An observational study of early heterosexual interaction at middle school dances. *Journal of Research on Adolescence, 17*, 613–638.

Pellerin, L. A. (2005). Student disengagement and the socialization styles of high schools. *Social Forces, 84*, 1159–1179.

Pennington, H. (2003). Accelerating advancement in school and work. In D. Ravitch (Ed.), *Brookings papers on education policy*. Washington, DC: Brookings Institution.

Pepler, D., Jiang, D., Craig, W., & Connolly, J. (2008). Developmental trajectories of bullying and associated factors. *Child Development, 79*, 325–338.

Perez-Febles, A., Allison, K., & Burton, L. (April, 1999). *Sociocultural context and the construction of research questions: The case of adolescent childbearing*. Paper presented at the biennial meetings of the Society for Research on Child Development, Albuquerque.

Perkins, D., Jacobs, J. E., Barber, B. L., & Eccles, J. (2003). Childhood and adolescent sports participation as predictors of participation in sports and physical fitness activities during young adulthood. *Youth and Society, 35*, 295–520.

Perkins, D., Luster, T., & Jank, W. (2002). Protective factors, physical abuse, and purging from community-wide surveys of female adolescents. *Journal of Adolescent Research, 17*, 377–400.

Perkins, D., Luster, T., Villarruel, F., & Small, S. (1998). An ecological, risk-factor examination of adolescents' sexual activity in three ethnic groups. *Journal of Marriage and the Family, 60*, 660–673.

Perkins, S. A., & Turiel, E. (2007). To lie or not to lie: To whom and under what circumstances. *Child Development, 78*, 609–621.

Perosa, L., Perosa, S., & Tam, H. (1996). The contribution of family structure and differentiation to identity development in females. *Journal of Youth and Adolescence, 25*, 817–837.

Perry, C., Williams, C., Veblen-Mortenson, S., Toomey, T., Komro, K., Anstine, P., McGivern, P., et al. (1996). Project Northland: Outcomes of a communitywide alcohol use prevention program during early adolescence. *American Journal of Public Health, 86*, 956–965.

Persson, A., Kerr, M., & Stattin, H. (2007). Staying in or moving away from structured activities: Explanations involving parents and peers. *Developmental Psychology, 43*, 197–207.

Peskin, H. (1967). Pubertal onset and ego functioning: A psychoanalytic approach. *Journal of Abnormal Psychology, 72*, 1–15.

Peskin, H. (1973). Influence of the developmental schedule of puberty on learning and ego functioning. *Journal of Youth and Adolescence, 2*, 273–290.

Petersen, A. (1988). Adolescent development. *Annual Review of Psychology, 39*, 583–607.

Petersen, A., Compas, B., Brooks-Gunn, J., Stemmler, M., Ey, S., & Grant, K. (1993). Depression in adolescence. *American Psychologist, 48*, 155–168.

Petersen, A., Sarigiani, P., & Kennedy, R. (1991). Adolescent depression: Why more girls? *Journal of Youth and Adolescence, 20,* 247–272.

Peterson, P., Hawkins, J., Abbott, R., & Catalano, R. (1994). *Journal of Research on Adolescence, 4,* 203–227.

Petraitis, J., Flay, B., & Miller, T. (1995). Reviewing theories of adolescent substance use: Organizing pieces in the puzzle. *Psychological Bulletin, 117,* 67–86.

Pettit, G., Bates, J., Dodge, K., & Meece, D. (1999). The impact of after-school peer contact on early adolescent externalizing problems is moderated by parental monitoring, perceived neighborhood safety, and prior adjustment. *Child Development, 70,* 768–778.

Phares, V., Steinberg, A. R., & Thompson, J. K. (2004). Gender differences in peer and parental influences: Body image disturbance, self-worth, and psychological functioning in preadolescent children. *Journal of Youth and Adolescence, 33,* 421–429.

Phelan, P., Yu, H., & Davidson, A. (1994). Navigating the psychosocial pressures of adolescence: The voices and experiences of high school youth. *American Educational Research Journal, 31,* 415–447.

Phillipsen, L. C. (1999). Associations between age, gender, and group acceptance and three components of friendship quality. *Journal of Early Adolescence, 19,* 438–464.

Phinney, J., & Chavira, V. (1995). Parental ethnic socialization and adolescent coping with problems related to ethnicity. *Journal of Research on Adolescence, 5,* 31–53.

Phinney, J., & Devich-Navarro, M. (1997). Variations in bicultural identification among African American and Mexican American adolescents. *Journal of Research on Adolescence, 7,* 3–32.

Phinney, J., Devich-Navarro, M., DuPont, S., Estrada, A., & Onwughala, M. (1994, February). *Bicultural identity orientations of African American and Mexican American adolescents.* Paper presented at the biennial meetings of the Society for Research on Adolescence, San Diego.

Phinney, J., Ferguson, D., & Tate, J. (1997). Intergroup attitudes among ethnic minority adolescents: A causal model. *Child Development, 68,* 955–969.

Phinney, J., & Ong, A. D. (2002). Adolescent–parent disagreements and life satisfaction in families from Vietnamese- and European-American backgrounds. *Journal of Behavioral Development, 26,* 556–561.

Phinney, J., Romero, I., Nava, M., & Huang, D. (2001). The role of language, parents, and peers in ethnic identity among adolescents in immigrant families. *Journal of Youth and Adolescence, 30,* 135–153.

Phinney, J., & Rosenthal, D. (1992). Ethnic identity in adolescence: Process, context, and outcome. In G. R. Adams, T. P. Gullotta, & R. Montemayor (Eds.), *Adolescent identity formation: Advances in adolescent development* (pp. 145–172). Newbury Park, CA: Sage.

Piehler, T., & Dishion, T. (2007). Interpersonal dynamics within adolescent friendships: Dyadic mutuality, deviant talk, and patterns of antisocial behavior. *Child Development, 78,* 1611–1624.

Pierce, J., & Gilpin, E. (1996). How long will today's new adolescent smoker be addicted to cigarettes? *American Journal of Public Health, 86,* 253–256.

Pietilainen, K. H., Kaprio, J., Rasanen, M., Winter, T., Rissanen, A., & Rose, R. (2001). Tracking of body size from birth to late adolescence: Contributions of birth length, birth weight, duration of gestation, parents' body size, and twinship. *American Journal of Epidemiology, 154,* 21–29.

Pike, A., McGuire, S., Hetherington, E. M., Reiss, D., et al. (1996). Family environment and adolescent depressive symptoms and antisocial behavior: A multivariate genetic analysis. *Developmental Psychology, 32,* 590–604.

Pilgrim, C., Luo, Q., Urberg, K. A., & Fang, X. (1999). Influence of peers, parents, and individual characteristics on adolescent drug use in two cultures. *Merrill-Palmer Quarterly, 45,* 85–107.

Pilkington, N., & D'Augelli, A. (1995). Victimization of lesbian, gay, and bisexual youth in community settings. *Journal of Community Psychology, 23,* 34–56.

Pillay, Y. (2005). Racial identity as a predictor of the psychological health of African American students at a predominantly White university. *Journal of Black Psychology, 31,* 46–66.

Pine, D., Cohen, P., Gurley, D., Brook, J., & Ma, Y. (1998). The risk for early-adulthood anxiety and depressive disorders in adolescents with anxiety and depressive disorders. *Archives of General Psychiatry, 55,* 56–64.

Pine, D., Wasserman, G., Coplan, J., Fried, J., Huang, Y., Kassir, S., et al. (1996). Platelet serotonin 2A ($5HT_{2A}$) receptor characteristics and parenting factors for boys at risk for delinquency: A preliminary report. *American Journal of Psychiatry, 153,* 538–544.

Pinquart, M., & Silbereisen, R. (2002). Changes in adolescents' and mothers' autonomy and connectedness in conflict discussions: An observation study. *Journal of Adolescence, 25,* 509–522.

Pintrich, P. (2000). Multiple goals, multiple pathways: The role of goal orientation in learning and achievement. *Journal of Educational Psychology, 92,* 544–555.

Pintrich, P., Roeser, R., & De Groot, E. (1994). Classroom and individual differences in early adolescents' motivation and self-regulated learning. *Journal of Early Adolescence, 14,* 139–161.

Piquero, A., & Chung, H. L. (2001). On the relationship between gender, early onset, and the seriousness of offending. *Journal of Criminal Justice, 29,* 189–206.

Piquero, A., Farrington, D., & Blumstein, A. (2003). The criminal career paradigm: Background and recent developments. *Crime and Justice: A Review of Research, 30,* 359–506.

Pitner, R. O., Astor, R. A., Benbenishty, R., Haj-Yahia, M. M., & Zeira, A. (2003). The effects of group stereotypes on adolescents' reasoning about peer retribution. *Child Development, 74,* 413–425.

Pittard, W., Laditka, J., & Laditka S. (2008). Associations between maternal age and infant health outcomes among Medicaid-insured infants in South Carolina: Mediating effects of socioeconomic factors, *Pediatrics, 122,* e100–e106.

Pittman, L. D., & Chase-Lansdale, P. L. (2001). African American adolescent girls in impoverished communities: Parenting style and adolescent outcomes. *Journal of Research on Adolescence, 11,* 199–224.

Planty, M., Bozick, R., & Regnier, M. (2006). Helping because you have to or helping because you want to?: Sustaining participation in service work from adolescence through young adulthood. *Youth and Society, 38,* 177–202.

Pleck, J., Sonenstein, F., & Ku, L. (1994). Problem behaviors and masculinity ideology in adolescent males. In R. Ketterlinus & M. Lamb (Eds.), *Adolescent problem behaviors: Issues and research* (pp. 165–186). Hillsdale, NJ: Erlbaum.

Plomin, R., & Daniels, D. (1987). Why are children in the same family so different from one another? *Behavioral and Brain Sciences, 10,* 1–60.

Plumert, J. (1994). Flexibility in children's use of spatial and categorical organizational strategies in recall. *Developmental Psychology, 30,* 738–747.

Pogarsky, G., Lizotte, A. J., & Thornberry, T. P. (2003). The delinquency of children born to young mothers: Results from the Rochester Youth Development Study. *Criminology, 41,* 1249–1286.

Pokorny, S. B., Jason, L. A., & Schoeny, M. E. (2006). Youth supplying tobacco to other minors: Evaluating individual and town-level correlates. *Journal of Youth and Adolescence, 35,* 705–715.

Pollack, C., & Bright, D. (2003). Caffeine consumption and weekly sleep patterns in U.S. seventh-, eighth-, and ninth-graders. *Pediatrics, 111,* 42–46.

Pomerantz, E. (2001). Parent–child socialization: Implications for the development of depressive symptoms. *Journal of Family Psychology, 15,* 510–525.

Pomerantz, E., Altermatt, E., & Saxon, J. L. (2002). Making the grade but feeling distressed: Gender differences in academic performance and internal distress. *Journal of Educational Psychology, 94,* 396–404.

Pong, S. (1997). Family structure, school context and eighth-grade math and reading achievement. *Journal of Marriage and the Family, 59,* 734–746.

Pong, S. (1998). The school compositional effect of single parenthood on 10th-grade achievement. *Sociology of Education, 71,* 23–42.

Pong, S., & Ju, D. (2000). The effects of change in family structure and income on dropping out in middle and high school. *Journal of Family Issues, 21,* 147–169.

Pope, A., & Bierman, K. (1999). Predicting adolescent peer problems and antisocial activities: The relative roles of aggression and dysregulation. *Developmental Psychology, 35,* 335–346.

Poropat, A. E. (2009). A meta-analysis of the five-factor model of personality and academic performance. *Psychological Bulletin, 135,* 322–338.

Poulin, F., Dishion, T., & Haas, E. (1999). The peer influence paradox: Friendship quality and deviancy training within male adolescent friendships. *Merrill-Palmer Quarterly, 45,* 42–61.

Poulin, F., & Pedersen, S. (2007). Developmental changes in gender composition of friendship networks in adolescent girls and boys. *Developmental Psychology, 43,* 1484–1496.

Prelow, H., Danoff-Burg, S., Swenson, R., & Pulgiano, D. (2004). The impact of ecological risk and perceived discrimination on the psychological adjustment of African American and European American youth. *Journal of Community Psychology, 32,* 375–389.

Prelow, H., & Loukas, A. (2003). The role of resource, protective, and risk factors in academic achievement–related outcomes of economically disadvantaged Latino youth. *Journal of Community Psychology, 31,* 513–529.

President's Science Advisory Committee. (1974). *Youth: Transition to adulthood.* Chicago: University of Chicago Press.

Prinstein, M. J., & Aikins, J. W. (2004). Cognitive moderators of the longitudinal association between peer rejection and adolescent depressive symptoms. *Journal of Abnormal Child Psychology, 32,* 147–158.

Prinstein, M. J., & Cillessen, A. H. (2003). Forms and functions of adolescent peer aggression associated with high levels of peer status. *Merrill-Palmer Quarterly, 49,* 310–342.

Prinstein, M. J., & La Greca, A. M. (2002). Peer crowd affiliation and internalizing distress in childhood and adolescence: A longitudinal follow-back study. *Journal of Research on Adolescence, 12,* 325–351.

Prinstein, M. J., Meade, C., & Cohen, G. (2003). Adolescent oral sex, peer popularity, and perceptions of best friends' sexual behavior. *Journal of Pediatric Psychology, 28,* 243–249.

Prosser, E., & Carlson, C. (April, 1999). *Ethnic differences in fluctuations in female self-esteem during early adolescence.* Paper presented at the biennial meetings of the Society for Research on Child Development, Albuquerque.

Public Agenda. (1997). *Getting by: What American teenagers really think about their schools.* New York: Public Agenda.

Public Agenda. (1999). *Kids these days '99: What Americans really think about the next generation.* New York: Public Agenda.

Punamäki, R., Qouta, S., & Sarraj, E. (1997). Models of traumatic experiences and children's psychological adjustment: The roles of perceived parenting and the children's own resources and activity. *Child Development, 68,* 718–728.

Punamäki, R., Wallenius, M., Nygård, C., Saarni, L., & Rimpelä, A. (2007). Use of information and communication technology (ICT) and perceived health in adolescence: The role of sleeping habits and waking-time tiredness. *Journal of Adolescence, 30,* 569–585.

Pungello, E., Kupersmidt, J., Burchinal, M., & Patterson, C. (1996). Environmental risk factors and children's achievement from middle childhood to early adolescence. *Developmental Psychology, 32,* 755–767.

Purdie, N., Hattie, J., & Douglas, G. (1996). Student conceptions of learning and their use of self-regulated learning strategies: A cross-cultural comparison. *Journal of Educational Psychology, 88,* 87–100.

Qin, D. B. (2008). Doing well vs. feeling well: Understanding family dynamics and the psychological adjustment of Chinese immigrant adolescents. *Journal of Youth and Adolescence, 37,* 22–35.

Qin, D. B., Way, N., & Mukherjee, P. (2008). The other side of the model minority story: The familial and peer challenges faced by Chinese American adolescents. *Youth and Society, 39,* 480–506.

Quadrel, M., Fischhoff, B., & Davis, W. (1993). Adolescent (in)vulnerability. *American Psychologist, 48,* 102–116.

Quatman, T., Sokolik, E., & Smith, K. (2000). Adolescent perception of peer success: A gendered perspective over time. *Sex Roles, 43,* 61–84.

Quillian, L., & Campbell, M. E. (2003). Beyond Black and White: The present and future of multiracial friendship segregation. *American Sociological Review, 68,* 540–566.

Quintana, S., Castaneda-English, P., & Ybarra, V. C. (1999). Role of perspective-taking abilities and ethnic socialization in development of adolescent ethnic identity. *Journal of Research on Adolescence, 9,* 161–184.

Radmacher, K., & Azmitia, M. (2006). Are there gendered pathways to intimacy in early adolescents' and emerging adults' friendships? *Journal of Adolescent Research, 21,* 415–448.

Raffaelli, M. (1997). Young adolescents' conflicts with siblings and friends. *Journal of Youth and Adolescence, 26,* 539–558.

Raffaelli, M., & Green, S. (2003). Parent–adolescent communication about sex: Retrospective reports by Latino college students. *Journal of Marriage and the Family, 65,* 474.

Raine, A., Loeber, R., Stouthamer-Loeber, M., Moffitt, T. E., Caspi, A., & Lynam, D. (2005). Neurocognitive impairments in boys on the life-course persistent antisocial path. *Journal of Abnormal Psychology, 114,* 38–49.

Ramchand, R., Ialongo, N. S., & Chilcoat, H. D. (2007). The effect of working for pay on adolescent tobacco use. *American Journal of Public Health, 97,* 2056–2062.

Ramirez-Valles, J., Zimmerman, M. A., & Juarez, L. (2002). Gender differences of neighborhood and social control processes: A study of the timing of first intercourse among low-achieving, urban, African American youth. *Youth and Society, 33,* 418–441.

Rampey, B. D., Dion, G. S., & Donahue, P. L. (2009). *NAEP 2008 Trends in Academic Progress.* Washington, DC: National Center for Education Statistics.

Randel, B., Stevenson, H. W., & Witruk, E. (2000). Attitudes, beliefs, and mathematics achievement of German and Japanese high school students. *International Journal of Behavioral Development, 24,* 190–198.

Rangel, M. C., Gavin, L., Reed, C., Fowler, M. G., & Lee, L. M. (2006). Epidemiology of HIV and AIDS among adolescents and young adults in the United States. *Journal of Adolescent Health, 39,* 156–163.

Rankin, J., Lane, D., Gibbons, F., & Gerrard, M. (2004). Adolescent self-consciousness: Longitudinal age changes and gender differences in two cohorts. *Journal of Research on Adolescence, 14,* 1–21.

Raskauskas, J., & Stoltz, A. D. (2007). Involvement in traditional and electronic bullying among adolescents. *Developmental Psychology, 43,* 564–575.

Rathunde, K. (1996). Family context and talented adolescents' optimal experience in school-related activities. *Journal of Research on Adolescence, 6,* 605–628.

Ravitch, D. (1995). *National standards in American education: A citizen's guide.* Washington, DC: Brookings Institution.

Ravitch, D. (2000). *Left back: A century of failed school reforms.* New York: Simon & Schuster.

Ravitch, D. (Ed.). (2001). *Brookings papers on education policy.* Washington, DC: Brookings Institution.

Ready, D. D., Lee, V., & Welner, K. G. (2004). Educational equity and school structure: School size, overcrowding, and schools-within-schools. *Teachers College Review, 106,* 1989–2014.

Ream, G., & Savin-Williams, R. (2005). Reciprocal associations between adolescent sexual activity and quality of youth–parent interactions. *Journal of Family Psychology, 19,* 171–179.

Ream, R., & Rumberger, R. (2008). Student engagement, peer social capital, and school dropout among Mexican American and non-Latino White students. *Sociology of Education, 81,* 109–139.

Rebellon, C. J. (2006). Do adolescents engage in delinquency to attract the social attention of peers?: An extension and longitudinal test of the social reinforcement hypothesis. *Journal of Research in Crime and Delinquency, 43,* 387–411.

Reddy, R., Rhodes, J. E., & Mulhall, P. (2003). The influence of teacher support on student adjustment in the middle school years: A latent growth curve study. *Development and Psychopathology, 15,* 119–138.

Redlich, A., & Goodman, G. (2003). Taking responsibility for an act not committed: The influence of age and suggestibility. *Law and Human Behavior, 27,* 141–156.

Redlich, A., Silverman, A., & Steiner, H. (2003). Pre-adjudicative competence in juveniles and young adults. *Behavioral Sciences and the Law, 21,* 393–410.

Reese-Weber, M. (2000). Middle and late adolescents' conflict resolution skills and siblings: Associations with interparental and parent–adolescent conflict resolution. *Journal of Youth and Adolescence, 29,* 697–711.

Reich, K., Oser, F., & Valentin, P. (1994). Knowing why I now know better: Children's and youth's explanations of their worldview changes. *Journal of Research on Adolescence, 4,* 151–173.

Reichhardt, T. (2003). Playing with fire. *Nature, 424,* 367–368.

Reimer, M. (1996). "Sinking into the ground": The development and consequences of shame in adolescence. *Developmental Review, 16,* 321–363.

Reinders, H., & Youniss, J. (2006). School-based required community service and civic development in adolescents. *Applied Developmental Science, 10,* 2–12.

Reiss, D., Hetherington, E. M., Plomin, R., Howe, G., Simmens, S., Henderson S., et al. (1995). Genetic questions for environmental studies. *Archives of General Psychiatry, 52,* 925–936.

Renken, B., Egeland, B., Marvinney, D., Mangelsdorf, S., & Sroufe, L. A. (1989). Early childhood antecedents of aggression and passive withdrawal in early elementary school. *Journal of Personality, 57,* 257–282.

Repetti, R. (1996). The effects of perceived daily social and academic failure experiences on school-age children's subsequent interactions with parents. *Child Development, 67,* 1467–1482.

Repetto, P. B., Zimmerman, M. A., & Caldwell, C. H. (2008). A longitudinal study of depressive symptoms and marijuana use in a sample of inner-city African Americans. *Journal of Research on Adolescence, 18,* 421–447.

Repinski, D., & Leffert, N. (1994, February). *Adolescents' relations with friends: The effects of a psychoeducational intervention.* Paper presented at the biennial meetings of the Society for Research on Adolescence, San Diego.

Resnick, M., Bearman, P., Blum, R., Bauman, K., Harris, K., Jones, J., et al. (1997). Protecting adolescents from harm: Findings from the National Longitudinal Study of Adolescent Health. *Journal of the American Medical Association, 278,* 823–832.

Resnicow, K., Ross-Gaddy, D., & Vaughan, R. (1995). Structure of problem and positive behaviors in African American youths. *Journal of Consulting and Clinical Psychology, 63,* 594–603.

Rest, J., Narvaez, D., Bebeau, M., & Thoma, S. (1999). *Postconventional moral thinking: A neo-Kohlbergian approach.* Mahwah, NJ: Erlbaum.

Reuman, D. (1989). How social comparison mediates the relation between ability-grouping practices and students' achievement expectancies in mathematics. *Journal of Educational Psychology, 81,* 178–189

Reviere, S., & Bakeman, R. (1992, March). *Measuring multicultural competence: American Whites, American Blacks, and immigrants.* Paper presented at the biennial meetings of the Society for Research on Adolescence, Washington, DC.

Reyes, O., & Jason, L. (1993). Pilot study examining factors associated with academic success for Hispanic high school students. *Journal of Youth and Adolescence, 22,* 57–71.

Reyna, V., & Farley, F. (2006). Risk and rationality in adolescent decision making: Implications for theory, practice, and public policy. *Psychological Science in the Public Interest, 7,* 1–44.

Reynolds, A., & Temple, J. (1998). Extended early childhood intervention and school achievement: Age thirteen findings from the Chicago Longitudinal Study. *Child Development, 69,* 231–246.

Reynolds, A., Temple, J., Robertson, D. L., & Mann, E. A. (2001). Long-term effects of an early childhood intervention on educational achievement and juvenile arrest: A 15-year follow-up of low-income children in public schools. *Journal of the American Medical Association, 285,* 2339–2346.

Reynolds, L. K., O'Koon, J. H., Papademetriou, E., Szczygiel, S., & Grant, K. E. (2001). Stress and somatic complaints in low-income urban adolescents. *Journal of Youth and Adolescence, 30,* 499–514.

Rhodes, J. (2004). *Stand by me.* Cambridge, MA: Harvard University Press.

Rhodes, J., Haight, W., & Briggs, E. (1999). The influence of mentoring on the peer relationships of foster youth in relative and nonrelative care. *Journal of Research on Adolescence, 9,* 185–201.

Rhodes, J., & Lowe, S. (2009). Mentoring in adolescence. In R. Lerner & L. Steinberg (Eds.), *Handbook of adolescent psychology* (3rd ed., Vol. 2, pp. 152–190). New York: Wiley.

Ricciardelli, L. A., & McCabe, M. P. (2001). Self-esteem and negative affect as moderators of sociocultural influences on body dissatisfaction, strategies to decrease weight, and strategies to increase muscles among adolescent boys and girls. *Sex Roles, 44*(3–4), 189–207.

Ricciardelli, L. A., & McCabe, M. P. (2004). A biopsychosocial model of disorder eating and the pursuit of muscularity in adolescent boys. *Psychological Bulletin, 130,* 179–205.

Rice, F., Harold, G., Shelton, K., & Thapar, A. (2006). Family conflict interacts with genetic liability in predicting childhood and adolescent depression. *Journal of the American Academy of Child & Adolescent Psychiatry, 45,* 841–848.

Rice, K., & Mulkeen, P. (1995). Relationships with parents and peers: A longitudinal study of adolescent intimacy. *Journal of Adolescent Research, 10,* 338–357.

Rich, L. M., & Kim, S.-B. (2002). Employment and the sexual and reproductive behavior of female adolescents. *Perspectives on Sexual and Reproductive Health, 34,* 127–134.

Richards, M., Boxer, A., Petersen, A., & Albrecht, R. (1990). Relation of weight to body image in pubertal girls and boys from two communities. *Developmental Psychology, 26,* 313–321.

Richards, M., Crowe, P., Larson, R., & Swarr, A. (1998). Developmental patterns and gender differences in the experience of peer companionship during adolescence. *Child Development, 69,* 154–163.

Richards, M., & Larson, R. (1993). Pubertal development and the daily subjective states of young adolescents. *Journal of Research on Adolescence, 3,* 145–169.

Richardson, J., Radziszcwska, B., Dent, C., & Flay, B. (1993). Relationship between after-school care of adolescents and substance use, risk taking, depressed mood, and academic achievement. *Pediatrics, 92,* 32–38.

Richardson, R. (1996, March). *Competence in the transition to adulthood: Exploring the influence of adolescent motherhood for low-income, urban, African-American women.* Paper presented at the biennial meetings of the Society for Research on Adolescence, Boston.

Ridenour, T., Cottier, L., Robins, L., Campton, W., Spitznagel, E., & Cunningham-Williams, R. (2002). Test of the plausibility of adolescent substance use playing a causal role in developing adulthood antisocial behavior. *Journal of Abnormal Psychology, 111,* 144–155.

Riegle-Crumb, C., Farkas, G., & Muller, C. (2006). The role of gender and friendship in advanced course taking. *Sociology of Education, 79,* 206–228.

Riggs, L., Holmbeck, G., Paikoff, R., & Bryant, F. (2004). Teen mothers parenting their own teen offspring: The moderating role of parenting support. *Journal of Early Adolescence, 24,* 200–230.

Rigsby, L., & McDill, E. (1975). Value orientations of high school students. In H. R. Stub (Ed.), *The sociology of education: A sourcebook* (3rd ed., pp. 53–74). Homewood, IL: Dorsey.

Ringwalt, C., Greene, J., Robertson, M., & McPheeters, M. (1998). The prevalence of homelessness among adolescents in the United States. *American Journal of Public Health, 88,* 1325–1329.

Risch, S., Jodl, K., & Eccles, J. (2004). Role of the father–adolescent relationship in shaping adolescents' attitudes toward divorce. *Journal of Marriage and the Family, 66,* 46.

Ritakallio, M., Koivisto, A., von, der Pahlen, B., Pelkonen, M., Marttunen, M., & Kaltiala-Heino, R. (2008). Continuity, comorbidity and longitudinal associations between depression and antisocial behaviour in middle adolescence: A 2-year prospective follow-up study. *Journal of Adolescence, 31,* 355–370.

Rivers, S., Reyna, V., & Mills, B. (2008). Risk taking under the influence: A fuzzy-trace theory of emotion in adolescence. *Developmental Review, 28,* 107–144.

Roberts, A., Seidman, E., Pederson, S., Chesir-Teran, D., Allen, L., Aber, J., et al. (2000). Perceived family and peer transactions and self-esteem among urban early adolescents. *Journal of Early Adolescence, 20,* 68–92.

Roberts, B., Caspi, A., & Moffitt, T. E. (2001). The kids are alright: Growth and stability in personality development from adolescence to adulthood. *Journal of Personality and Social Psychology, 81,* 670–683.

Roberts, B., & DelVecchio, W. F. (2000). The rank-order consistency of personality traits from childhood to old age: A quantitative review of longitudinal studies. *Psychological Bulletin, 126,* 3–25.

Roberts, B., O'Donnell, M., & Robins, R. (2004). Goal and personality trait development in emerging adulthood. *Journal of Personality and Social Psychology, 87,* 541–550.

Roberts, B., Walton, K., & Viechtbauer, W. (2006). Patterns of mean-level change in personality traits across the life course: A meta-analysis of longitudinal studies. *Psychological Bulletin, 132,* 1–25.

Roberts, D. (1993). Adolescents and the mass media: From "Leave It to Beaver" to "Beverly Hills 90210." *Teachers College Record, 94,* 629–644.

Roberts, D., Foehr, U., & Rideout, V. (2005). *Generation M: Media in the lives of 8–18-Year-olds.* Menlo Park, CA: Kaiser Family Foundation.

Roberts, D., Foehr, U., Rideout, V., & Brodie, M. (1999). *Kids & media @ the new millennium.* Menlo Park, CA: Kaiser Family Foundation.

Roberts, D., & Henriksen, L., & Foehr, U. (2009). Adolescence, adolescents, and media. In R. Lerner & L. Steinberg (Eds.), *Handbook of adolescent psychology* (3rd ed., Vol. 2, pp. 314–344). New York: Wiley.

Roberts, R., Phinney, J., Mâsse, L., Chen, Y., Roberts, C., & Romero, A. (1999). The structure of ethnic identity of young adolescents from diverse ethnocultural groups. *Journal of Early Adolescence, 19,* 301–322.

Roberts, R., Roberts, C., & Chen, Y. (1997). Ethnocultural differences in prevalence of adolescent depression. *American Journal of Community Psychology, 25,* 95–110.

Roberts, R. E., Roberts, C. R., & Duong, H. T. (2008). Chronic insomnia and its negative consequences for health and functioning of adolescents: A 12-month prospective study. *Journal of Adolescent Health, 42,* 294–302.

Roberts, R. E., Roberts, C. R., & Xing, Y. (2006). Prevalence of youth-reported DSM-IV psychiatric disorders among African, European, and Mexican American adolescents. *Journal of the American Academy of Child & Adolescent Psychiatry, 45,* 1329–1337.

Robins, R., John, O., Caspi, A., Moffitt, T., & Stouthamer-Loeber, M. (1996). Resilient, overcontrolled, and undercontrolled boys: Three replicable personality types. *Journal of Personality and Social Psychology, 70,* 157–171.

Robinson, N. (1995). Evaluating the nature of perceived support and its relation to perceived self-worth in adolescents. *Journal of Research on Adolescence, 5,* 253–280.

Roche, K. M., Ensminger, M. E., & Cherlin, A. J. (2007). Variations in parenting and adolescent outcomes among African American and Latino families living in low-income, urban areas. *Journal of Family Issues, 28,* 882–909.

Roche, K. M., Ensminger, M. E., Chilcoat, H., & Storr, C. (2003). Establishing independence in low-income urban areas: The relationship to adolescent aggressive behavior. *Journal of Marriage and the Family, 65,* 668.

Roderick, M. (1994). Grade retention and school dropout: Investigating the association. *American Educational Research Journal, 31,* 729–759.

Roderick, M., & Camburn, E. (1999). Risk and recovery from course failure in the early years of high school. *American Educational Research Journal, 36,* 303–343.

Rodgers, J., & Rowe, D. (1988). Influence of siblings on adolescent sexual behavior. *Developmental Psychology, 24,* 722–728.

Rodgers, J., & Rowe, D. (1993). Social contagion and adolescent sexual behavior: A developmental EMOSA model. *Psychological Review, 100,* 479–510.

Rodgers, K. (1999). Parenting processes related to sexual risk-taking behaviors of adolescent males and females. *Journal of Marriage and the Family, 61,* 99–109.

Rodgers, K., & Rose, H. A. (2002). Risk and resiliency factors among adolescents who experience marital transitions. *Journal of Marriage and the Family, 64,* 1024–1037.

Rodkin, P., Farmer, T., Pearl, R., & Van Acker, R. (2000). Heterogeneity of popular boys: Antisocial and prosocial configurations. *Developmental Psychology, 36,* 14–24.

Roe, K. (1995). Adolescents' use of socially disvalued media: Towards a theory of media delinquency. *Journal of Youth and Adolescence, 24,* 617–631.

Roenkae, A., & Pulkkinen, L. (1998). Work involvement and timing of motherhood in the accumulation of problems in social functioning in young women. *Journal of Research on Adolescence, 8,* 221–239.

Roenneberg, T., Kuehnle, T., Pramstaller, P., Ricken, J., Havel, M., Guth, A., et al. (2004). A marker for the end of adolescence. *Current Biology, 14,* 1038–1039.

Roeser, R., Eccles, J., & Freedman-Doan, C. (1999). Academic functioning and mental health in adolescence: Patterns, progressions, and routes from childhood. *Journal of Adolescent Research, 14,* 135–174.

Roeser, R., Eccles, J., & Sameroff, A. (1998). Academic and emotional functioning in early adolescence: Longitudinal relations, patterns, and prediction by experience in middle school. *Development and Psychopathology, 10,* 321–352.

Roeser, R., Lord, S., & Eccles, J. (1994, February). *A portrait of academic alienation in adolescence: Motivation, mental health, and family experience.* Paper presented at the biennial meetings of the Society for Research on Adolescence, San Diego.

Roeser, R., Midgley, C., & Urdan, T. (1996). Perceptions of the school psychological environment and early adolescents' psychological and behavioral functioning in school: The mediating role of goals and belonging. *Journal of Educational Psychology, 88,* 408–422.

Rogers, J., Boruch, R., Stoms, G., & DeMoya, D. (1991). Impact of the Minnesota parental notification law on abortion and birth. *American Journal of Public Health, 81,* 294–298.

Rogers, M., & Holmbeck, G. (1997). Effects of brief interparental aggression on children's adjustment: The moderating role of cognitive appraisal and coping. *Journal of Family Psychology, 11,* 125–130.

Rohde, P., Lewinsohn, P. M., Kahler, C. W., Seeley, J. R., & Brown, R. A. (2001). Natural course of alcohol use disorders from adolescence to young adulthood. *Journal of the American Academy of Child and Adolescent Psychiatry, 40,* 83–90.

Rohner, R., Bourque, S., & Elordi, C. (1996). Children's perceptions of corporal punishment, caretaker acceptance, and psychological adjustment in a poor, biracial Southern community. *Journal of Marriage and the Family, 58,* 842–852.

Roisman, G. I. (2002). Beyond main effect models of adolescent work intensity, family closeness and school disengagement: Mediational and conditional hypotheses. *Journal of Adolescent Research, 17,* 331–345.

Roisman, G. I., Aguilar, B., & Egeland, B. (2004). Antisocial behavior in the transition to adulthood: The independent and interactive roles of developmental history and emerging developmental tasks. *Development and Psychopathology, 16,* 857–871.

Roisman, G. I., Masten, A. S., Coatsworth, J. D., & Tellegen, A. (2004). Salient and emerging developmental tasks in the transition to adulthood. *Child Development, 75,* 123–133.

Romer, D., Black, M., Ricardo, I., Feigelman, S., Kaljee, L., Galbraith, J., et al. (1994). Social influences on the sexual behavior of youth at risk for HIV exposure. *American Journal of Public Health, 84,* 977–985.

Romero, A. J., Carvajal, S. C., Volle, F., & Orduña, M. (2007). Adolescent bicultural stress and its impact on mental well-being among Latinos, Asian Americans, and European Americans. *Journal of Community Psychology, 35,* 519–534.

Romo, L. F., Lefkowitz, E. S., Sigman, M., & Au, T. K. (2002). A longitudinal study of maternal messages about dating and sexuality and their influence on Latino adolescents. *Journal of Adolescent Health, 31,* 59–69.

Rong, X., & Brown, F. (2001). The effects of immigrant generation and ethnicity on educational attainment among young African and Caribbean Blacks in the United States. *Harvard Educational Review, 71,* 536–565.

Rönkä, A., & Pulkkinen, L. (1995). Accumulation of problems in social functioning in young adulthood: A developmental approach. *Journal of Personality and Social Psychology, 69,* 381–391.

Rosario, M., Salzinger, S., Feldman R., & Ng-Ma, D. (2008). Intervening processes between youths' exposure to community violence and internalizing symptoms over time: The roles of social support and coping. *American Journal of Community Psychology, 41,* 43–62.

Roscigno, V., & Ainsworth-Darnell, J. (1999). Race, cultural capital and educational resources: Persistent inequalities and achievement returns. *Sociology of Education, 72,* 158–178.

Rose, A. J. (2002). Co-rumination in the friendships of girls and boys. *Child Development, 73,* 1830–1843.

Rose, A. J., Carlson, W., & Waller, E. M. (2007). Prospective associations of co-rumination with friendship and emotional adjustment: Considering the socioemotional trade-offs of co-rumination. *Developmental Psychology, 43,* 1019–1031.

Rose, A. J., & Swenson, L. P. (2009). Do perceived popular adolescents who aggress against others experience emotional adjustment problems themselves? *Developmental Psychology, 45,* 868–872.

Rose, A. J., Swenson, L. P., & Waller, E. M. (2004). Overt and relational aggression and perceived popularity: Developmental differences in concurrent and prospective relations. *Developmental Psychology, 40,* 378–387.

Rose, S., & Feldman, J. (1995). Prediction of IQ and specific cognitive abilities at 11 years from infancy measures. *Developmental Psychology, 31,* 685–696.

Rosen, B., & D'Andrade, R. (1959). The psychosocial origins of achievement motivation. *Sociometry, 22,* 185–218.

Rosenbaum, J. (1996). Policy uses of research on the high school-to-work transition. *Sociology of Education,* Extra Issue, 102–122.

Rosenbaum, J. (2006). Reborn a virgin: Adolescents' retracting of virginity pledges and sexual histories. *American Journal of Public Health, 96,* 1098–1103.

Rosenbaum, J. (2009). Patient teenagers? A comparison of the sexual behavior of virginity pledgers and matched nonpledgers. *Pediatrics, 123,* e110–120.

Rosenbaum, J., Stern, D., Hamilton, M., Hamilton, S., Berryman, S., & Kazis, R. (1992). *Youth apprenticeship in America: Guidelines for building an effective system.* Washington, DC: William T. Grant Foundation Commission on Youth and America's Future.

Rosenberg, M. (1975). The dissonant context and the adolescent self-concept. In S. Dragastin & G. Elder, Jr. (Eds.), *Adolescence in the life cycle.* Washington, DC: Hemisphere.

Rosenberg, M. (1986). Self concept from middle childhood through adolescence. In J. Suls & A. Greenwald (Eds.), *Psychological perspectives on the self* (Vol. 3). Hillsdale, NJ: Erlbaum.

Rosenbloom, S. R., & Way, N. (2004). Experiences of discrimination among African American, Asian American, and Latino adolescents in an urban high school. *Youth and Society, 35,* 420–451.

Rosenblum, G., & Lewis, M. (1999). The relations among body image, physical attractiveness, and body mass in adolescence. *Child Development, 70,* 50–64.

Rosenthal, D. (1994, February). *Gendered constructions of adolescent sexuality.* Paper presented at the biennial meetings of the Society for Research on Adolescence, San Diego.

Rosenthal, D., & Feldman, S. (1990). The acculturation of Chinese immigrants: The effects on family functioning of length of residence in two cultural contexts. *Journal of Genetic Psychology, 151,* 493–514.

Rosenthal, D., & Smith, A. (1997). Adolescent sexual timetable. *Journal of Youth and Adolescence, 26,* 619–636.

Rosenthal, D., Smith, A., & de Visser, R. (1999). Personal and social factors influencing age at first sexual intercourse. *Archives of Sexual Behavior, 28,* 319–333.

Rosenthal, R., & Jacobson, E. (1968). *Pygmalion in the classroom.* New York: Holt, Rinehart & Winston.

Roseth, C. J., Johnson, D. W., & Johnson, R. T. (2008). Promoting early adolescents' achievement and peer relationships: The effects of cooperative, competitive, and individualistic goal structures. *Psychological Bulletin, 134,* 223–246.

Roth, J., Brooks-Gunn, J., Murray, L., & Foster, W. (1998). Promoting healthy adolescents: Synthesis of youth development program evaluations. *Journal of Research on Adolescence, 8,* 423–459.

Rotheram-Borus, M., & Koopman, C. (1991). Sexual risk behaviors, AIDS knowledge, and beliefs about AIDS among runaways. *American Journal of Public Health, 81,* 206–208.

Rotheram-Borus, M., Marelich, W., & Srinivasan, S. (1999). HIV risk among homosexual, bisexual, and heterosexual male and female youths. *Archives of Sexual Behavior, 28,* 159–177.

Rotheram-Borus, M., & Phinney, J. (1990). Patterns of social expectations among Black and Mexican-American children. *Child Development, 61,* 542–556.

Rotheram-Borus, M., Rosario, M., Van Rossem, R., Reid, H., & Gillis, R. (1995). Prevalence, course, and predictors of multiple problem behaviors among gay and bisexual male adolescents. *Developmental Psychology, 31,* 75–85.

Rouse, C. E., Brooks-Gunn, J., & McLanahan, S. (Eds.) (2005). *The future of children: School Readiness: Closing racial and ethnic gaps.* Brooking Institution and Woodrow Wilson School of Public and International Affairs, Princeton University.

Rousseau, J. (1911). *Emile* (B. Foxley, trans.). London: Dent. (Original work published 1762)

Rowe, D., Jacobson, K., & Van den Oord, E. (1999). Genetic and environmental influences on vocabulary IQ: Parental education level as moderator. *Child Development, 70,* 1151–1162.

Rowe, D., Rodgers, J., & Meseck-Bushey, S. (1992). Sibling delinquency and the family environment: Shared and unshared influences. *Child Development, 63,* 59–67.

Rowe, D., Rodgers, J., Meseck-Bushey S., & St. John, C. (1989). Sexual behavior and nonsexual deviance: A sibling study of their relationship. *Developmental Psychology, 25,* 61–69.

Rowe, D., Vazsonyi, A., & Flannery, D. (1994). No more than skin deep: Ethnic and racial similarity in developmental processes. *Psychological Review, 101,* 396–413.

Roye, C., & Balk, S. (1996). The relationship of partner support to outcomes for teenage mothers and their children: A review. *Journal of Adolescent Health, 19,* 86–93.

Rozin, P., Bauer, R., & Catanese, D. (2003). Food and life, pleasure and worry, among American college students: Gender differences and regional similarities. *Journal of Personality and Social Psychology, 85,* 132–141.

Rubin, K., Chen, X., McDougall, P., Bowker, A., & McKinnon, J. (1995). The Waterloo Longitudinal Project: Predicting internalizing and externalizing problems in adolescence. *Development and Psychopathology, 7,* 751–764.

Rubin, K., LeMare, L., & Lollis, S. (1990). Social withdrawal in childhood: Developmental pathways to peer rejection. In S. Asher & J. Coie (Eds.), *Peer rejection in childhood* (pp. 217–249). New York: Cambridge University Press.

Ruchkin, V., Henrich, C. C., Jones, S. M., Vermeiren, R., & Schwab-Stone, M. (2007). Violence exposure and psychopathology in urban youth: The mediating role of posttraumatic stress. *Journal of Abnormal Child Psychology, 35,* 578–593.

Ruck, M., Abramovitch, R., & Keating, D. (1998). Children and adolescents' understanding of rights: Balancing nurturance and self-determination. *Child Development, 64,* 404–417.

Ruck, M., Peterson-Badali, M., & Day, D. M. (2002). Adolescents' and mothers' understanding of children's rights in the home. *Journal of Research on Adolescence, 12,* 373–398.

Rudolph, K., & Hammen, C. (1999). Age and gender as determinants of stress exposure, generation, and reactions in youngsters: A transactional perspective. *Child Development, 70,* 660–677.

Rueter, M., & Conger, R. (1995a). Interaction style, problem-solving behavior, and family problem-solving effectiveness. *Child Development, 66,* 98–115.

Rueter, M., & Conger, R. (1995b). Antecedents of parent–adolescent disagreements. *Journal of Marriage and the Family, 57,* 435–448.

Rueter, M., & Conger, R. (1998). Reciprocal influences between parenting and adolescent problem-solving behavior. *Developmental Psychology, 34,* 1470–1482.

Rueter, M., & Kwon, H. (2005). Developmental trends in adolescent suicidal ideation. *Journal of Research on Adolescence, 15,* 205–222.

Ruggles, S. (1994). The origins of African-American family structure. *American Sociological Review, 59,* 136–151.

Ruiz, S., Roosa, M., & Gonzales, N. (2002). Predictors of self-esteem for Mexican-American and European American youths: A reexamination of the influence of parenting. *Journal of Family Psychology, 16,* 70–80.

Rumbaut, R. (1997). Assimilation and its discontents: Between rhetoric and reality. *International Migration Review, 31,* 923–960.

Rumbaut, R., & Cornelius, W. (Eds.). (1995). *California's immigrant children: Theory, research, and implications for educational policy.* San Diego: University of California, Center for U.S.-Mexican Studies.

Rumberger, R. (1995). Dropping out of middle school: A multilevel analysis of students and schools. *American Educational Research Journal, 32,* 583–625.

Rumberger, R., & Larson, K. (1998). Student mobility and the increased risk of high school dropout. *American Journal of Education, 107,* 1–35.

Rumberger, R., & Palardy, G. (2005). Test scores, dropout rates, and transfer rates as alternative indicators of high school performance. *American Education Research Journal, 42,* 3–42.

Rumberger, R., Ghatak, R., Poulos, G., Ritter, P., & Dornbusch, S. (1990). Family influences on dropout behavior in one California high school. *Sociology of Education, 63,* 283–299.

Rusby, J. C., Forrester, K. K., Biglan A., & Metzler, C. W. (2005). Relationships between peer harassment and adolescent problem behaviors. *Journal of Early Adolescence, 25,* 453–477.

Rushton, J., Forcier, M., & Schectman, R. M. (2002). Epidemiology of depressive symptoms in the National Longitudinal Study of Adolescent Health. *Journal of the American Academy of Child and Adolescent Psychiatry, 41,* 199–205.

Russell, S. (1994). Life course antecedents of premarital conception in Great Britain. *Journal of Marriage and the Family, 56,* 480–492.

Russell, S. (2002). Childhood development risk for teen childbearing in Britain. *Journal of Research on Adolescence, 12,* 305–324.

Russell, S., & Joyner, K. (2001). Adolescent sexual orientation and suicide risk: Evidence from a national study. *American Journal of Public Health, 91,* 1276–1281.

Russell, S., Elder, G. H., Jr., & Conger, R. (1997, April). *School transitions and academic achievement.* Paper presented at the biennial meetings of the Society for Research in Child Development, Washington, DC.

Russell, S., Franz, B., & Driscoll, A. (2001). Same-sex romantic attraction and experiences of violence in adolescence. *American Journal of Public Health, 91,* 903–906.

Rutter, M. (1983). School effects on pupil progress: Research findings and policy implications. *Child Development, 54,* 1–29.

Rutter, M., Graham, P., Chadwick, F., & Yule, W. (1976). Adolescent turmoil: Fact or fiction? *Journal of Child Psychiatry and Psychology, 17,* 35–56.

Ryan, A. M. (2001). The peer group as a context for the development of young adolescent motivation and achievement. *Child Development, 72,* 1135–1150.

Ryan, A. M., & Patrick, H. (2001). The classroom social environment and changes in adolescents' motivation and engagement during middle school. *American Educational Research Journal, 38,* 437–460.

Ryan, R., & Lynch, J. (1989). Emotional autonomy versus detachment: Revisiting the vicissitudes of adolescence and young adulthood. *Child Development, 60,* 340–356.

Ryan, S., Franzetta, K., & Manlove, J. (2007). Knowledge, perceptions, and motivations for contraception: Influence on teens' contraceptive consistency. *Youth and Society, 39,* 182–208.

Ryan, S., Franzetta, K., Manlove, J., & Schelar, E. (2008). Older sexual partners during adolescence: Links to reproductive health outcomes in young adulthood. *Perspectives on Sexual and Reproductive Health, 40,* 17–26.

Rys, G., & Bear, G. (1997). Relational aggression and peer relations: Gender and developmental issues. *Merrill-Palmer Quarterly, 43,* 87–106.

Sack, W., & Clarke, G. (1996). Multiple forms of stress in Cambodian adolescent refugees. *Child Development, 67,* 107–116.

Sackett, P. R., Kuncel, N. R., Arneson, J. J., Cooper, S. R., & Waters, S. D. (2009). Does socioeconomic status explain the relationship between admissions tests and post-secondary academic performance? *Psychological Bulletin, 135,* 1–22.

Safron, J., Sy, S., & Schulenberg, J. (2003). Wishing to work: New perspectives on how adolescents' part-time work intensity is linked to educational disengagement, substance use, and other problem behaviours. *International Journal of Behavioral Development, 27,* 301–315.

Sagar, H., Schofield, J., & Snyder, H. (1983). Race and gender barriers: Preadolescent peer behavior in academic classrooms. *Child Development, 54,* 1032–1040.

Sagrestano, L., McCormick, S., Paikoff, R., & Holmbeck, G. (1999). Pubertal development and parent–child conflict in low-income, urban, African American adolescents. *Journal of Research on Adolescence, 9,* 85–107.

Sale, E., Sambrano, S., Springer, J. F., Pena, C., Pan, W., & Kasim, R. (2005). Family protection and prevention of alcohol use among Hispanic youth at high risk. *American Journal of Community Psychology, 36,* 195–205.

Salekin, R. T. (2008). Psychopathy and recidivism from mid-adolescence to young adulthood: Cumulating legal problems and limiting life opportunities. *Journal of Abnormal Psychology, 117,* 386–395.

Salem, D., Zimmerman, M., & Notaro, P. (1998). Effects of family structure, family process, and father involvement on psychosocial outcomes among African American adolescents. *Family Relations, 47,* 331–341.

Salinger, J. D. (1964). *The catcher in the rye.* New York: Bantam Books. (Original work published 1951)

Salmivalli, C. (1998). Intelligent, attractive, well-behaving, unhappy: The structure of adolescents' self-concept and its relations to their social behavior. *Journal of Research on Adolescence, 8,* 333–354.

Samaniego, R., & Gonzales, N. (1999). Multiple mediators of the effects of acculturation status on delinquency for Mexican American adolescents. *American Journal of Community Psychology, 27,* 189–210.

Sameroff, A. J., Peck, S. C., & Eccles, J. (2004). Changing ecological determinants of conduct problems from early adolescence to early adulthood. *Development and Psychopathology, 16,* 873–896.

Sampson, R. (1992). Family management and child development: Insights from social disorganization theory. In J. McCord (Ed.), *Advances in criminological theory* (Vol. 3., pp. 63–93). New Brunswick, NJ: Transaction.

Sampson, R. (1997). Collective regulation of adolescent misbehavior: Validation results from eighty Chicago neighborhoods. *Journal of Adolescent Research, 12,* 227–244.

Sampson, R., & Laub, J. (1994). Urban poverty and the family context of delinquency: A new look at structure and process in a classic study. *Child Development, 65,* 523–540.

Sampson, R., & Laub, J. (2003). Life-course desistors? Trajectories of crime among delinquent boys followed to age 70. *Criminology, 41,* 555–592.

Sampson, R., Raudenbusch, S., & Earls, F. (1997). Neighborhoods and violent crime: A multilevel study of collective efficacy for children. *Science, 277,* 918–924.

Sanchez, B., Esparza, P., & Colón, Y. (2008). Natural mentoring under the microscope: An investigation of mentoring relationships and Latino adolescents' academic performance. *Journal of Community Psychology, 36,* 468–482.

Sandefur, G., McLanahan, S., & Wojtkiewicz, R. (1992). The effects of parental marital status during adolescence on high school graduation. *Social Forces, 71,* 103–121.

Sandfort, J., & Hill, M. (1996). Assisting young, unmarried mothers to become self-sufficient: The effects of different types of early economic support. *Journal of Marriage and the Family, 58,* 311–326.

Santelli, J., Abma, J., Ventura, S., Lindberg, L., Morrow, B., Anderson, J. E., et al. (2004). Can changes in sexual behaviors among high school students explain the decline in teen pregnancy rates in the 1990s? *Journal of Adolescent Health, 35,* 80–90.

Santelli, J., Carter, M., Orr, M., & Dittus, P. (2009). Trends in sexual risk behaviors, by nonsexual risk behavior involvement, U.S. high school students, 1991–2007. *Journal of Adolescent Health, 44,* 372–379.

Santelli, J., Lindberg, L., Abma, J., McNeely, C., & Resnick, M. (2000). Adolescent sexual behavior: Estimates and trends from four nationally representative surveys. *Family Planning Perspectives, 32,* 156–165.

Santelli, J., Warren, C., Lowry, R., Sogolow, E., Collins, J., Kann, L., et al. (1997). The use of condoms with other contraceptive methods among young men and women. *Family Planning Perspectives, 29,* 261–267.

Santelli, J. S., Lindberg, L. D., Finer, L. B., & Singh, S. (2007). Explaining recent declines in adolescent pregnancy in the United States: The contribution of abstinence and improved contraceptive use. *American Journal of Public Health, 97,* 150–156.

Santelli, J. S., Morrow, B., Anderson, J. E., & Lindberg, L. D. (2006). Contraceptive use and pregnancy risk among U.S. high school students, 1991–2003. *Perspectives on Sexual and Reproductive Health, 38,* 106–111.

Santesso, D. L., & Segalowitz, S. J. (2008). Developmental differences in error-related ERPs in middle- to late-adolescent males. *Developmental Psychology, 44,* 205–217.

Saporito, S., & Sohoni, D. (2006). Coloring outside the lines: Racial segregation in public schools and their attendance boundaries. *Sociology of Education, 79,* 81–105.

Sargent, J., & Dalton, M. (2001). Does parental disapproval of smoking prevent adolescents from becoming established smokers? *Pediatrics, 108,* 1256–1262.

Saunders, J., Davis, L., Williams, T., & Williams, J. H. (2004). Gender differences in self-perceptions and academic outcomes: A study of African American high school students. *Journal of Youth and Adolescence, 33,* 81–90.

Savage, M., & Holcomb, D. (1999). Adolescent female athletes' sexual risk-taking behaviors. *Journal of Youth and Adolescence, 28,* 595–602.

Savage, M., & Scott, L. (1998). Physical activity and rural middle school adolescents. *Journal of Youth and Adolescence, 27,* 245–253.

Savin-Williams, R. (1994). Verbal and physical abuse as stressors in the lives of lesbian, gay male, and bisexual youths: Associations with school problems, running away, substance abuse, prostitution, and suicide. *Journal of Consulting and Clinical Psychology, 62,* 261–269.

Savin-Williams, R. (2006). Who's gay? Does it matter? *Current Directions in Psychological Science, 15,* 40–44.

Savin-Williams, R., & Berndt, T. (1990). Friendship and peer relations. In S. Feldman & G. Elliott (Eds.), *At the threshold: The developing adolescent* (pp. 277–307). Cambridge, MA: Harvard University Press.

Savin-Williams, R., & Demo, D. (1983). Situational and transituational determinants of adolescent self-feelings. *Journal of Personality and Social Psychology, 44,* 824–833.

Scales, P. C., Benson, P. L., & Mannes, M. (2006). The contribution to adolescent well-being made by nonfamily adults: An examination of developmental assets as contexts and processes. *Journal of Community Psychology, 34,* 401–413.

Scales, P., Benson, P., Roehlkepartain, E., Sesma, Jr., A., & van Dulmen, M. (2006). The role of developmental assets in predicting academic achievement: A longitudinal study. *Journal of Adolescence, 29,* 691–708.

Scales, P., Blyth, D. A., Berkas, T. H., & Kielsmeier, J. C. (2000). The effects of service-learning on middle school students' social responsibility and academic success. *Journal of Early Adolescence, 20,* 332–358.

Scanlan, T., Bakes, M., & Scanlan, L. (2005). Participation in sport: A developmental glimpse at emotion. In J. Mahoney, R. Larson, & J. Eccles (Eds.), *Organized activities as contexts of development* (pp. 275–309). Hillsdale, NJ: Erlbaum.

Scaramella, L., Conger, R. D., Spoth, R., & Simons, R. L. (2002). Evaluation of a social contextual model of delinquency: A cross-study replication. *Child Development, 73,* 175–195.

Scharf, M., Shulman, S., & Avigad Spitz, L. (2005). Sibling relationships in emerging adulthood and in adolescence. *Journal of Adolescent Research, 20,* 64–90.

Scheier, L., & Botvin, G. (1998). Relations of social skills, personal competence, and adolescent alcohol use: A developmental exploratory study. *Journal of Early Adolescence, 18,* 77–114.

Scheier, L., Botvin, G. J., Griffin, K. W., & Diaz, T. (2000). Dynamic growth models of self-esteem and adolescent alcohol use. *Journal of Early Adolescence, 20,* 178–209.

Schellenbach, C., Whitman, T., & Borkowski, J. (1992). Toward an integrative model of adolescent parenting. *Human Development, 35,* 81–99.

Scherer, D., & Gardner, W. (1990). Reasserting the authority of science. *American Psychologist, 45,* 1173–1174.

Schiff, A., & Knopf, I. (1985). The effects of task demands on attention allocation in children of different ages. *Child Development, 56,* 621–630.

Schiller, K. (1999). Effects of feeder patterns on students' transition to high school. *Sociology of Education, 72,* 216–233.

Schilling, E. A., Aseltine, R. H. J., Glanovsky, J. L., James, A., & Jacobs, D. (2009). Adolescent alcohol use, suicidal ideation, and suicide attempts. *Journal of Adolescent Health, 44,* 335–341.

Schlegel, A. (2009). Cross-cultural issues in the study of adolescent development. In R. Lerner & L. Steinberg (Eds.), *Handbook of adolescent psychology* (3rd ed., Vol. 2, pp. 570–589). New York: Wiley.

Schlegel, A., & Barry, H. (1991). *Adolescence: An anthropological inquiry.* New York: Free Press.

Schmidt, J. (2003). Correlates of reduced misconduct among adolescents facing adversity. *Journal of Youth and Adolescence, 32,* 439–452.

Schmidt, J., & Padilla, B. (2003). Self-esteem and family challenge: An investigation of their effects on achievement. *Journal of Youth and Adolescence, 32,* 37–46.

Schmidt, J., Shumow, L., & Kackar, H. (2007). Adolescents' participation in service activities and its impact on academic, behavioral, and civic outcomes. *Journal of Youth and Adolescence, 36*, 127–140.

Schmidt, M. G., Reppucci, N. D., & Woolard, J. (2003). Effectiveness of participation as a defendant: The attorney-juvenile client relationships. *Behavioral Sciences and the Law, 21*, 175–198.

Schneider, B., & Stevenson, D. (1999). *The ambitious generations: America's teenagers, motivated but directionless.* New Haven, CT: Yale University Press.

Schneiders, J., Nicolson, N. A., Berkhof, J., Feron, F. J., van Os, J., & deVries, M. W. (2006). Mood reactivity to daily negative events in early adolescence: Relationship to risk for psychopathology. *Developmental Psychology, 42*, 543–554.

Schochet, T., Kelley, A., & Landry, C. (2004). Differential behavioral effects of nicotine exposure in adolescent and adult rats. *Psychopharmacology, 175*, 265–273.

Schochet, T., Kelley, A., & Landry, C. (2005). Differential expression of arc mRNA and other plasticity-related genes induced by nicotine in adolescent rat forebrain. *Neuroscience, 135*, 285–297.

Schoenhals, M., Tienda, M., & Schneider, B. (1998). The educational and personal consequences of adolescent employment. *Social Forces, 77*, 723–762.

Schofield, H. T., Bierman, K. L., Heinrichs, B., & Nix, R. L. (2008). Predicting early sexual activity with behavior problems exhibited at school entry and in early adolescence. *Journal of Abnormal Child Psychology, 36*, 1175–1188.

Schofield, J. (1981). Complementary and conflicting identities: Images and interaction in an interracial school. In S. Asher & J. Gottman (Eds.), *The development of children's friendships.* Cambridge: Cambridge University Press.

Scholte, R., van Lieshout, C., & Van Aken, C. (2001). Perceived relational support in adolescence: Dimensions, configurations, and adolescent adjustment. *Journal of Research on Adolescence, 11*, 71–94.

Schommer, M., Calvert, C., Gariglietti, G., & Bajaj, A. (1997). The development of epistemological beliefs among secondary school students: A longitudinal study. *Journal of Educational Psychology, 89*, 37–40.

Schooler, D. (2008). Real women have curves: A longitudinal investigation of TV and the body image development of Latina adolescents. *Journal of Adolescent Research, 23*, 132–153.

Schoon, I., Bynner, J., Joshi, H., Parsons, S., Wiggins, R. D., & Sacker, A. (2002). The influence of context, timing, and duration of risk experiences for the passage from childhood to midadulthood. *Child Development, 73*, 1486–1504.

Schoon, I., Parsons, S., & Sacker, A. (2004). Socioeconomic adversity, educational resilience, and subsequent levels of adult adaptation. *Journal of Adolescent Research, 19*, 383–404.

Schulenberg, J., & Bachman, J. (1993, March). *Long hours on the job? Not so bad for some adolescents in some types of jobs: The quality of work and substance use, affect, and stress.* Paper presented at the biennial meetings of the Society for Research in Child Development, New Orleans.

Schulenberg, J., Bryant, A. L., & O'Malley, P. (2004). Taking hold of some kind of life: How developmental tasks relate to trajectories of well-being during the transition to adulthood. *Development and Psychopathology, 16*, 1119–1140.

Schulenberg, J., Maggs, J., Dielman, T., Leech, S., Kloska, D., Shope, J., et al. (1999). On peer influences to get drunk: A panel study of young adolescents. *Merrill-Palmer Quarterly, 45*, 108–142.

Schulenberg, J., Wadsworth, K., O'Malley, P., Bachman, J., & Johnston, L. (1996). Adolescent risk factors for binge drinking during the transition to young adulthood: Variable- and pattern-centered approaches to change. *Developmental Psychology, 32*, 659–674.

Schwab, J., Kulin, H. E., Susman, E. J., Finkelstein, J. W., Chinchilli, V. M., Kunselman, S. J., et al. (2001). The role of sex hormone replacement therapy on self-perceived competence in adolescents with delayed puberty. *Child Development, 72*, 1439–1450.

Schwartz, S. J., Côté, J. E., & Arnett, J. J. (2005). Identity and agency in emerging adulthood: Two developmental routes in the individualization process. *Youth and Society, 37*, 201–229.

Schwartz, S. J., Pantin, H., Prado, G., Sullivan, S., & Szapocznik, J. (2005). Family functioning, identity and problem behavior in Hispanic immigrant early adolescents. *Journal of Early Adolescence, 25*, 392–420.

Schweder, R. (Ed.). (1998). *Welcome to middle age! And other cultural fictions.* Chicago: University of Chicago Press.

Schweingruber, H. A., & Kalil, A. (2000). Decision making and depressive symptoms in Black and White multigenerational teen-parent families. *Journal of Family Psychology, 14*, 556–569.

Scott, E., & Steinberg, L. (2008). *Rethinking juvenile justice.* Cambridge, MA: Harvard University Press.

Scott, L. D., & House, L. E. (2005). Relationship of distress and perceived control to coping with perceived racial discrimination among Black youth. *Journal of Black Psychology, 31*, 254–272.

Seaton, E., & Yip, T. (2009). School and neighborhood contexts, perceptions of racial discrimination, and psychological well-being among African American adolescents. *Journal of Youth and Adolescence, 38*, 153–163.

Seaton, E., Caldwell, C., Sellers, R., & Jackson, J. (2008). The prevalence of perceived discrimination among African American and Caribbean Black youth. *Developmental Psychology, 44*, 1288–1297.

Seaton, E., Scottham, K., & Sellers, R. (2006). The status model of racial identity development in African American adolescents: Evidence of structure, trajectories, and well-being. *Child Development, 77*, 1416–1426.

Seaton, E., Yip, T., & Sellers, R. (2009). A longitudinal examination of racial identity and racial discrimination among African American adolescents. *Child Development, 80*, 406–417.

Sebastian, C., Burnett, S., & Blakemore, S. (2008). Development of the self-concept during adolescence. *Trends in Cognitive Science, 12*, 441–446.

Segalowitz, S. J., & Davies, P. L. (2004). Charting the maturation of the frontal lobe: An electrophysiological strategy. *Brain and Cognition, 55*, 116–133.

Seginer, R. (1998). Adolescents' perceptions of relationships with older siblings in the context of other close relationships. *Journal of Research on Adolescence, 8*, 287–308.

Seguin, J., Arseneault, L., & Tremblay, R. (2007). The contribution of "cool" and "hot" components of decision-making in adolescence: Implications for developmental psychopathology. *Cognitive Development, 22*, 530–543.

Seidman, E., Aber, J., Allen, L., & French, S. (1996). The impact of the transition to high school on the self-system and perceived social context of poor urban youth. *American Journal of Community Psychology, 24*, 489–515.

Seidman, E., Allen, L., Aber, J., Mitchell, C., & Feinman, J. (1994). The impact of school transitions in early adolescence on the self-system and perceived social context of poor urban youth. *Child Development, 65*, 507–522.

Seidman, E., & French, S. E. (2004). Developmental trajectories and ecological transitions: A two-step procedure to aid in the choice of prevention and promotion interventions. *Development and Psychopathology, 16*, 1141–1159.

Seidman, E., Lambert, L. E., Allen, L., & Aber, J. L. (2003). Urban adolescents' transition to junior high school and protective family transactions. *Journal of Early Adolescence, 23*, 166–193.

Seiffge-Krenke, I. (2006). Leaving home or still in the nest? Parent–child relationships and psychological health as predictors of different leaving home patterns. *Developmental Psychology, 42*, 864–876.

Seiffge-Krenke, I. (2003). Testing theories of romantic development from adolescence to young adulthood: Evidence of a developmental sequence. *International Journal of Behavioral Development, 27*, 519–531.

Seiffge-Krenke, I., Aunola, K., & Nurmi, J. (2009). Changes in stress perception and coping during adolescence: The role of situational and personal factors. *Child Development, 80,* 259–279.

Seiffge-Krenke, I., & Beyers, W. (2005). Coping trajectories from adolescence to young adulthood: Links to attachment state of mind. *Journal of Research on Adolescence, 15,* 561–582.

Seiffge-Krenke, I., & Klessinger, N. (2000). Long-term effects of avoidant coping on adolescents' depressive symptoms. *Journal of Youth and Adolescence, 29,* 617–630.

Seiffge-Krenke, I., & Stemmler, M. (2002). Factors contributing to gender differences in depressive symptoms: A test of three developmental models. *Journal of Youth and Adolescence, 31,* 405–417.

Seitz, V., & Apfel, N. (1993). Adolescent mothers and repeated childbearing: Effects of a school-based intervention program. *American Journal of Orthopsychiatry, 63,* 572–581.

Seitz, V., & Apfel, N. (1994). Effects of a school for pregnant students on the incidence of low-birthweight deliveries. *Child Development, 65,* 666–676.

Selfhout, M., Branje, S., & Meeus, W. (2008). The development of delinquency and perceived friendship quality in adolescent best friendship dyads. *Journal of Abnormal Child Psychology, 36,* 471–485.

Sellers, R., Copeland Linder, N., Martin, P., & Lewis, R. (2006). Racial identity matters: The relationship between racial discrimination and psychological functioning in African American adolescents. *Journal of Research on Adolescence, 16,* 187–216.

Sellers, R., & Shelton, N. (2003). The role of racial identity in perceived racial discrimination. *Journal of Personality and Social Psychology, 84,* 1079–1092.

Sells, C., & Blum, R. (1996). Morbidity and mortality among U.S. adolescents: An overview of data and trends. *American Journal of Public Health, 86,* 513–519.

Selman, R. (1980). *The growth of interpersonal understanding: Developmental and clinical analyses.* New York: Academic Press.

Serovich, J., & Greene, K. (1997). Predictors of adolescent sexual risk taking behaviors which put them at risk for contracting HIV. *Journal of Youth and Adolescence, 26,* 429–444.

Sessa, F., & Steinberg, L. (1991). Family structure and the development of autonomy in adolescence. *Journal of Early Adolescence, 11,* 38–55.

Settersten, R., Furstenberg, F., Jr., & Rumbaut, R. (Eds.). (2005). *On the frontier of adulthood.* Chicago: University of Chicago Press.

Shahinfar, A., Kupersmidt, J. B., & Matza, L. S. (2001). The relation between exposure to violence and social information processing among incarcerated adolescents. *Journal of Abnormal Psychology, 110,* 136–141.

Shanahan, L., McHale, S., Crouter, A., & Osgood, D. W. (2007). Warmth with mothers and fathers from middle childhood to late adolescence: Within- and between-families comparisons. *Developmental Psychology, 43,* 551–563.

Shanahan, L., McHale, S., Crouter, A., & Osgood, D. W. (2008). Linkages between parents' differential treatment, youth depressive symptoms, and sibling relationships. *Journal of Marriage and Family, 70,* 480–494.

Shanahan, L., McHale, S., Osgood, D. W., & Crouter, A. (2007). Conflict frequency with mothers and fathers from middle childhood to late adolescence: Within- and between-families comparisons. *Developmental Psychology, 43,* 539–550.

Shanahan, M. J., & Bauer, D. J. (2004). Developmental properties of transactional models: The case of life events and mastery from adolescence to young adulthood. *Development and Psychopathology, 16,* 1095–1117.

Shanahan, M. J., & Flaherty, B. P. (2001). Dynamic patterns of time use in adolescence. *Child Development, 72,* 385–401.

Shanahan, M. J., Mortimer, J. T., & Krüger, H. (2002). Adolescence and adult work in the twenty-first century. *Journal of Research in Adolescence, 12,* 99–120.

Shanahan, M. J., Porfeli, E., Mortimer, J. T., & Erickson, L. (2005). Subjective age identity and the transition to adulthood: When do adolescents become adults? In R. Settersten, F. Furstenberg, Jr., & R. Rumbaut (Eds.), *On the frontier of adulthood* (pp. 225–255). Chicago: University of Chicago Press.

Sharabany, R., Gershoni, R., & Hofman, J. (1981). Girlfriend, boyfriend: Age and sex differences in intimate friendship. *Developmental Psychology, 17,* 800–808.

Shaw, M., & White, D. (1965). The relationship between child–parent identification and academic underachievement. *Journal of Clinical Psychology, 21,* 10–13.

Shaw, P., Greenstein, D., Lerch, J., Klasen, L., Lenroot, R., Gotgay, N., et al. (2006). Intellectual ability and cortical development in children and adolescents. *Nature, 440,* 676–679.

Shearer, D. L., Mulvihill, B. A., Klerman, L. V., Wallander, J. L., Hovinga, M. E., & Redden, D. T. (2002). Association of early childbearing and low cognitive ability. *Perspectives on Sexual and Reproductive Health, 34,* 236.

Shedler, J., & Block, J. (1990). Adolescent drug use and psychological health: A longitudinal inquiry. *American Psychologist, 45,* 612–630.

Sheeran, P., Abraham, C., & Orbell, S. (1999). Psychosocial correlates of heterosexual condom use: A meta-analysis. *Psychological Bulletin, 125,* 90–132.

Sheidow, A. J., Gorman-Smith, D., Tolan, P. H., & Henry, D. B. (2001). Family and community characteristics: Risk factors for violence exposure in inner-city youth. *Journal of Community Psychology, 29,* 345–360.

Sheidow, A. J., Strachan, M. K., Minden, J. A., Henry, D. B., Tolan, P. H., & Gorman-Smith, D. (2008). The relation of antisocial behavior patterns and changes in internalizing symptoms for a sample of inner-city youth: Comorbidity within a developmental framework. *Journal of Youth and Adolescence, 37,* 821–829.

Shek, D. (2007). A longitudinal study of perceived differences in parental control and parent–child relational qualities in Chinese adolescents in Hong Kong. *Journal of Adolescent Research, 22,* 156–188.

Sher, K. J., Gotham, H. J., & Watson, A. L. (2004). Trajectories of dynamic predictors of disorder: Their meanings and implications. *Development and Psychopathology, 16,* 825–856.

Shernoff, D. J., & Schmidt, J. A. (2008). Further evidence of an engagement-achievement paradox among U.S. high school students. *Journal of Youth and Adolescence, 37,* 564–580.

Shernoff, D. J., & Vandell, D. L. (2007). Engagement in after-school program activities: Quality of experience from the perspective of participants. *Journal of Youth and Adolescence, 36,* 891–903.

Sherrod, L., & Lauckhardt, J. (2009). The development of citizenship. In R. Lerner & L. Steinberg (Eds.), *Handbook of adolescent psychology* (3rd ed., Vol. 2, pp. 372–408). New York: Wiley.

Shih, T. (1998). Finding the niche: Friendship formation of immigrant adolescents. *Youth and Society, 30,* 209–240.

Shiner, R. L., Masten, A. S., & Tellegen, A. (2002). A developmental perspective on personality in emerging adulthood: Childhood antecedents and concurrent adaptation. *Journal of Personality and Social Psychology, 83,* 1165–1177.

Shoop, D., & Davidson, P. (1994). AIDS and adolescents: The relation of parent and partner communication to adolescent condom use. *Journal of Adolescence, 17,* 137–148.

Shope, J. T., Molnar, L. J., Elliott, M. R., & Waller, P. F. (2001). Early impact on motor vehicle crashes among 16-year-old drivers. *Journal of the American Medical Association, 286,* 1593–1598.

Shrum, W., Cheek, N., Jr., & Hunter, S. (1988). Friendship in school: Gender and racial homophily. *Sociology of Education, 61,* 227–239.

Shucksmith, J., Glendinning, A., & Hendry, L. (1997). Adolescent drinking behaviour and the role of family life: A Scottish perspective. *Journal of Adolescence, 20,* 85–101.

Shulman, S., & Laursen, B. (2002). Adolescent perceptions of conflict in interdependent and disengaged friendships. *Journal of Research on Adolescence, 12,* 353–372.

Shulman, S., Laursen, B., Kalman, Z., & Karpovsky, S. (1997). Adolescent intimacy revisited. *Journal of Youth and Adolescence, 26,* 597–617.

Shulman, S., & Scharf, M. (2000). Adolescent romantic behaviors and perceptions: Age- and gender-related differences, and links with family and peer relationships. *Journal of Research on Adolescence, 10,* 99–118.

Shulman, S., Tuval-Mashiach, R., Levran, E., & Anbar, S. (2006). Conflict resolution patterns and longevity of adolescent romantic couples: A 2-year follow-up study. *Journal of Adolescence, 29,* 575–588.

Shumow, L., & Miller, J. D. (2001). Parents' at-home and at-school academic involvement with youth adolescents. *Journal of Early Adolescence, 21,* 68–91.

Siebenbruner, J., Englund, M. M., Egeland, B., & Hudson, K. (2006). Developmental antecedents of late adolescence substance use patterns. *Development and Psychopathology, 18,* 551–571.

Siegel, A., & Scovill, L. C. (2000). Problem behavior: The double symptom of adolescence. *Development and Psychopathology, 12,* 763–793.

Siegel, J., Aneshensel, C., Taub, B., Cantwell, D., & Driscoll, A. (1998). Adolescent depressed mood in a multiethnic sample. *Journal of Youth and Adolescence, 27,* 413–427.

Siegel, J., Yancey, A., Aneshensel, C., & Schuler, R. (1999). Body image, perceived pubertal timing, and adolescent mental health. *Journal of Adolescent Health, 25,* 155–165.

Siegel, M., & Biener, L. (2000). The impact of an antismoking media campaign on progression to established smoking: Results of a longitudinal study. *American Journal of Public Health, 90,* 380–386.

Siegler, R. (1988). Individual differences in strategy choices: Good students, not-so-good students, and perfectionists. *Child Development, 59,* 833–851.

Sieving, R. E., Eisenberg, M. E., Pettingell, S., & Skay, C. (2006). Friends' influence on adolescents' first sexual intercourse. *Perspectives on Sexual and Reproductive Health, 38,* 13–19.

Sigler-Rushton, W. (2005). Young fatherhood and subsequent disadvantage in the United Kingdom. *Journal of Marriage and the Family, 67,* 735.

Silbereisen, R., Petersen, A., Albrecht, H., & Kracke, B. (1989). Maturational timing and the development of problem behavior: Longitudinal studies in adolescence. *Journal of Early Adolescence, 9,* 247–268.

Silbereisen, R., & Schmitt-Rodermund, E. (1995). German immigrants in Germany: Adaptation of adolescents' timetables for autonomy. In M. Hofer, P. Noack, & J. Youniss (Eds.), *Psychological responses to social change: Human development in changing environments* (pp. 105–125). Berlin: de Gruyter.

Silbereisen, R., Schwarz, B., Nowak, M., Kracke, B., & von Eye, A. (1993, March). *Psychosocial adversities and timing of adolescent transitions: A comparison of the former East and West Germanies.* Paper presented at the biennial meetings of the Society for Research in Child Development, New Orleans.

Silk, J., Morris, A., Kanaya, T., & Steinberg, L. (2003). Psychological control and autonomy granting: Opposite ends of a continuum or distinct constructs? *Journal of Research on Adolescence, 13,* 113–128.

Silk, J., Siegle, G., Whalen, D., Ostapenko, L., Ladouceur, D., & Dahl, R. (2009). Pubertal changes in emotional information processing: Pupillary, behavioral, and subjective evidence during emotional word identification. *Development and Psychopathology, 21,* 7–26.

Silk, J., Vanderbilt-Adriance, E., Shaw, D. S., Forbes, E. E., Whalen, D. J., Ryan, N. D., et al. (2007). Resilience among children and adolescents at risk for depression: Mediation and moderation across social and neurobiological context. *Development and Psychopathology, 19,* 841–865.

Silverberg, S., Marczak, M., & Gondoli, D. (1996). Maternal depressive symptoms and achievement-related outcomes among adolescent daughters: Variations by family structure. *Journal of Early Adolescence, 16,* 90–109.

Silverberg, S., & Steinberg, L. (1990). Psychological well-being of parents at midlife: The impact of early adolescent children. *Developmental Psychology, 26,* 658–666.

Silverberg, S., Tennenbaum, D., & Jacob, T. (1992). Adolescence and family interaction. In V. Van Hasselt & M. Hersen (Eds.), *Handbook of social development: A lifespan perspective* (pp. 347–370). New York: Plenum.

Silverman, J., Raj, A., Mucci, L. A., & Hathaway, J. E. (2001). Dating violence against adolescent girls and associated substance abuse, unhealthy weight control, sexual risk behavior, pregnancy, and suicidality. *Journal of the American Medical Association, 286,* 572–579.

Sim, H., & Vuchinich, S. (1996). The declining effects of family stressors on antisocial behavior from childhood to adolescence and early adulthood. *Journal of Family Issues, 17,* 408–427.

Sim, T. (2000). Adolescent psychosocial competence: The importance and role of regard for parents. *Journal of Research on Adolescence, 10,* 49–64.

Sim, T., & Koh, S. (2003). A domain conceptualization of adolescent susceptibility to peer pressure. *Journal of Research on Adolescence, 13,* 57–80.

Simmons, R. (2003). *Odd girl out.* New York: Harvest Books.

Simmons, R., & Blyth, D. (1987). *Moving into adolescence.* New York: Aldine de Gruyter.

Simmons, R., Blyth, D., & McKinney, K. (1983). The social and psychological effects of puberty on White females. In J. Brooks-Gunn & A. Petersen (Eds.), *Girls at puberty* (pp. 229–272). New York: Plenum.

Simmons, R., & Rosenberg, F. (1975). Sex, sex roles, and self-image. *Journal of Youth and Adolescence, 4,* 229–258.

Simmons, R., Rosenberg, F., & Rosenberg, M. (1973). Disturbance in the self-image at adolescence. *American Sociological Review, 38,* 553–568.

Simon, V. A., Aikins, J. W., & Prinstein, M. J. (2008). Romantic partner selection and socialization during early adolescence. *Child Development, 79,* 1676–1692.

Simons, L., & Conger, R. (2007). Linking mother–father differences in parenting to a typology of family parenting styles and adolescent outcomes. *Journal of Family Issues, 28,* 212–241.

Simons, R., Chao, W., Conger, R., & Elder, G. H., Jr. (2001). Quality of parenting as mediator of the effect of childhood defiance on adolescent friendship choice and delinquency: A growth curve analysis. *Journal of Marriage and the Family, 63,* 63–79.

Simons, R., Johnson, C., Beaman, J., Conger, R., & Whitbeck, L. (1996). Parents and peer group as mediators of the effect of community structure on adolescent problem behavior. *American Journal of Community Psychology, 24,* 145–171.

Simons, R., Lin, K., & Gordon, L. (1998). Socialization in the family of origin and male dating violence: A prospective study. *Journal of Marriage and the Family, 60,* 467–478.

Simons, R., Simons, L., Burt, C., Brody, G., & Cutrona, C. (2005). Collective efficacy, authoritative parenting and delinquency: A longitudinal test of a model integrating community- and family-level processes. *Criminology, 43,* 989–1029.

Simons, R., Whitbeck, L., Beaman, J., & Conger, R. (1994). The impact of mothers' parenting, involvement by nonresidential fathers, and parental conflict on the adjustment of adolescent children. *Journal of Marriage and the Family, 56,* 356–374.

Simons, R., Whitbeck, L., Conger, R., & Chyi-In, W. (1991). Intergenerational transmission of harsh parenting. *Developmental Psychology, 27,* 159–171.

Simons-Morton, B., Hartos, J., Leaf, W., & Preusser, D. (2005). Persistence of effects of the Checkpoints Program on parental restrictions on teen driving privileges. *American Journal of Public Health, 95,* 447–452.

Simpkins, S. D., Davis-Kean, P. E., & Eccles, J. (2006). Math and science motivation: A longitudinal examination of the links between choices and beliefs. *Developmental Psychology, 42,* 70–83.

Simpkins, S. D., Eccles, J., & Becnel, J. N. (2008). The mediational role of adolescents' friends in relations between activity breadth and adjustment. *Developmental Psychology, 44,* 1081–1094.

Simpson, J. A., Collins, W. A., Tran, S., & Haydon, K. C. (2007). Attachment and the experience and expression of emotions in romantic relationships: A developmental perspective. *Journal of Personality and Social Psychology, 92,* 355–367.

Singh, K., & Hernandez-Gantes, V. (1996). The relation of English language proficiency to educational aspirations of Mexican-American eighth graders. *Journal of Early Adolescence, 16,* 253–273.

Singh, S., & Darroch, J. (1999). Trends in sexual activity among adolescent American women: 1982–1995. *Family Planning Perspectives, 31,* 212–219.

Singh, S., & Darroch, J. E. (2000). Adolescent pregnancy and childbearing: Levels and trends in developed countries. *Family Planning Perspectives, 32*(1), 14–23.

Sinha, J. W., Cnaan, R. A., & Gelles, R. J. (2007). Adolescent risk behaviors and religion: Findings from a national study. *Journal of Adolescence, 30,* 231–249.

Sionean, C., DiClemente, R. J., Wingood, G. M., Crosby, R., Cobb, B. K., Harrington, K., et al. (2002). Psychosocial and behavioral correlates of refusing unwanted sex among African-American adolescent females. *Journal of Adolescent Health, 30,* 55–63.

Sirin, S. R., & Rogers-Sirin, L. (2004). Exploring school engagement of middle-class African American adolescents. *Youth and Society, 35,* 323–340.

Sisk, C. L., & Foster, D. L. (2004). The neural basis of puberty and adolescence. *Nature Neuroscience, 7,* 1040–1047.

Skeem, J., & Cauffman. E. (2003). Views of the downward extension: Comparing the youth version of the Psychopathy Checklist with the Youth Psychopathic Traits Inventory. *Behavioral Sciences and the Law, 21,* 737–770.

Skinner, B. F. (1953). *Science and human behavior.* New York: Free Press.

Skitch, S. A., & Abela, J. R. Z. (2008). Rumination in response to stress as a common vulnerability factor to depression and substance misuse in adolescence. *Journal of Abnormal Child Psychology, 36,* 1029–1045.

Skoog, T., Stattin, H., & Kerr, M. (2009). The role of pubertal timing in what adolescent boys do online. *Journal of Research on Adolescence, 19,* 1–7.

Skorikov, V. B., & Vondracek, F. W. (2007). Vocational identity. In V. B. Skorikov & W. Patton (Eds.), *Career development in childhood and adolescence* (pp. 143–168). Rotterdam, The Netherlands: Sense.

Slap, G., Goodman, E., & Huang, B. (2001). Adoption as a risk factor for attempted suicide during adolescence. *Pediatrics, 108,* Article E30.

Slap, G., & Jablow, M. (1994). *Teenage health care.* New York: Pocket Books.

Slyper, A. (2006). The pubertal timing controversy in the USA, and a review of possible causative factors for the advance in timing of onset of puberty. *Clinical Endocrinology, 65,* 1–8.

Small, S., & Luster, T. (1994). Adolescent sexual activity: An ecological, risk-factor approach. *Journal of Marriage and the Family, 56,* 181–192.

Small, S., & Memmo, M. (2004). Contemporary models of youth development and problem prevention: Toward an integration of terms, concepts and models. *Family Relations, 53,* 3–11.

Smetana, J. (1989). Adolescents' and parents' reasoning about actual family conflict. *Child Development, 59,* 1052–1067.

Smetana, J. (1995a). Conflict and coordination in adolescent–parent relationships. In S. Shulman (Ed.), *Close relationships and socioemotional development* (pp. 155–184). Norwood, NJ: Ablex.

Smetana, J. (1995b). Parenting styles and conceptions of parental authority during adolescence. *Child Development, 66,* 299–316.

Smetana, J. (2000). Middle-class African American adolescents' and parents' conceptions of parental authority and parenting practices: A longitudinal investigation. *Child Development, 71,* 1672–1686.

Smetana, J. (2005). Adolescent–parent conflict: Resistance and subversion as developmental process. In L. Nucci (Ed.), *Conflict, contradiction, and contrarian elements in moral development and education* (pp. 69–91). Mahwah, NJ: Erlbaum.

Smetana, J., & Asquith, P. (1994). Adolescents' and parents' conceptions of parental authority and personal autonomy. *Child Development, 65,* 1147–1162.

Smetana, J., & Bitz, B. (1996). Adolescents' conceptions of teachers' authority and their relations to rule violations in school. *Child Development, 67,* 1153–1172.

Smetana, J., Campione-Barr, N., & Daddis, C. (2004). Longitudinal development of family decision making: Defining healthy behavioral autonomy for middle-class African American adolescents. *Child Development, 75,* 1418–1434.

Smetana, J., & Chuang, S. (2001). Middle-class African American parents' conceptions of parenting in the transition to adolescence. *Journal of Research on Adolescence, 11,* 177–198.

Smetana, J., Crean, H. F., & Daddis, C. (2002). Family processes and problem behaviors in middle-class African American adolescents. *Journal of Research on Adolescence, 12,* 275–304.

Smetana, J., & Daddis, C. (2002). Domain-specific antecedents of parental psychological control and monitoring: The role of parenting beliefs and practices. *Child Development, 73,* 563–580.

Smetana, J., Daddis, C., & Chuang, S. (2003). "Clean your room!" *Journal of Adolescent Research, 18,* 631–650.

Smetana, J., & Gaines, C. (2000). Adolescent–parent conflict in middle-class African-American families. *Child Development, 70,* 1447–1463.

Smetana, J., & Gettman, D. C. (2006). Autonomy and relatedness with parents and romantic development in African American adolescents. *Developmental Psychology, 42,* 1347–1351.

Smetana, J., Metzger, A., & Campione-Barr, N. (2004). African American late adolescents' relationships with parents: Developmental transitions and longitudinal patterns. *Child Development, 75,* 932–947.

Smetana, J., Metzger, A., Gettman, D., & Campione-Barr, N. (2006). Disclosure and secrecy in adolescent–parent relationships. *Child Development, 77,* 201–217.

Smetana, J., & Villalobos, M. (2009). Social cognitive development in adolescence. In R. Lerner & L. Steinberg (Eds.), *Handbook of adolescent psychology* (3rd ed., Vol. 1, pp. 187–228). New York: Wiley.

Smetana, J., Yau, J., Restrepo, A., & Braeges, J. (1991). Adolescent–parent conflict in married and divorced families. *Developmental Psychology, 27,* 1000–1010.

Smith, A., & Lalonde, R. N. (2003). "Racelessness" in a Canadian context? Exploring the link between Black students' identity, achievement, and mental health. *Journal of Black Psychology, 29,* 142–164.

Smith, C., & Denton, M. (2005). *Soul searching: The religious and spiritual lives of American teenagers.* New York: Oxford University Press.

Smith, C., Denton, M., Faris, R., & Regnerus, M. (2002). Mapping American adolescent religious participation. *Journal for the Scientific Study of Religion, 41,* 597–612.

Smith, E. (1996, March). *Ethnic identity in African-American youth: Definition, components, and measurement.* Paper presented at the biennial meetings of the Society for Research on Adolescence, Boston.

Smith, E., & Zabin, L. (1993). Marital and birth expectations of urban adolescents. *Youth and Society, 25,* 62–74.

Smith, G., Goldman, M., Greenbaum, P., & Christiansen, B. (1995). Expectancy for social facilitation from drinking: The divergent paths of high-expectancy and low-expectancy adolescents. *Journal of Abnormal Psychology, 104,* 32–40.

Smith, P. H., White, J. W., & Holland, L. J. (2003). A longitudinal perspective on dating violence among adolescent and college-age women. *American Journal of Public Health, 93,* 1104–1109.

Smith, T. (1993, March). *Federal employment training programs for youth: Failings and opportunities.* Paper presented at the biennial meetings of the Society for Research in Child Development, New Orleans.

Smith, T. E., & Leaper, C. (2006). Self-perceived gender typicality and the peer context during adolescence. *Journal of Research on Adolescence, 16*, 91–103.

Smolak, L., Levine, M., & Gralen, S. (1993). The impact of puberty and dating on eating problems among middle school girls. *Journal of Youth and Adolescence, 22*, 355–368.

Smoll, F., & Schutz, R. (1990). Quantifying gender differences in physical performance: A developmental perspective. *Developmental Psychology, 26*, 360–369.

Smollar, J., & Youniss, J. (1985). *Transformation in adolescents' perceptions of parents.* Paper presented at the biennial meetings of the Society for Research in Child Development, Baltimore.

Snell, E. K., Adam, E. K., & Duncan, G. J. (2007). Sleep and the body mass index and overweight status of children and adolescents. *Child Development, 78*, 309–323.

Snyder, H., & Sickmund, M. (1995). *Juvenile offenders and victims: A national report.* Washington, DC: Office of Juvenile Justice and Delinquency Prevention.

Snyder, H., & Sickmund, M. (2006). *Juvenile offenders and victims: 2006 national report.* Washington, D.C.: Office of Juvenile Justice and Delinquency Prevention.

Snyder, J., Bank, L., & Burraston, B. (2005). The consequences of antisocial behavior in older male siblings for younger brothers and sisters. *Journal of Family Psychology, 19*, 643–653.

Sobesky, W. (1983). The effects of situational factors on moral judgments. *Child Development, 54*, 575–584.

Soenens, B., Vansteenkiste, M., Lens, W., Luyckx, K., Goossens, L., Beyers, W., et al. (2007). Conceptualizing parental autonomy support: Adolescent perceptions of promotion of independence versus promotion of volitional functioning. *Developmental Psychology, 43*, 633–646.

Soenens, B., Vansteenkiste, M., Luyckx, K., & Goossens, L. (2006). Parenting and adolescent problem behavior: An integrated model with adolescent self-disclosure and perceived parental knowledge as intervening variables. *Developmental Psychology, 42*, 305–318.

Solomon, R., & Liefeld, C. (1998). Effectiveness of a family support center approach to adolescent mothers: Repeat pregnancy and school drop-out rates. *Family Relations, 47*, 139–144.

Sommer, K., Whitman, T., Borkowski, J., Schellenbach, C., Maxwell, S., & Keogh, D. (1993). Cognitive readiness and adolescent parenting. *Developmental Psychology, 29*, 389–398.

Sommers, C. (2000). *The war against boys.* New York: Simon & Schuster.

Sontag, L. M., Graber, J. A., Brooks-Gunn, J., & Warren, M. P. (2008). Coping with social stress: Implications for psychopathology in young adolescent girls. *Journal of Abnormal Child Psychology, 36*, 1159–1174.

Sorensen, S., Richardson, B., & Peterson, J. (1993). Race/ethnicity patterns in the homicide of children in Los Angeles, 1980 through 1989. *American Journal of Public Health, 83*, 725–727.

Sourander, A., Elonheimo, H., Niemelä, S., Nuutila, A., Helenius, H., Sillanmäki, L., et al. (2006). Childhood predictors of male criminality: A prospective population-based follow-up study from age 8 to late adolescence. *Journal of the American Academy of Child & Adolescent Psychiatry, 45*, 578–586.

South, S. J., & Baumer, E. P. (2000). Deciphering community and race effects on adolescent premarital childbearing. *Social Forces, 78*, 1379–1407.

South, S. J., & Baumer, E. P. (2001). Community effects on the resolution of adolescent premarital pregnancy. *Journal of Family Issues, 22*, 1025–1043.

South, S. J., Baumer, E. P., & Lutz, A. (2003). Interpreting community effects on youth educational attainment. *Youth and Society, 35*, 3–36.

South, S. J., & Haynie, D. L. (2004). Friendship networks of mobile adolescents. *Social Forces, 83*, 315–350.

Spear, L. (2010). *The behavioral neuroscience of adolescence.* New York: Norton.

Spencer, G. A., & Bryant, S. A. (2000). Dating violence: A comparison of rural, suburban, and urban teens. *Journal of Adolescent Health, 27*, 302–305.

Spencer, M. B. (2005). Crafting identities and accessing opportunities post-Brown. *American Psychologist, 60*, 821–830.

Spieker, S., & Bensley, L. (1994). Roles of living arrangements and grandmother social support in adolescent mothering and infant attachment. *Developmental Psychology, 30*, 102–111.

Spielberger, C. (1966). The effects of anxiety on complex learning and academic achievement. In C. Spielberger (Ed.), *Anxiety and behavior.* New York: Academic Press.

Spingarn, R., & DuRant, R. (1996). Male adolescents involved in pregnancy: Associated health risk and problem behaviors. *Pediatrics, 98*, 262–268.

Spotts, E. L., Neiderheiser, J. M., Hetherington, E., & Reiss, D. (2001). The relation between observational measures of social problem solving and familial antisocial behavior: Genetic and environmental influences. *Journal of Research on Adolescence, 11*, 351–374.

Spriggs, A. L., & Halpern, C. T. (2008). Sexual debut timing and depressive symptoms in emerging adulthood. *Journal of Youth and Adolescence, 37*, 1085–1096.

Squeglia, L. M., Jacobus, J., & Tapert, S. F. (2009). The influence of substance use on adolescent brain development. *Clinical EEG and Neuroscience, 40*, 32–39.

Sroufe, L. A. (1979). The coherence of individual development. *American Psychologist, 34*, 834–841.

St. George, I., Williams, S., & Silva, P. (1994). Body size and menarche: The Dunedin study. *Journal of Adolescent Health, 15*, 573–576.

St. Lawrence, J., Brasfield, T., Jefferson, K., Allyene, E., & Shirley, A. (1994). Social support as a factor in African-American adolescents' sexual risk behavior. *Journal of Adolescent Research, 9*, 292–310.

St. Pierre, T., Mark, M., Kaltreider, D., & Aikin, K. (1997). Involving parents of high-risk youth in drug prevention. *Journal of Early Adolescence, 17*, 21–50.

Stack, S. (1994). The effect of geographic mobility on premarital sex. *Journal of Marriage and the Family, 56*, 204–208.

Staff, J., & Mortimer, J. T. (2007). Educational and work strategies from adolescence to early adulthood: Consequences for educational attainment. *Social Forces, 85*, 1169–1194.

Staff, J., Messersmith, E., & Schulenberg, J. (2009). Adolescents and the world of work. In R. Lerner & L. Steinberg (Eds.), *Handbook of adolescent psychology* (3rd ed., Vol. 2, pp. 270–313). New York: Wiley.

Stams, G. J., Brugman, D., Dekovic, M., van Rosmalen, L., van der Laan, P., & Gibbs, J. C. (2006). The moral judgment of juvenile delinquents: A meta-analysis. *Journal of Abnormal Child Psychology, 34*, 697–713.

Stanton, B., Romer, D., Ricardo, I., Black, M., Feigelman, S., & Galbraith, J. (1993). Early initiation of sex and its lack of association with risk behaviors among African-Americans. *Pediatrics, 92*, 13–19.

Stanton-Salazar, R., & Dornbusch, S. (1995). Social capital and the reproduction of inequality: Information networks among Mexican-origin high school students. *Sociology of Education, 68*, 116–135.

Stanton-Salazar, R., & Spina, S. (2005). Adolescent peer networks as a context for social and emotional support. *Youth and Society, 36*, 379–417.

Starr, L. R., & Davila, J. (2009). Clarifying co-rumination: Associations with internalizing symptoms and romantic involvement among adolescent girls. *Journal of Adolescence, 32*, 19–37.

Stattin, H., & Kerr, M. (2000). Parental monitoring: A reinterpretation. *Child Development, 71*, 1072–1085.

Stearns, E. (2004). Interracial friendliness and the social organization of schools. *Youth and Society 35*, 395–419.

Stearns, E., & Glennie, E. J. (2006). When and why dropouts leave high school. *Youth and Society, 38*, 29–57.

Stedman, L. (1998). An assessment of the contemporary debate over U.S. achievement. In

D. Ravitch (Ed.). *The state of student performance in American schools: Brookings papers on education policy, 1*, 53–121. Washington: Brookings Institution.

Steele, C. M. (1997). A threat in the air: How stereotypes shape intellectual identity and performance. *American Psychologist, 52*, 613–619.

Steele, J., & Brown, J. (1995). Adolescent room culture: Studying media in the context of everyday life. *Journal of Youth and Adolescence, 24*, 551–576.

Steffensmeier, D., Schwartz, J., Zhong, H., & Ackerman, J. (2005). An assessment of recent trends in girls' violence using diverse longitudinal sources: Is the gender gap closing? *Criminology, 43*, 355–406.

Stein, J., Newcomb, M., & Bentler, P. (1987). An 8-year study of multiple influences on drug use and drug use consequences. *Journal of Personality and Social Psychology, 53*, 1094–1105.

Stein, J., Newcomb, M., & Bentler, P. (1992). The effect of agency and communion on self-esteem: Gender differences in longitudinal data. *Sex Roles, 26*, 465–484.

Stein, J., & Reiser, L. (1994). A study of White middle-class adolescent boys' responses to "semenarche" (the first ejaculation). *Journal of Youth and Adolescence, 23*, 373–384.

Stein, N. (1995). Sexual harassment in school: The public performance of gendered violence. *Harvard Educational Review, 65*, 145–162.

Steinberg, L. (1986). Latchkey children and susceptibility to peer pressure: An ecological analysis. *Developmental Psychology, 22*, 433–439.

Steinberg, L. (1987). Single parents, stepparents, and the susceptibility of adolescents to antisocial peer pressure. *Child Development, 58*, 269–275.

Steinberg, L. (1990). Autonomy, conflict, and harmony in the family relationship. In S. Feldman & G. Elliott (Eds.), *At the threshold: The developing adolescent* (pp. 255–276). Cambridge, MA: Harvard University Press.

Steinberg, L. (1996). *Beyond the classroom: Why school reform has failed and what parents need to do.* New York: Simon & Schuster.

Steinberg, L. (2000). Youth violence: Do parents and families make a difference? *National Institute of Justice Journal*, April, 30–38.

Steinberg, L. (2001). We know some things: Adolescent–parent relationships in retrospect and prospect. *Journal of Research on Adolescence, 11*, 1–19.

Steinberg, L. (2003). The state of adolescence. In D. Ravitch (Ed.), *Brookings papers on education policy.* Washington, DC: Brookings Institution.

Steinberg, L. (2005a). Cognitive and affective development in adolescence. *Trends in Cognitive Sciences, 9*, 69–74.

Steinberg, L. (2005b). *The 10 basic principles of good parenting.* New York: Simon & Schuster.

Steinberg, L. (2007). Risk-taking in adolescence: New perspectives from brain and behavioral science. *Current Directions in Psychological Science, 16*, 55–59.

Steinberg, L. (2008). A social neuroscience perspective on adolescent risk-taking. *Developmental Review, 28*, 78–106.

Steinberg, L. (2009). Should the science of adolescent brain development inform public policy? *American Psychologist, 64*, 739–750.

Steinberg, L. (2011). *You and your adolescent: A comprehensive guide for ages 10 to 25.* New York: Simon & Schuster.

Steinberg, L., Albert, D., Cauffman, E., Banich, M., Graham, S., & Woolard, J. (2008). Age differences in sensation seeking and impulsivity as indexed by behavior and self-report: Evidence for a dual systems model. *Developmental Psychology, 44*, 1764–1778.

Steinberg, L., & Avenevoli, S. (2000). The role of context in the development of psychopathology: A conceptual framework and some speculative propositions. *Child Development, 71*, 66–74.

Steinberg, L., & Belsky, J. (1996). A sociobiological perspective on psychopathology in adolescence. In D. Cicchetti and S. Toth (Eds.), *Rochester Symposium on Developmental Psychopathology* (Vol. 7, pp. 93–124). Rochester, NY: University of Rochester Press.

Steinberg, L., Blatt-Eisengart, I., & Cauffman, E. (2006). Patterns of competence and adjustment among adolescents from authoritative, authoritarian, indulgent, and neglectful homes: Replication in a sample of serious juvenile offenders. *Journal of Research on Adolescence, 16*, 47–58.

Steinberg, L., & Cauffman, E. (1995). The impact of employment on adolescent development. In R. Vasta (Ed.), *Annals of Child Development* (Vol. 11, pp. 131–166). London: Jessica Kingsley.

Steinberg, L., & Cauffman, E. (1996). Maturity of judgment in adolescence: Psychosocial factors in adolescent decisionmaking. *Law and Human Behavior, 20*, 249–272.

Steinberg, L., Cauffman, E., Woolard, J., Graham, S., & Banich, M. (2009). Are adolescents less mature than adults? Minors' access to abortion, the juvenile death penalty, and the alleged APA "flip-flop." *American Psychologist, 64*, 583–594.

Steinberg, L., Dahl, R., Keating, D., Kupfer, D., Masten, A., & Pine, D. (2006). Psychopathology in adolescence: Integrating affective neuroscience with the study of context. In D. Cicchetti & D. Cohen (Eds.), *Developmental psychopathology: Vol. 2. Developmental neuroscience* (pp. 710–741). New York: Wiley.

Steinberg, L., & Dornbusch, S. (1991). Negative correlates of part-time work in adolescence: Replication and elaboration. *Developmental Psychology, 17*, 304–313.

Steinberg, L., Dornbusch, S., & Brown, B. (1992). Ethnic differences in adolescent achievement: An ecological perspective. *American Psychologist, 47*, 723–729.

Steinberg, L., Elmen, J., & Mounts, N. (1989). Authoritative parenting, psychosocial maturity, and academic success among adolescence. *Child Development, 60*, 1424–1436.

Steinberg, L., Fegley, S., & Dornbusch, S. (1993). Negative impact of part-time work on adolescent adjustment: Evidence from a longitudinal study. *Developmental Psychology, 29*, 171–180.

Steinberg, L., Graham, S., O'Brien, L., Woolard, J., Cauffman, E., & Banich, M. (2009). Age differences in future orientation and delay discounting. *Child Development, 80*, 28–44.

Steinberg, L., Lamborn, S., Darling, N., Mounts, N., & Dornbusch, S. (1994). Over-time changes in adjustment and competence among adolescents from authoritative, authoritarian, indulgent, and neglectful families. *Child Development, 65*, 754–770.

Steinberg, L., Lamborn, S., Dornbusch, S., & Darling, N. (1992). Impact of parenting practices on adolescent achievement: Authoritative parenting, school involvement, and encouragement to succeed. *Child Development, 63*, 1266–1281.

Steinberg, L., & Monahan, K. (2007). Age differences in resistance to peer influence. *Developmental Psychology, 43*, 1531–1543.

Steinberg, L., & Morris, A. (2001). Adolescent development. *Annual Review of Psychology, 52*, 83–110.

Steinberg, L., & Silk, J. (2002). Parenting adolescents. In M. Bornstein (Ed.), *Handbook of parenting: Vol. 1. Children and parenting* (2nd ed., pp. 103–133). Mahwah, NJ: Erlbaum.

Steinberg, L., & Silverberg, S. (1986). The vicissitudes of autonomy in early adolescence. *Child Development, 57*, 841–851.

Steinberg, L., & Steinberg, W. (1994). *Crossing paths: How your child's adolescence triggers your own crisis.* New York: Simon & Schuster.

Steinberg, S. J., Davila, J., & Fincham, F. (2006). Adolescent marital expectations and romantic experiences: Associations with perceptions about parental conflict and adolescent attachment security. *Journal of Youth and Adolescence, 35*, 333–348.

Steinman, K. J., & Zimmerman, M. A. (2004). Religious activity and risk behavior among African American adolescents: Concurrent and developmental effects. *American Journal of Community Psychology, 33*, 151–161.

Stephens, L. (1996). Will Johnny see Daddy this week? An empirical test of three theoretical perspectives of postdivorce contact. *Journal of Family Issues, 17*, 466–494.

Stern, D., Finkelstein, N., Stone, J., Latting, J., & Dornsife, C. (1994). *Research on school-to-work transition programs in the United States.* Berkeley, Calif.: National Center for Research in Vocational Education.

Sternberg, R. (1988). *The triarchic mind*. New York: Viking Penguin.

Sternberg, R., & Nigro, G. (1980). Developmental patterns in the solution of verbal analogies. *Child Development, 51*, 27–38.

Stevens, E. A., & Prinstein, M. J. (2005). Peer contagion of depressogenic attributional styles among adolescents: A longitudinal study. *Journal of Abnormal Child Psychology, 33*, 25–38.

Stevens, J. (1988). Social support, locus of control, and parenting in three low-income groups of mothers: Black teenagers, Black adults, and White adults. *Child Development, 59*, 635–642.

Stevenson, B., & Wolfers, J. (2007). Marriage and divorce: Changes and their driving forces. *Journal of Economic Perspectives, 21*, 27–52.

Stevenson, D., Schiller, K., & Schneider, B. (1994). Sequences of opportunities for learning. *Sociology of Education, 67*, 184–198.

Stevenson, H., & Stigler, J. (1992). *The learning gap: Why our schools are failing and what we can learn from Japanese and Chinese education*. New York: Simon & Schuster.

Stevenson, H., Jr. (1995). Relationship of adolescent perceptions of racial socialization to racial identity. *Journal of Black Psychology, 21*, 49–70.

Stevenson, H., Jr. (1998). Raising safe villages: Cultural-ecological factors that influence the emotional adjustment of adolescents. *Journal of Black Psychology, 24*, 44–59.

Stevenson, H., Reed, J., Bodison, P., & Bishop, A. (1997). Racism stress management: Racial social beliefs and the experience of depression and anger in African American youth. *Youth and Society, 29*, 197–222.

Stewart, E. B., Stewart, E. A., & Simons, R. L. (2007). The effect of neighborhood context on the college aspirations of African American adolescents. *American Education Research Journal, 44*, 896–919.

Stewart, S. D. (2003). Nonresident parenting and adolescent adjustment: The quality of nonresident father–child interaction. *Journal of Family Issues, 24*, 217–244.

Stice, E., & Barrera, M., Jr. (1995). A longitudinal examination of the reciprocal relations between perceived parenting and adolescents' substance use and externalizing behaviors. *Developmental Psychology, 31*, 322–334.

Stice, E., & Bearman, S. (2001). Body–image and eating disturbances prospectively predict increases in depressive symptoms in adolescent girls: A growth curve analysis. *Developmental Psychology, 37*, 597–607.

Stice, E., Burton, E., & Shaw, H. (2004). Prospective relations between bulimic pathology, depression, and substance abuse: Unpacking comorbidity in adolescent girls. *Journal of Consulting and Clinical Psychology, 72*, 62–71.

Stice, E., Cameron, R., Killen, J., Hayward, C., & Taylor, C. (1999). Naturalistic weight-reduction efforts prospectively predict growth in relative weight and onset of obesity among female adolescents. *Journal of Consulting and Clinical Psychology, 67*, 967–974.

Stice, E., & Gonzales, N. (1998). Adolescent temperament moderates the relation of parenting to antisocial behavior and substance use. *Journal of Adolescent Research, 13*, 5–31.

Stice, E., Hayward, C., Cameron, R. P., Killen, J., & Taylor, C. (2000). Body–image and eating disturbances predict onset of depression among female adolescents: A longitudinal study. *Journal of Abnormal Psychology, 109*, 438–444.

Stice, E., Presnell, K., & Bearman, S. (2001). Relation of early menarche to depression, eating disorders, substance abuse, and comorbid psychopathology among adolescent girls. *Developmental Psychology, 37*, 608–619.

Stice, E., Presnell, K., Shaw, H., & Rohde, P. (2005). Psychological and behavioral risk factors for obesity onset in adolescent girls: A prospective study. *Journal of Consulting and Clinical Psychology, 73*, 195–202.

Stice, E., & Shaw, H. (2003). Prospective relations of body image, eating, and affective disturbances to smoking onset in adolescent girls: How Virginia slims. *Journal of Consulting and Clinical Psychology, 71*, 129–135.

Stice, E., Shaw, H., & Marti, C. N. (2006). A meta-analytic review of obesity prevention programs for children and adolescents: The skinny on interventions that work. *Psychological Bulletin, 132*, 667–691.

Stice, E., & Whitenton, K. (2002). Risk factors for body dissatisfaction in adolescent girls: A longitudinal investigation. *Developmental Psychology, 38*, 669–678.

Stipek, D., & Gralinski, J. (1996). Children's beliefs about intelligence and school performance. *Journal of Educational Psychology, 88*, 397–407.

Stock, J., Bell, M., Boyer, D., & Connell, F. (1997). Adolescent pregnancy and sexual risk-taking among sexually abused girls. *Family Planning Perspectives, 29*, 200–203, 227.

Stocker, C. M., Burwell, R. A., & Briggs, M. L. (2002). Sibling conflict in middle childhood predicts children's adjustment in early adolescence. *Journal of Family Psychology, 16*, 50–57.

Stocker, C. M., Lanthier, R. P., & Furman, W. (1997). Sibling relationships in early adulthood. *Journal of Family Psychology, 11*, 210–221.

Stoller, C., Offer, D., Howard, K., & Koenig, L. (1996). Psychiatrists' concept of adolescent self-image. *Journal of Youth and Adolescence, 25*, 273–284.

Stoolmiller, M., Kim, H. K., & Capaldi, D. M. (2005). The course of depressive symptoms in men from early adolescence to young adulthood: Identifying latent trajectories and early predictors. *Journal of Abnormal Psychology, 114*, 331–345.

Storvoll, E. E., & Wichström, L. (2002). Do the risk factors associated with conduct problems vary according to gender? *Journal of Adolescence, 25*, 183–202.

Stouthamer-Loeber, M., Wei, E., & Loeber, R. (2004). Desistance from persistent serious delinquency in the transition to adulthood. *Development and Psychopathology, 16*, 897–918.

Strasburger, V., & Donnerstein, E. (1999). Children, adolescents, and the media: Issues and solutions. *Pediatrics, 103*, 129–139.

Straub, D. M., Hills, N. K., Thompson, P. J., & Moscicki, A. (2003). Effects of pro- and anti-tobacco advertising on nonsmoking adolescents' intentions to smoke. *Journal of Adolescent Health, 32*, 36–43.

Straus, M., & Yodanis, C. (1996). Corporal punishment in adolescence and physical assaults on spouses in later life: What accounts for the link? *Journal of Marriage and the Family, 58*, 825–841.

Strong American Schools. (2008). *Diploma to nowhere*. Washington, DC: Author.

Stroud, L., Foster, E., Papandonatos, G., Handwerger, K., Granger, D., Kivlighan, K., et al. (2009). Stress response and the adolescent transition: Performance versus peer rejection stressors. *Development and Psychopathology, 21*, 47–68.

Strough, J., & Berg, C. (2000). Goals as a mediator of gender differences in high-affiliation dyadic conversations. *Developmental Psychology, 36*, 117–125.

Strouse, J., Goodwin, M., & Roscoe, B. (1994). Correlates of attitudes toward sexual harassment among early adolescents. *Sex Roles, 31*, 559–577.

Stuart, E. A., & Green, K. M. (2008). Using full matching to estimate causal effects in non-experimental studies: Examining the relationship between adolescent marijuana use and adult outcomes. *Developmental Psychology, 44*, 395–406.

Studer, M., & Thornton, A. (1987). Adolescent religiosity and contraceptive usage. *Journal of Marriage and the Family, 49*, 117–128.

Stukas, A., Jr., Clary, E., & Snyder, M. (1999). Service learning: Who benefits and why. *Social Policy Report of the Society for Research in Child Development, 13*.

Sturmhöfel, S., & Swartzwelder, H. (2004). Alcohol's effects on the adolescent brain: What can be learned from animal models? *Alcohol Research and Health, 28*, 213–221.

Subrahmanyam, K., Smahel, D., & Greenfield, P. (2006). Connecting developmental constructions to the Internet: Identity presentation and sexual exploration in online teen chat rooms. *Developmental Psychology, 42*, 395–406.

Sue, S., & Okazaki, S. (1990). Asian-American educational achievements: A phenomenon in search of an explanation. *American Psychologist, 45,* 913–920.

Sui-Chu, E., & Willms, J. (1996). Effects of parental involvement on eighth-grade achievement. *Sociology of Education, 69,* 126–141.

Sullivan, H. S. (1953a). *The interpersonal theory of psychiatry.* New York: Norton.

Sullivan, H. S. (1953b). *Conceptions of modern psychiatry.* New York: Norton.

Sullivan, M. (1989). *Getting paid: Youth crime and work in the inner city.* New York: Cornell University Press.

Sullivan, T. N., Farrell, A. D., & Kliewer, W. (2006). Peer victimization in early adolescence: Association between physical and relational victimization and drug use, aggression, and delinquent behaviors among urban middle school students. *Development and Psychopathology, 18,* 119–137.

Summers, P., Forehand, R., Armistead, L., & Tannenbaum, L. (1998). Parental divorce during early adolescence in Caucasian families: The role of family process variables in predicting the long-term consequences for early adult psychosocial adjustment. *Journal of Consulting and Clinical Psychology, 66,* 327–336.

Sun, Y. (2001). Family environment and adolescents' well-being before and after parents' marital disruption: A longitudinal analysis. *Journal of Marriage and the Family, 63,* 697–713.

Sun, Y. (2003). The well-being of adolescents in households with no biological parents. *Journal of Marriage and Family 65,* 894.

Sun, Y., & Li, Y. (2002). Children's well-being during the parents' marital disruption process: A pooled time-series analysis. *Journal of Marriage and the Family, 64,* 472–488.

Super, D. (1967). *The psychology of careers.* New York: Harper & Row.

Supple, A. J., Ghazarian, S. R., Frabutt, J. M., Plunkett, S. W., & Sands, T. (2006). Contextual influences on Latino adolescent ethnic identity and academic outcomes. *Child Development, 77,* 1427–1433.

Supple, A. J., Peterson, G. W., & Bush, K. R. (2004). Assessing the validity of parenting measures in a sample of Chinese adolescents. *Journal of Family Psychology, 18,* 539–544.

Susman, E. (1997). Modeling developmental complexity in adolescence: Hormones and behavior in context. *Journal of Research on Adolescence, 7,* 283–306.

Susman, E., & Dorn, L. (2009). Puberty: Its role in development. In R. Lerner & L. Steinberg (Eds.), *Handbook of adolescent psychology* (3rd ed., Vol. 1, pp. 116–151). New York: Wiley.

Susman, E., Dorn, L., Inoff-Germain, G., Nottelmann, E., & Chrousos, G. (1997). Cortisol reactivity, distress behavior, and behavioral and psychological problems in young adolescents: A longitudinal perspective. *Journal of Research on Adolescence, 7,* 81–105.

Susman, E. J., Dockray, S., Schiefelbein, V. L., Herwehe, S., Heaton, J. A., & Dorn, L. D. (2007). Morningness/eveningness, morning-to-afternoon cortisol ratio, and antisocial behavior problems during puberty. *Developmental Psychology, 43,* 811–822.

Sussman, S., Dent, C., McAdams, L., Stacy, A., Burton, D., & Flay, B. (1994). Group self-identification and adolescent cigarette smoking: A 1-year prospective study. *Journal of Abnormal Psychology, 103,* 576–580.

Swahn, M. H., Bossarte, R. M., & Sullivent, E. E. I., II. (2008). Age of alcohol use initiation, suicidal behavior, and peer and dating violence victimization and perpetration among high-risk, seventh-grade adolescents. *Pediatrics, 121,* 297–305.

Swan, S., Juul, A., Sørensen, T., Dunkel, L., Himes, J., Teilmann, G., et al. (2008). Examination of US puberty-timing data from 1940 to 1994 for secular trends: Panel findings. *Pediatrics, 121,* S172–S191.

Swarr, A., & Richards, M. (1996). Longitudinal effects of adolescent girls' pubertal development, perceptions of pubertal timing, and parental relations on eating problems. *Developmental Psychology, 32,* 636–646.

Sweeten, G., Bushway, S. D., & Paternoster, R. (2009). Does dropping out of school mean dropping into delinquency? *Criminology: An Interdisciplinary Journal, 47,* 47–91.

Swenson, L. P., & Rose, A. J. (2003). Friends as reporters of children's and adolescents' depressive symptoms. *Journal of Abnormal Child Psychology, 31,* 619–631.

Syed, M., & Azmitia, M. (2008). A narrative approach to ethnic identity in emerging adulthood: Bringing life to the identity status model. *Developmental Psychology, 44,* 1012–1027.

Szeszulski, P., Martinez, A., & Reyes, B. (1994, February). *Patterns and predictors of self-satisfaction among culturally diverse high school students.* Paper presented at the biennial meetings of the Society for Research on Adolescence, San Diego.

Taga, K. A., Markey, C. N., & Friedman, H. S. (2006). A longitudinal investigation of associations between boys' pubertal timing and adult behavioral health and well-being. *Journal of Youth and Adolescence, 35,* 401–411.

Tang, C. S., Yeung, D. Y., & Lee, A. M. (2003). Psychosocial correlates of emotional responses to menarche among Chinese adolescent girls. *Journal of Adolescent Health, 33,* 193–201.

Tang, C. S., Yeung, D. Y. L., & Lee, A. M. (2004). A comparison of premenarcheal expectations and postmenarcheal experiences in Chinese early adolescents. *Journal of Early Adolescence, 24,* 180–195.

Tanner, D. (1972). *Secondary education.* New York: Macmillan.

Tanner, J. (1972). Sequence, tempo, and individual variation in growth and development of boys and girls aged twelve to sixteen. In J. Kagan & R. Coles (Eds.), *Twelve to sixteen: Early adolescence.* New York: Norton.

Tapert, S. F., Baratta, M. V., Abrantes A. M., & Brown, S. A. (2002). Attention dysfunction predicts involvement in community youths. *Journal of the American Academy of Child and Adolescent Psychiatry, 41,* 680–686.

Taradash, A., Connolly, J., Pepler, D., Craig, W., & Costa, M. (2001). The interpersonal context of romantic autonomy in adolescence. *Journal of Adolescence, 24,* 365–377.

Tasker, F., & Richards, M. (1994). Adolescents' attitudes toward marriage and marital prospects after parental divorce: A review. *Journal of Adolescent Research, 9,* 340–362.

Taylor, D., Jenni, O., Acebo, C., & Carskadon, M. (2005). Sleep tendency during extended wakefulness: Insights into adolescent sleep regulation and behavior. *Journal of Sleep Research, 14,* 239–244.

Taylor, R. (1996). Adolescents' perceptions of kinship support and family management practices: Association with adolescent adjustment in African American families. *Developmental Psychology, 32,* 697.

Taylor, R., & Roberts, D. (1995). Kinship support and maternal and adolescent well-being in economically disadvantaged African-American families. *Child Development, 66,* 1585–1597.

Taylor, R., Casten, R., Flickinger, S., Roberts, D., & Fulmore, C. (1994). Explaining the school performance of African-American adolescents. *Journal of Research on Adolescence, 4,* 21–44.

Taylor, R., Rodriguez, A. U., Seaton, E. K., & Dominguez, A. (2004). Association of financial resources with parenting and adolescent adjustment in African American families. *Journal of Adolescent Research, 19,* 267–283.

Taylor, T. J., Peterson, D., Esbensen, F., & Freng, A. (2007). Gang membership as a risk factor for adolescent violent victimization. *Journal of Research in Crime and Delinquency, 44,* 351–380.

Teachman, J. (1996). Intellectual skill and academic performance: Do families bias the relationship? *Sociology of Education, 69,* 35–48.

Teachman, J. (1997). Gender of siblings, cognitive achievement, and academic performance: Familial and nonfamilial influences on children. *Journal of Marriage and the Family, 59,* 363–374.

Teachman, J., & Paasch, K. (1998). The family and educational aspirations. *Journal of Marriage and the Family, 60,* 704–714.

Teachman, J., Paasch, K., & Carver, K. (1996). Social capital and dropping out of school early. *Journal of Marriage and the Family, 58,* 773–783.

Teachman, J., Paasch, K., & Carver, K. (1997). Social capital and the generation of human capital. *Social Forces, 75,* 1343–1359.

Teitler, J. O., & Weiss, C. C. (2000). Effects of neighborhood and school environments on transitions to first sexual intercourse. *Sociology of Education, 73,* 112–132.

Tejada-Vera, B., & Sutton, P. D. (2009). Births, marriages, divorces, and deaths: Provisional data for August 2008. *National Vital Statistics Reports, 57*(15). Hyattsville, MD: National Center for Health Statistics.

Telzer, E. H., & Fuligni, A. (2009). A longitudinal daily diary study of family assistance and academic achievement among adolescents from Mexican, Chinese, and European backgrounds. *Journal of Youth and Adolescence, 38,* 560–571.

Teti, D., & Lamb, M. (1989). Socioeconomic and marital outcomes of adolescent marriage, adolescent childbirth, and their co-occurrence. *Journal of Marriage and the Family, 51,* 203–212.

Tevendale, H., DuBois, D., Lopez, C., & Prindiville, S. (1997). Self-esteem stability and early adolescent adjustment: An exploratory study. *Journal of Early Adolescence, 17,* 216–237.

Theokas, C. (2009). Youth sport participation—A view of the issues: Introduction to the special section. *Developmental Psychology, 45,* 303–306.

Theokas, C., & Lerner, R. (2006). Promoting positive development in adolescence: The role of ecological assets in families, schools, and neighborhoods. *Applied Developmental Science, 10,* 61–74.

Thomas, J., & Daubman, K. A. (2001). The relationship between friendship quality and self-esteem in adolescent girls and boys. *Sex Roles, 45,* 53–65.

Thomas, L. A., De Bellis, M. D., Graham, R., & LaBar, K. S. (2007). Development of emotional facial recognition in late childhood and adolescence. *Developmental Science, 10,* 547–558.

Thomas, M., & Johnson, M. (2008). New advances in understanding sensitive periods in brain development. *Current Directions in Psychological Science, 17,* 1–5.

Thompson, R., & Zuroff, D. C. (1999). Dependency, self-criticism, and mothers' responses to adolescent sons' autonomy and competence. *Journal of Youth and Adolescence, 28,* 365–384.

Thomson, E., Hanson, T., & McLanahan, S. (1994). Family structure and child well-being: Economic resources vs. parental behaviors. *Social Forces, 73,* 221–242.

Thornberry, T., Freeman-Gallant, A., Lizotte, A. J., Krohn, M. D., & Smith, C. (2003). Linked lives: The intergenerational transmission of antisocial behavior. *Journal of Abnormal Child Psychology, 31,* 171–184.

Thornberry, T., Smith, C., & Howard, G. (1997). Risk factors for teenage fatherhood. *Journal of Marriage and the Family, 59,* 505–522.

Thornton, A., Orbuch, T. L., & Axinn, W. G. (1995). Parent–child relationships during the transition to adulthood. *Journal of Family Issues, 16,* 538–564.

Thurber, C. (1995). The experience and expression of homesickness in preadolescent and adolescent boys. *Child Development, 66,* 1162–1178.

Tilton-Weaver, L. C., & Galambos, N. L. (2003). Adolescents' characteristics and parents' beliefs as predictors of parents' peer management behaviors. *Journal of Research on Adolescence, 13,* 269–300.

Timmerman, G. (2002). A comparison between unwanted sexual behavior by teachers and by peers in secondary schools. *Journal of Youth and Adolescence, 31,* 397–404.

Tobian, A., Serwadda, D., Quinn, T., Kigozi, G., Gravitt, P., Laeyendecker, O., et al. (2009). Male circumcision for the prevention of HSV-2 and HPV infections and syphilis. *New England Journal of Medicine, 360,* 1298–1309.

Toch, T. (1993). Violence in schools. *U.S. News & World Report, 115,* 31–37.

Tolan, P., & Gorman-Smith, D. (2002). What violence prevention research can tell us about developmental psychopathology. *Development and Psychopathology, 14,* 713–729.

Tolan, P., Gorman-Smith, D., & Henry, D. (2003). The developmental ecology of urban males' youth violence. *Developmental Psychology, 39,* 274–291.

Tolan, P., Gorman-Smith, D., Henry, D., Chung, K., & Hunt, M. (2002). The relation of patterns of coping inner-city youth to psychopathology symptoms. *Journal of Research on Adolescence, 12,* 423–449.

Tolman, D. (1993, March). *"When my body says yes": Adolescent girls' experiences of sexual desire.* Paper presented at the biennial meetings of the Society for Research in Child Development, New Orleans.

Tolson, J., Halliday-Scher, K., & Mack, V. (1994, February). *Similarity and friendship quality in African-American adolescents.* Paper presented at the biennial meetings of the Society for Research on Adolescence, San Diego.

Tomal, A. (2001). The effect of religious membership on teen abortion rates. *Journal of Youth and Adolescence, 30,* 103–116.

Topolski, T. D., Patrick, D. L., Edwards, T. C., Huebner, C. E., Connell, F. A., & Mount, K. K. (2001). Quality of life and health-risk behaviors among adolescents. *Journal of Adolescent Health, 29,* 426–435.

Torney-Purta, J. (1990). Youth in relation to social institutions. In S. Feldman & G. Elliott (Eds.), *At the threshold: The developing adolescent,* pp. 457–478. Cambridge, MA: Harvard University Press.

Tough, P. (2008). *Whatever it takes: Geoffrey Canada's quest to change Harlem and America.* New York: Houghton Mifflin Harcourt.

Tram, J. M., & Cole, D. A. (2000). Self-perceived competence and the relation between life events and depressive symptoms in adolescence: Mediator or moderator? *Journal of Abnormal Psychology, 109,* 753–760.

Treaster, J. (1994, February 1). Survey finds marijuana use is up in high schools. *The New York Times,* pp. A1ff.

Tremblay, R., Mâsse, L., Vitaro, F., & Dobkin, P. (1995). The impact of friends' deviant behavior on early onset of delinquency: Longitudinal data from 6 to 13 years of age. *Development and Psychopathology, 7,* 649–667.

Tremblay, R., Pagani-Kurtz, L., Mâsse, L., Vitaro, F., & Pihl, R. (1995). A bimodal preventive intervention for disruptive kindergarten boys: Its impact through mid-adolescence. *Journal of Consulting and Clinical Psychology, 63,* 560–568.

Trent, K., & Crowder, K. (1997). Adolescent birth intentions, social disadvantage and behavioral outcomes. *Journal of Marriage and the Family, 59,* 523–535.

Trent, K., & Harlan, S. (1994). Teenage mothers in nuclear and extended households: Differences by marital status and race/ethnicity. *Journal of Family Issues, 15,* 309–337.

Trickett, P., McBride-Chang, C., & Putnam, F. (1994). The classroom performance and behavior of sexually abused females. *Development and Psychopathology, 6,* 183–194.

Trickett, P., Noll, J. G., Reiffman, A., & Putnam, F. W. (2001). Variants of intrafamilial sexual abuse experience: Implications for short- and long-term development. *Development and Psychopathology, 13,* 1001–1019.

Truong, K. D., & Sturm, R. (2009). Alcohol environments and disparities in exposure associated with adolescent drinking in California. *American Journal of Public Health, 99,* 264–270.

Trusty, J., Plata, M., & Salazar, C. F. (2003). Modeling Mexican Americans' educational expectations: Longitudinal effects of variables across adolescence. *Journal of Adolescent Research, 18,* 131–153.

Trzesniewski, K., & Donnellan, M. (2009). Reevaluating the evidence for increasingly positive self-views among high school students: More evidence for consistency across generations (1976–2006). *Psychological Science, 20,* 920–922

Trzesniewski, K., Donnellan, M., Moffitt, T., Robins, R., Poulton, R., & Caspi, A. (2006). Low self-esteem during adolescence predicts poor health, criminal behavior, and limited economic prospects during adulthood. *Developmental Psychology, 42,* 381–390.

Trzesniewski, K., Donnellan, M., & Robins, R. (2003). Stability of self-esteem across the life span. *Journal of Personality and Social Psychology, 84,* 205–220.

Tschann, J., & Adler, N. (1997). Sexual self-acceptance, communication with partner, and contraceptive use among adolescent females: A longitudinal study. *Journal of Research on Adolescence, 7,* 413–430.

Tschann, J., Flores, E., VanOss Marin, B., Pasch, L. A., Baisch, E., & Wibbelsman, C. J. (2002). Interparental conflict and risk behaviors among Mexican American adolescents: A cognitive-emotional model. *Journal of Abnormal Psychology, 30,* 373–385.

Tschann, J., Pasch, L., Flores, E., Marin, B., Baisch, E., & Wibbelsman, C. (2009). Nonviolent aspects of interparental conflict and dating violence among adolescents. *Journal of Family Issues, 30,* 295–319.

Tseng, V. (2004). Family interdependence and academic adjustment in college: Youth from immigrant and U.S.-born families. *Child Development, 75,* 966–983.

Tseng, V., & Fuligni, A. (2000). Parent–adolescent language use and relationship among immigrant families with East Asian, Filipino and Latin American backgrounds. *Journal of Marriage and the Family, 62,* 465–476.

Tubman, J. G., Montgomery, M. J., Gil, A. G., & Wagner, E. F. (2004). Abuse experiences in a community sample of young adults: Relations with psychiatric disorders, sexual risk behaviors, and sexually transmitted diseases. *American Journal of Community Psychology, 34,* 147–162.

Tucker, C., Barber, B., & Eccles, J. (1997). Advice about life plans and personal problems in late adolescent sibling relationships. *Journal of Youth and Adolescence, 26,* 63–76.

Tucker, C., McHale, S., & Crouter, A. (2001). Conditions of sibling support in adolescence. *Journal of Family Psychology, 15,* 254–271.

Tucker, C., McHale, S., & Crouter, A. (2003a). Dimensions of mothers' and fathers' differential treatment of siblings: Links with adolescents' sex-typed personal qualities. *Family Relations: Interdisciplinary Journal of Applied Family Studies, 52,* 82–89.

Tucker, C., McHale, S., & Crouter, A. (2003b). Conflict resolution links with adolescents' family relationships and individual well-being. *Journal of Family Influence, 24,* 715–736.

Tucker, J. S., Ellickson, P. L., Collins, R. L., & Klein, D. J. (2006). Are drug experimenters better adjusted than abstainers and users?: A longitudinal study of adolescent marijuana use. *Journal of Adolescent Health, 39,* 488–494.

Turkheimer, E., & Waldron, M. (2000). Nonshared environment: A theoretical, methodological, and quantitative review. *Psychological Bulletin, 126,* 78–108.

Turner, R., Sorenson, A. M., & Turner, J. (2000). Social contingencies in mental health: A seven-year follow-up study of teenage mothers. *Journal of Marriage and the Family, 62,* 777–791.

Tuval-Mashiach, R., & Shulman, S. (2006). Resolution of disagreements between romantic partners, among adolescents, and young adults: Qualitative analysis of interaction discourses. *Journal of Research on Adolescence, 16,* 561–588.

Twenge, J. (2000). The age of anxiety? The birth cohort change in anxiety and neuroticism, 1952–1993. *Journal of Personality and Social Psychology, 79,* 1007–1021.

Twenge, J., & Crocker, J. (2002). Race and self-esteem: Meta-analyses comparing Whites, Blacks, Hispanics, Asians, and American Indians and comment on Gray-Little and Hafdahl. *Psychological Bulletin, 128,* 371–408.

Twenge, J., & Nolen-Hoeksema, S. (2002). Age, gender, race, socioeconomic status, and birth cohort difference on the children's depression inventory: A meta-analysis. *Journal of Abnormal Psychology, 111,* 578–588.

Tyler, K. A., Hoyt, D. R., Whitbeck, L. B., & Cauce, A. (2001). The impact of childhood sexual abuse on later sexual victimization among runaway youth. *Journal of Research on Adolescence, 11,* 151–176.

Tynes, B. M. (2007). Role taking in online "classrooms": What adolescents are learning about race and ethnicity. *Developmental Psychology, 43,* 1312–1320.

Tyrka, A. R., Graber, J. A., & Brooks-Gunn, J. (2000). The development of disordered eating: Correlate and predictors of eating problems in the context of adolescence. In A. J. Sameroff, M. Lewis, & S. M. Miller (Eds.), *Handbook of developmental psychopathology* (2nd ed., pp. 607–624). New York: Kluwer Academic/Plenum.

Tyson, K., Darity, W., & Castellino, D. R. (2005). It's not "a Black thing." Understanding the burden of acting White and other dilemmas of high achievement. *American Sociological Review, 70,* 582–605.

U.S. Census Bureau. (2000). *Projections of the total resident population by 5-year age groups and sex with special age categories: Middle series, 1999 to 2100.* Washington, DC: Author.

U.S. Census Bureau. (2005a). *Current population survey.* Washington, DC: Author.

U.S. Census Bureau. (2005b). *Statistical abstract of the United States.* Washington, DC: Author.

U.S. Census Bureau. (2006). *Current population survey.* Washington, DC: Author.

U.S. Census Bureau. (2009a). *Educational attainment in the United States: 2007.* Washington, DC: Author.

U.S. Census Bureau. (2009b). *Statistical abstract of the United States.* Washington, DC: Author.

U.S. Census Bureau. (2010). *Statistical abstract of the United States.* Washington, DC: Author.

U.S. Department of Commerce, Bureau of the Census. (1940). *Characteristics of the population.* Washington, DC: U.S. Government Printing Office.

U.S. Department of Education. (2006). *No Child Left Behind.* Available at www.ed.gov.

U.S. Department of Education. (2009). Creating common standards, turning around schools. Retrieved from http://www.ed.gov/index .jhtml

Udry, J. (1987). Hormonal and social determinants of adolescent sexual initiation. In J. Bancroft (Ed.), *Adolescence and puberty.* New York: Oxford University Press.

Udry, J., Billy, J., Morris, N., Gruff, T., & Raj, M. (1985). Serum androgenic hormones motivate sexual behavior in boys. *Fertility and Sterility, 43,* 90–94.

Uhlenberg, P., & Eggebeen, D. (1986). The declining well-being of American adolescents. *Public Interest, 82,* 25–38.

Umaña-Taylor, A. J. (2004). Ethnic identity and self-esteem: Examining the role of social context. *Journal of Adolescence, 27,* 139–146.

Umaña-Taylor, A. J., Alfaro, E. C., Bamaca, M. Y., & Guimond, A. B. (2009). The central role of familial ethnic socialization in Latino adolescents' cultural orientation. *Journal of Marriage and the Family, 71,* 46–90.

Umaña-Taylor, A. J., & Bámaca-Gómez, M. Y. (2003). Generational differences in resistance to peer pressure among Mexican-origin adolescents. *Youth and Society, 35,* 183–203.

Umaña-Taylor, A. J., Bhanot, R., & Shin, N. (2006). Ethnic identity formation during adolescence: The critical role of families. *Journal of Family Issues, 27,* 390–414.

Umaña-Taylor, A. J., Gonzales-Backen, M. A., & Guimond, A. B. (2009). Latino adolescents' ethnic identity: Is there a developmental progression and does growth in ethnic identity predict growth in self-esteem? *Child Development, 80,* 391–405.

Umaña-Taylor, A. J., & Updegraff, K. A. (2007). Latino adolescents' mental health: Exploring the interrelations among discrimination, ethnic identity, cultural orientation, self-esteem, and depressive symptoms. *Journal of Adolescence, 30,* 549–567.

Underwood, M., Kupersmidt, J., & Coie, J. (1996). Childhood peer sociometric status and aggression as predictors of adolescent childbearing. *Journal of Research on Adolescence, 6,* 201–223.

Unger, J., Kipke, M., Simon, T., Montgomery, S., & Johnson, C. (1997). Homeless youths and young adults in Los Angeles: Prevalence of mental health problems and the relationship between mental health and substance abuse disorders. *American Journal of Community Psychology, 25,* 371–394.

Unger J., Molina G., & Teran, L. (2002). Perceived consequences of teenage childbearing among adolescent girls in an urban sample. *Journal of Adolescent Health, 26,* 205–212.

Unger, J., & Rohrbach, L. (2002). Why do adolescents overestimate their peers' smoking prevalence? Correlates of prevalence estimates among California 8th-grade students. *Journal of Youth and Adolescence, 31,* 147–153.

UNICEF (2001, July). *A league table of teenage births in rich nations.* Innocenti Report Card No. 3. UNICEF Innocenti Research Centre, Florence.

Upchurch, D., Aneshensel, C. S., Mudgal, J., & McNeely, C. (2001). Sociocultural contexts of time to first sex among Hispanic adolescents. *Journal of Marriage and the Family, 63,* 1158–1169.

Upchurch, D., Aneshensel, C., Sucoff, C., & Levy-Storms, L. (1999). Neighborhood and family contexts of adolescent sexual activity. *Journal of Marriage and the Family, 61,* 920–933.

Upchurch, D., Levy-Storms, L., Sucoff, C., & Aneshensel, C. (1998). Gender and ethnic differences in the timing of first sexual intercourse. *Family Planning Perspectives, 30,* 121–127.

Upchurch, D., & McCarthy, J. (1990). The timing of a first birth and high school completion. *American Sociological Review, 55,* 224–234.

Updegraff, K., Helms, H., McHale, S., Crouter, A., Thayer, S., & Sales, L. (2004). Who's the boss? Patterns of perceived control in adolescents' friendships. *Journal of Youth and Adolescence, 33,* 403–420.

Updegraff, K., Madden-Derdich, D., Estrada, A., Sales, L., & Leonard, S. (2002). Young adolescents' experiences with parents and friends: Exploring the connections. *Family Relations, 51,* 72–80.

Updegraff, K., McHale, S., & Crouter, A. (2000). Adolescents' sex-typed friendship experiences: Does having a sister versus a brother matter? *Child Development, 71,* 1597–1610.

Updegraff, K., McHale, S., Crouter, A., & Kupanoff, K. (2001). Parents' involvement in adolescents' peer relationships: A comparison of mothers' and fathers' roles. *Journal of Marriage and the Family, 63,* 655–668.

Updegraff, K., McHale, S., Whiteman, S., Thayer, S., & Crouter, A. (2006). The nature and correlates of Mexican-American adolescents' time with parents and peers. *Child Development, 77,* 1470–1486.

Urberg, K., Değirmencioğlu, S., & Pilgrim, C. (1997). Close friend and group influence on adolescent cigarette smoking and alcohol use. *Developmental Psychology, 33,* 834–844.

Urberg, K., Değirmencioğlu, S., Tolson, J., & Halliday-Scher, K. (1995). The structure of adolescent peer networks. *Developmental Psychology, 31,* 540–547.

Urdan, T. (2004). Predictors of academic self-handicapping and achievement: Examining achievement goals, classroom goal struc-

tures, and culture. *Journal of Educational Psychology, 96,* 251–264.

Usher, E. L. (2009). Sources of middle school students' self-efficacy in mathematics: A qualitative investigation. *American Educational Research Journal, 46,* 275–314.

Usher-Seriki, K., Bynum, M. S., & Callands, T. A. (2008). Mother-daughter communication about sex and sexual intercourse among middle- to upper-class African American girls. *Journal of Family Issues, 29,* 901–917.

Usmiani, S., & Daniluk, J. (1997). Mothers and their adolescent daughters: Relationship between self-esteem, gender role identity, and body image. *Journal of Youth and Adolescence, 26,* 45–62.

Valkenburg, P. M., & Peter, J. (2007). Preadolescents' and adolescents' online communication and their closeness to friends. *Developmental Psychology, 43,* 267–277.

Valkenburg, P. M., & Peter, J. (2009). Social consequences of the Internet for adolescents: A decade of research. *Current Directions in Psychological Science, 18,* 1–5.

Valois, R., Oeltmann, J., Waller, J., & Hussey, J. (1999). Relationship between number of sexual intercourse partners and selected health risk behaviors among public high school adolescents. *Journal of Adolescent Health, 25,* 328–335.

Van den Bulck, J. (2004). Television viewing, computer game playing, and Internet use and self-reported time to bed and time out of bed in secondary-school children. *Sleep, 27,* 101–104.

van den Eijnden, R., Meerkerk, G., Vermulst, A. A., Spijkerman, R., & Engels, R. (2008). On-line communication, compulsive Internet use, and psychosocial well–being among adolescents: A longitudinal study. *Developmental Psychology, 44,* 655–665.

Van der Berg, P., Neumark-Sztainer, D., Hannan, P. J., & Haines, J. (2007). Is dieting advice from magazines helpful or harmful? Five-year associations with weight-control behaviors and psychological outcomes in adolescents. *Pediatrics, 119,* 30–37.

Van der Geest, V., Blokland, A., & Bijleveld, C. (2009). Delinquent development in a sample of high-risk youth: Shape, content, and predictors of delinquent trajectories from age 12 to 32. *Journal of Research on Crime and Delinquency, 46,* 111–143.

van Hoeken, D., Lucas, A., & Hoek, H. (1998). Epidemiology. In H. W. Hoek, J. L. Treasure, & M. A. Katzman (Eds.), *Neurobiology in the treatment of eating disorders* (pp. 97–126). New York: Wiley.

Van Leeuwen, K. G., Mervielda, I., Braet, C., & Bosmans, G. (2004). Child personality and parental behavior as moderators of problem behavior: Variable- and person-centered approaches. *Developmental Psychology, 40,* 1028–1046.

Van Leijenhorst, L., Westenberg, P. M., & Crone, E. A. (2008). A developmental study of risky decisions on the cake gambling task: Age and gender analyses of probability estimation and reward evaluation. *Developmental Neuropsychology, 33,* 179–196.

van Lier, P., Wanner, B., & Vitaro, F. (2007). Onset of antisocial behavior, affiliation with deviant friends, and childhood maladjustment: A test of the childhood- and adolescent-onset models. *Development and Psychopathology, 19,* 167–185.

van Roosmalen, E. (2000). Forces of patriarchy: Adolescent experiences of sexuality and conceptions of relationships. *Youth and Society, 32,* 202–227.

van Wel, F. (1994). "I count my parents among my best friends:" Youths' bonds with parents and friends in the Netherlands. *Journal of Marriage and the Family, 56,* 835–843.

Vandell, D. L., & Ramanan, J. (1991). Children of the National Longitudinal Survey of Youth: Choices in after-school care and child development. *Developmental Psychology, 27,* 637–643.

Vandewater, E., & Lansford, J. (1998). Influences of family structure and parental conflict on children's well-being. *Family Relations, 47,* 323–330.

Vanfossen, B., Jones, J., & Spade, J. (1987). Curriculum tracking and status maintenance. *Sociology of Education, 60,* 104–122.

Vaughan, R., McCarthy, J., Armstrong, B., Walter, H., Waterman, P., & Tiezzi, L. (1996). Carrying and using weapons: A survey of minority junior high school students in New York City. *American Journal of Public Health, 86,* 568–572.

Vazsonyi, A. T., & Belliston, L. M. (2006). The cultural and developmental significance of parenting processes in adolescent anxiety and depression symptoms. *Journal of Youth and Adolescence, 35,* 491–505.

Vazsonyi, A. T., Hibbert, J. R., & Black, S. J. (2003). Exotic enterprise no more? Adolescent reports of family and parenting processes from youth in four countries. *Journal of Research on Adolescence, 13,* 129–160.

Vazsonyi, A. T., Trejos-Castillo, E., & Huang, L. (2006). Are developmental processes affected by immigration? Family processes, internalizing behaviors, and externalizing behaviors. *Journal of Youth and Adolescence, 35,* 799–813.

Vega, W., Khoury, E., Zimmerman, R., Gil, A., & Warheit, G. (1995). Cultural conflicts and problem behaviors of Latino adolescents in home and school environments. *Journal of Community Psychology, 23,* 167–179.

Ventura, S., Abma, J., Mosher, W., & Henshaw, S. (2008). Estimated pregnancy rates by outcome for the United States, 1990–2004. *National Vital Statistics Reports, 56,* Number 15.

Vera Institute of Justice. (1990). *The male role in teenage pregnancy and parenting.* New York: Vera Institute of Justice.

Verkuyten, M. (1995). Self-esteem, self-concept stability, and aspects of ethnic identity among minority and majority youth in the Netherlands. *Journal of Youth and Adolescence, 24,* 155–185.

Verkuyten, M., & Slooter, L. (2008). Muslim and non-Muslim adolescents' reasoning about freedom of speech and minority rights. *Child Development, 79,* 514–528.

Verma, S., & Larson, R. (Eds.). (2003). Examining adolescent leisure time across cultures. *New Directions for Child and Adolescent Development, 99.*

Vermeer, H. J., Boekaerts, M., & Seegers, G. (2000). Motivational and gender differences: Sixth-grade students' mathematical problem-solving behavior. *Journal of Educational Psychology, 92,* 308–315.

Vicary, J., Klingaman, L., & Harkness, W. (1995). Risk factors associated with date rape and sexual assault of adolescent girls. *Journal of Adolescence, 18,* 289–306.

Videon, T. M. (2002). The effects of parent–adolescent relationships and parental separation on adolescent well-being. *Journal of Marriage and the Family, 64,* 489–503.

Vieno, A., Perkins, D. D., Smith, T. M., & Santinello, M. (2005). Democratic school climate and sense of community in the school: A multilevel analysis. *American Journal of Community Psychology, 36,* 327–341.

Viljoen, J. L., Klaver, J., & Roesch, R. (2005). Legal decisions of preadolescent and adolescent defendants: Predictors of confessions, pleas, communication with attorneys, and appeals. *Law and Human Behavior, 29,* 253–277.

Vincent, G. M., Vitacco, M. J., Grisso, T., & Corrado, R. R. (2003). Subtypes of adolescent offenders: Affective traits and antisocial behavior patterns. *Behavioral Sciences and the Law, 21,* 695–712.

Vispoel, W. (1995). Success and failure in junior high school: A critical incident approach to understanding students' attributional beliefs. *American Educational Research Journal, 32,* 377–412.

Vitaro, F., Brendgen, M., & Tremblay, R. E. (2000). Influence of deviant friends on delinquency: Searching for moderator variables. *Journal of Abnormal Child Psychology, 28,* 313–325.

Vitaro, F., Tremblay, R., Kerr, M., Pagani, L., & Bukowski, W. (1997). Disruptiveness, friends' characteristics, and delinquency in early adolescence: A test of two competing models. *Child Development, 68,* 676–689.

Vitiello, B., Rohde, P., Silva, S., Wells, K., Casat, C., Waslick, B., et al. (2006). Functioning and quality of life in the treatment for adolescents with depression study (TADS). *Journal*

of the American Academy of Child & Adolescent Psychiatry, 45, 1419–1426.

Vloet, T. D., Konrad, K., Huebner, T., Herpertz, S., & Herpertz-Dahlmann, B. (2008). Structural and functional MRI-findings in children and adolescents with antisocial behavior. *Behavioral Sciences & the Law, 26,* 99–111.

Vo-Jutabha, E. D., Dinh, K. T., McHale, J. P., & Valsiner, J. (2009). A qualitative analysis of Vietnamese adolescent identity exploration within and outside an ethnic enclave. *Journal of Youth and Adolescence, 38,* 672–690.

Voelkl, K. (1997). Identification with school. *American Journal of Education, 105,* 294–318.

Volkow, N., & Ting-Kai, L. (2005). The neuroscience of addiction. *Nature Neuroscience, 8,* 1429–1430.

Voyer, D., Voyer, S., & Bryden, M. (1995). Magnitude of sex differences in spatial abilities: A meta-analysis and consideration of critical variables. *Psychological Bulletin, 117,* 250–270.

Vuchinich, S., Angeletti, J., & Gatherum, A. (1996). Context and development in family problem solving with preadolescent children. *Child Development, 67,* 1276–1288.

Vuchinich, S., Hetherington, E. M., Vuchinich, R., & Clingempeel, W. (1991). Parent–child interaction and gender differences in early adolescents' adaptation to stepfamilies. *Developmental Psychology, 27,* 618–626.

Vygotsky, L. (1978). *Mind in society.* Cambridge, MA: Harvard University Press. (Original work published 1930)

Wade, T. J., Cairney, J., & Pevalin, D. J. (2002). Emergence of gender differences in depression during adolescence: National panel results from three countries. *Journal of the American Academy of Child and Adolescent Psychiatry, 41,* 190–198.

Wadsworth, M. E., & Compas, B. E. (2002). Coping with family conflict and economic strain: The adolescent perspective. *Journal of Research on Adolescence, 12,* 243–274.

Wagner, B., Cohen, P., & Brook, J. (1996). Parent/adolescent relationships: Moderators of the effects of stressful life events. *Journal of Adolescent Research, 11,* 347–374.

Wainright, J. L., Russell, S. T., & Patterson, C. J. (2004). Psychosocial adjustment, school outcomes, and romantic relationships of adolescents with same-sex parents. *Child Development, 75,* 1886–1898.

Wainryb, C., Shaw, L. A., Laupa, M., & Smith, K. R. (2001). Children's, adolescents', and young adults' thinking about different types of disagreements. *Developmental Psychology, 37,* 373–386.

Waite, L., Goldscheider, F., & Witsberger, C. (1986). Nonfamily living and the erosion of traditional family orientations among young adults. *American Sociological Review, 51,* 541–554.

Waizenhofer, R., Buchanan, C. M., & Jackson-Newsom, J. (2004). Mothers' and fathers' knowledge of adolescents' daily activities: Its sources and its links with adolescent adjustment. *Journal of Family Psychology, 18,* 348–360.

Wakefield, M., Terry-McElrath, Y., Emery, S., Saffer, H., Chaloupka, F. J., Szczypka, G., et al. (2006). Effect of televised, tobacco company-funded smoking prevention advertising on youth smoking-related beliefs, intentions, and behavior. *American Journal of Public Health, 96,* 2154–2160.

Wakschlag, L. S., Gordon, R. A., Lahey, B. B., Loeber, R., Green, S. M., & Leventhal, B. L. (2000). Maternal age at first birth and boys' risk for conduct disorder. *Journal of Research on Adolescence, 10,* 417–441.

Walberg, H. (1998). *Spending more while learning less.* New York: Thomas B. Fordham Foundation.

Wald, M. (2005). Foreword. In D. Osgood, M. Foster, C. Flanagan, & G. Ruth (Eds.), *On your own without a net: The transition to adulthood for vulnerable populations,* pp. vii–xi. Chicago: University of Chicago Press.

Waldman, I. (1996). Aggressive boys' hostile perceptual and response biases: The role of attention and impulsivity. *Child Development, 67,* 1015–1033.

Walker, E., Sabuwalla, Z., & Huot, R. (2004). Pubertal neuromaturation, stress sensitivity, and psychopathology. *Development and Psychopathology, 16,* 807–824.

Walker, L., Gustafson, P., & Hennig, K. H. (2001). The consolidation/transition model in moral reasoning development. *Developmental Psychology, 37,* 187–197.

Walker-Barnes, C. J., & Mason, C. A. (2001). Ethnic difference in the effect of parenting on gang involvement and gang delinquency: A longitudinal, hierarchical linear modeling perspective. *Child Development, 72,* 1814–1831.

Walker-Barnes, C. J., & Mason, C. A. (2004). Delinquency and substance use among gang-involved youth: The moderating role of parenting practices. *American Journal of Community Psychology, 34,* 235–250.

Walkup, J. T., Albano, A. M., Piacentini, J., Birmaher, B., Compton, S. N., Sherrill, J. T., et al. (2008). Cognitive behavioral therapy, sertraline, or a combination in childhood anxiety. *New England Journal of Medicine, 359,* 2753–2766.

Wall, J., Power, T., & Arbona, C. (1993). Susceptibility to antisocial peer pressure and its relation to acculturation in Mexican-American adolescents. *Journal of Adolescent Research, 8,* 403–418.

Wallace, J. M., Forman, T. A., Caldwell, C. H., & Willis, D. S. (2003). Religion and U.S. secondary school students current patterns, recent trends, and sociodemographic correlates. *Youth and Society, 35,* 98–125.

Wallace-Broscious, A., Serafica, F., & Osipow, S. (1994). Adolescent career development: Relationships to self-concept and identity status. *Journal of Research on Adolescence, 4,* 127–149.

Wallerstein, J., & Blakeslee, S. (1989). *Second chances.* New York: Ticknor & Fields.

Wallerstein, J., & Kelley, J. (1974). The effects of parental divorce: The adolescent experience. In E. Anthony & A. Koupernik (Eds.), *The child in his family: Children as a psychiatric risk* (Vol. 3). New York: Wiley.

Walsh, B., Kaplan, A., Attia, E., Olmsted, M., Parides, M., Carter, J., et al. (2006). Fluoxetine after weight restoration in anorexia nervosa: A randomized controlled trial. *Journal of the American Medical Association,* i2605–2612.

Walsh, S., Shulman, S., Bar-On, Z. & Tsur, A. (2006). The role of parentification and family climate in adaptation among immigrant adolescents in Israel. *Journal of Research on Adolescence, 16,* 321–350.

Wang, L., Huettel, S., & De Bellis, M. D. (2008). Neural substrates for processing task-irrelevant sad images in adolescents. *Developmental Science, 11,* 23–32.

Wang, L., McCarthy, G., Song, A., & LaBar, K. (2005). Amygdala activation to sad pictures during high-field (4 Tesla) functional magnetic resonance imaging. *Emotion, 5,* 12–22.

Wang, Q., Pomerantz, E. M., & Chen, H. (2007). The role of parents' control in early adolescents' psychological functioning: A longitudinal investigation in the United States and China. *Child Development, 78,* 1592–1610.

Wångby, M., Bergman, L., & Magnusson, D. (1999). Development of adjustment problems in girls: What syndromes emerge? *Child Development, 70,* 678–699.

Ward, L. M. (2003). Understanding the role of entertainment media in the sexual socialization of American youth: A review of empirical research. *Developmental Review, 23,* 347–388.

Ward, L. M., & Friedman, K. (2006). Using TV as a guide: Associations between television viewing and adolescents' sexual attitudes and behavior. *Journal of Research on Adolescence, 16,* 133–156.

Ward, L. M., Hansbrough, E., & Walker, E. (2005). Contributions of music video exposure to Black adolescents' gender and sexual schemas. *Journal of Adolescent Research, 20,* 143–166.

Ward, M. (1995). Talking about sex: Common themes about sexuality in the prime-time television programs children and adolescents view most. *Journal of Youth and Adolescence, 24,* 595–615.

Warneke, C., & Cooper, S. (1994). Child and adolescent drownings in Harris County, Texas, 1983 through 1990. *American Journal of Public Health, 84,* 593–598.

Warner, S., & Moore, S. (2004). Excuses, excuses: Self-handicapping in an Australian adolescent sample. *Journal of Youth and Adolescence, 33,* 271–281.

Warr, M. (2007). The tangled web: Delinquency, deception, and parental attachment. *Journal of Youth and Adolescence, 36,* 607–622.

Warren, J. (2002). Reconsidering the relationship between student employment and academic outcomes: A new theory and better data. *Youth and Society, 33,* 366–393.

Warren, J. R., & Jenkins, K. N. (2005). High school exit examinations and high school dropout in Texas and Florida, 1971–2000. *Sociology of Education, 78,* 122–143.

Warren, J. R., Grodsky, E., & Lee, J. C. (2008). State high school exit examinations and postsecondary labor market outcomes. *Sociology of Education, 81,* 77–107.

Washburn-Ormachea, J. M., Hillman, S. B., & Sawilowsky, S. S. (2004). Gender and gender-role orientation differences on adolescents' coping with peer stressors. *Journal of Youth and Adolescence, 33,* 31–40.

Wasserman, G., Rauh, V., Brunelli, S., Garcia-Castro, M., & Necos, B. (1990). Psychosocial attributes and life experiences of disadvantaged minority mothers: Age and ethnic variations. *Child Development, 61,* 566–580.

Waters, E., Merrick, S., Treboux, D., Crowell, J., & Albersheim, L. (2000). Attachment security in infancy and early adulthood: A twenty-year longitudinal study. *Child Development, 71,* 684–689.

Watt, H. M. (2004). Development of adolescents' self-perceptions, values, and task perceptions according to gender and domain in 7th-through 11th-grade Australian students. *Child Development, 75,* 1556–1574.

Watt, T. T. (2003). Are small schools and private schools better for adolescents' emotional adjustment? *Sociology of Education, 76,* 344–367.

Watt, T. T., & Rogers, J. M. (2007). Factors contributing to differences in substance use among Black and White adolescents. *Youth and Society, 39,* 54–74.

Way, N., & Chen, L. (2000). Close and general friendships among African American, Latino, and Asian American adolescents from low-income families. *Journal of Adolescent Research, 15,* 274–301.

Way, N., & Greene, M. L. (2006). Trajectories of perceived friendship quality during adolescence: The patterns and contextual predictors. *Journal of Research on Adolescence, 16,* 293–320.

Way, N., & Pahl, K. (2001). Individual and contextual predictors of perceived friendship quality among ethnic minority, low-income adolescents. *Journal of Research on Adolescence, 11,* 325–349.

Way, N., & Robinson, M. G. (2003). A longitudinal study of the effects of family, friends, and school experiences on the psychological adjustment of ethnic minority, low-SES adolescents. *Journal of Adolescent Research, 18,* 324–346.

Way, N., Reddy, R., & Rhodes, J. (2007). Students' perceptions of school climate during the middle school years: Associations with trajectories of psychological and behavioral adjustment. *American Journal of Community Psychology, 40,* 194–213.

Weaver, S. R., & Kim, S. Y. (2008). A person-centered approach to studying the linkages among parent–child differences in cultural orientation, supportive parenting, and adolescent depressive symptoms in Chinese American families. *Journal of Youth and Adolescence, 37,* 36–49.

Weinfield, N., Ogawa, J. R., & Sroufe, L. A. (1997). Early attachment as a pathway to adolescent peer competence. *Journal of Research on Adolescence, 7*(3), 241–265.

Weinfield, N., Sroufe, A., & Egeland, B. (2000). Attachment from infancy to early adulthood in a high-risk sample: Continuity, discontinuity, and their correlates. *Child Development, 71,* 695–702.

Weinstein, S. M., Mermelstein, R. J., Hankin, B. L., Hedeker, D., & Flay, B. R. (2007). Longitudinal patterns of daily affect and global mood during adolescence. *Journal of Research on Adolescence, 17,* 587–600.

Weisner, T., & Garnier, H. (1995, March). *Family values and nonconventional family lifestyles: An 18-year longitudinal study at adolescence.* Paper presented at the biennial meetings of the Society for Research in Child Development, Indianapolis.

Weiss, R. (1974). The provisions of social relationships. In Z. Rubin (Ed.), *Doing unto others.* Englewood Cliffs, NJ: Prentice-Hall.

Weissberg, R., Caplan, M., & Harwood, R. (1991). Promoting competent young people in competence-enhancing environments: A systems-based perspective on primary prevention. *Journal of Consulting and Clinical Psychology, 59,* 830–841.

Weist, M., Freedman, A., Paskewitz, D., Proescher, E., & Flaherty, L. (1995). Urban youth under stress: Empirical identification of protective factors. *Journal of Youth and Adolescence, 24,* 705–729.

Weisz, J. R., Jensen-Doss, A., & Hawley, K. M. (2006). Evidence-based youth psychotherapies versus usual clinical care: A meta-analysis of direct comparisons. *American Psychologist, 61,* 671–689.

Weisz, J. R., McCarty, C. A., & Valeri, S. M. (2006). Effects of psychotherapy for depression in children and adolescents: A meta-analysis. *Psychological Bulletin, 132,* 132–149.

Wells, A., & Serna, I. (1996). The politics of culture: Understanding local political resistance to detracking in racially mixed schools. *Harvard Educational Review, 66,* 93–118.

Wentzel, K. (1994). Relations of social goal pursuit to social acceptance, classroom behavior, and perceived social support. *Journal of Educational Psychology, 86,* 173–182.

Wentzel, K. (1998). Social relationships and motivation in middle school: The role of parents, teachers, and peers. *Journal of Educational Psychology, 90,* 202–209.

Wentzel, K. (2002). Are effective teachers like good parents? Teaching styles and student adjustment in early adolescence. *Child Development, 73,* 287–301.

Wentzel, K. (2003). Sociometric status and adjustment in middle school: A longitudinal study. *Journal of Early Adolescence, 23,* 5–28.

Wentzel, K., & Asher, S. (1995). The academic lives of neglected, rejected, popular, and controversial children. *Child Development, 66,* 754–763.

Wentzel, K., Barry, C., & Caldwell, K. (2004). Friendships in middle school: Influences on motivation and school adjustment. *Journal of Educational Psychology, 96,* 195–203.

Wentzel, K., & Caldwell, K. (1997). Friendships, peer acceptance, and group membership: Relations to academic achievement in middle school. *Child Development, 68,* 1198–1209.

Werner, N., & Nixon, C. L. (2005). Normative beliefs about relational aggression: An investigation of the cognitive bases of adolescent aggressive behavior. *Journal of Youth and Adolescence, 34,* 229–243.

Werner, N., & Silbereisen, R. (2003). Family relationship quality and contact with deviant peers as predictors of adolescent problem behaviors: The moderating role of gender. *Journal of Adolescent Research, 18,* 454–480.

Whitaker, D., & Miller, K. (2000). Parent–adolescent discussions about sex and condoms: Impact on peer influences of sexual risk behavior. *Journal of Adolescent Research, 15,* 251–273.

Whitbeck, L., Conger, R., Simons, R., & Kao, M. (1993). Minor deviant behaviors and adolescent sexuality. *Youth and Society, 25,* 24–37.

Whitbeck, L., Hoyt, D., & Ackley, K. (1997). Abusive family backgrounds and later victimization among runaway and homeless adolescents. *Journal of Research on Adolescence, 7,* 375–392.

Whitbeck, L., Hoyt, D., & Bao, W. (2000). Depressive symptoms and co-occurring depressive symptoms, substance abuse, and conduct problems among runaway and homeless adolescents. *Child Development, 71,* 721–732.

Whitbeck, L., Hoyt, D., Miller, M., & Kao, M. (1992). Parental support, depressed affect, and sexual experience among adolescents. *Youth and Society, 24,* 166–177.

Whitbeck, L., Simons, R., & Kao, M. (1994). The effects of divorced mothers' dating behaviors and sexual attitudes on the sexual attitudes and behaviors of their adolescent children. *Journal of Marriage and the Family, 56,* 615–621.

Whitbeck, L., Yoder, K., Hoyt, D., & Conger, R. (1999). Early adolescent sexual activity: A developmental study. *Journal of Marriage and the Family, 61,* 934–946.

Whitbeck, L., Yu, M., Johnson, K., Hoyt, D., & Walls, M. (2008). Diagnostic prevalence rates from early to mid-adolescence among indigenous adolescents: First results from a longitudinal study. *Journal of the American Academy of Child & Adolescent Psychiatry, 47,* 890–900.

White, A. M., & Gager, C. T. (2007). Idle hands and empty pockets? Youth involvement in extracurricular activities, social capital, and economic status. *Youth and Society, 39,* 75–111.

White, H. R., Fleming, C. B., Kim, M. J., Catalano, R. F., & McMorris, B. J. (2008). Identifying two potential mechanisms for changes in alcohol use among college-attending and non-college-attending emerging adults. *Developmental Psychology, 44,* 1625–1639.

Whitehead, K. A., Ainsworth, A. T., Wittig, M. A., & Gadino, B. (2009). Implications of ethnic identity exploration and ethnic identity affirmation and belonging for intergroup attitudes among adolescents. *Journal of Research on Adolescence, 19,* 123–135.

Whiteman, S., & Buchanan, C. (2002). Mothers' and children's expectations for adolescence: The impact of perceptions of an older sibling's experience. *Journal of Family Psychology, 16,* 157–171.

Whitesell, N., & Harter, S. (1996). The interpersonal context of emotion: Anger with close friends and classmates. *Child Development, 67,* 1345–1359.

Whitesell, N. R., Mitchell, C. M., Kaufman, C. E., & Spicer, P. (2006). Developmental trajectories of personal and collective self-concept among American Indian adolescents. *Child Development, 77,* 1487–1503.

Whitlock, J. L., Powers, J. L., & Eckenrode, J. (2006). The virtual cutting edge: The Internet and adolescent self-injury. *Developmental Psychology, 42,* 407–417.

Wichstrøm, L. (1999). The emergence of gender difference in depressed mood during adolescence: The role of intensified gender socialization. *Developmental Psychology, 35,* 232–245.

Wichstrøm, L. (2001). The impact of pubertal timing on adolescents' alcohol use. *Journal of Research on Adolescence, 11,* 131–150.

Wickrama, K. A. S., Merton, M., & Elder, G. H., Jr. (2005). Community influence on precocious transitions to adulthood: Racial differences and mental health consequences. *Journal of Community Psychology, 33,* 639–653.

Wickrama, K. A. T., Wickrama, K. A. S., & Bryant, C. M. (2006). Community influence on adolescent obesity: Race/ethnic differences. *Journal of Youth and Adolescence, 35,* 647–657.

Widman, L., Welsh, D. P., McNulty, J. K., & Little, K. C. (2006). Sexual communication and contraceptive use in adolescent dating couples. *Journal of Adolescent Health, 39,* 893–899.

Widom, C., & Kuhns, J. (1996). Childhood victimization and subsequent risk for promiscuity, prostitution, and teenage pregnancy: A prospective study. *American Journal of Public Health, 86,* 1607–1612.

Wiesner, M., & Kim, H. K. (2006). Co-occurring delinquency and depressive symptoms of adolescent boys and girls: A dual trajectory modeling approach. *Developmental Psychology, 42,* 1220–1235.

Wiesner, M., Kim, H. K., & Capaldi, D. M. (2005). Developmental trajectories of offending: Validation and prediction to young adult alcohol use, drug use, and depressive symptoms. *Development and Psychopathology, 17,* 251–270.

Wigfield, A., Eccles, J., MacIver, D., Reuman, D., & Midgley, C. (1991). Transitions during early adolescence: Changes in children's domain-specific self-perceptions and general self-esteem across the transition to junior high school. *Developmental Psychology, 27,* 552–565.

Wight, R. G., Sepúlveda, J. E., & Aneshensel, C. S. (2004). Depressive symptoms: How do adolescents compare with adults? *Journal of Adolescent Health, 34,* 314–323.

Wilcox, W. (1998). Conservative Protestant childrearing: Authoritarian or authoritative? *American Sociological Review, 63,* 796–809.

Wilkinson, D., & Carr, P. J. (2008). Violent youths' responses to high levels of exposure to community violence: What violent events reveal about youth violence. *Journal of Community Psychology, 36,* 1026–1051.

Wilkinson, D., & Fagan, J. (1996). The role of firearms in violence "scripts": The dynamics of gun events among adolescent males. *Law and Contemporary Problems, 59,* 55–89.

Wilkinson, R. B. (2004). The role of parental and peer attachment in the psychological health and self-esteem of adolescents. *Journal of Youth and Adolescence, 33,* 479–493.

William T. Grant Foundation Commission on Work, Family, and Citizenship. (1988). *The forgotten half: Non-college youth in America.* Washington, DC: Author.

Williams, A. (2003). Teenage drivers: Patterns of risk. *Journal of Safety Research, 34,* 5–15.

Williams, K., & Guerra, N. (2007). Prevalence and predictors of Internet bullying. *Journal of Adolescent Health, 31,* S14–S21.

Williams, P., Holmbeck, G. N., & Greenley, R. N. (2002). Adolescent health psychology. *Journal of Consulting and Clinical Psychology, 70,* 828–842.

Williams, S. K., & Kelly, F. D. (2005). Relationships among involvement, attachment, and behavioral problems in adolescence: Examining fathers' influence. *Journal of Early Adolescence, 25,* 168–196.

Williams, S. T., Conger, K. J., & Blozis, S. A. (2007). The development of interpersonal aggression during adolescence: The importance of parents, siblings, and family economics. *Child Development, 78,* 1526–1542.

Williams, T., Connolly, J., & Cribbie, R. (2008). Light and heavy heterosexual activities of young Canadian adolescents: Normative patterns and differential predictors. *Journal of Research on Adolescence, 18,* 145–172.

Williams, W., Blythe, T., White, N., Li, J., Gardner, H., & Sternberg, R. J. (2002). Practical intelligence for school: Developing metacognitive sources of achievement in adolescence. *Developmental Review, 22,* 162–210.

Williamson, J., Borduin, C., & Howe, B. (1991). The ecology of adolescent maltreatment: A multilevel examination of adolescent physical abuse, sexual abuse, and neglect. *Journal of Consulting and Clinical Psychology, 59,* 449–457.

Willoughby, T. (2008). A short-term longitudinal study of Internet and computer game use by adolescent boys and girls: Prevalence, frequency of use, and psychosocial predictors. *Developmental Psychology, 44,* 195–204.

Willoughby, T., Chalmers, H., & Busseri, M. A. (2004). Where is the syndrome? Examining co-occurrence among multiple problem behaviors in adolescence. *Journal of Consulting and Clinical Psychology, 72,* 1022–1037.

Wills, T., McNamara, G., Vaccaro, D., & Hirky, A. (1996). Escalated substance use: A longitudinal grouping analysis from early to middle adolescence. *Journal of Abnormal Psychology, 105,* 166–180.

Wills, T., Sandy, J. M., Yaeger, A., & Shinar, O. (2001). Family risk factors and adolescent substance use: Moderation effects for temperament dimensions. *Developmental Psychology, 37,* 283–297.

Wilson, J. L., Peebles, R., Hardy, K. K., & Litt, I. F. (2006). Surfing for thinness: A pilot study of pro-eating disorder web site usage in adolescents with eating disorders. *Pediatrics, 118,* 1635–1643.

Wilson, M., & Daly, M. (1985). Competitiveness, risk taking, and violence: The young male syndrome. *Ethology and Sociobiology, 6,* 59–73.

Wilson, P., & Wilson, J. (1992). Environmental influences on adolescent educational aspirations: A logistic transform model. *Youth and Society, 24,* 52–70.

Wilson, R. (February 1, 2005). The six simple principles of viral marketing. *Web Marketing Today.* Retrieved from www.wilsonweb.com/wmt5/viral-principles.htm

Windle, M. (1994). A study of friendship characteristics and problem behaviors among middle adolescents. *Child Development, 65,* 1764–1777.

Windle, M., Miller-Tutzauer, C., & Barnes, G. (1991). Adolescent perceptions of help-seeking resources for substance abuse. *Child Development, 62,* 179–189.

Windle, M., & Wiesner, M. (2004). Trajectories of marijuana use from adolescence to young adulthood: Predictors and outcomes. *Development and Psychopathology, 16,* 1007–1027.

Winfree, J., L., Bäckström, T., & Mays, G. (1994). Social learning theory, self-reported delinquency, and youth gangs: A new twist on a general theory of crime and delinquency. *Youth and Society, 26,* 147–177.

Wintemute, G., Kraus, J., Teret, S., & Wright, M. (1987). Drowning in childhood and adolescence: A population-based study. *American Journal of Public Health, 77,* 830–832.

Winterbottom, M. (1958). The relation of need for achievement to learning experiences in independence and mastery. In J. Atkinson (Ed.), *Motives in fantasy, action, and society.* Princeton, NJ: Van Nostrand.

Wintre, M., Hicks, R., McVey, G., & Fox, J. (1988). Age and sex differences in choice of consultant for various types of problems. *Child Development, 59,* 1046–1055.

Wiseman, R. (2003). *Queen bees and wannabes.* New York: Three Rivers Press.

Witkow, M. R. (2009). Academic achievement and adolescents' daily time use in the social and academic domains. *Journal of Research on Adolescence, 19,* 151–172.

Wolak, J., Finkelhor, D., Mitchell, K., & Ybarra, M. (2008). Online "predators" and their victims: Myths, realities and implications for prevention and treatment. *American Psychologist, 63,* 111–128.

Wolak, J., Mitchell, K. J., & Finkelhor, D. (2003). Escaping or connecting? Characteristics of youth who form close online relationships. *Journal of Adolescence, 26,* 105–119.

Wolak, J., Mitchell, K., & Finkelhor, D. (2006). *Online victimization of youth: Five years later.* Durham: National Center for Missing and Exploited Children, University of New Hampshire.

Wolf, A., Gortmaker, S., Cheung, L., Gray, H., Herzog, D., & Colditz, G. (1993). Activity, inactivity, and obesity: Racial, ethnic, and age differences among schoolgirls. *American Journal of Public Health, 83,* 1625–1627.

Wolfe, D., Wekerle, C., Reitzel-Jaffe, D., & Lefebvre, L. (1998). Factors associated with abusive relationships among maltreated and non-maltreated youth. *Development and Psychopathology, 10,* 61–85.

Wolfe, S., & Truxillo, C. (1996, March). *The relationship between decisional control, responsibility and positive and negative outcomes during early adolescence.* Paper presented at the biennial meetings of the Society for Research on Adolescence, Boston.

Wolfson, A., & Carskadon, M. (1998). Sleep schedules and daytime functioning in adolescents. *Child Development, 69,* 875–887.

Wong, C., Crosnoe, R., Laird, J., & Dornbusch, S. (2003). *Relations with parents and teachers, susceptibility to friends' negative influences,* *and adolescent deviance.* Unpublished manuscript, Department of Sociology, University of Texas at Austin.

Wong, M., Nigg, J., Zucker, R., Puttler, L., Fitzgerald, H., Jester, J., et al. (2006). Behavioral control and resiliency in the onset of alcohol and illicit drug use: A prospective study from preschool to adolescence. *Child Development, 77,* 1016–1033.

Wood, D., Larson, R. W., & Brown, J. R. (2009). How adolescents come to see themselves as more responsible through participation in youth programs. *Child Development, 80,* 295–309.

Wood, P., & Clay, W. (1996). Perceived structural barriers and academic performance among American Indian high school students. *Youth and Society, 28,* 40–61.

Woods, L. N., & Jagers, R. J. (2003). Are cultural values predictors of moral reasoning in African American adolescents? *Journal of Black Psychology, 29,* 102–118.

Woodward, L., & Fergusson, D. (1999). Childhood peer relationship problems and psychosocial adjustment in late adolescence. *Journal of Abnormal Child Psychology, 27,* 87–104.

Woodward, L., Fergusson, D., & Belsky, J. (2000). Timing of parental separation and attachment to parents in adolescence: Results of a prospective study from birth to age 16. *Journal of Marriage and the Family, 62,* 162–174.

Woolard, J., & Scott, E. (2009). The legal regulation of adolescence. In R. Lerner & L. Steinberg (Eds.), *Handbook of adolescent psychology* (3rd ed., Vol. 2, pp. 345–371). New York: Wiley.

Wright, J., Cullen, F., & Williams, N. (1997). Working while in school and delinquent involvement: Implications for social policy. *Crime and Delinquency, 43,* 203–221.

Wu, L., & Anthony, J. (1999). Tobacco smoking and depressed mood in late childhood and early adolescence. *American Journal of Public Health, 89,* 1837–1840.

Wu, L., & Thomson, E. (2001). Race differences in family experience and early sexual initiation: Dynamic models of family structure and family change. *Journal of Marriage and the Family, 63,* 682–696.

Wu, L., Pilowsky, D. J., & Schlenger, W. E. (2004). Inhalant abuse and dependence among adolescents in the United States. *Journal of the American Academy of Child and Adolescent Psychiatry, 43,* 1206–1214.

Wu, L., Ringwalt, C. L., Mannelli, P., & Patkar, A. A. (2008). Prescription pain reliever abuse and dependence among adolescents: A nationally representative study. *Journal of the American Academy of Child & Adolescent Psychiatry, 47,* 1020–1029.

Wu, L., Schlenger, W. E., & Galvin, D. M. (2003). The relationship between employment and substance use among students aged 12 to 17. *Journal of Adolescent Health, 32,* 5–15.

Wu, T., Mendola, P., & Buck, G. (2002). Ethnic differences in the presence of secondary sex characteristics and menarche among U.S. girls: The Third National Health and Nutrition Examination Survey, 1988–1994. *Pediatrics, 110*(4).

Wyatt, L. W., & Haskett, M. E. (2001). Aggressive and nonaggressive young adolescents' attributions of intent in teacher/student interactions. *Journal of Early Adolescence, 21,* 425–446.

Xia, G., & Qian, M. (2001). The relationship of parenting style to self-reported mental health among two subcultures of Chinese. *Journal of Adolescence, 24,* 251–260.

Xu, J. (2004). Family help and homework management in urban and rural secondary schools. *Teachers College Review, 106,* 1786–1803.

Yamaguchi, R., Johnston, L., & O'Malley, P. (2003). Relationship between student illicit drug use and school drug-testing policies. *Journal of School Health, 73,* 159–164.

Yasui, M., Dorham, C. L., & Dishion, T. (2004). Ethnic identity and psychological adjustment: A validity analysis for European American and African American adolescents. *Journal of Adolescent Research, 19,* 807–825.

Yates, A., Edman, J., & Aruguete, M. (2004). Ethnic differences in BMI and body/self-dissatisfaction among Whites, Asian subgroups, Pacific Islanders, and African Americans. *Journal of Adolescent Health, 34,* 300–307.

Yates, M., & Youniss, J. (1996). Community service and political-moral identity in adolescents. *Journal of Research on Adolescence, 6,* 271–284.

Yau, J., & Smetana, J. (1996). Adolescent–parent conflict among Chinese adolescents in Hong Kong. *Child Development, 67,* 1262–1275.

Yau, J., & Smetana, J. (2003). Adolescent–parent conflict in Hong Kong and Shenzhen: A comparison of youth in two cultural contexts. *International Journal of Behavioral Development, 27,* 201–211.

Ybarra, M. L., Alexander, C., & Mitchell, K. J. (2005). Depressive symptomatology, youth Internet use, and online interactions: A national survey. *Journal of Adolescent Health, 36,* 9–18.

Yeh, H., & Lempers, J. D. (2004). Perceived sibling relationships and adolescent development. *Journal of Youth and Adolescence, 33,* 133–147.

Yip, T., Seaton, E., & Sellers, R. (2006). African American racial identity across the lifespan: Identity status, identity content, and depressive symptoms. *Child Development, 77,* 1504–1517.

YMCA. (2000). *Telephone survey conducted for the White House Conference on Teenagers.* Chicago: Author.

YMCA. (2006). Information on the history of the organization is available at www.ymca.net.

Yoon, J. S., Barton, E., & Taiarol, J. (2004). Relational aggression in middle school educational implications of developmental research. *Journal of Early Adolescence, 24,* 303–318.

Yoon, K., Eccles, J., Wigfield, A., & Barber, B. (1996, March). *Developmental trajectories of early to middle adolescents' academic achievement and motivation.* Paper presented at the biennial meetings of the Society for Research on Adolescence, Boston.

Yoshikawa, H. (1994). Prevention as cumulative protection: Effects of early family support and education on chronic delinquency and its risks. *Psychological Bulletin, 115,* 28–54.

Young, A. M., & D'Arcy, H. (2005). Older boyfriends of adolescent girls: The cause or a sign of the problem? *Journal of Adolescent Health, 36,* 410–419.

Young, J. F., Berenson, K., Cohen, P., & Garcia, J. (2005). The role of parent and peer support in predicting adolescent depression: A longitudinal community study. *Journal of Research on Adolescence 15,* 407–423.

Young, S. E., Friedman, N. P., Miyake, A., Willcutt, E. G., Corley, R. P., Haberstick, B. C., et al. (2009). Behavioral disinhibition: Liability for externalizing spectrum disorders and its genetic and environmental relation to response inhibition across adolescence. *Journal of Abnormal Psychology, 118,* 117–130.

Youngstrom, E., Weist, M. D., & Albus, K. E. (2003). Exploring violence exposure, stress, protective factors and behavioral problems among inner-city youth. *American Journal of Community Psychology, 32,* 115–129.

Youniss, J., & Smollar, J. (1985). *Adolescent relations with mothers, fathers, and friends.* Chicago: University of Chicago Press.

Yuan, A. S. V., & Hamilton, H. A. (2006). Stepfather involvement and adolescent well-being: Do mothers and nonresidential fathers matter? *Journal of Family Issues, 27,* 1191–1213.

Zabin, L., Astone, N., & Emerson, M. (1993). Do adolescents want babies? The relationship between attitudes and behavior. *Journal of Research on Adolescence, 3,* 67–86.

Zabin, L., Hirsch, M., & Emerson, M. (1989). When urban adolescents choose abortion: Effects on education, psychological status and subsequent pregnancy. *Family Planning Perspectives, 21,* 248–255.

Zaff, J. F., Moore, K. A., Papillo, A. R., & Williams, S. (2003). Implications of extracurricular activity participation during adolescence on positive outcomes. *Journal of Adolescent Research, 18,* 599–630.

Zaider, T., Johnson, J. G., & Cockell, S. J. (2002). Psychiatric disorders associated with the onset and persistence of bulimia nervosa and binge eating disorder during adolescence. *Journal of Youth and Adolescence, 31,* 319–329.

Zametkin, A. J., Alter, M. R., & Yemini, T. (2001). Suicide in teenagers. *Journal of the American Medical Association, 286,* 3120–3125.

Zametkin, A. J., Zoon, C. K., Klein, H. W., & Munson, S. (2004). Psychiatric aspects of child and adolescent obesity: A review of the past 10 years. *Journal of the American Academy of Child and Adolescent Psychiatry, 43,* 134–150.

Zapert, K., Snow, D. L., & Tebes, J. K. (2002). Patterns of substance use in early through late adolescence. *American Journal of Community Psychology, 30,* 835–852.

Zarrett, N., Fay, K., Li, Y., Carrano, J., Phelps, E., & Lerner, R. (2009). More than child's play: Variable- and pattern-centered approaches for examining effects of sports participation on youth development. *Developmental Psychology, 45,* 368–382.

Zavela, K., Battistich, V., Dean, B., Flores, R., Barton, R., & Delaney, R. (1997). Say yes first: A longitudinal, school-based alcohol and drug prevention project for rural youth and families. *Journal of Early Adolescence, 17,* 67–96.

Zavodny, M. (2004). Fertility and parental consent for minors to receive contraceptives. *American Journal of Public Health, 94,* 1347–1351.

Zeldin, S., & Topitzes, D. (2002). Neighborhood experiences, community connection, and positive beliefs about adolescents among urban adults and youth. *Journal of Community Psychology, 30,* 647–669.

Zeman, J., & Shipman, K. (1997). Social-contextual influences on expectancies for managing anger and sadness: The transition from middle childhood to adolescence. *Developmental Psychology, 33,* 917–924.

Zentner, M., & Renaud, O. (2007). Origins of adolescents' ideal self: An intergenerational perspective. *Journal of Personality and Social Psychology, 92,* 557–574.

Zhang, W., & Fuligni, A. (2006). Authority, autonomy, and family relationships among adolescents in urban and rural China. *Journal of Research on Adolescence, 16,* 527–537.

Zickler, P. (2004). Early nicotine initiation increases severity of addiction, vulnerability to some effects of cocaine. *NIDA Notes, 19,* 2.

Zillman, D. (2000). Influence of unrestrained access to erotica on adolescents' and young adults' dispositions toward sexuality. *Journal of Adolescent Health, 27,* 41–44.

Zima, B., Wells, K., & Freeman, H. (1994). Emotional and behavioral problems and severe academic delays among sheltered homeless children in Los Angeles County. *American Journal of Public Health, 84,* 260–264.

Zimiles, H., & Lee, V. (1991). Adolescent family structure and educational progress. *Developmental Psychology, 27,* 314–320.

Zimmer-Gembeck, M. (1999). Stability, change and individual differences in involvement with friends and romantic partners among adolescent females. *Journal of Youth and Adolescence, 28,* 419–438.

Zimmer-Gembeck, M., & Helfand, M. (2008). Ten years of longitudinal research on U.S. adolescent sexual behavior: Developmental correlates of sexual intercourse, and the importance of age, gender and ethnic background. *Developmental Review, 28,* 153–224.

Zimmer-Gembeck, M., Siebenbruner, J., & Collins, W. (2001). Diverse aspects of dating: Associations with psychosocial functioning from early to middle adolescence. *Journal of Adolescence, 24,* 313–336.

Zimmer-Gembeck, M. J., Siebenbruner, J., & Collins, W. A. (2004). A prospective study of intraindividual and peer influences on adolescents' heterosexual romantic and sexual behavior. *Archives of Sexual Behavior, 33,* 381–394.

Zimmerman, M., Bingenheimer, J. B., & Notaro, P. C. (2002). Natural mentors and adolescent resiliency: A study with urban youth. *American Journal of Community Psychology, 30,* 221–243.

Zimmerman, M., Copeland, L., Shope, J., & Dielman, T. (1997). A longitudinal study of self-esteem: Implications for adolescent development. *Journal of Youth and Adolescence, 26,* 117–141.

Zimmerman, M., & Schmeelk-Cone, K. (2003). A longitudinal analysis of adolescent substance use and school motivation among African American youth. *Journal of Research on Adolescence, 13,* 185–210.

Zimmermann, P., & Becker-Stoll, F. (2002). Stability of attachment representations during adolescence: The influence of ego-identity status. *Journal of Adolescence, 25,* 107–124.

Zimmerman, R., Sprecher, S., Langer, L., & Holloway, C. (1995). Adolescents' perceived ability to say "No" to unwanted sex. *Journal of Adolescent Research, 10,* 383–399.

Zimring, F. (1982). *The changing legal world of adolescence.* New York: Free Press.

Zimring, F. (1998). *American youth violence.* New York: Oxford University Press.

Zirkel, S. (2002). Is there a place for me? Role models and academic identity among White students and students of color. *Teachers College Record, 104,* 357–376.

Zito, J. M., Safer, D. J., DosReis, S., Gardner, J. F., Soeken, K., Boles, M., et al. (2002). Rising prevalence of antidepressants among U.S. youths. *Pediatrics, 109,* 721–727.

Zollo, P. (2004). *Getting wiser to teens: More insights into marketing to teenagers.* Ithaca, NY: New Strategist Publications.

Zuckerman, M. (Ed.). (1983). *Biological basis of sensation seeking, impulsivity, and anxiety.* Hillsdale, NJ: Erlbaum.

Zweig, J. M., Lindberg, L., & McGinley, K. (2001). Adolescent health risk profiles: The co-occurrence of health risks among females and males. *Journal of Youth and Adolescence, 30,* 707–728.

Credits

TEXT AND ILLUSTRATIONS

Chapter 1 Figure 1.1, page 25 From M. Grumbach, J. Roth, S. Kaplan & R. Kelch, 1974, "Hypothalamic-Pituitary Regulation of Puberty in Man: Evidence and Concepts Derived from Clinical Research," in *Control of the Onset of Puberty*, M. Grumbach, G. Grave & F. Mayer (eds.) Copyright © 1974 Lippincott Williams & Wilkins. Reprinted by permission. **Figure 1.2 a and b, page 29** From W. Marshall, 1978, "Puberty," in *Human Growth*, Vol. 2, F. Faulkner & J. Tanner (eds.). Copyright © 1978 Plenum Publishers. Reprinted with kind permission from Springer Science and Business Media. **Figure 1.3, page 30** From L. Dorn, R. Dahl, H. Woodward, & F. Biro, 2006, "Defining the Boundaries of Early Adolescence: A User's Guide to Assessing Pubertal Status and Pubertal Timing in Research with Adolescents," *Applied Developmental Science*, 1, pp. 30–56. Reprinted with permission from Taylor & Francis. **Table 1.1, page 31** From B. Goldstein, *Introduction to Human Sexuality*, Copyright © 1976. Reprinted by permission of Star Publishing Company, Belmont, CA. **Figure 1.4, page 32** From N. Morris & J. Udry, 1980, "Validation of a Self-Administered Instrument to Assess Stage of Adolescent Development," *Journal of Youth and Adolescence*, 9, pp. 271–280. Reprinted with kind permission from Springer Science and Business Media. **Figure 1.5, page 33** From W. Marshall & J. Tanner, 1969, "Variations in the Pattern of Pubertal Change in Girls," *Archive of Disease of Childhood*, 44, 130. BMJ Publishing Group. Reprinted with the permission of BMJ Publishing Group. **Figure 1.7, page 36** From P. Eveleth & J. Tanner, 1976, *Worldwide Variation in Human Growth*. Cambridge University Press. Reprinted with the permission of Cambridge University Press. **Figure 1.10, page 40** Snell et al., "Sleep and the Body Mass Index and Overweight Status of Children and Adolescents Child Development," 2007, Vol 78, Number 1, Page 315, Figure 2. Reprinted by permission. **Figure 1.11, page 46** From D. Dick, R. Rose, R. Viken & J. Kaprio, 2000, "Pubertal Timing and Substance Use: Associations Between and Within Families Across Late Adolescence," *Developmental Psychology*, 36(2), 180–189. Copyright © 2000 by the American Psychological Association. Reprinted by permission. **Figure 1.12, page 48** Adapted from "Prevalence of Obesity Among U.S. Children and Adolescents by Age Group and Selected Period, 1963–2002," from http://www.cdc.gov/nchs/products/pubs/pubd/hestats/overwght99.htm. **Figure 1.13, page 49** Nader et al., *Journal of the American Medical Association* (JAMA), July 16, 2008, Vol 300, p. 303, Figure 3.

Chapter 2 Figure 2.1, page 67 "Processing Speed in Childhood and Adolescence: Longitudinal Models for Examining Developmental Change" by Kail et al., *Child Development*, 2007, Vol 78, p. 1767. Figure 2, top panel only. Reprinted by permission. **Figure 2.4, page 72** "Why Do Many Psychiatric Disorders Emerge during Adolescence?" By Paus et al., from *Nature Review Neuroscience* 2008, Vol. 9, p. 953, figure 4. Reprinted by permission. **Figure 2.5, page 76** From N. Bayley, 1949, "Consistency and Variability in the Growth of Intelligence from Birth to Eighteen Years," *Journal of Genetic Psychology*, 75, 165–196. Reprinted with the permission of the Helen Dwight Reid Educational Foundation. Published by Heldref Publications, 1319 Eighteenth Street, NW, Washington, DC 20036–1802. Copyright © 1949. **Figure 2.6, page 84** From "Age Differences in Sensation Seeking and Impulsivity as Indexed by Behavior and Self-Report: Evidence for a Dual Systems Model" by Steinberg, Laurence; Albert, Dustin; Cauffman, Elizabeth; Banich, Marie; Graham, Sandra; Woolard, Jennifer in *Developmental Psychology*, November 2008. Reprinted by permission of American Psychological Association. **Figure 2.7, page 84** Reprinted from A. Williams, 2003, "Teenage Drivers: Patterns of Risk," *Journal of Safety Research*, Vol. 34, 5–15, Figure 13, with permission from Elsevier.

Chapter 3 Figure 3.1, page 93 Adapted from W. Osgood, G. Ruth, J. Eccles, J. Jacobs, & B. Barber, 2005, "Six Paths to Adulthood," in R. Settersten, F. Furstenberg, Jr., & R. Rumbaut (Eds.), *On the Frontier of Adulthood*, pp. 320–355. Chicago: University of Chicago Press. Reprinted with permission. **Figure 3.2 a and b, page 94** From N. L. Galambos, E. T. Barker, &

H. J. Krahn, 2006, "Depression, Self-Esteem, and Anger in Emerging Adulthood: Seven-Year Trajectories," *Developmental Psychology*, 42, 350–365. Copyright © 2006 by the American Psychological Association. Reprinted by permission. **Table 3.1, page 95** From J. E. Schulenberg, A. L. Bryant, & P. M. O'Malley, 2004, "Taking Hold of Some Kind of Life: How Developmental Tasks Relate to Trajectories of Well-Being During the Transition to Adulthood," *Development and Psychopathology*, 16(4), p 1124. Reprinted with the permission of Cambridge University Press. **Figure 3.7, page 111** Reprinted from V. J. Ebin, C. D. Sneed, D. E. Morisky, M. Rotherman-Borus, A. M. Magnusson, & C. Malotte, 2001, "Acculturation and Interrelationships Between Problem and Health-Promoting Behaviors Among Latino Adolescents," *Journal of Adolescent Health*, 28, Figure 1, 62–72, with permission from the Society for Adolescent Medicine and Elsevier. **Figure 3.8, page 113** "Welcome to the Neighborhood? Long-Term Impacts of Moving to Low-Poverty Neighborhoods on Poor Children's and Adolescents' Outcomes" by Fauth et al., *Journal of Research on Adolescence*, 2007, p. 270, Figure 3. Reprinted by permission of John Wiley & Sons. **Figure 3.10, page 115** Adapted from H. L. Chung & L. Steinberg, 2006, "Relations Between Neighborhood Factors, Parenting Behaviors, Peer Deviance, and Delinquency Among Serious Juvenile Offenders," *Developmental Psychology*, 42, 319–331. Copyright © 2006 by the American Psychological Association. Reprinted by permission.

Chapter 4 Figure 4.1, page 123 From R. Larson, M. Richards, G. Moneta, G. Holmbeck & E. Duckett, 1996, "Changes in Their Families From Ages 10 to 18: Disengagement and Transformation," *Developmental Psychology*, 32, 744–754. Copyright © 1996 by the American Psychological Association. Reprinted by permission. **Figure 4.2, page 126** From "Stage-environment Fit during Adolescence: Trajectories of Family relations and Adolescent Outcomes" by Gutman, Leslie Morrison; Eccles, Jacquelynne S. in *Developmental Psychology*, March 2007. Reprinted by permission of American Psychological Association. **Figure 4.3, page 129** From E. Maccoby & J. Martin, 1983, "Socialization in the Context of the Family: Parent-Child Interaction," in *Handbook of Child Psychology: Socialization, Personality and Social Development*, Vol. 4, E. M. Hetherington (ed.). This material is used by permission of John Wiley & Sons, Inc. **Table 4.1, page 130** Reprinted with the permission of Simon and Schuster Adult Publishing Group from *The Ten Basic Principles of Good Parenting*, by Laurence Steinberg, Ph.D. Copyright © 2004 by Laurence Steinberg, Ph.D. **Figure 4.5, page 133** "Longitudinal Course and Family Correlates of Sibling Relationships From Childhood Through Adolescence" by Kim et al., *Child Development*, 2006, p. 1753, Figure 1. **Figure 4.6, page 135** From "Parental Monitoring Moderates the Importance of Genetic and Environmental Influences on Adolescent Smoking" by Dick, Danielle M.; Viken, Richard; Purcell, Shaun; Kaprio, Jaakko; Pulkkinen, Lea; Rose, Richard J. from *Journal of Abnormal Psychology*, February 2007. Reprinted by permission of American Psychological Association. **Figure 4.7, page 137** Source: Tejada-Vera B., Sutton P. D. "Births, Marriages, Divorces, and Deaths: Provisional Data for August 2008." *National Vital Statistics Reports;* vol 57, no. 15. Hyattsville, MD: National Center for Health Statistics. 2009. **Figure 4.8, page 139** Apel & Kaukinen, *Criminology*, 2008, p. 49, Figure 1. **Figure 4.10, page 146** From R. Conger, K. Conger, G. Elder, Jr., F. Lornez, R. Simons & L. Whitbeck, 1993, "Family Economic Stress and Adjustment of Early Adolescent Girls," *Developmental Psychology*, 29, 206–219. Copyright © 1993 by the American Psychological Association. Reprinted by permission.

Chapter 5 Figure 5.1, page 150 From R. Larson & M. Richards, 1998, "Waiting for the Weekend," *New Directions for Child and Adolescent Development*, Winter, No. 82, 37–51. Reprinted by permission of John Wiley & Sons. Inc. **Figure 5.2 a and b, page 156** From R. Larson & M. Richards, 1991, "Daily Companionship in Late Childhood and Early Adolescence: Changing Developmental Contexts," *Child Development*, 62, pp. 284–300. Reprinted with permission of the Society for Research in Child Development and Blackwell Publishing. **Page 156** From D. Kinney, 1993, "From Nerds to

Normals: The Recovery of Identity Among Adolescents from Middle School to High School," *Sociology of Education*, 66, pp. 21–40.   **Figure 5.3, page 159** "An Observational Study of Early Heterosexual Interaction at Middle School Dances" by Pellegrini & Long, *Journal of Research on Adolescence*, 2007, p. 629, bottom panel only. Reprinted by permission.   **Figure 5.4, page 162** From B. Brown, 1990, "Peer Groups," in *At the Threshold: The Developing Adolescent*, S. Feldman & G. Elliot (eds.), Harvard University Press. Reprinted by permission.   **Figure 5.5, page 164** From "Developmental Changes in Gender Composition of Friendship Networks in Adolescent Girls and Boys" by Poulin, François; Pedersen, Sara in *Developmental Psychology*, November 2007. Reprinted by permission of American Psychological Association.   **Figure 5.6, page 166** From M. L. Greene, N. Way, & K. Pahl, 2006, "Trajectories of Perceived Adult and Peer Discrimination Among Black, Latino, and Asian American Adolescents: Patterns and Psychological Correlates," *Developmental Psychology*, 42, 227, Figure 2. Copyright © 2006 by the American Psychological Association. Reprinted by permission.   **Figure 5.8, page 175** From R. Macmillan & J. Hagan, 2004, "Violence in the Transition to Adulthood: Adolescent Victimization, Education, and Socioeconomic Attainment Later in Life," *Journal of Research on Adolescence*, 14, pp. 127–158. Reprinted by permission of Blackwell Publishing.   **Figure 5.10, page 177** "Developmental Trajectories of Bullying and Associated Factors" by Pepler et al., *Child Development*, 2008, p. 331, Figure 1. Reprinted by permission.

Chapter 6 Figure 6.1, page 183 From D. Tanner, 1972, *Secondary Education*. New York: Macmillan; William T. Grant Foundation Commission on Work, Family, and Citizenship. (1988*). The Forgotten Half: Non-College Youth in America*. Washington, D.C.: William T. Grant Foundation Commission on Work, Family, and Citizenship.   **Figure 6.2, page 192** "The Transition to High School as a Developmental Process Among Multiethnic Urban Youth" by Benner & Graham, *Child Development*, 2009, p. 368, Figure 6. Reprinted by permission.   **Page 196** From P. Phelan, H. Yu, & A. Davidson, 1994, "Navigating the Psychosocial Pressures of Adolescence: The Voices and Experiences of High School Youth," *American Educational Research Journal*, 31, pp. 415–447.   **Figure 6.3, page 197** Source: National Center for Education Statistics, 2002.   **Figure 6.4, page 200** "Parent Involvement in the Academic Adjustment of Latino Middle and High School Youth: Teacher Expectations and School Belonging as Mediators" by G. P. Kuperminc in *Journal of Adolescence*, Vol 31 (2008), pp. 469–483, figure 1, p. 474. Reprinted by permission.   **Figure 6.5, page 200** Source: National Center for Education Statistics, 2002.   **Figure 6.6, page 201** From R. Larson & M. Richards, 1998, "Waiting for the Weekend," *New Directions for Child and Adolescent Development*, Winter, No. 82, 37–51. Reprinted by permission of John Wiley & Sons, Inc.   **Figure 6.7, page 201** Source: National Center for Education Statistics, 2002.   **Figure 6.8, page 205** Source: National Center for Education Statistics, 2002.   **Figure 6.9, page 205** Source: National Center for Education Statistics, 2002.

Chapter 7 Figure 7.1, page 213 From R. Larson, M. Richards, B. Sims & J. Dworkin, 1999, "How Urban African-American Young Adolescents Spend Their Time: Time Budgets for Locations, Activities and Companionship," *American Journal of Community Psychology*, 29 (4), 565–597. Reprinted with kind permission from Springer Science and Business Media.   **Figure 7.3, page 217** Chapter 8 in Vol 2 of *Handbook of Adolescent Psychology* (3rd ed), pp. 279–280. Figure 8, panels a, b, c. Copyright © 2008. NY: John Wiley & Sons.   **Figure 7.4, page 223** From R. Larson & M. Richards, 1991, "Daily Companionship in Late Childhood and Early Adolescence: Changing Developmental Contexts," *Child Development*, 62. Reprinted with permission of the Society for Research in Child Development and Blackwell Publishing.   **Figure 7.5, page 224** From R. Larson, 2000, "Toward a Psychology of Positive Youth Development," *American Psychologist*, 55, 170–183. Copyright © 2000 by the American Psychological Association. Reprinted by permission.   **Figure 7.9, page 235** Reprinted by permission from J. Johnson, P. Cohen, E. Smailes, S. Kasen & J. Brook, 2002, "Television Viewing and Aggressive Behavior During Adolescence and Childhood," *Science*, 295(5564), 2468–2471. Copyright © 2002 American Association for the Advancement of Science.

Chapter 8, page 246 From S. Harter, 1999, *The Construction of the Self*. New York: Guilford. Reprinted by permission of Guilford Publications, Inc.

Page 248 Quote from S. Harter, 1990, "Identity and Self-Development," in *At the Threshold: The Developing Adolescent*, S. Feldman & G. Elliott (eds.), pp. 352–387. Harvard University Press. Reprinted by permission.   **Figure 8.1, page 252** From R. Larson, G. Moneta, M. Richards & S. Wilson, 2002, "Continuity, Stability and Change in Daily Emotional Experience Across Adolescence, *Child Development*, 73(4), pp. 1151–1165. Reprinted with permission of the Society for Research in Child Development.   **Figure 8.2, page 254** From S. Harter, 1999, *The Construction of the Self*, Guilford Press. Reprinted by permission of Guilford Publications, Inc.   **Figure 8.3, page 255** Reprinted from K. Brown, R. McMahon, F. Biro, P. Cranford, G. Schrieber, S. L. Similo, M. Waclawiw & R. Striegel-Moore, 1998, "Changes in Self Esteem in Black and White Girls Between the Ages of 9 and 14 years: The NHLBI Growth and Health Study," *Journal of Adolescent Health*, 23, 7–19, with permission from the Society for Adolescent Medicine and Elsevier.   **Figure 8.4, page 256** From M. L. Greene & N. Way, 2005, "Self-Esteem Trajectories Among Ethic Minority Adolescents: A Growth Curve Analysis of the Patterns and Predictors of Change," *Journal of Research on Adolescence*, 15, p. 165. Reprinted by permission of Blackwell Publishing.   **Page 259** From K.C. McLean, 2005, "Late Adolescent Development: Narrative Meaning Making and Memory Telling," *Developmental Psychology*, 41, 683–691. Copyright © 2005 by the American Psychological Association. Reprinted by permission.   **Table 8.1, page 271** From M. Herman, 2004, "Forced to Choose: Some Determinants of Racial Identification in Multiracial Adolescents," *Child Development*, 75, pp. 730–748, Table 2. Reprinted by permission of Blackwell Publishing.   **Figure 8.8, page 273** "The Development of Gendered Interests and Personality Qualities From Middle Childhood Through Adolescence: A Biosocial Analysis by McHale et al from Society for Research in Child Development 2009," *Child Development*, p. 488 (Figure 1) and p. 489 (Figure 3). Reprinted by permission.

Figure 9.1, page 282 From L. Steinberg & S. Silverberg, 1986, "The Vicissitudes of Autonomy in Early Adolescence," *Child Development*, 57. Reprinted with permission of the Society for Research in Child Development and Blackwell Publishing.   **Figure 9.3, page 288** From T. Grisso, L. Steinberg, J. Woolard, E. Cauffman, E. Scott, S. Graham, F. Lexcen, N. Reppucci, & R. Schwartz, 2003 , "Juveniles' Competence to Stand Trial: A Comparison of Adolescents' and Adults' Capabilities as Trial Defendants," *Law and Human Behavior*, 27, 333–363. Reprinted with kind permission from Springer Science and Business Media.   **Figure 9.4, page 290** "Leaders and Followers in Adolescent Close Friendships: Susceptibility to Peer Influence as a Predictor of Risky Behavior Friendship Instability and Depression" by Joseph P. Allen, Mary Frances R. Porter and F. Christy McFarland from *Development and Psychopathology*, Volume 18, Number 1, March 2006, pp. 155–172 (figure 1, p. 164). Reprinted by permission of Cambridge University Press.   **Figure 9.5, page 291** From A. Redlich & G. Goodman, 2003, "Taking Responsibility for an Act Not Committed: The Influence of Age and Suggestibility," *Law and Human Behavior, 27*(2), 141–156. Reprinted with kind permission from Springer Science and Business Media.   **Figure 9.6, page 293** From L. Steinberg & S. Silverberg, 1986, "The Vicissitudes of Autonomy in Early Adolescence," *Child Development*, 57, pp. 841–851. Reprinted with permission of the Society for Research in Child Development.

Chapter 10 Table 10.1, page 308 From *Conceptions of Modern Psychiatry*, by Henry Stack Sullivan. Copyright © 1940, 1945, 1947, 1953 by the William Alanson White Psychiatric Foundation. Used by permission of W. W. Norton & Company, Inc.   **Figure 10.1, page 312** From "Attachment and the Experience and Expression of Emotions in Romantic Relationships: A Developmental Perspective" by Simpson, Jeffry A.; Collins, W. Andrew; Tran, SiSi; Haydon, Katherine C. in *Journal of Personality and Social Psychology*, February 2007. Reprinted by permission of American Psychological Association.   **Figure 10.2, page 313** From J. Allen, C. Moore, G. Kuperminc & K. Bell, 1998, "Attachment and Adolescent Psychosocial Functioning," *Child Development*, 69, 1406–1419. Reprinted with permission of the Society for Research in Child Development.   **Figure 10.3, page 314** From B. J. Bigelow & J. J. LaGaipa, 1975, "Children's Written Descriptions of Friendship: A Multidimensional Analysis," *Developmental Psychology*, 11, 857–858. Copyright © 1975 by the American Psychological Association. Reprinted by permission.   **Figure 10.4, page 317** From N. Way & M. L. Greene, 2006, "Trajectories of Perceived Friendship Quality During Adolescence: The Patterns and Contextual Predictors," *Journal of Research on Adolescence*, 16(2), p. 308. Reprinted by permission of John Wiley & Sons.   **Figure 10.5, page 318** From D. Buhrmester, 1996, "Need Fulfillment, Interpersonal Competence and the Developmental Contexts of Early Adolescent Friendship," in *The Company They Keep: Friendship in Childhood and Adolescence*, W. Bukowski, A. Newcomb & W. Hartup (eds.), pp. 158–185. Cambridge University Press. Reprinted with the permission of Cambridge University Press.   **Figure 10.6, page 319** From G. M. Morrison, J. Laughlin, S. S. Miguel, D. C. Smith & K. Widaman, 1997, "Sources of Support for School-Related Issues: Choices of Hispanic Adolescents Varying in Migrant Status," *Journal of Youth and Adolescence*, 26(2), pp. 233–252. Reprinted with kind permission from Springer Science and Business Media.   **Page 319** From K. C. McLean & A. Thorne, 2003, "Late Adolescents' Self-Defining Memories About Relationships," *Developmental Psychology*, 39, 635–645. Copyright © 2003 by the American Psychological Association. Reprinted by permission.   **Figure 10.7 a–d, page 320** From A. Fuligni, 1998, "Authority, Autonomy, and Parent-Adolescent Conflict and Cohesion: A Study of Adolescents from Mexican, Chinese, Filipino and European Backgrounds," *Developmental Psychology*, 34, 782–792. Copyright © 1998 by the American Psychological Association. Reprinted by permission.   **Page 321** From R. D. Stanton-Salazar & S. U. Spina, 2005, "Adolescent Peer Networks as a Context for Social and Emotional Support," *Youth and Society*, 36(4), pp. 397–398; pp. 399–400.   **Page 327** From E. van Roosmalen, 2000, "Forces of Patriarchy: Adolescent Experiences of Sexuality and Concepts of Relationships," *Youth and Society*, 32(2), p. 207.

Chapter 11 Figure 11.2, page 344 Copyright © 2002 by the National Council on Family Relations, 3989 Central Avenue, NE, Suite 550, Minneapolis, MN 55421. Reprinted by permission of the National Council on Family Relations and Blackwell Publishing.   **Page 346** From L. M. Coleman & S. M. Cater, 2005, "A Qualitative Study of the Relationship Between Alcohol Consumption and Risky Sex in Adolescents," *Archives of Sexual Behavior*, 34, 649–661. Reprinted with kind permission from Springer Science and Business Media.   **Figure 11.5, page 357** From V. Lee, R. Croninger, E. Linn & X. Chen, 1996, "The Culture of Sexual Harassment in Secondary Schools," *American Educational Research Journal*, 33, pp. 383–417. Copyright © Sage Publications. Reprinted with permission.   **Figure 11.6, page 364** Source: Innocent Report Card, No. 3, Figure 11, p 15.

Chapter 12 Figure 12.1, page 379 "Implicit Theories of Intelligence Predict Achievement Across an Adolescent Transition: A Longitudinal Study and an Intervention" by Blackwell et al., *Child Development*, 2007, p. 257, Figure 3. Reprinted by permission of John Wiley & Sons.   **Figure 12.3, page 384** "Academic Achievement and Adolescents' Daily Time Use in the Social and Academic Domains" by Witkow from *Journal of Research on Adolescence*, 2009, pp. 162–163, Figures 1 and 2. Reprinted by permission.   **Page 388** From E. M. Horvat & K. S. Lewis, 2003, "Reassessing the Burden of 'Acting White': The Importance of Peer Group in Managing Academic Success," *Sociology of Education*, 76(4), pp. 270–272.   **Figure 12.6, page 396** From *Social Forces*, Vol. 80, No. 4. Copyright © 2002 by The University of North Carolina Press. Used by permission of the publisher. www.uncpress.unc.edu.

Chapter 13 Figure 13.3, page 409 Figure from L. Johnston, G. Bachman, & P. O'Malley, 2002, *Monitoring the Future*. Ann Arbor, MI: Institute for Social Research.   **Figure 13.4, page 411** From P. Zickler, 2004, "Early Nicotine Initiation Increases Severity of Addiction, Vulnerability to Some Effects of Cocaine," *NIDA Notes*, Vol. 19, p. 2.   **Table 13.1, page 413** Table: DSM-IV Diagnostic Criteria for Substance Abuse, from DSM-IV-R. Reprinted with permission from *The Diagnostic and Statistical Manual of Mental Disorders, Text Revision*, Copyright © 2000. American Psychiatric Association.   **Table 13.2, page 417** Table: DSM-IV Diagnostic Criteria for Conduct Disorder, from DSM-IV-R. Reprinted with permission from *The Diagnostic and Statistical Manual of Mental Disorders, Text Revision*, Copyright © 2000. American Psychiatric Association.   **Figure 13.5, page 418** "Testing an Idealized Dynamic Cascade Model of the Development of Serious Violence in Adolescence" by Dodge et al., *Child Development*, 2008, p. 1911, Figure 2. Reprinted by permission.   **Figure 13.6, page 419** From R. Loeber & D. P.

Farrington, 2000, "Young Children Who Commit Crime: Epidemiology, Developmental Origins, Risk Factors, Early Interventions, and Policy Implications," *Development and Psychopathology*, 12, 737–762. Reprinted with the permission of Cambridge University Press.   **Figure 13.7, page 422** "Sex Differences in Adolescent Depression: Stress Exposure and Reactivity Models" by Hankin et al., *Child Development*, 2007, p. 288, Figure 2. Reprinted by permission.   **Table 13.3, page 426** Table of Diagnostic Criteria for Mild Depressive Disorder (Dysthymic Disorder), from DSM-IV-R. Reprinted with permission from *The Diagnostic and Statistical Manual of Mental Disorders, Text Revision*, Copyright © 2000. American Psychiatric Association.   **Figure 13.8, page 428** From L. Wichstrøm, 1999, "The Emergence of Gender Difference in Depressed Mood During Adolescence: The Role of Intensified Gender Socialization," *Developmental Psychology*, 35, 232–245. Copyright ©1999 by the American Psychological Association. Reprinted by permission.   **Figure 13.10, page 430** From M. A. Rueter & H. Kwon, 2005, "Developmental Trends in Adolescent Suicidal Ideation," *Journal of Research on Adolescence*, 15, p. 211. Reprinted by permission of Blackwell Publishing.

PHOTOS

Introduction Page 2 © Purestock/Getty Images; **5** © The McGraw-Hill Companies, Inc./Christopher Kerrigan, photographer; **8** © BananaStock/PunchStock; **9** © Ryan McVay/Getty Images; **12** © Patrick Sheandell/Photo Alto; **16** © AP Photo/The Daily Sentinel, Andrew D. Brosig

Chapter 1 Page 21 © Royalty-Free/Corbis; **22** © Fancy/Veer; **27** © Clive Brunskill/Getty Images; **39** © Thinkstock/age fotostock; **41** © David Young-Wolff/PhotoEdit; **43** © Jeff Greenberg/Image Works; **49** © Donna Day/Getty Images

Chapter 2 Page 56 © The McGraw-Hill Companies, Inc./Photo and dissection by Christine Eckel; **61** © Rhoda Sidney/Image Works; **65(left)** © Photodisc/Getty Images; **65(right)** © Tim Pannell/Corbis; **69** © Brookhaven National Laboratory/Getty Images; **71** © Steve Gschmeissner/SPL/Photo Researchers; **75** © Steve Lyne, Rex Interstock/Stock Connection; **79** © PhotoAlto/PunchStock; **83** © Craig Prentis/Getty Images

Chapter 3 Page 86 © Royalty-Free/Corbis; **92** Courtesy of Seventeen Magazine. Photographed exclusively by Francesco Scavullo; **97** © AP Photo/The Oakland Press, Vaughn Gurganian; **100** © Carol Beckwith & Angela Fisher/HAGA/Image Works; **102** © Jeremy Woodhouse/age fotostock; **114** © AP Photo/Gaas

Chapter 4 Page 117 © Digital Vision/Getty Images; **118** © JupiterImages/Thinkstock/Alamy; **122** © Elizabeth Crews/Image Works; **124** © David Young-Wolff/PhotoEdit; **127** © Ryan McVay/Getty Images; **132** © Michelle D. Bridwell/PhotoEdit; **134** © Photodisc/age fotostock; **138** © John Moore/Getty Images; **144** © Michael Newman/PhotoEdit

Chapter 5 Page 148 © Punchstock/Brand X Pictures; **151** © Bob Daemmrich/Image Works; **153** © Monica Lau/Getty Images; **157** © Angela Hampton Picture Library/Alamy; **163** © Bob Daemmrich/Image Works; **165** © Danny Lehman/Corbis; **172** © Photodisc/Getty Images; **174** © Erin Patrice O'Brien/Getty Images

Chapter 6 Page 180 © Digital Vision/Getty Images; **184** © The Granger Collection; **186** © Will Hart/PhotoEdit; **188** © AP Photo/Medford Mail Tribune, Jim Craven; **194** © Michael Newman/PhotoEdit; **196** © Bob Daemmrich/PhotoEdit; **202** © David Lassman/Syracuse Newspapers/Image Works; **203** © BananaStock/PictureQuest

Chapter 7 Page 210 © Zefa RF/Alamy; **212** © Digital Vision; **215** © Peter Hvizdak/Image Works; **218** © BananaStock/PunchStock; **220** © Peter Hvizdak/Image Works; **226** © Royalty-Free/Corbis; **231** © Bob Daemmrich/Image Works; **237** © Punchstock/Brand X Pictures

Chapter 8 Page 243 © PhotoAlto; **244** © Rubberball; **247** © BananaStock/PunchStock; **249** © The McGraw-Hill Companies, Inc./Ken Karp, photographer; **253** © Angela Hampton Picture Library/Alamy; **257** © Sven Martson/Image Works; **260** © Ryan McVay/Getty Images; **264** © James Marshall/

Name Index

Subject Index